SEVENTH EDITION

Carper's Understanding the Law

John A. McKinsey
Partner, Locke Lord LLP, Adjunct Lecturer of Law, King Hall, School of Law, U.C. Davis, California

Debra D. Burke
Professor, College of Business, Western Carolina University

CENGAGE Learning®

Australia • Brazil • Japan • Korea • Mexico • Singapore • Spain • United Kingdom • United States

CENGAGE Learning

Carper's Understanding the Law, Seventh Edition
John A. McKinsey
Debra D. Burke

Vice President, General Manager Social Science & Qualitative Business: Erin Joyner

Product Director: Mike Worls

Senior Product Manager: Vicky True-Baker

Content Developer: Ted Knight

Product Assistant: Ryan McAndrews

Marketing Director: Kristen Hurd

Sr. Marketing Manager: Robin LeFevre

Marketing Coordinator: Christopher Walz

Art and Cover Direction, Production Management, and Composition: Cenveo Publisher Services

Senior Media Developer: Kristen Meere

Senior IP Director: Julie Geagan-Chevez

IP Project Manager: Anne Sheroff

Manufacturing Planner: Kevin Kluck

Cover Image(s): © Images.com/Corbis

Library of Congress Control Number: 2013953074

ISBN-13: 978-1-285-42842-0

ISBN-10: 1-285-42842-0

Cengage Learning
200 First Stamford Place, 4th Floor
Stamford, CT 06902
USA

Cengage Learning is a leading provider of customized learning solutions with office locations around the globe, including Singapore, the United Kingdom, Australia, Mexico, Brazil, and Japan. Locate your local office at: **www.cengage.com/global**

Cengage Learning products are represented in Canada by Nelson Education, Ltd.

To learn more about Cengage Learning Solutions, visit **www.cengage.com**

Purchase any of our products at your local college store or at our preferred online store **www.cengagebrain.com**

Printed in Mexico
Print Number: 04 Print Year: 2018

Brief Contents

Contents

Preface

In the seventh edition of *Understanding the Law,* we continue to provide a text that can be used in many different law courses. We still presume that the student lacks a prior law course and that this text is their first instruction specifically related to law. Our focus has been to make the text timely and current. Our goal always has been to provide a textbook that is interesting, and even fun, as well as scholarly. Most drama is about conflict, and nothing is more dramatic than law, the rationale and rules devised to address conflict.

The seventh edition of *Understanding the Law* includes a new chapter, Chapter 13, Consumer Rights, Privacy, and Protection, and several chapters have undergone additions or restructuring. These changes offer new, relevant material that instructors and students alike should appreciate. The seventh edition also includes more ethical examples and dilemmas, student-related topics, and additional coverage of privacy issues. Some of the cases were replaced with new, fresh, and topical ones, and there has been a restructuring of chapter sequence. In each chapter, we provide one or more examples of applications of moral and ethical principles to the issues and law raised in that chapter. Connected with the primer on ethical perspectives contained in Chapter 1, these features allow students using this book to maintain a connection to the moral views on issues that are inherent in law.

We continue to use the Legal Focus feature, which provides background, examples, cases, and problems to break up long textbook discussion of topics that become dry if not considered with the human condition. Each Legal Focus is clearly identified in the textbook. Some problems are actual cases, and the case classification is used when there is an available appellate court citation. Many Legal Focuses present issues that remain unresolved, hopefully prompting reasoned class discussion and continued attention to the resolution of important legal issues. The use of Chapter Objectives at the beginning of each chapter in the fourth edition was well received and is continued. A detailed glossary has been a feature of this text, and terms also are provided in the text margin when first introduced. Appendix A, about how to brief a case, has been retained as a critical-thinking writing exercise to assist those using case summaries.

SUPPLEMENTS

Electronic Instructor's Manual and Test Bank

The Instructor's Manual and Test Bank continues to be provided. Each chapter of the manual provides a chapter overview, along with teaching suggestions. The test bank has a minimum of twenty multiple-choice, fifteen true or false, ten fill-in, and three essay questions. It is available on the text companion website, http://www.cengage.com/blaw/carper.

Text Web Site

Visit the Carper, *Understanding the Law*, companion website at http://www.cengagebrain.com, where you will find teaching resources for your course.

Accessing CengageBrain

1. Use your browser to go to http://www.CengageBrain.com.
2. The first time you go to the site, you will need to register. It's free. Click on "Sign Up" in the top right corner of the page and fill out the registration information. (After you have signed in once, whenever you return to CengageBrain, you will enter the user name and password you have chosen and you will be taken directly to the companion site for your book.)
3. Once you have registered and logged in for the first time, go to the "Search for Books or Materials" bar and enter the author or ISBN for your textbook. When the title of your text appears, click on it and you will be taken to the companion site. There you can choose among the various folders provided on the Student side of the site.

   Note: If you are currently using more than one Cengage textbook, the same user name and password will give you access to all the companion sites for your Cengage titles. After you have entered the information for each title, all the titles you are using will appear listed in the pull-down menu in the "Search for Books or Materials" bar. Whenever you return to CengageBrain, you can click on the title of the site you wish to visit and go directly there.

ACKNOWLEDGMENTS

We welcome our new author, Debra Burke, who has brought fresh and current perspective and energy to bear. Also, in renaming the text "Carper's Understanding the Law", we acknowledge not just Donald Carper, but all past authors of Understanding the Law who brought this book to life and preserved it's currency through the decades. It is an honor to continue in their footsteps.

Our reviewers for this edition are again an eclectic group, providing helpful comments and suggestions. They are as follows:

Ian Bolling, *Old Dominion University*
Jason Brandeis, *University of Alaska Anchorage*
Jerry Brask, *Portland Community College Paralegal Program*
Joe Bucci, *Philadelphia University*
Dr. Elizabeth A. Cameron, *Alma College*
Frank Carothers, *Somerset Community College*
Bruce Carroll, *Texas Christian University*
Richard Coffinberger, *George Mason University*
Joshua Coplen, *Laney College*
Stephanie Daniel, *Institute of Technology*
Lizbeth Ellis, *New Mexico State University*
Sharon Feder, *Nassau Community College*
Charles Forer, *The Wharton School*
Ken Gaines, *East-West University*

Nancy R. Gallo, *Sussex County Community College*
Ilene Goldberg, *Rider University*
Kathi Hall, *Erie Business Center South*
Jennifer Hammack, *Georgia College and State University*
Henry Hardt, *Buena Vista University*
Jane Hicks, *St. John Fisher College*
Georgia Holmes, *Minnesota State University, Mankato*
Hua-Lun Huang, *University of Louisiana*
Timothy Jackson, *University*
Edward Kaplan, *Davenport University*
John Keifer, *Ohio University*
Fred Kramer, *John Jay College of Criminal Justice*
Nance Kriscenski, *Manchester Community College*
Greg Lauer, *North Iowa Area Community College*
John Lewis, *Salve Regina University*
Avi Liveson, *Hunter College*
Robert Loomis, *Spokane Community College*
Henry Lowenstein, *Coastal Carolina University/Wall College of Business*
Bruce Marx, *SUNY College at Old Westbury*
Will Mawe, *Southeastern Oklahoma State University*
Delores McMorrin, *Montclair State University*
Margaret Zonia Morrison, *University of Missouri at St. Louis*
John J. Nader, *Davenport University*
Tim O'Dea, *Marist College*
Susanna Peters, *Michigan Technological University*
Jim Pingel, *Everest University – Brandon*
Walter C. Prentice, *Austin Community College*
Regina Robson, *St. Joseph's University*
Andree Rosen, *Midland College*
Nicole Stowell, *University of South Florida St. Petersburg*
Norman Todd, *New Mexico State University*
Diana Tsaw, *California Lutheran University*
Wendy Vonnegut, *Methodist University*
Shunda Ware, *Atlanta Technical College*
Edd Welsh, *Mesa Community College*
Judith Wright, *Indiana University Kelley School of Business – Indianapolis*

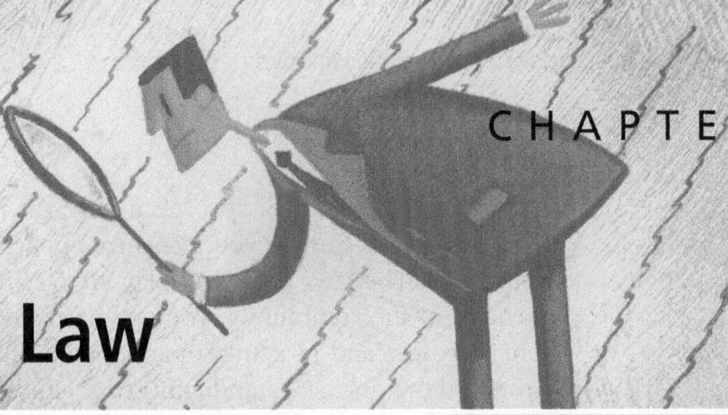

CHAPTER 1

Introduction to Law

Let reverence for the laws be breathed by every American mother to the lisping babe that prattles on her lap; let it be taught in schools, in seminaries, and in colleges; let it be written in primers, spelling-books, and in almanacs; let it be preached from the pulpit, proclaimed in legislative halls, and enforced in courts of justice. And, in short, let it become the political religion of the nation; and let the old and the young, the rich and the poor, the grave and the gay of all sexes and tongues and colors and conditions, sacrifice unceasingly upon its altars.

Abraham Lincoln, Address before the Young Men's Lyceum of Springfield, Illinois, January 1837

LEARNING OBJECTIVES

After reading and studying this chapter, you should be able to:

- Define "law" while understanding the varied meanings that legal concepts have across society.
- Understand the origins of the English common law system and its connection to the U.S. legal system.
- Describe the important sources of U.S. law and explain how they are interrelated.
- Explain the doctrine of *stare decisis* and understand how case law is related to other sources of law.
- Classify the law in a variety of ways, including federal and state law, criminal and civil law, private and public law, and procedural and substantive law.
- Be able to define ethics and distinguish ethics from law.
- Demonstrate familiarity with two forms of ethical reasoning and the ability to use them to consider an ethical problem.

Welcome to the study of law, specifically, the law of the United States. *Understanding the Law* is designed to help you recognize opportunities and overcome obstacles in reaching your goals. The laws of society play an ever-increasing role in our lives. As an educated member of the community, you will need to apply your understanding of our legal system in voting and in actively participating in local, state, and federal issues and affairs. From a more practical standpoint, your education of our legal system will help guide you toward a happier and more financially successful life.

Citizens of the United States engage with a myriad of businesses and with government, as consumers, as employees, and as active members of communities. Community leaders deal with difficult problems such as energy and resources, neighborhood crime, traffic, homelessness, and environmental protection. Already, you have learned something about the law, simply by experiencing life. For example, you know that stealing, damaging someone else's property, or intentionally injuring another person is "unlawful." But you may not completely understand what it means for something to be "unlawful." You also know that in an automobile collision, the careless driver is held responsible, and when both drivers are careless, they share the blame. You know that divorce creates issues of alimony, division of family property, and financial support for children and changes in their parental custody. You know that employers are expected to provide safe working conditions for their employees. You probably are aware of or are learning about the "property rights" that you interact with on a daily basis, such as software and music.

From these experiences, you probably can write a reasonable definition of the law. Perhaps you correctly would conclude that laws are rules that must be obeyed to avoid the imposition of sanctions (legal penalties). More precisely, **law** often is considered to be a body of rules of conduct prescribed by controlling authority and having binding legal force. But this traditional definition of law emphasizes the static perspective of law. Law is actually much more dynamic.

law
A body of rules of conduct prescribed by controlling authority and having binding legal force.

Consider law as continuously changing, always responding to society's need for solutions to new and evolving issues. There are many specific, written rules, such as speed limits. But also conflicts and questions arise when those static rules get applied to unique circumstances and evolving societal values. We often explain that legal rules follow rather than lead. Consider the Internet and the digital age that we live in today. It is challenging and changing traditional laws of privacy, free speech, property, and crime.

It is perfectly logical for laws to change continually in response to the evolving characteristics of, and the issues within, our society. That is, law changes as we change. Still, there is a fairly firm foundation behind all law in our society: the Constitution of the United States. All law must conform to the immutable principles of our Constitution or ultimately be discarded. Even within the Constitution, however, not all principles are expressed; many are implied. For example, the much-publicized "right of privacy," upon which issues like abortion and interracial marriage have been decided, does not actually appear as express words in the Constitution. The role of the Constitution and the U.S. Supreme Court, in defining the law of American society is explored more fully in Chapter 2.

Our legal system and laws are dynamic and respond to the legal issues that arise within our changing society. In a nutshell, the study of law is the study of a moving target. Some changes are quite immediate, as when legislatures respond to popular demands. In contrast, courts are structured to accommodate change more slowly, at a more reflective pace.

In the twenty-first century, we are experiencing a magnificent technological revolution, one focused on digital electronics, communication and microtechnology. In this revolution, the demands upon the legal system are reaching new heights of complexity, for example, the following:

- The Internet and digital technology is causing a reexamination of the principles of free speech, security, and privacy. The speed and worldwide, omniscient presence of communication is shrinking the earth and making local issues, national and international.
- Biotechnology is presenting our society and its legal system with momentous social and legal issues, such as genetic alteration of plant and animal life and human cloning.

In addition to the technology revolution, natural forces also are creating today's issues. Consider the following:

- Population continues to increase, causing a multitude of social issues, and the problem is growing exponentially. Consider, for example, the intense debate over health care, immigration policy, and energy. Additionally, our population is aging, setting the stage for fierce competition between workers and retirees for the nation's wealth and benefits.
- Environmental issues abound, many driven by increasing competition for a worldwide increasing thirst for and consumption of resources like water, trees, and fossil fuels. From global warming and energy reliability to air and water pollution, our society is facing problems it has yet to solve. Increasingly, most solutions seem to reach beyond the boundaries of the United States as well as the North American continent.
- In the United States, fundamental differences on many issues continue to divide us. Topics such as same-sex marriage, gun control, and the size and role of government are simultaneously both driving change to the law and creating inaction and stagnation within the government to change the law.

Historical perspective sharpens our understanding of the outlook for our laws and legal system in the early twenty-first century. It is said that if we ignore history, we are destined to repeat it. Here, we are not studying history, but we must take history into account when contemplating the role of law and our legal system as we tackle the issues of the twenty-first century.

From the time that our Constitution was established, our legal system has steadily accepted responsibility (jurisdiction) over an increasing variety of issues. Today, some prominent issues include gun control, sexual orientation, and abortion. There is a rationale that elected officials choose to avoid the tough and controversial issues that cost them votes and leave these no-win issues to the legal system in which the judges are brave, if for no other reason than because the electorate participates less in their tenure.

It is becoming increasingly important for well-informed citizens to be educated about our legal system, including the role of its judges and lawyers. Otherwise, citizens risk submission through ignorance and complacency to the latest sound bite or "spin" that seeks voter approval. Your understanding of the increasingly important legal system is critical over the long run, which is precisely why it is presented here.

Americans increasingly are turning to the courts to solve their problems—both public *and* private. This produces a great strain upon our legal system, as evidenced by the growth of alternative forums for dispute resolution (discussed in Chapter 4). The point here is that the future portends significant legal costs of doing business and of protecting consumers. These costs are indirectly reflected in the prices of products as well as taxes used to support courts, judges, and government offices charged with providing public or legal services.

There is no reason to suspect that the demand for attorneys (i.e., legal solutions) will lessen or that their services will cost less in the twenty-first century. Lawyers enjoy an oligarchy with the power (and willingness) to match their fees with the capabilities of their clients to pay. Increasing demand is producing more lawyers, who participate in an ever-wider scope of increasingly specialized tasks.

This is not to suggest that our dependence on law, courts, and lawyers is either good or bad. It is merely a well-understood phenomenon. Educators often speak of the legal system as being composed of laws and courts. The logic is that laws are the rules of our society, and courts ensure their enforcement. But what of attorneys? In reality, a person cannot hope to resolve a substantial conflict or commercial transaction without an attorney's professional help. Although citizens are entitled under law to self-representation, the reality is that to do so is ill advised for many obvious reasons. Thus, the attorney is the first person to become involved when legal issues, and many business opportunities arise. Attorneys give advice, most of which is followed. They also perform other services as described in Chapter 4. The point is that attorneys must be acknowledged as an integral part of the legal system because laws and judges are powerless until attorneys bring matters into court.

The adaptability of the Constitution, the courts, and lawyers to meet an ever-growing demand for services likely will continue. But at its roots, our American legal system still reflects its English origins.

THE ENGLISH SOURCE OF U.S. LAW

To understand American law, you must understand its origin, English law. Over hundreds of years, the law of England evolved into a framework of principles, found in both customs and statutes that were brought to the New World by the early colonial settlers. This body of law was called the common law. When the United States broke away from England after the Revolutionary War, it adopted the entire body of English common law as it existed in the eighteenth century—at least to the extent it did not conflict with U.S. federal and state law. That is still the situation today: Principles of the English common law are in effect throughout the country. Only Louisiana, purchased in 1803 from Napoleon, is different, retaining a variation of the Roman civil law that was then used in France. This California statute is representative of the continuing presence of English legal doctrine and process in the courts of the United States:

> *The Common Law of England so far as it is not repugnant to or inconsistent with the Constitution of the United States or the Constitution or laws of this state, is the rule of decision in all the courts of this state.*
>
> (California Civil Code, §22.2.)

So what is English common law? It arises from experience and custom and from the tacit consent of the people as evidenced from its development over a thousand years. The purpose of primitive English law was to keep the peace, and fact-finding processes were likely to provoke the population rather than calm it. So authorities avoided investigation and substituted mechanical tests that were believed to obtain the judgment of God. Among the favored tests were various ordeals an accused must suffer, including cold water, hot water, hot iron, and the morsel. Imagination probably suffices to picture all but the morsel ordeal so we offer this quote from the *Domesday Book* of the County of Norfolk, England, describing an ordeal by morsel.

LEGAL FOCUS—EXAMPLE

"May this morsel which is given him in order to bring the truth to light, stick in his throat and find no passage; may his face turn pale and his limbs be convulsed; and an horrible alteration appear in his whole body; if he is guilty. But if innocent of the crime laid to his charge, may he easily swallow it, consecrated in Thy Name, to the end that all may know."*

Before the eleventh century, England was an Anglo-Saxon society of unified and relatively prosperous people living mostly in villages. The economy was agricultural and the people were self-sufficient, growing grain, spinning wool, and even brewing beer for home consumption. Their kings headed powerful and wealthy aristocracies. Wealth was primarily tied to the landholding feudal system. Serfdom, in which people were born into vassalage and were required to work the aristocratic lords' hereditary lands, was widespread. Throughout the Saxon period, law was essentially a matter of local customs, and it changed very slowly.

In 1066, William, Duke of Normandy, led 5,000 men and 2,500 cavalry across the English Channel to defeat the Saxons in the Battle of Hastings. The Duke became known as William the Conqueror. The invasion was followed by decades of regional uprisings and resistance characterized by extensive murder, oppression, famine, and fear, despite William's zeal for law, order, and justice. The Normans (Vikings who originally came from Scandinavia via northern France) were French in viewpoint and culture. Their system of law was based on the ancient Roman civil law, which was expressed mostly in detailed codes (systematic collections of rules) imposed by the ruler from above, in contrast to the Saxon practice of developing rules from below, based on the customs of the people.

The Normans mostly retained the English common law of unwritten customs. England gradually underwent positive changes. A sense of national unity ensued, leading to a national system of law derived from both Anglo-Saxon and Norman influences. The conquest led to the introduction of elements of Roman civil law. As before, local justice continued to be the concern of local sheriffs, and the **common law** (law applied uniformly throughout the country) was characterized even then by equality before the law (the law applied the same to every person), respect for established rights, and impartial administration of justice.

common law: as a system of law
The total system of law that originated in medieval England and was adopted by the United States at the time of the American Revolution. Expressed originally in opinions and judgments of the courts, it is judge-made law that reflects the customs and usages of the people. Contrasted to Roman civil law, it is found throughout the English-speaking world. Common law is sometimes called unwritten law.

The king's courts dealt with civil and criminal legal matters, and new church courts dealt with canon law (ecclesiastical law governing internal relations of the Roman Catholic Church) and all aspects of marriage and succession. Disputes between common and canon law existed in some areas, such as legitimization of illegitimate children, which was not possible under canon law. Under common law, legitimization was accomplished by subsequent marriage of the parents. This was an important matter because it affected rights of inheritance and succession to land, the foundation of wealth and power in England.

By the twelfth century, judges, who periodically visited places in the country to dispense justice, were displacing sheriffs. These "circuits" were precursors of the present U.S. circuit and district courts. The itinerant judges dealt with such crimes as murder, robbery, forgery, and arson. One judge, Glanvil, is credited with writing *Treatise on the Laws and Customs of the Kingdom of England*, the first serious book on the evolving common law. In 1215, King John was forced to accept the Magna Carta (Latin: "Great Charter"), the basis of modern English constitutional liberty, commanding free elections

*Roscoe Pound, "Studying Law," in Arthur Vanderbilt, ed. *Introduction to American Law* (New York: New York University Press, 1955), p. 396.

and reform of the courts and barring imprisonment without a trial by a jury of peers. Trial by jury had evolved into permanency by way of the Magna Carta, and ultimately was incorporated into the U.S. Constitution. The Magna Carta essentially decreed supremacy of law over personal authority of the king and his aides. It was a precursor of our constitutional democracy.

For several hundred years, the English system of courts evolved, influenced by conflicts and political interventions. Over time, judges required formalities to be met before a matter could be brought to court. When these requirements were not met, courts were simply unavailable to a party. When the king's courts were unable or unwilling to provide a just solution to a legal problem, and a citizen (initially citizens of high status) appealed to the king, the matter would be referred to the lord chancellor for possible intervention. The lord chancellor served as the king's chief administrative officer, and the position was initially staffed by high churchmen. As a man committed to justice and fairness, the chancellor was authorized to decide the cases without the assistance of a jury.

action in equity
A civil trial held without a jury when relief sought by the plaintiff is equitable in nature, such as an injunction, or a divorce or dissolution of a marriage.

This alternative court became known as a *court of equity*. An example of an **action in equity** would be a dispute over the sale of a parcel of land in which the seller refused to transfer the title. The king's courts, by tradition, could do no more than award monetary damages. The chancellor (and, later, when the administration of these hearings was delegated to junior staff, courts of equity) could and would order the seller to relinquish possession. Ultimately, jurisdictional conflicts refined the fundamental distinction between courts at law and courts in equity. This distinction endures in the United States today and determines important questions. However, unlike England, where courts at law and in equity were physically separated, modern U.S. courts are empowered to render either equitable or legal relief. Equity is explained further in Chapter 3.

Modern Common Law and *Stare Decisis*

common law: as a type of law
That law that comes from the common courts as opposed to a legislature or court of equity.

The term **common law** might already be confusing to you because, like many English language terms, it is used in different ways to describe different things. For example, we have been using the term to describe law common to all of England. But we also have used the term to describe a legal system derived from English legal method, to describe law formulated by courts rather than legislatures, and to describe common law as distinguished from an action in equity. All the different expressions of the term *common law* are related. The use of the term to describe a type of legal system derives from a description of the unique nature of that legal system, the formulation of law by the courts. The distinction of law and equity derives from a historical accident within this lawmaking system. The uniqueness of the common law, or law developed by the courts, is what usually is meant when someone uses the term *common law*. In no other legal system do independent courts have the power to contribute to the law as they do in the common law system.

federalism
A government consisting of a union of more or less self-governing states under an umbrella of federal government.

When considering U.S. court-made or case law, it is important to note the important relationship between federal and state law. Our form of government is one of shared and often-overlapping power referred to as **federalism** (a union of states under a central federal government). The court systems include both federal and state courts, which function as either trial courts or appellate courts. These trial courts accept testimony and other evidence to determine guilt or innocence or to place financial responsibility. Appellate courts, on the other hand, review trial court procedures to ensure that correct laws were applied during trial. These appellate reviews, or written decisions, form the body of law also called the common law, or case law.

Both federal and state appellate courts review cases based on the constantly evolving principles of the common law that are expressed in the written decisions of courts. Who reads these written decisions? Members of the public often learn about new, unfolding laws from television, the Internet, newspapers, and news magazines (but hopefully not from tabloids). Lawyers and scholars read and study court decisions as part of their professional responsibilities. Of course, judges read and study prior court decisions upon which they may decide the trials or cases before them.

Some principles of law derived through the common law apply to both state and federal court systems. For example, the doctrine of ***stare decisis*** (Latin: "to stand by things that have been settled") mandates that once a rule of law is determined to be applicable to a particular set of facts involved in a case, it will be applied to all future cases that have similar facts. This doctrine binds courts of equal or junior rank to follow the senior court that first applied the rule or principle. Essentially, lower state courts are bound to the principles established by higher appellate courts within the same state; lower federal courts are bound to the principles established by higher appellate courts within their respective jurisdictions. (The hierarchy of courts is outlined in Chapter 3.)

stare decisis
The common law doctrine that binds an inferior (subordinate) court to follow and apply decisions and interpretations of higher courts when similar cases arise. Also called the *doctrine of precedents*.

This important doctrine of *stare decisis* leads to stability and predictability in the law. For example, if a high court establishes the principle that a promise to marry is not enforceable in court nor are damages allowed if broken, then routine legal research will alert all attorneys to the existence of that **precedent**. If a similar case arises, they will not waste time and money litigating the question; they know their court will be bound by the same earlier outcome under the doctrine of *stare decisis*. This doctrine also commonly is called the doctrine of precedents. Once a common law rule or principle is applied in a case, it becomes a precedent and is binding on other courts in similar future cases. The appellate court's decision thus has become a part of the common law of that particular state.

precedent
A court decision on a question of law that gives authority or direction on a similar question of law in a later case with similar facts. See also *stare decisis*.

Judges do not have the personal choice to disregard a binding precedent in the common law. Judges take oaths of office and are sworn "to comply with or be faithful to" the law.

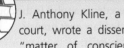

LEGAL FOCUS—PROBLEM

J. Anthony Kline, a justice of a state appellate court, wrote a dissenting opinion in which, as a "matter of conscience," he refused to vote consistently with a state supreme court precedent. Does such a declaration violate the doctrine of *stare decisis*?

Although the action of refusing to comply with a precedent flies in the face of the doctrine of *stare decisis*, it may be characterized as a "highly irregular and never to be lightly undertaken" exception based upon the conscience of the justice.

Stare decisis is not a straitjacket, however. If a principle has outlived its usefulness or has grown inapplicable because of changing social standards and circumstances, it may be overruled by a high court. Often, a current case is not controlled by a principle previously applied in an earlier case simply because the two cases are distinguishable on their facts. An example of an unenforceable and uncompensable promise to marry would be distinguishable from a case in which one of the prospective spouses had incurred considerable related expenses before the promise was broken. The earlier principle, therefore, would not apply to or bind the court's decision. Although the court, obviously, would not compel the parties to marry, it might establish a new principle in authorizing recovery of damages (an award of monetary compensation).

The common law of today is the body of rules derived from fundamental usages and customs of antiquity, particularly as they appeared in medieval England, and from modern judgments of appellate courts recognizing and applying those customs in specific cases. Since thousands of appellate cases are decided each year, the body of common law is enormous, even though most of these cases define no new principles. In preparing current cases, lawyers spend much time and effort searching earlier case records for principles of the common law that might be applicable. Thanks to modern information technology, the task is less physically laborious today, but the information at the attorney's fingertips is nonetheless overwhelming in volume, let alone complexity. Before lawyers can draft formal opinions or business documents or perform advocacy, they must perform legal research of the applicable common, statutory, and regulatory (administrative agency) law. Lawyers, thus, are responsible to their clients more for researching than for knowing the law. For those of you who are interested in learning more about, or in practicing, legal research, we have included a summary of basic steps in Appendix B.

unwritten law
A historically based reference to court- or judge-made law.

Originally, the common law of England was called **unwritten law**, because it evolved from judicial decisions that were based on the unwritten customs and usages of the people. Moreover, the decisions and opinions of the judges were not recorded or printed in books; often, judges talked with one another, exchanging their rulings through conversation. In contrast, codes and statutes (enacted by the king or a legislative body) were usually written (printed). Today, of course, most additions to the common law, made in appellate court decisions, are published chronologically in books, called **reporters**, and made available on the Internet. Such works are referred to as **case law**. If case law were not reported, both attorneys as well as the public would be unaware of decisions that had been made and of the appellate courts' rationale for those decisions. After centuries of relying on books, many lawyers and others are no longer using books as the primary way of finding information about cases. Instead, Internet-based databases and Websites provide much of the recorded case information.

reporter
A set of books that contains the written opinions of justices of specified appellate courts. These volumes contain the decisional, or unwritten, law. Volumes in the reporters and the cases they contain are arranged in chronological order and accessible by case name or subject matter index.

case law
All reported judicial decisions; the law that comes from judges' opinions in lawsuits. Also referred to as court law, judge law, and sometimes common law.

The application of the doctrine of *stare decisis* is a challenging process. For example, is a new fact situation the same as the suggested precedent, is it similar, or is it different? The adversary system allows each side a representative who argues what events occurred, what precedent should apply, and how it should apply. And what about the situation in which the facts are clear, the law is clear, and the result is absurd? What precedents apply? Is the court bound to come to an unjust decision, or is a decision based on settled law ever unjust?

In the search for precedent, the following possibilities exist:

1. The new case is identical or virtually identical to a case previously decided by a high court in the same court system. Result: Follow old decision. This is seen as binding precedent.
2. The new case is somewhat different from a case previously decided by a high court in the same court system, but the underlying policy and rationale for the old case also applies to the new one. Result: Reason from the old case and extend the previous holding to the new facts. This is known as using precedent to extend the rule of law to new situations.
3. The new case, although having some similarity to a case previously decided by a high court in the same court system, is not the same and the underlying rationale does not make sense in this case. Result: Distinguish new case from old case and limit the rule from the old case. This is known as using cases to limit the application of judicial doctrine.
4. The new case is identical or virtually identical to a case previously decided by a high court in the same court system but the underlying rule no longer makes sense. Result: Overrule previous precedent when strong reasons exist for doing so. This is not done often, but it is consistent with the doctrine of *stare decisis*.

LEGAL FOCUS—EXAMPLE

In 1954, the U.S. Supreme Court decided, in *Brown v. Board of Education*, that maintaining separate schools for black and white schoolchildren was unconstitutional. Some forty-eight years earlier, the U.S. Supreme Court had reached just the opposite conclusion in *Plessy v. Ferguson*. No laws had changed in the interim time between the two cases and both decisions evaluated the same Equal Protection Clause of the Fourteenth Amendment to the Constitution.

In overruling *Plessy v. Ferguson*, the Supreme Court determined that the previous reasoning, that separate facilities were equal, no longer made sense.

5. The new case presents problems that are not covered by an existing rule from a high court in the same court system. Possible Results: (a) The case will be dismissed and facts not considered because there is not a remedy in law for every perceived wrong; or (b) the case will be heard and decided based on extensions of doctrines of justice and fairness, and new law and rule will be developed. The deciding court may consider precedent from other states, the federal system, or even other countries when seeking guidance as to an appropriate rule to resolve the controversy.

MODERN SOURCES OF U.S. LAW

statutes
Laws enacted by Congress or by state legislatures.

ordinance
A written law enacted by a city or county (parish). An example is a zoning ordinance that governs the use of land.

written law
An old-fashioned reference to the statutes and ordinances of federal, state, and local governments, and the published rules of administrative agencies.

codes
Compilations of statutes that are grouped together by subject matter (e.g., a vehicle code).

Ours is a constitutional form of government. In one sense, our Constitution is the ultimate source of our laws because it contains principles by which our nation is governed. Here we are concerned with those institutions of government that create the laws of our land.

Most educated adults are familiar with the basic structure of our federal government, divided by our Constitution into the legislative, executive, and judicial branches. Knowledge of this structure facilitates an understanding of how and where our laws are made and of how they are classified for clarity and comprehensibility. State and local governments also are structured into these three branches, and they operate in a manner similar to the federal system. We explore government and these branches in greater detail in Chapters 2 and 5. Here we briefly consider the sources of our laws.

Lawmaking by Legislators

Legislators, both state and federal, enact laws called **statutes**.* Local legislative bodies (e.g., for cities and counties) enact laws called **ordinances**. Collectively, these statutes and ordinances are called the **written law**, as contrasted to case law (unwritten law). Compilations of statutes by topic are called **codes**. For example, a state legislature may enact a statute lengthening the previous jail sentence for the crime of making an obscene telephone call. This statute will be compiled with, indexed to, and become a part of the state's "criminal" or "penal" code. Numerous specialized codes in the states group together statutes pertaining to particular subjects, such as the Vehicle Code, Health and Welfare Code, Corporations Code, and Business and Professions Code. These codes (often with slightly different titles) are generally available in any public law library, usually located in county courthouses.

Statutory law covers a staggering number of subjects, such as crimes, civil rights, housing, health, and indeed all matters upon which the legislative branch has the

*Often, statutes are assigned titles, such as the Federal Racketeer Influence and Corrupt Organizations Act, commonly called RICO.

constitutional power to legislate. But it is important to understand that federal statutory law is limited to matters of federal jurisdiction. The term *jurisdiction* refers to the power or authority the federal government is given to enact statutes under the U.S. Constitution. State statutory law is limited to matters of statewide authority; a similar limitation is true for local ordinances. For example, Congress has jurisdiction to regulate the transportation of goods in interstate commerce; state legislatures do not. Court jurisdiction is explained fully in Chapter 3.

Some difficult conflicts over jurisdiction have occurred. The language in which Article I, Section 8 of the U.S. Constitution enumerates the federal government's areas of jurisdiction is open to interpretation. Some believe that the courts have interpreted it too expansively, letting the federal government intrude on states' rights. Others argue that the federal reach should be extended even further, perhaps into such matters as shelter for the homeless. (We consider constitutional law in greater detail in Chapter 2.) When conflicts arise between federal and state jurisdictions, the U.S. Supreme Court makes the ultimate judicial decision through its interpretation and application of the Constitution.

Similar jurisdictional conflicts exist between state and local governments. For example, local governments usually exercise exclusive jurisdiction over the zoning of real estate. Zoning laws restrict how land may be used. What if a state enacted a statute that authorized state officials to rezone real estate, regardless of local government rules? Does this differ from the common practice whereby state laws require suburban communities to accept construction of prisons and of treatment centers for drug addicts? Local ordinances may reflect NIMBY ("not in my back yard") attitudes of neighborhoods, but just as state law yields to federal law, local law yields to state law.

Although proposed statutes are studied before their enactment, and although the end sought is usually desirable and even necessary in the minds of proponents, the validity of a statute or ordinance still remains in doubt until it is challenged by some injured party and an appropriate court determines its validity. There is a presumption that an enacted statute or ordinance is constitutional, and courts hold few invalid. Nonetheless, a person could be sentenced to jail for violation of a statute that later is determined to be unconstitutional and therefore void. Even long-standing statutes or ordinances can be overturned by a person defying the law. Once the legislative branch enacts a law, uncertainty technically remains until the law is applied, then challenged in a trial, and finally judicially approved as constitutional. A court will not rule on the constitutionality of a statute or ordinance unless someone affected by its application files suit, because courts do not render decisions based on hypothetical conflicts. There must be a **case or controversy**, properly presented to a court, before judicial action will be taken.

case or controversy
A requirement that courts may decide only cases in which an actual conflict between persons exists.

LEGAL FOCUS—EXAMPLE

In 1955, Rosa Parks, an African American woman, refused to give up her seat in the front of public bus in Montgomery, Alabama, to a white man. She was sitting in an area of the bus designated for white people only. She was violating a law by doing so and was arrested. She lost her job but eventually was vindicated as such "Jim Crow" laws were overthrown as being unconstitutional.

Rosa Parks' action, though clearly a violation of law, is a modernly applauded event and such conduct often is referred to, nobly, as "civil disobedience." Without such cases or controversies before courts, no law, no matter how unconstitutional, can be overturned.

Lawmaking by the Executive Branch

The executive branch of government, at the federal, state, and local levels, collaborates with the legislative branch in the adoption of statutes. However, even if the president of the United States (or a state governor), as head of the executive branch, vetoes a proposed statute, the legislators have the power to override such action, usually with a two-thirds vote. This partnership in lawmaking is part of our system of checks and balances that encourages negotiation and compromise. The executive branch also independently can make certain laws. The president, state governors, and heads of local governments all have authority to issue certain directives that have the force and effect of law.*

The president also is authorized under both the Constitution and statutes of the United States to issue executive orders consistent with legal responsibilities of the office. An example is the executive order issued by President George W. Bush on October 8, 2001, establishing the new government agency, the Office of Homeland Security.

> *By the authority vested in me as President by the Constitution and the laws of the United States of America, it is hereby ordered as follows:*
>
> *Section 1. Establishment. I hereby establish within the Executive Office of the President an Office of Homeland Security (the "Office") to be headed by the Assistant to the President for Homeland Security.*
>
> *Sec. 2. Mission. The mission of the Office shall be to develop and coordinate the implementation of a comprehensive national strategy to secure the United States from terrorist threats or attacks. The Office shall perform the functions necessary to carry out this mission, including the functions specified in section 3 of this order.*
>
> (Executive Order Establishing Office of Homeland Security)

Often having greater impact on day-to-day life is the lawmaking power of other federal, state, and local administrative agencies, which are specialized bodies created by Congress and by legislation at the state and local levels to regulate specific activities. Administrative agencies investigate problems within their respective jurisdictions (an executive function), make laws called rules and regulations (a legislative function), and conduct hearings (similar to court trials) to determine whether their rules have been violated and, if so, what penalties should be imposed (a judicial function). There are many important federal administrative agencies, numerous state agencies in each state, and a lesser number of agencies within each sizable local government.

You probably have read or heard about such prominent federal administrative agencies as the Central Intelligence Agency (CIA), Drug Enforcement Administration (DEA), Environmental Protection Agency (EPA), Food and Drug Administration (FDA), and the Federal Trade Commission (FTC). Thousands of federal, state, and local administrative agencies continue to make and enforce innumerable laws each year on myriad subjects. You will learn more about lawmaking by administrative agencies in Chapter 5.

Lawmaking by Courts

As you have already partly learned earlier when studying the concept of "common law," courts create law. Federal and state courts resolve controversies that are brought before them by parties to legal disputes. At the end of each case proceeding, the presiding judge issues a judgment. Most judgments are never appealed to a higher court nor written down in a comprehensive decision that later courts can review. Occasionally, however,

*For example, in 1986 then-President Ronald Reagan ordered the random drug testing of certain employees working in interstate transportation. The subject of drug testing in other workplaces, and even in competitive sporting events, continues to be an important issue.

judicial activists
Judges whose judicial philosophy includes treating the law as a vibrant and active source of rules. When faced with new issues (e.g., social), such judges are likely to see the Constitution as a flexible document and *stare decisis* as challengeable when they believe important social needs must be addressed.

strict constructionists
Judges whose reading of the law narrowly interprets legal words and who subscribe to interpreting the law consistent with the believed meaning given it by the drafters.

dicta
Any part of a court opinion that is unnecessary to the resolution of dispute before the court. Such digression by a judge is not binding on later courts.

if the case is the first of its kind in that jurisdiction, the trial judge may formulate and apply a new rule of common law. An appellate court may then review such a rule. Upon the appellate court rendering a written opinion, all other trial courts in that jurisdiction then would follow the appellate court's decision.

In making rulings, appellate courts interpret and apply relevant statutory law together with appropriate rules of common law derived from prior cases under the previously discussed doctrine of *stare decisis*. If there is no controlling statute or principle of common law, which occasionally happens, the appellate court will create a new rule or extend an existing principle and apply it to the case. That new concept becomes a part of the continually evolving common law to be followed by other courts in future cases. Thus, new law is created.

Judges who purposefully expand on the law in their decisions often are referred to as **judicial activists**. Judges who narrowly interpret the law by relying heavily on the doctrine of *stare decisis* often are referred to as **strict constructionists**. Either way, the interpretations of law set forth by judges constitute "judge-made" law, or common law. Courts are reactive institutions; judges must wait for litigation to reach them before they can render a decision. Legislative bodies, on the other hand, can initiate new laws on any subject at any time they choose. Nonetheless, the judicial system has been responsible for many of the great social changes that have occurred in the United States. The following quote from political scientist Dennis D. Dorin is an enlightening reminder that labels used by others are not necessarily subscribed to by those who are so labeled.

> *I have interviewed fourteen United States Supreme Court Justices, on a spectrum ranging from "liberal" ones like Warren, Black and Douglas to "conservative" ones like Scalia and Thomas. Not one of them, I can report, has ever told me that he or she is an "activist." Not one has ever said that he or she is willing to violate the Constitution.*

Not all the language used by appellate courts in their written opinions becomes part of the common law. Much of it is explanatory, analyzing the facts of the case and elaborating on various legal principles that may or may not directly apply. Legal issues addressed in the opinion that are not logically necessary to support the ruling in the case are called **dicta** (Latin: "remarks"). Being unnecessary language, *dicta* do not become part of the common law, although they may provide clues about how that judge's philosophy might be applied in future cases.

Sometimes it is quite clear which statutory language or principle of common law is applicable to a case. But the issue of how it should be applied to the specific facts may be quite complex. For example, in a murder trial, there may be no disagreement about the applicability of a statute declaring that an unlawful killing with malice aforethought is murder. But the question of whether or not the particular defendant, who was severely impaired by illegal drugs at the time of the crime, can be legally capable of harboring "malice" (a state of mind prompting one to willfully kill the victim) may be open to argument. Following the trial (in which the trial court judge will have ruled one way or the other on the applicability of the issue), opposing appellate attorneys persuasively argue in favor of their contradictory positions when presenting their appeals to the court in written briefs and with oral arguments. Ultimately, an appellate court will decide the legal controversy and a precedent may be set.

Through this decisional process, both federal and state appellate judges are making new law on a daily basis. With judges throughout the country "making law," can we expect decisions to be consistent?

> *[C]ritical legal scholars—or simply "crits"— ... contend that decisions conflict with one another because they are based on different, and controversial, moral and political ideals. Lawyers cannot give a simple answer to a question, the crits say, because the legal system, like our society at large, cannot reconcile the contradictory instincts people feel when they confront social problems.**

Does this mean the rule of law is flexible, depending on who is declaring it? If so, does that give added significance to the political appointment process underlying the selection of judges?

To assist you in understanding the way our appellate courts make and apply the law, at least one edited appellate case is presented at the end of every chapter.

initiative
An electoral process for making new statutes or changing the constitution by filing appropriate formal petitions to be voted on by legislature (and governor) or by the people. The initiative is not available in all states.

Lawmaking by the People

Many states have provisions in their constitutions that authorize citizens to place proposed new laws on ballots for direct vote by the people. These **initiatives** have resulted in laws approved by voters who had been disappointed by the inaction of their legislatures. To qualify proposed new initiatives for the ballot, proponents must obtain the signature of a specified number of registered voters. Many of the most widely publicized initiatives in recent times have occurred in California. Proposition 209 dismantled affirmative action programs in public employment, education, and contracting. Like statutes, initiatives must pass the test of constitutionality as determined by courts. You will learn more about the initiative process in Chapter 2.

TYPES AND CLASSIFICATIONS OF LAW

We have briefly considered the historical sources and types of our contemporary law. We also have identified people and institutions that continually make and update our laws to help manage our highly complex modern society. We now turn to some definitions and classifications of U.S. law that will enhance your appreciation of its pervasiveness.

Federal and State Law

We have already distinguished between common law and statutory law. Federal law consists of the U.S. Constitution, statutes enacted by Congress, treaties and presidential orders, rules promulgated by federal agencies, and decisions of federal courts. State law consists of state constitutions, statutes enacted by state legislatures, rules promulgated by state agencies, and the decisions of state appellate courts.

LEGAL FOCUS—PROBLEM

Carl Copier believes he has a right to duplicate all music and videos he purchases, regardless of any "copyright stuff." The publishing industry disagrees and wants to stop him. Would this be a question of federal or state law?

*J. Frug, "Why Courts Are Always Making Law," *Fortune*, 25 September 1989, p. 245.

The Constitution grants the federal government the responsibility to regulate copyrights. Copyright protection is granted to the authors of literary works by federal statutory law and federal courts have interpreted it. Thus, the question must be answered by reference to federal law. That is not to say that state law also might be involved. State legal systems, too, may be utilized to enforce the law. But the core question of whether Carl has a right to copy music is a topic of federal law.

LEGAL FOCUS—PROBLEM

Richard Perkins, a firefighter, demands financial compensation from a fertility clinic for impregnating his former wife by using frozen embryos that previously had been fertilized with his sperm. What law should he consult to determine whether he can recover damages for child support and emotional distress?

civil law
The branch of law dealing with individual rights and duties and their enforcement. Civil law also refers to the total system of law, embracing civil and criminal matters, that was used in the ancient Roman Empire and copied on the continent of Europe in modern times. In ancient times, the law was defined by experts and imposed from above by the emperor. Roman civil law is contrasted to English *common law*.

Liability for wrongful birth, or negligence in handling fertilized embryos, is a subject governed by state statutory and case law. This question must be answered by reference to state law. We will further study the dichotomy between federal and state law in Chapter 2.

Civil and Criminal Law

Civil law is the body of law, both federal and state, that pertains to civil or private rights enforced by civil actions. For example, the laws governing contracts are civil laws. Breach of a contract may result in a civil action for money damages to reimburse the person wronged for any financial loss suffered. **Criminal law**, in contrast to civil law, is the body of statutory law, both federal and state, that declares what conduct is criminal and prescribes penalties for its commission. For example, a statute may define murder as an unlawful killing with malice aforethought. The precise definition of "malice aforethought" changes over the years through interpretation by courts, and thus courts have the continuing task of defining what conduct is criminal.

LEGAL FOCUS—PROBLEM

David Cash, Jr., entered a restroom in a gambling casino in Las Vegas a few minutes after his friend Jeremy Strohmeyer. Cash looked over a stall and saw Strohmeyer with his hand over a small girl's mouth. After telling Strohmeyer to let her go, Cash left and did not report the incident. Strohmeyer later pled guilty to rape and murder of the child and was sentenced to life in prison. Was Cash guilty of any civil or criminal offense?

criminal law
The branch of law dealing with crimes and their punishment.

Like many states, Nevada did not have a statute that criminalized the failure to report a crime in progress. Thus, Cash was not guilty of any state crime. Crimes between private persons ("persons" being a term that includes corporations) generally do not raise questions of federal law, and Cash was not guilty of any federal crime in this case. Under common law, there generally is no duty to protect strangers, and thus Cash probably was not liable for damages to the victim's parents for his conduct under the civil law of Nevada.* The law does not always criminalize immoral acts.

Despite the David Cash example, it is common for one act or a series of acts by a person to result in both criminal and civil penalties.

LEGAL FOCUS—PROBLEM

O. J. Simpson was acquitted by jury of the crime of murdering both his former wife Nicole and Ron Goldman, a rescuer acting as a Good Samaritan. Thereafter, Simpson was sued in a civil court for the wrongful death of the victims. In the civil proceeding, the jury found Simpson responsible for the killings and liable for monetary damages. Do all criminal acts also result in civil liability for monetary damages?

private law
That body of law regulating the rights and duties that exist between private persons (including private corporations). Contract law is an example of private law.

Not all criminal acts result in civil liability. For example, the crime of firing a handgun into the air within city limits may not injure any human, and there would be no victim to pursue a civil case. But many crimes do create victims who then are able to pursue separate civil remedies, as in the *Simpson* case.

The statutory criminal law of individual states is collected in books often called Penal Codes. Civil laws, in general, are collected in books often called Civil Codes. You will learn about the very important differences between civil and criminal laws and trials in several future chapters.

Private and Public Law

public law
That body of law directly concerned with public rights and obligations, such as constitutional, administrative, criminal, and international law.

Private law is the body of law regulating the rights and duties that exist between private persons. Contract law is an example of private law. **Public law**, on the other hand, includes constitutional, administrative, criminal, and international law, all of which are more directly concerned with public rights and obligations. Criminal law is of public concern because the next victim may be you or any other member of society. Administrative law, as will be seen in Chapter 5, protects consumers and the public from abuses by private businesses. It also protects the environment.

International and Domestic Law

international law
The branch of law governing relations between and among sovereign nations.

The law of a country, from within the country's boundaries is said to be that country's domestic law. Law that concerns relations among sovereign nations is called **international law**. Reliance on some form of international law dates to the Roman Empire or before and is typically based on custom. The precedents relied upon in international law are the acts of independent governments in their relations with one another, including treaties. When treaties or conventions (agreements between nations such as the Geneva Convention concerning human rights) exist, they contain a procedural machinery to enforce their terms.

*Many members of the public were outraged at what they believed to be a serious moral offense by David Cash. Protesters marched at the University of California, Berkeley, where Cash studied nuclear engineering, and demanded his expulsion from the public university. The University of California student senate held a hearing and voted narrowly (10–9) to condemn Cash. The student body president vetoed the measure.

LEGAL FOCUS—EXAMPLE

A U.S. EA-6B Marine jet, practicing low-level flying, hit and severed a ski gondola cable in the Italian Alps. Twenty people were killed. The United States claimed exclusive jurisdiction of the case under the North Atlantic Treaty Organization (NATO), an international mutual defense pact. Italy, spurred by the victims' families, claimed the jet had violated NATO's mandated flight patterns, and it therefore did not apply. Trial and punishment therefore should take place in Italy. However, an Italian judge threw the Italian manslaughter case out of court, ruling that there was no domestic jurisdiction because of NATO. Thus, the Marine pilot, Captain Richard J. Ashby, was returned to the United States for a military trial (called court-martial) where a jury of eight Marine officers acquitted him of all charges on March 4, 1999.

Certain rules and principles are acknowledged in international relations. These understood rules pertain to such matters as territorial boundaries, use of the high seas, limitations on war, telecommunications, diplomatic and consular exchange, and the use of air space. The difficulty is that sovereign nations, by definition, exercise exclusive power or government within their boundaries and may or may not comply with these understood rules.

The United Nations (UN) is the primary mechanism that creates international law. It brings diplomacy, negotiation, and even propaganda to bear on world affairs. Through agreements, even military observers and peacekeepers can be organized. In 1995, the UN established an International War Crimes Tribunal to prosecute persons accused of war crimes in the Bosnian war. All members of the UN comply with arrest warrants issued by the Tribunal. Many accused persons have been arrested and prosecuted. Thus, criminal law also can be and is a matter of international law.

Our legal system may be expected to face global problems differently than in the past, when the disputes of nations were resolved through negotiations, the UN, or war. During World War II, Japanese Americans were interred because of unfounded fears of espionage and disloyalty, presenting domestic constitutional issues. Presently, we are faced with the reality that the nature of war has changed. Wars may be less likely to involve countries than to involve unidentified groups of people who, through acts of terrorism, fight for the political, financial, and religious issues they support. Thus, public security measures may involve restrictions on individual liberty by construction of fences or walls with temporary or permanent exclusion of citizens from public places. Electronic eavesdropping, by court authorization, already is being dramatically increased because it is an effective weapon against terrorists and criminals. Airport security continues to increase—and passengers are subject to warrantless searches. Many searches are based on stereotypes of personal appearances and behavior. Freedom of speech not withstanding, jokingly mentioning a bomb while on or near an airplane is a criminal offense. Thus, international dangers affect both international and domestic law.

Procedural and Substantive Law

procedural law General principles and detailed rules that define the methods of administering substantive law.

Procedural law consists of all the rules or mechanisms, for processing civil and criminal and administrative matters through the applicable federal or state system. Some cynics call it "lawyers' law" since its complexities and technicalities provide employment for attorneys.

Procedural law may dictate the dates and time limits within which papers must be filed, the size of paper to be used by attorneys, the size of print to be used, what information must be contained in legal papers, how witnesses and parties can be orally examined before trial, what evidence may be offered to the jury, what actions an agency must take before issuing a new rule or regulation, and so on.

It is noteworthy that a separate body of procedural law governs the mechanics of processing appeals, that procedural law for civil cases differs from that for criminal cases, and that administrative agencies can each have their own procedural law. In short, the procedural law is as complex as it is vast, and cases that might have been won on their merits have been lost because of bad decisions regarding the applicable procedural law. A frequent type of attorney malpractice (professional negligence) involves procedural law mistakes, such as missing a critical deadline. If an attorney fails to comply with the civil procedural law, the court may, as a penalty, dismiss the case, with the result that the attorney's client loses. If a prosecutor fails to comply with the criminal procedural law, the court may dismiss the case and set the defendant free. Some of you may already have experienced this happy event when you went to court to challenge a citation for a traffic infraction. Because the citing officer was too busy with other duties and did not appear to testify, your case was dismissed.

Procedural law is so important that it receives basic constitutional protection in the Sixth Amendment to the U.S. Constitution (made applicable to the states by the Fourteenth Amendment, as explained in Chapter 2). The Sixth Amendment, as interpreted by the U.S. Supreme Court, requires that the government provide each citizen with procedural due process in criminal proceedings, including the right to have the advice of an attorney even if the accused is indigent, the right to confront accusers in a speedy and public trial by an impartial jury, and the right to be heard and to present a defense.

LEGAL FOCUS—PROBLEM

In 1985, Charles Ng was charged with torturing and murdering a dozen people in a California cabin where they had been kept as sex slaves. Ng fled to Canada, where he was arrested. But Canada refused to return him to California because California has a death penalty. After six years, the Canadian Supreme Court ruled that Ng must be extradited to the United States to stand trial. Meanwhile, the police had inadvertently destroyed some bullets and blood samples needed in the case. One key witness had died. Ng continued to use the procedural laws to challenge every attorney appointed for him and every judge assigned to preside over the trial. The files in the case were reported to weigh about six tons—which hopefully is an exaggeration. On February 24, 1999, he was found guilty of eleven murders and sentenced to death, marking with that date commencement of the appeals process. The exhaustion of appeals takes several more years. Was Ng deprived of his right to a speedy trial?

Charles Ng was not deprived of his right to a speedy trial. He waived his right to a speedy trial, believing, no doubt, that the passage of time was in his best interest. The public has no constitutional right to a speedy trial of criminal defendants. This case symbolizes a low point in the history of the procedural law.

substantive law General principles and detailed rules that define legal rights and duties.

Substantive law, in contrast to procedural law, defines duties, establishes rights, and prohibits wrongs. Substantive law prohibits murder, requires a real estate agent to be licensed, and imposes speed limits and registration requirements on automobile drivers. Earlier, it was observed that in 1998 Nevada had no law criminalizing inaction, and therefore David Cash, Jr., was not guilty of a crime for failing to render assistance to the young girl murdered by Jeremy Strohmeyer. Such conduct is a crime in some states under their criminal substantive laws. The issue of which state's law should apply to Cash, a California resident, and the time limits within which he must be prosecuted, are questions of the procedural law.

Subject Matter Classification

Law often is classified on the basis of subject matter. Consider these representative distinct categories of law: corporate, admiralty, business, real estate, intellectual property, family, environmental, constitutional, labor, probate, corporate securities, and immigration. There are dozens of other legal specialties, and the list keeps growing. For example, a recent addition is elder law, pertaining to unique rights and duties of senior citizens.

LEGAL FOCUS—PROBLEM

Sam Kroger, seventy-five years of age and a resident of Sun City, Arizona, uses his golf cart for trips to the store and a recreation center. Most residents of this retirement community also rely on golf carts for transportation. But cars also use the roads and accidents happen. Should Kroger be required by law to equip his golf cart with seat belts, turn signals, a windshield, and mirrors?

Under federal law, Sam Kroger is required to equip his golf cart as indicated. The National Highway Traffic Safety Administration (an administrative agency) has adopted rules to that effect, which some compare to similar state laws requiring motorcycle riders to wear helmets. Is it sufficient that a proposed law, in all likelihood, will protect family members from some perceived harm? Or should the potential good of a proposed law be balanced against its potential intrusiveness? But good, bad, or indifferent, golf carts are motor vehicles and, when on public streets, are subject to regulation like other vehicles.

THE RELATIONSHIP BETWEEN LAW AND ETHICS

To state the obvious, this textbook is about the law and that is an ambitious undertaking. It is ambitious because law is about almost everything. Most of all, the law is about people and the limitations and protections on and of their choices. But the law is not the sole source of community standards or even consequences regarding these choices. It is inevitable that the study of law raises questions about the fairness of a rule of law or the lack of a rule in situations in which you believe there should be law. These questions often rise from the differences between law and your moral beliefs. Although those who create law strive for fairness and justice, it is not surprising that the goal is not always met. It is thus important to be aware of ethics and morals as a separate but related topic when considering guidelines and restraints on behavior.

We also hope that your study of law will aid you in decision making. Is an action legal? What are the legal consequences of stated behaviors? What should you do? Concern about whether a decision is morally or ethically correct also should be an important part of decision making. Is an action ethically correct? Which choice is the morally correct choice? We thus believe a brief discussion of ethics is worthwhile to aid in developing your decision-making ability. As an educated person, you should be prepared to make, articulate, and defend the moral correctness of your decisions. Stating that an action is legally correct is usually not enough. Thus, it is helpful to define some terms and provide a few examples of ethical decision-making approaches used to assist people in choosing a correct or right action.

Part of one chapter in a book cannot teach a person to be ethical, but a conversation about ethics can

- Identify the nature of ethics;
- Provide some useful theories and tools for personal ethical decision making;
- Provide a framework for solving inevitable conflict, which results from differing moral standards and application abilities; and
- Provide information to help one evaluate the professional integrity of advisors and service providers (this discussion is part of Chapter 4).

What Are Ethics?

ethics
Standards of fair and honest conduct applied to social behavior.

The term **ethics** has several common meanings. The first is "the study of the general nature of morals and of the specific moral choices to be made by the individual in relationships with others; the philosophy of morals." This also is called "moral philosophy." A second meaning is "the rules or standards governing the conduct of the member of a profession, for example, the legal profession." Ethics is about doing the right thing when there is a sacrifice to be made. What we mean by sacrifice is that ethical behavior often entails overriding our self-interest in favor of preserving order in our society.

Why Study Ethics?

Moral issues feature again and again in the complex problems that we face in the world today. In a global economy with limited resources and unlimited consumer needs, we must grapple with issues of equitable distribution of products and services. As e-communication has become ubiquitous, we are now faced with the challenge of frequently interacting with people far removed from our culture, experience, and accessibility.

morals
Values concerning right and wrong.

There are many obstacles to making sound ethical decisions. Faulty reasoning, false premises, hidden values, unexamined beliefs, and double standards threaten the satisfactory conclusion to conflicts both complex and straightforward. Doing the right thing requires the disentanglement of a sometimes-complex web of interrelated values and viewpoints. Recognition and a more than cursory understanding of different theoretical perspectives are essential.

moral problem solving
Conflict-resolution process aimed at solving conflicts involving moral dilemmas through communication, education, and negotiation. The broad term describes interrelational rather than individual process.

Most of our discussion on ethics will focus on the nature of **morals** and **moral problem solving**. However, one should be aware that the law requires lawyers and judges to obey a code of conduct (**code of ethics**) in addition to, distinct from, and even sometimes at odds with generally applicable standards of conduct. In addition, effective management of one's affairs, both personal and commercial, may require the assistance of other professional advisors, such as accountants, insurance agents, and financial planners. As professionals, they, too, promise to conduct themselves according to a code of professional ethics. All professionals are required to vow to follow the rules of conduct of their respective professions. The discussions of legal ethics in this chapter and in Chapter 4 will serve as a guide to evaluating the professional integrity of the advisors you may hire one day.

code of ethics
A systematic statement of agreed-on moral rules for a profession, business, or group.

The following incident illustrates an important ethical dilemma. We will refer to it in developing the ability to formulate a logical reasoning process for moral problem solving.

LEGAL FOCUS—PROBLEM

A young woman, Kitty Genovese, returns from work just after 3:00 A.M. to a typical street in Queens, New York. She parks her car and begins the 100-foot walk to her apartment building. Concerned about a man standing between her path and the apartment building, she changes course and heads in the opposite direction. She was right to be concerned; he grabs her. She screams. No fewer than thirty-eight neighbors turn on their lights and open their windows. Again she screams. "He stabbed me!" "Help!" An observer shouts, "Leave the girl alone," and the attacker walks away. Then the lights all go out and windows are slammed shut. While the victim staggers to reach the nearest apartment building, the attacker returns and stabs her again. The victim yells, "I'm dying." The commotion again gets the attention of the apartment dwellers and again the attacker leaves. Again the lights go out and the windows close. The victim crawls toward the apartment house as the attacker returns again one last time to stab and kill her.

During that half hour, Kitty Genovese was stabbed three times. Had a call been made to police after the first attack, perhaps she could have been saved. (Actually, a call was made some thirty minutes after the first attack, but it was too late.)

Although the law often provides instructions for community behavior, no New York law required any witness to report the crime to police. No New York law required any bystander to come to the young woman's aid. Absent some relationship with the woman, no one had a legal obligation to save her life. But is there a moral obligation to help an innocent victim? Although this incident occurred many years ago, it continues to be addressed in books, articles, and Web sites. Questions focus on why the neighbors did not act.

For purposes of this text, the killing of Kitty Genovese provides a real-life situation for learning how to apply different standards of ethical behavior and reason through a moral dilemma.

The Nature of Ethical Inquiry

Ethical inquiry seeks to isolate the collection of moral judgments that society has made to govern behavior and to make moral judgments in daily life, in the political process, and in lawmaking.

The study of ethics is concerned not only with identification of societal values but with thinking logically about ethical challenges and developing practical approaches to moral problem solving. Other disciplines also are concerned with discovering society's moral precepts. For example, sociology and anthropology each study cultural norms.

Ethics departs from the other disciplines because ethics has another dimension. Whereas sociology and anthropology focus on identifying and accounting for societal norms, ethics goes beyond reporting. Ethics is concerned with value identification, moral problem solving, and behavior. Ethics entails action; it is not just a topic to mull or debate. In short, ethics is an applied science.

Whereas anthropology and sociology would ask whether Americans believe abortion is wrong, ethics is concerned with the question itself: Is abortion wrong? Is abortion always wrong? Should abortion be banned? As a technical matter, ethics is prescriptive ("Thou shall not kill"). Anthropology and sociology are descriptive ("There is a low homicide rate in Ireland").

The Object of Ethics

The object of ethics is to determine the right thing to do. This entails perceiving ethical distinctions and making difficult ethical choices. Making ethical choices requires clear thinking. Ethicists refer to this thinking process as **moral reasoning**. Ethics is concerned with the ability to discern right and wrong, to separate the ethical questions from the facts, and to scrupulously apply the moral standard to the circumstances. Moral reasoning is a rational approach to moral problem solving, and it can be learned.

moral reasoning
A rational thought process directed at testing whether action is right or wrong. The conclusion is a determination of moral responsibility or culpability.

Ethical Standards

Ethics are standards of fair and honest conduct. These standards guide our behavior. They are the indications of what we must do to remain in good standing as members of a group.

Ethical standards are the basis for moral judgment and personal action. They are derived from principles of right and wrong, from religious and philosophical beliefs concerning the nature of good and evil. Courts or legislatures do not create ethical standards; these standards come from life. However, the ability to know right from wrong is not innate; it must be learned.

Our family, teachers, and peers bequeath moral standards to us. They are transferred to us though immersion in society. We perceive values through observation and imitation.

At first, we conform to moral standards because there are consequences: admonishment, punishment, and ridicule. As we mature, we internalize the moral instruction of those around us. As we become more experienced with the consequences of our behavior, we decide what to believe in. We adopt some beliefs and reject others. The collection of beliefs we adopt becomes our own personal philosophy.

Ethical standards are often subjective. Since our personal philosophy is based on our unique circumstances and experiences, our ethical standards differ from those of our neighbors in some respects. Of course, universal acceptance of certain standards determines membership in a particular group.

Ethical schools and resources are available for guidance in determining ethical standards. Inquiry into the nature of "the good" is an age-old pursuit. Although there are many ethical schools of thought, our inquiry will be limited to two fundamental approaches. One approach defines ethical behavior as conforming to a set of duties. The other approach determines what is ethical or good by the consequences of any given action. We examine each of these approaches in the following section.

Duty-Based Ethics

LEGAL FOCUS—PROBLEM

Is it wrong to cheat on an examination? Assume that no one will ever know you cheated and that cheating will help you get into a good college. Further assume that you intend to devote yourself after college to the service of others.

This question weighs the "end or consequences" of the action against the "means" used to attain the end. With **duty-based ethics**, if you believe that you have an ethical duty not to cheat or lie, these acts can never be justified by the consequences. This is true even if the consequences are charitable or desirable. In American culture, the dominant duty-based ethical standards come from religious sources.

duty-based ethics
The doctrine that actions are morally correct if they comply with existing obligations owed another or ourselves.

Religious Ethics

The Western religious tradition—more specifically, the Judeo-Christian religious tradition—is rooted in the belief that certain absolute truths have been revealed through the prophets, the Torah, the Bible, and religious institutions. The "Thou shalt nots" of the Ten Commandments and Christ's instructions to help and care for others ("Love thy neighbor as thyself") are examples. These teachings establish for those who believe in them an absolute ethical duty. It is not the consequences of an act, but the nature of the act itself, that determines whether it is ethical.

LEGAL FOCUS—EXAMPLE

Leah Jordan decides to rob the rich to help the poor, like the English legend of Robin Hood. She has acted unethically despite her humane motive. She has "sinned" because stealing violates the Seventh Commandment ("Thou shalt not steal").

Religious ethical standards are absolute. When an act is prohibited by religious teachings, it is unethical. It should not be done, regardless of the consequences. Telling a lie for the sake of gaining a promotion is unethical—even if no one is harmed by the lie and the liar's future seems more promising.

Religious ethical standards, however, also involve an element of compassion. Therefore, although it might be profitable for a business to fire unproductive employees, those employees or their families may suffer. This potential suffering is given much weight by the decision maker. A compassionate manager or employer might decide to keep the employee. Another way to increase profits might be sought.

The Golden Rule ("Do unto others as you would have them do unto you") also expects compassionate treatment of others to a certain extent. This rule has been adopted in some form by most religions.

Kant and Duty-Based Ethics

A duty-based approach to ethics not expressly based on religion is characteristic of the philosophy of Immanuel Kant (1724–1804). Kant identified some general guiding principles of moral behavior. He believed in the fundamental worth of human beings and that each person was endowed with moral integrity and the capacity to reason and conduct their affairs rationally without resort to religious precept.

Kantian ethical reasoning gives philosophical weight to the Golden Rule. But the Golden Rule merely urges us to "do unto to others as we would have them do unto us." Kant's approach forces us to look at the larger picture and asks everyone to treat others as free individuals equal to everyone else. Thus, we have the duty to treat everyone with dignity and the right to expect such treatment from others. What would society be like if everybody acted as we did? Would it be positive or negative? Kant's theory forces us to look at and evaluate, from an objective point of view, social goals as well as our personal desires and welfare when considering our behavior.

The central premise in Kantian ethics is that the morality of conduct depends on the guiding principle, not on the results or consequences of the conduct. One must follow the guiding principle no matter what the circumstance. Kant called these no-matter-what principles *categorical imperatives*. They are absolute rules.

LEGAL FOCUS—EXAMPLE

You are thinking about whether to cheat on an examination. If you agree with Kant's categorical imperative, you will decide not to cheat because if everyone cheats, the examination is meaningless. Similarly, you would not cut in line to purchase a ticket for a music concert because if everyone else cut in line, the line would disappear and chaos would result.

The strength of Kant's duty theory lies in its relative simplicity. The Kantian model is easily applied. Determining the absolute rule and applying it to the real-world situation is all that is required to identify ethical conduct. Predictions about how others will be affected by one's actions are not necessary, although consequences do play an important role in defining the nature of conduct and formulating the categorical rule. Conduct is evaluated based on an unyielding rule: Either the rule was followed or it was not. The effect of conduct is not determinative when evaluating the moral correctness of a specific action.

Problems with Duty-Based Ethics

The efficacy of duty-based ethics is also its major shortcoming. Duty-based theory does not give clear guidance on resolving complex ethical dilemmas. Ethical decision making may involve fulfilling not just one ethical responsibility but several. When one ethical duty conflicts with another, you have to decide which is the most fundamental and act accordingly. Duty-based ethics provides no mechanism for prioritizing conflicting duties.

Duty-based ethics has other problems. There can be disagreements about which duties exist. Different religions, while often agreeing on many things, disagree fundamentally on others. Kant's formulas are not precise. Are there limits to obligations? If so, what are those limits? Is it morally correct to kill in order to survive? Sometimes, applying religious or Kantian ethics is difficult.

LEGAL FOCUS—PROBLEM

A business executive negotiating with another firm's representatives may feel it necessary to stretch the truth or hold back information. The reason may be to get the best deal for the executive's employer. Is this a violation of the religious teaching that one should not lie or of Kant's categorical imperative?

Yes, it is probably unethical in both religious and Kantian terms. Remember, however, that the executive also owes an ethical duty to his or her employer to make decisions that are profitable. Assume that the executive knows that, unless the deal is made, the employer will have to lay off several long-time employees. These employees depend on the firm for food on their table. Is "stretching the truth" consistent with the religious ethical duty to be compassionate toward others? Is it consistent with the Kantian imperative to act only as we would have all others act?

The executive may conclude that the ethical duty to be fully honest is more fundamental than the duty owed the business. This decision may include a personal cost, such as the loss of a raise, which may affect the executive's family. Alternatively, the executive might decide that the ethical duty owed to the business and its employees is the more fundamental one. The example illustrates that often ethical decisions are not clear-cut. Decisions involve choices, not between good and bad alternatives but between good and less good alternatives.

utilitarianism
An ethical doctrine holding that determining right conduct is based on consequences; that the purpose of the behavior should be the greatest happiness of the greatest number.

Utilitarianism

"Thou shalt act so as to generate the greatest good for the greatest number." This is a paraphrase of the major premise of **utilitarianism**. This philosophical theory was first developed by Jeremy Bentham (1748–1832). In contrast to duty-based moral theory, utilitarianism is outcome oriented. It focuses on the consequences of an action. It does not focus on the nature of the action itself or on any set of preestablished moral values or religious beliefs.

Right and Wrong in Utilitarianism

Under a utilitarian model of ethics, an action is morally correct or right when, among people it affects, it produces the greatest amount of good for the greatest number of people. When an action affects the majority adversely, it is morally wrong. Applying the utilitarian theory thus requires (1) a determination of the alternate actions available in a given situation; (2) a determination of who will be affected by these actions; (3) an assessment, or cost-benefit analysis, of the negative and positive effects of each alternative action on these individuals; and (4) a choice among the alternatives that will produce the maximum societal utility.

The major strength of utilitarian ethics is its flexible application. Duty-based ethics admits no exceptions or justifications for deviation from the moral standard. In contrast, utilitarians reject the notion that certain conduct is *always* right or *always* wrong. For example, utilitarians would deny that stealing is *always* wrong. Utilitarians consider the circumstances. A balancing of the harms resulting from unequivocal application of the moral standard is performed. Justifiable deviations are identified. Stealing would be morally acceptable if more good than harm would result from the theft. If a single mother of four, unemployed and starving, stole a loaf of bread from a supermarket, utilitarians would conclude that the theft was justified because five lives would be saved from starvation as weighed against the lost revenue (approximately $2.50) to the supermarket.

Another advantage of utilitarianism over absolutism is that utilitarianism may be applied in situations in which moral standards collide. Since the practical application of the absolute duty approach offers no scheme for resolving inevitable conflict among moral standards, the conflict is irresolvable under that model.

In situations that require a choice among competing moral values, the ranking of moral values is predicated on the consequences of alternative actions. The action resulting in the greatest social benefit or the least cost to society is deemed to be the proper course. Where the practical application of duty-based ethics would produce a moral predicament, utilitarian application produces a solution, however imperfect.

Problems with Utilitarianism

Utilitarianism also suffers from some problems. An accurate calculation of overall welfare, happiness, or utility requires knowledge of what the actual consequences, both negative and positive, of a given decision will be. Rarely, if ever, can all possibilities of a decision be accurately predicted. This is especially true with decisions that affect millions of people.

It is difficult to measure good and bad. What are your values? The cost-benefit method of measuring good and bad still requires the decision maker to assign values to expected outcomes. It isn't easy.

Another problem with utilitarianism is that it usually involves winners and losers. It is sometimes impossible to satisfy everyone with a policy action based on utility.

LEGAL FOCUS—PROBLEM

Tim Johnson, a manufacturer, owns many manufacturing plants. One of the plants is much older than the others. Equipment at the old plant is outdated and inefficient. The costs of production at the plant are twice that of any of Johnson's other plants. The product price cannot be increased because of competition. What should Johnson do about the plant?

In a utilitarian analysis of the problem, the costs of closing the plant, including the financial burden of laid-off employees, is weighed against the benefits of closing the plant. Benefits include the future financial security of the firm and the employees who retain their jobs at the other plants. If Johnson decides the issue from a utilitarianism perspective, he may close the plant. Closing the plant will yield the greatest benefit for the largest number of people. The winners are those helped by the decision. The losers are the workers now unemployed at the old plant.

situational ethics The term used disparagingly to describe an "end-justifies-the-means" maxim supplanting duty or obligation.

Utilitarianism is criticized because it is an objective, calculated approach to a problem. It reduces human beings to plus and minus signs on a cost-benefit worksheet. Utilitarian reasoning also has been used to "justify" human costs that many find unacceptable.

The strongest criticism of utilitarian theory is that an end-justifies-the-means maxim supplants the moral code. **Situational ethics** is a term often used disparagingly to describe such reasoning. In other words, ethical principle is minimized in favor of net social gain.

LEGAL FOCUS—PROBLEM

Is the execution of an innocent man ever justified? Consider the following hypothetical: An African American man is convicted of the rape and murder of a white woman in the Deep South. Should the governor commute the sentence of this death row inmate if he is convinced of the man's innocence?

Utilitarians would say no, if allowing the convict to be put to death would prevent a riot by the white community that likely would result in the killing of innocent African Americans. Here, execution of an innocent man would be justified under utilitarian theory because society's interest in saving more than one life (the predicted killing of innocent African Americans) trumps the rights of the individual.

There are other theories of moral responsibility, but all of them involve making difficult choices in a world in which information is imperfect. Ethical choices involve choosing between self-interest and perceived ethical obligations.

Deductive logic A method of logical reasoning from two or more propositions to a conclusion. Inferences are drawn from a general premise to a specific premise. The conclusion is valid if the propositions on which the conclusion is based are true.

Moral Reasoning

An important learning objective of this section is to help you develop a framework for moral problem solving. The following discussion will help you organize your thinking about what your personal philosophy is and how to apply it in an orderly fashion to circumstances for which you have little or no experience.

We present a rational approach to evaluating situations, but not the answers. We offer a method, not a conclusion. It is a compass with directions, not a roadmap.

Moral reasoning is a process of testing whether a given action is right or wrong. It also determines moral responsibility or culpability. It uses deductive logic. **Deductive logic** is a method of logical reasoning from two or more propositions to a conclusion. Inferences are drawn from a general premise to a specific premise. The argument is sound if the propositions on which the conclusion is based are true and if the inferences are valid.

syllogism A pattern of deductive logic that contains a major or general premise, a minor or specific premise, and a conclusion, always in that order. The conclusion follows from the premises but is not a premise itself.

Deduction may be understood as a pattern or **syllogism**. Syllogisms help to organize thinking so that a valid conclusion is reached. Syllogisms help to identify incorrect premises and flawed thinking. Moral reasoning follows the following pattern:

Proposition One	(general premise)
Proposition Two	(specific, factual, or situational premise)
Conclusion	(moral determination)

The general premise is the moral–ethical standard. The situational premise is the conduct ("what happened" or "what contemplated conduct") being scrutinized. The conclusion is the product of applying the ethical standard to the conduct. It is the evaluation as to whether conduct was proper or improper as measured against the moral standard.

Consider the *Kitty Genovese* case, discussed earlier, under the utilitarian model and compare it with the Kantian model. Under the utilitarian model, failing to come to the rescue could be morally justified.

General premise	One should come to the rescue of helpless living beings unless doing so would cause greater harm in the community.
Factual premise	Coming to the rescue of a helpless woman (Kitty Genovese) while her vicious attacker was stabbing her could have resulted in a multiple murder—greater harm. (*Note:* Predicting a likely result—a multiple murder—of the asserted failure to act, here a failure to come to the rescue—is necessary to reach a conclusion in utilitarian analysis.)
Moral determination	Failing to come to the rescue of Kitty Genovese was morally proper since coming to her aid could have meant more people would have been murdered.

Under duty-based models, failing to come to the rescue of Kitty Genovese is not morally acceptable.

General premise	Moral people must always come to the rescue of a helpless living being.
Factual premise	Kitty Genovese was helpless at the hands of her vicious attacker.
Moral determination	Since no one who witnessed the attack of Kitty Genovese, a helpless living being, came to her rescue, no witness acted morally.

Note that the different conclusions under the utilitarian and duty-based models are the result of the variation in the general premise, not a variation in the logical process. The pattern of reasoning remains the same; only the standard changed. To summarize, moral reasoning is a deductive process that follows the same pattern regardless of which ethical standard is applied: Determine the moral standard (general premise). Apply the moral standard to the situation (factual premise). Decide whether action was right or wrong.

Individuals are not born with the ability to understand and apply moral standards. People need to learn how to translate their personal philosophy into action. It requires inquiry, comparison, and reflection. It takes practice.

There are pitfalls to understanding ethics in general and moral problem solving in particular. Much of the terminology of ethics is used interchangeably. For example, the terms *morals* and *ethics* often are used synonymously. They are distinguishable, however. *Morals* are precepts or values held as beliefs. In contrast, *ethics* are the realization of those beliefs as standards of conduct or as evidenced by an act or failure to act.

Sometimes it is unclear whether one is referring to the moral standard (the rule) or the moral conclusion (the result of applying the standard to the situation). The two are distinct and especially so when one learns how to separate the steps of the moral reasoning process.

For learning purposes, it is critical to watch your language. For clarity, use vocabulary to distinguish conceptually distinct phases of the moral reasoning process and label the component terms carefully. For example, the statement "That's immoral" is an assertion that could mean the behavior is wrong. But, by what standard? It may not be a final conclusion, either. The behavior may be excused or justified.

Translating Moral Philosophy into Action

The process of moral problem solving must be broken down, step by step.

Step One First, you must break down the moral reasoning process. Separate facts from the moral premise (ethical rule or standard) and the moral premise from the moral judgment (application of the ethical rule). Be aware that moral standards are often implicit. Distinguishing among statements is helpful in separating the standard from the facts of the situation. Some statements are matters of fact. They do not assert a value judgment. Other statements are value laden.

Statements that reflect no value judgment are objective. They are what is so. These statements are referred to as positive or **nonnormative statements**.

nonnormative statements Statements that reflect no value judgment.

Statements that reflect what should be or how one should act are called **normative statements**. They tell what someone deems socially acceptable. The statement is subjective.

normative statements Statements that reflect what should be or how one should act.

Practice in developing the ability to recognize one's own values and those of others begins with distinguishing between normative and nonnormative statements. Again, it helps to watch your language and keep phases of the moral reasoning process separate.

Nonnormative Statements

- This legislative session, Congress lowered taxes.
- The new state building has more offices than the older one.

Normative Statements

- Lowering taxes is bad because it will fuel inflation.
- Producing oil is more important than protecting the environment.
- It was not necessary to build a new state building.

It is not always easy to recognize the difference between normative and nonnormative statements. One clue is that normative statements are asserted in a way that indicates both the conclusion and a justification or reason for the conclusion. The reason could be express or implied.

If we change the statement "Lowering taxes is bad because it will fuel inflation," to simply "Lowering taxes is bad," we are implying that if asked, we can provide some justification for the statement.

Nonnormative statements are matters of fact. They do not beg for reasons to validate their accuracy.

Another way to tell whether a sentence is normative or nonnormative is to ask, "Does it tell how? Why? Why not?" If the statement expressly or impliedly answers these questions, then it is probably normative.

Step Two Once you have isolated the moral standard, gather all relevant facts—just the facts. What happened? When? Where? Who? Be sure you have enough facts to determine the moral standard. It is critical to be accurate and complete, to use only relevant facts, and to separate the facts from the moral standard.

Step Three Using deductive logic, apply the moral standard to the facts of the situation. The result will be the moral determination.

This three-step process will result in a rational outcome, although it will not resolve all ethical dilemmas. Different people have differing moral philosophies and varying abilities to solve moral problems. However, this process will help you resolve moral conflicts in a coherent, rational way. Now you are prepared to articulate, defend, and negotiate for your moral conclusion. Let the moral problem-solving process begin.

Distinguishing between Laws and Moral Values

To answer the question of whether an action is legal does not necessarily answer the question of whether it is ethical. Not all moral standards are formalized or codified. Therefore, discerning between legal duties and moral obligations will simplify the moral problem-solving process.

positive law
The rules members of a society are obliged to obey to avoid punishment or penalty imposed by the government.

Many ethical decisions are made for us by our laws. In most cases, law reflects many of a society's ethical values. Virtually all of what you will read in this text involves **positive law**, sometimes called *black-letter law*. Positive law tells individuals which actions are prohibited. The law gives warning that society (through government) will punish the violators. Nonetheless, simply obeying the law does not fulfill all ethical obligations. In the interest of preserving personal freedom, as well as for practical reasons, the law does not—and cannot—make all ethical requirements legal requirements.

In all societies, ethics and the law go hand in hand. Law can never operate in a vacuum. It cannot be a series of rules imposed on society from outside the society. The law must reflect a society's customs and values. It must enforce principles of behavior that society thinks right and just. Law is thus an expression of the social forces at work in the society of which it is a part.

Criminal responsibility and civil liability imply failure to conform to a standard of conduct. Obviously, criminal responsibility and civil liability are not synonymous, and they are not coextensive with moral accountability. Significantly, moral accountability requires us to go beyond what the law requires.

In addition, the underlying rationale for criminal laws, civil laws, and moral standards and the consequences for violating or breaching them vary in important ways.

culpability
Behavior that is sufficiently wrongful to be at fault or to be responsible for proscribed conduct.

Criminal responsibility and civil liability are legal terms describing a duty to behave or refrain from conduct the failure of which results in a penalty. Criminal responsibility is concerned with the behavior of the criminal. The penalty for criminal conduct generally involves curtailment of basic civil liberties: loss of life (death sentence), liberty (prison time), and property (fines). Criminal behavior (**culpability**) also results in contempt for the wrongdoer. The primary justification for punishing criminals is to vindicate society's norms. Some argue that the purpose of such punishment is deterrence; some call it retribution; some believe the goal is (or should be) rehabilitation.

Civil liability is concerned with the victim. The object of civil liability is to put victims back in the position they were in before the wrongful act, or as nearly as possible. A determination that a person is liable necessitates compensation for the victim, usually in the form of monetary payment. In theory, the law's focus is on paying the victim back rather than on reproving the wrongdoer.

A moral breach may involve contempt, banishment, excommunication, or isolation. It may look and feel like punishment, but it does not entail imposition of penalty by the government.

USING COURT CASES

Although case law is but one source of American law, it has a special place in the study of law. Court cases are about the actual legal problems of people. Each case is an individual drama, in which parties seek help, justice, principles, and power. By reading cases, a student can see the legal problems of people and how the law is used to resolve these problems.

At the conclusion of each text chapter, we present a case to provide you with a real-life illustration of how courts interpret and apply the law. Some of the end-of-chapter problems are based on actual legal disputes. This section offers a brief introduction to case citations, the legal "shorthand" used to identify court cases.

Although the court system is discussed in detail in Chapter 3, one broad distinction is important. There are two types of courts, trial and appellate. In a trial court, two parties each present their version of the facts of a legal dispute and receive a decision or ruling. Appellate courts exist to review the actions of lower courts (trial or lower appellate courts) and to correct their mistakes of law.

Federal Court Decisions

Federal trial court decisions are published in West's *Federal Supplement* (F.Supp.). Opinions from the circuit courts of appeal are reported in West's *Federal Reporter* (F. or F.2d). Opinions from the U.S. Supreme Court are reported in West's *Supreme Court Reporter* (S.Ct.), the *United States Reports* (U.S.), the *Lawyers' Edition of the Supreme Court Reports* (L.Ed.), and other publications.

The *United States Reports* is the official edition of all decisions of the U.S. Supreme Court for which there are written opinions. Published by the federal government, the series includes reports of Supreme Court cases dating from 1791. Sample citations for federal court decisions are listed and explained in Exhibit 1.1.

State Court Decisions

Most state trial court decisions are not published. Usually, decisions from the state trial courts are filed in the office of the clerk of the court. The court clerk's job includes keeping court records and making the decisions of the court available for public inspection.

Written decisions of the state appellate courts, in contrast, are published and distributed. The reported appellate decisions are published in volumes called *Reports*. They are numbered consecutively.

State court appellate opinions also appear in regional units of the National Reporter System, published by West Publishing Company. Most libraries have the West reporters because they are published quickly and are distributed more widely than the state-published reports. Many states have eliminated their own reporters and use West's National Reporter System. The National Reporter System divides the states into the following geographic areas: Atlantic (A. or A.2d), South Eastern (S.E. or S.E.2d), South Western (S.W. or S.W.2d), North Western (N.W. or N.W.2d), North Eastern (N.E. or N.E.2d), Southern (So. or So.2d), and Pacific (P. or P.2d).

After appellate decisions have been published, they normally are referred to with the following information:

1. The name of the case
2. The volume, name, and page of the state's official reporter (if different from West's National Reporter System)
3. The volume, unit, and page number of the National Reporter
4. The volume, name, and page number of any other selected reporter

This information makes up what is called the **citation**. Citing a reporter by volume number, name, and page number, in that order, is common to all citations.

citation, legal
Abbreviated reference to a variety of legal authorities, including court cases.

EXHIBIT 1.1 National Reporter System—State/Federal

State Courts*

398 MASS. 254, 496 N.E.2d 827 (1986)

N.E. is the abbreviation for West's publication of state court decisions rendered in the northeastern region of the National Reporter System. *2d* indicates that this case was included in the second series of those reports.

MASS. is an abbreviation for *Massachusetts Reports*, Massachusetts' official reports of the decisions of its highest court, the supreme judicial court, which is comparable to other states' supreme courts.

The numbers 398 and 496 refer to reporter's volumes. The numbers 254 and 827 refer to the first pages in those volumes on which this case can be found.

59 Cal. 2d 428, 380 P.2d 644, 30 Cal. Rptr. 4 (1963)

Cal. Rptr. is the abbreviation for West's unofficial reports—titled *California Reporter*—of the decisions of California courts.

Cal. is an abbreviation for *California Reports*. This is the official state publication for the decisions of the highest California court, the state supreme court.

Federal Courts

477 U.S. 131, 106 S.Ct. 2240, 91 L.Ed.2d 110 (1986)

S.Ct. is an abbreviation for the *Supreme Court Reporter*, part of the West Publishing Company's National Reporter System, *L.Ed.* is an abbreviation for Lawyer's Editions *U.S. Supreme Court Reports*. Both of these publications are private unofficial reports of U.S. Supreme Court decisions.

U.S. is an abbreviation for the *United States Reports*. This is the official federal publication for the decisions of the highest U.S. court, the Supreme Court.

792 F.2d 1423 (9th Cir. 1986)

9th Cir. is an abbreviation denoting that this case was decided in the U.S. Court of Appeals for the Ninth Circuit.

F. is an abbreviation for *Federal Reporter*, a part of the West Publishing Company's National Reporter System. This publication reports cases from the U.S. Court of Appeal.

352 F.Supp. 1105 (S.D.N.Y. 1972)

S.D.N.Y. is an abbreviation indicating that the U.S. District Circuit for the Southern District of New York decided this case.

F.Supp. is an abbreviation for *Federal Supplement*, a part of the West Publishing National Reporter System. This publication reports cases from the U.S. district courts.

* The case names (for example, Roe v. Wade), have been deleted from these citations to emphasize the publications. It should be kept in mind, however, that the name of a case is as important as the specific page numbers in the volumes in which it is found. If a citation is incorrect, the correct citation may be found in a publication's index of case names. The date of a case is also important, both to provide a check on error in citations and because a recent case is likely to have more value as an authority than earlier cases.

When more than one reporter is cited for the same case, each reference is called a *parallel citation*. For example, consider the following case: *Quality Motors, Inc. v. Hays*, 216 Ark. 264, 225 S.W.2d 326 (1949). The opinion in this case can be found in volume 216 of the *Arkansas Reports* on page 264. The parallel citation is to volume 225 of the *South Western Reporter*, second series, page 326.

In cases presented in the text, we provide the citation, the name of the court hearing the case, and the year of the court's decision. A few of the states—including those with more than one appellate court, such as California, Illinois, and New York—have more than one reporter for the state court opinions. Sample citations are listed and explained in Exhibit 1.1.

Reading Court Cases

The cases in this text have been reworded and condensed from the full text of the courts' opinions. For those wishing to review court cases for future research projects or to gain additional information, the following sections will help you to read and understand case law.

Case Titles

In the title of a case, such as *Adams v. Jones*, the *v.* or *vs.* stands for versus, which means "against." If the case is at the trial court level, the plaintiff—the person who files the suit—would be the first name mentioned, Adams. The second name, Jones, would be the defendant—the person who is sued. If the case is an appellate court case, however, often the original plaintiff cannot be determined from the case title. Some appellate courts retain the trial court order of names, but many place the name of the party appealing the decision first, so the case might be called *Jones v. Adams*. You must read the facts of each case carefully to identify each party.

unanimous opinion A judicial decision with complete agreement by all judges.

Terminology

You frequently will find the following terms and phrases in court opinions and legal publications.

majority opinion A written opinion by a judge outlining the views of the majority of the judges of the court deciding the case.

Decisions and Opinions

Most appellate or reviewing court decisions are explained in writing. A decision contains the opinion (the court's reasons for its decision), the rules of law that apply, and the judgment. Appellate courts consist of a panel of three or more judges, and there are four types of written opinions for cases decided by these appellate courts.

concurring opinion A written opinion wherein a judge agrees (concurs) with the result reached by another judge, but for different reasons from those stated by the other judge.

1. When the judges unanimously agree on an opinion, the opinion is written for the entire court and is called a **unanimous opinion**.
2. When the opinion is not unanimous, a **majority opinion** is written. This opinion outlines the views of the majority of the judges deciding the case.
3. Often, a judge who feels strongly about making a point that was not made in the unanimous or majority opinion will write a **concurring opinion**. The judge agrees (concurs) with the judgment given in the unanimous or majority opinion, but for different reasons.
4. If the opinion is not unanimous, a **dissenting opinion** may be written by a judge who disagrees with the majority. The dissenting opinion is important because it may form the basis of arguments used years later to overrule the majority opinion.

dissenting opinion A written opinion by a judge or judges who votes contrary to the majority opinion and holding of the court.

Judges and Justice

The terms *judge* and *justice* are simply different names given to judges in different courts. All members of the U.S. Supreme Court, for example, are called justices. "Justice" is also the formal title given to judges of appellate courts. In New York, a justice is a judge of the trial court (which is called the supreme court), and a member of the court of appeals (the state's highest court) is called a judge. The term *justice* is commonly abbreviated to J., and *justices* to JJ.

A Supreme Court case might refer to Justice Kennedy as Kennedy, J., or to Chief Justice Roberts, Jr., as Roberts, C. J.

Appellants and Appellees

appellant or petitioner
The party who appeals to a higher court for review of a lower court ruling.

appellee or respondent
The party who, on appeal, defends the earlier court determination.

An **appellant** is a party who appeals a case to another court. An appellant is sometimes called a **petitioner**, usually when the case involves a matter in equity. An **appellee** is the party against whom an appeal is made. This party is sometimes called the **respondent**, usually when the case involves a matter in equity.

A Note on Abbreviations

In court opinions, and in other areas of this text, certain words in firm and organization names are abbreviated. Various terms for corporations, *Corporation, Company, Incorporated, and Limited,* for example, frequently appear in their abbreviated forms as *Corp., Co., Inc.,* and *Ltd.* Legislation and statutes often are referred to by their initials. To prevent confusion, we will give the complete name of each statute when it is first mentioned in the text. We also identify how we will refer to it in the future. For example, the Uniform Commercial Code is commonly referred to as the UCC.

We provide at least one case at the end of each chapter. We briefly introduce each case, but we leave the discussion of the case in the language of the court (although we have edited the court opinion for reasons of space and time). Knowing how to find and read a court opinion is an important step in legal research. A further step involves "briefing" the case to help one understand it. Legal researchers routinely brief cases by summarizing and reducing the opinions to their most important elements. A discussion on how to brief a case and a sample brief of the following case is provided in Appendix A.

CASE

Eric J. v. Betty M. The Court of Appeals Dist. 4

1 2

76 Cal. App. 4th 715, 90 Cal. Rptr. 2d 549 (1999)

3 4 5

6— *Robert brought home his new girlfriend, Helen, and her eight-year-old son, Eric, to meet his mother, father, brothers, sister, and their assorted spouses. The relationship between Robert and Helen continued and Helen and Eric were guests several times in various family homes. It was later discovered that Robert had sexually molested Eric during some of these visits at Robert's family's homes and that Robert was on parole for felony child molestation. Robert was convicted of molesting Eric and sent back to prison. Helen filed suit against Robert's family claiming they had a duty to warn her about Robert's criminal past and the potential danger to her child, and having failed that duty they were liable for monetary damages for the harm suffered by Eric. The trial court judge granted the defendant's motion to dismiss the case (nonsuit motion) after the completion of the evidentiary portion of the trial.*

7— **Justice Sills delivered the opinion of the court:**

When Robert was released from prison on rehabilitative parole after having been convicted of felony child molestation four years earlier, his family might have disowned him, but they didn't. They accepted him back. And when he found a girlfriend named Helen—who had an eight-year-old boy named Eric—they did not tell Helen about Robert's previous conviction, no doubt hoping against hope that he had reformed himself.

8— Unfortunately, and unbeknownst to any members of the family or Helen herself, Robert began molesting Helen's son early on in his relationship with her.

Facts and Litigation Background

In 1978 Robert was arrested for the misdemeanor of "annoying" a minor. He pled no contest and served six months, and was on probation for the next three years. During that time he committed one probation violation for taking four high school freshman boys to dinner without supervision. Again he served some time in jail and was placed on probation.

Then in 1984 he was arrested for molesting a 10-year old boy. He again pled no contest, this time to a felony count. He served four years in state prison, getting out in August 1988.

In June 1989, Robert met Helen and her eight-year-old son Eric at Magic Mountain. A relationship developed between Robert and Helen, and, by Thanksgiving 1989, Robert invited Helen and Eric for an overnight stay at the home of his mother Dorothy in Big Bear so she and Eric could meet some of the rest of his family. Besides Dorothy, Robert's family consists of his father Edwin, his father's wife Betty, Robert's three brothers Frank, Phillip and Eddie, and a sister named Diane.

The members of Robert's family concluded that Helen was his "girlfriend." Their relationship continued until early 1992, when Robert moved to Las Vegas.

Later that year, one of Helen's friends saw a special on television regarding convicts on parole, which showed a picture of a younger, beardless Robert and revealed that he was a convicted molester. She told Helen about the program, and a few days later, Helen took Eric to a police station. There, Helen learned that Robert had been molesting Eric. In June 1993 Robert was convicted of 23 counts of child molestation. He had never told Helen of his criminal history. —8

Helen, acting as guardian ad *litem* [Latin: "for purposes of the suit"] for Eric, sued various members of Robert s family. The case came to trial, during which it was learned that on several occasions Eric was molested on property owned by some of Robert's family members.

Each of the relatives had various degrees of knowledge of Robert's history. Father Edwin knew the most. He knew about the 1978 and 1984 convictions. Robert came to live with him and Betty for a short period after Robert's release from prison in 1988 and was visited by a parole officer shortly thereafter; she told Edwin that in her opinion Robert was a "pedophile." The parole officer also told Edwin that Robert had agreed to be put on a state parole rehabilitation program obligating him to report for psychiatric counseling, obtain gainful employment, not be alone with an unsupervised child, and allow for unannounced inspections of his residence.

Edwin also believed that his son was, as he would later testify in trial "truly repentant of his unfortunate situation back in 1984 that he was trying to adhere to his parole very, very vigorously." Indeed, Robert had voluntarily "participated" in the television special regarding convicts on parole against his father's advice because, as he told his father, "Dad, I want to do it to show we can succeed...."

The testimony was uncontroverted that none of the defendant family members ever told Helen about Robert's convictions.

After the evidence had been completed the trial court granted nonsuit motions made by the defendants in this appeal; Helen then filed a timely notice of appeal from the judgment in their favor. On appeal Helen now argues that the evidence was susceptible to liability based on either premises liability or general negligence theories. [We have omitted the discussion about premises liability.]

Discussion

Absent a "special relationship," one cannot be held liable for
8– mere nonfeasance, such as not protecting another from a criminal attack by a third party. (See *Totten v. More Oakland Residential Housing, Inc.* (1976) 63 Cal.App.,134 Cal. Rptr. 29 ["As a basic general principle, in the absence of a special relationship or circumstance, a private person has no duty to protect another from a criminal attack by a third person."].) The basic idea is often referred to as the "no duty to aid rule," which remains a fundamental and long-standing rule of tort law. As the Supreme Court said in *Williams v. State of California* (1983) 34 Cal.3d 18, 23, 192 Cal.Rptr. 233, 664 P.2d 137: "As a rule, one has no duty to come to the aid of another. A person who has not created a peril is not liable in tort merely for failure to take affirmative action to assist or protect another unless there is some relationship between them which gives rise to a duty to act."

> *[Helen's] claim essentially requires this court to depart from the rule against liability for mere nonfeasance. That rule is foundational in California tort jurisprudence. The tort law of California does not impose mandatory good samaritanism.*

Helen argues that *Soldano v. O'Daniels* (1983) 141 Cal. App. 3d 443, 190 Cal. Rptr. 310 modified the no duty to aid rule. As one commentator has noted, *Soldano* stands out as the only case in the United States during the thirty-year period since the death of Kitty Genovese that could "be read" as adopting a duty to aid rule, though the commentator who made that statement also noted that the "court's apparent holding [was] to the contrary." (See Payne, *Linking Tort Reform to Fairness and Moral Values* (1995) 1995 Det. C.L. Rev. 1207, 1237.) *Soldano* did not abrogate the rule against liability for mere nonfeasance. Rather like Justice Scalia's observation about the famous contracts case of *Hadley v. Baxendale* (1854) 156 Eng.Rep. 145 it is an instance of a court knowing the right rule but simply not applying it correctly. The time has come to explain why the result in the case is an aberration in American tort jurisprudence.

In *Soldano* a saloon patron ran across the street to a restaurant to try to phone the police about a threat that had been made in the bar. The patron requested the bartender of the restaurant (in the fairly neutral language which the opinion used to describe the actual facts) to "either call the police or allow him to use the [restaurant] phone to call the police. The [bartender] allegedly refused to call the police and allegedly refused to allow the patron to use the phone to make his own call." The threat in the saloon eventually escalated into a lethal shooting.

The appellate court reversed the judgment entered after a summary judgment motion when the son of the
man who was shot and killed in the saloon sued the res– –8
taurant across the street. The appellate court began its substantive discussion by saying the "facts" of the case before it "come very nearly within section 327" of the Restatement Second of Torts, which the court then paraphrased for the rather noncontroversial point that if you know a third person is going to render aid to another you shouldn't "prevent" that person "from doing so." The opinion then ... added the idea that you shouldn't "interfere" with another person's attempt to give aid as well as "prevent" it.

The problem with the court's analysis is that it subtly equated the concepts of prevention and interference with the fact that the bartender had *refused to allow* a saloon patron from across the street use the *restaurant's* phone. "Interference" and refusal to allow one's property to be commandeered, even for a good purpose, are simply two different things. If the English words "prevent" and "interfere" still mean anything, they necessarily convey the notion of some sort of affirmative action, not just refusal to turn one's property over to someone else.

The judgment in favor of the respondents is affirmed –9

RYLAARSDAM, J. and BEDSWORTH, J. concur. –10

Based on Eric J. v. Betty M. The Court of Appeals Dist. 476 Cal. App. 4th 715, 90 Cal. Rptr. 2d 549 (1999).

Case Notes

1. The name of the case is *Eric J. v. Betty M.* Eric J. is the plaintiff, although as he is a minor, his mother brought the case on his behalf; Betty M. was the first-named defendant. Other defendants are not named in the title.
2. The court deciding the case was the California Court of Appeals District 4, an intermediate-level court in the California state court system.
3. This citation is from the state of California official reporter and indicates that this case can be found in Volume 76 California Appellate Reporter, fourth series, on page 715.
4. This citation is a parallel citation to a West's state reporter and indicates this case also can be found in Volume 90 of the California Reporter, second series, on page 549.
5. The case was decided in 1999.
6. The authors prepare a short summary of the important facts, decision in the law court, and issues to be decided in the case.
7. The name of the judge or justice writing the majority or unanimous opinion and his or her recitation of important facts, history of this court case, and indication of issues in the case to be decided by the court.
8. The court addresses the legal questions posed by the case facts. This is the analysis portion of the case and the part that shows the use of prior court decisions and the specific reasoning leading to the court's ultimate decision.
9. The holding or decision of the court.
10. The remaining members of the panel concur, so this is a unanimous opinion. If one of the judges had disagreed with the result, he or she could write a dissenting opinion to explain why. A judge who agreed with the decision but not the reasons behind it could write a concurring opinion.

For Critical Analysis

1. What do you think of Robert's family's conduct? Should they have disclosed what they knew to Helen? Use both Kantian and utilitarian methods of ethical analysis to determine the duty to disclose, and compare results.
2. Is the rule determined by the court a substantive rule or procedural rule? Is this a criminal law case or civil case? Is this a state law or federal law matter?
3. Several of Robert's earlier pleas to criminal charges were "no contest." What does that mean? Why would that choice of a plea be made? Use the text index, glossary, or the Internet to find the answer.

CHAPTER QUESTIONS AND PROBLEMS

1. Consider a current issue lacking a clear legal resolution. What activities are occurring within American society to address the issue? Is Congress considering passing a new law? Is a case headed toward or at a higher court? Are candidates for political offices declaring a position on the issue? What do you think will be legal outcome of the issue? How do you think it will be resolved?
2. Contrast statutory law and case law. How are they different? What would be some strengths and weaknesses of each form of law? Texas is one of a few states that recognize common law marriage. Does that mean the law recognizing the marriage is statutory or case law?
3. Assume a fifty-first state called Columbia enacts the following statute sections during its 2008 session:
   a. Makes it illegal for anyone under age twenty-three to possess a can of aerosol spray paint unless that person is licensed by the state to do so.
   b. Establishes an application form and sets a filing fee to obtain a spray paint possessor's license.
   c. Defines the tort of spray-paint trespass and indicates the circumstances under which victims can sue and recover damages from spray painting violators.
   d. Provides that owners whose properties are wrongfully spray-painted can sue in small claims court for damages not to exceed $25,000.
   e. Makes it a misdemeanor to sell or give a spray paint can to any unlicensed person under age twenty-three.

   With regard to each of the above statute sections, characterize each as either civil or criminal law, public or private law, and procedural or substantive.
4. Explain to a friend the following types of court opinions: majority, concurring, and dissent.

5. Attorneys do not have a monopoly upon the legal issues within our society because everyone, individual or corporation, has the constitutional right to represent themselves without an attorney. Is this an accurate generalization?
6. Identify which of the following acts are crimes and which are civil wrongs (called torts).
   a. Dirk, brandishing a gun, robs a convenience store.
   b. Dirk captures and rapes Monica in the parking lot of a mall.
   c. Dirk shoplifts clothes from his employer's store.
   d. Dirk seduces Monica, age seventeen.
   e. Dirk carelessly drives his car into a school bus, killing one child.
   f. Dirk crudely asks Monica to engage in a sex act with him.
7. Which of the following issues most likely would be decided by both state and federal appellate courts?
   a. Proper selection of jurors.
   b. Whether or not a witness lied during trial.
   c. Whether or not a jury came to the correct decision.
   d. Whether or not certain evidence should have been produced by attorneys during trial.
   e. Whether or not the trial court judge made erroneous rulings on objections to evidence.
8. There are nine U.S. Supreme Court justices today, just as there were in 1900 when our population was 76 million. Today, the U.S. population is more than 300 million. Which of the following do you think should be done to rectify this situation?
   a. More justices should be appointed to share the workload.
   b. A new specialized court should be created to handle specified kinds of cases (say criminal appeals, only).
   c. Our justices should be paid more.

   Can you think of any other possible remedy?
9. Pam, a seventeen-year-old high school student, was spending Friday night at her friend Kristie's house. Both decided to go to a party at a fellow student's home. The parents of the host were away for the weekend. Marijuana and Ecstasy were said to have been used at the party. It was reported that Pam told a group of friends, including Kristie, that she had taken some Ecstasy, although no one actually saw her take the drug.

   Kristie went home without Pam. As the evening wore on, Pam complained of feeling sick. She was given lots of water to drink. (Dehydration is a common side effect of Ecstasy.) Soon Pam vomited and was moved to a bedroom to rest.

   The next morning, Kristie awoke to find that Pam had not returned to sleep at Kristie's house. Kristie ran back to the house where the party had taken place. She arrived just in time to see Pam taken away by ambulance. She was taken to the nearby hospital and pronounced dead on arrival.

   Who will be held responsible for allowing Pam to die? Kristie? The students at the party? The student whose house was the site of the party? Could Kristie's parents be held responsible? The host's parents? Is there any criminal responsibility? Civil liability? Would your answer be different if Kristie gave Pam the drug? As a matter of morality, who would be held responsible under utilitarian theory? Kantian ethics?
10. Why are the thousands of often-complex state and federal appellate decisions totaling tens of thousands of pages annually printed in expensive, hardcover books to collect dust in libraries? Why are they made available on the Internet? Who reads these long and, frankly, often-boring recitals of the law, precedents, and legal theory? Surely, all of these volumes cannot contain only significant and important cases. Why do we need volumes on the law of the 1800s, or of the 1920s?

CHAPTER 2

The Constitution

The layman's Constitutional view is that what he likes is Constitutional and that which he doesn't like is unconstitutional. That about measures up the Constitutional acumen of the average person.

Hugo Black, U.S. Supreme Court Justice, *New York Times*, February 26, 1971

LEARNING OBJECTIVES

After reading and studying this chapter, you should be able to:

- Define "constitutionalism."
- Distinguish between natural and positive law and provide examples of each.
- Explain the concept of judicial review.
- Describe how power and authority are divided among the branches of the government under the doctrine of separation of powers.
- Explain the organization of the national government and identify important attributes of each branch.
- Understand and define "federalism."
- Identify the major processes of citizen legislation.
- Define and provide examples of police power, the Supremacy Clause, and the power to tax.
- Explain what the Commerce Clause is and describe its effects.
- Understand the nature of the Bill of Rights and provide some examples of restrictions on federal government and, through the doctrine of incorporation, state government.
- Discuss the application of the First Amendment to expressions of free speech and religion.
- Understand the major contentions involving the "right to bear arms."
- Understand and be able to discuss the Due Process and Equal Protection Clauses and the right to privacy.

Does a woman have a legal right to an abortion?
Does a person have a right to burn the American flag?
Do gay couples have a right to marry?
Can the government take a citizen's property?
What rights do citizens have regarding firearms?
What rights do persons have to assemble or give speeches?
Can persons be denied or granted rights or privileges based on the color of their skin?

In the United States, questions about these important issues usually are answered by the U.S. Constitution or its interpretation by the courts. Many fundamental concerns related to social existence are about human rights, and the U.S. Constitution is a seminal document in the legal recognition of human rights. The U.S. Constitution is the foundation of the democratic institutions that define and provide our freedom and rights.

Our Constitution is a voluntary agreement among our citizens that specifies national rules of governance and expresses our fundamental principles of justice. It also lists the inalienable rights of the people that bind them to cooperate for their general welfare. Written eleven years after the Declaration of Independence, the Constitution became operative in 1789. It is the world's oldest effectively functioning written constitution. Current issues, such as fear of terrorism, abortion, firearms, and gay rights, may appear to challenge the durability of a document written before these issues arose. However, U.S. history is filled with eras like the present, and the Constitution has persevered due to its legitimacy and flexibility.

The U.S. Constitution ultimately derives its legitimacy from the guaranteed right of the people to vote in selecting their government representatives. This is also true of the written constitutions in all fifty states of the union. However, a democracy in which all of the qualified voters participate directly is obviously feasible only in very small political entities, such as some early New England towns. Our populous nation is a **republic**, meaning that its sovereign (supreme) power resides in the people but is exercised by representatives chosen through direct votes cast by voters. The Constitution did far more than create a democratic republic. The Constitution of the United States of America provides the means to protect important, enduring, and sometimes-competing values through the concept of constitutionalism.

republic
A system of government with the supreme power in the people, exercised by representatives chosen through the votes of qualified voters.

WHAT IS CONSTITUTIONALISM?

constitutionalism
The principles of constitutional government; adherence to them, including, notably, restrictions and limitations on government power.

arbitrary and capricious
Action taken impulsively or in bad faith and without good or valid reason.

Constitutionalism refers to a system of government wherein officials are subject and held accountable to a body of fundamental law as opposed to ruling from their arbitrary judgment. The United States, through the U.S. Constitution has historically demonstrated constitutionalism. Constitutionalism imposes limits on the exercise of government power. Many nations have constitutions, but that does not necessarily mean their citizens enjoy the fruits of constitutionalism. For example, a constitution that permits unlimited political power, whether in the hands of one, few, or many, does not provide constitutionalism. The Fascists' constitutions of Italy and Germany in the 1930s are examples. Neither included limitations on **arbitrary and capricious** uses of political power by the rulers. Arbitrary and capricious behavior can be characterized as willful and unreasonable action taken without consideration of or in disregard of facts or without determining principle. Even a constitution that provides limited political power, but establishes no mechanism to restrain the ruler's exercise of that power, fails to provide constitutionalism. For instance, a "freedom of the press" mandate in the Argentinean constitution did not prevent Juan Perón (president, 1945–1955) from destroying the world's largest Spanish-language newspaper, *La Prensa*, in Buenos Aires.

People enjoy constitutionalism only to the degree that their constitution limits power by specific provisions that effectively control the behavior of the rulers. One such control is having the judiciary serve as an enforcing watchdog on the exercise of powers by the executive and legislative branches, and even the lower levels of the judicial branch of government. "Separation of powers," as it exists in the United States, is discussed more fully later in this chapter. A good example of its application occurred in 1952 when President Harry S. Truman ordered the Secretary of Commerce to seize and operate the country's privately owned steel mills after the United Steel Workers Union threatened to strike. Corporate managers retaliated by a "lockout" that kept the workers off their jobs. The president believed that a shutdown would impair the nation's ability to conduct the Korean War. Was the seizure order within the president's power? No, it was not. The Supreme Court held that "this seizure order cannot stand" for the following reasons:

1. The president's power to issue the order had to stem either from an act of Congress or from the Constitution itself. The U.S. Supreme Court could find no congressional statute or constitutional provision that expressly authorized the president to take possession of private property as he did in the steel mill case.
2. Moreover, before that controversy, when the Taft-Hartley Act was under consideration in 1947, Congress had refused to adopt a law authorizing the seizure method of settling labor disputes that Truman used.
3. The order could not be sustained as an exercise of the president's military power as commander-in-chief of the armed forces. The commander-in-chief did not have the power to take possession of private property for the purpose of keeping labor-management disputes from stopping production. The nation's lawmakers, not military authorities, should regulate labor disputes, declared the Court.

The separation of powers inherent in the Constitution set the limit on the president's authority. The power and ability of the U.S. Supreme Court to dictate to President Truman, and have him obey, demonstrates how constitutionalism helps to protect the people of the United States from abuses of executive power, however well intended such abuses may be.

Another example of separation and limitation of power took place in 1974 when the Supreme Court ordered President Richard M. Nixon to release tape recordings of discussions concerning a politically inspired burglary in the Watergate apartment house in Washington, D.C. Initially, the president refused to release the tapes, claiming as "executive privilege" the right to withhold recorded information he deemed important to the exercise of his presidential duties. The tapes showed that he had halted an investigation of the Federal Bureau of Investigation, a serious obstruction of justice.

LEGAL FOCUS—CASE

In 1997, Paula Jones filed a civil lawsuit for money damages against President William J. Clinton, alleging sexual harassment while he was governor of Arkansas. President Clinton asserted an executive privilege as justification for his request to suspend the litigation until after his presidency ended. Does the U.S. Constitution provide presidents with such an "executive privilege" to delay civil litigation?

Clinton v. Jones, 520 U.S. 681, 117 S.Ct. 1636 (1997).

No, the president cannot delay civil litigation. The president had contended that ongoing civil litigation would impair his ability to lead the nation—thus, it should be suspended by executive privilege. The president was subpoenaed (ordered by the court) to appear and testify in that litigation, and he ultimately agreed to do so.

WHAT IS CONSTITUTIONAL LAW?

natural law
The higher law believed by some ethicists to be above and beyond man's power to change.

natural rights
Inalienable rights of every human being that exist by virtue of natural law, notably to life, liberty, and property.

positive law
Law enacted by government authority, such as legislatures, courts, and administrative agencies, as distinguished from natural law.

Constitutional law in the United States has a variety of meanings. To the founders of our nation, it had to do with a concept known as **natural law** and its corollary concept of **natural rights**. From the founders' perspective, natural law was the higher law, in accordance with nature, applicable to all men, and unchangeable and eternal.* Natural rights are rights of human beings that exist regardless of any other law. The founders believed they had incorporated natural law principles into the Constitution in a manner consistent with the necessities of government or **positive law**. Positive law is defined as any law enacted by the sovereign (supreme power) and deemed necessary to regulate an ordered society.† The natural law doctrines found in the Constitution are reflected in the following fundamental beliefs, and they dictate the parameters within which legitimate government positive law must be exercised:

1. The *rights of man* are inalienable and indestructible.
2. Paramount is the natural law doctrine that the most fundamental rights of all human beings are life, liberty, and property.
3. Legitimate governments are obligated (by natural law) under their social contracts (constitutions) to protect and guarantee these rights to every person within their respective jurisdictions.
4. The higher law acknowledges and promotes the principle of *private domain* into which governments should not intrude. Under this doctrine, the individual is free to do anything he chooses, unless specifically prohibited or circumscribed by reasonable positive law. This means that one may violate ethical standards, hallowed conventions, and Holy Writ, and yet not be answerable to the state unless the behavior involved has been prohibited or circumscribed by reasonable positive law. By contrast, many countries in today's turbulent world allow their citizens to do only that which is permitted by their manmade rules and decrees. All else that conflicts therewith is deemed prohibited.
5. No person is allowed to be a judge in his or her own cause. Thus, a justice of the U.S. Supreme Court who has a personal interest in a controversy under appeal

*See Marcus Tullius Cicero, *De re publica*, trans. George Sabine and Stanley Smith (Indianapolis, New York, Dobbs: Merrill, 1960). Cicero's definition of natural law reads thus:

> *True law is right reason, harmonious with nature, diffused among all, constant, eternal; a law which calls to duty by its commands and restrains from evil by its prohibitions.... It is a sacred obligation not to attempt to legislate in contradiction to this law; nor may it be derogated from nor abrogated. Indeed, by neither the Senate nor the people can we be released from this law; nor does it require any but ourselves to be its expositor or interpreter. Nor is it one law at Rome and another at Athens; one now and another at a later time; but one eternal and unchangeable law binding all nations through all time.*
>
> Based on Marcus Tullius Cicero, reported in Lactantius, *Divina institutiones*, trans. Roberts and Donaldson (1871), vi, 8, 370

†As is often true with philosophies, there is an inherent conflict between the pure precept of positive law and natural law. As proffered by Thomas Hobbes (1588–1679), positive law is essential to protect people from their primitive state, so when a law is enacted, people are duty-bound to obey it. Natural law presupposes a system of law grounded on its intrinsic truth rather than on any power of compulsion, and it is held to exist irrespective of and sometimes inconsistent with manmade laws. The tension between individual belief in and respect for natural law versus the positive laws of the state is not the subject of an abstract debate. One justification often given for civil disobedience is that the violator is actually complying with a higher law, namely natural law.

before the Court will refuse to participate in the case. A long-standing philosophical bias is not a disqualifying conflict of interest.

6. No person is above the law—not legislators, not presidents, not judges.

In Chapter 1, we used the following case to describe the difference between civil and criminal law and concluded that neither was applicable to the situation.

ETHICAL FOCUS—PROBLEM

Late one night, David Thomas Cash, Jr., age nineteen, observed his friend Jeremy Strohmeyer, age twenty, escort a very young girl into a restroom inside the Primadonna casino near Las Vegas. Shortly thereafter, Cash followed them inside, where he peered over the top of a stall. He saw Strohmeyer grappling with the girl, but said nothing and left. Later, Strohmeyer rejoined Cash in the casino. After discussing the killing of the girl, Cash and Strohmeyer continued their evening of conviviality and gambling. Strohmeyer ultimately pled guilty to the rape and murder of the victim and is serving life imprisonment without the possibility of parole. Did Cash have a natural law right to choose to assist, or to ignore, the victim?

Yes, Cash did have a natural law right to choose. Recall from paragraph 4 earlier: "[O]ne may violate ethical standards, hallowed conventions, and Holy Writ, and yet not be answerable to the state unless the behavior involved has been prohibited or circumscribed by reasonable positive law." Under the natural law principle of private domain, Cash was free either to help the victim or to ignore her plight. Nevada had no statute (positive law) criminalizing a refusal to prevent a crime from occurring. Furthermore, it is unclear whether a law requiring citizens to intervene in criminal conduct would be constitutional.

Important elements of the natural law and natural rights were included in the second paragraph of the Declaration of Independence:

> *We hold these truths to be self-evident, that all men are created equal, that they are Endowed by their Creator with certain unalienable Rights, that among these are Life, Liberty and the pursuit of Happiness. That to secure these rights, Governments are instituted among Men, deriving their just powers from the consent of the governed. That whenever any Form of Government becomes destructive of these ends, it is the Right of the people to alter or to abolish it, and to institute new Government, laying its foundation on such principles and organizing its powers in such form, as to them shall seem most likely to effect their Safety and Happiness.*

In January 1776, George Washington wrote of "the propriety of separation [from England on the basis of] … the sound doctrine and unanswerable reasoning contained in the pamphlet *Common Sense*." The author of *Common Sense*, Thomas Paine, summed up the spirit of the time in these lofty words:

> *But where, say some, is the King of America? I'll tell you, Friend. He reigns above, and does not make havoc of mankind like the royal brute of Britain. Yet, that we may not appear to be defective even in earthly honors, let a day be solemnly set apart for proclaiming the charter; let it be brought forth placed in the divine law, the word of God; let a crown be placed thereon, by which the world may know, that so far as we approve of monarchy, that in America the law is king. For as in absolute governments the king is law, so in free countries the law ought to be king; and there ought to be no other.*

When we speak of constitutional law today, we mean the fundamental law or the supreme law of the land. Constitutional principles accorded special designation as constitutional laws are (1) judicial review, (2) separation of powers, (3) federalism, and (4) civil rights and liberties. These four special categories contain the most publicized and exciting principles of constitutional law.

WHAT IS JUDICIAL REVIEW?

judicial review Power of the U.S. Supreme Court to declare unconstitutional an act of Congress, a presidential order, or a state law.

Judicial review is the power and duty vested in the U.S. Supreme Court to declare null and void (i.e., of no validity or effect) any statute or act of the federal government or of any state government that violates the U.S. Constitution. (State supreme courts possess similar powers to nullify laws of their own legislatures that violate their respective state constitutions.) Although not specifically authorized in Article III (the Judicial Article of the Constitution), some form of judicial review presumably was envisioned by the framers of the Constitution. According to Alexander Hamilton, the Supreme Court is the "least dangerous branch" because it controls neither sword nor purse. He said the Supreme Court and not the Congress or the president should be the custodian of the Constitution. Furthermore, he referred to "the medium of the courts of justice, whose duty it must be to declare all acts contrary to the manifest tenor of the constitution void. Without this, all the reservations of particular rights or privileges would amount to nothing." What *judicial review* meant, however, was not articulated until 1803, in the case of *Marbury v. Madison.* This case did more than validate (i.e., give legal force to) the judicial review of legislative and executive enactments and orders. Chief Justice Marshall enunciated a major power for the Supreme Court, recognizing it as the sole interpreter and custodian of the Constitution, to the exclusion of the president and Congress. With this declaration came the awesome duty of defining what the Constitution means and what it does not mean.

Although the exclusive judicial power of review has engendered heated controversy over the years, it also has been a stabilizing force for a growing and changing society. As national economic, social, and political conditions have changed, so, too, have attitudes and opinions of the people. This evolution is reflected in the leaders the people elect to office and in the Supreme Court justices who are appointed. As a result, some long-standing Supreme Court decisions have been changed. What once was ruled constitutional thereafter is declared unconstitutional. For example, as the twentieth century began, racial segregation in schools was accepted and even endorsed by the separate but equal rule of *Plessy v. Ferguson.* In 1954, however, the "separate but equal" rule was rejected by *Brown v. Board of Education of Topeka.*

Besides judicial review effectuating the equivalent of a change to the Constitution through interpretation, there is a way to directly change the Constitution. The people can and do make changes through the more difficult process of formal amendment. For example, women obtained the right to vote in 1920 by the Nineteenth Amendment to the Constitution, and in 1971, the Twenty-Sixth Amendment lowered the voting age in national elections to eighteen.

WHAT IS SEPARATION OF POWERS?

separation of powers The granting of the various powers of government among three branches so that each branch checks the other two.

Separation of powers is an indispensable element of our charter of government. The Constitution allocates powers of government according to function. The functional branches are legislative (law making), executive (law enforcing), and judicial (adjudicating). Separation of powers provides an effective balance of power among the three branches of government. Different officials have unique and specific powers, and each branch operates under the direction of different persons. Each branch checks the other two to prevent them from garnering or exercising power illegally. This institutional structure restrains a natural human tendency toward expansion of personal power. While preventing possible tyranny (i.e., despotic abuse of authority), the separation of powers provides officials sufficient independence to faithfully execute their constitutionally delegated powers.

The constitutional doctrine of separation of powers speaks of the relationships among the divisions of government. Although, indeed, exclusive functions are assigned to each (e.g., tax bills must begin in the House of Representatives), much of the work engaged in by the three branches of government is shared.

Congress may pass a bill; the president may sign or veto it. Congress may override the veto and enact the bill as law. The Supreme Court may strike down the statute as unconstitutional. If necessary, Congress may initiate a campaign to have the Constitution amended to accomplish the purpose of the statute, or more likely it may attempt to pass a new statute that is in conformity with the Constitution. Note, too, that the president may be able to appoint new members to the Supreme Court (with the advice and consent of the Senate) who are sympathetic to his or her views.

Most members of the public probably would approve of a litmus test (single-issue test that determines result) for nominees to the Supreme Court. Over a lifetime, however, a justice will face an extraordinary number of important issues involving significant values, and most people, no doubt, also would prefer the appointment of highly qualified persons rather than persons sympathetic to one specific controversial issue—unless that issue was of supreme importance to the individual. This obvious conundrum typically is resolved by the refusal of candidates to respond specifically to such questions, reciting their loyalties to follow the rule of law.

LEGAL FOCUS—EXAMPLE

In 2005, Sandra Day O'Connor announced her intent to retire from the U.S. Supreme Court. President George W. Bush nominated Judge John Roberts, then a federal court of appeals judge for the District of Columbia Circuit to fill the vacancy. On September 4, 2005, before the confirmation hearing, Chief Justice Rehnquist passed away. The president then changed Roberts' nomination to instead nominate him to replace Rehnquist as chief justice. After Justice Roberts was confirmed by a vote of 78–22, President Bush nominated Harriet Miers for the still-vacant seat of Justice O'Connor.

Ms. Miers eventually withdrew her nomination before the formal confirmation process began, and President Bush nominated U.S. Court of Appeals Judge Samuel A. Alito, Jr., for the position. Eventually, Justice Alito was confirmed, albeit by a much tighter vote of 58–42. Along the way, both Roberts and Alito endured Congressional hearings in which repeated questions about their views on controversial topics including abortion were asked. Many felt that they repeatedly avoided answering those questions directly. Specifically, on the abortion-related questions, Justice Roberts' responses included: "I should not, based on the precedent of prior nominees, agree or disagree with particular decisions … I'm reluctant to do that," "I didn't [then] have a position," and "I feel the need to stay away from a discussion of particular cases."

It is reassuring to note that, in the final analysis, the power to decide most issues rests with the people, who may use their votes—the power of the ballot box—to elect representatives who are expected to comply with the expressed will of the people. However, elected representatives are not legally obliged to do so. Even if they were, public opinion often is divided and sometimes fragmented on controversial issues.

The presidential veto procedure is prescribed by Article I, Section 7 of the Constitution, which states, "Every Bill which shall have passed the House of Representatives and the

Senate shall, before it becomes a Law, be presented to the President." Thereupon, "if he approves he shall sign it, but if not he shall return it, with his Objections to that House in which it shall have originated." If, after reconsideration it is approved by two-thirds of both houses, it shall become a law. Note that

> *if any Bill shall not be returned by the President within ten Days (Sundays excepted) after it shall have been presented to him, the Same shall be a Law, in like Manner as if he had signed it, unless the Congress by their Adjournment prevent its Return, in which Case it shall not be a Law.*

Each year, Congress presents a budget to the president for signature into law. Typically, some of the proposed expenditures in the budget are intended primarily as political patronage. These so-called pork barrel budget items are added by the most powerful legislators in Congress, a tactic that assists them in their reelection campaigns.

LEGAL FOCUS—PROBLEM

Congress presented the fiscal year budget for the year 2004 to the president for signature or veto. Included was an item for $10 million for "parks and recreation" projects in Congresswoman Peavy's hometown. For years, Peavy had been a very vocal critic of the president. Can the president approve the budget yet, in retaliation, veto the proposed appropriation for Peavy?

No, the president cannot. The power to make partial vetoes (called *line-item vetoes*) would have the practical effect of amending enactments by Congress. The president is not authorized by the Constitution to amend laws proposed by Congress. Thus, the separation of the legislative and executive powers cannot be blurred by line-item vetoes.

HOW IS THE NATIONAL GOVERNMENT ORGANIZED?

Legislative Branch (Congress)

Article I of the Constitution provides the organization and functions of the legislature. The legislative branch is *bicameral* (having two parts), with an upper house (the Senate) and a lower house (the House of Representatives). Members of the Senate originally were appointed by state legislatures, but in 1913 the Seventeenth Amendment changed the system to direct selection by popular vote. The Senate has 100 members, two from each state. Members of the House of Representatives are elected to 435 seats that are allocated to the states on the basis of population, as determined in the decennial national census.

The basic function of the legislative branch is to enact laws. This usually is accomplished by a majority vote for or against enactment, amendment, or repeal. In both the House and the Senate, a quorum consists of a majority of the members who have been elected and sworn (i.e., taken an oath of office) to serve. Powers of the Congress are spelled out in Article I, Section 8 of the Constitution. They include the power to tax and borrow money, to regulate interstate commerce, to make laws regulating bankruptcies, to coin money, to establish post offices, to establish courts inferior to the Supreme Court, to declare war, and to govern the District of Columbia (the area of the nation's capital). However, Congress has great latitude in the detailed application of its enumerated powers by virtue of its blanket authority "to make all Laws which shall be necessary and proper for carrying into Execution" its stated powers.

Once the legislature enacts a law, its job is usually done. All persons subject to the newly enacted law then are required to comply. If necessary, lower-level government officials in the executive branch (e.g., police) enforce compliance. If and when the constitutionality of a statute is challenged, the dispute ultimately may be resolved by decision of the Supreme Court.

Sometimes newly enacted laws never actually become law.

LEGAL FOCUS—EXAMPLE

Congress passed a law releasing alien Chinese students who were studying in the United States from the requirement of returning to China upon the expiration of their visas. (A visa is a document that grants a citizen of a foreign country legal permission to live, work, or study in the host country.) This was done because Congress believed that the Chinese government would punish most of these students for supporting the 1989 student uprising in Tiananmen Square and elsewhere in China. The proposed law was sent to the White House for signature by the president.

President George H. W. Bush vetoed the legislation on the grounds that Congress was interfering with foreign policy matters, a presidential responsibility. Moreover, the students already were protected against forced repatriation by his executive order, which directed the Immigration and Naturalization Service to extend the Chinese student visas indefinitely. When the bill was returned to the Congress, the House voted to override the veto, but the Senate did not; thus, the president's veto stood.

The only constitutional method to remove a president from office is by a congressional proceeding called *impeachment*. Impeachment is a process potentially leading to removal from office certain federal officers, including the president. The process for the president is provided for in the U.S. Constitution Article II, Section 4: "The President, Vice President and all civil Officers of the United States, shall be removed from Office on Impeachment for, and Conviction of, Treason, Bribery, or other high Crimes and Misdemeanors." Impeachment requires a majority vote in the House of Representatives. The impeached office-holder is then subject to trial in the Senate with removal from office requiring a two-thirds majority vote of the Senate after trial. In 1998, the U.S. House of Representatives voted to impeach President William Jefferson Clinton for obstruction of justice and perjury relating to his conduct following the infamous "Monica Lewinsky affair." The U.S. Senate, with Supreme Court Chief Justice William Rehnquist presiding, conducted an impeachment trial. On February 12, 1999, it voted 50–50 and 45–55 on the respective charges, thereby declining to remove the president from office.

Executive Branch (Presidency)

The president and vice president are each elected to a term of four years, with a limit of two consecutive full terms.* The constitutional process for choosing the chief executive

*"No person shall be elected to the office of the president more than twice, and no person who has held the office of president, or acted as president for more than two years of a term to which some other person was elected president, shall be elected to the office of the president more than once." (U.S. Constitution, Twenty-Second Amendment)

and his or her running mate is cumbersome because the method is indirect, with state electors actually electing the president by casting electoral votes. The number of electors in each state is determined by the number of representatives the state has in the House, plus its two senators. After the 2000 census, each of seven states (Alaska, Delaware, Montana, North and South Dakota, Vermont, and Wyoming) and the District of Columbia had three votes, for a total of twenty-four; populous California alone had fifty-five; and New York had thirty-one.

In total, there are 538 electoral votes: 435 based on members of the House, 100 based on members of the Senate, and three from the District of Columbia. To win requires a majority (270) of the electoral votes. Note that presidential elections and vacancies are further regulated by technical amendments to the Constitution.

The unique Electoral College has survived despite repeated efforts to alter or abolish it. This survival may be because it maintains the viability of political parties, which "in turn serve to identify issues and support candidates committed to advancing identified policies and programs." A new Electoral College is created for every presidential election; that is, the people who serve as electors (casting votes) in the Electoral College are different for each election.

Powers of the President

Section 2 of Article II of the Constitution specifies the following presidential powers. First and foremost, and of momentous importance during most of the twentieth century, is the power of the president as "Commander in Chief of the Armed Forces of the United States and of the militia of the several states, when called into actual service of the United States."

Although Congress retains to itself the power to declare war, the power "to make war" is granted solely to the president. It was during the Civil War that the commander-in-chief was declared to be the sole determiner of whether the hostilities were of "such alarming proportions as will compel him to accord to them the character of belligerent" and whether he would engage the armed forces of the United States in such hostilities. Advanced technology has changed the nature of modern warfare, thus further justifying the presidential power to respond quickly with military force to a military attack without congressional approval.

The president has the duty and power to make treaties, but they must be approved by a two-thirds vote of the Senate. For example, three controversial yet vitally important treaties entered into by our country in the twentieth century were the Charter of the United Nations (1945); the North Atlantic Treaty Pact (1948), which created NATO (North Atlantic Treaty Organization), a defensive military alliance; and the North American Free Trade Agreement (NAFTA) among Canada, Mexico, and the United States. All three of these treaties were duly voted on and approved by the Senate. The president also may sign *executive agreements*, which do not require Senate ratification. For example, during the early months of World War II, when German submarines were sinking many supply ships in an attempt to starve England into surrender, President Franklin D. Roosevelt signed an executive agreement giving the British fifty 1914-type destroyers in exchange for eight naval bases. This was entirely constitutional, despite the fact that the United States had not yet declared war on Germany.

With the "advice and consent" of the Senate, the president appoints ambassadors, public ministers and consuls, Supreme Court justices, and presidential advisors. Congress has empowered the president to choose other federal officers and commission heads. The

Judiciary Act of 1789 gave presidents the power to nominate appellate and district court judges for the federal courts. Congress must approve these appointments, a function that is another example of shared power between the branches of government.

Some scholars contend that the power to nominate Supreme Court justices, who serve for life, is the single most important power of the president.

LEGAL FOCUS—CASE

In the case of *Roe v. Wade*, the U.S. Supreme Court held for the first time that women have a constitutionally protected right to choose whether or not to have an abortion. Following this declaration, the states could no longer abolish abortion within their borders. Four justices voted against the majority in *Roe v. Wade*. Could the replacement of one justice cause reversal of *Roe*, thereby altering or even eliminating the abortion law?

Roe v. Wade, 410 U.S. 113, 93 S.Ct. 705 (1973).

Yes, one justice could cause reversal. Many of the most controversial Supreme Court cases are decided by 5–4 votes. Nonetheless, presidential candidates historically have not announced the names of persons they would, if elected, nominate to the Supreme Court if the opportunity should arise. Nor do presidential candidates announce the names of possible appointees to their cabinets (department heads with the highest authority in an administration). Thus, voters make assumptions about their future based on the campaign statements and track records of presidential candidates.

Judicial Branch (Courts)

Article III of the Constitution, the judicial article, declares, "The Judicial power of the United States shall be vested in one Supreme Court, and in such inferior courts as the Congress may from time to time ordain and establish." Compared with detailed mandates given to the executive and legislative branches, Article III is sparse in providing guidance to the judiciary. Despite this lack of a closely defined role, the federal courts have become central to the doctrine of separation of powers. The U.S. Supreme Court has created and refined the "proper" place of the court within the federal government, beginning with its landmark case of *Marbury v. Madison* mentioned earlier.

The power to determine the constitutionality of federal and state legislative enactments, as well as judicial review of actions taken by the executive branch, has given the U.S. Supreme Court major responsibility for maintaining the integrity of the Constitution. The Supreme Court commonly is thought to be the branch of government least likely to be swayed by political pressures and popular whims. One reason for this is that, like all federal judges, Supreme Court justices hold office for life, contingent only on good behavior.

All courts are empowered to issue orders to compel compliance with their rules and procedures. For example, courts authorize the issuance of subpoenas (orders to appear at a certain time and place) upon proper request by officials or lawyers (for their clients) who are engaged in litigation or investigation. Failure to comply with such a judicial order can prompt a court to hold the witness in "contempt" of court. The court's penalty for contempt may range from a monetary fine to jail time.

LEGAL FOCUS—PROBLEM

In 1971, the Supreme Court approved the legality of a subpoena served upon President Richard Nixon (executive branch) to deliver to the Congress (legislative branch) certain tape-recorded conversations that Nixon most certainly knew would end his term of office. He could have refused to obey the subpoena and destroyed the tapes. If Nixon had refused to comply with the subpoena and had destroyed the tapes, what would have happened?

Most likely, the Congress would have impeached President Nixon for failure to comply with a lawful subpoena approved by the U.S. Supreme Court. But it is not clear that disregard of a subpoena issued by Congress is a legal basis for impeachment. We never will know what would have happened then. But it is important to know how the three powers of government must interact, and that the gravity of the crisis then related to the president's willingness to comply with an order of the judicial branch of government.

LEGAL FOCUS—PROBLEM

In 1998, President Clinton was subpoenaed to testify before a federal grand jury, not as a witness, but concerning his personal conduct. Again, rather than create a constitutional confrontation about the obligation of a president to respond to a subpoena, President Clinton ultimately agreed to testify, and did. Could the president personally have appeared at the time and place to testify, but then refused to answer questions?

In Chapter 6, you will review the fundamental principle in our society that no person is required to testify against himself in a criminal proceeding. A person may volunteer to do so, but he or she need not. President Clinton did not assert his privilege against self-incrimination, either because there was no criminal conduct about which he was concerned or because he simply waived his right. He became the first sitting president in history to testify before a federal grand jury (by closed-circuit television). But in either case, he ultimately chose the course of former President Nixon by complying with the dictates of the subpoena.

Federal judges can be removed from their courts only by death, voluntary retirement, or impeachment by the Congress of the United States.

LEGAL FOCUS—PROBLEM

The Honorable Harry E. Claiborne, a federal district judge in Nevada, was tried and convicted of cheating on his income tax by filing a false return. He was sentenced to federal prison for two years. Upon conviction, the judge refused to resign his office and continued to collect his $78,700 annual salary. He made clear his intent to resume his lifetime office after the completion of this term Can he be impeached?

Yes, he can. Eight months after returning to his job as a judge, Claiborne finally was removed from the court by impeachment.

Congress is reluctant to use the impeachment procedure to remove public officials from office because it is costly, cumbersome, and time consuming. But impeachment is the only way to remove federal judges from the public payroll even when they are proven guilty of criminal conduct. Fortunately, criminal acts by federal judges are rare.

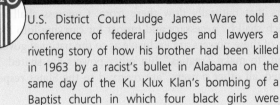

LEGAL FOCUS—EXAMPLE

U.S. District Court Judge James Ware told a conference of federal judges and lawyers a riveting story of how his brother had been killed in 1963 by a racist's bullet in Alabama on the same day of the Ku Klux Klan's bombing of a Baptist church in which four black girls were killed. Later, it was discovered and widely publicized that Judge Ware's story was a lie. What punishment, if any, do federal judges receive for conduct that goes to the heart of the credibility of the courts—honesty in public life?

Before his misrepresentation, Judge Ware had been nominated for promotion to the U.S. Court of Appeals. After publication of his falsehood, Judge Ware withdrew his nomination. He also was reprimanded publicly by a panel of federal judges who stated that his conduct "was prejudicial to the effective administration of the business of the courts." Judge Ware was not removed from office.

Under the Constitution, the Senate has the sole power to try all impeachments, and no person may be convicted without the concurrence of two-thirds of the members present. When political loyalty to the accused is involved, such a majority can be difficult to obtain unless the alleged offense is flagrant. Understandably, therefore, the practice is seldom used.

Congress sets the salaries for all federal employees, including judges. However, once the salaries for federal judges are set by Congress, they can never be reduced for any reason during the tenure of judges then on the court. This serves to forestall possible improper efforts to impose financial pressure on judges whose opinions are not favored.

WHAT IS FEDERALISM?

federalism
A form of government consisting of a union of more or less self-governing states under an umbrella of federal government.

Federalism may be defined as a political arrangement in which two or more levels of government provide a variety of services for a given group of citizens in a specified geographic area. For example, Iowans are served by the national government and by their state government as well as by a variety of local governance structures.

The United States is a case study in federalism. Scholars have estimated that more than 80,000 state and local governments* exist in the United States, each striving to meet the needs and wants of our complex, technologically driven society. This government profusion operates in a climate of political pressures, involving both competition and cooperation among various public officeholders. In effect, the U.S. Constitution created and endorsed some of this complexity when it reserved a large measure of sovereignty for each of the original thirteen states, in accordance with Article IV and the Tenth Amendment of the U.S. Constitution.

*All governments within states were (are) created by the state legislatures under provisions in their respective state constitutions. The governments of cities, boroughs, and counties are most commonly recognized by citizens. Other varieties of local governments are school districts, flood-control districts, mosquito-abatement districts, and park districts. Under their charters of government (granted by state legislatures), they have budgets, collect taxes, and perform various other government functions.

writ of *habeas corpus* [Latin: "you have the body"]
A formal written order that an arrestee be brought before a court.

bill of attainder
Act of the legislature inflicting capital punishment upon a named person or member of a specific group without trial and conviction. Forbidden by the U.S. Constitution.

***ex post facto* laws** [Latin: "after the fact"]
A statute that retroactively makes previously lawful conduct a crime. Such a statute is unconstitutional.

In any event, we are a people served by, but also subject to, government rules that range from taxation mandated by Congress to the narrowly defined standards for admission of toddlers to kindergarten mandated by local school boards.

The Constitution defines the boundaries between the national government and the state governments, providing that national government has only those powers delegated to it and such other powers that naturally flow there from. Congress shall have the power "to make all laws which shall be necessary and proper for carrying into Execution the foregoing powers." Some of these powers are exclusive as to the national government, such as "to coin Money" and "to make Treaties." But other powers are shared, such as taxing and spending. As noted, all other powers "are reserved to the States respectively, or to the people."

Our Constitution also limits the power of the national government; for example, it is prohibited from denying a request for a **writ of *habeas corpus*** (Latin: "you have the body"), a formal written order that an arrestee be brought before a court, usually to protect against abusive incarceration, without release on bail, pending a formal trial.

Under the Constitution, some powers also are denied to the states, such as the power to make a treaty. Finally, there are powers denied to both, such as the passage of **bills of attainder**, which are acts of the legislature punishing a named individual(s) or member(s) of a specific group without a judicial trial; and ***ex post facto* laws** (Latin: "after the fact"), which are retroactive laws that would punish alleged violators for acts lawful when committed or that would increase the punishment applicable at the time the act was committed.

LEGAL FOCUS—PROBLEM

David Cash (mentioned earlier in this chapter) was not guilty of any crime by declining to rescue a young girl from his friend's murderous acts. Assume that in response to public outcry, Nevada passed a statute that made failure to assist the victim of criminal behavior a felony (i.e., a serious crime). If the state of Nevada then arrested, prosecuted, convicted, and sent Cash to jail, what, if anything, could he do?

Under the preceding hypothetical example, Cash could sidestep the Nevada judicial system altogether and petition a federal court to protect him from this *ex post facto* law. The U.S. Constitution prohibits states from subjecting people to such laws regardless of the outcry or sentiment of most citizens. The federal court would order Nevada to release Cash.

WHAT CONSTITUTIONAL POWERS BELONG TO CITIZENS?

initiative process
An electoral process for making new statutes or changing the constitution by filing appropriate formal petitions to be voted upon by legislature (and governor) or by the total electorate.

Although much power is delegated to the national government, and great power is reserved to states, it is the people who possess the ultimate power in our free society with its constitutional system. One of the great powers of the people is found in their right to vote.

Every citizen wishing to govern personally must compete with political opponents and win this privilege by receiving a majority of the people's vote. It is by popular vote that lawmakers and governors are chosen. Some state constitutions give qualified voters the right and power to bypass customary lawmaking procedures of state and local governments and to make laws directly. This is called the **initiative process**. It enables groups

referendum
A democratic process whereby a state legislature submits (refers) proposed or existing laws to the electorate for approval or rejection.

recall
A democratic process for removing public officials from their elective positions by a vote of the people taken after filing of a petition signed by the required number of qualified voters.

of voters, if sufficient in numbers, to originate and pass statutes, ordinances, and amendments to their respective constitutions without recourse to the legislature. State legislatures may submit a **referendum** petition to voters for their approval or disapproval of an existing or proposed law. State constitutions as well as statutes can be created, amended, or disapproved through the referendum process. The **recall** petition enables voters to remove from office any elected state or local official before the expiration of his or her term. For most of the past hundred years, these three practices of direct democracy have given the people enhanced power of control over legislation and legislators.

These practices, especially the initiative process, are sometimes misused by well-financed special interest groups, businesses, and professions to secure enactment of laws that favor their own purposes. Such groups may hire public relations firms to run a campaign for passage of certain desired legislation. With the use of directmail fund-raising, and with payments offered to "vote hustlers" for each signature obtained, the public relations firms readily qualify their initiatives for the ballot. Later, absentee ballots may be mailed to persons who have signed the petitions to make it easy for them to vote on the particular proposal.

LEGAL FOCUS—EXAMPLE

Citizens have used the initiative process to establish a statewide lottery in California, to protect the moose in Maine, to encourage the death penalty in Massachusetts, to approve the sale of wine in local grocery stores in Colorado, to abolish daylight savings time in North Dakota, and to limit rights of gays in Colorado.

Critics have condemned the initiative process as it is presently used. Controversial issues make their way onto the ballot and often are written in a manner so verbose and confusing that most people cannot reasonably evaluate the relevant pros and cons or fairly understand how they should vote. The confusion frequently is increased by slick media advertising. Despite the potential abuse inherent in the initiative process, however, it has the big advantage of increasing voter interest and participation.

LEGAL FOCUS—CASE

In 1996, California voters approved by majority vote a bitterly contested initiative. The effect of Proposition 209 was to prohibit affirmative action in public education, employment, and other state programs. Lawsuits were filed in federal court by minorities affected by the change in the law on the grounds that it would deny them equal protection under the law as guaranteed by the U.S. Constitution. What was the result?

Coalition for Economic Equity v. Wilson, 110 F. 3rd 1431 (Ca.9, 1997).

In an *ex parte* (no opposition) hearing, a federal court judge initially suspended Proposition 209 pending a future trial. Shortly thereafter, a higher federal court overruled the decision, and Proposition 209 then went into effect. Thus, through the initiative process, the voter majority was able to create a new law that the state legislative branch was unwilling to enact. Proposition 209 raised the visibility of affirmative action and has been the catalyst for the creation and hardening of opposition groups on both sides of the issue.

THE POLICE POWER

police power
The inherent power of the government to make laws and impose reasonable regulations for the health, safety, morals, or general welfare of the public, even when this limits individual freedom.

Neither those who wrote the Constitution nor those who ratified it intended the national government to have authority over most details in the everyday lives of people. James Madison believed that limitation on the power of the national government was a major virtue of federalism, whereby the police power is implicitly reserved to the states under the Tenth Amendment. The **police power** is the right to enact and enforce laws for the prevention of fraud and crime and to promote order, safety, health, morals, and the general welfare of the people. Both state and local governments implement police power.

LEGAL FOCUS—CASE

The Virginia state entomologist ordered Julia Miller to cut down a large number of fungoid-infected ornamental red cedar trees growing on her property. The order was made to prevent the transfer of cedar rust disease to local apple orchards. The disease did not affect the value of the cedar trees but did threaten to destroy apple crops in the vicinity. Is Miller bound to comply with the order, and if so does she have a right to compensation for the loss of value to her property?

Miller v. Schoene, 216 U.S. 272, 48 S.Ct. 246 (1928).

It is not unusual for local governments to quarantine crops, create firebreaks, and delay people to respond to important or emergency situations. Persons subject to these actions may suffer significant losses without any legal right to recover these losses from government. Julia Miller had to comply with the order, and no reimbursement for her loss was required of government.

> *And where the public interest is involved preferment of that interest over the property interest of the individual, to the extent even of its destruction, is one of the distinguishing characteristics of every exercise of the police power which affects property.*

The police power is thus an essential attribute of government but is subject to the limitations of the federal and state constitutions. Under the Constitution, the national government's power to regulate, control, and circumscribe human conduct is tied specifically tied to one or more of its delegated powers.

LEGAL FOCUS—EXAMPLE

The Federal Aviation Administration (FAA) was established to provide for safety regulation in the manufacture of aircraft as a "necessary and proper" extension of Congress's power to "regulate Commerce ... among the several States," as prescribed in the Constitution:

> *The Congress shall have Power ... To regulate Commerce with foreign Nations, and among the several States.... And To make all Laws which shall be necessary and proper for carrying into Execution the foregoing Powers, and all other Powers vested by this Constitution in the Government of the United States, or in any Department or Officer thereof.*

Amendment XVI (ratified on February 3, 1913)

We will examine the Commerce Clause of the Constitution in more detail later in this chapter. Here, the point is that to create the FAA, Congress needed authority in the Constitution. They relied on the Commerce Clause. The FAA is an example of an administrative agency. Chapter 5 examines administrative agencies and administrative law in detail. The topic of what authority Congress or a state has or does not have is a persistent one.

WHAT IS THE SUPREMACY CLAUSE?

According to the U.S. Constitution:

> *This Constitution and the Laws of the United States which shall be made in pursuance thereof; and all Treaties made, or which shall be made, under the Authority of the United States, shall be the supreme Law of the Land; and the Judges in every State shall be bound thereby, any Thing in the Constitution or Laws of any State to the Contrary not withstanding.*

Thus, the Constitution and federal laws made under it, as well as decisions of the Supreme Court of the United States, together with related supporting opinions, are constituent parts of the "supreme law of the land." The significance of the **supremacy doctrine** is that it invalidates any conflicting state law by preemption, meaning that federal law takes precedence over state law in areas of control expressly delegated to the United States by the Constitution. The Supremacy Clause does not give the federal government additional authority, it just makes what authority it has the superior law. The Supremacy Clause, however, makes Commerce Clause authority very powerful.

supremacy doctrine
The judicial doctrine that holds that any state or federal law that is inconsistent with the U.S. Constitution is null and void.

LEGAL FOCUS—CASE

An Arizona statute made it unlawful to operate a train of more than fourteen passenger cars or seventy freight cars within the state. The law was a safety measure enacted under the state's police power. Was such state regulation of train lengths lawful?

Southern Pacific v. Arizona, 325 U.S. 761, 65 S.Ct. 1515 (1945).

No, the state regulation was not lawful. Trains move into and out of Arizona, from and to other states. Interstate commerce is subject to federal regulation under Article I, Section 8 and the Arizona statute unduly burdened interstate transportation. If the state regulation affects interstate commerce only slightly, or if national interests are served well by it, then states may regulate the particular interstate commerce and preemption is unnecessary.

Today, there is no argument about the supremacy of the national government. Most of the debate about proper state and federal roles has to do with "effectiveness." Should it be done nationally, or can it be done better locally? The availability of necessary funds and adequate resources are also important factors. States, counties, and cities that are "strapped for cash" eagerly seek federal funding for local projects such as public housing, mass transit construction, education, and indigent care. Also, major natural disasters require a national response. The terrible and devastating harm done by Hurricane Katrina probably will have a powerful effect on the direction of the debate over national versus local response, although which direction it will go is not so obvious.

WHAT ABOUT TAXES?

In the famous case of *McCulloch v. Maryland,* Chief Justice John Marshall observed that "[t]he power to tax involves the power to destroy." Although primarily revenue-raising measures, taxes also are used to influence the behavior of people and the production and distribution of goods and services. Income taxes and estate and inheritance taxes (so-called *death taxes* on the privilege of giving and receiving part of a decedent's estate) tend to redistribute wealth. So-called *sin taxes* on liquor and tobacco products presumably tend to discourage harmful use of such products. Credits against the payment of taxes otherwise due by renters tend to ease the costs of housing. Tax benefits accorded parents of dependent children tend to ease family costs. And so on.

The authority to tax is provided to the Congress in Article I, Section 8 of the Constitution.

> *The Congress shall have Power To lay and collect Taxes, Duties, Imposts and Excises, to pay the Debts and provide for the common Defence and general Welfare of the United States; but all Duties, Imposts and Excises shall be uniform throughout the United States.**

> The U.S. Constitution gives Congress

> *Power To lay (i.e., impose) and collect Taxes, Duties, Imposts (a generic term for taxes, usually referring to schedules of customs duties) and Excises (the term loosely applied to most taxes, including the sales tax, but excluding the income tax and the property tax).*

For most employees, the personal income tax is collected by their employers who are required to withhold proper amounts from wages or salaries earned. All wage-earners are reminded of this each payday when they compare the difference between their "gross" and "net" earnings. The difference is a wide range of federal and state income taxes.

For persons with incomes from various investments, and for business firms, the income tax has evolved into a monstrous maze of confusing regulations. Certified public accountants (CPAs) and tax lawyers often disagree as to the proper interpretation of many clauses. Huge national CPA firms employ both accountants and tax lawyers to offer their customers full tax services. Less wealthy individuals obtain assistance in preparing their returns from tax preparer businesses available in most cities in the United States. Computer programs also enable many people to prepare their own tax returns without professional assistance, and some file them electronically. Entire books are written on the topic of tax computation ideas, interpretations, rules, and controversies. The concept of a "tax shelter" (an investment or activity with at least one purpose being to reduce tax liability) constantly is tested in courts.

The income tax on individuals and corporations has become the most important single source of revenue for the federal government. It also is imposed by most states and by some local governments. Economists justify it as the most equitable, or progressive, of taxes, especially when rates are graduated, because the levy is imposed in accordance with apparent ability to pay.

*Significant limitations on how the federal government could tax were removed by constitutional amendment. "Congress shall have power to lay and collect taxes on incomes, from whatever source derived, without apportionment among the several States, and without regard to any census or enumeration." Amendment XVI (ratified on February 3, 1913).

MORALS AND ETHICS

Duty to Pay Taxes?

Paying taxes in the United States, with its myriad of credits, special exemptions, and other means to reduce one's taxes, presents a moral and ethical question. Although tax evasion is a crime, the past many decades have been filled with people finding a way to deduct an expense, only to see Congress "plug the hole" with a statute prohibiting such a "tax shelter." Americans often can be divided into two camps: Those who say it is your duty to pay your taxes and those who say it is your duty to pay the most minimal amount of taxes the law allows. These latter taxpayers strive to find interpretations or loopholes that allow them to exploit an exemption or obtain a credit. Corporations pay lawyers expensive fees for advice that a tax strategy is "reasonable." What it all comes down to is that paying taxes for many involves finding the gray line between a legal obligation to pay taxes and the moral justification not to pay them.

In contrast, the sales tax is regressive in that it imposes a disproportionately heavy burden on persons with *low* incomes. For example, the sales tax on an automobile is the same regardless of the purchaser's income. This sum may represent a substantial percentage of one person's disposable income yet hardly be noticed by another, more wealthy individual.

The ability to pay taxes is not necessarily related to income. Wealth and annual income are not the same thing. For example, large land holdings—although subject to real property taxes—may produce no taxable income for their land-rich owners. Likewise, persons of great wealth may own tax-exempt bonds issued by the federal or state governments or other public agencies. The interest rate on such bonds is generally lower than rates paid by private corporate borrowers. So the owner of tax-free bonds indirectly helps to support the government. Moreover, corporations that reinvest all earnings and pay no dividends (which are taxable income), gradually, may grow in value and increase the wealth of their shareholders, who pay no income taxes until their shares are sold, if ever, and then at reduced tax (capital gains) rates.

commerce
The exchange of goods or commodities for payment in cash, credit, services, or other goods.

Commerce clause
A part of the U.S. Constitution that provides Congress with the power to pass laws to provide for trade with foreign countries and among states.

Obviously, there is much to be considered in understanding income taxation. From a constitutional standpoint, there is no right to equality of wealth. That the more wealthy citizens may acquire more luxuries in life, or even better legal services, than less wealthy persons is of no constitutional significance. For example, criminal defendants are entitled constitutionally to *competent* legal services, not the best available legal services nor any particular lawyer of choice.

WHAT IS THE COMMERCE CLAUSE?

In Article I, Section 8, the Constitution expressly grants the federal government the power to "regulate Commerce with foreign Nations, and among the several States, and with the Indian Tribes." This power to "regulate Commerce" allows the federal government to regulate most business activities in the United States with uniform rules.

interstate
Activity that crosses state boundaries.

intrastate
Activity that occurs entirely within a state's boundaries.

Commerce includes the buying, selling, and transporting of things of value from place to place. The Supreme Court has held that Congress through the **Commerce Clause** has the power to regulate any activity, **interstate** or **intrastate**, that "affects" interstate commerce. Interstate means any activity that crosses state boundaries. Intrastate means any activity that occurs entirely within a state's boundaries. Thus, Congress can pass laws that regulate intrastate commerce if, but only if, interstate commerce is affected. From the 1930s until recent years, the Commerce Clause authority seemed unlimited. In 1995, however, the Supreme Court decided a case that defined limits, albeit vague ones, on the extent to which the Commerce Clause could be used as justification for federal authority to regulate.

LEGAL FOCUS—CASE

In 1990, the United States enacted the Gun-Free School Zones Act (GFSZA), which, among other things, prohibited the possession of a firearm in a local school zone. Congress relied upon the Commerce Clause for its authority to pass the law. Fred subsequently was convicted of possessing a handgun in a school zone. He appealed his conviction in part claiming Congress lacked authority to pass this law and it ultimately was heard in the U.S. Supreme Court. The government, in defending the law, essentially argued that guns around schools could cause a violent crime and that violent crime could adversely affect the national economy by either raising the cost of insurance or deterring interstate travel. Thus, the law regulated interstate commerce. Did the Supreme Court accept the interstate commerce basis of federal authority to ban firearms around schools?

No, the Supreme Court did not. The Supreme Court noted that

> *under the theories that the Government presents in support of [the Act], it is difficult to perceive any limitation on federal power.... Thus, if we were to accept the Government's arguments, we are hard pressed to posit any activity by an individual that Congress is without power to regulate.*

The Court held that Commerce Clause authority had to either directly regulate travel or movement across state borders, regulate the instruments of such interstate movement of goods or persons, or regulate "commercial activities that substantially affect interstate commerce." GFSZA did not regulate movement at all, and the activity it did regulate—possession of guns near schools—did not substantially affect commerce; thus, the law was unconstitutional and the conviction overturned.

When states seek to regulate local activities, they frequently collide with the Commerce Clause. As part of their inherent sovereignty (power to govern), states possess police powers to regulate private activities to protect or promote the public health, safety, or general welfare of their citizens. For example, states have a clear interest in keeping their local roads and highways safe. However, when a state regulates the use of its roads and highways, those laws also will affect interstate commerce. A law setting a top speed on a highway affects all drivers, including interstate truckers.

If the state law affects interstate commerce, the courts may be asked to balance the state's interests with those of the federal government. The question is, does a state's exercise of its police power interfere with the federal government's right to regulate interstate commerce? Recall that the Constitution provides that when state and federal law conflict, federal law is supreme. The courts try to answer this question by balancing the interests of the state with those of the federal government. The courts will consider several factors, including the following:

- What interest is the state furthering by its law?
- Does the state law burden (make more difficult) interstate commerce?
- Is there another way the state could accomplish its purpose without burdening interstate commerce?

LEGAL FOCUS—PROBLEM

Suppose Georgia passes a law requiring use of "contoured" rear-fender mudguards on trucks and trailers operating on its highways. All other mudguards are declared illegal. In thirty-five other states, including the neighboring state of Florida, "straight" mudguards are either legal or required. Evidence suggests that contoured mudguards are safer than straight mudguards. Is the Georgia statute constitutional?

No, the statue is not constitution. Truckers traveling through Georgia would have a problem. What is legal in Georgia is illegal in other states, including Florida, and vice versa. Clearly, the Georgia law would affect interstate commerce. Even though Georgia's purpose in passing the statute was to increase safety on the highways, a possible increase in safety would not justify requiring truckers to either avoid Georgia or change their mudguards before they pass through.

LEGAL FOCUS—CASE

The Direct Shipping Cases

Following the repeal of the federal prohibition on the sale, manufacture, and transport of intoxicating liquor with the enactment of the Twenty-First Amendment to the Constitution, states stepped into the void to regulate and control the sales of liquor. Many states developed a complex system of liquor regulation, and liquor law in the United States is now characterized by a maze of differing requirements from state to state. Many states include prohibitions on the sale and shipping of alcohol to consumers via mail or other third-party shipping services, so-called direct shipping. Gradually, many states made exceptions to the direct shipping prohibition for in-state wineries. Other states went farther and allowed out-of-state wineries to ship wine to their residents. New York and Michigan were two states that prohibited out-of-state wineries from shipping wine to in-state residents but allowed in-state wineries to do so. Residents desiring to receive wine shipments from out-of-state wineries sued, challenging the laws, and won. The states appealed to the Supreme Court. The states argued that safety concerns related to liquor and the fact that out-of-state wineries were more difficult to regulate combined to justify the ban on out-of-state winery shipping. Did the Supreme Court agree?

No, the Supreme Court did not. The Supreme Court held that the state laws burdened interstate commerce unnecessarily, and they invalidated the laws. Since then, many states have jettisoned their out-of-state shipping bans on wine and replaced them with tax and regulation structures that treat in-state and out-of-state shippers equally.

WHAT IS THE BILL OF RIGHTS?

Bill of Rights
The first ten amendments to the U.S. Constitution.

The **Bill of Rights** is the all-inclusive title popularly given to the first ten amendments to the U.S. Constitution (see Exhibit 2.1). The Bill of Rights mandates specific and general restraints on the national government to protect all persons from arbitrary and capricious acts by federal officials. Thus, the Bill of Rights originally applied only as a restraint on the national government. States were bound only by provisions on civil rights if and as specified in their own state constitutions.

Following the Civil War, several amendments were added to the U.S. Constitution to protect and assist the newly freed slaves. In 1865, the Thirteenth Amendment formally outlawed slavery. Previously, most African Americans had been denied liberty despite the contrary words of the Declaration of Independence, "We hold these Truths to be self-evident, that all Men are created equal, that they are endowed by their Creator with certain unalienable Rights, that among these are Life, Liberty, and the Pursuit of Happiness" and the mandate of the Fifth Amendment that "no person shall be deprived of life, liberty, or property without due process of law." Three years later, in 1868, the Fourteenth Amendment reiterated the right of all persons to liberty and extended the scope of its protection by binding all state and local governments with these words:

> *No state shall make or enforce any law which shall abridge the privileges or immunities of citizens of the United States; nor shall any state deprive any person of life, liberty, or property, without due process of law, nor deny to any person within its jurisdiction the equal protection of the laws.*

EXHIBIT 2.1 The Bill of Rights

First Amendment	Guarantees freedom of religion, speech, press, assembly, and petition.
Second Amendment	Guarantees the right to keep and bear arms, because a state requires a well-equipped citizen army for its own security.
Third Amendment	Prohibits the lodging of soldiers in peacetime without the dweller's consent.
Fourth Amendment	Prohibits unreasonable searches and seizures of persons or property.
Fifth Amendment	Prohibits deprivation of life, liberty, or property without due process of law, and fair payment when private property is taken for public use, such as in eminent domain; prohibits compulsory self-incrimination and double jeopardy (trial for the same crime twice).
Sixth Amendment	Guarantees the accused in a criminal case the right to a speedy and public trial by an impartial jury and with counsel; allows the accused to cross-examine witnesses against him or her and to solicit testimony from witnesses in his or her favor.
Seventh Amendment	Guarantees a trial by jury for the accused in a civil case involving $20 or more.
Eighth Amendment	Prohibits excessive bail and fines, as well as cruel and unusual punishments.
Ninth Amendment	Establishes that the people have rights in addition to those specified in the Constitution.
Tenth Amendment	Establishes that those powers neither delegated to the national government nor denied to the states are reserved for the states.

Due Process
The requirement that legal proceedings (including arrest, civil and criminal trials, and punishment) comply with the U.S. Constitution and other applicable substantive and procedural laws.

Equal Protection
The clause in the Fourteenth Amendment to the U.S. Constitution declaring that "no state shall ... deny to any person within its jurisdiction the equal protection of the laws."

incorporation doctrine
The Supreme Court's utilization of the Fourteenth Amendment to find Bill of Rights limitations on state and local governments.

The clauses guaranteeing due process of law and equal protection of the law were not defined at the time of the Fourteenth Amendment, leaving the work of definition and specific application to the judicial branch. The Due Process and Equal Protection Clauses have been used by the Supreme Court to restrict the constitutionally reserved powers of the states.

Simply stated, the Supreme Court defines **due process** as the equivalent of fundamental fairness and **equal protection** as the prevention of invidious discrimination (i.e., differentiating offensively or unfairly). Thus, states cannot violate the due process or equal protection guaranteed to the people, regardless of what is contained in their respective constitutions. But the application of those terms to specific examples of state action was to evolve through Supreme Court decisions using an interpretive process referred to as the **incorporation doctrine**.

Incorporation Doctrine

In its trailblazing decision in *Gitlow v. New York* in 1925, the U.S. Supreme Court announced, "[W]e may and do assume that freedom of speech and of press—First Amendment protections—are among the fundamental personal rights and 'liberties' protected by the Due Process Clause of the Fourteenth Amendment from impairment by the States."

With the *Gitlow* decision, the Supreme Court began a policy that it has maintained ever since. As selected cases reach it, the Court has systematically imposed on the states most of the guarantees found in the Bill of Rights by interpreting the Fourteenth Amendment's Due Process Clause to restrict state impositions on individual liberty. Its ongoing impact is to bind both the national and state governments to a similar standard of compliance regarding due process and equal protection.

THE FIRST AMENDMENT AND FREE SPEECH

First Amendment
"Congress shall make no law respecting an establishment of religion, or prohibiting the free exercise thereof; or abridging the freedom of speech, or of the press; or of the right of the people peaceably to assemble, and to petition the Government for a redress of grievances."

free speech
"Congress shall make no law ... abridging the freedom of speech, or of the press; or the right of the people peaceably to assemble, and to petition the Government for a redress of grievances."

The **First Amendment** contains what are known historically as *primary rights*. It is no accident that this amendment begins with the phrase, "Congress shall make no law." Nor is it accidental that first among our primary rights is freedom of speech and press. They are "the matrix, the indispensable condition, of nearly every other form of freedom." As Justice Hugo Black remarked,

> *Freedom to speak and write about public questions is as important to the life of our government as is the heart to the human body.... If that heart be weakened, the result is debilitation; if it be stilled, the result is death.*

Accordingly, the Supreme Court has decided incrementally, one case after another, that the states must also guarantee to their citizens First Amendment rights of freedom of speech and press.

The Court, however, has been unable to define **free speech** with precision. It has moved successively through certain legal expedients, or "tests," including the following:

1. The "clear and present danger" test under which speech could be regulated by government was explained in *Schenck*.
2. The "bad tendency" test was exemplified in *Abrams*. Here the Court accorded little importance to the guarantee of free speech, focusing almost solely on the impact of the challenged speech on the war (World War I) effort.
3. The "preferred position" test was articulated in Justice Harlan Stone's famous footnote in the *Carolene Products* case. Stone presented the view that free speech enjoyed a preferred position in relation to other constitutional guarantees, calling for a more precise and searching scrutiny of legislation that might curtail "political processes."
4. During the Cold War of the late 1940s and 1950s, the Supreme Court upheld the conviction of eleven leaders of the American Communist Party by enforcing the Smith Act of 1940, which made it a crime to teach or advocate the overthrow of government by force. In doing so, the Court adopted the "probability" statement of the "clear and present danger" rule, as expressed by the highly respected Chief Judge Learned Hand, writing for the lower court majority: "In each case [courts] must ask whether the gravity of the 'evil,' discounted by its improbability, justifies such invasion of free speech as is necessary to avoid the danger."
5. Political dissent during the late 1960s and early 1970s found the Court using the "ad hoc balancing" test. Using the "clear and present danger" test, the Court weighed the competing interests of free speech and law and order. Every ordinance attempting to serve the interests of the state must be drawn with "reasonable specificity toward the [speech] and conduct prohibited."

LEGAL FOCUS—CASE

Paladin Press published a book *Hit Man: A Technical Manual for Independent Contractors*, which provided instructions for would-be contract murderers. Lawrence Horn hired James Perry, a contract killer, to murder his ex-wife and their brain-damaged son, after which Horn expected to inherit a $2 million trust fund intended for the boy. Perry, using principles studied in the Paladin murder text, suffocated the boy and fatally shot the ex-wife and an overnight nurse. A sister of the ex-wife sued Paladin Press in a civil case for damages for aiding and abetting the murderer. Is the publication of an instructional book for murder protected by the First Amendment from a civil lawsuit?

Paladin Enterprises, Inc. v. Rice, 940 F.Supp. 836 (D. Md. 1996), rev'd, 128 F.3d 233 (4th Cir. 1997), cert. denied, 523 U.S. 1074, 118 S.Ct. 1515 (1998).

No, the Constitution does not shield from civil lawsuits such things as bomb-making guides, assassination manuals, or similar works that exhort people to take the law into their own hands. Nor does the Constitution prevent the publication of libelous (untruthful) material and any subsequent civil lawsuits that may follow. The **prior restraint** of speech that is offensive for any reason is a judicial power that is exercised only in the most extraordinary circumstances.

prior restraint
Restraints on a publication before it is actually published.

The Court has been careful to protect expressive activity and symbolic speech and has ruled that burning of the national flag of the United States, as political speech, can be restricted neither by the states nor by the Congress. Several attempts have been made to establish an amendment granting Congress specific authority to prohibit the physical desecration of the U.S. flag, but none have yet passed the Senate.

Is Commercial Speech Protected?

commercial speech
Oral, written, and other forms of communication used in advertising and in other business activities.

Commercial speech, which is defined as any communication that advertises a product or service for a business purpose to earn a profit, also is protected, but not as comprehensively as other speech.

LEGAL FOCUS—CASE

San Diego enacted an ordinance that prohibited commercial outdoor advertising signs within the city limits. Sign owners sued the city for injunctive relief, claiming that the law violated their rights under the First Amendment. Does the ordinance violate the Constitution?

Metromedia Inc. v. City of San Diego, 453 U.S. 490, 101 S.Ct. 2882 (1981).

Yes, the ordinance does. Speaking for the Court, Justice Byron B. White stated:

Prior to 1975, purely commercial advertisements of services or goods for sale was considered to be outside the protection of the First Amendment.... [But] in Virginia Pharmacy Board v. Virginia Citizens Consumer Council, 425 U.S. 748 (1976), we plainly held that speech proposing no more than commercial transaction enjoys a substantial degree of First Amendment protection. A State may not completely suppress the dissemination of truthful information about an entirely lawful activity merely because it is fearful of that information's effect upon its disseminators and its recipients.

LEGAL FOCUS—PROBLEM

U.S. Beverage Co. produced Phat Boy, an inexpensive malt liquor that was sold in bigger bottles with a higher alcohol content than competing beers. It also sported a funky red, black, and yellow label and contained ginseng, which some consider an aphrodisiac. ("Phat" is a 1990s version of the word "cool.") A public interest group contended that Phat Boy was targeted to underage African Americans, much like cigarette ads featuring Joe Camel allegedly targeted teenagers. Does the Constitution protect focused commercial advertising?

Yes, but to a lesser extent than other forms of speech. When alcohol is involved in any commercial activity, the states have an additional interest in protecting the public from harm. However, the North Carolina Alcoholic Beverage Commission received no complaints from the public, and the product was promoted and sold widely, not targeted in specific neighborhoods.

Is Symbolic Speech Protected? Even "Hate Speech"?

Although originally expressed as protection for spoken, written, or printed words, the First Amendment has been appropriately construed by the Court to embrace many forms of the communication of ideas.

Motion pictures, television programs, electronic tapes, digital disks, and electronic and fax transmissions have taken their place alongside the formerly dominant person-to-person speech and printed statements. In Des Moines, Iowa, the U.S. Supreme Court upheld the right of students to wear black armbands in school to show their opposition to the Vietnam War. The conduct was "a symbolic act that is within the Free Speech Clause … [and] was entirely divorced from actually or potentially disruptive conduct" that would interfere with appropriate discipline in the operation of the school. As noted earlier, the symbolic act of burning an American flag is likewise protected under the First Amendment.

As indicated by these cases, the U.S. Supreme Court zealously erects ramparts around the cherished First Amendment freedoms to communicate.

LEGAL FOCUS—PROBLEM

Stanford University, a private institution, adopted a code stating that "one student cannot with purpose vilify another with fighting words that are ugly gutter epithets like 'nigger' and 'kike'." The code also banned such hate-associated symbols as the swastika. Can a private university proscribe undesirable speech?

hate speech
Words spoken, written, or symbolized (e.g., by placing burning crosses on private lawns) that express irrational and false ideas that insult and demean certain persons or classes of persons.

No, a university cannot. Stanford students challenged the code in a state superior court (trial court) where the judge granted a preliminary injunction declaring Stanford's "**hate speech**" ban unconstitutionally broad. Basing his decision on a state law, the judge ruled that the university violated students' freedom of expression by prohibiting only certain "fighting words" linked to sex and race. Stanford defended their eighteen-months-in-the-making speech code by contending that [California's] Leonard Law, which extended free speech protections to private schools, "intruded on the university's right to govern itself and establish rules of proper behavior."

In 1992, the U.S. Supreme Court unanimously condemned a St. Paul, Minnesota, ordinance that outlawed any hate-motivated expression (e.g., burning crosses, displaying swastikas) that "one knows or has reasonable grounds to know arouses anger, alarm, or resentment in others on the basis of race, color, creed, religion or gender." In the hate speech case in question, a seventeen-year-old skinhead (i.e., an antisocial or delinquent youth who wears his hair closely cropped) was arrested after setting fire to a crude cross in the yard of an African American family that recently had settled in a predominantly white neighborhood. Justice Antonin Scalia noted that such conduct "is reprehensible.... But St. Paul has sufficient means at its disposal to prevent such behavior without adding the First Amendment to the fire." Note, however, that in the following year, the Court unanimously upheld a Wisconsin statute that imposes harsher penalties on a criminal who "intentionally selects the person against whom the crime ... is committed ... because of the race, religion, color, disability, sexual orientation, national origin or ancestry of that person." Most states now have similar "hate crime" penalty-enhancement laws.

In other cases, the Court has withheld the protective shield of the First Amendment from "fighting words," meaning words "which by their very utterance inflict injury or tend to incite an immediate breach of the peace" and conduct that is "directed to inciting or producing imminent lawless action and is likely to incite or produce such action."

Certain artists and their publishers have produced paintings, photographs, magazines, books, songs, videotapes, and compact discs that allegedly violate traditional and appropriate standards of morality and decency. Probably most people are not offended because they are not within the targeted markets for most of this bizarre art. However, programs on free television and cable television now enter most homes. Increasing numbers of viewers, both old and young, find excessive violence and perceived obscenity intolerable and are demanding government imposition of restraints or standards. But the practical difficulty of imposing effective controls is readily apparent from a reading of the 1973 case of *Miller v. California*, in which the U.S. Supreme Court decreed that to be legally condemned as obscene, the material must be such that

1. the average person,
2. applying contemporary community standards,
3. would find that the work taken as a whole appeals to the prurient (i.e., characterized by lustful thoughts) interest, and
4. the work depicts or describes in a patently offensive way sexual conduct proscribed by state law, and
5. whether—taken as a whole—it is lacking in serious artistic, political, or scientific value.

The inherently subjective nature of the listed criteria, coupled with potentially thousands of different problems or cases, every one of which is unique in at least some respect, makes any comprehensive policing effort predestined to fail, except in the most egregious cases.

What is known is that nearly nude dancing by females (wearing pasties and G-strings) is not inherently obscene and may be expressive conduct protected by the First and Fourteenth Amendments. Essentially, the determination of specifically what is obscene and, therefore, may be prohibited by state or local government is made by juries on a case-by-case basis.

Symbolic speech also sometimes may be deemed offensive because of historical implications related to race, religion, or other constitutionally protected classifications.

LEGAL FOCUS—PROBLEM

The mascot of Birmingham High School in Pontiac, Michigan, is a head-dressed American Indian based on Chief Pontiac, an Ottawa Indian who was an organizer of tribes against the invading English during the 1700s. The city of Pontiac is named after this chief. The high school's team name is the "Braves." In response to demands of American Indian activists, the local board of education chose to change the mascots of four high schools, including the "Mohicans" and the "Warriors." Removing the "Braves" logo from the Birmingham High School gym floor and track and purchasing new gym clothes and uniforms will cost $240,000. The activists argued that portrayal of an American Indian with a headdress is sacrilegious. Does the Constitution protect the use of insulting or sacrilegious speech?

Yes, it does. However, a public school may choose to avoid offensive language or symbols for other reasons. Even if offensive speech is protected from censorship by the Constitution, that does not mean it should be employed.

Public Employees and Free Speech

When a public employee makes statements, drafts letters, or otherwise "speaks" in the course of his or her duties, is such speech protected? Can a supervisor take an adverse action against the employee because of the content of the speech? The First Amendment could be interpreted to protect such speech. Under a recent Supreme Court decision, *Garcetti v. Ceballos*, however, speech in the course of official duties is not protected by the First Amendment. Thus, a deputy district attorney could be disciplined by his employer for stating in court that the police had made false statements while seeking an arrest warrant. When public employees speak outside of their official duties, such as a teacher sending a letter to a local newspaper about school funding, such speech can be protected under the First Amendment.

Free Speech and the Internet

Although the Internet is around forty years old, it is still very young in terms of governments applying control through legal rules. The Internet is a unique and wholly new medium of worldwide human communication, the use of which is posing new challenges to our Constitution and legal system. The growth of Internet use, with its attendant social and economic impacts, makes access and control very important to people and to governments. Issues such as individual privacy, spam, identity theft, and pornography are but some of the issues that send people to the government asking for rules. As electronic transmissions cross state and national boundaries, the potential legal problems are growing in number and complexity almost as fast as the Internet itself.

Among the important legal issues in the United States about the Internet are fundamental questions concerning free speech and pornography. Sexually explicit material on the Internet includes text, pictures, and chat that range from the modestly titillating to the completely explicit. Many people go looking for sexually explicit material but your authors know from experience that sometimes these sites show up in search requests for material totally unrelated to sex. In 1996, Congress adopted two acts, the

Communications Decency Act (CDA) and the Child Pornography Prevention Act (CPPA), in an attempt to regulate sexually explicit Internet content as it related to children. The CDA attempted to prohibit the knowing transmission of obscene or indecent messages to any recipient less than eighteen years of age. In 1997, the Supreme Court held the CDA to be an unconstitutional infringement of free speech guaranteed by the U.S. Constitution.

LEGAL FOCUS—CASE

The CPPA provided a federal prohibition against sexually explicit images that appear to depict minors produced without using any real children—virtual child pornography. The statute prohibited possessing or distributing these virtual images. Is the act constitutional, or does it violate the First Amendment protection against free speech?

Ashcroft v. The Free Speech Coalition, 535 U.S. 234, 122 S.Ct. 1389 (2002).

The Court stated:

> *[A]s a general principle, the First Amendment bars the government from dictating what we see or read or speak or hear. The freedom of speech has its limits; it does not embrace certain categories of speech, including defamation, incitement, obscenity, and pornography produced with real children.*

Among the arguments in favor of the statute was that to eliminate the market for pornography produced using real children necessitated a prohibition on virtual images. The Court's response to that argument was, "The Government may not suppress lawful speech as the means to suppress unlawful speech. Protected speech does not become unprotected merely because it resembles the latter." In holding the second of the two 1996 congressional attempts to control Internet pornography unconstitutional, the Court stated the provisions considered "are overbroad and unconstitutional."

Do these two cases mean that Internet content cannot be regulated? Hardly. But the cases do make clear that constitutional freedoms such as the First Amendment make regulation of the Internet and new technologies a challenging task for the legislatures. Still improper use of the Internet by individuals, such as by publishing libelous material (civil) or by conspiring to commit criminal offenses, can result in civil or criminal penalties. Free speech does not equate to freedom from personal responsibility to comply with laws enacted under proper exercise of the police powers of the states.

LEGAL FOCUS—CASE

"Approximately 10 percent of the Americans who use the Internet access it at public libraries. And approximately 95 percent of all public libraries in the United States provide public access to the Internet." Can Congress require public libraries to provide software filters to guard against sexually explicit content as a condition to the receipt of federal subsidies?

American Library Ass'n, Inc. v. United States, 201 F.Supp.2d 401 (E.D.Pa., 2002).

The United States was sued by a group of libraries, library associations, library patrons, and Website publishers alleging that the Children's Internet Protection Act (CIPA), requiring filtering of sexually explicit content, forces the libraries to violate their patrons' First Amendment rights. The district court agreed with the plaintiffs. The lower court decision ultimately was overturned, however, by the U.S. Supreme Court, which upheld CIPA. Though a plurality decision, the common thread in the justices' opinions related to ease or means by which patrons or libraries could defeat or bypass the filter.

THE FIRST AMENDMENT AND FREEDOM OF RELIGION

freedom of religion
"Congress shall make no law respecting an establishment of religion, or prohibiting the free exercise thereof."

It is not surprising that the Bill of Rights provides for the protection of religious liberty first, because many of the colonists came here to escape religious persecution. The First Amendment guarantees **freedom of religion** in two ways. The First Amendment *Establishment Clause* prohibits Congress from establishing a religion ("Congress shall make no law respecting an establishment of religion"). Additionally, the *Free Exercise Clause* prohibits government interference in the free exercise of religious beliefs ("Congress shall make no law … prohibiting the free exercise of [religion]"). Government action, both federal and state, is expected to be neutral toward religion. Regulation that does not promote religion or place a significant burden on religion is constitutional.

Religious pluralism is a hallmark of American life, together with our commitment to religious freedom. In many parts of the world, governments maintain "official" religions and official religions maintain governments. In the United States, a wall has been erected between church and state; any significant breach of that wall by either government or church, no matter how compelling, is generally suspect. Yet attempts to promote or dissuade certain religions are made from time to time in spite of the First Amendment. What should be the government's position respecting religion? The Supreme Court has answered. The First Amendment (on religion) means this:

> *Neither a state nor the federal government can set up a church. Neither can pass laws, which aid one religion, aid all religions, or prefer one religion to another. Neither can force nor influence a person to go to or to remain away from church against his will or force him to profess a belief or disbelief in any religion. No person can be punished for entertaining or professing religious beliefs or disbeliefs, for church attendance or nonattendance. No tax in any amount, large or small, can be levied to support any religious activities or institutions, whatever they may be called, or whatever form they may adopt to teach or practice religion. Neither a state nor the federal government can, openly or secretly, participate in the affairs of any religious organizations or groups and vice versa … the [religious] clause was intended to erect "a wall of separation between church and state.*
>
> *Everson v. Board of Education of the Town of Ewing*

Establishment Clause

Accordingly, the Supreme Court has declared unconstitutional various state attempts to promote "religious values" in public schools under the Establishment Clause. In 1962, in a controversial decision (*Engel v. Vitale*), the Court outlawed the recitation of a nonsectarian prayer in the public schools of New York State. The prayer was to be said aloud in class in the presence of a teacher at the beginning of every school day. The prayer provided by the New York Board of Regents was: "Almighty God, we acknowledge our dependence upon Thee, and we beg Thy blessings upon us, our parents, our teachers and our country." Speaking for the Court, Justice Hugo L. Black pointed out that the prayer violated the Establishment Clause of the First Amendment:

> *Its first and most immediate purpose [referring to the clause] rested on the belief that a union of government and religion tends to destroy government and to degrade religions.... [G]overnmentally established religions and religious persecution go hand in hand.... It was in large part to get completely away from this sort of systematic religious persecution that the Founders brought into being our Nation, our Constitution and our Bill of Rights.*

The Court said that even a one-minute period of silence for "meditation or voluntary prayer" is constitutionally impermissible.

Free Exercise Clause

The First Amendment's protection of religion is complicated because while it restricts any government establishment of religion it also restricts government from "prohibiting the free exercise" of religion. There clearly is a tension between these two admonitions. Do individuals have the right to act any way they want to on the basis of their religious beliefs? No. There is an important distinction between belief and practice. Although the government lacks authority to compel you to accept or reject any religious belief, the right to practice one's beliefs does have some limitations. Through the years, the Supreme Court has followed the general principle that people are free to believe and worship as they wish so long as their conduct violates no laws that validly protect the health, safety, or morals of the community.

LEGAL FOCUS—CASE

It is the 1870s in Utah, and Reynolds is a Mormon with two wives. The then territory of Utah prosecutes him for violation of a U.S. Territory statute stating

> *Every person having a husband or wife living, who marries another ... is guilty of bigamy, and shall be punished by a fine of not more than $500, and by imprisonment for a term of not more than five years.*

Among the defenses offered by Reynolds were that the church doctrine of the time made it "the duty of male members of said church, circumstances permitting, to practise [*sic*] polygamy," and the First Amendment restricts government from passing a statute that prohibits the free exercise of his religion. Was he correct?

Reynolds v. United States, 98 U.S. 145, 25 L.Ed. 244 (1878).

This U.S. Supreme Court case was one of the first to consider whether the Free Exercise Clause provides a defense to a criminal act. The Court bluntly said no.

> *To permit this would be to make the professed doctrines of religious belief superior to the law of the land, and in effect to permit every citizen to become a law unto himself. Government could exist only in name under such circumstances.*

In recent years, a number of cases have raised the question of allowing free exercise of religion in public schools as a counter to public school establishment of religion. In other words, although the public school cannot encourage a religious practice, must it allow it? In 1984, Congress passed the Equal Access Act, making it unlawful for any public high school receiving federal assistance (funds) to prevent student groups from using school facilities for religious activities. In addition, the Religious Freedoms Restoration Act was passed in 1993, stating that "governments should not substantially burden religious exercise without compelling justification." These statutes have been interpreted to authorize student-initiated religious activities if other types of student-initiated gatherings are permitted. The Supreme Court already had declared constitutional student-initiated religious worship at state universities and colleges.

Other activities involving religion are permissible in public schools. These include the following:

- Silent prayer before tests so long as other students are not persuaded to participate.
- The teaching of the history of religion as distinguished from teaching religion.
- The expression by students of their religious beliefs in the form of reports that are germane to their assignments.
- Participation in religious clubs.
- The wearing of religious garb including ceremonial knives.

CAN GUNS BE BANNED?

As this edition was being written, a series of violent shootings in the United States had raised the topic of gun control to the top of many agendas in government. What limits exist upon the government's right to restrict or ban gun ownership? According to the Second Amendment: "A well regulated Militia, being necessary to the security of a free State, the right of the people to keep and bear Arms, shall not be infringed."

When this amendment was penned, the common practice of states was to have large standing armies. There was a strong public sentiment that a large permanent army should not be part of the national government. Also, the amendment was designed to prevent Congress from disarming and abolishing state militias.

The Supreme Court had sustained this sentiment holding "The Second Amendment guarantees *no* right to keep and bear a firearm that does not have some reasonable relationship to the preservation or efficiency of a well-regulated militia." Then beginning with a case in 2008, the court established a doctrine that the Second Amendment gives citizens individual rights to own guns for self-defense. Most recently, the U.S. Supreme Court ruled that the Second Amendment rights to own and bear firearms apply to citizens. This case is presented as one of the featured cases in this chapter. *McDonald*, like many modern U.S. Supreme Court cases, is a plurality. The plurality agreed that Chicago's handgun ban was a violation of the Second Amendment, but left open the question of what level of restriction or control over the ownership of handguns or firearms would be constitutional.

FREEDOM FROM UNREASONABLE SEARCHES

The Fourth Amendment recognizes "[t]he right of the people to be secure in their persons, houses, papers, and effects against unreasonable searches and seizures." But note that *reasonable* searches and seizures are permitted. Consequently, search warrants may be issued "upon probable cause, supported by Oath or affirmation, and particularly describing the place to be searched, and the persons or things to be seized." In two cases, *Wolf v. Colorado* (1949) and *Mapp v. Ohio* (1961), the Supreme Court imposed on the states the same standards of care in search and seizure procedures and the exclusion of evidence illegally obtained as that imposed by the Constitution on

exclusionary rule
The court-made rule that precludes the use in criminal court proceedings of any evidence improperly obtained by the prosecution.

the national government. The Court said that citizens have a "right to privacy" and to be "free from unreasonable state intrusions.... We hold that all evidence obtained by search and seizures in violation of the Constitution is, by the same authority, inadmissible in a state Court." This is known as the **exclusionary rule**. The exclusionary rule has been narrowed in its applicability since. The exclusionary rule is discussed more fully in Chapter 6.

RIGHTS OF AN ACCUSED TO DUE PROCESS OF LAW

Fifth Amendment
"No person shall be held to answer for a capital, or otherwise infamous crime, unless on a presentment or indictment of a Grand Jury, except in cases arising in the land or naval forces, or in the Militia, when in actual service in time of War or public danger; nor shall any person be subject for the same offence to be twice put in jeopardy of life or limb; nor shall be compelled in any criminal case to be a witness against himself, nor be deprived of life, liberty, or property, without due process of law; nor shall private property be taken for public use, without just compensation."

The Due Process Clause of the U.S. Constitution is really two clauses: the **Fifth Amendment**, which restricts federal government power, and the Fourteenth, which restricts state government power. The clauses hold that no person shall "be deprived of life, liberty, or property, without due process of law." These few words have led to millions of words by courts, lawyers, and laypeople attempting to define what due process means. Due process means government is expected to use fair and reasonable methods when exercising power over individuals, which is a matter of procedural due process. The clause also has been used to limit government exercise of power over the content of the law, which is a matter of substantive due process.

Examples of procedural due process questions often arise in the processing of individuals in the criminal justice system. Among the due process rights recognized over the years is the right to be represented by a lawyer during police questioning. The right arises after one is taken into custody or otherwise deprived of freedom in any significant way. The representation by an attorney is necessary to protect against compelled testimony and self-incrimination, each a basic right mandated by the U.S. Supreme Court for compliance by federal government and all states.

LEGAL FOCUS—CASE

A police undercover agent was planted in a cell with prisoner Perkins, who had been jailed for aggravated assault. Perkins was also under investigation for murder. The undercover agent asked Perkins if he had ever killed anybody. In answering the question, Perkins made statements implicating himself in the murder. Is this testimony that was given voluntarily but unknowingly by Perkins to a police officer admissible as evidence despite the way it was obtained?

Illinois v. Perkins, 496 U.S. 292, 110 S.Ct. 2394 (1990).

Yes, it is admissible. The Supreme Court held that an undercover officer posing as an inmate has no obligation to warn an incarcerated suspect of any constitutional rights before asking questions, even though the response could be legally incriminating.

Fourteenth Amendment
In part, "All persons born or naturalized in the United States, and subject to the jurisdiction thereof, are citizens of the United States and of the State wherein they reside. No State shall make or enforce any law which shall abridge the privileges or immunities of citizens of the United States; nor shall any State deprive any person of life, liberty, or property, without due process of law; nor deny to any person within its jurisdiction the equal protection of the laws."

Through a series of decisions based on Section 1 of the **Fourteenth Amendment**, the Supreme Court has imposed an obligation on the states to honor the human rights identified in the Fifth and Sixth Amendments. Included is the right to a speedy and public trial by an unbiased jury, assuredly among the most vital of rights in a free society. To further guarantee a fair trial, the Court in other cases also incorporated the right to have **compulsory process*** for obtaining witnesses for the defense of the accused person and to the assistance of professional legal counsel in all cases and at all stages of criminal procedures to which the defendant is subjected. An exception is made as to counsel in appellate proceedings (although, in fact, appellants generally are assisted by state compensated counsel).

LEGAL FOCUS—CASE

Chicago adopted an antiloitering ordinance intended to curb the "expanding cancer" of urban gangs. Under the ordinance, people loitering (standing) in a public place could be ordered to move along if a police officer believed one or more was a gang member. Those who refused to move along could be arrested and sent to jail for up to six months, fined $500, and ordered to perform three weeks of public service—even without proof of criminal intent. Does the ordinance as applied deprive defendants of due process of law?

City of Chicago v. Morales, 527 U.S. 41, 119 S.Ct. 1849 (1999).

compulsory process
(a) The right guaranteed by the Sixth Amendment to every person accused of a crime to require witnesses to appear in his or her favor, by court order.
(b) Official action to force a person to appear as a witness in court, at an administrative hearing, or before a legislature.

Concern about criminal activity by members of urban gangs has prompted many local boards and councils to adopt ordinances designed to protect their residents. The Chicago ordinance is but one example. Ordinarily, a person cannot be convicted of a crime by mere association and without criminal intent. In *City of Chicago v. Morales*, the Illinois Supreme Court concluded that the Chicago ordinance did not provide sufficiently specific limits on the enforcement discretion of the police to meet constitutional standards for definiteness and clarity. In upholding the Illinois Supreme Court, the U.S. Supreme Court stated:

> *We recognize the serious and difficult problems testified to by the citizens of Chicago that led to the enactment of this ordinance. We are mindful that the preservation of liberty depends in part on the maintenance of social order. However, in this instance the city has enacted an ordinance that affords too much discretion to the police and too little notice to citizens who wish to use the public streets.*

*Compulsory process means the court, at the request of a defendant in a criminal prosecution, must use its legal powers to compel the appearance of witnesses in favor of the defendant (U.S. Constitution, Sixth Amendment).

The War on Terror that has grown from the September 11, 2001, terrorist attacks has raised controversy regarding the rights guaranteed under the Constitution to non-citizens, to terrorist suspects, and to enemy combatants. What due process do such persons deserve or have a right to when the U.S. government conducts proceedings to determine their fate or punishment? The answer is not clear. A recent Supreme Court decision held that certain proposed military tribunals for enemy combatants lacked sufficient protections of the accused's rights but did not fully explain the rights such persons had. The Court did make it clear that enemy combatants might not be entitled to the same due process protections to which criminal defendants are entitled. Chapter 6 addresses this topic in part as it more fully addresses the rights of persons accused of a crime.

EQUAL PROTECTION OF THE LAW IN EDUCATION

The Fourteenth Amendment of the U.S. Constitution also provides that "no state shall ... deny to any person within its jurisdiction the equal protection of the laws," commonly called the Equal Protection Clause. Understanding this expectation of equal treatment requires context. As college students, some of you received government grants and loans, but many of you did not. Virtually no one is paying the same for their college education. Faculty, administrators, and handicapped persons probably have a better parking place at universities than others. The Equal Protection Clause has not been interpreted to afford equality among persons; instead, it requires equal treatment of persons in similar situations. In other words, government must treat people similarly if they are "similarly circumstanced." Note again the requirement of government action, as the Constitution protects against government, not private, conduct.

The Supreme Court has developed a three-stage test based on the nature of the right (e.g., to vote) or the class of individuals (e.g., gender) being affected when considering equal protection challenges. The Court begins with presumption of legislative validity.

1. **Strict scrutiny test.** Is the nature of the right or the class of individuals being affected inherently suspect? Distinctions based on race, alienage, national origin, ethnicity, religion, marriage, and voting have been held inherently suspect. Government must demonstrate that any law providing for differential treatment serves a compelling state interest and is narrowly tailored to serve that interest.
2. **Intermediate scrutiny test.** Is the right or classification similar to a protected fundamental right? If so, the court provides for "heightened scrutiny." The standard has been used for gender- and legitimacy-based discrimination cases. Government must show that the discriminating law or policy bears a "substantial relationship" to an "important" government interest.
3. **Minimal scrutiny or rational basis test.** Does the challenged law involve neither a suspect classification nor a fundamental right? In that case, government need show only that the law is rationally related to a legitimate state interest. Usually, classifications based on economic and social status fall within this minimal scrutiny range.

The equal right to education is arguably the first key to providing an opportunity for all students to realize their potential. The second would be employment, and the third would be housing. The three are interdependent, forming a repeating cycle.

To give disadvantaged minorities benefits of education that others routinely have enjoyed, the U.S. Supreme Court acted in the *Brown v. Board of Education of Topeka* cases discussed shortly. Implementation, however, has been difficult and time consuming. Education problems remain despite much progress. When they married, many children of older residents in large cities found more desirable housing at affordable prices in new suburban subdivisions, readily accessible by private automobiles on new superhighways. This pattern accelerated the decline of the aging city neighborhoods, which now attracted low-income families, often minorities. Thus, the minority literally became the majority in the inner cities of a large number of metropolitan areas. Government attempts to integrate white and African American students in elementary and secondary schools were resented by many whites (and also by some African Americans), and in large measure were effectively frustrated by the migration to the suburbs.

The nationalization of equal opportunity continues to be a major priority of our legislatures and courts. Nowhere is this commitment by the federal government more evident than in the field of education at all levels. In 1954, a unanimous U.S. Supreme Court decreed that separation of the races in schools violated the right to *equal protection of the laws* guaranteed by the Fourteenth Amendment. Chief Justice Earl Warren declared that

> *segregation of children in public schools solely on the basis of race, even though the physical facilities and other "tangible" factors may be equal, deprives the children of the minority group of equal educational opportunities.... To separate them from others of similar age and qualifications solely because of their race generates a feeling of inferiority as to their status in the community that may affect their hearts and minds in a way unlikely ever to be undone.*

A year later, the Court ordered all public school districts to desegregate "with all deliberate speed."

In 1976, the Court extended the principles of the Brown cases to private schools. It held that federal civil rights laws prohibited private nonsectarian schools from refusing to admit prospective students because they were black.

Congress passed the Civil Rights Act of 1964, which is divided into subject matter sections called titles. Title VI requires that all federal funds must be withdrawn from any school, college, or university that is guilty of discrimination on the "grounds of race, color, or national origin in any program or activity receiving federal financial assistance." (Gender, disability, age, Vietnam veteran status, and disability of veterans were later added to the list.)

LEGAL FOCUS—CASE

Grove City College, a private, coeducational liberal arts institution, declined all state or federal financial assistance in order to preserve its autonomy. However, many of its students received Basic Educational Opportunity Grants (BEOGs) from the U.S. Department of Education. The department required every participating institution to file a report certifying that no sex discrimination existed on its campus. Grove City College refused to file the report and brought suit to prevent the department from canceling all BEOGs. What was the result?

Grove City College v. Bell, 465 U.S. 555, 104 S.Ct. 1211 (1984).

Grove City College gained a partial victory. The Supreme Court found that even though Grove City did not directly distribute the students' awards, the BEOGs clearly augmented the college's financial aid program. Therefore, Grove City must assure the U.S. Department of Education that no discrimination exists in the college's financial aid program. The receipt of the BEOGs by some of Grove City's students, however, was not determined to trigger institution-wide coverage under nondiscrimination statutes. Grove City challenged the conditioning of federal assistance on compliance with the nondiscrimination requirements, claiming it infringed on the First Amendment rights of the college and its students. "Congress is free to attach reasonable and unambiguous conditions to federal financial assistance that educational institutions are not obligated to accept." In other words, the college can avoid compliance requirements by not allowing students attending to accept BEOG awards. In similar cases involving tax-exempt organizations, such as religious schools, a failure to comply with legal orders to eliminate discrimination has resulted in threats from the Internal Revenue Service (IRS) to remove their tax-exempt status.

LEGAL FOCUS—CASE

Bob Jones University (BJU) is a private learning institution whose founding principles include a specific religious belief. BJU receives no government assistance, but the IRS denied its tax-exempt status because of the school's policy prohibiting interracial association and intermarriage. Can the IRS cause a private, religious university to pay income taxes (by denial of exempt status) while other religious organizations are exempt?

Bob Jones University v. United States, 461 U.S. 574, 103 S.Ct. 2017 (1983).

Yes, the IRS can. Even though all races can enroll, discrimination by racial affiliation (e.g., ban on intermarriage) is against public policy. The state has a compelling interest in banning racial discrimination in any form. The intent of the tax law is that entitlement to tax exemption depends on meeting "certain common-law standards of charity—namely that an institution seeking tax-exempt status must serve a public purpose and not be contrary to established public policy," which could not be satisfied by less restrictive means. Loss of tax-exempt status could cause the closure of many otherwise-worthwhile organizations.

Segregation in public schools due to socioeconomic factors does not, in itself, violate the Constitution. For example, in one case, the Court ordered removal of a court order that required busing of students to achieve integration goals in Oklahoma City—if as much had been accomplished as was practical. But schools must adopt policies that remove the effects of past discrimination. Race-neutral policies are not enough. Otherwise, the courts will intervene.

AFFIRMATIVE ACTION IN EDUCATION

affirmative action
Policies and practices designed to ensure employment of women and of minorities until their percentages in the workforce approximate their percentages in the community.

African Americans in particular have been victims of discrimination in education, employment, and housing. **Affirmative action** is a process to eliminate continued discrimination (e.g., based on arbitrary classifications, such as race or sex) through the conscious adoption and implementation of policies favoring minorities in university admissions, public employment, and housing. Proponents argue that preferences are essential to erase the effects of prior and long-continued discrimination. Opponents argue that preferences themselves are an invidious form of discrimination—the claim is essentially that two wrongs do not make a right. There are other more sophisticated arguments concerning the possible indirect and psychological effects of preferential treatment.

Critics of racial preferences in education claim that what began as reasoned argument to overcome past discriminatory practices soon emerged as a series of numerical goals, quotas, and timetables created to bring African Americans, Asian Americans, Hispanic Americans, and Native Americans into the nation's colleges and universities. Although there is much opposition to the way it is being done, there is no question that affirmative action is alive and well throughout the country. But is it constitutional?

LEGAL FOCUS—CASE

The Medical School of the University of California, Davis (UCD) set aside sixteen class admissions for minority applicants. Allan Bakke, a white male and a top undergraduate student at the University of Minnesota and Stanford University, applied for admission to the UCD Medical School and was rejected twice. On both occasions, minority students with lower admission test scores, lower grade-point averages, and less impressive interviews were nonetheless admitted.

Bakke sued the university claiming he had been rejected because of his race, in violation of the Fourteenth Amendment and of Title VI of the Civil Rights Act of 1964. The trial court and the California Supreme Court found that UCD's admission plan did indeed violate the constitutional requirement of equal protection under the law. The U.S. Supreme Court accepted the case. How should it rule?

University of California Regents v. Bakke, 438 U.S. 265, 95 S.Ct. 2733 (1978).

The U.S. Supreme Court found for Bakke and declared the UCD admissions plan unconstitutional, thus affirming the decision of the California Supreme Court. The Court also held—with five votes and five different rationales—that ethnic diversity among medical students is an appropriate goal and therefore race can be one of the factors considered when students apply for admission.

There have been no decisions by the Court to clarify this language. U.S. Supreme Court Justice Byron White summarized the situation accurately when he wrote: "Agreement upon a means for applying the Equal Protection Clause to an affirmative action program has eluded this Court every time the issue has come before us."

As noted earlier in this chapter, California eliminated all affirmative action policies through the initiative process (direct vote of the people). Although the U.S. Supreme Court has authorized race-conscious admissions policies, California has chosen to achieve racial balance through other practices, such as improved outreach programs to fully qualified students. Other states have variations of processes in admissions and employment to achieve racial equality.

RIGHT TO PRIVACY

The right to privacy is the right to be left alone by other persons and by government. It generally is recognized as an essential component of personal dignity, peace of mind, and independence. Nevertheless, a right to privacy has not always been implicitly recognized and respected as a constitutionally protected right. There is no reference to privacy, as such, in the Constitution or the Bill of Rights. Indeed, it was not until 1965 that the U.S. Supreme Court recognized "the new constitutional right of privacy," in the words of Justice William O. Douglas. In the case of *Griswold v. Connecticut*, the Court held invalid a Connecticut statute that made it a criminal offense for married persons to use any drug or instrument to prevent conception. The Court held that the statute violated the First, Third, Fourth, Fifth, and Ninth Amendments, plus the Equal Protection Clause of the Fourteenth Amendment.

The nation's highest court subsequently has used the declared and implicit right of privacy to affirm (1) the right of unmarried persons to have access to contraceptives, (2) the right of persons of different races to intermarry (also protected by the Due Process and Equal Protection Clauses of the Fourteenth Amendment), (3) the right of a woman to have an abortion under certain conditions, and (4) the right to possess obscene materials in one's home.

LEGAL FOCUS—CASE

Ohio passed a law making it a crime to possess obscene materials that depict minors having sex in any form or manner. Osborne was arrested for having photographs of children having sex. Does Osborne have a constitutional right of privacy to possess this particular matter in his home?

Osborne v. Ohio, 495 U.S. 103, 110 S.Ct. 1691 (1990).

No, he does not. Osborne's right of privacy allowing possession of obscene materials is not absolute. The state's interest in protecting "the victims of child pornography" is paramount and sufficient to ban its possession. The U.S. Supreme Court upheld the accused's conviction.

The Court has held that the right of privacy does not extend to "places of public accommodation" and therefore adults do not have a constitutional right to acquire pornographic materials in bookstores or theaters. In 2003, the Supreme Court held, in *Lawrence v. Texas*, that private homosexual sexual relations are protected as a liberty right. In the past, cases involving sexual relations between persons of the same sex usually had focused on the sexual activity itself. In *Lawrence*, however, the Supreme Court focused on the relationship that the sexual activity might be a part of, rather than the sexual act.

Do "coerced" polygraph tests administered by private employers violate the right to privacy? Yes, they do, at least in California. In a huge out-of-court settlement, the Federated Groups agreed to pay $12.1 million to job applicants forced to take polygraph (lie detector) tests as a condition of employment.

The reliability of lie detectors is sufficiently uncertain that they are not accepted as evidence in court over a defendant's objection. This factor of unreliability differentiates lie detector tests from others, such as blood, urine, or breath-analyzer tests.

LEGAL FOCUS—PROBLEM

Certain U.S. companies desire to sell encryption (secret code) software internationally. The software encodes e-mail and files to protect them from prying eyes. A supercomputer would need 10,000 years to break the code of a file with 128-bit encryption. The U.S. Commerce Department requires that such companies provide them with a key with which to decipher the code. Does the Constitution's right of privacy guarantee citizens and companies the right to make private and secret encoded communications?

The specific issue presented may never arise because encryption software is generally available on the international market. The right of government to ban encryption software unless a key is provided involves balancing national security interests against those of privacy and free speech.

Congress long ago banned the manufacture, sale, advertisement, and use of devices intended to secretly listen to and record telephone and oral communications.

Yet today sophisticated electronic spy equipment is accessible in "spy shops" and from mail-order companies. A stranger can monitor conversations inside a bedroom from a mile away, and spouses can track the movements of each other in the family car. Employers can listen to the conversations of every employee on the job. Although laws prohibiting the sale of spying equipment are on the books, lax enforcement, rapid changes in technology, and lack of public complaint have distorted (lowered) the public's expectation of privacy. Government cannot make wiretaps or otherwise perform searches without a prior search warrant, as will be discussed further in Chapter 6. But the Constitution does not guarantee a right of privacy to its citizens in the sense that they are protected from the intrusiveness of one another. The Constitution restrains only government from unreasonable intrusiveness.

DUE PROCESS AND EQUAL PROTECTION AND MEDICAL TESTING

The 1980s saw the emergence of a number of hotly contested issues pitting individual rights against the police power of the state to protect the public. State constitutions can require more stringent protective laws than are required by the U.S. Constitution. However, no state constitution or law can relax standards established by federal law, because of the doctrine of supremacy.

Among these problems, none are more difficult to resolve than the issues surrounding AIDS (acquired immune deficiency syndrome). For example, should individuals be subject to a mandatory AIDS testing program, especially those who work in certain high-risk areas or with high-risk persons? The general answer is no.

LEGAL FOCUS—CASE

Nebraska requires state health care workers with the mentally retarded to submit to blood tests for AIDS. Is such a requirement an unreasonable search of a person's body?

Glover v. Eastern Neb. Community Office of Retardation, 686 F.Supp. 243, 250 (D. Neb. 1988), aff'd, 867 F.2d 461 (8th Cir.), cert. denied, 493 U.S. 932 (1989).

Yes, it is unreasonable. The Nebraska statute is unconstitutional. The Supreme Court, without comment, upheld a lower court's decision that blood tests for AIDS did violate the Fourth Amendment. For now, the Supreme Court seems content to accept the doctrine that AIDS testing must meet the same constitutional requirements of reasonableness as other warrantless search and seizure practices.

Critics of universal blood testing charge that the Fourth Amendment "right of the people to be secure in their persons, houses, papers and effects, against unreasonable searches and seizure" is violated by indiscriminate blood testing (i.e., taking blood from one's body is a "search"). However, the Supreme Court said it was not unconstitutional to take blood from a person without permission if that person is believed to be driving under the influence of alcohol. (In this case, the person in question was convicted of drunk driving on the basis of the amount of alcohol in his blood.)

Another area of constitutional conflict is mandatory drug testing. The legal status of drug testing in the private sector varies from state to state. While the Supreme Court has ruled that certain government drug-testing plans are constitutional, some authorities believe that the states will have to make their own decisions about drug testing. As long as drug testing meets a "reasonableness" test as to safeguards, such as providing sufficient notice and keeping the test results secret, the business community apparently will be permitted to continue testing employees and job applicants.

LEGAL FOCUS—CASE

Lawrence Berkeley Laboratory is a research institution jointly operated by state and federal agencies. Several African American employees allege that as part of mandatory employment medical examinations, Lawrence tested their blood and urine for intimate medical conditions—namely, syphilis, sickle cell trait, and pregnancy—and that this was done without their knowledge or consent. Assuming the factual contentions are correct, would such tests violate their right to privacy as guaranteed by the U.S. Constitution?

Norman-Bloodsaw v. Lawrence Berkeley Laboratory, 135 F.3d 1260 (C.A.9, 1998).

The court stated it did:

> *The constitutionally protected privacy interest in avoiding disclosure of personal matters clearly encompasses medical information and its confidentiality. One can think of few subject areas more personal and more likely to implicate privacy interests than that of one's health or genetic make-up.*

CASE

Thomas et al. v. Chicago Park District

534 U.S. 316, 122 S.Ct. 775 (2002)

The Chicago Park District operates the Chicago public parks and is responsible for group use. It adopted an ordinance requiring park users to get permits before any public assembly, parade, picnic, or other event involving more than fifty people, or events using amplified sound. The applications are processed in order of receipt, and the Park District decides whether to grant or deny most applications within fourteen days. Applications can be denied on any of thirteen specified grounds. A denial requires written explanation and, when feasible, suggestions as to how to prepare a successful application. If a denial is given, one can appeal to the Park Superintendent, who has seven days to respond. If the Park Superintendent denies the appeal, the applicant may seek judicial review in state court.

Petitioners have applied to the Park District on several occasions for permits to hold rallies advocating the legalization of marijuana. The Park District granted some permits and denied others. Unsatisfied, the petitioners filed suit in U.S. District Court, alleging that the ordinance is unconstitutional. The district court granted summary judgment for the Park District, and the U.S. Court of Appeals for the Seventh Circuit affirmed.

Justice Scalia Delivered the Opinion of the Court

II

The First Amendment's guarantee of the freedom of speech, or of the press, prohibits a wide assortment of government restraints upon expression, but the core abuse against which it was directed was the scheme of licensing laws implemented by the monarch and Parliament to contain the evils of the printing press in 16th- and 17th-century England. The Printing Act of 1662 had prescribed what could be printed, who could print, and who could sell. It punished the publication of any book or pamphlet without a license and required that all works be submitted for approval to a government official, who wielded broad authority to suppress works that he found to be heretical, seditious, schismatical, or offensive. The English licensing system expired at the end of the 17th century, but the memory of its abuses was still vivid enough in colonial times that Blackstone warned against the restrictive power of such a licenser—an administrative official who enjoyed unconfined authority to pass judgment on the content of speech.

In *Freedman v. Maryland* (1965), we confronted a state law that enacted a strikingly similar system of prior restraint for motion pictures. It required that every motion picture film be submitted to a Board of Censors before the film was shown anywhere in the State. The Board enjoyed authority to reject films that it considered obscene or that tend[ed], in the judgment of the Board, to debase or corrupt morals or incite to crimes, characteristics defined by the statute in broad terms. The statute punished the exhibition of a film not submitted to the Board for advance approval, even where the film would have received a license had it been properly submitted. It was no defense that the content of the film was protected by the First Amendment.

We recognized in *Freedman* that a scheme conditioning expression on a licensing body's prior approval of content presents peculiar dangers to constitutionally protected speech. [T]he censor's business is to censor, and a licensing body likely will overestimate the dangers of controversial speech when determining, without regard to the film's actual effect on an audience, whether speech is likely to incite or to corrupt [the] morals. In response to these grave dangers of a censorship system, we held that a film licensing process must contain certain procedural safeguards in order to avoid constituting an invalid prior restraint: (1) any restraint prior to judicial review can be imposed only for a specified brief period during which the status quo must be maintained; (2) expeditious judicial review of that decision must be available; and (3) the censor must bear the burden of going to court to suppress the speech and must bear the burden of proof once in court.

[T]he licensing scheme at issue here is not subject-matter censorship but content-neutral time, place, and manner regulation of the use of a public forum. The Park District's ordinance does not authorize a licensor to pass judgment on the content of speech: None of the grounds for denying a permit has anything to do with what a speaker might say. The picnicker and soccer-player, no less than the political activist or parade marshal, must apply for a permit if the 50-person limit is to be exceeded. As the Court of Appeals well put it: [T]o allow unregulated access to all comers could easily reduce rather than enlarge the park's utility as a forum for speech.

We have never required that a content-neutral permit scheme regulating speech in a public forum adhere to the procedural requirements set forth in *Freedman*. [T]he [permit] required is not the kind of prepublication license deemed a denial of liberty since the time of John Milton but a ministerial, police routine for adjusting the rights of citizens so that the opportunity for effective freedom of speech may be preserved. Regulations of the use of a public forum that ensure the safety and convenience of the people are not inconsistent with civil liberties but [are] one of the means of safeguarding the good order upon which [civil liberties] ultimately depend. Such a traditional exercise of authority does not raise the censorship concerns that prompted us to impose the extraordinary procedural safeguards on the film licensing process in *Freedman*.

III

Of course even content-neutral time, place, and manner restrictions can be applied in such a manner as to stifle free expression. Where the licensing official enjoys unduly broad discretion in determining whether to grant or deny a permit, there is a risk that he will favor or disfavor speech based on its content. We have thus required that a time, place, and manner regulation contain adequate standards to guide the official's decision and render it subject to effective judicial review. Petitioners contend that the Park District's ordinance fails this test.

We think not. As we have described, the Park District may deny a permit only for one or more of the reasons set forth in the ordinance. It may deny, for example, when the application is incomplete or contains a material falsehood or misrepresentation; when the applicant has damaged Park District property on prior occasions and has not paid for the damage; when a permit has been granted to an earlier applicant for the same time and place; when the intended use would present an unreasonable danger to the health or safety of park users or Park District employees; or when the applicant has violated the terms of a prior permit. Moreover, the Park District must process applications within 28 days, and must clearly explain its reasons for any denial. These grounds are reasonably specific and objective, and do not leave the decision to the whim of the administrator. They provide narrowly drawn, reasonable, and definite standards to guide the licensor's determination. And they are enforceable on review first by appeal to the General Superintendent of the Park District and then by writ of common-law *certiorari*[*] in the Illinois courts.

For the foregoing reasons, we affirm the judgment of the Court of Appeals.

For Critical Analysis

1. What was the importance of the court's determination that the Chicago Park District's procedures were content neutral?
2. Why is the court applying a federal constitution test to a state governmental entity?
3. Are the petitioners attempting to argue that actions by the Park District are a prior restraint? If so, did they succeed? Do you believe it is a prior restraint? What requirements are necessary for a prior restraint to be held valid?

*A writ or order by which an appellate court exercises its discretionary power to decide which lower court cases it will hear. Writs of certiorari are discussed in more detail in Chapter 3.

McDonald v. Chicago

130 S.Ct. 3020 (2010)

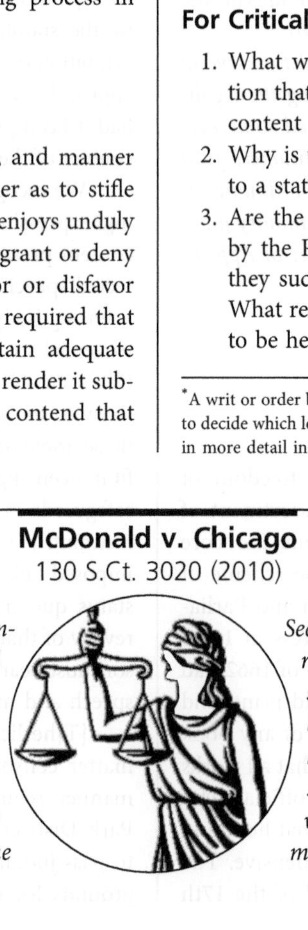

The Second Amendment's prohibition on infringing the "right of the people to keep and bear Arms" has long been controversial. Some feel it applies only to local government and militias. Others feel it protects individual rights. In 2008, the Supreme Court (District of Columbia v. Heller, 554 U.S. 570, 128 S.Ct. 2783, 171 L.Ed.2d 637) held that the Second Amendment protected an individual's right to keep and bear arms for the purpose of self-defense. That was a watershed decision, but it left open the question of whether and how the Second Amendment applied to the states' right to regulate firearms. One question was whether and how the Fourteenth Amendment had made the Second Amendment also

protect citizens as to state and local laws that attempted to restrict firearm ownership. Because many municipalities had severely restricted or banned various forms of firearm ownership in the latter half of the Twentieth Century, the Second Amendment question has been a brooding issue of basic constitutional law only partly answered by the 2008 Heller decision.

The City of Chicago essentially had banned the ownership of handguns since 1983. Otis McDonald and other residents challenged the law in federal court. The District Court upheld the law as did the Seventh Circuit Court of Appeals. The petitioners appealed to the Supreme Court.

Justice Alito Announced the Judgment of the Court

Two years ago we held that the Second Amendment protects the right to keep and bear arms for the purpose of self-defense and we struck down a District of Columbia law that banned the possession of handguns in the home. The City of Chicago and the village of Oak Park, a Chicago suburb, have laws that are similar to the District of Columbia's, but Chicago and Oak Park argue that their laws are constitutional because the Second Amendment has no application to the States. We have previously held that most of the provisions of the Bill of Rights apply with full force to both the Federal Government and the States. Applying the standard that is well established in our case law, we hold that the Second Amendment right is fully applicable to the States.

Chicago enacted its handgun ban to protect its residents "from the loss of property and injury or death from firearms." The Chicago petitioners and their *amici*, however, argue that the handgun ban has left them vulnerable to criminals. Chicago Police Department statistics, we are told, reveal that the City's handgun murder rate has actually increased since the ban was enacted and that Chicago residents now face one of the highest murder rates in the country and rates of other violent crimes that exceed the average in comparable cities.

Several of the Chicago petitioners have been the targets of threats and violence. For instance, Otis McDonald, who is in his late seventies, lives in a high-crime neighborhood. McDonald and the other Chicago petitioners own handguns that they store outside of the city limits, but they would like to keep their handguns in their homes for protection.

Petitioners argue that the Chicago and Oak Park laws violate the right to keep and bear arms. Petitioners contend that the Fourteenth Amendment's Due Process Clause "incorporates" the Second Amendment right. Chicago maintains that a right set out in the Bill of Rights applies to the States only if that right is an indispensable attribute of *any* "civilized" legal system.

The Bill of Rights, including the Second Amendment, originally applied only to the Federal Government. The constitutional Amendments adopted in the aftermath of the Civil War fundamentally altered our country's federal system. The provision at issue in this case, § 1 of the Fourteenth Amendment, provides, among other things, that a State may not abridge "the privileges or immunities of citizens of the United States" or deprive "any person of life, liberty, or property, without due process of law."

Four years after the adoption of the Fourteenth Amendment, this Court was asked to interpret the Amendment's reference to "the privileges or immunities of citizens of the United States." The case involved challenges to a Louisiana law permitting the creation of a state-sanctioned monopoly on the butchering of animals within the city of New Orleans. Justice Samuel Miller's opinion for the Court concluded that the Privileges or Immunities Clause protects only those rights "which owe their existence to the Federal government, its National character, its Constitution, or its laws." The Court held that other fundamental rights—rights that predated the creation of the Federal Government and that "the State governments were created to establish and secure"—were not protected by the Clause.

The Court wrote that the right of bearing arms for a lawful purpose "is not a right granted by the Constitution" and is not "in any manner dependent upon that instrument for its existence." "The second amendment," the Court continued, "declares that it shall not be infringed; but this … means no more than that it shall not be infringed by Congress."

We see no need to reconsider that interpretation here. For many decades, the question of the rights protected by the Fourteenth Amendment against state infringement has been analyzed under the Due Process Clause of that Amendment and not under the Privileges or Immunities Clause. The Court held that the general "right of the people peaceably to assemble for lawful purposes," which is protected by the First Amendment, applied only against the Federal Government and not against the States. Nonetheless, over 60 years later the Court held that the right of peaceful assembly was a fundamental right safeguarded by the due process clause of the Fourteenth Amendment. We follow the same path here and thus consider whether the right to keep and bear arms applies to the States under the Due Process Clause.

In the late 19th century, the Court began to consider whether the Due Process Clause prohibits the States from infringing rights set out in the Bill of Rights. Employing this approach, the Court overruled earlier decisions in which it had held that particular Bill of Rights guarantees or remedies did not apply to the States.

With this framework in mind, we now turn directly to the question whether the Second Amendment right to keep and bear arms is incorporated in the concept of due process. In answering that question, we must decide whether the right to keep and bear arms is fundamental to *our* scheme of ordered liberty, or as we have said in a related context, whether this right is "deeply rooted in this Nation's history and tradition,"

Our decision in Heller points unmistakably to the answer. Self-defense is a basic right, recognized by many legal systems from ancient times to the present day and in Heller, we held that individual self-defense is "the *central component*" of the Second Amendment right. Explaining that "the need for defense of self, family, and property is most acute" in the home, we found that this right applies to handguns because they are "the most preferred firearm in the nation to 'keep' and use for protection of one's home and family". Thus, we concluded, citizens must be permitted to use handguns for the core lawful purpose of self-defense.

After the Civil War, many of the over 180,000 African Americans who served in the Union Army returned to the States of the old Confederacy, where systematic efforts were made to disarm them and other blacks. The 39th Congress concluded that legislative action was necessary. Its efforts to safeguard the right to keep and bear arms demonstrate that the right was still recognized to be fundamental. The Civil Rights Act of 1866 sought to protect the right of all citizens to keep and bear arms. In debating the Fourteenth Amendment, the 39th Congress referred to the right to keep and bear arms as a fundamental right deserving of protection. Senator Samuel Pomeroy described three "indispensable" "safeguards of liberty under our form of Government." One of these, he said, was the right to keep and bear arms. The right to keep and bear arms was also widely protected by state constitutions at the time when the Fourteenth Amendment was ratified. In 1868, 22 of the 37 States in the Union had state constitutional provisions explicitly protecting the right to keep and bear arms.

In sum, it is clear that the Framers and ratifiers of the Fourteenth Amendment counted the right to keep and bear arms among those fundamental rights necessary to our system of ordered liberty.

In Heller, we held that the Second Amendment protects the right to possess a handgun in the home for the purpose of self-defense. Unless considerations of *stare decisis* counsel otherwise, a provision of the Bill of Rights that protects a right that is fundamental from an American perspective applies equally to the Federal Government and the States. We therefore hold that the Due Process Clause of the Fourteenth Amendment incorporates the Second Amendment right recognized in Heller. The judgment of the Court of Appeals is reversed, and the case is remanded for further proceedings.

It is so ordered.

Justice Scalia and Justice Thomas wrote concurring opinions. Chief Justice Roberts and Justice Kennedy concurred at least in part in the judgment, thus establishing a plurality.

Justice Stevens and Justice Breyer wrote dissenting opinions.

Justice Stevens dissent: In Heller the Court answered the question whether a federal enclave's "prohibition on the possession of usable handguns in the home violates the Second Amendment to the Constitution." The question we should be answering in this case is whether the Constitution "guarantees individuals a fundamental right," enforceable against the States, "to possess a functional, personal firearm, including a handgun, within the home." That is a different—and more difficult—inquiry than asking if the Fourteenth Amendment "incorporates" the Second Amendment. The so-called incorporation question was squarely and, in my view, correctly resolved in the late 19th century.

This is a substantive due process case. Section 1 of the Fourteenth Amendment decrees that no State shall "deprive any person of life, liberty, or property, without due process of law." The Court has filled thousands of pages expounding that spare text. As I read the vast corpus of substantive due process opinions, they confirm several important principles that ought to guide our resolution of this case.

The first, and most basic, principle established by our cases is that the rights protected by the Due Process Clause are not merely procedural in nature. At first glance, this proposition might seem surprising, given that the Clause refers to "process." But substance and procedure are often deeply entwined. The second principle woven through our cases is that substantive due process is fundamentally a matter of personal liberty. The third precept to emerge from our case law flows from the second: The rights protected against state infringement by the Fourteenth Amendment's Due Process Clause need not be identical in shape or scope to the rights protected against Federal Government infringement by the various provisions of the Bill of Rights.

So far, I have explained that substantive due process analysis generally requires us to consider the term "liberty" in the Fourteenth Amendment, and that this inquiry may be informed by but does not depend upon the content of the Bill of Rights. How should a court go about the analysis, then? Our precedents have established, not an exact methodology, but rather a framework for decision making. In this respect, too, the Court's narrative fails to capture the continuity and flexibility in our doctrine.

The basic inquiry was described by Justice Cardozo more than 70 years ago. When confronted with a substantive due process claim, we must ask whether the allegedly unlawful practice violates values "implicit in the concept of ordered liberty."

If the practice in question lacks any "oppressive and arbitrary" character, if judicial enforcement of the asserted right would not materially contribute to "a fair and enlightened system of justice," then the claim is unsuitable for substantive due process protection.

The question in this case, then, is not whether the Second Amendment right to keep and bear arms (whatever that right's precise contours) applies to the States because the Amendment has been incorporated into the Fourteenth Amendment. It has not been. The question, rather, is whether the particular right asserted by petitioners applies to the States because of the Fourteenth Amendment itself, standing on its own bottom.

What petitioners have asked is that we "incorporate" the Second Amendment and thereby establish a constitutional entitlement, enforceable against the States, to keep a handgun in the home. Of course, owning a handgun may be useful for practicing self-defense. But the right to take a certain type of action is analytically distinct from the right to acquire and utilize specific instrumentalities in furtherance of that action.

The right to possess a firearm of one's choosing is different in kind from the liberty interests we have recognized under the Due Process Clause. Despite the plethora of substantive due process cases that have been decided, I have found none that holds, states, or even suggests that the term "liberty" encompasses either the common-law right of self-defense or a right to keep and bear arms. I do not doubt for a moment that many Americans feel deeply passionate about firearms, and see them as critical to their way of life as well as to their security. Nevertheless, it does not appear to be the case that the ability to own a handgun, or any particular type of firearm, is critical to leading a life of autonomy, dignity, or political equality. Although it may be true that Americans' interest in firearm possession and state-law recognition of that interest are "deeply rooted" in some important senses it is equally true that the States have a long and unbroken history of regulating firearms.

The fact that the right to keep and bear arms appears in the Constitution should not obscure the novelty of the Court's decision to enforce that right against the States. By its terms, the Second Amendment does not apply to the States; read properly, it does not even apply to individuals outside of the militia context. The Second Amendment was adopted to protect the *states* from federal encroachment. And the Fourteenth Amendment has never been understood by the Court to have "incorporated" the entire Bill of Rights. There was nothing foreordained about today's outcome. I cannot accept either the methodology the Court employs or the conclusions it draws. Although impressively argued, the majority's decision to overturn more than a century of Supreme Court precedent and to unsettle a much longer tradition of state practice is not, in my judgment, built

> *upon respect for the teachings of history, solid recognition of the basic values that underlie our society, and wise appreciation of the great roles that the doctrines of federalism and separation of powers have played in establishing and preserving American freedoms.*

Accordingly, I respectfully dissent.

For Critical Analysis

1. Is the court interpreting the scope of the Second Amendment and the right "to keep and bear Arms" or is it evaluating the meaning of the Fourteenth Amendment? Or both?
2. In Justice Steven's dissent, he considers the case a question of substantive due process. What does he mean. Does Justice Alito disagree with that characterization? Does the question of whether the issue is procedural or substantive due process determine the outcome?
3. How do Justice Alito and Justice Stevens disagree on how the Incorporation doctrine is to be enforced? Is that disagreement, ultimately, the dividing line between their opposite conclusions?

CHAPTER QUESTIONS AND PROBLEMS

1. Wayne Gerber, an inmate at Mule Creek State Prison, is serving a sentence of 100 years to life, plus eleven years as a habitual felon under California's three-strikes law. Although conjugal visits are allowed in California, they are not allowed to prisoners serving life terms. As his prospects of walking among the general public are slim, so are his prospects of impregnating his wife. Gerber requested that he be allowed to package his semen in a plastic collection container and mail it to a laboratory, eventually to artificially inseminate his wife. His request was denied.
   a. Does a prisoner lose all constitutional rights?
   b. Does a prisoner have a constitutional right to conjugal visits? What constitutional provisions would be argued?
   c. Is the warden's denial of Gerber's right to provide sperm samples a violation of the Equal Protection Clause because the state allows conjugal visits for some prisoners but not others?
2. Organizers of the annual Fiesta Bowl football game held in Arizona proposed establishing a race-specific scholarship fund for players of the competing teams. Are such scholarships unconstitutional because they are awarded only to members of one race? Would your answer be any different if the scholarships were awarded in schools that had a history of intentional racial segregation?
3. Can government constitutionally regulate the content (i.e., censor) of e-mail by banning "spam" (unwanted advertisements) and Web sex or pornography available on Websites? What constitutional arguments would you make pro and con?
4. Do state laws that criminalize sodomy between members of the same or opposite sex violate the constitutional right of privacy? Equal Protection Clause? Are such laws necessary in a free society?
5. In the Seattle School District, students are allowed to choose which high school they wish to attend. If too many students choose the same school, the district has to turn some students away. To assist in this determination, the district uses tie-breakers. The first tiebreaker tries to keep families together—a student with a brother or sister at the chosen school is given preference. The second tie-breaker tries to keep the racial mix in each high school equal to the racial mix in the district—if a school has too many white students, nonwhites are given preference, and vice versa. Is this use of race constitutionally permissible? What other selection criteria might the district use to make the decision? [*Parents Involved in Community Schools v. Seattle School Dist., No. 1,* 285 F.3d 1236 (C.A.9 Wash. 2002).]
6. Several recent counterterrorism measures raise constitutional questions. Discuss the constitutional questions that can reasonably be raised in each situation. What is the probable outcome if the challenge is made?
   a. Visitors to the United States who hold visas from Iran, Iraq, Libya, Sudan, and Syria will be fingerprinted and photographed. Visitors from other countries will not be unless the immigration service believes they represent a security risk.
   b. A presidential order allows trials by special military commissions for non-U.S. citizens who are suspected of involvement in international terrorism.
   c. Police or federal agents eavesdrop on phone calls between detained suspected terrorists and their lawyers without seeking judicial approval.
7. The City of Oakland passed an ordinance that prohibited the burning of all substances in residential yards within the city limits on days when a fire hazard warning was in effect. Violation was made a misdemeanor crime with a minimum fine of $500. Harry Haggerty, a political science major, invited student friends to his home in Oakland where, among other backyard activities, he intended to burn an American flag in protest of U.S. involvement in Iraq. If a fire warning were in effect, could Harry be convicted of the misdemeanor offense?
8. In an editorial comment, the highly respected British journal The *Economist* (27 March 1992, p. 15) opined, "Short of declaring war, nothing an American President can do has as much effect as appointing a justice to the Supreme Court." Do you agree? Why or why not?
9. The principal of Nathan Bishop Middle School in Providence, Rhode Island, invited Rabbi Leslie Gutterman to deliver prayers at the public school graduation ceremony. The rabbi agreed to deliver a nonsectarian prayer at the ceremony. Weisman, the father of a student, sued to prohibit school officials from including prayer in the ceremony. He was unsuccessful, and the

ceremony took place with the Weismans in attendance. Weisman then sued to permanently bar prayers at future ceremonies, including his daughter's high school graduation. Does including a nonsectarian prayer in a public high school graduation ceremony constitute the establishment of a religion by government in violation of the First Amendment? [*Lee v. Weisman*, 505 U.S. 577, 112 S.Ct. 2649 (1992).]

10. Many changes in human rights law in the United States have occurred only because somebody broke the law, was convicted, and then appealed their case. Rosa Parks, an African American who died in 2006, was famous for refusing to surrender her seat on a bus to a white person as required at the time. This is partly a result of the fact that a court usually must have a true controversy before it to decide. Is it fair to force individuals to risk imprisonment and fines to vindicate their civil rights? Does this make it morally acceptable to break the law when you believe the law is wrong? Consider the effect, however, if anybody could require a court to review a law for constitutionality whenever they chose.

CHAPTER 3

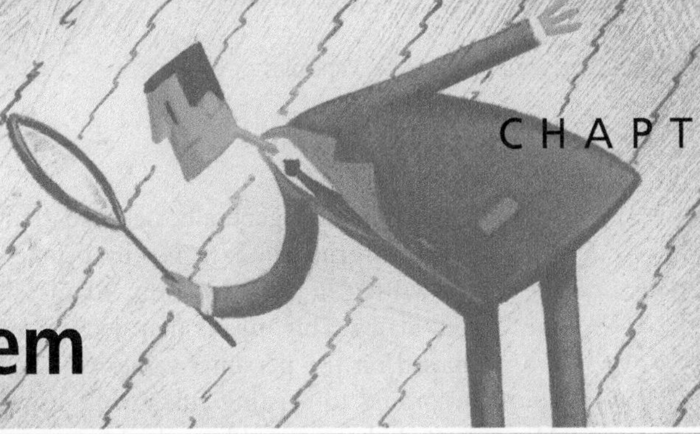

The Court System

Sir Thomas More: *The law, Roper, the law. I know what's legal and not what's right. And I'll stick to what's legal.*

William Roper: *Then you set man's law above God's.*

Sir Thomas More: *No, far below; but let me draw your attention to a fact—I'm not God. The currents and eddies of right and wrong, which you find such plain sailing, I can't navigate.*

William Roper: *So ... you'd give the Devil benefit of the law!*

Sir Thomas More: *Yes. What would you do? Cut a great road through the law to get after the Devil?*

William Roper: *I'd cut down every law in England to do that!*

Sir Thomas More: *Oh? And when the last law was down and the Devil turned round on you where would you hide, Roper, the laws all being flat? Yes, I'd give the Devil benefit of law, for my own safety's sake.*

Robert Bolt, slightly and reverently edited from his play
A Man for All Seasons

LEARNING OBJECTIVES

After reading and studying this chapter, you should be able to:

- Explain what a "court" is and distinguish between a trial court and an appellate court.
- Understand the concept of jurisdiction and explain the various types of jurisdiction.
- Recognize challenges to concepts of jurisdiction raised by new technologies.
- Describe a typical state court system.
- Describe the federal court system.
- Understand how a typical civil case is processed though the court system.
- Understand the nature of juries and be able to discuss jury size, jury selection, and a litigant's right to a jury trial.
- Explain and provide examples of actions or causes in equity.
- Understand the various ways a trial might conclude.

It is often stated and generally believed that persons residing in the United States of America are governed by law, not by people. "A government of laws, and not of men" are words written in 1774 by John Adams, first vice president and second president of the United States. This means that decisions establishing and affecting rights and duties are not based on the personal values of certain individuals but rather are made by the courts according to existing rules while using fair and impartial processes. Sir Thomas More, quoted above, would no doubt approve of the United States' emphasis on established rules rather than individual discretion. The American court system is still one created by and administered by individuals, however.

rule of law
Principle that decisions should be made by the application of established laws without the intervention of individual discretion.

Indeed, providing a fair, impartial and consistent application of the **rule of law** is a difficult task, especially in the United States, which contains such a diversity of ethnic origins and cultural backgrounds. Yet, it is that very diversity that makes the rule of law so vitally important for the resolution of disputes with "equal justice under law" for all.

> *We are going to have to decide what kind of people we are—whether we obey the law only when we approve of it or whether we obey it no matter how distasteful we may find it.*
>
> —Harry S. Ashmore, "On Integration of Little Rock High School," *Arkansas Gazette,* September 4, 1957

Probably no other country is more reliant on its judges and its courts than the United States. One hundred and fifty years ago, French political scientist Alexis de Tocqueville noted the unique importance of courts in the American political system. "Restricted within its limits, the power granted to American courts to pronounce on the constitutionality of laws is yet one of the most powerful barriers ever erected against the tyranny of political assemblies."

Although the power of courts can and does restrict arbitrary abuse of power, bias can creep into the court system. As an example, consider the following episode in traffic court:

> *The traffic court judge found himself facing two attorneys, both of whom he knew very well. Both were charged with speeding violations. "Gentlemen," he said, "I could not be truly objective in either of your cases, so I'm going to let you judge each other's case." Both lawyers agreed. Attorney Number One climbed to the bench. "You are charged with driving 40 in a 25 mph zone. How do you plead?" he asked Attorney Number Two. "Guilty," was the response. "I fine you $50," said Number One. Then they exchanged places. "You are charged with driving 40 in a 25 mph zone," said Number Two. "What is your plea?" "Guilty," said Number One. "Then I fine you $200," said Number Two. "Hey! That's unfair," said the first. "I fined you only $50." "Yes," was the reply, "but there is too much speeding going on. This is the second case we've had like that today."*

bias
A preconceived belief affecting neutrality.

Although the purpose of the story is to amuse, it illustrates the injustice of an inconsistent and unfair decision made by a biased judge. **Bias** is a preconceived belief about some person or fact that makes it difficult to be neutral, dispassionate, or fair in evaluating that person's rights and duties, guilt, or innocence. A judge is biased when he or she has a personal interest in the outcome of a case or has reached a conclusion about a case before hearing the evidence and legal arguments. The U.S. system of justice strives to provide both reasonable consistency and neutrality.

WHAT IS A COURT?

Clearly, it is important and useful to know where our courts are located, how they function, and the important role they play in our society. Court-based drama permeates American culture and media. Significant decisions of appellate courts, especially the

U.S. Supreme Court, receive widespread media coverage and drive the thought and conversations of citizens over important issues. For example, courts recently have affected issues ranging from the right to keep a handgun in your home to the right for same-sex couples to marry. The public's acute interest in such decisions prompts lively debate on the Internet, in coffee shops, on talk radio, and so on. Because the actions of courts receive such expansive notoriety, it is obvious that you, as educated citizens, must be familiar with the functions of courts.

court
(a) A government body that administers justice by applying laws to civil controversies and criminal offenses. (b) The place where trials are held.

Courts are public facilities, available to private persons, business organizations, and government agencies, where legal disputes are heard and decided. Courts offer their tax-supported services practically free to users. Under the U.S. Constitution, courts are essentially independent of the other branches of government.* This independence protects the courts from potential interference by the executive or legislative branches.

A court is both a place and a system. It is a place where you may go to peacefully resolve your legal disputes with others ("I'll see you in court!"). The word *court* also is used to describe all the court system participants, including judges, attorneys, clerks, witnesses, parties, and the public ("Court is in session"), and sometimes only the presiding judge or justice ("If the court please, may I be heard at this time?").

Courts are also part of a system, as there are different courts for different types of legal disputes, each with different specified procedures. Some courts determine the facts of individual disputes (trial courts); others review decisions of lower courts for correctness, consistency, and fairness (appellate courts). Under the common law system, appellate judges, both in the state and federal systems, have the power to make new law. To understand the courts, it is useful to recognize some of their different functions, including those of trial and appellate courts.

What Is a Trial Court?

trial court
The initial court that hears evidence and applies the law to decided facts.

Trial courts conduct the initial proceedings in legal disputes. These proceedings have three distinct purposes: (1) to determine the facts of the dispute ("What happened between the competing parties?"), (2) to determine what rules of law should be applied to the facts, and (3) to apply those rules to the facts.

LEGAL FOCUS—PROBLEM

Marya Martinez signed up for ski instruction at Heavenly Mountain in Idaho. Gary Graf, a certified ski instructor, fitted Martinez with rental skis. He then taught her how to snowplow (a beginning maneuver for turning, reducing speed, or stopping). Later that afternoon, Martinez was showing her new skills to Luther Thomas, whom she had just met during lunch. Her show was short. Martinez fell and suffered a spiral fracture of her right leg, just above the ankle. Her bindings had failed to release her boot from the skis when she fell. She sued Graf in a civil action for damages, alleging that he had carelessly adjusted the bindings too tightly. Can she win?

Maybe, but maybe not. The outcome will turn on the facts, the applicable law and the decision by the judge or jury based on those facts and the applicable law. The "facts"

*The courts are not totally independent of the other two branches. For example, the executive branch of government makes judicial appointments, collects taxes, and distributes funds necessary to pay judges and otherwise operate the judicial system. The legislative branch sets salaries and benefits of judges and often confirms judicial appointments.

plaintiff
In trial, the person trying to recover money damages or other relief from a defendant.

damages
Money awarded by a court to a plaintiff for injury or economic loss caused by the defendant.

defendant
(a) In a civil trial, the person from whom money damages or other relief is sought by the plaintiff. (b) In a criminal trial, the accused.

lawsuit or litigation
A court process at law or in equity to determine the legal merits of a controversy.

civil dispute
A lawsuit commenced for the purpose of resolving a civil conflict.

kangaroo court
A farce trial—one that lacks proper procedure and fairness and where the outcome is predetermined. Origin of the term is thought to be the bizarre appearance of the animal after which it is named.

you just read above are likely not all the facts, and the court might not even allow all of the facts you read above to be considered. The court also has not determined the applicable law yet. As the lawsuit progresses many other issues likely are to be considered. Did Graf secure the bindings too tightly? Did Martinez, or anyone else, tamper with the bindings after Graf set them? Did the bindings fail because they were too tight or because Martinez had allowed ice to accumulate beneath her boot? Was Graf responsible for the binding setting? Was there a contract that disclaimed or limited Graf's liability? Were the bindings themselves defective? A civil trial will determine the answers to these and other relevant factual and legal contentions. In the trial, Martinez is the **plaintiff** (person seeking relief in a civil trial) because she is seeking to recover **damages** (money) from Graf, the **defendant** (in a civil trial, the person whom a lawsuit is brought against). The entire process, designed to resolve (i.e., decide or settle) the legal controversy, is called a **lawsuit or litigation**.

Martinez's attempt to collect damages from Graf is an example of a *civil dispute* (also called a *civil action* or *civil lawsuit*). **Civil disputes** are private controversies between persons.* A civil dispute is sometimes defined broadly by stating what it is not. It is not a matter involving criminal law. A **criminal dispute** (also called a *criminal action* or *criminal case*) is brought by government to determine whether an accused (also called a defendant) is guilty of an act committed against the public and in violation of a penal statute.

Civil matters and criminal matters are separate fields of law; in large cities, attorneys and judges often specialize in one or the other. The dependence of courts upon attorneys is such that it would be foolhardy for a civil case attorney to defend an accused murderer even before an impartial jury. There are similarities as well as differences between civil and criminal matters. Both involve formal proceedings before a court. Both are conducted to resolve disputed questions of fact and law that, in turn, will define applicable rights and duties of the parties involved. Different terminology, however, often is used. For example, a defendant found to be responsible in a civil trial is said to be *liable*, while in a criminal trial such a person is said to be *guilty*. The accused in both processes, though, is called a *defendant*.

In a criminal trial, a prosecutor (e.g., a public prosecutor or district attorney) from the local governing unit (county) represents the public on behalf of the state. If a federal crime is involved, an attorney from the Department of Justice, a division of the federal government, represents the public. While government can be a party in either a civil or criminal matter, only the government can prosecute a criminal action, because *crimes*—although usually committed against private persons—are prosecuted as public offenses against all society. Procedures differ substantially in criminal actions from those used in civil actions. The focus of this chapter is on the civil court system, although we make some references to the criminal system. (See Chapter 6 for a more complete discussion of criminal law and criminal procedure.)

Most court proceedings and court records are open to public scrutiny, thereby assuring us that no secret **kangaroo court** sessions take place. However, public attendance at a trial can be restricted or barred for security reasons. Sometimes one or both parties request privacy, and the court will agree when there is an overriding reason for the public to be excluded from hearing the details of the dispute or seeing witnesses whose privacy ought to be protected. Even if the proceeding is closed to the public, a verbatim transcript of the trial is prepared so reviewing courts may know precisely

*The term *persons,* for most situations in law, also includes artificial persons, such as government bodies and business entities including corporations.

what was said and by whom. Moreover, the press follows important and interesting cases and often has an investigative posture when dealing with government, including courts.

LEGAL FOCUS—CASE

The attorney general of Maryland filed a civil suit against Cottman Transmissions Systems, Inc., relating to allegations of fraudulent activities. Cottman was accused of removing automobile transmissions for inspection and maintenance when this costly action was unnecessary. The attorney general distributed news releases elaborating on the charges against Cottman. When the attorney general made additional claims, Cottman asked the court to close the courtroom except for parties directly involved in the proceeding. Did the court agree to do this?

Maryland v. Cottman Transmissions, Inc., 75 Md.App. 647, 542 A.2d 859 (Md., 1988).

Initially, yes, the court agreed to close the courtroom. Cottman's counsel convinced the trial court judge that the press releases harmed their client's ability to obtain a fair trial, and so the public was barred. Before trial began, however, a higher court overruled this decision. A request for a closed proceeding is most likely to be favorably considered in domestic and family relations matters.

Restricting access to civil law proceedings is unusual and restricting access to criminal law proceedings is rare. The possibility of secret trials resulting in loss of individual liberty through a jail sentence is an abomination in our democracy. Criminal proceedings may be conducted in private only in extraordinary situations that are demonstrated to, and then justified by, the trial court judge. An exception to the openness in most court cases is the juvenile court proceeding, which is conducted privately in most states to protect youthful offenders.

WHAT IS AN APPELLATE COURT?

appeal
Formal request to a higher court to review any action of a lower court.

appellate court
Court that reviews decisions of prior courts for substantive and procedural correctness.

Within a specified time following the trial court's final determination (a *judgment*), the losing party can **appeal**, which is a formal request to a higher court to review the trial judge's ruling. These review courts are called **appellate courts**. Consisting of three or more judges, called justices, these courts review decisions of trial court judges for substantive and procedural correctness. In civil cases, there is no automatic right to have the state's highest court consider an appeal. In criminal cases resulting in the death penalty, the right to an appellate review by the state's highest court is guaranteed. This is a safeguard against imposing an irreversible penalty without thorough review of all aspects of the conviction. Lawyers research the written opinions of appellate courts to determine what law should be applied in the trial courts to the problem facing their clients. This is one example of how trial courts depend on attorneys.

The appellate court works from a verbatim record (court transcript) of what was said and what *evidence* was accepted in the lower court. Appellate courts do not listen to witnesses, accept new evidence,* make new determinations of fact, or utilize a jury.

*Examples of evidence are testimony of witnesses, photographs, documents, handwriting samples, dented fenders, and so on. In weighing the believability of testimony evidence, the finder of fact also considers the demeanor, eye contact, dress, and mannerisms of a witness.

briefs
Written arguments addressed to the appellate court.

Instead, the court receives written **briefs**, prepared by lawyers, that contain legal arguments as to how the law was correctly or incorrectly stated or applied to the facts as presented to the trial court. This is an example of how appellate courts rely on attorneys. The appellate court accepts as true the facts found by the trial court, which considered all the testimony of all witnesses along with all other evidence and, upon so doing, decides whether rules of substantive and procedural law were properly applied by the trial judge. However, appellate judges may also weigh, or evaluate, the factual evidence as presented in the trial court and then decide whether, as a matter of law, the facts presented were sufficient to justify the judgment.

If the appellate court justices conclude that the trial court erroneously applied or interpreted the law, it may modify or reverse the judgment or decision, and either enter a new judgment or *remand* (return) the case to the trial court for a new trial or other proceedings in compliance with the appellate court's instructions. In other words, the trial court is instructed to "do it right this time." Merely finding an error at the trial court level is not sufficient to overturn the trial court's judgment. If an error is minor, it is believed unlikely to have affected the case outcome. The error found must be serious, requiring correction by the appellate court to avoid a miscarriage of justice. Therefore, it can be concluded that when a reversal occurs, the trial court judge is deemed to have made a serious error in one or more legal rulings.

In the previously discussed *Cottman* case, the trial court judge's decision to ban the press was appealed and reversed even before the trial took place. The Maryland appellate court stated:

> *To close a court to public scrutiny of the proceedings is to shut off the light of the law. How else will the citizenry learn of the happenings in the courts—their government's third branch—except through access to the courts by the people themselves or through reports supplied by the media? A ... corporate entity involved as a party to a civil case is entitled to a fair trial, not a private one.*

Relative to the number of cases heard in trial court, very few cases are appealed. The cost to appeal can be prohibitive in time, money, and peace of mind. Although the losing party may not be pleased with the outcome of the trial, he or she nonetheless has had one's "day in court."

Thus, to win a corrective action by an appellate court, the appellant or petitioner, the party who appeals the case to a higher court, must show that an error by the court prejudiced the appellant's cause. The appellee or respondent, the party against whom the appeal is brought, will contend that no error was made, or that any error did not affect the outcome of the trial. Clearly, the trial is the crucial, potent, and final source of justice for most persons involved in litigation.

WHAT IS JURISDICTION?

jurisdiction
The power of a court to decide a controversy and to award appropriate relief.

To understand courts, we must understand the concept of **jurisdiction**. The power to speak the law is the broad meaning of the term *jurisdiction*. It refers to the geographic area within which a court has the right and power to operate (that is, "speak"). It also refers to the persons over whom and the subject matter about which a court has the right and power to make decisions that are legally binding. Obviously, the term is used many ways, but always in relation to the right and power of the courts to act. Jurisdiction is about (1) political boundaries (states, federal government, territories, foreign countries, etc.), (2) the type of dispute and dollar amount involved, and (3) persons and property. In other words, jurisdiction is about a plaintiff choosing the right place to sue and choosing the right court in that place, and about compliance with rules of fairness governing when a person must appear in court to defend his or her liberty or property.

Political Boundaries of State and Federal Courts

Government power begins and ends at geographic boundaries. It is clear to most that the courts of one sovereign power ordinarily have no authority over someone present in another sovereign power, absent extraordinary reason. The United States is, however, a country with shared political boundaries, and the states are not entirely sovereign. Federalism exists in the U.S. court system as well as in the executive and legislative branches of government. Simply put, we have both federal and state court systems. There are fifty-one court systems—one for each of the fifty states, and the federal government.* They have much in common and are interrelated, but each is still an independent system.

concurrent jurisdiction
Power of more than one court to hear a case.

Interestingly, a party seeking judicial resolution of a dispute often may have the choice of which court system, federal or state, he or she wishes to use. When both a federal court and a state court have the power to hear a case, they have **concurrent jurisdiction**. Which court, federal or state or both, has power or authority over a given matter is a question of jurisdiction, as provided for in the constitutions and statutes of the federal government and of the respective states.

LEGAL FOCUS—PROBLEM

While walking along a busy street in Tallahassee, Florida, Jorge Cepada, a citizen of Florida, was struck by a crate that flew off a move-yourself rental driven by Laura Alexander, a new resident of Oklahoma. Desiring compensation for his injuries, Cepada intends to sue Alexander in the convenient Florida courts. May he do so? Could he instead sue in a federal court?

When Alexander allegedly injured Cepada in Florida, the Florida state courts and the U.S. District Court had concurrent jurisdiction. An injured victim has the right to use the courts of the state where harm occurs. A plaintiff also generally has the right to bring suit in the courts of the state in which he or she is a resident.

A right also may exist to use a federal court when the parties to a dispute are each citizens of different states. When such diversity of citizenship exists, a plaintiff may file an action in federal court if the claimed damages exceed $75,000. The party could also choose to file in a state court. The federal basis for jurisdiction in this example is called *diversity of citizenship* (discussed further later in this chapter). In diversity of citizenship cases, the federal court applies the substantive law of the state in which it sits, such as the state's law of negligence. Different procedural rules apply in federal civil courts than in state courts, and attorneys may seize on advantages sometimes available in this regard. Note that diversity jurisdiction allows people to use the federal courts when their claims are based on state law. Claims based on federal law may be filed in a federal court without the need for diversity jurisdiction.

*Federal courts include courts for the District of Columbia and the U.S. Territories, Puerto Rico, Virgin Islands, Canal Zone, Guam, and the Northern Mariana Islands.

Jurisdiction over Subject Matter

Subject matter jurisdiction determines which types of cases a court can hear. Probate courts—courts that handle only wills and estate matters—are examples of courts of **limited jurisdiction**, meaning courts authorized to hear limited types of cases. A court of **general jurisdiction** is a court that can hear and decide almost any type of case.

The subject matter jurisdiction of a court usually is defined in the constitutional or statutory law that creates the court. This creating law may refer to the type of case, its seriousness as reflected by the amount of money requested by the person bringing the lawsuit, or the type of relief requested of the court. For example, a court may be able to hear only cases in which the damages requested are $50,000 or less, or when the court is asked to compel a person to do or not do something (an equitable remedy).

In criminal matters, the seriousness of a crime often determines which court hears a case. For example, a murder trial is held in the trial court of general jurisdiction rather than one of limited jurisdiction. Whether the proceeding is a trial or an appeal is perhaps the most obvious subject matter limitation on jurisdiction.

subject matter jurisdiction
The power of a court to hear and decide cases of the general type to which the subject in question belongs.

limited jurisdiction
Limitation on a court as to the types of cases it can hear and decide.

general jurisdiction
Authorization of a court to hear and decide virtually any type of case occurring within the political boundaries of the geographic area in which it is located.

Venue

The proper place for a trial that otherwise has appropriate subject matter jurisdiction for either a civil or criminal case is called its venue (French: "to come"). **Venue** is the local place, within the geographic boundaries of a larger political jurisdiction, where a case is most appropriately tried. Proper venue reflects a policy of closeness—that is, a court trying a suit should be close to where the incident leading to the suit occurred or close to where the defendant resides.

All things being equal, the following are typical of state venue rules:

- In divorce cases, proper venue is the county of the family residence.
- In automobile accident cases, proper venue is the county where the accident occurred or where the defendant resides.
- In breach of contract cases, proper venue is where the contract was made, where it was breached, or where the defendant lives.
- In criminal cases, proper venue is the county in which the crime occurred or where the defendant was apprehended.

All things are not equal, however, when a significant event occurs that makes a different venue more likely to produce a just result. For example, excessive publicity in the county where a crime occurred may unreasonably prejudice an accused person's right to a fair trial. Under such circumstances, courts will grant a **motion for change of venue** and order that the case be tried in a more appropriate place.

venue
The local place, within the geographic boundaries of a larger jurisdiction, where a case is generally most appropriately tried.

motion for change of venue
Request to a judge by counsel to transfer the trial to a different geographic location within the jurisdiction of the court.

LEGAL FOCUS—PROBLEM

It is difficult to predict what will catch the attention of the nation, but the disappearance of attractive pregnant Laci Peterson on Christmas Eve in Modesto, California, in 2002 did just that. A concerned and curious nation kept track of her handsome husband, Scott Peterson, and the community of Modesto mobilized in the search for Laci. After the bodies of Laci and her unborn child were discovered four months later in the San Francisco Bay, Scott was charged with two counts of murder. Scott Peterson's attorneys requested that the trial be moved, claiming that news coverage of the murder made a fair trial in the local courts impossible. Prosecutors countered that as the media coverage was national, the local courts were as likely to be unbiased as anywhere in the state. What did the trial court rule?

Citing the extraordinary media coverage locally, as well as nationally, the court agreed with the defense and granted the motion for a change of venue.

Jurisdiction over Persons and Property

In our earlier example, if Laura Alexander can be served with a *summons*—an order informing her that a lawsuit has been filed against her—within the boundaries of Florida, the Florida state court has the power and right to hear the case. Under such circumstances, Jorge Cepada's Florida court would have ***in personam* jurisdiction** over Alexander, meaning power over her. The most common means of obtaining *in personam* jurisdiction in a civil case is by personal service of a summons and complaint on the defendant who is within the boundaries of the state in which the suit is commenced.

***in personam* jurisdiction**
The power of a court over a person.

LEGAL FOCUS—PROBLEM

Assume the address given to Cepada by Alexander shows her new home is in Oklahoma, and by the time the suit is filed, she lives in Oklahoma. Can Cepada still sue Alexander in Florida, or must he now sue in Oklahoma?

Clearly, if the process server (a person in the business of serving summons upon defendants) can find Alexander within Florida, Cepada can sue in the Florida court. But, if Alexander had returned to Oklahoma before Cepada engaged the services of a lawyer and began litigation, the question is whether or not the Florida court could obtain jurisdiction over an Oklahoma citizen who never returns to Florida. The answer is yes, because Florida, like all states, has a **long-arm statute** and because it would be "fair" to Alexander, under due process rules, to hear the case in Florida.

long-arm statute
A state law authorizing a court to hear cases brought against nonresidents under specified circumstances.

Two requirements must be met before a plaintiff can obtain jurisdiction over an out-of-state defendant. First, the state must have a statute that authorizes it to get jurisdiction under the particular circumstances. Second, the Constitution requires that the basis for jurisdiction must satisfy procedural due process. Is it fair to require the defendant to come to the state to defend the lawsuit? A three-pronged test has emerged for determining whether the exercise of specific personal jurisdiction over a nonresident defendant is appropriate: (1) the defendant must have sufficient "minimum contacts" with the forum state, (2) the claim asserted against the defendant must arise out of those contacts, and (3) the exercise of jurisdiction must be reasonable.

Long-arm statutes subject nonresident defendants to local jurisdiction for wrongful activities they engage in while physically within a state even if they have left the state before they are sued. Long-arm statutes also can be used to obtain jurisdiction over some activities of a defendant that occur outside the state but that caused harm within the state. If a person drives a motor vehicle within a state, he is deemed to give his agreement to appear and answer for any harm he causes while driving in that state (called *implied consent*). Cepada will not even be required to hire a process server in Oklahoma, although that would be permissible; service of the summons by registered mail to Alexander's home typically would be adequate. Defendants also give implied consent to jurisdiction of states in which they do business. Thus, consumers in Florida can use their local courts to sue out-of-state companies who do business in their state. When defendants are not subject to long-arm statutes, plaintiffs can always sue a defendant in the state of the defendant's residence.

in rem jurisdiction
The power of a court to declare rights against the world rather than solely against the named defendant(s).

Although *in personam* jurisdiction is the most common way to get jurisdiction over a defendant, sometimes a dispute involves ownership or title to property. In these cases, plaintiffs will seek ***in rem* jurisdiction** (Latin: "against a thing"). *In rem* jurisdiction empowers courts to declare rights against the world rather than just the named defendant(s). If the legal question involves ownership of real property located in Washington, for example, the appropriate court to hear the case would be the trial court where the property is located in Washington. Parties known to the plaintiff, who have an interest in the property, have a due process right to receive fair notice of any proceeding based on *in rem* jurisdiction, as well as a right to participate in the case.

Jurisdiction and the Internet

The Internet in the digital, connected age has challenged many settled concepts of law. This is true for jurisdiction. The challenge comes from the sheer number and variety of communications, exchanges, and transactions involving people from different places who do not know one another by any other means. An Internet transaction seems local to each party, but it may even be international. The dilemma posed by the Internet to jurisdiction is easy to understand. Any consumer or party considered aggrieved would prefer to sue where they reside. The party with whom they have a dispute could be anywhere in the world. A long list of possible disputes can arise, including consumer contracts (an unsatisfactory purchase), an intellectual property dispute (someone using a company's trade name), or a Website disparaging a name or product.

LEGAL FOCUS—CASE

Although the law is not settled as to what Internet activities are sufficient to confer jurisdiction, this list, found in the case of *Morantz, Inc.*, v. *Hang & Shine Ultrasonics, Inc.*, is helpful.

- [A] mere presence on the World Wide Web does not establish the minimum contacts necessary to subject a corporation to personal jurisdiction on a worldwide basis.
- [T]he minimum contacts analysis in cases involving the Internet is conducted on a "sliding scale," on which the constitutionality of the exercise of personal jurisdiction is directly proportional to the level of commercial interactivity on a corporation's Web site.
- [A] Web site targeted at a particular jurisdiction is likely to give rise to personal jurisdiction.
- Court[s] will consider the quality and quantity of contacts with the plaintiff's jurisdiction to which the Internet site has given rise in determining whether personal jurisdiction may be exercised.

Most courts have categorized Internet contacts in three ways.

1. Passive Websites: A passive Website that does little more than make information available is not grounds for the exercise of personal jurisdiction.
2. Interactive Website: In cases in which people interact on a Website, jurisdiction is determined by the level of interaction and the commercial nature of the exchange of information.
3. Commercial Website: Contracts with residents of a foreign jurisdiction involving knowing and repeated transmission of computer files renders jurisdiction proper.

HOW ARE STATE COURT SYSTEMS ORGANIZED?

The typical state court system consists of both trial and appellate courts. Consider the typical state court system shown in Exhibit 3.1. It has three main levels: (1) trial courts of general or limited jurisdiction,* (2) intermediate appellate courts, and (3) the highest court (usually named the supreme court). Although most state court systems provide two levels of appeal, some states have but one appellate court. Also, unfortunately, titles of state courts are not uniform; names of courts in one state frequently apply to quite different courts in another state. Confusion can be avoided by focusing on the function a court performs: trial or appellate.

The typical state will have a trial court of general jurisdiction, often called the *superior court.* That court may hear money matters with unlimited dollar limits and serious criminal matters. Most states have courts with limited subject matter jurisdiction, often called special *inferior trial courts or minor judiciary courts.* A small claims court, discussed shortly, is an example of an inferior trial court of limited jurisdiction. Small claims courts hear claims involving relatively small dollar amounts. A domestic relations court, which handles only divorce actions and child custody cases, is another example of a court of limited jurisdiction. Local municipal courts handling, for example, misdemeanors and civil cases of modest dollar amounts are also courts of limited jurisdiction.

EXHIBIT 3.1 A Typical State Court System

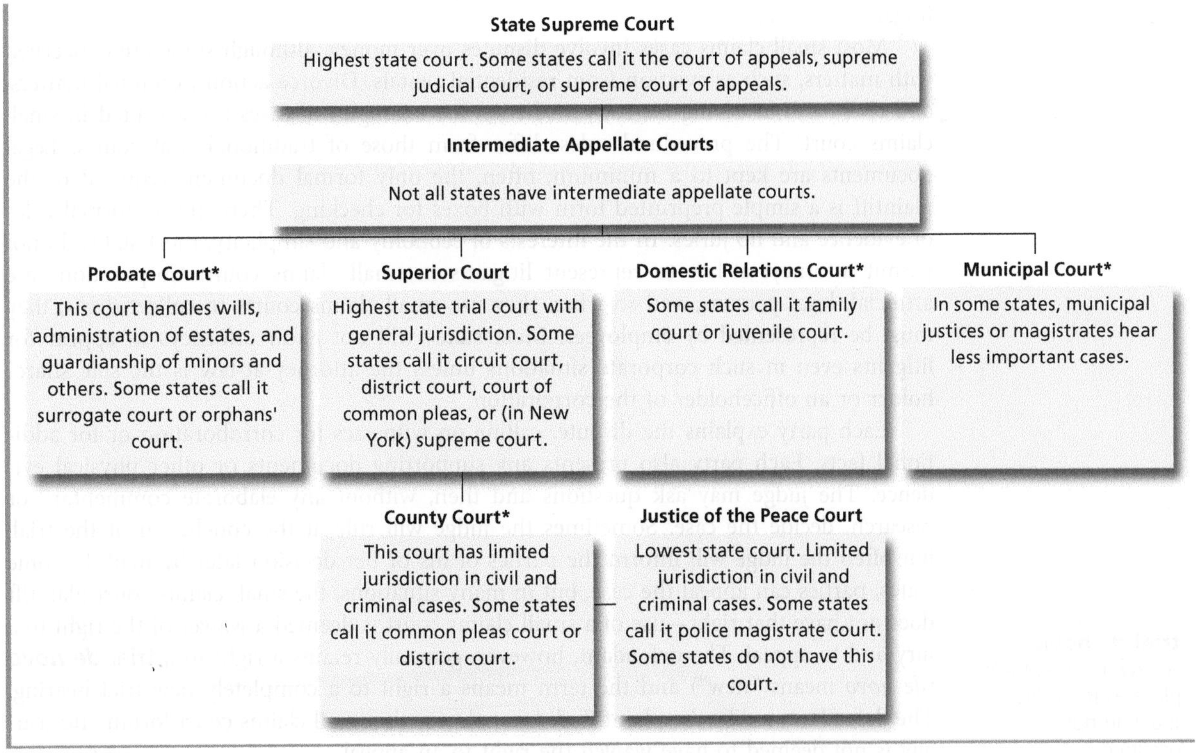

* Courts of limited jurisdiction, such as probate, domestic relations, municipal, or county courts, may be separate courts or may be part of a trial court of general jurisdiction.

What Are Small Claims Courts?

Court procedures are devised to handle a great variety of legal problems ranging from the most complex to the simplest. Not surprisingly, the usual manner of handling legal matters is inefficient for small or simple cases. If you have a legal claim for $2,000 worth of minor damage to your automobile in an accident, the cost of hiring an attorney to help you recover that amount through court action would no doubt exceed your hoped-for recovery.

small claims court
A court with jurisdiction to decide civil controversies of a relatively minor nature.

To promote peaceful resolution of disputes for which a conventional lawsuit is prohibitively expensive, states have created a special trial court, called the **small claims court**. Jurisdiction of this court usually is limited to disputes involving small sums of money damages. They often are referred to as the people's court, because an average adult with limited formal education may obtain resolution of minor civil legal disputes in a speedy, informal, and user-friendly forum.

The small claims court may be a separate court, or a designated subdivision of another court. Because they are the creation of each state, particulars vary widely. The maximum amount of recoverable damages ranges from $1,500 to $25,000, depending on the state, and the most common maximums are between $5,000 and $10,000.

The purpose of the small claims court is the same as any other trial court: to determine facts and apply the law. The dynamics of the small claims court, however, are more relaxed, proceedings usually are faster, and procedures to use the court are less complicated than those found in other courts. This is not to say it is uncomplicated or that the small claims court is a social gathering—only that it is less intimidating to the average litigant.

Most small claims cases involve disputes over money, although some are concerned with matters, such as eviction from residential rentals. Divorce actions, criminal matters, and civil cases involving *in rem* jurisdiction are examples of cases not accepted in small claims court. The procedural rules differ from those of traditional trial courts. Legal documents are kept to a minimum; often, the only formal document required of the plaintiff is a simple preprinted form with boxes for checking. There are no formal rules of evidence and no juries. In the interests of economy and simplicity, most states do not permit attorneys-at-law to represent litigants in small claims court. Corporations are artificial, legal persons, and so when they use small claims courts to collect debts, they must be represented by employees. Most states will not allow attorneys to appear for litigants even in such corporate situations unless the attorney-at-law is the sole shareholder or an officeholder of the corporation.

Each party explains the dispute, calling on witnesses for corroboration or for additional facts. Each party also presents any supporting documents or other physical evidence. The judge may ask questions and then, without any elaborate commentary or research, decide the case. Sometimes the judge will rule at the conclusion of the trial, but often the judge will inform the parties of his or her decision later by mail. In some states, parties can appeal the case, but in many situations, the small claims court plaintiff does not have that right—use of a small claims court is deemed a waiver of the right to a jury and to appeal. The defendant, however, generally retains a right to a ***trial de novo*** (*de novo* means "new") and the term means a right to a completely new trial hearing. The defendant, unlike the plaintiff, did not choose the small claims court forum and usually is not deemed to have waived the right to an appeal.

trial *de novo*
A new trial that takes place as if the first trial had not occurred.

In the normal appeal, the trial record is reviewed to determine whether the trial judge made an error. If a party has a right to a trial *de novo*, the prior court record is not considered (note that small claims courts do not keep a record of transcripts), and the defendant automatically is given a new day in court. Although the new trial occurs at a higher level court, the trial usually remains informal and is decided by a judge without a jury.

Small claims courts help "the little person" get his or her "day in court" without the delays and costs that accompany use of traditional courts. Because business firms often have a substantial number of small claims, they appear most frequently as plaintiffs in small claims court actions.

Various television programs have popularized small claims courts. Technically, these proceedings are *arbitrations* (a private third party is selected by the parties to hear and resolve the dispute) designed to look like a small claims court trial, but they illustrate the types of disputes heard and resolved in small claims courts. What they do not do is illustrate usual judicial behavior. The cases heard are chosen for entertainment value and the television judge's questions and decisions often are rendered in a sarcastic and condescending fashion.

WHAT IS THE FEDERAL COURT SYSTEM?

Like the state court system, the federal court system consists of both trial and appellate courts. The two principal appellate courts are the U.S. Courts of Appeals and the U.S. Supreme Court.

Federal Trial Courts

The federal government has one trial court of general jurisdiction called the U.S. District Court. The country is divided into ninety-four districts. Each district consists of a number of judges doing business in a number of different courtrooms and even in different buildings. How many judges are "sitting" (i.e., conducting the court's business) is related to the population within each district. In populous areas, the districts are geographically small; in rural areas, they are large. There is at least one U.S. District Court in every state and territory in the United States.

U.S. District Courts conduct trials concerning federal matters, such as federal crimes and enforcement of federal statutes. Most federal crimes involve crimes against the government or crimes occurring on federal property. One crime, kidnapping, is a federal crime even though it does not occur on federal land. This federal law was passed after the notorious kidnapping of the son of famous aviator, Charles Lindbergh, in 1932. Federal jurisdiction for the crime of kidnapping is based on the taking of the victim across state or country lines.

diversity of citizenship
A basis of jurisdiction in federal courts requiring that plaintiff and defendant be involved in an actual controversy, that they be citizens of different states, and that a minimum of $75,000 be sought in damages.

As discussed earlier, it is possible to sue in a federal court even though the claim is based on state law when the plaintiff and defendant are from different states or countries. **Diversity of citizenship** jurisdiction exists when a plaintiff is a citizen of one state and the defendant is a citizen of another state, or when one party is a foreign country or a citizen of a foreign country and the other is a citizen of the United States. The amount of claimed damages in a diversity of citizenship case must be at least $75,000. In settling such controversies, the particular U.S. District Court involved applies federal *procedural law* (which involves the manner in which rights and duties are to be enforced) and the *substantive law* (which involves the defining of rights and duties) of the appropriate state, usually the state where the court is located. When a federal court hears a case because of diversity jurisdiction, an example of *concurrent jurisdiction* exists because at least one state court also would have had the power to hear the case, if the plaintiff had chosen to file the case there.

LEGAL FOCUS—PROBLEM

Jorge Cepada, a resident of Florida, wishes to sue Laura Alexander, an Oklahoma resident, to collect damages for injuries and losses arising from the motor vehicle accident that occurred in Florida (see page 91). If the amount of damages requested exceeds $75,000, Cepada can sue in a U.S. District Court sitting in either Florida or Oklahoma. Can he alternatively file the case in a state court?

Yes, as noted earlier, he can file the case in a state court. Because the accident occurred in Florida, the most convenient state court would be Florida's. Using a long-arm statute, he could get jurisdiction over Alexander through the mail. Cepada also could file the lawsuit in Oklahoma, Alexander's resident state, and obtain jurisdiction there. This accident provides an example of a legal dispute in which concurrent jurisdiction exists.

exclusive jurisdiction
The sole power a court has over the particular subject matter of a case.

When cases can be tried only in federal courts or only in state courts, **exclusive jurisdiction** exists. A person filing for a discharge in bankruptcy, which is a constitutional legal right that releases one from the duty to pay one's debts, can file the petition (a petition is the appropriate filing to institute a bankruptcy proceeding) only in a federal court. States also have exclusive jurisdiction in certain subject matter areas—for example, in divorces and adoptions. The concepts of concurrent and exclusive jurisdiction are illustrated in Exhibit 3.2.

EXHIBIT 3.2
Exclusive and Concurrent Jurisdiction

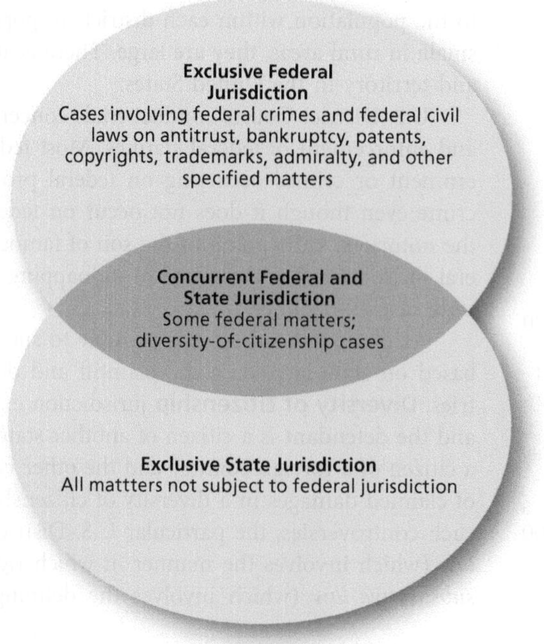
Exclusive Federal Jurisdiction
Cases involving federal crimes and federal civil laws on antitrust, bankruptcy, patents, copyrights, trademarks, admiralty, and other specified matters
Concurrent Federal and State Jurisdiction
Some federal matters; diversity-of-citizenship cases
Exclusive State Jurisdiction
All matters not subject to federal jurisdiction

Federal Appellate Courts

U.S. Courts of Appeals

The U.S. Courts of Appeals review the decisions of the U.S. District Courts located within their respective circuits. The country is divided into thirteen circuits, or geographic areas, each with a U.S. Court of Appeals. The number of judges, courtroom-building locations, and geographic size of the circuits vary greatly.*

As with state appellate courts, the U.S. Courts of Appeals review cases brought to the court's attention by parties contending that the federal trial judge made an error of law. The federal system also has a U.S. Court of Appeals for the federal circuit, which has nationwide jurisdiction to hear appeals from all district courts in patent cases, as well as certain claims against the federal government. Also heard before this court are appeals from specialized courts (e.g., the U.S. Claims Court and the U.S. Court of International Trade) and claims arising from decisions of federal administrative agencies.

U.S. Supreme Court

The highest level of the federal court system is the U.S. Supreme Court. Under the U.S. Constitution, there is but one such court. The court consists of nine justices.† It has original, or trial, jurisdiction in rare instances. Most often, it acts as the court of final appeal for federal courts of appeals and, in less frequent situations, the highest state appellate courts when they have decided cases on the basis of federal law.

Many cases compete for the attention of the U.S. Supreme Court. The selection process is accomplished by the *rule of four*, which means that the case is selected to be heard if four of the nine justices so choose. When the Court selects a case for review, it issues an order (writ of *certiorari*) to the court of appeals, or highest state court, requesting the record of the case. A **writ of *certiorari*** (Latin: "to be informed of") is an order by which the U.S. Supreme Court exercises its discretionary power to decide which lower court cases it will hear. To be among these cases, an important federal question must be raised, such as one involving a constitutional issue (e.g., freedom of speech). Also, any case in which different lower federal courts have issued conflicting rulings on the same issue would be one the Court would seriously consider hearing. When the Supreme Court declines review of a case, the practical effect is an agreement with the lower court decision, which continues binding the parties. The Court is able to hear only a small percentage of the appeals filed annually, and formal opinions are delivered in only about 115–130 cases.

writ of *certiorari*
A procedural document whereby an appellate court exercises its discretionary power to accept jurisdiction of a pending case.

Exhibit 3.3 depicts the federal court structure, which, in addition to the principal courts, includes the U.S. Court of International Trade, U.S. Claims Court, and U.S. Tax Court. Each of these is a special jurisdiction court restricted to hearing particular types of cases.

*The Washington, D.C., circuit is the smallest circuit in geographic size and is responsible only for the nation's capital. The largest geographic circuit is the ninth (Alaska, Arizona, California, Guam, Hawaii, Idaho, Montana, Oregon, Nevada, the Northern Mariana islands, and Washington). The number of judges per circuit ranges from six sitting circuit judges in the first circuit (Maine, Massachusetts, New Hampshire, Puerto Rico, and Rhode Island) to twenty-eight authorized judges in the ninth circuit.

†The Constitution does not specify the number of Supreme Court justices, and since its inception the number has varied. However, since 1869 the number has remained at nine. In 1937, an attempt was made by President Franklin D. Roosevelt to "pack the court" with six additional justices who presumably would be sympathetic to his New Deal reform legislation. This maneuver was opposed vigorously and rejected by Congress.

EXHIBIT 3.3 The U.S. Court System

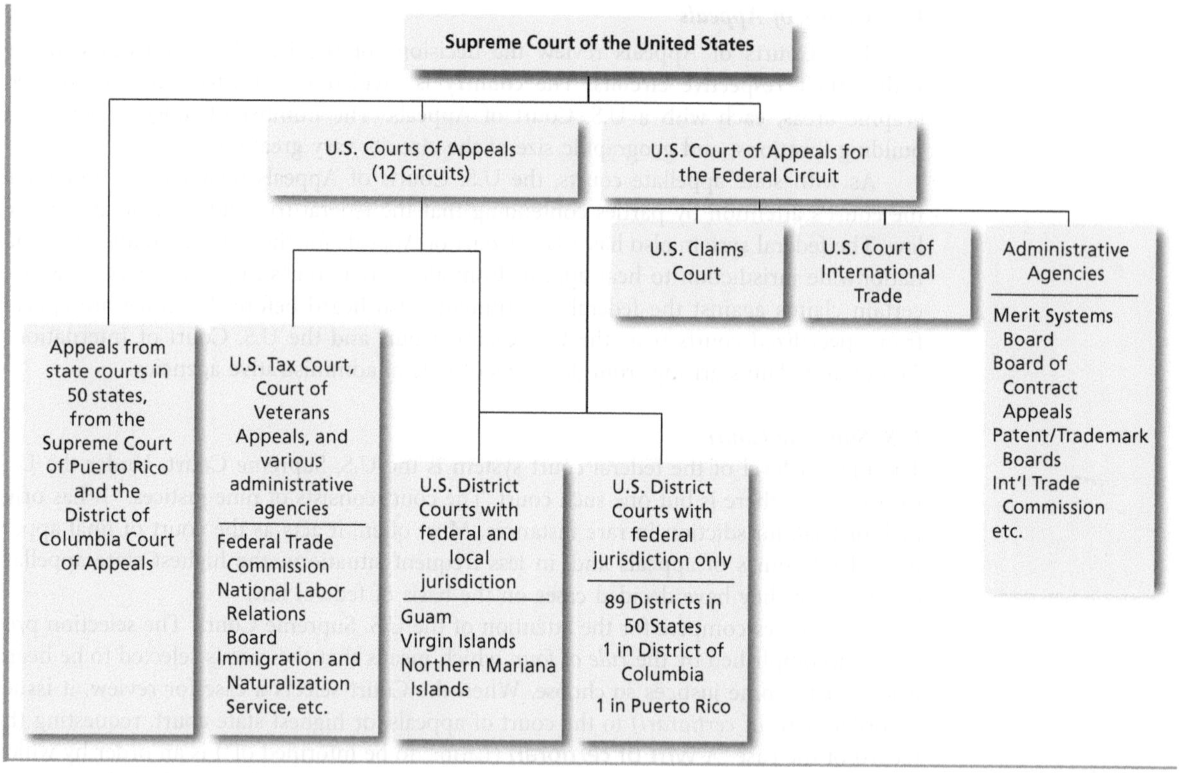

Source: Administrative Office of the U.S. Courts.

TRIAL PROCEEDINGS

complaint
A document stating the facts constituting an alleged cause of action.

American trial procedures are complex, byzantine, and, often, expensive. The outcome of even an open-and-shut case is uncertain. Meritorious cases can be lost because of errors made in the procedures that are necessary in maneuvering a civil case through the court process. Some litigants with a strong case nevertheless may pay their opponents a sum of money, often called "nuisance money," to settle a case and thus avoid the cost and risk of proceeding through a trial.

cause of action
An existing right to seek and to receive judicial relief, assuming the factual allegations of the plaintiff are true.

How Is a Civil Case Started?

Recall the example in which Marya Martinez was injured in a skiing accident that she believes would not have occurred but for the carelessness of her ski instructor, Gary Graf (page 87). If Martinez decides to sue Graf, her attorney will begin the case by filing a document called a **complaint** with the county clerk. The complaint briefly states the facts she believes justify her claim, the basis for jurisdiction of the court, and the request for damages or other relief she seeks. Martinez is the plaintiff, and the complaint is almost always prepared by her attorney, who is satisfied that she has a **cause of action** (legally appropriate basis for suing).

summons
A document issued by a clerk of the court inviting the defendant to respond to a complaint.

County clerks maintain files, generally in alphabetical and numerical order, of every case filed in their respective counties. These records are open to the public. A filing fee (from $100 to $250 or more) is charged at the time of filing. When the complaint is filed, the clerk issues a **summons** (prepared by the plaintiff's attorney) by endorsing it on behalf of the court. The summons is a notice of a lawsuit; it informs the defendant that a lawsuit has been filed against him or her in the named court and that the defendant has a prescribed time (e.g., thirty days) to personally appear or respond to the complaint. You may recall the importance of the summons in obtaining jurisdiction over the defendant, as described earlier in the case involving Jorge Cepada and Laura Alexander. If the defendant fails to respond, the plaintiff may win the case by default (forfeit), and a judgment, the final decision of the court, may be awarded to the plaintiff.

process server
A person who serves (delivers) a copy of the summons and complaint, or other legal document, upon a party or witness at the request of the opposing party to civil litigation.

Martinez's attorney will arrange with a **process server** or a local official, such as a sheriff, to have a copy of the summons and complaint personally served on the defendant, Gary Graf, to obtain *in personam* jurisdiction. As discussed earlier, a process server is in the business of serving legal documents on defendants or plaintiffs and witnesses. If Graf cannot be found, or if he evades service of the process, he nonetheless may be served by alternative methods such as "constructive service" through a notification to the defendant by mail and the publication of a summons in a local newspaper. Serving a copy of the summons and complaint (or publication of summons) gives Graf notice that he has been sued and gives the proper court jurisdiction (or power) over his person to decide the controversy. The court, of course, also must be the appropriate forum (have jurisdiction) over the subject matter and type of dispute involved.

answer
A document containing a defendant's denials, admissions or allegations of fact in response to a complaint.

pleadings
The complaint of the plaintiff and answer of the defendant in a lawsuit.

Upon receipt of the summons and complaint, Graf typically would hire a lawyer to represent him to uphold his interests. Graf's lawyer would file a responsive pleading, called an **answer**, with the county clerk and mail a copy to the plaintiff's lawyer. The answer is a document containing a defendant's denial and personal allegations of fact. In the answer, Graf may admit to any parts of the complaint that he believes are true and deny the rest. The complaint and answer together are called the **pleadings**.

demurrer or motion to dismiss
A motion filed by a defendant in response to a summons and complaint alleging the complaint, even if true, is insufficient to state a cause of action.

motion
A formal request by counsel addressed to a court or other tribunal for a particular decision or act.

Instead of an answer, Graf's attorney might be able to file another type of responsive document, asking for a dismissal of the complaint. This is called a **demurrer** or **motion to dismiss** and is used when the complaint, even if true, is legally insufficient to justify an answer. A **motion** is a formal request to a court for some action by the judge. The demurrer or motion to dismiss often is called a so-what motion, as its legal effect is to say that even if all of the plaintiff's allegations are true, no legal duty was breached by the defendant. To provide an example of a motion to dismiss, let us consider an illustrative dispute.

LEGAL FOCUS—PROBLEM

Plaintiff Archibald Cantwell alleged in his complaint that the defendant professor "wrongfully, viciously, and wantonly pointed at and called on the plaintiff, while in class, causing great and severe mental anguish." Did Cantwell state a cause of action in his complaint?

sustained
Agreement by the judge with request by an attorney-at-law.

No, Cantwell did not state a cause of action. Even if the plaintiff's claims were admitted by the defendant, there would be no legal recovery (judgment) possible for the plaintiff, simply because asking questions and pointing at a student is not against the law. Therefore, the defendant should file a demurrer or motion to dismiss, which would be **sustained** (agreed to) by the court, and the complaint would be dismissed. If Cantwell chose instead to file an answer, the case would continue on to trial, wasting the time and money of both the defendant and the court.

statute of limitations
A statute that bars civil or criminal proceedings unless brought within a specified period of time after the act occurred.

default judgment
Court-awarded judgment based on the defendant's failure to answer the summons and complaint or to appear at the trial to contest the claim of the plaintiff.

***ex parte* trial**
A legal action in which only one side of the dispute is heard.

accusation
Formal commencement of a criminal case by a specified public official such as a district attorney or by a grand jury.

information
An accusation of a criminal offense issued following a preliminary hearing.

grand jury
An appointed body of citizens formed both to investigate the operations of government and to issue indictments against persons suspected of criminal conduct.

indictment
An accusation of felony filed by a grand jury.

A demurrer also can raise procedural defenses, as, for example, a claim that the action is barred by a **statute of limitations**—a statute requiring that particular legal actions be commenced within a stated period of time. Late claims are barred (i.e., prohibited) by statutes of limitations even if they are otherwise meritorious. The reasoning for statutes of limitation is that memories fade and other evidence becomes scarce and less reliable, all of which diminishes the possibility of a just resolution of the dispute by a court. Such statutes also serve to eliminate what could be an ongoing threat of suit that otherwise would interfere with the defendant's life.

Once Martinez's complaint and Graf's answer are filed, the factual contentions of each party are stated on the record. Plaintiffs and defendants almost always disagree with each other's version of what had happened; these factual disagreements are much of what must be resolved at trial.

Following receipt of summons and complaint, Graf might voluntarily or unwittingly do nothing. Doing nothing is rarely a smart choice; here it would pave the way for Martinez to obtain an uncontested judgment, called a **default judgment**. As explained earlier, a judgment is a final expression by the court telling who wins and who loses. Unlike a judgment following a trial, a default judgment may be issued by the judge following a trial in which the defendant is absent, and who, it is therefore assumed, does not contest the accuracy of the plaintiff's claims. The judge simply takes minimal evidence from the plaintiff to ensure that the claim is not frivolous or improper in some respect. Following such an ***ex parte* (Latin: "with one party") trial**, which often takes only minutes of the court's time, a judgment typically is awarded to the plaintiff. So, doing nothing can be a costly mistake. Even if he is going to concede fault and liability, Graf would be wise to file an answer to the complaint and then try to negotiate a compromise limiting the damages he must pay or providing a reasonable payment schedule. Default judgments are surprisingly common occurrences, particularly in small claim actions.

How Is a Criminal Case Started?

In contrast to a civil case, a criminal case formally begins with the issuance of an **accusation**, which formally charges a specified person with commission of a particular crime. An accusation usually is initiated by the district attorney (under which circumstance it is called an **information**) or by a body called the **grand jury** (under which circumstance it is called an **indictment**). The grand jury is a body composed of a number of jurors that varies from state to state, sometimes six, sometimes twelve, and occasionally more than twelve. It inquires into crimes committed in the city or other geographic region from which the members are drawn, makes determination of the probability of guilt, and then issues indictments against supposed offenders. Misdemeanor cases typically are initiated by the filing of a complaint. These terms and criminal procedures are discussed in Chapter 6.

What Are Pretrial Procedures?

Once a civil lawsuit begins by the filing of pleadings, a year or more may elapse before the trial. In some crowded metropolitan areas, the volume of cases filed, together with shortages of judges and courtrooms, cause seriously congested calendars, which in turn necessitate undesirable delays in setting cases for trial. In rural and less populous jurisdictions, the trial may occur as soon as the opposing attorneys are prepared. In populous urban areas, delays of three to four years sometimes occur. Courtroom delay is one of the most serious problems facing this country's legal system. Many states experiment with new administrative methods to expedite the process and actively encourage alternatives to litigation, such as arbitration. The legal system is flexible enough to allow for

alternative dispute resolution
Any of various methods of resolving disputes through means other than the judicial process.

alternatives to the courts in many situations. Alternatives to litigation are called **alternative dispute resolution** (ADR) and are discussed in Chapter 4.

Discovery

discovery
Group of methods used during the period between commencement of a lawsuit and the date of trial to learn facts about the dispute.

One of the most time-consuming, expensive, intrusive, and sometimes-frustrating aspects of going through civil trials today involves a process called discovery. **Discovery** includes the use of a group of methods to learn facts about the dispute. Nonexistent early in the twentieth century, many believe that discovery has escalated into an arsenal of weapons that often is abused by attorneys. Should discovery be streamlined to keep pace with life and times in the twenty-first century? Many business contracts today contain arbitration agreements (discussed in Chapter 4) to avoid going to court if and when future disputes arise between the contracting persons. Many, perhaps most, financial businesses (e.g., banks, stock brokerages) and HMOs (health maintenance organizations) choose this judicial bypass to attempt to avoid the costs, intrusiveness, and delays associated with discovery procedures.

Although courtroom availability is the most common reason for a delay in a trial date, counsel for one or both of the parties may seek delay because more time is needed for discovery procedures. The stated goals of discovery are to

- Educate each party as to the facts surrounding the controversy,
- Promote voluntary settlement of the controversy by revealing strengths and weaknesses in the cases of each party, and
- Eliminate surprises that otherwise might arise during the trial, possibly leading to a miscarriage of justice.

deposition
Questioning of a witness or adverse party to an action, under oath, by the opposing attorney before the trial.

Depositions and interrogatories are the most common types of discovery. A **deposition** is the questioning of a witness or adverse party by the opposing attorney, long before the trial, under oath, in the presence of a court reporter and the other party's attorney. **Interrogatories** are a form of discovery in which written questions are directed to a party, who must then reply under oath with written answers.

LEGAL FOCUS—PROBLEM

Marya Martinez hired Sally Sharpe as her attorney in the case against Gary Graf. Sharpe's complaint and summons issued by the court were served personally on Graf. He promptly hired a lawyer, Scott Sagedevan, who prepared and filed an answer. In the answer, Graf contended that he had adjusted Martinez's bindings carefully and properly and was not negligent. He also alleged that Martinez was negligent in two respects: (1) being under the influence of alcohol at the time of her injury and (2) being careless in allowing ice to form beneath her boots. The pleadings were filed, joining the issues of fact. What is the most likely next step by the attorneys?

interrogatories
A form of discovery consisting of written questions directed to a party or witness who is expected to reply with written answers under oath.

Attorney Sharpe is seeking a money judgment against Graf to compensate Martinez for her injury on the theory that Graf was negligent. Attorney Sagedevan, on behalf of Graf, is contending that Graf was not negligent and that even if he was, Martinez was equally careless as to her own safety and so she should be denied a money judgment. Both attorneys will need more information to prepare for trial.

Depositions

Sharpe wants to know the exact setting Graf used in adjusting Martinez's bindings, and then she will seek expert advice as to the proper setting. Sharpe could mail a notice of taking deposition to Graf's attorney, requesting that Graf appear in Sharpe's office at a stated time to be questioned under oath with a court reporter present. The court reporters will use mechanical shorthand to record all testimony. In many states, electronic shorthand equipment and recording machines also are used. During this deposition, which Graf must attend, Sharpe could ask him, among other things, what setting he had used on Martinez's bindings. Of course, Graf's attorney will respond by taking Martinez's deposition.

LEGAL FOCUS—PROBLEM

At the deposition, attorney Sagedevan asked the following question: "Ms. Martinez, do you date frequently?" Attorney Sharpe immediately objected, shouting that she would not allow her client to be subjected to irrelevant questions by Sagedevan. Must Martinez answer the question?

At the deposition, Sagedevan cannot force Martinez to answer a question if she refuses. He could, however, seek a court order requiring her to answer the question if the question is deemed appropriate by the judge. Courts have the power to compel the parties to comply with the discovery procedures. If the order is granted and Martinez still refuses to answer, her entire case may be dismissed or another sanction (penalty) imposed. Attorney Sagedevan will need to explain to a judge why the question is appropriate, because its relevance to the case is not obvious.

After the deposition, the court reporter prepares a hard (paper) copy of all questions and answers. This document is made available to the witness, who makes any necessary corrections before signing and returning it. If the witness is unavailable at the trial, or is present but changes the version of the story given at the deposition, the transcript itself may be introduced as evidence and used to **impeach** (i.e., discredit) the witness. In complex cases, depositions may require several days of testimony under oath. The cost of taking depositions is a major expense of litigation and one significant reason why alternatives to litigation are often sought. As undeniably useful as discovery is, it is costly and can be subject to abuse. Litigants can request large quantities of documents based on possible relevance, and the expense of this production of documents is borne by the person producing them. The federal courts and many state court systems have experimented with discovery rules in an attempt to preserve discovery's value while limiting its excesses. Examples include requiring a party to provide relevant discovery without it being requested by the other party and harsher penalties (sanctions) available to the courts for instances in which abuse of discovery rules exist. Some have suggested eliminating discovery altogether.

impeach
To discredit, dispute, disparage, or contradict a witness's testimony.

Written Interrogatories

After the deposition, attorney Sagedevan thought of some additional questions that he would like to ask. He sent the following written interrogatories to Martinez through her attorney:

1. Please state the address of Luther Thomas.
2. Please state each date you visited a doctor and your total medical bill expenses.
3. Please state whether or not your medical bills are being paid by an insurance company. If so, please state the company's name and the applicable policy number.

If Martinez fails to answer the written interrogatories, Graf's attorney may seek an order from the court compelling answers. Attorneys may serve hundreds of written interrogatories in preparation of a complex case. They are less expensive than depositions because no court reporter is needed, and since they are written, they tend to be more concise than the ramblings that frequently accompany oral interrogations. Furthermore, parties responding to interrogatories must search their files and records for information they "cannot recall." A disadvantage is that they allow a witness to consult with counsel and draft an answer that, while true, discloses as little as possible and states even that as favorably as possible. The questioning attorney is not present to detect signs of uneasiness and possible evasion or concealment, nor is he or she able to immediately pursue promising leads suggested by oral responses during depositions.

motion to produce
Request to a judge by counsel to compel the opposing party to provide specified evidence to the court.

Motion to Produce

The **motion to produce** may result in an order made by a judge. It compels the opposing party to provide specified evidence that he or she currently controls or possesses and that is believed to be relevant in the case.

LEGAL FOCUS—PROBLEM

Sagedevan believed that Martinez's diary might provide important information. He therefore filed a motion to produce with the court after his request to produce it had been refused. The motion requested an order compelling Martinez to deliver her diary to Sagedevan for his inspection. Will the motion be granted?

Sagedevan's motion will not be granted unless he can demonstrate to the court specifically what may be contained in the diary that would be relevant to the issues in the case. That appears doubtful unless, for example, Sagedevan can offer proof that Martinez has been deceitful and he has reason to believe that the diary would confirm the deceit.

subpoena
An order directing a person to appear at a certain time and place for the purpose of giving testimony as a witness.

At the time of trial, either attorney may ask the court for a **subpoena** (Latin: "under penalty"), a written order directing a person to appear in court and testify as a witness. If it is believed that the witness has books or documents needed for a full disclosure of the facts, the court may issue a **subpoena *duces tecum*** (Latin: "under penalty bring with you"), requiring that identified documents or physical evidence be brought to court.

subpoena *duces tecum*
A judicial order to bring specified documents or physical evidence to court.

Discovery in Criminal Matters

In a criminal case, discovery is limited because of the defendant's **privilege against self-incrimination** (a privilege is a legal right). This legal right, in brief, provides that a defendant cannot be compelled to testify against himself or herself in a criminal case. The privilege is derived from the Fifth Amendment to the U.S. Constitution, and colloquially, it often is referred to as "taking the Fifth."

privilege against self-incrimination
The right of any person, including one accused of a crime, to remain silent when what might be said could indicate criminal guilt.

The government prosecutor does not have this same right, as the prosecutors are not on trial. The Sixth Amendment to the U.S. Constitution gives the accused the right "in all criminal prosecutions ... to be confronted with the witnesses against him." Therefore, the government prosecutor must allow examination of the evidence against the defendant, including names of witnesses against the defendant. However, physical evidence (such as weapons, clothing, and stolen goods) may be impounded (seized and held) by the district attorney, pending trial. The defendant, however, does have the right to inspect all such evidence before trial. The apparent advantage of one-way discovery for the criminal defendant is more than counterbalanced by the state's greater resources to independently investigate and discover facts surrounding alleged criminal activity.

motion for summary judgment
Request to a judge by counsel to award judgment because there are no significant questions of fact in the lawsuit.

Motion for Summary Judgment

If there are no disputes over facts that need to be resolved, it is possible that the case can be decided without a trial. In a **motion for summary judgment**, the moving party argues that there are no significant questions of fact and that the applicable law requires that the moving party be awarded judgment. This motion might be made to the court after discovery, when a party believes discovery has shown that there is no real dispute as to the facts. If the motion is granted, no trial takes place. The party against whom a motion for summary judgment is granted (or any other adverse order that terminates the case) would have the right to appeal.

pretrial hearing or conference
Hearing occurring before a trial.

The Pretrial Hearing or Conference

Either party or the court can request a **pretrial hearing or conference**, which usually takes place after the discovery process is over. The conference consists of an informal discussion between the judge and the attorneys. Its purpose is to identify the matters that are in dispute and to plan the course of the trial. At the pretrial hearing, the judge may encourage the parties to settle without a trial (an out-of-court settlement). These "settlement conferences" sometimes are attended by the parties to the litigation, as well as by their attorneys. Possible "before trial" steps in a civil dispute are set forth in Exhibit 3.4.

What Is a Jury?

Jury duty [is] a bog of quicksand on the path to justice.

—Sidney Bernard, "The Waiting Game,"
New York Journal-American, December 30, 1965

jury
A group of men and women sworn to declare the truth based on evidence presented to them.

A **jury** is a group of men and women selected according to established procedures to ensure lack of bias, who are sworn under oath to inquire of certain matters of fact and declare the truth based on evidence presented to them. This broad definition of a jury includes many types of juries used in the United States, including grand jury, petit jury, special jury, coroner's jury, and sheriff's jury. Our discussion focuses on those juries selected to hear and decide specific legal disputes rather than investigative juries, such as grand juries.

In the United States, litigating parties often request a jury trial. Whether the request is granted will depend on whether the requesting party has a legal right to a jury trial. Many U.S. citizens believe that they have a right to a jury trial in all legal matters, but they are wrong. Litigants, however, do have a right to a jury trial in many matters. Whether they have a right to jury trial may depend on whether the trial is criminal or civil, raises matters "in equity" or "law," or whether it takes place in state or federal courts.*

LEGAL FOCUS—CASE

People's Bank, a Connecticut corporation, filed an action to foreclose on a home owned by William and Nadine Podd, husband and wife, alleging the Podds failed to pay their monthly mortgage payments. The Podds requested a trial by jury. People's Bank objected. Do the Podds have a right to jury trial in this lawsuit?

People's Bank v. Podd, 1993 WL 382514, 10 Conn. L. Rptr. 83 (Conn. Super.).

*Article III, Section 2 of the Constitution provides that "the Trial of all Crimes … shall be by Jury." The Sixth and Seventh Amendments also provide for the right to a jury trial. The Sixth Amendment, referring to criminal cases, provides that "In all criminal prosecutions, the accused shall enjoy the right to a speedy and public trial." The Seventh Amendment states, "In Suits at common law, where the value in controversy shall exceed twenty dollars, the right of trial by jury shall be persevered."

EXHIBIT 3.4 Steps in a Civil Case—Before Trial

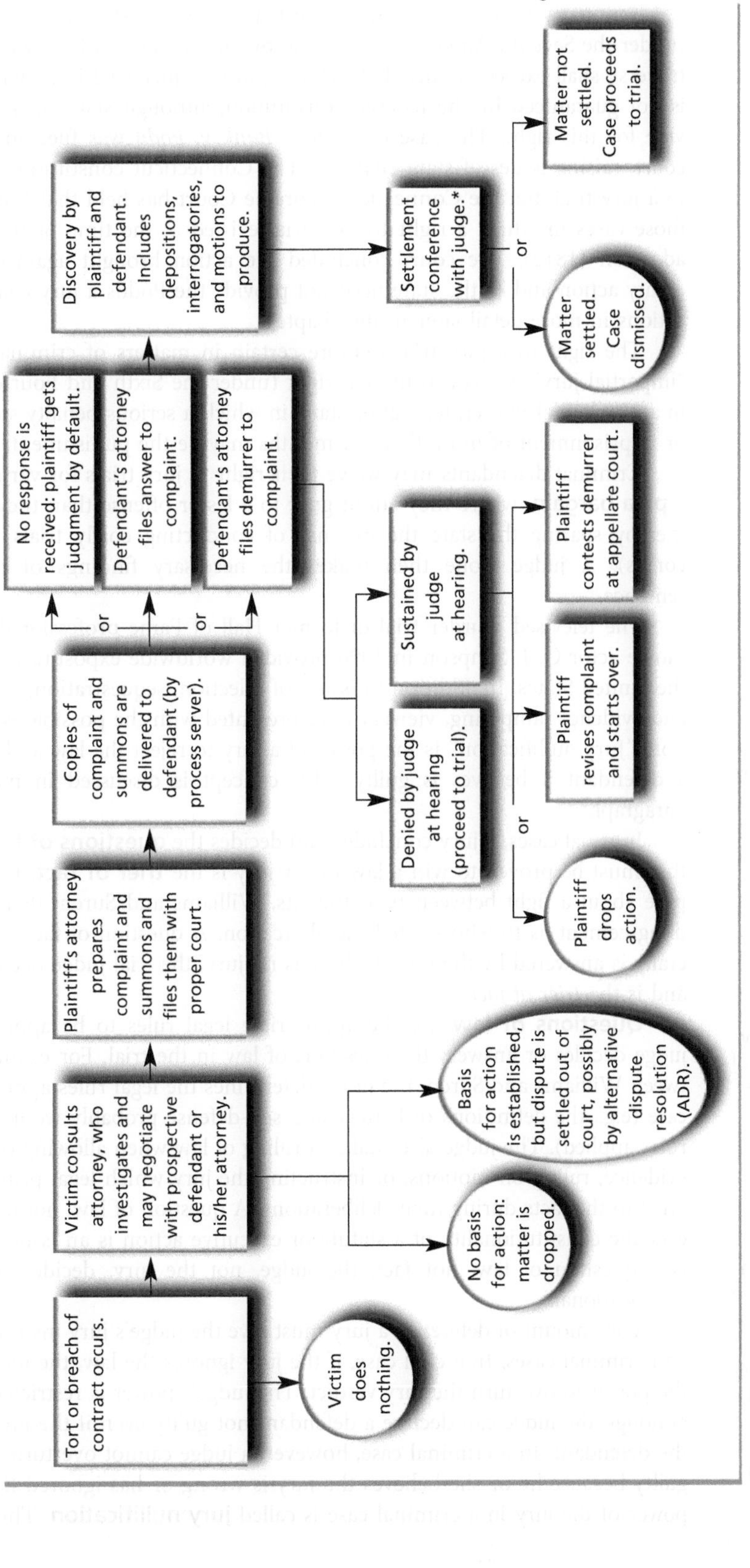

* In many states, nonbinding arbitration may be required in addition to or in lieu of the settlement conference.

Any party to a civil lawsuit in the federal court system has the constitutional right (under the Seventh Amendment) to trial by jury in cases at law "where the value in controversy shall exceed twenty dollars." A right to a jury trial in a civil case in state courts is not guaranteed by the federal Constitution, although state constitutions usually provide for this right. The case of *People's Bank v. Podd* was filed in a Connecticut state court, raising issues of state civil law. The Connecticut constitution provides for a right to a jury trial, but the Connecticut Supreme Court has held that this right exists only in those cases in which a right to jury trial existed at the time of the state constitution's adoption (1812). The court concluded the action brought against the Podds was an equity action and so the state need not provide the Podds a jury trial. We discuss equity actions in more detail later in the chapter.

The right to a jury trial is more certain in matters of criminal law. A trial by an "impartial jury" is a constitutional right (under the Sixth and Fourteenth Amendments) in any criminal matter, federal or state, in which a serious penalty such as a jail sentence or imprisonment of more than six months may be the punishment.

plea bargain
A binding agreement in which an accused agrees to plead guilty if the court agrees to a specified charge and punishment in advance.

Criminal defendants may waive their right to jury trials for various reasons (such as a **plea bargain**, where they admit guilt to a lesser offense than they were charged with, thereby sparing the state the expense of conducting costly trials with uncertain outcomes). A judge alone then makes the necessary findings of fact and imposes a sentence.

The televised murder trial of former Hall of Fame professional football player and movie actor O. J. Simpson in 1996 provided worldwide exposure to the role of juries in the United States. In addition to issues of selection, sequestration, crime scene visitation, and evidence tampering, viewers were presented with the possible issue of jury nullification. "Jury nullification" is the power of a jury to reject the law and evidence and acquit a defendant it believes is guilty. This concept is discussed in more detail in a few paragraphs.

questions of fact
Circumstances or matters surrounding and involved in a case that is being tried by a court.

trier of fact
Jury or judge acting as the finder of issues of fact.

In usual cases, a jury concludes and decides the **questions of fact**—historical events that must be proved to win a lawsuit. A jury is the **trier of fact**. For example, in a dispute about a fight between two students, Williams and Suren, there probably will be a disagreement as to who started the altercation. A question of fact is presented and generally is answered by the jury. If there is no jury, the trial judge decides questions of fact and is the *trier of fact*.

questions of law
Principles and rules of human conduct determined by the judge to be applicable in a case being tried by a court.

Questions of law are the appropriate legal rules to be applied in the trial. The judge decides or answers the questions of law in the trial. For example, in the fight between Williams and Suren, the judge determines the legal rules appropriate to decide the case (e.g., the definitions of battery and self-defense probably would be among the legal rules applied). The judge also makes a ruling of law when allowing or disallowing certain evidence, ruling on motions, or instructing the jury which legal principles should be applied to the facts during their deliberations. A question of law, not fact, also arises whenever the constitutionality of a statute or executive action is an issue. As constitutionality is a question of law, not fact, the judge, not the jury, decides whether a statute is constitutional.

jury nullification
The power of a jury in a criminal trial to disregard the law and unanimously find the defendant innocent, although there is ample evidence to support a verdict of guilty.

The amount of deference a jury must give the judge's jury instructions differs in civil and criminal cases. In a civil case, if the jury ignores the law, the judge has the duty and the power to overturn the jury verdict. The judge's power is restricted in a criminal case, although the judge can declare a defendant not guilty even if the jury decided to convict the defendant. In a criminal case, however, a judge cannot overturn a jury verdict of not guilty because he or she believes the jury is wrong or has ignored the law. This residual power of the jury in a criminal case is called **jury nullification**. Thus, for example, in a criminal case, although a jury could not find a law unconstitutional, it could legally refuse to convict a defendant because the jurors think the law is unconstitutional, or unfair, or for any other reason. A judge is not free to disregard the jury's verdict of not guilty unless the judge finds jury corruption or misconduct (e.g., one or more jurors had been bribed).

LEGAL FOCUS—CASE

Defendant Anthony Edwards was charged with and admitted to committing fraud by using other people's credit cards to purchase gasoline. His defense was his self-proclaimed status as "The Black Shadow of Robin Hood." He claimed "he was motivated by the need to redistribute wealth in a system he perceived as racist." At trial, he requested that the judge issue the following jury instruction: "if collectively you decide that despite the acts of the [defendant] which you may find the government proved beyond a reasonable doubt, you believe that the [defendant's] actions should not be considered to be criminal by society, you may find him not guilty." The instruction if granted would advise the jury of its power of nullification. The judge refused. Was the judge correct?

United States v. Anthony Edwards, 101 F.3d 17 (E.D.N.Y., 1996).

The judge was correct to refuse the instruction, and did so stating, "While juries have the power to ignore the law in their verdicts, courts have no obligation to tell them they may do so. It appears that every circuit that has considered this issue agrees." In a later case, another court explained this curious position as follows:

> *[I]n language originally employed by Judge Learned Hand, the power of juries to "nullify" or exercise a power of lenity is just that—a power; it is by no means a right or something that a judge should encourage or permit if it is within his authority to prevent. It is true that nullification has a long history in the Anglo-American legal system, and that the federal courts have long noted the de facto power of a jury to render general verdicts "in the teeth of both law and facts." However … it is the duty of juries in criminal cases to take the law from the court and apply that law to the facts as they find them, courts have consistently recognized that jurors have no right to nullify.*

Prospective Jurors

The jury is a group of persons selected from a panel of randomly designated citizens of the local region to decide a particular civil or criminal case. A jury is considered the fairest instrument of justice on the theory that it tends to neutralize individual bias from the courtroom by drawing together a number of persons of diverse interests and backgrounds. No single person—not even a highly educated, coldly analytical, scrupulously honest, professional scientist—is totally objective, so it is hoped that the combination of differing perspectives will provide the balance needed for just decisions. Judges, lawyers, witnesses, scholars—and most important, litigants themselves—generally agree that the jury system works well most of the time.

Usually, litigants in emotionally charged cases, both civil and criminal, prefer the consensus of a jury of their peers (equals) to the decision of one judge. On the other hand, many attorneys believe that in complex business litigation, for example, a jury can be overwhelmed and thoroughly confused by a flood of technical language. Thus, they often think that in such cases their clients will fare better by waiving their right to a jury trial and relying on the expertise of the judge or an arbitrator.

It is important that the jury selection process be random. Otherwise, people justifiably would suspect its integrity. In criminal cases especially, the jury is sometimes the sole barrier between the individual and the awesome power of the prosecuting government. The selection begins with preparation of a list or panel of prospective jurors. Most states prepare such lists from voter registrations. Because minorities, the poor, and young adults do not register to vote at the same rate as the rest of the population, these groups are likely to be underrepresented on juries. For this reason, many states use other sources of names for prospective jurors, such as driver-registration records, telephone directories, hunting and fishing license lists, utility customer lists, or census rolls. Some accept volunteers for jury duty.

The Jury Selection and Service Act regulates jury selection in federal cases. This act provides that names selected from voter registration lists should be supplemented with names from additional lists to help ensure selection of juries that better represent a diverse community.

Exemptions from Jury Service

A few classes of people are automatically exempt, or disqualified, from jury duty in many states. In federal courts, disqualified groups include noncitizens; minors; residents of less than one year; persons unable to read, write, and understand English; persons with mental or physical infirmities that would impair their capability as jurors; and convicted felons. States have adopted similar exemptions. In addition, persons may be excused temporarily or indefinitely exempted when absence from a job or family would cause an unreasonable hardship.

It is illegal for an employer to penalize or discriminate against an employee for serving as a juror by docking vacation time. Some employers continue to pay the salaries or wages of jurors, less the modest fees received from the court, but this is not compulsory. Jurors are presently paid $40 per day in the federal court system and usually less in state courts. Such small sums are inadequate pay for most jurors who are not receiving any income from their employers. Consequently, jury duty that may last for weeks or longer may mean a significant financial sacrifice. Yet, jury service is a citizen's duty in a democracy. Persons refusing to serve without an acceptable excuse can be found in contempt of court, resulting in fines or imprisonment.

Voir Dire

The French phrase ***voir dire*** (pronounced *v'wah deer* and meaning "to speak the truth") refers to the questioning of prospective jurors to find possible bias. Understandably, attorneys try to *seat* (select) jurors whom they believe to be sympathetic to their clients' position. Thus, an accountant accustomed to arithmetic precision may not be welcomed as a juror by a defendant relying on an unverified alibi in a criminal trial, or a clerk who earns a low salary may be considered undesirable by the plaintiff in a civil action where damages sought for loss of future earning power exceed $1 million.

voir dire
Process of questioning prospective jurors to ascertain whether they have any bias that would make difficult or unlikely their impartiality in determining questions of fact during a trial.

In large cities, private companies are available to research potential juror lists for cases when a sizable amount of money is at stake. Such research firms provide "jury books" containing past juror voting records and other personal information. These books are sold to attorneys to assist them in identifying favorable prospective jurors. In major trials, where the stakes are high, sociologists and psychologists have been hired by lawyers to analyze the physical appearance, education, social status, economic condition, personality, and general cultural background of each prospective juror. The idea is to predict attitude and probable voting conduct in the forthcoming trial. Such assistance in jury selection raises many questions about the accuracy of character evaluation and the ethical propriety of this practice, especially if only one side has access to such information. Legal consulting firms provide pretrial opinion polls, profiles of "ideal jurors," mock trials, and shadow juries. They also coach lawyers and witnesses and prepare designs for courtroom graphics. When such assistance is utilized, critics suggest that the jury is not composed of one's peers.

LEGAL FOCUS—PROBLEM

On behalf of Marya Martinez, attorney Sharpe demands a jury trial. On the day set for trial, Sharpe and attorney Sagedevan meet with Judge Miller in chambers. Sharpe requests permission to personally *voir dire* the prospective jurors. Sagedevan does not object. Will Judge Miller grant this request?

The judge possibly will grant the request. Historically, judges have had the power to either conduct *voir dire* themselves or to allow the attorneys to do so. Most states follow the lead of the federal court system where *voir dire* is conducted by the judge, but only after considering specific questions offered by the attorneys. Using a judge usually expedites the questioning and serves to preclude the use of inappropriate questions. Some attorneys try to argue their case in *voir dire*, which is not a valid purpose of the jury selection process.

LEGAL FOCUS—PROBLEM

Judge Miller grants Sharpe's request and orders that the two attorneys conduct the *voir dire*. One of the questions Sharpe asks each prospective juror is whether he or she has ever been a ski instructor. One person answers "yes." Is this sufficient evidence of juror bias? If so, what recourse does Sharpe have against it?

Prior experience or knowledge of a situation does not necessarily mean that the person is biased. Everyone possesses inclinations and opinions consistent with his or her culture, education, family background, experience, and so forth, but not everyone allows these to prejudice his or her thinking. What matters is whether a certain experience or inclination tends to make a person unable to decide fairly a particular case. Some types of experience are more likely than others to do this. If bias is evident or likely, the judge may excuse the prospective juror using a **challenge for cause** (bias or the appearance of bias is shown). In Martinez's trial, a prospective juror who was once a ski instructor probably would not be as impartial as someone without this experience. Thus, bias is likely. The judge might properly excuse that prospective juror for cause.

challenge for cause
Ability to exclude a prospective trial juror if bias or prejudice is indicated.

There is no limit on the number of challenges for cause, which can be granted for a showing of bias. In jury selection for a trial concerning a highly publicized Brink's warehouse robbery in Boston, some 1,000 prospective jurors were excused for cause. Because of newspaper accounts over the years before the first arrest in the case, most of those excused had definite opinions as to the guilt of the defendants.

peremptory challenge
Ability to exclude a prospective juror for any reason other than race or gender.

Even if no bias is demonstrable, each attorney in either a civil or criminal action can challenge peremptorily (without cause) and thereby excuse from service a limited number of prospective jurors (six, for example, in civil actions, and generally more in criminal actions). The purpose of a **peremptory challenge** (dismissal of a juror for an undisclosed personal reason of the dismissing party) is to permit parties to eliminate some prospective jurors for any reason or for no reason. Some clients simply do not like the looks of a particular prospective juror. A well-known ditty goes:

I do not like thee, Dr. Fell;
The reason why I cannot tell.
But this I know and know full well,
I do not like thee, Dr. Fell.

Although no reason need be stated for a peremptory challenge, such challenges cannot be used to accomplish the illegal and impermissible purpose of excluding persons on the basis of their race or gender. Once peremptory challenges are exhausted or waived (given up or unused), the designated number of jurors are sworn to fulfill their duty faithfully, and the trial begins. If the trial is expected to last very long, one, two, or more extra jurors (called *alternates*) are selected and remain in the courtroom throughout the trial. In the infamous criminal trial of O. J. Simpson, for the first time in U.S. history, more alternate jurors (fifteen) were selected than jurors (twelve). Alternate jurors vote only if a regular juror dies or withdraws because of illness, family hardship, misconduct, or other conflict. If, by the end of a trial, there are not enough jurors remaining to render a verdict, a mistrial results unless both parties agree to accept the verdict of the smaller panel.

LEGAL FOCUS—PROBLEM

A preschool molestation case in Los Angeles took more than two and a half years before the jury adjourned to consider their verdicts. By that time all six alternate jurors had replaced vacancies that occurred during trial. If the jury had lost another juror before the verdicts were rendered, a mistrial would have occurred in a trial that cost more than $15 million. After three months of deliberations, the jury reached verdicts on sixty-five counts (separate criminal charges) against two defendants. One defendant was found not guilty on all charged counts. The other defendant was found not guilty on all but thirteen counts. As to these counts, the jury was unable to reach a verdict. As the jury finished its deliberations without losing another juror, there was no mistrial.

Jury Size and Vote

Since the middle of the fourteenth century, juries in England have been composed of twelve people. Probably for that reason, laypersons as well as scholars in the United States had long assumed that the Constitution, when referring to a jury, meant a jury of twelve people. In federal criminal court trials, twelve jurors are required, although criminal verdicts have been upheld with eleven jurors. In civil cases, the number of jurors required has been reduced to six in many district courts. According to the U.S. Supreme Court, this reduction to six jurors in a civil case satisfies the Seventh Amendment.

The U.S. Supreme Court has also held that the Fourteenth Amendment does not require that state court juries (as opposed to federal ones) be composed of twelve people in either civil or criminal cases. As few as six members have been found constitutional in a state court, although a jury of five in a criminal case has been disallowed. For reasons of efficiency and economy, about one-fourth of the states have reduced the size of juries to six or eight jurors in both civil and criminal matters. Currently, no state provides for fewer than twelve jurors in cases in which the death penalty could be imposed, although that may be constitutionally permissible.

The number of jurors required to agree on a verdict is an additional important question in American jurisprudence. Historically, to reach a verdict in criminal cases, the jury vote had to be unanimous. Thus, in criminal actions, one juror has been able to block the prosecutor's attempt to convict the accused. Such power is an affirmation of the importance of each juror. The requirement of the unanimous jury is the rule in federal and most state criminal prosecutions. A few states allow for a guilty verdict without requiring a unanimous jury (e.g., Oregon permits a conviction by ten out of twelve jurors), although a unanimous vote for a verdict in a state six-person jury criminal case is required. In most civil cases, however, a three-fourths majority (nine of twelve jurors) is sufficient. On the other hand, in the federal court system, civil juries are required to render unanimous verdicts.

LEGAL FOCUS—CASE

After considerable deliberation, the six-person jury informed the judge they could not reach a unanimous opinion in the criminal assault and battery case against Kevin Nobles. The Palm Beach County Circuit Court judge and the attorneys for Nobles and the state discussed the limited options available, including a suggestion from Nobles' attorney that Nobles could accept a majority verdict and waive his state right to a unanimous jury rather than begin again after a mistrial. Can a defendant waive his right to a unanimous verdict?

Nobles v. Florida, 786 So.2d 56 (Fla., 2001).

Kevin Nobles agreed to waive his right and was rewarded for his impatience by the jury finding him guilty by a vote of 4–2. Obviously, he reconsidered his waiver and on appeal argued that

> *the trial court erred when it accepted his request for a majority verdict because even though waivers of the right to a unanimous verdict have been accepted for super majorities of five to one, there is no authority that expressly approves a four to two majority verdict.*

The trial court upheld the conviction, stating,

> *[T]he following requirements [were] met in Nobles' trial: (1) the waiver is initiated by the defendant, not the trial judge or the prosecutor; (2) the jury has informed the court that it is unable to reach a verdict, after having had a reasonable time to deliberate; (3) the trial judge explains to the defendant his/her right to a unanimous jury verdict and the consequences of a waiver of that right; and (4) the trial judge questions the defendant directly and determines that the waiver is being made knowingly and voluntarily.*

LEGAL FOCUS—EXAMPLE

The instructions from the judge in the Nobles' case:

JUDGE: It is possible to waive one's constitutional rights if the waiver is a knowing waiver. It's my understanding that after conferring with counsel, and without knowing how the jury is split in this case, that it's your desire to waive or give up your right to a unanimous verdict and to agree to a, what we call a majority verdict, which means there are six jurors, if four of them or more vote one way or another as to any count, that would be the verdict in the case. Is my understanding correct?

APPELLANT: Yes, Sir.

Clearly, a reduction in jury size together with relaxed voting percentages for a verdict will do much to change the role of the jury in our society. In addition, some states have limited the types of cases in which a jury is considered appropriate. For example, states with no-fault automobile insurance plans largely bypass the jury process in automobile-related personal injury cases. Many states have decriminalized such matters as minor traffic offenses and have removed a person's right to a jury trial in such cases. In the federal system, there is a presumption that offenses punishable by incarceration for six months or less are petty offenses for which jury trials are unavailable. In addition, there is an important area of U.S. jurisprudence in which the Constitution does not require jury trials and legal history has not provided them, namely all matters "in equity." Recall the Legal Focus on page 106, in which the Podds were unsuccessful in their request for a jury trial in the foreclosure action brought against them. Most laypersons are uninformed on the important subject of equity, which we address next.

What Is an Action or Cause in Equity?

The U.S. legal system, like that of the United Kingdom, distinguishes between what are called disputes *at law* and *in equity*. The distinction between law and equity is based not on logic but on history. As discussed in Chapter 1, in medieval times, certain types of cases in England were decided by chancellors (government administrators) rather than in the king's court. The chancellors were often also religious aides to the king. In most disputes, an aggrieved person could seek and obtain monetary relief from a regular king's court. In the king's court, a judge would decide the case, sometimes with the assistance of a jury. Such were matters "at common law," and monetary damages usually were the only relief available from the king's courts.

A person unable to obtain relief from a regular court would appeal to the king, who would refer the citizen to the king's chancellor. As a general proposition, chancellors became involved only when there was no adequate remedy at law and when monetary damages were not sought or did not satisfy the need of the party seeking relief. These actions became known as actions "at equity." The chancellors decided matters brought before them based on their conscience, community norms of conduct, and principles of equity, or fairness.

specific performance
An equitable remedy allowing a buyer to get possession and title to real property and to goods that are unique when the seller refuses to deliver under a valid sales contract.

Today, all but a few U.S. courts have combined powers of law and equity. Delaware's Court of Chancery may not hear any case in which a sufficient remedy may be had by common law or statute. However, differences between the two methods of relief remain in the handling of certain types of disputes, available remedies, and the procedural rules applied to the actions. For example, matters involving the family were and are matters in equity, and they are an example of a type of dispute heard only as a matter in equity. Thus, if a dispute involves a divorce or dissolution of marriage, adoption, name change, or juvenile problem, a court sits in equity without a jury and usually applies different procedural rules.

rescission
An equitable remedy that annuls a contract and returns the parties to the relationship they had before the contract was made.

Other civil cases in equity based on the claimant seeking a different remedy include the following:

- An action requesting the court to order the defendant to comply with a contract by performing as promised (e.g., when the subject of the sales contract is unique, such as an original painting by van Gogh or a parcel of land), and the buyer wants performance, not monetary damages (**specific performance**).
- An action requesting the court to rescind an agreement to sell one's home, because of the undue influence of a relative (**rescission**).
- An action to bar a person from continuing to hunt unlawfully on someone else's property, or to end an unlawful strike by a union (**injunction**).

injunction
An order of a court of equity to someone to do or not do some act.

Note that in each example of equity, money damages are not sought. The monetary remedy at law was either inadequate or unavailable. However, today most courts, even in an equity action, strive to give full relief requested, including monetary damages if appropriate. Except in a few states, a modern court can grant both a remedy at law and a remedy at equity. For example, an aggrieved songwriter might be awarded an injunction barring the infringer (wrongful user) from using her copyrighted song without permission and also may be given dollar damages for the prior illegal use. Equitable remedies contrast with remedies at law, such as recovery of money for (1) injury caused by negligence of the defendant, (2) loss of earnings caused by defamation of character by the defendant, (3) money lost as the result of the defendant's fraud and deceit, and (4) profits lost due to breach of contract by the defendant. Exhibit 3.5 provides a contrast between matters at equity and at law.

Criminal cases are not matters in equity with one exception, juvenile crimes. If a juvenile commits an act that is criminal if committed by an adult, the matter generally will be considered a matter in equity. It technically is not considered a criminal matter, although a deprivation of liberty can and often does result if the minor is found responsible. Although an equitable matter, some due process protection still applies because of the potential for deprivation of liberty. However, there is no right to a jury trial. Many states provide for criminal prosecution of a minor as an adult in certain situations. If the minor is tried as an adult, the case is transferred from the court of equity to the criminal courts and all rights and jeopardy of criminal defendants apply.

There is no right to trial by jury in equity cases. The constitutional right to a jury was limited in the Seventh Amendment of the Constitution to civil matters, which are "suits at common law." The distinction between *common law* and *equity* was well known by the drafters of the Constitution. Jury trials in equity matters did not exist in England, as the chancellor relied on his own good conscience and sense of what was just. Since juries were available at law, a person who sought relief in equity waived the right to common law procedures, including the jury. In some states, a judge in equity may use an advisory jury but is not obliged to apply its verdict.

equitable maxims
General rules applied by courts to cases in equity.

A judge sitting in a matter in equity has awesome power. The judge is both the finder of fact and law and controls the powerful remedies available only in equity. Courts of equity not only provide different remedies but also often operate using different procedures and guidelines, including what are called **equitable maxims**—propositions or statements that provide a guide to a judge's exercise of his or her discretion. A few examples of equitable maxims are provided and explained in Exhibit 3.6.

EXHIBIT 3.5 Contrast between a Matter in Equity and a Matter at Law

	Equity	Law
Subject Matter	Family law Probate Trust When remedy at law is inadequate	Everything that is not a matter in equity
Nature of Trial	No jury	Jury
Remedies in Contracts	Reformation Rescission Specific performance Injunction Restitution	Money damages

EXHIBIT 3.6 Equitable Maxims

A maxim is a proposition or general statement. Some common maxims relating to actions in equity follow:

1. Whoever seeks equity must do equity. (Anyone who wishes to be treated fairly must treat others fairly.)
2. When there is equal equity, the law must prevail. (The applicable law will determine the outcome of a controversy in which the merits of both sides are equal.)
3. One seeking the aid of an equity court must come to the court with clean hands. (Plaintiffs must have acted fairly and honestly.)
4. Equity will not suffer a right to exist without a remedy. (Equitable relief will be awarded when there is a right to relief and there is not adequate remedy at law.)
5. Equity regards substance rather than form. (Equity is more concerned with fairness and justice than with legal technicalities.)
6. Equity aids the vigilant, not those who rest on their rights. (Equity will not help those who neglect their rights for an unreasonably long period of time.)

contempt of court
Willful defiance of the authority of a court, affront to its dignity, or willful disobedience of its lawful orders.

Defiance of a judge's order can place a person in **contempt of court** and subject him or her to summary arrest and imprisonment. Contempt of court is willful disobedience of a judicial order or obstruction of the work of the court. Some of the most controversial cases in the history of law have involved the exercise of a judge's equitable power.

LEGAL FOCUS—PROBLEM

Dr. J. Elizabeth Morgan was a party to a legal action involving visitation rights concerning her minor female child, Hilary. She maintained that the child's father had sexually abused her daughter. Although the husband strenuously denied this allegation, Morgan refused to obey an unsupervised visitation order in favor of her husband and placed the girl in hiding. Judge Herbert Dixon held Morgan in contempt of court. How could the court enforce its order?

Morgan was taken to the District of Columbia jail, where she spent the next 759 days for refusing to disclose the whereabouts of her child. She finally was released after a special law requiring her immediate release was passed by Congress and signed by then-President George H. W. Bush. As the court matter was in equity, no jury had been involved. Morgan had been jailed for her continuing refusal to follow the court's order, even though she had committed no crime. During the late 1990s, Susan McDougal spent eighteen months in jail for civil contempt for her refusal to answer questions posed by Special Prosecutor Kenneth Starr about President William J. Clinton's involvement in the Whitewater Development Corporation.

burden of proof
The duty to produce evidence as a trial progresses.

Returning to Martinez's case against Graf, we can see that since it is an action at law, either party may demand a jury trial. If neither party demands a jury, the right is waived, and the trial will proceed with the judge alone determining the truth of all factual contentions.

HOW IS A TRIAL CONDUCTED?

After the jury is selected in a civil case, the plaintiff's attorney proceeds first because the plaintiff has the **burden of proof**. This is the duty to present evidence that supports the allegations in the complaint (the facts). In civil cases, the burden of proof is satisfied by presenting a **preponderance of evidence**. That is, according to the evidence, it is more likely than not that the allegations in the complaint are true. If the jury agrees that the plaintiff more likely than not is right, the burden is met, and they must return a verdict for the plaintiff. In a criminal case, however, the burden of proof is much greater. The government, represented by a prosecutor, has the burden of proving the guilt of the defendant **beyond a reasonable doubt**. This means the finder of fact must be firmly convinced of the defendant's guilt.* The proof of guilt must preclude any other reasonable interpretation of the facts and be inconsistent with any other rational conclusion.

preponderance of evidence
Standard of determining civil liability, that the weight of the evidence offered to prove a matter is more probable than not.

LEGAL FOCUS—PROBLEM

While Marya Martinez was in the hospital, she told her father that Gary Graf took her wallet after she fell. This incensed Hernando Martinez, Marya's father, who demanded that Graf be prosecuted for theft. The criminal case came to trial months before the civil case, and the jury found Graf not guilty. Does this mean that Martinez will lose her civil case?

No, this does not mean Martinez will lose her civil case. Martinez's civil case concerns the civil issue of negligence in adjusting her ski bindings. The criminal case dealt with subsequent independent, unrelated behavior. In some situations, however, a single act can result in civil liability and also a criminal penalty. For example, if Graf had deliberately struck Martinez in the face without legal excuse or justification, he should be found civilly liable for damages and criminally guilty of battery. Theoretically, though, the defendant Graf could win the criminal case and lose the civil case. Such a result could happen because of the different burdens of proof involved. Moreover, the trials take place at different times with different juries and different procedural rules. The law allows both victims (society at large and Martinez in particular) their "days in court"—society (the state) is hurt by the alleged public crime, and Martinez (a private party) is hurt civilly by the alleged private tort. Because one charge is civil and one is criminal, there is no **double jeopardy** (being tried twice for the same offense), which would be unconstitutional as violating the Fifth Amendment. A notorious example of this split possibility occurred after the not guilty verdict in the notorious O. J. Simpson criminal trial. The parents of Nicole Brown Simpson and Ron Goldman sued for the wrongful death of their children. The jury in the civil case found O. J. Simpson liable (legally responsible) for the deaths.

beyond a reasonable doubt
The quantum evidence that fully satisfies and entirely convinces the jury in a criminal trial that the defendant is guilty as charged.

double jeopardy
A second criminal prosecution against a person for the same single offense, after the person has been found innocent of the crime in the prior trial.

*"The beyond a reasonable doubt standard is a requirement of due process, but the Constitution neither prohibits trial courts from defining reasonable doubt nor requires them to do so as a matter of course," *Hopt v. Utah*, 120 U.S. 430, 99 S.Ct. 2781 (1887). Supreme Court Justice Kennedy referred to the following "beyond a reasonable doubt" jury instruction as "clear, straightforward and accurate" in his concurring opinion in *Victor v. Nebraska*, 511 U.S. 1, 114 S.Ct. 1239, 1253 (1994):

> *The government has the burden of proving the defendant guilty beyond a reasonable doubt. Some of you may have served as juror in civil cases, where you were told that it is only necessary to prove that a fact is more likely true than not true. In criminal cases, the government's proof must be more powerful than that. It must be beyond a reasonable doubt. Proof beyond a reasonable doubt is proof that leaves you firmly convinced of the defendant's guilt. There are very few things in this world that we know with absolute certainty, and in criminal cases the law does not require proof that overcomes every possible doubt. If, based on your consideration of the evidence, you are firmly convinced that the defendant is guilty of the crime charged, you must find him guilty. If on the other hand, you think there is a real possibility that he is not guilty, you must give him the benefit of the doubt and find him not guilty.*

opening statement Summaries by counsel of plaintiff and of defendant indicating what they expect to prove in the ensuing trial.

case-in-chief The case presented by each party in a trial.

evidence Everything presented by disputing parties and witnesses that the "finder of fact" is entitled to consider in arriving at a determination of the facts.

relevant evidence Evidence that is related to the facts in dispute.

irrelevant evidence Evidence that does not relate to or have a bearing upon a question of fact in dispute during a trial.

Separate criminal trials brought by different governmental entities even upon the same set of facts generally are not considered to be double jeopardy. For example, after police officers were accused of beating Rodney King, they were found not guilty of state criminal charges. The federal government was later successful in bringing federal criminal charges against two of the officers for depriving King of his civil rights.

Procedures in a criminal trial are essentially the same as those for a civil case. Under the U.S. Constitution (Fifth Amendment), however, a defendant in a criminal case cannot be compelled to testify. This is not true in a civil case, unless the testimony would tend to incriminate and possibly subject the defendant to prosecution for some crime.

Opening Statements

The plaintiff's attorney begins the trial by making an **opening statement**—a summary of what the plaintiff expects to prove in the trial. Then the defendant's attorney may, but need not, make an opening statement telling what the defendant expects to prove in the trial. Such statements often are used to inform the jurors, in broad outline, of what they can expect to hear as the trial unfolds.

Evidence

After the opening statements, the plaintiff's attorney presents the plaintiff's **case-in-chief**. This involves calling and questioning witnesses and introducing into evidence documents, photographs, or other things that bear on the issues. **Evidence** is everything that the "finder of fact" (the jury, or judge when there is no jury) is entitled to consider in arriving at a determination of the facts. For example, the oral testimony of witnesses presented under oath is evidence; commentary of the attorney about that evidence is not. Attorneys are hired after the events in question have taken place and thus are not competent to testify as witnesses. Their role is to elicit evidence, comment on it, and argue about its significance. Of course, if the attorney's interpretation of the testimony of the witnesses is persuasive, the jury will be influenced by it.

Whether evidence should or should not be admitted is a question of law; therefore, the judge rules on all objections attorneys may make as to the admission of particular evidence. Evidence is admitted if the judge believes it will be useful in resolving issues in the case. Many rules concern what evidence is and is not admissible. For example, to be admitted, evidence must be **relevant** (related to the fact in dispute). **Irrelevant evidence** (evidence not related to the fact in dispute) is not admissible.

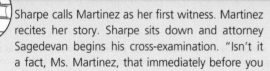

LEGAL FOCUS—PROBLEM

Sharpe calls Martinez as her first witness. Martinez recites her story. Sharpe sits down and attorney Sagedevan begins his cross-examination. "Isn't it a fact, Ms. Martinez, that immediately before you fractured your leg you got drunk on wine with a gentleman, Luther Thomas, who you picked up in the bar?" Sharpe objects to the question. Will the judge sustain or overrule the objection?

The objection will be sustained (the judge will not allow the question to be answered). The question is compound; that is, it contains two or more questions, one concerning sobriety, the other concerning whether, and where and how, she met Luther Thomas. It also contains a conclusion, which is inflammatory: "drunk." Attorney Sagedevan probably will be instructed to rephrase or drop the question. The question appears to be designed more to intimidate the witness than to extract information. The ruling by the judge is a ruling on a question of law.

A better form of questioning would be as follows:

Sagedevan: Isn't it a fact, Ms. Martinez, that immediately before you fractured your leg you were drinking wine?

Martinez: Yes, sir.

Sagedevan: With whom were you drinking wine?

Martinez: Luther Thomas.

Sagedevan: And did you know him previously?

Martinez: No.

expert witness
Anyone qualified by knowledge and skill, experience, training, or education to offer a credible and useful opinion upon some material issue in a trial.

Because the case may be decided based on the technical question of why Martinez's bindings did not release her skis, Sharpe may decide to include an **expert witness**. An expert witness is a witness with specialized knowledge or training in a field who is recognized as such by the court and allowed to testify about that topic, including opinion testimony. Expert testimony can be invaluable when technical or science-related questions of fact are at issue. Sharpe might decide to call an expert witness who can testify as to why the bindings failed. Ordinary witnesses are not allowed to give their opinion as that is a role of the finder of fact. However, an expert witness could testify that, in that expert's opinion, an improper adjustment of the bindings was the cause of the failure of the bindings to release.

Of course, when Sagedevan presents his case, he might have an expert witness who counters Sharpe's expert. Conflicting expert witness testimony about both fact and opinion is common. Thus, the jury may simply dismiss the expert testimony or decide which expert to believe. Thus, Sharpe and Sagedevan will attempt to undermine the credibility or accuracy of the opposing expert's testimony. They might do that by cross-examining the witness and also by eliciting testimony from their own witness. In the end, experts can make a case, but not managed well, they can distract, confuse, or worse yet, alienate a jury. They must be chosen and used wisely. After Sharpe has called all of the plaintiff's witnesses and introduced into evidence all relevant documents and other physical evidence (such as the ski boots and bindings), she *rests* (ends) the plaintiff's case. The defendant may now offer a *motion to dismiss* the case, claiming that the plaintiff has failed to establish a ***prima facie*** (Latin: "at first sight; on the face of it") case. A plaintiff is required to offer sufficient evidence of the defendant's wrongful conduct to justify an award of monetary damages or other relief. For example, if a preponderance of the evidence proved only that the defendant "thrust his middle finger in the air as an obscene gesture," the plaintiff could not win. There was no *prima facie* case and the judge would not permit the jury to return a verdict for the plaintiff. Under those circumstances, the defense need produce no evidence and can figuratively "point a finger" at the plaintiff.

prima facie [Latin: "on first appearance"]
Term describing facts legally sufficient to establish a fact or a case unless disproved by some contrary evidence.

If the plaintiff's motion to dismiss is denied by the judge, the defendant's attorney may make an opening statement (provided that it was not made at the beginning of the trial).

The defendant's case-in-chief also begins by calling witnesses. Of course, the plaintiff's attorney has the right to cross-examine the defendant's witnesses immediately after their direct examination, as the defendant's attorney did when the plaintiff's case was presented. After the defense rests, the plaintiff may offer additional evidence limited to rebutting the defense, but not opening new issues. And, of course, the defense has one final opportunity to rebut, limited to whatever was presented in the plaintiff's rebuttal.

motion for a directed verdict
Request to a judge by counsel to enter a particular verdict instead of allowing the jury to do so because there are insufficient facts to allow any other verdict.

Motion for a Directed Verdict

After the parties have rested their respective cases-in-chief, either may ask the judge to decide the matter by making a **motion for a directed verdict**. This motion is a request to a judge that he or she enter the requested verdict instead of allowing the jury to present its verdict. It is based on the alleged absence of sufficient facts to allow any other verdict than the requested one. The judge, for example, could properly direct a verdict in favor of the plaintiff if, despite the evidence presented by the defendant, no reasonable person could agree with the defendant. Granting such a motion is unusual; even if the evidence appears to be legally conclusive for one party, the judge normally allows the jury to provide its independent opinion.

> *When you have the facts on your side, argue the facts. When you have the law on your side, argue the law. When you have neither, holler.*
>
> —Albert Gore Jr., vice president of the United States (1993–2001)

summation
The review of the evidence presented to the court by each lawyer in oral argument at the close of the trial.

Summation

After all the evidence has been offered, each attorney argues the case before the jury. In other words, each attorney tells the jury what he or she believes was proved in the trial and tries to persuade the jury to agree. The **summation** is not evidence or even a discussion; rather, it is a speech made by the attorney designed to persuade the jury. In our civil case example, the plaintiff's attorney would begin, followed by the defendant's attorney, and then the plaintiff's attorney concludes. Martinez's attorney, Sharpe, might argue as follows:

> *Ladies and gentlemen of the jury, you have heard all the evidence. It is now your duty to determine the facts. I believe we have shown by a preponderance of the evidence that the injury was caused by Mr. Graf. I remind you that Marya's medical bills were $12,573.45. She missed one month of work, at her rate of pay of $5,195 a month. She had to wear a cast from her waist to her toes for six months. What is this worth in dollars? Put yourself in her shoes—excuse me, cast. Why all this expense and all this pain and anguish? Why? Because the defendant, this careless ski instructor, Gary Graf, fastened the bindings down on Ms. Martinez's foot with unprofessional disregard for her safety and well-being. The evidence is clear: Gary Graf was not thinking about bindings. Gary Graf did not pay attention to his serious duty. Gary Graf was clearly negligent. And so it is now your duty to lessen the harm he caused. Simple justice requires you to return a verdict in favor of Marya.*

Attorney Sagedevan might argue to the jury:

> *Ladies and gentlemen, it is our duty to pierce the veil of emotion with which counsel is attempting to surround us. Let us look at the facts. Unfortunately, the plaintiff was injured. No one feels good about that, especially Gary Graf. However, the fact that Ms. Martinez was injured is not a reason to hold Gary Graf responsible. Skiing is a sport with risks. Marya cannot transfer responsibility for her own safety to another person if the risk materializes. Marya decided to ski. She failed to exercise the appropriate care that would have prevented her accident. Feeling sorry for her is natural. We all feel sorry for her. But this does not justify a verdict against Mr. Graf. The simple facts are that Ms. Martinez was not thinking about skiing; she was more interested in impressing her date after spending a good part of the day drinking wine. She was injured not because of any negligence of Gary Graf. Bindings don't work if they are icy, and had she been sober she would have seen the ice when she put her skis back*

on. She was negligent. Now she is trying to obtain a bonanza at the expense of my client, a hard-working, sincere, very professional gentleman. Ladies and gentlemen of this jury, you know your duty: return a verdict for Gary Graf.

jury instructions
Rules of law and charges provided by the judge to the jury for guidance in reaching a verdict.

Instructions to the Jury

After the summation, the judge will instruct the jury on the law (**jury instructions**) that must be applied to the facts that the jury decides are true. Typically, each attorney will submit proposed instructions to the judge. The judge decides what instructions to give to the jury. The instructions might include the following, but would be considerably more exhaustive:

> *You are instructed that statements of witnesses, sworn to tell the truth, constitute evidence that you may consider. Comments of the attorneys are not evidence. You are instructed that if the defendant failed to use reasonable care and secured the bindings too tightly, he was negligent. You are further instructed that if the accident was caused by ice between the boot and ski, and not by the adjustment to the bindings, the plaintiff was negligent.*

deliberate
The review, discussion, and weighing of evidence presented at a trial by a jury.

verdict
The expressed decision of the jury on questions of fact submitted to it for determination, based on evidence presented during trial.

judgment *non obstante veredicto*
A decision by a judge that overrules the verdict of the jury.

Deliberation and Verdict

After the instructions, the jury will retire to a private room to **deliberate**, and return a **verdict** by vote, the jury's decision.

If the jury returns with a verdict deemed to be wrong as a matter of law, the judge in a civil case has the power to render a contrary judgment, sometimes called a judgment n.o.v., which is a **judgment *non obstante veredicto*** (Latin: "notwithstanding the verdict"). In effect, the judge is the thirteenth juror, with the power to veto the others' decision and to substitute a different one. (Recall that in a criminal case the judge cannot set aside a verdict of "not guilty.")

After a verdict, the judge may grant a motion made by the losing party for a new trial. The judge will not grant a *motion for a new trial* unless some serious mistake of law (called *error*) has occurred. Sometimes the judge may think that the damages awarded by the jury are excessive or inadequate and therefore may grant a motion for a new trial unless the plaintiff or defendant, as the case may be, agrees to a modified award. To avoid the costs and uncertainties of another trial, the parties may compromise and agree to the modified award. The steps in a jury trial are identified in Exhibit 3.7.

judgment
The final determination or decision of the court as to the rights and duties of the parties in a lawsuit.

How Is a Case Ended?

The concluding pronouncement of a court is its **judgment**. A judgment may declare a status (e.g., divorced), order one to do or not do something (e.g., pay money damages or transfer a title to land), impose a sentence (e.g., go to jail), or otherwise resolve a controversy.

LEGAL FOCUS—PROBLEM

In an auto accident case, the jury became convinced that the plaintiff should be compensated for harm to her left leg, which was crushed and had to be removed surgically. The accident was caused by the negligent operation of a truck by the defendant. The jury returned its verdict in the plaintiff's favor for $1.3 million. Is the verdict the voice of the court?

EXHIBIT 3.7 Steps in a Civil Case—Jury Trial

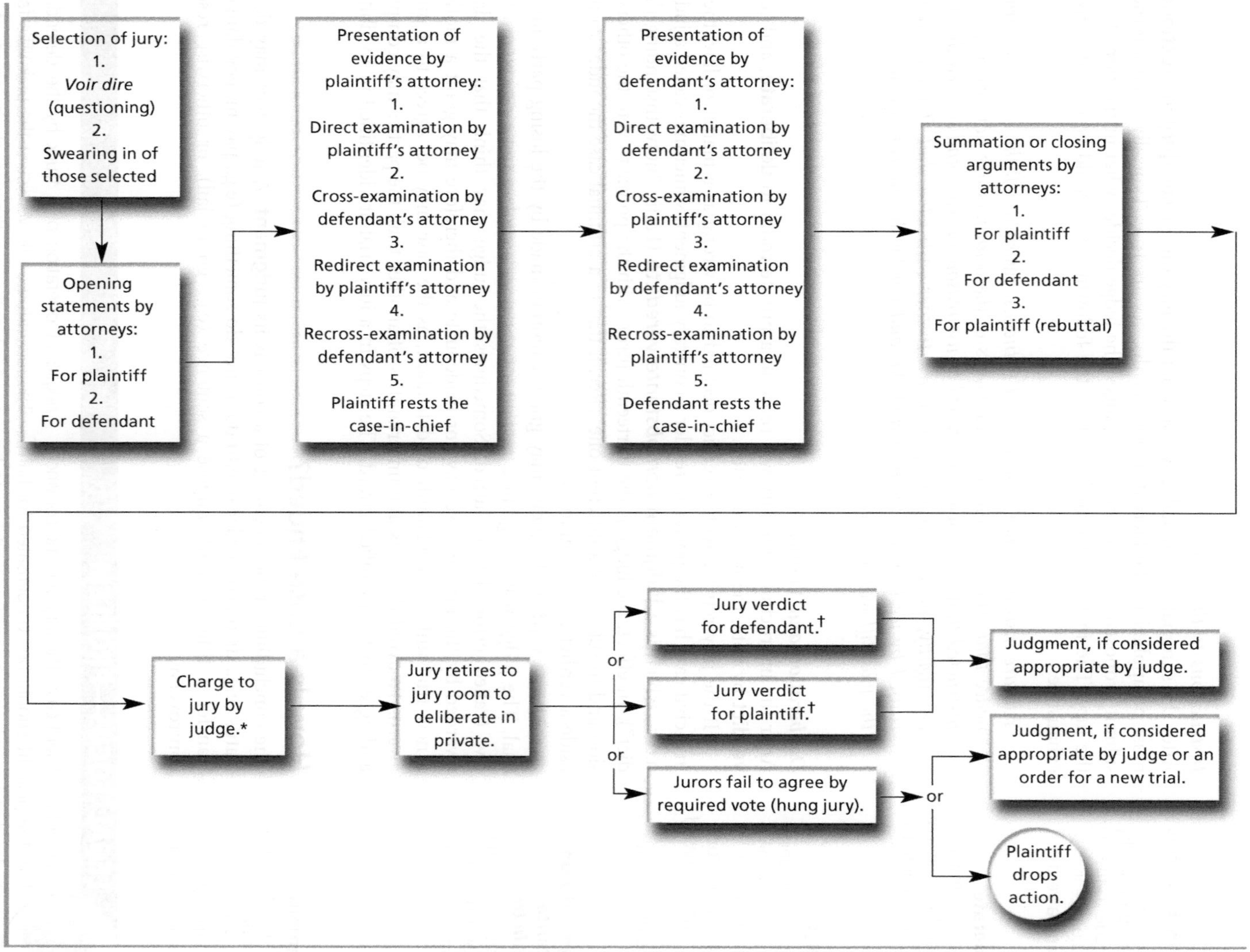

* A judge may direct a jury to return a certain verdict when, if all testimony on one side were believed, the other party nonetheless would be entitled to win.
† In rare cases, a judge may grant a judgment *non obstante veredicto* (Latin:"notwithstanding the verdict"), setting aside the jury's verdict because in the judge's opinion it is wrong as a matter of law.

No, the verdict is not the voice of the court. The verdict is the expressed opinion of the jury. On the basis of the verdict, the court usually will issue a judgment for damages. As noted earlier, if the court concludes that the jury verdict is unreasonable in the light of the evidence, it can prevent a miscarriage of justice by reducing the amount of damages, ordering a new trial, or granting a judgment notwithstanding a verdict.

In divorce proceedings, the judgment of the court will be termination of the marriage. In a paternity case, the judgment of the court will be a declaration that the defendant is or is not the natural father. In a suit to end mass picketing and violence in a strike, the judgment of the court will be an injunction. In a suit to compel someone to do something that was promised by contract, the judgment of the court will be a decree of specific performance.

In criminal cases, the verdict will be guilty or not guilty.* If it is "not guilty," the judgment of the court must correspond to the verdict. If the verdict is "guilty," however, the judge may overrule the jury and acquit the defendant, or the judge may order a new trial to avoid a miscarriage of justice. In most cases, the judge has the power to impose a sentence, then suspend it, and place the defendant on probation.

Once a party has received a judgment, the judicial branch of government has completed its work, unless the matter is appealed. Sometimes a party to the action may return to court if the order of the court is not obeyed. In divorce, for example, after support payments have been ordered, either party may return and request an increase or decrease in payments because of changed circumstances, needs, or ability to pay.

judgment debtor A person against whom a judgment for payment of money has been entered but who has not yet made or completed that payment.

judgment creditor A person who has won a judgment but has not been fully paid.

writ of execution Order of the court directing the sheriff to confiscate property of the defendant.

garnishment A legal proceeding in which a plaintiff-creditor gets a court order compelling a third party to pay monies earned by the defendant to the plaintiff.

Collecting a Judgment

If the defendant does not appeal and the time for appeal passes, a losing defendant is considered a **judgment debtor**, meaning one against whom a judgment has been entered but who has not paid the judgment. The judgment debtor may voluntarily pay the judgment, or pay the judgment after the plaintiff demands payment. If the judgment debtor fails to pay, however, the legal system provides a method of satisfying the debt provided the defendant has assets that can be identified and seized. State statutes generally call for payment of interest (usually at an annual rate between 6 and 10 percent) to accrue on the unpaid balance of the judgment until fully paid.

Assistance in collecting the dollar amount of the judgment is provided by the executive branch of government, usually through the office of the county sheriff or federal marshal. Officials will not do anything simply because you have won a lawsuit and have not been paid. A **judgment creditor**, one who has won a judgment but is as yet unpaid, must first provide a copy of the final judgment, identify assets owned by the judgment debtor, and give specific instructions to a sheriff or marshal before he or she will assist in collecting the judgment. The court order directing the sheriff to confiscate property of the defendant is called a **writ of execution**. Through a **garnishment** proceeding, such a writ may be used to garnish (confiscate) part of any debt owed to the judgment debtor by others, usually unpaid wages due from the debtor's employer(s). After being paid in full, the judgment creditor must provide the judgment debtor with a signed *satisfaction of judgment* document as evidence of that fact.

*Of course, it is possible that a jury will be unable to reach a decision. In 1994, a pair of criminal cases captured national media attention. Erik and Lyle Menendez were accused of the first-degree murder of their parents. At the trial, the fact that the brothers had killed their parents was admitted, but both brothers defended their action on the basis of self-defense. Two juries, one for each brother, heard the case; neither jury was able to agree on a verdict. The two brothers were retried, found guilty, and sentenced to life imprisonment without the possibility of parole.

order of examination
A judicially authorized inquiry as to the assets of a judgment debtor.

Judicial means exist for compelling cooperation of the judgment debtor in identifying his or her assets—namely, by means of an **order of examination**, which is a judicially authorized inquiry about the judgment debtor's assets.

What Happens if Either Party Appeals?

affirm
The confirmation of a lower court's judgment or order because the prior decision is deemed to be correct and free from prejudicial error.

As previously discussed, procedures before a federal or state appellate court differ greatly from trial court procedures. Appellate courts hear appeals from trial courts and do not conduct trials. The only question on appeal, as a general proposition, is whether or not the law was applied correctly by the judge during the trial proceedings. Appellate courts do not consider new evidence or hear witnesses. An appellate court has several options when an appeal is filed, including refusing to hear the appeal. If it accepts the appeal and concludes that the law was applied correctly at the trial court or that an error was made but that the error did not affect the verdict, the court will **affirm** (uphold) the judgment. If the court determines that the law was applied incorrectly, it can **reverse**, **modify**, or remand the decision. A reversal turns the loser into the winner, a modification changes the result in a less drastic fashion than a reversal, and a **remand** sends the case back to the trial court with instructions for the trial court judge, such as granting a new trial.

LEGAL FOCUS—PROBLEM

The jury found Jack Malum guilty of cocaine possession. During the trial, the judge instructed the jury, in part, as follows: "I instruct you that a crime is committed when one attends a party at which cocaine is being used, regardless of whether or not the defendant participated in such activity." Will an appeal by Malum be successful?

reverse
Appellate court sets aside the decision of a lower court.

modify
Appellate court alters the decision of a lower court.

remand
Appellate court sends case back to a lower court to take some further action.

Yes, an appeal by Malum would be successful. An appellate court would conclude that the court's instruction to the jury was an erroneous statement of the law. Jack Malum did not receive a fair trial, because mere attendance at a party is not in itself a crime, yet the jury was told that it was.

Appellate courts consist of three or more justices. Most of their work is done in private and consists of reading *transcripts* (official copies of the proceedings in the trial court) of cases on appeal. The appellate court assumes that all facts found by the trial court are true. To make the court's decision, they will study the applicable law and examine briefs filed by the attorneys for the appellant and the appellee and study the applicable law. A *brief* is a written legal argument addressed to the appellate court discussing or arguing why the judgment from below should be affirmed or reversed, modified, or perhaps remanded to the trial court for further specified action. Before the appellate court makes its decision, the respective attorneys may be allowed to make oral arguments to the appellate court, within limited allotted times. The concluding steps in a civil trial are provided in Exhibit 3.8.

EXHIBIT 3.8 Steps in a Civil Case—After Trial

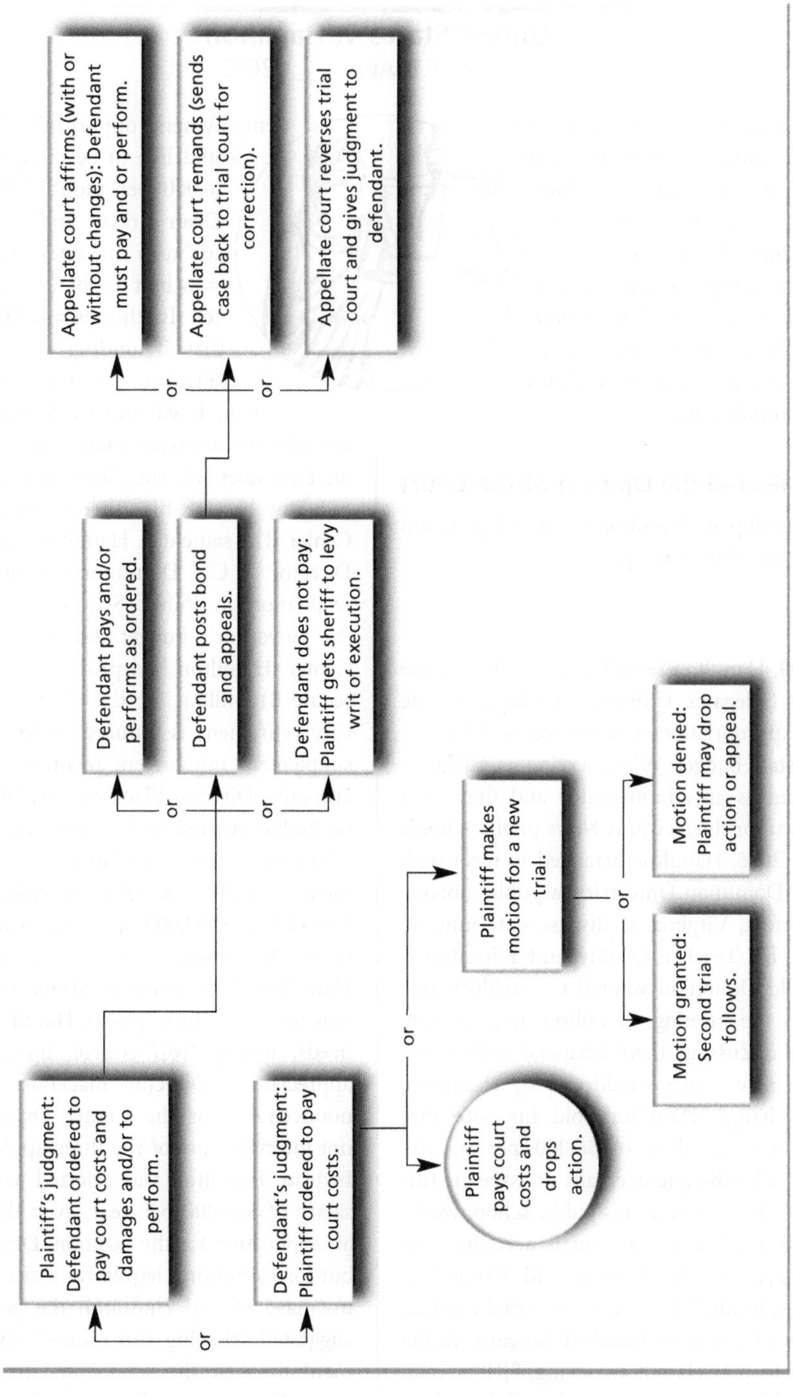
Plaintiff's judgment: Defendant ordered to pay court costs and damages and/or to perform.
Defendant's judgment: Plaintiff ordered to pay court costs.
or
Defendant pays and/or performs as ordered.
Defendant posts bond and appeals.
Defendant does not pay: Plaintiff gets sheriff to levy writ of execution.
Appellate court affirms (with or without changes): Defendant must pay and or perform.
Appellate court remands (sends case back to trial court for correction).
Appellate court reverses trial court and gives judgment to defendant.
Plaintiff pays court costs and drops action.
Plaintiff makes motion for a new trial.
Motion granted: Second trial follows.
Motion denied: Plaintiff may drop action or appeal.

CASE

United States v. Hamilton

____4th Ct. App. ____ 2012

The United States charged and convicted a Virginia state legislator with crimes of bribery and extortion for using his legislative position to obtain a paid position at a university. At issue in the case were emails from the legislator to his wife, using a "work" computer and whether those emails should have been allowed into court over the marital communications privilege that otherwise might have prevented them from being admitted into evidence.

Judge Motz Delivered the Opinion of the Court

A jury convicted Phillip A. Hamilton of federal program bribery and extortion. Hamilton appeals.

I.

From 1988 to 2009, Hamilton served as a member of the Virginia House of Delegates. Ultimately he became Vice Chairman of the Appropriations Committee, which is responsible for the state budget. While serving as a legislator, he also worked as an administrator and then as a part-time consultant for the Newport News public schools system. In August 2006, Hamilton arranged to meet with officials from Old Dominion University, a public university located in Norfolk, Virginia, to discuss state funding for a new Center for Teacher Quality and Educational Leadership that Old Dominion wanted to establish. Immediately prior to the meeting, Hamilton and his wife exchanged emails discussing their financial difficulties, and hope that the new Center would employ Hamilton. In their email exchange, Hamilton told his wife that he would "shoot for" a salary of $6,000 per month. Those emails, like all subsequent emails at issue in this case, were sent to or from Hamilton's public school workplace computer, through his work email account. The Dean of the College of Education at Old Dominion, Dr. William Graves, testified that, after the initial meeting with Hamilton, Old Dominion President Roseann Runte directed the Dean to hire Hamilton, saying, "[t]hat man wants a job, make him director or something." Hamilton emailed his wife that the meeting "went well" and that he had "reinforced" the idea that "if and when an employment opportunity became available," he would like to be compensated "in the area of $6,000 per month." Hamilton also emailed Dean Graves and, after advising the Dean to "keep this under the radar," he explained how best to obtain state funding for the Center. In this email, Hamilton further stated that, if funding for the Center was not included in the Governor's budget, "on my own, I will initiate legislation and/or a budget amendment to create such a center." Four months later, on December 21, Hamilton emailed President Runte, reminding her of his interest in employment with the Center. The same day, Hamilton emailed David Blackburn, Director of Old Dominion's Program for Research and Evaluation in Public Schools, explaining that, because the Governor's budget did not include money for the Center, Hamilton had proposed a budget amendment to secure $1 million for the Center. Hamilton added: "My City retirement is reduced in May 2007. I will need to supplement my current income ... by at least an equal amount." Director Blackburn replied: "Thanks for passing on budget request and specific salary need[.] I believe GA [General Assembly] will fund and you will be on board[.]" Soon thereafter, Hamilton introduced legislation for the first of two $500,000 appropriations for the Center, both of which ultimately passed. Director Blackburn emailed Hamilton: "Are congratulations in order? Are you our new director?" In response, Hamilton reiterated his salary needs, noting "[o]f course, more than that is always appreciated." Director Blackburn then posted an announcement for the Center Director position, but did not interview any of the three applicants for the position. Instead, Hamilton was selected as Center Director, at a salary of $40,000 per year, even though he had not filed an application for the position. Dean Graves testified that, but for Hamilton's legislative assistance, the Center would not have offered Hamilton the position. Hamilton later suggested "flowing the money" for his Center employment through the school system payroll and generally concealing his position as Director of the Center. Hamilton explained at one point in an email to Blackburn, "looks like they are digging."

On the basis of the above evidence, the Government charged Hamilton with bribery concerning federal program funds and extortion under color of official right. The jury convicted him of both crimes. The district court then sentenced him to 114 months' imprisonment. Hamilton noted a timely appeal.

II.

Hamilton challenges the district court's admission into evidence of emails he sent to and received from his wife. He maintains that the admission of these emails violated the marital communications privilege. We review evidentiary rulings, including rulings on privilege, for abuse of discretion, factual findings as to whether a privilege applies for clear error, and the application of legal principles de novo. "Communications between … spouses, privately made, are generally assumed to have been intended to be confidential, and hence they are privileged." *Wolfle v. United States*, 291 U.S. 7, 14 (1934). This is so because "marital confidences" are "regarded as so essential to the preservation of the marriage relationship as to outweigh the disadvantages to the administration of justice which the privilege entails." But, of course, to be covered by the privilege, a communication between spouses must be confidential; "voluntary disclosure" of a communication waives the privilege. The Government maintains that Hamilton waived the marital communications privilege by communicating with his wife on his workplace computer, through his work email account, and subsequently failing to safeguard the emails. *Wolfle*, the leading marital communications privilege case to have reached the Supreme Court, provides an analogy useful in resolving Hamilton's privilege claim. In *Wolfle*, the Court held that a defendant's communication with his wife did not come "within the privilege because of [his] voluntary disclosure" of the communication "to a third person, his stenographer." The Court explained that

> *[n]ormally husband and wife may conveniently communicate without stenographic aid, and the privilege of holding their confidences immune from proof in court may be reasonably enjoyed and preserved without embracing within it the testimony of third persons to whom such communications have been voluntarily revealed.*

Because "[t]he privilege suppresses relevant testimony," it "should be allowed only when it is plain that marital confidence cannot otherwise reasonably be preserved," and "[n]othing in this case suggests any such necessity." In Hamilton's case, email has become the modern stenographer. Like the communications to the stenographer in Wolfle's time, emails today, "in common experience," are confidential. But just as spouses can "conveniently communicate without" use of a stenographer, they can also "conveniently communicate without" using a work email account on an office computer. Therefore, as in *Wolfle*, it is hardly "plain that marital confidence cannot … reasonably be preserved" without according the privilege to the spousal communications at issue here. Accordingly, that one may generally have a reasonable expectation of privacy in email, at least before a policy is in place indicating otherwise, does not end our inquiry. Hamilton ignores this guidance from *Wolfle* and focuses solely on the fact that, in 2006, when he used his workplace email system to send the emails for which he claims privilege, his public school employer had no computer usage policy. This is true, but the school system adopted a computer policy well prior to the 2009 investigation of, and 2011 charges against, Hamilton. The computer policy, as revised in 2008, expressly provides that users have "no expectation of privacy in their use of the Computer System" and "[a]ll information created, sent[,] received, accessed, or stored in the … Computer System is subject to inspection and monitoring at any time." The district court concluded that Hamilton had waived any privilege he had in the emails. Hamilton contends that he did not waive the privilege because he "had no reason to believe, at the time he sent and received the emails, that they were not privileged," and he could not waive his privilege retroactively. Amicus, the Electronic Privacy Information Center, adds that it seems "extreme" to "require an employee to scan all archived emails and remove any that are personal and confidential every time the workplace use policy changes," when "employees may not even be aware that archived emails exist or know where to find them." In an era in which email plays a ubiquitous role in daily communications, these arguments caution against lightly finding waiver of marital privilege by email usage. But the district court found that Hamilton did not take any steps to protect the emails in question, even after he was on notice of his employer's policy permitting inspection of emails stored on the system at the employer's discretion. In similar circumstances, we have held that a defendant did not have an "objectively reasonable" belief in the privacy of files on an office computer after his employer's policy put him "on notice" that "it would be overseeing his Internet use." Thus, the district court's conclusion that the emails were not subject to the marital communications privilege constitutes no abuse of discretion. Rather, that conclusion accords with the admonition in *Wolfle* against freely extending the privilege to communications outside of which marital confidences can "otherwise reasonably be preserved," and with the principle that one who is on notice that then allegedly privileged material is subject to search may waive the privilege when he makes no efforts to protect it.

III.

Because we find Hamilton's claims on appeal to be without merit, we affirm the judgment of the district court. **AFFIRMED**

For Critical Analysis

1. Do you think that the marital communications at issue were key to convicting Hamilton? Stated differently, if the court had concluded that the emails to Hamilton's wife should not have been admitted, what would the appellate court do? Send the case back for a new trial? Affirm the conviction anyway?
2. The court seems to look for an analogy to an older "technology" (stenographer) to help decide how to handle a new technology (email). Do you agree with this approach? This analogy?
3. How did the appeals court resolve the fact that the policy declaring Hamilton's work email to not be private was issued several years after the email in question? Could Hamilton really have done anything after the policy had been issued to keep the previous email private? If not, then why do you think the court failed to consider that?
4. What was the "standard of review" that the appellate court applied to the appeal? What did that mean to how closely the appellate court scrutinized the lower court outcome?
5. Was the privilege question purely one of "law" or did the "facts" and evidence from the trial partly drive the outcome of the appellate court's decision?

CHAPTER QUESTIONS AND PROBLEMS

1. In regard to small claims court:
   a. Why do many states not allow attorneys to represent litigants in small claims court? (Note that in all states parties can consult counsel before and after the trial.)
   b. What should the appropriate maximum dollar amount be for small claims court (if any)? What should be the basis for determining the appropriate jurisdictional amount?
2. While driving her car in Colorado, Callie Norset, a resident of Alabama, negligently struck Jake Nguyen, a resident of Arizona. As a result of the accident, Nguyen suffered more than $22,000 in property damage, $40,000 in medical expenses, and $15,000 in lost wages. Nguyen wants to know whether he can obtain jurisdiction over Norset in the following courts:
   a. Federal District Court in Colorado
   b. Alabama State Trial Court
   c. Colorado State Trial Court
   d. District of Columbia Trial Court
   e. Federal Circuit Court of Appeals for the Ninth Circuit (includes Arizona)
3. In regard to courts and trials:
   a. Name each of the courts of your state and properly display them on an organization chart.
   b. What are the pros and cons of permitting each side in a case to exercise one peremptory challenge of the judge assigned to the case? Would your arguments be different depending on whether the case is criminal or civil?
   c. Do you believe a judge can influence a jury by such seemingly innocent conduct as smiling, eyebrow raising, grimacing, and so on, during the testimony of witnesses? How can any such effect be combated?
4. Sylvester is on trial for the assault and battery of his roommate, Arnold. Sylvester hit Arnold after Arnold refused to stop playing death metal music on his guitar. Sylvester was trying to study for a test. Sylvester intends to argue self-defense, arguing a physical noise attack. One of the prospective jurors has spiked green hair and a nose ring. Suggest a strategy that would best serve Sylvester's interests in dismissing the juror. Use the correct legal terms.
5. About jury nullification:
   a. What is it?
   b. Are jurors instructed by the judge as to existence of the power of jury nullification? Why or why not?
   c. Does the power of jury nullification exist in both civil and criminal trials?
   d. Can you think of any situation where if you were on a jury you would argue for jury nullification? No matter your answer, is it ethically correct? On what basis?
6. About trial and appellate courts:
   a. Define each.
   b. What is the purpose of each?
   c. Do juries assist both? Explain.
   d. Do both exist in state and federal systems?
   e. Do witnesses testify before each? Explain.
7. Thomas, William, and Ella McCollum were white defendants facing criminal charges of assault and battery against two African Americans. Before the trial began, the prosecution requested that the court prohibit these defendants from exercising their peremptory challenges in a racially discriminatory manner. The prosecution claimed that the defendants' attorneys intended to eliminate African American jurors from the panel through the use of peremptory challenges. The defendants argued that the law prohibiting the state from the discriminatory use of peremptory challenges was necessary to guarantee due process for a criminal defendant, but any restriction on defense use of peremptory challenges would deny defendants the right to a fair trial, The state argued that if it is prohibited from dismissing jurors on racial grounds, the defense should be similarly restrained. How did the court decide? [*Georgia v. McCollum*, 505 U.S. 42, 112 S.Ct. 2348 (1992).]
8. Walter Martin brought an employment discrimination suit against the New York Department of Mental Hygiene and Dr. Stuart Keill, a regional director of the department. Although Dr. Keill knew of the lawsuit and the nature of the claim, he was not served with a copy of the complaint and a summons. Could Martin pursue the case against Dr. Keill without such service? [*Martin v. N.Y. State Department of Mental Hygiene*, 588 F.2d 371 (N.Y., 1978).]
9. Martha Anderson obtained a contested divorce from her husband, Donald. The trial court judge entered judgment of divorce. Donald asked the trial court to "vacate" (rescind or erase) the judgment, but the court refused his request. On Donald's appeal, the appellate court agreed that the trial court judge was erroneous in his ruling. Does this mean that Donald and Martha

are married again? [*Anderson v. Anderson*, 869 S.W.2d 289 (Mo. 1994).]

10. Joshua Southard was cited for speeding and failing to yield to an emergency vehicle. He requested a trial in the Cape Girardeu County Circuit Court and was found guilty and fined. He appealed, claiming that the circuit court lacked subject matter jurisdiction. He was correct: The appropriate court was the municipal court. However, Southard, when requesting the hearing, told the circuit court that the municipal court previously had heard his case and rendered judgment. The circuit court did have the power to hold a trial *de novo*. The prosecution argued that because Southard "stated that judgment had been rendered against him in the municipal court, he should not be allowed to take advantage of an error of his own making." Did Southard win his appeal arguing that the court lacked subject matter jurisdiction? [*City of Jackson v. Southard*, 869 S.W.2d 280 (Mo. 1994).]
11. Timothy McVeigh was indicted by a federal grand jury for the planting of an explosive device in a truck next to the Alfred P. Murrah Federal Building in Oklahoma City, Oklahoma, on April 19, 1995. The explosion led to the deaths of 168 men, women, and children, and injuries to hundreds of other people. As the explosion occurred in Oklahoma City, the Oklahoma Western Federal District Court was the appropriate venue. McVeigh sought a change of venue. Why did he seek a change of venue? Why was the trial to be held in a federal rather than state court? Did he succeed in obtaining a change of venue? [*United States v. McVeigh*, 918 F.Supp. 1467 (W.D. Okl. 1996).]
12. Can you provide an example of a kangaroo court proceeding? Would the use of the term kangaroo court be normative or factual? Is that important?

CHAPTER 4

Attorney–Client Relationship and Dispute Resolution

A law firm receptionist answered the phone the morning after the firm's senior partner had died unexpectedly.

"Is Mr. Smith there?" asked the client on the phone.

"I'm very sorry, but Mr. Smith passed away last night," the receptionist answered.

"Is Mr. Smith there?" repeated the client.

The receptionist was perplexed. "Perhaps you didn't understand me. I'm afraid Mr. Smith died last night."

"Is Mr. Smith there?" asked the client again.

"Madam, do you understand what I'm saying?" said the exasperated receptionist. "Mr. Smith is dead."

"I understand perfectly," the client sighed. "I just can't hear it often enough."

Adapted from a statement made at a U.S. Senate confirmation hearing of a Supreme Court Justice

LEARNING OBJECTIVES

After reading and studying this chapter, you should be able to:

- Explain the adversary system.
- Explain how an attorney qualifies to practice law.
- Discuss ethics as it relates to lawyers and judges.
- Explain how attorneys are hired and fired.
- Recognize the nature of legal malpractice.
- Recognize, explain, and distinguish the various forms of alternative dispute resolution (ADR).
- Be able to discuss the pros and cons of mediation.
- Be able to discuss the pros and cons of arbitration and identify some important fairness issues related to the use of arbitration.

An ideal legal system meets the somewhat-inconsistent goals of stability and flexibility. In previous chapters, we have discussed constitutional law and the legal doctrine of *stare decisis*, both of which work toward balancing those two goals. In this chapter, we will consider the two additional goals of an ideal legal system: understandability and accessibility. Are the laws of the country known, comprehensible, and adequate? After a close look at lawyers and their role in the American legal system, we will discuss alternatives lawyers might use, alternatives to the use of lawyers, and, indeed, alternatives to the use of formal legal structures. Finally, we have included in Appendix D a reference to legal research methods.

LEGAL FOCUS—BACKGROUND

The first thing we do, let's kill all the lawyers.

Shakespeare's *Henry VI*, Part II

Lawyers have been targets of criticism in the guise of humor, and otherwise, throughout history, but this is the classic quotation. The use of this quote as a pejorative is ironic because within the context of the play, the words speak well, not ill, of lawyers. In the play, the Duke of York foments revolution through the use of Jack Cade, who fancies he will be king after a peasant revolution. As king, he intends to be worshipped as a god, to require all in the kingdom to dress alike, to "be the parliament of England," and to require all women to surrender their virginity to him before any marriage. In the ramblings between Cade and one Dick the butcher, the environment for his scheme of despotism is discussed. Dick opines that to advance Cade's evil goals, "The first thing we do, let's kill all the lawyers." Cade says, "Nay, that I mean to do."

Why is so much animosity displayed toward lawyers? In an era of sensitivity to affiliations and status, where jokes and comments about gender, ethnic origin, and sexuality are considered in bad form and even the basis of punishment (e.g., public apology or resignation from office), negative comments about lawyers are still common and socially acceptable. Who are lawyers, or attorneys-at-law, and what functions do they perform in our legal system? Is it necessary to use a lawyer to access the legal system? Before addressing these issues, the first question to ask is, what is the special importance of advocacy (i.e., pleading the cause of another person) within American jurisprudence? The answer: Advocacy is so important partly because of the adversarial nature of the legal system.

WHAT IS THE ADVERSARIAL SYSTEM?

adversarial system
The jurisprudential system in which the parties to a legal dispute are opponents. Their attorneys advocate a great variety of theories of benefit to the cause of their clients both before and during the trial, and on any appeal.

The backbone of the U.S. legal system is the adversarial method of resolving disputes. In an **adversarial system**, parties to legal actions are opponents. The judge is independent and neutral, unlike magistrates in so-called inquisitorial systems (discussed shortly). This fairly simple concept has enormous ramifications. Courts make decisions based on facts brought to their attention by the proponents and opponents in the legal conflict. Each party is responsible for producing evidence and rules of law that support its contentions. The competitors openly are biased and partial to their respective sides. Each party asserts every possible reason to merit victory. Every theory asserted or discovered is considered and subject to attack and counterattack. The judge acts much as a referee in a sporting contest, to ensure that the procedural rules, created to maintain civility and fairness, are followed.

Another distinguishing feature of the adversarial system is that a party must take action to get a case before the court. Legal questions are considered by a court only if a party brings a problem to the attention of the court by filing a lawsuit. Each party is independently responsible for presenting its case. Attorneys play a critical role organizing and arguing cases to the court. The moving party, or plaintiff, in a civil lawsuit must meet a required burden of proof before the defendant must respond. In a criminal case, the moving party is the prosecutor (e.g., a county district attorney). He is from the executive branch of government, not the judicial branch.

The adversarial system is the essence of what many consider to be the most just legal system the world has ever known. But it also has shortcomings and critics. The merits of a legal position are not necessarily related to one's ability to convince others, yet the adversarial system places a premium on advocacy skills. Arguments must be articulated clearly and presented in both written and oral form to convince decision makers of the merits of a case. Therefore, parties to a legal conflict generally hire advocates—lawyers—who possess the required talent.

Of course, access to the system is critically important—redress is not possible if access is denied. The means and methods used to seek legal redress are often complicated, specialized, and daunting to the casual user. Clerical personnel of courts do not assist parties to disputes. They dispense preliminary paperwork and receive new filings but do not give any advice. If they did, they could be punished for practicing law without a license. For this reason, parties may find court clerks unhelpful and sometimes even hostile. Parties who decide to file suit without representation are disadvantaged doubly; they are ignorant of the filing process (how to get a claim before the court), and they are ignorant of the rules of engagement (procedure, evidence, and advocacy).

inquisitorial system
A legal system used in some countries that allows the judge to investigate, question witnesses, and seek out evidence before a trial.

The contrasting **inquisitorial system**, mentioned previously, exists in many other countries as diverse as Argentina, China, and France. Under the inquisitorial system, judges need not depend on the testimony of the parties once the matter is before the court. Judges can investigate the dispute, question witnesses, and independently seek out evidence before a trial. Although attorneys are still necessary in countries with such systems, their role and the role of a trial often are seen as less critical to the administration of justice. In the interest of accuracy, it should be noted that in most modern legal systems the distinctions between adversarial and inquisitorial methods are not as great in practice as in theory. For example, in the adversary system judges, within limits, do ask witnesses questions and make limited suggestions to counsel about what evidence should be provided to the court. In inquisitorial systems, counsel represents parties, and the scope and degree of judicial inquiry often are limited.

ATTORNEYS-AT-LAW

attorney-at-law
A person licensed to practice law, and usually called a lawyer, attorney, counsel, or counselor.

An **attorney-at-law** (also called a *lawyer*) is a person authorized by law to represent clients in legal matters. Attorneys also draft documents involving legal rights and duties and give expert advice on legal questions. Countless businesses and public organizations routinely look to lawyers for such help. More than two-thirds of the adults in the United States have consulted attorneys for assistance with personal legal problems. Most of these problems involve the preparation of wills, the purchase or sale of real properly, divorce or marriage dissolution, serious personal injuries caused by other persons, consumer problems (e.g., disputes with landlords or lenders), criminal matters, or difficulties with government agencies. Every person during his lifetime should anticipate direct or indirect involvement with an attorney. Accordingly, one should be familiar with the legal profession and learn how to select, retain (hire), and cooperate with an attorney and evaluate her performance.

Lawyers are trained to sort through complicated descriptions of human events to determine which facts are important. They are highly skilled at analyzing the relationship of those facts to legal rules and principles. Lawyers have the special ability to advocate rational positions through oral and written argument.

Who May Practice Law?

Generally, only licensed attorneys may perform legal services for others, their clients. Most state legislatures have created state bar associations to regulate lawyers and the practice of law. The rules of such associations, together with applicable federal and state statutes, combine with the inherent powers of the court to regulate the legal profession. Each state sets its own qualifications for admission to practice law within its borders. However, all states permit attorneys to hire nonattorneys, often called **legal assistants**, to perform legal services under their indirect supervision. A considerable number of legal services are actually performed by nonattorneys.

legal assistant
Someone with specialized training who assists an attorney. Also called a "paralegal".

The practice of law is a licensed profession. Technical training, a commitment to public service, and a pledge to follow standards of practice distinguish a profession from a service or trade. The practice of law is regulated in part because legal representation is fiduciary in nature. A **fiduciary relationship** is one involving a person in a position of trust who undertakes to act for the benefit of another. The attorney as a fiduciary must exercise the utmost good faith, honesty, and fairness toward that client. Licensure is designed to protect the public by seeking to ensure that every attorney is competent, honorable, and worthy of that trust reposed by the client. Offering legal services without being duly licensed as an attorney is a criminal offense. Attorneys must have a separate license from each state in which they wish to practice law. Occasionally, attorneys will represent a client in the court of a state other than the one where they have a license. An attorney can do so after receiving permission from the court of that state. The granting of the right is referred to as *pro hac vice* (Latin: "for this occasion"). It is customary for a court to require that the out-of-state attorney associate with a local attorney for the duration of the case.

fiduciary relationship
A relationship between two persons wherein one has an obligation to perform services with scrupulous good faith and honesty.

A candidate for a license to practice law must possess good moral character, complete certain minimum education requirements, pass an examination on the law (called a *bar examination*), and take an oath to support the law and conform to rules of professional conduct of that state. The education requirements vary depending on the state. Most states require that any person wishing to take the state bar examination must be a graduate of a law school accredited by the American Bar Association (ABA). A law school is a professional institution offering a graduate-level degree program. Law students must possess a baccalaureate degree to gain admission to accredited law schools. Many states also require that each attorney complete a minimum number of continuing legal education courses within a prescribed time to retain the license.

Each federal court (e.g., U.S. Supreme Court, U.S. Courts of Appeals, U.S. District Courts) recognizes its own separate bar or group of attorneys permitted to practice before it. Admission is granted to attorneys licensed in the state where the federal court sits. Federal court rules impose separate preconditions for admission to the federal bar, although no further legal education or additional examination is required.

LEGAL FOCUS—CASE

Bonnie Cord and Jeffrey Blue, an unmarried couple, bought a home and resided together in a rural area of Warren County, Virginia. Bonnie, an attorney licensed to practice law in Washington, D.C., applied for a license in Virginia. Duncan Gibb, judge of the Circuit Court of Warren County, denied her application because her living arrangement "would lower the public's opinion of the Bar as a whole." Bonnie appealed to a higher court. What should have been the result?

At the time this case was heard, unmarried couples living together were uncommon and their behavior was considered by most Americans as socially unacceptable. Despite the social attitudes of the day, Bonnie won the case and her license because her conduct did not affect her fitness to practice law. The same result has been reached where an applicant disclosed a sexual preference for persons of the same sex.

With a few exceptions, no one is required to use a lawyer in a legal proceeding. A party to a case before a trial court may appear ***in propria persona*** (Latin: "in one's own person") or ***in pro se*** (Latin: "on one's own behalf"), that is, without the services of a lawyer. Generally, though, it is not advisable to go to court without a lawyer. A common saying even among lawyers is "one who serves as his own lawyer has a fool for a client!" Thus, lawyers usually are represented by another lawyer when they are sued. All of us, even lawyers, are emotionally involved in our own cases; we need educated, experienced, and rational counsel to analyze issues dispassionately and argue them persuasively before judge and jury. It is important to have an independent advocate.

in propria persona (in pro se)
Term meaning the person represents herself or himself in a legal action with out the appearance of an attorney.

An attorney's license can be suspended or revoked for failing to follow professional standards, for example, by breaking the law or providing services in an incompetent and unethical fashion. Attorneys, however, are not required to disclose to prospective clients whether or not they have ever been disciplined for unprofessional conduct, they are under treatment for any mental or addictive health problems, or former clients have sued them.

Specialization

As is a license to practice medicine, a license to practice law is a broad grant of power. It permits an attorney to undertake a wide variety of legal tasks. Common sense for both lawyer and client suggests that a general-practice attorney should undertake only routine matters for a client. A complex legal problem should be referred to a specialist, who will be familiar with the intricacies, procedures, and detailed rules in that particular area of law. All areas of law practice include unwritten norms, knowledge of which allows the specialist to bring a legal problem to a faster, more satisfactory conclusion than an attorney not well versed in the particular area.

Attorneys may choose to specialize in any one or more areas, such as divorce or family law, probate and estates, criminal law, administrative law, real properly law, personal injury law, small business law, and consumer law. These specialties usually correlate with the most common public needs. Other specialties include antitrust law, labor or employment law, tax law, bankruptcy law, intellectual property law, international law, workers' compensation law, water law, and elder law (a relatively new legal specialty serving America's aging baby boomers). Attorneys also may be classified as performing either transactional or litigation (court-related) services. For example, one attorney may perform transactional services, such as writing wills, contracts, articles of incorporation, and so on, whereas another primarily litigates cases in court.

Many states allow attorneys to identify themselves as certified specialists in a particular area of law if they have the requisite experience and have met the education standards set by the state bar. The availability of specialized legal services is determined, in part, by geography. For example, antitrust, patent, immigration, and securities specialists are found in populous urban areas, whereas general practitioners usually are found in suburbs and rural communities. Family, small business, criminal, and probate law attorneys are found in all communities of any significant size.

Associations of Lawyers

A lawyer may choose to practice alone, combine with one or more other attorneys in a law partnership, or (in most states) conduct business as a professional corporation.

Law partnerships and corporations currently range in size from 2 to more than 3,000 attorneys.

Most attorneys who associate with others do so in a general partnership, a limited liability partnership, or a professional corporation. When professionals, including lawyers, form organizations, they seldom gain all the advantages that exist for other businesses. For example, there are generally no restrictions on who may be a shareholder (part owner) in the usual corporation. But in a professional law corporation or limited liability partnership, nonlegal professionals (e.g., legal secretaries, legal assistants, and investigators) are not allowed to be shareholders. In addition, although many business forms protect a shareholder from all personal liability for the debts of the firm, such forms will not protect completely a professional in most states. To protect the public, most states will not shield attorneys (or other professionals) from liability for errors and omissions (malpractice).

Various statutory schemes protect clients of professional corporations. One type will not allow owners to have limited liability. Another requires professional corporations or limited liability partnerships to purchase insurance against professional malpractice (errors and omissions insurance). A third scheme requires all shareholders to personally guarantee all corporate obligations for malpractice as a condition for certification. Lawyers in all but the smallest "boutique" firms often are assisted by legal assistants or paralegals (persons qualified to perform a wide range of administrative and semilegal tasks), secretaries or personal assistants, investigators, and office managers.

Medium to large partnerships include attorneys offering a wide variety of specialized legal services. On the other hand, some law firms limit their entire practice to a single specially. For example, some firms specialize in the defense of automobile injury cases. These firms are employed by automobile insurance companies to represent their customers who are involved in automobile accidents.

Prestige within the legal community often is related to the size of the firm. The larger the firm, the greater its prestige and, usually, the higher the fees it charges its clients. This phenomenon is partly the result of large, well-established firms attracting top graduates from elite law schools. Members (owners or "equity-partners") of these firms often earn high personal incomes, serve wealthy clients, and occupy luxurious offices. The solo practitioner, rightly or wrongly, often is found at the bottom of the image and income ladder. Although the evolution of legal practice from solo practitioners to large firms has been going on for more than sixty years,* the establishment of the megafirm with offices in different cities, states, and countries is a more recent innovation.

Public attorneys (e.g., district attorneys, U.S. attorneys, and county counsels) represent various local, state, and federal governments. Public defenders are also public attorneys. They are paid by local, state, and federal governments to represent indigents accused of a crime. Attorneys in public service usually are bound by the same rules of professional conduct as attorneys in private practice. In some circumstances, public lawyers are held to a higher standard.

contingency fee
A fixed percentage of the monetary recovery obtained by a lawyer for a client. It is agreed on in advance and accepted in full payment for services rendered.

Generally, the government is not obligated to provide free legal counsel to low-income people in civil matters. Many communities, however, have established legal aid offices. They give assistance and limited legal advice in civil matters to people who cannot afford an attorney. Representation in personal injury cases is affordable because private attorneys charge on a **contingency fee** basis. The fee, a percentage of the amount recovered, is contingent on the outcome of the case. In other words, a fee is due and

*In the years immediately after World War II, approximately 65 percent of lawyers in this country practiced alone. Albert Blaustein, *American Lawyer* (Westport, CT: Greenwood Publishing, 1972).

payable only if the client wins. (Further discussion of attorney fees appears later in this chapter.)

Legal Services Corporation (LSC)
A federally funded corporation that distributes federal tax dollars to state programs that provide legal assistance in noncriminal proceedings to persons financially unable to afford such services.

The federal **Legal Services Corporation (LSC)** helps states provide legal assistance to the underprivileged through grants to local legal aid offices. It promotes equal access to justice and improves opportunities for low-income people through grants that provide civil legal assistance to persons unable to afford legal counsel. Created in 1964, the LSC has encountered some controversy because advocating for the poor often has unpopular political ramifications. Cases brought by the LSC grantees often name other government agencies as defendants, creating political backlash and resentment.

pro bono publico
When an attorney provides legal services free of charge to poor but worthy clients or causes.

Many bar associations and legal commentators urge lawyers to allocate part of their time to civil ***pro bono publico*** (Latin: "for the public good") services free of charge. Many attorneys do contribute their time and effort to serving poor people who have legal problems, but the need is far from being met to the satisfaction of all concerned. The ABA House of Delegates adopted new ethics rules requiring every lawyer to provide legal services to those unable to pay. Congress and state legislatures have enacted "fee shifting" statutes to encourage attorneys to represent the underprivileged: If the attorney wins the case, the government will pay all attorney fees. Fees are quite generous in civil rights matters and government overreaching cases. Victims who do not have to pay attorney fees in advance are more likely to proceed in vindicating their rights. To some, fee shifting is the only way to protect poor people. To others, fee-shifting statutes are like adding gasoline to the fires of litigation, which many believe already to be out of control.

LEGAL FOCUS—BACKGROUND

When an elderly couple faced eviction for amassing large amounts of clutter, Northridge professor Bruce Zucker and ten students agreed to clean and organize the couple's longtime rent-controlled apartment to keep the pair from losing their home. And when the landlord later reneged on the agreement, Zucker took the case to trial—and the couple, who were living on a fixed income, won the right to stay. That was just one of several recent cases in which Zucker, a full-time professor of real estate law and finance at California State University, Northridge, stepped in to assist low-income individuals in the midst of a crisis.

Assistance to indigent persons accused of crimes is provided without charge through state and federal public defenders' offices. Courts appoint private attorneys when public attorneys are not available. The state pays these private attorneys standardized fees. Under the Sixth Amendment, legal assistance is a constitutional right of all persons accused of crimes punishable by imprisonment, even if they cannot afford to hire private legal counsel. There is no constitutional right to counsel for defendants in civil suits.

MORALS AND ETHICS

As we examine next, many moral and ethical standards for lawyers exist as regulatory obligations. In essence, these ethics are codified. But some lawyer values exist outside of lawyers' ethical code. Serving pro bono clients is one of those values. Although lawyers are not required to perform pro bono work, they certainly are expected to do so. Law firms and judges praise lawyers who provide pro bono services to the needy, and many young lawyers are in part attracted to the profession because they expect to have the opportunity to serve clients who cannot afford their services. Still, the business pressure on private-practice lawyers increasingly is making such honorable service difficult.

Some "store-front lawyers" or "law clinics" operating out of strip malls and other such quarters provide routine legal services for reduced fees. This type of law practice began in the 1970s with the relaxation of rules prohibiting advertising. These clinics often limit representation to such areas as family law, criminal defense, and probate matters. To lower costs, they take on only those matters that lend themselves to simple procedures and use of standard legal forms. In recent years, many of these clinics have added other legal specialties to their services.

legal service plans
Insurance plans designed to make legal services available to members of unions or other organizations, such as business firms.

The cost of legal services, like the cost of medical care, has skyrocketed in recent years. For many, access to competent legal advice at an affordable rate has become elusive. Group and prepaid **legal service plans** are designed to make legal services available at reduced cost to members of associations. Increasingly, prepaid legal service plans are offered as part of employee benefits packages. These plans operate like group health insurance. Subscribers get free or reduced-fee legal services after a deductible has been met. The plans usually are limited in scope, but they do provide low-cost assistance for routine legal matters (e.g., simple wills, document review, and warranty enforcement). Criminal matters generally are excluded from coverage. Prepaid legal service plans have been criticized for violating attorney ethical rules (discussed next) respecting client confidentiality and for interfering with attorneys' professional judgment.

public interest law firm
A nonprofit law firm that offers assistance in areas such as employment, minority rights, civil rights, political rights, family law, and environmental law.

Public interest law firms became popular in the late 1960s. These firms offer assistance in such particular areas as employment, minority rights, civil rights, political rights, family law, and environmental law. Public interest law firms often are funded by grants from private charitable organizations. Public interest firms represent opposite sides of controversial legal issues.

WHAT ARE PROFESSIONAL ETHICS?

professional ethics
Written rules of conduct that are adopted by and binding upon members of a professional group.

As discussed in Chapter 1, ethics is about what is fair and just. It addresses the question, what is the right thing to do in a situation? **Professional ethics** are written rules of acceptable conduct that are adopted by and binding upon members of a professional group. They are established and enforced to protect the public and to preserve and improve the reputation of the profession. Recall that an oath to follow ethical rules is what distinguishes a profession from a service or a trade. Ethics and the law, although not identical, do go hand in hand.

legal ethics
Rules promulgated by lawyer-governing bodies to proscribe standards of professional behavior and regulate lawyer and judicial conduct.

Legal ethics is the set of rules promulgated by the governing bodies that regulate lawyer and judicial conduct. Legal ethics may embody moralistic choices, but not necessarily. *Rules of professional conduct* or *rules of professional responsibility* are more precise terms, as many of the rules do not directly concern moral issues. They relate to more practical aspects of legal practice, such as prohibiting unauthorized practice of law. The states are responsible for regulating lawyer conduct.

As a practical matter, the legal profession is self-regulating. The various state bar associations, under the auspices of the states' supreme courts, devise and publish the rules of ethics, determine admission eligibility and procedures, and decide who receives discipline and to what extent. These rules carry the force of law when they are codified by a legislature or are cited by courts in opinions. A breach of these rules may lead to discipline. It may take the form of (1) disbarment, (2) suspension from practice for a stated period of time, (3) probation, or (4) reproval (formal private or public censure).

The ABA is the preeminent source on legal ethics. Since the early twentieth century, the ABA has promulgated rules of ethics for legal practitioners. The first set of rules, the Canons of Professional Ethics, was introduced in 1908. It was intended as a practice guide, not a basis for discipline. A new set of rules, the Model Code of Professional Conduct, was introduced in 1969. It had two sets of rules: one aspirational and one disciplinary. In 1983, the ABA adopted the Model Rules of Professional Conduct. The aspirational component of the earlier codes was eliminated. The current major revision of the ABA Model Rules of Professional Conduct was adopted in February 2002.

Charging unconscionable or exorbitant fees, stealing a client's funds, improperly soliciting employment, neglecting a client's case, and misusing a client's funds are all examples of unethical conduct directly related to the attorney's profession. Other improprieties and bad behavior also can expose the attorney to ethics violations.

Attorneys may be disciplined for conduct involving *moral turpitude* (conduct contrary to justice, honesty, and good morals). Perjury, failure to pay income taxes, murder, larceny, participation in business fraud, child molestation, and sale of narcotics are all examples of crimes involving moral turpitude. Such acts subject the offending attorney to professional discipline, in addition to criminal charges and individual civil lawsuits. Disciplinary hearings may take place even if questionable conduct does not directly relate to the attorney's ability to practice law. For example, a former vice president of the United States, Spiro T. Agnew, was disbarred following his plea of *nolo contendere* (Latin: "I will not contest it"), a special form of guilty plea, to willful tax evasion (Maryland State Bar Assoc. v. Agnew, 318 A.2d 822 (Md. 1974).

LEGAL FOCUS—CASE

Grace Akinsanya retained Pineda, an attorney, and paid him $1,500, in advance, to represent her in a real estate matter. After a few months, Akinsanya became dissatisfied with Pineda's inaction and fired him. Pineda refused to sign a substitution-of-attorney form and would not return Akinsanya's files or refund any part of the fee. Can Pineda refuse to remove himself from the case and keep the client's files?

Pineda v. State Bar of Calif., 49 Cal.3d 753, 781 P.2d 1 (Calif. 1989).

An attorney-at-law has no right to continue to represent a client who no longer wants the lawyer's services. Pineda finally did withdraw from the case and returned Akinsanya's files, but only after the Superior Court sanctioned (punished) him for his actions. On the basis of these acts and six other similar acts of failure to perform services for clients, Pineda was suspended from the practice of law for two years and placed on probation for five years.

There is an important difference between private and public attorneys. Both are ethically bound to zealously represent a client. They are advocates, and the object is to win the client's case. In litigation, each attorney works with the record of historical events, which lawyers refer to as *facts*. Each must resolve all doubts about the facts (and law) in the client's favor. Significantly, a public attorney, such as a prosecutor or other government lawyer, is held to a higher standard. A government lawyer is duty bound to see that justice is carried out, not simply to win the case. For example, a prosecutor must notify the defense of any obvious evidence in a criminal case that tends to show the defendant's innocence. Private attorneys are not obligated in the same way. They are not responsible for passing judgment. However, they may not destroy, nor present as true, any evidence that is known to be false, nor solicit or condone perjury to win a case.

LEGAL FOCUS—PROBLEM

Attorney Tak Sharpe represented the plaintiff in an automobile accident case that was nearing trial. To encourage a compromise, Sharpe telephoned the defendant, Sandra Broderik, instead of calling Broderik's attorney. Sharpe told Broderik that $17,500 would be a fair settlement. Broderick responded that she would prefer to discuss the matter with her attorney. Has Sharpe acted ethically?

No, Sharpe has not acted ethically. The Rules of Professional Conduct do not allow opposing counsel to communicate directly with another attorney's client without the other lawyer's consent. Sharpe should have telephoned Broderik's lawyer. The purpose of this rule is to prevent an opponent's lawyer from intimidating the opposition or undermining the advice given by that client's counsel.

Questions of professional ethics are sometimes complex and susceptible to misunderstanding. The attorney's job is to represent the client vigorously while honoring the law. For example, a criminal attorney must attempt to persuade a judge and jury to free a client, even if he or she personally believes that the client is guilty of the offense. This advocacy is considered ethically correct because the lawyer's duty is to represent—not to judge—the client. Everyone is entitled to all available legal advantage. Even following conviction, the attorney will argue for probation rather than prison. A tax attorney will look vigilantly to find a loophole (an ambiguity in the law), allowing a client to reduce or avoid tax payments. This action is proper, as a matter of legal ethics, so long as no fraudulent practice is involved. Congress often authorizes loopholes or tax shelters to encourage certain types of socially desirable investments. For example, Congress allows interest paid on home mortgages to be deducted from taxable income, reducing the income taxes paid by homeowners. (Of course, the taxpayer must request the deduction.)

LEGAL FOCUS—CASE

Tammy Forsberg was injured in a motorcycle accident. Her attorney, John Casey, obtained a settlement, of which her portion was $23,233. Casey paid her $5,000 and refused to pay the rest. Forsberg hired a second lawyer, James Himmel, on a contingency fee basis to recover the remaining balance from Casey. Himmel sued Casey and won a judgment of $100,000 for Forsberg. Himmel did not report Casey to the state bar. What are the ethical implications of Casey's and Himmel's conduct?

In re James H. Himmel, 125 Ill.2d 531, 533 N.E.2d 790 (Ill. 1989).

The Illinois state bar disbarred Casey for keeping Forsberg's money. Apparently, Casey had treated the money as if it were his own. He put his desire for fees above the interests of his clients and the legal system. Himmel exacerbated the misconduct by not reporting it. Under ethical rules, lawyers are required to report another lawyer's misconduct to the proper authority. The Illinois Supreme Court held that Himmel, by not reporting Casey's activities, had contributed to the misappropriation of other clients' funds. Although Himmel had practiced law without complaint for eleven years, he was suspended from the practice of law for one year (*In re* Ethics Advisory Panel Opinion 92-1, 627 A.2d 317 (1993)).

The public and even some lawyers have trouble understanding the ethical rules despite the continuing effort to update and clarify them. One influential source of ethical guidance is a body of published ethics opinions written by ethics committees of the ABA and state or local bar associations. An ethics committee is convened to consider how the rules of professional conduct apply in a specific circumstance. The committee debates the ethical issues and writes an opinion resolving the matter. Although influential, the opinions do not carry the force of law. Ethics Hotlines, operated by state and local bar associations, are a source of guidance for lawyers. Lawyers may make a confidential telephone inquiry about an ethical dilemma and receive advice on how to solve the problem. Again, such advice may be helpful but is not binding on any court.

Confidentiality and the Attorney–Client Privilege

attorney–client privilege
The right of clients to keep communications with their attorneys confidential and free from disclosure.

confidentiality
A private communication with an attorney-at-law in which the attorney is under a duty to keep the information secret.

The **attorney–client privilege** is a rule of evidence that protects all communications between a client and her attorney from disclosure in a legal proceeding. An attorney cannot be compelled by statute or court order to reveal such information except in a few narrow circumstances. The client may waive the privilege, but the attorney may not. The attorney–client privilege applies in all states.

The attorney–client privilege often is confused with the broader duty of **confidentiality**. The duty of confidentiality is a lawyer's ethical obligation to protect any information learned from or about a client during the course of representation. It applies in any forum or context, not just in judicial proceedings. Whereas the duty of confidentiality protects any information a lawyer learns about the client from any source from disclosure to anyone, anywhere, the attorney–client privilege protects the client's information *only* if the attorney learns it directly from the client. Some exceptions to the confidentiality rule apply. Although there is wide variation among the states, the most common exceptions are to defend a malpractice case or fee dispute, to warn of a client's contemplated crime, and to avoid assisting with the commission of a crime.

The attorney–client privilege and the duty of confidentiality were designed to accomplish competent representation. To build a strong case, attorneys need full disclosure and open communication with their clients. Clients will share information freely with counsel only if they believe their confidences are safe.

LEGAL FOCUS—PROBLEM

A criminal defense attorney learned from his client, Derrick Vaughn, that in addition to the present crime with which Derrick was charged, he previously had murdered two young girls, recently reported as missing. The lawyer even learned the specific location of their bodies. Yet the attorney did not report this information to the authorities, to the parents of the girls, or to anyone else. Did the attorney behave ethically?

Yes, according to generally understood legal ethics, the attorney behaved ethically. An attorney cannot breach the duty of confidentiality, without the client's consent. Rule 1.6 of the ABA Model Rules of Professional Conduct prohibits a lawyer from revealing "information relating to the representation of a client unless the client gives informed consent, the disclosure is impliedly authorized in order to carry out the representation." The attorney cannot waive the privilege. The client, however, may do so. Cases involving situations such as this have brought the rule to the public's attention, if not understanding, over the years.

LEGAL FOCUS—CASE

An anonymous client (referred to as J. Doe) contacted an attorney following Doe's involvement in a fatal hit-and-run accident. Doe instructed the attorney to offer a plea to the prosecutor in exchange for a reduced criminal charge while Doe remained anonymous. The prosecutor refused to bargain without revelation of Doe's identity. The victim's family sued the attorney to force disclosure of the client's name. Can the family get Doe's real name?

Baltes v. Doe, 57 U.S.L.W. 2268 (Fla. Cir. Ct. 1988).

No, the family cannot get the real name. The Florida Circuit Court held that the information was privileged, and the attorney was not required to disclose the client's name. Courts understand the natural public resentment that arises with such rulings. Nevertheless, if the privilege is not respected, people will be reluctant to seek counsel.

LEGAL FOCUS—CASE

In 1993 Deputy White House Counsel Vincent W. Foster, Jr., met with attorney James Hamilton seeking personal legal representation. Hamilton took handwritten notes at the meeting. Nine days later, Foster committed suicide. Subsequently, a federal grand jury, at the request of Independent Counsel Kenneth Starr, issued subpoenas for the notes as part of an investigation of President Clinton and his staff. Hamilton sought to quash the subpoena, arguing that the notes were protected by the attorney–client privilege. Starr's contention was that the attorney–client privilege does not apply after the client has died, particularly if the information is relevant to a criminal proceeding. Did Starr get the notes?

Swidler & Berlin and James Hamilton v. United States, 524 U.S 399 (1998).

No, Starr did not get the notes. In reversing the Court of Appeals for the District of Columbia Circuit, the U.S. Supreme Court stated,

> *[W]e think there are weighty reasons that counsel in favor of posthumous application [of the attorney-client privilege]. Knowing that communications will remain confidential even after death encourages the client to communicate fully and frankly with counsel. Clients may be concerned about reputation, civil liability, or possible harm to friends or family. Posthumous disclosure of such communications may be as feared as disclosure during the client's lifetime.*

The privilege, however, has not been held to cover all communications in all situations; for example, there is no protection if the communication is made in the presence of others, if the communication indicates an intent to commit a future crime, or if there is a statute requiring specified communications to be disclosed.

Conflicts of Interest

A quality attorney–client relationship depends on trust. Clients develop trust in their attorney if they believe their attorney will treat them in an honest, fair, and loyal manner. It is virtually impossible for an attorney to represent clients competently unless clients are completely candid. The natural inclination to avoid disclosing embarrassing or incriminating information cannot be overcome unless clients are confident their attorney will not use confidential information without permission. If clients believe confidences will be respected, then they will communicate openly with their attorney. A relationship of trust forms when the attorney is first engaged and continues throughout the representation and even after the representation ends.

conflict of interest
When a client's interests are at odds with another's because the attorney serves, might serve, or is tempted to serve the other.

Conflicts of interest breach this trust. A **conflict of interest** occurs when one client's interests are at odds with the interests of another person because the attorney either serves, might serve, or is tempted to serve the other. Any situation that compromises or has the potential to compromise an attorney's loyalty to clients is a conflict of interest. The rules of professional conduct forbid conflicts of interest. These rules are intended to foster trust in individual attorney–client relationships and to build confidence in the legal profession.

Obviously, a conflict arises when an attorney seeks to be named a beneficiary in a client's will or trust (called a breach of trust or breach of fiduciary duty). Attorneys may not use financial information about a client to their own advantage. Conflicts of interest can arise between two or more clients or between a new client and a current or former client. For this reason, lawyers may not represent two defendants accused of commission of the same crime. An attorney faced with a potential conflict of interest can contact the local bar association's Ethics Hotline for guidance. An advisory opinion may be published if the bar believes the issues in the case require general guidance.

LEGAL FOCUS—EXAMPLE

Problem:

The inquirer asks if it is a violation of the Rules of Professional Conduct for a retired judge, now volunteering for a local legal aid office, to represent a client in an ongoing child custody–parenting dispute when that same client appeared before him in Drug Court while he was still on the Superior Court bench. He had signed an agreed order in the child custody–parenting dispute, which was the result of a hearing in front of another judge when the other judge assigned to the case was out of town.

The Rule:

A lawyer shall not represent anyone in connection with a matter in which the lawyer participated personally and substantially as a judge or other adjudicative officer; as a law clerk to such a person; or as an arbitrator, mediator, or other third-party neutral, unless all parties to the proceeding give informed consent confirmed in writing.

Analysis:

The committee cannot comment on potential violations of the Code of Judicial Conduct. Nonetheless, if the judge did not have any substantial participation while he was on the bench in the matter in which he now wishes to represent the client, representation of that client does not appear to be a violation of the Rules of Professional Conduct 1.12. The retired judge's involvement in drug proceedings involving his current client may be deemed "personal and substantial" participation in a related matter but, if so, they can be addressed by the informed consent of his client. Under the facts of this case, it does not appear that the retired judge had "personal and substantial" participation in the child custody–parenting dispute so as to require the consent, after disclosure, of the other party to the child custody proceedings.

Informal Opinion 2092 issued in 2005 from the Washington State Bar Association.

Conflicts are created when attorneys change employers, either from one private law firm to another or from government service to private practice. The magnitude of this problem has increased with the growth in law firm size. Performing detailed conflicts checks is now critical to escaping malpractice suits and violations of ethical rules. When taking on new clients, attorneys must be vigilant in determining that the new representation does not conflict with obligations owed to other clients (even previous ones). To serve the best interest of clients, even the appearance of a conflict needs to be avoided.

LEGAL FOCUS—CASE

Judge Bennie Boles appointed Victor Haley to represent Larry Christopher, an indigent defendant charged with a crime. Haley asked to withdraw on the basis of a conflict of interest, stating his law partner was married to the county district attorney, Karren Price. Judge Boles held that no conflict of interest existed. Haley requested judicial review on the question. Did a conflict of interest exist?

Haley v. Boles, 824 S.W.2d 796 (Tex. 1992).

The Texas appellate court held that because indigent criminal defendants are not required to pay attorney fees, they are not free to discharge appointed counsel, even upon discovery of a conflict of interest. Ignoring the marital relationship between the district attorney and the defense counsel, however, would undermine public confidence in the criminal justice system. The court found this apparent conflict of interest sufficient to dismiss Haley as Christopher's counsel.

Frivolous Lawsuits

Claims without legal justification, solely intended to retaliate or punish, are regarded as frivolous. They are costly to society. Defendants incur attorney fees and expenses. Time is wasted and minds are preoccupied unnecessarily. Courtrooms are occupied, and the attention of judges is diverted from valid cases. Meritless lawsuits clog the court system. Arguably, access to justice is denied when meritorious cases cannot be tried on a timely basis. Perhaps surprising to the public, it is unethical for lawyers to file baseless lawsuits. In fact, the ABA Model Rules of Professional Conduct and states' rules prohibit attorneys from taking on any legal work of a frivolous nature.

A lawyer may not write a demand letter or place a telephone call on behalf of a client if there is no validity to the claim. The costs of defending a frivolous lawsuit are recoverable under statute, case law, and court rules. Federal Rule of Civil Procedure 11 permits the court to sanction attorneys and *pro se* litigants for filing frivolous lawsuits. A signature on any moving paper (motions, answers, and so on) is a certification to the court that the signer believes, based on investigation, the allegations to be true. If the courts find that the suit has no basis in law or fact, it may dismiss the case and order that the defendants be paid their litigation costs, including attorney fees. Plaintiffs beware: The court system may not be used to facilitate bad-faith attempts at seeking justice.

DEALING WITH AN ATTORNEY

Is an Attorney Necessary?

Lawyers are expected to assist with a seemingly endless stream of problems for private persons, businesses, government agencies, and other organizations. Obviously, many clients consider attorneys an essential source of information, advice, and representation in numerous situations. Nonetheless, people routinely resolve some legal problems without the assistance of an attorney. Among these are simple divorces, settlement of "fender-bender" car-crash cases, simple handwritten wills, consumer purchase and sale contracts (such as "pink-slip" certificates of vehicle ownership), and simple real estate purchase agreements. Numerous disputes involving small sums are within the jurisdiction of the small claims court (recall that attorneys may not appear in small claims court unless they are parties in a case). The Internet is a useful tool for gathering legal information. There are excellent self-help books such as those published by Nolo Press* and legal software such as Quicken Lawyer. Unfortunately, too often persons in genuine need of legal advice or assistance fail to seek it, or they delay consulting an attorney. The result may be a permanent loss of a valuable legal right. A decision about self-help should be made carefully.

The Internet has made legal information easily available, so why consult an attorney? Finding the law is only one of many critical services that an attorney performs. Attorneys have legal insights that only years of study and experience can engender. In addition, attorneys are skilled orators and writers. They are expert problem solvers, negotiators, and advocates. Not every dispute or problem ought to be taken to an attorney. Indeed, elementary economics militates against such petty litigiousness. The potential impact of events on one's life should be considered when considering the need for an attorney's services.

Some general guidelines may help you decide whether or not to consult an attorney for a matter. Do consult an attorney if the matter can be characterized in any of the following ways:

- The matter involves the risk of losing or possibility of obtaining a sum of money that is significant to you.
- The matter involves the risk of losing your freedom or suffering harm to your reputation.
- The matter involves actual or possible physical or mental injury, suffered or threatened, that can be characterized as significant.
- The matter seems important for any other reason (e.g., a major impact on your life or that of a dependent, such as in a child custody dispute).
- The area of law is complex or you lack the time to carefully preserve or pursue your rights.

In recent years, many critics have claimed that the United States has too many lawyers. The number of lawyers in our society allegedly has a negative effect on economic productivity and has engendered dissatisfaction among citizens. Indeed, lawyers have the dubious distinction of inspiring an anti–fan club called HALT (Help Abolish Legal Tyranny), set off in part by dishonorable lawyer conduct. Such criticisms are difficult to evaluate because they measure productivity as a function of the number of lawyers in a country. This measure is flawed because qualifications of legal practitioners vary significantly among countries, making comparisons unreliable. Thus, studies purporting to measure productivity as a function of the number of lawyers are at best misleading.

How Do You Find a "Good" Attorney?

Time, energy, and resourcefulness spent finding an attorney will help create a satisfactory relationship and final result. Too often, the presence of a serious problem that prompts

*We frequently cite Nolo Press in this textbook. Nolo Press began publishing self-help legal resources in the late 1960s, and in our opinion, has set the standard for accurate, easy-to-understand legal materials As their publishing philosophy has been motivated in part by social goals, the materials they provide seem reasonably priced to the authors.

the search also prompts great haste in the selection process. A cavalier approach to the selection process increases the chance of retaining an attorney who may not perform as well as others who are equally qualified. An exhaustive search should not be necessary to avoid a "bad" attorney; to the contrary, in populous areas, a number of qualified attorneys are ready, willing, and able to perform the required service.

Paid Advertisements

In the not-so-distant past, lawyers were prohibited by law and professional rules from advertising their services. Marketing legal services in this manner was considered not only unethical but also unbecoming. Many in the legal profession feared that advertising would lead to false and misleading claims. Promotional practices were thought to foster rather than resolve conflict. Many attorneys also believed that advertising tarnishes the general reputation of the profession.*

Rules of conduct regarding publicity and advertising were changed dramatically in the past quarter of the twentieth century. In 1977, the U.S. Supreme Court ruled that the public had a right to information as to the availability and cost of routine legal services, and attorneys had a right to furnish that information. The Supreme Court also has held that lawyers cannot be prohibited from sending direct mail solicitations and communications informing potential clients of their certification as specialists.

The ABA Model Rules of Professional Conduct concerning advertising have been liberalized. States have reformulated rules regarding advertising, although many issues are still debated. In the legal profession, claims made concerning an individual's competence or ability to achieve results are considered unethical.

National law firms with outstanding reputations traditionally declined to advertise, but in recent years, even they have begun to do so. Still, they avoid commercial television in favor of simple announcements, news releases, brochures, public television sponsorship, newsletters, and advertisements in magazines targeted to special audiences. Legal directories have been available for many years and never have been considered advertising. Bar associations, private organizations, and law firms maintain lists of attorneys, often with detailed information about each individual and areas of practice. These lists are accessible over the Internet. Most public libraries maintain directories of attorneys with biographical information, including practice specialties and lists of representative clients. Finally, group legal services relieve clients of the burden of finding a qualified attorney. In this sense, they serve a marketing function for member lawyers.

Word-of-Mouth Advertising

Generally, the most reliable advertising is word of mouth. An attorney's reputation, however, is more than simply "good" or "bad." Better questions concerning the reputation of a particular attorney include the following:

- What is the attorney's specialty?
- How long has the attorney been in practice?
- Does the attorney have a reputation for being a problem solver? Thorough? Expensive? Aggressive? Sincere? Or any other quality thought to be appropriate or inappropriate for the case?
- Do judges and attorneys generally think highly of the individual or firm?

*"Marketplace lawyer advertising, using all the sights, color, sounds, subliminal messages and not so hidden persuaders of commercial television, adversely affects not only the public's perception of those court officers, but also of the courts and the total judicial system." Justice Reynoldson, retired chief justice of the Iowa Supreme Court, "The Case against Lawyer Advertising," *ABA Journal* 75 (January 1989), p. 60.

- Is the attorney active in the community?
- Has the attorney been disciplined by the bar or been a defendant in malpractice cases?
- Is the attorney in good health?
- Does the attorney have a reputation for consuming alcohol to excess or taking harmful drugs?
- Does the attorney usually win cases?
- Does the attorney make the fee arrangement clear?
- Does the attorney have a reputation for communicating with the client, returning phone calls promptly, keeping the client informed on case progress?
- Does the attorney work on the case personally or delegate the work to others?

The selection of an attorney should be accompanied by some introspection by the client. Clients should consider their own attitudes, goals, and objectives, and, as dispassionately as possible, the nature of their claims. Some attorneys are problem solvers and others are "gladiators" (problem winners). A problem solver might complete the task in a short period of time, but the resolution may require considerable compromise on the part of the client. The gladiator might be victorious and provide more of what the client wanted (or less) but may take considerably more time and require a different emotional commitment by the client. (Fewer than 5 percent of all civil cases actually go to trial, so even gladiators typically compromise; they just do it later in the process.) The problem solver may preserve a friendly, mutually profitable relationship for the client with the other party, which is seldom possible with a gladiator who may embarrass, anger, or even humiliate the opposing party.

Most attorneys are listed somewhere on the Internet and in the Yellow Pages, some times with large ads. Such listings do not guarantee competence, however. A person with a legal problem should ask friends, family, and neighbors to recommend an attorney. Business managers, bankers, title company officers, educators, merchants, stockbrokers, insurance executives, real estate personnel, and, of course, lawyers are likely to have direct communication with and know of attorneys by their reputation. Employers and government officials are also good sources.

Meeting with the Attorney

Once a prospective client gets the name of one or two attorneys as possible selections, an office appointment should be made with each by telephone. Many attorneys will consult with a prospective client for a modest fee or at no charge. It is prudent to ask how long the initial appointment will last and if there is a charge. A prospective client will have many questions about which laws apply to her case. Several laws may be relevant to the case, so the attorney will necessarily be noncommittal. No attorney is capable of explaining all the legal ramifications of a situation without careful research and preparation; nor is any attorney capable of predicting with certainly the outcome of any complex case.

No commitment to hire needs be made at the first meeting; a simple "Thank you, I would like to consider the matter for a couple of days" permits a graceful departure. During the initial meeting, much can be learned by asking the attorney a few questions:

- Do you frequently handle cases like mine?
- Is this area your specialty? If not, how many cases of this type have you handled?
- Will you be doing all the work, or will other persons be involved?
- Will you refer my case to another attorney in the firm or handle it yourself?

- Will this case conflict with any of your other obligations, court calendars, or appointments?
- Is it best to settle this matter now, even at a loss, rather than to be embroiled in a lengthy legal battle?
- May I have a copy of your standard retainer agreement?
- Can you give me an estimate of my likely trial costs and fees for handling this matter to its conclusion?
- How will I be kept informed about the progress of the matter in your office?

Much can be learned about the prospective attorney by arriving for your meeting early and observing the law office in operation. Confusion and disorganization often suggest a lower quality of service. An office cluttered with files, papers, and books does not engender confidence. After you leave, will your file simply be part of the mess?

You should be aware that not all attorneys will appreciate being asked all of the questions in the previous list. Some will interpret your inquiries as an indication that you will be a "problem" or malcontent client. However, consumers of any service, including legal services, have the right to be informed and assured of the nature of the service they are to receive. If in the process of protecting your interests you are reasonable and courteous, a responsible attorney should not resent your questions. And if the two of you decide to do business together, you will be off to a good start, with mutual respect for each other.

Attorney Referral Services

Referral services are a means of indirect advertising. Bar associations in some communities administer attorney referral services. They are listed in telephone directories and on websites. The association maintains a list or panel of attorneys in various specialties. Referrals are made alphabetically or by type of case. No special qualifications are required to get on the list. Newer members of the bar, in particular, may join the panel, and possibly charge reduced rates for their services, to gain clients.

Some attorney referral services are operated by private businesses. These are quite similar to the bar panels. The service places advertisements seeking a particular kind of client—for example, a personal injury victim. Responses to the advertisement then are referred to panel members. Attorney members pay a registration fee to participate on the panel.

Public Defenders

As noted earlier, a defendant accused of a serious crime (i.e., one for which the possible punishment is incarceration) has a constitutional right to be represented by a competent attorney at all stages of legal proceedings. If a defendant is indigent (unable to afford the services of a private attorney), the court will appoint an attorney, often called a **public defender**, to represent the accused without charge. Contrary to some popularly held views, attorneys in public defender roles generally are competent and zealous advocates. They are specialists. They handle a heavy caseload, develop vast experience in a short time, spend much time in court, and know the judges and court staff. Because they handle many criminal matters, they know the probable results of a plea negotiation or plea bargain. Records of numerous convictions reflect not incompetence on the part of the public defender but rather the fact that these lawyers are unable to choose their clients. Public defenders by inclination fight for the underdog, and they usually fight well. On the negative side, public defenders often are given too many cases to be able to devote the time and attention to any one case that a client accused of a crime might wish.

public defender
A lawyer provided by the community for a person who is accused of a serious crime (felony) and cannot afford to hire counsel.

Solicitation

Most methods of solicitation, in which lawyers aggressively seek clients, are considered unethical. Public policy frowns on efforts to promote litigation, such as "ambulance chasing." There, an accident victim is coerced to sign a retainer agreement at a time of great vulnerability. More sophisticated forms of solicitation, through "cappers" or "runners" who frequent such places as hospitals and police stations in search of potential clients, are likewise unethical. Investigators, as well as nurses in emergency wards, have been used as cappers. They may receive an illegal referral fee from the attorney. Such payments frequently are made in cash in an attempt to prevent detection of the conspiracy and evade taxes. In most cases, direct solicitation by an attorney is unethical and should be reported to the local or state bar association. Schemes involving cappers are illegal and should be reported to law enforcement and the appropriate bar association.

LEGAL FOCUS—CASE

David Barrett, the managing partner of a Tallahassee, Florida, law firm, hired Chad Cooper, an ordained minister, as a "paralegal." Barrett told Cooper to "do whatever you need to do to bring in some business" and "go out and ... get some clients." To assist Cooper in finding personal injury clients, Barrett paid Cooper to attend a hospital chaplain's course. In March 1994, Molly Glass's son was injured by an automobile while riding a bicycle. At the hospital, Cooper identified himself as a chaplain and consoled Molly Glass, prayed with her, and gave her the business card of the firm. Barrett's firm ultimately represented Glass and received a settlement. Cooper was paid a salary and bonuses for this case and other similar referrals. Was it ethical and legal to use Cooper to attract potential clients?

The Florida Bar v. Barrett, 897 So.2d 1269 (Fla. 2005).

This arrangement was neither legal nor ethical. Citing violations of several ethical rules regarding professional behavior and solicitation of clients, the Florida Supreme Court stated:

> *This type of violation brings dishonor and disgrace not only upon the attorney who has broken the rules but upon the entire legal profession, a burden that all attorneys must bear because it affects all of our reputations. Moreover, such violations harm people who are already in a vulnerable condition, which is one of the reasons these types of solicitations are barred. Therefore, this Court will strictly enforce the rules that prohibit these improper solicitations and impose severe sanctions on those who commit violations of them.... Molly Glass, infuriated that someone would attempt to take advantage of her while in the midst of such a tragedy, turned to somebody she thought she could trust to help her, an attorney that was recommended to her by a hospital chaplain, only to realize years later that her attorney also exploited this same vulnerability in order to obtain her business.*

The court approved the referee's findings of fact and recommendations as to guilt and went beyond the referee's recommendation of a more lenient suspension and chose to disbar Barrett.

HOW DO YOU HIRE AND FIRE AN ATTORNEY?

The attorney–client relationship is determined by contract. The attorney promises to represent the client in exchange for a promise of compensation. The ABA Model Rules and many states require that contingent fee agreements be in writing and signed by the client. Whether or not the law requires an agreement, the client should request a written agreement and ask that it be fully explained. Attorneys have an ethical obligation to reject a frivolous case or a case raising issues where they lack competence. Filing of frivolous and defamatory litigation justifies disciplinary action. The attorney is also vulnerable to a civil lawsuit for malicious prosecution, although such actions are seldom successful. See the previous discussion concerning frivolous lawsuits.

The agreement necessarily will have limitations. It cannot guarantee any particular result or any particular completion date, and it usually will not detail the step-by-step procedures the attorney ultimately will take. This lack of detail is not sinister but instead realistic. Even the most common legal problem or case may entail many unpredictable complications. The client should carefully ask questions until all ramifications of the problem or case are at least generally understood. Examples of questions a prospective client might ask include the following:

1. On what basis is the fee calculated? If hourly, is the "meter" running at the same rate while junior attorneys or paralegals are working on the case? How much library or computer research is anticipated, and at what cost? Will the fee statement be itemized as to hours spent and tasks accomplished? How often will a bill be issued?
   a. If the fee is contingent (client and attorney share in any recovery), are costs to be deducted from the award before or after computation of the attorney's share? If the matter is settled quickly (and so the attorney's involvement is less than was anticipated) is the fee division altered commensurately?
   b. What happens if the lawyer's work increases greatly—for example, when a new trial is granted or an appeal must be initiated?
   c. If a flat fee is charged, how will costs be paid? What does the fee include? What happens if there is an appeal? There should be a careful delineation of the work to be performed.
2. Specifically, what important actions and events does the attorney predict, and when are they most likely to happen?
3. What are the possible outcomes of the action, good and bad? Is there any point of no return; that is, a point beyond which the client cannot practically withdraw from the matter?
4. Will there be a need to refer all or any part of the case to another attorney? If so, how will the fee and work be affected and divided?
5. What will be the means (telephone, e-mail, and letter) and frequency of communications with the attorney or secretary? Will copies of all documents and correspondence routinely be sent to the client?

A client generally has the right to dismiss an attorney at any time for any reason. Difficulty may arise with respect to how much of the fee, if any, has been earned at the time of the discharge. The rule is easy to state but difficult to apply: The attorney is entitled to be paid the reasonable value of work done before discharge. In a contingent fee case, the attorney is entitled to be paid the agreed amount or proportionate share only if and when a recovery is obtained.

If the client is unable to pay all fees the attorney has earned up to the time of discharge, a serious conflict may arise. The attorney demands payment and the client demands return of all documents (the file) connected with the case. The attorney pressures the client for payment of accrued fees by refusing to release the file. In the absence of a statute giving the attorney the right to do so (called a *statutory or common law retaining lien*), such conduct is illegal and probably unethical. Many states, however, do authorize such a lien.

As a general rule, an attorney can terminate representation of a client if there is a reasonable basis for the withdrawal. For example, the client's failure to pay the agreed fee is grounds for withdrawal. An attorney, however, must (1) give reasonable notice to the client of intention to withdraw, (2) obtain court permission to withdraw if pleadings have been filed, (3) return the client's papers, and (4) refund any unearned fees. An attorney *must* withdraw from the employment when continued representation would require the attorney to violate a disciplinary rule. Other good reasons for withdrawal include failure of the attorney's health, materially affecting his ability to continue, or an awareness that a conflict of interest exists.

Attorney Fee Arrangements

Fees are earned based on an hourly rate (e.g., $250 per hour), a flat fee for a service (e.g., $15,000 payable in two installments), a contingency fee (e.g., 35 percent of net recovery), or a combination of these methods. Tradition, business practice, and law tie certain types of fee arrangements to certain types of legal matters. For example, the contingency fee is common in personal injury actions but is considered an unethical method of billing in a family law matter.

retainer fee
(a) A sum of money paid to an attorney for a promise to remain available to the client for consultation when needed and requested. (b) Fees paid in advance that are held in a trust account to be drawn down (taken) by the attorney as work progresses.

A **retainer fee** is an advance payment for legal services on a flat or continuing basis. A lawyer may require advance payment on any fee and is obliged to return the unearned portion. A common form of retainer is a monthly or yearly fee paid in exchange for the lawyer's promise to remain available to the client for consultation. Such agreement should be in writing and clearly define the services it covers, the term it covers, and the hourly rate at which additional services will be billed. Group legal service plans may be understood as a type of retainer. If the client seeks legal advice through the plan, minor, specified legal services will be rendered without charge. If requested services are complicated or time consuming (such as conduct of a trial), additional charges are billed as "earned" fees. At universities and colleges, it is common for the student government association to enter a retainer contract with an attorney to be available for a certain number of hours a week to assist students with minor legal problems. Many attorneys simply will not take a case without a retainer. They are reluctant to sue a client to collect a fee because they believe doing so will create bad publicity. So they require payment upfront.

Some attorneys include arbitration clauses in their fee agreements. This clause allows them to go after clients for unpaid fees without the negative publicity associated with a public trial because arbitration proceedings are private and arbitration awards are confidential. (See the discussion of arbitration later in this chapter.)

LEGAL FOCUS—PROBLEM

Elaine Taylor's husband, Buck, a young doctor, was killed in the crash of a commercial "commuter" airplane. Buck was not in the airplane; he was in his medical office in San Luis Obispo, which was destroyed by the crash. Attorney Ian Page offered to represent Taylor on a contingent fee basis for one-third of any net recovery. Page indicated no fees would be charged "unless and until" a recovery was made. Should Taylor hire Page?

Whether or not Taylor should hire Page depends on several factors. Charging contingency fees in matters in which liability is clear and some recovery expected is not an ethical violation *per se*. The real issue is whether the fee is reasonable and the client has been fully informed of the availability of alternative billing arrangements. In most calamitous events, there is no issue of "if" as to liability. Recovery is ensured because defendants in such cases are held strictly liable. Only the amount is arguable. Obtaining a settlement will require negotiations, but one-third of, for example, a $3 million settlement is excessive for the perhaps 100 hours necessary to represent Taylor. Competent attorneys undoubtedly would take her case for an hourly fee with payment deferred. It could be argued that contingent fees in calamitous personal injury or death cases in which liability is certain (or even probable) are unethical because clients do not fully understand the arrangement or its alternatives and the fees are excessive. It is not uncommon for personal injury attorneys to refer to such cases as "jackpots" or "retirement" cases.

Several states impose maximums on the percentage that may be charged in contingency fee contracts. Similar statutory limitations exist in matters processed by administrative agencies rather than by courts (e.g., veterans' benefits, Social Security claims, and workers' compensation cases).

The flat fee is common for certain types of routine matters, such as family law, criminal law matters, real estate title searches, trusts, and wills. The hourly fee, however, is still the dominant form of attorney billing and is used for all types of legal services.

Attorney fee agreements should describe how the fee will be calculated (hourly, flat rate, and so on) and, when feasible, specify the total amount of the fee. Attorneys are free to negotiate fee arrangements with clients, so long as they are reasonable. In some in stances, attorney fees are limited by statute or by the courts. Furthermore, when fee disputes arise, courts tend to give the benefit of any doubt to the client because of the usual bargaining superiority of the attorney. In some states, the law presumes overreaching by the attorney if representation is begun before the fee is negotiated and the client signs a written fee agreement. In such instances, the attorney is hard pressed to justify and collect more than a minimal reasonable fee.

Although attorneys are free to charge their "going rate," the client's case must not be delayed deliberately for the purpose of coercing payment of a delinquent installment, nor may an attorney charge an unconscionable or clearly excessive legal fee. The attorney is subject to discipline for making such an attempt.

class actions
When all members of a group of persons who have suffered the same or similar injury join together in a single lawsuit against the alleged wrongdoer. The group must be so numerous that it is impracticable to bring all members before the court individually.

Actual fees charged for legal services are difficult to compare because of the many factors used in setting fees in specific cases. Different fee rates exist in different parts of the country. Hourly fees are higher in large cities than in rural areas. Fees change over time and are at least somewhat related to the general economy. A flat fee for a simple divorce, with no significant property or child custody dispute, may be $1,000; complex divorces for wealthy clients, on the other hand, may command fees in the tens of thousands of dollars. Contingency fees are rarely less than 25 percent of the net recovery or more than 50 percent. Astronomical fees may be charged in celebrated cases involving **class actions**. In a class action lawsuit, the plaintiff represents the interests of a group (persons who are similarly situated) that otherwise is too unwieldy for courts to handle on an individual, case-by-case basis. Overhead costs prevent large firms from profitably handling legal matters in which small sums (less than $25,000–$50,000) are in dispute.

The following important factors normally are taken into consideration in setting an attorney's fee:

- The time required
- The degree of legal skill needed and novelty of the legal question presented
- The customary fee charged in the locality for similar services

- The experience, reputation, and ability of the attorney
- The amount of money involved in the case
- The result obtained for the client
- Whether or not the case precluded the lawyer from accepting other legal work
- The nature and length of the attorney's relationship with the client
- Time constraints imposed by the client
- Whether the fee is fixed or contingent

The client should understand the possible conflicts inherent in various fee arrangements. With a contingency fee arrangement, depending on how it is structured, either the attorney or the client "wants" a quick settlement, whereas the other would be better off by proceeding through trial. In a flat fee arrangement, the lawyer may have an incentive to dispose of the case as quickly as possible. An attorney paid by the hour might be tempted to overwork the case (i.e., with exhaustive research and discovery).

In addition, a fee charged by an attorney may be set by, or subject to the approval of, the court. An example of this would be fees of attorneys appointed to represent indigents or minors. When a fee limitation is applicable (by statute or court order), the client should ask whether the fee is prescribed or is a maximum allowed by law. In many cases, the statutory fee is a maximum, and the client is free to negotiate payment of a lower fee (e.g., a probate fee).

Many countries, including Great Britain, provide that attorney fees (as well as court costs) are to be paid by the loser in a case.* In contrast, in the United States, parties usually are responsible for their own attorney fees, unless they agreed otherwise. For example, a landlord suing a renter for past-due rent might benefit from a lease providing that the renter is to reimburse the landlord for any attorney fees incurred in collecting rent or enforcing the lease (this clause is commonly found in rental agreements). Many state statutes provide that if such a provision exists in the contract, it will be construed to give the victor in the legal dispute, be it the landlord or the tenant, the right to reimbursement of legal fees. Even if a contract states that it only protects the landlord, the tenant will be awarded attorney fees upon winning the lawsuit. The statute trumps the contract provisions. The loser always pays the court costs. Who pays the attorney fees, however, can end up having important ramifications.

A person who is unable to settle a fee dispute with an attorney through direct negotiation should contact the local bar association. Many state or local bar associations sponsor attorney fee arbitration programs. Often a mutually satisfactory result can be achieved without further legal action. In California, for example, arbitration is voluntary for the client and mandatory for the attorney if commenced by the client.

LEGAL FOCUS—PROBLEM

John Tyson, owner of a Burger King franchise, wanted to fire Jason Yohn. He suspected Yohn of repeatedly failing to wash his hands after using the bathroom. A posted policy required all employees to wash their hands after using the bathroom. Tyson hired attorney Lisa Beck to advise him. Beck explained that the law had to be researched and that a written opinion would be prepared.

*Like most things, what appears simple at first blush is not quite so. In the United Kingdom, the general rule is that the loser is responsible for reasonable attorney fees (and costs) of the prevailing party. Many low-income persons in Great Britain, however, are eligible for a government-funded legal aid program. Such persons are not subject to the cost-shifting rule.

Convinced of Beck's self-proclaimed expertise, Tyson left her office. Unbeknownst to Tyson, Beck assigned the Tyson file to a summer law student intern. The intern did all the research and prepared an opinion as to whether or not Tyson could fire Jason based upon the firm's database of hundreds of letters to previous clients on the subject of when employees may be fired. Beck glanced at the report and asked her secretary to send it to Tyson under her signature with a bill showing seven hours at $250 per hour for a total of $1,750. Beck's law firm paid its summer interns $20 per hour. Has Beck violated any ethical rules?

Tyson would have no basis to suspect that anything was out of the ordinary. Oftentimes, the lawyer with whom a client meets does not perform all the legal services for the client. As far as the billing is concerned, attorneys are free to charge whatever they choose for their services and do not disclose routinely the names of persons to whom the work is delegated. The point is that you should enter into a legal service agreement like any other service agreement, understanding your rights and being vigilant in protecting your interests.

Financing Attorney Fees

In some instances, a client may need to borrow money to pay attorney fees. A loan may be procured from a lending institution, a third person (e.g., a relative), or the attorney. If the attorney finances the debt, the client must sign a promissory note. This arrangement may create a conflict of interest, because the attorney becomes both a creditor and an agent of the client. An attorney may not use unreasonable collection methods; such conduct is unethical. Some attorneys refuse to extend credit to clients for the same reason that attorneys take cases only on retainer: They do not want to sue their client.

Financing the Client's Case

As a legal case progresses, costs often are incurred long before any recovery is possible. The following are costs in a typical personal injury case:

- *Medical examination:* The physical and sometimes mental condition of the victim is an issue in an injury case. Before trial, a physician probably will make one or more medical examinations. Some physicians specialize in examination of injury victims (and later provide testimony in court) rather than the treatment of patients, for a fee.
- *Court costs:* The court charges fees (e.g., $300) to cover at least some administrative costs of processing the paperwork connected with litigation. Other court charges are made for items such as daily fees paid to each juror in a jury trial (e.g., $20).
- *Investigation:* Most attorneys lack the time, skill, or inclination to inspect personally the accident scene, photograph it, and talk to potential witnesses. These and similar tasks often are performed by a professional investigator.
- *Discovery:* Sworn testimony is taken before a court reporter, usually in the office of the attorney who made the request. The session may be recorded, either in audio or video form. Discovery is usually expensive, involving transcription costs as well as attorney fees.
- *Expert witness fees:* Court testimony from experts is often necessary, and they are well paid for their time.

These expenses can total many thousands of dollars. Most of these expenses are incurred whether or not—and certainly long before—any recovery is awarded and received.

Under the ABA Model Rules of Professional Conduct, an attorney is permitted to "advance" litigation costs even though she or he arguably is invested in the outcome of the client's case. The attorney might be tempted to suggest an early settlement not because it is in the client's best interest, but rather to recapture costs advanced as well as to participate in the recovery. In the past, ABA rules permitted this practice only if the client was ultimately responsible for reimbursing the attorney. The reimbursement requirement was believed to militate against possible conflict of interest between the attorney and the client. The requirement that the client remain ultimately liable for such expenses has been eliminated. The attorney's duty to require reimbursement raises interesting ethical questions. Strictly speaking, payment of court costs for the client is **maintenance**, which is maintaining, supporting, or promoting the litigation of another. Maintenance is considered unethical and illegal because it encourages litigation.

maintenance
Assisting a party to a lawsuit with money or otherwise, to prosecute or defend the lawsuit.

Assuming the fee is contingent and the lawsuit is successful, litigation costs may be shared by the plaintiff and plaintiff's attorney. For example—

Gross recovery (in damages or settlement)		$200,000
Less net litigation costs incurred by the plaintiff's lawyer		
Total out-of-pocket litigation costs incurred (e.g., filing fees, investigation costs)	($35,000)	
Portion of court costs recovered from unsuccessful litigant (e.g., jury fees reimbursed by defendant)	$5,000	($30,000)
Net recovery		$170,000
Less attorney's fee (35 percent of net recovery)		($59,500)
Client recovery after deduction of all expenses		$110,500

Litigation costs may be modest in some types of cases, such as a simple divorce, whereas litigation costs in antitrust cases may be hundreds of thousands or even millions of dollars in celebrated cases involving major corporations.

LEGAL FOCUS—PROBLEM

Charles Hall brought a lawsuit against several defendants, alleging patent infringement regarding his waterbed innovations. To finance the lawsuit, he syndicated interests in the possible outcome of the suits. He raised $750,000. May he finance his lawsuit in this fashion?

champerty
An illegal agreement with a party to a suit for a portion of any recovery in exchange for paying the litigant's lawsuit expenses.

No, he may not finance his lawsuit in this fashion. The doctrine of **champerty** forbids one from financially participating in the lawsuit of another. Champerty is an illegal agreement between a litigant and someone who agrees to finance the litigation in return for a portion of the outcome if the litigant is successful. Society's concern is that investment in cases by outsiders encourages gambling and litigation.

WHAT IS LEGAL MALPRACTICE?

legal malpractice
Violation of a duty of due care by a professional person.

Legal malpractice is a civil cause of action that may be brought by a client against an attorney for negligence or intentional wrongdoing. Negligence arises, in this context, out of attorney carelessness or professional misconduct. A wrongful act is not sufficient to prove malpractice. The client must have suffered a loss as a consequence of the bad act. The remedy for negligence is money damages. The tort of negligence, of which legal malpractice is but one example, is discussed in detail in Chapter 7. In all states, attorneys have a legal duty of care to the client. The standard of care has been described in various ways, but generally, an attorney is required to possess legal knowledge and skill and exercise due care and diligence. Attorney specialists are held to higher standards than other attorneys. If the attorney fails to meet the standard of care and this failure has caused the client to suffer a loss, legal malpractice has occurred.

To recover damages for attorney malpractice, the client probably will hire a second attorney to pursue the case against the first. This prospect is undoubtedly unpleasant for a client who already has suffered a loss. A malpractice suit must be initiated within the applicable statute of limitations, usually within one to three years from the time of the negligent act(s).

At trial, the plaintiff must prove that, but for the attorney's negligence, the result in the earlier matter would have been more favorable to the client. The accused may deny the charge or contend, "Yes, I may have been negligent, but the result was fair, adequate, and reasonable." Legal malpractice cases are difficult to prove. Even when clients win a case, they still face the problem of collecting the judgment. Attorneys who commit serious malpractice also may be the least able to pay a sizable judgment and the least likely to have purchased adequate malpractice insurance. In many states, lawyers are not required to carry malpractice insurance, although many do. When selecting an attorney, it is reasonable and prudent to ask whether the attorney carries malpractice insurance.

It is important to distinguish between legal malpractice and disciplinary actions against an attorney. Legal malpractice actions are brought in civil court by the client seeking compensation for loss caused by the attorney's failure to exercise due care. Professional misconduct actions are brought by the state disciplinary authority, usually the state bar, seeking punishment of the attorney for ethical rules violations. The client does not normally receive any compensation as a consequence of a disciplinary action. An ethical rule violation is relevant to show failure to meet the standard of care, but it is not conclusive.

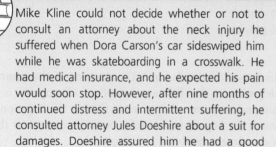

LEGAL FOCUS—PROBLEM

Mike Kline could not decide whether or not to consult an attorney about the neck injury he suffered when Dora Carson's car sideswiped him while he was skateboarding in a crosswalk. He had medical insurance, and he expected his pain would soon stop. However, after nine months of continued distress and intermittent suffering, he consulted attorney Jules Doeshire about a suit for damages. Doeshire assured him he had a good case and prepared a contingency fee retainer agreement, which Kline signed. Several months later (thirteen months after the accident), attorney Doeshire contacted Kline and said that after further study he concluded that Kline really did not have a good case after all. "But don't worry; I won't charge you a cent," Doeshire told Kline. What should Kline do?

Mike Kline should be suspicious and request a complete explanation of why the matter should be dropped. Kline should consult another attorney, as it appears that Doeshire committed malpractice by failing to file the complaint within the statute of limitations. Once attorneys accept cases, it is their obligation to comply with procedural requirements. Failure to file documents within statutory time limits is one of the most common acts of malpractice. An attorney is not guilty of malpractice just because a case is lost. In every case with two or more adversaries, someone must lose and someone must win. A strategic decision that subsequently turns out to be disastrous is not necessarily malpractice.

Attorney malpractice encompasses a wide variety of negligent acts and omissions: failure to apply settled principles of law to the case, failure to protect the right to appeal, failure to draft pleadings (court-related documents) properly and promptly, failure to appear and defend, failure to assert all possible claims or defenses, failure to act in accordance with professional ethical standards, failure to present relevant evidence, lack of diligence in prosecuting a case once initiated, and improperly drafting a will. An ounce of prevention in the careful selection of an attorney is worth a pound of cure.

UNAUTHORIZED PRACTICE OF LAW

Practicing law without a license is a crime, just as practicing medicine or dentistry without a license is a crime. Contracts for legal services by a nonattorney are void as matter of law and are unenforceable. A nonlawyer may not use the courts to collect a fee for legal services. Any payment made by the client is recoverable.

As discussed earlier in the chapter, licensure is a prerequisite to practice in all states. A person who does not have, or who fails to maintain, a license to practice law is forbidden to practice. It is sometimes difficult to decide whether a given act constitutes the practice of law or simply the performance of related activities. Different states provide different answers. For example, in some states, it is common for title companies to conduct title searches when real property is sold (albeit with the aid of in-house staff attorneys). In other states, independent attorneys perform this activity. Nonlawyers (such as real estate brokers) generally are permitted to complete blanks on forms that may affect legal rights. These must be standard forms, however, and no legal advice may be offered with the forms. Accountants prepare tax returns and suggest probable tax consequences but must be careful not to interpret tax statutes, rules, or cases or render tax planning legal advice.

Today there is popular support for relaxing the historical prohibition against the unauthorized practice of law arguing that legal assistants, paralegals, and legal technicians should be permitted to handle routine legal matters. Legal assistants under the direction of lawyers already often perform such work. Lawyer supervision adds to the cost of such services, causing some consumers and nonlawyer providers to question whether the public is being protected or exploited. Routine matters usually include uncontested divorce pleadings, simple wills, eviction notices, simple bankruptcy filings, and probate of small estates. Exhibit 4.1 identifies the "practice of law" and other related legal work done by legal assistants under supervision of lawyers.

Some critics contend that routine legal services can be delivered to the consumer at lower cost, with higher pay for the legal service technician, by eliminating a superfluous middle person—the attorney. There is, however, strong opposition to the relaxation of unauthorized-practice laws. The concern is that the dividing line between what is and what is not the practice of law will become even more confused and risky for consumers.

Many people do not know or appreciate the difference in the education backgrounds of legal assistants and attorneys. Others disregard the difference and hire nonattorneys because their fees are lower. These choices can and often do compromise the consumer's ability to succeed at law. Furthermore, it is difficult if not impossible to predetermine what is simple and routine. Every attorney has been told by a client, "I just want a simple will,"

EXHIBIT 4.1 Legal Work Requiring a Law License and Legal Work That Can Be Performed by Nonlawyers under Lawyer Supervision

Practice of Law	Work That May Be Done by Nonlawyers When Supervised by Lawyer*
Accept a case	Obtain facts from client and other sources
Negotiate a fee agreement	Communicate information to client
Evaluate a case and determine strategy	Interview witnesses
Provide legal analysis	Perform legal research to assist lawyer with legal analysis
Give legal advice	Obtain documents (e.g., police reports, medical records, photographs, employment records, deeds, plans, probate records, weather records)
Represent a client in court (e.g., depositions, hearings, trials)	
Supervise legal assistants	Prepare chronologies and summaries
Appear at administrative hearings	Prepare itemization of claims
Select, explain, draft, or recommend the use of any legal document to any client	Prepare outlines for lawyer to use in deposing witnesses
Contract with a client to provide paralegal services	Prepare drafts of judicial documents, such as pleadings or discovery
	Index deposition transcripts and prepare summaries of the evidence
	Prepare exhibit lists
	Analyze collected information and make an in dependent decision and recommendation to a supervising attorney
	If permitted by state statute, court rule, or administrative rule, represent clients before a state or federal administrative agency

*But performed under the supervision of a lawyer.

Sources: Adapted from American Bar Association, Section of Law Practice Management, "Leveraging with Legal Assistants" (Chicago: ABA, 1993), 20.

only to discover that either the client's circumstances or more detailed desires make that impossible.

Do-it-yourself probate kits (designed to assist the personal representative, executor, or administrator with necessary procedures following death) and divorce kits are not considered to be the practice of law because the information is generalized and not tailored to the needs of a particular client. In recent years, many self-help books and software in a variety of legal areas have become available.

ALTERNATIVE DISPUTE RESOLUTION

Discourage litigation. Persuade your neighbors to compromise whenever you can. Point out to them how the nominal winner is often a real loser—in fees, expenses, and waste of time. As a peacemaker the lawyer has a superior opportunity of being a good man.

Abraham Lincoln (1809–1865), U.S. president

These words of Abraham Lincoln remain true. They suggest that persons who are considering litigation should think twice and consider alternatives to litigation such as negotiation, mediation, and arbitration whenever possible. **Alternative dispute resolution (ADR)** is a broad term used to describe methods of resolving disputes through means other than the traditional judicial process. When clients seek the advice of counsel in a civil matter, attorneys have an obligation to inform them about the availability and appropriateness of ADR. Failure to do so may be a violation of ethical rules or the basis for attorney malpractice.

alternative dispute resolution (ADR)
Various methods of resolving disputes through means other than the judicial process.

As stated earlier, courts are available to resolve all manner of disputes, be they complicated or simple. U.S. courts seek to protect the fundamental liberties of free speech, press, assembly, and religion, and they are available to decide such trivia as who gets to keep the dog in a dissolution of marriage. The traditional justice system requires parties to delegate resolution authority to a judge or jury who considers the issue of law. Typically, one side wins, and the other loses. Often, neither side is truly satisfied.

Litigation is complicated and burdensome. It is costly in terms of time, money, goodwill, peace of mind, and lost productivity. Small claims courts provide relief from complicated and costly legal procedures, but only in matters involving small sums of money. There are times when it is not feasible or desirable to seek justice through the courts. Sometimes, the law fails to recognize rights or wrongs. (Recall from Chapter 1 the killing of Kitty Genovese.)

In the latter years of the twentieth century, significant developments in ADR occurred in response to lengthy court delays. Efficiency-conscious business managers have been active in the search for effective dispute resolution methods for just this reason. Businesses can suffer financial losses from delays.

One of the primary causes of court delay has been increased court filings coupled with a shortage of judges and other court personnel. Population growth, too much crime, too many persons wanting to sue, too many laws, and complex government regulations have contributed to increases in filings. Budget deficits have made it difficult to hire more judges. The number of criminal matters brought to court has grown faster than civil cases. Because criminal matters take priority over civil matters, judges who otherwise would be available to hear civil cases are hearing criminal cases. The increased volume of filings has extended greatly the time necessary to resolve civil disputes, especially in major metropolitan areas. The courts and legislatures have acted in response to the enormous economic, social, and emotional costs that delay imposes. A myriad of statutes and court rules at the state and federal levels expressly encourages or requires the use of alternative dispute resolution. Fast-track programs designed to streamline the litigation process and bring cases to trial quickly have been implemented in many court systems. They have not relieved the problem completely, however.

Although delay has provided the motivation for government to encourage the use of ADR, many believe that a commonsense approach to resolving disputes suggests its use as well. Not all disputes are best resolved using litigation, which raises the important question of which methods are best for what disputes. A common saying among ADR proponents is, "The forum should fit the fuss."

LEGAL FOCUS—PROBLEM

Tanda Holden not only liked rap music, she liked it loud and late. Occupying her first house, she really appreciated freedom from repeated parental insistence that she "turn that thing down." Evan and Juanita Jenkins lived next door in the house they had lived in for forty years. After one week of 3:00 A.M. concerts, Evan Jenkins was unable to hide his anger. Dressed in his robe, he stormed over to Holden's house and shouted, "Turn the blessed thing off!" Holden was annoyed and shouted back, "I didn't move to get new parents. Anyway, it's a free country!" Then she turned the volume even higher. How do the Jenkinses get some sleep?

The Jenkinses have a number of legal options. They can phone the police, who will ask Holden to show more consideration for her neighbors. Holden is probably disturbing the peace, and the Jenkinses could file a criminal complaint against her. They also can seek civil redress by suing Holden and claiming nuisance—a tort. In such an action, the Jenkinses can claim money damages for past harm and request an injunction (equitable relief) prohibiting the loud music as a continuing nuisance.

The practical problem with all of these remedies is that they are costly in time, money, and tranquility. The Jenkinses could go to small claims court, where the cost of litigation is minimal, but it still will be time consuming and a drain on their peace of mind. Moreover, courtroom resolution ignores the fact that the parties will still live next door to each other after legal actions conclude. The root of many problems referred to the courts is a defective human relationship, and such a relationship may continue and worsen after judicial intervention. The adversarial nature of a trial usually aggravates and exaggerates existing hard feelings. Neighboring parties thus often find new reasons to argue and land in court again.

Likewise, court resolution of business-related disputes may not be in the best interest of the contesting parties. Examples include consumer product disputes that affect company public relations and product reception, disputes over medical care in health maintenance organizations (HMOs), and environmental disputes that will affect community-government relations for years. With increasing frequency, business and government agencies are using ADR techniques in such cases instead of and in addition to the courts. Not only are such techniques usually easier and cheaper to use than the courts, they are more likely to lead to improved long-term understandings and harmony. The most common types of ADR are as follows:

- Negotiation
- Mediation
- Arbitration
- Med-arb
- Private judging
- Ombudsperson
- Expert fact-finding
- Early neutral evaluation
- Mini-trial
- Summary jury trial
- Collaborative law practice
- Partnering

Exhibit 4.2 compares the three most common types of ADR with a lawsuit.

Negotiation
Communication between disputing parties for the purposes of persuasion and settlement or resolution.

Negotiation

Negotiation is defined as two-way communication for the purpose of persuasion. It is a bargaining process in which parties plan the future, structure a transaction, or fix a problem. It is voluntary and informal. Parties communicate directly with each other or

EXHIBIT 4.2 Comparison of Alternative Dispute Resolution Methods with a Lawsuit

Characteristic	Negotiation	Mediation	Arbitration	Court Trial
Private or public process?	Private	Private	Private	Public
Who decides?	Parties	Parties	Arbitrator	Judge or jury
Adversary or cooperative?	Cooperative	Cooperative	Adversary	Adversary
Elapsed time to conclusion?	As long or short as it takes	As long or short as it takes	Usually two to eighteen months	Usually one to five years (plus appeal, if any)
Cost of process?	Low	Low	Medium to high	High
Appeal?	Unnecessary	Unnecessary	Few grounds	Full right of appeal
Procedural rules?	Decided by parties	Decided by parties	Few and simple	Complex
Need attorney?	No	No	Yes	Yes
Discovery process?	No	No	Minimal allowed	Extensive allowed
Right to jury?	Unnecessary	Unnecessary	No	Yes, in most cases
Permanent record in files?	No	No	No	Yes

through representatives and agents. All manner of agreements and disagreements are negotiated. It is a common, everyday occurrence. Lawyers constantly negotiate on behalf of clients. Typically, by the time a dispute is referred to a lawyer, negotiation is thought to have failed. Negotiation that continues after a lawsuit is filed is then considered part of litigation strategy, and it may be premised on adversarial objectives and tactics. But as an ADR process, negotiation is based on a collaborative or problem-solving viewpoint. When parties approach negotiations from a collaborative perspective, the process is more pleasant, the agreement more satisfying, and the commitment to the agreement more solid.

Although we all negotiate, most people can substantially improve their negotiation skills by observing a few rules. In recent years, several books (perhaps the most significant is Fisher, Ury, and Patton's *Getting to Yes*) have stressed the importance and art of negotiation. Because the point of negotiation is to persuade, careful consideration of how best to present your views and seek acceptable results is important. Thus, effective negotiation requires preparation.

Negotiation, like most skills, can be improved. Indeed, it can be improved continually. Skilled athletes do not stop trying to improve when they reach a certain level; in the same manner, one can always refine one's negotiating skills. Many effective negotiation techniques can be learned, including using supportable arguments, avoiding personalizing the dispute, giving as well as taking, and attempting to establish a relationship with the other party. The skills can be utilized in legal disputes or everyday matters. Using even a few such techniques can improve most people's success rates.

There is utility in characterizing negotiation as a form of ADR. It legitimizes informal problem solving in the eyes of clients and lawyers. It may encourage the lawyer to negotiate earlier in the dispute, perhaps even before filing. Doing so enhances the possibility of success.

In contentious situations, parties often begin by demanding recognition of rights and a remedy of grievances by the other side. The response is generally a counter, demanding similar recognition. At this point, neither party is really negotiating with the other. Neither is attempting to persuade; instead, they are talking at, not with, each other, although attempts at persuasion may follow.

In our hypothetical problem, Evan Jenkins did not try to persuade Tanda Holden to turn down the volume of her music; he issued an ultimatum. Negotiation might have been more successful. If Jenkins tried negotiating, with or without the assistance of a neutral party, and failed, he could still complain to the authorities (criminal action) and bring suit (civil action). Only if Jenkins and Holden agreed to arbitrate the claim would Jenkins irrevocably substitute ADR for the traditional trial process. In other words, Jenkins, like most persons with legal problems, would have had little, if anything, to lose by attempting to negotiate a resolution to the dispute.

Mediation

mediation
The use of a neutral third party to assist parties in voluntarily resolving their dispute(s).

The preservation of relationships, which is valued in negotiation, is also a goal of mediation. **Mediation** is a facilitative process in which contending parties negotiate their own resolution to a problem with the assistance of a third-party neutral, the mediator. The mediator is not a judge and cannot decide the case. The mediator sets the tone for the mediation and controls the process, but the parties control the result. The mediator uses open-ended, nonthreatening questions, which expose facts and feelings, which is the information needed to resolve the conflict. Questions such as, "How do you feel about what happened?" open points for discussion and resolution, and they can be effective to show a willingness to cooperate.

The process and the resolution are confidential unless the parties agree otherwise. To encourage settlement, statements made in the course of mediation are inadmissible in a subsequent adjudicative proceeding. The neutral may be an individual (mediator) or a panel of two or three members (panel). The defining feature of the mediation process is that the parties themselves determine how to structure their interactions (procedural matters) and decide the outcome (settlement).

Mediation works best when the parties participate voluntarily and in good faith. (There is precedent for mandatory mediation, but most agree that the process is less satisfying and compliance with settlements is more elusive.) The mediator convenes a meeting of the parties and helps them to get started. When negotiations break down, the mediator encourages the parties to continue. Unlike judges, who are assigned to cases at random, mediators are selected carefully by mutual agreement of the parties. Mediators are chosen for their skills in facilitating conflict analysis, bargaining, and consensus building. A mediator is not necessarily trained as a judge or even as a lawyer. In commercial cases, it is not uncommon to find architects, engineers, and general contractors serving as mediators. In family law cases, the mediator may have training as a social worker or psychologist. The individual must be a good listener and an effective communicator. The parties' perception of the individual's integrity, fairness, and subject-matter expertise is critical. Significantly, the mediator has no power to impose a resolution to a dispute. This feature distinguishes mediation from trials and arbitrations. In practice, different mediators apply varying amounts of pressure to get parties to settle.

Conciliation
Use of a third party to lower tensions, improve communications, and explore possible solutions to a conflict.

Sometimes, mediation is confused with conciliation. **Conciliation** is an ADR process, similar to mediation, in which the neutral actively attempts to get acceptance of proposals for settlement. In both conciliation and mediation, the third party attempts to lower tensions, improve communications, and explore possible solutions to a conflict. In mediation, the neutral is less involved in finding the resolution to the conflict. The mediator helps the parties develop, communicate, and bargain for solutions on their own. Theoretically, the mediator does not advocate a position. In practice, conciliation and mediation are difficult to discern because the terms often are used interchangeably.

caucus
A private confidential meeting between disputants and a third-party neutral.

Some mediators meet with the parties separately in a private meeting called a **caucus**. Others do not. A caucus is a safe place for parties to disclose information that they would be reluctant to reveal in a joint session. It provides an opportunity for parties to avoid confrontation and save face, and a way for the mediator to do a reality check—all in confidence. The mediator can act as a messenger—in a sort of shuttle diplomacy—to convey one party's concession(s) and offer to the other side. Sometimes, the parties permit the mediator to divulge secrets or proprietary information. Service providers and professional organizations have developed standards of practice in an effort to ameliorate some differences in form and to gain wider acceptance of the process.

American Arbitration Association (AAA)
A private nonprofit organization with the purpose of providing education, training, and administrative assistance to parties who use nonjudicial methods—that is, alternative dispute resolution (ADR)—for resolving disputes.

Parties generally split the cost of mediation. Mediators usually charge an hourly rate for their services, although some charge a flat rate or *per diem*. Service provider organizations, such as the **American Arbitration Association (AAA)**, charge an additional administrative fee, which may either be a flat amount or be tacked on to the mediator's hourly rate. In major metropolitan areas, it is possible to engage the services of a mediator at no or low cost through community-based organizations known as neighborhood dispute centers. These centers provide mediation training and services in neighbor–neighbor, landlord–tenant, and family conflicts. Although mediation has been used in labor and insurance disputes for many years, its acceptance in commercial and other types of disputes has grown significantly only since the 1980s.

The most serious barrier to use of mediation is ignorance of the features and benefits of the process. It is a challenge to get parties to agree to mediation when they have been socialized to believe that the only way to resolve a dispute, once and for all, is to let a judge or jury decide it. Attorneys are sometimes reluctant to mediate a case. They believe they are at a disadvantage if they mediate and later proceed to trial, because their trial strategies will be discovered during the mediation process.

The mediation process usually involves some compromise, and people often are stubborn. They either do not want to compromise or believe no compromise is possible. The dispute between Tanda Holden and the Jenkinses is the type that usually is best solved through mediation. A local neighborhood dispute center could be the resolution forum for a neighbor–neighbor conflict like loud nighttime music. The mutual understanding that is required for a long-term solution is seldom achieved through a criminal or civil court process. The record of neighborhood mediation on such cases has been excellent—substantially more effective than court resolution. The most difficult task in mediation is getting both parties to agree to use the process.

Arbitration

arbitration
An alternative to litigation whereby conflicting parties select a neutral third party (or parties) to hear and decide their dispute. Arbitration can be binding or nonbinding.

award
The final decision of an arbitrator or other nonjudicial officer in the resolution of a dispute.

Arbitration is the most formal of the ADR processes. **Arbitration** is a process of dispute resolution in which one or more impartial third persons (arbitrator) renders a decision after a hearing at which both parties have an opportunity to be heard. Whereas mediation is facilitative and conciliatory, arbitration is adjudicative and adversarial, like a court proceeding. Notably, arbitrators have the power to impose a resolution; they are private judges. The arbitrator conducts a hearing and acts as finder of both law and fact (as both judge and jury). Attorneys usually present their clients' case: The claimant first and then the respondent. Then, the arbitrator decides the case and issues a written disposition, known as an **award**, usually within thirty days. There is little direct negotiation between the parties.

The Federal Arbitration Act (FAA) provides for the enforceability of a written arbitration provision in any maritime transaction or contract involving interstate commerce, and declares that such agreements "shall be valid, irrevocable, and enforceable, save upon such grounds as exist at law or in equity for the revocation of any contract" (9 U.S.C. § 2). Supreme Court precedents sanction arbitration as a dispute resolution mechanism, as well. Commercial business, consumer, and employment disputes are arbitrated by such organizations as the National Arbitration Forum (NAF) and the AAA.

LEGAL FOCUS—CASE

A provision in an employee's application for work at an electronics retailer required all employment disputes to be settled by arbitration. The employee subsequently filed a state-law employment discrimination action against his employer. The employer claimed that the Federal Arbitration Act (FAA) permitted the dispute to be arbitrated, but the employee countered that employment contracts could not be arbitrated because of an exemption in the FAA, which provides that the Act shall not apply to "contracts of employment of seamen, railroad employees, or any other class of workers engaged in foreign or interstate commerce." What is the scope of the exemption?

Circuit City Stores, Inc. v. Adams, 532 U.S. 105 (2001).

The Supreme Court interpreted the phrase "engaged in commerce" broadly in light of the pro-arbitration purposes of the FAA, and confined the exclusion to contracts of employment of transportation workers, rather than all employment contracts. Other statutory claims, such as those involving securities law and consumers, can be resolved through arbitration, as well. In determining whether or not federal statutory claims may be arbitrated, courts first must examine whether the parties agreed to submit their claims to arbitration, and then decide whether Congress intended to preclude a waiver of judicial remedies for the statutory rights at issue.

Compared with other forms of ADR, arbitration is formal, but it is less formal than a court trial. Arbitration rules are more flexible than court rules. Procedural rules are determined by the parties. Discovery is limited, and the rules of evidence are relaxed dramatically. Virtually any commercial matter can be submitted to arbitration. It commonly is used to resolve complex cases, including international commercial disputes. The number of businesses that use arbitration grows every year.

In its pure form, arbitration is a voluntary process that concludes with a final resolution of the dispute, outside the public court system. So long as there is mutual assent, the parties have wide discretion in deciding when arbitration is appropriate, who will hear and decide the case, the time and location of the hearing, what arbitration rules will apply, and whether or not the decision will be binding. Parties typically agree to arbitrate before a claim arises by including an arbitration clause in their contract. Parties also may agree to arbitrate after a claim arises. (*Note:* Arbitrations are convened less often in tort cases because parties usually do not have a prior contractual relationship.) Exhibit 4.3 shows some sample arbitration clauses. Most arbitration clauses provide for binding arbitration, meaning the award is final. All state and federal courts have the power under statute to enforce an arbitrator's award, if that becomes necessary. A losing party may appeal an arbitrator's decision to a court. Courts seldom overturn arbitration awards, however, except in cases of serious arbitrator misconduct—for example, fraud or oppression. Even a clear mistake of law is not grounds for overturning an arbitration award. Parties who have agreed to binding arbitration are not allowed to change their minds if they lose the case—not for any reason.

The parties generally are free to set the rules in arbitration. The AAA and other service provider organizations have created procedural rules and provide administrative

EXHIBIT 4.3 Sample Arbitration Clauses

Predispute Clauses
Any controversy or claim arising out of or related to this contract, or the breach thereof, shall be settled by arbitration administered by the American Arbitration Association (AAA) under its Commercial Arbitration Rules, and judgment on the award rendered by the arbitrator(s) may be entered in any court having jurisdiction thereof.

Postdispute Clause
We, the undersigned parties, hereby agree to submit to arbitration administered by the American Arbitration Association under its Commercial Arbitration Rules the following controversy: (Cite briefly).

We further agree that the above controversy be submitted to (one) (three) arbitrator(s). We further agree that we will faithfully observe this agreement and the rules, that we will abide by and perform any award rendered by the arbitrator(s), and that a judgment of the court having jurisdiction may be entered on the award.

Source: Reprinted with permission of the American Arbitration Association.

assistance for parties seeking arbitration. Parties are free to incorporate these standardized rules into their contracts or adopt them when a dispute arises. Parties also may modify the rules or develop their own.

Unlike judges, who are assigned to cases at random, arbitrators are selected by mutual agreement of the parties. Arbitrators are chosen for their integrity, fairness, and subject-matter expertise. Arbitrators are not trained as judges or even lawyers necessarily, but most are. Parties may agree on any number of arbitrators; it is common to have one arbitrator in a small dispute and three arbitrators when dollar damages are high. Because arbitration awards can be binding and appeals are seldom successful, the choice of arbitrator is critical.

In common usage, the term *arbitration* means binding arbitration. However, there are forms of nonbinding arbitration. In addition, there are hybrids that use arbitration in conjunction with other processes. One needs to be familiar with the hybrid to discern whether the component arbitration process is binding. ADR terms are used interchangeably by practitioners, in part because the processes are so adaptable. To avoid confusion, it is important to ask whether or not the process is binding and to watch your language.

court-annexed arbitration
A type of nonbinding arbitration required by some courts before the parties may proceed to trial.

med-arb
An alternative dispute resolution (ADR) process that combines mediation and arbitration.

Two common types of arbitration are court-annexed arbitration and med-arb. **Court-annexed arbitration** is a mandatory, usually nonbinding process, required by statute prior to trial. Awards may be appealed and a *trial de novo* granted. Nonbinding awards may become binding if neither side appeals. **Med-arb** combines mediation and arbitration in one proceeding. A neutral party is appointed to mediate the dispute. If mediation fails, the neutral party is authorized to resolve the dispute with a binding award. Med-arb is utilized when parties who prefer to bargain directly want assurance that if they reach an impasse, a neutral third party will decide the case. Some believe that the possibility of proceeding to the arbitration phase of the process changes the dynamics of the mediation. Parties are thought to be less candid for fear that disclosures made during the mediation will be used against them in the arbitration. Statements made in the course of mediation, however, are confidential and thus protected under law.

LEGAL FOCUS—CASE

Greene agreed to construct a residence for homeowners Hundley and Butt. The construction contract provided that "[a]ny controversy relating to the construction of the residence or any other matter arising out of the terms of this contract shall be settled by binding arbitration … conducted pursuant to the Rules of the American Arbitration Association with regard to the

Construction Industry Arbitration Rules." A construction dispute arose and was submitted for arbitration. After a two-day hearing, the arbitrator found for both parties and awarded $17,000 to the homeowners and $20,400 to Greene. The award lacked any explanation, and the homeowners contested the award. Must the arbitrator provide support for his or her award?

Greene et al., v. Hundley et al., 266 Ga. 392, 468 S.E. 2d 350 (Ga. 1996).

No, the arbitrator does not have to support his or her award. "[T]he Arbitration Code does not require that an arbitrator enter written findings of fact in support of an award; nor does the Code require an arbitrator to explain the reasoning behind an award." Of course, the terms of the parties' agreement to arbitrate or the applicable arbitration rules may require the arbitrator to give a reason for the decision. Some arbitrators will issue a reasoned award upon request, but rarely. Although arbitration can be less expensive than litigation, some costs are associated with arbitration that are not present in litigation. Costs can include filing fees and administrative fees, as well as the fees of the arbitrators, which can be a substantial financial burden, especially if the arbitration agreement requires a panel of arbitrators. In contrast, the salaries of judges are paid by the government in the civil justice system. Also, fee-shifting statutes, which require courts to award attorney fees to the prevailing party, may or may not be applicable in an arbitration proceeding to mitigate costs.

LEGAL FOCUS—CASE

A consumer challenged an arbitration clause in a financing agreement for the purchase of a mobile home, contending that it was unenforceable due to potentially prohibitive costs. The consumer argued that the arbitration agreement's silence with respect to costs and fees created a risk of prohibitively high arbitration costs, which would result in the inevitable abandonment of any right to assert her statutory rights. Would such a possibility make the arbitration clause unenforceable?

Green Tree Financial Services Corp. v. Randolph, 531 U.S. 79 (2000).

The Supreme Court determined that, although the existence of substantially arbitration costs could preclude litigants from effectively vindicating federal statutory rights under the Truth in Lending Act (TILA) in an arbitration forum, the record in the case failed to show the amount of such costs. The Court suggested that the party seeking to avoid arbitration bears the burden of establishing that arbitration would be prohibitively expensive, as well as the likelihood of incurring such costs.

Legal Issues in Arbitration

Binding agreements to arbitrate raise important legal issues. When parties agree to binding arbitration, parties may unwittingly waive their right to some critical traditional due process (fairness) protections. We address these issues in a question and answer format below.

An agreement to arbitrate exists, but a party files a lawsuit rather than beginning arbitration. What are the responding party's options? The responding party could file an answer and proceed with the litigation. If both parties agree to litigate, they are free to do so. The right and obligation to arbitrate is created by contract and not imposed by law. Parties may thus waive the right to arbitration. The respondent is more likely to respond by filing a motion to compel arbitration. The court will decide whether a valid agreement to arbitrate exists. If so, the court will stay the litigation and order the plaintiff to proceed to arbitration. Statutes exist in all state and federal jurisdictions to permit such removal of cases from courts to arbitration. The underlying purpose of these rules is to require parties to comply with their agreement to arbitrate and to encourage the use of arbitration.

Can you conduct discovery in an arbitration process? The answer depends on whether or not the agreement to arbitrate provides for discovery. Most arbitration clauses are silent with respect to discovery. Sometimes, the right to perform discovery is incorporated into an agreement to arbitrate by reference to the arbitration rules of a specific provider (e.g., the AAA). Some state statutes provide that discovery must be allowed in certain types of claims, such as employment claims. If the agreement does not provide for discovery and it is not required by statute, it cannot be compelled.

Can witnesses be compelled to appear at an arbitration? In most states, arbitrators have the power to subpoena witnesses. State statutes that authorize judicial enforcement of arbitration awards also grant subpoena power to arbitrators.

Will the arbitrator provide a reasoned, written decision? The standard award states who the prevailing party is and the amount of damages. It does not explain how or why the arbitrator reached the decision. As with discovery, whether or not an arbitrator will write a reasoned decision depends on the terms of the agreement to arbitrate. If the agreement to arbitrate requires a reasoned award, then the arbitrator is bound to provide one. By tradition, reasoned decisions usually are provided in labor arbitrations but not in commercial arbitrations.

The arbitrator has decided the case, the award has been issued, and it is good news. You won a handsome sum. The losing party is not a good sport and refuses to pay. What do you do? The prevailing party may file a motion to confirm the award in all state and federal courts. If the motion is granted, the prevailing party may have the award entered as a final judgment. Entry as final judgment permits the prevailing party to enforce the award just as if the case had been decided by a court.

Can an arbitrator's award be appealed? Final arbitration awards may be appealed on limited grounds, under statute. Whereas most court decisions are challenged because the trial judge made an error of law, appeals of arbitration awards are rarely successful on these grounds. To successfully appeal an arbitration award, the losing party must allege and prove that the arbitration process was unfair (e.g., the arbitrator committed fraud or oppression). For example, a successful appeal could be based on the failure of an arbitrator to disclose a conflict of interest (prior dealings with one of the parties).

In recent years, predispute arbitration agreements have been subject to special scrutiny by the courts. Because arbitration is a creature of contract, parties to arbitration are free to devise the arbitration process in any way they see fit. Parties with greater bargaining power draft agreements that change the dispute resolution forum from a court to arbitration and present it to the weaker party on a "take-it-or-leave-it" basis. What appears to be a mere change in venue is a critical waiver of the weaker party's right to due process. Agreements like these favoring the interests of the stronger party are called adhesion contracts (see Chapter 8).

private judging
The use of a legally trained arbitrator who follows formal judicial procedures in hearing a case outside a court.

Private Judging

Private judging, also called *rent-a-judge*, allows parties to bypass the formal court system and take their cases to a private court. The proceedings have all the formalities of a public court. Private judging is permitted in many but not all states. Cases are tried before a referee who is selected and paid by the parties. Referees are often retired judges. In some states, including California, any member of the state bar can be a referee. Jurors can be selected from the public jury rolls to participate in such trials. State statutes authorize the referee to enter the decision in the trial court as a final judgment, if the parties choose. If so entered, the final judgment can be appealed to a state appellate court.

Private judging, much like arbitration, provides more flexibility and privacy than a court trial. With private judging, parties do not need to wait for a court date—if a referee is available, they can schedule the trial immediately. Parties are free to determine the procedural rules, but usually they agree to apply the formal rules used in the public courts, including the rules of evidence. Unlike with arbitration, however, parties have the right to appeal adverse rulings to the appellate courts.

The use of private judging is widespread, yet is the most controversial of the ADR processes. The rent-a-judge system has been disparagingly referred to as "Cadillac justice." Because the referees are paid entirely by the disputants, private judging allows disputants to bypass the public trial calendar only if they can afford to pay the judge. Parties who cannot afford it must wait their turn in the public courts. Private courts also are criticized because it is feared they may lure judges away from the public courts through early retirement. Judges are paid substantially more in fees by private clients than they earn as salaried public servants. Furthermore, hearings in private courts are not open to the public or the press. Wealthy corporations and other parties can shield their activities from the public eye and keep judgments confidential. Finally, some observers believe that this private justice system may delay or even relieve the legislature and the courts from making needed legal reforms.

Ombudsperson

ombudsperson
A proactive neutral party who investigates and determines facts and suggests resolutions to disputes.

An **ombudsperson or ombud** is a consultant or permanent employee of an organization hired to resolve conflicts that arise within the organization. This concept was developed in Scandinavia. There, an ombudsman was a public official appointed to investigate and hear citizen complaints against the government. In the United States, ombuds are present in both public and private institutions. The ombuds investigate, propose, and advocate solutions and often make public their independent findings and recommendations. The role of the ombud, like the mediator, is to facilitate resolution through better communication among the members of the group. Neither has authority to impose a settlement. Ombuds are distinguishable from mediators in that the ombud becomes actively involved in determining the facts and advocating solutions. Whereas mediators are expected to maintain neutrality throughout their service, ombuds start out neutral but are not required to remain so. Usually, the ombud is selected by one of the disputing parties and paid solely by that party. In contrast, mediator fees generally are shared by the disputants.

Expert Fact-Finding

expert fact-finding
A nonbinding process in which an appointed expert investigates or hears facts on selected issues. At the conclusion, he or she makes findings of fact.

Expert fact-finding is a process by which a neutral party with subject-matter expertise is appointed to conduct an independent investigation or take evidence on selected factual is sues in highly technical matters. The expert does not decide the case. The sole object is to determine what happened. Like other adjudicatory processes, attorneys present evidence to the neutral. At the conclusion, the expert makes an evaluation and issues findings of fact. The findings can be binding or nonbinding. Parties may adopt them in a subsequent conciliatory process or even admit them in arbitration or at trial. In a similar process, a special master, selected for his or her legal expertise, will determine the factual issues in cases set for trial. Negotiated settlements are more likely once the factual issues have been settled.

Early Neutral Evaluation

early neutral evaluation
An ADR process providing disputing parties with an early and candid evaluation by an objective observer of the merits of a case.

Early neutral evaluation is an evaluative process and typically is nonbinding. The objective of the process is to facilitate negotiations, not to decide the case. A neutral third party conducts a hearing and issues an opinion as to the merits of the case and the strengths and weaknesses of evidence and assesses the likely outcome at trial. The proceeding is not unlike a trial, but it is brief. Oral presentations are limited to a summary of the key issues in the case. Written submissions are extremely limited in length. The attorney plays a critical role in this process. Because the proceeding is expected to be brief, the attorney must be skilled in oral advocacy. Early neutral evaluation is appropriate for cases in which parties have valued a case unrealistically and in which fault has been established but damages are hotly contested.

Mini-Trial

mini-trial
A private, voluntary, informal form of dispute resolution in which attorneys for each disputant make a brief presentation of their best case before officials for each side who have authority to settle.

A **mini-trial** is a voluntary, nonbinding process used primarily by large business organizations to better inform themselves of the merits of a case. A trial-like proceeding is conducted with high-ranking company officials who have settlement authority acting as jurors. The parties agree on rules of procedure and exchange of information and select a neutral advisor. Attorneys for each side present a case summary to the jury. There is no examination of witnesses. As jurors, the officials hear both sides and gain insight about the dispute. Now well-informed, the parties can negotiate a settlement with or without the assistance of the neutral advisor and avoid an actual court trial. Because preparation and presentation of a case, even in summary form, can be expensive, mini-trials are used when large amounts of money are at stake.

Summary Jury Trial

summary jury trial
A nonbinding alternative dispute resolution (ADR) process in which parties present their cases to a private mock jury, which then gives the parties an advisory verdict.

mock jury
A panel of lay citizens selected and paid to mirror the role of an actual jury.

The **summary jury trial** is similar to both the mini-trial and early neutral evaluation. The object is to facilitate settlement in lawsuits that have been filed but not yet tried by providing parties with a realistic jury reaction. An abbreviated case is presented to a **mock jury**. The jury returns its verdict quickly. After the verdict, attorneys for each side are permitted to query each juror about how and why they reached their decision. Parties then negotiate a settlement, each equipped with insights gained from the jury. The process is nonbinding: If a settlement is not reached, both sides have the right to a full trial. Procedurally, a summary jury trial is more relaxed than an actual trial. Because attorneys for the parties put on an abbreviated case, including examination of the parties as witnesses, it is more formal than a mini-trial. Summary jury trials are also more expensive than mini-trials. The presentation of a case, although abbreviated, requires more attorney research and preparation than presentation of a case summary. Also, it costs more to compensate a number of jurors as contrasted with a single neutral third party.

Collaborative Law Practice

Minnesota lawyer–mediator Stu Webb became dissatisfied with the acrimony resulting from lost love and the adversarial nature of family law practice. Rather than continue to do what he disliked, he challenged the status quo and introduced a practice innovation called **collaborative law practice**. Since its development in the early 1990s, it has evolved to include these attributes:

collaborative law practice
A method whereby the parties agree to resolve their disputes without court intervention using interest-based negotiation practices.

1. A participation contract between a client and the attorney where they agree to resolve issues in contention without resort to using courts.
2. Agreement that if resolution requires going to court, the attorney will cease representation of the client who then will need to get a new lawyer.
3. Commitment to candor, including early and full disclosure to the other party of all important information.
4. Agreement to advocate interests of the clients not positions.
5. Agreement that all information obtained and conversations made in the process are confidential and cannot be used in contentious proceedings.

To work, the process requires that the other side's client and attorney must commit to this process and sign a collaborative practice participation contract. For this dance, it takes at least four to tango. It began in family law (i.e., divorce, child custody), but proponents believe it has benefits in other areas of civil law practice. The converts of collaborative practice have taken its principles to most states, Canada, Australia, and some European countries.

Partnering

Partnering is a dispute prevention process. Parties to complex undertakings, such as large construction projects, land use planning, or agency rulemaking, meet before commencement of the project. The objective of the meeting is to identify potential sources of conflict and design a system to resolve problems at the earliest stage possible. Partnering is similar to mediation and other dispute resolution processes as a neutral third party facilitates discussions. The key difference is that the partnering meeting is convened before, rather than after, any conflict has arisen. Attorneys typically participate in negotiations as advisors rather than as advocates.

partnering
A team-building process designed to improve contract performance and reduce or eliminate contract litigation through common understanding of goals and improved communication. The process is used in large, complicated, and expensive contracts and has its roots in the construction industry.

Conclusions Regarding ADR

People tend to accept and live more graciously with a voluntary agreement than with a court-imposed solution, which often will rankle for years. Litigation is risky because the outcome is uncertain. It is time consuming for attorneys and clients, and it is costly. Participants likely will suffer stress from drawn-out litigation. In the end, most lawsuits are settled before trial, but often after years of waiting. Litigation is necessary to vindicate rights or clarify the law, but litigation is not required to resolve all disagreements. A trial usually aggravates and exaggerates existing hard feelings. A decision to sue or defend a suit through trial should be carefully thought out. In addition to the obvious costs associated with litigation, such as attorney fees, court costs, witness expenses, and discovery costs, indirect or hidden costs must be taken into account. Finally, the cost for the state to provide justice must not be overlooked.

LEGAL FOCUS—EXAMPLE

Kevin Banks rejected a settlement offer of $22,500 in his breach of contract and tort action against eight former associates. He believed he was entitled to $500,000 in punitive damages. The case went to trial. The "good news" was that Banks won a jury verdict of $50,000. The "bad news" was that it took three years to resolve, during which time he was unemployed. His single-minded concern with the case alienated friends and relatives. The case cost him $105,000 in litigation expenses. During the prolonged dispute, he employed seven different lawyers, one at a time—six of them quit. Despite winning at trial, he continued to be consumed by the case. He accused the judge, defendants, defense attorneys, and his own attorneys of a conspiracy against him.

Often, the nominal winner is the real loser. Banks won his case, so one could assume he had been wronged. Had he accepted the settlement offer, he would have had a positive net recovery, rather than a negative victory with an out-of-pocket loss of at least $55,000 (litigation recovery of $50,000 minus litigation costs of $105,000). Was his pursuit of "justice at any price" too high a personal price to pay? Some people who win at trial feel vindicated despite a negative net recovery. Was the public harmed in any way?

For certain purposes, access to our public courts may be wholly inappropriate. Banks sought more than justice. He sought vengeance through the public court system in a civil matter. The civil courts are designed to shift the burden of compensating victims to the wrongdoer, not to mete out punishment. Use of our civil courts for vengeance is a breach of public trust and a squandering of public resources.

CASE

Equal Employment Opportunity Commission v. Waffle House, Inc.

534 U.S. 279, 122 S.Ct. 754 (2002)

Waffle House fired Eric Baker when he suffered a seizure on the job within a month of being hired. He filed a discrimination complaint with the Equal Employment Opportunity Commission (EEOC) alleging that his discharge violated the Americans with Disabilities Act of 1990 (ADA). The EEOC pursued the claim and filed suit in federal court requesting injunctive relief to prevent Waffle House from discriminating against other employees now and in the future, to get Baker reinstated on the job, to collect damages on behalf of Baker, and to punish Waffle House for discriminating against Baker. Waffle House moved to stay the EEOC's suit and compel arbitration based on Baker's employment contract that required employment disputes to be settled by binding arbitration. The district court denied Waffle House's request for relief. The Fourth Circuit Court of Appeals also held for the EEOC but limited the EEOC to injunctive relief against Waffle House and precluded the agency from seeking victim-specific relief. The court held that the Federal Arbitration Act (FAA), which favored enforcement of private arbitration agreements, outweighed the EEOC's right to enforce private, rather than public, interests. In other words, EEOC could proceed but Baker's arbitration agreement limited Baker's recovery to that which would be determined in an arbitration.

Justice Stevens Delivered the Opinion of the Court

The question presented is whether an agreement between an employer and an employee to arbitrate employment-related disputes bars the Equal Employment Opportunity Commission (EEOC) from pursuing victim-specific judicial relief, such as backpay, reinstatement, and damages, in an enforcement action alleging that the employer has violated Title I of the Americans with Disabilities Act of 1990 (ADA).

In his application for employment with respondent, Eric Baker agreed that "any dispute or claim" concerning his employment would be "settled by binding arbitration." As a condition of employment, all prospective Waffle House employees are required to sign an application containing a similar mandatory arbitration agreement. Baker began working as a grill operator at one of respondent's restaurants on August 10, 1994. Sixteen days later he suffered a seizure at work and soon thereafter was discharged. Baker did not initiate arbitration proceedings, nor has he in the seven years since his termination, but he did file a timely charge of discrimination with the EEOC alleging that his discharge violated the ADA.

After an investigation and an unsuccessful attempt to conciliate, the EEOC filed an enforcement action against respondent in the Federal District Court for the District of South Carolina. Baker is not a party to the case. The EEOC's complaint alleged that respondent engaged in employment practices that violated the ADA, including its discharge of Baker "because of his disability," and that its violation was intentional, and "done with malice or with reckless indifference to [his] federally protected rights." The complaint requested the court to grant in junctive relief to "eradicate the effects of [respondent's] past and present unlawful employment practices," to order specific relief designed to make Baker whole, including backpay, reinstatement, and compensatory damages, and to award punitive damages for malicious and reckless conduct.

Congress has directed the EEOC to exercise the same enforcement powers, remedies, and procedures that are set forth in Title VII of the Civil Rights Act of 1964 when it is enforcing the ADA's prohibitions against employment discrimination on the basis of disability.

The FAA directs courts to place arbitration agreements on equal footing with other contracts, but it "does not require parties to arbitrate when they have not agreed to do so." Because the FAA is "at bottom a policy guaranteeing the enforcement of private contractual arrangements," we look first to whether the parties agreed to arbitrate a dispute, not to general policy goals, to determine the scope of the agreement. Although ambiguities in the language of the agreement should be resolved in favor of arbitration, we do not override the clear intent of the parties, or reach a result inconsistent with the plain text of the contract, simply because the policy favoring arbitration is implicated. "Arbitration under the [FAA] is a matter of consent, not coercion." Here there is no ambiguity. No one asserts that the EEOC is a party to the contract, or that it agreed to arbitrate its claims. It goes without saying that a contract cannot bind a nonparty. Accordingly, the proarbitration policy goals of the FAA do not require the agency to relinquish its statutory authority if it has not agreed to do so.

[T]he statutory language is clear; the EEOC has the authority to pursue victim-specific relief regardless of the forum that the employer and employee have chosen to resolve their disputes. Rather than attempt to split the difference, we are persuaded that, pursuant to Title VII and the ADA, whenever the EEOC chooses from among the many charges filed each year to bring an enforcement action in a particular case, the agency may be seeking to vindicate a public interest, not simply provide make-whole relief for the employee, even when it pursues entirely victim-specific relief. To hold otherwise would undermine the detailed enforcement scheme created by Congress simply to give greater effect to an agreement between private parties that does not even contemplate the EEOC's statutory function.

It is true, as respondent [has] argued, that Baker's conduct may have the effect of limiting the relief that the EEOC may obtain in court. If, for example, he had failed to mitigate his damages, or had accepted a monetary settlement, any recovery by the EEOC would be limited accordingly. As we have noted, it "goes without saying that the courts can and should preclude double recovery by an individual."

But no question concerning the validity of his claim or the character of the relief that could be appropriately awarded in either a judicial or an arbitral forum is presented by this record. Baker has not sought arbitration of his claim, nor is there any indication that he has entered into settlement negotiations with respondent. It is an open question whether a settlement or arbitration judgment would affect the validity of the EEOC's claim or the character of relief the EEOC may seek. The only issue before this Court is whether the fact that Baker has signed a mandatory arbitration agreement limits the remedies available to the EEOC. The text of the relevant statutes provides a clear answer to that question. They do not authorize the courts to balance the competing policies of the ADA and the FAA or to second-guess the agency's judgment concerning which of the remedies authorized by law that it shall seek in any given case.

Moreover, it simply does not follow from the cases holding that the employee's conduct may affect the EEOC's recovery that the EEOC's claim is merely derivative. We have recognized several situations in which the EEOC does not stand in the employee's shoes. And, in this context, the statute specifically grants the EEOC exclusive authority over the choice of forum and the prayer for relief once a charge has been filed. The fact that ordinary principles of *res judicata**, mootness, or mitigation may apply to EEOC claims does not contradict these decisions, nor does it render the EEOC a proxy for the employee.

The judgment of the Court of Appeals is reversed, and the case is remanded for further proceedings consistent with this opinion.

It is so ordered.

Justice Thomas, with Whom the Chief Justice and Justice Scalia Join, Dissenting

Because Congress has not given the EEOC the authority to usurp the traditional role of courts to determine what constitutes "appropriate" relief in a given case, it is necessary to examine whether it would be "appropriate" to allow the EEOC to obtain victim-specific relief for Baker here, notwithstanding the fact that Baker, by signing an arbitration agreement, has waived his ability to seek such relief on his own behalf in a judicial forum. For two reasons, I conclude it is not "appropriate" to allow the EEOC to do on behalf of Baker that which Baker is precluded from doing for himself.

To begin with, when the EEOC litigates to obtain relief on behalf of a particular employee, the Commission must take that individual as it finds him. Whether the EEOC or an employee files a particular lawsuit, the employee is the ultimate beneficiary of victim-specific relief. The relevance of the employee's circumstances therefore does not change simply because the EEOC, rather than the employee himself, is litigating the case, and a court must consider these circumstances in fashioning an "appropriate" remedy.

As a result, the EEOC's ability to obtain relief is often limited by the actions of an employee on whose behalf the Commission may wish to bring a lawsuit. If an employee signs an agreement to waive or settle discrimination claims against an employer, for example, the EEOC may not recover victim-specific relief on that employee's behalf.

Not only would it be "inappropriate" for a court to allow the EEOC to obtain victim-specific relief on behalf of Baker, to do so in this case would contravene the "liberal federal policy favoring arbitration agreements" embodied in the FAA.

By allowing the EEOC to pursue victim-specific relief on behalf of Baker under these circumstances, the Court

*Latin: "a matter [already] adjudicated." A party may not sue again on a matter that has been settled by judicial decision.

eviscerates Baker's arbitration agreement with Waffle House and liberates Baker from the consequences of his agreement. Waffle House gains nothing and, if anything, will be worse off in cases where the EEOC brings an enforcement action should it continue to utilize arbitration agreements in the future. This is because it will face the prospect of defending itself in two different forums against two different parties seeking precisely the same relief. It could face the EEOC in court and the employee in an arbitral forum.

I respectfully dissent.

For Critical Analysis

1. Waffle House requested a stay and a motion to compel arbitration. What was it asking for?
2. Do you agree with Waffle House's argument that although the EEOC was not a party to the arbitration agreement, it is still effectively bound by it (Justice Thomas's dissent)? Or do you agree with the EEOC that Waffle House is free to pursue all remedies without regard to whether an employee has signed an arbitration agreement (Justice Stevens' majority opinion)? Explain which position you agree with and why.
3. When Baker was given the pre-employment agreement with the arbitration clause, do you think he understood what he was signing? Does it matter?
4. If Baker had refused to sign the employment agreement, would he still have been hired? If he had simply struck the clause and then signed, would he have been hired?
5. Why did Waffle House require the arbitration clause in its employment contracts? Why might an employee be concerned about such a clause? Why might an employee be pleased with such a clause?

Tillman v. Commercial Credit Loans, Inc.

655 S.E.2d 362 (N.C. 2008)

The plaintiff in this case challenges a binding arbitration clause in a loan agreement, on the grounds that the term was unconscionable, alleging that the costs involved in conducting the arbitration would essentially deny her access to justice and any resolution of her dispute.*

J. Timmons-Goodson Delivered the Opinion of the Court

The question chiefly presented is whether the arbitration clause contained in the loan agreements that serve as the basis for the instant case is unconscionable. Because the clause is one-sided, prohibits joinder of claims and class actions, and exposes claimants to prohibitively high costs, we hold that the trial court did not err in concluding as a matter of law that the clause is unconscionable.

I. BACKGROUND

On 22 September 1998, Fannie Lee Tillman obtained a loan for a term of 120 months with a principal amount of $18,253.68. In connection with the loan, Commercial Credit† sold Mrs. Tillman single premium credit life and disability insurance with premiums of $1,058.80 and $1,005.95, respectively. On 4 June 1999, Shirley Richardson obtained a loan for a term of 180 months with a principal amount of $20,935.57. In connection with the loan, Commercial Credit sold Mrs. Richardson single premium credit life, disability, and involuntary unemployment insurance with premiums of $1,871.54, $1,109.49, and $1,227.72, respectively. Plaintiffs' loan principal amounts included their insurance premiums, which were financed over the life of the loan.

It is undisputed that both plaintiffs have limited financial resources. Mrs. Tillman's weekly after-tax take-home pay is approximately $258.00. Her husband is deceased, and as a result, Mrs. Tillman also receives $285.60 per month in pension benefits and $1063.00 per month in Social Security benefits. Mrs. Richardson works two jobs where she earns $12.70 per hour and $12.00 per hour. For both plaintiffs, their home is their most significant asset.

*An unconscionable term is one that "shocks the consciousness." A court may refuse to enforce an unconscionable term in a contract under some circumstances, such as are discussed in this case. Unconscionable terms in contracts are addressed in Chapter 8, Contracts: Enforceable Agreements.

†In text that was edited from this case, the court explained that CitiFinancial Services acquired the assets of Commercial Credit following the execution of the involved loans.

Plaintiffs' loan agreements contained the standard arbitration clauses that defendants have included in their loan agreements since 1996. The arbitration clause was drafted by defendants, and plaintiffs were given no opportunity to negotiate regarding the clause.

In June 2002 plaintiffs commenced this suit against defendants asserting claims for violations of North Carolina's Unfair and Deceptive Trade Practices Act, unjust enrichment, and breach of the duties of good faith and fair dealing.

Beginning in May 2003, defendants filed a series of motions to compel arbitration pursuant to the arbitration clause contained in plaintiffs' loan agreements. The trial court denied defendants' motion to compel arbitration in an order that included the following findings of fact:

- The Commercial Credit arbitration clause is a standard-form contract of adhesion. The borrower is given no opportunity to negotiate out of the arbitration provision, and CitiFinancial Services would not make a loan if the loan agreement did not include the arbitration provision. The loan documents, including the arbitration provision at issue, were drafted by Defendant.
- Since the time CitiFinancial Services, Inc. began including an arbitration clause in its loan agreements, the lender has made more than 68,000 loans in North Carolina. During that time, CitiFinancial Services has pursued lawsuits in civil court against more than 3,700 borrowers in North Carolina, including over 2,000 collection actions and more than 1,700 foreclosure actions. There have been no arbitration proceedings in North Carolina involving CitiFinancial Services, and any of its borrowers. Since introduction of the arbitration clause, no North Carolina borrower has requested arbitration of any dispute with CitiFinancial Services, Inc. The only legal redress sought has been the collection and foreclosure actions pursued in civil court by Defendant against its borrowers.
- The only persons present at the loan closings involving Plaintiffs Tillman and Richardson were Plaintiffs and a Commercial Credit loan officer. [Mrs.] Tillman and [Mrs.] Richardson were rushed through the loan closings, and the Commercial Credit loan officer indicated where [Mrs.] Tillman and [Mrs.] Richardson were to sign or initial the loan documents. There was no mention of the arbitration clause at the loan closings.
- The compensation rates for American Arbitration Association ("AAA") arbitrators in North Carolina range from $500.00 to $2,380.00 per day. The average daily rate of AAA arbitrator compensation in North Carolina is $1,225.00.
- Plaintiffs Fannie Lee Tillman and Shirley Richardson entered into contingency fee contracts with the attorneys representing them. The contingency fee contract is typical of such agreements. The contingency fee agreement entered into by Plaintiffs provides that their attorneys will not be entitled to any fee unless there is some monetary recovery obtained on behalf of Plaintiffs, either by way of settlement or verdict. The agreement further provides that the law firm representing Plaintiffs shall advance the costs and expenses incurred in prosecuting the action.
- Based upon the 1998 North Carolina Bar Association Economic Survey, the most recent survey published, the average hourly rate for attorneys working on litigation matters such as this is between $150.00–$250.00 per hour. Based upon the limited financial resources of Plaintiffs and other similarly situated borrowers, they could not afford to hire an attorney to be paid on an hourly basis. The only realistic means by which persons in the position of Plaintiffs can prosecute their claims is by entering into a contingency fee agreement.
- Defendant's arbitration clause contains features which would deter many consumers from seeking to vindicate their rights. These features include the cost-shifting ("loser pays") provision with respect to the initial arbitration proceeding to the extent it exceeds eight hours, the cost-shifting provision associated with the de novo appeal from that initial arbitration proceeding, and the prohibition on joinder of claims and class actions. The prohibition on class actions and the cap of $15,000.00 on the value of claims that can be pursued outside of the arbitration process designed by Defendant make it unlikely that borrowers would be able to retain lawyers willing to pursue litigation against a large commercial entity, such as CitiFinancial Services, Inc.

Ultimately, the trial court denied the motion to compel arbitration based on its conclusion that the arbitration clause contained in plaintiffs' loan agreements is unconscionable and unenforceable due to the prohibitively high arbitration costs borrowers might face in pursuing claims through arbitration, the fee-shifting ("loser pays") provisions which expose borrowers to excessive arbitration and appeal costs and because the arbitration clause is excessively one-sided and lacks mutuality in that it preserves access to the courts for the lender while prohibiting joinder of claims and class actions on the part of borrowers and restricts what claims of borrowers can be pursued in civil court.

II. ANALYSIS

Because unconscionability is a question of law, this Court will review de novo the trial court's conclusion that the arbitration agreement contained in plaintiffs' loan agreements is unconscionable. In the instant case, many of the trial court's findings are uncontested. Furthermore, after extensive review of the record, we conclude that the eight findings of fact contested by defendant are supported by competent evidence.

Arbitration is favored in North Carolina. As with any contract, however, "equity may require invalidation of an arbitration agreement that is unconscionable." A court will find a contract to be unconscionable only when the inequality of the bargain is so manifest as to shock the judgment of a person of common sense, and where the terms are so oppressive that no reasonable person would make them on the one hand, and no honest and fair person would accept them on the other.

An inquiry into unconscionability requires that a court "consider all the facts and circumstances of a particular case," and "[i]f the provisions are then viewed as so one-sided that the contracting party is denied any opportunity for a meaningful choice, the contract should be found unconscionable."

Procedural unconscionability involves "bargaining naughtiness" in the form of unfair surprise, lack of meaningful choice, and an inequality of bargaining power. Substantive unconscionability, on the other hand, refers to harsh, one-sided, and oppressive contract terms. Therefore, we note that while the presence of both procedural and substantive problems is necessary for an ultimate finding of unconscionability, such a finding may be appropriate when a contract presents pronounced substantive unfairness and a minimal degree of procedural unfairness, or vice versa.

We conclude that, taken together, the oppressive and one-sided substantive provisions of the arbitration clause at issue in the instant case and the inequality of bargaining power between the parties render the arbitration clause in plaintiffs' loan agreements unconscionable.

A. PROCEDURAL UNCONSCIONABILITY

The trial court made the following finding of fact, which is supported by evidence in the record: "[Mrs.] Tillman and [Mrs.] Richardson were rushed through the loan closings, and the Commercial Credit loan officer indicated where [Mrs.] Tillman and [Mrs.] Richardson were to sign or initial the loan documents. There was no mention of credit insurance or the arbitration clause at the loan closings." In addition, defendants admit that they would have refused to make a loan to plaintiffs rather than negotiate with them over the terms of the arbitration agreement. Finally, the bargaining power between defendants and plaintiffs was unquestionably unequal in that plaintiffs are relatively unsophisticated consumers contracting with corporate defendants who drafted the arbitration clause and included it as boilerplate language in all of their loan agreements. We therefore conclude that plaintiffs made a sufficient showing to establish procedural unconscionability.

B. SUBSTANTIVE UNCONSCIONABILITY

The trial court found the arbitration clause to be substantively unconscionable because (1) the arbitration costs borrowers may face are "prohibitively high"; (2) "the arbitration clause is excessively one-sided and lacks mutuality"; and (3) the clause prohibits joinder of claims and class actions. We agree that here, the collective effect of the arbitration provisions is that plaintiffs are precluded from "effectively vindicating [their] … rights in the arbitral forum." In terms of ability to pay, the evidence of plaintiffs' limited financial means is uncontested. Plaintiffs live paycheck to paycheck and usually have very little money left in their bank accounts after paying their monthly bills. The arbitration clause specifies that AAA will administer any arbitration between the parties to the loan agreement, and evidence in the record indicates that the average daily rate of AAA arbitrator compensation in North Carolina is $1,225.00. According to the arbitration clause, when an arbitration lasts more than eight hours, the loser will be charged with costs. Moreover, the clause provides for a de novo appeal before a panel of three arbitrators, and again, the loser pays the costs. For example, at the average rate, a two-day appeal would cost the losing party $7,350.00 in arbitrator fees. Plaintiffs simply do not have the resources to risk facing these kinds of fees.

The trial court also found that [t]he only realistic means by which persons in the position of Plaintiffs can prosecute their claims is by entering into a contingency fee agreement with lawyers willing to advance the costs and expenses of the litigation and with the law firm assuming the risk that there might be no recovery.

Because plaintiffs' damage amounts are so low (under $4,500 each), the trial court found that it is "unlikely that any attorneys would be willing to accept the risks attendant to pursuing [these] claims." The likelihood that an attorney would take a case controlled by the arbitration clause at issue here is even less because the arbitration clause prohibits the joinder of claims and class actions. Therefore, neither attorneys nor plaintiffs are able to share the risks attendant to pursuing this litigation.

In order to find unenforceability due to excessive costs, the cost differential between litigation and arbitration must be so great that it deters individuals from bringing claims under the arbitration clause. Evidence in the record indicates that no arbitrations have been brought under the clause that defendant has included in over 68,000 loan agreements in North Carolina. Based on this evidence and the above analysis, it appears that the combination of the loser pays provision, the de novo appeal process, and the prohibition on joinder of claims and class actions creates a barrier to pursuing arbitration that is substantially greater than that present in the context of litigation. We agree with the trial court that "[d]efendant's arbitration clause contains features which would deter many consumers from seeking to vindicate their rights."

In the instant case, the clause excepts from arbitration foreclosure actions and actions in which the total damages, costs, and fees do not exceed $15,000. Plaintiffs argue that the arbitration clause preserves defendants' ability to pursue its claims in court while denying plaintiffs that same option. Evidence in the record indicates that since 1996, defendants have brought over 2,000 collection actions with an average "payoff" of under $7,000. In addition, it appears that defendants have not initiated arbitration in North Carolina. In other words, every time defendants have taken legal action against a borrower, they have managed to avoid application of the arbitration clause. This arbitration clause is not as egregious as some that specifically carve out an exception for the corporate drafter of the clause to pursue collection actions in court. Practically speaking, however, the exceptions appear to be designed far more for the benefit of defendants than for plaintiffs. The one-sidedness of the clause therefore contributes to our overall conclusion that it is unconscionable.

In conclusion, we hold that the provisions of the arbitration clause, taken together, render it substantively unconscionable because the provisions do not provide plaintiffs with a forum in which they can effectively vindicate their rights.

For Critical Analysis

1. Why did the court find the clause to be procedurally unconscionable?
2. Why did the court find the contract to be substantively unconscionable?
3. Do you agree with the court's ruling?
4. If the arbitration clause is invalid, what can Ms. Tillman do now?

CHAPTER QUESTIONS AND PROBLEMS

1. The legal profession is in the process of change. Following are some questions involving changes that have impact on the public interest:
   a. Should attorneys who participate in formal courtroom trials be trained differently from other lawyers?
   b. Should charges concerning the unprofessional conduct of an attorney be heard and decided by attorneys, by nonlawyers, or by both?
   c. What limitations, if any, should be imposed on the right of attorneys to advertise for and to solicit legal business?
   d. Should there be limits to the fees charged by attorneys for legal services?
   e. Should current rules requiring all partners or owners in law firms to be lawyers be changed?
   f. Should lawyers be allowed to associate and share fees with nonlawyer professionals? Would such multidisciplinary associations benefit the general public?
2. Contingent fee arrangements are said to make legal services available to persons who otherwise would be unable to pay, but contingent fee arrangements are also said to promote litigation unnecessarily because potential plaintiffs (victims) have nothing to lose by suing. What do you think of these contentions?
3. Our founding fathers adopted (or, more correctly, retained) the English common law after the American Revolution. However, we have consistently refused to adopt the so-called English Plan for the payment of legal fees. The English Plan requires the losing party to pay the plaintiffs and the defendant's attorney fees (as well as court costs). Presently, losers in the United States always pay court costs and their own attorney fees (unless otherwise agreed by contract), but they do not pay the attorney fees of their opponents. Some observers strongly recommend we adopt the English Plan. Do you agree?
4. Liability insurance is available to cover potential attorney malpractice. As with most liability insurance, the premiums charged have increased significantly in recent years. Malpractice insurance coverage for attorneys is usually not required either by law or by the Professional Rules of Conduct. As in many other liability situations, those who can most afford a major loss carry ample insurance, whereas those who have little financial ability are more likely to be without insurance. Should malpractice insurance or other proof of financial responsibility be required as a condition for the practice of law? Discuss.
5. The typical arbitration clause requires binding arbitration. That means that the arbitrator's decision cannot be appealed except for limited reasons. What are the negative and positive aspects of arbitration resulting from this lack of appeal? Assume that during arbitration the attorney representing one party becomes angry, screams obscenities at the arbitrator, and finally throws the exhibits onto the floor. Can the arbitrator hold the attorney in contempt?
6. In January 1991, Gail P. Carr-Williams, an attorney licensed to practice law in Michigan, applied for admission, without examination, to the State Bar of Ohio. After an initial recommendation that Carr-Williams's application be approved, the Board of Commissioners on Character and Fitness of the Supreme Court of Ohio appointed a panel to investigate Carr-Williams's application. The panel concluded that Carr-Williams had not satisfied her federal income tax obligations for several years and owed the Internal Revenue Service approximately $98,000 in taxes, interest, and penalties. She also owed state taxes of $14,000. Should the Board of Commissioners recommend she be licensed to practice law in Ohio? [*In re* Application of Carr-Williams, 63 Ohio St.3d 752, 591 N.E.2d 693 (Ohio 1992).]
7. Attorney Edward M. Cooperman was retained to represent a client in a criminal matter. The client signed Cooperman's fee agreement: "My minimum fee for appearing for you in this matter is fifteen thousand dollars ($15,000). This fee is not refundable for any reason whatsoever once I file a notice of appearance on your behalf." One month later, the client discharged Cooperman, but Cooperman refused to refund any portion of the fee. In the past, Cooperman had been told by the local bar association grievance committee to stop using nonrefundable fee agreements. The attorneys' Code of Professional Conduct and Responsibility provides that an attorney "shall not enter into an agreement for, charge or collect an illegal or excessive fee" and upon withdrawal from employment "shall refund promptly any part of a fee paid in advance that has not been earned." Did Cooperman's fee arrangement violate the code? [*Grievance Committee for the Tenth Judicial District*

v. *Edward M. Cooperman*, 83 N.Y.2d 465, 633 N.E.2d 1069, 611 N.Y.S.2d 465 (N.Y. 1994).]

8. John E. Mallard, an attorney who practiced bankruptcy and securities law, was selected by the U.S. magistrate to represent indigent inmates who were suing prison officials for maltreatment. He was compelled to represent the inmates under a federal statute authorizing federal courts to "request" an attorney to represent any person claiming poverty status. Claiming that he was not competent to handle complex trial matters, Mallard filed a motion to withdraw. The magistrate denied his request, and his appeal to the district court and court of appeals was unsuccessful. Can the court compel attorney Mallard to represent an indigent civil litigant? [*Mallard v. U.S. District Court for Southern Dist. of Iowa*, 490 U.S. 296, 109 S.Ct. 1814 (1989).]
9. Richard Shapero, a Kentucky attorney, applied to the state Attorneys' Advertising Commission for approval of a letter that he proposed to send "to potential clients who have had a foreclosure suit filed against them." The letter advised the clients that federal law may prevent creditors from taking immediate action and that the recipients of the letters could call Shapero's office for free information on how to keep their homes. The commission would not approve the letter because Professional Conduct Rules prohibited direct-mail solicitation by lawyers if the mail was directed to *specific recipients* rather than to *a general group of persons* known to need the particular kind of legal services offered. The Kentucky Supreme Court affirmed the commission's finding. Shapero appealed to the U.S. Supreme Court, claiming that the rule violated attorneys' rights to free speech. Did Shapero succeed in his claim? [*Shapero v. Kentucky Bar Association*, 486 U.S. 466, 108 S.Ct. 1916 (1988).]
10. The Hembrees purchased a home. The purchase contract included the following clause: "Any controversy or claim arising out of or relating to this contract, or the breach thereof, shall be settled by arbitration in the city of contract origin, in accordance with the rules of the American Arbitration Association." A claim that the home they purchased had a defective roof was arbitrated and the arbitrator found for the Hembrees on the theory of implied warranty. An implied warranty is a guarantee imposed by law that the seller will stand behind the item even though the contract is silent with respect to warranties. The seller and seller's real estate agent challenged the arbitrator's award in state court. They claimed the arbitrator exceeded his authority because the contract did not expressly provide for a remedy based on warranty. They argued the arbitrator's finding was a clear error of law. Is the arbitrator's authority strictly limited to the terms of the contract? If the arbitrator is clearly wrong as to the application of law, will the award be overturned by the court? [*Hembree v. Broadway Realty Trust Company, Inc.*, 151 Ariz. 418, 728 P.2d 288 (Ariz. 1986).]
11. Edward Kuhnel, a correctional officer for the New York Correctional Services Department ("Department"), flew a Nazi flag from the front porch of his home commemorating the 55th anniversary of Hitler's declaration of war against the United States. His actions received a great deal of media attention. The Department suspended Kuhnel from his job for violating two sections of the Department's employee manual. Kuhnel contested his suspension, and the claim was submitted to arbitration under a collective bargaining agreement. Both parties agreed that the arbitration procedure would be final and binding. The arbitrator concluded that Kuhnel was not guilty of the charges and reinstated Kuhnel with full back pay and benefits. The Department appealed. May the courts revisit the evidence and consider whether the arbitrator erred in determining the facts or applying the law? [*New York State Correctional Officers and Police Benevolent Association, Inc. v. State of New York*, 94 N.Y.2d 321, 726 N.E.2d 462, 704 N.Y.S.2d 910 (N.Y. 1999).]
12. Florida lawyer Shane Stafford arranged for Roy Blevins, a West Palm Beach police officer, to solicit personal injury cases for him. In an eighteen-month period, Blevins referred ten or eleven cases to Stafford, including three automobile accident cases he investigated as a police officer. Stafford gave 15 percent of his legal fees to Blevins, who received approximately $11,000 total. Is such a referral arrangement legal and ethical? [*The Florida Bar v. Stafford*, 542 So.2d 1321 (Fla. 1989).]
13. Weaver agreed to buy a house from builder McGill Homes for $181,900. The contract provided "that all claims arising out of or related to the purchase agreement would be settled by arbitration in accordance with the commercial arbitration rules of the American Arbitration Association." After moving into the home, Weaver was dissatisfied with the builder and claimed the home was worth less than the agreed-upon price. He petitioned for an arbitration to hear

his claim of defective construction. He received an award of $12,755.50 for defective and incomplete construction from the arbitrator. McGill Homes moved to vacate the arbitration award, claiming that the arbitrator manifestly disregarded the law. To support its contention, it attached affidavits of its construction foreman and a project worker. Do you expect the court to overturn the arbitrator's award? [*McGill Homes, Inc. v. Weaver*, 278 Ga.App. 622, 629 S.E.2d 535 (Ga. 2006).]

CHAPTER 5

Administrative Law

The rise of administrative bodies probably has been the most significant legal trend of the last century and perhaps more values are affected by their decisions than by those of all the courts.

Justice Robert H. Jackson, U.S. Supreme Court Justice, 1941–1954

LEARNING OBJECTIVES

After reading and studying this chapter, you should be able to:

- Define and explain the term administrative law. Distinguish between the two different ways in which the term is used.
- Explain what an administrative agency is, how an agency gets its authority, and what the general purposes of administrative agencies are. Describe the importance of the Administrative Procedure Act and the enabling statute relative to agency authority and purpose.
- Explain the importance of agency procedures.
- Distinguish between an independent administrative agency and an executive department.
- Identify leading administrative agencies and the areas they regulate.
- Explain what a regulation is and identify the major rulemaking steps required by the Administrative Procedure Act.
- Describe the major investigatory methods and powers of administrative agencies.
- Briefly explain the degree and type of control that each branch of the federal government has over independent administrative agencies.
- Identify and explain some methods by which the public may scrutinize agency action.

Most of us have seen recreations of dramatic courtroom showdowns and perhaps even viewed video of grand oratory in Congress. You probably also have seen live broadcast of a speech by the president. Courts, Congress and the presidency are the three faces of government, the three separate branches of U.S. government. The fourth important face to the law, the face you are most likely to encounter on a daily basis, however, is administrative law. Administrative agencies enforce administrative law. Administrative law gets less attention in media and culture that the three branches of government, but it arguably is much more important. For some, this fourth face of government conjures up an image of a powerful agency able to both make and execute law, and one subject to less oversight or review than a court, legislature, or police officer might have. **Administrative law** is the body of law that governs what administrative agencies are allowed to do, how they can do it, and what they cannot do. This chapter prepares you to better understand administrative law and its place in American governance.

LEGAL FOCUS—EXAMPLE

On August 24, 2009, a Sun Country Airlines flight waited on the tarmac for more than six hours with passengers and crew trapped on the hot plane. Earlier that month, on August 8, a Continental Express Airlines flight kept passengers on a plane overnight under terrible conditions of overflowing toilets, no water, and no food. Congressional inquiries and public outrage led the Department of Transportation to adopt new rules that took effect in 2010, setting three hours as the maximum time that passengers can be kept on a locked airplane. Many airlines claim that this rule will hurt passengers more than it will help them as the time period is too short; that it will result in cancelled flights and unnecessarily stranded passengers. Passenger advocates claim otherwise.

administrative law
The body of law concerned with the power of administrative agencies. Administrative law consists of rules, regulations, orders, and adjudications. Also the composite body of substantive law created by the various administrative agencies in the performance of their assigned tasks.

Do you agree with the airlines or the passenger advocates? What gives the Department of Transportation the authority to decide what is too long of a stay in an airplane on a runway? The answer is "administrative law," specifically in this case, the federal laws creating the Department of Transportation and authorizing it to regulate the Airline Industry. We will present the structure and processes of administrative law, both in the federal government as well as in several states. Our particular focus will be on the power wielded by agencies and the constraints on this power. You should come to understand why administrative law is a topic so unique and important. Hopefully, you will be better prepared to solve problems of government involvement (perhaps interference) in your life and better able to obtain the services, rights, and benefits you seek from the government.

A final word before our discussion of administrative law: This chapter is mostly about process—that is, the process that agencies use when enforcing the law—presented earlier as procedural law. That process can deny a right or grant a privilege just as surely as any substantive law. To understand its importance, you need only speak with someone who has just dealt with a government process and felt confused and powerless to help shape the outcome. For example, trying to survive in a courtroom without understanding the complex rules for evidence and procedure, or dealing with an agency without understanding how it makes decisions, both are efforts likely to result in frustration, anger, and long-lasting disappointment.

WHAT IS ADMINISTRATIVE LAW?

Often, the term *administrative law* is used to describe two very different subjects of law. One is the law governing agency process and procedure. The other type is the law that

EXHIBIT 5.1
Types of Agency Law

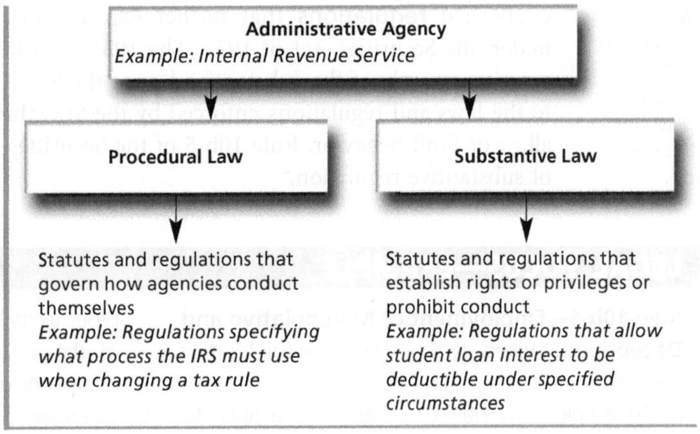

agencies create and apply, the "substantive law" of agencies. In this chapter, we focus on the process and procedure of agencies rather than on the subject matter of the laws agencies create or of the statutes that agencies enforce. Exhibit 5.1 provides examples of procedural and substantive administrative law.

Agency Process

A body of law governs how agencies can or must conduct themselves and their processes. As you will learn, policies of fairness and constitutional principles have established significant restraints and limits on agency power, particularly on the way in which an agency may act. Agencies, however, often are given significant authority to independently execute laws, make decisions, and otherwise do their business. Collectively, laws and rules governing how agencies can or must conduct themselves can be referred to as the *procedural law* of agencies.

Some laws and regulations that appear procedural in nature really directly control the rights, privileges, or benefits of others. Consider the following regulation of the U.S. Department of Education.

LEGAL FOCUS—EXAMPLE

Obtaining a loan. (a) *Application for a Direct Subsidized Loan or a Direct Unsubsidized Loan.* (1) To obtain a Direct Subsidized Loan or a Direct Unsubsidized Loan, a student must complete a FreeApplication for Federal Student Aid and submit it in accordance with instructions in the application.

A strict reading of the above regulation shows that a student could be denied a loan for merely failing to follow instructions in the application. Thus, this regulation and those instructions in the loan application, while procedural, have substantive effect. In any case, this is the realm of administrative law, where rights and benefits such as these are affected every day through the creation and application of the laws and regulations of agencies.

Substantive Law of Agencies

Every agency has a purpose, usually to enforce or apply a particular set of laws. For instance, the U.S. Securities and Exchange Commission (SEC) is tasked with enforcing, among other laws, the Securities Act of 1933. Besides that federal statute, the SEC has

regulations
Rules promulgated by an administrative agency under authority given to the agency by the enabling statute.

established **regulations** that further explain and apply the broader statute they are under, the Securities Act of 1933. The 1933 Securities Act and its associated regulations are one example of the substantive law of the SEC. The term *substantive law* here refers to the laws and regulations enforced by the SEC that describe or proscribe conduct, that allow or limit behavior. Rule 10b-5 of the Securities Exchange Act of 1934 is an example of substantive regulation.

LEGAL FOCUS—EXAMPLE

Rule 10b-5—Employment of Manipulative and Deceptive Devices. It shall be unlawful for any person.

a. To employ any device, scheme, or artifice to defraud,
b. To make any untrue statement of a material fact or to omit to state a material fact necessary in order to make the statements made, in the light of the circumstances under which they were made, not misleading, or
c. To engage in any act, practice, or course of business which operates or would operate as a fraud or deceit upon any person, in connection with the purchase or sale of any security.

Rule 10b-5 is the so-called Securities Fraud regulation that some believe should proscribe the type of conduct alleged to have occurred in the 2001 Enron Corporation collapse. It is a great example of a substantive regulation that has had a colorful and rich history of enforcement. Its reach goes beyond brokers and traders and touches, theoretically, every person who buys or sells a stock or bond.

LEGAL FOCUS—CASE

In December of 2001, Martha Stewart sold 3,928 shares of ImClone Systems Incorporated. The SEC later accused her of insider trading in relation to that sale, alleging that she had been told of a pending denial of approval of an important new drug being developed by ImClone. Though the Department of Justice sought criminal "securities fraud" charges against her, the court rejected the charge. Martha Stewart was convicted of crimes related to attempting to hide the circumstances of the sale. While serving a sentence for her crimes, the SEC brought civil charges of "insider trading," a form of securities fraud. Though she initially fought the charges, Martha Stewart eventually settled with the SEC agreeing to pay approximately $195,000 and to not serve as an officer or employee of a public company for five years.

Focus on Agency Process

In this chapter, we do not focus on the substantive law of agencies for several reasons. First, the substantive law of a particular agency is usually a particular topic or type of law. For instance, the SEC enforces "Securities" laws. Second, the substantive law of administrative agencies is a topic as broad as law itself. This is because nearly every statute, state or federal, involves at least one agency in its application. In this chapter, we focus on understanding agency process. Along the way, we will discuss what administrative agencies are, how they are created, what they do, what they cannot do, how they affect our lives, and what we can do when we disagree with their decisions.

LEGAL FOCUS—PROBLEM

Dan and Linda Dixon bought a parcel of land on which to build their dream home. Upon retirement, they met with an architect and commissioned plans. They found a contractor to build their home. Unfortunately, the land they owned had been rezoned, and they were told by the city planning commission that they had to apply for a conditional use permit (CUP), which they did. The planning commission denied their CUP application, stating that the Dixons' proposed house did not reflect the values intended for the land. The Dixons felt it would be a waste of time to appeal the decision to the city council and engaged an attorney to file a lawsuit. Their attorney advised them that there was really nothing they could do.

The Dixons have just participated in an administrative process. Local governments also have agencies such as city planning commissions that must apply the law. The limits and powers of agencies that we study in this chapter reach down to the city level. That is one reason why understanding administrative law may be far more important than understanding trial procedures.

What Is an Administrative Agency?

Understanding administrative law and how it affects your life requires that you first understand what an administrative agency is and what the various types of agencies are. Recall that the United States is a federal form of government, meaning it is made up of numerous governments that coexist; namely, a federal government and fifty state governments. Each of those governments has its own body of administrative law complete with numerous agencies. In the case of the federal government, the number of agencies is too vast to cover in this chapter, even summarily. The supremacy of federal law over state law adds a layer of complexity to this as well. In any given state, there will be offices of federal agencies as well as those of the state's agencies. Some state agencies may serve similar purposes as federal agencies, such as environmental protection, or public health. Exhibit 5.2 depicts a simplified version of this federal–state federalism structure of administrative law.

EXHIBIT 5.2
Federal and State Administrative Law

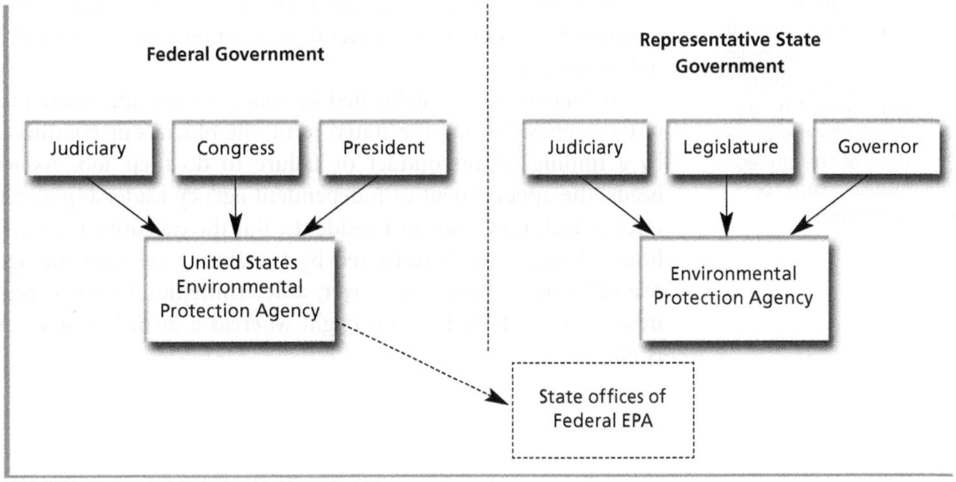

administrative agency
Collectively, subbranches of the executive branch of federal, state, and local governments. Administrative agencies may possess legislative, executive, and judicial powers in specialized technical areas where appropriate regulation requires action by experts.

An **administrative agency** is a subbranch of the executive branch of the federal, a state, or a local government. Usually, federal agencies are used as examples to explain and teach administrative law. States usually are organized in a similar, if less complex, structure as the federal administrative government system. So it is useful to use the federal government as an introductory tool. To fully understand administrative law requires a review of state structures as well.

Two important categories of federal agencies are executive departments and independent administrative agencies. Exhibit 5.3 shows a sampling of administrative agencies within the federal government system. It also outlines offices of the judiciary and the legislature branches, but those normally are not defined as agencies. The main constitutional and policy concern arises with agencies that have powers of the other branches in addition to executive power.

Executive Departments

executive departments
Generally, administrative bodies headed by single persons ultimately answerable to one person, the chief executive.

Some agencies are nothing more than a department of the executive branch of the federal government. These **executive departments** were created by Congress to allow the president to better execute the laws of the United States. Examples include the Department of the Interior, the Department of Justice, the National Security Council, and the Department of Defense. These agencies are controlled more directly by the president and thus exist as an arm of the executive department. The Department of Homeland Security is a recent addition to the list of executive department administrative agencies. The executive departments that are part of the cabinet of the president of the United States are headed by a secretary appointed by the president with the advice and consent of the Senate. The president may remove department heads at will.

Independent Administrative Agencies

independent administrative agency
An administrative body empowered to regulate some policy area led by officials who cannot be dismissed by the president of the United States except for good cause.

Most of the agencies referred to in this chapter are not executive departments. Instead they are independent administrative agencies. **Independent administrative agencies** are government units with delegated powers commonly found in the other branches of government. Applying the Separation of Powers doctrine, the Supreme Court of the United States generally has allowed agencies to collect the powers of multiple branches of the federal government only when there is some guarantee of independence.

Independence is established by making term appointments of the persons in charge of the agency. During the stated term, the officials or commissioners are removable only by a finding of misconduct or failure to do their job. As with executive department heads, the appointment of independent agency leadership generally is made by the executive branch (governor or president). But the executive branch's ability to remove agency heads at will (fire) is restricted by the statute creating the agency generally to reasons related to misfeasance. Moreover, a determination by the executive of good cause to dismiss is subject to judicial oversight whereas a dismissal of an executive department head is not.

EXHIBIT 5.3 The Government of the United States

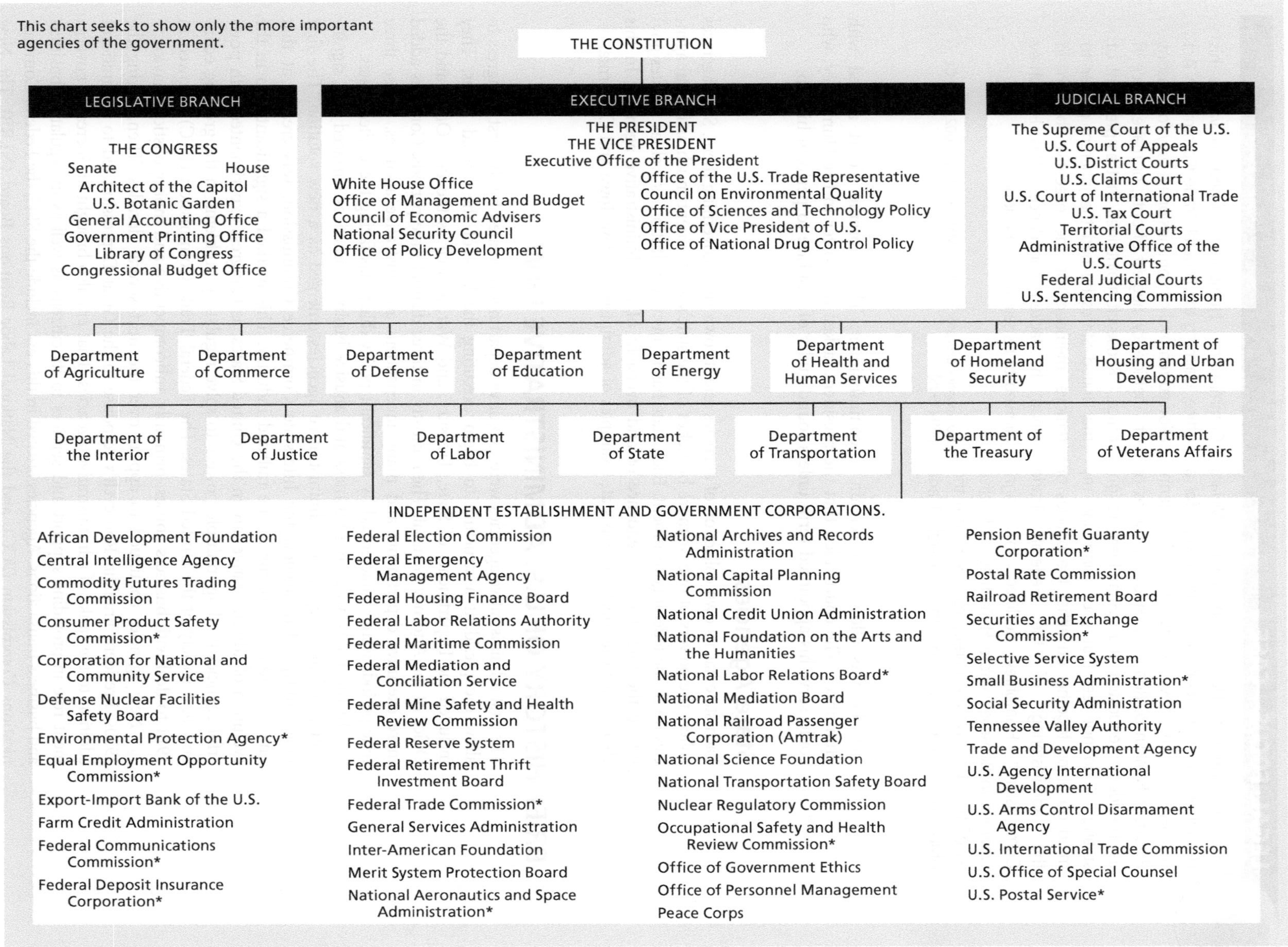
This chart seeks to show only the more important agencies of the government.
THE CONSTITUTION
LEGISLATIVE BRANCH
THE CONGRESS
Senate House
Architect of the Capitol
U.S. Botanic Garden
General Accounting Office
Government Printing Office
Library of Congress
Congressional Budget Office
EXECUTIVE BRANCH
THE PRESIDENT
THE VICE PRESIDENT
Executive Office of the President
White House Office
Office of Management and Budget
Council of Economic Advisers
National Security Council
Office of Policy Development
Office of the U.S. Trade Representative
Council on Environmental Quality
Office of Sciences and Technology Policy
Office of Vice President of U.S.
Office of National Drug Control Policy
JUDICIAL BRANCH
The Supreme Court of the U.S.
U.S. Court of Appeals
U.S. District Courts
U.S. Claims Court
U.S. Court of International Trade
U.S. Tax Court
Territorial Courts
Administrative Office of the U.S. Courts
Federal Judicial Courts
U.S. Sentencing Commission
Department of Agriculture
Department of Commerce
Department of Defense
Department of Education
Department of Energy
Department of Health and Human Services
Department of Homeland Security
Department of Housing and Urban Development
Department of the Interior
Department of Justice
Department of Labor
Department of State
Department of Transportation
Department of the Treasury
Department of Veterans Affairs
INDEPENDENT ESTABLISHMENT AND GOVERNMENT CORPORATIONS.
African Development Foundation
Central Intelligence Agency
Commodity Futures Trading Commission
Consumer Product Safety Commission*
Corporation for National and Community Service
Defense Nuclear Facilities Safety Board
Environmental Protection Agency*
Equal Employment Opportunity Commission*
Export-Import Bank of the U.S.
Farm Credit Administration
Federal Communications Commission*
Federal Deposit Insurance Corporation*
Federal Election Commission
Federal Emergency Management Agency
Federal Housing Finance Board
Federal Labor Relations Authority
Federal Maritime Commission
Federal Mediation and Conciliation Service
Federal Mine Safety and Health Review Commission
Federal Reserve System
Federal Retirement Thrift Investment Board
Federal Trade Commission*
General Services Administration
Inter-American Foundation
Merit System Protection Board
National Aeronautics and Space Administration*
National Archives and Records Administration
National Capital Planning Commission
National Credit Union Administration
National Foundation on the Arts and the Humanities
National Labor Relations Board*
National Mediation Board
National Railroad Passenger Corporation (Amtrak)
National Science Foundation
National Transportation Safety Board
Nuclear Regulatory Commission
Occupational Safety and Health Review Commission*
Office of Government Ethics
Office of Personnel Management
Peace Corps
Pension Benefit Guaranty Corporation*
Postal Rate Commission
Railroad Retirement Board
Securities and Exchange Commission*
Selective Service System
Small Business Administration*
Social Security Administration
Tennessee Valley Authority
Trade and Development Agency
U.S. Agency International Development
U.S. Arms Control Disarmament Agency
U.S. International Trade Commission
U.S. Office of Special Counsel
U.S. Postal Service*

* Major administrative agency.
Source: U.S. Government Manual, 2002–2003.

LEGAL FOCUS—CASE

President Herbert Hoover appointed William Humphrey to the Federal Trade Commission for a seven-year term. Two years into the term, President Franklin D. Roosevelt, Hoover's successor as president, requested that Humphrey resign, stating, "I do not feel that your mind and my mind go along together on either the policies or the administering of the Federal Trade Commission." Humphrey declined to resign, whereupon Roosevelt wrote Humphrey, "Effective as of this date you are hereby removed from the office of Commissioner of the Federal Trade Commission." Humphrey refused to vacate his office, claiming the Federal Trade Commission Act allowed removal of commissioners only for reasons of "inefficiency, neglect of duty, or malfeasance in office." Roosevelt maintained that as president of the United States he had the inherent power to remove members of the executive branch in whom he lacked confidence. Was Humphrey allowed to remain a commissioner?

Humphrey's Executor v. United States, 295 U.S. 602, 55 S.Ct. 869 (1935).

Yes, he was allowed to remain a commissioner. The Supreme Court agreed with Humphrey. The court ruled that the president lacked the power to fire Humphrey, who could serve his appointed term unless found guilty of a failure to perform his job.

State Agencies

Each state has its own collection of agencies and its own rules governing them. State agencies collect the powers of one or more branches of the state's government much as federal agencies do in the federal government. Each state has its own constitution as well as statutes governing the rules for independence of and oversight of its administrative agencies. In this chapter, we will touch on two state examples of administrative law, Iowa and California.

BRIEF HISTORY OF U.S. ADMINISTRATIVE LAW

The first administrative agencies were executive departments created by the first Congress to allow the president a structure to begin executing the laws of the United States. They included the Departments of State, Treasury, and War, as well as the Post Office and the Office of the Attorney General. Then, mostly in three distinct time periods, Congress added more executive departments and many independent administrative agencies. Those three time periods were characterized by significant policy dilemmas facing the United States.

In the 1880s, when big business and abusive business practices surfaced as a significant problem, independent administrative agencies emerged as a new solution. The first major independent agency, the Interstate Commerce Commission, was created at that time to address problems in the railroad industry. This marked a significant step in the evolution of administrative law in the United States, as Congress experimented with powerful agencies holding multiple powers to solve regulatory problems in the growing economy and society of the United States. The Federal Trade Commission (FTC) followed in 1914 to deal with business abuses, primarily anticompetitive and monopolistic behavior.

New agencies continued to appear over the next several decades. Then, during the 1930s, President Franklin Roosevelt's response to the Great Depression led to a significant addition to the ranks of administrative agencies. That era also brought an increased government role in providing support and services to its citizens as well as in regulating business and business transactions. Agencies created in this era include the SEC, the Federal Communications Commission (FCC), and the National Labor Relations Board (NLRB). The New

Deal era embodied more than just an increase in government; it was a paradigm shift of the role of the government in regulating the economy and business and supporting workers. Administrative agencies were the workhorses for government expansion in that era.

The third wave of administrative agencies occurred during the 1960s and 1970s. Many of these agencies focused on protecting and managing the environment and its resources (e.g., the Environmental Protection Agency [EPA]), ending racial discrimination (e.g., the Equal Employment Opportunity Commission [EEOC]), or establishing safe and stable working conditions (e.g., the Occupational Safety and Health Administration [OSHA]).

deregulation
A process of eliminating, reducing, or restructuring the regulation of an industry.

Today, the U.S. government had evolved into a vast labyrinth of administrative agencies making up a bureaucracy that most citizens encounter on a regular basis. During the later decades of the twentieth century, **deregulation** swept through numerous industries. Deregulation symbolically means reducing the extent to which the government regulates an industry. In practice, however, nearly all efforts to deregulate have, in fact, simply been "re-regulation," that is, a change in the way industry is regulated.

LEGAL FOCUS—BACKGROUND

A notorious experiment in deregulation swept through the electricity industry at the close of the 1990s. It began in California in 1997, as the largest state economy removed the utility monopoly over the generation of electricity. Left unchanged was the manner in which electricity was distributed and delivered to customers, which stayed in the hands of large investor-owned utilities. Within a few years, the wholesale price for electricity soared; mysterious shortages appeared; and controversial marketing, accounting, and sales practices came to light. Other states followed suit in deregulation, but not all. Although government and business press releases and media accounts usually referred to the events as the "deregulation experiment," it was, in fact, a change in the way the electricity industry was regulated. As part of California's supposed deregulation, two new agencies were created, the California Independent System Operator and the California Consumer Power Financing Authority.

CREATION OF ADMINISTRATIVE AGENCIES

enabling statute
A statute that creates an administrative agency and typically also authorizes it to perform specified actions.

An administrative agency is usually created by a statute, known as the **enabling statute**. The enabling statute typically will name the agency and specify its purpose, powers, limits, and structure. The statute may call for a board or commission, or it might call for a single individual to head the agency. Some agencies are required by a state constitution. Those usually are called "constitutional agencies." Even then, the agency may be described only briefly in the state constitution, allowing the state legislature the ability to better define it and modify it over time. When dealing with any particular agency, the first step should be to understand its powers and limitations, as well as its structure. Studying the enabling statute or constitutional authority for the agency is critical to understanding any agency.

Administrative Procedure Act

Administrative Procedure Act (APA) of 1946
Law that mandates procedures for federal administrative agencies.

In 1946, the **Administrative Procedure Act (APA)** established a set of rules governing most federal agency conduct. The APA was enacted in response to numerous charges of inconsistent or reckless procedures and inconsistent standards being used by the numerous federal agencies created before World War II. The APA created a structure that categorized various agency conduct and set rules for each category. Agency conduct that was defined as either "rulemaking" or "adjudication" was given basic minimum requirements to ensure a fair and accurate action. Rulemaking and adjudication are explored later in this chapter. Most states have enacted laws similar to the federal APA to govern state administrative agencies.

Delegation of Power

When an enabling statute grants a power to an agency that is otherwise a power assigned to Congress in the U.S. Constitution, there is a legitimate question as to whether Congress and the president have made a constitutional delegation. The U.S. Supreme Court has ruled on this issue several times, usually allowing delegations. The most often cited case arose during the Great Depression as the New Deal sought to create numerous new administrative agencies.

LEGAL FOCUS—CASE

In the midst of the 1930s depression, Congress enacted the National Industry Recovery Act (NIRA). The NIRA authorized the president of the United States to approve codes of fair competition that had been prepared and submitted to him by trade and industry associations or had been created upon the president's own initiative. The act provided that violations of these codes would be punishable as crimes. The Schechter Poultry Corporation was held criminally liable for violation of one such code, the "Live Poultry Code." Schechter challenged the code by challenging the constitutionality of Congress's delegating to the president the power to approve codes. How did the Supreme Court rule?

Schechter Poultry Corp. v. United States, 295 U.S. 495, 55 S.Ct. 837 (1935).

A unanimous Supreme Court held that the delegation by Congress to the president in the NIRA was too broad, because it allowed the president to impose any regulation he chose. This "unfettered" power was "an unconstitutional delegation of legislative power." *Schechter* is a rare overturning of a delegation by Congress, but it helped define how and when Congress could delegate its power without running afoul of the U.S. Constitution.

LEGAL FOCUS—BACKGROUND

The creation of the Federal Trade Commission (FTC) is an example of a lawful delegation by Congress. The FTC was created by the Federal Trade Commission Act of 1914, which prohibits unfair and deceptive trade practices. The act describes the procedures the agency must follow to charge violators, provides for the judicial review of agency actions, and grants the power to investigate and to make rules and regulations. The FTC may force a company to stop an advertising campaign if it considers the advertisements to be "unfair or deceptive" to consumers. The FTC may even require a company to make announcements or advertisements to correct the false statements made in earlier advertisements.

State Administrative Agencies

California

The state of California has an administrative bureaucracy that many argue rivals the federal government. In a state famous for its protective statutes, numerous agencies exist to carry out those laws. California also has its own Administrative Procedure Act

(CAL-APA). Yet another administrative agency was created just to enforce the CAL-APA, the Office of Administrative Law (OAL). Like the federal government, California has an Environmental Protection Agency (CAL-EPA), numerous other environmental protection agencies, health and welfare agencies, business and trade regulation agencies, and consumer protection agencies. In California, there is a state-equivalent agency for nearly every federal agency. In many cases, California law more strictly regulates economic transactions than federal law does. For instance, the U.S. EPA might allow a particular chemical to be discharged into the ground, whereas the CAL-EPA might prohibit it. Such duplicative state law generally is allowed by federal statute when it does not unduly interfere with federal regulation of interstate commerce.

Iowa

California's administrative law contrasts greatly with Iowa's law. Iowa has its own version of the APA, but it has a simpler and smaller labyrinth of administrative agencies. Less duplication exists with federal agencies. Still, there is a significant administrative law system within the Iowa state government. Iowa regulates business, protects the environment, and regulates its professional trades. It also has administrative agencies for building code development, organized labor, and employment disputes.

LEADING AREAS OF ADMINISTRATIVE LAW

Administrative law touches on nearly every aspect of government; moreover, administrative agencies of the federal and state governments do the majority of the work of enforcing the law in several major areas. This section introduces several substantive areas of administrative law. Every agency was created in response to a specific need. Gradually, as government regulation became more common, and perhaps more expected, the *laissez-faire* (French: "allow to act") capitalism conceived by the early economist Adam Smith gradually was replaced with a regulated economy.

Business Finance

By definition, in a free economy, the government does not interfere in business at all. But the health and function of business can greatly affect the economy and the general welfare of the United States; left unregulated, business practices have shown themselves to be highly vulnerable to abuse and exploitation with drastic consequences for the economy as well. Since the Great Depression of the 1930s, the United States has maintained a strong regulatory oversight of the financial sector, including investment, banking, securities, accounting, and trading. Three large and important agencies in this arena are the SEC, the Commodity Futures Trading Commission (CFTC), and the Federal Reserve Board.

The SEC (1934) regulates organized securities markets and the securities traded there. It also thus regulates every company that uses securities for finance purposes. Because "security" is defined very broadly, the SEC reaches many investments beyond traditional securities like stocks and bonds. The SEC controls and regulates the dissemination of information by regulated companies and investigates and prosecutes violations of securities laws and regulations. The SEC also regulates traders, brokers, and other professionals who work in securities. The CFTC (1974) is similar to the SEC but focuses on the commodity futures and options markets. The Federal Reserve Board (1913) supervises and regulates most of the nation's banks and helps to ensure a stable money currency, to hedge against inflation, and to control the flow of money in the economy.

LEGAL FOCUS—BACKGROUND

In 2001, Enron, a large energy and technology company, collapsed under admissions of manipulating debt and hiding losses of billions of dollars. MCI, a communications company, followed suit in 2002. HealthSouth was next in 2003. Eventually, the senior officers of Enron and MCI were convicted of securities crimes, but the chief executive officer of HealthSouth, Richard Scrushy, escaped criminal liability. The political and economic fallout from these collapses has been tremendous. A new law, the Sarbanes-Oxley Act, was created, that requires chief executive officers and chief financial officers to certify periodic disclosure reports filed at the SEC.

Communications

The roaring economic growth of the 1990s was fueled in part by tremendous growth in the communications sector. From cellular phones to the Internet, from cable to the radio, the FCC is the agency at the center of this sector. Created in 1934 to regulate the then-stressed radio communications business, the FCC regulates the companies that own, operate, or trade capacity in wire and radio communication systems. Much regulation of the communications business deals with the dividing up of the limited electromagnetic spectrum in the bands used for communication. In that sense, cellular telephone systems are the latest growth industry that the FCC has managed. Without a regulating central agency, the communication industry would be chaos at best and war at worst. The industry includes common carriers, such as the telephone and telegraph services. Currently, the Internet is not regulated directly in the United States. By virtue of regulating the telephone industry and cable industries, the FCC is the closest any government office comes to regulating the Internet.

A key function the FCC performs is the issuance of licenses to radio, telephone, and cellular telephone systems. The FCC assigns operating frequencies, where appropriate, and investigates and enforces regulations covering, for example, the use of unauthorized frequencies. The FCC also regulates radio and television content as to "decency" and suitability for its audience.

Employment Practices

Employment law is substantially affected by administrative law. The government regulates working conditions, pay, hiring and firing of employees, health, pension and retirement benefit plans, and organized labor and its relationship with employers. Many disputes involving the employer–employee relationship are resolved through state or federal labor boards.

The NLRB was created in 1935 to supervise the union–employer relationship. Among other functions, the NLRB is charged with preventing unfair labor practices.

Some state labor boards focus on labor disputes such as overtime pay. Employees often are surprised to find out they can file a complaint with the local labor board and have their matter heard in an administrative hearing rather than file a lawsuit.

The EEOC was created in 1964 to investigate and resolve complaints of discrimination filed by employees. The Employee Retirement Income Security Act (ERISA) was enacted in 1974 to regulate pension and retirement benefit plans following the prominent failure of numerous plans. The Pension and Welfare Programs Office of the Labor Department enforces ERISA.

Environment

Government protection of the environment began with agencies such as the EPA, established in 1970. Numerous laws protect the environment and restrict what individuals, property owners, and businesses can and cannot do that might affect the health of the environment. The Endangered Species Act, the National Environmental Protection Act, the Clean Air Act, and the Clean Water Act are just a few of the many statutes that obligate numerous agencies to work vigorously to protect the environment. Besides the EPA, other agencies that work to enforce these and other environmental laws include the U.S. Fish and Wildlife Service, the Bureau of Land Management, and the National Forest Service. Many state agencies are delegated the authority to enforce federal environmental protection laws.

The EPA is the single agency at the core of environmental protection. Exhibit 5.4 is the formal statement of the EPA's purpose. Through the EPA and affiliated federal and state agencies, the government strives to reduce water- and airborne pollution, clean up contaminated land, reduce destruction of habitat, and save species from extinction. Most of this work is accomplished by controlling development and enforcing regulations against violators. Nearly every environmental protection statute requires a tremendous amount of detail in the form of regulations to make it effective. For instance, to enforce the Clean Air Act, the EPA had to establish standards for healthy air. Today, a hot political topic is global warming. One question is whether the EPA has the authority to and will directly regulate carbon dioxide emissions, the largest contributor to global warming.

Energy

The United States consumes more energy per capita than any other nation. It relies primarily upon fossil fuels (oil, natural gas, and coal) and to a smaller extent on hydroelectric dams and nuclear, geothermal, solar, and wind power. The United States is highly dependent on foreign sources of fossil fuels, such as oil from the Middle East and natural gas from Canada and Mexico. About one-third of the oil consumed in this country is used in the transportation sector. This foreign dependency, combined with the core economic need for an adequate, safe, and reliable supply of energy, has led to creation of agencies at both

EXHIBIT 5.4 EPA Statement of Purpose

The EPA's purpose is to ensure that

- All Americans are protected from significant risk to human health and the environment where they live, learn, and work.
- National efforts to reduce environmental risk are based on the best available scientific information.
- Federal laws protecting human health and the environment are enforced fairly and effectively.
- Environmental protection is an integral consideration in U.S. policies concerning natural resources, human health, economic growth, energy transportation, agriculture, industry, and international trade, and these factors are similarly considered in establishing environmental policy.
- All parts of society—communities, individuals, business, state and local governments, tribal governments—have access to accurate information sufficient to effectively participate in managing human health and environmental risks.
- Environment protection contributes to making our communities and ecosystems diverse, sustainable, and economically productive.
- The United States plays a leadership role in working with other nations to protect the global environment.

the federal and state levels. Further complicating the situation is that nearly all energy consumed in the United States has environmental impact considerations, thus drawing federal and state environmental agencies into the energy sector.

The Federal Energy Regulatory Commission (FERC), created in 1977, is responsible for regulating electricity generation and transmission, numerous federally owned large hydroelectric facilities, and natural gas and oil production and transmission. Nuclear energy is regulated by the Nuclear Regulatory Commission (NRC), established in 1974. The NRC licenses and supervises all nonmilitary nuclear power plant, research, test, and training reactors. It is also responsible for regulating all medical, academic, and industrial uses of nuclear materials.

Free Enterprise and Healthy Competition

The United States was founded on the modern economic thought of Adam Smith. Adam Smith promoted the idea that the invisible hand of the market naturally would guide a capitalistic economy far better than the artificial efforts of government ever could. That model survived intact only briefly, as the United States steadily found circumstances in which the economy was not functioning adequately. In every instance, the solution involved new laws or regulations designed to protect competition from itself.

The chief federal administrative agency tasked with protecting competition is the FTC, established in 1914. Another agency that regulates in this area is the SEC, with its supervision of the financing of business. The primary concern of the FTC is controlling unfair competition by administering various *antitrust* statutes. Antitrust describes government efforts to control the collusion of businesses to manipulate markets and also the development and wielding of market power by gaining monopoly status. The FTC shares responsibility with the Justice Department in this area.

LEGAL FOCUS—CASE

The Superior Court Trial Lawyers Association of Washington, D.C. (SCTLA), went on a one-month strike for higher wages (higher hourly rates). SCTLA members are criminal defense lawyers in private practice. They are registered with courts, indicating their availability to represent indigent defendants in cases assigned by the court.

After an investigation and hearing, the FTC ruled that the SCTLA boycott was illegal and barred any future similar action. The SCTLA appealed. A federal appeals court ordered the FTC to reconsider its decision and determine whether the SCTLA had sufficient control of the market to make its boycott anticompetitive. The FTC appealed to the U.S. Supreme Court. Should the FTC be compelled to reconsider its ruling?

FTC v. Superior Court Trial Lawyers Ass'n, 493 U.S. 411, 110 S.Ct. 768 (1990).

No, they should not. The Supreme Court said, "The social justification[s] proffered for [this] restraint of trade … do not make it any less unlawful." The Court applied the toughest antitrust rule, the *per se* (Latin: "in itself") rule. This means that the Court recognized that some business activities, such as price fixing, are so anticompetitive that they are automatically (*per se*) prohibited. Thus, these activities do not require proof that conspirators (in this case, SCTLA members) had a motive, or the power, to control the market. The Supreme Court overturned the appeals court order and upheld the FTC ruling that the SCTLA strike was inherently illegal. Therefore, evidence of SCTLA power to control the market was not required.

Other Areas of Administrative Law

Recall that administrative law is as vast as the subject of law itself. Thus, the foregoing discussion identifies only some major leading areas of administrative law. The transportation sector, medical facilities, and the licensing of the professional trades are all handled with administrative agencies. Welfare programs and other government benefits such as unemployment and disability insurance are supervised by administrative agencies. Suffice it to say that administrative law touches nearly every subject of law.

AGENCY POWER, PROCESS, AND ACTION

You have learned that administrative law is vast and pervasive and the agencies that create and apply the law are numerous. Now we will study the basic ways in which agencies perform their duties and functions. As mentioned earlier, our focus is on the federal system. Most states have similar structures, processes, and rules.

Generally speaking, important agency actions are classified as rulemaking, investigation, or enforcement. Adjudication can be part of an enforcement proceeding. Exhibit 5.5 illustrates the relationship between agency actions and agency products. Rulemaking and adjudication are the two significant and powerful tools that an administrative agency wields to accomplish its purposes.

The Independence of Agencies

It can be said that agencies act as "judge, jury, and prosecutor," a description that well describes the independent power and action of many agencies. It also illustrates what happens when powers from all three branches of the government are placed within one agency. Most independent administrative agencies and some executive departments make regulations to enforce statutes, choose how and to whom to apply those regulations, and then apply them. Agencies can fine, take property, issue permits, and give benefits to

EXHIBIT 5.5
Agency Authority, Purpose, and Action

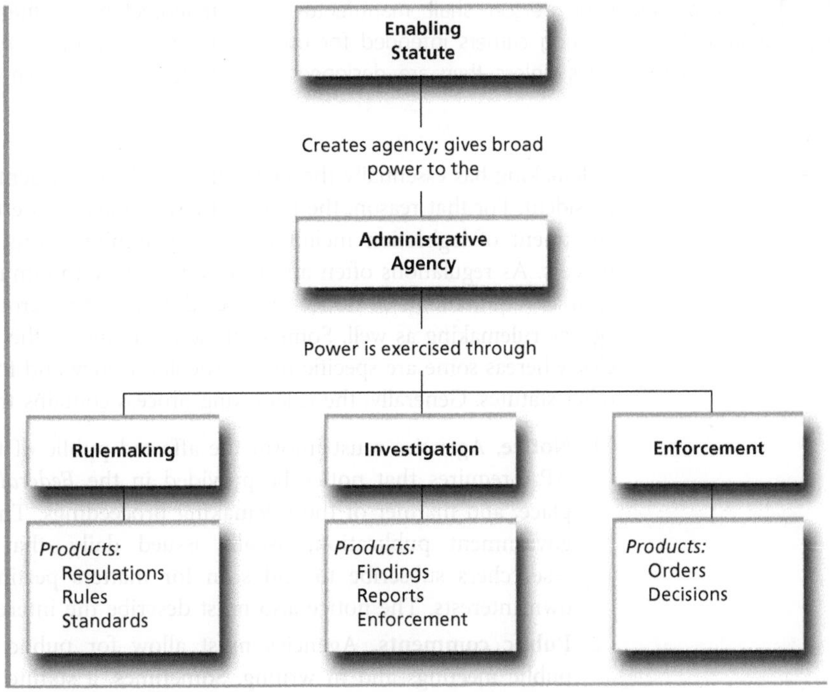

businesses and individuals. They do much of this without leaving the confines of their own buildings. Hence, they operate very independently. Congress can do little to stop or control an agency's action. The president has some control over executive departments, but little if any direct control over independent administrative agencies. The judiciary exercises some oversight and review of agency conduct, but as we will see later, that review is very deferential. Thus, successful interaction with administrative agencies requires good working knowledge and management of agency structure and procedure.

Regulations and Rulemaking

Rulemaking is, obviously, the making of rules or regulations. Rules and regulations are the laws made by agencies that implement, interpret, or prescribe law or policy. Historically, rules and regulations represented two distinctly different types of law. *Rules* are procedural laws that describe agency processes, such as the conduct of hearings. *Regulations*, on the other hand, are the laws that guide agency decision making, that determine rights and duties. Today, the distinction between rules and regulations has blurred significantly in many agencies, federal and state. Agencies often create a type of regulation known as a *standard*. Standards are regulations designed to establish norms or guidelines. Another type of regulation is an *interpretive rule*, which explains how an agency interprets a rule or intends to apply it. Interpretive rules do not have the force of law that other regulations do. They, however, do have considerable weight in court, should someone challenge an agency action or decision. Courts give significant deference to agency expertise. When interpretive rules are published, courts seldom apply a different interpretation.

Below is a regulation passed by the EPA that prohibits ring carriers (the plastic that holds six-packs of soda together) unless they will degrade in accordance with specified testing standards.

LEGAL FOCUS—EXAMPLE

No processor or person shall manufacture or import, in bulk, ring carriers intended for use in the United States unless they are designed and manufactured so that the ring carriers degrade to the point of 5 percent elongation at break, when tested in accordance with [testing standards].

Rulemaking has essentially the same effect as the enactment of a law by Congress and the president. For that reason, the process by which agencies establish regulations is similar to enactment of legislation including meeting minimal constitutional requirements of due process. As regulations often affect personal rights, minimum standards of fairness apply, such as requirements of notice to affected parties. Numerous other requirements apply to agency rulemaking as well. Some of these are found in the APA and apply to most agencies, whereas some are specific to a particular agency and found in the enabling statute or other statutes. Generally, the rulemaking process contains these fundamental elements:

1. **Notice**. Agencies must inform the affected public of the intended rulemaking. The APA requires that notice be provided in the *Federal Register*, including the time, place, and manner of the rulemaking proceedings. The *Federal Register* is a federal government publication, usually issued daily, that administrative lawyers and researchers subscribe to and scan for matters pertinent to their clients' or their own interests. The notice also must describe the interests being affected.
2. **Public comments.** Agencies must allow for public comments, usually orally at public meetings and in writing. Sometimes, a statute requires that rules cannot be

enacted without a public hearing. Hearings often are conducted around the country to receive comments. If a hearing is not required, the agency usually provides an address to which written comments can be sent.

3. **Publishing of the regulation.** Final federal regulations are printed in the *Federal Register*, taking effect thirty days after publication. After the thirty-day period, the regulations are published in the Code of Federal Regulations (CFR). The CFR is a huge, growing document that includes all federal regulations. States often have an equivalent to the CFR for state regulations, though they are often organized very differently. States may have an equivalent to the *Federal Register* as well.
4. **Response to comments.** Sometimes, agencies are required to respond in writing to significant comments made by other parties. When this is the case, the agency publishes a comprehensive explanation of how each comment was addressed.
5. **Written record.** An agency may be compelled to maintain a rulemaking record in case a regulation is challenged in the courts. The regulation process results in numerous written documents including the initial rulemaking notice, comments by parties and the agency, and a final rule, sometimes with an explanation.

Exhibit 5.6 provides a general outline of the rulemaking process for the FCC. The specific process in each federal agency varies slightly, but stays within the requirements of the APA. Each state has its own version of the rulemaking process as well. The above components represented in Exhibit 5.6 are nearly always present, however, though perhaps with different names. Notice that public comments are invited after each step in the FCC's process. Note also the extensive use of acronyms (NOI, NPRM, etc.). Administrative agency rulemaking, like many government activities, uses acronyms liberally.

EXHIBIT 5.6
FCC Rulemaking Process

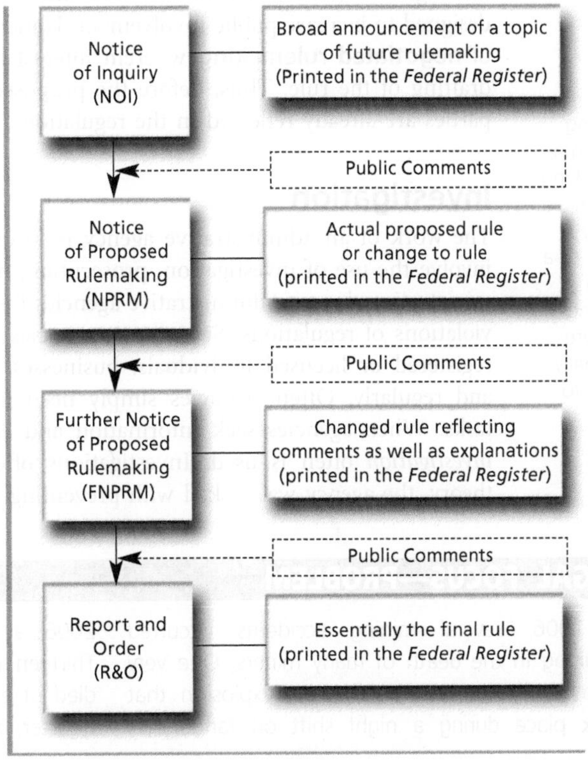

LEGAL FOCUS—PROBLEM

The Internal Revenue Service decides to create a new regulation to discourage tax evasion. The new regulation, published in the latest edition of an IRS publication, requires any taxpayer who is selected for an audit to pay the IRS $10,000. Failure to do so will be considered an admission of illegal tax evasion. An enraged taxpayer challenges the regulation in the courts. Is it an enforceable regulation?

No, it is not enforceable. A court will conclude that the regulation was not properly created. The IRS did not provide public notice and did not receive and reflect on public comments. The IRS did not tailor the regulation to reflect legitimate public concerns or respond to comments. The alleged regulation was not published in the CFR. Even if the IRS had done all of these things, a court likely would conclude that the regulation exceeded the authority and power granted to the IRS. Judicial review of agency action is covered later in this chapter, but this is an easy case.

Negotiated Rulemaking

Even with notice protections, the rulemaking process is often unsatisfactory to the agency or the interested parties. In some cases, the overwhelming amount of written information frustrates participants. Sometimes, the formulaic process of publish-comment-publish leaves interested parties feeling ignored. Often, different interests make comments reflecting opposite viewpoints on numerous issues. This leaves agencies in a difficult position: They cannot satisfy all parties. The formal rulemaking process limits give-and-take dialogue that might help find common ground. The Negotiated Rulemaking Act (NRA) allows an alternative method for creating regulations that is designed to increase public involvement. Under the NRA, agencies can conduct a process of **negotiated rulemaking** wherein interested parties are invited to participate in the drafting of the rule. Thus, before the proposed rule is even published, the concerns of parties are already reflected in the regulation.

negotiated rulemaking
A process to bring together representatives of a rulemaking agency and stakeholders to jointly prepare the text of a proposed rule in a consensus-seeking negotiation before the agency formally submits the rule to the rulemaking process.

Investigation

The work of an administrative agency is to execute its administrative tasks. That may involve the use of investigation, prosecution, negotiation, and any number of other administrative chores. Administrative agencies frequently respond to information regarding violations of regulations. Sometimes, agencies conduct inspection programs wherein all registered or licensed individuals, businesses, or facilities are inspected systematically and regularly. Often, agencies simply need information to fulfill their administrative tasks. When agencies seek information and engage in fact-finding activities, the term *investigation* often is used. Investigations often follow accidents or disasters that, in theory, the agency was tasked with preventing.

LEGAL FOCUS—PROBLEM

In 2006, several mining accidents occurred resulting in the death of many miners. One very high profile incident involved an explosion that took place during a night shift on January 2, 2006, at the Sago coal mine in West Virginia. Thirteen miners were trapped, and all but one died of exposure and suffocation. Following the disaster, a federal agency responsible for mine safety, the Mine Safety and Health Administration (MSHA), initiated an investigation into the causes of the accident. Some became openly critical of how ineffectively MSHA had been in routinely investigating mine safety and assessing fines. Some called for the immediate closure of all mines until mine safety was established. The Sago mine reopened, partially, on March 11, 2006. Could MSHA have ordered all mines to shut down temporarily?

You might try to answer those questions from a legal perspective. If you did, you likely would cite the Due Process Clauses of the U.S. Constitution. But, even after citing those clauses, you probably still would be pressed to conduct a moral judgment regarding the meaning and extent of those clauses.

subpoena
An order directing a person to appear at a certain time and place for the purpose of giving testimony as a witness.

When parties fail to cooperate with an agency, or when an agency believes it is necessary, subpoenas can be used. A **subpoena** is an order to produce a witness or a thing. Using a subpoena, the administrative agency can compel testimony or production of documents, papers, records, and physical objects. Failure to comply with a subpoena can lead to a contempt citation punishable by fine or imprisonment.

Search and Seizure by Administrative Agencies

Administrative agencies, like police authorities, have the power to search and seize property. Searches can be part of an investigation for an enforcement proceeding. Some inspections are used in place of formal processes, as when a person being inspected is shown a problem and allowed to fix it. Nevertheless, the search and seize power is useful, but it clashes with a person's right to privacy, due process, and freedom from self-incrimination under the U.S. Constitution. Because of that, the Supreme Court has ruled that administrative agencies must comply with the search and seizure provisions of the Fourth Amendment.

The requirements for agencies are less stringent than those for criminal warrants, and warrants are not always required. Some agencies are not required by statute to obtain a warrant. Such warrantless searches have been challenged in courts. The Supreme Court has held that commercial property can be searched by an administrative agency without a warrant in certain situations involving heavily regulated businesses such as mining, liquor, or weapons.

LEGAL FOCUS—CASE

Craig and Marilyn Lessor of Union Grove, Wisconsin, were licensed dealers of long-eared, short-tailed lagomorphs—that is, rabbits. Their rabbitry was subject to regulation and inspection under federal law by government agents. They were found to have unlawfully refused to allow inspections of their rabbitry on five occasions and were fined by the department secretary. The Lessors sought judicial review of the sanction, claiming that by inspecting and attempting to inspect their rabbitry without a warrant, their right to be free from unreasonable searches guaranteed by the Fourth Amendment was violated. Was a warrantless inspection of their rabbit farm lawful?

Lessor v. Epsy, 34 F.3d 1301 (7th Cir., 1994).

The inspections were held to be lawful. Although the U.S. Supreme Court has yet to articulate clear guidelines for warrantless searches, generally these three guidelines apply:

1. Administrative searches of heavily regulated industries are less likely to require a warrant. Industries such as nuclear power or mining fall in this category.

2. A warrantless search might be reasonable, or not even considered a search but merely an inspection. In that case, it is lawful. When searches are tailored narrowly to minimize the invasion of privacy or not connected to enforcement-specific efforts, they are likely to be allowed.
3. A reasonable expectation of privacy increases the need for a warrant. This last guideline is the most difficult. The privacy of one's home requires the highest protection from warrantless searches, but what if a regulated business is run from one's home? Most farmers would be among those so classified.

It should be clear that these general guidelines fall far short of covering all the possible situations involving warrantless searches. For that reason, warrantless searches often create the risk for the agency that an enforcement action may be overturned. The best way to avoid the issue is to get permission to search, something the Lessors refused to grant in the preceding example.

Enforcement

After concluding an investigation, the agency may start an administrative action. These actions may be brought against individuals or organizations. Enforcements are used to gain compliance with the law. Sometimes, enforcement does not follow an investigation. Sometimes, private citizens and organizations are allowed under statute to initiate complaints precipitating the enforcement action. Usually, the agency has discretion to decline a complaint or dismiss it. In any case, the enforcement is brought by the agency itself.

In enforcement actions, the agency acts as prosecutor, judge, and jury. To protect persons subject to administrative investigations, there are procedural safeguards against possible abuse of power by the agency. When procedural safeguards are found inadequate, Congress may hold hearings and pass new laws constraining administrative powers.

Enforcement can take one of several paths. The problem might be resolved through negotiation between the accused and the agency. It might go to a hearing before an administrative law judge (ALJ). Finally, the full commission might review the ALJ's decision or act as the decision maker itself. Every agency has its own procedures, and enforcement processes vary significantly from agency to agency. The APA is silent on this topic, addressing only the adjudication aspect of enforcement. As a result, when an individual faces enforcement proceedings, the first step is to seek assistance from a lawyer or consult the agency's regulations, or both. In any case, the individual should become knowledgeable about the agency's procedures.

Exhibit 5.7 shows a map of a generic agency enforcement process. Many administrative law practitioners advise that someone subject to administrative action attempt to negotiate an agreement in a cooperative manner early on in the process. As agencies have huge workloads, cooperative individuals often can obtain a reasonable negotiated settlement. If that fails, most agency enforcement processes will lead to adjudication (i.e., a hearing). Sometimes, alternative dispute resolution programs are offered.

Alternative Dispute Resolution

In the federal system, several statutes have authorized alternative dispute resolution (ADR) methods in agency processes. The 1990 Administrative Dispute Resolution Act was renewed by passage of the Administrative Dispute Resolution Act of 1996. The ADR Act of

EXHIBIT 5.7
Administrative Agency Enforcement

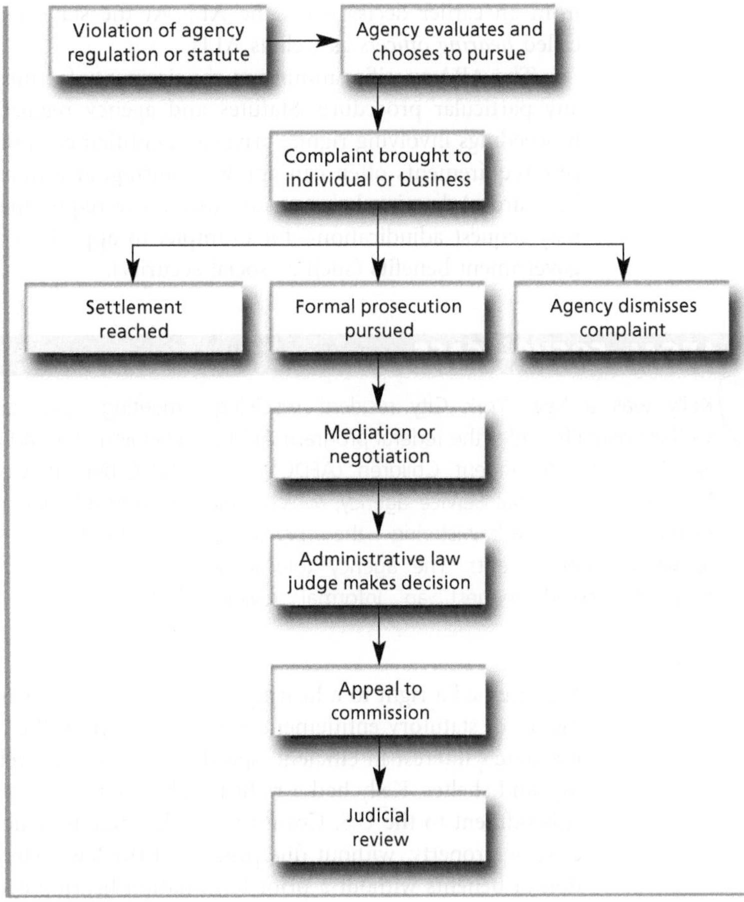

1996 expressly authorizes agencies to utilize ADR methods to supplement existing procedures. The act gives discretion to the agencies to choose how to use ADR, but it does require that all federal agencies develop an ADR policy, appoint and train a senior "dispute resolution specialist," and train key employees in ADR. The ADR Act of 1996 added binding arbitration as a dispute resolution method available to agencies. In the future, it is likely that agency enforcement proceedings will offer negotiation, mediation, or even binding arbitration as an optional or perhaps mandatory step in the resolution processes. In any case, should ADR (if offered) fail to resolve a matter, the next step is adjudication.

Adjudication

administrative law judge
A government employee appointed to hear and decide matters in administrative agency hearings.

Most agencies provide a hearing as an alternative to a court action when a person is threatened with the loss of denial or some license, right, entitlement, or privilege. The agencies not only create rules consistent with their task but also enforce their rules through trial-like proceedings before an **administrative law judge (ALJ)**. An ALJ is a government employee, usually an attorney, appointed to hear administrative cases.* Sometimes, the appointed heads of the agency hear the cases instead of, or on appeal

*Some ALJs are employees of the very agency prosecuting the case. When such is the case, safeguards are in place to separate the ALJ from the investigative and prosecutorial staff. Private communication between the ALJ and anyone who is a party to an agency proceeding while the matter is pending is forbidden.

from an earlier decision by, the ALJ. At the state level, similar quasi-judges are often called *hearing officers* as well as ALJs.

The APA specifies minimum requirements for these hearings but does not mandate any particular procedure. Statutes and agency regulations usually specify hearings for proceedings involving rights, privileges, entitlements, or licenses. Constitutional due process requirements often can apply, requiring, at a minimum, notice and opportunity to be heard. A hearing helps ensure that those requirements have been met. Citizens, too, may request adjudication—for example, to appeal an agency's denial of their claim for government benefits (such as social security).

LEGAL FOCUS—CASE

Kelly was a New York City resident receiving welfare benefits under the federal program Aid to Families with Dependent Children (AFDC). The New York City Social Service agency, which was responsible for administering the program, terminated her benefits. The agency told Kelly that she could request an informal review meeting and a formal hearing. She sued, claiming she had a right to a hearing before her AFDC benefits were terminated. Did Kelly have a right to a hearing before the AFDC benefits were terminated?

Goldberg v. Kelly, 397 U.S. 254, 90 S.Ct. 1011 (1970).

Yes, she had a right to a hearing. The U.S. Supreme Court held that where benefits are a matter of statutory entitlement, the importance to the recipient must be weighed against the state's interest in efficient, speedy processes. As welfare benefits provide food, clothing, and shelter, Kelly had a right to a hearing before termination. Under the Fourteenth Amendment to the U.S. Constitution, the state may not "deprive any person of life, liberty, or property, without due process of the law." Here, the Court held that a termination of benefits without a prior termination hearing denied Kelly due process.

Since the *Kelly* case, agencies have been much more sensitive to when a hearing might be required. Accordingly, agencies often offer to hold a preliminary hearing when the agency's contemplated action would deny a person some right, license, or privilege.

Many agencies use the ALJ-led hearing as a first step in the adjudication process. It is followed by a review by the head of the agency or by the full commission or board of the agency. Other agencies treat the ALJ decision as the final decision, but they allow for an appeal to the head of the agency or to the full board or commission. Another variance is to assign a few members of the board or commission to work as a committee in reaching a decision. In those cases, the ALJ conducts the hearing and advises the committee members, but the ultimate decision is made by the committee. State agencies use a similar variety of approaches to adjudication.

cease-and-desist
A command from an administrative agency that the subject party refrain from specified activities.

A final order may compel payment of monetary damages or can provide a **cease-and-desist** order to prohibit a certain activity. In the case of benefits, such as welfare or unemployment, the order might reverse an agency staff's decision to deny the benefit.

LEGAL FOCUS—ETHICAL PROBLEM

In separate incidents over a period of several months, three employees died in a steel mill owned by USX Corp.: one from burns, one from crushing, and one from suffocation. OSHA, an administrative arm of the U.S. Department of Labor, was asked to investigate. After a finding of safety violations, OSHA recommended fines of $7.3 million. OSHA prevailed in a legal challenge of their authority to assess and collect fines without USX having an opportunity to contest the findings. How much due process does a company or person deserve? Should all circumstances require the same due process, or does an emergency situation justify less due process?

No, all circumstance do not require the same due process. Although the agency did have the power to impose a fine, it could not deny USX the opportunity to have a fact-finding hearing before an ALJ. At the eventual hearing, USX pleaded guilty to the violations and promised to correct the problem and follow OSHA's recommendations. The negotiated fee resulted in a much-reduced fine.

Fair Hearings and Due Process

Administrative hearings are conducted much like trials. Lawyers may represent parties, and evidence is presented using witness testimony, documents, and authentication. Cross-examination usually is allowed. There are significant differences, however, between a trial and an administrative hearing. Administrative hearings do not have juries. Likewise, evidence and procedural rules can be somewhat different and often slightly less formal. For instance, hearsay often is admitted.

fair hearing
An oral proceeding before an administrative agency to hear and decide some factual question related to agency action.

The APA requirements for a **fair hearing** are simple. The APA requires that each side have the opportunity to submit and have evidence considered. The APA also requires that the ALJ be neutral and unbiased. Most agency regulations go farther than that, mostly to ensure a fair fact-finding process. These fairness protections primarily are driven by due process considerations under the U.S. Constitution.

Judge Henry Friendly, in an influential article still as timely and accurate now as when he wrote it in 1975, described eleven attributes that make up a fair hearing. Not all of these attributes are required constitutionally, but many of them are what an American citizen expects as fair treatment, not only from government but also from any large organization. With some editorial license, Judge Friendly's list is reproduced with a brief discussion of how each attribute affects an administrative hearing and contrasts with court processes:

1. **An unbiased tribunal.** In a court proceeding, a tribunal is a neutral court with a judge or a jury deciding a case. In the usual administrative hearing, an agency employee who was not a party to the original decision is considered sufficiently unbiased to decide the case.
2. **Notice of the proposed action and the grounds for the action.** In a judicial process, a complaint and summons are used to notify the party sued of the nature of the adverse claim. In an administrative action, some additional statement is expected about what government action is proposed, along with the legal reasons for the action.
3. **An opportunity to present reasons why the proposed action should not be taken.** Fundamental to all fair processes is opportunity to tell, and justify with evidence, your view of the facts to the person making the decision.
4. **The right to call witnesses.** In a court trial, you have the right to subpoena witnesses. This means you can force a witness to attend your trial. While a party to an administrative hearing can call witnesses, they may not always be compelled to attend.
5. **The right to know the evidence against you.** A person subject to a government action should be aware of all evidence used by the ALJ to make the decision. A hearing

officer or an ALJ should not receive evidence or opinions without sharing that information with the affected party. Nevertheless, there are some administrative hearing situations in which parties are not allowed to know all evidence against them. For example, a hearing to discipline a prisoner is an administrative hearing, but if testimony used to discipline the prisoner were provided to the prisoner, the adverse party, usually another prisoner, could face reprisals. For that reason, the prisoner subject to discipline often is not given complete information regarding the source and nature of the evidence.

6. **A decision based on evidence presented at the hearing**. If the decision is based on information presented at the hearing, then one has the opportunity to rebut it. If the ALJ makes a decision on facts learned outside the hearing, the claimant is denied a fair opportunity to contest the information. This right is almost always required.
7. **The right to counsel**. Most administrative hearings will allow counsel but will not pay for it. Also, unlike in court proceedings, counsel is not required to have legal training.
8. **Making of a record**. A written record needs to be available to allow a party a fair ability to contest a hearing. Administrative requirements regarding the type of record vary, whereas court records are transcribed consistently from tapes or created in shorthand contemporaneously.
9. **Statement of reasons for the decision**. If reasons for the decision are given, faulty reasoning can be challenged and appealed. A statement of reasons, even though brief, usually is expected as part of the administrative hearing process.
10. **Public attendance**. Open attendance in court trials is permitted on the general belief that the activities of government officials should be open to the public to protect individuals from possible abuse of government power. In administrative hearings, open attendance may be allowed, but often it is not.
11. **Judicial review**. As court decisions, results of administrative hearings can be appealed. Experience has shown that courts seldom overturn administrative rulings or actions. Usually, the best chance for appeal is within the agency. When appeals are taken outside the agency, courts involved are more likely to grant relief if the agency violated due process in some way. Courts seldom challenge agency interpretation and application of the facts, because the agency is presumed to have expertise in the application of the facts presented. Nevertheless, judicial review is an important component of administrative law.

LIMITS ON AGENCY POWER

Several restraints counteract the broad power and independence of administrative agencies. Some of these already have been discussed, such as the limits on delegating power to agencies and the constitutional due process requirements that apply to administrative processes. Other chief restraints are political control, constitutional guarantees, laws enforcing public accountability, and—probably the most important means of controlling agency behavior—judicial review.

Political Control

The separation of powers in the U.S. government drives a certain degree of independence in agencies, but Congress and the president still have ability to control agencies politically. One way is by amending the statute that gives an agency its power. Another avenue of control, if slower and less direct, is through the appointment process for new board or commission members. The budge process may be the president's and Congress's most crucial power over independent administrative agencies. Funding levels from year to year affect an agency's activity just as well as direct supervision can.

Constitutional Guarantees

The role of constitutional due process on agencies was described earlier. Agencies must provide notice and opportunity to be heard. They generally must receive and respond to comments when making regulations. Agencies also must respect due process in the adjudication role. Finally, as described earlier, the Fourth Amendment restricts agency search and seizure efforts.

Public Accountability

Several laws hold government accountable to the public and require that it conduct itself in accordance with the law and in a manner responsible to the public's expectations. The laws discussed next are federal and apply only to the federal government, but many states have state equivalent laws for some of these federal laws.

Freedom of Information Act (FOIA)
A federal law requiring the federal government to disclose most public records to any person on request.

Freedom of Information Act

The **Freedom of Information Act (FOIA)** requires that the federal government disclose most "records" to "any person" on request. Under this act, government agencies are expected to publish most statements of policy and staff manuals that affect the public and are not already published in the *Federal Register.* Agencies also are required to state how much unpublished information may be obtained and to designate a contact person in their office to handle such requests. The person requesting the information need not disclose why it is wanted. Certain records, such as information related to security risks or ongoing criminal investigations, are not retrievable. The news media and business firms make the most frequent requests under the FOIA. A refusal by a government agency to provide requested information could be challenged in court.

Government in the Sunshine Act
A federal law requiring that most meetings of federal agencies be open for public observation and that advance notice be given of agency meetings, listing the expected topics of discussion.

Government in the Sunshine Act

The **Government in the Sunshine Act** prohibits secret agency meetings. It is an open-meeting law. Not only must most meetings be open for public observation, but also advance notice must be given of the meetings, along with the expected topics of discussion. Administrative hearings are not covered by the Sunshine Act, so they usually are conducted in private.

Regulatory Flexibility Act
Federal law requiring federal agencies to consider the effects of their regulatory actions on small businesses and other small entities and to minimize any undue disproportionate burden.

Regulatory Flexibility Act

Whenever a new regulation will have a "significant impact upon a substantial number of businesses," the **Regulatory Flexibility Act** requires that the agency conduct a "flexibility analysis." This means that the agency must estimate and disclose the costs of the rule on small businesses. It also must consider any less burdensome alternatives. The act requires notice to small businesses about the proposed regulations.

judicial review
The power of the courts to review administrative agency action.

Judicial Review of Agency Action

The courts, with their ultimate power to declare the law, provide a direct avenue for the **judicial review** of agency action. The ability of the judicial branch of government to hear complaints regarding agency actions, to review agency conduct, and to correct violations and wrongs is a critical part of the balancing of agency power with restraint. Judicial review is not an unlimited control from illegal agency processes or decisions, however, because various constraints on judicial review can limit its effectiveness.

Scope of Judicial Review

The APA allows judicial review of most agency actions. That means a court may prevent or undo any unauthorized action by an agency. Likewise, courts may compel agency action that has been withheld unlawfully. In reviewing administrative actions, however, courts are reluctant to review questions of fact. This deference is based partly on the judicial attitude that those who hear and see the evidence firsthand are best able to evaluate it. Also, the agency is considered an expert on the topic that it hears, and as such, usually is more knowledgeable about the topic contested than a reviewing judge would be. Finally, courts generally believe that wholesale review of agency actions would destroy the value of the more efficient agency process and worsen the problem of already crowded court calendars.

de novo review
A complete reevaluation of an issue, finding, or case as if the original decision had never been made.

A ***de novo* review** (new proceeding), however, will be granted if (1) a review is required by statute, (2) the agency's fact-finding proceeding was inadequate, or (3) new facts not heard in the original proceeding are to be raised.

Standing to Sue

standing to sue
A person's right or capacity to bring a lawsuit because he or she has a legally protected interest at stake in the litigation.

The challenging party must have **standing to sue**. Standing requires that a challenger have a direct stake in the outcome of the judicial proceeding. The best way to show this is to demonstrate that the agency's action had a substantial effect on the challenger. An injury to an economic interest, or even in some cases to an emotional, environmental, or aesthetic interest, is sufficient to show standing to sue. One reason for the requirement of standing to sue is to discourage petty lawsuits. The courts will require that a plaintiff show an actual injury by, or because of, an agency action. Protest lawsuits or lawsuits from taxpayers who are simply angry about some government action are dismissed because of lack of standing to sue.

LEGAL FOCUS—CASE

The trustees of the Loudoun County Public Library in Virginia instituted a policy to block access to sexually explicit material through the library's publicly provided Internet access sites. An association of library patrons, Mainstream Loudoun, challenged the regulation in court. The library trustees defended on several bases, among them that

> *neither the individual plaintiffs nor Mainstream Loudoun have suffered an actual injury as a result of the Policy. Specifically ... no member of the Mainstream Loudoun has attempted to access blocked Internet materials in Loudoun County libraries, or petitioned a library to unblock a blocked site.*

Mainstream Loudoun contradicted this claim in its complaint. Does Mainstream Loudoun have standing to sue the library trustees?

Loudoun v. Trustees of the Loudoun County Library, 2 F.Supp.2d 783 (E.D., Virginia 1998).

The court said that Mainstream Loudoun had standing to sue. Because the group's complaint contradicted the library trustees' claim, stating that several members had in fact attempted to access blocked sites, they had standing. For an association to have standing to sue on behalf of its members,

> *(1) its own members would have standing to sue in their own right; (2) the interests the organization seeks to protect are germane to the organization's purpose; and*

(3) neither the claim nor the relief sought requires the participation of the individual members in the lawsuit.

All three criteria were found to exist.

exhaustion of remedies
A doctrine requiring that a person attempt all available options within an administrative agency before taking a claim to a court.

Exhaustion of Administrative Remedies

Courts are reluctant to interfere with the regulatory process, preferring that the agency correct its own mistakes. Until recently, courts had been unwilling to review an action until the challenging party had exhausted all possible alternative means of resolving the controversy within the agency, known as **exhaustion of remedies**. This stance, however, has come under challenge.

LEGAL FOCUS—CASE

R. Gordon Darby was a South Carolina real estate developer specializing in the development and management of multifamily rental projects. In the 1980s, working with a mortgage banker's plan, Darby was able to obtain mortgage insurance from the Department of Housing and Urban Development (HUD). The plan was later determined to be inconsistent with a department regulation. The assistant secretary proposed to debar (suspend) Darby from further participation in HUD programs. Darby contested the suspension, but following an administrative hearing, an ALJ upheld an eighteen-month debarment from all federal programs. Darby failed to request a review from the HUD secretary within fifteen days of receipt of the ALJ's determination. He later sought a judicial review of the ALJ's action. Did Darby's failure to avail himself of a HUD secretary review forestall his right to judicial review?

Darby v. Cisneros, 509 U.S. 137, 113 S.Ct. 2539 (1993).

No, it did not forestall his right. In a decision that surprised many administrative law scholars, the Supreme Court held that, under the APA, a plaintiff need not exhaust available administrative remedies unless a statute or specific agency rule requires it, and in this case, none did. Said the Court,

> *It is perhaps surprising that it has taken over forty-five years since the passage of the APA for this court to definitively address this question. But where the APA applies, an appeal to "superior agency authority" is a prerequisite to judicial review only when expressly required by statute or when an agency rule requires appeal before review and the administrative action is made inoperative pending that review.*

Knowledge of the requirement is still important because the law often requires that administrative options be exhausted before seeking judicial relief at both the federal and state levels.

Defenses to Agency Action

The following are the usual defenses the party might raise when seeking judicial review of an agency decision. The party's goal, of course, would be to overrule the agency determination:

- The agency exceeded the authority conferred on it by its enabling legislation.
- The agency improperly interpreted laws applicable to the agency action under review.

- The agency violated a constitutional provision.
- The agency acted in violation of the procedural requirements.
- The agency acted in a manner that was arbitrary or capricious, or constituted an abuse of discretion.
- The conclusion drawn by the agency was not supported by substantial evidence.

These criteria offer a solid base for judicial review. Other grounds for review are unlikely to suffice.

LEGAL FOCUS—CASE

Environmentalists persuaded a court to require the Nuclear Regulatory Commission (NRC) to reconsider its decision to grant an operating license to the Vermont Yankee Nuclear Power Corporation. The court held that the NRC was not adequately considering the dangers of nuclear fuel reprocessing and nuclear waste management. The NRC appealed to the U.S. Supreme Court, claiming that the lower court had no power to interfere in the administrative process. Could the lower court legally interfere?

Vermont Yankee Nuclear Power Corp. v. NDRC, 435 U.S. 519, 98 S.Ct. 1197 (1978).

No, the lower court could not. The courts do not have power to prescribe procedures that regulatory agencies must follow; at most, they may analyze whether the agency followed its own procedures and gathered sufficient evidence to support its actions. This decision reflects the Supreme Court's expectation of deferential treatment toward administrative agencies.

CASE

If your university is a public institution, the due process rules applicable to administrative agencies and discussed in the chapter apply to it. If you are accused of cheating or otherwise run afoul of university administrators—or, dare we say it, professors—you can expect certain minimum protection from expulsion or other treatment detrimental to your continued beneficial enrollment. The following case discusses due process protections available in such a hearing. Consider the case in reference to the discussion of Judge Friendly's article. If your university is a private school, you probably will find that it has provided rules very similar to those available at public institutions. After all, due process protections are minimum requirements; universities whether they be public or private are free to provide more expansive protections, and they often do.

Nash v. Auburn University

812 F.2d 655 (11th Cir., 1987)

Two students, David Nash and Donna Perry, were accused of cheating on their anatomy examinations at Auburn University's School of Veterinary Medicine. At a university hearing to determine the merits of the charge, faculty members and student witnesses testified that they observed Nash and Perry examining specimens together in laboratory examinations and moving together from question to question at those exams. At the exams, Nash and Perry were seen suspiciously to signal each other and to exchange glances: on written exams, they were seen to look on each other's papers. Appellants frequently sat together at written exams in seats not assigned to them at the rear of the exam rooms. The students were suspended from the university at the conclusion of the hearing. Nash and Perry filed suit, arguing that Auburn University suspended them based on constitutionally inadequate procedures that violated their rights under the Due Process Clause of the Fourteenth Amendment. The U.S. District Court for the Middle District of Alabama entered judgment in favor of the university, and the students appealed. The court of appeals agreed with the district court, holding that the students were provided with a fair hearing—notwithstanding the lack of advance notice of statements from accusing witnesses and the lack of opportunity to directly cross-examine witnesses. The court also ruled that the students had been given adequate time to prepare for the disciplinary hearing.

Senior District Judge James E. Doyle Delivered the Opinion of the Court

Appellants were advised in writing on June 6, 1985, that they were charged with a violation of the Student Code of Professional Ethics (the code) of the Auburn University School of Veterinary Medicine. They were given "at least 72 hours to prepare a defense for the charge of academic dishonesty, in that while taking examinations during the 1984–1985 school year, information was allegedly obtained in an unethical manner." Appellants appeared with counsel at the hearing [and] objected that the notice was inadequate and too general to advise them of the charge[s]. [Counsel] requested a more specific notice and one additional day to prepare their defense. The following day each appellant received a written memorandum, dated June 11, 1985, advising them that they were charged with a violation of the code in "giving or receiving assistance or communication between students during the anatomy examination given on or about May 16, 1985." Included in the memorandum was a list of students and anatomy faculty witnesses who were expected to testify at the hearing in support of the charge against appellants.

A disciplinary hearing … was held on June 12, 1985. Both Nash and Perry attended, in the company of their attorney. The hearing was conducted by the non-voting student chancellor of the board, in the presence of appellants, witnesses, and student justices. There was no attorney for the board present. The chancellor allowed appellants' counsel to advise his clients during the hearing, but he was not permitted to participate in the proceedings. Appellants were to be allowed to question the adverse witnesses by directing their questions to the chancellor, who would then pose their questions to the witnesses.

After all of the testimony was presented supporting the charge, appellants were granted a short recess and then given an opportunity to present their defense. Appellants were allowed to present statements responding to the charge against them and rebutting the testimony of the student and faculty witnesses. They brought witnesses in their behalf who also made statements to the board and answered questions of the justices. After all of the presentations, the board again questioned appellants and the witnesses. After the board completed its questioning, appellants were given the opportunity to question the opposing witnesses by submitting questions to the chancellor, who would then direct the questions to the witnesses. Appellants instead asked the board several questions. Appellants asked for a recess, which was denied by the chancellor, and the hearing was concluded. After deliberating in private, the board decided unanimously that appellants were guilty of the charge of academic dishonesty. The justices recommended that appellants be suspended from school, with the opportunity to apply for admission again in one year. Appellants were notified of the board's decision and recommendation.

Appellants … appealed to the dean on June 13, 1985. Pursuant to the code, the dean referred the case to the school's faculty Committee on Admissions and Standards for its review and recommendation. On June 19, 1985, the committee held a day-long meeting to consider the appeal. The committee reviewed a copy of the materials presented to the board at its June 12 hearing and listened to an audio recording of the June 12 hearing. Appellants presented oral and written statements in their defense and answered questions from the committee. After deliberating, the committee voted unanimously to recommend that the dean uphold the board's findings and recommendation. The dean accepted the committee's recommendation and upheld the action of the board. Appellants later appealed to the president of Auburn University, who reviewed the written file in the case and concurred in their suspension.

Under the Fourteenth Amendment to the United States Constitution, no state may "deprive any person of life, liberty, or property, without due process of law." It is alleged and not disputed that Auburn University is a creature of the state of Alabama. Further, it is assumed by the parties and by the district court that appellants have property and liberty interests in their continued enrollment at Auburn University and that their interests enjoy the protections of due process.

The Procedural Due Process Claims

"The Fundamental requirement of due process is the opportunity to be heard at a meaningful time and in a meaningful manner." *Goss v. Lopez*. What process is due is measured by a flexible standard that depends on the practical requirements of the circumstances. That flexible standard was translated by the Goss court to mean that high school students facing the deprivation of a property right by suspension from school must, at a minimum, "be given some kind of notice and afforded some kind of hearing." [W]e broadly defined the notice and hearing required in cases of student expulsion from college: "[A] n opportunity to hear both sides in considerable detail is best suited to protect the rights of all involved. This is not to imply that a full-dress judicial hearing, with the right to cross-examine witnesses, is required."

The adequacy of the notice and the nature of the hearing vary according to an "appropriate accommodation of the competing interests involved." [T]hree factors are important when considering the constitutional adequacy of the procedures afforded in a given situation: First, the private interest that will be affected by the official action; second, the risk of an erroneous deprivation of such interest through the procedures used, and the probable value, if any, of additional or substitute procedural safeguards; and finally, the [g]overnment's interest, including the function involved and the fiscal and administrative burdens that the additional or substitute procedural requirement would entail. The due process clause is not a "shield … from suspensions properly imposed," nor does it ensure that the academic disciplinary process is a "totally accurate, unerring process;" it merely guards against the risk of unfair suspension "if that may lie done without prohibitive cost or interference with the educational process."

Nash and Perry argue that [Auburn] engaged in procedures, which deprived them of constitutionally protectable rights in their continued enrollment as veterinary students. They argue that inadequate notice failed to provide them the opportunity for a meaningful response to the charge of academic dishonesty. Specifically, they claim that the interval of time between the notice and the hearing was too short, and the notice did not apprise them of the substance of the evidence against them. They argue also that the hearing was inadequate to protect their interests from erroneous deprivation in that they were denied the opportunity to cross-examine witnesses. Further, they argue that the tribunal was unfairly prejudiced by the existence and the participation of a justice with knowledge of the charge. Appellants argue also that they were denied a meaningful appeal and that the cumulative effect of these individual abridgments of their rights denied them due process of law.

1. The Notice

a. Timing: There are no hard and fast rules by which to measure meaningful notice. "An elementary and fundamental requirement of due process ... is notice reasonably calculated, under all the circumstances, to apprise interested parties of the pendency of the action and afford them an opportunity to present their objections."

Appellants urge ... that a coercive atmosphere pervaded the June 10 hearing, providing appellants and their counsel no choice but to agree to the board's proposed timing of the restated notice and the rescheduled hearing. However, in the record of the June 10 hearing we find no evidence of coercion to give us concern that appellants' waiver might not have been knowingly given. In sum, appellants were given four days by the June 6 notice and an additional one day by the June 11 notice, for a total of about six days from the June 6 notice to prepare their defense at the June 12 hearing. Despite the severity of the charge of academic dishonesty and the severe sanction it carries, the time allowed appellants was reasonable. It enabled them to retain counsel who successfully argued in their behalf at the June 10 hearing for a more specific notice of the charge as well as for a delayed hearing. Further, appellants had sufficient time to appear at the June 12 hearing with witnesses in their behalf, bringing documentation to support their defense.

b. Content: Appellants argue that the notice in this case was deficient because it did not advise them of the nature of the testimony to be presented against them or of the facts underlying the charge of academic dishonesty. Appellants urge that the analysis by [anatomy professor Donald] Buxton of their May 16 examination answers was persuasive, complex testimony and came as a surprise. They argue that they were entitled to a summary of the testimony expected from Buxton and the other accusing witnesses at the June 12 hearing, because only such notice would have provided safeguards against their surprise at the testimony and would have ensured them a fair opportunity to respond. Had they known of Buxton's analysis before he testified, appellants suggest they would have presented expert, statistical testimony to rebut the inference that they cheated on the May 16 neuroanatomy exam.

There is no constitutional requirement that, to provide them an opportunity to respond, appellants must have received any more in the way of notice than a statement of the charge against them. Although the June 6 notice in their case was rudimentary, the June 11 notice specified that appellants were accused of academic dishonesty on the May 16 neuroanatomy exam and it included a list of accusing witnesses. On that notice, appellants obtained the assistance of counsel and brought to the June 12 hearing students and a faculty witness who testified as to their own interpretations of appellants' conduct throughout the school year and at the May 16 exam. Appellants were present at the entire June 12 hearing to hear the evidence against them, made a cogent defense, and undertook to discredit the adverse testimony, including Professor Buxton's analysis of their exam answers.

Despite the serious charge against appellants, who were hard-working students on the threshold of their careers, and the severity of the sanction imposed on them, we find that appellants were afforded constitutionally adequate notice and were adequately prepared by the notice to defend the charge against them.

2. The Hearing

a. Right to cross-examination: "The fundamental requisite of due process of law is the opportunity to be heard." However, the nature of the hearing "will depend on appropriate accommodation of the competing interests involved." Appellants rely on *Goldberg v. Kelly* (1970) to challenge the constitutional adequacy of their hearing on the ground they were not allowed to cross-examine the accusing witnesses. *Goldberg* taught us that "[i]n almost every setting where important decisions turn on questions of fact, due process requires an opportunity to confront and cross-examine adverse witnesses." However, we have not expanded the *Goldberg* procedural requirements for quasi-judicial termination of welfare benefits in student disciplinary hearings. Where basic fairness is preserved, we have not required the cross-examination of witnesses and a full adversary proceeding. Due process requires that appellants have the right to respond, but their rights in the academic disciplinary process are not coextensive with the rights of litigants in a civil trial or with those of defendants in a criminal trial.

Although appellants were not allowed to ask questions directly of the adverse witnesses at the June 12 hearing, it is clear that they heard all of the testimony against them. Appellants were told they could pose questions of the accusing witnesses by directing their questions to the presiding board chancellor, who would then direct appellants' questions to the witnesses.

We do not suggest that the opportunity to question witnesses would not have been valuable in this case. Although an important notion in our concept of justice is the cross-examination of witnesses, there was no denial of appellants' constitutional rights to due process by their inability to question the adverse witnesses in the usual, adversarial manner.

3. Fairness of the Tribunal

An impartial decision maker is an essential guarantee of due process. "[B]asic fairness and integrity of the fact-finding process are the guiding stars." Appellants argue that the board was unfairly prejudiced at the June 12 hearing by the failure of a student justice to recuse himself. Appellants argue that the active presence of one student justice unfairly prejudiced the June 12 hearing and the deliberations of the board in this case, because that justice had prior knowledge of the charge of academic misconduct against appellants. They argue that a fair hearing and an unbiased decision were not possible in their case because the justice had not recused himself.

There is no evidence in the record, however, which suggests bias on the part of the student justice in question, such that he should disqualify himself from performing his duties on the board. He was familiar with appellants' conduct and with the general comments made about them by their classmates. In his contact with some potential student witnesses prior to the June 12 hearing, he explained the method of bringing information about violations of the code before the board chancellor. We agree with the district court that just "any prior knowledge of the incident" does not disqualify a decision maker; neither this student justice's knowledge of the suspicions about appellants nor his contact with potential witnesses appear to have rendered him a biased decision maker or to have denied appellants a tribunal free of bias.

4. The Appeal

[A]ppellants argue that their case was given only "perfunctory, fleeting review" by the dean of the school and the president of the university, both accepting the recommendations of the board and the committee, in violation of appellants' constitutional right to a meaningful appeal. We do not agree. The possibility that an erroneous decision may have been made by the board was diminished by the extensive review by the faculty committee. To impose two additional layers of de novo review, as appellants seem to request, would not have changed the nature of their opportunity to respond to the charge against them.

The Combination of Violations

The Student Code of Professional Ethics at Auburn University School of Veterinary Medicine provides rudimentary protections for students facing suspension on a charge of academic dishonesty. As we have explained, where appellants have challenged the adequacy of the notice and hearing provided them, Auburn's procedures met the constitutional minimum, but no more. They were given notice of the specific violation with which they were charged and were allowed an opportunity to respond at a hearing before an impartial tribunal, held within a reasonable time following the notice. Appellants were allowed to speak in their own behalf, to bring witnesses to support their defense, to confront their accusers, and to appeal their adverse decision to a committee of faculty members and then to officials of the school and the university. The judgment of the district court is affirmed.

For Critical Analysis

Considering this case and the text discussion, answer the following questions about the hypothetical Mid-State University:

The policies of Mid-State University provide that students who disrupt class activities are subject to expulsion. Before expulsion can occur, however, the student is entitled to a conference with the dean of students. Jim Landry is a student who has been accused of obstructing the administration of the school by engaging in a sit-in demonstration. He asserts that he is entitled to more procedural protection than afforded by the conference with the dean of students.

1. Mid-State says that Landry enrolled at the university and therefore has waived any further protections than those granted him in the rules and regulations. Is this position well taken?
2. Landry asserts that he is entitled to have his lawyer present during any procedures designed to expel him. Is this position reasonable?
3. Landry states that he has the right to cross-examine the witnesses against him. Is he correct?
4. Landry maintains that the dean of students is biased against him because of statements the dean has made to the effect that Landry is a menace and should be removed from the university. Is Landry's objection allowable?
5. Would it make any difference to Landry if the university in question were a private rather than a public university? Restrict your answer to the right to a hearing and the general nature of such a hearing.

CHAPTER QUESTIONS AND PROBLEMS

1. What is the distinguishing characteristic of an independent administrative agency? What are the checks and balances on an administrative agency by the executive, legislative, and judicial branches of government?
2. Legal scholars have pointed out that "the sheer volume of law generated by all types of administrative agencies exceeds the volume produced by both the legislatures and the courts combined." Yet comparatively few cases involving the work of administrative agencies appear in the docket of the U.S. Supreme Court or in the dockets of the lower courts. Can you suggest a reason for this phenomenon?
3. Following the 9/11 terrorist attacks, the U.S. government, through the National Security Administration (NSA), began a program of systematically monitoring communications suspected to be related to terrorism. The NSA did so without obtaining search warrants. One justification offered was that the War on Terror made necessary warrantless searches legitimate under the Fourth Amendment. What reasons might the federal government have for not seeking warrants prior to monitoring phone or e-mail communications?
4. What recourse does a citizen have when an administrative agency such as the Environmental Protection Agency, in its enthusiasm and dedication, imposes what one might consider to be unreasonable standards—for example, for clean air, where the cost of eliminating perhaps the last 5 percent of pollution may be as high as the cost of eliminating the first 95 percent?
5. Several unrelated deaths occurred in a chemical plant owned by Rivercity Chemical Corporation over a period of several months in 1999. The Occupational Safety and Health Administration (OSHA)—an administrative arm of the U.S. Department of Labor—was asked to investigate. After a finding of safety violations, OSHA fined Rivercity $8.3 million. Does an administrative agency such as OSHA have the power to assess and collect fines?
6. Martin Mazurie, a non-Indian, operated a bar on land he owned near an Indian reservation. A federal statute authorized Indian tribes to control the distribution of alcoholic beverages on their reservations. Mazurie, after being denied a tribal liquor license, was convicted of introducing spirituous beverages into Indian country. Mazurie appealed, claiming that as a non-Indian landowner he was not subject to Indian authority and that the federal statute authorizing tribal regulation of alcoholic beverages was an unconstitutional delegation of authority by Congress to a private body. The U.S. Court of Appeals agreed with Mazurie, holding: "Congress cannot delegate its authority to a private, voluntary organization, which is obviously not a governmental agency, to regulate a business on privately owned lands, no matter where located." The Indian tribe appealed. Can Congress delegate power to an Indian tribe to regulate non-Indians on the reservation? [*United States v. Mazurie*, 419 U.S. 544, 95 S.Ct. 710 (1975).]
7. An organization of criminal-defense lawyers known as the Federal Defenders of San Diego brought suit to challenge the constitutionality of sentencing guidelines issued by the U.S. Sentencing Commission. The commission challenged the plaintiffs' standing to bring the lawsuit. The plaintiffs argued that their members appear as counsel in 60 percent of federal criminal cases that continue after an initial appearance. Do the Federal Defenders have standing to bring the lawsuit? [*Federal Defenders of San Diego, Inc., et al., v. U.S. Sentencing Commission*, 680 F.Supp. 26 (D.C. 1988).]
8. Ulmer G. Wilson, a New Orleans realtor, was unhappy when he discovered an immobilizing "boot" on his car. A note on the car's window gave a number to call to retrieve the car. After calling, Wilson became even more unhappy. He was expected to pay $630 for previous parking violations and a $30 boot-removal fee. Wilson refused to pay, and the car was stored. The decision to boot Wilson's car had been made by Datacom, a private business under contract with the city to collect unpaid parking violations, receiving a commission on all it collected. The decision to boot was made by Datacom based on a city ordinance allowing for immobilization of vehicles with three or more unpaid parking violations. Wilson had at least twenty parking tickets; nevertheless, he contested the booting as a taking of his property without due process of law. He contended that the booting took place without proper notice and that Datacom's determination to boot was made by a partial decision maker who did not offer Wilson a hearing before booting the car. Was Wilson denied his right to a fair hearing with an impartial decision

maker? [*Ulmer G. Wilson v. The City of New Orleans*, 479 So.2d 891 (Louisiana, 1985).]

9. As a general rule, administrative searches of businesses require a search warrant. The Department of Alcohol, Tobacco and Firearms (ATF) officials inspected Colonnade Catering without either a warrant or permission. The inspection was based on information provided by an ATF agent who, while a guest at a party held at the establishment, noted possible violations of federal law (not paying tax on alcoholic beverages). The catering service owner claimed that the officers conducted the search in violation of his Fourth Amendment rights as they searched without a warrant or his permission. The ATF claimed that the catering service store is part of a "pervasively regulated industry" and as such there is a substantial government interest in warrantless searches. Can the department conduct the warrantless search? [*Colonnade Catering Corp. v.* U.S., 387 U.S. 72, 90 S.Ct. 774 (1970).]
10. Save The Dolphins is a nonprofit corporation whose primary purpose is to stop the incidental killing of dolphins in tuna fishing. The National Marine Fisheries Service (NMFS) made a film on an experimental tuna-fishing cruise. Save The Dolphins requested a copy of the film under the Freedom of Information Act. The NMFS declined to release the film because at the time the film was made the government had assured tuna boat captain Medina that "the film would not be shown to anyone but those involved in the research, since the scenes therein would depict fishing trade secrets and commercial information used by Medina's crew." Will NMFS be required to make the film available to Save The Dolphins? [*Save The Dolphins v. U.S. Department of Commerce*, 404 F.Supp. 407 (N.D.Ca., 1975).]

CHAPTER 6

Crimes: Public Wrongs

If there were no bad people there would be no good lawyers.

Charles Dickens, *The Old Curiosity Shop*, 1841

LEARNING OBJECTIVES

After reading and studying this chapter, you should be able to:

- Define the term *crime* and describe the usual elements of a criminal act.
- Define and explain *corpus delicti*.
- Explain the various crimes against the person and against property.
- Recognize various valid defenses to crimes.
- Discuss the Fourth Amendment to the U.S. Constitution and identify situations in which a warrantless search might be permitted.
- Describe common procedures used in a criminal trial.
- Discuss the rights of the criminal accused, including Miranda warnings and the Fifth Amendment.
- Explain the various punishments available for crimes and when a punishment might be considered cruel or unusual.

No area of law provokes more intense public reaction than criminal law. And the media capitalizes on the public's interest in crime, which borders on morbid fascination. Publicized cases frequently focus on issues that are controversial, perplexing, and provocative. Unfortunately, as a result, important but controversial issues are frequently obscured by emotions.

Criminal behavior patterns constantly have been evolving and changing since the United States was founded. New ways to commit old crimes have emerged, and new crimes have been defined statutorily to enable the government to stop or control undesired behavior. Carjacking; homicide and serial killers; child victim crimes, including molestation, kidnapping, and rape; drug crimes; terrorist bombings; electronic crimes, such as identity theft; and white-collar crimes, such as securities fraud, exist in the twenty-first century. The sheer magnitude and cost of the prison systems in the United States are straining the ability of government to keep the criminal system functioning smoothly.

Punishment is the direct consequence for apprehended criminals, but there also are indirect consequences of criminal law enforcement. For example, marijuana and its cousin, hemp, are illegal contraband under federal law (Controlled Substances Act), although bills have been introduced in Congress to exclude industrial hemp from the definition of "marijuana" in the statute. Thus, hemp cannot be grown legally in this country unless the Drug Enforcement Agency (DEA) issues a permit for its cultivation. A few states have applied for such a license, but none have been granted by the DEA for industrial hemp production. Like soybeans, hemp can be used to produce an oil that in turn can be used in a wide variety of beneficial products, including cooking oil, cosmetics, and plastics. Hemp fiber can be used to make paper, cloth, and even structural panels stronger than plywood. Hemp seed can be ground for flour and even livestock feed. When grown in rotation with other crops, such as cotton, hemp increases their yields and reduces the need for pesticides. In short, hemp is a potentially beneficial and valuable crop that is grown successfully in other countries, such as Canada, France, Germany, and England. On the other hand, hemp contains a small amount of the same chemical found in marijuana. Existence of the chemical may not be significant, but hemp looks like marijuana and would make law enforcement more difficult, so some officials argue its legalization is a thinly veiled attempt to legalize marijuana. In fact, two states (Washington and Colorado) already have legalized and regulated recreational marijuana to some degree, even though its possession and distribution remains a crime under federal law. The controversy surrounding legalization of hemp is both an example of how crime and its enforcement affect our society and an example of how the complexities of our legal system are increasing.

Society also seems increasingly willing to treat minors as adults relative to punishments for criminal behavior. In most states, the move toward harsher treatment of juveniles is politically popular. But there also is concern that juveniles in adult prisons may be abused, labeled as criminals, and denied access to rehabilitative services. The following questions illustrate many of the criminal law issues attracting intense public scrutiny:

- Is the public victimized by repeat offenders who are punished too leniently?
- Is blue-collar, back-street crime condemned whereas white-collar, "Wall Street" crime is implicitly condoned? Does the theft of a wallet lead to imprisonment and the theft of millions lead to fines?
- Are there different standards of justice for the rich and poor?

- Is capital punishment barbaric, justified, or both?
- Should so-called victimless crimes (e.g., prostitution and gambling) be prosecuted?
- Why can insanity excuse even the most heinous criminal conduct?
- Are too many nonviolent offenders being sentenced to prison?
- Is criminal law being applied unfairly, producing a prison population disproportionately composed of young African American males?
- Can we afford to offer the fairness protections provided by the Constitution in our quest to protect ourselves from terrorist threats? How can we distinguish an accused terrorist from someone accused of another form of criminal activity?
- How do we bring to justice those who commit criminal acts over the Internet, sometimes from another country?

These are tough questions, and easy answers are not forthcoming. People like you will be required to answer these questions either by choice or default.

This chapter will familiarize you with the pervasiveness and complexity of some of these dilemmas through a survey of selected concepts of criminal law. There are no perfect solutions or antidotes for antisocial criminal behavior, but after studying the chapter, you should understand better the dynamics involved and sharpen your thinking about what might be the best ways of dealing with the problem. Crime and punishment—or what happens when prevention fails—are the subjects addressed here.

WHAT IS A CRIME?

A crime is a wrong against society, as defined by statute, and punishable by society. Certain human behavior is deemed to be so offensive and objectionable that it threatens the safety or common good of society. Such objectionable and antisocial conduct therefore is prohibited by statute. A crime has occurred when a prohibitory statute has been violated.

Two elements must exist simultaneously before a person can be convicted of a crime: (1) a specified state of mind or intent on the part of the person and (2) the performance of a prohibited act.* Even where both elements exist, there may be defenses to the criminal conduct. If arrested and convicted, criminals face a wide range of possible penalties, including monetary fines and forfeitures, incarceration, and even death, although they sometimes are given the choice of performing some act beneficial to society, such as community service.

It is important to note the dual consequences of most wrongful behavior. That is, most crimes are also civil wrongs: A person who burglarizes a home is committing the crime of burglary, as well as a civil wrong called *trespass*, and probably also the civil wrong called *conversion* (theft) of another's properly. In such a situation, the victim has the right to seek monetary compensation in the civil law whether or not society, through criminal law, punishes the wrongdoer. This principle was dramatized vividly in the mid-1990s by the globally publicized case involving a retired Hall of Fame professional football player and actor, O. J. Simpson.

*Some criminal statutes are mandatory—for example, those that command: "You must file a tax return and pay your income taxes without evasion" or "You must serve your country if drafted in time of war." Even these can be expressed as prohibitions of antisocial conduct.

LEGAL FOCUS—EXAMPLE

In a criminal proceeding, O. J. Simpson was found not guilty of the double murder of his former wife, Nicole Brown, and her friend Ronald Goldman. In a subsequent civil proceeding, however, Simpson was found liable, or legally responsible, for those wrongful deaths and was ordered to pay $35 million in monetary damages to the families of the victims. Thus, the criminal law and the civil law acted independently of each other concerning a single wrong. There was no issue of "double jeopardy" in this case because double jeopardy is a safeguard that applies only to successive *criminal* trials for the same offense.

Under the U.S. Constitution, criminal statutes must describe the forbidden conduct clearly and precisely, so that all persons may know, after reasonable investigation or reflection, what is prohibited. For example, a law prohibiting "loitering," but without specifically defining the prohibited conduct, is unconstitutionally vague. The underlying principle of justice is that no one shall be held criminally liable for conduct that reasonably could not be recognized as forbidden. In general, we are entitled to a "fair warning" of the existence of a criminal law so we can avoid the behavior it proscribes. The fair warning precondition requires the following:

- The statute must be clear and specific.
- Statutes will be construed "strictly" (interpreted) by courts to limit their scope as specifically as possible.
- Courts cannot adopt a novel or creative interpretation of a statute to sweep certain behavior into its literal terms.

LEGAL FOCUS—CASE

Tennessee Judge David Lanier was convicted of violating the constitutional rights of five women by sexually assaulting them. The federal statute the judge allegedly violated provided that it is a crime to "deprive a person of rights protected by the Constitution." Under the federal statute, if the deprivation of protected rights includes bodily injury, the prison sentence is enhanced to ten years. The jury found that two oral rapes by Judge Lanier caused the victims "bodily injury" and he received a twenty-year sentence as a result of that finding. But Judge Lanier appealed, contending that he was ignorant that the words in the statute covered sexual assault. What was the result on appeal?

Judge Lanier won on appeal because he could not "reasonably anticipate" that his sexual assaults would violate the statute. The U.S. Supreme Court held that the "unlawfulness must be apparent." In other words, Judge Lanier may have known that his behavior was improper, but he did not know that his sexual assaults deprived the victims of their constitutional rights. At first blush, this result may appear to violate the principle that "ignorance of the law is no excuse." The Court, however, ruled only that "ignorance of a *nonspecific and vague law* is an excuse." This requirement of clarity and specificity protects citizens from being prosecuted by zealous moralists, but it often creates an opportunity for exploitation by those who take advantage of statutory gaps created by new challenges, such as technological and scientific advances.

The difficulties inherent in clearly specifying in a statute what conduct is prohibited is dramatized by so-called loitering statutes. The definition of loitering has frustrated legislators who wish to prohibit undesirable conduct associated with homelessness activities, such as aggressive begging, urinating in public, and sleeping on sidewalks, along with gang activities such as hanging out, dealing drugs, and provoking other gangs. How can such conduct be defined and then prohibited when our freedom of association, that is, to "hang out," is protected by the Constitution? Can police logically separate harmless loitering from activity that leads to drug dealing, drive-by shootings, and other violence that the ordinance is intended to prevent?

LEGAL FOCUS—CASE

A Chicago city ordinance made loitering a criminal offense punishable by imprisonment for up to six months. To loiter under the ordinance required (1) a police officer to reasonably believe that at least one of the two or more persons present in a public place is a criminal street gang member, (2) the person to remain in place with no apparent purpose, (3) an order by the officer that all of the persons disperse and leave the area, and (4) disobedience of the officer's order. Any person, gang member or not, who is found to have disobeyed the officer's order is guilty of violating the ordinance. Does the ordinance provide sufficient specificity of criminal conduct to meet constitutional requirements?

Chicago v. Morales, 687 N.E.2d 53 (Ill., 1997) and *City of Chicago v. Morales*, 527 U.S. 41, 119 S.Ct. 1849 (1999).

criminal intent
The requisite guilty state of mind [Latin *mens rea*: "guilty mind"] to hold a person responsible for a particular crime.

infraction
Any minor crime (for example, parking violation) that is not punishable by incarceration, but only by fine. Accordingly, trial by jury is not required or permitted.

specific intent
In criminal law, the intent to accomplish the precise act and harm that the law prohibits.

general intent
In criminal law, the intent to do the prohibited act without the necessity of proving intent to cause the precise harm.

No, the ordinance does not provide sufficient specificity. The Illinois Supreme Court held that the ordinance was unconstitutional, and the U.S. Supreme Court affirmed. The ordinance failed to articulate sufficiently specific limits on the enforcement discretion of the police to meet constitutional standards for definiteness and clarity. How would any citizen of Chicago standing in a public place with a group of people know if he or she had an *apparent purpose*?

Every criminal statute prohibits certain behavior. Most crimes require an act. That is, a person must *do* something (a guilty act) to commit a crime. Mere thoughts are not crimes. The *guilty* act requirement is based on the idea that a person should be punished only for actual harm done to society. Thinking about killing someone or stealing a car may be wrong morally, but the thoughts do no actual harm. The harm happens when thoughts are translated into action. In a few situations, *not* doing something (an omission) is a crime, for example, when the law commands a person to do something and the person chooses not to do it. Examples include failure to file a tax return or to report causing a serious automobile accident.

A wrongful mental state, **criminal intent**, is also a usual requirement for criminal responsibility. The limited exceptions include certain types of regulatory offenses, often called **infractions** (e.g., failing to keep a restaurant kitchen adequately clean), and criminally negligent conduct (e.g., driving a vehicle while under the influence of alcohol). There is no universally accepted definition of criminal intent; however, it generally means evil or wrongful purpose or design. Sometimes criminal statutes require **specific intent**. Specific intent crimes require proof that an accused had a particular purpose in mind when engaging in illegal conduct (e.g., the crime of theft generally requires proof that the perpetrator intended to permanently deprive the victim of his property). Sometimes, criminal statutes require **general intent**, which requires an intentional act but no specific knowledge of particular circumstances is required (e.g., rape and assault are usually general intent crimes).

LEGAL FOCUS—PROBLEM

Derick Dagger thought about murdering his wife, Glynda, so he could inherit her money. Over a period of time, he developed and refined an elaborate scheme to commit the murder. He even wrote a step-by-step plan that he kept in his filing cabinet. Is he guilty of any crime?

motive
A reason for committing, or failing to perform, an act. Motive is not synonymous with criminal intent. Intent is essential for proof of crime; motive is not.

No, he is not guilty. Criminal intent in the absence of any supportive overt act (i.e., an open, outward, manifested act) is not a crime, even if one confesses to such intent. The written plan could be hypothetical and is an insufficient overt act on which to base a conviction. The desire to inherit money was Dagger's motive, but a motive is not a crime. Intent is different from **motive**, which is a need, desire, or purpose that impels a person to act. A prosecutor need not prove the existence of an evil motive; however, a good motive never justifies a criminal act. Thus, a "mercy killing" is a crime regardless of its underlying noble motive.

LEGAL FOCUS—PROBLEM

Marilyn Harrell, a real estate broker in Maryland, publicly admitted unauthorized diversion of $5.7 million in proceeds from sales of federally insured properties that had been foreclosed. But she insisted that the bulk of the stolen money was used to provide housing for needy families as well as food for the poor. She had been entrusted with the money by the U.S. Department of Housing and Urban Development (HUD). Are her commendable purposes a legal defense to the crime of theft (which, under these circumstances, is also called embezzlement)?

criminal negligence
Conduct that is without criminal intent and yet is so careless, or occurs in such reckless disregard of another's safety, that criminal penalties are prescribed by statute.

No, they are not a legal defense. Robin Hood's classic motive to help the poor was no defense for Marilyn, who has been dubbed "Robin HUD." She was convicted and sentenced to a prison term of forty-six months, which she served.

Criminal negligence is conduct that is without criminal intent and yet is sufficiently careless or reckless to be punished as a crime. Driving a vehicle while under the influence of drugs or alcohol is an example of criminal negligence. Leaving a handgun in one's home that is accessible to a child or leaving a child for a long period in a parked car are other examples.

Violation of state food quality regulations by a restaurant is an example of a **regulatory offense**, in which proof of criminal intent is unnecessary. Failure to get a required business or professional license is also an example of a regulatory offense.

LEGAL FOCUS—PROBLEM

In furtherance of his plan, Dagger asked his lifelong friend, Patrick O'Leary, to assist him in murdering his wife. O'Leary declined to assist but lent his revolver to Derick for use in accomplishing the murder. Have any crimes occurred?

regulatory offense
A violation of a rule promulgated by an administrative agency.

Yes, a crime has occurred. Dagger has committed the crime of **solicitation**. Criminal solicitation is to strongly urge, entice, lure, or proposition another to engage in the commission of a crime. O'Leary is guilty of **criminal facilitation** because he knowingly and substantially increased the probability that the crime would be committed; that is, he made it easier for Dagger to effectuate his plan. Unlike a gun dealer in a normal

solicitation
The crime of encouraging another person to commit a crime.

criminal facilitation
The crime of assisting another person in the commission of a crime.

retail sale, O'Leary knew of Dagger's intended crime and voluntarily assisted in its commission.

Suppose Patrick O'Leary had responded that he would be "happy to assist in the plan." Has another crime occurred? No. An agreement to commit a crime, standing alone, is not a crime. There is a constitutional limitation in criminalizing mere thought when there is no conduct in furtherance of the conspiracy. There must be some manifestation of the conspiratorial intent by what is called an *overt act.* But suppose that O'Leary then demonstrated how to load and fire his gun, and Dagger and O'Leary agreed to divide the inheritance. Has another crime occurred? Yes, Dagger and O'Leary would be guilty of the crime of **conspiracy** under these circumstances. An agreement to commit a crime becomes a criminal conspiracy once a substantial act of preparation is performed by one or more of the conspirators in furtherance of their plan. Teaching how to load and use the gun is such an overt act.

LEGAL FOCUS—PROBLEM

Early that evening, while Glynda Dagger was preparing supper, Derick aimed the loaded gun at her through the kitchen window, but she kept moving, providing a poor target. He did not fire. Have any more crimes occurred?

conspiracy
An agreement by two or more persons to commit a crime coupled with an overt act by one party toward commission of the agreed crime.

attempt
Intention of the accused to commit a crime and a substantial step toward its commission.

Yes, more crimes have occurred. Derick Dagger also committed the crime of **attempt** to commit murder because he committed an act of perpetration—that is, he took a substantial step toward the commission of the crime. Because conspirators share each other's guilt, O'Leary is also guilty of attempted murder.

If Dagger and O'Leary actually did all of the assumed acts, they would not be chargeable with, nor punishable for, each separate act necessarily. Some crimes are said to be included within, and merge into, the ultimate crime. For example, the crime of solicitation would merge into, and become a part of, the ultimate crime of attempted murder, for which both O'Leary and Dagger would be guilty.

Federal versus State Crimes

A crime is conduct that is proscribed by a statute enacted by the legislative branch of government. For example, Congress has the power to pass statutes criminalizing drug transactions because such transactions involve interstate commerce. If the conduct violates a federal statute, it results in a federal crime punishable by the U.S. government. Federal crimes are prosecuted in a federal court and, if conviction follows, result in confinement in a federal prison. The case involving Judge Lanier is a prosecution of a federal crime.

Examples of federal crimes are transportation of contraband (illegal property, such as certain harmful drugs) across state lines; kidnapping; bank robbery; forgery of a federal check; violation of certain civil rights protected by federal laws; wrongful interference with, or theft of, mail; evasion of federal income taxes; theft of U.S. government property; violation of securities laws; and physical violence on government property. In recent years, Congress has stiffened penalties for drug-related and various violent federal crimes.

If the conduct violates a state statute, it is a state crime punishable by the state. In a highly publicized case in 1991, police officers Stacey Koon and Laurence Powell were charged with violating a state statute forbidding excessive force while arresting suspects.

principal
One who is present and participates in a crime or persuades another to commit a crime.

A bystander videotaped the events surrounding the arrest of Rodney King, who had been fleeing the police at high speeds on a freeway. Despite the provocative video, a state jury found the police officers not guilty of violating the state statute.

Soon after the acquittal Koon and Powell were charged with violating the federal Civil Rights Act of 1964 for the same offensive conduct. The federal court jury found them guilty. Thus, one act can be both a state and a federal crime. Double jeopardy does not apply because the federal and state governments are separate and distinct entities under the Constitution.

WHO ARE PARTIES TO A CRIME?

accessory
A person who, though not present at the scene of a crime, aided and abetted the principal in its commission.

accessory before the fact
Person who encourages or assists a perpetrator of a crime but is not present at its commission.

To define the degree of culpability (blameworthiness) of a participant in a crime, criminals historically have been classified as either a **principal** or an **accessory**. A principal is a person directly involved in committing a crime. An accessory is a person who helps or assists a criminal activity without being present during commission of the crime. Principals receive more severe sentences than accessories. Under such classifications, a person who actually commits the crime, such as robbing a liquor store, is a principal in the first degree. Another person not as directly involved, the driver of the getaway car, for example, is classified as a principal of the second degree. A person who participated in the planning but who was not present in person at the scene of the crime is an **accessory before the fact**. One who assists the principals in evading capture is called an **accessory after the fact**.

A recent trend in many states, as in the federal system, is to classify all participants in a crime—the planner, the actual perpetrator, and the **aider or abettor**—as principals. A "lookout" is aiding and abetting in a crime and would be considered a principal. Anyone who knowingly hides a fugitive, under this modern view, is called an "accessory".

LEGAL FOCUS—PROBLEM

In a notorious case in California in 1971, Charles Manson was charged with the murders of the pregnant movie star Sharon Tate and others. Although not present at the scene of the crime, Manson, possessing hypnotic-like powers over members of his cult, commanded certain followers to commit the atrocity. Is Manson a principal or an accessory?

accessory after the fact
Person who harbors, conceals, or otherwise voluntarily and intentionally aids a known perpetrator of a crime to escape arrest or punishment

Although Manson never appeared at the scene of the crime, he was convicted as a principal to the crime of murder and sentenced to death. How a state classifies participation in criminal activity is not as important as the fact that in all states even slight participation in the commission of a crime may subject one to grave criminal penalties.

WHAT IS THE *CORPUS DELICTI*?

aider or abettor
One who encourages, incites, persuades, or sets another on to commit a crime.

The ***corpus delicti*** (Latin: "body of a crime") sounds like, but is not, the body of the deceased. The term refers to two essential elements of every crime: (1) the material being, or substance, upon which a crime has been committed (as, in homicide, a dead person; in arson, a burned building) and (2) evidence of some person's criminal conduct (as, in homicide, a bullet hole in the corpse; in arson, glass fragments from a Molotov cocktail found at the scene). Evidence that a person is missing does not alone satisfy the requirement of a *corpus delicti*.

LEGAL FOCUS—PROBLEM

Margaret Lesher, widow and heiress of a $100 million estate, married professional buffalo rider T. C. Thorstenson following a whirlwind courtship. Thorstenson concealed from Lesher his previous marriage and allegations of domestic violence. Six months after their wedding, Lesher and Thorstenson were camping one evening by a desolate lake, sleeping in separate bags. In the morning, Lesher was missing. Thorstenson looked "everywhere" to no avail and then called the police. Lesher was found dead, floating in the lake near the campsite. An autopsy revealed only that Lesher had drowned. Thorstenson claimed his inheritance under Lesher's recently drafted will. Can Thorstenson be prosecuted for murder?

corpus delicti
The two essential elements of every crime: evidence that (a) harm has occurred, (b) most probably because of a criminal act.

No, he cannot be prosecuted for murder. The law requires that no person be tried for any crime unless the prosecutor has established a *corpus delicti*. In the *T. C. Thorstenson* case, there was no clear evidence that a crime had occurred; therefore, the *corpus delicti* could not be established. The drowning could have been accidental. If the corpse had a head injury apparently inflicted by a weapon, however, Thorstenson could have been investigated and, if corroborating evidence were presented, he could have been charged with and tried for **homicide** (an unlawful taking of a human life).

LEGAL FOCUS—CASE

Goldie Millar's $340,000 ranch home was discovered burned to the ground. Her body was never found. Her grandson, Michael Pyle, lived in the vicinity and was shown to have believed that he was the sole beneficiary of her will. The sole evidence of wrongdoing was a telephone call by Pyle to his wife reporting the fire and death of his grandmother two hours before these events actually took place. Can Pyle be convicted of homicide even though no trace of Millar's body was ever found?

State v. Pyle, 216 Kan. 423, 532 P.2d 1309 (Kan., 1975).

homicide
The killing of a human being by another human being.

Yes, he can be convicted, because neither the body of the missing person nor evidence of the means used to cause death is essential to establish the *corpus delicti* or to sustain a murder conviction. Pyle's premature display of knowledge of the fire, the fire itself, and his grandmother's absence were critical factors supporting the first-degree murder conviction. Whenever a victim's body is missing, the *corpus delicti* must be established by other evidence that a crime occurred (e.g., the testimony of an eyewitness). In any crime, the *corpus delicti* must be established before a criminal prosecution can take place against anyone.

As noted, the "body of the crime" must be proved before the defendant can be prosecuted. But what if the only evidence of the "body of the crime" comes from a confession by the accused?

LEGAL FOCUS—CASE

Dennis Creutz admitted that he "might have touched" a three-year-old girl in the vaginal area but "never thought he was doing anything wrong." The only other evidence of the crime were statements from the three-year-old girl to the effect that she had been inappropriately touched with the hands and mouth of the defendant. Can the case proceed to trial?

Creutz v. People, 49 Cal.App.4th 822, 56 Cal.Rptr. 2d 870 (1996).

felony
A serious crime (such as murder) that is punishable by death or imprisonment for more than one year.

capital crime
A crime for which the death penalty may be imposed in states where authorized and at the federal level.

No, the case cannot proceed to trial. In most types of criminal cases, prosecution cannot occur unless the *corpus delicti* is established by evidence other than a confession by the accused to prevent convictions of persons who would confess to anything in order to obtain attention or perhaps food and shelter in a prison.

In crimes against minors who are too young and therefore incapable of testifying in court, confessions of the accused can be used to establish the *corpus delicti*. In other words, the out-of-court corroboration by a witness who is too young to testify is sufficient to justify use of a confession for a *corpus delicti*. In the preceding example, however, the mere incriminating statements of Creutz do not constitute a confession. A confession is a complete acknowledgment of guilt and must encompass all the elements of the crime. The mere admission that he "might" have touched the girl is not a confession and therefore cannot be used to establish a *corpus delicti*.

FELONY, MISDEMEANOR, OR INFRACTION?

noncapital crime
A homicide for which the death penalty may not be imposed even if such penalty is authorized for other crimes by the state in which the crime is committed.

misdemeanor
A crime punishable by fine or by incarceration in a county jail up to a year, or both.

violations
Any minor crime (for example, parking violation) that is not punishable by incarceration, but only by fine. Accordingly, trial by jury is not required or permitted.

States generally classify crimes on the basis of blameworthiness as either felonies or misdemeanors. The determinant is usually the gravity of the criminal act, which in turn determines the severity of the penally imposed. Generally, a **felony** is a crime that is punishable by death or imprisonment in a state prison for a year or longer. If the statute is silent as to the gravity of the crime, but incarceration in a state prison is the prescribed punishment, the crime usually is a felony. Sometimes, felonies are divided into **capital crimes** (punishable by death or imprisonment) and **noncapital crimes** (punishable by imprisonment only). The term *capital* derives from the Latin word *capita*, which means heads; so a capital crime is a crime for which you could lose your head.

A **misdemeanor** typically is punishable either by fine or incarceration in a jail for less than a year, or both. Some states have an additional classification for petty offenses, called infractions or **violations**. These carry no moral stigma and are punishable only by fine. Common infractions are gaming illegally, disturbing the peace, possessing alcohol as a minor, and presenting false evidence of age. Like felonies, misdemeanors may be divided into categories or classes as well, in a legislative attempt to distinguish criminal acts on the basis of culpability (degree of wrongfulness), leading to appropriate differences in the penalties imposed.

States vary widely in the severity of punishment that may be imposed by the sentencing judge for a particular crime. Some statutes prescribe determinate sentences, with a range of minimums and maximums. In all jurisdictions, a felony is substantially more blameworthy and more severely punished than a misdemeanor. It is not unusual for states to reexamine their sentencing laws in response to demand for harsher penalties for crimes and recurring questions about the nature of imprisonment.

WHAT ARE CRIMES AGAINST THE PERSON?

To be free of physical attack is of paramount value to all members of society. The right to life and physical security is the matrix of all the other inalienable rights of a person. Therefore, crimes of violence against persons warrant the severest penalties. Yet violence often grows out of emotions that are difficult to control. As a result, in the United States, there are distinctions in moral culpability, and they are often subtle and difficult to apply. A discussion of the general rules follows.

Murder

murder
The unlawful killing of a human being with malice aforethought.

malice
The highest degree of criminal culpability, characterized by a cold and malignant heart and a mental predetermination to do the wrongful act without legal justification or excuse.

first-degree murder
Premeditated murder perpetrated with malice aforethought.

second-degree murder
A measurement in law of the degree of culpability of the perpetrator of a murder of less than first degree.

Murder is the unlawful killing of a human being with **malice** (sometimes called malice aforethought), which denotes the highest degree of moral culpability or blameworthiness—an evil, cold-blooded state of mind. To kill with malice aforethought is to act intending to kill or in such a way that death or serious harm to another is virtually certain to occur (extreme disregard for human life). Both a paid killer and the person who did the hiring provide examples of such a state of mind.

State laws classify murder into at least two categories—typically, murder in the **first degree** (or capital murder) and murder in the **second degree** (noncapital murder). Murder in the first degree may be punishable by death or by imprisonment for life with or without the possibility of parole. Murder in the second degree may be punishable by imprisonment for less than life.

Generally, any murder perpetrated by means of poison or torture, by ambush, during the commission of a dangerous felony (e.g., during rape or robbery), or by any other kind of willful, deliberate, or premeditated killing is murder of the highest degree. All other kinds of murder, as when some provocation exists, are deemed murder of a lesser degree. Premeditation is an important factor in determining the highest degree of murder and does not necessarily require any certain period of time to occur. A cold, calculated decision to kill may be arrived at in a short period of time. On the other hand, a sudden rash impulse, even though it includes intent to kill, is not sufficient deliberation and premeditation to render an unlawful killing as "murder one." To be guilty of a deliberate and premeditated killing with malice aforethought, the slayer

1. must have weighed and considered the question of killing, including the reasons for and against such a choice, and
2. having in mind the consequences, decided to commit the crime, and
3. actually perpetrated the unlawful act causing death.

These components are difficult to apply, as demonstrated by the following case.

LEGAL FOCUS—CASE

Ernest Martinez was at a party when he learned his live-in girlfriend had gone home with another man. Martinez ran to his apartment, climbed in the bathroom window, and chased the two out the front door into the streets. Martinez managed to hit the man on the head several times with a shower curtain rod and then cornered his girlfriend, nude, in the rear alley. He beat her savagely until a neighbor asked what was going on. Martinez replied that he had "caught her in the act." He then dragged her back into his apartment, turned up the stereo, and beat her to death. Martinez was jealous and often had warned his girlfriend about infidelity. Martinez contends he is guilty only of voluntary manslaughter because of the passion and rage he felt under the circumstances. How should the jury decide?

People v. Martinez, 193 Cal.App.3d 364, 238 Cal.Rptr. 265 (1987).

Martinez was found guilty of murder in the first degree on two separate theories: (1) there was evidence of premeditation and (2) his acts were murder by torture. The intervention of the neighbor coupled with the act of turning up the stereo deprived the defendant of that intensity of passion that alone could have sufficed to reduce murder to voluntary manslaughter. There had been a "cooling-off period," supporting the finding of malice.

The Malice Requirement

The presence of malice aforethought may be implied from the conduct of the accused. Without malice, there is no murder. Under such circumstances, the homicide is generally manslaughter.

LEGAL FOCUS—CASE

Robert Rosenkrantz, age 18, was a "closet" homosexual, primarily because he feared reprisal from his father and the rest of his family. His brother, Joey, discovered the truth and, along with his friend Steven Redman, revealed it to the family. Rosenkrantz, under great mental strain, purchased an Uzi semiautomatic carbine, tracked down Redman, and killed him with a fusillade of bullets. Psychiatrists agreed that Rosenkrantz was suffering from acute emotional disturbance. Rosenkrantz appealed a second-degree murder conviction, arguing he was guilty only of voluntary manslaughter because there was no evidence of malice. What should be the result?

People v. Rosenkrantz, 198 Cal.App.3d 1187, 244 Cal.Rptr. 403 (1988).

manslaughter
The unlawful killing of another person without malice aforethought. Usually classified as *voluntary* or *involuntary*, depending on the degree of culpability involved.

The second-degree murder conviction was affirmed on appeal. Malice may be implied when, as here, the jury determines that insufficient provocation existed.

The Personhood Requirement

Malice is not the only statutory requirement of murder. The unlawful killing must be of a "human being." What constitutes a human being or "person" is among the more controversial issues in law.

For purposes of the Fourteenth Amendment to the U.S. Constitution, a fetus is not yet a person. Therefore, the respective states are free to define, as a matter of state law, when life begins, for the purpose of defining the crime of murder. The vast majority of states do not consider a fetus to be a person in a criminal law context; that is, there can be no murder of a fetus. A few states have amended their traditional murder statutes to include a fetus as a human being.

voluntary manslaughter
The wrongful and intentional killing of another person during the heat of passion, or under the influence of alcohol or drugs, or while engaged in some reckless and dangerous activity.

The U.S. Supreme Court has declared abortion legal throughout the country and also has ruled that the states can regulate abortion in the interest of protecting the "potentiality" of life. Any distinction between a "human being" and a "potentiality of life" does not render unconstitutional the respective states' definitions of murder. The issue of abortion is discussed in Chapter 9.

Manslaughter

involuntary manslaughter
The unintentional killing of another person because of gross negligence, or as a result of dangerous and unlawful conduct.

There are two general categories of **manslaughter**, both involving an unlawful killing of a person under some variety of emotional circumstances. **Voluntary manslaughter** is the most blameworthy because it is an intentional killing of a person. **Involuntary manslaughter** is an accidental killing. There is one other category in many states, **vehicular manslaughter**, specifically related to deaths caused by the reckless driving of motor vehicles.

Voluntary manslaughter is an intentional killing—although without malice—in the heat of passion, as a result of severe provocation. As discussed earlier in the *Rosenkrantz*

vehicular manslaughter
The wrongful killing of another person by a perpetrator driving a vehicle in a reckless and dangerous manner (e.g., in some cases while under the influence of alcohol or other drugs).

case, there must be a considerable heat of passion at the time of the killing from some substantial provocation. Otherwise, the homicide is murder. Robert Rosenkrantz simply was not in the heat of passion at the time of the killing. For example, he purchased the Uzi many days before the killing, allowing plenty of time to "cool off."

LEGAL FOCUS—CASE

Robert Watson, while intoxicated, ran a red light at high speed and narrowly missed hitting another car by skidding to a stop. He accelerated again at high speed, and collided with a Toyota at another intersection, skidding 292 feet before coming to a stop. The driver of the Toyota and his six-year-old daughter were killed. Watson's blood alcohol was 0.23 percent. Watson was charged with murder, but contended he could be tried only for manslaughter because there was no proof of malice. Was Watson correct?

People v. Watson, 30 Cal.3d 290, 637 P.2d 279, 179 Cal.Rptr. 43 (1981).

rape
An unlawful act of sexual intercourse, against the will of the victim.

No, he was not correct. Malice may be implied from any conduct that has a high probability of resulting in a death and when it is done in wanton disregard for human life. Watson was speeding through city streets while intoxicated, an act presenting a great risk of death. He narrowly avoided one accident, only to cause another. These factors support a finding of implied malice. The jury verdict, guilty of murder in the second degree, was affirmed.

LEGAL FOCUS—PROBLEM

Michael Costin was refereeing his son's summer hockey game when an argument ensued with Thomas Junta, a parent of one of the other players. Junta was unhappy with the on-ice roughhousing, and the two parents had words. After the match, the two men fought, and Costin suffered an injury leading to his death two days later. Junta at 275 pounds outweighed Costin by 100 pounds. Prosecutors presented evidence that Junta hit Costin many times and twice slammed his head against the floor. Was the charge murder or manslaughter?

statutory rape
Sexual intercourse between an adult, usually eighteen years or older, and a consenting minor, usually seventeen years or younger.

In the highly publicized Boston "sideline rage" case, Junta was charged with and later convicted of manslaughter and sentenced to six to ten years in prison. Prosecutors charged manslaughter rather than murder because there was no indication that Junta intended to kill Costin.

informed consent
Actual and complete knowledge by a person of risks involved in a situation.

Rape

Sexual intercourse without the consent of the adult victim is the definition of the crime of **rape**. Rape statutes ordinarily apply to persons of opposite gender, whereas special statutes govern unlawful sexual conduct between same-sex adults. If the victim is a minor, the crime is often called **statutory rape**. The purpose of statutes prohibiting sexual intercourse between adults and minors is to protect children. Presumably, children cannot, because of their minority, give **informed consent**.

LEGAL FOCUS—PROBLEM

Mary Kay LeTourneau, thirty-five years old, a popular teacher in Seattle, and the mother of four children, pleaded guilty to having sex with a thirteen-year-old boy who had been a student in her sixth-grade class. The two originally met in her second-grade class. According to the victim, they had exchanged rings and planned the pregnancy that produced their daughter. Was LeTourneau guilty of rape?

Yes, she was guilty. LeTourneau was sentenced to seven years in prison, but the sentence was suspended after six months and probation granted. Promptly following her release from jail in early 1998, LeTourneau violated probation by again having sex with her underage victim. Her probation violated, LeTourneau went back to jail to finish serving her seven-year sentence, although she was pregnant. Her daughter Georgia was born in October 1998—the same month a book coauthored by LeTourneau and her underage victim was published in Europe. This stranger-than-fiction story continued after LeTourneau's release from prison when she married her now adult victim in 2005. This bizarre case exemplifies how seriously the law recognizes the distinction between apparent and informed consent.

rape shield statute
A statute that protects victims from courtroom questioning about prior sexual experiences with persons other than the defendant.

Many states have enacted **rape shield statutes** protecting victims from courtroom questioning about prior sexual experience(s) with persons other than the defendant.

LEGAL FOCUS—PROBLEM

Ignacio Perea kidnapped an eleven-year-old boy in Florida, took him to a deserted warehouse, and raped him. Perea had a clinic receipt in his pocket indicating that he had tested positive for the deadly AIDS virus, HIV. Of what crimes is Perea guilty?

A jury found Perea guilty of kidnapping (a felony discussed later in this chapter), rape, and attempted murder. This case represents the first time a jury considered the AIDS virus to be a deadly weapon. Other states have created new, specific crimes for those who engage in sexual contact while knowingly infected with the AIDS virus.

LEGAL FOCUS—CASE

During trial for forcible **date rape**, there was evidence that the victim, M., initially consented to sexual intercourse with defendant David Vela but changed her mind during the act. She told him to "stop." Vela nonetheless forcibly continued against her will. Is Vela guilty of any crime?

People v. Vela, 172 Cal.App.3d 237, 218 Cal.Rptr. 161 (1985).

date rape
Nonconsensual sexual intercourse by a friend or acquaintance.

Vela is not guilty of forcible date rape because M. consented when penetration first occurred. The essence of the crime of rape is the offense felt by the victim at being violated. If she retracts her consent during intercourse, but the male continues, she may certainly feel violated, but of less magnitude than from nonconsensual intercourse. The male who persists once consent is withdrawn, however, may be guilty of another crime, such as assault and battery.

Extortion

extortion
Obtaining something of value from a person by force, intimidation, or undue or other illegal acts.

Extortion is the crime of obtaining money by the wrongful use of force or fear. Extortion is recognized as an inherently vicious crime. Some states confine the meaning of extortion to the unlawful taking by an official under color of his office (e.g., "pay me now or I'll have you arrested"), whereas **blackmail** refers to an unlawful taking of money by a private person under some threat. The threat may be to accuse the victim of a crime, or to expose some deformity, previous crime, or important secret of the victim.

LEGAL FOCUS—PROBLEM

Autumn Jackson demanded $40 million from Bill Cosby to keep secret his alleged parenthood and then signed a $24 million payoff agreement that was negotiated in a Federal Bureau of Investigation (FBI) sting. Although Jackson's mother had had a sexual liaison with Cosby approximately nine months before Jackson's birth, Cosby's paternity is denied and unproven. Is it extortion to demand money to keep quiet a fact you believe to be true?

blackmail
Obtaining something of value from a person by threatening to reveal substantially true information about that person.

Yes, it is extortion. What Jackson believed is not relevant (nor is Cosby's alleged parentage) to her wrongful demand for hush money in exchange for withholding a civil paternity claim. Note that the FBI was involved because the threat was forwarded across state lines, thereby invoking federal jurisdiction. Notice that this example involved an attempt to extort money out of fear of publicity, not out of fear of physical harm to anyone.

LEGAL FOCUS—CASE

Richard Alday telephoned the father of a seven-year-old boy to say that he had kidnapped his son. Alday demanded $15,000, threatening that the child would be "hurt bad" unless the money was paid. Before the payment of any ransom, it was discovered that the boy had not been kidnapped, but had become lost when he wandered away from the family summer cabin. Alday was arrested. During prosecution for extortion, his attorney argued that no crime had been committed because no kidnapping had occurred. Did a crime occur?

People v. Alday, 10 Cal.3d 392, 315 P.2d 1169, 110 Cal.Rptr. 617 (1973).

Yes, a crime occurred. Alday committed extortion when he tried to obtain money by threatening injury to the son. This example of threatening physical injury is unlike the Cosby example of threatening publicity. Although there was no actual kidnapping in this case, it would have been a separate crime if it had occurred. And, of course, as in the *Alday* case, any threat to injure a person is also extortion. It is no defense to extortion that the "facts" upon which the threats were based are later revealed to be untrue. It is the threat to reveal them if the wrongdoer is not paid that is a criminal act.

Kidnapping

kidnapping
The crime of unlawful seizure and transport of a victim against his will.

Kidnapping involves the use of force (or threat of force) in taking a person from one place to another against his will. Kidnapping is both a state and federal crime. Kidnapping is a federal crime if the victim is taken across state lines or if facilities of interstate commerce (such as the mail or wire service) are used for ransom demands. Aggravated kidnapping occurs when an additional crime is involved, such as kidnapping to commit robbery, or to collect a ransom or reward, or to commit extortion. A typical sentence for aggravated kidnapping, without serious injury, is life imprisonment with the possibility of parole. Any homicide occurring during a kidnapping will trigger the felony murder rule in many states, enhancing the crime to murder in the first degree. The felony murder rule mandates that all participants in a dangerous felony, during which a killing occurs, are guilty of murder in the first degree.

LEGAL FOCUS—BACKGROUND

The kidnapping of the infant child of Charles and Anne Lindbergh was considered at the time to be the crime of the twentieth century. Colonel Lindbergh was the first person to fly solo nonstop across the Atlantic, and he was a world hero to a degree that is difficult to comprehend in the twenty-first century. In 1932, his 20-month-old son was taken out of a second story bedroom; a ransom demand was made and eventually paid. Later, the infant was found dead in a decomposing state in a field only four miles from the Lindbergh home. An illegal German immigrant named Bruno Richard Hauptmann was later arrested, tried, convicted, and executed for the crime. A by-product of the case was the federalization of kidnapping when Congress passed the "Little Lindbergh Law" making kidnapping a federal crime if the victim is taken across state lines or if the mail service is used for ransom demands.

robbery
The crime of stealing property from another person in her immediate presence through the use of force or fear.

armed robbery
Robbery committed with the use of a lethal weapon, such as a gun or a knife.

Robbery

Robbery is the taking of money or other personal property of another from her person or immediate presence by means of force or fear. A specific intent to steal is a necessary element of the crime. Robbery commands a greater penalty than theft (stealing without confrontation, discussed later) because there is a greater possibility of violence when the victim and offender are face to face. **Armed robbery** (use of a dangerous weapon) typically results in an enhanced penalty.

Recall that even an accidental killing that occurs during the commission of a dangerous felony, such as armed robbery, elevates the homicide to murder of the first degree under the felony murder rule in many states, and that all participants, even the getaway driver, are equally guilty.

mayhem
The crime of unlawfully depriving the victim of some member of his body; disfiguring, disabling, or rendering the member useless or otherwise permanently disfiguring the body.

Mayhem

The crime of **mayhem** occurs when someone gives another a serious permanent wound or dismembers, disfigures, or maims another person (e.g., cuts the tongue, severs a finger, puts out an eye, slits the nose, etc.).

LEGAL FOCUS—PROBLEM

Lorena Bobbitt sliced off the penis of her sleeping husband, John Wayne Bobbitt, then fled from their home and ultimately tossed his member from her car into the street. Found by a passerby, Mr. Bobbitt's member was reattached surgically. Is the crime reduced to battery because the dismemberment was not permanent?

No, the crime is not reduced to battery. Once the crime of mayhem occurs, the success of a subsequent surgical or other repair does not reduce the crime. The permanency and nature of dismemberment may affect the penalty imposed by the sentencing judge, however.

LEGAL FOCUS—CASE

Bernie Lopez threw a beer bottle into a car, hitting Raul Morales and rendering him legally blind in the left eye. Lopez did not intend to damage Morales seriously, let alone render him partially blind. Is he guilty of battery or mayhem?

People v. Lopez, 176 Cal.App.3d 545, 222 Cal.Rptr. 101 (1986).

Lopez is guilty of mayhem. Specific intent to maim is not an element of the crime. All that is necessary is a general wrongful intent, such as Lopez had when he threw the beer bottle.

Assault and Battery

criminal assault
The threat of violence upon another person.

criminal battery
The unlawful application of force to another human being without excuse or consent.

Criminal assault is an unlawful attempt, coupled with a present ability, to commit a violent injury upon the person of another. A **criminal battery** occurs if the assault is successful resulting in injury. There can be no battery in criminal law without an assault, because battery is a completed assault. For assault, there must be a present ability to injure. A menacing gesture with an unloaded gun is not an assault in the criminal law, although the result is different in the civil law (see Chapter 7). An unloaded gun cannot injure the victim unless it is used to pistol-whip or to club. Otherwise, there is no present ability to cause physical injury. On the other hand, one who fires at a service station attendant who is protected by bulletproof glass is guilty of assault. The shooter has the ability to strike out, and by shooting does in fact strike, even though the bullets cannot reach the intended victim. Waving an unloaded gun toward another person may be a lesser crime than assault, such as brandishing a firearm.

Hate Crimes

hate crime
Any crime for which the motivation was persecution of a victim because of race, religion, sexual orientation, or political beliefs.

Violence directed at victims because of their race, religion, political affiliation, or other personal beliefs (e.g., supporting abortion rights) is loosely referred to as a **hate crime.** A hate crime may be a separately defined crime, but it usually provides for a sentence enhancement if the elements are proven. Some states have included within their penalty-enhancement laws those crimes that are based on hatred of the victim's sexual orientation. International terrorism or any antigovernment crime directed at randomly selected victims also might be classified within this category.

LEGAL FOCUS—PROBLEM

Pretending they were gay, Aaron McKinney and Russell Henderson lured twenty-one-year-old University of Wyoming student Matthew Shepard from a local bar. After robbing Shepard, they tied him to a fence post and beat him. He died of head injuries five days later. Would this homicide qualify as a hate crime?

Whether or not a crime is a hate crime depends on the motivations of the perpetrators. Was Shepard killed because he was gay or incident to a robbery? As Wyoming lacked a hate-crime statute, the prosecution charged felony murder and kidnapping. To avoid the probable finding of the death penalty, Henderson pled guilty before trial, agreed to two life sentences, and promised not to appeal the verdict. A jury found McKinney guilty of felony murder, kidnapping, and aggravated robbery. This tragedy, along with several others, increased lobbying efforts for hate-crime legislation. Many states and the federal government now provide penalty enhancements for hate crimes. Opponents of hate-crime legislation argue that the reason why crimes are committed does not affect the victim nor reflect the egregiousness of the act and, therefore, should be ignored.

Terrorism

Terrorist activities overlap other criminal definitions and create special challenges to U.S. law enforcement. For example, a terrorist may commit murder, but instead of one victim, there may be a hundred or a thousand. The motivation may be political gain or revenge instead of jealousy or a desire to steal. Terrorism may be against citizens or interests of the United States in a foreign country or be by foreign nationals or U.S. citizens in the United States itself. Long-standing jurisdiction distinctions between state and federal authorities and the various federal authorities themselves (the FBI, the Treasury Department, and the Central Intelligence Agency) are challenged by terrorist activities. Distinctions between criminal investigation and national defense become important and perplexing, as well.

Following the September 11 terrorist-perpetrated attacks, the federal government passed the Patriot Act, which was designed to increase the ability of the federal government to combat terrorism. The Act was renewed and amended in 2006. The Patriot Act contains the following provisions:

- Gave law enforcement and intelligence officers greater authority to gather and share evidence particularly with respect to wire and electronic communications.
- Amended federal money-laundering laws, particularly those involving overseas financial activities.
- Created new federal crimes and increased punishment for existing crimes. The definition of "domestic terrorism" was expanded. Domestic terrorism now includes criminal acts "dangerous to human life" intended to intimidate or coerce a civilian population, influence government policy through intimidation or "affect the conduct of a government by mass destruction, assassination, or kidnapping."
- Increased the federal government's ability to prevent terrorists from entering the country and to detain or deport foreign terrorist suspects.

stalking
An unwelcome or intrusive long-term pattern of threat or harassment directed repeatedly toward a specific individual that triggers fear or concern in that person.

Stalking

Stalking involves repeatedly being around or even secretly watching a person, making uninvited written or verbal communications, or making implied threats. It often involves telephone harassment or the act of waiting for someone to appear. Victims typically are women between nineteen and thirty-nine years old, and they are stalked repeatedly, some for years. Stalkers often are former husbands, boyfriends, or roommates. A late twentieth-century crime, whose notoriety was ensured by the film *Fatal Attraction*,

arson
The intentional and malicious burning of a building or other property for unlawful purposes.

stalking is prohibited in all states. Court restraining orders are available to potential victims before any physical harm is inflicted. Although known to be widespread (about one in every twelve women reports having been stalked), most stalking is not reported by the victims.

LEGAL FOCUS—PROBLEM

Jonathan Norman was arrested for attempting to enter filmmaker Steven Spielberg's home while carrying a "rape kit" containing handcuffs and duct tape among other paraphernalia. Norman's former lover, Charles Markovich, testified that it was Norman's secret intention to bind and rape Spielberg in the presence of his wife. In defense, Norman's public defender contended that it is not a crime to have "weird thoughts" about someone famous, that Norman never entered Spielberg's property, and that when told to leave, he did. Is Norman guilty of stalking?

burglary
The crime of unlawfully entering premises, structures, or vehicles with intent to commit larceny (theft) or any other felony.

Yes, he is guilty. Although conduct may fall short of an attempted crime, it nonetheless may constitute stalking under state statutes. This stalking example is not the usual one because the victim was a male.

WHAT ARE CRIMES AGAINST PROPERTY?

Arson

home invasion burglary
The intentional breaking and entering into a person's occupied residence using violent means to take property of the occupant.

Arson is the wrongful burning of real or personal property, either intentionally or recklessly—simple negligence is not enough. It is the classic crime against property. Punishment for arson typically varies with the type of property burned. For example, arson of an inhabited structure is more serious than arson of a vacant storage building. It is not arson to burn one's own properly unless there is some fraudulent purpose (e.g., obtaining casualty insurance proceeds) or damage to the property of others.

Burglary

theft
The taking of property without the owner's consent. Depending on the nature or value of the property stolen, it is either petty theft (*misdemeanor*) or grand theft (*felony*).

Burglary is the unlawful entry into premises and structures with the intent to commit larceny (theft) or any other felony. Common law definitions of crimes against property vary among the states, and many specialized property crimes exist. For example, one specialized crime that triggers enhanced sentences is **home invasion burglary**, in which gang members burst into a victim's home and quickly overpower all occupants. Unfortunately, a variety of other crimes usually ensue, such as murder, rape, or robbery. In some states, burglary includes breaking into a vehicle for the purpose of committing larceny or theft—crimes we will examine next.

Theft

larceny
The crime of stealing property from another.

Theft is the modern catchall term that embraces the unlawful taking of another's personal property with the intent to permanently deprive the person thereof. It includes the common law crime of **larceny**, which is the wrongful taking of another's property

embezzlement
The crime of stealing property that, before the theft, was lawfully in the possession of the thief.

larceny by trick
Theft accomplished by deceit or subterfuge wherein the victim turns over property, especially money, to the perpetrator.

grand theft
Theft of personal property of substantial value, as declared by statute.

petty theft
Theft of a thing of little value, as specified by statute.

without the use of force or fear. The wrongful taking of property through the use of force and fear is the crime of robbery (see previous discussion). **Embezzlement** is a common law form of larceny in which an employee steals money from his employer. In embezzlement, access to the money is lawful, as by a bookkeeper or government officer, but the money is diverted wrongfully and secretly to the personal use of the embezzler. **Larceny by trick** is the common law crime of wrongfully obtaining property through some dishonest scam or fraudulent scheme. In all of these definitions, the modern term is simply *theft,* and its definition includes the conduct previously called *larceny* under common law.

Theft also can be defined by degree. The purpose in classifying criminal acts is to make the penalty fit the crime. **Grand theft** is a felony involving the taking of something of substantial value, as defined by statute (e.g., $400 or more in some states), or the taking of a certain kind of property, such as motor vehicles, firearms, or farm animals. Theft of personal property worth less than the statutory definition of substantial value, such as $400, is a misdemeanor and is called **petty theft**. Thus, for example, shoplifting may be either a felony or a misdemeanor depending upon the value of the stolen merchandise. Not surprisingly, grand theft results in a harsher penalty than petty theft.

Receiving Stolen Property

Knowingly **receiving stolen property** is a crime. To be responsible for the offense, the accused must have known, or should have known, the property was stolen. Proof of knowledge may be inferred from the circumstances, such as adequacy of the price paid, the character of the vendor, the time and place of delivery, and so on. Ownership of the stolen property does not change; an innocent purchaser of stolen property must return it to the real owner and may seek reimbursement only from the person (generally the thief) who sold it.

LEGAL FOCUS—PROBLEM

Sam Vreeland purchased a car radio and CD player from Jaspar Malloy at the Greater Tuna Flea Market. The price was attractive, but it was not unusually low. Vreeland installed the unit and proudly showed it off to some of his friends at school. Donna Janeway noticed how similar the unit looked to one that had been stolen from her mother's car. She wrote down the serial number and took it home for comparison with her mother's warranty registration documents. The numbers were the same. Is Vreeland guilty of a crime? Who gets to keep the radio and CD player?

receiving stolen property
The crime of knowingly receiving property of another.

Vreeland is innocent of any wrongdoing. He did not know, and had no reason to suspect, that the radio had been stolen. Janeway's mother still owns the radio and is entitled to its return. Vreeland theoretically could sue Malloy for return of his money. More likely than not, Malloy will be gone. He may or may not be guilty of a crime, depending on how he obtained the radio.

Misuse of a credit card, issuing a check knowing there are insufficient funds at the bank, and malicious mischief (vandalism) are examples of other crimes against property. "Keying" a car (scratching its painted surfaces with a key) and spray-painting graffiti are examples of costly vandalism that can provoke widespread concern and public outrage. When crimes such as these involve small amounts of money or damage, they are misdemeanors. When victims suffer significant financial loss as a result of the crime, courts usually impose a penalty and order the convicted defendant to make full restitution.

Identity Theft

LEGAL FOCUS—PROBLEM

Marsha Jones used Mari Franket's name, Social Security number, and driver's license number to purchase a red Mustang convertible on credit. Unfortunately, while Franket continues to defend herself from the collection agency that is attempting to collect the Mustang's selling price, Jones continues to possess and drive the flashy car. Is it a crime to steal another person's identity?

identity theft
The wrongful or false use of another person's identification or the commission of a crime using the identification of another.

Yes, it is a crime. **Identity theft** is a growing problem. In 1998, nine states had identity theft statutes; today, almost all states have specific identity theft laws. In states where stealing identification is not a specific crime, other statutes may apply if the stolen identification is used to defraud a merchant. If the offense involves interstate commerce, it also is a federal crime punishable by up to fifteen years in prison.

WHAT ARE CRIMES AGAINST PUBLIC HEALTH, SAFETY, AND WELFARE?

All states have adopted either the Uniform Controlled Substances Act or the Uniform Narcotic Drug Act. These laws classify drugs in schedules depending upon their harmfulness. For example, Schedule I drugs have a high potential for abuse and no generally accepted medical use. They include heroin, LSD (lysergic acid diethylamide,), marijuana, mescaline, peyote, PCP (phencyclidine), and cocaine base, as well as crack. Many states have passed so-called medical marijuana laws. These statutes exempt patients who use marijuana under a physician's supervision from state criminal penalties. There is an organized effort to use these laws to legalize a restricted availability of marijuana on the grounds that it is an effective painkiller for certain patients, such as cancer and AIDS sufferers. This effort was dealt a significant setback when the U.S. Supreme Court ruled in 2005 that the federal government could enforce federal laws (Controlled Substances Act) against marijuana possession despite state laws that allow its use. The U.S. Supreme Court also has ruled that there is no medical necessity exception to the federal Controlled Substances Act's prohibitions on manufacturing and distributing marijuana.

Schedule II drugs, such as opium, codeine, morphine, and amphetamines, have some accepted medical use. Further down the scale, Schedule V drugs, such as Buprenorphine and Lomotil, have a low potential for abuse but may lead to some psychological or physical dependence. Penalties are related to the activity (such as selling or manufacturing versus using), the class of drug involved in the crime, its quantity, previous offenses, and sale to children or around schools and range from misdemeanors to felonies.

Much controversy surrounds the implications of imposing long prison sentences for drug offenses involving the less-expensive, yet potent, crack cocaine. Because poor, inner-city youths are more likely to be involved with crack than more affluent adults, the overwhelming majority of those imprisoned for its use are young African American males. Are there disparate penalties for users of inexpensive drugs compared with users of expensive narcotics? Perhaps.

LEGAL FOCUS—EXAMPLE

Actor Robert Downey, Jr., was arrested in 1996 when police stopped his speeding pickup truck and found cocaine, crack, heroin, and a pistol. He pleaded guilty and was sentenced to three years probation. In 1998, Downey's probation was revoked for use of drugs and alcohol in violation of the court's previous order. He then was sentenced to six months in jail. However, he received four all-day furloughs from jail to complete the movie *In Dreams*. Deputy sheriffs had been asking for and receiving autographs from Downey, posing for pictures with him, and even letting the actor buy them lunch at the movie studio. Downey also was permitted to visit a plastic surgeon after a jailhouse fight. Are these "celebrity perks" legal?

No, these perks are not legal. Judges do have discretion to tailor sentences and to modify state incarceration procedures. It is not clear that a "furlough" to participate in a movie is a proper exercise of that discretion. The judge in the *Downey* case was directed by a higher court to stop further "furloughs" pending review, but Downey's sentence ended before a more definitive ruling could be made. You might consider whether an innercity African American youth, or any noncelebrity, would have received similar perks from the judge.

States prohibit the buying or possession of certain kinds of implements that primarily can be used as weapons. So-called brass knuckles and switchblade knives are examples. But what of a key ring that happens to be shaped like a cat's head and, therefore, has pointy ears?

LEGAL FOCUS—PROBLEM

Marcy Allen walked through a metal detector in a public building. The bell sounded, and her purse was searched. Marcy was carrying a key ring that was designed also as a can opener, windshield scraper, and hair lifter. It was in the shape of a cat head with two holes for eyes and sharp triangles for ears. If one placed one's fingers through the "eyes," the key ring doubled as a sort of brass knuckles with sharp points (the ears of the cat). Allen was charged with carrying an illegal weapon. What was the result?

The jury sided with the state and convicted Allen of a misdemeanor. She was placed on probation for six months. With modern tensions, it is unlikely that juries will be sympathetic to careless defendants.

WHAT ARE CRIMES AGAINST PUBLIC DECENCY AND MORALS?

One of the most controversial classifications of criminal behavior involves crimes against public decency and morals. Examples in this category are unlawful sexual intercourse, sodomy, and oral copulation. Illinois was the first state that decriminalized sexual activities between consenting adults in private places, but some states have prohibited all "unnatural and lascivious" acts whether in private or not. These laws are considered by some to infringe on liberty rights guaranteed in the Constitution.

LEGAL FOCUS—CASE

Responding to a telephone complaint that a burglary was taking place, police burst into a home discovering, instead of a burglar, the residents John Lawrence and Tyrone Garner engaging in sodomy. They were arrested, booked, and jailed overnight for violation of the Texas misdemeanor sodomy law. Lawrence and Garner pleaded "no contest," were fined $125 each, and then filed an appeal on the grounds that the law was unconstitutional.

The U.S. Supreme Court, in a 6–3 decision, declared the Texas law prohibiting sexual acts between same-sex couples unconstitutional. The Court held that the right to privacy, as a liberty right under the Due Process Clause, protects an adult's right to engage in private, consensual homosexual activity.

Sex perversion is a catchall crime that includes sodomy between consenting adults as well as lewd or lascivious acts with a child. In some states, conviction of sex perversion or any other crime involving lascivious activity (such as rape, pimping, or prostitution) has for many years resulted in a continuing duty, after release from jail, to register with the local police as a sex offender. Such registration is intended to provide law enforcement with a list of "usual suspects" to be checked when sex crimes occur, but it has been difficult to enforce, often is ignored by law enforcement agencies, and has not proved to be an effective deterrent.

Megan's Law
A state law that protects children and families by allowing or requiring law enforcement to publicize information about the identity and location of convicted sex offenders.

In 1996, following the notorious murder of seven-year-old Megan Kanka, Congress passed a law encouraging states to adopt procedures disclosing the identity and residences of sex offenders. In response, the states have adopted statutes referred to as **Megan's Law**. These statutes authorize law enforcement to publicize the identification and residential address of convicted sex offenders who are on parole or have served their sentences. The purpose is to protect families through disclosure. Names and addresses of convicted sex offenders are made available by CD-ROM, held at local police stations, distributed by hand to households in the neighborhood, or published on the Internet; sometimes photographs also are distributed to aid identification by neighbors.

MORALS AND ETHICS

Critics of Megan's Law question the fairness of subjecting persons who have served their time and paid their debt to society to a lifetime of harassment. Disclosure may prevent the former offender from retaining employment or enjoying the life available to others living in the suburbs without public shame. There are also fears of vigilantism, and some people question the potential results when sex offenders repeatedly are "pushed" from one neighborhood to another, perhaps until finally locating in the inner cities in high-density apartments and public housing. With the increased anonymity found in densely populated cities, the risk to poor children may be increased as more-affluent children in the suburbs become more protected.

Regardless, the public strongly favors implementation of Megan's Law, and courts have upheld its application, ruling that it does not constitute additional punishment.

LEGAL FOCUS—PROBLEM

Jonathan Hawes, twenty-nine years old, planned to live with his mother in the small town of Dilley, about twenty-five miles from Portland, Oregon, upon his release from prison where he had served five years for sexually abusing two 10-year-old girls. Upon notification under Megan's Law, community members had a meeting with Hawes's mother. Tempers flared; there was talk of guard dogs, burning down the home, even killing Hawes. One resident shouted in the face of Hawes's mother, "When can I kill him?" The home where Hawes planned to live is isolated from children in the middle of twenty-seven acres of pasture. Ultimately, members of the community offered to purchase the home to get rid of Hawes, and then to sell the home later to a more acceptable person. Is Hawes legally obligated to sell and move?

No, she is not obligated to sell. An agreement of sale was reached, however, and Hawes moved on. The right of free speech is not absolute. Not protected is speech that is lewd or obscene, profane, libelous, or insulting—"fighting" words.

LEGAL FOCUS—CASE

John V., sixteen years of age, screamed obscenities at his neighbor, Nancy W., who was driving past his house. A complaint was made, and John was charged with violating a statute that prohibits "offensive words in a public place which are inherently likely to provoke an immediate violent reaction." Nancy had become first angry and then furious. She was incoherent, enraged, and humiliated, although she admitted she had "flipped off" John on prior occasions. John was convicted and placed on probation. He contends the law is unconstitutionally overbroad and vague and has appealed. What should be the result?

People v. John V., 167 Cal.App.3d 761, 213 Cal.Rptr. 503 (1985).

John lost. For fighting words to be a crime, they must be uttered, as here, in a provocative manner, so there is a clear and present danger that an immediate breach of the peace will erupt. Such words are not protected because they are of such slight social value as a step to truth that any benefit is clearly outweighed by the social interest in order and morality. Obviously, these distinctions are difficult to make, especially on a consistent basis, if only because the circumstances vary so widely.

WHAT ARE SOME EXAMPLES OF OTHER CRIMES?

White-Collar Crimes

white-collar crime
Illegal acts committed usually without violence by persons of comparatively high social status and economic wealth.

The term **white-collar crime** is applied to nonviolent illegal acts committed by individuals or corporations in a business setting. Typical examples include theft, fraud, bribery, illegal kickbacks, embezzlement of money or trade secrets, prohibited "insider" information exchanges among securities dealers and corporate managers, and bid-rigging of construction contracts.

Although business crimes can be complicated and difficult to prove beyond a reasonable doubt, prosecutors have pursued white-collar criminals and asked for tougher sentencing. Recent convictions of executives of WorldCom and Enron certainly have raised the visibility of accounting- and securities-related crime.

LEGAL FOCUS—PROBLEM

At age sixteen, Barry Minkow began a carpet-cleaning business in the family garage. Minkow became a youthful symbol of free enterprise by his early twenties as his company, ZZZZ Best, skyrocketed onto Wall Street and into homes across the United States through television advertising. On the way to this pinnacle of success, he swindled banks and investors out of $26 million with a pyramid of lies about company earnings and financial success. He essentially "cooked the books" of ZZZZ Best to obtain bank and investor monies. A jury convicted him of fifty-seven counts of fraud, carrying a maximum of 403 years in prison and $50 million in fines. Eleven other defendants were convicted with Minkow. Can Minkow's victims recover their losses?

The victims did initiate costly and long-lasting civil actions to recover their losses, but Minkow's financial resources made collection unlikely. The judge ordered full restitution of $26 million. Victims probably can deduct their losses on their tax returns and thereby reduce the income taxes they otherwise would be obligated to pay. Thus, indirectly, all other taxpayers share the loss because they have to pay more to offset the ultimate effect of those deductions.

White-collar crime can occur in securities markets in which stock markets can be used by insiders (owners and managers of businesses) to raise huge sums of money from investors seeking profits. The 2001 bankruptcy of the giant energy firm Enron and the 2002 financial irregularities of communications giant WorldCom led to criminal convictions of Bernie Ebbers (WorldCom), Kenneth Lay (Enron), and Jeff Skilling (Enron) in 2005 and 2006. The Sarbanes-Oxley Act of 2002 created new duties for executives of public corporations. Chief executive officers and chief financial officers now must certify periodic reports submitted to the Securities and Exchange Commission. Doing so improperly can be a crime. Supporters of the law hope that the potential for criminal liability for corporate executives will reduce the fraud and questionable accounting practices that contributed to the stock market collapse in 2001.

tax evasion
The intentional and illegal violation of federal and state tax laws.

Tax evasion probably is the most familiar white-collar crime. Simply stated, it involves knowingly cheating on your income taxes, and it can be a felony. It is widely remembered that the infamous Al Capone, whose evil ways during Prohibition could not be proven in court, ultimately was convicted for income tax evasion. The government pursued a less famous individual, Reuben Sturman, for some twenty-nine years, trying to convict him on obscenity charges. Sturman masterminded a pornography empire that gave him a net worth estimated by authorities at $100 million, much of which had been laundered (i.e., funneled through other organizations—in this case, through Swiss and Caribbean banks—to create the appearances of business profits). The government's first break came in 1989 when, like Al Capone, Sturman was convicted of income tax fraud and sentenced to ten years in prison. The Internal Revenue Service took twelve years to untangle Sturman's web of dummy corporations and foreign bank accounts; but that first tax evasion conviction led to other convictions for extortion and conspiracy.

Racketeer Influenced and Corrupt Organizations Act (RICO)
A federal law passed to control attempts by organized crime to invest money gained from illegal racketeering in legitimate business activities.

Under the **Racketeer Influenced and Corrupt Organizations Act (RICO)**, organized crime members who are involved in an "enterprise" that engages, at least twice within ten years, in any of numerous specified criminal acts are chargeable with "racketeering." The list of forty criminal acts that underlie RICO includes murder, robbery, securities fraud, and use of the mail or telephone for illegal purposes. Lying twice on the telephone concerning a business contract theoretically could trigger a RICO indictment or lawsuit. RICO penalties include heavy prison sentences (up to twenty years) and forfeiture of any ill-gotten monetary gains.

Federal prosecutors have utilized RICO widely against white-collar criminals, whether part of organized crime or not. RICO has been used with considerable success against violators of securities laws. For example, Michael Milken was convicted under RICO of charges of scheming to manipulate stock prices, of trading on inside information, and of defrauding customers. His employer, the investment banking firm Drexel Burnham Lambert, facing a RICO indictment, pleaded guilty to lesser charges and was fined $650 million. To qualify for a RICO prosecution, the accused must have been involved in a "pattern of racketeering activity." Abortion protesters who block access to abortion clinics can be sued by abortion-rights advocates for engaging in such a "pattern of racketeering activity." The decision does not prohibit *peaceful* protests outside abortion clinics, nor stop protesters who trespass on clinic property without threatening clinic employees.

Federal courts have expanded the applicability of RICO to just about any collective wrongful activity, whether for economic gain or not. RICO's deterrent effect can be real. For example, actual damages can be trebled in civil cases. In criminal cases, assets of an accused can be temporarily seized before a trial begins.

WHAT ARE SOME DEFENSES TO CRIMES?

Self-Defense

Violent conduct, which otherwise would be criminal behavior, is justified when used in defense of oneself or of certain other persons. All states recognize some form of the privilege of **self-defense**.

LEGAL FOCUS—PROBLEM

Cinnamon Clark and her boyfriend, Harry Holland, were listening to CDs in her apartment. A noisy party was under way next door. Suddenly, there was a banging on Clark's unlocked door, and it was flung open. There stood Butch Meen, butcher knife in one hand and beer bottle in the other. Holland's first thought was to run out the back door, but Clark grabbed her pistol from the table drawer, aimed it at Meen's heart, and stared him right in the eyes. When Meen lunged toward her, Clark, fearful of imminent and serious personal harm, killed him with a single well-aimed shot. Was the killing lawful?

self-defense
The legal right to use whatever force appears to be reasonably necessary to protect oneself (or specified others) from great and imminent bodily injury by an assailant.

Yes, the killing was lawful. The privilege of self-defense arises when one is confronted with a threat that causes a genuine and reasonable fear of imminent danger of great bodily injury. "Deadly resistance" is justified when the imminent peril is great. Because Meen held a butcher knife and bottle, Clark's fear of great and imminent harm, including possible death, was reasonable and her defense was reasonable. If Meen had retreated, stepping backward, the killing would not have been justified, and Clark would have been guilty of homicide, probably manslaughter. If Meen had lunged toward Holland alone, the killing would still be justified because she was entitled to defend Holland as well as herself.

Generally, the right to self-defense extends to members of one's immediate family or household and to others whom one is under a legal or socially recognized duty to protect. The fact that the acts occurred in Clark's apartment increases the scope of the privilege of self-defense. Defense of habitation is rooted in the ancient principle that one's home is one's castle. It does not mean that a killing is justified merely because it takes place in the home of the accused; however, when at home, one is not obliged to retreat. On the other hand, when one is outside one's house (or apartment), one might be expected to retreat if possible to do so without added risk of harm. Thus, there is a general duty to retreat rather than to kill in self-defense. Even in the home, the killing must be in defense of life or to prevent probable grievous bodily injury, such as rape.

LEGAL FOCUS—PROBLEM

John Booth was released from prison and promptly, the same day, got drunk and decided to burglarize a house. Michael Lanier, a college student, and his fiancée were upstairs when they heard glass shattering downstairs. Lanier grabbed a bat, went downstairs, and hit Booth, who was entering through the window. Immediately upon being struck by the bat, Booth began running away. Lanier chased him and continued to beat him into submission with the bat. Booth suffered a brain hemorrhage and fractured skull; his legs had been battered as well. Lanier was arrested for assault with a deadly weapon. Will the argument of self-defense work for Lanier?

The prosecutor dropped all charges against Lanier, citing (1) the outpouring of public support for Lanier, (2) the uncertainty of whether or not a jury from that community would convict, and (3) the fact that Lanier believed Booth to be a significant threat of death or serious physical injury. As a general proposition, lethal force cannot be used to chase down an intruder who no longer poses any threat of imminent harm. But prosecutors often, as in the *Lanier* case, make the decision as to whether or not self-defense under all of the circumstances was justified. If Lanier had been a former convict who had served time for assault and battery on a police officer while resisting arrest for drunken driving, would the district attorney have prosecuted him for assault? If so, would that prosecution tend to suggest a dual standard of justice through selective prosecution?

Deadly force may not be used in defense against nondeadly force, such as slapping. Nor may it be used in defense of property when life is not threatened. Thus, one may not set a deadly spring gun to fire if a door or window is broken into when one is not at home. If an intruder is hurt or killed, the person who set the gun is guilty of either murder or manslaughter and is also liable in a civil action for injury or wrongful death. Whether the crime was murder or manslaughter would be determined by the presence or absence of malice in the mind of the defendant who set the spring gun.

The right of self-defense is never a "license to kill." If less than deadly force is all that is reasonably required under the particular circumstances, then a killing in self-defense becomes unlawful and punishable as a crime. Once the danger is over, there is no justification for further retaliation.

duress
Any threat of, or actual, physical harm that deprives a person of the freedom of will to choose and decide.

Duress

Duress may negate the intent required to commit a crime. Duress is the forced participation in what otherwise would be a crime. It implies that a person's free will was overpowered, that she was coerced by threat of imminent death or serious bodily injury to herself or another person. It follows then, if the person alleging duress had an option not to committee the crime, then the coercion defense in unavailable.

LEGAL FOCUS—EXAMPLE

The heiress Pattie Hearst claimed that she was forced to commit crimes by the Symbionese Liberation Army (SLO), which had kidnapped her in the 1970s. She claimed they threatened to kill her if she did not commit the crimes, she feared the threat would be carried out, and she had had no reasonable opportunity to escape. In one photo of an armed robbery of a bank, Hearst appeared to be holding a weapon, and in another photo, she seemed to be in a car waiting without being guarded. How do those facts weaken her duress defense to criminal responsibility?

It would weaken her defense because the photos seemed to suggest that she had opportunities to escape, but maybe not. Hearst was tried and convicted for her involvement in the robbery. Her sentence was later commuted by President Carter, and her crime subsequently pardoned by President Clinton. Note, however, that killing another person is never excused or justified because it was committed under duress.

Is Lack of Mental Capacity a Defense?

An insane person is not legally responsible for criminal conduct. The rationale is that our society's collective conscience does not allow punishment in cases in which it cannot impose moral blame. Nonetheless, an insane person may be committed for an indefinite period to a hospital for the insane, an approach that satisfies society's need for protection and its duty to assist those who are ill.

The historic difficulty with the defense of insanity results from the lack of a satisfactory definition of the term, coupled with clear and reliable criteria to enable juries to evaluate the mental condition and conduct of the accused. The defense of "not guilty by reason of insanity" has been eliminated by statute in some states, and the U.S. Supreme Court has declined to review those laws. In California, an **insanity defense** is available if the jury, in a separate trial for that purpose, determines that the defendant, by a preponderance of the evidence, was incapable (1) of knowing or understanding the nature and quality of the act or (2) of distinguishing right from wrong at the time the act was committed. In New York, a defendant is not criminally responsible if she lacked substantial capacity to know or appreciate (1) the nature and consequences of her act or (2) that such conduct was wrong.

insanity defense
A defense to a crime based on some mental disease or defect.

Juries are accustomed to determining facts (e.g., did the gun belong to the defendant or not?). But when it comes to determining the sanity of the defendant, the jury must determine the correctness of an opinion. Insanity is an opinion expressed by psychiatrists until the jury says it is a fact. It is extremely difficult to determine that a certain state of mind is a fact, and its importance is questionable if the basic goal of society is to incarcerate defendants until they no longer are a threat to society. Some persons argue that all perpetrators of heinous crimes are insane.

LEGAL FOCUS—PROBLEM

Defendant Jeffrey Dahmer was convicted of serial killing, of drilling holes in his living victims' heads and then pouring in chemicals to "zombify" them, of having sex with the corpses' viscera, and of keeping some body parts in his refrigerator, occasionally eating them. Should Dahmer have been punished as a criminal or treated as a desperately sick human being?

"Crazy" is different from legally insane. The Wisconsin jury trying the *Dahmer* case concluded that Dahmer was not insane. But if Dahmer was not insane when he committed such grotesque and inhuman acts, one might ask, who *is* insane? As a matter of official policy, Wisconsin follows the Model Penal Code definition of mental responsibility: "A person is not responsible for criminal conduct if at the time of such conduct as a result of mental disease or defect he lacked substantial capacity either to appreciate the wrongfulness of his conduct or to conform his conduct to the requirements of law." Thus, Dahmer was judged able to appreciate the wrongfulness of what he did and able to refrain from doing it. The fact that he wanted to commit such "crazy" acts does not constitute legal insanity. Jeffrey Dahmer subsequently was murdered in prison.

diminished capacity
Reduced ability to exercise one's freedom of will or to choose between right and wrong.

temporary insanity
A passing or temporal mental disease or defect.

Insanity is to be distinguished from **diminished capacity**, which involves a different mental state. Some crimes are defined to require a specific intent on the part of the defendant. For example, capital murder requires the specific intent to kill. If by reason of delusion, narcotics, or alcohol, for example, the defendant's mental capacity is diminished to the extent that there can be no specific intent to kill, there can be no capital murder. The crime may be reduced to manslaughter because of the defendant's diminished capacity. This defense has been eliminated by constitutional amendment in some states. In some states, the defense of **temporary insanity** is possible, whereby the accused is innocent of the crime because of insanity, and yet, being sane after the act, need not be confined in a mental hospital.

It is possible that an accused, sane at the time of the alleged crime, subsequently becomes insane. Insanity at the time of trial is not a defense to a crime committed during a prior time of sanity. A trial cannot proceed, however, until the defendant is sane because a "fair" trial as guaranteed by our Constitution contemplates rational defendants who can understand the charges against them and assist in a proper defense, nor can a prison sentence be served by, nor an execution be administered to, an insane convict. In general terms, insanity suspends judicial proceedings as long as it continues. The defendant may be committed to a state institution for the insane until sanity is regained, at which time the criminal proceedings may resume.

LEGAL FOCUS—PROBLEM

Terrence Shulman was caught shoplifting a bottle of champagne from a supermarket. The champagne was to be a consolation gift to his girlfriend with whom he had just broken up because of his "addictive compulsive" shoplifting problem. Is kleptomania, or an "impulse control" disorder, or "addictive compulsive" behavior a defense to the crime of shoplifting?

No, they are not a defense to the crime. The United States has about 23 million shoplifters in the United States, who steal about $25 million worth of merchandise each day. Few shoplifters are believed to steal out of absolute financial need. Perhaps one-third of shoplifters steal for resale or to finance drug habits. But the vast majority of shoplifters (usually teenagers) steal as a response to personal or social pressures or in response to a compulsive impulse, such as kleptomania.

Criminal conduct is voluntary conduct. The defense of duress, discussed previously, is one example in which participation in criminal conduct is not voluntary. Are criminal acts while asleep another example?

LEGAL FOCUS—PROBLEM

Early one morning, Kenneth Parks drove fourteen miles to attack his wife's parents while they were asleep. He killed his mother-in-law with a butcher knife, severely injured his father-in-law, and then turned himself in to police. Parks had a sleep disorder and contended that, although perfectly sane, he simply had been sleepwalking while committing the homicide and attack. Is this defense sound?

Yes, at least in Canada. The *Parks* case occurred in Ottawa, where a judge ruled that the acts were involuntary. His acquittal was upheld on appeal. As difficult as it might be to persuade a jury, an involuntary stupor or trance, caused by some innocent involvement such as sleeping, presumably would negate the required voluntariness. Note that a stupor or trance caused by drugs is neither involuntary nor innocent if the use of the drugs is by personal choice.

What Is Entrapment?

entrapment
A defense to criminal charges if the crime was induced by police encouragement, but not if police merely provided an opportunity for the accused to commit the criminal act.

A defendant cannot be convicted of committing a crime if the government, acting through its law enforcement personnel, induced the criminal act. The defense of **entrapment** is an affirmative defense that must be proven by the defendant by a preponderance of the evidence, as in civil litigation; it does not have to be proven beyond a reasonable doubt. This defense, however, is narrow, limited in scope, and usually unsuccessful. It applies only when the conduct of the law enforcement agent was likely to induce a normally law-abiding person to commit the offense when such a person otherwise would not be disposed to do so. That is, the question is not whether or not the particular defendant was induced to commit the crime, but whether or not any reasonable, law-abiding person would have been so induced. There is no entrapment when undercover agents are merely negotiating the price of, and buying, illegal drugs from the defendant.

LEGAL FOCUS—CASE

Joe Shapiro, operating on Whidbey Island, Washington, negotiated with Richard Russell and others for the purchase of homemade methamphetamine or "speed." Russell needed the scarce, but legal, chemical phenyl-2-propanone to prepare the drug, which was supplied by Shapiro. A month after the batch was prepared and delivered, Russell was advised that Shapiro was an employee of the Federal Bureau of Narcotics. Arrest and trial followed in due course. Had Russell been entrapped?

United States v. Russell, 411 U.S. 423 (1973).

No, Russell was not entrapped. Entrapment occurs only if the government agent implants the criminal design or idea in the mind of the defendant. The U.S. Supreme Court held that Russell had a predisposition to commit the crime and that the mere affording of opportunity by Shapiro was not entrapment.

Even if the defendant is predisposed to criminal activity, the government may not engage in "outrageous" investigatory conduct, or evidence collected will be suppressed and the defendant set free.

LEGAL FOCUS—CASE

Ralph "Sonny" Barger, the recognized leader of the Hell's Angels, was convicted of conspiracy to violate federal explosives laws based upon the testimony of Anthony Tait, an FBI informant who participated in a "sting" operation (investigative activity in which a suspected criminal organization is infiltrated by a government witness). The government investigation followed the murder of a Hell's Angel by members of the Outlaws Motorcycle Club. Barger contended that the government was guilty of outrageous investigative conduct: by hiring Tait on a contingent fee basis; by having Tait travel from city to city throughout the country; by spending $150,000 of government expense money recruiting Hell's Angels to retaliate against the Outlaws by blowing up their clubhouse in Chicago; and by inciting Barger, personally, to retaliate. Should the conviction be reversed?

United States v. Barger, 931 F.2d 359 (1991).

No, it should not be reversed. The federal court acknowledged that the Due Process Clause of the Fifth Amendment requires fundamental fairness and that some police conduct may be so egregious as to violate that command. But in this case, the government merely responded to the real threat of gang retaliation, which could have caused great personal harm and property damage between two rival gangs with a history of violence. Barger also contended that he had been entrapped, arguing that he had no predisposition to engage in criminal activity. His predisposition, the court held, was refuted by his personal involvement in the retaliatory scheme both before and after Anthony Tait's proposed plan of action was revealed.

WHAT IS THE STATUTE OF LIMITATIONS FOR CRIME?

A **statute of limitations** is a legislative determination that legal proceedings in connection with various types of civil and criminal acts may not be commenced beyond specified periods of time. Accordingly, such a statute may be a valid defense for the defendant. Most criminal courts already are overcrowded with current cases. Such statutes are not intended to shield defendants from the law; rather, they prevent stale prosecutions in which witnesses' memories may have faded, making a "fair" trial exceedingly difficult, if not impossible, to obtain. Moreover, witnesses and principals may move, or die, and evidence may be obscured or lost. Furthermore, society is better served if wrongdoers resume normal, productive, law-abiding lives, without the psychological burden of possible arrest endlessly hanging over their heads. There is no statute of limitations for certain serious crimes, such as murder.

statute of limitations
A statute that bars civil or criminal proceedings unless brought within a specified period of time after the act occurred.

VICTIMS' RIGHTS

The last years of the twentieth century witnessed a gradual but pervasive trend to elevate the rights of crime victims. Congress enacted the Omnibus Victim and Protection Act of 1982, providing, among other things, for victim-impact statements at sentencing, protection from intimidation, restitution from offenders (e.g., return of stolen property), and a general tightening of bail procedures.

The states have not remained on the sidelines. Since 1985, most states have passed either legislation or constitutional amendments supportive of victims' rights in the criminal system. Most states now require that notice be provided to all victims, or to members of deceased victims' families, before sentencing proceedings. During these proceedings, victims or their families may express verbally (or in writing or by video) their views about the crime, about the convicted felon, and about the need for restitution for the judge's use in sentencing. They typically contain information about the victim's economic loss, physical and psychological injuries, and how the crime caused changes in the victim's employment.

LEGAL FOCUS—PROBLEM

Lawrence Singleton had been convicted by a Florida jury of murdering a hitchhiker he had picked up and taken to his home. Singleton claimed that the victim, Roxanne Hayes, attacked him with a knife, and that he was trying to grab the weapon when the blade plunged seven times into her body. In the penalty phase of the trial, when the jury must recommend either life imprisonment or death, the assistant state attorney reached back twenty years, to 1978, to call a previous victim of Singleton's as a witness in support of the death penalty. Do former victims have the right to testify in current proceedings to help persuade the jury to render the death penalty?

Yes, former victims have the right to testify in current proceedings. Mary Vincent traveled from California to Florida to testify and told the jury, "I was raped, and I had my hands cut off" in 1978 when she was only fifteen years old. Singleton used a hatchet and left Vincent to die in a ditch invisible to the road. Somehow, without hands, Vincent crawled up to the road, obtained help, and survived. Because Vincent survived, Singleton was hunted down and convicted. Paroled from a California prison after serving just ten years, Singleton moved to Florida because many California towns resisted his residency. The Florida jury, after listening to Mary Vincent, recommended the death penalty. Singleton died in December 2001 while on death row awaiting execution.

A plea bargain is an agreement under which an accused person agrees to plead guilty to a specified offense in exchange for a court-approved sentence. Some state statutes restrict plea bargaining in cases involving violence or serious felonies. These restrictive states will not agree in advance to any particular sentence in specified types of crimes, usually involving violence, such as rape.

Some states provide victims with information about possible civil remedies against the defendant, as well as the procedures to recover compensation from the innocent-victim restitution fund. Monies are collected for these innocent-victim funds from penalty assessments and restitution fines levied against convicted persons. Victims otherwise without financial means can apply for financial assistance for medical treatment, mental health counseling, loss of income, loss of support, funeral or burial costs, and rehabilitation.

Son-of-Sam Laws A law that limits the ability of a criminal offender to receive profits from the recounting of his crime.

So-called **Son-of-Sam Laws** impound the proceeds of sales by notorious criminals of their "story" to the media, such as movie and book rights.*

Funds are escrowed until victims have had ample opportunity to sue in civil proceedings and obtain a judgment that then may be satisfied from the impounded funds. Any excess is returned to the felon. New York also created a Crime Victims Board to administer all state programs dealing with crime victims. New York's Son-of-Sam law

*During 1977, New York was terrorized by multiple random shootings of young women and their companions committed by a killer dubbed the "Son of Sam" by the press. The killer, David Berkowitz, sold book rights to his story. This prompted the state to enact the first Son-of-Sam escrow law.

was declared unconstitutional, but New York and several other states subsequently have passed statutes to stop convicted criminals from profiting from their criminal behavior.

Some victims are found in jail. Those persons are victims of a judicial system that erroneously found them guilty.

LEGAL FOCUS—PROBLEM

Freddie Pitts and Wilbert Lee, both African American, were sentenced to death by an all-white jury for the murder of two white gas station attendants. After more than thirty years in jail, nine of which were on death row, Pitts, fifty-four, and Lee, sixty-two, were found innocent. A white man, Curtis "Boo" Adams, was the guilty person. As victims, can Pitts and Lee sue for compensation?

Persons who are wrongfully convicted of a crime often do not recover compensation. As long as prosecutors acted reasonably and witnesses were truthful, there is no wrong-doer to sue. Florida, however, is an example of a state that does pay compensation in such situations. Pitts and Lee each received $500,000 as compensation for their thirty years in jail.

Some victims of crime are witnesses to its commission.

LEGAL FOCUS—PROBLEM

Gloria Lyons and Denise Jones witnessed a homicide by Charles Lafayette, a member of the "Bloods" gang. The slaying occurred during an argument over a $5 rock of cocaine. Lyons and Jones were reluctant to tell what they saw, for fear of "wearing snitch jackets," which they consider to be targets on their backs. What can the prosecutor do to safeguard these witnesses from retaliation?

Some states have witness relocation laws that provide some financial help for relocating endangered witnesses to new neighborhoods. Unfortunately, many such witnesses become lonely for, and return to, their old neighborhoods. The problem of witness protection in gang member prosecutions is an unresolved problem. In the preceding case, Lyons and Jones did testify; Lafayette is in prison serving twenty-five years to life. Lyons was executed in an alley within three days of testifying; Jones returned to her former neighborhood and promptly was murdered on the street. No arrests were made. The tally: one murderer in jail and two witnesses dead with their murderer(s) still on the street.

WHEN ARE POLICE PERMITTED TO SEARCH AND SEIZE?

exclusionary rule The court-made rule that precludes the use in criminal court proceedings of any evidence improperly obtained by the prosecution.

The Fourth Amendment to the U.S. Constitution prohibits unreasonable searches and seizures by government officials. It is aimed at protecting the privacy of people from unreasonable government intrusions, but it does not provide for any penalty against government officials when they violate its shield. However, decisions of the U.S. Supreme Court have established the so-called **exclusionary rule**, which acts as a deterrent to unreasonable police searches by prohibiting prosecutors from using improperly obtained evidence in a trial.

Exclusionary Rule

Few criminal law rules generate more public outcry than the exclusionary rule. The public hears or reads that a clearly guilty person was released simply because incriminating evidence was gathered in an illegal search. To a limited extent and subject to certain immunities, the victim of an unreasonable search may even bring a civil suit against the officer involved. A recent trend in Fourth Amendment law may be reducing the scope of the exclusionary rule.

LEGAL FOCUS—EXAMPLE

Police officers approach a house with a search warrant. Upon approaching the house, the police officers announce "police" and after approximately three to five seconds break the door down. They do not knock or wait long for anyone to come to the door. The police enter, find illegal drugs and drug-making paraphernalia, and arrest the residents of the house. At their criminal trials, the residents move to exclude all evidence found in the house, claiming that a failure to "knock and announce" rendered the search illegal. What will the result be?

The evidence probably will be admitted under a recent decision of the U.S. Supreme Court. In *Hudson v. Michigan* the Court held that a failure to knock would not prevent use of evidence obtained, if the search was otherwise proper and legitimate. The Court noted that the exclusionary rule generates substantial social costs that sometimes include "setting the guilty free and the dangerous at large." The Court rejected "indiscriminate application" of the rule and held it to be applicable only "where its remedial objectives are thought most efficaciously served," that is, "where its deterrence benefits outweigh its 'substantial' social costs."

Search Warrants and Warrantless Searches

probable cause The standard by which a police officer may make an arrest, conduct a personal or property search, or obtain a warrant.

A search for, and seizure of, evidence may be authorized in advance by issuance of a search warrant. A proper judge or magistrate issues the warrant based upon **probable cause** that incriminating evidence will be found, which may include authorization to perform electronic or telephonic eavesdropping. Warrants are granted only upon preparation of a sworn (under penalty of perjury) affidavit, which must contain the basis (such as the statement of a reliable informant) upon which the requesting law enforcement agency believes there is probable cause that criminal conduct is taking place.

A search and seizure also may be justified and legal in the absence of a search warrant when circumstances necessitate prompt, decisive action. The various states have developed many different rules with fine distinctions as to when a warrantless search is permitted. The states are free to adopt more stringent rules restricting searches than are required under federal law, but no state can permit searches that are prohibited by the Fourth Amendment. Situations in which a warrantless search may be permitted are as follows:

- **Consent.** A person may freely consent to a search. Another occupant of one's apartment also may consent to a search of shared areas within the dwelling.
- **Incident to a lawful arrest.** During a lawful arrest, a defendant is taken into custody. The arresting officer then may make a search, generally limited to an arm's-length area in which the defendant could reach for a weapon or destructible evidence. Once at the police station, during booking procedures, the warrantless

search may take the form of a strip search for weapons or contraband. In many states, a person arrested for minor, misdemeanor offenses (such as unpaid parking violations) could be strip-searched at the police station. Because of the unlikelihood that such arrestees might possess weapons or contraband, however, such practices are rare.

- **Motor-vehicle search based on probable cause.** A vehicle may be searched if there is probable cause to believe it contains contraband. Mobility of the vehicle underlies this exception to the rule requiring a search warrant in advance. Note that a traffic offense, such as speeding, may not be used as a pretext to justify a search for evidence of a different crime, but the observation of something "in plain view" is not an unreasonable search. Indeed, it is not considered a search at all and, thus, is not subject to the confines of the Fourth Amendment. For example, a handgun lying on the floor behind the front seat, if seen by the officer, would justify a search of a vehicle that had been stopped for a routine traffic offense. The only restriction on the "plain view" doctrine is that the officer must have a right to be in that place when the observation is made.

Sobriety checkpoints set up by law enforcement to detect drunk drivers do not violate the Fourth Amendment despite the absence of any individualized suspicion that a particular driver is under the influence. (DUIs refer to driving under the influence of alcohol or drugs.) Neither the magnitude of the drunk-driving problem, nor the state's interest in eradicating it, can be disputed. The intrusion on the privacy of motorists stopped briefly at sobriety checkpoints is slight.

LEGAL FOCUS—CASE

Officer Studnicka observed a van sitting on the shoulder of a state highway in the early evening. Thinking the van's driver might be having mechanical trouble, Studnicka made a U-turn, turned on his flashing red lights, and came to a stop at the rear of the van. When asking driver Steven Hanson for his driver's license, Officer Studnicka observed an open can beer near the dashboard. He then asked Hanson to get out, smelled alcohol, administered an "Alcohol Sensor" test, and arrested him for DUI. The van was impounded, and 8.7 grams of marijuana were found. Hanson moved the court for an order suppressing all evidence on the grounds that an illegal seizure had occurred, in violation of his Fourth Amendment rights. What was the result?

State v. Hanson, 501 N.W.2d 677 (Minn. App. 1993).

Because the flashing red lights were a clear direction to Hanson, sitting in the van, not to drive away, there was an improper seizure. In effect, Hanson was detained by the flashing lights. Officer Studnicka admitted that he had no suspicion of criminal activity when he turned on the red lights. Therefore, Studnicka had restrained Hanson improperly. All evidence was ordered suppressed, and the charges against Hanson were dropped. If Studnicka had not turned on the flashing red lights, the subsequent visual search would have been proper. It is interesting to consider whether or not the ruling of the judge would have been the same if, instead of marijuana, the police found the dead body of Hanson's wife in the van.

Cases in which a search warrant is unnecessary include the following:

- **Stop and frisk based on reasonable suspicion.** If an officer has a reasonable suspicion of criminal activity, or if a dangerous misdemeanor is occurring, the object of that suspicion may be detained, questioned, and "frisked" or "patted down" for a weapon.

- **Hot pursuit.** A fleeing suspect may be pursued into a private building without a search (or arrest) warrant.
- **Emergency.** Under emergency conditions, it may not be possible to obtain a search warrant before acting. An example would be a break-in to rescue the victim of a crime, seen through the window, who is in need of immediate assistance. Other evidence of a crime in progress (such as wet blood or sounds of agony) also justifies immediate action by police.
- **Open field.** An officer may search an open field suspected to contain contraband as long as there is no reasonable expectation of privacy therein. Police may trespass in a neighbor's backyard and stand on their tiptoes to visually search a defendant's backyard. The defendant's reasonable expectation of privacy, or zone of privacy, is limited to observers who happen to be less than six feet tall, or the height of the fence. Observations from airplanes or helicopters (e.g., of fields suspected of being used to grow marijuana) generally do not require a search warrant. Use of a thermal imaging device (i.e., one that registers heat from electric sun lamps), however, cannot be used without a warrant to detect an underground marijuana farm at a targeted property.
  On the other hand, use of an infrared forward-looking device, aimed above a suspect's residence, to detect heat discharged by exhaust from lamps that might be used to grow marijuana inside the building does not violate the Fourth Amendment. The difference between these two examples is that there could be no reasonable expectation of privacy regarding heat discharged from the residence through a vent.
- **Abandoned property.** An officer may search an abandoned automobile or dwelling or personal properly discarded by a suspect.

LEGAL FOCUS—CASE

Jenny Stracner, a police investigator, examined the trash in a bag that Billy Greenwood and Dyanne Van Houten placed on the sidewalk near their home, and discovered evidence of narcotics use. She used this evidence to obtain a search warrant of the house, where quantities of narcotics were found. Was the warrantless search of the garbage constitutional?

California v. Greenwood & Van Houten, 486 U.S. 35 (1988).

Yes, the search was constitutional. There is no reasonable expectation of privacy of trash placed outside for collection. Therefore, the search does not violate the Fourth Amendment.

- **Customs and immigration.** Customs and immigration officers do not need a search warrant in certain situations. For example, searches near the border, or places of entry to the United States, are exempt from the general requirements of probable cause. That is, those officers can detain and search persons if they have a "mere suspicion." Body ("skin") searches must be based on "real, or reasonable, suspicion," and even a body cavity search (i.e., an intrusion beyond the body's surface) requires only a "clear indication," which is much less than probable cause. Conforming to a drug carrier's profile, behaving nervously, and wearing bulky clothing are typical bases for a strip search.

- **Mail to and from prisons.** Although domestic first-class mail cannot be searched without probable cause, an exception is made for U.S. mail to and from prisons, all of which is subject to search. Some states prohibit the search of prison mail that is addressed to judges or lawyers from prison inmates.
- **Searches by private citizens.** The Fourth Amendment is a restraint upon government, not upon individuals. Accordingly, evidence obtained from a search by a private citizen is admissible in court.
- **Administrative inspections.** Certain pervasively regulated businesses (e.g., food establishments) are subject to warrantless inspections by administrative personnel as part of public necessity and licensing rules, and evidence discovered during such a search is accordingly admissible, even if unrelated to the inspection.
- **Banks.** Banks and financial institutions supply information to government agencies pursuant to the Bank Secrecy Act without the necessity of a search warrant.
- **Probation and parole.** As a usual condition to the granting of probation or parole, convicted felons waive their rights to a search warrant, and searches can take place requiring no more than reasonable suspicion at any time and any place.

As discussed earlier, the states are free to establish more stringent restraints upon the police than are required by the U.S. Constitution. Many states originally did provide greater restraints upon warrantless searches. Through the adoption of victims' rights laws, as previously discussed, many states have relaxed their warrantless search rules to the federal standards. In some states, federal officers continue to possess somewhat more latitude in performing warrantless searches than state officials, but this is not the modern trend. Determining the validity of a search is one of the most perplexing legal problems. It involves weighing the interests of the state in preventing crime against the interests of each person in maintaining privacy and freedom from unwarranted intrusion.

The Patriot Act, discussed previously, strengthened and expanded the ability of federal intelligence and law enforcement agencies to conduct warrantless searches related to terrorism. Under the Patriot Act, the FBI can conduct a search by merely certifying to a judge that the search "protects against terrorism." Such broad authority has been controversial. Some praise it as needed to effectively fight the war on terror, and others fear the abuse of such authority.

WHAT PROCEDURES LEAD TO A CRIMINAL TRIAL?

Criminal court procedures affect the quality of justice dispensed by our legal system and so are important. But procedural safeguards can be frightening and mysterious to nonlawyers. The professional assistance of a qualified attorney for the accused person is thus advisable as early as possible in the criminal prosecution process. As soon as an investigation has included an individual, she should consult an attorney. The U.S. Supreme Court has declared that every accused person who cannot afford to hire a lawyer has a constitutional right to the services of professional counsel (usually a public defender) at public expense. Persons accused of minor crimes and infractions are excluded from this constitutional protection.

A discussion follows of the procedures that face those accused of serious crimes. All citizens should be generally familiar with these procedures. Exhibit 6.1 presents the typical steps in a criminal prosecution.

Accusatory Pleading

complaint, criminal
(a) A written statement filed by complainant containing facts that indicate a crime has been committed and that the accused committed it. (b) An accusation of a misdemeanor.

information
An accusation of a criminal offense.

indictment
An accusation of felony filed by a grand jury.

A person suspected of committing a state or federal crime becomes an accused following the issuance of an accusatory pleading. The most common types of accusatory pleadings are **complaint**, **information** (or affidavit), and **indictment**. Although the federal and state systems use documents with similar names, their procedures are somewhat different.

State Crimes

In some felony cases, the district attorney will prepare a complaint and file it with a judicial officer (usually called a *magistrate*), who is authorized to issue arrest warrants. If there is probable cause for the charges made against the accused, an arrest warrant will be issued. Following the arrest, a preliminary hearing will be conducted by a judge or magistrate to determine whether any information should be issued binding the defendant for subsequent trial in the designated trial court. During this period of time, the defendant may be free on bail, which is discussed later in this chapter.

In other felony cases, the district attorney will request that the local grand jury convene. Following a secret session, the grand jury may issue an indictment charging the suspect with commission of a crime. The indictment is issued only if the grand jury is persuaded that there is probable cause that the defendant committed a crime. Although the grand jury hears evidence before issuing an indictment, the process has been criticized widely as being a mere "rubber stamp" procedure because the evidence in defense, if any, may be deemphasized or even withheld by the prosecutor. A commonly heard quote whose source, if not meaning, is in doubt is "a good prosecutor could get a grand jury to indict a ham sandwich." Sometimes, the suspect is not even aware that the grand jury proceeding is taking place. After an indictment is issued, a warrant for the arrest of the accused will follow. Trial will follow apprehension and arraignment of the defendant.

Sometimes, a grand jury will identify (but decline to indict) a person as a coconspirator with the defendant. Such an unindicted coconspirator is neither arrested nor prosecuted, usually because of a lack of sufficient evidence to convict.

The decision to proceed against a suspect with the process of complaint, preliminary hearing, information, and trial—or more directly with indictment and trial—is left to the discretion of the prosecuting attorney. Frequently, if the suspect is a prominent person or political figure, the elected district attorney may prefer the indictment procedure, thereby delegating the decision to prosecute to a body of private citizens. In either process of accusation, there must be some kind of hearing to evaluate the prosecutor's case before the defendant is held for trial. Such a hearing prevents an overzealous prosecutor from arbitrarily subjecting an accused to a criminal trial.

Regardless of the name of the accusatory documents utilized in a given state, they all provide the defendant with a clear understanding of the offenses charged so he may prepare a defense. Misdemeanor suspects are accused by documents usually called *complaints* rather than indictments by a grand jury.

Federal Crimes

A complaint may be prepared by a federal official (such as a U.S. marshal or U.S. attorney) and submitted to a U.S. magistrate (i.e., a judicial officer, appointed by judges of federal district courts, having some powers of a judge) charging that there is probable cause to arrest a suspect. A private person cannot file such a complaint but may enlist the assistance of a U.S. attorney to instigate criminal proceedings. The magistrate then may issue a warrant for the arrest of the accused. For a crime committed in their presence, law enforcement persons can make an arrest without a warrant.

EXHIBIT 6.1 Typical Steps in a Criminal Prosecution

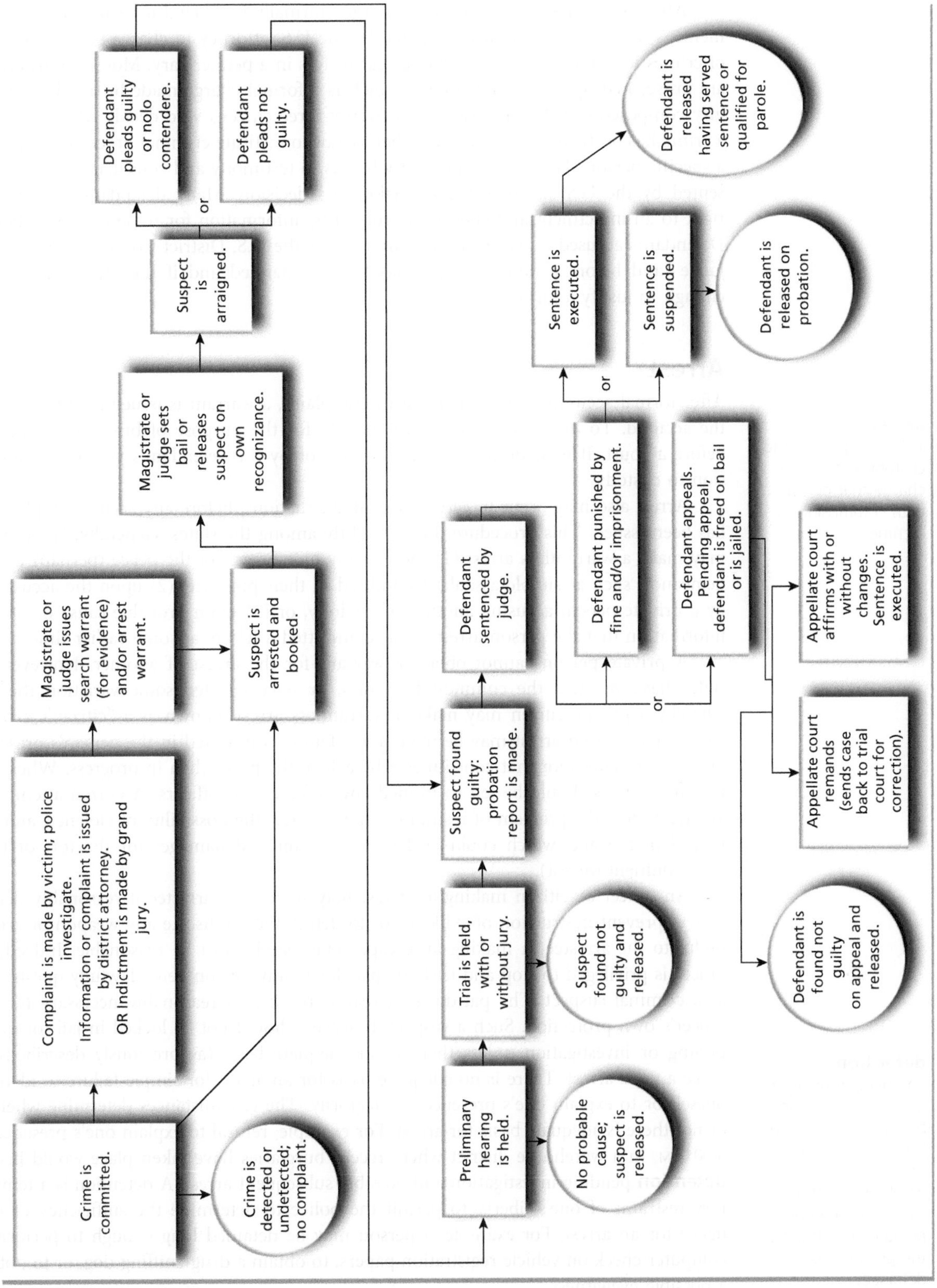

After arrest, the accused must be charged formally by federal information or indictment. A federal information is prepared by the U.S. attorney to charge persons accused of crimes for which the penalty is one year or less in a penitentiary. More serious crimes are prosecuted by federal indictment, which is a formal charge made by a federal grand jury composed of between sixteen and twenty-three citizens who decide whether or not a crime has been committed and whether or not to institute criminal proceedings against a specific person. The federal grand jury listens to testimony and considers evidence presented by the U.S. attorney before making its decision. Many defendants waive their right to an indictment and choose to proceed by information for reasons of expediency. Defendants accused of federal crimes are tried in the U.S. District Court before a federal judge (and before a jury, if a jury has been demanded and if the offense is serious enough to justify a jury).

Arrest

arrest
To take a person into custody in order to charge that person with commission of a crime.

After formal accusation by indictment or complaint, a warrant is issued for the arrest of the accused. To **arrest** is to take into custody for the purpose of bringing the person before a court. It is made by physical restraint or by the defendant's voluntary submission to custody.

Arrest also may occur in certain specified situations, before any accusatory pleading has been issued. This procedure differs slightly among the states. Generally, law officers may make a warrantless arrest (1) for a felony or a breach of the peace (perhaps a misdemeanor, such as simple assault) committed in their presence, (2) upon the accusation by a private person accusing another of a felony, or (3) upon probable cause or official information that the person arrested has committed a felony at some earlier time.

A private person cannot obtain a warrant for the arrest of another. However, all states have retained the common law rules, or have enacted some variation thereof, whereby a private citizen may make a warrantless arrest, known as a "citizen's arrest." Generally, such an arrest may be made for a felony committed in the person's presence or for a misdemeanor that constitutes a breach of the peace then in progress. Whenever possible, arrests should be left to trained law enforcement officers. A citizen attempting an arrest faces the problem of restraining the arrestee, the possibility of violence, and the hazard of mistake, which could lead to a civil suit and damages for the tort of false imprisonment (arrest).

detention
The brief stopping of a suspicious person by a police officer for the limited purpose of determining whether or not a crime has been or is being committed in the proximity of the detainee.

An officer or citizen making an arrest may search the arrestee if reasonably necessary to prevent destruction of evidence or to detect and confiscate any weapon or article useful to the arrestee in making an escape. The search must be reasonable. Indeed, an officer is privileged to stop and frisk, by pat-down, any person being lawfully questioned as a criminal suspect. The pat-down is reasonable if it is reasonably necessary for the officer's own protection. Such a suspect, however, should not be locked in jail for questioning or investigation unless there is an adequate basis (as previously described) to make a valid arrest. There is no adequate basis for an arrest for simple failure to identify oneself or to explain one's presence satisfactorily. The circumstances determine whether or not there is adequate basis for arrest. For example, refusal to explain one's presence at 3:00 A.M. in a warehouse district where recent burglaries have taken place would justify **detention** pending investigation and possibly subsequent arrest. A detention is a temporary restraint of one's liberty to permit the police to determine the sufficiency of evidence for an arrest. For example, a person may be detained long enough to perform a computer check on vehicle registration papers, to obtain a drug-sniffing dog, or to obtain a possible eyewitness.

An officer making an arrest may use the force reasonably necessary to accomplish the restraint. The modern view is to discourage the use of deadly force in making an arrest. A private citizen may not use deadly force in making an arrest except in the case of a violent felony (e.g., murder, arson, rape, or robbery). It is the legal duty of everyone, innocent or guilty, to submit to a lawful arrest, and improper resistance is a separate crime.

Arrests are not always necessary in situations involving misdemeanors, petty offenses, and infractions. One alternative to arrest is the ordinary traffic ticket, which is similar to the summons used in civil proceedings. The traffic violator is not a criminal and usually will appear in court after making a written promise to do so on the citation (the traffic ticket). In a growing number of misdemeanors, including shoplifting and some narcotics violations, the summons is being used instead of arrest to facilitate and streamline the procedures for handling large numbers of cases.

Booking

booked
The administrative practice that occurs when an arrested person is brought to a police station following arrest but before incarceration in jail.

After an arrest, the accused may be **booked**, which involves searching, fingerprinting, photographing, testing for alcohol or drugs, and reasonably related activities. With respect to crimes involving the operation of motor vehicles while under the influence of alcohol or drugs, states have statutes establishing prohibited levels of blood-alcohol concentration (BAC).

The practice of strip-searching arrestees for the purpose of confiscating any weapon, contraband (i.e., any property that is unlawful to produce or possess), or other evidence is often controversial. Under federal court rulings, an arrestee can be required to strip and be searched only if an officer has a reasonable suspicion the arrestee is concealing drugs or contraband that cannot be discovered in a pat-down. Some states prohibit strip-searching in nonviolent misdemeanor cases.

The accused has certain rights after arrest, including the right to be promptly taken before a judge or magistrate, the right to be allowed bail (except in certain cases), the right to remain silent, and, in serious criminal cases, the right to have an attorney present (a telephone call, without charge, must be permitted for this purpose). The right of an accused to be promptly taken before a judge or magistrate limits the possibility of unreasonable police interrogation and affords an opportunity for the accused to have bail set (if it has not already been set and stated in the arrest warrant), to have constitutional rights explained, and to have an attorney appointed if she cannot afford private legal services.

Bail

bail
Security posted with the court to ensure that the accused, if released before trial, will return voluntarily for further criminal proceedings.

An accused who is arrested is physically taken to jail. But the state has no right to punish the arrestee. Every person accused of a crime is presumed innocent under the Fifth Amendment until proven guilty beyond a reasonable doubt and to a moral certainty, and therefore is entitled to be released on bail with only limited exceptions. The purpose of **bail** is merely to help ensure the defendant's presence for trial. Bail refers to the security given the court by the accused to ensure the accused's later appearance for trial, in exchange for immediate release from custody. The amount of bail must be specified in the arrest warrant or, if arrest is without warrant, the magistrate will set bail after the arrest and booking. The court may deny bail in cases in which the likelihood the defendant will flee is great, such as when a capital offense has been charged and the evidence of guilt is overwhelming. But bail cannot be denied or set unreasonably high simply because a judge considers a defendant to be dangerous.

Bail will be denied a person accused of certain extremely serious federal crimes if the government demonstrates by clear and convincing evidence, after an adversary hearing,* that no release conditions will reasonably ensure the safety of the community. Bail for defendants accused of less serious federal offenses may be denied when, for example, there is a high degree of risk that the defendant will flee if released pending trial. When bail is denied, federal detainees are housed separately from convicted defendants, and other procedural safeguards apply. In all cases, the policy is to be liberal in setting bail before any conviction takes place. Freedom while appealing a conviction is easily distinguishable from the situation before trial because there is no longer a presumption of innocence.

bail bond
A document signed by both the accused and a bail bondsman, binding the bail bondsman to pay a specified sum of money to the state if the accused fails to appear in court as directed.

A **bail bond** is a document signed by both the accused and a bail bondsman binding them to pay to the state a specified sum if the accused fails to appear in court as directed. Bail bondsmen charge substantial fees in exchange for making such a promise, typically 10 percent of the sum specified as bail (e.g., a $1,000 fee when the bail is $10,000). They rarely lose money because they secure their risk with collateral (such as stocks, bonds, mortgages, jewelry, or other valuables) and later go to great lengths to recover from the clients who "jump bail" (i.e., fail to appear in court as promised).

recognizance
A written promise by the accused that if released without posting bail, that person will return voluntarily for further criminal proceedings.

Under the Eighth Amendment, a judge or magistrate may not demand "excessive bail," but any amount may be too much for a poor person. Accordingly, at the federal level and in a number of progressive states, reforms have been enacted to permit release of the poor on their own **recognizance**, whereby the accused person simply promises in writing to appear for the trial. The court can attach other conditions to the prisoner's release, such as a promise not to contact the victim of the crime. Failure to fulfill conditions of release may lead to rearrest and may involve an obligation to pay a specified sum of money to the court.

Arraignment

arraigned
To be formally charged with a crime in a court of law and to make a plea.

After being charged formally with a crime by the filing of an accusatory pleading (complaint, information, or indictment), the accused must be **arraigned**, meaning called into court, informed of the charge, and given an opportunity to make a response or plea. A public defender will be appointed to defend an accused who is unable to afford private counsel. In general, the defendant's plea may be either guilty, not guilty, *nob contendere* (Latin: "I will not contest it"), or not guilty by reason of insanity. A plea of *nolo contendere* in criminal law is comparable to a plea of guilty. The only real distinction justifying its use is that a guilty plea can be used against the defendant as an admission against interest in subsequent civil litigation, whereas a plea of *nolo contendere* generally cannot. A guilty plea standing alone presumes that the defendant was sane at the time the crime was committed. Hence, the question of insanity must be raised by special plea, namely "not guilty by reason of insanity." In felony cases, a preliminary hearing (unless waived by the defendant) and trial will follow the defendant's plea. There is no preliminary hearing in misdemeanor cases. If the plea is guilty, in either a felony or misdemeanor case, sentencing will then follow.

*The adversary hearing is a mini-trial, the purpose of which is to determine the potential danger to the community if the accused defendant is released on bail pending trial. The accused may have counsel, cross-examine witnesses, offer evidence, and so forth. There is no jury in these proceedings.

Plea Bargain

plea bargain
A binding agreement in which an accused agrees to plead guilty (or *nolo contendere*) if the court agrees to a specified punishment in advance.

Often, following arraignment, the district attorney or county prosecutor will decide that it is in the best interests of justice to offer a **plea bargain** to a defendant. Typically, the defendant agrees to plead guilty to some crime of lesser severity than the crime specified at the arraignment. In return, a judge agrees to a specified punishment and accepts the guilty plea on that basis. Once a judge has accepted a guilty plea, the judge cannot refuse to carry through the bargain that induced the plea.

The government's rationale for plea bargaining is that the interests of justice are better served when the time, expense, and uncertainly of a trial can be avoided. For example, it may be uncertain whether or not a conviction for murder in the second degree or voluntary manslaughter can be obtained. It may be preferable to accept a guilty plea to the lesser charge than to incur the expense and difficulty of trial. There is an unending stream of cases to be disposed, and plea bargaining can be of benefit to the defendants—who are in jeopardy of a more severe sentence—as well as to the people represented by the prosecutor's office.

Preliminary Hearing

preliminary hearing
An examination in open court by a judge to determine whether sufficient evidence exists to hold the accused for trial.

A **preliminary hearing** is an evidentiary proceeding after a felony accusation, done before a magistrate or judge, to determine whether or not there is probable cause that the specified felony has been committed by the accused. The district attorney will call witnesses and present evidence in support of the charges. The accused need not, and usually does not, present any evidence because he is presumed innocent. Most defendants' attorneys, however, take advantage of the opportunity and cross-examine prosecution witnesses at length to learn as much as possible about the case. In some states, a preliminary hearing is not conducted after an indictment, on the theory that there already has been an evidentiary hearing. This rule is subject to constitutional question because the grand jury is a one-sided proceeding with no judge or magistrate present.

After the preliminary hearing, assuming the prosecution has presented enough evidence to justify a trial, the matter will be set for jury or nonjury trial, to determine the guilt or innocence of the defendant. Preliminary hearings are not conducted in misdemeanor cases.

WHAT ARE THE CONSTITUTIONAL RIGHTS OF AN ACCUSED?

The legislative branch of government decides what activities are criminal and therefore prohibited. Commission of a proscribed act is a crime. The legislative branch of government has no power to prohibit that which the Constitution protects, such as the expression of opinion critical of government.

The executive branch of government, in turn, has the responsibility of arresting persons reasonably thought to have committed criminal acts.

The judicial branch has the responsibility for conducting trials of the accused. In the process, it is conceivable that the executive branch or the judicial branch could treat those accused of crimes in an unfair manner, thereby increasing the possibility that innocent persons may be convicted.

To minimize this possibility, certain fundamental rights are guaranteed by the U.S. Constitution, as well as by state constitutions, to every person suspected of involvement in criminal activity. For example, there is a right to be free from unreasonable searches and seizures, as described in a previous section of this chapter. State constitutions are free to be more demanding than the U.S. Constitution in guaranteeing such rights. Thus, in some states, persons who are accused of a crime may enjoy expanded rights of protection from unreasonable prosecutorial activities.

According to federal law, the police cannot arrest anyone without probable cause. Moreover, that person must be informed (1) of the right to remain silent, (2) that anything said can and will be used against him in a court of law, (3) that he is entitled to the presence and aid of a lawyer during questioning, and (4) that if he cannot afford to hire counsel, one will be provided free of charge. These **Miranda warnings** technically are not constitutional rights; rather they are "procedural safeguards" imposed by the courts to preserve the integrity of the judicial system. Therefore, if the arresting officer fails to inform the arrestee of these rights, the court subsequently may reject as evidence anything said by the defendant that is of an incriminating nature, such as a confession. Rejection of such evidence by the court may result in dismissal of the case if there is no other evidence sufficient to convict.

Miranda warnings
Warnings directed to a suspect by police before a *custodial* (while in custody) interrogation may occur.

Miranda warnings are required before custodial (while in custody) interrogation, but not before general investigatory questioning (e.g., Where do you live? What are you doing here? How did you get here?). The warnings relate to all offenses, regardless of their gravity (e.g., for DUI of alcohol or drugs). Police can detain persons, during an investigation, for a reasonable time for some reasonable purpose, without making any arrest. This "right to detain" can be based on a reasonable suspicion of criminal activity involving the detainee. The Miranda warnings need not be given until an arrest is contemplated. In petty misdemeanor cases or infractions (e.g., traffic violations), no arrest is contemplated, so Miranda warnings are inapplicable. The Supreme Court also has recognized a public safety justification for dispensing with the Miranda requirement in exigent circumstances, for example, in cases of terrorism when there is a continued threat to public safety and the Miranda warnings would deter the suspect from providing crucial information.

The accused is entitled to due process in all procedures following arrest. Bail, as previously discussed, is designed to prevent the punishment of one who is presumed innocent pending trial. There is a right to a speedy trial unless the defendant waives time and permits a later trial date. States typically provide that the defendant is entitled to commencement of trial within approximately sixty days of arraignment. But most defendants "waive time" to prepare better defenses, or even simply to stall as long as possible. There is a right to be arraigned—that is, informed of the specific charges pending.

During trial, the defendant is entitled to an impartial jury and judge and is presumed innocent until found guilty. The state, representing the people, always has the burden of proof to convict "beyond a reasonable doubt." The defendant is entitled to be present in court in ordinary clothing* and is entitled to confront and cross-examine adverse witnesses, including informants who are witnesses to the crime charged. A defendant has a right to conduct her own defense but must be able and willing to abide by rules of procedure and courtroom protocol. The Fifth Amendment provides that "no person shall … be compelled in any criminal case to be a witness against himself." This right is known as the **privilege against self-incrimination**. Accordingly, a defendant need not take the witness stand and testify in the proceeding. The prosecution must prove its case beyond a reasonable doubt without the use of the defendant's testimony.

privilege against self-incrimination
The right of any person, including one accused of a crime, to remain silent when what might be said could indicate guilt.

*A defendant cannot be compelled to be tried in jail attire because it may insinuate that the defendant has been arrested not only on the charge being tried but also on other charges for which he is being incarcerated. The presumption of innocence requires the civilian garb of innocence.

LEGAL FOCUS—PROBLEM

Michael Vega was charged with vehicular manslaughter. Antoinette Marie Joseph was the sole witness able to incriminate him. Just before his jury trial was scheduled to begin, Vega married Joseph, setting the stage for his wife not to testify against him. On motion of the defense attorney, Judge Carolyn Sweeney dismissed all charges, but noted that the timing of the marriage was a "terrible violation of ordinary moral decency." Was the judge correct to dismiss the case?

A variation of the privilege against self-incrimination is the privilege against incrimination by one's spouse. Thus, in most jurisdictions Joseph cannot testify against Vega without his permission—an unlikely circumstance.

In trying to meet its burden of proof, the prosecution cannot suppress evidence favorable to an accused. Thus, defendants may make a pretrial request for access to possibly favorable evidence. Furthermore, an involuntary confession made out of court is not admissible as evidence against the defendant, and a confession is involuntary if obtained by any form of compulsion, including false promises. Interestingly, the Fifth Amendment does not prevent police from requiring a defendant to participate in a lineup, repeat certain words that were uttered by a guilty person, submit to executing samples of handwriting, be fingerprinted, or be photographed. What about DNA?

LEGAL FOCUS—PROBLEM

Defendant was arrested and charged with assault for menacing a group of people with a shotgun. As part of a routine booking procedure for serious offenses, defendant's DNA sample was taken by applying a cotton swab to the inside of his cheeks. The DNA was found to match the DNA taken from a rape victim. Can he be arrested for the rape, or is such a search unreasonable under the Fourth Amendment?

Maryland v. King, 2013 U.S. LEXIS 4165 (June 3, 2013).

The Supreme Court determined that taking and analyzing a cheek swab of defendant's DNA was similar to fingerprinting and photographing, a legitimate police booking procedure that was reasonable under the Fourth Amendment. It concluded that the government had a legitimate interest in a safe and accurate way to process and identify persons taken into custody and that any privacy intrusion on the suspect was minimal.

A defendant is entitled to subpoena defense witnesses and to have a "fair" trial, generally in a place where publicity about the case has not unreasonably tainted the proceedings, which must be open to the public. Defendants may waive many of these rights if desired.

An accused cannot be placed twice in jeopardy for the same offense, but one wrongful act (such as rape) may be grounds for both criminal proceedings and a civil lawsuit for battery. A single criminal activity can involve violation of several statutory provisions and consequently result in several different crimes and punishments. The constitutional safeguard against double jeopardy protects against a second prosecution following acquittal or conviction for a single crime and against multiple punishments by the state for that offense.

Can Innocent Persons Be Convicted?

The basic purpose of the many constitutional safeguards we have considered is to minimize the risk of convicting innocent persons of crimes. In other words, the purpose is to ensure that justice is done to the extent possible. To err by releasing a guilty defendant is thought to be preferable to incarcerating one who is innocent. Nevertheless, grievous mistakes are sometimes made.

LEGAL FOCUS—PROBLEM

Kirk Bloodsworth was convicted of the brutal rape and murder of a nine-year-old girl. Bloodsworth was in prison and on death row for more than eight years when serious doubt of his guilt arose from the results of recent DNA testing of semen specimens, which excluded him. Should Bloodsworth be released because of these test results?

Bloodsworth, his innocence confirmed, was promptly released from prison. Like fingerprint comparison, DNA matching is admissible in evidence, although unlike fingerprint analysis, it is not always absolutely conclusive. The overwhelming statistical probability of unique identification, however, will be taken as conclusive in the minds of reasonable people. In a pioneering case, the court ruled that any evidence that generally was accepted in the applicable scientific community was admissible (acceptable) in court. Thus, DNA evidence has become widely acceptable.

Terrorism Issues

Some issues demand coverage because of their importance and timeliness and yet the complexity and uncertainly of the issues are difficult to cover in an introductory law text. Such are the legal issues raised by the war on terrorism. But a few issues can be raised briefly.

Law Enforcement, Military Defense, and Due Process

In 2001, President Bush issued a Military Order directing the Department of Defense to establish military commissions to decide the guilt of noncitizens suspected of involvement in terrorist activities. These commissions have raised additional legal and political questions about the long-term separation of military from law enforcement functions. In 2006, however, the Supreme Court struck down the tribunals, finding a lack of military necessity. Although the Court made it clear that military combatants might not be entitled to the same due process protections to which criminal defendants are entitled, the Court nevertheless noted that the tribunals did not guarantee sufficient due process. The Court noted that the president could choose to conduct trials pursuant to the Uniform Code of Military Justice.

Immigration Law

Some persons suspected of terrorist activities are in the United States illegally in violation of U.S. immigration law. The Illegal Immigration Reform and Immigrant Responsibility Act of 1996 created substantial penalties for persons who overstay their visas or enter the country illegally. In addition, violation of immigration status allows for detention of violators outside of normal criminal process.

WHAT IS THE PUNISHMENT OF CONVICTED PERSONS?

After conviction, judges impose sentences. Some state judges have more discretion in sentencing than federal judges, who must comply with specific guidelines. State statutes prescribe the ranges of punishments that may be imposed. To help juries determine the degree of guilt (e.g., first- or second-degree murder) and make sentencing decisions, courts allow "expert opinion" testimony on a wide range of topics, such as the psychological profile of the defendant. The personal characteristics of defendants may bear upon their personal responsibility or upon the sentence that ought to be imposed. Social scientists can and do offer an array of causes for crime: low verbal I.Q. (intelligence quotient) score, low levels of certain body chemicals and elevated levels of others, the presence of the XYY chromosome pattern in men, fetal alcohol and drug syndrome, a lack of religious involvement, extreme poverty, being raised in a single-parent family, the battered woman syndrome, and more.

Imprisonment and fines are two basic forms of punishment. Either or both may be ordered, depending on the statute and what a judge (and, in some cases, a jury) decides. Misdemeanants are confined in county jail, and felons are incarcerated in state prisons. Offenders guilty of federal crimes are incarcerated in federal penitentiaries.

Prison sentences are classified as either determinate or indeterminate. A determinate sentence is the confinement for a fixed or minimum period that is specified by statute. An indeterminate sentence provides for a range of years of imprisonment (e.g., one to five years) rather than a specific period. The indeterminate sentencing system gives judges broad discretion in setting the type and extent of punishment imposed. This discretion results in great disparities in time actually served as well as in sentences imposed because parole boards (officials with authority to set release dates) make actual release decisions tailored to the supposed amenability of each prisoner to rehabilitation.

Punishment for Misdemeanors

LEGAL FOCUS—PROBLEM

Ripley Offenbach tried to shoplift a pair of jeans from a department store. He was caught, entered a plea of guilty in the municipal court, and was sentenced to sixty days in jail. While confined, can Offenbach simply loaf, eat nourishing food, and—in some jails—watch television?

Not necessarily. A prisoner is entitled to be fed, to receive medical care, and to be kept free from physical abuse by prisoners or guards. There is scant management of prison guards, however, and little solid information on abuses within prison walls.

County jail prisoners can be made to work on public roads and trails or on other jobs for the benefit of the public. Some counties have road camps for such purposes. Commitment to such a camp, called the "farm," is selective, however, and Ripley Offenbach, in the preceding example, may or may not be selected by jail officials. In some states, under **work furlough** programs, a prisoner in a county jail may work at regular outside employment during working hours and remain in confinement at other times.

work furlough
A rehabilitative program for prisoners under which they may participate in part-time gainful employment even while they are serving time in a prison or jail.

Punishments can be tailored for a specific defendant and the circumstances surrounding the crime by offering probation, with conditions, in lieu of time in jail. The imposition of conditions to receive probation is loosely known as "creative sentencing." Conditions may involve community work, for example, but this option can be rejected by a defendant who prefers to go to jail.

LEGAL FOCUS—PROBLEM

As punishment, four crab poachers in Florida agreed to parade around town for four Saturdays wearing signs that said, "It is a felony punishable by five years in prison and/or a $5,000 fine to molest crab pots. I know because I molested one." Is this a constitutional punishment?

Yes, this is constitutional. This unique punishment was agreed to by the defendants, who preferred it to a more traditional punishment. There may be a limit, however, as to how far judges can go with their creative sentencing. Judges have assigned unusual conditions that many find offensive, for example, that prostitutes permanently move out of the county or that the names of "Johns" (men who have been convicted of soliciting prostitution) be printed in the local newspaper.

Commonly, a county jail sentence imposed by the court may be shortened for good conduct—for example, ten days off for each month of such behavior. Additional time off may be granted for satisfactory completion of work assignments and for blood donations made to a blood bank.

Punishment for Felonies

Traditionally, the legislative branch of government establishes either specified periods of confinement or minimum–maximum ranges for specified offenses. Egregious circumstances surrounding offenses usually suggest which end of the scale will be applied by the sentencing judge.

LEGAL FOCUS—EXAMPLE

Richard Rowold fired his shotgun at a dog, missed, and accidentally shot his neighbor who was in her backyard. Rowold was convicted of criminal recklessness for injuring his neighbor and was sentenced to three years in prison. However, the sentence was enhanced to eight years because he was a "habitual offender" guilty of two previous felonies; that is, the federal crimes of mail fraud in 1980 and fraudulent use of an access device (cable television decoder) in 1986.

Statutory penalties for crimes can and do vary widely among the states. Capital crimes (punishable by death) may be punished by life imprisonment with or without the possibility of parole, or death. Capital punishment, called the death penalty by many, is discussed later in this chapter under the heading "When Is Punishment Cruel and Unusual?" because of the controversy surrounding that issue. Under traditional statutes for noncapital felonies, a specified minimum sentence is increased automatically when certain aggravating circumstances are present. Statutes specify increased or enhanced penalties for crimes if, for example—

- The defendant has a prior conviction.
- A weapon was used during the commission of the crime.
- Great bodily harm was inflicted.
- A particular class of victim is involved (e.g., a police officer).
- The criminal motive was hatred of a protected class of persons (e.g., racial minorities).

recidivist
A repeat criminal offender.

Traditionally, three- or four-time felons face the impact of **recidivist** (repeat offender) statutes (as detailed in the discussion of cruel and unusual punishment). Some states have been echoing the former federal system by prescribing indeterminate sentences that authorize judges and parole boards to tailor the actual time served to the individual criminal. But changes in traditional sentencing formulas inevitably vary in response to ever-changing public demands. "Three strikes and you're out" has been adopted in many states in response to public outcry and provides that three felony convictions should result in incarceration for nothing less than twenty-five years to the maximum of life without possibility of parole.

These laws were passed in the 1990s, following the public fury over the kidnap and murder of Polly Klaas, a twelve-year-old from Petaluma, California. Polly was kidnapped from her bedroom and murdered in 1993 by a man with a long criminal record. Some persons contend, however, that enhancing prison sentences under three-strikes laws for *nonviolent* crimes is unfair and accomplishes little more than filling up the nation's prisons. Others rebut that contention by pointing to the recent downturn in crime rates, which they suggest is the direct result of harsher sentencing policies.

LEGAL FOCUS—PROBLEM

Andre Wilks, nineteen years, was arrested for breaking a car window and stealing a cell phone. He had a juvenile record of two purse-snatching convictions, crimes committed during one spree when he was sixteen years old. The district attorney offered him a plea bargain of seven years in prison; if convicted by a jury, he faced a three-strikes enhancement of twenty-five years to life in prison, even though it would be based on his juvenile record. Wilks, against the advice of his lawyer, his mother, his uncle, the prosecutor, and even the judge, refused to accept the offer and chose trial by jury. During trial, he perjured himself by denying everything. To his surprise and chagrin, the twelve-year-old accomplice in the car burglary testified against him. Wilks was convicted by the jury. Must the sentencing judge send Wilks to prison for twenty-five years to life for stealing the cell phone?

The judge could "expunge" one of the prior juvenile convictions and thereby avoid the "three strikes and you're out" law. But, because Wilks showed no remorse before conviction, and because he perjured himself, he was sentenced to twenty-five years to life in prison.

The publicized sentences imposed upon convicted defendants often are different from the time actually served in prison. Many persons contend that criminals are not serving enough time and that there is too much of a gap between sentences set by judges and the amount of time actually served. Early releases can occur for a variety of reasons, such as early parole (discussed later in this chapter), credits for time served for "good time" (prison time without disciplinary action), and even court-ordered release to relieve prison overcrowding. In reaction to public concern, more than half the states (and the District of Columbia) now require violent offenders to serve at least 85 percent of their prison sentences.

LEGAL FOCUS—PROBLEM

Ronnie Hawkins was convicted of petty theft, but it was his "third strike" and hence considered a felony. During his jury trial, although instructed by the judge to be quiet, Hawkins blurted out that he was HIV positive and was facing twenty-five years to life for petty theft—an apparent appeal to sympathy. He was considered disruptive. After his conviction, and during a sentencing hearing, Hawkins kept talking and interrupting the judge. Outraged, the judge ordered the bailiff to use a remote control device that caused 50,000 volts of electricity to surge into Hawkins. The jolt struck just above Hawkins's left kidney and continued for eight seconds, during which he "grimaced and sat stiff as a board." Can defendants be physically punished while in the courtroom even though they have not been held in contempt, are not behaving violently, or are otherwise not threatening to harm anyone?

Judges are in control of their courtrooms and can and do take precautionary steps to protect themselves and others from violence. Electronic security belts are not uncommon to restrain violent defendants. The *Hawkins* case was unusual because his disruption took the form of talking too much. Restraining or subduing a defendant in court is not considered "punishment" in the same way that "punishment" follows conviction. Rather, it is physical restraint or action that serves a nonpunishment purpose; in this case, order in the court. Nonetheless, upon petition by Hawkins, a U.S. District Court judge issued a preliminary injunction prohibiting the use of stun belts in Los Angeles courts, asserting that the use of a pain-infliction device, which could compromise an individual's ability to participate in his or her own defense, was inappropriate in a court of law.

Does punishment end upon release from prison? Recall the discussion earlier concerning disclosure of the identity and residential address of convicted sex offenders under state statutes known as Megan's Law (discussed earlier in the chapter). Does the public's fear that sex offenders are habitual also apply to other felons?

LEGAL FOCUS—PROBLEM

Glenn Barker, forty, served his sentence for murder, was released from prison, and obtained a job coaching youth basketball at the YMCA. But he was fired when police revealed his criminal record. He moved to another town, and according to his lawyer, "he's been employed, he's never had a parking ticket, and he's never been in trouble or charged. He doesn't smoke, drink, or dance the hoochie-coochie." The police then used Megan's Law as a basis to visit almost 1,000 homes distributing flyers of Barker's address and record. When does a criminal's sentence end?

This was the first instance when Megan's Law has been applied selectively by police to an ex-convict who was not a sex offender. Questions arise as to just which ex-convicts police will choose to expose repeatedly. What are ex-convicts supposed to do if they are excluded from employment and from neighborhoods? If one ex-convict is exposed, should law enforcement be required to disclose all former convicts who committed similar crimes? Can police use Megan's Law as an excuse to harass selected ex-convicts?

For federal crimes, sentencing guidelines, in the form of a table, were prepared by the U.S. Sentencing Commission pursuant to the Sentencing Reform Act of 1984. Rehabilitation was a primary goal of indeterminate sentencing until the Sentencing Reform Act rejected imprisonment as a means of rehabilitation. The act stated that punishment should serve the goals of retribution (punishment), education (preparation for legitimate employment), deterrence (discouragement of repetition through fear), and incapacitation (prevention of repetition through confinement). The law abolished parole (suspension of part of a jail sentence) and made all sentences determinate, with sentence reduction allowed only for credits earned by good behavior while in custody. The U.S. Sentencing Commission, an administrative agency within the judicial branch of government, established binding sentencing guidelines. The vertical axis is divided into forty-three units, each corresponding to a level of offense seriousness. The horizontal axis is divided into six units, each corresponding to a level of criminal history. Judges were supposed to base each sentence on where the unit representing the defendant's present crime intersects with that representing his past record. Opponents to this mechanical procedure referred to it as "sentencing by numbers" and decried the lack of judgment it allowed.

In 2005, the Supreme Court in *United States v. Booker* addressed some legal concerns about the Sentencing Reform Act. In the *Booker* plurality decision, the court found that mandatory federal sentencing guidelines required that a judge make factual determinations after the jury had established guilt. This process violated the defendant's Sixth Amendment right that he have a jury determine essential facts related to his punishment and thus violated a defendant's constitutional right to a jury trial. Currently, the federal sentencing guidelines are no longer mandatory but merely "advisory." In spite of *Booker*, the sentencing guidelines remain important because federal judges commonly still follow them. Under the federal sentencing guidelines, all those convicted of a felony serve some time in prison, including white-collar criminal defendants.

In addition to fines and imprisonment, some professional persons convicted of crimes involving moral turpitude (intentionally evil) may suffer penalties such as loss of professional license or employment. Teachers may lose their positions if convicted of criminal sexual misconduct on the basis of unfitness to teach or for lack of moral principles. Likewise, a license to practice law may be suspended or revoked for conviction of a crime involving moral turpitude, such as income tax evasion. In Chapter 4, you learned about lawyer discipline. Loss of professional license or position is not a substitute for a fine or imprisonment. It is an additional penalty that a professional person may suffer as the result of committing a crime.

WHAT ARE PAROLE, PROBATION, AND CLEMENCY?

parole
Release from a prison on specified conditions involving good behavior.

probation
Release of a convicted criminal before sentence begins on condition of good behavior and under supervision of a probation officer. If this condition is violated, incarceration begins.

Parole, probation, and clemency are three means by which punishment is reduced or rescinded. **Parole** suspends a sentence after incarceration has begun, as distinct from **probation**, which suspends the sentence before incarceration. Either a felon in a state prison or a misdemeanant in a county jail may be paroled. Officials designated under legislative authority (parole boards) make the decision to parole. The liberty of a parolee is conditional and may be suspended or revoked unilaterally for violation of conditions specified, such as avoiding certain company (e.g., former gang members) or activity (e.g., carrying a gun). Thus, parole consists of two parts. Parole *boards* are state administrative bodies that have the authority to decide when to release prisoners. If an indeterminate sentence exists (e.g., twenty-five years to life imprisonment), the board decides the exact time for release based on such matters as "good time" credits (reductions in sentence for time spent in prison without discipline), other prison records, and recommendations from prison officials, prosecutors, victims, and the prisoner's family and friends. Even if an indeterminate sentence does not exist, such boards often set the actual date of release and provide conditions for early release from prison, set the conditions of parole (e.g., refrain from consuming alcohol and from associating with known felons), and monitor the parolee's activities while on parole. Parole officers supervise convicts after their release.

To prevent the early release of prisoners, some states have abolished parole boards. One result of eliminating early release is the swelling of prison populations. Traditionally, parole officers were social workers who helped offenders find jobs. Entering the twenty-first century, parole officers are more like law enforcement officers concerned with surveillance, warrantless searches, and drug tests. Thus, even more parolees are returned to prison for various offenses.

The purpose of probation is to aid in rehabilitation. There is no absolute right to probation; it is a discretionary decision for the judge. After conviction and before sentencing, a probation officer will, at the court's discretion, thoroughly examine the defendant's background and circumstances. A recommendation to grant or deny probation is then made to the court. Probation depends on many events, such as compliance with all laws, search for gainful employment, restitution or return of stolen properly or its value, abstention from using intoxicants, and submission to periodic tests for drug addiction.

executive clemency
A formal act of kindness, mercy, and leniency by a governor or by the president in commuting a criminal penalty or granting a pardon.

reprieve
Postponement, or stay of execution (i.e., of enforcement), of the judgment after conviction for a crime.

commutation
Reduction, by a state governor or by the president, of punishment for a crime.

In many states, statutes limit probation. Thus, probation is not allowed for certain defendants, such as someone armed with a deadly weapon during a prison escape; or someone who committed the crimes of kidnapping, murder, or forcible rape; or someone who has two prior felonies. Traditional practices concerning probation are limited severely when "three strikes and you're out" legislation is adopted in a state.

When probation is granted, either the sentence is suspended pending successful completion of probation, or there is no imposition of any sentence at all during the period of probation. In either case, probation will be revoked if the defendant violates its terms or conditions. The original sentence then may become operative. Revocation of probation, however, may occur only after a hearing has been conducted to establish the fact of the violation. If probation is completed successfully, the defendant's conviction legally is erased.

A defendant has the right to refuse probation and accept the sentence, but that seldom happens. In addition, there are three kinds of **executive clemency**, meaning a formal act of mercy: (1) **reprieve** (delay in execution of judgment), (2) **commutation** (reduction of punishment), and (3) **pardon** (release from punishment with restoration of all rights and privileges—for example, voting rights). Governors of states possess the power of clemency over state criminals; the president of the United States possesses the power over persons guilty of federal crimes.

LEGAL FOCUS—PROBLEM

Joseph Yandle was convicted of first-degree murder for driving the getaway car for his accomplice, who entered the Mystic Liquor store in Medford, Massachusetts, and shot the store manager to death. Yandle was sentenced to life imprisonment without possibility of parole. After twenty-three years in prison, Yandle appeared on the television program *60 Minutes* and said his crime was prompted by heroin, which he used to "numb" his memories of fighting in the Vietnam War. In patriotic response, the Board of Pardons recommended commutation of sentence; the governor agreed and Yandle was set free. Five years later, it was learned that Yandle had been only a clerk in Okinawa, Japan, and had never fought in Vietnam. Yandle had lied because he "just wanted to go home." Can Yandle's commutation of sentence be revoked?

pardon
Release of a convicted criminal from all punishment for a crime through an act of the governor of the state or the president.

Yes, the commutation can be revoked. Yandle surrendered to officials and returned to custody while his commutation was in the process of revocation.

LEGAL FOCUS—PROBLEM

In December 1990, Taro, a five-year-old, one-hundred-ten-pound Akita dog, injured Brie Halfond, a ten-year-old girl. Taro was ordered "forfeited" and killed under the New Jersey vicious-dog law. Lonnie and Sandy Lehrer, Taro's owners, began legal proceedings ultimately costing some $30,000 in fees whereas the state incurred twice that amount in costs plus $18,000 to house and feed Taro. Taro's fate ultimately involved the courts, the state legislature, and gubernatorial candidates and gained an international following. The legal issue was whether or not Brie had provoked Taro into the attack. The case finally reached the New Jersey Supreme Court, which let stand a lower court's order to put Taro to death. Can the governor grant executive clemency to Taro?

Yes, the governor can. Then-Governor Christie Whitman, fulfilling a campaign promise, used an executive order to remove a "forfeiture order" on the dog in lieu of a "pardon," which is a remedy reserved for human beings. Taro's life was spared.

WHEN IS PUNISHMENT CRUEL AND UNUSUAL?

cruel and unusual punishment
Criminal punishment in which the punishment is totally disproportionate to the offense, or the prisoner is subjected to inhuman torture or merciless abuse, or the method of the punishment is unacceptable to society, or the punishment is arbitrary.

The Eighth Amendment to the U.S. Constitution prohibits government from inflicting **cruel and unusual punishment** upon persons convicted of crimes. Punishment can be cruel and unusual in any one of four ways:

1. The sentence can be totally disproportionate to the offense.
2. The prisoner may be subjected to inherently cruel abuse.
3. The method of punishment may be unacceptable to society.
4. The punishment may be inflicted arbitrarily.

LEGAL FOCUS—CASE

Defendant William James Rummel was sentenced to life imprisonment under the Texas recidivist statute. He was guilty of committing three felonies over a period of some fifteen years, as follows: (1) fraudulently using a credit card to obtain $80 worth of goods, for which a sentence of three years was imposed; (2) passing a forged check for $28.36 for which a sentence of four years was imposed; and (3) obtaining $120.75 by false pretenses, the third felony, for which a sentence of life imprisonment was required under the recidivist statute. Under Texas law, defendants may be paroled within twelve years if they earn maximum good-time credit and the parole board and the governor approve. Defendant Rummel contended that his penalty was so disproportionate to the crimes that it to violated the Eighth Amendment prohibition against cruel and unusual punishment. He appealed to the U.S. Supreme Court. What was the result?

Rummel v. Estelle, 445 U.S. 263 (1980).

The Court upheld Rummel's sentence by a 5–4 split decision. The Court noted that although the crimes did not involve much money, the crime of obtaining $120.75 by false pretenses standing alone is a felony in thirty-five states. Furthermore, his crime of passing a forged check of $28.36 theoretically would be punishable by some amount of imprisonment in forty-nine states. Thus, the Texas recidivist statute was allowed to apply. The sentence of life imprisonment without possibility of parole for a defendant convicted of possessing a large amount of drugs (650 grams of cocaine) is not cruel and unusual punishment either, according to the U.S. Supreme Court.

LEGAL FOCUS—CASE

Roger Davis was convicted by a Virginia jury of possessing nine ounces of marijuana, with a street value of $200, for distribution. He was sentenced to prison for forty years and fined $20,000. He appealed on the basis that the sentence was so disproportionate to the crime that it constituted cruel and unusual punishment. What was the result?

Hutto v. Davis, 454 U.S. 370 (1982).

The U.S. Supreme Court, in a 6–3 decision, repeated its earlier declaration that federal courts should be reluctant to review legislatively mandated terms of imprisonment and that successful court challenges to the proportionality of particular sentences should be exceedingly rare. The sentence was permitted to stand.

habeas corpus
A legal writ or court order to release a prisoner from allegedly unlawful confinement so that he can appear before a court for proper remedial action. The petitioner seeks release.

Prison officials properly may use force (e.g., tear-gassing, clubbing, or even shooting) in defense of themselves or other persons. On the other hand, corporal punishment (physical injury as punishment) constitutionally is prohibited. Generally, however, the remedy for an aggrieved prisoner remains inadequate. An abused prisoner presumably can obtain a writ of ***habeas corpus*** (Latin: "you have the body"), a procedure prompting a court hearing, or the prisoner may sue under civil rights legislation or in a common law tort action.

LEGAL FOCUS—CASE

William McKinney, a Nevada state prisoner, filed suit against prison officials claiming that his involuntary exposure to environmental tobacco smoke (ETS) from the cigarettes of his cellmate and of other inmates posed an unreasonable risk to his health, thus subjecting him to cruel and unusual punishment. There was no claim that injury already had occurred. What was the result?

Helling v. McKinney, 509 U.S. 25 (1993).

Justice Byron White, writing for the majority of the U.S. Supreme Court, held that McKinney was entitled to a trial on the issue of whether or not he was being exposed to unreasonably high levels of ETS that posed an unreasonable risk of serious damage to his future health. Justice Clarence Thomas, with Justice Antonin Scalia joining, dissented, stating, "I would draw the line at actual, serious injuries and reject the claim that exposure to the risk of injury can violate the Eighth Amendment."

capital punishment
Death penalty for a crime.

Critics of **capital punishment** (death by execution) insist that it is not a deterrent to crime, that it is "cruel and unusual," and that it "degrades and dehumanizes" all who participate in its administration. They claim that it discriminates against the poor and minorities, citing statistics showing that most persons sentenced to die, in recent years, have been poor, male, and members of minority groups. This latter argument was especially persuasive in the decision by the U.S. Supreme Court limiting capital punishment. It held that a state may not leave the decision whether or not to impose capital punishment upon a particular defendant to the unguided discretion of a jury.

As a result, there is usually a bifurcated proceeding in which guilt or innocence is determined, followed by a proceeding to determine punishment. To determine during the sentencing phase whether or not the imposition of capital punishment is warranted, mitigating circumstances (e.g., having no prior criminal record or a capacity to appreciate the wrongfulness of the conduct) are weighed against aggravating circumstances (e.g., knowingly creating a grave risk of death separate from the person murdered, or committing the murder in an especially heinous, cruel or depraved manner).

If a state wants to authorize the death penalty, it has a constitutional responsibility to tailor it and apply its law in a manner that avoids any arbitrary and capricious infliction of the death penalty. The implicit assumption is that prosecutors, juries, and judges, if left to their own discretion, would discriminate against defendants on the basis of irrelevant factors, such as race. In other words, if a statutory procedure specifies the factors to be weighed as mitigating and aggravating circumstances, along with the procedures to be followed in deciding when to impose capital punishment, or if it specifies a mandatory death penalty for specified crimes, then capital punishment is constitutional.

To sentence someone to death when the crime is "outrageously or wantonly vile, horrible and inhumane" is too vague because virtually all homicides fit this description. Also inadequate are the words "especially heinous, atrocious, or cruel." When "cruel" is defined to mean the defendant intentionally inflicted extreme pain or torture upon the victim, above and beyond the pain necessarily accompanying the victim's death, there is sufficient clarity of standard to justify imposition of the death penalty.

LEGAL FOCUS—CASE

Daryl Atkins was convicted of abduction, armed robbery, and capital murder. In the penalty phase of the trial, Dr. Evan Nelson, a forensic psychologist, testified that Atkins was "mildly mentally retarded" with an I.Q. of 59 (in the lowest one percent of the population). Nevertheless, the jury sentenced Atkins to death. He appealed, arguing that, as he is mentally retarded, a death sentence is cruel and unusual punishment. Was he correct?

Atkins v. Virginia, 536 U.S. 304 (2002).

Yes, it is cruel and unusual. The U.S. Supreme Court was persuaded by the fact that eighteen states recently had passed laws eliminating the death sentence for mentally retarded defendants.

> *We are not persuaded that the execution of mentally retarded criminals will measurably advance the deterrent or the retributive purpose of the death penalty. Construing and applying the Eighth Amendment in the light of our "evolving standards of decency," we therefore conclude that such punishment is excessive and that the Constitution "places a substantive restriction on the State's power to take the life" of a mentally retarded offender.*

LEGAL FOCUS—CASE

After convicting Russell Coleman of rape and capital murder, the jury was required to recommend death or life imprisonment without possibility of parole. The judge instructed the jury that the governor could commute (reduce) a sentence of life without possibility of parole, whereupon the jury recommended death. In truth, the governor does not have that sole authority and must first obtain the written consent of four state supreme court justices before reducing such a sentence. Was Russell Coleman denied a fair sentencing because of the incorrect information?

Calderon v. Coleman, 525 U.S. 141 (1998).

No, he was not denied a fair sentencing. Arguably the jury opted for the death penalty out of fear that Coleman might someday be released from prison by the governor. The U.S. Supreme Court held that even if the instruction was erroneous, there was no showing that it had a "substantial and injurious" effect on the jury. Under this 5–4 split decision, it is increasingly difficult for federal courts to reverse state death penalties.

Convicts may linger on death row for a dozen or more years pending the final outcome of appeals that determine the propriety of the procedures and laws applied in the original trial. Can living under the threat of a future death by execution for years itself constitute the prohibited cruel and unusual punishment? In one dissenting opinion, Justice Breyer suggested that a delay of twenty-three years between sentencing and execution may be cruel and unusual punishment.

The death penalty is unique among all forms of criminal punishment in (1) its rejection of rehabilitation as a fundamental purpose of our criminal justice system, (2) its total irrevocability, and (3) its conflict with our society's commitment to humane treatment of fellow human beings. Some who support it, however, ask whether there are reasonable alternatives for those few cases in which death is adjudged a proper penalty. Is life imprisonment without possibility of parole, and perhaps without possibility of pardon, actually less cruel than death?

Former U.S. Supreme Court Justice Harry A. Blackmun supported capital punishment throughout his legal career until 1994, when he reversed course in a case involving a man shot to death in a tavern. Blackmun, at this point, rejected capital punishment as being inherently unconstitutional. Justice Scalia, writing separately, noted that Blackmun did not select for his argument against capital punishment any of several more brutal murders pending before the Court as examples—such as the case of an eleven-year-old girl raped by four men who then killed her by stuffing her panties down her throat, noting, "How enviable a quiet death by lethal injection compared with that!" Sincerely held, yet divisive, conflicts of opinion engendered by capital punishment clearly are here to stay.

CAN A DEFENDANT'S RECORD BE CLEARED?

State legislatures provide for the sealing (erasing) of certain criminal records as an aid to rehabilitation of defendants who have "learned their lesson." In cases in which the sentence is probation and the defendant has successfully completed all the requirements of probation, the court may, upon motion, vacate the guilty plea or the finding of guilt and dismiss the accusation or information. Thus, most legal disabilities that arise in connection with the conviction are erased legally. Such convictions ordinarily cannot be used thereafter to enhance the penalty for a subsequent conviction, although this traditional rule may be modified by variations of "three strikes and you're out" legislation.

A defendant who was under age twenty-one at the time of conviction for a misdemeanor may, upon completion of the sentence or probation, obtain an order of the court sealing all records pertaining to the conviction. Although the records are sealed officially in this manner, some applications for professional licensure inquire whether or not records exist and have been sealed, and, if so, what circumstance surrounded the crime. Otherwise, the defendant can answer questions as if the crime never occurred. Some types of misdemeanor records or infractions typically cannot be sealed, such as those pertaining to vehicle code violations, those involving registration as a sex offender, and those involving specified drug offenses.

WHAT SHOULD YOU DO IF ARRESTED?

A person placed under arrest, whether innocent or guilty, would be well advised to comply with the following suggestions (in the absence of more specific legal advice):

1. Do not strike an officer or resist arrest. If the officer is abusive, get the badge number and (if possible) the name. Be attentive and try to remember the specifics of the abuse involved.
2. Do not resist the officer searching you (e.g., patting down your body) and your car.
3. Do cooperate with fingerprinting and booking procedures. Even if these procedures are personally offensive, such as a strip search, no good can come from physical resistance. If given the choice between certain sobriety tests, be sure you understand your state's penalty for refusing all such tests before making that decision.
4. Do request (if not offered) the right to make a telephone call and use it to contact someone (parent, relative, friend) who can get a lawyer or assistance in posting bail and taking you home. If you cannot afford a lawyer, tell the magistrate or judge before whom you will be required to appear. You can request release on your own recognizance, and the magistrate or judge will promptly make the decision on whether or not to grant your request.
5. Do not respond to detailed questions—beyond such harmless basics as name, address, and telephone number—until and unless you are advised to answer by your attorney. You cannot be penalized for remaining silent. As some attorneys advise, "put a zipper on your mouth."
6. When applicable, do immediately mention to the arresting officer any physical condition requiring medication, such as multiple sclerosis, epilepsy, or diabetes.
7. Be honest in explaining in confidence to your attorney exactly what happened. Counsel is bound by law to respect this confidence and will be better able to represent you if in possession of all the facts surrounding the incident. Your attorney cannot be compelled to reveal your conversation, even if it involves a confession of guilt.

CASE

Herring v. United States

111 U.S. 111 (2009)

Investigator Mark Anderson learned that Bennie Dean Herring had driven to the Coffee County Sheriffs Department to retrieve something from his impounded truck. Herring was no stranger to law enforcement, and Anderson asked the county's warrant clerk, Sandy Pope, to check for any outstanding warrants for Herring's arrest. When she found none, Anderson asked Pope to check with Sharon Morgan, her counterpart in neighboring Dale County. After checking Dale County's computer database, Morgan replied that there was an active arrest warrant for Herring's failure to appear on a felony charge. Pope relayed the information to Anderson and asked Morgan to fax over a copy of the warrant as confirmation. Anderson and a deputy followed Herring as he left the impound lot, pulled him over, and arrested him. A search incident to the arrest revealed methamphetamine in Herring's pocket, and a pistol (which as a felon he could not possess) in his vehicle.

There had, however, been a mistake about the warrant. The Dale County sheriff's computer records are supposed to correspond to actual arrest warrants, which the office also maintains. But when Morgan went to the files to retrieve the actual warrant to fax to Pope, Morgan was unable to find it. She called a court clerk and learned that the warrant had been recalled five months earlier. Normally when a warrant is recalled the court clerk's office or a judge's chambers calls Morgan, who enters the information in the sheriff's computer database and disposes of the physical copy. For whatever reason, the information about the recall of the warrant for Herring did not appear in the database. Morgan immediately called Pope to alert her to the mix-up, and Pope contacted Anderson over a secure radio. This all unfolded in 10 to 15 minutes, but Herring had already been arrested and found with the gun and drugs, just a few hundred yards from the sheriff's office.

Herring was indicted in the District Court for the Middle District of Alabama for illegally possessing the gun and drugs, violations of 18 U. S. C. §922(g)(l) and 21 U. S. C. §844(a). He moved to suppress the evidence on the ground that his initial arrest had been illegal because the warrant had been rescinded. The Magistrate Judge recommended denying the motion because the arresting officers had acted in a good-faith belief that the warrant was still outstanding. Thus, even if there were a Fourth Amendment violation, there was "no reason to believe that application of the exclusionary rule here would deter the occurrence of any future mistakes." App. 70. The District Court adopted the Magistrate Judge's recommendation, 451 F.Supp.2d 1290 (2005), and the Court of Appeals for the Eleventh Circuit affirmed, 492 F.3d 1212 (2007).

Chief Justice Roberts Delivered the Opinion of the Court

The Fourth Amendment forbids "unreasonable searches and seizures," and this usually requires the police to have probable cause or a warrant before making an arrest. What if an officer reasonably believes there is an outstanding arrest warrant, but that belief turns out to be wrong because of a negligent bookkeeping error by another police employee? Such suppression is not an automatic consequence. Instead, the question turns on the culpability of the police and the potential of exclusion to deter wrongful police conduct. Here the error was the result of isolated negligence attenuated from the arrest.

The Eleventh Circuit found that the arresting officers in Coffee County were entirely innocent of any wrongdoing or carelessness. The court assumed that whoever failed to update the Dale County sheriffs records was also a law enforcement official, but noted that the conduct in question was a negligent failure to act, not a deliberate or tactical choice to act.

II

When a probable-cause determination was based on reasonable but mistaken assumptions, the person subjected to a search or seizure has not necessarily been the victim of a constitutional violation.

A

The Fourth Amendment protects the right of the people to be secure in their persons, houses, papers, and effects, against unreasonable searches and seizures, but contains no provision expressly precluding the use of evidence obtained in violation of its commands. Nonetheless, our decisions establish an exclusionary rule that, when applicable, forbids the use of improperly obtained evidence at trial.

In analyzing the applicability of the rule, *Leon* admonished that we must consider the actions of all the police officers involved. The Coffee County officers did nothing improper. Indeed, the error was noticed so quickly because Coffee County requested a faxed confirmation of the warrant.

The Eleventh Circuit concluded, however, that somebody in Dale County should have updated the computer database to reflect the recall of the arrest warrant. The court also concluded that this error was negligent, but did not find it to be reckless or deliberate. That fact is crucial to our holding that this error is not enough by itself to require the extreme sanction of exclusion.

B

The exclusionary rule is not an individual right and applies only where it results in appreciable deterrence. We have repeatedly rejected the argument that exclusion is a necessary consequence of a Fourth Amendment violation. Instead we have focused on the efficacy of the rule in deterring Fourth Amendment violations in the future.

In addition, the benefits of deterrence must outweigh the costs. The principal cost of applying the rule is, of course, letting guilty and possibly dangerous defendants go free—something that offends basic concepts of the criminal justice system. These principles are reflected in the holding of *Leon:* When police act under a warrant that is invalid for lack of probable cause, the exclusionary rule does not apply if the police acted in objectively reasonable reliance on the subsequently invalidated search warrant.

Shortly thereafter we extended these holdings to warrantless administrative searches performed in good-faith reliance on a statute later declared unconstitutional. Finally, we applied this good-faith rule to police who reasonably relied on mistaken information in a court's database that an arrest warrant was outstanding. We held that a mistake made by a judicial employee could not give rise to exclusion for three reasons: The exclusionary rule was crafted to curb police rather than judicial misconduct; court employees were unlikely to try to subvert the Fourth Amendment. We left unresolved whether the abuses that gave rise to the exclusionary rule featured intentional conduct that was patently unconstitutional. In a foundational exclusionary rule case, the officers had broken into the defendant's home, confiscated incriminating papers, then returned again with a U. S. Marshal to confiscate even more. Not only did they have no search warrant, which the Court held was required, but they could not have gotten one had they tried. They were so lacking in sworn and particularized information that not even an order of court would have justified such procedure. Even the Government seemed to acknowledge that the seizure was an outrage.

Equally flagrant conduct was at issue in *Mapp* v. *Ohio,* which extended the exclusionary rule to the States. Officers forced open a door to Ms. Mapp's house, kept her lawyer from entering, brandished what the court concluded was a false warrant, then forced her into handcuffs and canvassed the house for obscenity. An error that arises from nonrecurring and attenuated negligence is thus far removed from the core concerns that led us to adopt the rule in the first place.

To trigger the exclusionary rule, police conduct must be sufficiently deliberate that exclusion can meaningfully deter it, and sufficiently culpable that such deterrence is worth the price paid by the justice system. As laid out in our cases, the exclusionary rule serves to deter deliberate, reckless, or grossly negligent conduct, or in some circumstances recurring or systemic negligence.

The pertinent analysis of deterrence and culpability is objective, not an inquiry into the subjective awareness of arresting officers. We have already held that our good-faith inquiry is confined to the objectively ascertainable question whether a reasonably well trained officer would have known that the search was illegal in light of all of the circumstances. We do not suggest that all record-keeping errors by the police are immune from the exclusionary rule. In this case, however, the conduct at issue was not so objectively culpable as to require exclusion.

If the police have been shown to be reckless in maintaining a warrant system, or to have knowingly made false entries to lay the groundwork for future false arrests, exclusion would certainly be justified under our cases should such misconduct cause a Fourth Amendment violation. We said as much in *Leon,* explaining that an officer could not obtain a warrant on the basis of a bare bones affidavit and then rely on colleagues who are ignorant of the circumstances under which the warrant was obtained to conduct the search. Petitioner's fears that our decision will cause police departments to deliberately keep their officers ignorant are thus unfounded. In a case where systemic errors were demonstrated, it might be reckless for officers to rely on an unreliable warrant system.

Petitioner's claim that police negligence automatically triggers suppression cannot be squared with the principles underlying the exclusionary rule, as they have been explained in our cases. In light of our repeated holdings that the deterrent effect of suppression must be substantial and outweigh any harm to the justice system, we conclude that when police mistakes are the result of negligence such as that described here, rather than systemic error or reckless disregard of constitutional requirement the criminal should not go free.

The judgment of the Court of Appeals for the Eleventh Circuit is affirmed.

It is so ordered.

For Critical Analysis

1. Does this case mark a radical change in the law, or simply note an extension of a principal?
2. Do you think it would be clear to a law enforcement officer when a search would be a result of negligence or reckless conduct? Consider that an officer in the field can only rely on the information presented to her.
3. Does the balancing between the competing interests of convicting criminals versus preserving civil liberties seem appropriate to you? Whether or not it does, does your view reflect a clear interpretation of the wording of the Fourth Amendment or is it an application of your personal values?

United States v. Jones

132 S. Ct. 945 (2012)

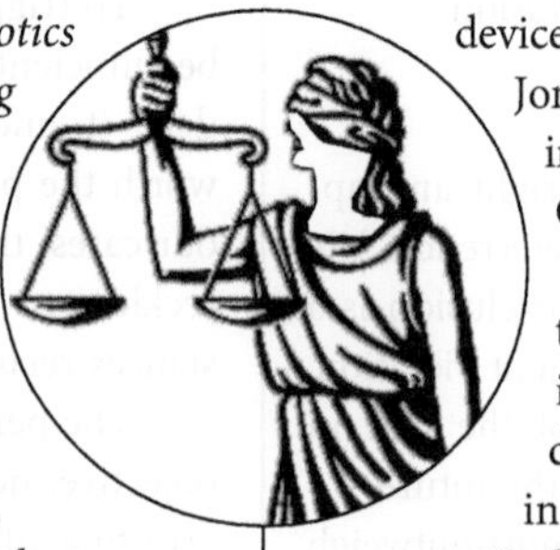

Defendant was suspected of trafficking in narcotics in violation of federal law. Without securing a warrant, government agents installed a global-positioning-system (GPS) tracking device on the undercarriage of a vehicle registered to defendant's wife while it was parked in a public parking lot. For the next twenty-eight days, the agents tracked the vehicle's movements. Defendant was convicted, but on appeal, argued that the admission of the evidence obtained by the use of the GPS device violated his rights under the Fourth Amendment. The Supreme Court had to decide whether or not the warrantless installation of the GPS and monitoring of the vehicle's movements constituted an unreasonable search.

Justice Scalia Delivered the Opinion of the Court

In 2004 respondent Antoine Jones, owner and operator of a nightclub in the District of Columbia, came under suspicion of trafficking in narcotics and was made the target of an investigation by a joint FBI and Metropolitan Police Department task force. Officers employed various investigative techniques, including visual surveillance of the nightclub, installation of a camera focused on the front door of the club, and a pen register and wiretap covering Jones's cellular phone.

Based in part on information gathered from these sources, in 2005 the Government applied to the United States District Court for the District of Columbia for a warrant authorizing the use of an electronic tracking device on the Jeep Grand Cherokee registered to Jones's wife. A warrant issued, authorizing installation of the device in the District of Columbia and within 10 days.

On the 11th day, and not in the District of Columbia but in Maryland, agents installed a GPS tracking device on the undercarriage of the Jeep while it was parked in a public parking lot. Over the next 28 days, the Government used the device to track the vehicle's movements, and once had to replace the device's battery when the vehicle was parked in a different public lot in Maryland. By means of signals from multiple satellites, the device established the vehicle's location within 50 to 100 feet, and communicated that location by cellular phone to a Government computer. It relayed more than 2,000 pages of data over the 4-week period.

The Government ultimately obtained a multiple-count indictment charging Jones and several alleged co-conspirators with, as relevant here, conspiracy to distribute and possess with intent to distribute five kilograms or more of cocaine and 50 grams or more of cocaine base, in violation of 21 U.S.C. §§ 841 and 846. Before trial, Jones filed a motion to suppress evidence obtained through the GPS device. The District Court granted the motion only in part, suppressing the data obtained while the vehicle was parked in the garage adjoining Jones's residence. It held the remaining data admissible, because "a person traveling in an automobile on public thoroughfares has no reasonable expectation of privacy in his movements from one place to another." Jones's trial in October 2006 produced a hung jury on the conspiracy count.

In March 2007, a grand jury returned another indictment, charging Jones and others with the same conspiracy. The Government introduced at trial the same GPS-derived locational data admitted in the first trial, which connected Jones to the alleged conspirators' stash house that contained $850,000 in cash, 97 kilograms of cocaine, and 1 kilogram of cocaine base. The jury returned a guilty verdict, and the District Court sentenced Jones to life imprisonment.

The United States Court of Appeals for the District of Columbia Circuit reversed the conviction because of admission of the evidence obtained by warrantless use of the GPS device which, it said, violated the Fourth Amendment. We granted certiorari.

The Fourth Amendment provides in relevant part that "[t]he right of the people to be secure in their persons, houses, papers, and effects, against unreasonable searches and seizures, shall not be violated." It is beyond dispute that a vehicle is an "effect" as that term is used in the Amendment. We hold that the Government's installation of a GPS device on a target's vehicle, and its use of that device to monitor the vehicle's movements, constitutes a "search."

It is important to be clear about what occurred in this case: The Government physically occupied private property for the purpose of obtaining information. We have no doubt that such a physical intrusion would have been considered a "search" within the meaning of the Fourth Amendment when it was adopted ... The text of the Fourth Amendment reflects its close connection to property, since otherwise it would have referred simply to "the right of the people to be secure against unreasonable searches and seizures"; the phrase "in their persons, houses, papers, and effects" would have been superfluous.

Consistent with this understanding, our Fourth Amendment jurisprudence was tied to common-law trespass, at least until the latter half of the 20th century.... Our later cases, of course, have deviated from that exclusively property-based approach. In Katz v. United States, we said that "the Fourth Amendment protects people, not places," and found a violation in attachment of an eavesdropping device to a public telephone booth. Our later cases have applied the analysis of Justice Harlan's concurrence in that case, which said that a violation occurs when government officers violate a person's "reasonable expectation of privacy."

The Government contends that the Harlan standard shows that no search occurred here, since Jones had no "reasonable expectation of privacy" in the area of the Jeep accessed by Government agents (its underbody) and in the locations of the Jeep on the public roads, which were visible to all. But we need not address the Government's contentions, because Jones's Fourth Amendment rights do not rise or fall with the Katz formulation. As explained, for most of our history the Fourth Amendment was understood to embody a particular concern for government trespass upon the areas ("persons, houses, papers, and effects") it enumerates. Katz did not repudiate that understanding. Less than two years later the Court upheld defendants' contention that the Government could not introduce against them conversations between other people obtained by warrantless placement of electronic surveillance devices in their homes ...

We have embodied that preservation of past rights in our very definition of "reasonable expectation of privacy" which we have said to be an expectation "that has a source outside of the Fourth Amendment, either by reference to concepts of real or personal property law or to understandings that are recognized and permitted by society."

The Government contends that several of our post-Katz cases foreclose the conclusion that what occurred here constituted a search. It relies principally on two cases in which we rejected Fourth Amendment challenges to "beepers," electronic tracking devices that represent another form of electronic monitoring. The first case, Knotts, upheld against Fourth Amendment challenge the use of a "beeper" that had been placed in a container of chloroform, allowing law enforcement to monitor the location of the container. We said that there had been no infringement of Knotts' reasonable expectation of privacy since the information obtained—the location of the automobile carrying the container on public roads, and the location of the off-loaded container in open fields near Knotts' cabin—had been voluntarily conveyed to the public. But as have discussed, the Katz reasonable-expectation-of-privacy test has been added to, not substituted for, the common-law trespassory test. The holding in Knotts addressed only the former, since the latter was not at issue. The beeper had been placed in the container before it came into Knotts' possession, with the consent of the then-owner. Knotts did not challenge that installation, and we specifically declined to consider its effect on the Fourth Amendment analysis. Knotts would be relevant, perhaps, if the Government were making the argument that what would otherwise be an unconstitutional search is not such where it produces only public information. The Government does not make that argument, and we know of no case that would support it.

The Government also points to our exposition in New York v. Class, that "[t]he exterior of a car ... is thrust into the public eye, and thus to examine it does not constitute a 'search.'" That statement is of marginal relevance here since, as the Government acknowledges, "the officers in this case did more than conduct a visual inspection of respondent's vehicle." By attaching the device to the Jeep, officers encroached on a protected area. In Class itself we suggested that this would make a difference, for we concluded that an officer's momentary reaching into the interior of a vehicle did constitute a search.

Finally, the Government's position gains little support from our conclusion in Oliver v. United States, that officers' information-gathering intrusion on an "open field" did not constitute a Fourth Amendment search even though it was a trespass at common law. Quite simply, an open field, unlike the curtilage of a home, is not one of those protected areas enumerated in the Fourth Amendment. The Government's physical intrusion on such an area—unlike its intrusion on the "effect" at issue here—is of no Fourth Amendment significance.

The Government argues in the alternative that even if the attachment and use of the device was a search, it was reasonable—and thus lawful—under the Fourth Amendment because "officers had reasonable suspicion, and indeed probable cause, to believe that [Jones] was a leader in a large-scale cocaine distribution conspiracy." We have no occasion to consider this argument. The Government did not raise it below, and the D. C. Circuit therefore did not address it. The judgment of the Court of Appeals for the D. C. Circuit is affirmed.

For Critical Analysis

1. Explain why the first warrant the police obtained did not cover the GPS device placed on the vehicle.
2. How does the tort of common law trespass support the Court's reasoning that Fourth Amendment rights had been violated? What constituted a search?
3. The Court did not consider whether or not the Government had probable cause to attach the device because it was not previously raised. How would that fact, if proved, have affected the outcome? Then could the evidence obtained through the GPS have been admitted even without a warrant?

CHAPTER QUESTIONS AND PROBLEMS

1. Theodore Kaczynski, known as the Unabomber, pleaded guilty to killing three people and wounding twenty-three others using handmade bombs over a seventeen-year crime spree. Sentenced to life without possibility of parole, Kaczynski is in "Super Max," the Colorado federal prison designed to house "the worst of the worst." In a cell larger than his former cabin in the mountains, Kaczynski enjoys a shower, a commode, an electric lamp, a concrete desk and stool, a cigarette lighter, and a thirteen-inch television. He can order books, including novels. Breakfast, lunch, and dinner are delivered to his cell, and he makes limited selections from a menu. Freshly laundered clothing and bedding arrive three times a week. Although he can write to his heart's content and receive five visitors per month, Kaczynski is isolated from other prisoners.
   a. Do you think Ted Kaczynski was wise to plea-bargain for a life sentence rather than to face the risk of a death penalty from the jury?
   b. Do you think the attorney general was equally wise to offer the bargain?
   c. What changes, if any, would you recommend be made to the prison lifestyle?
2. Prison officials may deprive prisoners of any right that is reasonably related to legitimate penological interests. Thus, many states forbid beards, long hair and ponytails, earrings, and long sideburns as well as letters, numbers, and designs shaved onto the heads of inmates. Can you identify how each of the following rules may relate to a legitimate interest? Or are these simply mean-spirited attempts to make the lives of prisoners miserable?
   a. no beards
   b. no long hair or ponytails
   c. no earrings or other pierced jewelry
   d. no letters, numbers, and designs shaved onto heads
   e. no body-building machines
   f. no television

   Should exceptions be made on the basis of religion? Some Sikhs view unshorn hair as a supplication to God—cutting their hair would make them a renegade. Some Native Americans believe that long hair is a link to their ancestors. Some Muslims hold that the Koran teaches that beards are a sign of manhood. What are the implications of such exceptions?
3. George, Milton, and Fernando, all eighteen years old, decided to rob a bicyclist on a trail in the early morning in Pacific Heights. They grabbed a bicyclist who, to their dismay, promptly produced a .25-caliber handgun and shot Fernando through the heart. George and Milton jumped in their car to speed away but promptly crashed. The bicyclist never has been found. Of what crimes are George and Milton guilty?
4. Assume a violent rape occurred in a small, rural community and that DNA evidence was collected at the scene of the crime. The victim could describe her assailant only as a young Caucasian man between eighteen and thirty years of age. Assume the police then ran a local newspaper advertisement requesting that all men in the suspected category come by the station to supply saliva samples for DNA matching. Approximately 15,000 males within the suspected category were believed to reside in the nearby communities. The police intended to test all DNA samples received and to question all males in the suspected category who declined to submit samples. What issues can you identify relative to this procedure of "blanket" testing of DNA as a police procedure?
5. What percentage of prospective jurors from across the nation do you assume would be "fair and impartial" if:
   a. one of the parties in the case was a gay man or lesbian?
   b. one of the parties was an African American?
   c. one of the parties was a Hispanic?
   d. one of the parties was an Asian?
   e. one of the parties was a tobacco company?
   f. one of the parties was a politician?
   g. one of the parties was a Muslim?

   What percentage of prospective jurors from across the nation do you assume would act on their own beliefs of right and wrong regardless of legal instructions from a judge?

   Do you believe that responses of prospective jurors about such matters would be different once they were seated and participating in the solemnity of an actual trial?
6. In this chapter you read how one act, such as the assault and battery by police upon the suspect Rodney King, could be both a state and a federal crime without violating the prohibition against double

jeopardy. You may recall that officers Koon and Powell, although acquitted of a state crime, were subsequently convicted of a federal crime—for the same offensive act. Under what circumstances do you think federal prosecutors should proceed against defendants who have been acquitted in state proceedings? Should federal prosecutors proceed against everyone suspected of committing a federal crime even though they previously were acquitted by a jury in a state trial? In forming your rationale, consider that every time a state police officer violates the constitutional rights of any accused, by false arrest, for example, a federal offense also has occurred (violation of constitutional rights).

7. Raymond Lara was convicted of first-degree murder for killing a rival gang member in a drive-by shooting. The murder was the result of an ongoing conflict between Lara's gang the Nortenos, and their rivals, the Surenos. The Nortenos got into two cars and drove by the home of a Sureno. The victim and two others were standing outside. According to some witnesses, the victim pointed a shotgun at the first car of Nortenos. Lara, in the second car, then shot the victim. Since first-degree murder requires the prosecution to generally prove extreme indifference to human life beyond a reasonable doubt, does the Lara have the burden of proving self-defense or must the prosecution disprove self-defense? How should a jury weigh the legitimacy of an accused's evidence of self-defense?
8. Generally speaking, statutes—and the prosecutors, juries, and judges who enforce them—treat crimes against the person more harshly than crimes against property. The rationale is that human life is much more important than property of any description. Is there validity to the proposition that by downplaying crimes against property, society implicitly invites more serious crimes against persons? Present arguments both pro and con regarding this proposition.
9. Are you in favor of Megan's Law, which authorizes police to inform residents that a former sex offender is living in their midst? Should maps showing the specific location of residences be distributed at public expense? Should photographs be distributed for ease in identifying such persons, for example, in the local supermarket? To what other kinds of former felons should the practice be extended, if any? What constitutional issues can you identify relative to these practices?
10. Stand-your-ground laws generally provide that persons may use force to defend themselves without first attempting to retreat from the danger. As a result, persons who "stand their ground" cannot be prosecuted for reasonably defending themselves without first attempting to retreat or avoid the conflict. What are some arguments in favor of and against these laws, which are often controversial?
11. On most Saturdays, Steve Mean played handball at a nearby park. He usually inline-skated via sidewalks and then across a pedestrian overpass above the nearby freeway. Noticing a hole in the cage like fencing along the overpass, Mean decided to drop a handball onto the freeway below to "see what would happen." Kristina Rey was driving to the mall when the ball struck and broke the windshield on her new Volkswagen. Startled, she jerked the wheel, sending her car directly into oncoming traffic. Rey was killed instantly when an eighteen-wheeler smashed into her Volkswagen head on. Of what kind of homicide is Steve Mean guilty?
12. It is 3:00 A.M. and the Brigham City police officers get a call about a loud party. Arriving at the house, they hear shouting inside. As they enter the yard, they see through a screen door and window a fight involving several persons. One officer opened the screen door and declared he was a police officer. He was ignored, and he then entered the room, eventually arresting several parties for contributing to the delinquency of a minor, a misdemeanor. At trial, the defendants moved to suppress all evidence, claiming the warrantless entry violated their Fourth Amendment right to a search warrant. The state court agreed with the defendant. How do you think the U.S. Supreme Court ruled when it heard the appeal from the state of Utah? [*Brigham City v. Stuart,* 547 U.S. 398 (2006).]

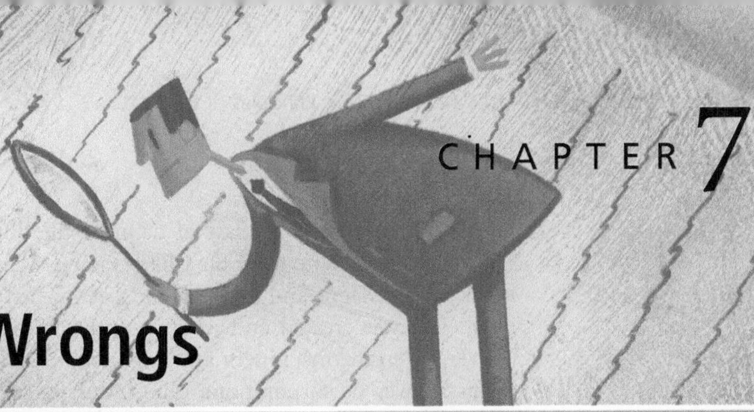

CHAPTER 7

Torts: Private Wrongs

That great principle of the common law which declares that it is your duty so to use and exercise your own rights as not to cause injury to other people.

Sir Charles James Watkins Williams, ***English jurist***

LEARNING OBJECTIVES

After reading and studying this chapter, you should be able to:

- Define a tort.
- Explain what an intentional tort is and define and identify examples of major types of intentional torts.
- Explain negligence and provide examples of negligent conduct.
- Discuss and provide examples of the elements of a negligence action.
- Discuss defenses to negligence including assumption of the risk.
- Differentiate between comparative and contributory negligence.
- Explain strict liability.
- List and explain the various types of damages.
- Identify difficulties that make the collection of damages problematic.

The law of torts is the law of defining the duties and rights people have to each other. The opening quote from Sir Charles James Watkins Williams captures the essence of tort law nicely. Here and now, in the twenty-first century, tort law is as relevant as it was when it was created and when it evolved. Some might argue it is more important than ever, given the machinery and engines and technology available to all Americans and the vast power of corporations. The industrial and technological revolutions, indeed, have made it much easier for a person to harm another.

Our tort law comes from the common law of England that was in general effect when the United States formed. We have since added new torts. These old and new torts form the basis of this chapter.

The modern law of torts (Latin: "to twist") concerns compensating victims for wrongful or unacceptable conduct and sometimes for public policy reasons. As we shall see in this chapter, tort law "tomorrow" faces—and must resolve—some very unique problems.

Everyone is familiar with the highly publicized awards of money to victims of a wide variety of acts that society, through its legal system, deems to be wrong or simply unacceptable. These plaintiffs (victims who bring civil actions) recover damages (money) from defendants (those held responsible) in amounts typically set by juries. Most of these monies paid to victims come from insurance companies, which expect to take in enough money from premiums to pay all claims and then, of course, to retain a profit.

Thus, the civil law of torts shapes our society often by shifting the risk of injury from victims to others who can better afford the costs (the "deep pockets"). Certain businesses (and sometimes persons) also are punished financially for actions deemed especially wrongful. These are punitive damage cases that discourage future wrongful conduct and, as well, enrich those victims whose lawyers can successfully pursue those kinds of claims. Thus, tort law is a vehicle through which both claims for compensation by victims, and sometimes demands for punishment, can be administered.

Most injuries, and hence torts, arise from the role of individuals as consumers, commuters, and employees. Thus, buying and using products, commuting to and from work, and being safe and humanely treated during employment are three major responsibilities of the civil tort law. We are consumers of products that may be defective, that may injure buyers and bystanders, that we never may see (breast implants), or that may disappear (food products). Other products, such as legal, medical, and personal services, or even investments, may not be as tangible as an automobile or a coffeemaker but still can cause considerable injury or financial loss. We buy and equip homes with a myriad of products and store recreational "toys" in our garages. In using and enjoying the products we acquire, we can and do injure one another, as in automobile and boating accidents. We are also employees in businesses, where we make and distribute our goods and may violate one another's rights.

In other words, tort law affects our everyday conduct, making "the good life" a possible dream. It has grown and served our society as it has evolved and advanced. But the tort system is imperfect. Manufacturers, retailers, insurers, and even doctors, being frequent defendants, contend that Americans are excessively litigious, file frivolous claims, and persuade juries to award excessive damages based on sympathy and emotions rather than on hard evidence. One notorious and well-known example of this contention took place in the mid-1990s and involved a woman who sued McDonald's for injuries suffered when hot coffee spilled on her lap.

LEGAL FOCUS—PROBLEM

Stella Liebeck, age seventy-nine, having just purchased a cup of coffee from a McDonald's drive-through window, tried to remove its lid to add cream. The coffee spilled, burning Liebeck. She sued and recovered damages of $200,000 plus punitive damages of $2.7 million. What can we learn from this example of the tort law in action?

We can learn that the media, responding to considerable public interest, focuses on the sensational aspects of tort cases, even at the expense of "the rest of the story." In the preceding ten years before this incident, McDonald's had some 700 claims for burns. McDonald's knew that its coffee at 180–190 degrees was capable of causing third-degree burns, as it did on Liebeck. And McDonald's knew that most competitors sold coffee at the household range of 135–140 degrees. Stella Liebeck suffered third-degree burns on her buttocks, inner thighs, and genitals and required skin grafts and eight days' hospitalization. The $2.7 million punitive damage claim equaled about two days of McDonald's coffee sales. Before the trial, McDonald's rejected an offer to settle the claim for $20,000. After the large verdict, the trial judge reduced the verdict to $160,000 general and $480,000 punitive damages. Additional important facts surround the matter, which may or may not change a person's mind about the fairness of the jury verdict. The lesson is that we, as educated persons, should not leap to conclusions based on media versions of tort law in action.

As noted earlier, tort laws are less than perfect. The McDonald's example is useful again. Most civil lawsuits settle after the case is initiated (and thus, after it has been reported in the media). That is, the people involved decide to resolve their dispute privately. No judge or trial is involved. Almost everyone agrees that private settlement is the preferable alternative. However, private settlements are not made public, usually as a condition of the settlement, and thus the public remains forever ignorant of how the important cases are resolved. The McDonald's "coffee" case settled out of court rather than continue appeals, and whether McDonald's eventually paid more or less to Stella Liebeck than the noted sums is unknown to the public.

What is the reason for the growth of tort law since World War II? First, courts have been expanding the scope of tort liability, for example, by determining that manufacturers and sellers of defective products could be sued for injuries without proof of negligence or fault. We discuss "product liability" later in this chapter. New statutes passed by Congress and state legislatures that are intended to relieve suffering and injustice are another reason for the growth of tort law. For example, the Civil Rights Act of 1964 has been interpreted to create tort liability for a wide range of violations of civil rights. These civil rights cases occur when the wrongdoer is a government employee, such as a police officer. As a counter to this trend, many states in recent years have passed statutes limiting damages and expanding defenses.

LEGAL FOCUS—BACKGROUND

In response to a noise complaint, about 100 deputy sheriffs responded to a bridal shower of a Samoan American family. A melee followed during which deputies hit partygoers with flashlights and clubs. These "torts" by police violated the civil rights of the victims. A jury returned a verdict for thirty-six plaintiffs of $16 million that, through interest earned while on appeal, grew to the $25 million actually paid by the County of Los Angeles.

Further expansion of tort law occurred with enactment of the federal Americans with Disabilities Act. The ADA allows lawsuits for violations of its terms. Many laws essentially benefit one group in society at the expense of another group, the latter group being better able to afford the solution. For example, businesses can afford to provide special accommodations to disabled customers who otherwise could not enjoy the same pleasures nor fulfill the same obligations of modern society without such accommodation. Thus, the tort law can and does shape social policy—indeed, some say it micromanages our lives.

MORALS AND ETHICS

The subject of torts is ripe with moral questions. The law decides when one person must compensate the other. Or not. On what criteria? In cases in which torts are used to implement social policy, especially when tort cases confront currently accepted behavior in society, individuals may feel unfairly punished for doing something that everyone does all the time. We will examine the types of torts. One type, negligence, frequently presents the fact finder with a moral judgment. Following the earlier note, is it fair to have a bias toward holding the party that can afford to pay responsible? Does this reward the correct behavior?

tort
A private wrong committed by one person (the tortfeasor) that injures another (the victim) in person or property and for which society allows the legal remedy of monetary damages.

Private lawsuits in tort law range in importance from the trivial to the profound. Most are overlooked or are settled through negotiation. But whatever the seriousness of the disputes, they may be resolved by legal action in accordance with the law of torts.

WHAT ARE TORTS AND HOW ARE THEY CLASSIFIED?

A **tort** is a private wrong (other than a breach of contract) committed by one that injures a person or property, for which the law allows a legal remedy (usually money damages).

tortfeasor
A wrongdoer who commits a private injury to another person by breaching a duty recognized by law.

The wrongdoer is called a **tortfeasor**. Sometimes, two or more persons, called *joint tortfeasors,* are liable for the particular injury to one or more victims, but any one of the joint tortfeasors may be required to pay all damages suffered by the victim(s). For example, assume an automobile accident happened because a curve on a state highway was not banked appropriately and because Steve Jones was driving with unsafe tires—he failed to make the turn. Both Jones and the state are joint tortfeasors and fully responsible, but any award of money damages to an injured victim could be collected entirely from either. If Steve Jones were indigent, the victim most likely would recover all of the damages from the state with its "deep pockets."

intentional tort
Occurs when the tortfeasor deliberately performs a wrongful act that injures an innocent victim.

Torts generally are classified into three groupings: intentional, negligent, and strict liability (including product liability).

An **intentional tort** occurs when a person purposely commits some act that injures the victim. As you might expect, most crimes are also torts because criminal acts almost always are intentional and cause injury to a victim. Thus, the state may prosecute the wrongdoer in a criminal action for the public wrong to society, while the victim may sue in a civil action for the private wrong. Earlier, you read about this dual role in the example of O. J. Simpson, who was found not guilty of murder but civilly responsible for damages for committing the tort of battery resulting in wrongful death.

negligence
Failure to act as a reasonable, careful person would act under the same or similar circumstances, thereby causing injury that was foreseeable.

But there are significant differences between crimes and torts. In crimes, the intent is evil. In torts, the intent of the actor may or may not be evil. For example, a practical joke may be intended with no underlying evil motive, but if injury to a victim results, an intentional tort has occurred.

LEGAL FOCUS—EXAMPLE

Yolanda Geersan excitedly fires a pistol into the air as part of a Fourth of July celebration. Later, she learns that the bullet on its inevitable descent killed a child. An intentional tort has occurred because the handgun was fired intentionally, even though Geersan lacked evil intent.

On the other hand, O. J. Simpson was found by the jury to have acted with evil intent when he committed the intentional tort of battery upon his victims. Thus, as noted, the intent behind the wrongful act necessary for tort liability may or may not be evil. Understandably, many intentional torts are not crimes because many people do not act with a *guilty mind* (i.e., with intent to commit a crime against the person or property of another).

strict liability
A tort theory available in special situations determined by public policy in which a person is held responsible for harm occurring to another without proof of fault (e.g., inherently dangerous activities, wild animals, explosives, sale of defective products).

A second kind of tort is negligence. **Negligence** means carelessness. By failing to act as a reasonable, careful person would act under the same or similar circumstances, the person inadvertently causes an injury that was foreseeable (one that a reasonable person could and should anticipate as being a possible consequence).

The third basic type of tort, **strict liability** (including **product liability**), arises when the victim need not prove that the defendant acted negligently or was guilty of an intentional tort. Indeed, strict liability often is referred to as "liability without fault." All the victim must prove is that an injury occurred, that damages were suffered, and that the injury was caused by a product or act to which strict liability attaches, such as an airplane crash or a defective consumer product.

TORTS BY INTENTIONAL CONDUCT

product liability
Law holding manufacturers and sellers of goods liable to buyers, users, and perhaps bystanders for harm caused by defective goods.

People sometimes are motivated by greed, anger, revenge, lust, a perverted sense of humor, a distorted sense of justice, a craving for costly drugs, or a desperate quest for a quick "solution" to poverty or unemployment. So motivated, a person purposely engages in antisocial conduct when they know or should know it may harm others. Deliberate conduct that is regarded by law as wrong and that causes injury to the person or property of another is an *intentional tort.* Because most persons do not deliberately commit acts that have a high probability of injury to others, intentional torts are encountered much less frequently than torts based on carelessness. Eight of the most significant types of intentional torts are described next.

assault
The tort of creating apprehension in the mind of the victim that he or she is about to be touched in a harmful or an offensive way. There is no requirement that the actor have the present ability to inflict actual harm.

Assault

Assault is an intentional threat or attempt that places the victim in fear or *apprehension* of an immediate harmful or offensive touching. It is one of several intentional torts protecting against invasion of a personal interest, in this case physical and psychological well-being.

LEGAL FOCUS—PROBLEM

Lonnie Shaqate was arguing loudly with "Spike" Lea over a debt. Finally, Lea said, "Listen, **** I've paid you off. Get lost!" He turned and began walking toward his pickup. Without uttering a word, Shaqate grabbed a baseball bat from the ground and swung violently at Lea's head, but missed. Oblivious of the act, Lea got into his pickup and drove away. Was Shaqate guilty of the tort of assault?

No, he was not guilty. Because Lea was not aware of the deadly attempt, he suffered no fear of immediate injury. Putting another person in apprehension or fear of immediate injury is the wrongful act of assault. (Note that Shaqate could be found guilty of the *crime* of assault, and possibly of attempted murder, neither of which requires proof of the victim's mental apprehension, as explained in Chapter 6.)

battery
Any harmful or offensive touching of another human being without excuse or consent. Usually (but not necessarily) battery involves violent infliction of injury.

Battery

A **battery** is the harmful or offensive touching of another person without justification, consent, or excuse. A successful right hook to the jaw of someone you do not like, as well as a slap in the face, are classic examples of a battery. A left hook that misses because the victim saw it coming and dodged in time is an assault. An assault often occurs before, but is not an essential element of, a battery. Criminal sexual attacks, including rape, are also civil law assaults and batteries.

LEGAL FOCUS—PROBLEM

In Angola, Indiana, defendant Muir pleaded guilty to two felony counts of sexual battery, for which he was sentenced to six years in prison and fined $5,000. After the prison sentence was suspended, the victim brought a civil action for the intentional tort of battery and was awarded $17.5 million in damages. Is the large judgment likely to be collectible?

Unfortunately, collection of such sizable judgments from irresponsible defendants is unlikely. Because many criminals do not have financial resources, their victims for practical rather than legal reasons do not commonly sue them.

LEGAL FOCUS—CASE

As part of a medical experiment, employees of the University of Chicago (in cooperation with drug manufacturer Eli Lilly & Co.) caused the drug diethylstilbestrol (DES) to be administered at its Lying-In Hospital to some pregnant patients without their knowledge. The drug was designed to prevent miscarriages. Subsequently, more than 1,000 of the women alleged that their female children had suffered an increased propensity for cancer as a side effect of the drug. Were the women victims of actionable batteries?

Mink v. University of Chicago and Eli Lilly & Co., 460 F.Supp. 713 (M.D. Illinois, 1978).

Yes, the women were victims. Batteries occurred because the women did not consent to the experiment. In medical practice, before administering experimental drugs, performing a surgical operation, or providing other treatment, doctors must obtain the **informed consent** of their patients. The patient must be told what risks are involved and what alternatives are available. The consent need not be in writing and may be implied by conduct. In cases of true emergency, when consent cannot be obtained, it is not required.

informed consent Actual and complete knowledge by a person of risks involved in a situation.

In the *Eli Lilly* & Co. case, the hospital's action was a tort, even though certainly the hospital personnel intended no harm (quite the contrary). But the act of administering the drug was intentional. Note that even if the drug had no harmful effects—indeed, even if it had beneficial effects—there would have been batteries. Such touching without prior permission would be offensive because, it offends a reasonable sense of personal dignity.

One is required to tolerate the proximity of other persons in crowded public places. Thus, for example, bodily contact with strangers—which may be unpleasant and offensive to some sensitive individuals—is quite legal when necessary or inadvertent, as in buses and trains during rush hours, even though similar touching might be actionable battery at other times of the day.

false imprisonment The wrongful restraint of the personal liberty of another.

false arrest Taking custody of another, without proper legal authority, to be held or restrained in order to answer a civil claim or criminal charge. Because this action restrains the person's liberty, it is also *false imprisonment*.

False Imprisonment and False Arrest

The wrongful restraint of the physical liberty of another is called **false imprisonment**. It involves detention of the victim and restraint of his or her freedom of movement. There must be confinement within a given area, large or small, by means of physical barriers or physical force or threatened force. **False arrest** by an officer with legal authority (or even by one who pretends to have such authority) is a variety of false imprisonment, although in some states no real distinction is made. False arrest by a police officer also may be a violation of the civil rights of the victim, a federal offense.

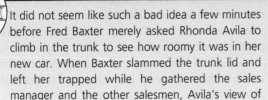

LEGAL FOCUS—PROBLEM

It did not seem like such a bad idea a few minutes before Fred Baxter merely asked Rhonda Avila to climb in the trunk to see how roomy it was in her new car. When Baxter slammed the trunk lid and left her trapped while he gathered the sales manager and the other salesmen, Avila's view of this adventure changed. She was released to the laughter of the group, and Baxter claimed his $100 prize from the sales manager for talking a customer into the trunk of her car. Does Avila have a claim for false imprisonment?

Although Avila's entry into the car trunk was voluntary, Baxter's closing the trunk and leaving her there restrained her movement without her privilege or consent.

Because of the prevalence of self-service in stores where merchandise is displayed openly, the crime of shoplifting reportedly costs merchants (and ultimately consumers) billions of dollars annually. The exact figure is unknown largely because some inventory shortages are also caused by employee theft. Attempts to reduce these losses through closer surveillance and the employment of plainclothes private security personnel have brought about many arrests—and, along with them, charges of false imprisonment. Legislatures and police, however, are generally sympathetic to the plight of the storeowners. To help protect affected business firms, legislatures in many states have enacted laws that establish the **shopkeeper's privilege**. These statutes permit a retail merchant or authorized employee to detain a person if there are reasonable grounds to believe that the suspect has shoplifted and if reasonable means of detection are used. To reduce the number of lawsuits and charges of abuse of privilege, prudent store security people use minimum restraint and promptly summon official police to conduct the search and make an arrest, if justified. As a further precaution, security people usually wait until the suspect has left the store and therefore cannot claim, "I'm still shopping," when detained.

shopkeeper's privilege
Legal right of a storekeeper to detain suspected shoplifters for a reasonable time in a reasonable way when there is probable cause to believe a theft has taken place.

LEGAL FOCUS—CASE

Lucia Resendez was at Wal-Mart shopping during a lunch break when she started eating from a bag of peanuts. The source and ownership of those peanuts were the crux of a lawsuit between her and Wal-Mart. Security guard Raul Salinas saw Resendez eat the peanuts from a Wal-Mart bag that she then discarded. He watched her pay for some items but not the peanuts and she then left the store. Salinas followed Resendez and asked her to return to the store and explain her actions. Resendez complied and told him she had bought the peanuts the day before at another Wal-Mart store. Within fifteen minutes, a police officer arrived to arrest her. A jury found her guilty of misdemeanor theft, but the conviction was overturned for procedural reasons. She sued Wal-Mart for false imprisonment. What was the result?

Wal-Mart Stores, Inc. v. Resendez, 962 S.W.2d 539 (Texas, 1998).

The court looked at three factors to determine whether the shopkeeper's privilege applied.

1. Was the detention based on a reasonable belief that the accused had stolen store merchandise?
2. Was the detention for a reasonable period of time?
3. Was the detention conducted in a reasonable manner?

The court answered "yes" to all three questions. Resendez was seen eating from a bag of peanuts marked with a Wal-Mart price sticker; because she did not pay for the peanuts before she left the store, probable cause existed to believe that the peanuts were stolen property. The court concluded that if a jury found probable cause to commence criminal proceedings, then reasonable cause in a civil proceeding existed as a matter of law. The court also concluded that Wal-Mart's fifteen-minute detention was not an unreasonable time and that the manner of detention was reasonable under the circumstances.

False imprisonment is often a crime. The crime of rape constitutes two intentional torts, battery and false imprisonment. The locking of a child in a closet for an extended period may become the crime of parental abuse and the intentional tort of false imprisonment.

Intentional Infliction of Mental Distress

intentional infliction of mental distress
Outrageous conduct that causes mental, if not immediate physical, suffering by the victim.

Intentional infliction of mental distress, or as some states name it, *outrageous conduct,* occurs when one intentionally acts in a manner that reasonably may be expected to cause severe mental distress to another, the victim. To be actionable, the wrongful conduct must be describable as atrocious, utterly intolerable in society, and exceeding the bounds of all decency. This kind of conduct is so extreme and outrageous that it causes severe emotional distress, even though there is no physical touching of the plaintiff (as in a battery) or apprehension of an immediate harmful or offensive touching (as in assault). Because of the absence of physical harm, or its immediate threat, such claims formerly have been rejected. Claims of mental distress that are not evidenced by some tangible injury are easy to make, yet difficult to disprove. Nevertheless, most courts now hold that in a proper case such injury is real and compensable.

LEGAL FOCUS—CASE

Mark Goldfarb, a student at Tennessee State University, was attending Professor Baker's class when an unidentified assailant surreptitiously entered the room and threw a pie that hit Baker. The professor immediately, but erroneously, accused Goldfarb of the offense. The next day, Professor Baker barred Goldfarb from the classroom and had him ejected from the building, still believing he was the culprit. Goldfarb claimed he suffered emotional distress, especially because he was an ex-prisoner attempting personal rehabilitation; the accusation of lawlessness was particularly offensive to him. Mark sued the professor for the tort of outrageous conduct. Will he prevail?

Goldfarb v. Baker, 547 S.W.2d 567 (Tennessee, 1977).

No, he will not prevail. The conduct was not actionable because the professor acted under provocation, and his conduct, although wrong, was the product of the sudden, unjustified, and humiliating attack. This type of reflexive encounter is simply one of life's frictions and irritations for which there is no legal remedy.

LEGAL FOCUS—PROBLEM

Brendan McVeasy, angry because his college girlfriend, Sara Phong, broke up with him, posted a nude photograph of Phong on the Internet and notified several friends. Word of the posting spread and before the photograph was removed, it was viewed by many on campus and elsewhere and downloaded by numerous viewers causing Phong humiliation and distress. Can Phong recover damages from McVeasy?

A jury would certainly agree that McVeasy's conduct was intentional and outrageous. McVeasy may be without funds to pay any court award, which could very well be huge. However, judgments often last from ten to twenty years, and sometimes more. Thus, if Phong obtained a judgment, she would be a creditor of McVeasy and, among other remedies, could take part of his earnings through a procedure known as *garnishment.*

The tort of outrageous conduct sometimes arises when creditors, often with the assistance of collection agencies, pursue debtors in an especially aggressive manner. The problem became so acute that the United States enacted the **Fair Debt Collection Practices Act**, which prohibits abusive tactics such as threats of violence or use of obscene language, harassing telephone calls, and publication of "shame" lists. In communicating with third parties to learn the location of a debtor, the creditor may not even state that the person owes a debt. Abused debtors may seek damages of up to $1,000 plus court costs and reasonable attorney fees. The act does not apply to creditors who do their own collecting, but under certain circumstances, they instead may be subject to claims for outrageous conduct.

Fair Debt Collection Practices Act
A federal law that outlaws certain unreasonably harsh collection practices previously used by professional debt collectors.

Torts committed by police often are characterized as violations of the victim's civil rights—but are common law torts nonetheless.

LEGAL FOCUS—PROBLEM

Elbert Poppell opened a "swingers' club" near San Diego. Guests donated $50 to attend weekend parties where they engaged in sex on mattresses throughout the house. Some guests were married couples, others were not, and still others were complete strangers. Poppell previously was denied a business license for his purple "love bus" that was outfitted with beds and a hot tub. But Poppell broke no California laws because no money was exchanged between sex partners. His business was something like renting out one motel room to a large group of "members." But the police opposed the sex club and often parked outside with lights flashing, ticketing guests for infractions such as broken taillights and illegal parking. Finally, Poppell sued the City of San Diego in federal court claiming outrageous harassment. What should the result be?

A unanimous jury awarded Poppell $200,000 in punitive and compensatory damages. Although the police ostensibly violated no laws, the jury believed their conduct outrageous. Would it be similar if police stopped and administered a sobriety test to every patron leaving a gay bar after midnight, but stopped no patrons leaving a sports bar in the same neighborhood? There undoubtedly is a strong temptation on the part of some police officers to carry out, through selective enforcement or other improper tactics, what they honestly believe is the will of the community. But the police, as well as other well-meaning persons, must express their political beliefs by working to change local laws, not by taking individual actions that may result in personal liability.

defamation
False statement injuring the reputation of the victim.

Serious actions taken to deprecate people because of their race, religion, physical characteristics, or sexual orientation, such as painting symbols on residences or etching epithets on plate-glass windows, usually will constitute the intentional infliction of mental distress upon the victim. Most victims of this tort do not file a lawsuit because the wrongdoers are insolvent as well as irresponsible.

slander
Oral defamation; the speaking of false words to a third person tending to cause injury to the reputation of the victim.

Defamation

The law imposes a general duty on all persons to refrain from wrongfully injuring another person's good reputation through false and harmful, unprivileged statements made to others. The breach of this duty is **defamation**. Breaching, or violating, this duty orally is the common law tort of **slander**; violating it in writing is the tort of **libel**. Defamation reduces the goodwill and respect a person previously enjoyed and may subject him or her to ridicule, contempt, or possibly hatred by others. The critical element is the effect on third parties, people in the community. Thus, there can be no civil defamation without

libel
A false statement of fact about a person in written or other permanent form causing harm to the reputation of that person and is further communicated to a third person.

publication, which means communication to at least one other, a third party. If one person lies about another to his or her face in private, or sends him or her a defamatory letter that only the victim reads, there is no civil defamation. If the letter is shared with an administrative assistant, there has been publication.

LEGAL FOCUS—PROBLEM

Anna Thompson writes Andrew Chin a private letter accusing him of embezzling funds. Edgar Peters calls Marilu Gordon dishonest and incompetent when no one else is around. All statements are false. Do these false communications result in civil liability for defamation?

No, they do not result in defamation. The letter is not libel, and the conversation is not slander. Neither Thompson nor Peters communicated their messages to a third party. If either Chin or Gordon later publishes the false statements, they voluntarily damage their own reputations and therefore cannot recover. If a third party, by chance, overhears defamatory statements, the courts usually hold that this is a publication. Anyone who republishes or repeats defamatory statements is liable even if that person reveals the source of the statements. Most broadcast outlets delay the transmission of live programs, such as talk shows, for several seconds to avoid this kind of liability.

Special state laws protect specified businesses involving perishable crops from defamatory publications about the crop. The theory is that irreparable damage is done when the crop perishes, which may be long before a trial can be obtained.

LEGAL FOCUS—PROBLEM

On her television program, Oprah Winfrey warned her audience that "mad cow" disease could spread to people and, according to her guest, "make AIDS look like the common cold." Winfrey added that she was "stopped cold from eating another burger." Within days of the show, cattle prices had plummeted to ten-year lows in what was dubbed the "Oprah crash."

"After the show, the price of finished cattle dropped as low as the mid-50s; the volume of sales also went down. The cattlemen assert that the depression continued for approximately 11 weeks." Cattle ranchers sued in federal court for violation of the Texas "veggie" laws that protect perishable products from false statements. Was this defamation of product? Are cattle a perishable product?

Perishable crops are extraordinarily vulnerable because their useful life as food is very short. Strawberries are an example of such a crop. The federal judge ruled that beef is not a perishable commodity, however, and that there was no liability for merely negligent misstatements. Thus, the cattle ranchers were required to prove, under ordinary business defamation rules, that Winfrey's guests and or her remarks were deliberate or at least reckless. The U.S. Court of Appeals upheld the trial court dismissal of the case stating, "When Ms. Winfrey speaks, America listens. But her statement is neither actionable nor claimed to be so." In short, the cattle ranchers could not show that Oprah acted deliberately or recklessly.

Slander

A false spoken or transitory gesture about the victim is *slander*. To succeed in proving slander, the plaintiff must prove actual monetary loss, technically called *special damages* (discussed later in this chapter). However, certain types of slander are so obviously harmful to reputation that special damages are presumed to exist and need not be proved. Such cases of **slander *per se***, defamatory as a matter of law, exist whenever the defendant falsely publishes that the plaintiff (1) has committed a crime punishable by imprisonment; (2) has an existing venereal disease; (3) is unfit for his or her lawful business, trade, profession, or office (public or private); or (4) is guilty of sexual misconduct. Not every false statement about another person is actionable, even though it may contain vituperative, derogatory, or disparaging terms.

slander *per se* Slander in itself; words not requiring proof of special damages.

LEGAL FOCUS—CASE

In the presence of other persons, Marjorie Taylor, a high school teacher, told Monty Standby, her principal, that he was "plain stupid ... not qualified ... a disgrace to the profession" and "just like Lee Harvey Oswald ... and Jack Ruby."* Principal Standby sued. Who won?

Stanley v. Taylor, 4 Ill.App.3d, 98, 278 N.E.2d 824 (Illinois, 1972).

Principal Standby won a jury verdict of $75,775 at the trial level. But judgment was reversed on appeal because Taylor's language was held to be not sufficiently defamatory, as a matter of law, to be slanderous. Perhaps the judge found the comparison to Oswald and Ruby, made in anger, to be so preposterous that it made the outburst laughable and not likely to damage the reputation of the principal.

LEGAL FOCUS—EXAMPLE

Tawana Brawley, age fifteen, claimed through her advisers, one of whom was the Rev. Al Sharpton, that she had been raped by a gang of white men that included state prosecutor Steven Pagones. The publicity surrounding this accusation was considerable. A grand jury later found Brawley's story to be false. Pagones sued Brawley and her advisers for slander. A jury awarded Pagones $345,000 damages against the advisers.

Libel

A false communication, written or printed, is *libel.* As such, it historically has been considered a more durable form of defamation than slander, with a stronger, longer-lasting impact. Accordingly, the cause of action may be successful even without proof of actual, out-of-pocket special damages, such as lost wages.

LEGAL FOCUS—EXAMPLE

McLibel—The Longest Trial in British History

Britons Helen Steel, a part-time bartender, and Dave Morris, an ex-postal worker, helped distribute a pamphlet claiming that McDonald's was cruel to animals and exploited children in its advertising, and that its low wages in Britain tended to depress salaries in the entire fast-food

*Lee Harvey Oswald was the assassin of President John F. Kennedy. Jack Ruby murdered Oswald shortly after his arrest while he was being transferred between jails.

industry. The pamphlet contained other charges about the treatment of chickens used in McNuggets and the fat and salt content of Big Macs. Many statements in the pamphlet ultimately were found to be false. McDonald's then sued Steel and Morris in what became known as the McLibel trial between David and Goliath. Without legal counsel, Helen and Dave called as expert witnesses vegetarians, environmentalists, libertarians, and animal rights activists from around the world. The English court took testimony involving some 60,000 pages of documents from 180 witnesses over 313 court days in a period of two and a half years. Lawyers for McDonald's were attired in wig and gown, as are traditional in English courts, while Helen and Dave wore jeans and sweatshirts.

The McLibel trial became the longest in the history of England. At its end, the judge found that Helen and Dave had committed libel and entered judgment for McDonald's for $96,000. The pair later sued the United Kingdom, filing the case at the European Court of Human Rights. Their claim was that their lack of access to legal aid breached their rights to a fair trial as guaranteed under Article 6 of the Human Rights Convention. On February 15, 2005, the EU court agreed, rendering a damage verdict against the United Kingdom. If McDonald's can collect none of the judgment, nor any of its huge legal fees from Helen and Dave, was the case an exercise in futility?

Sometimes, considerations other than money control the decision to pursue litigation. It might be deemed sensible for a company such as McDonald's to defend its reputation and thereby to dissuade others from publicizing untrue disparaging statements. On the other hand, many believe McDonald's suffered a public relations disaster through its litigation.

privilege
A legal right to do or refrain from doing something enjoyed by only some persons or classes.

Privilege to Defame Others

Truth is an *absolute* defense against a defamation lawsuit. In other words, if a statement is true, then even if it damages someone's character, it is not defamatory. Such a statement, however, may violate the person's right to privacy, which is another intentional tort discussed later in the chapter. A **privilege** also may be a defense, since it is a legal right to do something. A privilege may be absolute or conditional. An **absolute privilege** gives the holder a right to act under all circumstances. A **conditional or qualified privilege** gives the holder a right to act under certain circumstances.

absolute privilege
Total protection from liability for defamation. Legislators enjoy it for statements made during official sessions, and judges and others enjoy it during judicial proceedings.

Absolute Privilege

Public policy requires that certain persons be permitted and encouraged to express their ideas without restraint or fear of lawsuits for defamation. In our republic or representative democracy, legislative, executive, and judicial officers are encouraged to speak out for the common good. Legislators during legislative proceedings; judges, lawyers, jurors, and witnesses during judicial proceedings; top officials of the executive branch (notably the president and vice president, cabinet members, and major department heads); as well as high-level officials of administrative agencies, acting in the official performance of their duties, have an absolute privilege to say anything, even if it is false, malicious, or self-serving. The media (newspapers, magazines, and radio and television stations) have an absolute privilege in quoting the identified officials verbatim. Understandably, there is an absolute privilege between husband and wife for communications concerning third persons and for parents telling their children derogatory opinions about friends of the children.

conditional or qualified privilege
A partial immunity which protects one who makes a defamatory statement in the performance of a legal, moral, or social duty, to a person who has a corresponding duty or interest in receiving it.

Qualified Privilege

A qualified privilege, or conditional privilege, exists for creditors who may, in good faith, exchange otherwise-defamatory information about debtors whose creditworthiness is a mutual concern. A similar conditional privilege exists between employers with reference to qualifications of past and prospective employees. The privilege is qualified, or conditional, in the sense that the employer must act in good faith and without negligence. But note that the statements must be well founded. Nevertheless, many employers refuse to express any opinion about the quality of performance of former employees, because of a fear of lawsuits claiming defamation. Even when one is vindicated, legal defense is costly.

The furor caused by defamation is better understood when one realizes that a person's reputation or good name is usually a delicate mental image in the minds of other persons in the community. It is a priceless possession available to both poor and rich, taking years to develop. Yet it is very fragile and can be shattered in seconds by one false statement. Defamation has been likened to cutting open a down-filled pillow in a violent windstorm. Fully restoring the good reputation, through denial by the victim and retraction by the liar, is like gathering up all of the thousands of tiny feathers that have scattered far and wide in the storm—impossible.

Special Status of Newspapers

A very important expansion of the right of newspapers to print libelous materials was made by the U.S. Supreme Court in 1964, in a famous case involving the *New York Times*. The Court held that the common law of libel is superseded in part by the First and Fourteenth amendments to the U.S. Constitution, with reference to articles about public officials or public figures. In effect, it gives the media a right of freedom of expression that approaches, but does not equal, the absolute privilege enjoyed by government officials as previously noted. The *New York Times* rule bars public officials or public figures from recovering for defamatory falsehoods unless they can prove the statement was made with actual malice. *Actual malice,* here, means that it was made with prior knowledge that it was false or with reckless disregard as to whether it was true or false. Moreover, the defamation must be proved by clear and convincing evidence, which is more than the preponderance-of-evidence standard usually required in civil cases. Significantly, a number of state courts have applied the rule and extended it to nonmedia defendants as well.

Some 22 years later, in a 1986 case involving the *Philadelphia Inquirer,* the U.S. Supreme Court reinforced free speech–free press protection of the media. It held that under the U.S. Constitution, when a newspaper publishes a speech of public concern about a *private figure,* the plaintiff bears "the burden of showing falsity as well as fault (wrongfulness) before recovering damages." Generally, if a newspaper defames someone who is a private rather than a public figure, prompt retraction and apology are mitigating circumstances that may affect the award of punitive damages. The U.S. Supreme Court, to encourage freedom of expression, has ruled that punitive damages may not be awarded to private defamation plaintiffs in actions against media defendants (e.g., newspapers and radio and television stations) without proof of actual malice. The media defendant remains liable only for actual monetary special damages, and these are likely to be modest.

In 1990, the Supreme Court imposed a new restraint on the press. It held that statements of opinion, as well as statements of fact, can be libelous. In the words of the Court, saying "In my opinion Jones is a liar" is the same thing as saying "Jones is a liar." However, newspapers and other media may—without liability—publish reports containing defamatory statements that were absolutely privileged when made during legislative or judicial proceedings.

LEGAL FOCUS—EXAMPLE

It is difficult, but not impossible, for a celebrity to win a defamation lawsuit. Comedian Carol Burnett won a landmark libel lawsuit against the tabloid National Enquirer Inc. The *National Enquirer* is known for its vigorous defense of defamation lawsuits. The *National Enquirer* falsely implied that Burnett had been intoxicated and gotten into a loud argument with a well-known politician in a Washington, D.C., restaurant. Ms. Burnett had among other things been a national spokesperson on alcohol abuse. The *National Enquirer* defended, in part, that it was a newspaper and enjoyed special protection by state statute. The court rejected its claimed status as a newspaper: "[T]he National Enquirer should not be deemed a newspaper for the purposes of the instant litigation." Normal "lead time" for its subject matter is one to three weeks. Its owner claimed it did not generate stories "day to day as a daily newspaper does."

In the summer of 2006, one of the former stars of the popular television show "Friends" won a defamation lawsuit against charity fundraiser Aaron Tonken. Tonken falsely claimed David Schwimmer had demanded two Rolex watches to attend his own charity event. Schwimmer won a $400,000 judgment, and Tonken admitted his allegation was false.

Invasion of Privacy

Most states recognize the right of privacy by means of common law case decisions, by statutes, and by state constitutions. The *Restatement of Torts* recognizes four broad categories of **invasion of privacy** that may justify the award of damages:

invasion of privacy
Violation of the right of every person who has done no wrong to be left alone. Rights related to property interests in one's own person.

1. Unreasonable intrusion on the seclusion of another
2. Appropriation of the other's name or likeness
3. Unreasonable publicity given to the other's private life
4. Publicity that unreasonably places the other in a false light before the public

In one famous case, consumer advocate Ralph Nader's privacy was violated by General Motors Corporation (GMC) after he had criticized their automobiles. GMC employees threatened Nader, tapped his telephone, and attempted to entice him with women—all in a futile effort to silence him. In another notable case, former *Tonight Show* host Johnny Carson blocked the use of the phrase "Here's Johnny" (his nightly introduction signature) by a corporation engaged in renting and selling portable toilets. But generally, public personages, such as sports and entertainment stars, cannot claim a right of privacy in their public image, performance, or duties. Such figures usually need, want, and solicit publicity to advance their careers—thus, in effect, waiving some rights of privacy. Some advocates suggest that celebrities ought to be protected by statute from such apparent invasions of privacy as having their photographs taken in secluded but public places through high-powered telescopic lenses, or having any obnoxious behavior in crowded public places such as restaurants or sports events be reported on.

All states, as well as the federal government, have enacted laws that supplement the tort of invasion of privacy. These include legislation concerning the wrongful opening of mail, electronic eavesdropping and telephone wiretapping, and disclosure of income taxes paid and welfare payments received. The 1997–1998 recordings by Linda Tripp of private conversations she had with Monica Lewinsky in the scandal leading ultimately to the impeachment of President Bill Clinton raised the consciousness of the nation to the issues of telephonic privacy. In general, federal wiretap laws and the laws of a majority of states allow a person to tape a telephone call in which they are a party. However, in Ms. Tripp's case, she recorded the call in Maryland, one of twelve states that require both parties to approve the taping of the call. A prosecution of Ms. Tripp for surreptitious recordings in violation of Maryland law was dropped before trial.

The tort law of privacy is not limited to celebrities. Everyone is entitled to protection from unreasonable invasions of privacy.

LEGAL FOCUS—CASE

Sylvia Nistle noticed but thought nothing of small scratches in the bathroom mirror of her apartment. Unbeknownst to her, construction workers, who were engaged in repairing the neighboring apartment, made the scratches to serve as peepholes. Nistle suffered humiliation and severe distress after learning that strangers routinely had been violating her privacy. Can she sue the landlord for the intentional tort of invasion of privacy?

Based on *New Summit Associates Limited Partnership v. Nistle*, 73 Md.App. 351, 533 A.2d 1350 (Md., 1987).

No, she cannot sue her landlord. The next-door construction workers were not agents or employees of the landlord, who personally did not scratch the peepholes or use them. Nistle could sue the individual construction workers for the intentional tort of invasion of privacy, but they probably were without substantial wealth. She also might be able to sue the employer of the workers, but determining the success of such a case would require more knowledge about the employer's actions in hiring and supervising the workers.

Conversion (Civil Theft)

conversion
Unauthorized taking of the personal property of another and wrongfully exercising rights of ownership.

Any unauthorized taking of the personal property of another and wrongfully exercising rights of ownership is the tort of **conversion**. It can involve wrongfully taking such things as (1) a house trailer, (2) stock certificates sold by a broker without authorization, (3) architectural plans for a residence, even if the building is in public view, and (4) the re-recording and sale of recorded musical performances owned by a record label.

LEGAL FOCUS—PROBLEM

Alexis Marks finds a valuable digital camera in a leather case under a bench at Disney World in Orlando, Florida. A business card inside has the name, address, and phone number of Daniel Daze, with the words "Reward for Return." Marks recalls the ditty "Finders Keepers, Losers Weepers" from her childhood and decides to keep the camera. Has she committed a crime or a tort?

She has committed both a crime and a tort. Marks has committed the crime of larceny. She also is liable in damages to Daniel Daze for commission of the tort of conversion. Unfortunately for Daze, the crime and tort probably will go undetected and unpunished. Marks, the finder, is known in law as a constructive bailee of the goods. A *bailee* is a person to whom goods are entrusted for use, storage, or other purposes. The bailee has temporary possession, coupled with a duty to return or dispose of the goods in accordance with the trust. A restaurant with coat checking, a parking garage, and a laundry are examples of bailees. As a bailee, Marks should make a reasonable effort to find the owner, usually with the assistance of the local police. If no one claims the item within a

trespass to chattel
A brief, temporary, unauthorized interference with the personal-property rights of another.

fraud
A knowingly false representation of a material fact, made through words or conduct, with intent to deceive a victim, who is induced to contract in reliance on the lie, and who is thereby injured.

misrepresentation
A false statement made intentionally, knowing it is not true. A negligent misrepresentation is a false statement made carelessly.

reasonable time, the finder may keep the property. (See further discussion of personal property in Chapter 10.)

A brief, temporary, and unauthorized interference with the personal-property rights of another is termed a **trespass to chattel**. The owner is entitled to damages for the limited loss of possession and any actual harm to the property. But the wrongdoer is not compelled to pay the full market value. An example is the deliberate "keying" (scratching with a key) of a parked automobile (which is a tort and also the crime of malicious mischief). Repainting is costly and time consuming, but such tortfeasors are usually juvenile "hit-and-run" types who are not likely to be caught.

Fraud

Fraud is a tort most frequently committed in the sale of goods or services. It is also called *deceit* and sometimes **misrepresentation**. For fraud, the following elements must be present:

1. a false representation (i.e., a lie);
2. a factual matter (not personal opinion, unless the opinion is that of an expert on the subject);
3. material (i.e., important enough to affect the decision of the intended victim);
4. known by the wrongdoer to be false, or made with reckless indifference as to its truth;
5. made with intent to induce action by the victim, who is unaware of its falsity;
6. the victim acting reasonably does justifiably rely on the lie in his or her decision
7. victim is injured as a result.

In a simple, often-repeated type of case, a seller of a used car may misrepresent the mileage, the times and frequency of servicing and of overhaul, the number and identity of previous owners, or the number and nature of accidents, if any, in which the vehicle has been involved. A knowledgeable car buff might not be misled, but many amateurs would buy in trusting reliance and, if victimized, could therefore sue for damages.

LEGAL FOCUS—EXAMPLE

In a gross example of misrepresentation of mileage, Chrysler Corporation was fined $7.6 million by a federal district court judge for selling thirty previously damaged vehicles as new cars and for odometer violations. Chrysler previously had entered a plea of no contest to the criminal charges. The fine supplemented an earlier settlement of more than $16 million in a civil suit. Records showed that between 1949 and 1986, Chrysler personnel had disconnected the odometers on about 60,000 new cars that were driven for periods of one day to five weeks by Chrysler executives before being placed on sale as brand new. In the thirty specially noted cases, the cars had been damaged while being driven by the executives and repaired before sale as new.

Fraud also may occur under a wide variety of unusual circumstances, as the following cases indicate.

LEGAL FOCUS—CASE

Peter Roberts, an eighteen-year-old sales clerk at Sears, invented a quick-release socket wrench in his spare time. He applied for and received a patent in 1965. Thereafter, Sears negotiated to buy Roberts's patent rights. He was told that (1) the invention was "not new," (2) the production cost would be $0.40 to $0.50 per wrench (Sears knew it would be only $0.20), and (3) it would sell only to the extent promoted and, hence, was worth only $10,000. Roberts agreed to accept a $0.02 royalty up to a maximum of $10,000. Within days, Sears was manufacturing 44,000 of Roberts's wrenches per week. A half-million wrenches were sold in nine months. By 1975, more than 19 million wrenches had been sold for a net profit of more than $44 million, according to court records. Was Sears guilty of the tort of fraud?

Roberts v. Sears, Roebuck & Co., 673 F.2d 976 (7th Cir., 1978).

Yes, Sears was guilty. A jury awarded Roberts $1 million in damages. The U.S. Court of Appeals affirmed and also authorized Roberts to rescind (set aside) his contract and sue Sears for breach of his patent. In 1982, a federal jury awarded Roberts $5 million, and the judge increased this to $8.2 million on the grounds that the infringement was willful. In 1983, this decision was overturned by the court of appeals, which ordered a new trial. In September 1989, twenty-five years after receiving his patent, Roberts and his attorney finally confronted Sears again in court. This time on the fifth day of the trial the litigants reached a settlement, the terms of which were not disclosed.

LEGAL FOCUS—CASE

Dining at Yesterday's Restaurant in Mobile, Louisiana, Patrick Lamey ordered the "De La Mer" omelet. Afterwards, Lamey suffered nausea, vomiting, high fever, stomach cramps, and diarrhea. He was admitted to the hospital, where his condition was diagnosed as acute gastroenteritis. He was released in a few days. Lamey had no evidence that Yesterday's had been negligent or that the food was contaminated. But the menu stated that the "De La Mer" omelet contained crabmeat and trout when in fact it contained only codfish. Can Lamey simplify the proof needed by suing for misrepresentation?

Lamey v. Yesterday's Inc., 492 So.2d 988 (Louisiana, 1986).

Yes, Lamey can simplify the proof. Lamey easily could and did prove that the menu was a false misrepresentation of a material fact that he relied on and was damaged as a result. He recovered $27,500 in damages.

Tort law protects even the naive, the trusting, and the ignorant.

LEGAL FOCUS—CASE

Soldier Steven Malandris, a truck driver in Korea, met and married Jung Ja, who was illiterate. Returning to the United States, their marriage was dominated by a quest for financial security. Malandris worked as a baggage handler for United Airlines in Colorado; Jung Ja managed their money. They lived meagerly and saved $60,000, which they invested in United's stock. Malandris met John Barron, an account executive for securities firm Merrill Lynch, Pierce, Fenner & Smith, Inc. (a major securities firm), who suggested he forge his wife's name to get access to the family money held as stock and to invest it in commodity options. Barron told Malandris that there would be an "assured gain" and "no possibility" of any loss. Soon, however, $30,000 was gone. Jung Ja sustained permanent emotional injury, which allegedly "destroyed her ability to function as a human being." She was despondent about life and lived only in anticipation of life after death. May Jung Ja recover damages for fraud?

Malandris v. Merrill Lynch, Pierce, Fenner & Smith, Inc., 447 F.Supp. 543 (Colorado, 1977).

Yes, she can recover damages. A six-person jury in federal court awarded compensatory damages of $1.03 million plus punitive damages of $3 million. When denying a motion for new trial, the judge commented, "This is not a case of a lost investment; it is the tragedy of a lost life."

LEGAL FOCUS—PROBLEM

The children of Margaret Lesher, believing that her recent husband, buffalo rider T. C. Thorstenson, had murdered their mother to obtain part of her $100 million estate, sued him for fraud. They contended that Thorstenson intentionally had concealed one of his two previous marriages, the one in which he had been accused of spousal abuse. Lesher never would have married Thorstenson, her children contended, if she had known the truth. For their part, Thorstenson's attorneys argued that Lesher told their client a lie, that she was only fifty-five years old. Are lies told between spouses the proper basis for a lawsuit for fraud?

Lies concerning the affection one does or does not feel about the other, made just before marriage or without regard to marriage, are not ordinarily grounds for a lawsuit. Thus, if one person relies upon the statement "I love you" and therefore takes some action that ultimately turns out to be regrettable, there is no basis for court action. However, lies of material fact may form the basis of an action for misrepresentation or fraud, even if the consequent action was to become married. In the *Thorstenson* case, the outcome is not public because the case settled out of court.

Not all misrepresentations are torts. A person commits no tort when he or she innocently does not know the information is false, but mistakenly tells you that a dog being sold to you is two years old when in fact it is five. Generally, if you are the victim of an innocent or a negligent misrepresentation, you have the option of rescinding the contract (by returning the dog and getting your money back) or renegotiating the sale price. However, a professional veterinarian seller who knows, or should know, the true age of the dog could be guilty of fraud under these circumstances.

Opinions of quality in advertisements and sales talks ("the finest car on the road," "enjoy the pleasure of the best in international travel," "the best in cordless telephones just got better") are actual examples of customary commercial "puffing" and are not actionable. A dissatisfied purchaser of automobile insurance claimed that the seller violated the New Jersey Consumer Fraud Act because its service did not live up to its slogan. The state supreme court disagreed, explaining that the slogan "You're in Good Hands with Allstate" is "nothing more than puffery;" there was no fraud. Social fibs likewise are not actionable (e.g., "I'll be there at 5 P.M." and the person doesn't arrive until 6 P.M., or not at all).

Bad Faith

Persons pay premiums to insurance companies, which promise in exchange to pay money when some uncertain future calamity, such as an automobile accident, death, fire, or disability, occurs. If the insured person fails to make timely payment of premiums, the insurance coverage may be cancelled. And if the insurance company fails to make a promised payment when some calamity occurs, the insured may sue for breach of the insurance contract. In the next chapter (about contracts), you will learn that punitive damages are not available for ordinary breach of contract. But some courts have imposed a duty of "good faith and fair dealing" upon insurance companies, the violation of which may subject them to punitive damages. Violation of this duty is said to be the intentional tort of **bad faith**.

bad faith
The deliberate failure to fulfill some duty or contractual obligation owed to another (e.g., a purposeful failure by an insurance company to pay a lawful claim).

The tort of bad faith in actions against insurance companies generally involves either of two scenarios.

In the first scenario, Joe Levendowski pays premiums for automobile insurance with maximum liability coverage of, say, $100,000. Suppose Levendowski is involved in a car crash that seriously injures a victim, Diego Berka, in another car. Berka as the victim sues Levendowski for $150,000 but, learning of the insurance amount, agrees to settle out of court for the $100,000. Levendowski's insurance company rejects the offer, however, choosing instead to go to trial on a "roll of the dice" to see whether a jury might return a verdict of less than $100,000. Instead, the jury verdict is $150,000. The insurance company pays the $100,000 policy maximum, thinking, "Well, at least we had a chance of saving some money." But Levendowski now must pay the $50,000 personally. Levendowski's loss is caused in part by his insurance company, which violated its duty of good faith and fair dealing because it could have and should have paid its policy maximum to protect Levendowski. Courts in most states would permit Levendowski to sue his insurance company for bad faith and to recover the $50,000 above coverage limits plus punitive damages.

In the second scenario, the carrier delays payment of a legitimate claim. The reason may be to earn interest on delayed payments, a desire to gamble on a less costly award by a jury, or an attempt to induce a needy claimant to settle for less because he or she cannot afford to wait or litigate. Unreasonable delay in payment of a claim violates the duty of good faith and fair dealing and renders the insurance company liable for general and punitive damages. Some states provide for the recovery of bad faith claims by statute and provide a cap on recovery of such claims. The pertinent part of such a Georgia statute is provided here.

LEGAL FOCUS—BACKGROUND

In the event of a loss that is covered by a policy of insurance and the refusal of the insurer to pay the same within sixty days after a demand has been made by the holder of the policy and a finding has been made that such refusal was in bad faith, the insurer shall be liable to pay such holder, in addition to the loss, not more than 50 percent of the liability of the insurer for the loss or $5,000, whichever is greater, and all reasonable attorney's fees for the prosecution of the action against the insurer.

In theory, courts could impose a duty of good faith and fair dealing on any contract and permit a tort recovery of damages whenever a contract is breached under egregious circumstances. So far, courts are reluctant to extend tort recovery. When calamities occur, insurance companies have a tremendous negotiating power over their dependent customers, justifying the creation of a duty of good faith and fair dealing. Most other contractual relationships are not characterized by such unequal bargaining power and dependency. In some states, insurance companies have successfully lobbied the legislature or used the initiative process to limit the ability of the courts to award damages for bad faith claims.

TORTS BY NEGLIGENT BEHAVIOR

The Elements of Negligence

duty
The obligation enforceable in court to recognize and respect the person, property, and rights of others. Legal duty is the reciprocal of *legal right*.

Everyone has a **duty** (i.e., a mandatory obligation) imposed by law to behave with due care as a reasonable, prudent (i.e., cautious and careful) person would behave under the same or similar circumstances. If one fails to be legally careful and thus injures another's person or property, the victim may sue and recover damages from the wrongdoer for negligence.

Whether a particular act constitutes negligence depends on whether the elements of negligence exist. For that purpose, we can ask these questions:

- Did the defendant owe a duty of care to the injured victim?
- Did the defendant breach that duty through unreasonable conduct?
- Did the plaintiff suffer an injury as a result of the defendant's breach of the duty of care?
- Did the defendant's breach of duty cause the victim's injury?
- Is there any social policy under which the defendant's liability ought to be cut off? For example, was the injury so remote from the defendant's act that it would be unforeseeable by a reasonable person?

Duty and Breach of Duty

The duty of care that every person owes to all others is judged by the reasonable-person test. We all are duty bound to act as carefully or prudently as a so-called reasonable person would act under all of the circumstances existing at the time. Otherwise, we may be liable to any victim we injure—if we owe that victim a duty of care and if there is no social policy cutting off our responsibility. Whether or not a defendant acted reasonably is a question for the jury (or judge when there is no jury).

Determinants of duty include the foreseeability of harm to the victim, the proximity or closeness between the unreasonable act and the injury, and the moral blameworthiness of the defendant. Also relevant are the public policy of preventing future harm; the financial burden on the defendant and the community in imposing the liability; and the availability, cost, and prevalence of insurance for the risk involved. These considerations have evolved under common law. Special rules, discussed later, have been added by state statutes.

The standard of care required is usually called ordinary care: What would a reasonable person have done under the same or similar circumstances? The law does not demand perfection. But any judgmental errors must be understandable and excusable under the circumstances. Thus, for example, a "perfect" person driving on a busy highway and caught in a sudden and unusually heavy cloudburst, or a dense dust storm, would carefully drive off the highway and onto the shoulder, and wait there for the passing storm to subside. However, practically, a reasonable person—seeing other vehicles still moving in both directions—might assume that it was safe to drive on because the storm was only momentary and would shortly end. But the storm continues. Within seconds, our driver becomes one link in a chain reaction of rear-end crashes. Was the driver negligent? A jury would probably say, "No; it was an accident."

An accident is a sudden, unexpected, unintended happening that causes injury or death or loss of property. It may occur under circumstances in which nobody is at fault, as in an earthquake or natural landslide. However, in most "accidents," one (or more) of the parties involved is at fault because of what someone did or failed to do. Automobile "accidents" are common examples of events that usually are caused by negligence. One example of an excusable accident is when a driver unavoidably loses control of the vehicle because of the sudden attack and painful sting of a bee.

One expert on torts, Edward J. Kionka, explains that the

> *reasonable person ... is not the average or typical person, but an idealized image of such a person—a composite of the community's judgment as to how the typical community member ought to behave in each of the infinite variety of circumstances and activities in which there is a potential or actual risk of harm to the actor or others.*

Community members sit on the juries that determine how the defendant ought to have behaved; some suspect that jurors themselves might behave less carefully than the standards they impose on others.

LEGAL FOCUS—BACKGROUND

English legal humorist A. P. Herbert (1890–1971) wrote a series of misleading cases for the English magazine *Punch*. In his fictional case of *Fardell v. Potts*, he wrote this tongue-in-cheek account of the fictional reasonable person.

> Devoid, in short, of any human weakness, with not one single saving vice, sans prejudice, procrastination, ill-nature, avarice, and absence of mind, as careful for his own safety as he is for that of others, this excellent but odious character stands like a monument in our Courts of Justice, vainly appealing to his fellow-citizens to order their lives after his own example.

Failure to be reasonable may be seen in an act (e.g., setting fire to a building by flicking a cigarette butt) or an omission (e.g., neglecting to put out a small fire). It may be an intentional act (pushing the "pedal to the metal"), a careless act (talking on a cell phone while driving), or a carefully performed but dangerous act (down-hill skiing) that results in injury. Courts consider the nature of the act (whether it is outrageous or commonplace), how the act is performed (cautiously or carelessly), the relationship of the parties (landowner duty to trespasser), and the nature of the injury (serious or slight) to determine whether a duty of care has been breached.

The law of negligence has evolved by court decisions that arise in response to the injuries that occur as increasingly complex activities characterize our society.

LEGAL FOCUS—PROBLEM

Injo Kalen left a burning cigarette teetering on the edge of his girlfriend Amy Porubsky's ashtray, which was sitting on the arm of the couch in her apartment. While Kalen and Porubsky were dining in the other room, the cigarette became unbalanced as it burned and fell onto the cushions, which slowly began to burn. By the time the fire was noticed and extinguished, the couch and Porubsky's cashmere sweater were destroyed, and there were large burns in the carpet and smoke damage in the apartment. What are the legal consequences of this event?

Kalen owed a duty of reasonable care to Porubsky and her landlord. That duty was breached when Kalen failed to behave as a reasonable person by leaving the burning cigarette on the edge of the ashtray. Fire from a burning cigarette is a foreseeable consequence, and the damages were the proximate result of that negligence. Therefore, Kalen is liable to both Porubsky and her landlord. Porubsky can agree to accept a specified sum from Kalen for the value of her sweater (called *damages*). Porubsky's landlord, who owns the apartment and furniture, also could settle with Kalen. But if the parties cannot settle the problem, Porubsky or her landlord could begin civil tort proceedings against Kalen to recover damages. If Porubsky had renter's insurance, her insurance company also would compensate her for the sweater unless its value was less than the deductible portion of coverage. Most landlords carry fire insurance and would receive compensation from their casualty insurance company for damage to the building and couch as well. As a practical matter, both Porubsky and her landlord would probably accept payments by their insurance companies and take no further action.*

Causation: Actual and Proximate

Common sense tells us that one should be liable for conduct that injures others only when there is a logical cause-and-effect relationship between the defendant's negligent act (or failure to act) and the plaintiff's injury. In most fact situations, this principle is easy to apply. But when a sequence of events and persons is involved—as is sometimes the case—the determination of cause and effect is difficult.

If a person fails in a duty of care and someone suffers injury, the wrongful activity must have caused the harm in order for a tort to be committed. In deciding whether there is causation, two questions must be addressed:

actual cause
The negligent person's carelessness is the reason for the loss by the victim; in other words, when injury to person or property results from the tortfeasor's action or failure to act.

1. Is there **actual cause**? That is, did the injury happen because of the defendant's act, or would the injury have occurred anyway? If an injury would not have occurred without the defendant's act, then there is actual causation. Such causation usually can be determined by the descriptive but-for test: "*But for*" the wrongful act, the injury would not have happened.
2. Was the act the **proximate cause** of the injury? As a matter of social policy, how far should a defendant's liability extend or reach? The act not only was an important factor, but also it actually caused all the remote damages. But injuries can be so remote that, as a matter of public policy considerations of fairness, liability of the wrongdoer is simply cut off.

proximate cause
An action that, in natural and continuous sequence, unbroken by an intervening force or cause, produces the injury, and without which the effect or result would not have occurred. Furthermore, the result is not entirely outside the range of expectation or probability.

What if two independent forces combine to cause the injury? For example, suppose A builds an unreasonably large and roaring campfire near C's mountain cabin. B leaves an open container of gas on the ground at an adjoining campsite. Sparks from A's blazing campfire ignite B's gas can, causing a large enough fire to engulf and destroy C's cabin. Even if neither careless act alone could have produced that result, both A and B are liable under the *substantial-factor* test, since both contributed substantially to the destruction of the cabin and were the actual cause of the harm. The same is true if either careless act alone would have been sufficient to destroy the cabin.

To be "proximate," the cause need not necessarily be close or near to the resulting injury, in time or in space. But it must appear to be just and fair, and indeed feasible, to hold the defendant liable for the injury that did result. Theoretically—tongue in cheek—we

*In theory, either Porubsky's or the landlord's insurance company would have the right to sue Kalen for reimbursement of any claims paid. This right of an insurance company to seek reimbursement from a wrongdoer for a claim paid to their customer is called subrogation (substitution of creditors). As a practical matter, insurance companies usually do not seek subrogation, because the wrongdoer lacks financial resources.

might trace all events of human history in an unbroken chain back to Adam and Eve. The injury to the plaintiff must be reasonably related to the cause (the negligent act of the defendant). If it is not reasonably related, it is considered too remote. The proximate cause is the true cause which, in a natural and continuous sequence, unbroken by any efficient intervening cause, produces injury, and without which the result would not have occurred.

MORALS AND ETHICS

The proximate cause component of negligence interrupts the factual cause-and=effect process of actual cause and applies a moral judgment by asking whether it is "right" or "just" to hold the person responsible for the harm someone else incurred. Thus, proximate cause puts significant authority in the hands of the fact finder (judge or jury) to determine the reach of the tort of negligence. It is a rare instance in which the law is left fairly open-ended for fact finders to apply a moral or ethical judgment on the facts. Is it fair for a juror to decide the culpability of someone based on the juror's sense of right and wrong? Perhaps. Here, proximate cause acts as a limit to liability, not really an extension.

An attempt to thoroughly define proximate cause is probably futile, but examples can help with understanding.

LEGAL FOCUS—PROBLEM

Brent Starr was testing the power of his new sports car on a clear two-lane highway in good weather. When he reached 90 mph, he lost control and the car crashed through a fence and into a high-voltage electricity pole. This caused a short circuit and power failure throughout the city of Barclay, 100 miles away. Among the many persons affected were the staff and doctors in General Hospital. Just as the power went out, surgeon Ramona Ramirez was making a critical incision near patient Albert Johnson's heart during open-heart surgery. As a result of the darkness and loss of power to essential equipment, she had to stop abruptly. The machines supplying vital oxygen and pumping blood went silent. Within minutes, Albert Johnson was dead. Is Brent Starr liable for Johnson's death?

No, Starr is not liable. Starr's wrongful conduct was the actual cause of Johnson's death. Under the actual cause test mentioned previously, it can be said that "but for" Starr's folly, Johnson would not have died when he did. But Starr's act was not the proximate, legal cause because it was too indirect and remote from the death, which was not reasonably foreseeable by Starr.

Note that Starr would be liable for the damage to the fence and to the high-voltage electricity pole. It is also possible that General Hospital could be found guilty of negligence, and therefore liable, for failing to have a standby emergency electric power source available. (This is indeed standard practice in well-run hospitals, because power failures are not uncommon. But that is another case.)

LEGAL FOCUS—PROBLEM

Brent Starr's car, after ramming the pole, caromed into the brush nearby, striking and killing Tom Sneed, who was hunting quail. Starr did not know that Sneed was hunting there. Is Starr liable for Sneed's death?

Yes, he is liable for Sneed's death. Here, Starr's wrongful conduct was the actual and also the proximate or legal cause of the death. The negligent act was direct and close; there was no intervening cause. With his eyes glued to the road, Starr did not even see Sneed. Under the circumstances, however, the threat of injury or death from the speeding car to any person who happened to be in any of many potentially fatal locations on or along the highway was reasonably foreseeable in the law. What people really do and do not foresee is not decisive; what is foreseeable is a matter of law.

Thus, causation, both actual and proximate, must be proved to hold a defendant liable for negligence. There is proximate causation if there is "the ability to see or know in advance … that harm or injury is a likely result of acts or omissions." If, and only if, a reasonably prudent person, under similar circumstances, could and would have foreseen the likelihood of injury from the defendant's conduct to any person in the situation of the victim, does the defendant have the duty to exercise reasonable care to refrain from such conduct. This point is discussed in practically every law school in the nation by reference to the following famous case.

LEGAL FOCUS—CASE

Standing at one end of a railroad station platform, a woman waits for her train to arrive. Suddenly, there is a loud explosion at the distant other end of the platform. Vibrations resulting from the explosion cause some scales to fall on the woman, injuring her. Evidently, a railroad guard inside one car of a slowly moving train had reached out to grab a man who was running to get aboard. Another railroad guard—who was standing on the platform—gave the man a helping push from behind. The man happened to be carrying an unlabeled parcel, containing fireworks. When the parcel fell onto the railroad tracks, it exploded, whereupon Helen Palsgraf, the woman at the other end of the platform, suffered injuries. She sued the railroad for damages. The jury found the guards to be negligent toward Palsgraf, and the trial court awarded her damages against the railroad, as the responsible employer. The railroad company appealed. Should the appellate court affirm the judgment?

Palsgraf v. Long Island R.R. Co., 248 N.Y. 339, 162 N.E. 99 (New York, 1928).

No, the appellate court should not affirm the judgment. Palsgraf's complaint was dismissed. The injuries she suffered were not reasonably foreseeable—and certainly were not inflected intentionally—by the railroad guards. Therefore, there was no duty to her that was breached by the guards or by their employer. To prove negligence and to collect damages, Palsgraf would have had to show that the actions of the railroad guards "had possibilities of danger so many and apparent as to entitle" her to be protected against those very actions. This she could not prove.

Without foreseeability, there is no duty to act or refrain from action. Without duty, there can be no negligence. Without negligence, there can be no fault. Without fault, there can be no liability, regardless of the extent of the injury. William Prosser and Page Keeton, leading authorities on torts, unequivocally state, "The question of foreseeability is not an element of causation and does not arise until the issue of causation has been determined." Another legal scholar, Leon Green, properly points out that "Causation is a neutral issue, blind to right and wrong … but in absence of causal relation plaintiff has no case, and all other inquiries become moot." After all, the linkage of cause and effect in any series of events may be coldly analyzed and *objectively* determined. Thereafter, one may inquire into whether any involved person (e.g., the defendant) *subjectively* could.

Returning to Brent Starr's predicament in the earlier example, he could and should have foreseen that a person, such as Tom Sneed, might be in the bushes near the highway, perhaps hiking, hunting, resting, or bird-watching. But he could not reasonably have foreseen the tragic sequence of events in the hospital, nor could he have foreseen countless other resulting events at great distances from the scene of the crash, in areas served with electricity by the power line.

In summary, to prevail in a negligence action, the plaintiff must present a preponderance of evidence proving

1. existence of a legal duty to the plaintiff, and
2. breach of that duty by the defendant's action or failure to act, with
3. resulting legal causation, actual and proximate, of an alleged injury, which
4. justifies the award of damages in court.

Remember that the weight of required evidence in civil negligence cases is not as demanding as in criminal cases, where the trier of facts must be convinced of their truth beyond a reasonable doubt. The weight of the plaintiff's evidence must be such that what is alleged is more believable, more convincing, more probable than not.

LEGAL FOCUS—PROBLEM

Deborah Gaines arrived at the Preterm Health Services clinic to obtain her scheduled abortion. While sitting in the waiting room, John Salvi III opened fire and killed two receptionists. Gaines was left unharmed, but "emotionally messed up" and never could return to any clinic for an abortion. Gaines later gave birth to Vivian, who is learning disabled and hyperactive. Gaines has sued Preterm and the owner of the building for negligence that wrongfully caused the birth of Vivian. Gaines seeks damages with which to properly raise Vivian. Was the claimed negligence (failure to provide safe premises) the proximate cause of the birth of Vivian?

No, negligence was not the proximate cause. There was sufficient time following the Salvi shooting for Gaines to obtain an abortion at a different clinic. But, according to her lawsuit, she was unable to return because of emotional reasons. Unsafe premises may cause the foreseeable result of injury to the customer. But it is quite different to argue that unsafe premises may foreseeably result in the birth of a living child.

LEGAL FOCUS—PROBLEM

Chicago police were pursuing a car over a traffic violation. The speeding car crashed, killing Jamil Khouri, severely injuring his son Omar, and slightly injuring his daughter Ahlam. The Khouri estate and family sued the City of Chicago as employer of the police who, it was claimed, negligently pursued the traffic violator whose car was in the fatal crash. Is the act of pursuing a fleeing criminal the proximate cause of injury to an innocent bystander?

The City of Chicago settled the case, paying a total of more than $5.1 million to the Khouri family. After that case, the U.S. Supreme Court ruled that the sheriff was not responsible for the death of a passenger on a fleeing motorcycle who was killed when it crashed. The Court established a new rule that police essentially are not negligent nor is their conduct the proximate cause of resulting injuries during pursuits of suspects unless the actions of the police are so egregious that they "shock our conscience." The U.S. Supreme Court had jurisdiction in this case because the plaintiff alleged the federal civil rights of the deceased were violated.

LEGAL FOCUS—PROBLEM

Mukesh Rai, a devout Hindu, after ordering a bean burrito from Taco Bell, discovered to his dismay that he was eating beef, in violation of a fundamental religious principle. Rai contends that Taco Bell was negligent and must pay for psychiatry costs, for a trip to England for a purification ceremony with Hindu masters, for a trip to India for the ultimate purification of bathing in the waters of the Ganges River, and for emotional distress, pain, and suffering. Assuming that Taco Bell was negligent, were the damages claimed foreseeable?

On the one hand, there was a breach of contract when Rai did not receive the product he ordered. But damages from breach of contract are restricted to foreseeable and quantifiable monetary damages. The measure of damages in torts, as will be discussed later in this chapter, is more generous in that nonquantifiable losses, such as pain and suffering, are compensable. Still they also must be foreseeable. In today's multicultural society, is it unreasonable to require national retail organizations to be aware and protective of the differing religious and other beliefs, customs, and activities of customers?

LEGAL FOCUS—CASE

Darrell Parsons was riding his horse Poco along a bridle path when a garbage collection truck in a nearby restaurant parking lot picked up and emptied its trash-filled bin. The clanging noise spooked Poco, who began spinning, bucking, and finally bolting. Parsons was injured when he landed on the ground. Parsons sued the Crown Disposal Company for his injuries. What was the result?

Parsons v. Crown Disposal Company, 15 Cal. 4th 456, 936 P. 2d 70, 63 Cal.Rptr. 2d 291 (California, 1997).

The case was thrown out of court summarily and never reached the jury. Appeals continued until the case reached the California Supreme Court some six years after the incident. The defense attorney asked rhetorically, "Why should we be liable if a horse operates like a horse and a trash truck operates like a trash truck?" If you believe the answer to this case was easy, you may be surprised to learn that two dissenting justices on the five-member court believed that the victim was entitled to a trial.

LEGAL FOCUS—PROBLEM

Tired from an afternoon of drinking beer with friends while watching the Buffalo Bills on television, Will Brown was driving home. While passing down a street where homes were scattered among small warehouses, he did not notice a fairly large, dilapidated cardboard carton near the gutter in the road ahead. Weaving slightly, Brown's car hit the cardboard box. To his dismay and horror, he saw in his rear view mirror that the carton had concealed a child. Kathy Wellington, age three, had been walking on the curb, holding the carton over her head. She had evidently stumbled into the street, and the carton covered her completely. Her death was mercifully sudden. Kathy's parents now seek to hold Brown liable. Will they prevail?

No, they will not prevail. Although Brown's clearly negligent conduct was the actual cause of Kathy's death, he is not liable. While it is foreseeable that a pedestrian might be in the vicinity, it is not foreseeable that a tiny person would be inside an old cardboard carton in the street.

intervening cause
A cause of an accident or other injury that legally excuses the wrongdoer who originally sets a series of events in motion.

Intervening Causes and Shared Responsibility

An **intervening cause** is an independent force (either an act or a failure to act) that comes or happens after the defendant's negligent conduct has commenced. The natural sequence of events that could have caused the injury are interrupted. Instead, the end result is an injury that could not have been reasonably foreseen. Therefore, the original wrongdoer is not liable in damages.

LEGAL FOCUS—PROBLEM

Danny Pawar foolishly keeps a can of gasoline in the trunk of his car, thereby creating risk of a foreseeable injury from explosion or fire. Now lightning strikes the car, exploding the car's built-in gas tank as well as the portable can. Nearby pedestrians are injured. Is Pawar liable to the victims?

No, Pawar is not liable. The lightning, an unforeseeable natural phenomenon at that time and place, intervened, and the actual cause of the injuries from the explosion was the lightning.

Sometimes, intervention of a human actor expands the scope of a negligent wrongdoer's liability. Consider the following hypothetical situation.

LEGAL FOCUS—PROBLEM

Isaac York and Thor Waller are among a group of teenagers who walk to the end of a pier along the Atlantic coast in Florida. Waller objects when York engages in horseplay, but York persists, and with a quick push accidentally sends Waller into the deep water. Waller cannot swim. He flounders but is rescued by Connie Himaet and is revived by prompt resuscitation. Himaet also was injured when a high wave tossed her against the piling of the pier. Is York liable for the injury to Waller? To Himaet?

York is liable for injuries to Waller for negligently pushing him off the pier. He also is liable to Himaet under the doctrine that "danger invites rescue." Thus, the intervention of "Good Samaritan" Himaet expanded York's liability.

Whereas the law does not ordinarily require that a person, "the Good Samaritan," intervene (no legal duty), what happens if they choose to do so? At common law, if one decides to act, then they are expected to be careful under the circumstances; failing that, they are liable for their own negligence. This can happen, as it did when the U.S. Coast Guard (USCG) temporarily abandoned a search for a fisherman who subsequently died on a life raft five days after his boat had sunk. The death resulted because the USCG had negligently fouled up its own rescue-message transmission.

Good Samaritan laws
Statutes that protect volunteers from liability for ordinary negligence while aiding persons in need.

To deal with the moral dilemma of being legally immune if you do nothing but liable if you provide aid but fall short of providing the quality of assistance expected, most states have enacted some type of so-called **Good Samaritan laws**. These statutes shield doctors and others from liability they may incur to an injured person when they stop along the way and render emergency aid. Obviously, if all goes well, no protection is needed for the volunteer, but if the provided assistance aggravates the person's injuries, then the Good Samaritan statute provides immunity from liability. These statutes vary from state to state as to who is covered and in the protection provided. Some state statutes protect any emergency volunteer, and other state statutes protect only named emergency providers such as doctors, nurses, police, and firefighters; furthermore, some statutes distinguish between free assistance and paid providers. Volunteers still are expected to use reasonable care under the circumstances, but they cannot be found liable if they fail to do so.

LEGAL FOCUS—EXAMPLE

Utah Statutes 78-11-22 (1) Good Samaritan Act

A person who renders emergency care at or near the scene of, or during an emergency, gratuitously and in good faith, is not liable for any civil damages or penalties as a result of any act or omission by the person rendering the emergency care, unless the person is grossly negligent or caused the emergency. As used in this section, "emergency" means an unexpected occurrence involving injury, threat of injury, or illness to a person or the public, including motor vehicle accidents, disasters, actual or threatened discharges, removal, or disposal of hazardous materials, and other accidents or events of a similar nature. "Emergency care" includes actual assistance or advice offered to avoid, mitigate, or attempt to mitigate the effects of an emergency.

gross negligence The failure of even slight or scant care.

These immunity statutes generally do allow recovery by the injured person if the Good Samaritan is grossly negligent in the assistance provided. A wrongdoer is guilty of **gross negligence** "when he inflicts injury intentionally or is so utterly indifferent to the rights of others that he acts as if such rights did not exist." Good Samaritan statutes are just one form of statutory immunity; there are many others. The state of Maryland purportedly has twenty-four separate statutory immunities in the Maryland Civil Code protecting individuals for their negligent acts. Included within other immunity protections are state officers and employees acting within the scope of their employment. These other immunity protections also do not protect against grossly negligent acts.

Violation of a Statute as Proof of Negligence

negligence *per se* The unexcused violation of a statute or ordinance which is automatically deemed to be negligent conduct without argument or proof as to the particular surrounding circumstances.

Legislation or administrative regulation—at the federal, state, and local levels—often describes standards of conduct designed to prevent injuries. Violation of such statutes or rules may be both proof of duty and breach thereof. In most states, when a court determines that the particular statute applies to the facts of a case, its violation is *prima facie* (Latin: "on first appearance") negligence. An example would be harm flowing from exceeding the well-posted speed limit on a winding mountain road. Unless the defendant produces evidence that excuses the violation, negligence is conclusive. A possible excuse would be a sudden emergency, such as unexpected brake failure caused by another's defective repair. The application of this rule is called **negligence *per se***.

LEGAL FOCUS—CASE

Shaun and Alex O'Guin were killed when a section of pit wall collapsed while they were playing at the Bingham County landfill. The children had left a summer lunch program at Ridgecrest Elementary School and entered the closed unattended landfill through an unlocked gate after crossing a privately owned empty field. Applicable state rules required that access to a landfill be limited to those times when an attendant is on duty and "the site shall be fenced or otherwise blocked to access when an attendant is not on duty." The children's parents sued in negligence, claiming that violation of the state rule established that the county was negligent per se. The county countered that the O'Guin children were trespassers and the claim should be barred.

O'Guin v. Bingham County, 122 P.3d 308 (Idaho, 2005).

The court answered the first three of the following four questions in the affirmative.

> *In order to replace a common law duty of care with a duty of care from a statute or regulation, the following elements must be met: (1) the statute or regulation must clearly define the required standard of conduct; (2) the statute or regulation must have been intended to prevent the type of harm the defendant's act or omission caused; (3) the plaintiff must be a member of the class of persons the statute or regulation was designed to protect; and (4) the violation must have been the proximate cause of the injury.*

As to the fourth element, the court held there is at least a disputed issue of fact remaining and remanded the case back to the trial court.

Professional Malpractice

malpractice Violation of a duty of due care by a professional person.

Few areas of legal conflict have caused as much heated debate as **malpractice**. Malpractice is negligence committed by a professional person. It is the failure to use that degree of care, learning, and skill ordinarily possessed and applied by the average prudent member of the profession in the same locality. Thus, a general practitioner of law or medicine in a small town is not expected to have the skills or facilities of a group of specialists in a large city.

Physicians and surgeons have been the prime targets of plaintiffs, but dentists, lawyers, accountants, architects, and engineers have comparable professional duties to those they serve and increasingly are being sued. Lawsuits also have been brought against other similar public-service types, such as pharmacists, chiropractors, insurance and real estate agents, and investment advisers. Some contend that many doctors routinely order costly laboratory tests and X-rays, even when they are not essential for proper patient care, as "security blankets" to help protect themselves against possible lawsuits.

Harvard University researchers examined some 31,000 medical records in a four-year-long study of malpractice (conducted in fifty-one hospitals in the state of New York), with results disclosed in 1990. They found 1,133 "adverse events" ranging from patients falling down to patients being infected during surgery. Twenty-five percent of the adverse events could be traced to negligence, yet only one lawsuit was filed for every 9.6 cases of detected negligence. If these figures are extrapolated to the entire total of 2.7 million patients who were hospitalized in New York state during 1984, about 100,000 patients were injured by improper medical treatment, and as many as 7,000 died. In 2006, a leading health care reporting agency reported that

> *medical errors are a leading cause of injury and death in the United States.... Approximately 1.24 million total patient safety incidents occurred in almost 40 million*

hospitalizations in the Medicare population. These incidents were associated with $9.3 billion of excess cost during 2002 through 2004.

Thus, it could be that medical malpractice suits are less frequent than they should be, not the other way around. Or, another means of assuring patient safety must be found.

Premises Liability

trespass
Wrongful interference with the real or personal property of another.

The common law duty of care that is owed to all persons generally is modified relative to the owners or occupiers of property. Owners and occupiers of real property (land and buildings) owe special care to certain classes of potential victims. We review the duties owed by landowners to those who **trespass**, by homeowners to guests, and by businesses to their customers.

Trespassers on Land

Adult trespassers to real property are by definition uninvited, generally unexpected, and unwanted. To them, minimal duty is owed—the owner (or occupier) must not set traps or spring guns to thwart or hurt trespassers or burglars, nor otherwise intentionally harm them. A landowner need not warn trespassers of dangerous natural conditions, but if trespassers are known to be on the premises, the landowner has a duty to warn of unforeseeable man-made risks (e.g., an attack guard dog).

LEGAL FOCUS—PROBLEM

It was the first day of the summer holiday. Jimmy Parker and Tom Rouble, both ten years old, rode their bicycles into the country. They spotted an unattended tractor near the road, on the farm of Jensen Dairy, Inc. Tom said, "Let's see if we can start it!" Within minutes, they were over the fence and fiddling with the controls of the machine. The engine started and in a sudden forward lurch, Jimmy was thrown off and broke his arm. Is Jensen Dairy liable?

attractive-nuisance doctrine
The doctrine under which minors who trespass may collect damages if attracted on to the defendant's premises where they are injured by a man-made instrumentality that has special appeal to children (such as a railroad turntable or an unfenced swimming pool).

Young children are an exception to the rules regarding trespassers. When children trespass because of natural curiosity about an **attractive nuisance** and are injured, the owner is liable. The tractor could be considered such an attraction. A common attractive nuisance is a swimming pool. Many cities now have ordinances that specify the type of fencing that must safeguard pools from trespassing children. Attractive nuisances that are highly dangerous to children have included the second floor of a house under construction, from which a seven-year-old girl fell; an abandoned, burned-out semitrailer, with melted remnants of red-taillights, that fell on an eight-year-old boy; and an open sewer drain where a nineteen-month-old child was found drowned. The earlier case example illustrating negligence *per se* on page 308 involved two minor children and an unfenced unguarded county landfill. The children were trespassers, but the landfill was a tempting playground for some children.

In deciding whether the attractive-nuisance doctrine applies, courts consider (1) whether the defendant knew, or should have known, of the likelihood of trespassing children, and of the unreasonable risk of death or serious injury to them from an artificial (i.e., man-made) condition; (2) whether the children, because of their youth, do not realize the risk involved; and (3) whether the benefit of maintaining the condition, coupled with the burden or cost of eliminating the hazard, is slight compared with the risk to the children.

LEGAL FOCUS—CASE

Pacific Bell installed two public telephone booths on the sidewalk within twenty feet of the parking attendant's booth for the adjacent parking lot. The telephone booths attracted young drug dealers who loitered nearby often harassing passers-by. Pacific Bell refused to relocate the booths after Alfonso Martinez, parking attendant, complained. After Alfonso was robbed and shot in the hand and back, he sued Pacific Bell on the theory that the telephone booths were an attractive nuisance. Does Pacific Bell, under any theory, have a duty to protect a nearby parking attendant from harm by third parties?

Martinez v. Pacific Bell, 225 Cal. App. 3d 1557, 275 Cal.Rptr. 878 (1990).

Even if telephone booths were an attractive nuisance, Pacific Bell would not be liable for the wrongful acts of those who were attracted to the area. These criminals were not children, and they did not injure themselves. As to the parking attendant, Pacific Bell had no special duty to someone working on the adjoining property.

Guests of Property Owners—Licensees

licensee
A person who enters another's land with permission (implied or express) of the owner or possessor, for the visitor's convenience.

Those on property with implied or express permission of the owner are **licensees**. Social guests are obvious licensees but so are U.S. Postal Service employees, public utility employees (e.g., meter readers), and building and health inspectors. Generally, the occupier of land owes the licensee a duty of reasonable care, but it has no duty to inspect premises for dangerous conditions that are not obvious. Once dangers are known, however, they must be repaired or the licensee must be warned.

Police officers and firefighters generally are considered licensees under a special rule called the fireman's rule. Probably the vast majority of fires are caused by negligence; once started, they also threaten the property of neighbors. Thus, public policy generally bars suits by firefighters for injuries suffered in performing their work in an emergency situation. The owner is, however, duty-bound to warn the firefighters of any known hidden hazards, if there is an opportunity to do so. Failing this duty, the owner is liable for injuries to the firefighter. Also the possessor of land is liable "to a public officer or employee who enters the land in the performance of his public duty, and suffers harm because of a condition of a part of the land held open to the public" in the same fashion as if that person is an invitee (see the following discussion).

Many homeowners erroneously believe they will be held liable for any injury that occurs on their property. But homeowners have no duty to warn of a condition of which they are unaware. If a social guest stumbles on concrete stairs leading to the front door, there is no liability. On the other hand, if a social guest slips on a throw rug that carelessly was placed on a newly waxed hardwood floor, there may be liability for failure to warn of the rather obvious danger.

Customers in Business Premises—Invitees

invitee
One who enters another's land with the permission (implied or express) of the owner or occupier, for a matter of business benefiting the owner or occupier.

Shoppers and customers in retail stores and patrons of restaurants, hotels, theaters, and amusement parks are called property **invitees**. They are there for business purposes, and the owner or occupier of the premises is seeking to earn a profit from their presence. To them, the owner owes a high duty of care for their safety. He or she must routinely inspect for dangerous conditions and either correct them or clearly warn the invitees.

If a homeowner invites guests to a "lingerie party" hoping to make sales, the guests likewise have become business invitees to whom a high duty of care is owed.

LEGAL FOCUS—PROBLEM

Viola Velour was walking in the aisle of a supermarket, wearing her new high-heeled pumps for the first time. Suddenly, her left ankle twisted, and she tumbled to the floor. As she fell, she grasped at an empty shopping cart nearby, and it came down on her head. The impact broke her dentures and caused a painful, unsightly gash in her face. She sued the owner of the supermarket for damages. Is there liability?

No, the owner does not have liability. Velour was an invitee, but the market is still not an insurer of her safety. The accident resulted from her inability to use high-heeled shoes safely. To recover damages, she would have to prove that (1) the premises were in a dangerously defective condition; (2) this condition was the result of the store owner's conduct, or that it existed long enough for the owner to be alerted and to correct it; and (3) the usual rules of causation were satisfied.

Sometimes, produce in markets ends up on the floors, causing slippery spots. Customers who fall and are injured may bring "slip and fall" suits, which are fairly common. The question always arises as to the frequency with which the market inspects the floors for such spots and cleans them. A market is not reasonably required to inspect the floors every five minutes, and thus a "slip and fall" can occur under circumstances when the market simply is not negligent.

The Injury Requirement and Damages

There is no negligence if there is no injury. To recover damages (receive compensation), a person must suffer a loss, harm, wrong, or invasion of a protected interest. Essentially, the purpose of tort law is to compensate people for legally recognized injuries that result from unreasonable behavior. If no harm or injury results from a given action, there is no tort. Thus, the drunk driver of a speeding vehicle may be careless, but until injury occurs, there is no tort. This distinguishes a tort from a crime, which seldom requires an injury.

LEGAL FOCUS—PROBLEM

Patricia Burns, who had advanced multiple sclerosis, claims that her doctor, Thomas Hanson, negligently failed to detect her pregnancy in time for her to obtain an abortion. She thus gave birth to Molly, whom she loves very much. But Burns requires substantial funds (she asks for $1.6 million) to assist her with hiring in-house child care and other workers to help her raise a healthy Molly. Is having a healthy child a "wrongful birth" for which damages should be allowed?

In this case, the jury returned a verdict for the doctor. However, the trial judge refused to permit Burns to testify to the jury that she would have had an abortion if she had known promptly of her pregnancy. The difficulty is, of course, in defining a new life as a measure of damages suffered by the parent. On the other hand, if a doctor commits negligence that proves to be disruptive and costly to the victim, shouldn't there be compensation? And if so, by what standard should the amount of damages be measured?

What Is a *Res Ipsa Loquitur* Case?

res ipsa loquitur A doctrine under which negligence is inferred when the instrumentality causing the injury was under control of the defendant and an injury occurred that normally would not occur in the absence of negligence by the defendant. This doctrine is frequently relied on by victims of medical malpractice.

In negligence lawsuits, the injured victim is required to prove that the defendant has breached a duty. In certain situations, however, courts infer that the duty was breached. In this type of case, the burden shifts to the defendant, who must prove that he or she was not negligent. In other words, negligence can be found in situations lacking direct evidence of wrongdoing. This inference of the defendant's breach of duty is called the doctrine of ***res ipsa loquitur*** (Latin: "the thing speaks for itself").

The *res ipsa loquitur* doctrine applies when both of the following conditions exist:

1. The event is one that ordinarily does not occur without someone being negligent.
2. The agency or instrumentality creating the injury is under the exclusive control of the defendant.

LEGAL FOCUS—PROBLEM

Mike Hubell is walking on the sidewalk alongside a building with a penthouse apartment on the tenth floor. The penthouse has an open terrace with a railing three feet high and six inches deep, decorated by a line of potted plants on the railing. Hubell is knocked unconscious when he is hit on the head by a potted plant. It is later proven that the pot that hit him is similar to others on the penthouse railing, where one pot is missing. Hubell is unable to prove how the pot happened to fall on him. Is this a *res ipsa loquitur* case?

This is a classic situation for application of the doctrine that "the thing speaks for itself." The pot evidently came from that penthouse terrace, which was under the exclusive control of the occupants of the apartment. It ordinarily would not have fallen unless someone was either careless or, possibly, intended to be funny.

The doctrine has been applied by patients after undergoing surgery. If the patient suffers an injury that ordinarily does not occur without negligence (as when a sponge is not removed from the surgical area), the doctrine can be used to shift the burden to the defense to show they were not negligent. Thus, as the burden of proof shifts, the surgeon, surgical nurses, staff, and others will have to sort out the events among themselves.

LEGAL FOCUS—CASE

Seventy-eight-year-old Margaret Frostick was admitted to Porter Memorial Hospital for a right carotid endarterectomy. (Ouch!) Anesthesia was given to permit the patient to be in a sedated state but still be responsive. Supplemental oxygen was given to her through a mask. During surgery, the oxygen mask caught on fire and Frostick's face and chest were burned as a result. Not surprisingly, she sued the medical providers. Is she entitled to an instruction of *res ipsa loquitur* against the medical providers?

Gold v. Ishak, 720 N.E.2d 1175 (Ind., 1999).

The court of appeals held that the plaintiff had presented evidence that the oxygen mask was

> *under the exclusive control of the Medical Providers and that the fire was such that the ordinary course of things would not happen if those who used these devices*

exercised proper care. The conditions surrounding the surgery have met the underlying elements of the doctrine of res ipsa loquitur, and therefore, the inference of negligence is applicable.

What Are Defenses to Negligence?

Under certain circumstances, a defendant who otherwise might be liable because of his or her negligence can avoid payment of all or some of the damages by proving that the injured victim did one of the following:

- Also was negligent and, in most states, is entitled only to reduced damages, if any, under the doctrine of *comparative negligence*
- Also was negligent and therefore, in a few states, is entitled to no damages under the doctrine of *contributory negligence*
- Assumed the risk

These three defenses are discussed next.

comparative negligence
Negligence of the plaintiff that does not bar recovery of damages but may reduce the amount of recovery proportionally.

Comparative and Contributory Negligence

Most states have adopted the rule of **comparative negligence**, under which a victim who is negligent may nevertheless recover damages from a defendant who is more negligent. Damages allowed are simply reduced in proportion to the amount of negligence attributable to the plaintiff. In other words, liability for damages is allocated to the parties in proportion to the fault each contributed to causing the injury, as determined by the jury (or judge when there is no jury).

LEGAL FOCUS—PROBLEM

T. Ray Vitesse was driving home in his heavy-duty pickup truck at dusk on a residential street, about an hour after sunset. He had several beers that afternoon. He later claimed he was not drunk, although he had forgotten to turn on his headlights. It was raining heavily at the time, and he felt mellow and refreshed as the raindrops splashed on his face through an open window. "Just cruising along" at only ten mph over the posted speed limit (of twenty-five mph), his reverie suddenly ended as he crashed into the left side of Art Aritroso's sedan. Aritroso was backing out of his driveway, but had failed to look both ways and had not turned on his lights until he was in the street. Vitesse suffered no injuries and his truck required no repairs, but Aritroso's sedan was extensively damaged and he was badly injured. Aritroso sued and the jury decided that his negligence constituted 25 percent of the total. Aritroso's damages total $200,000. How much is he entitled to under the comparative-negligence rule?

The total damages recognized are reduced by the amount of the plaintiff's negligence, as long as it is not as great as the defendant's. Under this process, Aritroso would get $150,000 (100 percent − 25 percent = 75 percent). He would have received $102,000 if his negligence had been 49 percent (100 percent − 49 percent = 51 percent), but nothing if it had been 50 percent or higher. (This is the case in Wisconsin, one of the first states to adopt comparative negligence.) In a number of states, however, under the "pure" comparative-negligence rule, negligence by the plaintiff never bars recovery. Damages are reduced in proportion to the amount of the plaintiff's negligence. In those states, even if his negligence had been 99 percent, Aritroso would nevertheless have received $1,000 (100 percent − 99 percent = 1 percent).

contributory negligence
The negligence of a plaintiff that helped to cause a tort. In states accepting the doctrine, a contributory negligence plaintiff usually is barred from claiming damages if injured.

Previously, the rule of **contributory negligence** generally determined whether damages could be awarded at all for negligence. If two persons were involved in an accident and both were negligent, neither could recover any damages. Contributory negligence was held to be a complete bar to a negligence lawsuit. This was the rule even if one party "contributed" almost all of the negligence. Determination of contributory negligence is a question for the trier of fact. Not infrequently, a jury will temper strict application of the rule with compassion and common sense and simply overlook minimal amounts of negligence by an otherwise-deserving plaintiff. Moreover, the contributory negligence of a plaintiff is no defense for a defendant found guilty of willful and wanton misconduct (acting with reckless disregard for the plaintiff's safety, as by drunk driving).

This harsh rule of contributory negligence originated in England and was commonly applied in the United States during the 1800s, when railroads were introduced. "Establishment-oriented" courts were interested in helping the new industry, and they applied the doctrine as a matter of law to collisions at grade crossings. The doctrine survived into the twentieth century and frequently blocked recovery of damages in automobile accident cases (where it is not unusual to find at least some negligence on the part of both drivers).* More recently, most states have abandoned the doctrine of contributory negligence in favor of comparative negligence.

Is the failure to use an automobile seat belt or shoulder harness (or airbag that inflates on impact) evidence of contributory negligence? This issue is somewhat confusing. Belts generally reduce the severity of injury, but in some cases, can cause internal injury. There is no documented proof, however, that any person has died in a fiery accident because he or she could not unbuckle the seat belt. Indeed, the crash victim, if belted, is more likely to be conscious and better able to escape. If in the driver's seat, he or she is more likely to minimize further damage by maintaining better control of the car. Most states have mandated by statute the installation of seat belts, but not all require their use. Moreover, there is really no logical connection between a collision and the failure to use a seat belt. Consequently, many jurisdictions, including those of such populous states as New York and Texas, have ruled that failure to use a seat belt does not constitute sufficient negligence to bar the plaintiff's lawsuit. In a growing number of states, such failure is negligence that may reduce damages if expert testimony proves how much less the injuries would have been had the belt been used. A further discussion of negligence pertaining to automobile accidents is included in Chapter 10.

Assumption of Risk

assumption of risk
When a plaintiff with knowledge of the facts of a dangerous condition voluntarily exposes himself or herself to the particular risk of injury.

A person who voluntarily puts himself or herself in a risky situation, who knows the risk involved, and who is then injured is not allowed to recover damages. This is the defense of **assumption of risk**. A plaintiff who knows and appreciates a given risk may assume it, thereby absolving the defendant of liability if injury results. In sports, especially, the hazards may be serious for both spectators and participants, and both may assume the risks of customary hazards of such games as baseball, basketball, football, and hockey.

In contact sports, participants assume the risk of injuries that are common and expected, even when an opponent is violating a rule of the game (e.g., when a jockey carelessly changes lanes during a horse race—a violation of a foul-riding rule). But this

*A few states apply the doctrine of "last clear chance" to deny recovery if, despite the negligence of the defendant, the injured victim had the last clear chance to avoid the injury but failed to do so. Thus, a driver who foresaw an approaching car straddling the white line, and who reasonably could pull over to the right, but who continued ahead with a resultant crash, would have had the last clear chance to avoid the injury and thus could not recover damages.

does not give the contestants a *carte blanche* (French: "blank check") waiver of all violations of the rules. Conduct that is substantially outside the ordinary play of the game, especially if it is intentional, may give rise to tort liability.

To prove that a potential plaintiff had knowledge of the risk undertaken, many activity providers will require express assumption of the risk by having each participant sign a document that explains the hazards of a particular activity. (The clause also may serve as a contract waiver of that person's legal rights; we will discuss such waivers in Chapter 8.) Whether the document effectively waives legal rights or not, it can clearly establish knowledge of the risk and establish the doctrine of assumption of risk. Absent an express waiver, the defense also exists if the defendant can show a plaintiff assumes the dangers that are inherent in and necessary to the particular sport or activity.

LEGAL FOCUS—CASE

Moser and Ratinoff were participants in an organized, long-distance bicycle ride on public highways involving hundreds of cyclists. Event organizers required that participants sign a waiver and release form. Moser complied. The document stated that Moser expressly assumed the risk of injuries, including those caused by other participants. During the ride, Ratinoff swerved into Moser, causing a crash and injuries to Moser. When Moser sued Ratinoff for negligence, Ratinoff moved for summary judgment, arguing that a collision between bicycle riders was an inherent risk in the ride, and therefore no duty was owed Moser because of assumption of risk.

Moser v. Ratinoff, 105 Cal.App.4th 1211, 130 Cal.Rptr.2d 198, 2003 WL 203255 (Cal., 2003).

The court agreed with the defendant Ratinoff that by "knowingly participating in a sporting event in which what occurred is an evident risk, Moser is not entitled to a recovery. In its analysis, the court considered cases in which assumption of risk had been found to exist, including snow skiing, collegiate baseball, off-roading, skate-boarding, golf, lifeguard training, tubing behind a motorboat, wrestling, gymnastics stunt during cheerleading, little league baseball, cattle roundup, sport fishing, ice skating, football practice drill, judo, rock climbing, river rafting, snow skiing, and sailing. In considering for the first time a long-distance bicycle ride, the court stated, "activity is done for enjoyment or thrill, requires physical exertion as well as elements of skill, and involves a challenge containing a potential risk of injury."

Many states classify assumption of risk as either primary or secondary. The doctrine of primary assumption of risk was discussed earlier. Its effect is to eliminate the duty a defendant owes the plaintiff because the plaintiff knowingly and voluntarily assumed the risk of the activity in which both parties were engaged. Secondary assumption of risk is a failure to exercise reasonable care for one's own safety. Secondary assumption of risk is not a complete defense but instead is merged into the definition of comparative negligence.

STRICT LIABILITY TORTS

As a matter of public policy, certain businesses are required by law to compensate persons who are injured by their products, services, or activities. In these situations, the victimized plaintiff need not prove intent or negligence—the defendant is liable even if not at fault. This is true, for example, in the comparatively rare cases in which the defendant keeps a wild animal, with dangerous propensities, that injures someone. Circus and carnival elephants, lions, and tigers may have been trained or tamed, but they remain wild. In contrast, some wild animals—such as deer, oxen, and monkeys—are excluded if they have been domesticated to live peaceably in the service of humans. Nevertheless, the owner of domestic animals, including dogs, is strictly liable for injuries inflicted by the animal if the owner knows of their dangerous propensities. Thus, a guard dog known to be vicious is not entitled to a first "free bite."

Of course, the owner of an ordinary dog or cat, one not believed to be abnormally dangerous, would be liable if he or she directed the animal to harm another or negligently failed to prevent the harm. Animal behavior is often unpredictable and uncontrollable, and it is difficult to prove prior knowledge of viciousness. Therefore, some thirty states have enacted statutes that impose strict liability on owners of dogs that injure others, or specify that negligence need not be proved (e.g., as in roving dog cases and when leash laws are violated).

Certain activities are deemed to be so hazardous as to justify imposition of strict liability on the person so engaged. Examples of such ultrahazardous activities are fumigating buildings with poisonous gases and blasting with explosives in populated areas. Operating a nuclear reactor is another example of an ultrahazardous activity. To date, there has been no Chernobyl-type disaster with loss of life in the United States. Nevertheless, Congress has responded to the potential threat with the Price-Anderson Act of 1957, which placed a liability limit on the nuclear power industry of $710 million in damages, with any additional claims to be paid by the federal government. The limit was raised in 2005 to $10 billion, and over the years, coverage has been extended to include university research reactors, nuclear weapons plants, and nuclear waste repositories. The determination of absolute liability is a question of law for the courts rather than one for the jury. The legal question is decided in most states using the *Restatement of Torts* balancing test.

LEGAL FOCUS—BACKGROUND

In determining whether an activity is abnormally dangerous, the following factors are to be considered:

a. existence of a high degree of risk of some harm to the person, land or chattels of others;
b. likelihood that the harm that results from it will be great;
c. inability to eliminate the risk by the exercise of reasonable care;
d. extent to which the activity is not a matter of common usage;
e. inappropriateness of the activity to the place where it is carried on; and
f. extent to which its value to the community is outweighed by its dangerous attributes.

Restatement of (Second) Torts—Torts § 520 Abnormally Dangerous Activities.

Workers' Compensation

workers' compensation
Medical treatment, rehabilitation benefits, and disability payments for workers injured on the job.

Another important category of strict liability is imposed on employers when a worker is injured or killed on the job. In all states, workers' compensation insurance laws now cover most employees, although farm or agriculture workers and domestic servants in homes are still often excluded. Under **workers' compensation**, workers receive (1) all medical treatment necessary to cure or provide relief from effects of employment-caused injuries or illness, (2) temporary or permanent disability payments, (3) vocational rehabilitation and retraining benefits when unable to return to the former job, and (4) legal assistance without charge. The benefit payments are not lavish, but they are reasonably certain, and the injured worker is not required (nor, indeed, permitted) to sue in court to obtain prescribed benefits. Claims, however, are subject to review and approval in special administrative hearings.

Requirements for a successful workers' compensation claim are simple (at least in theory): (1) the claimant must be an employee, (2) the injury must be a work-related one, and (3) the employee must file a timely claim.

If someone other than the employer is responsible for the workplace injury, the worker may be able to sue and recover damages without limit in a conventional negligence action. A typical example would be when the injury is caused by defectively designed or built equipment that was used on the job. The injured worker cannot sue his or her own employer, but can sue the third-party equipment manufacturer. Also, coworkers may be liable for injuries caused by intentional attacks or by willful or wanton negligence. Limited circumstances under which workers' compensation benefits would be denied are when the injury was the result of voluntary intoxication on the job or was intentionally self-inflicted, or when the injured worker was the aggressor in a fight.

Generally, workers' compensation is the exclusive remedy available against the employer in covered businesses. This is a major practical improvement over the old common law rules, which permitted the worker to sue his or her employer—a costly and seldom prudent thing to do. For starters, the worker (if still alive) could be fired. Thereafter, in court, the employer could avoid liability by proving that either (1) the worker knew the hazards involved and assumed the risk (perhaps in exchange for a higher wage), (2) the worker was guilty of contributory negligence, or (3) a coworker's negligence caused the accident.

LEGAL FOCUS—PROBLEM

It was a glorious spring day as Willie Jon Fisher climbed to his workstation 125 feet above the bay. As a steelworker, he was paid premium wages for assuming the risk of his hazardous job on the new Silver Gate Bridge. In a burst of youthful exuberance, he removed his hard hat, waved to his pal Don Jones twenty feet above, and danced a quick jig on the beam where he stood. Jones shouted, "Simmer down and get to work!" But Willie fell, hitting a cross beam before the safety net caught his unconscious body. His injuries were permanent, and he never returned to the job. Does his carelessness preclude his recovery of benefits?

No, it does not preclude recovery. Any covered employee injured on the job is entitled to benefits under the state's workers' compensation law.

Employers complain that health care and workers' compensation premiums are too high, and workers complain that benefit payments are too low. Fortunately for employers, insurance premiums are a deductible business expense, and they can pass the cost along to their customers. On the receiving end, no federal income tax is assessed on workers' compensation insurance benefits (although Social Security disability payments may be subject to income tax).

Defective Products That Cause Injury

Every year, millions of consumers are injured and thousands are killed by familiar products used in daily life. Usually, nothing is wrong with the product, but the user has been careless or has failed to follow instructions for proper use and maintenance.

Examples include trucks and automobiles; power boats; skis, bats, hardballs, and other sports equipment; guns and firecrackers; knives; and patent and prescription medicines. The most innocent-appearing and useful product, however, in fact may be lethal. For example, a child's pajamas may be made of highly flammable fabric, a sleek sedan may have a steering mechanism prone to failure, and a wonder drug that prevents miscarriages may cause cancer in any female child born to the patient.

Under common law rules, a person injured by a defective product may recover damages by proving that the product was made negligently. The negligence may be in the design, a lack of safety features, faulty materials or manufacture, or a failure to explain proper use and maintenance. Proving negligence in such cases is usually extremely difficult and costly and often nearly impossible. The suspect product may be made with thousands of interrelated component parts; these may have been assembled many years before, in a factory located thousands of miles away, possibly in a foreign land.

An injured plaintiff also might allege a breach of a contractual warranty (see Chapter 8). However, there might be no warranties, or they may have expired, or recovery may be barred by failure to give proper prompt notice of the breach. Moreover, limited warranties often provide for no more than repair or replacement of the product if defective, or at best for a refund of the purchase price.

LEGAL FOCUS—BACKGROUND

In 1962, the California Supreme Court provided a new legal solution to the deficiencies of negligence and warranty theories by defining the new tort of strict liability for the manufacturer when a defective product is sold that injures a user. In this case, the product involved was an ingenious multipurpose power tool that could be used as a saw, a drill, and a wood lathe. It was purchased by the plaintiff's wife. Later, the plaintiff bought the attachments necessary to use the tool as a lathe to trim a large piece of wood. He had worked on a piece of wood several times without difficulty when it suddenly flew out of the machine and hit his forehead, causing a serious injury. Experts testified that an inadequate set of screws had been used by the manufacturer to hold parts of the machine together, and the machine's normal vibration caused the screws to be loosened, which brought about the accident. The court held, "A manufacturer is strictly liable in tort when an article he places on the market, knowing that it is to be used without inspection for defects, proves to have a defect that causes injury to a human being."

Greenman V. Yuba Power Products, Inc., 377 P.2d.897 (Calif. 1962).

The *Restatement of Torts* expanded the strict product liability doctrine to include injuries to any user or consumer or to his property, but qualified it by providing that the seller must be "one engaged in the business of selling or otherwise distributing products who sells or distributes a defective product is subject to liability for harm to persons or property caused by the defect." Many jurisdictions, including such populous states as Illinois, Pennsylvania, and Texas, have adopted the doctrine of strict liability for defective products. Contributory negligence of the plaintiff does not defeat a case. Some states, however, using comparative negligence, allow a reduction in damages. Also, in some jurisdictions, if the product was produced in accordance with the then-existing state of the art, the injury-causing design is not considered a defect.

The rule of strict liability for defective products shifts the burden of resulting injuries from the user to the manufacturer. Intermediaries such as wholesalers and retailers also are held responsible as they are better equipped to pursue the manufacturer. The manufacturer may purchase added insurance, which becomes a routine cost of production.

But, in any case, producers of products can pass along added costs to all customers in the form of slightly higher prices. Manufacturers are encouraged, moreover, to be more careful in product design, presale testing, inspection, quality control in production, post-sale follow-up of performance, and prompt recall and repair when defects are disclosed. In recent years, many automobile models have been recalled for appropriate modifications to forestall costly strict liability litigation.

The following is a selection of products for which liability has been imposed.

- Accutane (an antiacne drug linked to birth defects)
- All-terrain vehicles
- Bendectin and other teratogens (chemicals linked to birth defects)
- Chymopapain (a drug used to treat herniated disks)
- Zyprexa (a drug used to treat schizophrenia)
- Dalkon shield (contraceptive device associated with inflammatory disease and spontaneous abortion in users; removed from the market in 1974)
- Aspirin (lack of warning labels relating a child's use of aspirin to Reyes syndrome)
- DES (a drug used to prevent miscarriages but discontinued because of increased risk of cancer in women who had fetal exposure)
- Halcion (a drug used to induce sleep)
- Intrauterine devices (a contraceptive device)
- Silicone gel breast implants
- Tobacco products
- Vehicle transmissions and gas tank placement
- Vehicle tires

LEGAL FOCUS—BACKGROUND

Dow Corning Corporation helped develop and sold tens of thousands of silicone gel breast-implant devices. Thousands of women sued in a class action contending that their breast implants were defective, leaking silicone into their bodies and impairing their immune systems. Dow Corning, disputing the injuries, filed for bankruptcy due to the crush of claims. Later, under federal bankruptcy court rules, Dow Corning settled the cases, agreeing to pay \$3.2 billion to those women who claimed to be injured by its product.

class action
When all members of a group of persons who have suffered the same or similar injury join together in a single lawsuit against the alleged wrongdoer. The group must be so numerous that it is impracticable to bring all members before the court individually.

Class actions are procedural devices whereby groups of injured persons who are similarly situated can obtain redress in a single lawsuit, rather than filing hundreds or even thousands of separate cases. The silicone gel breast-implant case is an excellent example of how large groups of victims are handled by the civil law tort system. Shortly after the Dow Corning settlement, a court-appointed panel of neutral scientists concluded after two years of study of more than 2,000 cases that there was no credible evidence that breast implants cause disease. Silicone gel implants were introduced in the 1960s, and more than a million women had the procedure until it was banned by the U.S. Food and Drug Administration (FDA) in 1992. In 2006, the FDA reversed its ban and approved the marketing of silicone gel-filled breast implants made by two companies for breast reconstruction in women of all ages and breast augmentation in women ages twenty-two and older. The news release stated the "the products have been determined to be safe and effective."

The largest and most notorious cases of strict liability in the early years of the twenty-first century involve tobacco products. Smoking presents many dilemmas to society. There is no longer a debate that smoking is addictive (as are many other substances) and that it carries a high probability of contributing to lung diseases, especially cancer. Individuals generally cannot successfully sue cigarette companies effectively because of the difficulties in engaging enough experts to prove causation. Although it is one thing to show statistically that smoking contributes to lung cancer in the population, it is quite another thing to show that smoking (and not something else) caused an individual's lung cancer. Meanwhile, taxpayer-funded (via Medicaid) hospitals incur substantial costs in treating persons afflicted with diseases that likely were caused or exacerbated by cigarette smoking. Given these premises, almost all states joined together in filing litigation against the nation's four largest cigarette manufacturers.

LEGAL FOCUS—BACKGROUND

The tobacco industry settled lawsuits filed by most states by agreeing to pay about $206 billion as reimbursement for the Medicaid payments that had been incurred caring for patients of smoking-related diseases, and for future such costs through 2025. The states will receive portions of the $206 billion each year. Tobacco manufacturing companies agreed to pay the states a portion of their proceeds from cigarette sales. The states represented that they will use the money to pay some hospital and other expenses of those who are afflicted with tobacco-related diseases and who are unable to care for themselves. For example, California is slated to receive $23.9 billion each year, although estimated health costs of smoking-related diseases there are $42.5 billion each year. Furthermore, there is no requirement that the money actually be spent on smoking-related deaths. Thus, the settlement, spread out over more than twenty-five years, is a social policy akin to a "user tax" whereby cigarette users provide the funds with which to care for the illnesses created by cigarettes. Other provisions in the settlement restrict the kinds of advertising that will be permissible (no cartoon ads).

Immediately following the settlement, and to nobody's surprise, tobacco manufacturers announced a substantial price increase in cigarettes to offset the costs of the settlement. Since the price increase, Internet cigarette sales—some advertising no sales tax, discount prices, and free shipping—have been booming, as have sales of black-market cigarettes bought in low-tax states. Professional smuggling of "tax-free" export cigarettes has increased.

LEGAL FOCUS—PROBLEM

Marie Schwartz's husband brought a wrongful death action against Philip Morris after Schwartz died of lung cancer. She had smoked Merit cigarettes for twenty-three years, having chosen the brand as a "low-tar alternative" that she hoped would help her quit. Her husband argued that Merits had kept her from giving up cigarettes entirely and were the cause of her lung cancer. He also argued that Philip Morris had engaged in deceitful practices to suggest the low-tar cigarettes were a safer and healthier alternative in order to keep smokers as customers. Philip Morris claimed that Schwartz knew smoking was dangerous and that when she still chose to smoke she assumed the health risks. What was the result?

In this 2002 Oregon case, the jury found for the plaintiff and awarded $168,000 for compensatory damages and punitive damages of $150 million: $115 million for fraud,

$10 million for strict liability, and $25 million for negligence. The case has been appealed several times since then. In 2007, the U.S. Supreme Court vacated the $150 million punitive damages award finding that the jury had improperly consider punishing Phillip Morris for all potentially affected Oregon citizens and not just the person before the court. In 2012 a new trial resulted in an award of $25 million in punitive damages.

Lawsuits focused on the tobacco industry are not the only high publicity area of strict liability in tort. Everyone knows that guns can cause injury. According to the National Rifle Association, some 30,242 persons died of gun-related injuries in 2001. Under what circumstances might a gun manufacturer be held responsible for a defective gun?

LEGAL FOCUS—PROBLEM

Michael Soe, age fourteen, took his father's Beretta 92 Compact L handgun from a camera bag and replaced its loaded ammunition magazine with an empty one. Unbeknownst to Michael, a cartridge remained in the gun's chamber. Michael then, while playing with the gun, shot his best friend Kenzo Dix in the heart, killing him instantly. Kenzo's parents sued Beretta Corp. for $7.5 million on the theory that the red dot on the gun's barrel that is raised one millimeter when a cartridge is in the chamber was too subtle and inadequate a warning. Beretta blamed Michael's father for keeping the gun readily available and loaded. Beretta argued that a defense verdict would mean "personal responsibility is still a healthy concept in this society." Was the gun defective?

This was the first jury trial involving the question of whether or not a handgun is defective in its design or warnings. In the *Kenzo Dix* case, the jury returned a verdict for Beretta. Many other similar suits are pending in the United States with several having been decided against the plaintiffs. In 2005, the gun manufacturer Smith & Wesson agreed to settle a lawsuit brought by the parents of Royce Ryan alleging a handgun was defective because it did not provide childproof protections. Royce was shot with a gun thought to be unloaded by one of his friends and left with permanent disabilities and extensive brain damage.

In the late twentieth century, several major cities, including Chicago, New York, New Orleans, Miami, Boston, Atlanta, and Los Angeles, filed lawsuits against gun manufacturers to recoup the cost of urban gun violence. The contention was that guns are inherently defective products, unreasonably dangerous to the public health, much like cigarettes. In October of 2005, President George W. Bush signed the Protection of Lawful Commerce in Arms Act. This act exempts firearm manufacturers, distributors, dealers, and importers from civil liability for injuries and deaths caused by their products. It allows lawsuits alleging defective firearms but prohibits lawsuits based on public nuisance. Many, but not all, of these public lawsuits have been dismissed because of this 2005 statute.

statute of repose
A type of statute of limitations that specifies an absolute time from the date of sale during which the cause of action must be brought to collect damages for defects in the product.

Statutes of Repose

A **statute of repose** is a special statute of limitations that applies to specified defective products. Statutes of limitation (discussed fully later in this chapter) set time limits within which lawsuits must be commenced. Because knowledge that a product is defective may not arise for many years, there is a public policy to extend the time for victims to begin their lawsuits to recover for their injuries. It would be unfair, however, to businesses to allow an unlimited number of years to pass before claims are asserted. Statutes of repose are a compromise of the interests of consumers on the one hand and of manufacturers and sellers on the other. A statute of repose cuts off liability for a defective product for a specified number of years following its manufacture or sale, regardless of when the victim's injury occurs or is discovered. Statutes of limitation, on the other hand, do not begin to run until an injury has been discovered, or should have been discovered by a victim using reasonable care. There is no general federal statute of repose. State statutes vary, but all cut off the time allowed for specified lawsuits pertaining to, for the most part, consumer products.

In addition to consumer products, statutes of repose may apply to medical and legal malpractice, to workers who are injured in the workplace, and even to renters who are injured by a defective product that is installed in their apartment. In malpractice cases, when they are applicable, statutes of repose typically cut off liability of the physician regardless of when the defect or harm is discovered by the victim. Thus, the "clock starts running" for possible liability for malpractice from the date the injury was inflicted. For example, one state's statute of repose cuts off medical malpractice lawsuits if they have not been commenced within five years of the physician's negligence, regardless of when the harm was discovered. The clock starts running for construction or architectural design defect cases from the date of completion of the project, regardless of when the victim is injured.

LEGAL FOCUS—PROBLEM

Tom Urquhart worked for the Acme Excavating Company performing maintenance duties on heavy equipment. In September 2002, a steel roller on a hydraulic conveyor that was transporting rock broke free, causing a large rock to severely break Urquhart's right leg. The conveyor was manufactured in 1972 by Zeland Equipment Co. and sold to Acme in 1985. Urquhart was covered by workers' compensation insurance and received medical and other financial assistance. His attorney advised him to sue Zeland under a defective product "strict liability" theory. Can Urquhart recover damages from Zeland?

The statute of limitations is usually one year from the date of the injury, so Urquhart had until September 2003 to commence litigation. But thirty years have elapsed since the conveyor was built by Zeland Equipment Co. and seventeen years since it was sold to Acme. If there were a twenty-five-year statute of repose, Urquhart's case would be barred.

Most statutes of repose are applied to lawsuits brought upon the theory of a defective consumer product. For example, Oregon cuts off a manufacturer's liability for a defective product after eight years with only limited exceptions. Victims generally have been unsuccessful in claiming that statutes of repose deny them equal protection of the law if their claim is barred at any time within the useful life of the product.

WHAT ARE DAMAGES?

The word *damage* often is used to mean the loss caused by an injury. Perhaps just as often it is used to mean the injury itself (to a person, his or her property or rights). In the law, however, the plural word *damages* means the money awarded by a court to a plaintiff in a civil action for loss or injury caused by a defendant's wrongful conduct. Damages may be awarded for a breach of contract to put the plaintiff in the position he or she would have been in had the contract been performed as promised (see Chapter 8).

They also may be awarded to a plaintiff because of a tort; for example, an injury suffered in an accident caused by the defendant's negligence. The money received reimburses the plaintiff for medical bills (of doctors and hospital), property loss (a "totaled" car), lost wages, or future "lost" income that cannot be earned because of the plaintiff's injuries. Damages also are designed to compensate for physical impairment (e.g., spinal injury or broken arm), mental anguish, or pain and suffering (both present and prospective, because they are expected to continue into the indefinite future).

compensatory damages
Amount awarded by a court to make good or replace the actual loss suffered by a plaintiff.

Compensatory Damages

Compensatory damages are also called *actual damages* because they consist of money awarded to the plaintiff for real (i.e., actual) loss or injury.

If two or more tortfeasors are responsible for a given injury, each is fully liable to pay the entire amount of any judgment, but of course the plaintiff is entitled to only one full recovery. In most states, a tortfeasor who pays all or more than his or her share of the damages is entitled to contribution or partial reimbursement from the other wrongdoers. Compensatory damages may consist of two types of compensatory damages, special (or economic) and general.

special damages
Amount awarded by a court to pay for monetary out-of-pocket losses resulting from the specific or special circumstances of the plaintiff (e.g., for medical expenses, loss of wages, and destruction of property).

Special or Economic Damages

Special damages often are called *economic damages* or *out-of-pocket* costs because they can be specified and precisely measured in terms of money. Common examples are the cost of a hospital stay, income lost because of absence from work, and the cost of repairing a car that was rear-ended. In awarding special damages for anticipated future losses, a jury may award the present value of such future sums, using an appropriate discount interest rate. The plaintiff gets a sum of money that, if invested at the selected interest (discount) rate, will grow over the years to precisely the amount that had been determined to be the total future monetary loss. Since World War II, inflation has caused a continuing decline in the purchasing power of the dollar. This fact of life also may be taken into consideration in calculating future expenses resulting from the injury. Special damages are the actual result of the particular loss or injury; they flow from it naturally and proximately because of the unique combination of circumstances in any given case.

general damages
Amount awarded by a court to pay the plaintiff for nonmonetary losses (e.g., pain and suffering) that resulted from an injury, without reference to any special circumstances of the plaintiff.

General or Noneconomic Damages

General damages, the second kind of compensatory damages, are also the actual and proximate result of the particular loss or injury. General damages compensate victims for other than out-of-pocket monetary losses suffered. Prime examples include compensation for pain and suffering and compensation for mental distress caused by physical injuries.

LEGAL FOCUS—PROBLEM

Annette Blenker, age thirty-seven, was shopping at Berry's Market when a six-pack of long-necked beer bottles fell on her foot—she was wearing socks and sandals. Two months later, she contacted Berry's and complained of her injury. She then sued for $2.5 million. According to her claim, Annette suffers from a rare nerve disorder that leaves her in constant pain. She walks on crutches, takes painkillers, and has trouble sleeping. Her doctors report that she is likely to suffer from RSD (reflexive sympathetic dystrophy) for the rest of her life. She consulted eleven different doctors, including podiatrists, neurologists, anesthesiologists, an orthopedic surgeon, and a psychiatrist. What is the proper amount of damages?

The jury returned a verdict to Blenker of $388,000 for past and future economic damages and $87,000 for her pain and suffering. Jurors found no negligence in stacking the beer, but found that the store employees failed to preserve an in-house videotape of the incident and that the store neglected to have a written policy on how to handle injured customers. The owner of Berry's Market was "shocked" at the verdict and cites it as an example of "lawsuit abuse" and the need for "tort reform." His expert witness testified that Blenker's pain may be psychosomatic (bodily symptoms caused by mental or emotional disturbance).

In certain cases, a plaintiff may recover special and general damages for personal loss suffered as the result of harm done by the defendant to a third party, such as a spouse or child. For example, a spouse may recover for loss of **consortium** with the injured or deceased mate. *Consortium* includes companionship, affection, and sexual relations. Damages for consortium have not been recoverable by unmarried persons, regardless of the intimacy or duration of the relationship.

consortium
The reciprocal legal right of companionship, cooperation, aid, affection, and sexual relations of each spouse from and to the other.

In early common law, if a victim died because of someone's tort, the death ended all claims for damages. Today, however, **wrongful-death statutes** allow compensation for immediate dependent relatives for loss of companionship and financial support resulting from the death. The award may be as high as millions of dollars, such as when the victim is a highly paid executive who leaves a surviving dependent spouse and children. On the other hand, the death of a single person with no children or other dependents could result in no cause of action. Some states, however, have **survivor statutes** that provide that a decedent's cause of action survives the death. It is owned by the decedent's estate, rather than by the surviving dependents (if any). Damages recovered by the estate then are distributed in accordance with the decedent's last will or by intestate distribution (see Chapter 14).

wrongful-death statutes
A law allowing the heirs of a deceased person to sue whoever caused the decedent's death and to collect any court-awarded damages. The damage sued for is the damage to the heirs for the loss of the loved one's life.

survivor statutes
Law allowing a lawsuit even after the death of the victim perhaps permitting recovery for damages to the victim.

Punitive Damages

In certain cases, the civil law resembles the criminal law as sanctions are imposed. Damage awards can punish especially blameworthy wrongdoers who intentionally hurt other persons. It does this through **punitive damages** (also called *exemplary damages*) awarded to the victim, in addition to compensatory damages. The avowed purpose is not to enrich the plaintiff, who already has been compensated fully for his or her loss or injury; rather, the award is to punish and make an example to deter a wrongdoer and others from a repetition of the offense.

punitive damages
Amount awarded by a court, to the victim of an intentional tort, in addition to compensatory damages; designed to punish the tortfeasor and serve as an example to others.

Punitive damages are not awarded in breach-of-contract cases, unless they also involve an intentional tort by the defendant, such as fraud or bad faith. They are awarded

> *where the wrong done ... was aggravated by circumstances of violence, oppression, malice, fraud, or wanton and wicked conduct ... and are intended to solace the plaintiff for mental anguish, laceration of his feelings, shame, degradation, or other aggravations of the original wrong, or else to punish the defendant for his evil behavior, or to make an example of him.*

Generally, punitive damages are available in cases of intentional tort, such as assault and battery, defamation, and fraud. They also may be awarded (1) in product-liability cases, but only those in which the defendant acted despicably with willful and conscious disregard of the rights and safety of others; (2) in premises-liability cases, in which a tenant of an apartment building is the victim of criminal attack when the landlord knew of the danger of such attacks yet failed to take corrective action (e.g., by excluding unauthorized persons or preventing their access); and (3) in cases in which the defendant consumes alcohol to the point of intoxication when he or she plans to later operate a motor vehicle, and thereby harms another.

Punitive damages have been likened to fines imposed on convicted criminals. But critics point out that fines are always paid to the state, and thus benefit all of society. By the same logic, they say, punitive damages should be paid to the state, for the benefit of all. At the time of this writing, a number of states take a portion of punitive damages awarded in civil cases. Constitutional challenges to this scheme have been upheld by the U.S. Supreme Court. Most states, however, do not take any portion of the civil recovery. In a case involving a gold scam in Texas, the trial court judge approved an award of $75 million in compensatory damages and $100 million in punitive damages to the three victims. Although affirming the result on appeal, one justice of the Texas Supreme Court made the following observation:

> *I write separately to recommend that the Legislature enact a law apportioning one-half of punitive damage awards to the State. Presently, plaintiffs receive the entire award of punitive damages in Texas. For example, in this case three plaintiffs will share $100 million in punitive damages even though they were fully compensated for their injuries when the trial court awarded them more than $31 million in actual damages and $43 million in attorneys fees. Yet, the primary purposes for awarding punitive damages are to punish a defendant for reprehensible behavior and to deter similar conduct in the future. [citations] Also, punitive damages are generally awarded in situations in which the defendant's conduct has damaged society as a whole as well as the individual plaintiff. [citations] Thus the goal in awarding punitive damages is not to compensate the victim. Actual damages perform that function. Nevertheless, our law creates a windfall for plaintiffs by allowing them to recover the entire award of punitive damages. I question whether this is a wise public policy.*

LEGAL FOCUS—EXAMPLE

Municipalities often raise capital to build public improvements by issuing (selling) bonds to investors. These bonds create debts for the municipality; investors are the creditors. Monthly interest is paid to the investors as their bonds are repaid. Banks, acting as trustees, offer the administrative service of receiving monthly bond payments and then distributing them to the rightful bond owners. Over the years, some payments on bonds are unclaimed by bond owners. Patrick Stull, manager of the corporate trust department for Bank of America, noticed that unclaimed bond payments were being taken by the bank instead of being returned to the municipalities. In 1995, after being discharged, Stull filed a "whistleblower" lawsuit alleging that his discharge was retaliatory. "Whistleblower" laws protect employees who "blow the whistle" on fraudulent or illegal activities. Stull was joined by defrauded bond issuers and the City of San Francisco who filed suit against Bank of America. The key issue in the case was whether or not Bank of America deliberately siphoned off the cash or simply could not keep its bookkeeping straight. Facing this issue, Bank of America, denying any wrongdoing other than poor bookkeeping practices, settled the case by payment of $187.5 million to the various plaintiffs. What role did punitive damages play in this settlement?

If a jury had believed that Bank of America, with its sophisticated computer systems and accounting staff, could not have made such an obvious and huge error, and therefore the bank was deliberately stealing money, it may have awarded punitive damages in an astronomical amount. The threat of punitive damages often influences the decision to settle. Generally, punitive damages may not be awarded in the absence of compensatory damages.

Judges or juries determine the proper amount of punitive damages by considering the nature and gravity of the offense as well as the defendant's ability to pay and the amount of compensatory damages awarded. Damage awards that are grossly inflated as a result of prejudice against large corporations, or passion, are typically substantially reduced or even rejected on appeal.

LEGAL FOCUS—PROBLEM

In a widely publicized case in 1989, a Los Angeles jury awarded the male lover of actor Rock Hudson $14.5 million in compensatory damages and $7.25 million in punitive damages, in an action against the estate of the deceased star. The jury found that Hudson, who died of AIDS, was guilty of conspiring with his personal secretary to keep the fatal affliction secret so that the plaintiff would continue his sexual relationship with the movie star. Is an award of damages justified?

Yes, the award is justified. However, the trial judge reduced the compensatory damages to $5 million and the punitive damages to $500,000, saying he would order a new trial on damages if the plaintiff refused to accept the reductions.

In 2007, the U.S. Supreme Court in a 5–4 opinion decided the case of *Philip Morris v. Williams*. The court majority opinion held that a $79.5 million punitive damage award amounted to a taking of property from the defendant Philip Morris without due process of law:

> *In our view, the Constitution's Due Process Clause forbids a State to use a punitive damages award to punish a defendant for injury that it inflicts upon nonparties or those whom they directly represent, i.e., injury that it inflicts upon those who are, essentially, strangers to the litigation.*

nominal damages Insignificant amount (such as $1) awarded by a court when the defendant has violated the rights of the plaintiff but no monetary loss has been suffered or can be proved.

Nominal Damages

A victim who has suffered no actual loss or injury may recover **nominal damages** (usually $1). The awarding of nominal damages recognizes a technical injury when there is no actual loss by the plaintiff. An example might be a "Peeping Tom" whose gaze caused no monetary loss to the plaintiff. Ordinarily, if there is not harm there is no tort, but if the conduct is particularly wrongful the victim's recovery of nominal damages will support an added award of punitive damages.

LEGAL FOCUS—EXAMPLE

The Critic's Last Word

As an example of nominal damages, we offer a rather notorious case (at the time) involving American painter James Abbott McNeill Whistler known by even the art challenged for his portrait "Whistler's Mother." In 1877, British art critic John Ruskin published a letter about an exhibition of Whistler's work at London's Grosvenor Gallery.

> For Mr. Whistler's own sake, no less than for the protection of the purchaser, Sir Coutts Lindsay ought not to have admitted works into the gallery in which the ill-educated conceit of the artist so nearly approached the aspect of willful imposture. I have seen, and heard, much of cockney impudence before now; but never expected a cox-comb to ask two hundred guineas for flinging a pot of paint in the public's face.

Whistler sued Ruskin claiming the injury to his reputation was libel. The case was heard at the Old Bailey and the good news for Whistler is that he won. The bad news is that he learned about nominal damages the hard way; as his reward was one farthing (old British coin valued at one-quarter of a penny). To add insult to recovery, he was required to pay his own court costs.

WHAT BARRIERS CAN PREVENT COLLECTION OF DAMAGES?

A person with a good cause of action may fail recovery if (1) litigation is not commenced promptly, and thus the victim is barred from suing by an applicable statute of limitations or (2) a judgment is obtained from a judgment-proof defendant.

Statutes of Limitation

Statutes of limitation "wipe the slate clean" for a wrongdoer after specified periods of time have elapsed without the filing of a lawsuit by the victim. These statutes specify the period of time during which the victim must formally initiate an action for legal relief, or, in the case of a crime, during which the government must prosecute the accused. (Chapter 6 more fully discusses statutes of limitations for crimes.)

It is strategically counterproductive and ethically questionable to keep a potential civil lawsuit or criminal indictment hovering over a wrongdoer indefinitely. It discourages personal reform and tends to limit the individual's peace of mind as well as his or her social and economic productivity.

Statutes of limitation are designed to prescribe reasonable periods of time during which civil claims for damages may be filed. Normally, persons become aware of the breach or injury within the specified time and are expected to sue for damages within that time. With the passage of time, evidence is lost, memories fade, witnesses move away or die, and it becomes very difficult, if not impossible, for a court to determine "the whole truth."

In most jurisdictions, an action to recover damages for a tort injury must be commenced within one year from the date of commission of the negligent tort. The period is generally the same for intentional torts, except for fraud. The defrauded victim may not be aware of the injury until much later, and so the time limit is usually three years from time of discovery of the fraud. Generally, in medical and legal malpractice actions, the statutory time does not begin to run until the plaintiff becomes aware of the injury suffered. Statutes of limitation are tolled and "the clock stops" while the defendant is out of the jurisdiction and during a plaintiff's minority. Recall the earlier discussion of statutes of repose: Even though repose statutes are usually for a longer period of time, they begin to run as soon as the negligence occurs, and thus they often will terminate a right to sue earlier than a shorter statute of limitations will.

In certain types of cases, the doctrine of strict liability effectively supersedes traditional statutes of limitation, allowing a suit for damages many years after the allegedly defective product was sold. This is permitted even if the product, when sold, had been manufactured conscientiously and was of acceptable quality as measured by the state of the art at the time. Because lawsuits are now being filed under principles of strict liability well beyond the statutory periods of limitation, substantial damages awarded to plaintiffs have been affecting the price and availability of domestic products. There is a considerable political movement favoring "tort reform" that focuses on elimination of stale cases, punitive damage limitations, and other issues.

It is noteworthy that the statutory time limit for breach of contract (see Chapter 8) is typically two years for oral contracts and four years for written contracts and credit accounts. With crimes (see Chapter 6), the statutory periods of limitation reflect the gravity of the offenses. For felonies, three years from the date of commission is typical; for misdemeanors, one year. For murder, there is no time limit.

Judgment-Proof Defendants

judgment-proof
Financial condition of a person who lacks the assets to pay any judgment rendered against him or her.

Another barrier to collection of damages is that, even if found liable, the defendant may be **judgment-proof**, that is, without sufficient liability insurance (if any) or other resources to pay. Under state laws, however, a judgment survives for years, perhaps ten years on average, and may be renewed or extended for a like period. Meanwhile, the judgment continues to grow from the effect of accruing interest, typically at 10 percent. Earnings made and other assets acquired by the debtor (e.g., through gifts or by inheritance) during the life of the judgment may be levied on by the unsatisfied judgment creditor. A *levy* is a process whereby a court official confiscates assets of a judgment debtor to satisfy the judgment. The creditor must first locate the debtor and identify the property to be confiscated—an easier task now that computer-assisted asset-search services are readily available. Nonetheless, socially irresponsible debtors often "skip," sometimes leaving the city, state, or country and providing no forwarding address. The difficulty the Federal Bureau of Investigation has in tracking down most-wanted criminals suggests the cost and practical impossibility of locating and collecting money from a determined skip. Winning a money judgment in court, unfortunately, is not an assurance the winner will collect.

CASE

Randi W. v. Muroc Joint Unified School District

14 Cal.4th 1071, 60 Cal.Rptr.2d 263 (Calif., 1997).

Robert Gadams sought assistance from his placement office at Fresno Pacific College, where he had received his teaching credentials. Former employers were asked to provide references.

One former employer, Mendota School District, provided a letter of recommendation prepared by an official, Gilbert Rosette. Rosette's recommendation to Fresno Pacific College's placement office noted Gadams's "genuine concern" for students and his "outstanding rapport" with everyone, and concluded "I wouldn't hesitate to recommend Mr. Gadams for any position." Rosette allegedly knew, but did not mention, Gadams's history of improper contacts with female students. The contacts included hugging some female junior high school students, giving them back massages, making "sexual remarks" to them, and being involved in "sexual situations" with them.

Another former employer, Tranquility High School District, provided a letter of recommendation prepared by an official there, Richard Cole. Cole's recommendation to Fresno Pacific College's placement office was positive, but he did not mention information he allegedly possessed about Gadams while he was employed at Golden Plains Unified School District. Specifically, Cole knew that Gadams had been the subject of various parents' complaints, including charges that he "led a panty raid, made sexual overtures to students, sexual remarks to students." Nonetheless, Cole recommended Gadams for "almost any administrative position that he wishes to pursue."

Yet another former employer, Muroc Unified School District, provided a letter of recommendation prepared by an official there, David Malcolm. Malcolm's recommendation to Fresno Pacific College's placement office was positive. Malcolm described Gadams as an "upbeat, enthusiastic administrator who relates well to the students" and recommended him for "an assistant principalship … without reservation." Malcolm allegedly knew that during Gadams's employment, disciplinary actions were taken against him for "sexual touching" of female students that caused him to resign.

Robert Gadams then was hired by Livingston Union School District as vice principal. Randi W., age thirteen, a student at Livingston Middle School, was in Gadams's office when he offensively "touched, molested, and engaged in sexual touching" of her.

Randi W. brought suit against the school districts that recommended Gadams for employment on the theory, among others, that they were negligent for failing to disclose negative background information in their letters of recommendation to the placement office that provided them to her school's district.

The trial court dismissed the negligence aspect of Randi's action on the basis that the recommending school districts did not owe any duty to protect Randi because their recommendations were made only to a placement office.

Associate Justice Chin Delivered the Opinion of the Court

[N]o California case has yet held that one who intentionally or negligently provides false information to another owes a duty of *care to a third person* who did not receive the information and who has no special relationship with the provider.…

Although the chain of causation leading from defendants' statements and omissions to Gadams's alleged assault on plaintiff is somewhat attenuated, we think the assault was reasonably foreseeable … [D]efendants could foresee that Livingston's officers would read and rely on defendants' letters in deciding to hire Gadams. Likewise, defendants could foresee that, had they not unqualifiedly recommended Gadams, Livingston would not have hired him. And finally, defendants could foresee that Gadams, after being hired by Livingston, might molest or injure a Livingston student such as [Randi W.]….

As for public policy, the law certainly recognizes *a policy of preventing future harm* of the kind alleged here. One of society's highest priorities is to protect children from sexual or physical abuse. [citations] Defendants urge that *competing social or economic policies* may disfavor the imposition of liability for misrepresentation or nondisclosure in employment references. They observe that a rule imposing liability in these situations could greatly inhibit the preparation and distribution of reference letters, to the general detriment of employers and employees alike. We have recently stated that "when deciding whether to expand a tort duty of care, courts must consider the potential social and economic consequences." [citations] Defendants argue that a rule imposing tort liability on writers of recommendation letters could have one very predictable consequence: Employers would seldom write such letters, even in praise of exceptionally qualified employees. In defendants' view, … an employer would be better advised … merely to confirm the former employee's position, salary, and dates of employment.

In response, plaintiff asserts it is unlikely that employers will decline to write reference letters for fear of tort liability, at least in situations involving no foreseeable risks of physical injury to someone.

… [W]e hold … that that the writer of a letter of recommendation owes to third persons a duty not to misrepresent the facts in describing the qualifications and character of a former employee, if making these misrepresentations would present a substantial, foreseeable risk of physical injury to the third persons.

Note: The case was returned to the Superior Court for trial by jury. The decision of the justices was split 4–3 on other issues in the case, but all agreed upon the portion quoted above in which new tort law was created.

For Critical Analysis

1. Suppose an employer knew that an ex-employee had an arrest record of assault and battery that grew from a bar fight. Must the employer reveal that information every time a prospective employer asks for references? Or must only sexual offenses be reported? Would the complete withholding of such information violate the duty "not to misrepresent the facts"? Isn't failure to reveal some fact as damaging as actually misrepresenting it?
2. Would the former employers in the *Randi W.* case have escaped liability if they had reported only the dates of Robert Gadams's employment? Or, to escape liability, must they reveal whatever sordid details they possess to future employers? What if the information the former employers passed on was only rumor and unsubstantiated reports—could Gadams sue them for libel?
3. If the former employers reported the unsubstantiated information they possessed to all future prospective employers of Gadams, whether schools or any other businesses, would anybody employ him? Is it fair to warn only prospective employers who ask for references, and not others who accept prospective employees at their word? If your answer is "no," would you recommend publishing the names of such persons in some database available to all future employers?

Reider v. Louisiana

897 So.2d 893, 2005 WL 545142 (La., 2005)

Heather Reider was struck in her right eye by an errant foul ball as she approached the main entrance ticket booth along the third base line of McNeese State University's baseball field. The impact caused a complete fracture and implosion of the zygomatic structure of her right eye, laceration of the inner part of her right eyelid, and permanent macular blindness resulting in permanent 10/200 vision in her right eye. Ms. Reider sued McNeese for her personal injury. The district court entered judgment upon jury verdict in favor of Reider. The university appealed, raising the following issues: (1) whether the jury correctly found an unreasonably dangerous condition existed at its baseball park; (2) whether the jury correctly found McNeese had prior knowledge of said unreasonably dangerous defect; … and (5) whether the jury abused its discretion and incorrectly awarded general and special damages to plaintiff.

Circuit Judge McKay

The matter proceeded to trial by jury …, with the jury awarding damages as follows:

Past and present pain, suffering, physical and mental anguish	$ 75,000
Future pain, suffering, physical and mental anguish	25,000
Loss of enjoyment of life	200,000
Permanent disability	100,000
Medical expenses, past and future	85,000
Total	$485,000

… [T]he issue to be resolved by a reviewing court is not whether the trier of fact was right or wrong, but whether the factfinder's conclusion was a reasonable one.

After a thorough review of the voluminous record, we find that there was sufficient proof for reasonable persons to resolve the liability question in favor of the Plaintiff and in accordance with the substantive law.

The standard of care owed by McNeese to patrons of its baseball park is found in La.R.S. 9:2800. Under this statute, to carry her burden, Plaintiff must show: (1) the baseball field was in the care, custody and control of the Defendant; (2) the baseball park had a vice or defect which created an unreasonable risk of harm; (3) Plaintiff's injury was caused by the defect; and (4) the Defendant had actual or constructive knowledge of the dangerous condition.

There is no dispute that the baseball field was in the care, custody, and control of the Defendant; however, Defendant argues that an unreasonable condition did not exist at the McNeese State University baseball park, and if one did, they had no prior knowledge of said unreasonably dangerous defect. McNeese argues that the Plaintiff was an experienced softball player herself and, therefore, was sufficiently aware of the dangers involved in attending such a sporting event. McNeese further argues that in twelve years since the construction of the baseball park, an accident of this nature has never occurred, thus, even if a dangerous condition existed, they had no prior knowledge of the defect.

Plaintiff contends that regardless of the dangers assumed by attending this sporting event, she had not yet entered the field and had not yet assumed any risk associated therein. Plaintiff further contends that in order to enter the baseball park she had to purchase the ticket by walking to the ticket booth through a dangerous area known by the Defendant to be susceptible to foul balls down the third base line.

Plaintiff testified she could not see the field of play. At the time she was struck, Plaintiff was not yet inside the baseball park, but was approaching the main entrance preparing to present her student identification card to the ticket booth operator.

The Director of Facilities and Planning Operations for McNeese State University, Mr. Richard Rhoden, testified that he was in charge of the design and construction of the McNeese baseball field during the relevant time period. Mr. Rhoden, a defense witness, admitted in his testimony on direct examination that he knew the entranceway to the baseball field was likely to be struck by errant foul balls. Mr. Rhoden admitted that the ticket booth was purposely designed with extra wide eaves in order to protect its windows from being hit by foul balls. When Mr. Rhoden was asked by Plaintiff's counsel on cross examination if his design of the ticket booth with extra wide eaves meant he recognized the possibility that foul balls would be hit in the immediate area of the ticket booth, Mr. Rhoden stated, "[w]e knew that there's a possibility of foul balls, yes, sir." Thus, Defendant cannot successfully argue it did not have notice of the defect when it specifically constructed extra wide eaves on the ticket booth to protect against errant foul balls. Defendant chose to protect the building but not the patrons.

Defendant's liability expert, Mr. Gene Moody, testified that a wooden, decorative fence constructed along the third base line in September of 1996, only seven months prior to this accident, completely obscured the view of the playing field from patron's entering at the main entrance. McNeese built the wooden decorative fence at a cost of $19,400.00. Plaintiff's liability expert, Dr. Leonard Lucienko, testified that a protective fence from ten feet to fifteen feet high along the entrance walkway would cost between $4,500.00 to $13,500.00. When asked by Plaintiff's counsel if he agreed that the construction of a protective fence as proposed by Dr. Lucienko would provide protection to patrons entering the park, Mr. Moody admitted, "[y]es … if they stayed under the overhang of the fence up close to it, then that would be a protection from fly balls—foul balls." The burden of prevention is slight and the gravity of the harm is great. There will be foul balls as long as there are baseball games. Ballpark owners cannot be held legally responsible for every foul ball in common areas of the ball park. But, there are certain areas of a ballpark where protection is required. Obviously, the area behind home plate must be protected from anticipated foul balls. The area where people gather to purchase food and drink or go to the restroom should be protected. Another such area would be the main entrance ticket booth where people must go to purchase a ticket to enter the ballpark to see the game. There is an unreasonable risk of harm, and an unreasonably dangerous condition, when patrons have to purchase their ticket at the main entrance ticket booth of the ballpark along the third base line where one knows or should know, and can reasonably anticipate, numerous and errant foul balls. This is an area, like the concession area, restroom area, and the area behind home plate, where there should be a reasonable expectation of protection. In the case at bar, Plaintiff, an innocent

McNeese baseball fan outside the baseball park and in line to buy a ticket at the main entrance ticket booth, was unreasonably unprotected and struck by an errant foul ball down the third base line thereby sustaining a serious and permanent eye injury.

We are satisfied that the record contains a sufficient factual basis to support the jury's finding that the McNeese baseball park presented an unreasonably dangerous condition to patrons and that McNeese had notice of the existence of said defect. There was no manifest error and the jury was not clearly wrong.

Finally, McNeese argues the record does not support the jury's award of $85,000.00 for Plaintiff's past and future medical expenses, and $400,000.00 for her general damages. We disagree.

In appellate review of general damage awards, the court must accord much discretion to the trial court judge or jury. The role of an appellate court in reviewing awards of general damages is not to decide what it considers to be an appropriate award, but rather to review the exercise of discretion by the trial court. Only if the reviewing court determines that the trial court has abused its "much discretion" may it refer to prior awards in similar cases and then only to determine the highest or lowest point of an award within that discretion.

Because discretion vested in the trial court is "great," and even vast, an appellate court should rarely disturb an award of general damages. Reasonable persons frequently disagree about the measure of general damages in a particular case. It is only when the award is, *in either direction,* beyond that which a reasonable trier of fact could assess for the effects of the particular injury to the particular plaintiff under the particular circumstances that the appellate court should increase or reduce the award. (Citations omitted.)

Dr. Samuel Stahl testified that the Plaintiff suffered a "very painful" injury from a "zygomatic complex fracture that involved the connection of the facial bones to the skull" and "fairly extensive wide fractures of her nasal bones." Dr. James Patrinely testified that the Plaintiff suffered "a high degree of pain" from multiple fractures of her facial bones, a rupture of the eye itself, and a torn eyelid. Dr. Patrinely also testified there is a likelihood that the Plaintiff will develop complications in the future, such as, serious sinus infection, sagging of the eye socket, and post-traumatic fibrosis around the reconstructed tear duct. Finally, Dr. Patrinely also testified that should Plaintiff develop a serious sinus infection, surgery may be required to remove the implant placed in the orbit of her eye socket. If such a surgery is required, such a procedure would cost from $7,000.00 to $15,000.00.

Dr. Michael Lambert testified as to the risk of injury to the Plaintiff's left eye. Dr. Lambert testified that the Plaintiff runs a greater risk of injury to her left eye, and that she may develop recession glaucoma. Should she develop recession glaucoma, the estimated cost of an operation is approximately $10,000.00. We find no manifest error and the jury was not clearly wrong in its general and special damage award to Plaintiff.

For the foregoing reasons, the jury verdict is affirmed in its entirety. Costs of this appeal are assessed against the Defendant, the State of Louisiana through its Board of Trustees for State Colleges and Universities through McNeese State University. **AFFIRMED.**

For Critical Analysis

1. What tort theory did the plaintiff use to establish liability? What doctrine was applied to establish the duty owed by the university?
2. What defense is being argued by the university? What facts can the university use to support this defense? What facts are used by the plaintiff to counter the defense's claim? Who was successful?
3. The court provides a breakdown of the damages awarded by the jury in this case. Classify each damage award as either general or special damages. Explain how you made your characterizations. How would a plaintiff attempt to prove each type? Did the appellate court agree with the damage amounts? Is that the critical question posed to the court about damages?

CHAPTER QUESTIONS AND PROBLEMS

1. Sarah Gramling, an expert in the use of explosives, obtained a city permit to level a ten-story building in the center of town by implosion. The explosives were placed carefully throughout the structure so that it would collapse inwardly and leave a heap of rubble on the site. Unfortunately, for unknown reasons, one charge on the third floor caused fragments of brick, concrete, and glass to fly outward. As a result, extensive and costly damage was done to plate glass in nearby buildings and to parked automobiles in the vicinity. There were also personal injuries. Is Gramling liable, even though she acted with a city permit and there was no evidence or claim of negligence?
2. Assume a jury rules that John Forsyth was driving negligently and caused an automobile crash that injured the plaintiff.
   a. Does moral fault attach to Forsyth?
   b. Would your answer in (a) be different if John were uninsured and unable to pay the judgment? If your answer is yes, what is the fault—driving negligently or being uninsured?
   c. Assuming Forsyth had adequate insurance, what consequences does he personally suffer as a result of his negligence? Does the accident go into his permanent employment records? Into a national database of negligent drivers? Or can he conceal it in all of his future personal transactions?
   d. Can society reasonably expect Forsyth to become a more careful and accident-free driver following his first accident?
   e. Is the law of negligence more about social policy or more about providing for compensation to injured persons?
3. Nick Dekker went into the Black Oak Restaurant for dinner. When leaving, he mistakenly took George Walton's hat from the coat rack and walked out the door. Walton observed the incident, ran outside, and yelled "Stop thief!" just as Dekker was driving out of the parking lot. Walton jumped into his own car and gave pursuit. He overtook a car driven by a man who looked like Dekker, although it was really Ferdinand Sinzant. Walton pulled alongside and forced Sinzant onto the shoulder of the road by easing his car along the front left side of Sinzant's car. When the cars stopped, Walton leaped out and smashed Sinzant in the mouth, knocking him unconscious. He put Sinzant into his car and drove back to the restaurant, where he phoned the police. When the squad car arrived, Sinzant regained consciousness, and Walton said, "Arrest this man, he's a thief!" The police refused to make the arrest because they had not observed any crime. They advised Walton that if he made a citizen's arrest, they would book Sinzant. Walton thereupon placed Sinzant under arrest. Meanwhile, Harry Hightower was injured when his car ran into, and badly damaged, the left rear of Sinzant's car, which was protruding slightly into the street with its lights out. At the time of the accident, Hightower was under the influence of marijuana. What torts have occurred?
4. During a wild party on the Fourth of July, Harry Hammer went outside and fired his nine-millimeter pistol several times into the dark Los Angeles sky. Unfortunately, unlike the fabled arrow shot into the sky, Hammer's bullet descended, hitting and penetrating Penelope Marsh's head and causing her modest but permanent injuries. Following the incident, Marsh lacked enthusiasm, complained of headaches, and was frightened easily by loud noises. Hammer had homeowner's liability insurance that would cover his negligent acts and a good, permanent job paying him $8,000 a month. Would Hammer's insurance policy pay for Marsh's injuries? Could Marsh obtain punitive damages from Hammer?
5. Vera Babbitt, a mischievous prankster, called and told her friend Michelle Fleischer that Michelle's fiancé Gary Dunn was in a booth at the Hardball Sports Bar making out with an old girlfriend. Before Babbitt could explain that her message was a joke, Fleischer slammed down the telephone, jumped into her RV, and sped off to catch Dunn in the act. Unfortunately, Fleischer cut off another driver and caused an accident, seriously injuring Billie Bellweather. What tort liabilities have arisen and against whom?
6. Harriet Robicheaux made a batch of brownies and donated them to the Girl Scouts to be sold as part of a fundraiser. Unfortunately, several purchasers of the brownies became ill and died. Does the product-liability rule establish that Robicheaux is strictly liable for all injuries caused by the brownies?
7. Assume that a state enacted the following statute: "There shall be no recovery of damages based upon

the commission of ordinary negligence." What ramifications can you think of that might flow from this statute?

8. Johnson entered the defendant's store carrying her small child in an infant seat. When she tried to leave the store, she was stopped in a public place by a security officer who said that another employee had reported seeing her steal the infant seat. To show ownership, Johnson pointed to cat hair, food crumbs, and stains on the seat. After a twenty-minute delay, the security officer apologized to the defendant and permitted her to leave. The trial court dismissed her action for false imprisonment, and Johnson appealed. Did the defendant have probable cause to detain Johnson, and was the twenty-minute detention of Johnson reasonable in these circumstances? [*Johnson v. K-Mart Enterprises, Inc.*, 98 Wis.2d 533, 297 N.W.2d 74 (Wisconsin, 1980).]
9. Peter Wallis, a real estate broker, contends that before having sex, his girlfriend Kellie Clarke represented that she would use birth control pills. But Clarke purposefully got pregnant, according to Wallis. He is suing Clarke for fraud and for conversion (civil theft) for wrongfully acquiring and misusing his sperm. Clarke contends that she was using birth control pills and that his sperm given during sexual intercourse was not stolen or misused and should be considered a "gift" in the law. Clarke refused to obtain an abortion, moved out of their apartment, and gave birth to their daughter, Taylor. Has Clarke converted Wallis's sperm? Assuming that Wallis is correct in his contentions, what legal damages has he sustained?
10. The Carters traveled to a concert at the Birmingham Civic Center and checked into the Birmingham Civic Center Travelodge. That afternoon, they purchased fast food and went back to their room to eat, relax, and enjoy a romantic interlude away from home. The wall on one side of the room was covered by a mirror. Concerned about noises (not theirs) while they were enjoying the room, the Carters investigated and discovered a large hole in the wall behind the mirror. It would be possible for someone to look into their room from the adjoining room. Without specific proof that anyone observed the Carters, could they recover for invasion of privacy? [*Carter v. Innisfree Hotel, Inc.*, 661 So.2d 1174 (Ala.,1995).]
11. Wanda Birdsong went shopping at the Hopkinsville, Kentucky, Wal-Mart. She bought some items and began to exit the store along with several other customers. A theft control device set off a sensor alarm. A Wal-Mart employee asked all the customers to reenter the store and, after inspecting their bags, she asked them to walk through the sensor alarm one at a time. The only one who triggered the sensor alarm a second time was Birdsong. After a second search, Birdsong was asked to pass through the alarm a third time. Again the alarm was activated. Birdsong claims that the Wal-Mart employee then told her to sit down and stay at an area near the front door entrance where a shopping cart was placed to block her from leaving. A supervisor then determined that Birdsong's purse was tripping the alarm, whereupon Birdsong volunteered to let them search the purse. The Wal-Mart employees declined, saying they were not allowed to do so. Birdsong claims she was detained another fifteen minutes until the store manager arrived and told her she was free to go. Birdsong claims that she was detained a total of forty-five minutes and that she was humiliated by her placement at the front of the store. Wal-Mart claims her detention lasted no more than thirty minutes and was conducted reasonably. Would the shopkeeper's privilege protect Wal-Mart from Birdsong's false imprisonment and intentional infliction of emotional distress lawsuit? [*Birdsong v. Wal-Mart Stores, Inc.*, 74 S.W.3d 754 (Ky. App., 2001).]
12. Identify the tort that corresponds to each of the following crimes:
    a. Date rape
    b. Robbery
    c. Murder
    d. Manslaughter by vehicle
    e. Physical child abuse by a parent
    f. Burglary
    g. Shoplifting a dress
    h. Crawling over a backyard fence and peeping through a bedroom window
    i. Posting a naked picture of a former lover on the Internet
    j. Practicing medicine without a license
13. Mary Lou Miller underwent successful surgery to remove kidney stones and repair a malformed right kidney. A Penrose drain (a piece of soft tubing to drain off fluid) was placed to facilitate postoperative healing. A few days later the drain purportedly was removed. During the postsurgery follow-up, Miller reported pain in her right flank and abdomen. A diagnostic imaging report showed there was "radiopaque material in the soft tissues adjacent to the … right kidney." Part of the

Penrose drain remained. Is this an appropriate case for the doctrine of *res ipsa loquitur.* [*Miller v. Jacoby,* 145 Wash.2d 65, 33 P.3d 68 (Wash., 2001).]

14. Tort claims survive the death of the tortfeasor, and the damages are payable from the wrongdoer's estate. Assume a wrongdoer commits a tort that meets the requirements for punitive damages, but before a lawsuit is brought or concluded, the wrongdoer dies. Could the plaintiff recover punitive damages against the estate? Consider the rationale for punitive damages when answering the question. What if the lawsuit was completed but uncollected and the tortfeasor dies? Would that make any difference?

CHAPTER 8

Contracts: Enforceable Agreements

If, on tracing the right to contract, and the obligations created by contract, to their source, we find them to exist anterior to, and independent of society, we may reasonably conclude that those original and pre-existing principles are, like many other natural rights, brought with man into society; and, although they may be controlled, are not given by human legislation.

Chief Justice John Marshall, *Ogden v. Saunders*, 25 U.S. 213, 251–52 (1827)

LEARNING OBJECTIVES

After reading and studying this chapter, you should be able to:

- Define a contract and distinguish a contract from a tort, a crime, and a nonlegally binding moral obligation.
- Appreciate the importance of legally binding obligations in the U.S. and world economy.
- Understand the importance of the Uniform Commercial Code in business transactions and especially Article 2 (sales), in commercial transactions.
- Identify and discuss the various elements necessary to form a contract, including competent parties, mutual agreement, consideration, genuine assent, legality, and proper form.
- Discuss contract rights of parties in privity and third parties.
- Identify important issues involving performance of contract obligations, including satisfactory performance, substantial performance, breach, and discharge.
- Identify contract remedies, including compensatory damages and equitable remedies.

Contracts make promises enforceable and allow reliance. The law of contracts reflects our social values (commitment), interests (consumerism), and expectations (keeping promises) regarding the enforcement of promises. When are promises or commitments between two or more persons legally binding? What excuses justify breaking a legal commitment? Are there promises that are contrary to public policy and, therefore, void or invalid? If a promise violates the interests of society at large, will courts enforce it? If a child or an incompetent person makes a promise, can it be enforced? Answering these and other related questions is what contract law is about.

Contracts allow parties to create greater certainty as to the predictability of future acts. The parties can create rights and duties upon which each might rely and each might perhaps enforce through the legal system. Contracts also help parties reach clear agreement on the acceptable standards of performance expected of each other and how each party is expected to behave in situations that might occur.

LEGAL FOCUS—PROBLEM

Joseph Yonan needs 3,000 pumpkins for his innercity pumpkin patch by late September to celebrate the Halloween season. He is acquainted with Paula Felps, a local farmer, who is interested in selling the pumpkins. How can Yonan increase the probability of getting the pumpkins he needs, when he needs them, and at a price he can afford?

A contract entered into with Felps in July for a September delivery of those pumpkins will increase the likelihood that Yonan will have the pumpkins when and where he needs them and at a price he can afford. Felps, on the other hand, no longer needs to worry about selling her "ripe" pumpkins. If Felps fails to make delivery, Yonan will have rights against her to correct his losses because of her failure to perform. The parties can arrange by the contract the responsible party for delivery, the expected grade and condition of the pumpkins upon arrival, the payment method, credit or cash, and on and on.

Contract law allows parties to make enforceable promises. If you think about it, you will realize that many promises that people make do not create legal obligations. Sometimes, the promises create moral, rather than legal, obligations. A moral obligation defines what you should do. Failure to perform a moral obligation, such as an agreement to give a friend a ride, usually does not create a legal liability. Sometimes promises create both a moral and a legal obligation (as when a friend promises to pay you for gas expenses to drive her to a neighboring city).

MORALS AND ETHICS

Rosalie Chu invited an acquaintance, Jonathan Kaplan, to a fund-raising dinner dance for a U.S. senator at an extravagant restaurant in the city. Kaplan accepted the offer and, eager to please Chu, spent $750 lavishly preparing for the evening. He got a haircut and purchased a new jacket, new shoes, and flowers. On the evening of the dance, Kaplan arrived at Chu's house and found out that she had gone out of town for the weekend. Kaplan is considering suing Chu for breach of contract to recover his expenses. Does he have a lawsuit?

Agreements to go on dates are not contracts; they are social arrangements. Although Chu may have breached a moral obligation, she is not required to pay Kaplan's expenses even though she did not keep the date. We will see later that such moral obligations sometimes can be enforced through means other than contract law.

contract
A legally enforceable agreement to do or not to do a specified thing.

One short, snappy definition of a **contract** is "an agreement that can be enforced in a court." The definition is accurate and easy to remember but not especially helpful. The authoritative *Restatement of Contracts* expands the definition of a contract to say it is a promise or a set of promises for the breach of which the law gives a remedy, or the performance of which the law in some way recognizes as a duty. Contracts are the intelligent response to the human need to get things done with the cooperation of other human beings. The U.S. Constitution expressly provides that "no State shall … pass any … Law impairing the Obligation of Contracts."*

Ordinarily, a contract is made when two (and sometimes more than two) parties exchange binding promises. In a promise, each party declares that he will (or will not) take a specified action in the future.

If the contractual promise is not performed, the contract has been breached, and the party who failed to keep the promise must compensate the party to whom the promise was made. The nonperforming party usually is required to pay money damages for failure to perform. In some situations, money damages cannot make the victim of the failure to perform "whole," and so a court of equity may require actual performance of the promised act. In either case, the law seeks to give the party the benefit of the promise that was made. Understandably, punitive damages are not awarded; there is no crime and no tort, and generally no moral stigma attaches to the breach of contract. When a contractual promise is breached, in the vast majority of cases, the parties agree to some acceptable alternative without litigation and the payment of damages.

promisor
The person who makes a contractual promise.

promisee
The person to whom a contractual promise is made.

Most people keep promises because of a sense of duty. Furthermore, keeping their promises is usually in the self-interest of both parties. Often, the **promisor** (the person making the promise) and the **promisee** (the person to whom the promise is made) are not aware of the rules of contract law. They may rely on the good faith—the honesty and fairness—of the other persons who are involved. In business situations, however, parties should follow the rules of contract law carefully to avoid potential misunderstandings and disputes.

Contracts generally are entered into privately, between private parties. Government agencies—local and federal—are not involved directly unless the government is a party to the contract. Of course, this happens often in our time of big government. Collectively, government is the nation's biggest employer, always under contract. It is the biggest buyer of goods and services, all under contract. It is also true that government statutes and court decisions prescribe the rules for creation, performance, and enforcement of contracts. Private contracts stay private unless one of the private parties must use the court system to enforce the contract.

What Is the Uniform Commercial Code?

Elements of contract law vary from state to state and among major types of business enterprise. Many contracts are based on the common law, notably personal service agreements. Specialized statutes affect contract rights and obligations in security markets (for

*U.S. Constitution, Art. I, §10. In the famous *Dartmouth College* case, the first chief justice of the U.S. Supreme Court, John Marshall, held that a charter of incorporation granted by King George III to Dartmouth College in 1769, which gave its trustees the right to govern the college forever, was indeed a contract. As such, it could not be rescinded, as was attempted by the New Hampshire state legislature, which had voted to transfer control of the college to a new board of overseers. *Dartmouth College v. Woodward*, 4 Wheaton 518 (1819).

goods
Tangible, movable personal property.

Uniform Commercial Code
A uniform code drafted by the National Conference of Commissioners of Uniform State Laws governing the conduct of business, sales, warranties, and other commercial matters.

sale
A contract in which title (ownership) of property passes from seller to buyer. Possession usually transfers at the time of sale.

stocks and bonds), corporate financial transactions, and real estate dealings. Many contracts involve the sale or purchase of **goods** (i.e., all movable personal properly that consists of things—other than money and securities), and these contracts are governed by the **Uniform Commercial Code (UCC)**.*

In the twentieth century, a movement began to create various "uniform" acts or codes to make laws more consistent throughout the fifty states. The most pervasive and thus most significant uniform code is the UCC, which has been adopted, at least in part, by all fifty states as part of their statutory law. Although the UCC is uniform throughout the United States, it is not a federal law; state legislatures passed this proposed model act a part of their states' statutory law. Because the UCC does not attempt to answer every contract question, generally accepted common law rules still provide answers to most contract questions.

An important thing to know about any investigation of commercial law is whether or not the UCC governs a contract. Article 2 (Sales) is the most important part of the UCC for our discussion of contracts. Article 2 defines the rights and duties of contracting parties if the subject matter of the contract is a sale of goods. A **sale** is a transfer of ownership of goods in exchange for a price. Nonsale transfers of personal properly, leases, are covered in Article 2A of the UCC.

Also important to note is the emergence of expanded world markets and the law related to international sales transactions. The United Nations Convention on Contracts for the Sale of Goods became part of the law of the United States in 1988. More than two-thirds of the world's countries have adopted this convention. The convention applies to sales concluded by citizens of any two of the signatories, and it deviates from the UCC in some details. For example, unlike the UCC, the convention provides that any sales contract may be oral, whereas under the UCC, contracts for the sale of goods in excess of $500 must be evidenced by a written document. The contracting parties, however, may opt out of all or any part of this United Nations law.

HOW ARE CONTRACTS CLASSIFIED?

offeror
In contracts, the party who makes an offer.

offeree
In contracts, the party to whom an offer is made by the offeror.

Generally, just two parties are involved in a given contract, but there may be multiple parties when appropriate. One person (and a "person" could be a corporation or partnership), the **offeror**, makes an offer to a second person, termed the **offeree**. The offeree then may respond to the offer with an acceptance. In effect, each party promises to do (or in some cases, promises *not* to do) something the other party wants to have done (or not have done). Generally, no special words need be used. Often, there is preliminary negotiation or bargaining. With a few exceptions (discussed later in this chapter), the contract may be oral, written, or implied from conduct or from some custom or usage of the particular trade; the agreement also may result from a combination of these methods of expression. Contracts may be classified as to method of expression, parties bound, legal effect, and extent of performance. A summary of these classifications is represented in Exhibit 8.1.

*The UCC, as amended, replaced seven other "uniform" acts and a variety of other legislative acts governing commercial activities. Currently, the following articles constitute the bulk of the official text: (1) General Provisions; (2) Sales; (2.A) Leases; (3) Commercial Paper; (4) Bank Deposits and Collections; (4.A) Funds Transfer; (5) Letters of Credit; (6) Bulk Transfers–Bulk Sales; (7) Warehouse Receipts, Bills of Lading, and Other Documents of Title; (8) Investment Securities; (9) Secured Transactions.

EXHIBIT 8.1
How Are Contracts Classified?

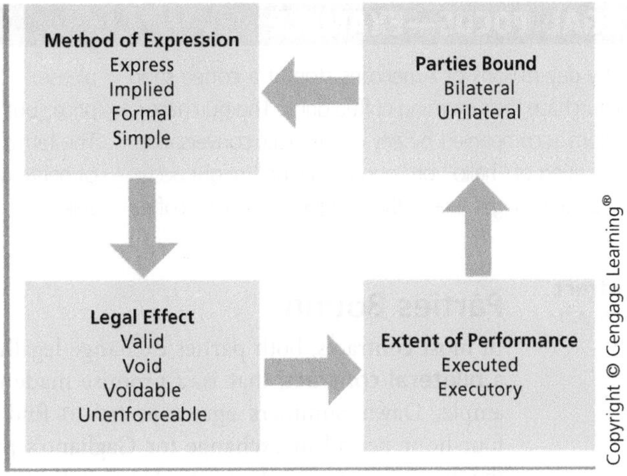

express contract
An agreement stated in words, spoken, or written.

implied in fact contract
Contractual agreement manifested by conduct or body language (e.g., purchase of items from vendors in noisy stadiums during sporting events).

quasi contract
Not a true contract, but an obligation imposed on one party to prevent unjust enrichment of another. Also called "implied in law contract."

formal contract
Agreement that must use prescribed language or be in prescribed form.

Method of Expression

Contracts are **express** when made in words spoken or written, and are **implied in fact**, when manifested in conduct or body language (e.g., an arm waved at a vendor in a stadium during a football game followed by the toss of money and a return toss of a bag of roasted peanuts). Contracts seldom are simply express or implied but combine express and implied terms.

Sometimes, the law will imply and enforce an obligation even when there is no true agreement, either express or implied, between the parties. Such an obligation is called a **quasi contract**. The law creates a quasi contract when, under the circumstances, there would be unjust enrichment of one person unless she was required to pay value for a benefit received from someone else. The law provides that recovery in court is the reasonable value of the benefit received. Thus, a person may be required to perform as though a contract exists, even though no promise was made and no intent to be bound was manifested. A fairly common example of how a quasi contract may come into being follows.

LEGAL FOCUS—EXAMPLE

A surgeon stops her car at the scene of an automobile collision. She gives needed emergency aid to an unconscious victim at the accident. There was no agreement, yet the doctor has a legitimate claim in quasi contract for the reasonable value of her services. In contrast, a passerby with some knowledge of first aid performing similar services is not entitled to any payment. Such an act would be that of a helpful volunteer, not of a professional who customarily is paid for such services.

simple contract
All oral and written contracts not classified as formal contracts.

Generally, the parties to an express contract or an implied in fact contract can use any language they please. In some cases, however, statutes prescribe the terms and exact language. Examples are negotiable instruments such as bank checks and promissory notes. These special types of contracts are called **formal contracts**; all other types of contracts are called **simple contracts**, whether they are oral or written.

LEGAL FOCUS—EXAMPLE

Every day millions of Americans stop at a coffee shop to purchase their morning coffee drink. The purchase is seldom accompanied by any commercial conversation. A greeting of "hello" or "good morning" might occur. Purchasers might state their request, "Large coffee please." There might not even be a mention of the price, but clearly a contract for the purchase occurs. The terms are implied through conduct and a pattern of behavior between the coffee drinker and the coffee seller.

bilateral contract Agreement in which both parties exchange binding promises.

unilateral contract A contract in which the promisor seeks performance of a requested act. Upon performance of the act, the contract is formed and the promisor is obligated to fulfill the promise.

Parties Bound

In most contracts, both parties exchange legally binding promises. Such an agreement is a **bilateral contract**, that is, a promise made in exchange for another promise. For example, Dawn Summers agrees to try to find Angie Gagliano's dog during a twenty-four-hour period in exchange for Gagliano's promise to pay $50. If Summers looks for the dog as promised, she is entitled to collect the $50 whether or not she succeeds in her search.

Note that at the time the contract is created neither party has performed the promise they made to the other. In contrast, in an offer for a **unilateral contract** one party makes a promise or offer to induce some completed act by another party. For example, Brandon Tore promises to pay $50 to anyone who will find and return his dog, dead or alive. No one is legally obliged to join in the search, nor is Tore obliged to pay unless the requested act is done and the dog is returned.

LEGAL FOCUS—EXAMPLE

In May 1927, Charles A. ("Lucky") Lindbergh became the first person to fly across the Atlantic Ocean solo and nonstop from New York to Paris, using a single-engine monoplane, *The Spirit of St. Louis*. Lindbergh was responding to a unilateral contract offer made by a St. Louis businessman to pay $25,000 to the first person(s) to perform the feat. After Lindbergh was aloft and on his way to Paris (a substantial effort to perform), the offer could not be revoked or canceled. Once the offeree clearly has started to perform, the law requires that the offeree have a reasonable time to complete the act, even though the offeree legally is not obliged to finish. Remember, this caveat only makes the offer irrevocable. The only way Lindberg actually can accept the offer is to complete the requested performance.

valid contract An agreement that complies with all requisites of the law for enforceability.

void agreement Without legal force or binding effect.

Legal Effect

If a contract complies with all essential elements (described in the next section), it is a **valid contract**. Sometimes, the attempt to create a contract may be totally ineffective, and so there is no contract; in such a case, there is a **void agreement**. An example is an agreement to commit a crime or a tort. Sometimes, an essential element of a valid contract is missing, and a party to the contract has the power to perform or withdraw without liability. Such contract is said to be **voidable**. For example, a minor (under age eighteen years) generally may invalidate or void a contract even if freely and intentionally made. A parent or guardian also may take such action on the minor's behalf.

Finally, some contracts are valid yet **unenforceable**. A proper contract claim for money or performance may have become stale and unenforceable because enforcement was not sought before the time provided under the statute of limitations had passed. For example, a creditor may have a right to be paid the balance due on a retail store credit account. The typical statute of limitations requires that such creditors sue within four

voidable contract
An agreement that may be legally enforced or may be rejected by a party. For example, a contract between a minor and an adult is voidable or valid at the option of the minor.

unenforceable contract
A valid contract that for some reason cannot be enforced, for example, because of the running of a statute of limitations.

years of the due date; otherwise collection is barred. Another example is a contract that is required to be in writing (Statute of Frauds) before one or more of the parties can sue successfully to enforce the contract. The contract is valid but unenforceable. Often, an unenforceable contract can become enforceable because of some later event (e.g., as to statute of limitations, a new promise to perform, and as to Statute of Frauds, a subsequent written promise).

Extent of Performance

If a contract has been performed fully by both parties, it is an **executed contract**. Sometimes, parties to a contract say that they have "executed the agreement" when they simply have signed the written contract. But the parties must perform the promises contained in their contract before it is truly an executed contract.

If something remains to be done by either or both parties, it is an **executory contract**. Often, sales contracts for goods, such as automobiles, are coupled with warranties as to performance for specified periods of time or extent of use (e.g., warranty for three years or 30,000 miles, whichever comes first). Although the basic contract may be executed, obligations created by the warranty remain for the specified time. Also, as noted in Chapter 7, if the user is injured by some defect in the product, the manufacturer may be held strictly liable in tort for damages whether or not the warranty period has expired.

WHAT ARE THE REQUISITES OF A VALID CONTRACT?

executed contract
A contract that has been performed fully by both parties.

executory contract
A valid contract in which something remains to be done by either or both parties.

competent parties
Parties who are legally qualified (that is, have the capacity) to make a binding contractual agreement.

There are six requirements for a valid contract: *competent parties* who make a *mutual agreement* with *genuine assent* supported by *reciprocal consideration* and which is legal in *formation and execution* and in the *form prescribed by law.* Let us examine each requirement.

Competent Parties

The first essential requirement for validity is **competent parties**, meaning that the parties who contract must have *legal capacity* to do so. The law generally expects that human beings will act as rational beings with freedom of will or of choice among alternative courses of action. Thus, the apparent agreement of a party may be negated by (1) infancy or minority (under age eighteen years in most states), (2) incapacitating mental condition that prevents the person from knowing the nature and consequences of a contract, or (3) incapacitating intoxication (from alcohol or drugs). Although most persons have full capacity (i.e., legal qualification or power) to contract, some persons do not. The law denies them the rights that flow from contracting, primarily to protect them from the burdensome duties of performance in foolish or improvident agreements. The restrictive denial also serves to protect them from possible exploitation by unscrupulous persons who might take unfair advantage of their ignorance, naiveté, or incapacity. In all three basic types of incapacity, the contract made usually is voidable, but only at the option of the incompetent person (or parent or guardian in control). Exhibit 8.2 illustrates the parallel status of minors, the mentally incompetent, and intoxicated persons. For example, minors can disaffirm contractual obligations during their minority and for a reasonable time thereafter; they only must return the consideration received, if they are able to do so. Disaffirmance must be of the entire contract, not just an objectionable part. Understandably, for big-ticket items, prudent retailers often require parental acknowledgment or approval and financial responsibility (e.g., by requiring the parent to cosign a promissory note or security agreement).

EXHIBIT 8.2 General Patterns of Effects of Incapacity on Agreements (caveat: in some states variations exist in definitions and effects)

Contracting Party	Valid Contract	Voidable Contract	Void Agreements
Minor	• *All* contracts, if married. • *All* contracts, if emancipated.* • *All* court-approved contracts. • Contract to enlist in armed service (at age seventeen years). • In some states, contracts for loans incurred to pay for necessaries, including education and medical care.	• *Most* contracts. • To avoid liability, any goods received must be returned if still available. • *Some* states do no require a full refund even if goods cannot be returned, and even if minor lied about age; in most states the minor may disaffirm the contract, but is liable for any depreciation and wear and tear or use. • The contract may be ratified or avoided within a reasonable time after person reaches majority age.	• *Some* attempts to contract (e.g., an apparent contract to name an agent or to dispose of real property).
Mentally incompetent person	• *All* contracts, if person is merely neurotic. • *All* contracts made during a lucid interval of full sanity.	• *All* attempts to contract made when person is entirely without understanding. • Any goods received must be returned, unless they are no longer available and other party acted in bad faith.	• *All* attempts to contract, if person has been judicially declared insane and a guardian has been appointed.
Intoxicated person	• *All* contracts, if the person is sober enough to understand the nature of the contract (even if he or she would not have made the contract if sober).	• *All* attempts to contract made when person is too intoxicated to understand the nature of the contract. • Avoidance, to be effective, must be prompt after regaining sobriety and learning of the agreement.	• *All* attempts to contract, if person has been judicially declared a victim of habitual intoxication and a guardian has been appointed.

*Living separate from consenting parents and managing own financial affairs.
In most states this will be a quasi contract rather than a "valid" contract.

LEGAL FOCUS—PROBLEM

Last week Ruby bought a new restaurant van and sold her old one to a university student named Bud, who told her he was nineteen years old and a sophomore. A week later, he brought it back—turns out he is a seventeen-year-old university student who wants to return the van to Ruby—wrecked. Must Ruby give him his money back?

Whether or not Rudy must give back the money depends on state law, but the common law rule has held that falsely representing that one has capacity does not confer capacity. So Ruby would receive the wrecked car and the minor would get his money back. Now, however, there is usually a greater obligation to make restitution in cases of misrepresentation. So some states would require the minor to pay damages to compensate for the wrecked vehicle. Other states do not allow avoidance when the minor has falsely represented his or her age.

Exception for Necessaries

necessaries
Goods and services ordinarily required by and appropriate to an incompetent person's station in life, yet not available and/or not provided by parent or guardian.

An agreement to purchase goods or services that are **necessaries** is enforceable as a quasi contract. In such a case, no valid contract exists, but a contractual remedy of reasonable compensatory damages is allowed to prevent unjust enrichment of the person who received the necessaries. Only the fair price would have to be paid, which might be different from the bargained-for price. Necessaries include such things as food, clothing, shelter, and medical care at the level at which the person is accustomed. They truly must be needed yet not be available from or provided by the parent or guardian of the incompetent.

LEGAL FOCUS—EXAMPLE

Brian Schall, the former lawyer of *High School Musical* star Vanessa Hudgens sued her for $150,000 in legal fees. Schall said that Hudgens signed a contract in October 2005, when she was sixteen years old, agreeing to pay him five percent of her earnings in exchange for his legal representation. Hudgens disaffirmed the agreement on December 14, 2007, and turned eighteen years old on October 9, 2007. Although minors can disaffirm contracts during their minority and for a reasonable time thereafter, could Schall still make a valid argument that for a minor in her position, legal representation is a necessary? If so, then she still may not be liable for the price of the legal services established by the contract, but for the *reasonable* value of those services.

Mutual Agreement

objective theory of contracts
A theory that the words and conduct of an offeror mean whatever a reasonable person in the offeree's position would think they mean, as opposed to what the offeror actually may have meant.

The second essential element of a valid contract is self-evident: The parties must come to a mutual agreement. One party must make an offer, and the other must accept. The parties must agree to the same thing. This agreement sometimes is referred to as a "meeting of the minds." The law requires external or objective manifestation, in words or actions, of a willingness to deal. Intent is decided by the **objective theory of contracts**. A party's intent to enter into a contract is judged by outward objective facts; persons are bound by what they express, either by their words or by their conduct. Internal, subjective thoughts remain secret. Before, during, and after an agreement of any complexity is entered, the parties seldom disclose the full content of their mental thinking about the terms of the contract.

The Offer

Three elements are necessary for an offer to be effective:

1. The offer must manifest an intention to be legally bound.
2. The terms of the offer must be reasonably definite and certain so a court can fashion a remedy.
3. The offer must be communicated to the offeree.

LEGAL FOCUS—PROBLEM

Adam Steinberg and three other students ride to college each day in Judy Naylor's new-to-her automobile. Her car is worth $10,000. One cold morning just after everyone got into her car, it would not start. Naylor yelled in anger, "I'll sell this car to anyone for $20!" Steinberg immediately dropped $20 in her lap. Does Steinberg, the offeree, have a contract with Naylor and a right to the car? Did Naylor, the offeror, intend to create a contract?

offer
A promise by one person (the offeror) to do or to give consideration (something of value) in exchange for sought-for consideration through acceptance by another person (the offeree).

For a valid **offer**, the person making the offer must manifest intent to be bound, to make a business agreement, a contract. The offer must be serious, not in obvious jest or in panicky fear. Naylor's expression obviously is made in anger, excitement, or jest, and it does not meet the objective-intent test. Because the offer is not effective, Steinberg's attempt to accept does not create an agreement. Likewise, an invitation to a social engagement or date is not a legal offer. If accepted, either party may cancel it without legal liability.

Most advertisements by custom are not legal offers to sell; instead, they are considered to be invitations to the world to come into the store and make offers to buy, to negotiate. Thus, under contract law an advertiser generally cannot be compelled to sell goods on the terms stated in an ad. Of course, if the ad is deliberately false or misleading, the advertiser may be liable for a tort or criminal act or may be in violation of some other duty as an advertiser. Catalogs, price lists, circulars, and other pricing vehicles used by companies are treated in the same fashion as advertisements.

LEGAL FOCUS—EXAMPLE

On a website allowing "for sale" advertisements, you put an ad offering to sell your favorite guitar for $75. Seven people e-mail and "accept" your "offer." If the ad is truly an offer, you would be bound by seven contracts to sell your guitar. But because initial advertisements are treated as invitations to make offers rather than as offers, you would have seven offers from which to choose. You could accept one without assuming any liability for the six you reject.

The offer must be reasonably definite and certain. In case of a dispute, a court must be able to determine what the parties agreed to do.

Among the terms the court expects to find in a valid offer are

- Parties—who and how many
- Subject matter—what and how many
- Time of performance—when, delivery terms, warranties
- Price—how much and when to be paid

Many common contracts are considered sufficiently definite and certain even though important terms are left unsettled. An example is a contract in which one is hired to work, and the duration of the employment is not stated; such a contract is considered employment at will. Also, contracts for the professional services of a doctor, dentist, lawyer, or accountant often are made without clear knowledge of the full scope of the time and effort that will be needed, and so no fixed fee is given. In these situations, when the price is finally set, it must be reasonable in light of all the circumstances. When such uncertainly is troubling or unacceptable, one can insist on a specific figure or an hourly rate, stated in advance.

Finally, the offer must be communicated to the person to whom it is made, the offeree. Only the offeree or an authorized agent of the offeree may accept. In daily life, the parties to contracts usually identify themselves more precisely than as offeror–offeree. They may be known as university–student, seller–buyer, doctor–patient, employer–employee, lawyer–client, landlord–tenant, bailor–bailee, and so forth.

The Acceptance

acceptance
Affirmative response to the terms of an offer, creating a contract.

To create a contract, the offeree must accept the offer by making a positive response to the offeror. General rules of contract law require that **acceptance** be a mirror-image response to the offer. It must be a timely, responsive, and unequivocal affirmation of a desire to enter into the contract on the terms of the offer. It also must be communicated to the offeror or to the offeror's authorized agent.

Under the UCC, the rules of acceptance for contracts involving the sale of goods are more flexible as to what constitutes an acceptance. For all types of transactions, the courts look for a timely response showing that the offeree wishes to be contractually bound.

Under the UCC, on offer to make a contract for the sale of goods is "construed as inviting acceptance in any manner and by any medium reasonable in the circumstances." Generally, unless otherwise specified, the offeree may accept by the same or faster means than were used by the offeror. When an offer is made by U.S. Postal Service mail, the offeror impliedly authorizes the offeree to respond by mail, unless otherwise specified. The acceptance is effective, and a contract arises, when the acceptance is properly posted (i.e., placed in the custody of the U.S. Postal Service with the correct ad dress and proper postage), even if the letter of acceptance is lost in transit. The rule often is called the *deposit acceptance rule* or *mailbox rule.** Similarly, if private overnight express delivery services are used, the acceptance is effective when the offeree gives the document to the delivery service.

LEGAL FOCUS—BACKGROUND

Today, many communications of offers and acceptances are made by telephone, fax machines, e-mail, or overnight express delivery services. The mailbox rule anticipates and applies to methods of delayed communication such as mail or telegraphs. Use of telephones, faxes, and e-mails do not quite fit the legal construct of the mailbox rule, and there is little judicial guidance as to how they will be treated. Obviously, when actual communication of the acceptance has occurred while the offer is timely, a contract exists. Faxes and e-mails can be sent and not seen for some time and, indeed, they can be misdirected or not received for a variety of reasons. Do you think the mailbox rule should apply to e-mails and faxes?

**Restatement (Second) of Contracts,* §30, provides that an offer invites acceptance "by any medium reasonable in the circumstances," unless the offer is specific about the means of acceptance. Under §65, a medium is reasonable if it is one used by the offeror or if it is one customary in similar transactions, unless the offeree knows of circumstances that would argue against the reasonableness of a particular method (the need for speed because of rapid price changes, for example).

How Long Does an Offer Last?

An offer, once made, does not last forever. It is ended by the *lapse of time,* if specified (e.g., "Let me know before Friday the 27th"). If no time is stated, then it ends after a reasonable time—an elastic concept that varies with the circumstances (e.g., a farmer's offer to sell fresh strawberries may be good for a few hours; an offer made in June to sell loads of firewood may be good for several months).

An offer also is ended by the destruction of the subject matter. For example, Annabel Leeds offers to sell her pickup truck to Salix Waukem. Before Waukem accepts the offer, the truck is damaged beyond practicable repair. Death or mental incompetence of either party also precludes acceptance and ends the offer.

LEGAL FOCUS—PROBLEM

On Saturday, Fred Arthur mailed Kim Trang an offer to sell his car for $1,000. On Monday, Arthur changed his mind and, not having heard from Trang, sent her a letter revoking his offer. On Wednesday, before she had received Arthur's letter of revocation, Trang mailed a letter of acceptance to Arthur. Trang demands that Arthur sell his car as promised, but Arthur claims that no contract exists because the offer was revoked prior to Trang's acceptance. Is Arthur correct?

No, Arthur is not correct. As previously noted, when an offer is made by mail, a contract exists when the acceptance is posted properly. In sharp contrast, although the offeror may notify the offeree at any time that the offer is revoked, such **revocation** is generally effective only upon receipt by the offeree. If this fact were not so, the offeree never could be sure that an offer received in the mail still was open to acceptance. Trang's acceptance was sent by an authorized and reasonable means (the same means used by Arthur) before she received or was aware of the attempted revocation of the offer. Because of the deposit-acceptance rule, the acceptance was good when sent.

revocation
The taking back of an offer.

If a week originally was specified "to let you think it over," the offeror nevertheless generally can revoke the offer, without liability, before acceptance. Remember that promises are enforceable only when a contract is formed, so a promise to keep an offer open usually can be broken without recourse. To avoid such possibility, the offeree may pay the offeror to keep the offer open for an agreed length of time by entering into an **option contract**. An enforceable option is a separate, but related contract. The option contract gives the offeree a fixed time to accept the offer. During this period, the offeror does not have the legal right to revoke. The offeree pays the offeror something of value to create the option contract. An option contract often is used in the negotiation of real estate sales.

option contract
An agreement concerning the right to buy or sell something to another at a certain price within a certain time.

As to contracts involving the sale of goods, a merchant may make a binding firm offer to keep the offer open for a stated time up to three months. It is not essential that the offeree pay for such a right, but the agreement must be in writing and signed by the merchant. As the rule specifically applies to merchants, it does not apply to causal sellers of goods, e.g., someone having a yard sale..

Subsequent incompetence, or even death, does not terminate an offer made in an option contract (unless the offeror's personal performance is essential). In such cases, generally a personal representative fulfills the contract, as by delivering goods or paying the price.

Now the offeree-option holder knows that he has the agreed-on option time to reflect, look at alternatives, or arrange financing. If the offeree-option holder decides to accept the original offer, any money paid for the option might be applied to the purchase price, if the parties had so agreed. If she rejects the offer, the offeror simply keeps that money as compensation for keeping the offer open.

The parties may haggle over the terms of the contract. In doing so, an unequivocal rejection of the offer by the offeree would end it. The rejection may take effect immediately, if made during oral negotiations; if mailed, unlike an acceptance, it is effective only when received. Similarly, a *counteroffer* terminates an offer.* Noncommittal words such as, "Your price sounds too rich for my diet, but let me sleep on that offer," would have no effect. Understandably, death or insanity of either party, or destruction of the subject matter, ends the offer.

Genuine Assent

genuine assent
When consent of both parties to be bound by a contract is given freely and is not negated by fraud, duress, undue influence, or certain mistakes.

The third essential element of a valid contract is that the agreement be made with the **genuine assent**, or real consent, of both parties. Assent is negated when either party acts under duress or because of undue influence. Assent, although given, is fatally flawed if it resulted from fraud or certain types of mistakes.

Duress

duress
Any threat of, or actual, physical harm that deprives a person of the freedom of will to choose and decide.

Duress happens when one party is prevented from exercising judgment and free will by some wrongful act or threat of the other party. It could result from threat of imprisonment (e.g., "I'll keep you locked up until you sign this contract!") or of physical injury to the other party or to a close relative or friend (e.g., "Sign here or I'll bash you so hard you'll never ever sign anything again!"). In addition, blackmail to induce consent to a contract is duress. The victim of the duress generally can choose to carry out the contract or to avoid the entire transaction, although duress involving a serious threat of violence leads to no contract at all, a void agreement. A threat of criminal prosecution would be duress; not so the comparatively common threat of filing a civil suit to collect a debt. Why the difference? The first is a form of extortion or menace; the second is the voicing of a legal right to sue for money owed.

Economic need generally is not a basis for a finding of duress, even when one party charges a high price for an item the other party needs. If the party charging the price also creates the need, however, economic duress may be found.

LEGAL FOCUS—PROBLEM

The Internal Revenue Service (IRS) assessed a large tax and penalty against Sam Thompson. Thompson retained Earl Eyman to represent him to reduce the tax and penalty. The last day before the deadline for filing a reply with the IRS, Eyman refused to represent Thompson. He said he would reconsider if Thompson signed an agreement to pay a much higher fee than previously agreed. Is the agreement enforceable?

No, the agreement is not enforceable. Although Eyman threatened only to withdraw his services, something he could do legitimately if done in proper time, he delayed his withdrawal until the last day. It would have been practically impossible at that late date for Thompson to get adequate representation elsewhere. Because Thompson was forced into

*Between merchants, an acceptance may be valid and binding on both parties "even though it states terms additional to or different from those offered or agreed upon." However, this provision of the UCC, §2-207, is subject to a number of conditions that effectively maintain the offeror's control and ability to require that acceptance comply with his terms if there is to be a contract, assuming the offeror is paying attention to the acceptance and the degree to which it differs from the offer.

signing the contract or losing his right to challenge the IRS assessment, the contract is voidable by him.

undue influence
Wrongful persuasion, often by a fiduciary or other trusted individual, that deprives the victim of freedom of will in making a contract.

Undue Influence

Although more subtle than duress, **undue influence** has the same effect: depriving a party of freedom of will in choosing a course of action. Wrongful persuasion and persistent pressure accomplish it. Typically, the wrongdoer asserts a position or authority or exploits the victim's misplaced confidence in the wrongdoer's apparent good faith and wisdom and, for example, obtains property from the victim at a price well below fair market value.

LEGAL FOCUS—EXAMPLE

When Mabel Taylor reached her eightieth birthday, she was no longer able to drive her car. Her nephew, Johnny Ray, convinced Taylor that she should sell him the car for $50. Ray told Taylor that if she did not agree, then he would no longer visit her. The actual value of the car was $7,000. This agreement is not enforceable because Ray is taking advantage of his special relationship with Taylor.

A suspicion of undue influence arises when parties are in a confidential or fiduciary relationship. Examples include that of parent and child, client and lawyer, guardian and ward, conservator and elderly conservatee, and principal and agent. Because one party relies so heavily on the other, the law requires the utmost good faith, scrupulous honesty, and full disclosure by the dominant party in dealings between the parties. To overcome a presumption of undue influence, the dominant party should make a full disclosure of all relevant facts; insist that the other party get the advice of qualified, independent counsel; and make honest, fair contracts.

fraud
A knowingly false representation of a material fact, made through words or conduct, with intent to deceive a victim, who is induced to contract in reliance on the lie, and who is thereby injured.

Fraud

The essential elements of **fraud** are (1) false representation, a lie, (2) of a material (important) (3) fact (generally not a personal opinion, unless an expert is expressing it) (4) known to be false (or made with reckless indifference as to its truth or made with blameworthy ignorance of its falsity), (5) made with intent to deceive the victim and in duce the victim to contract, as a result of which (6) the victim is deceived and contracts in reliance on the lie, and (7) the victim is thereby injured.

LEGAL FOCUS—PROBLEM

Peter Pride, proprietor of "Cars You're Proud to Own," sold a used car to Lilly Lee, a first-car buyer. Pride, who knew otherwise, said the car had one previous owner (actually, there had been two); had never been in an accident (actually, a rear fender, the trunk, and a bumper had been replaced after a collision); and had the original paint (the car had been repainted). The odometer showed 52,000 miles, and Pride said the engine had been overhauled (in fact, the odometer had been turned back from 66,000 miles, and the engine had been given only a tune-up). Pride also claimed the car had new tires (they looked new to Lee but were actually retreads). Pride claimed the car was worth $15,000 but because he was trying to reduce his inventory, he'd let Lee "steal it" for only $9,500. Relying on Pride's sales pitch, Lee bought the car for the asking price. She soon learned that in its actual condition, it was worth no more than $5,500. Is Peter Pride liable for fraud? If so, what can Lee do?

Yes, Pride is liable for fraud. He made a series of misrepresentations of fact, known to be false, intending to deceive Lee and to induce her to buy. Lee was deceived and, relying on the lies, bought the car to her injury. She paid more than she would have had she known the truth.

Lee has several options. She could *rescind* (cancel or undo) the contract, return the car, and demand a full refund of her $9,500. In addition, she could sue in tort for compensatory and punitive (or exemplary) damages. In a minority of states, Lee's compensatory damages would be the *out-of-pocket loss* suffered (i.e., the difference in value between what she gave—$9,500—and the value of what she got—$5,500—or a net $4,000). In most states, her compensatory damages would be the difference between the value of what she received ($5,500) and the value of performance as misrepresented by the defendant Pride ($15,000), or a net $9,500. In either case, in most states, Lee also could sue for punitive damages in addition to the compensatory damages because of Pride's intentional tort of fraud. Here the jury might award as much as $50,000 or more.

LEGAL FOCUS—PROBLEM

Tom Cullen contracts to purchase a hearing assistance dog from Manny Estacio. The dog is blind in one eye, but when Estacio shows the dog, he skillfully conceals this fact by turning the dog's head so Cullen cannot see the defect. All of the dog's senses are important in fulfilling the hearing assistance tasks. Is this concealment fraud?

Yes, this knowing concealment constitutes fraud. Another example of misrepresentation by conduct is the false denial of knowledge or information concerning facts that are material to the contract when such knowledge or information is requested. It is important that a purchaser ask many questions.

The use of deception to extract money or property from others unfortunately is not new or uncommon. And new forms of doing business attract the unscrupulous as well as the adventuresome who try new and old schemes with new features to mislead the trusting and naive among us. Use of the Internet and mobile phones are among those business ventures of which consumers need be wary.

LEGAL FOCUS—EXAMPLE

A $3.50 "rebate" check was sent to millions of small businesses and consumers. The check came with an attached form that looked like an invoice and used terms like "reference number," and "discount taken," making it look like there was a previous business relationship. Upon cashing the check, the consumers unknowingly were agreeing to allow the defendants to become their Internet service provider, and the defendants placed monthly charges of $19.95 to $29.95 on the consumers' telephone bills. They also made it difficult to cancel future monthly charges and receive refunds. A judge found

that, as a matter of law, check/invoice combinations that do not clearly and conspicuously disclose the effects of cashing the check and/or clearly state the check is an offer for the sale of Internet services on the face of the document constitute material representations that are likely to mislead consumers acting reasonably under the circumstances.

mutual or bilateral mistake
Where both parties to a contract labor under the same error about an important fact in their agreement.

Mutual Mistake

When both parties have an erroneous idea or understanding about some fact that is an important element of the contract, there is a **mutual or bilateral mistake** that generally renders their agreement void, or voidable, by either party. When both parties are mistaken about a material (i.e., important) fact, either party may rescind (i.e., cancel or annul the contract without liability). If the error was not obvious, the same court would not excuse the mistaken party.

LEGAL FOCUS—CASE

Defendant Wichelhaus contracted to buy 125 bales of cotton from plaintiff Raffles. They agreed that the cotton would come from Bombay, India, to Liverpool on the ship *Peerless*. Buyer Wichelhaus reasonably thought the goods would arrive on a ship named *Peerless* that was scheduled to sail in October. Seller Raffles reasonably thought of another ship, which also happened to be named *Peerless*, but which was scheduled to sail from Bombay in December. When the cotton finally arrived, much later than expected by Wichelhaus, he refused to accept or pay for it. Was Wichelhaus legally bound by the alleged contract?

Raffles v. Wichelhaus, 159 Eng. Rep. 375 (1864).

No, according to this landmark English case, the buyer was not legally bound. Acting in good faith, the parties referred to different ships, sailing at significantly different times. The mutual mistake of fact rendered the agreement voidable. Note that different opinions as to value (e.g., of a parcel of land, a jewel, or a share of stock) or expectations of future value do not affect the validity of the contract. Likewise, a **unilateral mistake** (by one party) about value, expectations, or the applicability of a statute, such as a zoning law, generally does not affect the contract. Suppose, however, one party is mistaken or errs in submitting a bid on a construction job. The other party recognizes the obvious error but says nothing and quickly signs the contract. A court of equity would permit the mistaken party to withdraw without liability.

unilateral mistake
A situation in which one of the parties to a contract labors under some error about an important fact in the agreement.

LEGAL FOCUS—PROBLEM

Jane Collins contracts to purchase one of two antique washing machines owned by Mike Heimer. Collins thinks she has purchased the white one, a premier model. Heimer thinks she has purchased the beige one, his less valuable washing machine. Does a contract exist?

No, a contract does not exist. Collins and Heimer have made a genuine mutual mistake of fact. Collins believes the contract subject matter is the white washing machine, whereas Heimer believes it is the beige one. Nothing is more material than the subject matter of the contract. Because both parties are mistaken about the subject matter, no contract exists.

LEGAL FOCUS—PROBLEM

Suppose instead that Collins contracts to buy the white washing machine, believing it to be worth $1,000 when it really is worth only $250. Can Collins escape the contract because of her mistake?

No, Collins cannot escape the contract. Collins's mistake is one of value or quality, not fact. A mistake of this nature does not normally affect the enforceability of the contract.

Reciprocal Consideration

When a man keeps hollering, "It's the principle of the thing," he's talking about the money.

—*Frank Hubbard*, American humorist, 1868–1930

The fourth requisite of a valid contract is the presence of *reciprocal consideration.*

consideration
The price or inducement (e.g., reciprocal promises) to enter a contract.

Consideration, in this context, is simply the value given in exchange for a promise or an act. The parties "bargain"—that is, they freely negotiate an exchange of promises or acts whereby each party ultimately enjoys some legal benefit and each suffers some legal detriment. Each party gives; each party receives. What is given and received must have legal value; generally, it need not be equal or adequate by any other person's standards of valuation. Thus, a promise of a gift is not legally enforceable because the donor is promised nothing of legal value in return. To say "Gee, thanks!" or "I love you!" is not bargained for consideration.

In a bilateral contract, each party is both promisor and promisee. Consideration may be (1) a return promise (e.g., to pay money or to give some service or property); (2) an act other than a promise (as in unilateral contracts); (3) a forbearance (where one party refrains from doing what she has a legal right to do); or (4) the creation, modification, or destruction of a legal relationship (e.g., where the parties agree to become associated as business partners).

LEGAL FOCUS—PROBLEM

Jerry Revcik says to Max Harris, "If you paint the garage green, I will pay you $100." Harris paints the garage green. Can Harris legally require Revcik to pay the $100? Is consideration present?

The answer to both questions is yes. The act of painting the garage is the consideration requested and in this case given in return for Revcik's promise to pay.

MORALS AND ETHICS

Suppose instead that Revcik says to Harris, "In consideration of you not being as wealthy as my other friends, I will pay you $500 next Tuesday." Can Harris legally require Revcik to pay him the $500? Does consideration exist? If it does not exist, how can such an outcome morally be justified?

No, consideration does not exist. Revcik's promise is not enforceable, because consideration is absent. Harris did not pay anything (give consideration) for the $500 promised. Jerry simply stated his motive for an intended *gift* to Harris. Such an outcome can be justified because Harris did not sacrifice anything in return; he has little reason to claim that he deserves the $500.

Note that use of the term *consideration* does not, alone, mean that consideration was given. Consideration is the sweetener that induces both parties to perform as promised. It conforms to the natural and customary human tendency to expect to receive something in exchange for something given, unless a gift is intended.

In so-called illusory agreements, there is no reciprocal consideration and therefore no contract. Examples include when the parties "agree to agree" or when a supplier agrees to sell all goods of a given type that the buyer "may want," which actually may be none at all. This situation is distinguishable from a deal in which the seller agrees to sell and the buyer agrees to buy all of the specified types of goods that the buyer actually and measurably may need or require during a stated period of time.

Similarly, there is no consideration when the promisor already is bound to do the act (e.g., when a police officer, for a promised fee, agrees to try to apprehend a burglar) or when some past consideration is involved (e.g., when A rescues B from drowning and *subsequently* B promises to pay A $5,000).

Under some special circumstances, consideration is not required as a matter of public policy. An illustration is a pledge or charitable subscription to a church or nonprofit hospital or school. The pledge states that it is for the purpose of erecting a library building, and it is made, in part, to induce others to contribute. Such a promise is legally binding in most states, even if the donor gets no valuable consideration in return. The charity, however, must act in reliance on the pledge, for example, by contracting for construction of the new facility. Likewise, no consideration need be given by a creditor for a new promise by a debtor to pay a debt that has been barred by the statute of limitations.

LEGAL FOCUS—PROBLEM

A police offer on duty apprehended Eric Rudolph, who was rummaging through a trash bin. Rudolph was wanted in conjunction with the bombing of abortion clinics and the Olympic bombing in Atlanta in 1996. As a result, there was a substantial reward offered for his apprehension and conviction. Is the police officer entitled to the reward?

No, the officer is not entitled to the reward. Even though the reward was an offer for a unilateral contract, which could be accepted by apprehending Rudolf, there was no consideration for the officer's capture of Rudolph as he already was under a preexisting legal duty to apprehend criminals within his jurisdiction.

Legality in Formation and Execution

As the fifth and, in many cases, the final requisite for validity, the contract must be legal in its formation and in its proposed execution. Generally, an agreement may fail to qualify because it is either (1) contrary to some statute or (2) contrary to public policy (i.e., prevailing community standards as to what is contrary to the public good, or commonwealth).

Violations of Statutes

The gangland expression "There's a contract out on him" refers to an agreement to kill a designated victim. Such agreement obviously is illegal and void. The same summary condemnation would apply to any agreement to commit a tort. Not so clear is the legal status of agreements (1) to gamble or conduct illegal lotteries, (2) to practice a trade or profession without a license, (3) to engage in profit-seeking business on Sundays, and (4) to charge interest rates that might be usurious. Consider the confusing status of these practices.

Gambling

Traditionally, gambling agreements, lotteries, and games of chance have been illegal when they involve three elements: (1) some payments by the gambler (2) for a chance

(3) to win some prize. Many states, however, now have certain legal forms of gambling. Pressure to raise public revenues in recent years has led to this legalization (according to some observers, a highly regressive form of taxation). Critics object to such activity as economically wasteful (unless one regards the dubious entertainment effect to be a valuable product). They say that the gullible and the ignorant thereby squander money that would be better spent for necessities and that gambling promoters cynically pander to greed and unfounded hope by suggesting that "you, too, can get rich quick," despite astronomical odds against such a result.

Sometimes, it is difficult to distinguish a gambling contract from the risk sharing inherent in most contracts.

LEGAL FOCUS—PROBLEM

Jaime Zavala takes out a life insurance policy on an acquaintance, Pete Botello. Zavala names himself as the beneficiary (the person to be paid) under the policy. Is this a legal contract or a gambling agreement?

insurable interest
A sufficient interest in property such that its loss or destruction would cause an economic loss to the owner or possessor.

The life insurance policy contract appears legal; however, Zavala is simply gambling on how long Botello will live. To prevent this type of contract, only someone with an **insurable interest** is allowed to recover on an insurance contract. An insurable interest exists when a person has a real economic risk related to the property or person insured. If your watch is stolen or damaged, for example, you suffer a real loss. If someone else's watch is stolen or broken, you may feel bad, but you suffer no direct economic loss. Thus, you have an insurable interest in your watch, but not in the other person's. Zavala cannot collect on an insurance policy on Botello's life (or home or auto) because he does not have an insurable interest in Botello or his property. If Zavala were a part owner of Botello's automobile, however, he legally could collect on an insurance policy on the auto because he has a property interest.

If an insurance company is aware that a person applying for insurance lacks an insurable interest, the company should refuse to sell the policy. An insurer that sells a policy unaware that the holder lacks an insurable interest will claim lack of insurable interest as a defense to a claim for payment upon learning the truth. An innocent claimant will get a return of the premiums paid but not a payment on the policy.

LEGAL FOCUS—EXAMPLE

One way scam artists get around the insurable interest rule is to persuade a person to purchase the life insurance policy himself but name the evil doer as the beneficiary. Or easier yet, they persuade a policy holder to change beneficiaries. Thus, there is no contract problem and, unless someone raises the question, no obvious criminal behavior. In May 2006, two women, one seventy-five and the other seventy-three, were arrested in Los Angeles and charged with mail fraud for allegedly participating in such a scheme involving homeless men. As a civil legal matter, the insurance companies would raise fraud as a defense to payment on the policy to these named beneficiaries.

Licensing

Many professions and trades require a license to practice (engage in business). Traditionally, the legitimate objective of such licensing laws has been to protect the public against unqualified practitioners. Typically, the government regulates the competency of practitioners by requiring prospective practitioners to pass a licensing exam and to complete coursework. Critics complain that the real objective is to limit entry to reduce competition in service and price. Nevertheless, contracts made by unlicensed persons generally are unenforceable; they cannot collect for services rendered. However, when the true objective of the licensing is to raise government revenues, the failure to obtain a license does *not* render the contracts of the parties unenforceable or void. For example, a business license, sometimes referred to as a privilege license, is designed to raise funds for general municipal purposes, including public safety, refuse collection, parks, and recreation. Payment of this fee authorizes the privilege of operating the business; however, a failure to pay the fee would not necessarily render contracts of the business void.

LEGAL FOCUS—CASE

Paris was a real estate broker licensed in the state of Georgia. Paris contacted Cooper, a Florida resident who was interested in purchasing some Gulf County, Florida, acreage. Paris visited the property in Florida, helped prepare Cooper's written offer of purchase, worked with Cooper's attorney on the sales contract, and attended the closing of the sale in Panama City, Florida. As a result of this sale, Paris received a $315,070 commission. Can Cooper recover the commission on the basis that the contract is unenforceable because Paris was not licensed to conduct real estate transactions in Florida?

Cooper v. Paris, 413 So.2d 772 (Fla.App., 1st Dist., 1982).

Yes, Cooper can recover the commission. An agent must have a real estate license to represent a client in a real estate transaction and expect to collect a fee. Such licenses are granted by each state to protect the citizens of that state. A license in Georgia does not authorize the agent to practice in Florida. The agent could not collect the commission, and if the commission had been paid, the client could sue for its return.

Blue Laws

blue laws
Statutes that regulate or prohibit commercial activities and amusements on Sundays.

In some states, strong support continues for traditional observance of the Sabbath as a day of rest and worship as mandated by the Mosaic Code. Accordingly, **blue laws** restrict the right to make or perform various contracts on Sundays. Blue laws originally referred to strict rules in colonial New England that outlawed such practices as working, dancing, and drinking intoxicating liquors on Sundays. The term now refers to statutes that regulate commercial activities and amusements on Sundays. When blue laws have been challenged as a violation of the First Amendment respecting establishment of religion, the U.S. Supreme Court has refused to interfere. Such observance is justified for needed rest and relaxation, the Court's reasoningexplains; any day of the week could be designated for the purpose. States retaining blue laws generally only restrict certain types of contracts, the most likely restriction being purchase of alcohol.

Usury

Most states regulate the maximum rates of interest that may be charged for certain loans of money. *Usury* is the practice of charging excessively high rates on loans. In the twenty-first century, most states maintain some control over how much interest may be charged, but, for example, they allow rates as high as forty percent a year or more on loans of no more than a few hundred dollars made by pawnbrokers and small loan companies. The extra interest charge is justified by the higher unit cost of processing such loans and by a higher risk of defaults by borrowers. The availability of such loans also helps to keep the borrowers out of the clutches of loan sharks, who may charge interest rates of 100 percent a year or more. Civil sanctions for usury vary among the states. In some states, the usurer is barred from collecting either principal or interest; in others, only the principal is payable; additional variations exist. But observers suggest that many violations are unreported, often because of ignorance or fear of violent retaliation.

interest
The price, usually expressed as an annualized rate (percentage), for use of a sum of money (principal) obtained from a lender.

The purchase of goods on credit, subject to a carrying charge (some states call it **interest**) on the unpaid balance, has not been considered usury because there is not a direct loan of money. As this practice has become widespread, however, legal limits often are imposed on the percentage rate that may be imposed. The typical carrying charge (or "interest rate") hovers around and sometimes exceeds twenty percent a year. This is a heavy levy, in light of the fact that the ordinary saver seldom earns as much as three to five percent in a bank savings account.

Violations of Public Policy

subornation of perjury
Crime of persuading another person to commit perjury.

Some agreements are obviously contrary to public policy and therefore are illegal and void. The list includes attempts to obstruct justice in court by bribing jurors, paying a witness to lie under oath (this is the crime of **subornation of perjury**), or paying a witness more than the modest legal fee prescribed by statute. (Note that counsel may engage experts for both the plaintiff and the defendant to study and render their opinions about facts of the case. They often are called on to testify during the trial. Such expert witnesses legitimately may receive fees for their services far in excess of payments made to other witnesses.) Also included in attempts to obstruct justice is paying bribes to influence legislators, administrators, and judges. The federal Foreign Corrupt Practices Act also has banned bribes to obtain contracts with foreign governments.

lobbying
Efforts by individuals and representatives of special-interest groups to persuade legislators (and sometimes administrators) to enact, amend, or rescind specified laws.

Lobbying, properly practiced, can be beneficial to the democratic process of legislation. Lobbyists outnumber legislators in Congress and in most state houses. They usually are employed under contracts with special-interest groups to persuade legislators to vote in a certain way on legislation. To many persons, *lobbyist* is a term of infamy, no doubt because the practice of lobbying too often in the past has been corrupted by bribery or veiled purchases of favors. Nevertheless, lobbyists serve a useful purpose in providing important information on the pros and cons of present and proposed legislation. Any person may lobby on his or her own behalf; however, federal and state statutes generally require persons who lobby for other individuals or groups to register, identify their clients, and disclose the source and amounts of payments received and dispensed.

covenant not to compete
A promise not to engage in a competing business or profession. Such covenants generally are illegal unless they are part of an otherwise-enforceable contract for the sale of a business or for employment. In such cases, they are legal only if they are drafted to be reasonable regarding time, scope, and geographic area and are necessary to protect the interests of the contracting parties.

Agreements that restrict trade and competition are generally illegal. Such contracts, called **covenants not to compete**, often violate one or more federal or state statutes and often are construed as common law torts as well. These restraints of trade are against the public interest, which favors free competition. The two major potential exceptions to this rule of illegality are as follows:

1. When the restraint of free trade is part of an otherwise-enforceable contract for the sale of a business and where a partner agrees not to compete in anticipation of dissolution of a partnership
2. When a new employee agrees, as part of the employment contract, not to accept another employment position with any other employer who is a competitor of the present employer

To be legal, such agreements must involve a legitimate business need and can be no more extensive in time, scope, and distance than reasonably necessary to protect the future related interests of the protected parties (i.e., the buyer of the business and the first employer). Courts also consider the effect of enforcement of such agreements on the public good—the restriction on the freedom to purchase goods and services cannot be excessive and is balanced against the contracting party's legitimate business need.

A promise by a person selling a business not to open a competing business close to the old one is an example of a covenant not to compete. A shoe retailer selling her business might appropriately agree not to open a competing business anywhere in a sparsely populated county for perhaps a year; a seller of a company manufacturing heavy-duty earth-moving machines, headed by a brilliant inventor whose unique products are sold worldwide, might properly agree not to open a competing business anywhere for three or more years. Thus, the buyer properly gets the benefit of the price paid for the goodwill* value of the going concern.

In employment contracts, it is common for middle- and upper-level managers to be asked to agree not to work for competitors or start new competing business firms for a specified time after leaving the current employment relationship. Such noncompete clauses in employment contracts are subject to even more scrutiny than those in the sale of business. The restriction on competition must be reasonable, be necessary to protect confidential information or trade secrets obtained during employment, and not be any greater than necessary to protect a legitimate business interest.

LEGAL FOCUS—CASE

Thomas Rector and four other employees of Paramount Termite Control Company agreed not to compete with their employer if they quit. The agreement stated they would refrain for two years after leaving Paramount employment from soliciting

> *business from any customer of Paramount where the purpose thereof is to provide the services of pest control with which customer the employee established contact while in the employ of Paramount at any time during the two years next preceding the termination of the Employment Agreement.*

The restriction covered the geographic areas the employees serviced as Paramount employees. Later, the employees resigned from Paramount and began working for a Paramount competitor that solicited business in the counties prohibited by the noncompetition agreement. Paramount sought to enforce the promise. Did Paramount succeed?

Paramount Termite Control Co. v. Rector, 238 Va. 171, 380 S.E.2d 922 (Va., 1989).

Yes, Paramount succeeded. The Supreme Court of Virginia declared the restriction on competition was reasonable in time (two-year period) and in the geographic area covered. The court applied three criteria: (1) From the standpoint of the employer, was the restraint greater than necessary to protect a legitimate business interest of the employer? (2) From the standpoint of the employee, was the restraint reasonable—not unduly harsh and oppressive in limiting the employee's ability to earn a living? and (3) Was the restraint reasonable as sound public policy? The court concluded that the restraint was no greater than reasonably necessary to protect Paramount's legitimate business interest. The five employees "had frequent contacts with Paramount's customers" and "were familiar with Paramount's methods of estimating the cost of its work, its specifications

*Goodwill is the valuable intangible asset of a business that is developed over a prolonged period of time through successful contractual relations with satisfied customers and suppliers. Thus, an established business with goodwill normally enjoys higher profits than a new business of the same size but lacking such goodwill.

for doing the work, and its techniques of pest control." The court also found the geographic restriction reasonable, as it applied only to those counties in which the employees had worked previously and not in all counties within the state. Finally, because there was sufficient competition in the area, the court held the restrictions did not unreasonably restrain trade or violate public policy.

Hold harmless agreement or Exculpatory clause
A hold harmless agreement or exculpatory clause releases one party to the agreement from liability.

Hold harmless agreements or Exculpatory clauses are another type of contractual arrangement that courts frequently evaluate on public policy grounds. An exculpatory clause or hold harmless agreement is designed to insulate or release the entity seeking exculpation from liability, which usually involves negligence. The term derived from the Latin root *culpa*, meaning blame or fault, and the prefix, *ex*, suggesting not; in other words, do not blame me or consider me to be at fault. There are two competing public interests at stake in evaluating the validity of such clauses. The first consideration is the notion that the law desires to hold parties accountable for their negligent actions that lead to another person's injury or result in damage to his or her property. After all, the law seeks to hold one's conduct to the standard of a reasonably prudent person. If one's conduct is substandard and is the proximate cause of another person's loss, then damages are owed under tort law. One the other hand, freedom of contract is a revered principle in our jurisprudence; therefore, if the parties wish to bargain about and include an exculpation clause in their agreement, why shouldn't courts enforce it?

In evaluating whether exculpatory clauses are valid or instead unenforceable and against public policy, courts will examine several factors: Is the release the result of bargaining or attached to a contract of adhesion, or did the parties bargain about its inclusion? Is the clause seeking to exculpate a party from personal injury or property damage? Did the clause use clear language and was its intent obvious? If negligence was involved, was the defendant's conduct reckless, or did it involve gross negligence?

Some courts also follow the criteria enunciated in a leading case involving a physician's release of liability when the patient subsequently died allegedly as a result of the doctor's negligence (*Tunkl v. Regents of University of California*, 383 P.2d 441 (Cal., 1963)). Those criteria are as follows: (1) the agreement concerns an endeavor of a type generally thought suitable for public regulation; (2) the party seeking exculpation is engaged in performing a service of great importance to the public, which is often a matter of practical necessity for some members of the public; (3) such party holds itself out as willing to perform this service for any member of the public who seeks it, or at least for any member of the public coming within certain established standards; (4) the party seeking the exculpation possesses a decisive advantage of bargaining strength against any member of the public who seeks the services; (5) in exercising a superior bargaining power, the party confronts the public with a standardized adhesion contract of exculpation and makes no provision whereby those receiving services may pay additional reasonable fees and obtain protection against negligence; and (6) the person or members of the public seeking such services must be placed under the control of the furnisher of the services, subject to the risk of carelessness on the part of the furnisher, its employees, or its agents.

LEGAL FOCUS—PROBLEM

The Escape Outdoor Center operates a facility that provides whitewater rafting excursions, mountain bike rentals, and a zipline course to area vacationers. Participants are required to sign a waiver of liability so as to hold the Center harmless in the event of property loss or personal injury. Is the agreement valid?

Of primary importance is the fact that the covered activities are recreational in nature. As such, rafting excursions, bike rentals, and zipline courses involve activities that are neither essential nor heavily regulated, compared with public transportation and health care. In the absence of gross negligence, the release of liability should be valid, providing that the risks are sufficiently disclosed so that the participant can make an informed decision. Of course, to secure the protections afforded by the clause, the Center must ensure that the equipment is maintained adequately and that their employees neither recklessly nor intentionally subject participants to known perils that exceed the normal expectation of risk.

There are some key differences between rafting excursions, zipline courses, and bike rentals. One basic difference is the fact that potential risks are posed by a river over which the center and its employees would have no control. A sudden downpour of rain could render rafting much more treacherous than originally anticipated. But the potential for such a development generally is known. On the other hand, a zipline course is designed and maintained by the Center, so from a responsibility perspective, the Center operates a ropes course more than it operates the river. Also, although the Center bears responsibility for maintaining the bikes, once rented, the operation of a functional bike is under the control of the cyclist. So in addition to evaluating the activity generally, the facts surrounding how any harm occurred should be considered as well.

Exculpatory agreements sometimes are characterized by courts as being *unconscionable*. Unconscionable clauses, those that "shock the conscience" of a court, are more likely to be found in preprinted form contracts than those in which the parties truly bargained over terms. When one party has vastly superior bargaining power over another, they often draft their contracts without consultation with the other party. Such a contract is called an **adhesion contract**, defined as a contract drafted by a dominant party and then presented to the weaker party—the adhering party—on a "take it or leave it" basis. If the powerful party used his or her bargaining advantage to include unfair or surprising terms in the contract, a court has the power to consider such terms or the entire contract unconscionable and to refuse to enforce it as against public policy. This unconscionability defense has been raised with respect to consumer contracts, and we will look closer at consumer transactions in Chapter 13.

adhesion contract
A contract drafted by a dominant party and then presented to the other party—the adhering party—on a "take it or leave it" basis.

What Is the Effect of Illegality?

An illegal agreement is void, and courts normally will not aid either party to the transaction in any way. Exceptions are made and damages in tort or other relief may be awarded (1) when the violated law is intended to protect one of the parties (e.g., this is true when one party is the victim of usury), (2) when the parties are not equally blameworthy (e.g., when one party is the victim of fraud in illegal securities dealing, or when one party acts under duress or undue influence), and (3) when one of the parties repents and withdraws before the time set for performance (as in illegal bets over the outcome of a football game).

It is also possible that instead of holding an entire contract void an offending paragraph might be considered void or reformed (rewritten). Some states refer to this as the "blue pencil" doctrine, which allows a judge to ignore or rewrite an offending provision and uphold the contract. Whether, when, and how the blue pencil rule applies differs significantly from state to state, but if the contract is indivisible (dependent on the void provision to make sense or be of value to the parties), the court would not apply the doctrine.

Form Prescribed by Law

The last requisite of a contract is that contracts be in the form prescribed by law to be enforceable. This requirement exists only for those contracts so identified by statute.

Interestingly, such contracts may be deficient in form, yet otherwise be valid. Thus, if the party who is entitled to raise the issue of form does not object, the contract may be routinely performed (executed) by both parties. After the contract is performed, the question of proper form is usually moot (no longer open to argument).

Statute of Frauds
A state statute requiring certain types of contracts to be evidenced by writing and to be signed by the party to be charged, or by her or his authorized agent.

A verbal contract isn't worth the paper it's written on.
—*Samuel Goldwyn*, movie producer, 1882–1974

What Is the Statute of Frauds and Perjuries?

By statute, certain specialized contracts, such as fire and homeowners' insurance policies, must contain prescribed language. It is also true of contracts for loans and for sales of goods on credit under the Truth in Lending Act. But the most important legislation governing form in contracts was originated in 1677 in the English **Statute of Frauds and Perjuries**. In essence, this statute provided that certain designated important contracts, to be enforceable in court, must (1) be in writing and (2) be signed by the party against whom enforcement is sought, or by her agent. Note that no problem as to form arises if the party *seeking* to enforce the contract has not signed. Such a party could simply and promptly sign the document if the other party points out the lack of a signature.

property
Anything that may be owned.

real property
Land and things permanently attached to it. Includes air space above, surface water, and subsurface waters, gases, and minerals.

The English statute is the original model for many versions adopted in most American states, all designed to prevent parties from subsequently fraudulently misrepresenting the actual terms of their agreements.

Writing important agreements encourages more careful draftsmanship and thus reduces potential misunderstandings and costly litigation. The requirement of a signature permits free and open negotiation and exchange of unsigned tentative drafts of the contract without fear of unintended or premature commitment. Including a sentence requiring the losing party, in the case of litigation, to pay all court costs and reasonable attorney fees of the winner can discourage breaches of contracts and spiteful lawsuits. Better still, the written contract can provide for arbitration or some other specified alternative method of dispute resolution (see Chapter 4). Although the Statute of Frauds should encourage careful draftsmanship, any writing satisfies the requirement if it sufficiently expresses the agreement. Of course, the party against whom enforcement is sought must sign it. The writing could consist of a memorandum or letters, for example.

personal property
All property that is not real property, that is, property other than land and things permanently attached to it.

tangible property
Property that has physical existence and can be touched. An automobile is tangible personal property; a house is tangible real property.

intangible property
Property recognized by law even though it has no physical existence.

The following rules are better understood if certain technical words are first defined. The word **property** has a double meaning. It usually means the thing that is owned; in a strict legal sense, however, *property* means the rights of the owner to possess, use, and dispose of that thing. Property is classified broadly as real or personal. **Real property** is the land and things "permanently attached" to the land, such as buildings. It includes rights to airspace above the land, to water on the surface, and to the materials below the surface (e.g., oil, gas, and minerals). **Personal property** includes all movable property other than land. Both real and personal properly appear in tangible and intangible forms. **Tangible property** has physical existence—it can be touched or seen. In contrast, **intangible property** has conceptual existence; an example is your reputation. Examples of *tangible real property* are the ground or land and buildings erected on the land. An example of *intangible real property* is an easement. An *easement* is the right to use another person's real properly within prescribed limits and without removing anything from the property. An example would be an easement to go across another's land to get to the shore of a lake or river. Examples of *tangible personal property* include this book, your watch, and a Big Mac at a McDonald's restaurant. Examples of *intangible personal property* are the copyright on this book, the design patent on your watch, and the goodwill enjoyed by owners of McDonald's fast-food restaurants. The person who has *title* owns the properly. Personal property is discussed further in Chapter 10 and real property in Chapter 9.

What Contracts Must Comply with the Statute of Frauds?

The Statute of Frauds applies to the following kinds of contracts:

- *A contract for the sale of land (real property) or an interest therein.* Some states also require a lease for more than one year to be in writing. Thus, a month-to-month lease, or a lease as long as one year, is valid even if oral. Under what is called the *equal-dignities rule,* the real estate broker's employment agreement (sometimes called a *listing*) to search for a purchaser of real properly also must be in writing and properly signed.
- *A contract for the sale of tangible goods for the price of $500 or more.* Under the UCC, *goods* means items that are movable, as well as the unborn young of animals and growing crops.

Remember, not all contracts in which the consideration exchanged is $500 or more must be in writing—the $500 provision applies only to contracts for the sale of goods. Certain important exceptions are made to this rule by the UCC, as well. An oral contract for goods priced at $500 or more nevertheless is enforceable "if the goods are to be specially manufactured for the buyer and are not suitable for sale to others in the ordinary course of the seller's business." An example would be a unique and elaborate cabinet made with costly imported woods to hold a variety of audiovisual equipment, complete with a wet bar and built-in refrigerator. Before notice of repudiation of the contract is received, the seller must have "made either a substantial beginning of their manufacture, or commitments for their procurement." Furthermore, the buyer is bound "with respect to goods for which payment has been made and accepted or which have been received and accepted." Finally, buyers are bound if they admit in their pleading, testimony, or otherwise in court that a contract was made. The contract in such case would be enforceable, but only for the quantity of goods admitted.

LEGAL FOCUS—BACKGROUND

The UCC provides a special rule for merchants. Assume that between merchants a writing in confirmation of the sales contract and sufficient *against* the sender (who has signed) is received within a reasonable time, and the recipient has reason to know its contents. This will satisfy the requirement of a signed writing against the recipient (even though the recipient has not signed), unless the recipient gives written notice of objection to its contents to the sender within ten days after it has been received.

- *A contract that is not to be performed, and cannot possibly be performed within one year from the date of the agreement.* In calculating the time, the law ignores fractions of days, including any fraction of the date of the agreement. Thus, an oral contract for one year, to begin tomorrow, is enforceable. If it is to begin two or more days hence, it must be in writing and signed.

LEGAL FOCUS—PROBLEM

Samer Jamal is set to graduate from college. An employer orally contracts with Jamal to employ him for two years at $2,000 per month. Is this contract required to be in writing?

Yes, the contract is required to be in writing. Because the terms of the contract exceed one year, this contract must be proved by written evidence to be enforceable. The oral agreement is insufficient proof of the existence of the contract. The one-year period begins to run the day after the contract is made, even if performance is not expected to begin until later. Remember, the fact that the salary exceeds $500 is insignificant because the contract does not involve the sale of goods. It is the one-year provision of the Statute of Frauds that applies in this case.

- *A secondary, or underlying, contract* under which one person promises to pay or answer for the debt or duty of another, if such person fails to perform, or one in which an executor or administrator of an estate promises to pay a debt of the estate with his own money.
- *A promise made in consideration of marriage* (e.g., "If you marry me, I will support your parents until they die"). Note that a contract to marry, and the actual contract of marriage, may be and usually are expressed orally: "Will you marry me?" "Yes." "I now pronounce you husband and wife."
- *For the sale of kinds of personal property not otherwise covered* (in an amount or value beyond $5,000).
- This provision does not apply to contracts for the sale of goods, securities, or security agreements, all of which are covered separately.

Sufficiency of the Writing

The Statute of Frauds does not require a complete written contract signed by both parties. The statute also can be satisfied with a far less extensive writing—a memorandum. The memorandum can consist of any confirmation, invoice, sales slip, check, or telegram. Such items, singly or in combination, may be writings sufficient to satisfy the Statute of Frauds. Requirements of the statute for the memorandum are as follows:

- It must be signed by the party against whom enforcement is sought.
- It must contain at least the essential terms of the contract.

It is not required that both parties sign the memorandum. The essential signature is the signature of the person against whom enforcement is sought (person being sued).

LEGAL FOCUS—PROBLEM

Shelly Moon agreed to lease Eric Almendral's house for three years for $600 a month rent. Moon found an old standard-form lease, filled out the terms, signed it, and gave it to Almendral saying, "Please sign this lease, Eric." Almendral responded that he had changed his mind and now would like $750 a month rent. Can Moon enforce Almendral's oral promise to lease the property for three years at $600 a month? Does the lease she signed satisfy the Statute of Frauds?

Moon cannot enforce Almendral's promise, as a lease for a three-year term must be in writing to be enforceable. Although Moon prepared the lease, Almendral did not sign it, and he is the party against whom enforcement is sought. In other words, for a party to enforce a contract, the writing must be signed by the other party. Thus, it is possible for a contract to be enforceable by one party, but not by the other.

The signature can be placed anywhere on the writing. It need not be at the end. And a signature can be initials or even a mark rather than a full name. The law does not require a witness, although without a witness, it is hard to prove who created a mark and that the mark was intended as a signature. Moon could have made a deposit by check (noting purpose of the payment on the check) and then Almendral's signature as an endorsement undoubtedly would have satisfied the Statute of Frauds.

LEGAL FOCUS—CASE

Can an e-mail contain a signature and satisfy the Statute of Frauds? Think about how one would sign an e-mail. In a California case heard in federal court between inventor Stewart Lamle and Mattel, Inc., Mattel argued that an e-mail did not satisfy the Statute of Frauds, particularly the requirement that the writing be signed by the party against whom enforcement is sought. The court concluded that an e-mail sent by a Mattel employee was sufficient:

> *California law ... provide[s] that typed names appearing on the end of telegrams are sufficient to be writings under the Statute of Frauds. California law also provides that a typewritten name is sufficient to be a signature. We can see no meaningful difference between a typewritten signature on a telegram and an e-mail. Therefore, we conclude that under California law the June 26 e-mail satisfies the Statute of Frauds ... and that the e-mail includes all the material terms of that agreement.*

Lamle v. Mattel, Inc., 394 F.3d 1355 (Ca.Fed. 2005).

Uniform Electronic Transactions Act (UETA)
A uniform state act providing a legal framework for electronic transactions giving electronic signatures and records the same validity and enforceability as manual signatures and paper-based transactions.

The Uniform Electronic Transactions Act (UETA) has been adopted by forty-seven states since its completion in 1999. Three states, Illinois, New York, and Washington, have not adopted the UETA, but they have state laws addressing electronic transactions. The UETA was designed to support the use of electronic commerce. The National Conference of Commissioners on Uniform State Laws stated "the primary objective of this act is to establish the legal equivalence of electronic records and signatures with paper writings and manually signed signatures, removing barriers to electronic commerce." Perhaps the most important section of the law is Section 7, which provides that an electronic record or signature can be sufficient to provide for enforceability of the contract.

PAROLE EVIDENCE RULE

Although certain categories of contracts must be in writing under the Statute of Frauds, a great number of oral contracts can be enforced in court. As a practical matter, however, many people prefer to reduce their agreements to writing so that terms can be proven more easily if a dispute arises. The Parole Evidence Rule provides that, if there is a written contract, then evidence from outside the four corners of the agreement cannot be admitted into court to change its terms. The court presumes that the written contract was intended to be the final expression of the agreement between the parties, so it cannot be contradicted by evidence of any prior agreement or of a contemporaneous oral agreement. Evidence can be introduced, however, to explain any ambiguity in the contract, as well as to prove a subsequent modification of the contract.

LEGAL FOCUS—PROBLEM

Tony entered into a complete and final written lease agreement for an apartment. The lease specified in bold, "NO PETS." At the time the parties signed the agreement, Tony pleaded with the landlord to allow him to keep Fluffy his cat. The landlord promised Tony orally that he could keep the cat. Tony's friends can attest to the fact that the landlord made this oral promise, but now the landlord wants to terminate the lease agreement. The lease provides for early termination with a penalty provision if pets are found on the premises. Can Tony introduce evidence of the oral agreement?

privity of contract
Applies to a direct contractual relationship between parties, as exists, for example, with a consumer-buyer dealing with the retail-seller but not with the wholesaler or manufacturer of the goods.

No, he cannot introduce the oral agreement. Evidence cannot be admitted to show that there was an oral agreement inconsistent with the terms of the written contract, so the written agreement stands, and Fluffy must go. If instead the parties had modified the agreement, for example, Tony agreed to pay a pet deposit and in exchange the landlord agreed to allow the cat to stay in the apartment, then evidence of that oral modification would be admissible. Or, if the lease had allowed "pets" and Tony wanted to start a breeding kennel over the landlord's objection, then evidence regarding what the parties meant in using the term "pets" could be introduced to assist in interpreting the agreement.

DIRECT INVOLVEMENT OF THIRD PARTIES IN CONTRACTS

Third-Party Donee and Creditor Beneficiaries

If a contract is valid and legally enforceable, attention turns to the rights and duties of the parties. The relationship created between parties to a contract is called **privity of contract**. Parties in privity of contract have rights and duties because of the contract. Usually, third parties not in privity have no rights under the contract.

third-party beneficiary
A third party who receives the benefit of a contract between two other persons.

Most bilateral and unilateral contracts directly involve only the two original contracting parties. However, from the inception of their agreement, one party may name and provide for a **third-party beneficiary**. For example, a parent in a contract for ordinary life insurance may name a child as a beneficiary of the policy. Because the main purpose is to confer a gift upon a third party, the child who has paid nothing therefore qualifies as a *donee beneficiary*. As such, the child may enforce the contract and collect the proceeds of the policy upon the death of the parent. If the main purpose of the promisee buying the policy is to pay a debt or extinguish an obligation owed to a third party, then the third party is a *creditor beneficiary*.

LEGAL FOCUS—PROBLEM

When Kirby Nikkel sold his gift and novelty shop to Cathy Oddeon, there were accounts payable (money owed to creditors) on the books with a total of $12,000 owed to five suppliers. Oddeon agreed to pay the balance due as part of the purchase price of the shop. Thus, the five suppliers were third-party creditor beneficiaries in the sales contract, and they have legal claims under the contract against Oddeon.

Beneficiaries of contracts (whether donee or creditor) can sue to enforce a contract that was made purposely for their benefit. Not all persons who benefit from contracts are given the right to enforce beneficial promises, however. The courts distinguish between intended beneficiaries (who can sue to enforce the contract) and incidental beneficiaries.

An incidental beneficiary is a person who benefits from a contract but is not named and has no legally enforceable rights or duties under the contract. An example would be the benefit that people enjoy when the government builds a road under contract, or when private developers build a shopping center. Probably everyone has been an incidental beneficiary in many contracts.

Assignment of Contract Rights and Delegation of Duties

assignment
The transfer of some or all rights under a contract to another person.

After a contract has been made, the original parties generally may transfer their contractual rights and duties to others. The transfer of a *right* to a third person is an **assignment**. When rights under a contract are assigned, the rights of the *assignor* (the party making the assignment) usually end. The third party—the *assignee,* the party receiving the assignment—has a right to demand performance from the other original party to the contract, the *obligor.* Most rights can be freely assigned, but there are exceptions. For example, unless otherwise agreed, one may not transfer rights to personal services. Also, a transfer of rights may not be made if it could materially increase the burden of performance on the other party to the contract. Thus, you cannot transfer your fire insurance policy to someone who buys your house, nor your automobile insurance to someone who buys your car. Indeed, such contracts specifically prohibit assignment to another party.

delegation
Transfer of some or all contractual duties to another person.

Parties also can transfer duties. Duties are not assigned—they are *delegated.* Normally, a **delegation** of duties does not release the party making the delegation (the *delegator*) from any obligations. If the party to whom the duty has been delegated (the *delegatee*) fails to perform, the delegator—who is the original obligor—must perform. No special form is required to delegate duties. In special situations, such as those involving uniquely personal services, the duties may not be delegated. Thus, without consent of the patient, a surgeon may not transfer an accepted duty of performing an operation.

LEGAL FOCUS—PROBLEM

On June 1, 2005, Able Construction Co., a general contractor, agrees to build and sell a particular house to Susie Baker on land it owns, for a contract price of $350,000. Promised delivery date is on or before November 1, that year. Daniel Able and a small crew of his employees prepare the site and lay the foundation. In separate contracts, on and after June 8, 2005, Able delegates all other construction work to independent contractors who are trade specialists in their fields (carpentry, plumbing, electrical work, painting, and so forth) for various prices. Able remains liable to Baker for the completed job as promised. On July 1, 2005, Baker learns that she is to be promoted and transferred by her employer to another city. Therefore, she sells the house to a friend, Jessica Newcomer, on August 10, 2005. She does this by assigning her rights and delegating her duties in the project to Newcomer. These contracts are portrayed graphically in Exhibit 8.3.

Valid transfers of contractual rights and duties occur with regularity. A common example that often involves multiple transfers is a contract for the construction of a private residence.

Note that Able might have assigned the right to part of or the entire $350,000 price to a bank for a construction loan. Also, both Baker and Newcomer could have negotiated separate loan contracts, with the house as security, to finance the purchase (see Chapter 9).

EXHIBIT 8.3 Example of Contract with Subsequent Delegation of Duties and Assignment of Rights

Original Contract	ABLE CONSTRUCTION CO.	June 1, 2005  → ← $350,000	BAKER
	Able agrees to construct house on lot.		Baker agrees to pay price of $350,000
Subcontracts	ABLE CONSTRUCTION CO.	June 8, 2005 (and other dates) various $ amounts → ← various labor and material	VARIOUS SUBCONTRACTORS (e.g., Charles & Co., carpenters; Eduardo & Co., plumbers; Linda & Co., electricians; Paul & Co., painters; etc.
	In a series of separate contracts, Able *delegates* many duties to independent subcontractors.		Various specified construction subcontractors agree to do work required to build house, supplying necessary materials.
Delegation of Duties and Assignment of Rights	BAKER	August 10, 2005  Assigns to Newcomer her rights to the house and delegates to Newcomer her duty to pay Able $350,000 →	NEWCOMER
	Baker *delegates* to Newcomer duty of paying $350,000 to Able (Baker remains contingently liable and must pay if Newcomer fails to do so). Concurrently, Baker *assigns* to Newcomer her right to the finished house.		Newcomer agrees to pay $350,000 to Able because this gives her the right to take possession of the house when finished.

Note, too, that Baker might have asked Newcomer to pay more or less than $350,000, but the parties agreed to the transfer at the original price.

HOW ARE CONTRACTS DISCHARGED?

performance
That which each party to a contract promises to do.

The usual way of discharging contracts is by **performance**. The reciprocal rights and duties of the parties are terminated legally when the parties have done what they have promised to do. Sometimes, the performance is not precisely as promised, but the minor deviation may be a good-faith oversight or failure. In the home construction example,

substantial performance
When a party to a contract honestly performs most essentials of the contract, but there is some minor omission or deviation that can be corrected, or compensated for in a reduction of the price.

assume the paint used was the proper quality and color but the wrong brand, or the garage door may have been a half-foot wider than specified The buyer must still "perform" by paying for such **substantial performance** by the general contractor but may deduct an appropriate amount because of any deficiency in the builder's performance. The buyer need not pay extra for any improvements "volunteered" by the builder. Often, businesspersons as well as ultimate consumers will accept an alternative or a variation of a promised performance simply because the deviation is not significant or does not reduce the value of consideration received. To insist on absolute compliance may end a mutually beneficial relationship.

waive
To give up a right.

Rather than engage in costly and acrimonious arguments and litigation, a party may **waive** (give up) or renounce legal contract rights. For example, an employer may do so when an employee under a one-year contract quits without just cause after a couple of months. Occasionally, a party will agree to accept some substitute for the consideration originally promised.

LEGAL FOCUS—EXAMPLE

Malcolm Defft, a dentist, never refused to treat a patient, regardless of her ability to pay promptly for the service. When the charges for dental care of Earl Gartner, an unemployed gardener, and his wife Hildy reached $600, they offered to redo Defft's lawn and trim all the trees and bushes on his lot in full payment or satisfaction of the debt. Defft agreed. This agreement was an executory *accord*. When the work was completed, the debt was discharged by *accord* and *satisfaction*.

accord and satisfaction
A party agrees (by accord) to accept some substitute for the promised performance of a contract, which is then provided (the satisfaction).

An accord is an agreement to perform an act to satisfy an existing contractual duty. A satisfaction is the performance of the accord agreement. For a contract to be discharged by **accord and satisfaction**, the parties must agree to accept a performance different from the performance originally promised. An accord and its satisfaction, or performance, discharge the original contractual obligation. Until satisfaction, the parties do not give up the rights they had before the accord.

LEGAL FOCUS—EXAMPLE

Peter Benton gets a judgment against Kris Lorie for $6,000. Later, both parties agree that the judgment can be satisfied (paid) by Lorie's transferring her motor home to Benton. This agreement to accept the motor home instead of $6,000 in cash is the accord. If Lorie transfers her motor home to Benton, the accord agreement is fully satisfied, and the $6,000 debt is discharged. If Lorie refuses to transfer her motor home, the accord is breached. Because an original obligation is merely suspended in an accord, Benton can bring a lawsuit to enforce the judgment for $6,000 in cash.

novation
A three-party agreement in which a creditor accepts a new party who agrees to assume the debt and to release the prior debtor.

In the hypothetical house construction, buyer Baker's contractual obligation might have been discharged if Able, the general contractor, had agreed with Baker and Newcomer to a **novation** (i.e., substitution of a new contract, debt, or obligation for an existing one between the same or different parties). Typically, a new contract is created with the same terms as the original one, but the novation substitutes a new party and discharges one of the original parties by agreement of all three parties. A novation would allow Newcomer to be substituted for Baker in the contract.

EXCUSES FOR NONPERFORMANCE

Other means of discharging a contract by operation of law include (1) subsequent illegality—as when the Eighteenth Amendment prohibited "manufacture, sale, or transportation of intoxicating liquors"; (2) bankruptcy (the debts are not extinguished, but they cannot be enforced unless reaffirmed by the debtor with approval by the court); (3) running of the statute of limitations (again, the debts are not extinguished, but they cannot be enforced unless reaffirmed by the debtor); (4) objective impossibility (as where a contract requires personal service and the individual dies); and (5) commercial impracticability amounting to much more than economic hardship, which is precipitated by an event unanticipated by either party. Sudden outbreak of war, the surprise discovery of solid granite throughout much of the anticipated site of an underground garage, and a major earthquake are examples of circumstances in which performance might be excused because the contract is rendered commercially impracticable.

As a practical matter, however, there are few legal excuses for failing to perform a valid contract. Generally, claims of impossibility of performance or commercial impracticability will not discharge contractual obligations because the parties are deemed to have assumed the risk of encountering potential difficulties when they contracted. Subjective factors that may make the contract difficult for one party to perform will not discharge the agreement. If Edna loses her job, it may be impossible for her to make her car payments as a practical matter, but legally she still is bound. To the extent possible, parties should risk-manage contingencies that could make the promised performance more difficult or less profitable by the inclusion of terms and conditions in the agreement.

For example, you can guard against price increases in raw materials by including a flexible pricing term in the contract. Then, if the price of raw materials rises dramatically, you will not lose money on the deal because the price in the contract will adjust accordingly. Because the law provides few excuses for contractual obligations to be discharged other than by performance, parties should write conditions into their contracts to provide for contingencies. An example of such a contractual condition is a morals clause in an endorsement contract. Such a clause is important because revelations that an endorser has drug or alcohol issues, has domestic violence concerns, or is engaged in criminal activity can have far-reaching financial impact on a company and its products. Morals clauses operate as a condition subsequent in the contract, and if violated by the celebrity, can terminate the endorsement contract and the obligation of the company to retain and pay the celebrity as an endorser. Without such a clause, there would be no excuse for the company's failure to pay the celebrity unless the contract could not be performed, for example, because the celebrity was incarcerated. Although contractual conditions are the enemies of a promise to perform, they are crucial in managing foreseeable risks.

breach
Failure without legal excuse to perform a promise made in a legally binding agreement.

rescission
The unmaking of a contract by the mutual agreement of the parties.

If a party fails to perform and that failure is not legally excused, then the aggrieved party may sue for damages. When there is a material (important) **breach**, or failure or refusal to perform a contract, the victim may cancel the contract with no liability in addition to suing for damages. The right to sue, if utilized successfully, may be superseded by a judgment of the court, which serves to discharge the contract by operation of law.

Circumstances can be such that both parties "want out." In such a case, a voluntary **rescission** mutually is agreed upon. Anything already received is returned, and the previous situation is restored.

WHAT REMEDIES ARE AVAILABLE FOR BREACH OF CONTRACT?

Vigorous contract activity is essential to a healthy economy. Through its laws, society seeks to encourage people to enter contracts and to perform as promised. Failure to do

compensatory damages
In the case of a breach of contract, this amount is equivalent to the actual dollar loss suffered because the defendant did not perform as promised.

so damages goodwill and continued relations. But a breach of contract is not a crime and, except in unusual circumstances (e.g., when there is a breach of covenant of good faith and fair dealing), it is not a tort. In a sense, contracting parties usually can regard a breach as a possible alternative to performance; it surely is not morally reprehensible if the victim of the breach is promptly "made whole" by being provided with money or some alternative performance that offsets any loss suffered.

If litigation becomes necessary, the defaulting party generally is obliged by a court to pay **compensatory damages**, sufficient to place the victim in essentially the same economic position or condition that would have resulted from performance of the contract. Only if the agreement were corrupted by a related tort, such as fraud, would punitive damages be awarded.

LEGAL FOCUS—EXAMPLE

Pete Armond agreed to sell his used Harley-Davidson motorcycle to Candy Bushnell for $6,500. When Armond changed his mind and refused to complete the deal, Bushnell promptly bought a comparable model for $7,500 from Pat Caldwell. Armond is liable to Bushnell for $1,000 in compensatory damages. If Bushnell was lucky enough to find a similar model priced at $6,000, she still could sue for *token or nominal damages* (typically for $1). Armond would also be liable for court costs, but not for Bushnell's attorney fees, unless that was provided for in the original sales contract.

liquidated damages
Amount of damages that contracting parties have previously agreed would be fair payment in case of breach. This amount will be unacceptable by a court if it is so large as to constitute a penalty.

Sometimes, the parties to a contract specify in advance what the damages shall be in case of breach. Such **liquidated damage clauses** often are used in contracts for the construction of public buildings or commercial structures where damages are difficult to determine and prove. Courts will enforce such terms as long as the damages are not in fact penalties. They must be reasonable in light of the anticipated or actual injury or harm caused by the breach.

LEGAL FOCUS—EXAMPLE

When Metropolitan College contracted for its new classroom building (price $6 million), the general contractor promised to have it ready for occupancy two years thereafter, when the fall semester would begin on August 28. A liquidated damage clause called for the payment of $600 per school day (Monday through Saturday) of delay in completion beyond the promised date of August 28. Losses incurred would include rental costs for temporary portable buildings and the monetary value of burdens imposed on students, faculty, and staff from overcrowding and required reassignments. Therefore, this clause would be enforceable.

In some cases in which money damages are inadequate, courts provide an *equitable, nonmonetary remedy*. For example, because every parcel of land is unique, a buyer of land can compel delivery of possession by the owner who promised to sell. So, too, with unique works of art. For example, in 1989, an unidentified Japanese bidder at an auction agreed to pay $45.9 million for *Pierrot's Wedding*, a masterpiece from Pablo

Picasso's famed "blue period." Under U.S. law, a seller who refuses to deliver such a painting could be compelled to do so by a buyer who obtains a *specific performance decree* from a court of equity. Of course, if the painting already has been sold to another person who, unaware of the prior contract, bought in good faith and received good title, the victimized buyer would have to be satisfied with a money judgment. When appropriate, courts of equity may also issue *injunctions* (sometimes called *restraining orders*), which may prohibit a defendant from doing a specified act or command the defendant to do some positive act.

LEGAL FOCUS—PROBLEM

The talented and temperamental opera star Matilda Nocallara contracted—a full year in advance—to perform at a gala concert in New York City. The event was promoted by Joy Jordane. A month before the scheduled date, Nocallara told Jordane that she was "indisposed" and planned instead to make "a less strenuous television appearance" that week in Los Angeles. What did Jordane do?

Jordane obtained an injunction from a court of equity, forbidding Nocallara to perform in Los Angeles on the day of the scheduled concert. The court would not directly compel her appearance in New York because that would smack of involuntary servitude and would be difficult to enforce. In addition, the court would award Jordane dollar damages if Nocallara failed to keep her New York commitment.

CASE

Hamer v. Sidway

124 N.Y. 538, 27 N.E. 256 (N.Y., 1891)

At a family celebration, in the presence of witnesses, William E. Story, Sr., promised to pay his nephew William E. Story, II, $5,000 if he would refrain from drinking, using tobacco, swearing, and playing cards or billiards (all legal activities for the nephew at that time) until he turned twenty-one. The nephew assented and fully performed the conditions of the promise. When he turned twenty-one, not quite six years later, he wrote a letter to his uncle, explaining that he had performed his part of their agreement and thereby was entitled to the $5,000. The uncle wrote a letter in response, reaffirming his promise. Unfortunately for the nephew, his uncle died some twelve years later without having paid him any money. The nephew assigned his claim to Hamer (the plaintiff in this case), but Sidway, the executor of the uncle's estate and the defendant in this action, rejected the claim. The executor's refusal was based on his belief that there was no consideration for the uncle's promise to pay because the uncle received no benefit from the nephew's performance. The following opinion of the New York Court of Appeals is a landmark statement on the rules of consideration, made in an interesting factual context. Keep in mind that $5,000 in 1891 is equivalent to more than $105,000 today.

J. Parker Wrote the Following

The uncle received the letter, and a few days later he wrote and mailed to his nephew the following letter:

> *Dear Nephew: Your letter of the 31st ult. came to hand all right, saying that you had lived up to the promise made to me several years ago. I have no doubt but you have, for which you shall have five thousand dollars, as I promised you. I had the money in the bank the day you was twenty-one years old that I intend for you, and you shall have the money certain. Now, Willie, I do not intend to interfere with this money in any way till I think you are capable of taking care of it, and the sooner that time comes the better it will please me. I would hate very much to have you start out in some adventure that you thought all right and lose this money in one year. The first five thousand dollars that I got together cost me a heap of hard work. You would hardly believe me when I tell you that to obtain this I shoved a jack-plane many a day, butchered three or four years, then came to this city, and, after three months' perseverance, I obtained a situation in a grocery store. I opened this store early, closed late, slept in the fourth story of the building in a room 30 by 40 feet, and not a human being in the building but myself. All this I done to live as cheap as I could to save something. I don't want you to take up with this kind of fare. I was here in the cholera season of '49 and '52, and the deaths averaged 80 to 125....*
>
> *Mr. Fisk, the gentleman I was working for, told me, if I left them, after it got healthy he probably would not want me. I stayed. All the money I have saved I know just how I got it. It did not come to me in any mysterious way, and the reason I speak of this is that money got in this way stops longer with a fellow that gets it with hard knocks than it does when he finds it. Willie, you are twenty-one, and you have many a timing to learn yet. This money you have earned much easier than I did, besides acquiring good habits at the same time, and you are quite welcome to the money. Hope you will make good use of it. I was ten long years getting this together after I was your age. Now, hoping this will be satisfactory, I stop. One thing more. Twenty-one years ago I bought you 15 sheep. These sheep were put out to double every four years. I kept track of them the first eight years. I have not heard much about them since. Your father and grandfather promised me that they would look after them till you were of age. Have they done so? I hope they have. By this time you have between five and six hundred sheep, worth a nice little income this spring. Willie, I have said much more than I expected to. Hope you can make out what I have written. Today is the seventeenth day that I have not been out of my room, and have had the doctor as many days. Am a little better today. Think I will get out next week. You*

> *need not mention [this] to father, as he always worries about small matters. Truly yours, W. E. STORY. P.S. You can consider this money on interest.*

The nephew received the letter, and thereafter consented that the money should remain with his uncle in accordance with the terms and conditions of the letter. The uncle died on the 29th day of January, 1887, without having paid over to his nephew any portion of the said $5,000 and interest....

The question which provoked the most discussion by counsel on this appeal, and which lies at the foundation of plaintiffs asserted right of recovery, is whether by virtue of a contract, defendant's testator, William E. Story, became indebted to his nephew, William E. Story, 2d, on his twenty-first birthday in the sum of $5,000. The defendant contends that the contract was without consideration to support it, and therefore invalid. He asserts that the promisee, by refraining from the use of liquor and tobacco, was not harmed, but benefited; that that which he did was best for him to do, independently of his uncle's promise—and insists that it follows that, unless the promisor was benefited, the contract was without consideration—a contention which, if well founded, would seem to leave open for controversy in many cases whether that which the promisee did or omitted to do was in fact of such benefit to him as to leave no consideration to support the enforcement of the promisor's agreement. Such a rule could not be tolerated, and is without foundation in the law. The exchequer chamber in 1875 defined "consideration" as follows: "A valuable consideration, in the sense of the law, may consist either in some right, interest, profit, or benefit accruing to the one party, or some forbearance, detriment, loss, or responsibility given, suffered, or undertaken by the other." Courts

> *will not ask whether the thing which forms the consideration does in fact benefit the promisee or a third party, or is of any substantial value to anyone. It is enough that something is promised, done, forborne, or suffered by the party to whom the promise is made as consideration for the promise made to him.*

Anson, Cont, 63. "In general a waiver of any legal right at the request of another party is a sufficient consideration for a promise." Pars. Cont. "Any damage, or suspension, or forbearance of a right will be sufficient to sustain a promise." 2 Kent, Comm. (12th Ed.)

Pollock, in his work on Contracts (page 166), after citing the definition given by the exchequer chamber, already quoted, says:

> *The second branch of this judicial description is really the most important one. "Consideration" means not so much that one party is profiting as that the other abandons some legal right in the present, or limits his legal freedom of action in the future, as an inducement for the promise of the first.*

Now, applying this rule to the facts before us, the promisee used tobacco, occasionally drank liquor, and he had a legal right to do so. That right he abandoned for a period of years upon the strength of the promise of the testator that for such forbearance he would give him $5,000.

We need not speculate on the effort which may have been required to give up the use of those stimulants. It is sufficient that he restricted his lawful freedom of action within certain prescribed limits upon the faith of his uncle's agreement, and now, having fully performed the conditions imposed, it is of no moment whether such performance actually proved a benefit to the promisor, and the court will not inquire into it; but, were it a proper subject of inquiry, we see nothing in this record that would permit a determination that the uncle was not benefited in a legal sense....

The order appealed from should be reversed, and the judgment of the special term affirmed, with costs payable out of the estate. All concur. [Hamer, the nephew's assignee, was found entitled to the $5,000 plus interest.]

For Critical Analysis

1. If "drinking, using tobacco, swearing, and playing cards or billiards" were illegal for minors in New York at the time of William Story, Sr.'s offer, would consideration have been present?
2. Why do you suppose the nephew did not demand payment from his uncle at the time he received his uncle's letter?
3. Could Sidway (the executor) argue that the Statute of Frauds applies in this case? How would Hamer counter that claim?

Vian v. Carey
1993 U.S. Dist. LEXIS 5460 (S.D.N.Y. Apr. 26, 1993)

This case involves a question about whether the parties intended to be bound in contract. One party argued that a contract was reached to make dolls in Mariah Carey's likeness, but the singer argued that she thought her father-in-law was just kidding.

J. Mukasey Delivered the Opinion of the Court

Defendant Mariah Carey is a famous, successful and apparently wealthy entertainer. Plaintiff Joseph Vian was her stepfather before she achieved stardom, but at the start of this litigation was in the process of becoming divorced from defendant's mother. He claims defendant agreed orally that he would have a license to market singing dolls in her likeness, and sues for breach of that agreement. Defendant claims that no contract existed and that the damages plaintiff seeks are not recoverable as a matter of law.

The alleged basis of the oral contract is that on at least three occasions, twice in the family car and once on **Vian's** boat, **Vian** told Carey, "Don't forget the Mariah dolls," and "I get the Mariah dolls." According to Vian, on one occasion Carey responded "okay" and on other occasions she merely smiled and nodded. Although Carey admits Vian mentioned the dolls two or three times, she testified that she thought it was a joke. For 30 years plaintiff has been in the business of designing, producing, and marketing gift and novelty items.

Plaintiff claims that he had an oral contract with defendant. In determining whether a contract exists, what matters are the parties' expressed intentions, the words and deeds which constitute objective signs in a given set of circumstances. It is well settled that for a contract to be valid, the agreement between the parties must be definite and explicit so their intention may be ascertained to a reasonable degree of certainty.

Therefore, the issue is whether the objective circumstances indicate that the parties intended to form a contract. Without such an intent, neither a contract nor a preliminary agreement to negotiate in good faith can exist. In making such a determination, a court may look at whether the terms of the contract have been finally resolved. In addition, a court may consider "the context of the negotiations." Id. Plaintiff has adduced no evidence that defendant ever intended by a nod of her head or the expression "okay" to enter into a complex commercial licensing agreement involving dolls in her likeness playing her copyrighted songs. The context in which this contract between an 18-year-old girl and her stepfather allegedly was made was an informal family setting, either in the car or on plaintiff's boat, while others were present. Vian's own version of events leads to the conclusion that there was no reason for Carey to think Vian was entirely serious, let alone that he intended to bind her to an agreement at that time. He admits he never told her he was serious. The objective circumstances do not indicate that Carey intended to form a contract with plaintiff. Although plaintiff's five-page memorandum of law (including two virtually textless pages) fails to raise the possibility, plaintiff also has not shown that Carey intended to be bound to negotiate with plaintiff at some later date over the licensing of "Mariah dolls."

There can be no meeting of the minds, required for the formation of a contract, where essential material terms are missing. Thus, even if the parties both believe themselves to be bound, there is no contract when the terms of the agreement are so vague and indefinite that there is no basis or standard for deciding whether the agreement had been kept or broken, or to fashion a remedy, and no means by which such terms may be made *certain*.

Licensing contracts such as the one Vian claims a right to exploit normally are intricate business. They involve details. Even if the agreement was merely to agree on terms at some future time, under New York law, a mere agreement to agree, in which a material term is left for future negotiations, is unenforceable. The word "license" was not even used. As defendant points out, no price or royalty term was mentioned, nor was the duration or geographic scope of the license, nor was Carey's right to approve the dolls. Plaintiff admits he would not have gone ahead without defendant's approval, thus conceding the materiality of that term.

In sum, plaintiff has not raised a triable issue of fact as to the existence of a contract. Viewing the facts in the light most favorable to plaintiff, as I have done in deciding this motion, there is no evidence that defendant thought, or should have thought, that plaintiff was serious about entering into a contract, nor that she believed she had bound herself to a licensing agreement for "Mariah dolls" by saying "okay" and nodding her head when her stepfather made passing references to the idea. The objective circumstances as portrayed by plaintiff do not indicate the existence of a legally binding agreement, and consideration is lacking.

For Critical Analysis

1. The question in the case is about whether or not there is an evidenced intent to be bound expressed by the parties. Intent is one of the three requirements for an offer. List the facts that suggest the parties intended to be bound in contract. List the facts that suggest that the parties did not intend to be bound in contract.
2. Do you agree with the court's holding? Why or why not?
3. What might Mariah Carey have done or said to evidence an intent to be bound?

Baker v. Adidas Am., Inc.

335 Fed. Appx. 356, 2009 U.S. App. LEXIS 14162 (4th Cir. N.C. 2009)

In this case a minor is attempting to avoid an endorsement contract. She claims the shoes caused injury, although she continued to receive payments pursuant to the agreement. Issues include the minor's ability to disaffirm a contract and the effect of conduct inconsistent with disaffirmance.

Per Curiam

Baker, a resident of Raleigh, North Carolina, was an outstanding junior tennis player who achieved national and international success as an amateur. While she was a junior, Adidas provided free merchandise for her to use during tournaments. Subsequently, on or about April 10, 2003, Baker—still a minor—signed an endorsement agreement with Adidas International Marketing BV. Pursuant to this agreement (the "Adidas Agreement"), Baker agreed to wear Adidas footwear and apparel for $20,000 in the first year of the contract and for $25,000 per year for each of the final two years, and Adidas agreed to pay certain performance bonuses … Finally, the Adidas Agreement provided that any claim of Baker's arising out of, or relating to the agreement would be governed by the law of the Netherlands and settled by Amsterdam courts. In 2003, the first year of the Adidas Agreement, Adidas International wired two $10,000 payments to SFX for Baker. Adidas also shipped shoes and clothes to Baker, which she wore while playing tennis.

In January 2004, Baker began experiencing problems with her left foot and withdrew from her tournament schedule. In April, Adidas International sent a representative from Portland, Oregon to North Carolina to examine Baker's foot and the shoes she was using. During this timeframe, Adidas International also made payment for Baker's travel expenses for a training camp. On April 10, 2004, Baker turned 18.

On April 19, 2004, Adidas International sent another payment to Baker in the amount of $12,500. In May 2004, the company flew Baker to Portland to try a redesigned shoe and gave her additional merchandise while she was there. The redesigned shoes did not help Baker. In October 2004, Adidas International wired $12,500 to SFX for Baker, thus completing its contractual obligation to pay Baker a $25,000 endorsement fee for the 2004 contract year.

In November 2004, with Baker still injured, Adidas International suspended further payments to her under Section 10 of the Adidas Agreement, which permitted suspension of payments "[w]ithout prejudice to the right to terminate th[e] Agreement" if Baker became unable to compete at world-class level for six months or more. J.A. 39. After undergoing surgeries and therapy, Baker was unable to recover and retired in 2005.

On August 4, 2005, Baker and SFX entered into an agreement and release terminating the Representation Agreement and "settl[ing] all issues between them." J.A. 149. In a letter dated December 20, 2006, from Baker's attorney to Adidas International, counsel stated, "Now that Ms. Baker has reached the age of majority, you are hereby notified that she has elected to declare the Agreement void. Accordingly, the jurisdictional provisions and limitations of liability set forth in the Agreement are unenforceable." In 2007, Baker brought this action against Adidas America in North Carolina state court, alleging that the shoes selected for her caused her injuries and ended her career. The complaint asserts a negligence claim and claims alleging breaches of the implied warranty of fitness for a particular purpose and the implied warranty of merchantability.

Adidas America removed the action to federal court and moved to dismiss under Rule 12(b)(3) for improper venue, pointing to the forum-selection clause contained in the Adidas Agreement. In her deposition, Baker stated that she did not remember signing the Adidas Agreement although she acknowledged that her signature is on it. She also stated that she was not aware of the payments that were made to her under that agreement. The court reasoned that since Baker entered into the Adidas Agreement —which contained the forum-selection clause—when she was a minor, it was voidable at her election under North Carolina law within a reasonable time after she reached the age of 18. The court also noted that, after Baker turned 18, she allowed Adidas International to attempt to redesign shoes for her and to fly her the next month to Portland, Oregon, for the same purpose. The court concluded that Baker's

> *failure to undertake the steps necessary to disaffirm the [Adidas] Agreement within a reasonable time, combined with defendant's continued performance of the contract through payments requires this court to reject plaintiff's arguments that the contract is avoidable due to age or proper disaffirmation.*

Under North Carolina law, "agreements or contracts, except for those dealing with necessities and those authorized by statute, are voidable at the election of the infant and may be disaffirmed by the infant during minority or within a reasonable time of reaching majority." *Creech v.* Melnik, 147 N.C. App. 471, 556 S.E.2d 587, 591 (N.C. Ct. App. 2001) (internal quotation marks omitted). What constitutes a reasonable time in this context "depends upon the circumstances of each case, no hard-and-fast rule regarding precise time limits being capable of definition." Nationwide Mut. Ins. Co. v. Chantos, 25 N.C. App. 482, 214 S.E.2d 438, 444 (N.C. Ct. App. 1975). "The privilege of disaffirmance may be lost where the infant affirms or otherwise ratifies the contract after reaching majority." Bobby Floars [*360] *Toyota, Inc. v. Smith,* 48 N.C. App. 580, 269 S.E.2d 320, 322 (N.C. Ct. App. 1980).

Here, after turning 18, Baker accepted two payments from Adidas International totaling $ 25,000. The second payment was received more than six months after her eighteenth birthday. 3 She also accepted Adidas International's attempt to redesign her shoes, [**9] as well as other merchandise at no charge to her one month after her birthday. After receiving all of these benefits, it was not until two years later—more than 32 months after she achieved the age of majority—that Baker communicated to Adidas International that she wished to void her contract. Under the facts of this case, this delay constituted an unreasonable length of time to elect disaffirmance. 4 Cf. Bobby Floars Toyota, 269 S.E.2d at 322-23 (holding that minor waited an unreasonable length of time to void purchase money security agreement to finance automobile when he continued to drive the vehicle and make payments on it for 10 months after reaching majority). In any event, Baker's acceptance of the two payments and other benefits after turning 18 "constituted a ratification of the contract, precluding subsequent disaffirmance." Id. at 323; see *McCormic v. Leggett,* 53 N.C. (8 Jones) 425, at *2 (1862) (holding that when minor sold real property, he ratified the sale by accepting payment after reaching age of majority).

For Critical Analysis

1. What agreement is Baker attempting to avoid? Why does she want to avoid the agreement? Is the fact that she did not remember signing the agreement a valid defense?
2. Was it entered into when she was minor? Can she disaffirm the agreement? Could she just disaffirm the forum selection clause and ratify the rest?
3. Could she have disaffirmed the contract before April 10, 2004? If so, what would her obligations to the company have been upon disaffirmance?

CHAPTER QUESTIONS AND PROBLEMS

1. Regarding the elements of a valid contract:
   a. What are the five, and sometimes six, elements that are said to be essential for a valid contract?
   b. In which of the six elements does the law permit performance or execution at the option of one of the parties who might have legally withdrawn without liability? Explain.
2. Regarding breach of contract:
   a. Is breaching a contract comparable in moral culpability and legal effect to committing a tort

or committing a crime? If not, how do these actions differ?

b. Under what circumstances can a party who breaches a contract also be guilty of committing a tort?

3. Identify three contracts you have experienced or observed. Select one that is expressed in writing, one expressed orally, and one implied in fact from con duct. Classify each as to parties bound, legal effect, and extent of performance.
4. Clearly distinguish between a valid contract, a voidable contract, and a void agreement. Provide an example of each type of agreement and demonstrate how the court would treat each of your situations if they were litigated.
5. When is an acceptance to an offer sent by mail effective to form a contract if the acceptance was returned by mail?
   a. When it arrives at the offeror(s)?
   b. When you decide you intend to accept?
   c. When the acceptance is given to the secretary to mail?
   d. When your check clears the bank?
   e. When your letter of acceptance is mailed?

   What are the legal consequences, if any, if a timely sent, properly addressed, and stamped letter is lost by the postal service?
6. Anne Marcie and Bob Bruce entered into a binding bilateral contract. The terms of the contract included that Marcie was to build a hang glider for Bruce and that Bruce was to pay Marcie $18,000 upon its completion. After formation of the contract, Bruce decided he did not want the hang glider; because the contract was advantageous, however, he assigned all of his rights thereunder and delegated his duty of payment to his friend Marc Shadoe. Shadoe paid Bruce $1,400 for the transferred right and immediately informed Marcie of the assignment. After Shadoe took delivery of the glider, he fled without paying Marcie. He was last seen by reliable sources gliding into Canada singing, "I did it my way." Characterize the contractual relationships of the parties and explain their respective rights.
7. Evelyn Millie, a university psychology professor, says to her students, "All of you have worked hard, and if you continue to perform at a high level, I will pay for a pizza party for the class at the end of the year—if I think it is warranted." The students insist that they continued to "work hard," and they claim that the class grades "are high," but Millie gives no party. Can the students enforce Millie's promise?
8. Plaintiff, a minor, alleged that his grandfather Schultz had made an oral contract with the plaintiff through his mother. In this alleged contract, Schultz agreed to give the plaintiff certain real estate if the plaintiff's mother would name the plaintiff after him. The plaintiff's parents accepted the proposal because they had in fact already named their son after Schultz. Schultz, however, never arranged for the title of the property to pass to the plaintiff. He did deliver possession of the real estate to the plaintiffs parents. The plaintiff requested that the court determine that he is the absolute owner of the real estate. Was the alleged contract between Schultz and the plaintiff's mother supported by consideration and therefore enforceable? [*Lanifer v. Lanifer,* 227 Iowa 258, 288 N.W. 104 (Iowa, 1939).]
9. On its webpage, Best Buy listed a fifty-two-inch set at a price of $9.99 for several hours, a great price for a Samsung set that typically costs $1,699.99. Some web shoppers ordered as many as ten sets in the hopes of getting what would be a very rare deal for a high-definition television. Best Buy, however, refused to honor the price. What result?
10. Lucy and Zehmer spoke while having dinner in a restaurant. During the course of their conversation, Lucy apparently offered to buy Zehmer's 471.6-acre farm for $50,000 cash. Although Zehmer claims that he thought the offer was made as a joke, he wrote the following on the back of a pad: "We hereby agree to sell to W.O. Lucy the Ferguson Farm complete for $50,000, title satisfactory to buyer." Zehmer then signed the writing and induced his wife Ida to do the same. She claims that she signed only after Zehmer assured her that it was only a joke. Can there be a contract even if she thought it was a joke? Would this contract need to be evidenced by a writing? [*Lucy v. Zehmer,* 84 S.E. 2d 516 (Va., 1954)]
11. Treasure Salvors and the State of Florida entered into a contract concerning the salvage of the *Atocha*, a Spanish ship that sank in 1622 loaded with treasure worth millions. Under the agreement, Treasure Salvors agreed to give Florida twenty-five percent of the items recovered in return for the right to salvage on state owned lands. Both parties thought the ship lay on land owned by Florida. After Treasure Salvors delivered to Florida its share of the bounty, the Supreme Court ruled that the land upon which the

ship rested was not owned by Florida. Does Treasure Salvors have a valid defense to the contract? [*Florida v. Treasure Salvors,* 458 U.S. 670 (1982)]

12. Howard entered into a contract to represent a hockey player, who was accused of plotting to kill his agent, in court proceedings. Howard, however, is an ex-con who has never been to law school and is not licensed to practice law. The hockey player paid a retainer fee to Howard as part of the agreement. Does the failure to have a law license affect the contract for legal representation?
13. Triangle Leasing Company, Inc. rents automobiles, trucks, and vans in western and central North Carolina. The company was ready to expand and hired defendant McMahon to manage their new regional office in the eastern part of the state. As part of the employment contract between Triangle and McMahon, the parties agreed that if McMahon's employment with Triangle was terminated for any reason, he would not "solicit or attempt to procure the customers, accounts, or business of [Triangle]" for a period of two years in North Carolina following his termination. Two years later, McMahon informed Triangle that he was terminating his employment and would be establishing a competing car rental business, Wilmington Auto Rental, Inc. in the same town. In an effort to enforce the no-solicitation clause of its employment contract with McMahon, Triangle sought an injunction. Should a court issue the injunction, or is the clause an illegal restraint of trade? [*Triangle Leasing Co. v. McMahon,* 393 S.E.2d 854 (N.C. 1990)]
14. The Teambuilding Ropes Course is a state-of-the-art training tool, designed and built to industry standards and is professionally inspected and maintained. It is operated by Have Fun Learning Services (HFLS). Participants in the challenge course must sign a release that provides:

    In consideration of the services of HFLS, I agree to release, indemnify, and discharge HFLS, and agree to indemnify and hold harmless HFLS from any and all claims, demands, or causes of action, which are in any way connected with my participation in this activity or my use of the equipment or facilities, including any such claims which allege negligent acts or omissions of HFLS.

    Would the hold harmless agreement more likely be deemed invalid or invalid in each of these situations on the ropes course and why?

    a. A participant's I-phone™ fell out of his pocket and was ruined.
    b. A participant broke her leg after grabbing a rope that HFLS knew was rotten and failed to replace.
    c. A participant slipped and fell after failing to follow clear directions.
    d. A participant suffered sunburn from being in the sun for three hours trying to complete the course.
15. Jill was hosting a conference at a local hotel. The written contract specified, among other things, the room rate, the guestroom block, the catering services to be provided, function space assignment and rental rate. A provision in the contract also specified,

    NO FOOD OR BEVERAGES OF ANY KIND WILL BE PERMITTED TO BE BROUGHT INTO THE HOTEL BY THE PATRON OR ANY PATRONS, GUESTS OR INVITEES FROM ANY OUTSIDE SOURCE. FURTHER, THE HOTEL RESERVES THE RIGHT TO CHARGE A SET-UP FEE FOR SUCH FOOD AND/OR BEVERAGE.

    The written agreement was intended to be the complete expression of the agreement between Jill and the Hotel. At the time the written agreement was signed, the hotel's manager and agent orally promised Jill that she could bring into her Executive Parlor any liquor or hors d'oeuvres she wished to serve conference attendees without charge. Subsequently, the hotel, upon learning of a soiree she hosted in her room, added the usual setup fee to her bill. Would the Parole Evidence Rule preclude the admission of the agent's promise? Would the Parole Evidence Rule also preclude the admission of an alleged oral agreement reached after the written contract was signed that added a cocktail party to the conference agenda for a specified fee?

CHAPTER 9

Real Property and Homeownership

Mid pleasures and palaces though we may roam, be it ever so humble, there's no place like home.

John Howard Payne

LEARNING OBJECTIVES

After reading and studying this chapter, you should be able to:

- Compare advantages and disadvantages of homeownership.
- Distinguish among the various types of agreements with real estate agents and brokers.
- Understand the important considerations to keep in mind when buying or selling a house.
- Understand the major legal considerations in a home sale contract.
- Identify and distinguish among the various methods of financing available for home sale contracts.
- Explain the legal ramifications of foreclosure and transfer of real estate security mortgages.
- Identify the important aspects of the escrow process, including title insurance.
- Identify the types of real property deeds.
- Distinguish among the various methods of joint title ownership.
- Explain how real property is taxed.
- Identify important attributes of fire insurance.
- Identify important attributes of covenants, conditions, and restrictions and other neighbor-to-neighbor legal issues.

The first home purchase is usually the biggest transaction a consumer has entered into at that point in his or her life. It also can be the most bewildering and confusing. Homes, whether single-family dwellings, townhouses, or condominiums, involve the complex and sometimes-archaic law of real property and significant numbers of traditions and customs. The decision of whether to rent or own is significantly complicated as well. The choice of a where and what to buy, how to go about purchasing the home, and who is responsible for what disclosures and issues is even more complicated.

LEGAL FOCUS—PROBLEM

Joe and Stephanie DiMarco and their two young children purchased a lovely home in the suburbs. They were unaware that a neighbor, Joshua Cox, previously had been convicted for a violent sexual assault upon a minor, had served five years in prison as a result, and had been released only two months before the DiMarco family arrived. Was the seller obligated to tell the DiMarcos about the neighbor?

Today in most places in the United States, sellers must reveal all relevant known information that might bear upon the decision to purchase a home. The current address of felons who have been convicted of specified violent sexual assaults is public information—but must sellers tell prospective buyers? The answer is uncertain, but with the trend as a guide, the most probable answer is that the DiMarcos should have been told by the seller. We consider the practices, economics, and laws of buying and selling homes in this chapter.

Homes are expensive and almost invariably, you will borrow money to purchase your home, adding a third party, the lender, to the mix in the transaction. Furthermore, because homes involve real property, the transaction will be complicated by topics of title, insurance deeds, agents, and the like. This chapter explores the process and reality of purchasing and owning your own home. We will begin by asking the first key question.

SHOULD I OWN MY OWN HOME?

The decision of whether to rent or own one's home is mostly an economic decision that has to be balanced against the advantages and disadvantages of each path. Exhibit 9.1 provides a comparison of advantages and disadvantages of homeownership against renting. Generally speaking, the monthly cost of ownership is greater than that of renting,

EXHIBIT 9.1 Advantages and Disadvantages of Homeownership

	Advantages	Disadvantages
Home ownership	Property builds equity	Responsible for maintenance
	Sense of community, stability, and security	Responsible for property taxes
	Free to change decor and landscaping	Possibility of foreclosure and loss of equity
	Not dependent on landlord to maintain property	Less mobility than renting

especially at the onset of a new home mortgage. But, over time, the monies put toward mortgage payments are partly going toward purchasing an asset that has value. If home values rise over the time of the mortgage, then the asset also appreciates. If the homebuyer does not take out additional or new loans and chooses a fixed interest rate loan, then payments usually can be expected to stay the same whereas other costs of living, including foregone rent, rise with inflation.

The higher monthly cost of homeownership at the beginning of a home purchase is derived from the usual necessity to make a down payment and the taking on of insurance, utility, tax, and repair payments. Although normally this cost is offset by equity and appreciation, a major consequence of frequent job change and the accompanying relocation and financial instability is that the traditional economic benefits of homeownership—equity buildup and appreciation—might never be realized.

LEGAL FOCUS—PROBLEM

Anne and Joe Fledsoe bought their first family home. It steadily appreciated in value, but they succumbed twice to mailed offers to refinance, each time pulling out their accumulated equity. Then, they took out a second mortgage to pay off a credit card and vehicle loan debt. Now Joe's employer has told him that he must relocate to another region of the country if he wishes to keep his job. At this point, their first and second mortgage payments are consuming a significant portion of their after-tax income. A realtor, in part because of a recent drop in home values, has just told the Fledsoes that they probably cannot sell their home for the balance of their first mortgage, let alone the combined amount of their first and second mortgages. The Fledsoes have two children and have accumulated new credit card debt. What options do the Fledsoes have?

The Fledsoes are typical of families who are dismayed to discover that their home equity has dissipated after buying and selling, refinancing, or taking out second mortgages. Often, these activities were based upon inflated home values at a peak market, which was followed by a market retraction. Sometimes equity loss is simply incurred costs (i.e., home improvements or repairs) that have not yet been paid back. The Fledsoes could sell for a loss or at a break-even price and move, with Anne seeking a new job in their new area. They could choose to have the family stay behind in their home and have Joe live in temporary quarters at his new location. Joe could decide not to move and look for a new job in their current area and avoid having to sell. In any case, the Fledsoes' potential job relocation has been greatly complicated by their homeownership, and they will have some difficult decisions ahead.

real estate broker
One who acts as an intermediary for real estate transactions on behalf of others for a fee or commission.

In later sections of this chapter, we will consider other examples of this unhappy phenomenon dealing with property taxation, other new financial burdens, and transaction costs (burdens placed upon sellers)—all of which are helping to erode traditional economic benefits of homeownership. First we are going to examine the home-buying process, starting with the role of the real estate agent.

WHAT IS THE ROLE OF A REAL ESTATE AGENT?

The real estate sales business is composed primarily of brokers and sales agents. **Real estate brokers** must obtain a state license that authorizes them to hire sales agents. Brokers need not be, but often are, corporations that hire many agents to perform the necessary services to sellers and buyers. Brokers act as managers and rarely meet with

real estate agent
A person licensed by the state to negotiate the buying and selling of real property while employed and supervised by a licensed real estate broker.

buyers or sellers, whose personal contact almost always is with a sales agent. **Real estate agents (sales agents)** also are licensed by the state and perform all of the day-to-day services and provide information as necessary to bring sellers and buyers of homes together and to make sales transactions happen. The success of home purchasers and sellers is affected by the services they receive from real estate sales agents.

Sales agents seldom receive salaries from the brokerage firms that employ them. Instead, they receive a portion, say 50 percent or more, of the sales commissions they generate. Thus, if a sales agent produces a commission of $18,000 by handling a home sale with a price of $300,000 (a 6 percent commission), she will be paid $9,000 by the broker, who will retain the other half. Top sales agents command commission splits with their brokers of 60 to 80 percent.

Service to Sellers

listing agent
A licensed agent who enters into an employment contract with the owner of real property to hunt for a buyer of the property on specified terms.

An owner desiring to sell usually hires a real estate brokerage company by negotiating with a sales agent. The owner understands that all future dealings will be directly with the sales agent—not with the broker. The employment of the agent, who is called the **listing agent**, is accomplished by using a form of employment contract that usually is presented to the homeowner by the agent. The employment contract, or listing, serves to hire the real estate broker (acting through the sales agent) to hunt for a suitable buyer.

The effect of the standard employment contract, or listing, subject to many regional variables, is that the prospective seller and the real estate agent exchange promises as follows: The seller promises to pay a commission of a negotiable percentage (often 6 percent) of the actual sales price if an acceptable offer to purchase is made by a qualified buyer (regardless of who finds the buyer) within a prescribed time period (often three to six months). The real estate broker promises to use "diligence" in hunting for a buyer. It is difficult, if not impossible, to prove in court that an incompetent agent failed to "use due diligence" in hunting for a buyer. That is why few sellers who become disenchanted with their listing agents sue them in court.

LEGAL FOCUS—PROBLEM

Samuel and Kimberly Yamshon signed a standard exclusive listing with Acme Real Estate for the sale of their home on specified terms. Shortly thereafter, at a social gathering, they met a couple, the Auburns, who were interested in buying a house similar to the Yamshons' home. The Auburns came by and decided to make an offer to purchase the home for an amount that was satisfactory to the Yamshons. Samuel telephoned their agent to cancel the listing because they had found their own buyer. Their sales agent, Jasdeep Saltsman, responded: "Fine, you may mail me a check for the 6 percent commission you owe." Do the Yamshons owe a commission even though their sales agent did no work and did not find the buyer?

exclusive listing
Employment contract in which the owner of real property agrees to pay a licensed agent a certain commission regardless of who finds the buyer to whom the property is sold. Also called *an exclusive right to sell.*

Yes, the Yamshons owe a commission. The commission is owed because the variety of service contract known as an **exclusive listing** requires payment of a commission regardless of who finds the buyer. Sometimes owners find their own buyers, sometimes buyers simply appear on their own accord, sometimes other sales agents find buyers, and, of course, sometimes the hired agent finds a buyer. In each of these situations, the commission is owed to the exclusive listing agent. The Yamshons would not owe any commission if they had asked for and signed a different kind of employment

exclusive-agency listing
Employment contract between an owner of real property and a licensed agent in which the owner may find a buyer and sell the property without liability for payment of commission, but must pay the listing agent if that agent or any other licensed agent finds the buyer.

multiple listing service
An organization of real estate brokers who exchange information about listings of property they have obtained.

contract—an **exclusive-agency listing**—under which owners who find their own buyers do not pay commissions, are widely available to sellers who are smart enough to ask for them. Such a listing is preferable from the seller's standpoint because, through luck or accident, a buyer may be found or appear without any agent.

As noted, listing agents promise to use diligence in hunting for a suitable buyer. This is accomplished by submitting data about the new seller's home to a regional database called the **multiple listing service**. All real estate brokers subscribe to this service and thereby gain access to specific data (address, square footage, number of baths and bedrooms, all amenities, and so on) about all homes in the region that are on the market. Thus, the subscribing broker has available for the firm's sales agents all of the information necessary to present to prospective buyers. Putting a home into multiple listing alone probably satisfies the promise by the listing agent to use due diligence.

Recall that the listing agreement is a fully negotiable employment contract. Before hiring a real estate broker to sell your home, you are well advised to negotiate for some, if not all, of the following provisions:

- The right to pay no commission if you find your own buyer. Often, a potential buyer may transfer to your workplace or surface through recommendations of your friends and acquaintances.
- A short listing period, perhaps as few as thirty days, with the understanding it will be extended in thirty-day increments if the agent is satisfactorily "pushing" the property. Remember, once your agent is hired, you have no legal right to end the listing early. How can you be sure your agent will provide good service?
- A reduced commission, perhaps 5 or even 4 percent, if the property is readily saleable and market conditions are good. Always calculate what percentage of your equity a 6 (or other) percent commission of the sales price represents. You will be surprised and probably shocked. Use this information in negotiating for a reduced commission percentage rate.
- Restrictions on when sales agents and their prospects will be permitted to enter the house, especially if you are still residing there. You can require the presence of your agent on each occasion your house is shown to others. (The sign in front of your house can read "shown by appointment.") Or you can accept a lock box arrangement whereby any agent can enter at any time.

The greatest benefit from hiring an agent to assist in the sale of your home is the experience of the agent (1) in directing you how to prepare your home for sale, (2) in knowing and explaining the market data in general and how they specifically affect the price of your home, and (3) in aggressively urging all other agents in the community to show your home to their prospects and providing them with a professional brochure of its features.

There are risks in hiring a listing agent. Your property may be placed in multiple listings and be quietly forgotten, with your agent doing nothing more than hoping that some other agent somewhere will stumble upon it (out of the thousands that are multiple listed). If your agent knows what your absolute lowest possible acceptable price is, that often will be the top offer you will receive. If your agent knows that your job has changed and you are desperate to sell, that information may find its way to prospective buyers who then will "bottom fish" (offer below-market prices). If no prospects appear as the weeks and months drift by, you cannot fire your listing agent for inactivity. If your listing agent is not competent and experienced, you may face problems with disclosing or withholding material information, with obtaining a reasonable termite clearance, and with demands by prospective buyers for repairs, fix-ups, and other costly changes. Care in employing a listing agent should be no less than the obvious care required in employing any professional person who will be charged with important responsibilities on your behalf.

Service to Buyers

Real estate sales agents usually take prospective buyers to and show them homes that are on the market. This often is referred to as the selling function. By tradition, the commission paid by the seller is split evenly between the brokers in charge of the listing and selling functions. It is important to distinguish between these two functions and to understand how the seller's commission is distributed. An example may clarify this distinction.

LEGAL FOCUS—PROBLEM

Sam Seller employed Larry Lister of Cold Realty to hunt for a buyer for his home on Shady Tree Lane and promised to pay a 6 percent commission if a ready, willing, and able purchaser was found who agreed to pay a $300,000 purchase price. Sallie Saleslady noticed Seller's home in the electronic multiple listing service while she was sitting at her desk at Tigar Realty Co. Saleslady thought this might be the right home for Betty Buyer, with whom she had been working, and arranged to show Seller's home to her. Buyer loved the home and asked Saleslady to prepare an offer to purchase and handle all the necessary details. As a result, Buyer bought Seller's home, and a commission of $18,000 was payable. Who gets the money?

In the listing agreement, Seller promised to pay the brokerage firm, Cold Realty, the $18,000 commission. But because the buyer was found by Tigar Realty Co., it received half, $9,000, directly from Cold Realty. Cold Realty splits commissions 50–50 with its agents and paid Lister his share, $4,500. Tigar Realty, however, had agreed to a 60–40 split with its leading producers, and so paid $5,400 to Saleslady for her efforts in finding the buyer and kept $3,600 for itself.

HOW IS AN OFFER TO PURCHASE A HOME MADE?

The agent representing the buyer will prepare a written offer to purchase. The buyer's agent will negotiate with the seller's agent by exchanging counteroffers. Once a real estate **purchase agreement** is signed by seller and buyer, the agents will play a less active role. The agents will assist in arranging for a home inspection, a termite inspection, and any other service providers who may be needed. Sellers and buyers typically rely on their agents for a wide variety of suggestions and information but also should read all documents and give the transaction the personal attention that its importance deserves.

purchase agreement
A contract by which a seller agrees to sell, and the buyer agrees to buy, a specified parcel of real property at a specified price and upon specified terms.

An offer to purchase real property, such as a home, should be made in writing. Otherwise, under the Statute of Frauds, it is unenforceable should either party dispute its terms or even deny its existence. The offer must state essential terms, such as a description of the property, the purchase price, and payment terms.

Sales agents usually then assist the process of negotiating back and forth on behalf of the seller and buyer, thereby avoiding the intransigence that typically is created by eye-to-eye dealings. This negotiation is the single most valuable service provided by agents.

Some contend that preparation of the written purchase agreement is the primary service rendered for sellers and buyers.

What Is the Effect of an Accepted Offer?

When a written purchase contract is prepared for and signed by the buyer, it becomes a formal offer to purchase and is delivered to the seller's agent. A good-faith deposit made by the buyer usually accompanies a purchase agreement. In theory, the deposit is to assure the seller that the buyer is not a mere "tire kicker" and intends to purchase the property. **Liquidated damages** are an amount of money agreed upon between contracting parties to fairly represent all losses of the innocent party if the contract is wrongfully broken. Such a provision is common and should eliminate the necessity of litigation because the parties already have agreed upon a solution. The earnest money serves as liquidated damages in the event of a broken contract. If the buyer wrongfully fails to complete the purchase, the deposit can be retained by the seller as liquidated damages for the breach of the contract of purchase. There is no legal requirement that a buyer include a deposit with the offer, but it is a customary sign of serious intent and ability to buy, and a seller most likely would refuse to accept an offer without one. Often, the earnest money deposit will approximate 1 percent of the purchase price. But there is one fly in the ointment for the seller who attempts to retain the earnest money deposit after a buyer defaults.

liquidated damages
Amount of damages that contracting parties previously have agreed would be fair payment in case of breach.

LEGAL FOCUS—PROBLEM

Sam Seller signed a contract to sell his home to Betty Buyer. A $3,000 earnest money deposit had accompanied the deposit receipt and was on deposit at the Acme Escrow and Title Company. Then Buyer found a home she liked better and bought it. Seller never saw her again. A few days later, Seller telephoned Acme and asked them to send the now-forfeited $3,000 deposit to him. To his dismay, Acme declined and referred him to the listing agent, Larry Lister. Seller immediately called Lister asking about the money. What do you suppose Lister said?

In all likelihood, Lister said, "Like it says in the listing, I get one-half of the forfeited deposit money for my troubles in finding the buyer." Seller learned, by reference to the listing contract, that Larry was indeed entitled to one-half of the money for finding the "deadbeat" buyer. If Seller had bothered to read the listing form before signing it, he could have deleted that provision.

LEGAL FOCUS—PROBLEM

Audra Acquirer made a written, signed offer to purchase Tom Holden's home. Holden signed and returned the offer, thereby creating a binding contract. Subsequently, pending "close of escrow" (the usual moment when ownership passes to the buyer), Holden refused to complete the transaction. Acquirer believed that Holden did this because he found out that his house was worth a lot more money than his selling price. Acquirer contacted her attorney. What advice will she receive?

Acquirer's attorney will advise her that she has two legal remedies. In the first, she can proceed "in equity" and request the court to order Holden to comply with the agreement. This remedy is called *specific performance* and is available when dollar damages would be inadequate. Money damages would be inadequate here because the courts consider every parcel of land to be unique (no two parcels can be in the same place) and unable to be substituted for in the marketplace, as can, for example, an automobile. If Acquirer won such a lawsuit, the court would order Holden to convey ownership as promised. Acquirer, of course, would have to pay the price, as promised.

In the alternative remedy, Acquirer can sue "at law" and request the court to assess damages against Holden in an amount equal to her out-of-pocket expenses plus the benefit of her bargain, if any. (This "benefit of the bargain" could be the difference between the low purchase price of the home and its higher fair market value.) Acquirer's choice of remedy—to sue for the property or the money—would depend primarily on how special the property was to her and what amount of monetary damages she could expect to recover.

In addition, and as a separate matter, if Holden had listed the property with a real estate brokerage firm and signed the customary form, he would be obligated to pay the firm a commission, even though the sale was never completed. This is so because the broker had found in Acquirer a "ready, willing, and able buyer" who had signed a written offer to buy on terms originally specified by the seller.

WHAT ARE DISCLOSURE LAWS?

In common law, the seller of a home is not required to disclose patent (visible) defects to a buyer, the theory being that the buyer should be alert enough to see and discover such defects. Latent (hidden) defects that were known to the seller need not be revealed; if asked, the seller cannot lie, but ordinary sales "puffing" is legal. In a general sense, common law holds "let the buyer beware." Under this version of common law, many cases have evolved that distinguish between those lies by sellers for which there was liability.

LEGAL FOCUS—PROBLEM

C. J. Thomas and his wife, Joan, were home when their real estate sales agent brought a prospective buyer, Art Shab, for a viewing. During introductions, Shab asked whether the neighbors ever made unusually loud noises or otherwise caused problems and whether the house was insulated. Thomas answered that the neighbors "were quiet" and "yes, the building was well insulated." In truth, as Thomas knew, the neighbors were extremely boisterous, often screaming profanities at each other in the early hours of the morning, and their children were known to break neighborhood windows with BB guns, empty garbage cans over neighbors' fences, and race their motorcycles up and down the street. Likewise, as Thomas also knew, the house was not insulated. Shab purchased the home and shortly thereafter learned the truth about the neighbors and the insulation. He contacted his attorney seeking to revoke the purchase, claiming fraud. Will Shab succeed?

Shab will succeed with the fraud claim if the seller (1) made a representation (2) of a material fact, (3) knowing the statement to be false, (4) which asserted fact was reasonably relied upon by the buyer, and (5) induced the buyer to consummate the purchase. Under the common law, the falsehood concerning the quiet neighbors is irrelevant because it is only a personal opinion. What is admirable to some is anathema to others. However, the presence or absence of insulation is a fact. If the absence of insulation would be obvious (patent) to an ordinary layman, Shab would again be out of luck—a buyer cannot close his eyes to the obvious and then complain after the sale. But the presence or absence of insulation usually is not readily ascertainable. Therefore, Shab may pursue either of two common law remedies. He may seek to recover the cost to cure the defect (by installing insulation) as compensatory damages, and he could also seek, and might receive, an additional sum as exemplary or punitive damages, where available, because of the intentional deception or fraud by Thomas. Alternatively, Shab may rescind the purchase, give up possession of the house to Thomas, and receive reimbursement for his down payment and other monies expended in the purchase.

Note that the remedies available to Shab are based on the common law tort of fraud (also called *deceit*). Some states have modern disclosure statutes, discussed shortly, that change the common law under which Thomas would be responsible for both misrepresentations.

Following are examples of statements of personal opinion, often exaggerated. A seller may make them to a prospective buyer without fear of liability for damages or of a demand for rescission:

- This house is really worth much more than I'm asking.
- This is the finest home in the area.
- This is the best-constructed home you will ever live in.
- Will taxes go up in this neighborhood? Never!
- The value of this house will increase at least 5 percent per year.

Statements such as the following *may* justify a rescission or action for damages, if they are false:

- A new roof was installed on this house two years ago.
- During the rainy season, all excess surface water drains off almost immediately.
- There are no termites, no dry rot.
- The foundation was not damaged by the earthquake.
- There is no asbestos in the house.

A more difficult question arises when a seller, knowing of some important latent defect, such as a fractured foundation, simply does not say anything to the prospective buyer. No lies are told, but important information is withheld. Under the common law and in some states, a seller has no general duty to speak. The rationale is that the buyer is free to investigate and to inquire; if asked, the seller's answers must be truthful. The problem is that most buyers are not qualified or prepared to ask all possibly relevant questions. For example, how many buyers would be likely to ask whether there is radon gas emission within the premises, if the neighbors have threatened to sue about the location of the new backyard fence, or whether there is landfill on the property?

Many state laws require sellers to disclose information beyond the traditional material questions of fact. The typical law requires sellers to disclose, in writing and as soon as practicable before close of escrow, information that they either know or can ascertain. For example, one category of disclosure requires preparation of a checklist of items on the premises, such as a range, dishwasher, washer and dryer hookup, burglar alarm, and so forth. Another category of disclosure requires notice to the buyer if any of the systems or appliances are not in good working order. Yet another category requires notice of any defects or malfunctions in the roof, ceiling, floor, foundation, driveway, plumbing, sewer and septic system, and so on. A final category calls for disclosure of general knowledge the seller has about any easements, absence of a building permit for any additions that have been made, a landfill under the house, settling or sliding incidents, flooding or drainage problems, zoning violations, and even neighborhood noise problems. Often, both the seller's agent and any buyer's agent must inspect the property and report to the prospective buyer any problems they observe. Unlike the seller, if the agent does not observe a defect, she is not responsible to discover and disclose it.

If the seller is negligent or dishonest in making any disclosure that later comes to the buyer's attention, a suit for money damages is usually authorized by statute. The sale, however, cannot be rescinded (undone).

LEGAL FOCUS—PROBLEM

Brent and Lorri Lanfield, having lived frugally for several years while accumulating sufficient money for a down payment, purchased their first home from the Maxwell family. A month after escrow closed, while Lorri was mowing the lawn, a next door neighbor dropped by, introduced himself, and asked, "Did you know that the Maxwells' grandson committed suicide in the upstairs bedroom of your new house?" The Lanfields were shocked by this discovery, and in the ensuing weeks became increasingly ill at ease because of it. They consulted Monica Smith, attorney-at-law, for advice. Should the law provide the Lanfields with a remedy against the Maxwells?

It is unfortunately true that occurrence of a human being's death in a house can have an adverse effect on its future resale value. In times past, for some people, a house was not a home unless and until both births and deaths had occurred within its walls. Today, rightly or wrongly, knowledge of a death by suicide may affect potential buyers differently than natural death from old age. Death on the premises from any cause may adversely affect the willingness of some people to purchase the property. Under common law principles, the Maxwells probably had no duty to reveal the fact of their grandson's death because it was not a material defect in the real property as distinguished from the subjective attitudes of members in the buying public. In states where the common law has been modified by comprehensive disclosure statutes, however, sellers must disclose the occurrence of prior deaths (statutes differ and may exclude certain types of deaths) or face the likelihood of an action for damages measured by the impact of such fact upon the market value of the property.

HOW CAN A BUYER FINANCE THE PURCHASE OF A HOME?

promissory note
A written promise to pay to a named person or to the bearer of the note a certain sum of money in the future.

Few buyers have the cash to pay the entire purchase price of a home. Even if they do, they may prefer to make a relatively low down payment and borrow the balance of the purchase price because they then can invest the rest of their savings elsewhere. The assumption is that with climbing wages or salaries, it is progressively easier to pay off the fixed amount of the loan as time goes by.

Buyers desiring to borrow money to purchase a home will be required to sign, and to be legally bound by, two important documents: the **promissory note** and the mortgage.

maker
The creator of a promissory note.

The Promissory Note

payee
Person in whose favor a check, draft, or promissory note is drawn.

A promissory note evidences the loan (see Exhibit 9.2). It is signed by the borrower, called the **maker**, and delivered to the lender, called the **payee**, when the sale is completed. As evidence of the debt, the note contains important information pertaining to the loan. The note is not a contract; rather, it is evidence of the existence of a debt. The most important information it contains is as follows:

- The names of the maker and the payee
- The amount of the debt

- The interest rate
- The amount of the monthly payments (of principal and interest)
- The due date of payments
- The delinquency date of payments after which a penalty is charged
- The penalty for delinquent payments
- The obligation of the debtor to pay the creditor's collection and attorney fees, if applicable

collateral
Money or other property made available as security by a debtor to a creditor, through physical possession or legal right, to guarantee repayment of a loan.

foreclosure
Process by which secured real property is confiscated at the direction of the unpaid creditor and sold to the highest bidder.

mortgage (or real mortgage)
The contract in which the buyer of real property typically gives a lender a lien or claim against the real property that serves as collateral for a loan of money, often borrowed to pay part of the purchase price.

mortgagor
The borrower of funds secured by a mortgage.

mortgagee
The lender of funds secured by a mortgage.

deed of trust
A deed used by a borrower (called *trustor*) to transfer the legal title to real property to a disinterested stakeholder (the *trustee*) to hold as security or collateral for the benefit of the lender (the *beneficiary*).

The Mortgage

The lender will not trust the borrower as the sole source for repayment of the loan. Too much money is involved. The lender will require the home to be put up as **collateral**, or security. If the borrower defaults (fails to make the proper monthly payments in repayment of the loan), the lender may take the home, sell it, and apply the proceeds of the sale to pay off the balance of the loan. This procedure is called **foreclosure**. The document that establishes the home as collateral is called a **mortgage**. The borrower or debtor is called the **mortgagor**; the lender or creditor is called the **mortgagee**.

When the home mortgage loan is paid off by the homeowner, the lender will return the mortgage to the borrower, who then may "burn the mortgage" or, perhaps, frame it. In the case of a **deed of trust**, the full repayment will be evidenced by a deed of reconveyance, or simply "recon" as it is called in the trade.

EXHIBIT 9.2 Example of Promissory Note for $200,000

PROMISSORY NOTE SECURED BY DEED OF TRUST

$200,000 June 1, 2013

FOR VALUE RECEIVED, I PROMISE TO PAY TO__________ (the lender/payee) __________, OR ORDER, AT __________ (lender's address) __________THE PRINCIPAL SUM OF $200,000, WITH INTEREST FROM THIS DATE UNTIL PAID AT THE RATE OF __________ PERCENT A YEAR ON THE BALANCE REMAINING FROM TIME TO TIME UNPAID. PRINCIPAL AND INTEREST SHALL BE DUE AND PAYABLE IN MONTHLY INSTALLMENTS OF $ __________ OR MORE,* COMMENCING ON THE DAY __________ OF __________, 200____, AND CONTINUING THEREAFTER UNTIL THE PRINCIPAL AND INTEREST ARE FULLY PAID.

UPON ANY DEFAULT IN THIS NOTE OR IN THE TERMS OF THE DEED OF TRUST SECURING THIS LOAN, THE UNPAID PRINCIPAL AND ACCRUED INTEREST SHALL AT ONCE BECOME DUE AND PAYABLE, WITHOUT NOTICE, AT THE OPTION OF THE HOLDER OF THIS NOTE.

MAKER AGREES TO PAY COURT COSTS AND REASONABLE ATTORNEY FEES INCURRED BY PAYEE IN CONNECTION WITH THE ENFORCEMENT OF THIS NOTE.

IF ANY MONTHLY INSTALLMENT IS RECEIVED BY PAYEE MORE THAN 10 DAYS AFTER ITS DUE DATE, LATE CHARGES OF ________ PERCENT OF SAID PAYMENT, BEING THE SUM OF $ ______________ EACH PAYMENT, ALSO WILL BE DUE AND PAYABLE.

PRIVILEGE IS RESERVED TO MAKE ADDITIONAL PRINCIPAL PAYMENTS NOT TO EXCEED A TOTAL OF $ __________ IN ANY TWELVE-MONTH PERIOD DURING THE FIRST 36 MONTHS OF THIS LOAN.

____
/s/Maker

*The phrase "or more" gives the borrower the option to make additional payments of principal. Technically, if the phrase is not included in the note, the loan is said to be "locked in," meaning that the borrower cannot make larger or additional monthly payments to retire the debt earlier. However, most states have declared that "locked in" home-purchase loans are against public policy, and unenforceable; therefore, lenders customarily add a provision, such as found at the bottom of this exemplar note, specifically authorizing additional principal payments in specified amounts.

What If a Homeowner Defaults on Monthly Loan Payments?

nonjudicial foreclosure
The involuntary sale, without court proceedings, of an owner's real property to raise money to satisfy the unpaid balance of the loan that is in default.

foreclosure sale
Sale of a debtor's real property to raise cash with which to reduce or retire the unpaid debt. A foreclosure sale may be of two varieties, by a court official following judicial foreclosure or by a trustee following nonjudicial foreclosure.

right of reinstatement
The right of a defaulting debtor to reinstate the loan by payment of all money due for prior months including late charges, even though the note and mortgage declare that the *entire* unpaid balance is immediately due in full upon any default.

acceleration clause
A provision in a loan agreement that allows the lender to declare the entire unpaid balance due and payable immediately if a given event occurs.

Upon default by the owner, the lender may simply do nothing for a while, giving the homeowner extra time to pay, or may start foreclosure proceedings. Both deeds of trust and mortgages contain many formal promises of the homeowner, such as to pay property taxes as they come due, to keep casualty insurance in force, to maintain the property, and to comply with all applicable laws. The mortgage lenders require these promises because they may have to foreclose on the property in the future and want it to be in good condition at that time.

A breach of any of these promises or of the promise to make monthly payments is called a *default,* for which the lender's basic remedy is foreclosure. Lenders do not like foreclosure any more than borrowers do. As a practical matter, long before foreclosure will be commenced by an unpaid lender, many attempts will be made to help solve the debtor's financial problem. See Exhibit 9.3 for advice on avoiding foreclosure.

If the remedy of foreclosure becomes necessary, most lenders choose foreclosure by private sale, which is called **nonjudicial foreclosure**, under which no court proceedings are necessary. Mortgages (and deeds of trust) contain a provision, called the *power-of-sale clause,* that authorizes a private **foreclosure sale** without court supervision. The date and place where the foreclosure sale will occur must be advertised in a local newspaper, and a notice will be posted in the county courthouse. Before the sale, the homeowner may reinstate the loan by paying all delinquent monthly payments as well as late-payment charges and any costs and fees to date. This valuable **right of reinstatement** exists even though the borrower may have agreed within the terms of the promissory note that upon default the entire unpaid balance becomes immediately due and payable. Such a provision is called an **acceleration clause** (because the loan due date is accelerated to the present), but its impact is overridden by the right of reinstatement.

If the defaulting homeowner does not reinstate (or, alternatively, completely pay off) the loan, a foreclosure sale will occur after about four months from the date the borrower's default was formally recorded. At the sale, the trustee accepts the highest cash bid and conveys title to the successful buyer by deed. If no bidders offer cash in at least the amount of the unpaid balance of the mortgage loan, the lender will bid its debt, that is, cancel its loan in exchange for ownership of the property. Thus, the lender either obtains payment of its loan in full from some cash bidder, or cancels its loan and acquires ownership of the house.

EXHIBIT 9.3 Avoiding Foreclosure

Avoiding Foreclosure

- Immediately contact your lender to discuss any problems regarding mortgage payments.
- Marshall your assets to pay your mortgage payments. Consider drawing on emergency funds.
- Read all important documents and pay attention to communications from your lender.
- Contact local government or government-approved counseling programs to consider all your options and receive explanations about the foreclosure process and your rights.
- Take advantage of any federal or state programs designed to avoid foreclosure. Many of these were established following the real estate declines that began in 2008.

short sale
The sale of property (such as a home) for less than the unpaid balance of a loan for which the property serves as security.

deficiency judgment
Judgment against a debtor for the unpaid balance still due after repossession and resale of goods that were sold on credit, or after judicial foreclosure of a real estate mortgage.

Houses owned by institutional lenders that have been acquired through foreclosure are called real estate owned (REOs) and make attractive purchase opportunities for homebuyers. Often, institutional owners of REOs will provide buyers with attractive financing to complete the purchase, as well as keep the price at an attractive level. These REO owners are not in the business of owning homes and usually work with interested homebuyers who may "take them off their hands." In recent times, a glut of homes on the market has caused many homes to sit empty and unsold for extended periods.

Sometimes a home is sold before foreclosure occurs, for less than the unpaid balance of its original mortgage in what is called a **short sale**. A short sale is any sale during foreclosure where the asking price is less than the unpaid amount of the mortgage on the home. Short sales were frequent in the early 1990s and again during the period of 2008 to 2012 when home prices fell, leaving many people saddled with homes worth less than the mortgages they owed. Many simply "walked away," leaving the banks with the choice of proceeding through foreclosure and then selling the homes as REOs, or simply accepting short sales during foreclosure to cut their losses.

MORALS AND ETHICS

During the recent real estate downturn, the morality of short sales was heavily debated. Advocates argued that the law grants the right to homeowners to escape any deficiency judgments in which a lender is owed more than a home is worth. They also noted that many lenders were really at fault, at least partly, for those circumstances because of shoddy due diligence in making lending decisions. Others, however, decried the spate of short sales and argued that borrowers had a moral responsibility to use a short sale only as a last resort. Such arguments seemed to have little effect on the psyche of Americans and short sales boomed.

judicial foreclosure
The forced sale, following a court proceeding, of an owner's real property to raise money to satisfy the creditor's claim for the unpaid balance of the loan that is in default.

right of redemption
Right of a debtor to recover, within one year, the property sold at a judicial foreclosure sale.

Homeowners who are not making their monthly mortgage payments receive advance notice of the date and place of their foreclosure sale and are entitled to remain in possession of the home until the sale takes place and a new owner of the property takes possession.

Proceeds of foreclosure sales go to the creditor to satisfy the homeowner's debt. Any excess (unlikely) belongs to the homeowner whose home was sold. But if there were any significant potential excess (i.e., equity) at the time of the foreclosure sale, it is likely the homeowner would sell the property and pay off the loan rather than suffer foreclosure.

The creditor may be entitled to a **deficiency judgment**, a court judgment against the debtor for the difference between the unpaid mortgage balance and the fair market value of the property. This represents the amount of money lost by the creditor as a result of the foreclosure. But such a judgment can be obtained only through a court-ordered and supervised foreclosure called **judicial foreclosure**, and most lenders prefer nonjudicial foreclosures by private sale because they are quicker, are less expensive, and do not require the services of an attorney. Furthermore, following judicial foreclosure, the debtor has one year within which to reclaim the property—called the one-year **right of redemption**—by fully reimbursing the person who made the winning bid at the judicial-foreclosure sale. So the only advantage to a judicial foreclosure is the possibility of a deficiency judgment, which could be uncollectible anyway (because the debtor lacks funds or assets).

Sometimes borrowers facing foreclosure offer a deed to the property to the lender to avoid the bad-credit implications of foreclosure. Such a deed is called a *deed in lieu of foreclosure*. Although these are more common in commercial property finances, they can offer advantages and disadvantages to other borrowers and lenders. From the homeowner's perspective, a deed in lieu of foreclosure can avoid the impact of a foreclosure upon his credit history. On the other hand, unless otherwise agreed, possession must be given to the lender immediately instead of several months later, following foreclosure sale. A deed in lieu of foreclosure also cancels any possibility of a deficiency judgment by the lender. From the lender's perspective, one advantage is that the delay and possible deterioration of the property while foreclosure is pending are avoided. If no deficiency judgment is possible or desirable, the deed in lieu of foreclosure should be satisfactory. The lender acquiring title by a deed in lieu of foreclosure, however, takes the property subject to any junior liens, such as a **mechanic's lien**, an unpaid home-equity loan, or a carryback mortgage, that are on the property. Mechanic's liens protect claims of persons who improve property by giving them claims on the owner's property. Such liens would be wiped out if the title were obtained by foreclosure sale. The decision to use a deed in lieu of foreclosure should be supported by professional advice.

mechanic's lien
A legal claim of a contractor or material supplier who helped or supplied materials to construct, improve, or repair a building.

Depending on the state involved, **homestead** laws may protect homeowners' rights or interests in their homes from unsecured creditors—that is, creditors other than the mortgage providers. State homestead laws vary in many details, including the scope of protection they afford homeowners. For instance, in California, a creditor can force a sale of a debtor's home, but a portion of any sales proceeds that exceed the mortgages goes to the debtor to buy a new home. In Florida, on the other hand, creditors cannot force the sale of a home for the lifetime of the debtor. The purpose of all homestead laws is to protect a family's ability to obtain a place of residence free from the threat of existing creditors.

homestead
A declaration of a debtor's exemption in a specified amount of the equity of the homeowner's residence from levy and execution by a creditor.

Types of Financing

Three general sources of financing are available for homebuyers: new financing, assumption of existing financing, and seller's financing. We discuss these alternatives in order.

New Loans

Several different types of new, or original, loans are available to persons who desire to purchase a home. Most loans are made by savings and loan associations, banks, mortgage brokers, and mortgage bankers. **Mortgage brokers** prepare loan packages (applications and other documents) for borrowers, which they send to other lenders who actually advance the funds and make the loan. These brokers often work with a pool of many lenders and try to find the most attractive loan terms for borrowers. **Mortgage bankers**, on the other hand, make loans that they may later resell for cash, which is used again as working capital.

mortgage broker
A person licensed to engage in the business of bringing together borrowers and lenders of mortgage funds. Mortgage brokers typically are paid a commission based upon the volume of loans they originate.

Often, applicants pay loan application fees, and sometimes appraisal charges, even if they fail to qualify for, or abandon, the loan commitment. A loan commitment is a lender's written agreement to make a loan to the borrower upon specified terms and conditions. Lenders, however, do not ordinarily make loan commitments until the buyer has signed a purchase agreement. Then the prospective lender can have the home appraised and make other lending evaluations.

mortgage banker
A business that makes real estate loans with its own capital, as well as with institutional funds, and then sells the loans in the secondary mortgage market.

It is increasingly popular for prospective buyers to be either preapproved or prequalified for financing. For preapproval, lenders will require a credit check and often written verification of employment. Prequalification is an estimate of the borrowing power of the prospective buyer based upon hypothetical information. Neither of these is a legal commitment by the lender to make a loan. Only a written loan commitment is binding. Preapproval and prequalifying are useful, however, because they tend to assure sellers that the buyer is financially able to purchase the home that is for sale.

Loan terms often are said to be negotiable, but in reality, lenders advertise the terms of loans they are willing to make and rarely depart from such limitations. Nevertheless, those astute borrowers who take the time to comparison shop for available financing often will save a considerable sum of money. Many mortgage brokers and even lenders advertise online the up-to-the-hour terms of available loans and offer assistance in making applications. Lenders compete aggressively to make loans to home purchasers, who are well advised to shop around and to fully discuss the opportunities with their sales agent.

Once loans are made (or "originated") in the primary market—that is, the market composed of savings and loan associations, banks, and others that issue new loans—they often, but not always, are sold to buyers in the secondary mortgage market, which is a market of agencies and buyers who are competing to purchase new loans. Selling home loans gives lenders the cash with which to make additional new loans to buyers in the primary mortgage market. The major buyers in the secondary mortgage market are government-enacted agencies known widely by their nicknames, Fannie Mae (FNMA), Freddie Mac (FHLMC), and Ginnie Mae (GNMA).* Because these buyers purchase home mortgages, they can specify the terms of the loans that they will purchase, by interest rate, length for repayment, loan-to-value ratio, qualifications of borrower, and so on. Nonconforming loans will not be purchased. Institutions then will make only those kinds of loans they can sell in the secondary market. These guidelines by mortgage buyers are reviewed regularly and updated to keep pace with changing market conditions and emerging social policies.

Buying loans is one way these three agencies—FNMA, FHLMC, and GNMA—are supposed to fulfill their responsibility to stabilize the mortgage-money market. For example, when money is "tight" (difficult to borrow and with rising interest rates), these agencies purchase loans from lenders, thereby making more cash available to them for new loans. When money is "loose" (easy to borrow and with declining interest rates), these agencies will sell loans at attractive prices, thereby taking money out of effective circulation. Such transactions help prevent wide fluctuations in interest rates that would endanger the health of the economy.

In the real estate and economic downturns and turmoil that have roiled the home loan markets during the past decade, there has been much criticism about the role of the secondary market in furthering the systematic problems of increasingly risky loans being made to unqualified borrowers.

conventional loan
A home-purchase mortgage, the repayment of which is not guaranteed by an agency of the federal government.

portfolio lender
A lender of home purchase funds that does not expect to sell its mortgages in the secondary mortgage market. Because such lenders keep their loans within their own portfolio of loans, they can be more flexible (liberal) in terms of the loans they offer prospective homebuyers.

private mortgage insurance (PMI)
Insurance to protect a lender in the event that a borrower defaults in the repayment of a mortgage loan.

Conventional Loans

A **conventional loan** is one in which the terms are not directly influenced by government regulations or subsidies. A bank that is not going to sell its mortgages can make the loan on any terms it desires. Such a lender is called a **portfolio lender** because the loan is retained in the lender's own portfolio of outstanding loans. Lenders usually require a larger down payment for these loans than for loans to be sold.

Most conventional loans, however, are sold in the secondary market, in which case the buyer must qualify for the guidelines of Fannie Mae or Freddie Mac. These guidelines declare that if the down payment is less than 20 percent, the buyer must purchase **private mortgage insurance (PMI)** to guarantee the loan purchaser against loss in case of default by the homeowner–borrower. The premium for PMI is collected monthly along with principal and interest payments. Thus, PMI achieves the same security for the ultimate holder of the homebuyer's mortgage loan as does government insurance, as explained shortly. In effect, mortgage buyers invest in risk-free mortgages, which are paid either by the homeowner or by an insurance company.

*These quasi-government agencies buy and sell mortgages to influence interest rates and to provide for the availability of funds for new mortgage lending. For example, if Fannie Mae announced that it would purchase mortgage loans made to recent college graduates for 100 percent of the purchase price of homes they bought, with interest at 6 percent, banks would immediately make such loans. Thus, public policy is influenced by the secondary mortgage market.

Veterans Administration (VA) loan
A home-purchase mortgage loan made to any eligible veteran by the federal Veterans Administration. The VA was established in 1944 by the Serviceman's Readjustment Act to assist veterans in becoming homeowners.

fixed-rate mortgage
A traditional home purchase mortgage in which the interest rate and the monthly payment do not fluctuate during the life of the loan.

Variable interest-rate mortgage (VIRM)
A home-purchase mortgage and promissory note in which the interest rate may fluctuate, up or down, in sync with a published index. Also called *adjustable-rate mortgage*.

amortize
To repay a note secured by mortgage through agreed-upon monthly payments of principal and interest over the life of the loan.

PITI
An acronym for principal, interest, taxes, and insurance, which represent the four basic repetitive expenses of buying real property with borrowed funds.

Federal Housing Administration Loan

In a Federal Housing Administration (FHA) loan, repayment is insured by the U.S. government, and so the lender (or current mortgage holder) is not likely to lose its money. In a sense, the U.S. government "cosigns" the borrower's loan. Because the loan is insured, lenders are able to accept transactions in which the down payment is as little as 3 percent of the purchase price. The FHA establishes limits, or ceilings, on the loan amount that it will insure. The ceilings vary, depending on whether the home is in a low-cost housing area or an expensive area and are changed periodically.

Veterans Administration Loan

In a **Veterans Administration (VA) loan**, repayment to the lender is guaranteed by the U.S. government because the borrower is a qualified veteran. No down payment is required for these loans unless the price paid for the home exceeds its "reasonable value" as determined by the VA appraisal (a professional estimate of value). In such cases, the excess must be paid in cash by the veteran. The VA does not have loan ceilings, but lenders adhere to guidelines set by Ginnie Mae and Fannie Mae.

Selecting the Best New Financing Some factors a borrower should consider in determining which loan is best are the repayment term, interest rate, qualification requirements, and amount of the loan.

Loans for which the interest rate remains the same during the life of the loan are called **fixed-rate mortgages**. Types of loans in which the interest rate may (will) fluctuate are called **variable-interest-rate mortgages (VIRMs)**, also called *adjustable-rate mortgages* (*ARMs*). Borrowers should examine carefully what caps, or limits, are placed on periodic fluctuations. Caps may restrict how high the interest rate ultimately can go, how much it can increase at any one adjustment, and how often adjustments can be made. Careful borrowers understand the parameters of any ARM they are considering. All real estate sales agents should be able to explain the pros and cons of an ARM.

Repayment Term The longer the time span during which the loan must be repaid, the lower the monthly payment. For example, the monthly payment to **amortize** (pay off) an 8 percent loan of $100,000 over 15 years is $955.70. (We are using the $100,000 figure because it is easy to follow the math, not because one can purchase a house at that price). In addition to principal and interest of $955.70, the borrower also must pay property taxes and casualty insurance (both discussed later). Lenders often require those payments on a monthly basis, which then are held in "impound accounts" until remitted to the appropriate insurance company and tax collector. Principal, interest, taxes, and insurance often are referred to by the acronym **PITI**. If PMI (private mortgage insurance), discussed earlier, is required by the lender, its premium is also tacked onto the monthly payment.

The same $100,000 loan repaid over a thirty-year period at 8 percent interest requires a monthly payment of $733.80, which is $221.90 a month less than the fifteen-year loan. These "savings" in monthly payments are offset by the increased amount of total interest that must be paid because of the longer-term loan. For example, the purchaser who borrows $100,000 of the purchase price at 8 percent will pay $172,026 ($955.70 × 12 × 15) over fifteen years, whereas the total cost would be $264,168 ($733.80 × 12 × 30) if the term of the $100,000 loan were thirty years. This $92,142 difference is interest paid because of the longer term.

A long-term loan can, of course, be paid off much earlier if the borrower chooses to make extra principal payments each month. Most loans permit an additional payment of principal each month without penalty. After five years of payments, there typically is no limit on the size of extra principal payments that may be made. The long-term loan gives the borrower the choice to pay extra principal, whereas a short-term loan requires the larger payment each month regardless of changing financial circumstances.

There are limits on the available term, typically thirty years for FHA and VA loans. Conventional lenders who sell their loans in the secondary mortgage market also are limited to thirty-year terms; however, loans allowing up to forty years for repayment are possible with portfolio lenders.

interest
The price, usually expressed as an annualized rate (percentage), for use of a sum of money (principal) obtained from a lender.

Interest Rate The price of borrowing money is **interest**. The higher the interest rate, the higher the monthly payment (which includes both principal and interest). For example, a real estate loan of $100,000 over thirty years at 8 percent interest requires a monthly payment of $733.80. If the interest is reduced to 7 percent, the monthly payment decreases to $665.31, which is a savings of $68.49 each month. Thus, the total payments under the 8 percent loan would be $264,168 ($733.80 × 12 × 30) and only $239,512 ($665.31 × 12 × 30) for the 7 percent loan, a savings of $24,656.

There are many variations from the simple fixed rate loan. As noted, an ARM provides for periodic increases or decreases in the interest rate depending on prevailing interest levels. Because lenders of ARMs are protected against being locked into a low rate if prevailing rates increase, they are willing to begin the loan at an interest rate lower than is available for fixed-rate mortgages. These "teaser" rates may last for only a year or two before automatically "triggering" up to the market rate. If market interest rates decrease, the borrower is protected against being locked into a higher rate. One contributor to the recent homeownership crisis was a wave of loans with teaser rates that expired just as home markets were declining and the unemployment rate was rising.

A refinancing occurs when a homeowner replaces the existing mortgage with a new mortgage at a lower interest rate, and sometimes for a greater amount of money that produces cash for other purchases or needs or even for investment. In refinancing, a smart borrower often switches to a fixed-rate loan right when interest rates are at a low, thus locking in an interest rate that cannot rise regardless of prevailing rates. Interest rates fluctuate upward and then downward over time, making the question, "Should I apply for a fixed-rate or a variable-rate mortgage?" impossible to answer with scientific precision. Everyone desires a VIRM when interest rates are falling and a fixed-rate mortgage when interest rates are rising.

negative amortization
A monthly increase in the unpaid principal balance of a mortgage loan resulting when the borrower does not make the required monthly interest payments in full.

To avoid the possibility that the monthly payment may become unbearably high, the loan contract can call for maintenance of the same monthly payment even when the interest rate automatically increases in step with the relevant index, simply by extending the term of the loan. Other VIRMs may maintain the same monthly payment, even though the variable interest rate has increased, by adding the monthly difference owed but unpaid to the unpaid balance of the loan. This is called **negative amortization** because the unpaid principal balance of the loan is actually getting larger each month. If you do not pay what you owe this year, you end up owing more next year. Consequently, the owner's equity is decreasing each month, unless the amount of negative amortization is exceeded by gains in appreciation. The large number of negative amortization loans at a time when the real estate market and the economy faltered was another contributor to the recent real estate market crisis.

graduated-payment mortgage
A home-purchase mortgage and promissory note that features artificially low monthly payments for the initial few years as an inducement for borrowers whose incomes and creditworthiness are expected to improve in the future.

Another variation is the **graduated-payment mortgage**, where early payments are kept artificially low (through reduced interest rates), and then are increased later to artificially high levels (above-market interest rates). This arrangement is geared to young persons who are beginning their careers. Much of the interest is deferred to later years when income has risen and interest can be repaid without undue hardship.

points
A one-time charge made by a lender when a home loan is originated. One point is 1 percent of the loan.

loan origination fee
A lump-sum fee paid by a mortgage borrower to the lender, who in turn pays all or a portion of it to the mortgage broker who introduced the borrower to the lender.

annualized percentage rate (APR)
The rate of interest a borrower is paying to a mortgage lender when points and lender's fees are considered as interest rather than mere expenses of the transaction.

appraised value
Opinion of a real estate expert "professional appraiser" of the fair market value of property, usually stated in a formal writing.

loan underwriting
The process of evaluating the acceptability of a prospective borrower's loan application.

Points and Annualized Percentage Rate Interest rates should not be confused with loan charges, called **points**, which are one-time charges made by a lender at the time the home loan is made (originated). These charges are computed much like any percentage commission. They have ranged from about 0.5 percent to 3 percent. Thus, two points on a $100,000 loan would mean a charge of $2,000. Points are said to be a payment designed to bring the effective, or true, profit of the loan in line with prevailing interest rates. They also serve to generate cash for the lender to pay a loan broker's commission. Often, the seller pays the points to the lender to avoid losing the sale, because on FHA and VA loans the buyer-borrower cannot be charged more than one point, which is considered a **loan origination fee**. This limitation reduces buyers' closing costs (which are discussed in detail later), but sellers who can do so may boost their sales price to make up the difference, thus indirectly passing this added cost to their buyers.

To show borrowers more clearly what their borrowing costs are, points are computationally treated as additional annualized interest. A loan that is 8 percent with no points charged may have an 8.75 percent **annualized percentage rate (APR)** if points are charged. When shopping for loans, prospective borrowers should compare the APRs of loans and not their stated interest rates. All lenders must, by law, provide to prospective borrowers the APRs of each of their available financing packages.

Amount of Loan The greater the amount of money that can be borrowed to purchase a home, the lower the required down payment. Lenders will loan up to a specified percentage of the **appraised value** of the home—that is, the value assigned by a professional appraiser chosen by the lender. Conventional lenders might lend up to 90 percent of the appraised value and require the borrower to guarantee its repayment through the purchase of PMI. Thus, to purchase a home appraised at and selling for $250,000, a loan of $225,000 can be made, requiring a $25,000 down payment. Other portfolio lenders may require a larger down payment. FHA loan limits are adjusted from time to time by government regulation, but always are more liberal than conventional loan limits. For example, the FHA typically permits (will insure) loans with as little as a 5 percent down payment. Current FHA and market data may be obtained from any real estate sales agent or lending institution. Online mortgage services, mentioned earlier, also publish the terms of available financing.

Loan Qualification Requirements To obtain a loan to purchase a home, a borrower must meet the creditworthiness criteria set by the lender. For a conventional loan, for example, a lender may require that monthly payments of principal and interest not exceed 40 percent of the borrower's total monthly income. Spouses or unrelated co-owners of a home may pool their respective incomes and credit standings to qualify for a loan. For government-subsidized loans, such as FHA and VA loans, qualifications are set by administrative regulation. Furthermore, purchasers of mortgages in the secondary mortgage market dictate borrower-qualification requirements as a precondition to purchase their loans. The process of evaluating a borrower's qualifications for a specified loan is called **loan underwriting**. All of these qualifying rules use ratios that compare the borrower's anticipated monthly housing expense and total monthly obligations with monthly gross income.

Mortgage borrowers must have good credit histories, or their applications may be denied. Often, loan applicants are categorized by *alphabet lenders* as either A, B, C, or D, depending on their credit histories. B and C borrowers have histories reflecting significant financial problems (missed payments), but they are not "deadbeats" (persons with disastrous credit histories). When even regional recessions occur, tens of thousands of homeowners may slip from category A to categories B and C. Unfortunately, these rating changes occur to victims of corporate downsizings, plant closings, regional economic slumps, and similar catastrophes that do not truly reflect upon their character as borrowers. B and C borrowers can qualify for mortgage loans, but will face higher than usual loan-to-value (LTV) requirements, meaning that larger down payments are required (e.g., 25 percent for B and 35 percent for C applicants). To assist these borrowers, many lenders typically permit a larger percentage of their income to be absorbed by monthly payments (up to 45 and even 50 percent is common, whereas category A borrowers often are not allowed to commit more than 38 percent of their income to PITI). This permits credit-impaired B and C borrowers to qualify if they are willing to commit both a larger down payment and a substantial portion of their income to homeownership.

assumption of mortgage
An agreement by one person (usually a buyer) to assume (i.e., take upon herself) all the obligations of an existing secured real property loan of another person (usually the seller).

Yet another cause of the recent real estate crisis was questionable evaluations of buyer creditworthiness by lenders. During the long run up of real estate prices in the opening years of the twenty-first century, many borrowers made their way into homes they probably could not afford. Many received ARM loans with a teaser rate (discussed earlier) and were dependent upon increasing their income levels or refinancing their homes to lock in a lower rate. As result of that period of questionable conduct by the real estate lending industry, there has been scrutiny of the industry, strict and heightened loan qualification criteria, and direct and indirect government regulation of the lending industry.

equity
The net interest of a homeowner in the property, representing the excess of the value of the property over loans or other legal claims outstanding against it.

Assumption of Existing Loan The obligation of an existing mortgage may be transferred from the debtor (homeowner who desires to sell) to another person (a prospective buyer) who desires to become obligated to its monthly payments. This transfer of obligation is called an **assumption of mortgage.**

Equity is the market value of a property minus the unpaid balance of loans against it. Frequently, sellers of a home have only a small equity in their property. In such a situation, the purchasers may not need to borrow directly; rather, they may desire to assume the loan of the sellers, especially if its interest rate is attractive.

LEGAL FOCUS—PROBLEM

Laura Shields wanted to sell her home for $400,000. She still owed $352,000 against it, as represented by a promissory note payable to the bank. The note was secured by a deed of trust on the home. Mark Hendricks offered to buy the house by paying Shields $48,000 for her equity and assuming her loan for the balance of the purchase price. Shields contacted her attorney, Colleen Strong, to find out what would happen if she accepted Hendricks's offer and if, at some future time, Hendricks failed to make his newly assumed monthly payment. What would attorney Strong advise her?

Shields's attorney would advise her that when Hendricks assumed the bank loan, he would become a debtor of the bank. The bank could either accept him as the sole debtor, and release Shields from the loan, or keep both as debtors. In either case, if the bank is not paid each month on time, the trustee (or mortgagee) can cause the house to be sold at public auction with the proceeds going to the bank in satisfaction of the debt. This may not bother Shields because she already would have received $48,000 for her equity; however, her credit rating could be affected adversely if the bank foreclosed in the future because her name would remain on the defaulted note. In addition, if the loan were federally insured, such as an FHA loan, and the sales price at foreclosure was less than the unpaid balance due on the loan, Shields could be made to pay the bank any deficiency (unpaid balance) on the loan remaining after a foreclosure sale. For this reason, most sellers whose mortgage is being assumed by a buyer request a release of liability from the lender at the time of the sale. A release will be given by the lender only if the assuming purchaser has a satisfactory credit record, or if the loan balance is small compared with the value of the security (the house). Generally speaking, it is easier for a prospective buyer to qualify for assumption of an existing loan than to qualify for a new loan.

antideficiency laws State laws protecting a homeowner from payment of any deficiency (or unpaid balance) if a mortgage foreclosure sale fails to produce sufficient money to satisfy the underlying debt in full.

Some states have **antideficiency laws** that apply to conventional purchase-money loans, which are any loan the proceeds of which are used by the borrower to purchase a home. As their name implies, antideficiency laws prohibit the collection of any deficiency by the creditor following foreclosure sale. A deficiency would arise if the proceeds of the foreclosure sale were less than the amount then owed on the defaulted loan, plus certain costs. These debtor laws date back to the Great Depression of the 1930s, when many people lost their homes and substantial equities through foreclosures but ended up still owing money to their lenders. If a home is fully paid, and then a mortgage is given for a loan, this statutory protection generally is not available. No doubt, legislators believe such borrowers are not vulnerable seekers of shelter, but rather they are sophisticated borrowers for profit.

construction loan A short-term real estate loan, secured by mortgage, intended to finance building costs.

refinance loan A loan, secured by mortgage, the proceeds of which are used primarily to pay off, or retire, an existing mortgage loan. Refinancing occurs when interest rates drop, encouraging homeowners to pay off existing high interest rate loans with new lower interest rate loans.

For the same reason, **construction loans** for the purpose of building a house generally are not protected, nor are **refinance loans** that are taken out to replace an existing loan. Another type of unprotected loan is the home-equity loan, whereby a homeowner borrows for miscellaneous purposes, such as traveling, paying tuition, or buying expensive consumer goods. As stated, these home-equity loans are subject to deficiency judgments if a foreclosure sale should fail to generate enough cash to pay them in full.

Seller's Financing

Sometimes, prospective buyers do not have sufficient funds for a substantial down payment, or are unable to qualify for a new loan under then-existing underwriting (borrower qualification) requirements. As an alternative to "hard" money loans from institutional lenders in which cash is borrowed for the purchase price, a "soft" money (paper) loan from the seller may be appropriate. Soft money here refers to simply paying the purchase price by giving the seller a promissory note for the amount owed. The seller takes on the role of a creditor, receives a note secured by deed of trust, and conveys title to the buyer.

carryback mortgage financing A credit sale of real property in which the seller takes a promissory note and security in the property (mortgage) from the buyer.

Carryback Mortgage Financing Sellers of homes that are free and clear of any loans may themselves finance, or "carry," their buyers, which is called **carryback mortgage financing**. In this situation, the buyer usually makes a small down payment and signs a promissory note in favor of the seller. The seller, like a bank, will not be content with the mere promise of the buyer to pay the unpaid balance but will want the home as collateral. The seller then will require the buyer to execute a carryback mortgage (or deed of trust).

If the buyer fails to make payments when due, the trustee (or mortgagee) will sell the property in a foreclosure auction and apply the cash proceeds to satisfying the defaulted debt. This would be a purchase-money mortgage (or deed of trust), and the seller could not obtain a deficiency judgment against the buyer-debtor if the proceeds of the sale were inadequate to pay off the loan. The seller simply would absorb any such loss.

Contract for Deed or Installment-Land Contract As an alternative method of financing, the buyer and seller may enter into an installment-land contract, also called a contract for deed. Under this arrangement, the seller will not immediately convey title to the buyer, who simply moves in and begins making monthly payments. Rather, title is retained by the seller until the buyer has made monthly payments for many years. This method is used when a buyer cannot qualify for a loan and has no money for a down payment. In these circumstances, the buyer simply makes monthly payments to the seller for, say, 20 years, at which time the seller conveys title to the buyer in exchange for payment of the balance of the purchase price.

From the buyer's standpoint, this generally is not a good way to buy a home, but when no other financing is available, it does solve the immediate problem. This type of transaction may be tempting to a budget-conscious buyer because closing costs can be eliminated, no legal assistance is necessary, the cost of title insurance (discussed later) may be avoided, and appraisal fees and lender's upfront fees (points) are avoided. Even the down payment may be small. Some of these are false savings, however; the seller may inflate the price of the house as compensation for the other munificent terms offered to the buyer.

LEGAL FOCUS—PROBLEM

Mona Morales entered into contract for the deed to a ten-acre parcel of land with the New Horizon Land Company. Her contract required her to make monthly payments for thirty years. The contract terms gave her the right to physically occupy the premises and make improvements. She was also obligated to pay all taxes and utility payments related to the property. Last, at the end of the thirty years, she would receive the deed conveying the title to the land. Thereafter, Mona installed a mobile home on the property, fenced it, and lived there peacefully for fifteen years while operating a small farm. Then, during a tough economic period, she no longer was able to make the required monthly payments. New Horizon Land Company threatens to evict her from the land. Can they do so?

As a buyer under a contract for deed, Mona theoretically can be evicted, as would a defaulting tenant, and would have no asset to show for the payments made to date. Because Mona did not receive title, there is no apparent need for the company to foreclose and regain title. Simple eviction theoretically is a potent remedy for the unpaid seller. If payments have been made regularly for a long time under an installment-land contract, however, a court of equity, in the vast majority of states, will require the seller to recognize that the buyer has acquired some reasonable amount of equity in the property. This remedy, however, requires a lawsuit by the buyer, who could be out of possession of the residence pending the litigation. Following litigation, there would be a foreclosure sale; any balance received in excess of the unpaid balance on the contract would go to the defaulting buyer. Here, Mona's improvement to the land, the addition of the mobile home, and the farm-related improvements would give her other equitable grounds to seek compensation.

As a practical matter, buyers under land contracts who have been in possession for only a short period probably will not profit from a lawsuit to establish equity in the property, because most payments during early years go primarily to interest and do not reduce the principal amount of the loan much.

Lease with Option to Buy

A buyer who has inadequate funds for a down payment and who may have difficulty qualifying for a new loan sometimes may be able to purchase a home by leasing it with an option to buy. This gives the renter an absolute right to purchase the property at a future date at a fixed price upon established terms. The renter who would like to buy now hopes to be better able financially to complete the purchase a few years in the future. A typical lease would be for five years. A portion of each month's lease payment would be "credited" to and earmarked as down payment on the purchase price. This gradual buildup of equity helps reduce or even eliminates the need for a down payment when the option is exercised. Any appreciation in the value of the residence above the agreed-upon option price would further benefit the buyer. Meanwhile, lease payments are made, equity is growing, and opportunity exists for the buyer to enjoy her future home while saving for a down payment. The seller, on the other hand, receives the advantage of delaying income taxes by delaying the sale to some future year, and receives tax deductions permitted for rental property (depreciation, interest, taxes, maintenance if applicable, insurance, supplies, and so forth) while waiting. Because a future sale already is in the works, a real estate commission may be avoided. What is more, tenants with an option to buy probably will be excellent residents, making improvements and caring for the property as if it were their own.

Leases with options to buy can be a panacea for buyers and sellers alike. Lease-option forms are readily available from stationery stores and sellers of legal forms. But, as in most transactions involving a considerable sum of money, precautions should be taken by both parties. For example, if the seller should go into bankruptcy or foreclosure during the term of the lease, and consequently be unable to deliver title in the future, the tenant-buyer could lose her rent credit. Professional legal assistance is advisable before entering a lease-option purchase contract.

WHAT IS ESCROW?

To complete the purchase of a house, many things need to be done at the same time. At the moment title passes, the buyer wants to be certain that title insurance and fire insurance (discussed later) are in effect; the seller wants to receive the amount of the sales price; the lender wants the promissory note and mortgage or deed of trust; the real estate broker wants the earned commission, and so forth. Because it would be impractical for all of these persons to meet and hand out some documents with the left hand while simultaneously taking other documents in with the right, the practice of hiring a third-party intermediary (called the **escrow agent**, or simply **escrow**) developed.

escrow agent
A person paid to perform all the administrative tasks necessary to close a real estate escrow.

Title companies, escrow departments of banks, escrow companies, and sometimes real estate brokers and attorneys may act as escrow agents. The escrow agent collects the required monies and documents from all the interested persons as necessary, and then, at the close of escrow, disburses and distributes them to the appropriate persons. Close of escrow is execution of the contract; title is conveyed to the buyer, cash is delivered to the seller, and so forth.

escrow
An arrangement common in real estate transactions whereby the buyer and seller (and/or the borrower and lender) designate a neutral third party as an agent to carry out instructions for gathering and distributing documents and funds as necessary.

Each party interested in a real estate transaction signs escrow instructions that are prepared from standard forms by escrow agents, or by attorneys for the parties. The escrow instructions command the escrow agent as to what each person will put into escrow and what is expected out of it upon its close. For example, in simplified form, the seller may instruct the escrow officer as follows: "I hand you a duly executed grant deed that you are authorized and instructed to record and deliver to the buyer upon receipt on my behalf of $175,000, the sales price." The escrow agent who complies with all of the instructions will not be liable for any losses suffered by any of the parties.

LEGAL FOCUS—CASE

On or about December 4, 1998, Darryl S. Anderson agreed to sell and Kathy Falcon and Adam Ferrecchia agreed to buy real estate for $99,000. The sale agreement called for a closing date of January 22, 1999, with "time being of the essence." The agreement also contained a mortgage contingency clause wherein the buyers agreed to make diligent efforts to obtain FHA financing for up to $96,000. It was also agreed that if the buyers failed after diligent efforts to obtain financing, they were entitled to a return of the $5,000 deposit. They were, however, required to notify the seller in writing by January 4, 1999, of failure to get financing. Furthermore, under the contract, if the buyers failed to comply with the contract, they would forfeit the $5,000 deposit as liquidated damages. The buyers did not get financing and also failed to notify the seller by the agreed date. Both the seller and buyer are demanding the $5,000 from the escrow agent. What is the escrow agent to do?

Kotseas v. Anderson, 13 Mass. L. Rptr. 232, 2001 WL 881471 (Mass. Super., 2001).

The escrow instructions must dovetail or the escrow cannot close. For example, if a mistake is made such that the instructions direct the escrow agent to accept $175,000 for the seller, but for the buyer to pay only $172,000, there is a conflict and the escrow cannot close. Sometimes errors are made and instructions of the buyer and seller conflict as to how some of the money should be disbursed by the escrow officer. Or situations arise, such as the in the previous case, in which the parties make conflicting demands on the escrow agent. Facing conflicting demands or instructions that do not dovetail, the escrow officer may file a court action called an **interpleader**, deposit the contested funds with the clerk of the court, and withdraw completely, leaving the buyer and seller with the problem of settling their dispute in court. The rationale is that the escrow officer is a mere stakeholder who is obligated to follow instructions as received and when instructions conflict, the stakeholder should be allowed to withdraw. In the preceding Massachusetts case, the escrow agent filed an interpleader action, and the court awarded the remainder of the deposit after costs of escrow to the seller.

interpleader
A legal proceeding to resolve conflicting claims (e.g., conflicting claims to funds in an escrow account).

The escrow officer is a disinterested stakeholder owing allegiance to neither seller nor buyer. Therefore, you should not rely on escrow agents for advice about the merits or consequences of any real estate transaction. In fact, escrow agents are reluctant to say anything to anybody that might be construed as advice. This "mere stakeholder" concept is so clearly defined in the law that even if an escrow officer knows that the buyer is about to be defrauded in a transaction pending in escrow, nothing can be said and no warning can be given. The theory underlying such law is that if escrow officers were permitted to offer advice or suggestions, it would lead to claims of negligent advice (malpractice), bias, and deal wrecking by disappointed consumers. As a practical matter, sellers and buyers do sign many important papers (standard forms) in the presence of the escrow agent, who generally explains their meanings. These papers include written escrow instructions, deeds, and even promissory notes and mortgages provided by the buyer's lender. Do buyers and sellers rely on escrow agents? Yes, most do.

In some states, such as New York, attorneys commonly perform all services necessary to close escrow—that is, they serve as escrow officers. More commonly, banks, professional escrow companies, or title companies provide escrow services. Escrows charge fees for their services—it is up to the parties to negotiate how they will be allocated between buyer and seller. Usually, the parties agree to allocate escrow costs "in accordance with the customs and practices" of the county.

Closing Costs

Buyers and sellers negotiate how to share a variety of costs that are necessary to close escrow when homes are sold. This array of expenses commonly is called **closing costs**.

LEGAL FOCUS—PROBLEM

Michelle Chen was buying Henry Foster's home for $225,000. She had arranged financing of $200,000 from a savings and loan association and anticipated putting down $25,000 of her savings to make the purchase price. Will she be required to pay more than $25,000 into escrow?

closing costs
Charges for various services that arise in connection with the purchase and sale of a home.

Yes, the buyer will be required to pay more. The seller likely will have prepaid real property taxes and fire insurance premiums, some amount of which will have to be reimbursed by the buyer. Thus, if the seller has prepaid, say, $1,000 for the period that extends six months after the close of escrow, the buyer must reimburse that sum. The buyer is responsible for property taxes following the sale.

The same sort of allocation results with prepaid casualty (fire) insurance. Furthermore, the buyer probably will pay the cost of a boundary survey if needed, termite inspection, loan fees (points), and perhaps title, notary, and recording fees. All of these costs and more make up what commonly are called closing costs. Some participants call them garbage fees.

It is customarily the responsibility of the seller to pay any transfer taxes (taxes imposed upon the transfer of ownership of real property, based upon its sales price) and to pay for any corrective repairs determined to be necessary because of damage by termites or dry rot (wood damage from water penetration). Almost all details of the purchase of a home are appropriate matters for inclusion in the contract between seller and buyer and are freely negotiable. Real estate sales agents should be capable of estimating closing costs for their clients.

The Legal Significance of Close of Escrow

recordation
The act or process of recording title to real property in a public registry.

The term close of escrow already has been defined as the final distribution of cash and documents to the seller and buyer. At the close of escrow, the deed to the buyer and mortgage to the lender are recorded in the official records of the county. **Recordation** is a process by which a county official dates and time stamps deeds and mortgages, then files copies in the official records. These records are open to the public and are the records relied upon by attorneys or title companies when a title search is made. The original documents are returned to the parties.

Before close of escrow, the buyer has promised to buy, the seller has promised to sell, the lender has promised to lend, the broker has earned a commission, and so forth. All of these contractual promises are executory, that is, still to be performed. Upon the close of escrow, the buyer has received title to and possession of the home and is its owner; the seller has sold, received the net purchase price, and no longer owns any interest in the property; the lender has made the loan, which the buyer has promised to repay; and the broker has received the agreed-on commission. Most of the promises have been executed or performed. Sometimes, in complicated transactions, the parties will be present with their attorneys at a final meeting called the closing. Many of the documents will be reviewed for the last time and then signed. Although the transaction is completed at close of escrow, the buyer, as borrower, must continue to make future payments on the loan as required by the note.

In brief, the sale is a *fait accompli* (French: "fact or deed accomplished," presumably irrevocably) when escrow closes. Some rights and responsibilities, however, linger beyond close of escrow. For example, buyers and sellers continue to have the right to sue each other for fraud or deceit up until the statute of limitations extinguishes their claims. But generally speaking, most buyers and sellers consider the transaction completed when escrow closes.

What Is a Deed?

deed
Any document used to transfer any ownership interest in real property. Many types of deeds are used in a variety of property transfers.

warranty deed
A type of deed with several warranties implied by law to protect the buyer.

grant deed
A document that conveys the ownership of real property, and impliedly warrants that the grantor previously has not conveyed the property to another and that the property is free from undisclosed encumbrances.

quitclaim deed
A deed to real property in which the transferor conveys whatever ownership interest he may possess, which may be none.

cloud on title
Any dormant or actively pursued claim to the possession of or title to real property that is unresolved or contested.

A **deed** is the document that transfers or conveys title (ownership) of real property from one person to another. A valid deed must contain the following:

- The names of the seller (grantor) and the buyer (grantee)
- Words evidencing an intent to transfer title (e.g., I hereby "grant" or "convey" to)
- A legally sufficient description of the real property deeded
- The grantor's (and usually the spouse's) signature(s)

Finally, to be valid, a deed must be delivered from the grantor to the grantee. Most deeds are recorded in the official records of the county in which the property is located and must be recorded if title insurance is to be purchased. But unrecorded deeds are legally valid.

Different types of deeds provide different degrees of protection for the buyer against potential problems affecting title. A **warranty deed** provides the greatest protection. In most states, a warranty deed requires special language. A warranty deed includes a promise to protect the buyer against all claims of ownership of the property by another. By its use, the grantor impliedly makes certain covenants or promises:

- The grantor has full ownership of the exact interest being conveyed.
- The property is free of liens or claims of third persons except as disclosed in the deed.
- The title will not be challenged by third persons.
- The grantor will execute any further documents that may be required to perfect the grantee's title.

In states in which title insurance policies provide considerable assurance that there will be no surprises found in the official records, the simple **grant deed** commonly is used. By use of the word *grant,* the grantor (seller) impliedly warrants that (1) he previously has not conveyed the property to someone else and (2) the estate (ownership) conveyed is free from prior encumbrances by the grantor, unless disclosed. A **quitclaim deed** offers the least protection against defects in the title. Basically, it conveys to the grantee whatever interest the grantor had. If the grantor has no interest, then the grantee receives no interest. A quitclaim deed seems strange to most people. After all, what value is a deed in which the person transferring it to you is not promising they own anything? Actually, quitclaim deeds often are used in situations in which ownership rights are uncertain. The transfer of such a deed can help clarify ownership interests. The quitclaim deed is appropriate when land is transferred by gift or to clear some possible "**cloud on title**"—some obstacle to clear title, such as an abandoned leasehold that otherwise might be the basis for a later lawsuit.

Married persons can change the form of ownership of property held as community property to tenancy-in-common or joint tenancy, or vice versa, by deed. Under some circumstances, courts have held that even though property is held in joint tenancy, the husband and wife actually intended to and did hold the property as community property. The result of such a ruling is a tax advantage, in that surviving owners of community property pay considerably less income tax on any future sale than do surviving joint tenants.

LEGAL FOCUS—PROBLEM

Lee and Patricia Mietus own a house in California. The house was owned by Lee Mietus as his separate property before his marriage to Patricia. Improvements were made to the house after the marriage and were paid for by community property funds. Remember, California is a community property state, and most property acquired during a marriage is community property. Assume that Don Burgunder wishes to buy the property from Lee Mietus. Lee will want to be sure that all interests in the property are conveyed to him. Ownership records will show that Lee Mietus is the sole owner. Lee, however, would be right to be concerned that Patricia may have some interest in the house because of the community property improvements to it. What type of deed should Don expect from the Mietuses to protect his interests?

Don would like a warranty or grant deed from Lee, which will include promises to protect Don from all claims of ownership from others. He would like more than a promise to protect as to Patricia's interest, however; he would like a quitclaim deed. Patricia should be willing to convey this deed; after all, it only transfers what she has and does not guarantee she owns anything. Quitclaim deeds are useful to transfer an interest in cases such as this, when a person may have an interest, but no formal records document its existence.

WHAT IS TITLE INSURANCE?

abstract of title
A chronological history of recorded documents that affect the title to a parcel of real property.

standard title insurance
Customary title insurance coverage that does not include the special coverage included within the more expensive American Land Title Association policy, which includes physical inspection of the premises as well as a review of the official records in a title search.

In some states, such as New York, attorneys perform title searches and render legal opinions regarding the quality of title to property. These opinions are called **abstracts of title**. In most states, however, title insurance companies guarantee property purchasers that they have accurately searched the public records. **Standard title insurance** is a policy of insurance whereby the owner of a home may ensure that there are no surprises lurking in the official records that pertain to her newly acquired property. The insurance covers a narrow range of losses, up to a specified face amount of the policy. Title insurance is unlike any other variety of insurance, such as life insurance, where the event of loss is unpredictable. Title insurance does not insure against unpredictable losses. Rather, it insures against losses that may occur from the failure to reveal to the owner any recorded documents—which should have been found absent negligence by the title insurance company.

At the time the title insurance policy is issued, the owner is given a list of recorded documents pertaining to the property, which might include earlier deeds, mortgages, and liens. As briefly noted earlier, recorded documents have been physically date-time stamped and copies have been filed in the public records, indexed alphabetically by the surnames of the parties to the document. You can visit the recorder of your county and examine any recorded document. The process of recording permanently establishes the sequence in which the documents pertaining to a particular parcel of real property were recorded (date-time stamped). In general, claims that are first in time are first in right, so such formal recording in the official records obviously is important.

notarized
Signed in the presence of a person licensed by the state to perform identification services as a notary public.

In addition to the accuracy of a list of recorded documents, standard coverage title insurance covers a few losses that may arise from matters not readily ascertainable from the official records, such as forgery of a deed in the chain of title, lack of capacity of parties who are grantors (perhaps through mental incompetency), or lack of delivery of a deed to a former owner. Losses from forgery are unlikely because documents must be **notarized** (signed in the presence of an official who is called a notary public) before being recorded. Losses from the lack of capacity of previous owners also are unlikely because court judgments declaring a person incompetent (lacking in capacity) are available in the official records. Nor is a lack of delivery of deed a likely defect because the law presumes delivery whenever a document, such as a deed, is recorded.

LEGAL FOCUS—PROBLEM

Percy Fairchild bought a one-acre homesite in the country, on which he planned to build a home and enjoy a "gentleman's farm" with an extensive garden and a variety of animals. In connection with the purchase, he acquired a standard policy of title insurance. Thereafter, he began leveling the land for a foundation for his home and outbuildings. He promptly was served with a lawsuit in which a neighbor to the rear, Georgette Simpson, was the plaintiff. Simpson alleged that she owned an easement (right to use) across the middle of Fairchild's lot because she had used it for 15 years for access to the county road. She requested the court to enjoin the construction to protect her easement. Fairchild asked his lawyer to cross-complain against the title insurance company for the apparent defect in his title. Will he win?

easement
The right to use the real property of another for a limited purpose (e.g., access to a beach or public road).

prescriptive easement
An easement, usually of access, over the land of another person, created by a continuous, open (visible) use without the consent of the landowner for a long period of time, usually five years or more in most states.

Fairchild probably will lose his case with Simpson and certainly will lose his cross-complaint against the title company. Among defects in title that are not covered by standard title insurance are unrecorded **easements**. An easement is a right a person has to make limited use of another person's property. An easement, for example, can be the right to walk across another's property or run a telephone line across it. An unrecorded easement is a legal right to use the land of another that is not recorded in the official records. Some easements are prepared by deeds and are recorded in the official records. But many easements do not appear in the public records. They are created by adjacent landowners who repeatedly use neighboring land for access over many years. Such an easement is called a prescriptive easement. Such an easement can arise when one person uses another person's land for a time equal to the applicable statute of limitations. If the owner of the land did not object to the use of the land during this period, the person using the land has an easement by prescription. These **prescriptive easements** are not evidenced by any documents and therefore do not appear in the public records. In Simpson's case, the court would not bar Fairchild from any use of his land but could order him to make suitable some portion of his land for continued periodic access by Simpson. If a defect is disclosed by the title insurer in its policy, any losses from that defect are not covered by insurance. That is, the risk of loss is that the insurer (title company) will negligently overlook a recorded document and thus fail to inform the insured (homeowner) of its existence.

Other exclusions from coverage in standard title insurance policies are boundary discrepancies and errors about how many acres or square feet are contained within the parcel.

extended coverage
Coverage for title defects as described within the American Land Title Insurance form.

American Land Title Association insurance policy
A standardized form of extended title insurance coverage that is more comprehensive than the customary policy.

Many lenders require **extended coverage** insurance (also called an **American Land Title Association (ALTA) insurance policy**) against loss from any defect, including such unrecorded matters as the presence of tenants or adverse possessors who may assert a future claim of ownership in the property. An **adverse possessor** is anyone who physically occupies and pays taxes on someone else's property for a number of years, such as five, under some color or claim of ownership. Such interlopers can be awarded ownership rights by judicial proceeding even though they never paid a cent for the property. Extended insurance (ALTA) costs more than standard coverage because the title insurance company must make an on-site physical inspection in addition to the customary search of the official records. Presumably, such an on-site inspection would reveal to the title insurer that someone is adversely possessing the property or encroaching its boundaries, causing that fact to be noted as an exception to coverage and thereby placing the risk of loss upon the buyer. As a practical matter in the buying and selling of homes, adverse possession would be extraordinarily unlikely and on-site inspections are not made.

ROLE OF ATTORNEY IN HOME TRANSACTIONS

adverse possessor
A person who creates ownership of real property through its possession for a prescribed number of years without the consent of its owner.

On the one hand, it would be prudent to simply advise all prospective sellers and buyers of homes to consult with an attorney to draft or at least to review all documents involved. It is unrealistic to engage the services of an attorney for each step in the process, however, because the steps occur at different times and places. As a general proposition, most buyers and sellers of homes do not consult attorneys; rather, they rely on the advice and recommendations of their real estate sales agents who, in turn, rely on standard forms and customs and practices they have followed for years. And, yes, many sellers and buyers end up unhappy or even outraged by how they feel mistreated following a home purchase. The more costly the transaction, the more likely the services of attorneys should be considered.

LEGAL FOCUS—PROBLEM

Dave and Kathy McDaniel were in the market for a home priced around $285,000. While deciding whether to buy a preowned or newly built home, they contacted their attorney, Colleen Strong, for advice about available financing. What would attorney Strong's advice likely be?

Their attorney probably would advise the McDaniels that financing is primarily an economic, not a legal, question. The most knowledgeable persons concerning the availability of home loans and their terms are found in real estate sales and loan brokerage firms. Additional useful information is obtainable from local banks, savings and loan institutions, and the FHA. Attorney Strong might properly suggest, however, that she review all significant documents before they are signed. Sales agents loathe the involvement of attorneys, who never seem to be available at critical times when the parties are ready to sign a document and who raise many questions, some of which may create buyers' or sellers' remorse. Agents often refer to attorneys as "deal killers." Nonetheless, Strong might review any purchase agreement.

The advice of attorneys always is essential in complex arrangements in which one party is in a position to take advantage of the other. The hiring of a building contractor to build a custom home is one important example.

Because most questions that arise in buying homes are simple and repetitive, real estate agents develop considerable expertise and usually are qualified to assist buyers in the preparation of purchase agreements without the need for legal assistance. Agents are primarily in the business of selling, however, and are not qualified or authorized to render

severalty
Separate or individual ownership of property by one person or ownership as separate property by a married person.

legal opinions to prospective buyers or sellers. A prudent buyer who asks questions and receives fuzzy, nonresponsive, or incomplete answers would be well advised to obtain legal assistance before signing any contracts. Fees for contract review are likely to be modest because attorneys can perform such routine services in a short time—if that is their specialization.

One decision that more often than not should be made carefully, perhaps requiring the services of an attorney, concerns choice in legal form of title, which we consider next.

HOW MAY TITLE TO YOUR HOME BE HELD?

tenancy in common
A form of coownership of property by two or more persons. Upon the death of any co-owner, that person's percentage interest passes by intestate succession or by last will.

joint tenancy
A method of co-ownership of property by two or more persons. Upon the death of any co-owner, that person's percentage interest goes to the surviving joint tenant (s) regardless of the decedent's last will. This right of survivorship is the basic incident of joint-tenancy ownership.

tenancy by the entirety
A form of co-ownership of property between husband and wife in some states. As with joint-tenancy ownership, the spouses have a right of survivorship.

If only one person owns property, it is owned in **severalty**. If persons share ownership rights in property, they are said to be concurrent owners or tenants. There are four principal types of *concurrent ownership:* tenancy in common, joint tenancy, tenancy by the entireties, and community property.

Each form of co-ownership has different characteristics and serves different purposes. A **tenancy in common** is the form of co-ownership most appropriate for unrelated owners. Tenants can own unequal shares and get their interests at different times. The shares of ownership can be transferred easily. If any tenant dies, that tenant's interest passes to her heirs. Any tenant can transfer her interest to a third person.

Another common form of joint ownership, called **joint tenancy**, provides for a different result upon a joint owner's death. Joint tenancy is co-ownership with the right of survivorship. If any joint tenant dies, the deceased joint tenant's interest passes to the surviving joint tenant(s). The deceased tenant's interest expires at death and cannot pass to her heirs. A joint tenant does, however, have the right to transfer her ownership before death. The transfer will terminate the joint tenancy.

A joint tenancy requires a written document and cannot be created casually or accidentally. Because of its survivorship feature, many states require the words "with right of survivorship" to be included in the instrument creating the interest.

About half of the states permit a variation of joint tenancy between husband and wife called **tenancy by the entirety**. Unlike joint tenancy, a tenancy by the entirety usually can be between only a husband and wife, and both parties have full ownership of the property. Thus, neither party can unilaterally terminate the tenancy by the entirety or dispose of the property without the other party's concurrence except when subject to the other's right of survivorship.

Some states (Arizona, California, Idaho, Louisiana, Nevada, New Mexico, Texas, and Washington) have community property and a few have marital property, both are a variation of co-ownership by married couples.

When two or more persons decide to purchase a residence, a decision must be made as to the legal form of joint ownership to be used.

LEGAL FOCUS—PROBLEM

Robert and Clarissa Ramirez, a married couple, were buying their first home. Just before close of escrow, they were advised by their real estate agent to take title in joint tenancy. Should they do so? What alternatives should they consider?

Owning a home in joint tenancy is a common form of ownership by married couples. Upon the death of one joint tenant, transfer of ownership to the survivor is expedient because the property need not go through probate (discussed in Chapter 15). Joint tenancy property is not affected by a will and may be vulnerable to death tax problems in large estates. The advice the real estate agent gave in this problem is dangerously close to the unauthorized practice of law. A more prudent agent would provide clients with published material generally describing the alternatives available and suggest they get further advice from an attorney.

In some states, the Ramirezes would probably take title as tenants by the entirety, with essentially the same effect as if they were joint tenants. In any of the states where available, they might consider taking title as community property, so that each spouse's one-half share could be disposed of by will, if so desired. Community property ownership also offers income tax advantages to the surviving spouse when her highly appreciated house is sold following the other's death. One community property state, Washington, requires that married couples own their home as community property.

If two or more unrelated persons decide to pool their resources to improve their quality of life by purchasing a home, they would, no doubt, prefer to retain the right to individually will their undivided interests to their respective relatives or loved ones. They would accordingly select the tenancy-in-common form of homeownership.

LEGAL FOCUS—PROBLEM

Jinna Roberts and Kathy Jennings, unrelated, owned Sky High Ranch as joint tenants. Upon learning that their respective interests would go to the survivor of them regardless of their respective wills, they decided to change their ownership form. May they do so?

Yes, they may do so. Roberts and Jennings can simply convey the property to themselves as tenants in common. Then, both may will their respective equal shares to anyone they choose. For example, if Roberts should die without leaving a will, her undivided one-half interest would go to her closest surviving heirs. Such surviving heirs, under law, would become tenants in common with Jennings.

HOW IS A HOME TAXED?

market value
The price property would bring if offered for sale in a fair market (not at auction or in a forced sale) by a willing and fully informed (but not compelled) seller, after ample time to find a willing and fully informed (but not compelled) buyer.

A home may be located within the boundaries of both a county and a city as well as within various municipal taxing districts, all of which may impose taxes on property to finance schools, colleges, flood control districts, mosquito abatement districts, air pollution control districts, parks, water systems, sewers, and so on. Generally, these needs are expressed in a combined budget, which reflects the money local government must obtain from its residents to function for another fiscal year.

In most states, taxation of real property, including homes, is the principal method by which local governments obtain needed funds. Theoretically, all properties are taxed in proportion to their current values, whether they are residential, commercial, industrial, or whatever. The county assessor appraises each property at its **market value** (called *full cash value)* and declares a uniform fraction of that amount

assessed value The value assigned to real property by a local official called an assessor for the purpose of levying a property tax.

to be its **assessed value**. Some states assess at full cash value. These values are approximations of fair market values because assessors cannot possibly keep all properties within a jurisdiction currently appraised on a year-to-year basis.

Whether a full cash value or fractional assessment (some arbitrary portion, or fraction, of full cash value) is used has no effect on the amount of property tax paid by the homeowner. These "assessed" values are listed on the assessment roll.

The applicable combined budget then is divided by the total assessed value of all taxable property in the county to arrive at the property tax rate—the percentage that must be applied to the assessed value of each parcel of taxable property in the county to determine how much its share of the entire budget should be.

In this way, property owners are taxed in proportion to the value of the property they own. A property worth 30 percent more than another property will be liable for 30 percent more in taxes, if both are within the same municipal taxing districts. Also, a home worth $275,000 will be liable for exactly the same amount of tax as a service station worth $275,000, if both are within the same district.

Owners who believe their taxes are unfairly high in comparison with similar properties may informally request a reappraisal by the tax assessor, or formally appeal to the specified appeals body (such as the local Board of Equalization). If unsuccessful, they can appeal to a court, but courts generally do not overrule administrative agencies, especially on matters of taxation.

Any individual's property may be reappraised, and if its assessed value goes up, its specific tax bill will rise. Conversely, a person whose property goes down in assessed value in relationship to other properties will pay a lower tax. Increases or decreases in assessed values or tax rates have nothing to do with increased total taxes, which can occur only when government expenditures increase. In other words, if all assessed values rise, but budgeted expenses remain constant, total taxes collected will remain constant. Rising and falling property taxes are a function of rising and falling combined county budgets.

Typically, all assessed values in a county are increased annually by some percentage to reflect estimated general inflationary pressures. A constant tax rate thus will produce an increase in the budget, producing, in turn, higher taxes for everyone's property. Some states, California for instance, have adopted property tax limitations that apply to older but not recently sold properties. Therefore, a home that recently sold for $250,000 may be chargeable with more property tax than a home or service station also worth $250,000 but that has been owned a number of years. In effect, new homeowners subsidize owners who have owned their homes for some years. This result of higher taxes for newer homes of comparable values is another example of how the traditional economic benefits of homeownership are eroding in the early twenty-first century.

impound account An account held by a mortgage lender in which to accumulate sufficient funds to pay all annual property taxes and property and liability insurance premiums.

Property taxes typically are paid twice a year, in December and April, although they accrue daily. Some lenders require their borrowers to pay taxes monthly, along with their payments of principal and interest. These lenders then forward the collected property taxes to the local tax collector twice a year. The funds collected monthly are held in an **impound account** by the lender until disbursed to the tax collector. A small amount of interest is paid to the borrower by some lenders for these prepayments of taxes. The reason lenders prefer impounds is that it gives them an assurance that the homeowner has set aside enough money to pay the taxes when due. When negotiating for a home mortgage, borrowers can ask that they pay all property taxes and insurance bills directly, avoiding the impounding process. This gives the homeowner use of the cash until the periodic tax and insurance bills arrive.

WHAT IS FIRE INSURANCE?

A private home is the costliest single asset the typical adult is likely ever to acquire. The greatest hazard both buyer and lender face is the possibility that a fire may break out and damage or completely destroy the building and contents. There are basically two types of insurance policies for a home: standard fire insurance policies and homeowners policies. Additional coverage for other perils, such as for damages from windstorm, hail, an explosion, or earthquake or flood, is available for added premiums.

Standard Fire Insurance Policies

The standard fire insurance policy protects the homeowner against fire and lightning and damage from smoke and water caused by the fire or the fire department. Paying a slightly higher amount will extend the coverage to damage caused by hail, windstorms, explosions, and so on. Personal theft insurance and a comprehensive liability policy also can be added to fire insurance. Liability insurance in a fire policy protects a homeowner from obligations that might arise because of a tort by the homeowner, for example, if a neighbor slipped and hurt herself because of a toy left on a homeowner's entrance stairway.

As in all forms of insurance, the terms of the policy determine the insurer's liability. Most policies, however, limit recovery to losses resulting from a *hostile*—not a *friendly*—*fire*. A *friendly fire* is one intentionally set and burning where it is supposed to burn, for example, in a fireplace. A *hostile fire* is one that was not intended.

Fire insurance policies require the insured to file a claim within a specified time. The claimant must prove loss within this time or risk revocation of coverage.

Homeowners Policy

homeowners policy
Insurance that typically covers losses of the homeowner's property from specified casualties, such as fire and water damage, as well as the possible liability of the owner for specified damages she may cause to another person through negligent behavior (other than with a motor vehicle or boat).

A **homeowners policy** provides protection against several risks under a single policy. This allows the policyholder to avoid the cost of buying each protection separately. There are two basic types of coverage in a homeowners policy.

1. Property coverage includes garage, house, and other private buildings on the policyholder's lot. This coverage also protects the personal possessions and property of the policyholder at home, in travel, or at work. A claim can pay additional living expenses for living away from home because of a fire or some other covered peril (dangers). Some perils commonly are excluded from coverage unless specifically requested and with payment of an additional premium. Among the types of perils that are sometimes excluded are war, earthquake, flood, and nuclear hazard.
2. Liability coverage protects for personal liability if someone is injured on the insured's property. This coverage also protects the insured who damages someone else's property or injures someone else. Two major exclusions from coverage are harm caused to others while in an automobile and liability for professional malpractice.

An insured also can pay a slightly higher premium to insure specific and expensive personal articles or protection for certain events. Adding items to a policy is done with what is called a *floater*.

Additionally, the value of coverage is as important as the scope of coverage. If an insured has an extensive policy but low liability limits, he will have considerable risk. For example, if you are covered for most types of liability but only in the amount of $25,000, you still would have limited coverage.

Coinsurance Clauses

Both fire and homeowners insurance usually have a *coinsurance clause* as standard language in the insurance contract. A coinsurance clause requires that the owner insure her property up to a specified percentage—usually 80 percent—of its value. If the owner insures for less than the required percentage, the owner is paid only a proportionate share of her loss. It is important for homeowners to keep track of the current replacement value of their home to ensure that they have sufficient insurance.

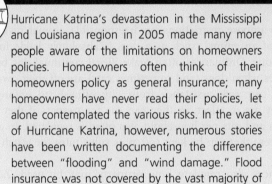

LEGAL FOCUS—PROBLEM

Hurricane Katrina's devastation in the Mississippi and Louisiana region in 2005 made many more people aware of the limitations on homeowners policies. Homeowners often think of their homeowners policy as general insurance; many homeowners have never read their policies, let alone contemplated the various risks. In the wake of Hurricane Katrina, however, numerous stories have been written documenting the difference between "flooding" and "wind damage." Flood insurance was not covered by the vast majority of homeowners, so only wind damage qualified for compensation. As this edition was being written, some of the first cases testing claims that insurance companies have failed to pay justified claims are reaching resolution, which are unsatisfactory to many of the insured. Many victims have expressed anger and frustration that they paid for insurance, in some cases for many years, only to receive little or no payment following the hurricane.

WHAT IS NEIGHBOR LAW?

Disputes between neighbors frequently center around noise, encroachments of tree roots and limbs, boundary lines, and obstruction of views. Various laws, both statutory and common law, comprise **neighbor law**. Court decisions are infrequent largely because the picayune nature of many neighbor squabbles does not justify spending the substantial sums that are required to pursue formal litigation remedies. Neighbor disputes, however, are notable for their intensity and longevity. Lawyers and judges alike prefer to remain uninvolved, knowing that even after a court rules the neighbors will find something else to fight about. Most neighbor quarrels are resolved by local officials in small claims courts (fully discussed in Chapter 3), and many are resolved by simple resignation and tolerance of annoyances that are part of life. Renters, of course, simply move.

neighbor law
The body of laws and rules found in state statutes; in county and city ordinances; in covenants, conditions, and restrictions (CC&Rs); and in court decisions that govern the legal issues that arise between residential neighbors.

Help from Local Officials

Many common neighbor disputes have been anticipated and are regulated by local ordinance. Ordinances prohibit allowing city property to become blighted (in a condition of disrepair), and they often prohibit the accumulation of weeds, debris, rubbish, and so forth. Antiblight ordinances may apply to fences, sidewalks, windows, and driveways as well as structures. Graffiti may be considered a form of blight. Some local ordinances address possible public health problems, such as garbage, debris, and weeds or other rubbish that encourages the breeding of rats and insects or is conducive to fires. Offended neighbors can obtain assistance from city officials, who will compel repairs of unsightly messes or impose fines upon persons responsible. Local ordinances also prohibit unreasonably loud noises, sometimes applying to such activities as late-night basketball, blaring outdoor stereos, and even screaming and fighting neighbors. Police can be called upon to enforce such ordinances. What is reasonable sound is sometimes determined by measurement of decibels and their relationship to the time of day ("quiet times" may be included within the ordinance) and the type of applicable zoning. Some states have criminal statutes prohibiting noise that is so loud that it "disturbs the peace."

The traffic, crime, and fear engendered by continual drug dealing in a house also may be prohibited by ordinances that provide neighbors with small claims court remedies against landlords and owners of such nuisances. Courts have imposed damages upon landlords of such crack houses, and this ultimately leads to evictions to forestall future penalties.

Local ordinances also impose restrictions on irresponsible animal owners. Under common law, the owner of an animal, such as a dog, is absolutely liable for damages caused when it bites someone. Ordinances often make illegal continual dog barking and howling and require leashes when dogs (and sometimes cats) are off their owner's property. Offended neighbors can seek assistance from city officials to enforce "pooper scooper" ordinances if they are in effect, or they can sue for trespass if they are not in effect. The number of dogs and cats per household also often is regulated. In at least one instance, the number of geese that can be kept (often as substitutes for watch dogs) also is regulated.

Local zoning ordinances also regulate how property may be used. Zoning laws typically prohibit running a business at a residence if it attracts customers and creates traffic. Persons who perform "outsource" work at home do not violate residential ordinances unless repeated customer and car traffic is thereby generated. Even running garage sales every weekend is probably illegal in most residentially zoned communities. Ordinances also regulate the use and storage of motor vehicles. For example, recreational vehicles sometimes must be shielded by fencing or vegetation. Under many ordinances, cars cannot be stored in driveways in a state of disassembly and disrepair for indefinite times. And most communities prohibit the continual parking of cars on public streets.

Help from CC&Rs

Condominium projects and planned unit subdivisions are regulated by deed restrictions, called **covenants, conditions, and restrictions (CC&Rs)**. These restrictions are binding upon the owners and occupants of homes within the subdivision. The purpose of CC&Rs is usually to maintain property values within the community and to contribute to a safe, neat, and pleasing environment. A wide range of neighbor disputes may be solved by application of the CC&Rs to the problem. For example, CC&Rs almost always cover noise problems, regulate the time of day when swimming pools may be used, restrict when basketball may be played and whether a court may be lighted, and so on. Colors of fences as well as their style, height, material, and location usually are regulated, both by local ordinance and by applicable CC&Rs.

covenants, conditions, and restrictions (CC&Rs)
A written set of limitations, in deeds or other recorded documents, on the future use of real property.

When a dispute arises, the CC&Rs include a mechanism, or procedure, by which complaints can be brought to the attention of the homeowners association (HOA).

Earlier in this chapter, a general comparison of the amenities between owning and renting a home was presented. HOAs and the rules they enforce are considered by many to equal, or at least to resemble, the restrictive rules found in apartments. In other words, the owned home is less like a "castle" and more like a rented apartment.

LEGAL FOCUS—PROBLEM

Phyllis Hammond was living in Taromina, a ninety-two-unit oceanfront cooperative in Florida, when its HOA ended its ban on cats. Hammond scurried out and bought a ten-pound cat named Sam for $100. Weeks later, the co-op board of directors reinstated its prior ban on cats as pets and ordered Hammond to get Sam out of her one-bedroom apartment. Legal battles ensued, and before long, Hammond, who was living on a modest pension and Social Security, had spent $8,063, mostly in attorney fees; the co-op board had spent $11,000. The governing rules provided that in legal skirmishes, the prevailing party was entitled to reimbursement of attorney fees from the losing side. In disgust, Hammond offered to get rid of Sam, sell her apartment, and end the dispute if each side would pay its own attorney fees. The board refused "on principle" according to its lawyer. How can Hammond end the dispute?

Hammond cannot end the dispute. All too often, attorney fees become the tail that wags the dog (or cat, in this situation) in litigation. HOA rules typically provide that the prevailing party is entitled to recover attorney fees, which may greatly exceed the amount in controversy, as the *Hammond* case demonstrates. Because of the frequency and ferocity of litigation between owners and HOAs, some states require that such disputes be submitted to nonbinding arbitration before litigation can be pursued. The theory is that the nonbinding arbitration decision will give the parties third-party input that may lead to some compromise.

Help from Court

encroachment
Construction (e.g., building or fence) or vegetation (e.g., tree limb or ground cover) that physically intrudes upon or overlaps the real property of another.

Many people develop zealously protective attitudes about their trees. As trees grow, their limbs may extend across lot lines, offering both their fruit to the neighbor (sometimes welcome) as well as their dripping sap, falling leaves and limbs, and bird droppings (seldom welcome). Furthermore, your neighbor's trees can be counted on to clog up your rain gutters and downspouts (never welcome). Roots can and do extend across lot lines, and sometimes even a tree's trunk will cross the line. Any physical protrusion across a boundary line is called an **encroachment**. Problems arise when neighbors want to cut limbs off their neighbor's tree or cut the tree down, especially if its roots are uprooting the fence, driveway, or even a nearby structure. Of equally provoking concern is loss of sunlight, allergic reaction to drifting pollen, and, of course, loss of an ocean, valley, or mountain view. The location of a tree's trunk determines its ownership. If the trunk overlaps a lot line, it is jointly owned by both homeowners whether they like the idea or not. If a wrongdoer (whether or not a neighbor) kills a landowner's tree, the victim may recover compensatory damages (cost of replacement or diminution in value of the land, plus out-of-pocket costs) and punitive damages if applicable. Many states have adopted statutes prescribing damages for crimes against trees, doubling or trebling compensatory damages, and sometimes permitting the recovery of attorney fees. In some states, wrongful tree killing is a crime, a misdemeanor punishable by fine or imprisonment.

In common law, there is a right of self-help. Under the doctrine of self-help, a person has the right to personally secure or enforce some legal right so long as no violent confrontation is involved. But, in a modern application of the rule, neighbors simply can cut off any encroaching limbs or roots of trees. This conduct may offend the tree's owner, but it is permitted in all states under common law. The trimming, however, is generally at the neighbor's expense and cannot result in killing the tree—if it does die, the neighbor can be sued for damages for loss of the tree. This is noteworthy because some trees can add a substantial amount to the value of a home. In most states, the neighbor has no other remedy than to trim the tree back to the boundary, unless real damage has been caused (e.g., by partially falling onto the roof). When substantial injury has occurred, or is threatened, the encroaching tree qualifies as a **nuisance**. Any unreasonable interference with the use and enjoyment of real property is called a nuisance; it may be enjoined by court (through its issuance of an injunction) or damages may be awarded. Tree owners clearly must keep their trees from becoming a nuisance, that is, from encroaching on and damaging their neighbors' property.

nuisance
Any unreasonable and continuous interference with the use and enjoyment of real property.

The owner of a fruit tree owns its fruit, even if the fruit is growing on a limb that is overhanging the boundary fence. This rule makes it clear that the public cannot legally pull off a road to pick fruit from orchard trees that overhang onto the public right of way. If the owner of a fruit tree desired to enter upon the neighbor's property to retrieve fruit, the issue of trespass would arise. It is unclear whether the law would uphold an owner's fundamental right to exclude persons from the property or would create a limited right in the owner of a fruit tree to trespass on another's property to retrieve fruit.

LEGAL FOCUS—PROBLEM

Janice Turner was angry that her neighbor's Strawberry Blush cling peach tree was overhanging the fence. She said nothing to her neighbor, Baylor Scott, during the following months. In August the tree was laden with beautiful ripe fruit, much of which was clinging to the limbs overhanging Turner's property. Turner then smugly trimmed the limbs back to the fence line and, after the limbs were severed, picked the peaches, canning some and simply enjoying the others. Scott learned of the timely trimming and sued in small claims court for the value of the peaches Turner had taken. What arguments support each side, and what decision should the judge make?

Turner would argue that she exercised her common law right of self-help by trimming the encroaching limbs back to the property line. Scott might counter that her real intention was to steal his fruit. He could argue that the limbs and fruit remained his property even after they were trimmed, and that Turner is guilty of the tort of conversion. (Conversion was explained in Chapter 7.) The law on this point is nonexistent; the judge would simply have to make a decision without the benefit of the doctrine of *stare decisis*. What decision would you make as judge?

Homeowners enjoy sunlight, free-flowing breezes, and sometimes good views. In common law, however, there is no right to light, air, or view, which may be impaired from growing trees (or even buildings) on neighboring property. This harsh rule has been modified by local ordinances in some areas near the ocean or with other scenic-view potential. These ordinances do not prohibit growing trees that may someday obstruct a neighbor's view. The court is authorized to balance the owner's rights with the desirability of a view for the neighbor, whether or not trimming to the extent of providing a filtered view, or even topping or windowing (cutting out a window to provide a partial view) would be a satisfactory solution. CC&Rs also may regulate the protection of views from growing trees.

Disputes in connection with fences, as noted previously, may be resolved by resort to local officials, who will enforce ordinances regulating fences, or by resort to HOA officials, who will enforce applicable CC&Rs. Sometimes, however, a property owner will erect a spite fence, creating a dispute that will require going to court for relief. Any fence that is built to annoy or vex a neighbor, and that has no reasonable value to its owner, is called a **spite fence**. Many states have statutes defining spite fences as nuisances and authorizing lawsuits for their removal and recovery of damages.

spite fence
A fence erected primarily to vex, annoy, or "spite" a neighbor.

Proof that a fence is intended to annoy or vex may be easier to produce than it seems. Often, a spite fence deliberately is made to look like a monstrosity, to further annoy the neighbor. The existence of ongoing hostility between the neighbors is evidence of a malicious intent. If a fence does not contribute materially to needed privacy, or does not effectively fence anything inside, or does not effectively stop intruders, strong evidence exists that it is a spite fence. Made-up reasons, such as "needed to support my climbing roses," are not likely to be persuasive. Courts can order the removal of spite fences and award compensatory damages and even punitive damages in outrageous cases.

Neighbor disputes can make life less enjoyable. Prospective homebuyers are well advised to extend their inquiries beyond the four corners of the lots they are considering for purchase. Much about the neighborhood can be learned from asking nearby residents pertinent questions. Letter carriers also are available for questions and often are experts in any ongoing neighborhood disputes. The location of trees, condition of fences, establishment of boundary lines through survey, as well as a late-night visit on Friday or Saturday can all contribute to making a well-informed purchase.

Sometimes, families rent homes in subdivisions in which most homes are owned. This situation can exacerbate problems on occasion when renters are less concerned than owners with long-term neighbor relations. Some think that renters are less likely to maintain proper outside appearances of the home they rent, as by storing old vehicles or not making repairs in front or by not picking up loose papers, and so on. Owners of homes that are rented often are accused of ignoring exterior appearances through marginal landscaping services, deteriorated paint and roof conditions, and permissiveness toward all **blight**. Blight in real estate refers to any condition that negatively affects property values in a neighborhood. Examples of blight include foil in or bars over windows, toys constantly left asunder, motorcycles on lawn areas, moss growing on roofs, cracked windows, makeshift visible repairs, exposed garbage cans, and so on. Neighbors who are offended by nearby blight have little recourse in the law, no recourse in CC&Rs if none are applicable, and little assistance from government officials unless more serious violations of law also are taking place.

blight
An extremely adverse condition affecting the value of real property, such as disrepair or garbage in the yard.

Sometimes, the American dream can become an American nightmare—it pays to be a smart buyer.

CASE

Antrim, Piper, Wenger v. Lowe

37 Kan.App.2d 932, 159 P.3d 215 Kansas Court of Appeals, 2007.

David Lowe signed a nonexclusive right to sell agreement with Einer Johnson, a real estate agent for Antrim, Piper, Wenger, Inc. (Antrim), to sell the Lowes' ranch near Sedan, Kansas. This contract allowed Antrim to list and sell the property with a commission of 5 percent. Alan Lewis called Johnson to inquire about the ranch but told Johnson not to come to the ranch because he just wanted to look around. Johnson then stated that he gave Lewis directions to the ranch but Lewis seemed confused. After talking to Lewis, Johnson called the Lowes and spoke to Lowe's wife, Deborah. He told her that people interested in the property were staying at the Ranch Motel in Sedan and that she might want to help them find the ranch. Deborah called the Ranch Restaurant, which is next to the hotel, and gave them her number. Around noon, Lewis and Logan entered the restaurant and the waitress gave them the number. Once they arrived, David showed them around the land. When Lewis decided to buy the property, David wrote a contract for sale, which Lewis signed. Later that evening, Johnson called and spoke to David, who told him that Lewis and Logan bought the property. Although Johnson offered to write a contract for the sale, David refused his assistance. The parties closed the sale of the ranch, but the Lowes refused to pay Antrim a commission on the sale. In June, Antrim sued the Lowes. Antrim moved for summary judgment, which the court granted ordering the Lowes to pay Antrim its commission.

Justice Green Delivered the Opinion of the Court

On March 31, 2004, David W. Lowe signed a nonexclusive right to sell agreement with Einer Johnson, a real estate agent for Antrim, Piper, Wenger, Inc. (Antrim), to sell the Lowes' ranch near Sedan, Kansas. The Lowes contend that the trial court erred in granting Antrim's motion for summary judgment. The Lowes first argue that summary judgment was inappropriate because they had retained the right to personally sell the property to an interested buyer. David showed the property and wrote the contract for sale. Deborah helped find the buyers and directed them to the ranch. Therefore, David maintains that Antrim did not earn a commission because he and Deborah completed the actual sale.

Because the brokerage contract between Antrim and David was a nonexclusive right to sell, David retained the right to sell his property. Nevertheless, this rule does not apply when the owner uses a buyer procured by a real estate agent hired by the owner. If the agent efficiently produces a buyer who is ready, willing, and able to purchase the property and if the agent is the procuring cause of the deal, the agent is entitled to receive a commission. The agent is not required to introduce the parties or to bring them together personally. Nor is the agent required to procure a binding contract signed by the purchaser.

Here, despite the fact that the Lowes found the buyers in Sedan, showed them the property, and wrote the contract for sale, the key undisputed fact remains that the Lowes knew that Lewis and Logan had been sent to them through the efforts of Johnson, Antrim's salesperson. Moreover, without Antrim's website listing, Lewis would not have learned of the ranch. Without the website, Lewis would not have called Johnson and Johnson would not have alerted Deborah to the fact that buyers were in the area. Antrim was the procuring cause (a term apparently used interchangeably with "efficient cause" and "proximate cause") of the Lowes' deal with Lewis. David cannot defeat Antrim's right to a commission by closing the deal himself. Therefore, since the Lowes do not dispute that they sold the property to a purchaser whom they knew was sent to them by Antrim's salesperson, there is no genuine issue of material fact and summary judgment was appropriate.

The Lowes next argue that the agreement allows Antrim to receive its commission only if the contract closed before November 22, 2004. The agreement, which expired on August 22, 2004, stated:

> *In addition, if within ninety (90) days after the expiration or termination of this Agreement ... Seller enters into an agreement to sell or exchange said*

property to any person ... with whom Broker has negotiated for the purchase or exchange of such property during the term hereof and Seller shall have knowledge of such person and negotiations, Broker shall be entitled to receive the full brokerage fee. (Emphasis added.)

Thus, contrary to Lowes' contentions, the language does not require the sale to be completely closed. It requires only an "agreement to sell or exchange."

In summary, there is no doubt that ordinarily when an owner of property lists the property with a broker for sale, and the broker produces a buyer to whom the owner's terms of sale are satisfactory, the owner expects to pay the brokerage fee indicated in the brokerage contract.

The Lowes' other argument asserts that Johnson did not have the permission of Deborah to list and sell the ranch even though she had a one-half ownership interest. The Lowes argue that the trial court abused its discretion in granting summary motion since an issue of fact exists on whether Antrim would be entitled to a commission on Deborah's interest in the property because it never had her consent for the sale.

The Lowes did not raise the issue of Deborah's interest in the property before the trial court. Generally, issues not raised before the trial court cannot be raised upon appeal. There are several exceptions to this general rule: (1) where the newly asserted theory involves only a question of law arising on proved or admitted facts and is finally determinative of the case; (2) where consideration of the theory is necessary to serve the ends of justice or to prevent denial of fundamental rights; and (3) where the judgment of the trial court may be upheld on appeal although that court may have relied on the wrong ground or assigned a wrong reason for its decision. None of those exceptions apply here. Because Deborah's alleged lack of consent to the sale of the ranch was not before the trial court when it entered the summary judgment, the trial court properly resolved this case Affirmed.

For Critical Analysis

1. This case could be interpreted as a contract law case as much as it is a real estate law case. How did the customs and practices of the real estate industry influence how the court interpreted the contract?
2. This case involved a nonexclusive right to sell agreement. If it had been an exclusive right to sell, would there have been any issue? Can you concisely describe the line the court drew where this sale fell under the broker's right to sell contract?
3. If the buyer had merely seen a listing or a webpage created by the broker but had completed all communications solely with the seller, do you think this court would still have held for the broker?

Van Camp v. Bradford

63 Ohio Misc. 2d 245, 623 N.E.2d 731 (Ohio, 1993)

Buyer filed her complaint alleging that the defendant's seller and real estate agent and broker knew of the unsafe character of the residence and neighborhood, failed to disclose, and concealed these material facts, which would have influenced her decision to buy the property. Plaintiff sought damages from all defendants for mental stress and anguish, for the decreased value of the property, for fraud and negligence, and for equitable relief.

The defendants filed for summary judgment, arguing that the doctrine of caveat emptor *is a complete defense in a suit seeking recovery for the "stigma" attached to or the "psychological impairment" of a piece of property. Defendants also claimed that a cause of action for property defects that are neither a physical nor legal impairment does not exist in Ohio.*

The trial court held that (1) latent nature of alleged stigmatizing defect in property which resulted from rape in residence rendered defense of caveat emptor *inapplicable; (2) material issue of fact as to whether purchaser in fact inquired regarding safety of premises precluded summary judgment; and (3) real estate agents had no affirmative duty to speak up and disclose knowledge of crimes simply because they were in room at time inquiry regarding safety of residence was made.*

Ordered accordingly.

Michael J. Sage, Judge

I

This case arises from the sale of a residence located at 6027 Arcade Drive, Fairfield, Ohio. On or about October 30, 1991, a renter's daughter was raped at knifepoint in the residence owned by defendant Bradford. On or about December 20, 1991, another rape occurred in a neighboring home. That same day, defendant Bradford listed the house for sale with defendant Realty World.

Plaintiff Kitty Van Camp submitted a written offer to purchase the home on February 4, 1992. Before closing and during a walk-through inspection of the premises with defendant Bradford and defendant Patton (listing agent) and defendant Hoff (cooperating agent) present, plaintiff noticed bars on the basement windows. In response to plaintiff's inquiry regarding the purpose and necessity of the bars on the windows, defendant Bradford stated that a break-in had occurred sixteen years earlier, but that there was currently no problem with the residence. Plaintiff stated that she would like to remove the bars for cosmetic purposes, but Bradford advised her not to do so, as it was in plaintiff's best interests to leave the bars in place.

The closing on the property took place on February 21, 1992. At this time, the perpetrator of the crimes was still at large. While moving into the home, a neighbor informed plaintiff that the daughter of the last occupant had been raped in October, and that another brutal rape had occurred shortly before Christmas, in 1991. Two more rapes occurred in June and August 1992 at a nearby home. Plaintiff's house was burglarized on April 8, 1992, and threatening phone calls were received by plaintiff in July 1992. Police reports submitted by plaintiff confirm that all of these crimes did in fact take place.

Plaintiff, after being informed of the rapes in her home and the surrounding neighborhood, confronted defendant Campbell (owner of Realty World) who acknowledged that he, defendant Patton, and defendant Hoff were all aware of the rapes, including the rape at the subject property.

II

The rule that a seller is generally under no duty to disclose material facts about the subject matter of a sale unless a specific exception exists originates from the doctrine of *caveat emptor.* At least since 1956, the principle of *caveat emptor* has been consistently applied in Ohio to sales of real estate relative to conditions discoverable by the buyer, or open to observation upon an investigation of the property. [In 1979], however, the Supreme Court of Ohio held that latent defects do give rise to a duty on the part of the seller, and constitute an exception to the application of *caveat emptor.* When latent defects are coupled with misrepresentations or concealment, the doctrine of *caveat emptor* does not preclude recovery for fraud. Fraudulent concealment exists in cases in which a vendor fails to disclose sources of peril of which he is aware, if such a source is not discoverable by the vendee. Thus, the Supreme Court of Ohio held that the plaintiffs could sue for termites discovered after the real estate agent made the representation that the house was a "good solid home," especially since the seller was personally aware of the problem prior to the sale. The nature of the defect and the ability of the parties to determine through a reasonable inspection that a defect exists are key to determining whether or not the defect is latent.

In contrast to the national trend, Ohio has recently upheld the doctrine of *caveat emptor* with regard to real estate sales. Conditions traditionally limiting the application of the doctrine, however, were also vigorously upheld in the court's opinion: the property defect must be open to observation or discoverable upon a reasonable inspection, the purchaser must have an unimpeded opportunity to examine the property, and the vendor may not engage in fraud. The court held that, unlike a latent defect, the structural defect of the basement wall at issue was "highly visible," and the corrective I-beams supporting the wall were open to observation by the plaintiffs.

With the recent enactment of R.C. 5302.30, the Ohio legislature has taken a bold step toward ameliorating the harsh application of *caveat emptor* in even patent defect real estate transactions. For sales conducted on or after July 1, 1993, the statute requires a seller of residential property to provide each prospective buyer, or his/her agent, with a prescribed disclosure form regarding various aspects of the property. Even though the official disclosure form has not yet been formally established, preliminary drafts indicate that its purpose is to disclose material matters regarding not only the physical condition of the property, but also title, survey and other matters. If the seller fails to provide the disclosure form, the statute grants the buyer the powerful remedy of rescission. With this initiative, the Ohio legislature has seriously undermined the doctrine of *caveat emptor* as previously applied.

Virtually all of the case law regarding the buyer's duties under *caveat emptor* focuses on physical property defects. Thus, the case at bar is unique in that it presents issues regarding duty and liability for a so-called psychological defect in the property, namely, that the property was rendered unsafe for habitation by the plaintiff due to the serious crimes that had occurred in and near the residence.

The stigma associated with the residence at 6027 Arcade Drive is analogous to the latent property defects that have become an exception to the strict application of *caveat emptor.* Due to the intangible nature of the defect at issue here, a prospective buyer would have been unable to determine from a walk-through of the house in 1992 that it was the site of a serious, unsolved violent crime. Clearly, any psychological stigma that may be attached to a residence is even more undiscoverable than the existence of termites in a home, or a defect in the title to the property, both of which have been deemed latent defects despite the fact that they could have been discovered through a professional inspection or title search.

Defendants' argument that the defect at issue here was readily discoverable lacks merit. Checking police records in order to ascertain the relative safety of a neighborhood or a particular residence would not be an action undertaken by even the most prudent of purchasers. When viewed in conjunction with a potential misrepresentation or concealment on the part of defendant Bradford regarding the relative safety of the home, the latent nature of the defect at issue here renders the defense of *caveat emptor* inapplicable.

III

The case *subjudice* raises the question whether Ohio should recognize a cause of action for residential property tainted by stigmatizing events that have occurred on and near the premises. The only reported case involving a psychological property defect was heard in California and involved a house that had been the site of multiple murders ten years prior to its sale to the plaintiff. The Third District held that the plaintiff buyer did have a cause of action capable of surviving the seller's motion to dismiss. The determinative issue in that case was whether the failure to disclose the murders was material.

The California court "saw no principled basis for making the duty to disclose turn upon the character of the information," and held that the failure to disclose the murders was a material fact that could conceivably depress the value of the property.

IV

Clearly defining the cause of action for stigmatized property is necessary in order to protect the stability of contracts and prevent limitless recovery for insubstantial harms and irrational fears: misrepresentation, concealment or nondisclosure of a material fact by a seller of residential property in response to an affirmative inquiry is evidence of a breach of duty on the part of the seller. After inquiry, if the buyer justifiably relied on the misrepresentation or nondisclosure, or was induced or misled into effecting the sale to his/her detriment and damage, the buyer has met the burden of proof required to withstand a summary judgment motion.

When a seller receives an affirmative inquiry regarding the condition of a piece of property, the buyer is entitled to a truthful answer. One who responds to an inquiry is guilty of fraud if he gives equivocal, evasive or misleading answers calculated to convey a false impression, even though the answer may be literally true. Responding honestly to an affirmative inquiry regarding the condition of a residence is a lighter burden than the voluntary disclosure of a defect mandated by caveat emptor, particularly when knowledge of a stigmatizing defect is within the ready personal or actual knowledge of the seller at the time of the inquiry.

A seller who is under a duty to disclose facts and fails to do so will be held liable for damages directly and proximately resulting from his silence. A person injured by fraud is entitled to such damages as will fairly compensate him for the wrong suffered. As an additional safeguard, objective tangible harm must be demonstrated to still the concern that permitting cases of this nature to go forward will open the floodgates to rescission on subjective and idiosyncratic grounds.

V

The defendants in this case have argued that the prevailing trend across the nation regarding property disclosure is evidenced by the nondisclosure statutes that have been enacted in twenty states and the District of Columbia. Defendants also contend that these statutes imply that a cause of action for tainted property in Ohio is necessarily barred.

These statutes generally state that sellers of real estate are not liable for failing to disclose stigmatizing events, such as the fact that a homicide, suicide, felony or death by AIDS occurred in the residence. Ohio has not adopted a nondisclosure statute of this nature.

It is the opinion of this court that the nondisclosure statutes as enacted in other states still require a good faith response to an inquiry regarding a potential psychological impairment: these statutes were enacted solely to insulate sellers from liability for any failure to *voluntarily* and automatically disclose information regarding potential stigmas associated with property. As aptly stated by Representative Prague during the public hearings discussing Connecticut's newly adopted nondisclosure statute, "It seems to me that anybody selling a house would have to answer truthfully when a buyer asks a question. I mean, why should we tell you what the realtor should say or shouldn't say, or should reveal and shouldn't reveal. He should reveal anything that is asked of him."

VI

A cause of action for stigmatized property, as previously defined and limited, is warranted in the case at bar. At this point, it is necessary to analyze the elements of the cause of action for stigmatized property in the context of the defendants' summary judgment motions.

A motion for summary judgment shall be granted when there is no genuine issue of any material fact and the moving party is entitled to judgment as a matter of law. It must be awarded with caution, resolving doubts and construing evidence against the moving party, and granted only when it appears from the evidentiary material that reasonable minds can reach only an adverse conclusion as to the party opposing the motion.

Construing the evidence in the light most favorable to the plaintiff, the court finds that the plaintiff has met her initial burden of proof. The court must accept plaintiffs evidence that a rape occurred in the residence at 6027 Arcade Drive, and that several other crimes occurred in close proximity to the property. Further, the court must accept plaintiffs allegation that all of the defendants involved knew that these crimes had occurred, yet failed to disclose this knowledge to the plaintiff.

Reasonable minds could construe the plaintiff's question regarding the bars on the basement windows as an affirmative inquiry directed at ascertaining the safety of the premises, and defendant Bradford's statements regarding the reason for the bars to be a misrepresentation or a nondisclosure of their current purpose. Upon the plaintiff's inquiry, defendant Bradford was simply required to tell the truth. A more difficult case would arise had there been no evidence to indicate that the plaintiff had solicited information regarding the safety of the residence.

Numerous questions of material fact remain regarding the conversation that took place between plaintiff and defendant Bradford, and these questions preclude a granting of summary judgment. [Defendant Bradford's motion for summary judgment is hereby DENIED.]

By contrast, however, the court finds as a matter of law that the inquiry of plaintiff was directed solely to the homeowner, defendant Bradford: she alone responded to plaintiff's question regarding the safety of the residence. The real estate defendants had no duty to affirmatively speak up and disclose their knowledge of the crimes simply because they were in the room at the time the inquiry was made. Had the real estate agents similarly misrepresented or failed to disclose a material fact upon an inquiry directed to them, summary judgment in their favor would not be warranted. Even construing the facts in the light most favorable to the plaintiff, however, the court must nevertheless find that this factually distinguishable situation simply did not transpire in this case. Thus, since reasonable minds could come to but one conclusion regarding the evidence, and that conclusion is adverse to the plaintiff, the summary judgment motions of defendants Realty World, Campbell, Patton, and defendants West Shell and Hoff are hereby GRANTED.

So ordered.

For Critical Analysis

1. Distinguish latent from patent defects. Which type is discussed in the case? Explain.
2. Was the response by the seller to the buyer about the reason for the bars on basement windows made before the contract to buy the house was entered into or was it made afterward? Should that make a difference? Did it?
3. Whose real estate agents were being sued? The seller's or buyer's? Does it make any difference?
4. How did the court resolve the issue of whether *caveat emptor* applied?
5. Would you analyze this case differently if you were applying ethical rules rather than legal rules?
6. When was the Ohio disclosure statute enacted relative to this case? Is that important? Why?

CHAPTER QUESTIONS AND PROBLEMS

1. What is the amount of the standard real estate commission charged by brokerage firms in your community? Assume you own a home in which your equity is $25,000, and that you are about to sell for $125,000. If your agent's commission rate is 6 percent, what is the commission rate expressed as a percentage of your equity? How much difference in effort do you suspect a sales agent expends in listing a home in which the owner has a $50,000 equity? What conclusions can be drawn from your analysis? Would a prospective seller be wise to engage the services of a listing agent on an hourly basis? Why or why not?
2. What specific services are rendered to a homeowner by a licensed real estate agent who has "listed" the property?
3. What questions should you ask the seller, or the seller's agent, before buying a house for your personal residence?
4. In 1950, Michael and Albina Klos purchased a lot from the Molenda family, who continued to live right next door. Rather than survey the property, the buyers and sellers paced off the lot and placed stakes in the ground as boundary markers. After Mr. Molenda's death in 1983, his widow hired a surveyor to determine the exact property line. The property line turned out to be thirty inches closer to the Kloses' house. Mrs. Molenda immediately dug up thirty inches of the Kloses' grass and erected a fence on the true property line. Should the court require dismantling of the fence and award ownership of the thirty-inch strip to the Kloses? [*Klos v. Molenda,* 355 Pa. Super. 399, 513 A.2d 490 (Perm., 1986).]
5. If you were selling your home, and a prospective buyer offered an attractive price, and suggested the use of a land contract with only a $1,000 down payment, what factors would you take into consideration?
6. If you were applying for a loan at a savings and loan association for the purpose of buying a home, which three of the following factors would be the most important to you?
   a. A relatively low interest rate.
   b. A relatively long repayment term.
   c. The right to prepay principal payments without penalty.
   d. A relatively low "late payment" penalty.
   e. The right to have someone else assume your loan without any assumption fee and without any increase in the interest rate.
   f. The absence of the requirement that you pay the lender's attorney fees incurred by the lender because of your default in making monthly payments.
   g. The absence of an acceleration clause that made the entire unpaid balance of the loan due upon any default in monthly payments.
7. As a prospective buyer of your first home, what dis advantages would there be in leasing with an option to buy?
8. Would you prefer to finance the purchase of your home with a fixed-rate mortgage or with a variable-rate mortgage that begins with an interest rate one full percentage point rate lower than the former? Why?
9. Would you prefer to own a single-family detached home or a condominium? What are your perceptions of the advantages and disadvantages of each?
10. What is the primary reason you hope to be a homeowner in the future? If you will buy and sell a home on five different occasions over your working career, would you still prefer to be a homeowner? Explain.

CHAPTER 10

Intellectual and Personal Property Including Motor Vehicles

My words and my ideas are my property, and I'll keep and protect them as surely as I do my stable of unicorns.

Jarod Kintz in *This Book Is Not For Sale*

LEARNING OBJECTIVES

After reading and studying this chapter, you should be able to:

- Understand the concepts of personal property and intellectual property and be able to identify examples of each.
- Explain the nature of a contract to buy or lease an automobile.
- Discuss the warranties arising in a sale or lease of a motor vehicle and how such warranties are disclaimed.
- Explain what a lemon law is and how it might affect a vehicle contract.
- Explain product liability as it is applied to motor vehicles.
- Identify the basic types of automobile insurance coverage.
- Explain the application of negligence to motor vehicle incidents and accidents.
- Define a bailment and describe various bailment situations.
- Distinguish between the legal requirements of ownership by possession, production, gift, and inheritance.
- Distinguish between lost, abandoned, and mislaid personal property.
- Explain how intellectual property rights are created
- Identify situations in which a person has limited rights regarding intellectual property.

Property is a word often associated with land, a type of property referred to as "real property." Real property is covered in Chapter 9. This chapter is about the other major category of property, personal property. For the most part, an entirely different body of law and set of rules apply to personal property than to real property. Furthermore, a very specialized form of personal property, called intellectual property, has specialized laws and rules for each specific form of intellectual property. Finally, motor vehicles are a form of tangible personal property subject to many other special laws, rules and customs. We will introduce you to the law surrounding all of these types of property.

You may be thinking that much of this chapter is not applicable to you. For instance, you may not yet own a car. But, you are likely to own one at some point in your life. You might also be thinking that you are not interested in, or involved at all, with intellectual property. In today's modern, digital, and technical world, however, nothing could be further from the truth about your life and property. You are probably a walking, talking, breathing example of intellectual property in use.

LEGAL FOCUS—EXAMPLE

Ivana owns a sedan that she uses to drive to and from school and work. Inside her car she usually has her textbooks, purse, and music CDs that she plays in the CD player installed in the dash of her car.

What types of property does Ivana have regarding her vehicle?

The answer is many. Her car, as well as her purse, books, and CDs, are her personal property. The CDs contain music that is intellectual property, copyrights, owned by others. She has a license to listen to the music and perhaps to make one copy of it for certain limited uses. The books also contain copyrighted material that she has some limited rights to duplicate. Ivana's purse might be a name-brand purse with a special logo or trademark on it. It might also be an illegal "knockoff," meaning someone reproduced that trademarked logo, or perhaps the design of the purse, without permission. The vehicle probably includes many components and systems covered by patents, another form of intellectual property. Although the car itself is her personal property, the ideas and innovations contained within the design of the vehicle do not belong to her, she merely has a right to use them. She cannot reproduce those systems and components at all.

property
The legally protected rights and interests a person has in anything with an ascertainable value that is subject to ownership.

personal property
Movable property; any property that is not real property.

Intellectual property
Information or property, such as patents or copyrights, that provides the owner a competitive advantage

Property is an aggregate of rights to a thing which are protected and guaranteed by government, including and especially ownership. Property is classified in many ways, most importantly, as either real or personal. **Personal property** is property not permanently attached to land, such as vehicles, merchandise in stores, food products, skis, boats, and backpacks. Personal property is further classified as being either tangible property or intellectual property. Often the term "personal property" means tangible personal property that you can touch and can move. That mental image usually works until one tries to move a 52-inch high-definition television or a piano. The general idea is that if property is not land or that which is permanently affixed to land, it is personality (personal property). **Intellectual property** is property that exists as an idea, data or expression. It includes patents, copyrights, trademarks, and trade secrets.

Intellectual Property versus Personal Property

Intellectual property cannot be physically touched or handle, in its true form, but it often is reduced to a physical form or is used to produce a tangible, physical object, which then is simple personal property. Imbedded in the personal property are rights regarding its use that are intellectual property rights. Ivana's music CDs in the previous example are but one example of that relationship between intangible intellectual property and **tangible personal property**. Sometimes, the distinction between intellectual property and tangible personal property can seem confusing, But try to keep in mind the previous definition of property. Property, in the legal sense, is about rights to use something. This is true whether it is the right to use an idea or to use an object.

tangible personal property
Property in a physical form.

Once you are through studying this chapter, you will better understand all the ways in which you interact with personal property laws on a daily, if not constant, basis. We will use the motor vehicle to introduce you to and explain most of the laws of tangible personal property. Then we will look at some of the generic laws and rules surrounding how we obtain ownership or rights to use personal property. Following that exploration of personal property, we will examine the types of intellectual property.

MOTOR VEHICLES AND PERSONAL PROPERTY

A motor vehicle is an example of personal, rather than real, property. There is not a body of law called "motor vehicle law." Previously discussed areas of law, however, such as contracts, torts, and crimes have application, sometimes specialized application, to motor vehicles.

Is a Special Contract Required to Purchase a Motor Vehicle?

The sale of a motor vehicle is an ordinary contractual transaction subject to the law of contracts relating to personal property. The contract involves a sale of goods (tangible personal property) and is subject to the Uniform Commercial Code (UCC) (see Chapter 8). The UCC relaxes some of the otherwise-formal rules of common law contract formation and performance, and motor vehicle sales law is mostly uniform throughout the states.

Motor vehicles, of course, usually cost more than $500, and so the Statute of Frauds applies to such purchases. Thus, to provide evidence of an executory contract, there must be a writing signed by the party to be obligated. This requirement usually is met with a standard-form contract prepared by commercial sellers. Standardized (preprinted) form agreements, including automobile sales contracts, are adhesion contracts. Recall that adhesion contracts are drafted by a dominant party and then are presented to the other party—the adhering party—on a "take-it-or-leave-it" basis. Unconscionable clauses, those that "shock the conscience" of a court, are more likely to be found in adhesion contracts than contracts in which the parties truly bargain over terms. If language in an adhesion contract is ambiguous, courts often will interpret the language to favor the buyer, the party who did not draft the contract. Nevertheless, the buyer should be aware that the contract is written primarily to protect the interests of the seller and is unlikely to have ambiguous terms or clauses. (See additional discussion of Statute of Frauds, adhesion contracts, and unconscionable clauses in Chapter 9.)

LEGAL FOCUS—PROBLEM

The trunk of the car seemed too small to Bill Clark as he viewed the car he was thinking about buying. The salesperson, Frank, assured him there was adequate room in the trunk for luggage for a family of four. Frank also said, "If there isn't enough room, bring the car back and we will install a luggage rack." Bill signed a standard-form automobile purchase contract that did not include any reference to the luggage rack. A few months later, Bill, unable to load four suitcases in the trunk, returned to the dealership expecting a new luggage rack free of additional charge. Does Bill have an enforceable right to a luggage rack?

Bill's claim would be thwarted by the parol evidence rule. This rule holds that when people have signed a contract as their final and complete expression of intention (integrated contracts), then neither party may introduce in court any evidence of prior or contemporaneous oral or written material that adds to or modifies that written contract. The rule does not apply to less formal contracts—those not portending to be the final and complete expression of the agreement. Standard-form automobile purchase contracts, however, do purport to be final and complete agreements. The lesson is clear and crucial: If important promises are made to you (e.g., warranties, credit terms, additional equipment), be sure they are included as part of the written contract.

In motor vehicle sales transactions, there are standard sales customs and techniques, and some states regulate contracts written by commercial sellers. A complete discussion of this topic is beyond the scope of this text. Buyers are well advised, however, to consult reliable sources for help in selecting the appropriate vehicle (especially if previously owned) and for information on negotiating the best deal.

The Statute of Frauds and parol evidence rule also apply to purchases from private owners. If there are warranties, any other promises, or an extension of credit, a written contract should be prepared containing these terms and the signatures of both the seller and the buyer to satisfy these requirements.

Warranties for Motor Vehicles

The seller of a new motor vehicle transfers title with any express warranties made and with several implied warranties. Express warranties are created by statements of fact made by the seller about quality, condition, description, and performance potential.

LEGAL FOCUS—PROBLEM

Praneel X. Singh expressed his interest in a new model SRV. Steve Walters, the number one salesperson at Autoworld, claimed, "This is the best new vehicle to be introduced in 40 years." Is Walters's statement an express warranty?

puffing
Seller's talk; claims about the quality of goods, usually exaggerated; not considered fraud.

Walters's *opinion* that the vehicle is "the best new vehicle to be introduced in 40 years" is not a warranty; it is **puffing**, the word used to describe normal sellers' exaggerations about goods for sale. Similarly, statements such as, "It's worth a fortune" or "Anywhere else you'd pay more for it," do not usually create warranties. Whether the buyer's reliance on the seller's statement is reasonable is often the controlling factor. For example, a salesperson's statement that a car "will never break down" and "will last a lifetime" is so improbable that no reasonable buyer should rely on it. The how and where of the statement are also important in determining the reasonableness of the buyer's reliance. For example, it is generally more reasonable for a buyer to rely on a statement made in a written advertisement than on a salesperson's oral statement.

Also recall from Chapter 8 that *implied warranties* are warranties that arise in a sales transaction unless specifically disclaimed. The most important implied warranties in automobile sales transactions are usually the warranty of title, the warranty against encumbrances, and the warranty of merchantability. The implied warranty of title promises to the buyer that the seller possesses good title to the motor vehicle and can rightfully transfer title to the buyer. The implied warranty against encumbrances promises the buyer that the title to the vehicle is free of secured debt (no creditor has a right to the vehicle for failure to pay off a loan). The implied warranty of merchantability refers to quality and is a promise that a vehicle is of usual and customary quality and as such is fit for its ordinary and intended use. Implied warranties of merchantability are made only by merchants. Of course, an auto dealer is a merchant. Given the value of a motor vehicle and its intended use, the implied warranty of merchantability is very extensive, unless limited by the seller. As you will see and should note, implied warranties of quality are almost always limited in some fashion by the seller.

LEGAL FOCUS—PROBLEM

When Betty Orra bought her new automobile, she expected 100,000 or more miles of carefree motoring. She carefully maintained and serviced her vehicle. The car was sold with a written warranty from the dealer that included this language: "This warranty is in lieu of and excludes all other warranties, express or implied, including the warranty of merchantability." The warranty covered defects in materials or workmanship "for one year or 12,000 miles, whichever occurs first." Did Orra lose anything when she received this warranty?

Yes and no. The dealer statement is an attempted disclaimer sufficient to deny an implied warranty of merchantability in most contracts except those involving consumer goods. An automobile for personal use is certainly consumer goods. A disclaimer is a specific statement indicating that a particular warranty does not exist or limiting the warranty as to nature or duration. In a transaction for consumer goods, you can make a total disclaimer of the implied warranty of merchantability, but not a partial disclaimer. Total exclusion of an implied warranty of merchantability requires specific, legally acceptable language of disclaimer. The most common methods of a total disclaimer for an implied warranty of merchantability are (1) use of the terms "as is" or "with all faults" or (2) a statement that no other warranty, including that of merchantability, exists. The dealer did not use the "as is" form of disclaimer but rather relied on the alternative method. Although in a nonconsumer transaction this disclaimer would be effective, the federal Magnuson-Moss Warranty Act preempts the UCC in consumer transactions involving warranties.

The Magnuson-Moss Warranty Act (see Chapter 13) allows sellers of consumer goods to limit, but not eliminate, warranties of merchantability if any express warranty is provided. Thus, the dealer cannot disclaim the warranty in the manner attempted. A merchant cannot give an express warranty and include an "as is" clause to eliminate the implied warranty of merchantability. Under Magnuson-Moss, a seller making an express warranty in a sales contract is not allowed to disclaim or modify either the implied warranty of merchantability or the implied warranty of fitness for a particular purpose. Sellers, however, can impose a time limit on the duration of an implied warranty. The time limit must be no less than the duration of the express warranty. Any limitation also must be reasonable, conscionable, and stated in clear and conspicuous language on the face of the warranty. All motor vehicle manufacturers provide express warranties, and the implied warranty of merchantability often is limited in time as part of the express warranty provision in the sales contract.* An acceptable limitation might read, "Any implied warranty of merchantability or fitness for a particular purpose applicable to this vehicle is limited to the duration of this written warranty."

Thus, Betty Orra did not lose her implied warranty of merchantability, but its limitation to twelve months was effective. The extent of the express warranty, as to both scope and length of coverage, is a very important issue when determining which motor vehicle to buy and how much to pay.

Motor vehicle dealers often offer (at an additional cost) extended warranties to vehicle buyers. These warranties typically extend the time and expand the coverage provided by manufacturer warranties. These policies can be purchased from companies other than the original dealership and often at more favorable prices. Before deciding whether to purchase an extended warranty, one should become an informed consumer by studying the need for the product and the available extended warranties and prices. There are substantial differences in price, scope, and length of coverage and possible restrictions on who may service the vehicle.

A manufacturer providing a written warranty is also required to comply with Magnuson-Moss and applicable state laws. Remember Magnuson-Moss does not require that the manufacturer or seller provide a warranty, but rather it governs the wording of and extent of warranties when express warranties are given. If a seller makes an express written warranty involving consumer goods costing more than $10, the Act controls how the warranty is to be given. Any warranty under the Act must be labeled as "full" or "limited." In addition, if the cost of the goods is more than $15, the warrantor (the person making the warranty) must make certain disclosures in language that is easy to understand. The disclosures must state the names and addresses of the warrantor and must identify the product warranted, the procedures for enforcement of the warranty, and any limitations on warranty remedies.

A *full warranty* may not cover every problem arising from use of a consumer product, but it must give the buyer rights to free repair or replacement of any defective part. If the product cannot be repaired within a reasonable time, the consumer can choose a refund or a replacement without charge. The warranty does not cover damage that is caused by the consumer. A written consumer warranty that does not meet all the requirements of a full warranty is a *limited warranty.* The seller must state clearly that only a limited warranty is given. The Federal Trade Commission (FTC) has the power to enforce many provisions of Magnuson-Moss and may sue businesses that fail to honor their written warranties.

Used cars purchased from dealers also carry implied warranties of merchantability because the dealers are still merchants even though the goods are used. Used cars purchased from private parties do not carry any warranty of quality unless the nonmerchant seller makes one (get these assurances in writing). Note that the implied warranty of merchantability is disclaimed by the words "as is." This is true even under Magnuson-Moss as long as no express warranty of quality is given.

*Some states have statutes that further restrict the ability of a seller to disclaim or limit implied warranties in consumer transactions. These state laws are upheld as long as they add to those rights provided by Magnuson-Moss.

What Are Lemon Laws?

LEGAL FOCUS—PROBLEM

Maggie O'Malley was very excited when she bought her new convertible Aardvark Seven from Autoworld. She drove it off the lot and headed toward Slim's Health Club to show it to her friends. Two blocks from the dealership, the engine died. The car needed to be towed back to Autoworld. A very angry O'Malley was not mollified when the sales representative said, "We'll be happy to repair or replace that cracked engine block." O'Malley snapped back, "I expect to get a new and different Aardvark Seven. I am a consumer who won't be satisfied with a lemon." Will O'Malley get a new car, or must she allow the repair or replacement of the engine block?

The legal question is, did the dealership perform its contractual obligations when it delivered the vehicle? If the delivery is legally sufficient, Autoworld need only honor the warranty—either repair or replace the defective part. If, however, the delivery is insufficient under key UCC provisions, Autoworld must replace the defective car with a new one.

O'Malley had a right to inspect her purchase before accepting it. What is considered an appropriate inspection depends on the circumstances and the nature of the goods. In this situation, although O'Malley received and took possession of the vehicle, a normal inspection would not have shown that the engine had a cracked block. Since she discovered that the vehicle was nonconforming almost immediately after she took possession, she can return it and make a reasonable argument that she never really accepted it. O'Malley really did indeed get a lemon (sour deal), and she has a legal right to a full refund or a new vehicle under the UCC.

Additional rights under the UCC also may be claimed to assist a buyer when there is a major contract breach by the seller. Perhaps even if O'Malley accepted the vehicle after a careful inspection, she could revoke her acceptance and enjoy the same rights (of replacement or full refund) as if she had rejected it initially. It is necessary that she revoke within a reasonable time after she discovers (or should have discovered) a sufficient reason for revocation, and before there is any substantial change in the condition of the goods (not caused by the defect).

lemon laws
Statutes designed to assist the buyer of seriously defective goods to obtain a replacement or full refund.

Most problems with new cars are not as dramatic or immediate as the problems suffered by O'Malley. All states have passed so-called **lemon laws** to provide protection for angry consumers who are dissatisfied with extensive warranty work and instead demand a new car or their money back. A lemon law provides that if a car is determined to be a lemon, the dealer must refund to the customer the purchase price of the car, plus sales tax, registration, and license fees, minus a reasonable allowance for use. The problem, of course, is to define a "lemon" with sufficient precision and to enforce consumers' rights in a fair and prompt manner.

A lemon often is defined as a major problem not permanently fixed after a reasonable number of attempts (i.e., four or more), or if a car is out of service for repairs for a certain number of days within a certain period (i.e., thirty calendar days during a twelve-month period). The covered period in different states ranges from the written warranty period, or twelve months to two years; sometimes coverage is based on miles driven (e.g., 18,000 miles). Many lemon laws allow for the use of alternative dispute resolution methods, such as nonbinding arbitration, to assist in the resolution of the dispute (see Chapter 4).

LEGAL FOCUS—CASE

John L. Hughes's new Dodge Caravan qualified as a lemon. His first year of ownership required seven separate trips to the dealer to repair transmission defects. Attempts to get Chrysler to replace the car within the time provided by the lemon law were unsuccessful. Hughes filed a lawsuit. The court entered judgment for Hughes in the amount of $74,371, double the amount he paid for the vehicle and attorney fees. Do lemon laws always provide for a recovery that exceeds the price of the vehicle?

John L. Hughes v. Chrysler Motors Corp., 197 Wis. 2d 973, 542 N.W.2d 148 (Wis., 1996).

Wisconsin does provide for such a recovery, but most states do not. The Wisconsin statute specifically allows a court to award twice the customer damages plus attorney fees. The court opinion recites the transactional dilemma well:

> *We realize that car manufacturers do not deliberately set out to manufacture a lemon. Quite the opposite. In fact, it is in their own best interest not to do so. However, an unfortunate fact of life, seemingly as inevitable as night following day, is that occasionally a 'lemon' will slip through the line. And when that happens, another unfortunate fact of modern-day life is that the cost to the unlucky consumer who purchases that 'lemon' is far more than the cost of the car: interrupted, delayed, or even cancelled schedules; the time and the trouble, as well as the anxiety and stress that accompany those changes; the apprehensions that result every time the consumer gets back into that automobile wondering 'what next?' Dependability is a prime objective of every new car buyer. When that is taken away, the loss is far greater than the cost of the car. It is this fact that the legislature recognized when they enacted the lemon law. Its principal motivation is not to punish the manufacturer who, after all, would far prefer that no 'lemons' escape their line. Rather, it seeks to provide an incentive to that manufacturer to promptly return those unfortunate consumers back to where they thought they were when they first purchased that new automobile.*

What Are Automobile Leases?

Leasing is a popular alternative to purchasing a vehicle. Technically, a "lease" is a **bailment** for use. A bailment is a common legal relationship created when personal property is temporarily delivered into the care of another without transfer of title. Thus, a bailment is created when you lend your car to a friend. Any personal property can be bailed. The legal specifics of bailment are discussed later in this chapter.

bailment
A delivery of personal property to another by which that person has the right to temporary possession. Often, though not always, bailment is created by contract.

Virtually every study and analysis concludes that buying an automobile is less expensive than leasing over the full term of ownership. Monthly costs of leasing are reasonably low, however, and if the lease deposit is small, the consumer may believe there is a lower cost. Many consumers are also happy that at the end of the lease the car is simply returned to the dealer, or lessor. Although strings are attached to the car's return, most people view them as a very distant and unimportant problem. A person contemplating a lease should consider the following:

- What is the term of the lease, and what are the up front, monthly, and end-of-lease charges?
- What additional charges, such as responsibility for repair, are occasioned by what events?

- What limitations are imposed on total miles driven during the lease? What extra costs are incurred if the mileage limit is exceeded?
- What warranty is offered with the leased automobile?
- How and at what cost can the lease be terminated before it expires?

Anyone who leases an automobile should realize that the usual and normal costs of automobile ownership still exist in a lease. For example, costs such as license registration, liability and property insurance, emission certificates, gasoline, and maintenance remain costs of the buyer or lessee and are not changed by the normal lease. Also, bailment law and lease contracts require that personal property be returned in good condition. Thus, while an owner may neglect an automobile, a lessee does so with peril. There undoubtedly will be additional costs at lease return for excess mileage or wear and tear. Some leases contain important options at the end of the lease. If the car is worth more or less than a specified amount at the end of the lease, the consumer will receive a credit (unlikely) or pay a differential (likely) to guarantee the leasing company from any unpredicted depreciation or loss in value.

Leases are covered by Article 2A of the UCC. Article 2A provides rules similar to provisions in the sales code for contract formation, performance, and warranties. Special protection under the UCC is provided for consumer leases that are defined as "a lease that a lessor regularly engaged in the business of leasing or selling makes to a lessee who is an individual and who takes under the lease primarily for a personal, family, or household purpose." Some states provide that a consumer lease cannot exceed a maximum amount, but states with a maximum have varied the amount.

The federal Consumer Leasing Act also covers personal property leases lasting more than four months if the total contractual obligation does not exceed $25,000. The Act requires the lessor to make several disclosures to the lessee:

- Total amount of any upfront payment
- Number and amount of monthly payments
- Payments for other fees, such as registration and taxes
- Any penalty for default or late payments
- The annual mileage allowance and the amount of extra charges for exceeding the allowance
- What counts as excessive wear and tear
- If the lease can be ended early, and if so, are there any extra charges
- Provisions for purchase at lease conclusion, and for what price
- Any responsibility for the difference between the estimated value of the auto and its market value at the end of the lease
- Any extra payments at the end of the lease

Some consumers who use their automobiles in their businesses, such as traveling salespersons and real estate agents, assume that they obtain tax benefits by deducting from their taxes the full amount of lease payments, plus all other related expenses. The tax laws, however, do not play favorites with leased automobiles. Owners also can deduct their business travel expenses, including interest payments, and can depreciate (deduct) the cost of their vehicles gradually and proportionally over the years. Many states levy a "use" tax against buyers in lieu of the sales tax they otherwise would pay if they had purchased the vehicle.

LEGAL FOCUS—CASE

Potente leased a new Peugeot through Peugeot Motors of America, Inc. (PMA). A few months later, after experiencing problems with the vehicle, he sought relief under Ohio's "lemon law." PMA moved for summary judgment on the lemon law claim, arguing that Potente, as lessee, had no standing to bring an action under Ohio's lemon law. What was the result?

Potente v. Peugeot, 62 Ohio Misc.2d 335, 598 N.E .2d 9907 (Ohio, 1991).

The court held that any consumer entitled to enforce contract warranties against the manufacturer had the right to enforce the state lemon laws. "A lease agreement which extends the manufacturer's warranty and the ability to enforce the warranty to the lessee falls within the protective ambit of Ohio's Lemon Law." Most state lemon laws do extend to automobile leases, but not all.

What Are Automobile Recalls?

Even after motor vehicles are sold, manufacturers have a continuing obligation to ensure their safety in normal use. Under federal law, manufacturers are required to notify consumers and the National Highway Traffic Safety Administration (NHTSA) of discovered safety defects and how they propose to eliminate or "cure" them. Recalls can be voluntary or mandated by the NHTSA. The manufacturer generally has the option of repairing the defect, replacing the vehicle, or refunding the price paid. Obviously, repairing the defect is the usual means of correction chosen by the manufacturers.

Recalls are common and usually only noticed by affected parties. Some notices, however, are accompanied by significant media attention because of the number of vehicles involved or because they involve a significant risk to life. As this edition was being prepared, Toyota was undergoing nationwide scrutiny from consumer to Congress over

EXHIBIT 10.1 Firestone Recall Notice

NHTSA CAMPAIGN ID Number: 00T005000
Component: TIRES: TREAD
Manufacturer: BRIDGESTONE/FIRESTONE, INC.

Year: All years	Make: FIRESTONE	Model: WILDERNESS AT	Recall Date: 08/10/2000

Type of Report: Tire

Potential Number of Units Affected: 14400000

Defect Summary:
TIRE DESCRIPTION: FIRESTONE WILDERNESS AT, SIZE P235/75R15, PRODUCED AT THE DECATUR, ILLINOIS TIRE PLANT AND ALL FIRESTONE RADIAL ATX AND RADIAL ATX II TIRES, SIZE P235/75R15. OPERATION OF THESE TIRES AT LOW INFLATION PRESSURES, HIGH SPEED, AND IN HOT WEATHER, CAN CONTRIBUTE TO SEPARATION OF THE TIRE TREAD.
Consequence Summary:
IF THE TREAD SEPARATES FROM THE TIRE, THE DRIVER CAN LOSE CONTROL OF THE VEHICLE, POSSIBLY RESULTING IN A CRASH CAUSING INJURY OR DEATH.
Corrective Summary:
THE REPLACEMENT/REIMBURSEMENT PROGRAM FOR THIS CAMPAIGN EXPIRED ON AUGUST 29, 2001. HOWEVER, CUSTOMERS SHOULD CONTACT FIRESTONE CUSTOMER SERVICE AT 1-800-465-1904 FOR POSSIBLE ASSISTANCE.

sudden, uncontrolled acceleration problems. Toyota's executives appeared before a congressional committee to answer questions regarding the timing and extent of its recall efforts and how well it reported information to the NHSTA. A number of cases were filed against Toyota for injuries caused by sudden acceleration. Toyota had frequently claimed that the sudden acceleration was caused by a combination of either or both floor mats becoming stuck under gas pedals and drivers mistaking the gas pedal for the brake. In July, 2013 the first case went to trial in Los Angeles, California.

Such lawsuits and claims for injury are discussed in the following sections. Firestone Tires also underwent high levels of attention in 2000. Exhibit 10.1 shows the Firestone recall notice sent out for the problem.

Product Liability

LEGAL FOCUS—BACKGROUND

In early 1993, the National Highway Traffic Safety Administration (NHTSA) requested that General Motors (GM) recall 4.7 million pickup trucks equipped with side-saddle gasoline tanks. "Since the side-saddle trucks were introduced in 1973, their gas tanks have sometimes ripped open and exploded in side-impact collisions. According to NHTSA, the GM trucks are 2.4 times as likely as pickups made by Ford Motor Co. to be involved in deadly crashes with fires. This translates into about five deaths a year out of more than 40,000 on the nation's highways." GM was the defendant and loser in two cases with multimillion-dollar product liability verdicts based on accusations of defective side-saddle gasoline tanks. In GM's defense, the NHTSA acknowledged that the vehicles passed all NHTSA safety tests in existence at the time the vehicles were manufactured. On December 2, 1994, four days before a public hearing to consider making the recall mandatory, the government dropped its recall effort. In exchange, GM agreed to spend $51 million on a variety of vehicle safety programs.

Manufacturers and sellers of goods, including automobiles, can be held liable to consumers, users, and bystanders for physical harm or property damage caused by the goods. This liability is called **product liability**. Legal theories of product liability include the contract theory of warranty and dual tort theories of negligence and strict liability (Chapter 7).

product liability
A general area of law holding manufacturers and sellers of goods liable to buyers, users, and perhaps bystanders for harm caused when goods are defective.

Product Liability Based on Warranty

An important part of product liability law is the breach of warranty theory. A person suffering physical injury or injury to other property because of substandard goods can seek recovery based on breach of warranty. The general rule is that consumers, purchasers, and even users of goods can recover from any seller for losses resulting from breach of implied and express warranties. In other words, most parties who are injured by goods can sue any seller of the goods, including the manufacturer on warranty theory.

This extensive right to recover is an exception to the usual requirement that a party be in *privity* of contract (direct contract relationship) with another to sue on a contract theory. The UCC has addressed the problem of privity by eliminating the requirement of privity for certain types of injuries and for certain third-party beneficiaries.

Product Liability Based on Negligence

In Chapter 7, we discussed *negligence* as a failure to use the degree of care that a reasonable, prudent person would have used under the circumstances. If a seller does not

EXHIBIT 10.2 Requirements of Strict Product Liability

The basic requirements of strict product liability are as follows:

- The product is sold in a defective condition.
- The defendant is in the business of selling that product.
- The product is unreasonably dangerous to the user or consumer because of its defective condition.
- The plaintiff (who need not be the purchaser) must suffer physical harm to self or property by use or consumption of the product.
- The defective condition must be the proximate cause of the injury or damage.

exercise reasonable care and injury results, he or she is liable for negligence. A manufacturer must exercise due care to make a product safe. This due care must be exercised in all aspects of manufacturing the product. It includes product design and selection of the materials to make the product. It includes appropriate production, assembly, and testing of the product. It includes placing adequate warnings on the label to inform the user of potential dangers of which he or she might not be aware. And, it extends to the inspection and testing of any purchased products used in the final product sold by the manufacturer. The failure to exercise due care is negligence. A manufacturer is liable to any person who is injured by a negligently made (defective) product. The manufacturer is liable for harm regardless of whether a sale or a contract to sell was involved.

Product Liability Based on Strict Liability

Under strict liability (introduced in Chapter 7), persons are responsible for their products regardless of the intentions or the exercise of reasonable care. The doctrine of strict liability applies to manufacturers, wholesalers, and retailers (also processors, assemblers, packagers, bottlers, and distributors) of personal property. A product may be defective because of production errors, design deficiencies, improper packaging, or failure to warn of dangers or to provide safety devices or instructions. A seller of any product in a defective condition that is unreasonably dangerous is subject to liability for physical harm caused to the ultimate user or to his property if (1) the seller is in the business of selling such a product and (2) the product is expected to and does reach the user without substantial change from the condition in which it was sold. See Exhibit 10.2 for the requirements to prove strict product liability.

Thus, under this theory, in any action against a manufacturer or seller, the plaintiff need not show how the product became defective. The plaintiff must, however, show that at the time of the injury, the condition of the product was essentially the same as it was when it left the hands of the defendant manufacturer or seller. All courts extend the strict liability of manufacturers and other sellers to injured bystanders.

LEGAL FOCUS—PROBLEM

The motor of a car exploded, producing a cloud of steam. The steam caused a series of multiple collisions, since it prevented other drivers from seeing well. The motor was defective. Is the automobile manufacturer liable for injuries caused by the explosion of the car's motor?

Yes, the manufacturer is liable because the car motor was determined to be defective and the cause of the harm to the innocent third parties. Strict liability also has been expanded to include suppliers of parts and lessors of movable goods. Liability for personal injuries caused by defective goods extends also to those who lease such goods. Most courts hold that a leasing agreement creates an *implied warranty* that the leased goods will be fit for the duration of the lease. Under this view, if a Rent-a-Car Company leases an improperly maintained automobile, a passenger who is injured in an accident can sue the Rent-a-Car Company. (Liability here is based on the contract theory of warranty, not tort, because the lease is an ongoing contract.)

Frequently, a product injures a person because he or she did not use it carefully. Misconduct or misuse by a claimant can be a defense to reduce the claimant's recovery or to deny it altogether.

Registration of Motor Vehicles

The government requires that ownership of most types of motor vehicles be registered and that formal documents of ownership be properly executed. Similar requirements do not exist for most other types of personal property, such as stereos and backpacks, although some state registration laws exist for some types of guns.

Advantages of Registration

Registration provides a method by which a state government can ensure vehicle owner compliance with safety and environmental requirements. To be registered initially, the vehicle must comply with minimal safety and pollution standards governing brakes, lights, and exhaust emissions. Registration of ownership also ensures orderly transfer of title. By requiring presentation and release of the certificate of ownership signed by the seller, the buyer has a better assurance of receiving a good title and becoming the true owner. If the vehicle is stolen, the certificate of ownership and registration facilitates identification and restitution to the rightful owner. If a vehicle is involved in an accident in which property is damaged or a person is injured or killed, vehicle license numbers help trace the party responsible and facilitate follow-up measures. The issuance and renewal of the certificate of registration also serve as a convenient means of raising tax revenues for a variety of purposes, including highway construction and maintenance. Moreover, annual motor vehicle registration lists also aid selection of jury panels and the collection of unpaid traffic fines.

Licensing and Registration Procedures

Generally, a state will issue two certificates to the owners of motor vehicles: a certificate of ownership, or title, showing who owns the vehicle; and a certificate of registration, permitting operation of the vehicle on the highways of the state. License plates, or annual renewal tags, also are issued in conjunction with the certificate of registration.

With a few exceptions, such as U.S. government vehicles, a motor vehicle is licensed in the state where it usually is driven. When you move to another state, your vehicle registration generally remains valid for a limited period of time (thirty to ninety days) before a local vehicle registration and license is required. At the time of yearly license registration, states commonly provide for emissions control device inspections and sometimes vehicle safety inspections. Some states require that the primary driver of the vehicle offer proof of financial responsibility (e.g., through ownership of an automobile liability insurance policy) before vehicle license plates are renewed.

Many counties and cities require the registration and periodic licensing of bicycles. The money generated from bicycle licensure commonly is used to maintain records that facilitate the recovery and return of stolen bikes.

LEGAL FOCUS—PROBLEM

Kitty Horrigan was carefully riding her new imported British motorcycle along a city street when Dick Guarno negligently lost control of his automobile and crashed into her. Guarno now claims Horrigan was also guilty of negligence because she failed to register her motorcycle as required by law. Is it considered negligence to drive an unlicensed motor vehicle on a public road?

No, driving an unlicensed vehicle is not considered negligence. Horrigan's failure to register her motorcycle had nothing to do with Guarno's negligence and will not prevent her from recovering damages for her injuries.

Horrigan is guilty of the infraction of driving an unregistered vehicle on a public street. Failure to sign title over to a new owner when delivering possession of a motor vehicle may leave the original owner liable to strangers who are injured by the motor vehicle in a later accident. Some states provide that the registered owner is liable (usually limited to some specified amount) for damage caused by the negligence of any authorized user of the vehicle.

registered owner The buyer of a car on credit, who, as the equitable owner, gets possession and use of the vehicle while making payments.

legal owner An owner who has legal title, for example, as security for repayment of a loan or payment of the purchase price of real property or personal property, such as an automobile.

equitable owner An owner who has possession and use of the property although someone else may retain the legal title.

Usually, a certificate of ownership of a newly purchased vehicle lists two owners: a **registered owner** and a **legal owner**. Most automobiles are purchased on credit, and the lender retains a security interest in the vehicle. The purchaser–borrower is the registered owner (also called the **equitable owner**), with an ownership interest in the vehicle to the extent that the loan has been paid. Persons who refer to their equity in a vehicle mean the difference between the automobile's market value and the amount still owed to the lender. The lender (or creditor), having advanced the purchase money or sold the car on credit, retains a security interest in the vehicle and remains the legal (technical) owner until the loan is paid in full. A legal owner generally is not responsible for the manner in which the equitable owner uses or misuses the vehicle. The legal owner primarily is concerned with timely monthly payments. The lender's singular interest is in protecting the value of the collateral, increasing the probability that the loan will be repaid in full. For protection in the event that the car is damaged or stolen, the lender (legal owner) requires the equitable owner to carry adequate collision and comprehensive automobile insurance. The former covers damages to the vehicle caused by collision; the latter covers theft of the vehicle or damage caused by vandals. Careful and socially responsible owners also carry liability insurance to protect themselves from liability for possible injuries to others. Many states also require this latter liability insurance.

Because a registered owner has potential tort liability, it is very important to change registration simultaneously with the transfer of the vehicle. Requirements for a valid transfer of registration vary from state to state. It is common to require both a signed transfer of a certificate of ownership and a notification to the department of motor vehicles requesting a change in the registered owner of the vehicle. The seller should file the notice of change of ownership, transferring potential liability to the buyer along with the ownership.

Each automobile has a unique seventeen-character vehicle identification number (VIN) found on vehicle dashboards and title documents. VIN numbers have enabled the creation of a new and useful national business. Carfax has created a national registry of historic information about most automobiles in the United States and Canada. Carfax claims a database of "two billion unique records compiled from hundreds of separate data sources including motor vehicle departments in the United States and Canada, vehicle inspection stations, auto auctions, fleet management and rental agencies, automobile manufacturers and fire and police departments." Use of the VIN information database can disclose the following critical information about a vehicle:

- Totaled in an accident/Salvaged
- Flood damage
- Odometer rollbacks
- Lemon histories
- Junked titles
- State emissions inspection results
- Lien activity
- Vehicle use (taxi, rental, lease, etc.)

When and How May an Automobile Be Repossessed?

It is unusual for people to have sufficient cash to buy an automobile outright. Yet, sellers still wish to sell automobiles and buyers still wish to buy them. Article 9 of the UCC provides a way for sellers to grant credit with low risk. Payment is guaranteed, or *secured*, by the car being purchased by the debtor. This is a type of **secured transaction**, meaning any transaction regardless of its form that is intended to create a security interest in personal property.

secured transaction
Any transaction, regardless of form, that is intended to create a security interest in personal property.

The importance to the creditor of being a secured creditor cannot be overemphasized. State laws that protect debtors generally do not hamper secured creditors. They have a preferred position if the debtor becomes bankrupt. Business as we know it would not exist without secured transaction law.

If the debt is paid, full legal ownership is returned or transferred to the purchaser. If, however, the debt is not paid, the creditor may exercise a right to seize or repossess the vehicle. Failure to pay a credit debt is called **default**. After default, a secured creditor can sue to collect the balance due on the debt, or enforce a security interest in the car by any available judicial process. The most common remedy is to take back the collateral. The debtor may simply return the collateral at the request of the secured party or the creditor may surreptitiously confiscate the car. When the secured party seizes the collateral, care must be taken to ensure that no *breach of the peace* (as determined by state law) occurs. In other words, the creditor or the creditor's agent cannot forcibly enter a debtor's home, garage, or place of business without the permission of the debtor.

default
Failure of a party to do what is legally required.

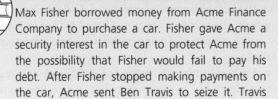

LEGAL FOCUS—PROBLEM

Max Fisher borrowed money from Acme Finance Company to purchase a car. Fisher gave Acme a security interest in the car to protect Acme from the possibility that Fisher would fail to pay his debt. After Fisher stopped making payments on the car, Acme sent Ben Travis to seize it. Travis sneaked onto Fisher's property in the dead of night and made his way up the driveway where the car was parked. Travis jimmied a window of the car, hot-wired it, and drove it off. Is this a lawful repossession?

It appears to be a lawful repossession, as there was no confrontation with Fisher and no breach of the peace. And although Travis did go onto Fisher's property, he did not forcibly enter any building. To avoid possible confrontations with defaulting debtors, however, most car repossessions occur when the car is parked on a street or in a parking lot.

The secured party sometimes can keep the goods in satisfaction of the debt by following strict notice requirements under the UCC. Alternatively, the secured party can resell the goods and apply the proceeds (money received from the sale) toward the debt. Proceeds from a sale of retaken collateral must be applied in the following order:

1. Reasonable expenses stemming from the retaking, holding, or preparing for sale are covered first. When authorized by law and if provided for in the agreement, these can include reasonable attorneys' fees and legal expenses.
2. Satisfaction of the balance of the debt owed to the secured party.
3. Payment to owners of other security interests who have made a written demand received by the secured party before the proceeds have been distributed.
4. Return of any surplus amount received from the sale to the debtor.

Often, after proper disposition of the collateral, the secured party has not collected all that is owed by the debtor. Unless otherwise agreed, the debtor may be sued for any deficiency.

The debtor may be able to exercise the right of *redemption* of the collateral. The right of redemption is the right to have the collateral returned to the debtor. Redemption obviously must occur before the secured party disposes of the collateral. The debtor can exercise the right of redemption by paying the underlying debt. All expenses related to the enforcement of the security interest by the secured party also must be paid.

DRIVING A MOTOR VEHICLE

Why Must Drivers Be Licensed?

LEGAL FOCUS—PROBLEM

Colleen Callahan's license to drive had been revoked for proper cause. (She had been convicted of speeding on three occasions within eighteen months.) She resented this interference with her freedom of movement and decided to drive anyway—but with extra care to avoid any trouble. As luck would have it, while driving safely and in compliance with the rules of the road, another motorist negligently ran a red light and rammed into her car. Will her lack of a driver's license have any effect on civil and criminal court proceedings?

No and yes. Unless there is some cause–effect relationship between the lack of the driver's license and the accident, the lack of license is immaterial. Callahan's rights in a civil action for damages resulting from the accident are not affected by her lack of a driver's license. She would be guilty of the offense of driving without a license, however, and for this she could be fined or jailed.

Driving is a privilege, not a constitutionally protected right, and it is regulated by state or local government as an exercise of government police power. Prospective drivers must demonstrate an ability to drive in traffic and must understand the rules of the road. A license to drive may be suspended or revoked for violating the rules of the road, or even for an inability to demonstrate financial responsibility after an accident. Demerit points are assigned for each infraction, and a person's license can be suspended or revoked if too many points have been accumulated in a specific time period. Point systems vary from state to state. Exhibit 10.3 shows an example of the South Dakota Driver's License Point System. Many states have much more complicated charts.

Auto insurance companies check government records for information about the driving records of people who apply for insurance or have policies with the company. The insurance companies routinely charge higher premiums or cancel coverage after one or more "moving" violations (an infraction based on the car's motion). The individual then must purchase a minimum coverage policy at a premium price under what is called an *assigned-risk program.* Most states have an assigned-risk program under which insurance companies are required to sell insurance to high-risk drivers on a rotating basis. They are allowed to charge higher premiums to cover their risk.

Computer tracking has assisted some states in collecting payments for unpaid parking tickets. The department of government that renews vehicle registrations is kept informed by computer and simply withholds new license plates or tags until all fines are paid.

Generally, any competent adult may qualify for a driver's license upon passing a written test, a driving test, and a vision test. A minor of proper age (typically sixteen) also may qualify, but often must, in addition to the requirements for an adult, complete a driver education or driver training course. Several states have adopted a graduated licensing procedure for youths. Typically such graduated licensing involves a mandatory learner permit for at least six months, followed by an intermediate licensing phase restricting night driving or driving with other youths in the vehicle.

Some states require that parents sign and verify a minor's application and consent to be responsible for harm caused by their child while driving on a highway. Fortunately for most parents, this liability is usually limited. The amount of liability often is tied to the state's financial responsibility laws (e.g., $15,000 for injury or death, payable to any one person, and $30,000 payable to any number of persons, plus $5,000 for property

EXHIBIT 10.3 South Dakota Point System

South Dakota Point System	
Conviction	Points
Driving While Intoxicated	10*
Reckless Driving	8
Eluding/Attempting to Elude	6
Drag Racing	6
Failure to Yield Right of Way	4
Improper Passing	4
Driving Wrong Side of Roadway	4
Stop Sign/Light Violation	3
Other Moving Offenses	2
*State law requires revocation of license for Driving While Intoxicated.	
Any operator who accumulates fifteen (15) points in any twelve (12) consecutive months, or 22 points in any 24 consecutive months is subject to Driver License suspension.	
Periods of Suspension	
First Suspension	60 Days Maximum
Second Suspension	6 Months Maximum
Subsequent Suspension	1 Year Maximum

Source: http://state.sd.us/dcr/dl/sddriver.html.

damage as the result of any one accident for which their minor child is found to be legally responsible). The requirement that an owner purchase insurance may be mandated by statute; if not, prudence and concern for others who may be injured by a child's negligence would dictate that a parent purchase at least the minimum coverage.

Parental liability for a child's damages caused with motor vehicles deviates from the general rule that parents are not vicariously responsible for their child's torts. Of course, parents are liable if the wrongful conduct of the child was committed at the parent's command, or in the course of the parent's business. In recent years, some states have extended the motor vehicle exception to include limited liability of parents for the willful misconduct of minor children. Even in states where statutes create this parental liability, the minor wrongdoer is likewise liable. Realistically, however, the minor usually lacks the financial resources to pay the injured victim. Moreover, in cases of negligence, the minor could escape a heavy judgment by bankruptcy, unless drunken driving caused the accident.

What Standard of Care Does the Law Prescribe for Drivers?

The standard of care necessary when operating a motor vehicle is one example of the rules of negligence discussed in Chapter 7. The duty to act as a reasonable person requires that you, whether on or off the highway, refrain from carelessly injuring others. The question always is, were you as careful as a hypothetical reasonable person would have been under all circumstances surrounding the event? This broad duty may be violated willfully or negligently. From time to time, most of us are careless. We fail to exercise reasonable care. We do not behave as an ordinary, prudent man, woman, or child of comparable age should behave under the same or similar circumstances. If someone is injured as a result of our negligence, we are generally liable for monetary damages.

Sometimes, of course, we may injure someone while we are acting without negligence or willful intent to harm. Then there is no liability. Such an injury could happen in a pure accident, a casualty that is sudden, unexpected, unforeseeable, and unplanned—perhaps the result of an unknown cause or the unpredictable result of a known cause. There is no liability, for example, when an injury results from a natural calamity (a violent storm) or from the victim's own carelessness (when a person, walking along while reading a paper, steps off a curb into a stream of traffic and suddenly is injured or even killed).

Must Drivers Stop at Accident Scenes?

LEGAL FOCUS—PROBLEM

Gus Shikel, an expert in first aid, was driving along a lonely country road when he came upon the scene of a one-car accident. The wrecked vehicle had collided with a utility pole. Inside were two adults and a child, all unconscious or in shock. One was bleeding profusely. Not wanting to get involved, Shikel drove on. Was he legally obliged to stop and render aid?

He was not obligated in most states. We visited the issue of strangers failing to help Kitty Genovese in Chapter 1 and David Cash failing to help a young girl in deadly peril in Chapters 1 and 2. Generally, the law does not require one to be a good neighbor. The victims were strangers to whom Shikel legally owed no duty. The same result would apply in most states if Shikel were a medical doctor. Shikel's retreat is likely an ethical violation, but not a legal one. If Shikel had in any way caused or contributed to the accident (as by drifting across the center line and forcing the oncoming driver into defensive maneuvers that resulted in the crash), however, he would be obligated to stop and would be criminally and civilly responsible for failure to do so.

In any event, if he does stop—and one hopes that he would—and renders first aid, under common law, he has the duty to provide help with reasonable care under emergency situations. Conceivably, if one stops and renders aid, injured persons could sue the person providing assistance if that person failed to exercise reasonable care and thus aggravated the injuries. Such lawsuits are rare and recovery rarer still, but they create the anomaly that ethical behavior creates a legal peril that unethical behavior does not.

Good Samaritan statute
Statute that protects volunteers from liability for ordinary negligence while aiding persons in need.

As discussed in Chapter 7, most states have enacted **Good Samaritan statutes** to shield volunteers from actions for ordinary negligence. North Carolina has a typical statute, stating that no person shall be liable for damages for injuries or death claimed to result from the rendering of first aid or emergency health care treatment when the circumstances require prompt decisions and actions, and when the necessity is "so reasonably apparent that any delay … would seriously worsen the physical condition or endanger the life" of the patient. As stated in Chapter 7, immunity is not available when the act is gross negligence, wanton conduct, or intentional wrongdoing. Nor does the statute relieve persons of liability for damages "while rendering health care services in the normal and ordinary course of a business or profession."

Does a Traffic Citation Prove Civil Liability for an Accident?

LEGAL FOCUS—PROBLEM

Kevin Harper was driving on the wrong side of a two-lane highway when he was involved in a head-on collision with Lisa Bowden. Bowden was proceeding legally in the opposite direction. Harper was cited by the state patrol for violation of the vehicle code. Is he guilty of negligence *per se* (Latin: "of itself") because he was apparently violating a statute at the time?

presumption
A rule of law permitting one to assume a fact is true until such time as there is a greater weight of evidence that disproves or outweighs the assumed fact.

He probably is guilty. **Negligence *per se*** means that proof of the act establishes the duty. Violation of a statute raises a *prima facie* (Latin: "at first sight") **presumption** or inference of negligence. A presumption is an important procedural rule affecting how certain facts can be proved. A presumption allows a court to infer a new fact by the proof of another. If the plaintiff proves that the statute was violated and caused the accident, and the defendant introduces no contrary evidence, then the defendant is negligent. Violation of the statute must bear some relationship to the accident and be the cause in fact and proximate cause of the accident. For instance, violation of a statute requiring the driver to be licensed would not bear any relationship to Kevin's accident and would not be its cause. Violation of a statute established to protect against driving the wrong way down a road and injuring others driving on the proper side of the road would be negligence *per se.* That very type of harm occurred, and it appears Kevin is liable.

Although difficult to do, a presumption of negligence can be rebutted by proof of excuse or justification. It is possible that Kevin diverted his car because of conditions beyond his control (such as an object in the road, an unforeseeable failure of his steering mechanism, a sudden heart attack, or an illegal action by another car squeezing by on his right side).

Are Owners Liable for Negligence of Other Drivers?

vicarious liability
The responsibility of one person for the wrongful acts of another.

Clearly, an owner-driver is liable for injuries to others caused by his or her own negligent driving. Under the principle of **vicarious liability** (liability for acts of another), the owner also may be liable for harm caused when someone else is the driver, if one of the following conditions applies:

- The driver is the employee or agent of the owner and is acting within the scope of his or her employment. See the discussion of the doctrine of *respondeat superior* in Chapter 12.
- The owner is negligent in lending or giving the car to someone who is not qualified to drive or is known by the owner to be an unsafe driver. The owner is also negligent if he or she lends or gives an automobile to another in a condition (e.g., with faulty brakes) that makes it unsafe to drive.
- In a number of states, owners are responsible whenever a member of their immediate family or household drives and a third party is injured because of the negligence of the driver. This is called the **family purpose doctrine**.
- In several states, parents or guardians who sign a minor's application for a driver's license become liable for damage caused by the minor's negligent operation of the vehicle. As discussed earlier, there are usually dollar limits to the amount of this liability.
- Many different variations and combinations of state statutes impose liability when an owner permits another to use the vehicle (called *permissive use*). In several states, owners are liable when a person they allow to use the vehicle negligently injures a third party. In a few states (e.g., Maine, Pennsylvania, and Utah), owners are liable for permissive use when they have furnished a car to a minor who negligently injures a third party.

family purpose doctrine
A law in some states that holds the owner of a motor vehicle vicariously responsible whenever a member of his immediate family or household drives and a third party is injured because of the negligence of the driver.

If the driver is an employee of the owner and is acting within the scope of employment, the owner-employer is liable without limit under the doctrine of *respondeat superior*. A driver, even though an employee, is always liable (without limit) for his or her own torts.

LEGAL FOCUS—PROBLEM

Walter Johnson was driving down Main Street on his way to deliver a package for Racehorse Delivery Service. Unfortunately, Johnson was momentarily distracted and collided with the rear of Marisa Steinbacher's new automobile. Luckily, Steinbacher was not hurt, but the car was damaged and repairs cost $8,000. Who is legally responsible for the harm to Steinbacher's car?

Johnson is, of course, liable for his own negligence. Walter Johnson was also an employee of Racehorse, and he injured another while driving the automobile on company business. As Johnson was within the scope of his employment, Racehorse Delivery Service is also liable under the doctrine of *respondeat superior*. Steinbacher can sue both or either Johnson and Racehorse, but she can collect her actual damages only once.

LEGAL FOCUS—PROBLEM

Karl Mellon parked his car in the street and ran into the post office to mail a parcel. In his haste, he forgot to remove the ignition key. When he returned, the car was gone. The police later reported that his stolen car had been in a collision with a motorcycle, injuring its rider, Joanna Denton. Denton later sued Mellon. Is he liable?

No, he is not liable. Although leaving the key in an unattended car is negligent and, in some states, a violation of a statute, the owner has no duty to protect the public from unexpected and illegal activities of thieves. The theft and negligent use of stolen property is an intervening and supervening act. A contrary argument can be advanced that Mellon's carelessness created a danger and a result that was predictable. Most states, however, have rejected such an extension of liability to a careless automobile owner theft victim.

LEGAL FOCUS—CASE

Luella Wilson, a ninety-one-year-old Vermont grandmother, enjoyed her own home, friends, and family and had more than $500,000 in the bank. She lent her grandnephew, Willard Stuart, money to buy a car. After a night of drug and alcohol use, he was involved in a serious accident. A passenger in his car, Mark Vince, was paralyzed from the waist down and lost a leg. Stuart had no driver's license, no assets, and no automobile insurance. The victim sued Wilson, alleging that she knew Stuart did not have a license and used drugs and that she was therefore negligent in lending him the money to buy the car. Luella did not appear at the trial because she was ill. What was the verdict?

Vince v. Wilson, 151 Vt. 425, 561 A.2d 103 (Vermont, 1989).

The jury held for the plaintiff against Luella Wilson in the amount of $950,000. This case of negligent lending attracted considerable attention and was appealed. The Vermont Supreme Court did not reverse the trial court verdict, but it did order a new trial to determine whether the automobile dealership and the salesperson who sold Stuart the car should share Wilson's liability. At the new trial, the parties reached an out-of-court settlement, with the plaintiff dismissing his claim against Wilson. The out-of-court settlement relieved Wilson of her liability, but it did not change the rule of law in this case, which found liability for a person other than a driver in a case of negligent entrustment (loan of the car or in this case the means to get the car).

A common extension of liability to persons who neither own nor were driving the car involved in an accident occurs under a **dramshop statute**, a state law making it a crime for a tavern proprietor or employee to serve intoxicants to an obviously drunk patron or someone under the legal drinking age. Injured victims of accidents caused by these patrons have successfully sued the bars and restaurants when they can prove that a dramshop statute was violated. A few cases have found liability against social hosts of parties where intoxicating beverages or drugs were served and shortly afterward the guests were involved in automobile accidents. Wisdom and prudence dictate: If you drink, don't drive. Arranging for a designated driver, one who does not drink alcoholic beverages or take any mood-altering substances, avoids the problem. Furthermore, as a host or hostess, do not have "open bars" or serve drinks of alcoholic beverages to the point of intoxication of your guests.

dramshop statute
A state law making it a crime for a tavern proprietor or employee to serve intoxicants to an obviously inebriated customer.

Are Drivers Liable for Injuries to Guests in Their Cars?

Generally, a driver has a responsibility not only to persons outside the vehicle but also to passengers inside the vehicle. The duty is that of ordinary and usual care for the safety of others. Issues of comparative negligence and assumption of the risk also must be considered when appropriate. In years past, a driver usually could not be held liable to guest passengers for injuries caused by the driver's ordinary negligence, because of special

guest statutes
Law that pertains to guests of a driver of a motor vehicle. In some states, a guest cannot sue the driver if injured, unless the driver is guilty of intoxication, willful misconduct, or gross negligence that causes the accident and resulting injury or death. In other states, a guest may sue the driver for ordinary negligence.

protective statutes called **guest statutes**. Today, only a minority of states have retained guest statutes. Idaho's guest statute is representative of the content of such protections for motor vehicle drivers.

> ***Liability of Motor Owner to Guest***
> *No person transported by the owner or operator of a motor vehicle as his guest without payment for such transportation shall have a cause for damages against such owner or operator or for injuries, death or loss, in case of accident, unless such accident shall have been intentional on the part of the said owner or operator or caused by his intoxication or gross negligence.*
> *The provisions of this section shall not relieve a public carrier or any owner or operator of a motor vehicle while the same is being demonstrated to a prospective purchaser of responsibility for injuries sustained by a passenger being transported by such public carrier or by such owner or operator.*

Proponents of guest statutes argue that when the drivers are insured, there can be collusion in staged accidents to defraud insurance companies. Even in the absence of fraud, a negligent driver who is a relative (e.g., a parent) of the guest (e.g., a child) who receives dollar damages would indirectly profit from his or her own negligence. Guest statutes also prevent possible fraudulent claims by guests who may be the only witnesses to a single-car accident. As social views have changed, most states have abolished guest statutes. The rationale for change has been that the recovery probably will come from an insurance company, and if you buy insurance to compensate strangers whom you might injure, you probably would want to have the same protection for relatives and friends who are your guests.

Even when a state has a guest statute, liability exists when the plaintiff can prove that death or injury resulted from intoxication or willful misconduct of the driver. Thus, in our earlier example, Luella Wilson's nephew Willard Stuart, who was high on drugs and alcohol, was not protected from the lawsuit by a guest statute. He was, however, judgment-proof, which led the injured plaintiff to seek other possible defendants who were not judgment-proof.

Driving Under the Influence

People who drive under the influence (DUI) of mind-altering chemicals are a major social problem in the United States. Drunk driving is the major cause of accidents on the highways and is an ingredient in most fatal accidents. Several organizations try to protect the rights of people who are victims of such criminal activity. These organizations include MADD (Mothers Against Drunk Driving) and SADD (Students Against Drunk Driving). They have had a significant effect on public attitudes and on the enactment of laws concerning driving under the influence. All fifty states have set twenty-one as the minimum age for purchasing alcohol. The penalties for DUI have increased with longer jail sentences, driver's license revocations, and bigger fines.

LEGAL FOCUS—PROBLEM

Several friends were at Lawrence Harberson's apartment celebrating the end of the school year. Beer was flowing freely. Harberson, a 260-pound star tackle on the college football team, had just finished his first twelve-ounce beer when he opened a second. Waving the beer can, he jumped into his car and rammed the pedal to the metal, burning tire rubber as he sped off to collect his girlfriend Marcie Jasper at the nearby airport. While en route, he was stopped by a highway patrol officer for exceeding the posted speed limit by 20 mph or more. Is he also guilty of driving under the influence of alcohol?

Probably not, although he could be required to demonstrate he is sober. One beer is not likely to intoxicate or adversely influence a 260-pound person's body mechanisms. He could be cited, however, for carrying an open container of alcoholic beverage in his car. It is also true that alcohol affects persons, genders, and those using medications differently.

When stopped under suspicion of intoxication, a driver is required to submit to a **field sobriety test**. It is a preliminary test at the scene, where the driver may be asked to walk a straight line, stand on one foot, or perform some other similar act. A person who appears intoxicated may be taken to a police station and asked for a sample of breath, blood, or urine to be analyzed for alcoholic or drug content.

field sobriety test A simple test used to determine the reactions of a motor vehicle driver who is suspected of driving under the influence of alcohol or another drug. The test is administered at the scene of the arrest.

Refusing to submit to a chemical test by exercising your constitutional right against self-incrimination may cause forfeiture of your driver's license. Every person who accepts a license to drive impliedly consents to sobriety tests upon police suspicion, with probable cause, of the driver's intoxication. The driver has a right to a proper warning of the possible effect of the law, and a right to a court or administrative hearing, before the license is revoked.

In all states, driving with a blood-alcohol concentration of 0.08 percent or above establishes the crime of DUI. It need not be proven that the driver is intoxicated. Driving with a blood-alcohol content level at or above the stated percentage is a *per se* violation of law and therefore cannot be contested. In other words, it need not be shown that a person is impaired; instead, having the prohibited blood-alcohol content while driving completes the crime. The means of measurement varies, but almost all states provide for blood, breath, or urine tests or some combination of tests. Also, all states have adopted what is referred to as a "zero tolerance" for a minor. These laws make it illegal for drivers under the age of twenty-one to operate a motor vehicle with either any blood-alcohol level or a 0.02 percent or more level; the presence of alcohol or a refusal to test leads to an automatic suspension of the minor's driver's license.

LEGAL FOCUS—EXAMPLE

Any driver under the age of twenty-one who tests positive for the presence of alcohol or refuses testing upon a police officer's proper request is subject to summary suspension of his or her driving privileges.

[T]he Illinois Vehicle Code provides that drivers under the age of 21 who are arrested, as evidenced by a Uniform Traffic Ticket for any violation of the Illinois Vehicle Code or similar provision of a local ordinance, shall be deemed to have given consent to chemical tests of blood, breath, or urine for the purpose of determining the alcohol content of the person's blood, provided the police officer has probable cause to believe that the driver has consumed any amount of an alcoholic beverage. The officer requesting the test must warn the driver that refusal to submit to the test, or submission to the test resulting in an alcohol concentration more than 0.00, may result in the suspension of driving privileges. The length of the suspension ranges from three months to two years, depending on whether the driver is a first offender, and whether the driver refuses the test or submits to a test that discloses an alcohol concentration more than 0.00.

Arvia v. Madigan, 209 Ill.2d 520, 283 Ill.Dec. 895 (Ill., 2004) citing 625 ILCS 5/11-501.8(a) and (d).

Criminal penalties for driving under the influence can be severe. In a representative state, a jail sentence of from two days to six months is imposed if one is convicted two or more times for drunk driving within five years; a judge who fails to send the defendant to jail must write a formal opinion justifying such leniency. It is also common that a first conviction leads to an automatic driver's license suspension of 90–120 days. A fine of from $500 to $2,500 or more also is assessed. Under certain circumstances, the vehicle may be impounded or even forfeited. In addition, the defendant's automobile insurance premiums will rise.

A single DUI can lead to cancellation of insurance and an inability to rent an automobile when out of town or on vacation for up to three years after conviction. It is clear that the cost of a DUI starts at about $6,000–$10,000 the first year (not including court costs and attorneys' fees) and continues for several years while your new insurance company surcharges cover premiums. Deaths resulting from a DUI can subject the wrongdoer to various degrees of homicide charges (usually vehicular homicide), but convictions also have included second-degree murder. Penalties for multiple DUIs usually become substantially more severe.

It should be noted that the legal tolerance of drinking while boating has lessened in many states in recent years. In 1998, Georgia's new tougher boating law provided for a loss of boating privileges, up to a $1,000 fine, and one year of jail upon conviction of the first offense.

LEGAL FOCUS—BACKGROUND

Unfortunately, bad decision making by people who drink is not confined to automobile drivers. Two pilots, Thomas Cloyd and Christopher Hughes, just wanted to carry their coffee through the security checkpoint, but security personnel had other plans. While discussing their differences, security smelled alcohol on their breath. The pilots continued to the America West plane, but air traffic controllers ordered the aircraft back to the gate before it could take off on a scheduled flight to Phoenix. They were arrested after tests showed Cloyd's blood-alcohol level was 0.091 and Hughes's was 0.084. Both pilots had their licenses revoked by the Federal Aviation Administration and were fired by America West. They ultimately were convicted of operating an aircraft while intoxicated and sentenced to jail.

Must Owners Maintain Their Vehicles in Good Repair?

Owners of motor vehicles are legally required to maintain them in safe operating condition. One appellate court stated this generally applicable duty in the following words:

> *Generally speaking, it is the duty of one driving a motor vehicle along a public highway to see that it is properly equipped so that it may be at all times controlled to the end that it be not a menace to the safety of others or of their property. The law requires that such a vehicle be equipped with brakes adequate to its quick stopping when necessary for the safety of its occupants or of others, and it is equally essential that it be maintained in such a condition as to mechanical efficiency and fuel supply that it may not become a menace to, or an obstruction of, other traffic by stopping on the road. But if the person in charge of such vehicle has done all that can be reasonably expected of a person of ordinary prudence to see that his vehicle is in proper condition, and an unforeseen failure of a part of his equipment occurs, it does not necessarily follow that he must be deemed guilty of negligence as a matter of law.*

A driver is not liable for injuries suffered by strangers from an unforeseeable mechanical failure of his or her automobile. Furthermore, if the driver is injured, he or she might recover damages from the manufacturer (or an intermediary) on the theory of strict product liability. The driver must prove that the defendant placed the product (automobile or component part thereof) on the market, knowing that it was to be used without inspection for defects by the consumer. The driver additionally must show personal injury as a result of a defect in the design or manufacture of the article while it was being used properly. There can be no recovery, however, if the driver was aware that such defect made the article unsafe for its intended use.

LEGAL FOCUS—PROBLEM

When Alberta Ayers stopped for a cup of coffee at the Summit Cafe, she mentioned a "short pedal" on the hydraulic brakes of her heavy-duty truck. She had to "pump" the brake pedal to get a braking response. Nevertheless, after her coffee break, she proceeded down the mountain road until the brakes did not hold and the rig went out of control, ultimately careening over the side of the road and landing 200 feet below. Was the manufacturer or seller of the truck or of the brakes liable?

No, the manufacturer and the seller were not liable. Even if the brakes were defective in design or manufacture, Ayers knew of the condition and was negligent by returning to the highway, especially in the mountains without a checkup, adjustment, or repair.

Both federal and state governments assist owners by prescribing a variety of safety standards for motor vehicles. Not only are manufacturers required to manufacture motor vehicles meeting minimum safety standards, but also in recent years, many states (through court opinions and legislative statutes) have increased the responsibilities of drivers for their own safety. The most common personal safety equipment is the mandatory use of safety seat belts. With respect to motorcycles, about twenty states require helmets for all riders and another protective headgear must be worn while driving.

LEGAL FOCUS—BACKGROUND

In the late spring of 2006, wearing motorcycle helmets was in the national news. Helmetless Pittsburgh Steelers quarterback Ben Roethlisberger was in an accident when his team "Suzuki motorcycle" lost to "car." He was injury-free after his earlier February Super Bowl victory but not from this encounter, where it took seven hours of surgery to repair his jaw, nose, and teeth. Wearing helmets is optional in Pennsylvania, but Roethlisberger was still fined as he lacked a motorcycle license. Laws requiring that helmets be worn are a source of contention between state governments and many motorcycle riders. Some riders argue that the use of a helmet should be a personal decision; many even view helmet use as a freedom issue. States counter that although helmets do not prevent accidents they reduce the severity of the harm. Government taxes often pay some of the health care costs of brain-damaged indigent motorcycle drivers.

Are There Special Laws for Rented Vehicles?

When you rent an automobile, you contract for the use rather than the ownership of personal property. The legal term for this relationship is a *bailment*, which, as explained earlier, is a temporary right of possession of the goods of another. In a sale or a gift, title is transferred; in a bailment, possession is transferred, but not title. Any personal property can be bailed, and automobile rentals are bailments. The rental car company is a **bailor**, and the renter a **bailee**. Although bailment law has very well-defined rights and duties, the most important determinant of the relationship is the language of the rental agreement, which is the controlling written contract.

bailor
One who transfers temporary possession of personal property to another, the bailee.

bailee
One who rightfully receives temporary possession of personal property from another, the bailor, in a bailment.

Most bailments are created by agreement, but not necessarily by contract. For example, if you loan your bicycle to a friend, a bailment is created. Because there is no payment (or other type of consideration), it is not a contract. Most bailments, however, are based on contract (e.g., the delivery of your sleeping bag or dress to the cleaners for dry cleaning).

Elements of a Bailment

For a transfer of property to be a bailment, the following three conditions must be met:

1. **Personal property.** Bailments involve only personal property. A bailment of your luggage is created when it is taken to an airline. The airline passenger is not subject to a bailment. Real property cannot be bailed; thus, renting a house is not a bailment.
2. **Delivery of possession.** The property must be transferred to the bailee. There are two requirements for effective delivery: (a) the bailee must be given both exclusive possession and control over the property and (b) the bailee *must knowingly* accept the personal property.

LEGAL FOCUS—PROBLEM

Millie Banks took Billie Saven out to dinner at an expensive restaurant. Upon arrival at the restaurant, Banks turned over her car to the parking attendant, who parked the car. Did a bailment of Banks's car occur?

Yes, valet parking is usually a bailment. Self-parking is not. The difference is who controls the car keys. If Banks parked the car herself, locked it, and kept the keys, it is considered a lease of space. The owner of the parking lot is a *lessor*, and Banks is a lessee of the space. Self-service parking lots generally are not considered bailments because the parking lot owners do not take control or possession of the automobile. Even if a bailment exists, the bailee often will limit or disclaim liability by posting signs and including disclaimer language on the claim ticket.

3. **Bailment agreement.** A bailment agreement can be express or *implied*. A written agreement usually is not required for a bailment. It is, however, a good idea to have one when valuable property is involved. Remember that not all bailment agreements are contracts. If you loan your next-door neighbor your hedge trimmer, it is an agreement and a bailment, but it is not a contract unless the neighbor pays for the use.

A bailment agreement expressly or impliedly expects the return of the property to the bailor. An agreement might provide for the return of the property to a third person or for disposal by the bailee. The bailee is expected to also return the identical goods given by the bailor. In certain types of bailments, only equivalent property must be returned, for example, a bailment of *fungible*, uniformly identical, goods.

LEGAL FOCUS—EXAMPLE

Holman stores his grain (*fungible goods*) at Joe's Warehouse. At the end of the storage period, the warehouse does not have to return the exact same grain. The warehouse bailee must, however, return grain of the same *type*, *grade*, and *quantity*.

Laws relating to rental car bailments vary significantly among the states, but two rules are uniform. The first uniform rule is that the rental car company has a duty to provide a vehicle that is safe to use and in good driving condition. A bailee has rights both in contract and tort if harmed because of a breach of this duty. Second, the bailor has a right to expect the car to be returned in the same condition in which it was rented, minus ordinary wear and tear. The bailee is responsible for harm to the car even if it was not the bailee's fault. Rental companies suggest special collision insurance (called *collision damage waivers*) to cover this risk. As this insurance is very costly (rental companies make a sizeable profit with this add-on fee), many states have restricted rental car company practices promoting such special coverage. If you have collision insurance on your own automobile, your policy typically will cover this risk (minus the deductible) on any rental car (however, check your specific policy to determine your specific coverage). Credit card companies often provide collision waiver coverage as an important fringe benefit for their customers. Of course, for the benefit to apply, the customer must use the credit card when renting the vehicle.

LEGAL FOCUS—PROBLEM

Joua Landini landed at Metropolitan Airport and walked over to the Maxi Car Rental agency to pick up his reserved auto. After he provided his license and credit card to the rental company, the agent refused to rent him an automobile. She told Landini that the two speeding violations found when she did a computer search of his driving disqualified him from renting from Maxi. Landini insists that Maxi rent him a car, arguing that the search was an invasion of his privacy.

The rental company has a legitimate interest in public information, which lets it determine the level of risk it takes when renting to a particular customer. If the renter has certain types of recent traffic violations or a certain violation "point level," the rental company may refuse to rent or may charge a higher rental amount. This has become a common business practice of rental car companies, and neither court case nor legislation has curbed this practice.

Are There Special Laws for Common Carriers?

common carrier
A carrier that transports for payment all persons who apply for passage, assuming space is available and there is no legal excuse for refusal.

A **common carrier** of passengers agrees to transport, in exchange for money, anybody applying for passage, assuming there is available space and no legal justification for refusal. Bus lines, taxicabs, railroads, airlines, and subway systems are all classified as common carriers. Common carriers are required to be licensed and are regulated by federal, and sometimes state, agencies. Regulations usually cover routes, safety measures, operating methods, rates, passenger contracts and treatment, and luggage handling. At the heart of the relationship are two legal concepts: (1) specific obligations or duties are owed to passengers created by a contract of transport and (2) general duties are also owed as a matter of public policy. These general duties are independent of private contract and arise from the carrier's position as a public utility. These common carrier legal duties are very important for passenger safety and baggage care.

LEGAL FOCUS—CASE

Mark Oglesby and Mark Finken, both seventh graders, were riding on a Milwaukee County bus. A group of about twenty youths stormed the bus, some entering through its windows. The hoodlums demanded money of Finken; when he refused, they beat him. Oglesby and Finken eventually were able to flee the scene. During the entire course of events, the bus driver, although watching in her rear-view mirror, made no attempt to intervene. Did the bus driver breach a duty owed Oglesby and Finken?

Kasanof v. Embry-Riddle Co., 157 Fla. 677, 26 So. 2d 889 (Florida, 1946).

Yes, the driver breached a duty owed. Common carriers are responsible for the safety of their passengers. Because common carriers are open to everyone, the public reasonably expects to be safe. Although the carriers are not insurers of the passengers' safety, their duty is described as either a high, or the highest, duty of care. This duty includes inspection of equipment, safe means of access and departure, use of protective restraints such as seat belts in airlines and possibly even in buses, and protection from fellow passengers. In the preceding case, the court stated, "It was reasonable to infer … that the assault would not have occurred had the driver ordered the youths off the bus for their rowdiness, warned them, or notified them she was summoning the police."

A common carrier is also responsible for the safe transport and return of a passenger's baggage, as covered by that passenger's ticket or fare. If there is no extraordinary excuse (such as confiscation of the baggage by police), the carrier is responsible for loss or damage to the baggage, without proof of fault. Statutes regulating baggage transport typically provide that although liability may not be eliminated, it may be limited by contract to certain defined amounts. Such partial disclaimers are allowed as long as the passenger is given the right to have the monetary limit raised after paying an additional fee. As baggage transport contracts generally include a disclaimer, it behooves the passenger to protect valuable goods through a suitable declaration of higher value and payment of an additional fee.

financial responsibility law
A statute requiring that after an automobile accident of specified severity, driver not covered by insurance must post specified cash or equivalent bond.

What Is the Financial Responsibility Law?

LEGAL FOCUS—PROBLEM

Jill Searle and Bob Ranney were in an automobile collision that occurred when their speeding cars collided at the campus entrance on the way to morning classes at Nashville University. The collision created a terrible traffic jam, and several hundred students missed their first morning class. Many regarded the event as a festive occasion because no one was hurt and everyone had an excuse from class. Each car sustained at least $500 worth of damage. Searle and Ranney notified their respective insurance companies and relaxed with the thought that both had adequate coverage. Have they overlooked anything important?

Yes, they have. Although proof of insurance is important and notifying their insurance companies is wise, they also must notify the state about the accident. Tennessee, like most states, has a **financial responsibility law**. Such laws require that within a set period each driver involved in an automobile accident, regardless of fault, must provide proof of financial responsibility and also report to the state any accident that causes more than a modest amount of property damage (such as $1,000) or in which someone is injured (no matter how slightly) or killed. The financial responsibility requirement is usually met by purchase of a minimum amount of automobile insurance. Drivers who do not have automobile insurance usually must either pay a cash deposit or post a bond. The cash deposit or bond (a form of guarantee) is proof of financial responsibility.

Failure to report a serious accident (e.g., $1,000 damage, injury, or death) can lead to suspension or revocation of your driver's license. If you do not have insurance and cannot establish financial responsibility, your driver's license will be suspended in most states until proof is presented. The minimum financial responsibility requirements vary among the states. A common required amount is $25,000 for injury to or death of any one person in any one accident, $50,000 for injury to or death of more than one person, and $10,000 for property damage. Many states have compulsory insurance laws in addition to financial responsibility laws. All states have at least one or the other. Insurance salespersons and brokers should know your state's minimum coverage requirements.

Financial responsibility requirements, as the name suggests, are designed to provide some assurance that persons who use the highways and negligently injure others will pay resulting claims. Damages awarded by a court may far exceed the statutory responsibility limits. Furthermore, since financial responsibility need not be demonstrated until after an accident has occurred, there is no guarantee that any particular driver is complying with the law. Indeed, socially irresponsible persons who violate the rights of others are the least likely to buy the needed insurance. Even states that require motor vehicle insurance are left with many liability issues unresolved. The minimum coverage required is typically low, unregistered (and uninsured) automobiles are still driven, and unlicensed (and uninsured) drivers still drive.

LEGAL FOCUS—PROBLEM

Negligently backing his car and house trailer from a parking spot across a mountain road, Malcolm Maclede caused a major accident in which three persons were seriously injured and two $27,000 automobiles were totally wrecked. Medical expenses alone exceeded $70,000 within a year, and one victim had to be confined to a bed, presumably for the rest of her life. All three victims were adults with families, and none could work for a year or longer. Maclede had the minimum insurance coverage required by the financial responsibility law. Is Maclede guilty of a crime? Will he lose all his assets in civil litigation? Can he escape punishment through bankruptcy?

exempt assets
Property that a debtor can protect against seizure resulting from execution of judgment by a judgment creditor or a trustee in a bankruptcy distribution.

Maclede is not guilty of a crime because he was not criminally negligent. If he had been intoxicated, and had any of the victims died, he would have faced manslaughter and possibly even murder charges (see Chapter 6 for examples). He will, no doubt, lose all of his assets not otherwise subject to preexisting creditors' claims, unless he is very wealthy. He can escape his civil liability through bankruptcy, but all his nonexempt assets could be seized. **Exempt assets** are assets that every debtor is permitted to keep, such as an inexpensive automobile, personal clothes and effects, tools of his or her trade, a television, and a residential homestead. The moral is that all drivers should carry adequate public liability coverage for bodily injury to others as a matter of prudent self-interest as well as of social justice and concern for other human beings.

PURCHASING AUTOMOBILE INSURANCE

Owners of a car absolutely, unequivocally, and without reservation need to protect themselves against losses that may arise from, for example, a collision, vandalism, or theft, and especially against the overwhelming losses that could arise from injury to oneself or others as a result of an auto accident. The typical family automobile insurance policy covers the named insured (and spouse, if any) and residents of the same household (including children, even when they are temporarily away from home, as when attending a distant school). The policy also covers other persons when they are using the vehicle with the permission of the named insured. Persons in the household other than the named insured cannot give permission to others to use the family car with continuing coverage by the policy. When an insured person drives another owner's car with permission, the driver's policy provides additional supplementary coverage if the owner's policy is insufficient to cover a valid claim or judgment.

What Types of Automobile Insurance Are Available?

LEGAL FOCUS—PROBLEM

When Tosh Takimota celebrated his twentieth birthday, his parents gave him his first new car. "Remember," his father said, "you won't be driving one horse, you'll be driving 150 of them. That can be worse than a stampede. So before you use these keys, let's see our insurance agent and make sure you're adequately covered." What sort of insurance coverage does Takimota need?

liability insurance Coverage sold to protect against claims based on the insured's negligence that has caused bodily injury or property damage to the claimant.

Takimota needs all four basic types of automobile insurance—liability, medical payments, uninsured motorist, and physical damage—to meet the hazards caused by motor vehicles and those who drive them.

Liability Insurance

A policy of **liability insurance** (also called personal liability or PL *insurance*) will pay a specified amount of money for bodily injury and property damage (also called PD *insurance*) to other persons for which any insured is legally responsible. If your state mandates that all drivers have insurance coverage, this is the coverage required. PL and PD coverage compensates others who are injured by the negligence of the insured. PL coverage pays claims against the insured for losses resulting from the injury or death of the victims. PD coverage pays claims resulting from damage to the car or other property of the victims. PL and PD coverage can be purchased in most states with a single liability limit, such as $50,000. In other words, the insurance company provides $50,000 coverage for both personal and property losses suffered by injured victims. Some policies are written with "split limits," such as $10,000/$20,000/$5,000 (i.e., in any one accident the company pays up to $10,000 for injury or death to any one person or $20,000 to all persons, and $5,000 for property damage).

medical-payments insurance Coverage available in conjunction with automobile insurance—for example, to pay medical, surgical, dental, and funeral expenses suffered by the insured or any member of the insured's household who is injured while occupying or being struck by an automobile.

Medical-Payments Insurance

Medical-payments insurance covers medical and funeral expenses incurred by the insured and others riding in the car. Payments are made without reference to fault. If the named insured or family members are injured by a motor vehicle while they are pedestrians, or if they are injured while occupying another motor vehicle, they also will be protected by this coverage.

If a person already has adequate health insurance, this additional coverage may be unnecessary. Of course, guests in the insured's car may not have health insurance, and for their sake, this comparatively inexpensive coverage should be considered.

LEGAL FOCUS—PROBLEM

Stranded in downtown Atlanta without his wallet, which had been picked from his pocket, Dean Labordee desperately needed a ride to the airport for a return flight to Detroit. (His airline ticket was safely tucked in his breast pocket.) Frantically, he "hot-wired" the first idle car he came upon (an Oldsmobile owned by Thad Turner) and headed for the airport. Labordee had been drinking, and within a block, he crashed into a telephone pole. Before it was all over, his medical payments totaled $18,789. Will Thad Turner's medical-payments policy (limit $20,000) have to cover Labordee's damage?

uninsured-motorist insurance Automobile insurance that protects against the risk of loss from bodily injury and property damage suffered by an insured driver because of the negligence of either an uninsured, an underinsured, or a hit-and-rundriver.

No, Turner's policy will not cover the damage. For Turner's medical-payments insurance to apply, he must have given the driver, Labordee, permission to use his vehicle. Labordee did not have Turner's permission; he had stolen Turner's car. Labordee's own medical-payments coverage is inapplicable, as is the rest of his automobile insurance policy, because, as a thief, he was using a vehicle without a reasonable belief of permission. If, however, Labordee also carried ordinary health insurance, his medical expenses would be covered.

Like other forms of automobile insurance, a certain limit of coverage will identify the responsibility of the insurance company. The limit applies to each covered person in the accident.

Uninsured Motorist Insurance

This type of insurance pays for injuries or property damages to the insured, family members, and guests in a covered vehicle resulting from accidents involving hit-and-run drivers and uninsured or underinsured drivers.

LEGAL FOCUS—PROBLEM

Pedro Perez was at the wheel of his car, patiently waiting for a green light, when he was rear-ended with a horrendous crash. He was wearing a shoulder harness, but his neck and back were snapped in a violent whiplash. Although conscious, he was dazed and could not identify the hit-and-run driver or car that backed off, made a U-turn, and then sped away. What type of automobile insurance protects Perez in this situation?

deductible A provision in an insurance policy whereby the insured bears modest losses up to a prescribed sum (for example, $50, $100, or a little more) in exchange for reduced premiums.

Perez can recover his medical expenses and his property damages up to the agreed limits under **uninsured-motorist insurance**. For a relatively modest premium, this policy typically pays between $15,000 and $25,000 for bodily injury suffered by the insured as a result of being struck by a hit-and-run driver who escapes without being identified, or by an identified but uninsured or judgment-proof driver who is at fault. Some states require uninsured-motorist insurance to be included in all PL and PD policies.

Physical-Damage Coverage

Two types of insurance are available to pay for damages to your own automobile in excess of any agreed **deductible**. Most physical-damage coverage is divided into two parts:

collision insurance
Automobile insurance that protects against the risk of loss from damages to one's own automobile in a collision regardless of who is at fault.

collision and comprehensive. **Collision insurance** pays for damage to the insured's motor vehicle caused by a collision, no matter who is at fault. If the other party was at fault, your automobile insurance company will have a right of subrogation. **Subrogation** is the right to succeed to or substitute for the rights of another. In insurance law, if the insurance company pays a claimant, it has the right to reimbursement from the wrongdoer.

Comprehensive insurance (also called *other-than-collision loss*) protects against any losses to the insured's vehicle except those caused by collision. Thus, comprehensive applies if the vehicle is stolen, vandalized, or otherwise damaged (as by fire, earthquake, flood, or sandstorm). The policy does not pay for loss caused by theft of personal effects (e.g., clothing, cameras, or luggage) left in the vehicle or for the theft of radio or stereo equipment, although these may be covered by special endorsement or addition to the policy.

Who Is Protected by Automobile Insurance?

LEGAL FOCUS—PROBLEM

Sally and Ben McFarland have a teenage daughter, Karen. All drive the family car. Are all covered by the couple's automobile insurance policy?

subrogation
The substitution of a third party for the creditor in a claim against a debtor.

comprehensive insurance
Automobile insurance that protects against losses from having one's car stolen or damaged other than by collision (for example, by falling trees, sandstorm).

Yes, if the insurance company is properly informed that everyone drives the family car. As all family members are likely to be significant drivers, the insurance company has a right to be told which members of the family drive in order to properly estimate its risk and charge the appropriate insurance premium (price paid for the policy). With respect to an owned automobile identified in a policy, the following persons normally are insured:

- The named insured and spouse, if residing in the same household.
- Declared residents of the same household. (This applies even if the person is temporarily away from the residence; for example, if Karen goes to school in another state.)
- Other persons who use the automobile with the permission of the named insured. This coverage is provided to nonresident drivers who infrequently drive the insured vehicle.
- Other persons who might be liable because of negligence of the insured. This could be the employer of the insured, if Sally or Ben McFarland got into an accident while on company business.

Under most policies, if you sell your car and buy another, your automobile coverage continues for at least thirty days, or at most until the next policy anniversary date. Thus, you are fully protected in case you are in an accident during the short transition period. The company should be notified promptly, however, so it can make the necessary changes to your policy, including an adjustment in the premium.

LEGAL FOCUS—PROBLEM

While on vacation in Glacier National Park, Nelson Salbeck borrowed a four-wheel-drive vehicle from some friends and took off on a cross-country trip. Does his automobile insurance policy cover him while he drives the borrowed vehicle?

nonowned automobile
An automobile or trailer not owned by, or furnished for, the regular use of the named insured.

Yes, it does. Salbeck and relatives who reside in his household are all covered when they drive nonowned passenger automobiles with the permission of the vehicle's owner. A **nonowned automobile** is defined as an automobile or trailer not owned by, or furnished for, the regular use of the named insured. Insurance carried by the owner of the vehicle provides the basic coverage. Salbeck's insurer would pay only amounts in excess of the owner's policy limits.

LEGAL FOCUS—PROBLEM

When Nelson Salbeck came home, he learned that his adult son, Jack, who still lived with his parents, had bought a new car with a manual gearshift and had insured it in his own name. Salbeck asked if he might try it out; Jack said yes, and Nelson took off. He had an accident in which the car was damaged, and both a pedestrian and Nelson were injured, all because of his negligence in shifting gears. Did Nelson's insurance cover him?

Nelson's insurance would be secondary or excess. The son's car does not fit the definition of nonowned since a resident relative, the son, owns it. Since Salbeck drove with his son's permission, however, the son's policy will cover the accident. Unfortunately, this might be much less coverage than he considers adequate; he is vulnerable to a sizable claim for damages by the pedestrian. An exception to this rule exists if Salbeck borrows his son's car while his own is being serviced or repaired. The son's car then would be considered a temporary substitute automobile, and both policies would cover the loss.

LEGAL FOCUS—PROBLEM

Aaron Dittmar bought a stand-alone trailer for camping trips and mounted a light trail motorcycle to the rear of the trailer. Are these vehicles covered by Dittmar's automobile insurance policy?

The trailer is covered, without an added premium, for PL and PD only if it is designed for use with a private passenger automobile and is not used for business or commercial purposes. Motorcycles, dune buggies, all-terrain vehicles (ATVs), mopeds, motor homes, and other similar vehicles generally are excluded from coverage unless specially added to the policy. Of course, individual policies may be written directly for a motorcycle or other vehicle.

A policy effective within the United States generally does not cover the insured in other countries unless specially endorsed in exchange for an extra premium. Most U.S. policies apply to travel while in Canada, but U.S. drivers need to carry proof of insurance coverage while driving there. Most U.S. insurance is not sufficient in Mexico. Before driving in Mexico, a driver should purchase a policy covering Mexican travel. Such policies are sold in both countries. It is extremely important that you review your automobile liability and property-damage coverage with your insurance agent before you leave to travel by car in foreign countries. Otherwise, you could be burdened with a noncovered judgment and might even be jailed pending trial because of lack of local insurance to cover possible damages.

What Is the Insurance Company's Duty to the Insured?

The insurance company is obligated under the policy to act fairly toward its insureds in handling their claims. It is expected to pay rightful claims up to the policy limits and provide legal defense to the insured against claims made that are covered by the policy. The cost of defending claims is covered under the policy over and above any policy limits.

What Is No-Fault Insurance?

no-fault
A type of automobile insurance, generally mandatory for all motorists in adopting states, that provides benefits to the insured, regardless of fault of parties to the accident.

No-fault is a type of insurance requiring each driver to look to his or her own insurance carrier for reimbursement of losses after an accident. Injured victims cannot sue negligent drivers. Under no-fault, every driver is required to buy insurance. After an accident, each company pays the physical injury damages suffered by its insured up to some prescribed limit, regardless of fault. The label "no-fault" means that the insured will be paid even if he or she caused the accident. There are different versions of no-fault insurance, but in its purest conceptual form, neither party may sue the other, nor may the insurance companies sue by right of subrogation after making payment. With pure no-fault, the insured may not recover any damages for pain and suffering, which is often the largest portion of jury verdicts. If there is a dispute as to the proper amount of damages to be paid, an administrator decides after a hearing. Each party collects from his or her own company for medical or funeral expenses and lost wages (usually for a limited time), both for themselves and for other occupants of the cars.

No-fault insurance replaces the typical method of establishing responsibility for wrongs related to automobile accidents. It replaces the tort fault system and thus it is a system itself. The closest existing parallel is workers' compensation insurance, which replaced the fault system for most work-related injuries. All states that have adopted no-fault systems have implemented modified versions of the pure concept. For instance, in a modified plan, if an accidental death, permanent injury, or disfigurement results, or if medical expenses exceed a specified minimum (such as $2,500 or $5,000, or ninety days of disability or a specific type of injury such as the loss of a limb), it is called the "threshold for suit." When the "threshold" is met, the general prohibition against suits is waived. If it then is proved that the other party's negligence caused the accident, a larger sum may be recovered, including all special damages (for medical expenses, loss of wages, or destruction of property) and payment of general damages for pain, suffering, and disfigurement.

Massachusetts pioneered no-fault in 1971, and several states followed with a variety of no-fault plans. Some states have adopted plans and then abandoned or modified them. Other states have considered the idea but rejected it. At the federal level, repeated unsuccessful efforts have been made to enact a comprehensive national plan, excluding only those states that have acceptable equivalent plans. Individuals who are not satisfied with recovery schedules under no-fault can, of course, buy additional health or medical-payments, accident, and disability insurance coverage for themselves. Most no-fault plans exclude property damage, so drivers should continue to buy such protection, both comprehensive and collision.

What Should You Do If Involved in an Accident?

The following suggestions are made to help protect your legal rights in the event that you have an accident while driving a car. More important, they may help to protect human lives, including your own.

1. If your car is not stopped by the accident, park it in a safe place, immediately ahead of the accident area and preferably off the highway. To hit-and-run is a serious criminal offense and morally wrong. If possible, post someone to warn oncoming

vehicles, place warning flares, or do both. If you hit an unattended car or damage other property, leave your name, address, telephone number, and automobile license number on a note inside the car or under the windshield wiper.

2. Provide first aid to anyone injured if you are qualified to do so. Do not move anyone unless absolutely necessary, lest you aggravate injuries.
3. Call, or have someone call, for an ambulance, if necessary. As soon as practical, see a doctor if you or others have been injured. This is important because some serious injuries are not immediately apparent.
4. Call, or have someone call, the highway patrol or local police when anyone is injured or killed, or if there is serious property damage. Get the name or number of the officer who investigates the accident. Although the officer's name will be on the police report, you will not receive this report for several days. Persons protecting your interests (e.g., your insurance company or your attorney) will want to begin their investigation of the accident immediately.
5. Even before the police arrive, write down (or have someone else write down) the vehicle license numbers, names, addresses, and phone numbers of all witnesses (they might leave the scene after a few minutes). Get the same information from the driver and occupants of the other vehicle. Also ask the other driver for the name of his or her insurance company.
6. Do not admit responsibility for the accident. Any such admission of fault would be later held against you in court. Right after an accident is not the time to make dramatic conclusions, especially since they may be wrong.
7. Notify your insurance company if the other party is injured or has suffered property damage, or if you intend to submit a claim for personal injuries or for damages to your car.
8. As soon after the accident as possible, write down the full details of what happened immediately before, at the time of, and immediately after the accident. A map or sketch of the scene may help. Note the weather and road conditions, visibility (sun, moon, lights), time, speed estimates, and skid marks. If you can, get pictures of the cars and any skid marks.
9. If the accident was serious, have your family contact an attorney as soon as possible. If you do not have an attorney, find one. (Methods of attorney selection are discussed in Chapter 4.) The attorney may have a professional photographer take pictures of the scene, including skid marks, aided by your notes of the event.
10. Notify the appropriate government agency, using its preprinted forms, to comply with the state's financial responsibility law.
11. If an insurance claims adjuster for the other driver contacts you or your family, refer them to your attorney. Be careful not to admit fault to the adjuster, who openly or with concealed equipment may be recording any conversation. Do not make any settlement until you know the extent of your damages. You cannot know that information until after you have been released by your doctor and have received legal advice. If you are an innocent victim of another driver's negligence, you may be entitled to damages sufficient to cover (a) medical and hospital expenses, present and future; (b) damage to property (car, clothing); (c) loss of wages, actual and prospective; and (d) payment for pain, suffering, and disfigurement. When damages are high, you are well advised to hire an attorney. Even after the attorney's fee, you probably will receive a sum larger than any direct offer from an insurance claims adjuster.

12. You probably will want to have your damaged car repaired. The insurance company may require two or more written estimates from reliable repair shops. The insurance company will pay you on the basis of the lower estimate. If it seems that a defect in your vehicle caused the accident, consult your attorney before you repair the car. The attorney may arrange to have an expert examine the suspect parts to preserve them as evidence.

OTHER METHODS OF ACQUIRING OWNERSHIP OF PERSONAL PROPERTY

As discussed earlier in the chapter, ownership of personal property can occur in several ways. These methods include possession, purchase, production, gift, will or inheritance, and accession. Property also can be acquired when it is lost, abandoned, or mislaid. Purchase is the most likely method for a motor vehicle although other methods are possible. We will discuss these other methods of personal property ownership even though they occur more commonly with other types of personal property than motor vehicles.

Possession

The person who finds abandoned property generally becomes the owner of it. A person who finds lost property may become the owner of that property if the true owner does not come forward. The first person to take possession of a wild animal normally owns it.

gift
A voluntary transfer of property ownership by one under no duty to transfer the ownership.

Production

Production—the fruits of one's labor—is another means of acquiring ownership of personal property. For example, writers, inventors, and manufacturers all produce personal property and get title to what they have produced.

donor
A person who makes a gift in life or by will.

Gifts

donee
The person to whom a gift is made in life or by will.

A **gift** is a voluntary transfer of property ownership. The very essence of a gift is giving someone something without expecting anything in return. A promise to make a gift is not enforceable. The gift must be actually delivered to be an effective transfer of ownership. The person giving the gift is called a **donor**. The person receiving a gift is called a **donee**.

LEGAL FOCUS—PROBLEM

Katrina Brown's favorite aunt, Valerie Karnes, tells her when she graduates from college she is going to give her a new Ford Mustang convertible. What are Brown's rights if any to the new car upon her graduation?

Aunt Valerie has made a gratuitous promise, but the Mustang does not become Brown's until and unless Karnes delivers it to her. The aunt's choice of words could be critical to Katrina's rights. In Chapter 8, we explained what constitutes a unilateral offer to form a contract. Had the aunt promised Katrina the car if she graduates from college and her actions suggested she is bargaining for Katrina to continue her education, the aunt might have made a unilateral offer and Katrina might have a right to receive the car upon completion of the required task.

LEGAL FOCUS—PROBLEM

Linda Ector wishes to make a gift to Patricia Nguyen of some old rare coins stored in a safety deposit box at Lone Star Savings and Loan. Ector is the donor. The intended beneficiary of Ector's generosity, Nguyen, is the donee. How can Ector effectively transfer ownership of the rare coins to Nguyen?

There are three requirements to an effective gift: donative intent, delivery, and acceptance.

donative intent
Present intent to make a gift.

1. **Donative intent.** There must be evidence of the donor's intent to give the donee the gift. **Donative intent** is determined from the language of the donor and the surrounding circumstances. Ector can tell Nguyen that she wishes to give her the coins. Writing down her intention provides even better proof.
2. **Delivery.** Delivery is giving up *complete control and dominion* (ownership rights) over the subject matter of the gift. Delivery is obvious in most gift situations. In the rare coin example, delivery could take place in several ways. Ector could go get the coins and deliver them to Nguyen. Ector may, however, be reluctant to take the coins out of the bank. When a physical object cannot be delivered, a symbolic, or *constructive,* delivery is sufficient.

   Constructive delivery is a term used to describe acts that the law holds to be the equivalent of a real delivery. In our rare coin example, the delivery of the key to the safety deposit box to Nguyen would be a constructive delivery of the contents of the box. The delivery of intangible property—such as stocks, bonds, insurance policies, contracts, and so on—is always accomplished by symbolic, or constructive, delivery.
3. **Acceptance.** The final requirement of a valid gift is acceptance by the donee. This rarely presents any problems since most donees readily accept their gifts. The courts generally assume acceptance unless shown otherwise.

constructive delivery
Acts that are the equivalent of actual delivery such as delivering the key to the safety deposit box with the present intent to give the person the contents of that box.

Will or Inheritance

Ownership of personal property may be transferred by will or by inheritance under state statutes (see Chapter 14). These transfers are called *bequests* (personal property), *devises* (real property), or *inheritances* (any or all property rights transferred at death).

Accession

Accession means "adding on" to something. It happens when someone adds value to a piece of personal property by either labor or materials. The installation of a stereo system in an automobile adds value to the automobile and becomes part of it.

If accession occurs without the permission of the owner, the ownership rights in the improved property usually depend on the good faith of the improver. If the improver is a wrongdoer, most courts will not allow him or her to be reimbursed for the value added. For example, if a car thief put new tires on a stolen car, he or she would not be paid for the value of the new tires.

LEGAL FOCUS—PROBLEM

Roberto Juarez is walking in a large country field. He discovers a huge stone shaped somewhat like a horse lying near a fence. Juarez works on the stone for twenty-seven weeks. He eventually transforms it into a replica of the Lone Ranger's horse, Silver. Juarez's artist friends are very impressed and convince him to move the stone horse to a gallery. The gallery appraises the art at $50,000. The owner of the field where Juarez found the stone now claims title to it. Who gets the statue of Silver? Who is that masked man, anyway?

Juarez should get title to the stone statue because the changes he made greatly increased its value and the accession was performed in good faith. Juarez is, however, responsible for paying the owner of the field the reasonable value of the unaltered stone. If the increase in value is not significant, the original owner would keep title to the property. Many courts require the original owner to compensate an honest mistaken improver for the value he or she has added to the property.

Confusion

confusion
Mixing of one person's personal property with another's, resulting in the goods becoming indistinguishable.

fungible
Each item of personal property is identical to every other item.

Confusion is the mixing of one person's personal property with another's, resulting in the goods becoming indistinguishable. This frequently occurs when the goods are **fungible**. "Fungible" means that each individual item is identical to every other item; this is the case with grain and oil. For example, if two farmers put their number 2-grade winter wheat into the same silo, confusion occurs.

If the confusion of goods was done to deceive or take advantage of another, the innocent party gets title to the whole. If the confusion occurs as a result of agreement, an honest mistake, or the act of some third party, the owners share ownership as *tenants in common.*

Mislaid, Lost, and Abandoned Property

If you find someone's property, it is important to learn whether the owner mislaid, lost, or simply abandoned the property because it affects who has what rights to the property. We define and discuss each below.

LEGAL FOCUS—PROBLEM

While at the movie theater, Dawn Waller went to the concession stand to purchase some popcorn and a cola. She accidentally left her gloves on the concession stand. The next day, she realized they were gone. What are Waller's rights to a return of her gloves?

Mislaid Property

mislaid property
Property that has been voluntarily placed somewhere by the owner and then forgotten.

Property that has been voluntarily placed somewhere by the owner and then forgotten is **mislaid property**. Her gloves are mislaid property. Assuming the theater employees found the gloves, Waller has a right to the return of the gloves. The theater owner has the duty to care for the goods in a reasonable way. The finder does not get title to mislaid property; instead, he or she becomes an *involuntary bailee.* The law presumes the true owner will return for the property.

lost property
Property that is involuntarily left and forgotten by the owner.

Lost Property

Property that is involuntarily left and forgotten is **lost property**. The finder of the property can claim title to the property against everyone but the true owner. If the true owner demands that the lost property be returned, the finder must return it. The finder, however, has better title than anyone else.

If the finder knows who the true owner is, the property should be returned to him or her. Failure to return such property is the tort of *conversion* (see Chapter 7). Many states require the finder to make a diligent search to locate the true owner of lost property.

estray statutes
Laws requiring finders of lost personal property to report their discovery to authorities.

Many states have **estray statutes** to encourage and aid the return of lost property. A common estray statute requires finders to report their discovery, whereupon the county clerk will advertise that property is found to try to find the owner. After a specified time, if the true owner does not claim the property, the finder becomes the new owner.

abandoned property
Property discarded by the true owner, who has no intention of reclaiming it.

Abandoned Property

Property discarded by the true owner, who has no intention of reclaiming the property, is **abandoned property**. Generally, the person who finds the abandoned property and takes possession of it has title. This title is good against everyone, *including the original owner*. If the finder is trespassing and finds abandoned property, title belongs to the owner of the land.

LEGAL FOCUS—PROBLEM

On October 7, 2001, at PacBell Park in San Francisco, Barry Bonds hit his seventy-third home run. In anticipation of this record-breaking blast, Alex Popov and Patrick Hayashi bought tickets for the arcade section of the ballpark and brought their ball gloves. Barry Bonds came to bat in the first inning. With nobody on base and a full count, Bonds swung at a slow knuckleball. He connected. The ball sailed over the right-field fence and into the arcade. Now the facts are disputed. Popov attempted to catch the ball and either did or did not, but he was pummeled by the crowd. The ball came loose and ended up in the sole possession of Hayashi, a nonaggressor. There was video of the event and lots of witnesses but how Popov lost the ball was not clear from the evidence. Who has the property right to the ball? Major League Baseball? The San Francisco Giants? Barry Bonds? Alex Popov? Patrick Hayashi? Your humble baseball-loving author?

Mr. Popov filed suit against Hayashi claiming Hayashi wrongfully took possession of the ball (conversion) from Popov. Prior to the time the ball was hit, it was possessed and owned by Major League Baseball. At the time it was hit it became intentionally abandoned property. The first person who came in possession of the ball became its new owner. The judge proffered that the case hinged on the definition and facts regarding possession. "Mr. Hayashi's claim is compromised by Mr. Popov's pre-possessory interest. Mr. Popov cannot demonstrate full control. Their legal claims are of equal quality and they are equally entitled to the ball." Rather than split the ball (rendering it valueless), the judge ordered it sold with the "proceeds divided equally between the parties." The ball ultimately sold for $450,000, netting less than half of the ball's estimated $1 million value even before the serious allegations of steroid use by Bonds. The attorney's bill for Mr. Popov was $473,530.32, over twice his $225,000 share.

INTELLECTUAL PROPERTY

Up to this point we have focused on tangible personal property, especially motor vehicles. Now we examine a special form of personal property that is intangible: intellectual property. As explained earlier, intellectual property consists of the rights related to ideas, data, and expression that individuals can possess. These rights usually take the form of restricting what nonpossessors can do to replicate or sometimes use the ideas, data or expressions that are protected. We will examine four distinct types of intellectual property: patents, copyrights, trademarks, and trade secrets.

Patents

patent
An exclusive privilege which allows the holder to manufacture, use, or sell a product for a fixed, non-renewable period of 20 years.

A **patent** is a form of a form of intellectual property consisting of a unique idea, design, or invention. Like most intellectual property, the valuable rights are usually thought of to be those that allow you to prevent others from using the property. Here, that means preventing others from using your idea or design. This allows you, the holder of the patent, to completely control how the patent is used. In other words, you have a form of a monopoly over your invention. Patents only exist for a certain amount of time. This is to push the holder of a patent to take advantage of it before it is gone and goes into the public domain. Sometimes, the original design undergoes changes to improve it resulting in new patents.

LEGAL FOCUS—PROBLEM

Proctor & Gamble obtained what might have been one of its most valuable patents for an improvement on the then-standard cloth diaper. The first patent was granted in 1967 and a continuous stream of improvements to the original design allowed the company to continue to get new patents throughout the 1970s and 1980s. Since the term of its patents ran seventeen years, the first patent expired in 1983. But patents received on improved designs in the 1980s reached into the new century. Was it correct for Proctor & Gamble to be able to enjoy more than forty years of monopoly over its diaper inventions?

utility patent
Issued for the invention of a new and useful process, machine, manufacture, or composition of matter.

Yes, it was correct, because each new patent was only granted if it added a new, unique, and valuable characteristic to the Pampers diaper. The original patent expired in 1983, and at that time, competitors then could replicate that idea. The story of Pampers is not unique. In almost every industry, when a new product is introduced, everyone, including the holder of the patent, begins trying to invent and patent something that is a uniquely different improvement to the original patent. In fact, Huggies, a competitor to Pampers reached the market in the mid-1970s.

design patent
Issued for the visual ornamental characteristics embodied in, or applied to, an article of manufacture.

Types of Patents

there are three types of patents: utility, design, and plant. A **utility patent** is granted for a new and useful process, machine, article of manufacture, or composition of matter. As explained, a utility patent can be granted for any new and useful improvement of an earlier utility patent. A **design patent** can be granted to anyone who invents a new, original, and ornamental design for an article of manufacture. A **plant patent** may be granted to anyone who invents or discovers and asexually reproduces any distinct and new variety of plant. Of these three types, the most common type of patent that usually is also the most talked and written about is the utility patent. The utility patent is usually at the heart of all innovation and improvement.

plant patent
Issued for a distinct and new variety of plant invented or discovered and asexually reproduced.

Duration of Patents

Since 1995, patents have had a duration of twenty years as measured from the earliest filing date. This is derived from the 1994 Uruguay Round Agreements Act (1995), to which most countries of the world have ascribed. Before 1995, the term in the United States was seventeen years from the date of patent approval. As described previously, few patents are actively produced or used for their full life. Instead, improvement patents and gradual, infringing competition cause patent holders to aggressively pursue a patent the moment it is applied for and simultaneously to begin developing and obtaining an improvement patent.

Obtaining a Patent

The U.S. Patent and Trademark Office (USPTO) accepts and approves patent applications. You can visit http://www.uspto.gov to learn more about the patent process. Many people, and nearly all companies, conclude that having an attorney who specializes in patents is a valuable and sometimes essential part of obtaining a patent. In the United States, a special bar association exists for attorneys who pursue patents called the patent bar. To become a member of the patent bar, attorneys must have a science or engineering or technical background or education, have experience with patents as lawyers, and pass a special examination. Patent attorneys help applicants navigate the complex rules and requirements of patent eligibility.

Copyrights

An old saying goes that "you patent ideas but you copyright expression," and this is not far off from reality. Where patents apply to ideas that can take tangible form, copyrights ascribe to human expression, whether that expression be word, visual, or sound in nature. You can copyright literary, musical, visual, and artistic expression. Interestingly, software, because it consists of words (or at least characters), found primary protection in copyright as a strange form of a literary work. As with patents, the primary "property" right that a copyright holder gains is the right to prevent others from duplicating, or copying, the expression.

LEGAL FOCUS—PROBLEM

Delisa Durn took copious notes throughout her American law class. At the end of the course, she and her friends used these notes to study for the final exam. One of her friends commented "You know, Delisa, you should sell copies of your notes for students next semester. You could make a lot of money." Delisa, being the good student that she was, recognized this opportunity and promptly printed up sets of the notes and advertised them on the student web pages for sale. As the next semester started, she sold a few copies, but then noticed more copies in students' hands than she had sold. Furious, she realized that one student, Carl Copycat, bought one from her and promptly duplicated it for his entire class. Could Carl do that? Can Delisa stop him? Can she get compensation for her lost profits or his "ill-gotten" gains?

Perhaps. Which remedies are available to Delisa will turn in part on what steps she took to give notice or register her work. She also might have a problem if she gave copies to her friends when they were studying without making it clear that she was asserting her copyright to the work. Ideally, Delisa would have put "Copyright, © Delisa Durn, 2012, All Rights Reserved" on the first page of all the copies she gave away or sold. She also might have taken the time to register her work with the Library of Congress. These actions would strengthen her ability to preserve and protect the copyright that she has or had on her work.

Copyright includes the following rights and protections:

- Reproduce the work
- Prepare derivative works
- Distribute copies to the public
- Perform the work publicly
- Display the work publicly

Thus, the holder of a copyright can stop others from doing any of the noted actions. The ability to stop others from such activities is the heart of the value of a copyright. But as Delisa may have learned, there are some actions you should take to maximize the value of your copyrighted material.

What Can be Copyrighted?

Although copyrights generally can be described as applying to expression, all copyrights must fall into one of several specific categories of expression to copyright, including the following:

- Literary works, including computer software
- Musical works, including any accompanying words
- Dramatic works, including any accompanying music
- Pantomimes and choreographic works
- Pictorial, graphic, and sculptural works
- Motion pictures and other audiovisual works
- Sound recordings
- Architectural works

Although this list can be viewed narrowly, it is interpreted broadly. Thus, computer software was allowed to fall within "literary works" even though it hardly is intended to be read, at least by humans. The author of an original expression should look to this list for places where his or her expression can fit.

How Do You Obtain Copyrights?

Unlike patents, copyrights technically accrue automatically, that is, you do not have to submit an application and get that application approved. Your rights and ability to defend against infringers, however, are improved significantly by taking some actions beyond your authorship. The Library of Congress is the primary government agency that manages data and rights related to copyrights.

Generally, the creator of an original expression is thus well advised to "publish" their work. In some situations, publishing then triggers a mandatory deposit of copies with the Library of Congress. By depositing the work, an author establishes very clearly exactly what was created and when. Authors are no longer required to provide notice of copyright to others. Providing notice does enhance potential damages and penalties against infringers, however, so many authors still choose to do so.

When Can You Reproduce Copyrighted Material?

The very essence of copyright is the right to prevent a "copy" from being made. Public policy, however, led to the development of a doctrine, called "Fair Use," which now is codified. Under fair use, one can make partial copies or perhaps a single copy, of copyrighted works.

fair use
A defense to claim of copyright infringement that allows the use of copyrighted material without owner's permission.

The doctrine of **fair use** allows limited reproduction of copyrighted material for certain uses, such as scholarship, research, or criticism. The doctrine generally is limited to uses that will not injure the economic value of the copyright. Thus, for example, one might be able to copy one chapter of a book for research, but be infringing if he or she copied the entire book. Teachers can duplicate copyrighted material to distribute to students under some circumstances but not others. You generally are allowed to make a copy of music or software for purposes of preserving it. Should you attempt to sell, even that backup copy, you probably would be violating the rights of the copyright holder. If you wish to duplicate material in a manner that might exceed the fair use doctrine, then you need to get permission from the copyright holder.

license
Permission to use copyrighted work granted by the holder of the copyright.

royalty
A share in the proceeds paid to a copyright holder.

The primary tool for allowing others to duplicate copyrighted material involves the granting of a license or permission to copy the product. An author of a novel, for instance, in essence, grants his or her publisher a **license** to reproduce the novel and sell it in exchange for a **royalty** on each sale. Although a license can allow repeated copying and sales, a single instance of the use of copyrighted material or perhaps multiple copies of part of a work usually are handled through a granting of permission from the holder of the copyright. In cases in which a potential duplication is in the gray area of the fair use doctrine, one is advised to seek and obtain permission for the duplication to ensure that the holder of the copyright is satisfied that the use is acceptable.

How Can You Protect Your Copyrights?

Although copyrights accrue automatically, the previous information has made it clear that some actions can increase the ability to protect against infringement. These actions include publishing your work, registering it with the Library of Congress and perhaps depositing copies, and proving notice of copyright on copies of the work. Beyond that, diligence and monitoring against infringement is necessary in the digital age. Digital duplication on the Internet can spread rapidly, making pursuit of legal remedies against the original infringer pointless. Stopping infringement at its nascent moment is more important than ever.

LEGAL FOCUS—EXAMPLE

Roman is author of a how-to book on setting up a home theater titled "Super Good Secrets of Home Theater." Soundy Books published the book and included a copyright statement on the information page inside the book. Roman is surfing the Internet and notices what appears to be his book, but with a slightly different name, for sale by a home theater equipment seller called "Better Home Theater 4U." He orders a copy and when it arrives, he realizes it is a duplication of his book almost word for word. Furious, he calls Soundy Books and informs them. Soundy Books promptly sends a letter to the president of Better Home Theater 4U. In the letter, Soundy instructs them to immediately stop selling the product. It also explains that Soundy expects a full accounting of all sales and will expect "satisfactory compensation" for "blatant copyright violation." Soundy knows that they have an easy case to win and that if Better Home Theatre 4U is smart, they will cooperate immediately and completely.

When infringement occurs, the normal first action traditionally has been a "cease and desist" letter. In recent times, however, nearly immediate legal action has paralleled the communication to the infringer. Perhaps even more important, when the infringement is posted on the Internet, reaching out to the enablers of the infringer, the website hosting entities, has become a standard action.

Trademarks

A **trademark** is a form of intellectual property consisting of unique sound, color, logo, or other symbol or other mark that distinguishes merchandise and services. A trademark is a brand name or the symbol associated with that brand name. A trademark or service mark includes any word, name, symbol, device, or any combination, used or intended to be used to identify and distinguish the goods and services of one seller or provider from those of others, and to indicate the source of the goods and services.

What Can Be Trademarked?

Distinctive symbols, phrases, sounds, scents, and even colors can be trademarked. To be distinctive, the mark must distinguish one product from another. Generic names and marks cannot be trademarked, however. Thus "cola" cannot be trademarked by itself because it generally is used to identify a soda with a particular color and flavor. But "Coca-Cola" is, of course, a trademark. Descriptive words also usually cannot be used if the description describes the product. Thus, "crisp" cannot be used by a lettuce supplier as a protected trademark, because crisp would be used to describe the lettuce. But "Blue Diamond" is an allowed trademark for almonds because those two descriptive words have no actual descriptive relation to almonds.

How Do You Obtain a Trademark?

In essence, you obtain a trademark by being the first to use it to identify your good or service. But there are steps you should take to most effectively establish your trademark.

1. **Identify your mark.** Choose a distinctive mark that qualifies as a trademark.
2. **Identify your goods or service.** List the services or goods that you wish the mark to identify.
3. **Search the database.** The USPTO provides a searchable database on its website for words and phrases. Searching for each combination of words, including similar words, is called a "knockout" search. Sounds, colors, and symbols are more challenging to knock out as searching for them requires more time to search similar industries. Internet access, however, has made doing knockout searches much more feasible. Doing a knockout search is essential. Very large companies have made the mistake of assuming a mark is available simply because no one has noticed it in use.
   Microsoft settled on the eve of trial, purchasing the mark from SyNet. In all likelihood, Microsoft realized that "winning" in court would simply ruin their ability to use the mark since it would result in a decision that the mark could not be protected. We may never know, but the argument Microsoft was making was reasonable. Microsoft never would have found itself in that situation had they completed an adequate knockout search.

LEGAL FOCUS—PROBLEM

Microsoft released its first Internet browser software, Internet Explorer, with significant investment in the new product. It was at the core of its newest focus: the Internet. Unfortunately, Microsoft failed to complete an adequate knockout search. A company called SyNet had actually trademarked the name a year earlier. Microsoft could not initially reach an agreement with SyNet and decided to sue SyNet claiming the name "Internet Explorer" could not be protected because it was "descriptive" not "distinctive." What was the result?

4. **File application.** You should begin using the mark as soon as you have completed your selection. Using the mark first is what establishes your rights against others as to the mark. You then can register the trademark with the USPTO by filing an application. Registration of a mark is not required, but it has several advantages. Registering the mark makes the mark effective nationwide and internationally as well. Registration also ensures that you have provided adequate notice to the public that the mark is protected. After five years of use following registration, your rights to the mark become nearly uncontestable because most challenges are prohibited after that. You also gain stronger damages claims.

How Are Trademarks Enforced?

You must protect your mark by watching for and stopping infringing uses. Failure to do this could result in uses being allowed that otherwise might be considered infringement. The ultimate failure to protect a mark can result in the mark becoming a "generic" mark. Xerox was a mark that was lost to its holder because it became synonymous with "copying." When you register a mark with the USPTO you can then use the ® symbol each time you use the mark. You should do so, because failure to use the ® symbol is one way to let your mark begin a path toward becoming generic.

Ultimately, when you identify an infringing use, you must take action to stop it. This usually begins with a "cease and desist" letter that allows the infringer an opportunity to stop use. If the infringer fails to stop, the next step is to sue them for infringement. To succeed in the suit you must show that the use is likely to cause consumers or purchasers to confuse your product with that of the infringer. If you succeed in court, you can obtain multiple damages and attorneys' fees and force the infringer to disgorge its profits.

Trade Secrets

trade secret
Confidential data or other information that has economic value because it is not generally known.

A final category of intellectual property consists of secret information. A **trade secret** is data or other information, such as a formula, that has economic value because it generally is not known or easily discoverable. To be considered a trade secret, efforts have to be made to maintain the secrecy of the information. Unlike the other types of intellectual property discussed thus far, there is almost no government role in approving, regulating, or protecting trade secrets. Instead, it is up to the holder of the trade secret to take the steps necessary to create and maintain the value in a trade secret. Trade secrets are recognized in various ways under state law. Similarly, most states give the holder of a trade secret the authority to use the court and law enforcement system to protect that right by stopping unauthorized use or disclosure and also to obtain compensatory damages for such use or disclosure. The Uniform Trade Secrets Act has been adopted in part by thirty-three states.

Criminal law can provide some protection. The U.S. attorney general has the authority to prosecute any person or company involved in trade secret misappropriation and can punish intentional stealing, copying, or receiving of trade secrets. Penalties for violations are severe: Individuals may be fined up to $500,000 and corporations up to $5 million. A violator also may be sent to prison for up to ten years. All property used and proceeds derived from the theft can be seized and sold by the government.

What Can Trade Secrets Protect?

Trade secrets can include formulas, recipes, special methods of doing business, inventions kept secret, ways to manufacture goods and even the algorithms imbedded in software. Generally, trade secrets can protect ideas that could give a business a competitive advantage, such as the following:

- Keep competitors from learning that a product or service is under development and from discovering its functional or technical attributes—for example, how a new software program works;
- Protect valuable business information, such as marketing plans, cost and price information, and customer lists—for example, a company's plans to launch a new product line;
- Protect "negative know-how"—that is, information you have learned during the course of research and development on what not to do or what does not work optimally—for example, research revealing that a new type of drug is ineffective; and
- Protect any other information that has some value and generally is not known by your competitors—for example, a list of customers ranked by the profitability of their business.

Protecting Trade Secrets

You gain a trade secret by keeping it secret. You protect your trade secret by doing the same thing: Keeping it secret. This means you must take actions to preserve the secrecy of the information.

LEGAL FOCUS—EXAMPLE

Coca-Cola keeps the formula for its famous soda locked in a bank vault that can be opened only by approval of the company's board of directors. Supposedly, only two employees ever know the formula at the same time. In 1919, a group of investors who had purchased the company arranged a loan. As collateral, they produced documentation of the formula that was placed in a bank vault in New York until the loan was repaid. Then the formula was moved to Atlanta and placed in a bank vault there. Today, the formula is in a specially built vault on display at the company's visitor center in Atlanta.

The Uniform Trade Secrets Act established numerous enforcement rights, such as court orders and injunctions. To win a trade secret infringement suit, the trade secret owner must show that the information provides a competitive advantage and really is kept secret. The trade secret owner also must show that the information was either improperly acquired or disclosed. But, if someone discovers the trade secret on their own and without violating any laws or agreements, then his or her use of the secret is allowed.

CASE

Jamison v. The Pantry, Inc.

301 S.C. 443, 392 S.E.2d 474 (South Carolina, 1990)

After attending a football game, Willis DeBruhl, a minor, drove to a convenience store and bought some beer. It is illegal in South Carolina for a minor to purchase alcohol. He apparently returned to the car and shared the beer with his buddy. Sometime later, DeBruhl was involved in a head-on collision with another vehicle, killing himself and the driver of the other vehicle and injuring passengers in that vehicle. An action was brought on behalf of the deceased driver and passengers against the convenience store. The trial court granted a directed verdict for the defendant on the grounds that the plaintiffs failed to prove that "any beer purchased at The Pantry was ever consumed prior to this accident [and] that any beer purchased from The Pantry was [a] proximate cause of the accident in question." The plaintiffs appealed.

Goolsby, Judge

These personal injury actions against The Pantry, Inc. arise out of an alleged unlawful sale of beer. The actions were consolidated for trial. The trial court directed a verdict in The Pantry's favor. The question on appeal concerns only the sufficiency of the evidence as to proximate cause. We reverse and remand.

The three complaints, among other things, allege that The Pantry sold beer to Willis Dean DeBruhl, a minor, that DeBruhl's consumption of the beer resulted in a head-on collision that injured Jamison and Kyle Ruff and fatally injured Opal Ruff, and that the sale of the beer by The Pantry was a proximate cause of the collision and of the injuries the collision brought about.

At trial, the trial judge granted The Pantry's motion for a directed verdict, finding simply that "as a matter of law there [is] insufficient evidence to submit the case to the jury." The grounds for The Pantry's motion were that Jamison and the Ruffs failed to prove that "any beer purchased at The Pantry was ever consumed prior to this accident [and] that any beer purchased from The Pantry was [a] proximate cause of the accident in question."

In determining the question of whether the trial judge properly granted The Pantry's motion for a directed verdict, we are required, as was the trial judge, to view the evidence and all reasonable inferences that can be drawn therefrom in the light most favorable to Jamison and the Ruffs and if there is even a "scintilla of evidence" tending to prove the allegations of the complaints, the motion should have been denied. Because a direction of a verdict is not favored, a case must be clear, certain, or indisputable to warrant a trial judge's granting of a motion seeking a directed verdict.

A review of the evidence and its reasonable inferences in the light most favorable to Jamison and the Ruffs follows.

On September 5, 1986, Mark Uggiano talked to DeBruhl, a nineteen-year-old, at a high school football game and arranged to meet him after the game at The Pantry. Thirty or forty minutes after leaving the game, Uggiano met DeBruhl and Richard Derodo in Dusty Bend at The Pantry, a convenience store. DeBruhl, who was not intoxicated at the time, bought a case of beer from The Pantry.*

*We infer from the following that DeBruhl was not intoxicated:

Q. (By Mr. Hardaway): Did you see Willis Dean DeBruhl on September the 5th, 1986?

A. (By Mr. Uggiano): Yes, sir.

Q. When did you first see him?

A. I saw him at the football game at Camden High.

Q. Did he appear to be drunk?

A. No, sir, he didn't.

Q. When you saw Willis Dean DeBruhl at The Pantry when he came there that night, describe what he looked like then.

A. Nothing out of the ordinary, same way.

Q. Was he drunk?

A. Not that I could tell.

And from the following:

Q. (By Mr. Pulliam): ... In your opinion, as an eyewitness, was he drunk or intoxicated when he went into [The] Pantry?

A. (By Mr. Uggiano): As far as I know, no.

The beer, which The Pantry was licensed to sell, was put into a paper bag and DeBruhl carried it to his car. DeBruhl got into the car and handed the beer to Uggiano who sat on the back seat. The beer DeBruhl purchased was the only beer in the car.**

**We infer from the following that the beer bought by DeBruhl from The Pantry was the only beer in the car:

Q. (By Mr. Hardaway): Was there any particular reason for ya'll to meet at this particular Pantry?

A. (By Mr. Uggiano): To buy beer so that we could head out to sorority night.

Q. How much beer did he buy?

A. A case.

Q. How much beer did Willis Dean DeBruhl buy that night?

A. I only saw a case.

Q. (By Mr. Mathews): Now, when Dean went into The Pantry and he came back out, did he give you something in the back seat?

A. He gave me the beer.

Q. Did you see any other beer in the car at that time?

A. No, sir. I didn't.

Q. (By Mr. Hardaway): When ... Willis Dean DeBruhl bought that beer and brought it back to the car, was there any other beer in the car?

A. Not that I could see.

Q. Were there any other coolers in the car?

A. Not that I know of.

At 10:45 P.M., a mile from The Pantry, DeBruhl's car collided head-on with another car. The collision killed both DeBruhl and the driver of the other car, Opal Ruff, and injured the passengers in her car, Jamison and Kyle Ruff. DeBruhl was the at-fault driver.

A highway patrolman found opened beer cans inside the car, along with unopened beer cans in a paper bag and inside an ice chest. DeBruhl's blood alcohol level was determined to be .135. This amount of alcohol is sufficient to bring a person under its influence to such an extent as to impair the person's faculties. (A person is under the influence of alcohol or drugs when the ingestion of alcohol or drugs results in the impairment of the person's faculties.)

We think the evidence just recited supports the inferences that DeBruhl purchased beer at The Pantry no later than about 9:58 P.M., or approximately 47 minutes before the accident at 10:45 P.M., that the beer sold DeBruhl by The Pantry was the only beer in the car, that DeBruhl consumed from the opened cans found in his car some of the beer purchased from The Pantry, and that his consumption of the beer caused him to be under the influence of alcohol and impaired his driving ability.***

***We determined the time this way: the game ended at approximately 9:30 P.M.; a quarter of high school football is 12 minutes; Uggiano left the game either at the end of the third quarter or at the start of the fourth; assuming it actually took only 12 minutes to play the 12-minute quarter, which is highly unlikely, Uggiano left the game at approximately 9:18 P.M.; and he met DeBruhl at The Pantry 30 or 40 minutes later, or at approximately 9:48 or 9:58 P.M. Had it taken longer than 12 minutes to play the fourth quarter, then Uggiano, obviously, would have left the game earlier than approximately 9:18 P.M. and would have met DeBruhl earlier than approximately 9:48 or 9:58 P.M. Viewing the evidence as suggesting that Uggiano left the game at approximately 9:18 P.M. and not earlier favors The Pantry and not Jamison and the Ruffs.

We also think the evidence just recited supports the inference that The Pantry's sale of beer to DeBruhl, a minor, in violation of Sections 61-9-40 and 61-9-410 of the South Carolina Code of Laws* was a proximate cause of the

*Section 61-9-40 of the South Carolina Code of Laws (1976) (Rev.1990) provides in part as follows:

*(A) It is unlawful for any person to sell beer ... to a person under twenty years of age and effective September 14, 1986, under twenty-one years of age. Any person making such unlawful sale must be, upon conviction, fined not less than one hundred dollars nor more than two hundred dollars or imprisoned not less than thirty days nor more than sixty days, or both, in the discretion of the court....

*Section 61-9-410 provides in part as follows:

*No holder of a permit authorizing the sale of beer ... or any servant, agent, or employee of the permittee shall knowingly do any of the following acts upon the licensed premises covered by the holder's permit:

*(1) sell beer or wine to a person under twenty years of age and effective September 14, 1986, under twenty-one years of age; ...

*A violation of ... the foregoing provision[ ] is a ground for the revocation or suspension of the holder's permit.

injuries suffered by Jamison and the Ruffs. It was reasonably foreseeable that a nineteen-year-old who was sold a case of beer by a convenience store in violation of statutes would consume a portion of the beer, would become intoxicated, would drive an automobile, would collide with another vehicle, and would injure or kill someone.

A jury issue existed, therefore, regarding whether The Pantry's sale of the beer to DeBruhl in violation of Sections 61-9-40 and 61-9-410 was a proximate cause of the injuries sustained by Jamison and the Ruffs. REVERSED AND REMANDED SANDERS, C. J., and SHAW, J., concur.

For Critical Analysis

1. Willis DeBruhl was the negligent driver. Why is The Pantry the defendant?
2. The case was reversed and remanded in favor of the plaintiffs—is the case over?
3. Assuming that DeBruhl has automobile insurance, what type of coverage applies to this type of claim? If his policy limits are less than damages proved, would his estate be personally liable? His parents?
4. Assume that when DeBruhl purchased the beer from The Pantry he used a fake identification that showed he was of legal age. Would it make any difference as to the case against The Pantry?

CHAPTER QUESTIONS AND PROBLEMS

1. Scott Noojin had not quite mastered the stick shift in his new four-wheel-drive truck. While parking in a shopping center lot, he shifted into forward when he wanted reverse. With a sickening crunch, his truck rammed into the side of a new limousine, causing \$5,000 in damages. His own vehicle needed \$2,000 in repairs. Scott purchased his car with a loan from Schools Credit Union. Since he had repaid only 25 percent of the loan, Schools Credit Union was listed as the legal owner of the truck. Who is liable for the damages to the limousine?
2. Darryl Galloway is fourteen years old, but he has been driving autos, trucks, and all-terrain vehicles on his family's 3,000-acre cattle ranch for more than five years without a driver's license. Sometimes he drives on a neighbor's land and sometimes on nearby U.S. Forest Service land. Is he or are his parents guilty of violating the state's vehicle code?
3. A driver was seated behind the steering wheel of her car, which was stopped in the fast lane of the highway. The car started drifting backward, its transmission in neutral, while the driver was trying to start the car. Officers tried without success to find out what she was doing. A field sobriety test showed probable cause for a breath test, which she failed with a 0.13 reading. What criminal offenses might the driver face, if any? [*People v. Garcia,* 214 Cal.App.3d. Supp.1, 262 Cal. Rptr. 915 (Calif., 1989).]
4. As Alyse Brooks was easing from her tight parking space in the three-story "Park Yourself" garage, she creased the side of the neighboring vehicle, a 1975 Pinto, with her front bumper. She stopped, looked, and left, thinking it was an old car not even worth spending the \$100 it would take for repairs. Has Brooks violated any law?
5. David Kelynack was the proud purchaser of a new Yamaha motorcycle from Anderson Vehicle Sales with a six-month limited warranty. About two and a half months and 3,115 miles after the purchase, a tapping noise in the engine caused Kelynack to bring the cycle in for repairs. The seller agreed that the repairs were under warranty, but through misdiagnosis, a wait for parts, and another wait for additional parts, the cycle was in the shop for two months. At that time, Kelynack informed Anderson Vehicle Sales that the limited warranty was inadequate and he was exercising his right to revoke under the UCC. Three and a half months after repairs began, the cycle was as good as new. Could Kelynack revoke his acceptance and demand his purchase price returned? [*Kelynack v. Yamaha Motor Corporation,* 152 Mich. App. 505, 394 N.W.2d 17 (Mich., 1986).]
6. Following an extra-inning baseball game, thousands of fans were pouring onto the local highways, where visibility was poor due to fog. On the main highway, thirty-seven vehicles smashed into one another in a massive chain collision. If it is established that Douglas Burham, driver of the second car in line, was at fault because he rear-ended the first car, is he liable for damages to all the other damaged vehicles?
7. Lisa Dunning borrowed John Brady's car with his permission. Due to carelessness in making a U-turn, Dunning was involved in a collision. The driver of the other vehicle was faultless and neither his person

nor his heavy-duty truck suffered damage. Brady's car needed $1,500 worth of bodywork. Both Dunning and Brady have collision insurance coverage, each providing for a $250 deductible. Which policy, if either, will pay for Brady's loss?

8. Joann Earley liked Ford Grenadas so well that she purchased a used one three years newer than her previous Grenada. Within three days, the car needed valve work, relocation of the radiator, and various other repairs. O'Neal Ford agreed to make these repairs under a limited guarantee that appeared in the contract of sale. Earley sent O'Neal Ford a letter revoking acceptance under rights provided by the UCC and requested a return of her payments. Can a buyer revoke acceptance of a used car under the UCC? Does the fact that she was given a limited warranty prohibit her claim of revocation? [*O'Neal Ford, Inc. v. Earley*, 13 Ark. App. 189, 681 S.W.2d 414 (Ark., 1985).]
9. D. J. Parthworthy owned the Old Eagle Tavern, located with a beautiful view overlooking Deadman Canyon. One Saturday night, the bartender, Tran Ong, was serving Craig Hamada "Long Island Iced Teas" (an especially potent alcoholic drink) from 8:00 P.M. UNTIL 2:00 A.M. Ong knew that Hamada would have to drive some fifteen miles to get home. Hamada left for home at 2:00 A.M., after "one more for the road," and had gone only two miles before crashing into an oncoming car driven by Toni Shelia. Shelia was killed; the relaxed Hamada was uninjured. Shelia's mother brought a wrongful death action against Craig Hamada, Tran Ong, and the Old Eagle Tavern. Discuss.
10. You intend to drive your automobile into a foreign country for a four-month vacation. What legal issues regarding the car's use should you consider prior to your trip?
11. Leases defined as consumer leases often are limited to a $25,000 maximum for the special protections to occur. Are dollar limitations for such qualification good public policy? Is that amount sufficient?
12. Does your state have a point system for driver license suspension or revocation? Check online to see.

CHAPTER 11

Renters and Landlords

The Landlord is a gentleman who does not earn his wealth. He has a host of agents and clerks that receive for him. He does not even take the trouble to spend his wealth. He has a host of people around him to do the actual spending. He never sees it until he comes to enjoy it. His sole function, his chief pride, is the stately consumption of wealth produced by others.

David Lloyd George, British Prime Minister, 1863–1945

LEARNING OBJECTIVES

After reading and studying this chapter, you should be able to:

- Compare the advantages and disadvantages of renting your dwelling.
- Identify the legal terms used in real estate leases.
- Identify the legal rights and duties of landlords and tenants.
- Describe the legal requirements and types of real estate leases.
- Discuss major issues in leases such as deposit or security use and return, eviction, habitability, and quiet enjoyment.
- Discuss legal theories for landlord liability for injuries of the tenant on the premises.
- Distinguish and explain subletting and assignment of apartment leases.
- Use the guidelines for tenants to make good choices and create a positive landlord–tenant relationship.

Many of you probably rent an apartment now. Some of you may be preparing to enter into a rental agreement. You might be a renter now, but unsure if you completely understand your rights and duties as a tenant. You might also be wondering if renting is a great idea or whether you should buy your first home soon. Questions related to renting your home, whether it be a house, apartment, condominium, or townhouse, are common. As an example, does a landlord (the owner or representative of the owner) have to change the locks when a new tenant moves in?

LEGAL FOCUS—PROBLEM

Jamie O'Quinn moved into an apartment near the university she was attending. O'Quinn did not know, did not ask, and was not informed that the prior resident in her unit had been evicted for failure to pay rent following his arrest on charges of forcible rape. She also did not know that the apartment door lock had not been changed. Does the law require landlords to provide new door locks when apartments are rented to new tenants?

No, the law does not require the landlord to provide new locks. But if O'Quinn had asked, the landlord would have been placed in the precarious position of either lying or telling the truth and re-keying the apartment. Most likely, the landlord would tell the truth, and O'Quinn would discover useful information. If the landlord opted to lie, and if O'Quinn became the victim of a crime following an entry into her apartment, the landlord then would be liable for substantial compensatory and punitive damages.

tenant
A party to a lease who pays rent to the landlord in exchange for the possession and use of real property (e.g., a person who rents an apartment).

Like others around the world, millions of Americans live in dwellings they do not own. Called **tenants**, these people rent their living quarters, mostly in cities and suburban areas. As cities in the United States grew, so too did the problems of crime, unhealthy living conditions, and victimization of renters. Many renters are and were poor and not as able to defend their interests.

New York was the first city to appoint a Tenement Commission to solve the problems of poor living conditions for renters. Many cities today have commissions responsible for administering laws, such as rent controls, that are designed to protect renters. The plight of the poor who rent was, and some believe still is, unfortunate. But as you will learn, renters now are protected by numerous legal rights. Rent gouging in the early twentieth century set the tone for future conflicts between landlords and their tenants. That issue continues into the twenty-first century but is expressed as a landlord's right to a fair return on the investment. Regardless of how the issue is expressed, a solution that is satisfactory to both sides continues to elude society.

Why do people rent their living accommodations? Lack of funds to buy is usually the primary reason, although personal preference influences many. In some desirable areas, home prices have escalated to the extent that fully employed families cannot afford to live close to downtown employment centers. These families therefore either must choose to rent in unglamorous, high-density apartment buildings or commute to suburban areas where home prices are lower. As a result, many choose to buy and commute rather than to rent and walk or take public transportation.

Traditionally, it has been understood that the financial benefits of renting are poor. The rent that tenants pay edges upward, reflecting continuing inflation (or, more precisely, the rising costs of new construction and increasing expenses of operation and maintenance). As the demand for apartments increases, new construction must occur or vacancies become impossible to find; rents respond accordingly by increasing further.

The cost of homeownership also is high, largely because of population increases and demographic shifts that occur as more people become parents and new buyers in the housing marketplace. Many young people in metropolitan areas who desire to own their homes cannot qualify as purchasers because of the prices and down payments required. These reluctant renters contribute to overall low vacancy rates, and thus to the economic pressure for higher rents. One result of demand for homeownership in urban locations has been the conversion of apartment units into condominiums, thereby further reducing the number of apartments available for rent. See Exhibit 11.1 for a chart comparing advantages and disadvantages of renting versus buying.

When housing shortages intensify, causing rents to escalate, a clamor for government remedial action is heard. Some local governments, especially in crowded metropolitan areas and university towns, respond with rent controls; others restrict condominium conversions. Government-subsidized apartment-building programs for poor families are demanded in populous areas. In response, some frightened communities curtail the rental housing supply by enacting growth-limitation laws, out of fear that any new growth will disturb existing lifestyles and may reduce property values in the city's core or vicinity. Subsidizing high-density housing also requires expanding public services (e.g., police and fire protection and community services), which are financed, at least in part, by higher taxes. So the desire to avoid higher taxes fuels the resistance to uncontrolled growth, even though new development contributes to the revenues of local governments in many ways (e.g., property tax and sales tax revenues).

Renters traditionally lament that each month they are "throwing their money away" while homeowners are "buying equity." Renters may take some solace in our observation that the efficacy of this classic theory is in doubt. The recent downturn in home values clearly shows that owning is not always better than renting.

EXHIBIT 11.1 Advantages and Disadvantages of Renting

	Advantages	Disadvantages
Rent	Little or no responsibility for maintenance	No tax benefits
	Easier to move	No building of equity
		No control over rent increases
		Possibility of eviction

Source: Adapted from a comparison chart provided by Ginnie Mae (http://www.ginniemae.gov), a wholly owned corporation within the Department of Housing and Urban Development (HUD).

The overall inventory of available housing and the laws that guarantee at least minimum health and safety standards to renters have improved indescribably since the early 1900s. Suburban apartment buildings are characterized by many amenities, such as recreational and laundry facilities. A great deal of substandard housing still exists, however, usually within our large cities, much of which is rented to the elderly and the poor.

From the foregoing discussion, it should be clear that laws affecting housing necessarily reflect some kind of social policy. Almost everyone agrees that the housing industry, both rental and homeowner, must be regulated by law.

landlord
The owner of residential property who leases it to a tenant, or renter, in exchange for rent.

Unfortunately, the relationship between tenants and owners of rental properties, legally called **landlords**, often is characterized by misunderstanding, controversy, and even ill will. Many of the legal problems experienced by these parties may be anticipated simply from the nature of the relationship. Landlords desire to control rent and maintenance standards and to choose selectively from among tenant applicants who, in turn, rely on civil rights and consumer laws for protection against discrimination. Tenants also benefit from the forces of competition when vacancy factors are high and landlords accordingly are anxious to rent.

Once in occupancy, tenants do not have any compelling economic incentive to maintain the rented premises. They have no proprietary interest in the property; all monetary benefit goes to the landlords. And landlords have an incentive to maintain their rental premises only if the expenditures are covered by rental receipts. Rising maintenance costs, taxes, and utility charges lead to rent increases, which can be onerous for the poor and create hostility even in tenants who are well able to pay. No tenant appreciates a rent increase. Moreover, tenants often are considered, by some, to be in a lower social position because they rent rather than own. This erosion of self-esteem is heightened by the insecurity caused by the landlords' continuing ability to remove tenants under certain circumstances.

Sometimes, the economic realities of housing favor landlords; some landlords lack common decency and take advantage of tenants who are unlikely to avail themselves of legal protections.

LEGAL FOCUS—EXAMPLE

Moving day came, but Maria Taylor never received the key to her newly rented apartment. The landlord told her to go in through the window. So Maria crawled through a side window, into a place filled with piles of trash, wires jutting from electrical sockets, and mold in the refrigerator. Upstairs, the electricity did work at all. But Maria felt she had no choice. She had paid the first month's rent and deposit for the apartment two months earlier from her wages as a temporary worker. Maria had been staying in a motel with her two teenage daughters. "I'd run out of money and had no place to go," she said, "so I moved into this filthy, nasty apartment."

lease
A contract, usually written, by which the relationship of landlord and tenant is created and a property interest is created.

The law governing the landlord–tenant relationship evolved from concepts, now archaic, that related to an agrarian, feudal society in England. Those concepts are largely irrelevant to the relationship as it is, or as reformers think it should be, in our urbanized, egalitarian democracy. For example, in the law, a **lease** of a dwelling historically was considered primarily a conveyance of a property interest, not a traditional contract with reciprocal rights and duties. Accordingly, the landlord owed no continuing duty of maintenance because the tenant had the right of exclusive possession of the "leasehold" or "property." Thus, repairs had to be made by the tenant if they were to be made at all. The rule of *caveat emptor* (Latin: "let the buyer beware") clearly applied to tenants then.

In modern times, though, legislatures and courts increasingly approach the landlord–tenant relationship in a more enlightened manner. For example, most states now consider a lease to be primarily a contract with reciprocal rights and duties. Therefore, a landlord now may be required by law to repair and maintain the rented premises. In most states, legislatures have adopted comprehensive statutory schemes that have replaced or modified the historic common law rules. The following laws now in effect in many states exemplify significant departures from the common law:

- The landlord must maintain the premises in *habitable* (reasonably livable) conditions, unless the tenant agrees otherwise. The tenant's agreement cannot be coerced.
- If the landlord fails to maintain the premises, the tenant, under specified conditions, may do so—spending (typically) up to one month's rent, which then may be deducted from the next installment of rent due.
- The landlord cannot evict a tenant in retaliation for exercising any tenant right; if the attempt is made, the landlord may be held liable for punitive damages up to a specified cap.

security deposit
A lump sum of cash paid by a tenant to his or her new landlord as security that the tenant will pay rent as agreed and will not damage the rented premises.

Landlords must refund **security deposits** promptly (often within two weeks of vacancy). The deposits may be retained by the landlord only to repair or clean the premises, and then only by following procedures typically set forth by statute. Statutory damages may be imposed for a failure to comply with these laws. Nonrefundable security deposits are not legal in modern law.

Charges by the landlord for cleaning or damage repair, if withheld from security deposits, must be itemized and explained. The landlord typically has the burden of proving, in court, the reasonableness of each levy contested by the former tenant.

Landlords owe their tenants and perhaps their guests a continuing duty of safety under certain circumstances.

LEGAL FOCUS—PROBLEM

Richard Cory, in Unit 5 of Shady Tree Apartments, had plugged a portable space heater, television, and hot plate for coffee into a long extension cord that was designed for low amperage use, such as a radio. It was plugged into the bedroom socket. Hours after Cory fell asleep with all three appliances turned on, the electric socket overheated and started a fire. Extensive damage occurred before the fire was extinguished, partly because the nearby fire extinguisher in the hallway was not operative. What liabilities have arisen?

Tenants, as well as landlords, are obligated by law to use reasonable care. In this example, Cory's negligence was primarily responsible for the fire damage. He is lucky that other tenants were not injured or even killed. The landlord, however, must share liability to the extent the damages are attributable to negligently maintaining the fire extinguisher.

Unfortunately, rental property reform has moved slowly, which has led to various disruptive developments: organizations of militant tenant groups, legislatively imposed rent controls, and increasing reluctance of investors and lenders to become involved in the purchase or operation of rental properties in certain geographic areas, thus aggravating the shortage of needed housing (especially for low- and moderate-income tenants). Another trend has been the willingness of public interest attorneys to misuse procedural laws to further exacerbate the landlord–tenant relationship. Even with reform, the amounts of money in dispute are relatively small, and many tenants simply move away without claiming or enforcing their rights.

Many apartments are constructed especially for low-income renters. These apartments are subsidized under programs authorized by the U.S. Housing Act. Administered by the Department of Housing and Urban Development (HUD), these programs seek to improve landlord–tenant relations in many ways—for example, by eliminating onerous clauses from its leases and rental agreements. For example, *distraint clauses* (which authorize the landlord to seize the tenant's property for unpaid rent) and *exculpatory clauses* (which immunize the landlord from responsibility for all injuries or losses caused by negligence), discussed later, have been eliminated from standard HUD leases. Even so, tenants of public housing projects still must rely on state law to protect other basic legal rights as renters.

Clearly, there are opposing public policy issues—for example, housing for everyone in our nation and respect for property rights of owners of rental properties. Legislatures and enlightened courts will no doubt continue the movement toward uniformity in landlord–tenant laws of the various states. Meanwhile, prospective tenants need to bargain carefully and effectively with landlords to minimize the risk of possible future costly conflict. State laws protect you primarily after you become a tenant. It is the responsibility of prospective tenants to fend for themselves in negotiating rental terms and in obtaining the often-specific and detailed protections that are provided by state statutes. Without any doubt, an "ounce of prevention" in making rental commitments is worth a "pound of cure" for both landlords and their renters.

THE CONFLICTING PERSPECTIVES OF RENTERS AND LANDLORDS

After all, the three major sources of apartments are death, divorce, and transfer.

Cornelius Gallagher, New York City real estate agent

The landlord and tenant are involved in a business relationship. One must accept this fact in order to understand landlord–tenant law. The landlord's primary concern is that total rent received be sufficient to cover all cash outlays, including periodic major expenditures to replace carpets and appliances, to repair roofs, and to repaint building interiors and exteriors. As cash outlays rise with inflation, pressure grows to raise rents sufficiently to cover these outlays. The renters of modern projects often enjoy rising incomes and are able to pay higher rents, with the result that the owners' project continues to appreciate in value. (Note this declaration pertains primarily to multifamily projects renting to more affluent segments of society.)

Millions of other dwelling units are rented by low-income persons who cannot afford any increases in their rent, which already represents a formidable portion of their total income. Some multifamily dwellings languish in disrepair and gradually become uninhabitable. Mainstream thinking is that laws designed to force landlords to spend money for adequate maintenance and repair actually would hurt low-income tenants, who could not afford to pay necessary resulting increases in rent. They would be forced to move, possibly onto the streets, joining the ranks of the homeless. This conundrum prompted the production of huge housing projects for low-income renters under government subsidies.

Typically, the owner, especially of a large apartment complex, hires an on-site manager to handle the day-to-day business of the apartment, collecting rent, paying bills, maintaining the building, or employing others to perform some, or all, of these tasks. The on-site manager, or *resident manager*, is the person with whom the residents must deal, at least initially, in solving whatever problems arise. Unfortunately, some resident managers try to do as little work as possible in exchange for the customary rent-free apartment and small salary. Thus, tenant complaints may fall upon "deaf ears" where the owner-landlord is a passive investor, secure in anonymity and absence from the premises.

Owners of larger or many complexes frequently hire property management firms that specialize in managing apartments. These organizations supervise the resident manager, the collection of rents and payment of bills, and maintenance and repairs.

They often charge a percentage of the gross rent collected for their services, which tend to be more systematic and efficient than those found in owner-supervised projects.

The manager, whether an individual or a professional organization, is the owner's representative, and agency law governs the relationship. It extends to all activities connected with the conduct of the rental business, including the receipt of notices and complaints. It therefore is a wise policy for tenants to make complaints in writing to the resident manager, retaining a copy for themselves as well.

The nature of the rental business obviously places the landlord and tenant in conflicting financial positions. On the one hand, as owner of the property, the landlord is in the superior position, having both business experience and the availability of professional help from attorneys and accountants. On the other hand, government regulation, modernization of applicable state laws, and enlightenment of the renting public have done much to equalize the strength of the parties. But to bargain effectively over the terms of a lease, a tenant should understand what terms are negotiable and what potential problems can be solved in advance. Unfortunately, the bargaining power often is so lopsided in favor of the landlord that the tenant has little choice but to "sign on the dotted line" or "keep on looking." This is so because most consumer protection laws become operative only after one becomes a tenant—the negotiating process is left to the prospect and landlord. Often, the landlord presents a form lease full of disclaimers and frequently printed in difficult-to-understand legalese: a classic *adhesion contract* (discussed in Chapter 8). Many state laws protect tenants from unfair provisions within the leases they sign, on the basis of public policy. State laws are found in statutes and in the common law decisions of courts.

LEGAL FOCUS—PROBLEM

Kristin Benet moved into the Berkshire Arms apartment complex during registration week at the University of Washington. Vacancies at rental rates that Benet could afford were scarce, and she was especially pleased to be able to walk to school because she did not own a car. Harry Hammer, the owner and manager, began "hitting" on Benet the day she moved in. At first, Hammer made remarks about her "fine body" and what a "sensational lover" he was, and how "she could have the time of her life with him." Week after week, the harassment continued, becoming more graphic in its innuendos and more threatening to Benet. Fearing the need to abandon her coveted apartment, Benet visited the campus legal adviser, Sherlock, and asked what she could do, if anything. Sherlock advised her that apartments were not businesses and tenants are not employees, therefore the sexual harassment laws did not apply to protect her. Until she was "assaulted" or "battered" by Hammer, there was nothing she could do. Was Sherlock right?

Sexual harassment against persons in their homes may be more oppressive than at their workplaces, but it is far less protected under law. Being forced to abandon a desirable apartment or home is a considerable loss. But what statutory laws protect Benet from

Hammer's obnoxious behavior? Federal laws apply to larger employers whose business affects interstate commerce. State employment laws protect *employees* of local (intrastate) businesses, and many extend specified protections to tenants. Under the common law, if the harassment became very obnoxious and offensive, Benet could bring an action for the tort of intentional infliction of mental distress and seek punitive damages as well as compensation for her anguish.

LEGAL FOCUS—PROBLEM

Sidney Chaudhry owns the Laguna Apartments, an exclusive oceanfront complex. Appealing to upper-class retirees, Chaudhry charges high rents and restricts the behavior of his tenants with clauses in the lease agreements and in exhaustive written "rules." These rules are intended to assure privacy, to maintain the quiet and peaceful coexistence of the tenants, and to preserve the aesthetics of the structures. One of the restrictions prohibits the installation of any kind of antenna or satellite dish on the balconies or in the patios of apartments. Chaudhry also is the principal shareholder of the local cable television corporation that services his apartments. Stanley Craig installed a satellite dish in his Laguna Apartments patio to assist him in his work. Chaudhry, after repeatedly demanding removal of the dish, instigated eviction proceedings. Can Chaudhry evict Craig?

lessor
A party to a lease who receives rent from a tenant in exchange for the possession and use of real property by the tenant. The lessor more commonly is called the *landlord*.

No, he cannot evict Craig. Despite Craig's agreement not to install any antennae, his behavior is protected by rules of the Federal Communications Commission (FCC). The FCC, a federal administrative agency, bans the blanket prohibition of viewers to use competing technologies. Reasonable rules of how such a satellite dish may be used would be appropriate. Under the doctrine of supremacy, the rules of the FCC supersede all contrary state laws or private contracts, such as Chaudhry's lease.

WHAT KINDS OF LEASES ARE AVAILABLE?

lessee
A party to a lease who pays rent to the landlord in exchange for the possession and use of real property, such as a person who rents an apartment. The lessee more commonly is called the tenant.

rent
The tenant's payment to the landlord for the tenant's use of the landlord's real property.

A lease transfers possession of a dwelling or apartment unit from the owner (called **lessor** or landlord) to the renter (called **lessee**) in exchange for **rent**. With a lease, the landlord transfers to the tenant the exclusive right to use and possess a designated space (apartment unit) for a period of time in exchange for a promise to pay rent periodically. A lease usually is, and always ought to be, in written form. Leases for more than one year (or three years, in some states) must be in writing and signed by the obligated party to be enforceable under state statutes of frauds. Ideally, both parties should sign. No law is violated, however, if a landlord and tenant choose to abide by an oral lease, even though it may be unenforceable if taken to court. If there is no complaint, there is no consequence. A lease contains the mutual promises of the parties. Because a lease involves both the transfer of a property interest (possession) and reciprocal agreements, it is both a conveyance of a property interest and a contract.

A resident's occupancy (or tenancy) commonly is called a lease if it continues for a fixed period of time (e.g., "I have a one-year lease"). On the other hand, if the tenancy is agreed to last indefinitely, usually renewing automatically from month to month, it

rental agreement
A contract, usually written, between a landlord and tenant. Technically, it is a lease.

commonly is called simply a **rental agreement** (e.g., "I have a month-to-month rental agreement"). Technically, both tenancies are created by a lease and are called a *tenancy for years* and a *periodic tenancy*, respectively. Both types are discussed later in this chapter.

Legal Requirements of a Lease

A lease document must (1) express the intention to establish the landlord–tenant relationship; (2) state that exclusive possession transfers to the tenant at the beginning of the lease term; (3) provide for the landlord to retake possession of the property upon termination of the lease; (4) describe the leased premises, usually with its street address and unit number; and (5) provide for the length of the lease (its term), the amount of rent, and payment dates. Most lease documents are supplied by landlords who obtain them from trade associations or from purveyors of business forms. In addition to the minimum legal requirements of a lease, as noted previously, most lease forms contain many difficult-to-understand clauses regarding legal remedies for the landlord. Prospective tenants are well advised to read lease forms completely and to insist on clarification of any words and phrases they do not understand. But realistically, most prospective tenants will gloss over most of this "fine print" and trust that they are protected adequately by law. At the end of this chapter, a checklist is provided for prospective tenants to help them in negotiating with landlords about the standardized or customized forms.

There are four types of tenancies: (1) a tenancy for years, (2) a periodic tenancy, (3) a tenancy at will, and (4) a tenancy at sufferance. All, except a tenancy at sufferance, involve the transfer of the right to possession. The owner or lessor (landlord) conveys the property to the lessee (tenant) for a certain time. The tenant has a qualified right to exclusive possession. The tenant's right to exclusive possession is qualified by the landlord's right to inspect the premises to ensure that the tenant is properly caring for the property.

Tenancy for Years

tenancy for years
Tenancy for a specified time period stated by express contract.

The unique characteristic of an estate or **tenancy for years** lease is that it is always for a stated period of time, usually one year.*

The main advantage of such a lease to the lessee-tenant is that all terms, including the amount of rent and duration of occupancy, are fixed by the lease and cannot be changed by the lessor-landlord until the lease expires. The lease, however, may authorize the landlord to change the detailed *operating rules* for the rental premises during the period of the lease. For example, the hours during which a swimming pool may be used may be changed during the leasehold. Nonetheless, the tenant can rely on a fixed, or predictable, rent for a stated period while enjoying occupancy of the dwelling.

The main disadvantage to tenants is the inability to move during the lease term without ensuring that the landlord will continue to collect the agreed-upon rent. Likewise, a main advantage to the lessor is that rental income is uninterrupted for the term of the lease; there will be no need to advertise the premises or to prepare them for another resident. This is a significant advantage, since new tenants rarely can be found to replace departing tenants precisely when vacancies occur. Consequently, even brief periods of vacancy, during which apartments are readied and replacement tenants are sought, contribute to a *vacancy factor*. When tenant turnover is high, vacancy factors are larger and the financial return to the owner is less.

*Technically, a lease for a fixed period of time is called an estate for years, even when it terminates in less than one year. Thus, a six-month lease creates an estate for years, also called a tenancy for years.

A disadvantage to the owner is that the rent is locked for the duration of the lease and cannot be increased to reflect increases in operating expenses. Some landlords, however, include an adjustable rent feature in their leases that limits annual increases to some percentage, say 4 percent, as an alternative to an absolutely fixed amount of rent. Or, in very long-term leases, the rent may fluctuate with a standard cost-of-living index. This protects landlords from a decline in their net cash flow caused by increasing operating expenses. And tenants thus know they will, or may, face an increase in rent each year, but at least it is limited in amount.

Periodic Tenancy

periodic tenancy
Tenancy for a period often determined by frequency of rent payments; automatically renewed unless proper notice is given.

A **periodic tenancy** is commonly called a *month-to-month tenancy* because most landlords prefer to do business on a monthly basis rather than, for example, a weekly basis. The defining attribute of a periodic tenancy is that the agreement states a measuring period. For example, "Landlord agrees to lease a unit in Rivercity Acres to tenant on a month-to-month basis." A month-to-month tenancy continues indefinitely for successive monthly periods until properly terminated, again in writing, by the lessor or the lessee.

At common law, to terminate a periodic tenancy, the landlord or tenant must give one period's notice to the other party. If the tenancy is month to month, one month's notice must be given. If the tenancy is week to week, one week's notice must be given. State law often provides the notice that is required to end a periodic tenancy, and it might require a minimum notice period no matter what the expressed term in the lease. In 2002, California statutory law was changed to require a minimum notice of 60 days in many rental situations before a landlord can terminate a tenancy without cause. The law requires an owner of a residential dwelling to give at least 60 days' notice to a tenant of intent to terminate the lease or 30 days' notice if the tenant has resided in the dwelling for less than one year. The law only applies to a few specified California cities, including Los Angeles. The bill had popular political support after a foreign investor gave 30 days' notice to around 1,000 northern California tenants, most of whom were in single-family dwellings. A public uproar ensued.

The main advantage of a month-to-month tenancy to the resident is the freedom to vacate without further liability for rent by giving a relatively short notice. The main advantage to the landlord is the freedom to increase the rent or to evict a "problem" tenant by giving the same short notice. The tenant who is faced with an unacceptable rent increase simply may choose to move elsewhere.

Tenancy at Will

tenancy at will
Tenancy for as long as both parties agree; no notice of termination is required.

If a landlord rents an apartment to a tenant "for as long as both agree," the tenant receives a **tenancy at will**. At common law, either party can terminate the tenancy without notice. This type of estate may come about when a tenant keeps possession after the termination of a tenancy for years with the landlord's consent. Before the tenancy is converted into a periodic tenancy (by the periodic payment of rent), it is a tenancy at will. The death of either party terminates a tenancy at will.

Tenancy at Sufferance

tenancy at sufferance
Continued possession of land by a tenant without legal right.

If a tenant remains in possession after another form of tenancy ends without the owner's permission, a **tenancy at sufferance** is created. A tenancy at sufferance is not a true tenancy, as it is created by a tenant wrongfully retaining possession of property. The tenant is, however, in a different position from a trespasser, someone with no right to be on the property. A trespasser can be arrested summarily; a tenant at sufferance must be evicted. The eviction process, discussed later, provides protection for the person accused of wrongfully possessing the property that is unavailable for the trespasser.

LAW AND PUBLIC POLICY IN THE LANDLORD–TENANT RELATIONSHIP

Under basic principles of contract law in former years, landlords were generally free to rent to whomever they pleased upon whatever terms they pleased. Of course, then and now, the marketplace dictates a cap on maximum rent, as it must be competitive if vacancies are to be minimized. But in addition to market forces, many metropolitan areas now have comprehensive **rent-control** or rent-stabilization laws that regulate increases of rent and criteria for eviction. Restrictions on eviction are thought to be necessary to prevent landlords from avoiding rent restrictions by periodically evicting tenants for no reason, and then renting to new tenants at increased rates. Valid cause to evict in jurisdictions that regulate eviction would include such defaults as failure to pay rent or deliberate damage to the premises.

rent control
A law that places limits on the amount of rent a landlord can charge for an apartment.

Rent control repeatedly has been ruled constitutional despite the contention that it constitutes the compulsory "taking" of private property without "just compensation." The constitutionality of rent control depends upon the actual existence of a housing shortage with its concomitant ill effects. Under those circumstances, rent control is deemed to be a rational curative measure. Opponents of rent control contend that it is a disguised tax on landlords, discriminating unfairly against them by taking their wealth to subsidize renters, a burden that should be imposed on the total society. Still others argue that rent controls result in the deterioration of rental units because artificially low rents are not sufficient to cover the increasing costs of maintenance and repairs. The buildings are not maintained and often finally are abandoned and permitted to become veritable urban wasteland.

Almost all rent-control laws exempt new construction from coverage to avoid the possibility of discouraging new residential developments. Landlords can recapture some of their losses from rent control by setting very high rents for new tenants when vacancies occur. For example, university towns such as Berkeley, California, are characterized by rental accommodations because streams of students come and go on a regular basis. Thus, strict rent control, called "vacancy control," under which landlords cannot raise the rents on newly vacated apartments to their market value, was in effect in Berkeley for more than twenty-five years. This angered landlords and triggered attempts to preempt the Berkeley city laws with a new state law permitting increases to market value of all vacancies. The landlords were successful: In 1999, a state law preempted local rent control, allowing landlords throughout California to raise the rents on vacant units to market demand.

One alternative to rent control allows government agencies to make direct cash subsidies (e.g., through rent vouchers) to qualified low-income renters who then can pay market rental rates. This alternative shifts the burden of subsidized housing from landlords to taxpayers in general. Needless to say, landlords prefer voucher systems to rent control.

The landlord generally is free to include in the lease limitations on noise, parking regulations, restrictions on wall hangings, restrictions on the number of guests and frequency of parties, and so on. Some landlords are strict in such matters and others are lax. Renters generally are informed about restrictions when their tenancy begins, although the enforcement policy often is not spelled out. Nevertheless, the remedy available to the landlord for violation of such rules is the same as for nonpayment of rent: eviction, plus monetary damages when appropriate.

The power of the landlord to exclude prospective tenants is not without limitation. Although illegal for many years, racial discrimination in housing still exists. This phenomenon is attributable to weak enforcement as well as to apparent regional preferences for segregated lifestyles by persons of different races. The Fair Housing Amendments Act of 1988 allows the award of generous damages (no limit is specified), as well as necessary reasonable attorney fees, coupled with an overall expanded role of the federal government for proven, illegal discrimination. Persons now protected from exclusionary discrimination are children, the physically disabled, and the mentally impaired. AIDS sufferers also are protected. Qualified senior citizen complexes, however, may discriminate on the basis of age. Traditional protection from discrimination in housing is continued in the categories of sex (gender), race, color, religion, ancestry, and national origin. Other areas of historical discrimination that are ignored by the act are lack of wealth (minimum income restrictions), marital status (unmarried couples), family size (separate bedrooms for each child), and sexual preference (homosexual relationships). State civil rights or human rights laws, however, now protect some of these categories. California, for example, has long protected against discrimination on the basis of sex (gender), sexual orientation, race, color, religion, ancestry, national origin, blindness or other physical disability, and children.

Certain terms in leases or rental agreements generally are declared to be against public policy and unenforceable by landlords. Nonrefundable security deposit clauses* and exculpatory clauses—explained later in this chapter—are examples.

LEGAL FOCUS—CASE

Timothy Whalen, attorney-at-law and former state legislator, owns the Shannon Rose Apartments in Billings, Montana. John Taylor, a forty-eight-year-old janitor, was renting an apartment from Whalen. When Taylor was late for the payment of rent, Whalen changed Taylor's locks, refused to accept the late rent when Taylor returned, and gave him a small part of his deposit. Taylor moved to the Esquire Motor Inn that night. Whalen personally moved into Taylor's apartment and then sued him for damages and attorney fees. Taylor countered, asking for damages and possession, but was confronted with a clause in the rental agreement that said: *Acceptance of a refund of deposit shall constitute a full release of landlord from any claims of tenants whatsoever.* Is Taylor's claim for damages for wrongful eviction waived?

Whalen v. Taylor, 925 P.2d 462 (Montana, 1996).

No, Taylor's claim in not waived. Such a waiver is against public policy. Under the Montana statutes, Taylor was entitled to three months' rent because attorney Whalen used the clause knowing it was illegal. Furthermore, Whalen was evicted from the apartment, and possession was awarded to Taylor. How this interesting example ultimately worked out is not public information. Presumably, Taylor moved back in. Under these circumstances, Whalen would, no doubt, be tempted to serve Taylor with a thirty-day notice to vacate—a normal eviction procedure. Attorney Whalen might then face an

*Even where it is against public policy to have a nonrefundable cleaning deposit, it may be possible to have a nonrefundable cleaning fee. See, for example, Washington Statutes, Landlord and Tenant, 59.18.130.

action by Taylor for retaliatory eviction, however, a variety of wrongful eviction that is discussed later.

Unfortunately, a tenant may unwittingly sign rental papers that include an unenforceable provision and submit to its consequences not realizing that the lease provision is not enforceable. For example, an unsophisticated or illiterate tenant who agrees in a written contract that the security deposit is nonrefundable might fail to request the deposit. The unscrupulous landlord who obtained the illegal waiver is not likely to volunteer a refund that the tenant does not request.

Prospective tenants always should read and obtain explanations for the lease and rules forms with which they are presented. For example, many states require the landlord to pay interest on the amount of security deposit that is refunded at the end of the lease term. A trusting tenant, however, who does not understand this benefit simply may not receive it. Thus, a tenant should ask at the beginning about the landlord's policy in this regard and a record should be made of the answer.

LEGAL REMEDIES FOR LANDLORDS

Substantive and procedural law benefits and protects landlords over tenants, creditors over debtors, lenders over borrowers, and the poor are seldom among the favored parties.

John Turner, former attorney general of Canada

Damages and Eviction

abandonment
When a tenant leaves rented premises with no intent to return or to honor legal obligations under the lease.

If a tenant fails to pay rent (defaults) and leaves the premises (**abandonment**), the landlord may sue the tenant for accrued rent and damages. Damages may include the cost of repairs for physical damage to the premises, as well as the rent the landlord would have received if the tenant had completely performed the rental contract. In a month-to-month tenancy, for example, the landlord typically is entitled by state statute to one month's notice of the tenant's intention to terminate (not necessarily on the first day of the month) and also is entitled to receive rent for that full period. Reciprocally, the tenant has the same legal right to receive notice of the landlord's intention to raise the rent or to terminate the lease.

In a tenancy for years (a lease with fixed term), the landlord is entitled to rent payment for the entire unexpired portion of the lease term. The landlord, however, would have to deduct from that amount any rent actually received from any successor tenant. In other words, the landlord is not entitled to obtain double rent for the premises: once from the tenant who abandoned and once again from a replacement tenant. As a practical matter, a tenant who simply "buys himself out of the lease" by paying rent for the full unexpired term would be unlikely to learn if his former landlord in fact collected double rent. Sometimes landlords do not sue for damages because their defaulting tenants "skip" out, leaving no forwarding address, or are without financial resources and therefore are "judgment-proof." Many rental agreements also include a provision allowing the landlord to recover reasonable attorney fees incurred in settling the matter after abandonment. In many states, the inclusion of a clause giving a landlord the right to recover attorney fees in a lease dispute is interpreted, as a matter of law, to allow for the recovery of reasonable attorney fees by the prevailing party, landlord or tenant.

When the tenant remains in possession after default in the payment of rent, the situation becomes more complex. The tenant may have defaulted in the payment of rent because of some personal circumstance and remained in possession simply because there

forcible eviction
An illegal eviction technique, by which a landlord confronts a tenant, forcibly removes all personal items, and changes locks on the unit.

was nowhere else to go. Or, the tenant may have defaulted in rent because of what the tenant believed was just cause, such as a continuing failure of the landlord to maintain habitability (e.g., to repair the heating system). Regardless of why the tenant-in-possession defaulted in the payment of rent, the landlord typically will seek to reclaim possession by evicting the tenant.

Under common law rules, a landlord could forcibly evict (expel) tenants who were in default and then literally throw their possessions into the street. **Forcible eviction** is now prohibited in all states. Another possible method of self-help eviction is a "peaceable eviction."

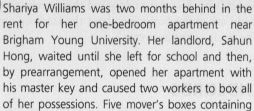

LEGAL FOCUS—PROBLEM

Shariya Williams was two months behind in the rent for her one-bedroom apartment near Brigham Young University. Her landlord, Sahun Hong, waited until she left for school and then, by prearrangement, opened her apartment with his master key and caused two workers to box all of her possessions. Five mover's boxes containing all of Williams's belongings were carefully set on the ground outside her former apartment. Hong changed the lock to the apartment. When Williams returned after classes and discovered what had happened, Hong was nowhere to be found. Has Williams been evicted lawfully for nonpayment of rent?

peaceable eviction
An improper eviction technique by which a landlord surreptitiously enters the absent tenant's apartment, removes the tenant's belongings, and changes locks to the unit. It is peaceable in the sense that no eye-to-eye, person-to-person confrontation takes place, as in a forcible eviction.

No, she has not been evicted lawfully. The self-help remedy of **peaceable eviction** is also prohibited in all states. Although the landlord is entitled to possession of the property ultimately, statutory remedies compel the landlord to follow court procedures. In this case, Williams could sue her landlord for *wrongful eviction* and, in many states, could recover punitive damages even though she was behind in her rent. Note that Williams's situation is different from those situations in which tenants abandon their rental unit and leave their personal property behind.

LEGAL FOCUS—PROBLEM

Salvatore Smith rented a small apartment in Butte, Montana. He lost his job and was looking for work and missed his December 1 rent payment. Landlord Gene Dudley repeatedly demanded the overdue rent, threatening eviction. Smith, finding no work, traveled to Chicago to visit his niece and to look for work over the Christmas holiday. When the rent was due again on January 1, a bitter cold front had hit the area, dropping temperatures to 20 degrees below zero. Dudley, angry about the late rent, turned off the heat to Smith's apartment and left a note on the table that said: "no rent—no heat." Smith, returning on January 5, abandoned the freezing apartment within days and took up residence in a downtown homeless shelter. Can Dudley sue Smith for the unpaid rent?

Yes, Dudley can sue for the unpaid rent. The apartment, however, was not habitable from the date the heat was cut off. Thus, no rent would accrue for that period. Also, to Dudley's chagrin, Smith, like Williams in the previous example, could sue for wrongful eviction. Landlords cannot indirectly evict a tenant by cutting off services, such as water, heat, electricity, and so forth. Unless a tenant voluntarily complies with a request or demand to vacate the premises, court remedies must be obtained. As a practical matter, Dudley probably would not pursue litigation against the insolvent Smith.

All states provide for statutory remedies that enable a landlord to resolve the problem of a defaulting tenant who remains in possession. These proceedings generally are *summary proceedings,* and different terms for the process are used in different states. Other common titles are **unlawful detainer**, *dispossessory warrant* proceedings, and *forcible entry* proceedings.

unlawful detainer
A statutory remedy for a landlord to evict a renter who has defaulted in the payment of rent or who has broken the terms of the lease in some other manner. It is not a full-blown trial on all issues before a jury.

Uniformly, the purpose of summary proceedings is to secure possession of the premises quickly, pending any subsequent and time-consuming litigation concerning collection of unpaid rent, forfeiture of deposits, or monetary damages. Because summary proceedings for eviction are so important, involving a person's shelter, most states—

- Require a notice to precede the litigation, giving the tenant a grace period to cure the default.
- Make trial by jury available to decide disputed factual contentions, although this option imposes expenses upon the tenant and landlord and practically requires hiring attorneys.
- Permit the tenant who acted in good faith to continue occupancy by paying all overdue rent and court costs even after loss of the case.
- Give the proceedings priority of hearing time on court calendars, which frequently are crowded.

Eviction, when decreed by the court, is accomplished by the marshal, sheriff, or other designated officer who physically removes the tenants (if necessary) and places their personal belongings, if abandoned, in a municipal warehouse or other designated place. Personal property may be redeemed by the tenant upon payment of storage fees. Some states give landlords a *lien* (a formal, legal claim) on all of the tenant's property abandoned in the apartment. The practical effect is to guarantee the landlord that the value of the property ultimately will be applied to unpaid rent as well as to storage costs. The landlord, however, must instigate court proceedings to cause the property to be sold.

Although the disposition of abandoned personal property may sound unreasonably harsh at first blush, the tenant has the opportunity and responsibility to make other arrangements. Only under exceptional circumstances are valuable goods left behind by an evicted tenant. Warehouses that store belongings must be paid for their services and usually enjoy a statutory **possessory lien** to help ensure payment of storage fees through the sale of the goods, if necessary. Either way, the handling of such a tenant's property is unpleasant for all persons who are involved.

possessory lien
A lien that empowers a creditor to retain possession of the collateral until the debt is paid or until it is sold to the highest bidder in accordance with law.

The typical defense to a summary proceeding for eviction is exemplified by the tenant who testifies: "Yes, I admit I did not pay the rent. But that was because the toilet does not work," or "There's a big leak in the roof." This response may or may not be a proper defense to the eviction proceedings, depending on who has the duty to repair and maintain under the contractual terms of the lease, or under applicable statutes. Unfortunately, most tenants are not adequately informed as to the laws of their state and do not know whether they can successfully resist eviction on the grounds that the premises are not habitable. The tenant facing summary eviction is in a difficult position. It is possible to simply appear in court at the designated time and testify as to the conditions that render the premises uninhabitable. But many lease forms provide for the recovery of attorney fees in addition to rent and court costs. In some metropolitan areas, public interest attorneys are available through nearby law schools or legal aid services, but they are restricted to low-income tenants. Hiring a private attorney is an expensive proposition, although specialists can be identified from advertisements and may be priced reasonably due to the volume of these routine cases they handle. Unfortunately, many tenants with proper defenses of nonhabitability probably give up the fight and simply move on.

MORALS AND ETHICS

Landlord can suffer from "tenants from hell" who do not pay their rent on time or at all. Many public interest lawyers are experts in resisting evictions, both properly and improperly. It is unethical for an attorney to use legal procedures to stall an eviction that is legally justified; court-ordered sanctions (monetary fines) can be imposed to punish such unethical behavior. But as a practical matter, it is almost impossible to determine whether an attorney is employing judicial tactics for ethical or unethical reasons. Because lawyers' ethical standards are enforceable, however, the immoral behavior of using legal procedure to bar an otherwise-legal process is prohibited.

Security Deposits

LEGAL FOCUS—BACKGROUND

In June 2002, the following appeared in *The Buffalo News:* Nick Sidoti's nose itched at the rancid smell. A stench of urine, smoke, mold and spoiled food hung in the air as cut-up winter blankets filtered the cold spring sunlight through the windows. The Riverside neighborhood apartment was littered with garbage bags, uneaten food, glasses filled with furry mold, empty beer bottles and an open box of macaroni and cheese. In the bedroom, a pristine Holy Bible sat beside a table of burnt marijuana stems. Sidoti, the landlord, took a good look around. "I hate to say this," he said, "but this is not bad."

Security deposits are lump-sum cash payments commonly demanded by landlords to protect them from various forms of loss that may result when a renter defaults or if unpaid rent is due when the lease ends. The legal right to the return of a security deposit depends on how it is characterized by the court interpreting the documents involved. It may be considered (1) an advance payment of rent, (2) a bonus for the landlord for renting to the tenant, (3) liquidated or agreed-upon damages that may later be owed to the landlord, or (4) security for the tenant's performance. Let's look at each of these interpretations.

LEGAL FOCUS—BACKGROUND

"Security deposit" means value given, in money or its equivalent, to secure the payment of rent by the tenant under a leasehold agreement or to secure payment for damage to and cleaning of the leasehold premises. If a leasehold agreement or an agreement incident thereto requires the tenant or prospective tenant to provide or maintain in effect any deposit to the landlord for part or all of the term of the leasehold agreement, the deposit shall be presumed to be a security deposit. A fee or charge for cleaning and damages, no matter how designated, is presumed to be a security deposit.

Montana Statutes 70-25-101 (4).

First, the deposit may be designated as an advance payment of rent (called *prepaid rent*), usually for the first and last month of the occupancy. It serves to give the landlord security because the tenant has something to lose if the premises are abandoned. In such an event, the rental unit is paid for while the landlord locates another tenant. But advance rent is rent; it cannot be retained by the landlord as compensation for damage or cleaning.

Another use of the security deposit is as a "bonus" or "key money" paid to a landlord when desirable rental quarters are hard to find. It is owned by the landlord and is not refundable under any circumstances. Currently, this use generally is prohibited.

liquidated damages Amount of damages that contracting parties have previously agreed would be fair payment in case of breach. A court will not accept this amount if it is so large as to constitute a penalty.

A third use is as **liquidated damages**, an amount of money the parties agree will compensate the landlord for any property damages that may occur in the future, whether or not the actual amount for repairing the damage turns out to be more or less. Liquidated damage clauses are seldom found in leases because state laws limit their use, for example, to situations in which actual damages would be difficult to prove.

On the other hand, a security deposit commonly is used as a security fund held by the landlord to be applied against any actual losses incurred by the landlord from any default by the tenant. Any portion of the security deposit in excess of actual damages must be refunded to the tenant; if actual damages exceed the amount of deposit, the tenant remains liable for their payment.

The prospective tenant should insist that a clearly understandable provision in the lease explains the ultimate disposition of the security deposit. Although a true security deposit (as distinguished from prepaid rent) is the tenant's money until properly applied to damages, the landlord is not, in most jurisdictions, obligated to pay any interest on it to the tenant.

Disputes often arise in connection with the return of security deposits because of disagreement as to the condition of the premises at the beginning and end of the term. Also, there can be differences in opinion as to what constitutes ordinary wear and tear, which generally is defined as deterioration attributable to the passage of time and reasonable use by a tenant rather than abuse or wrongful conduct.

LEGAL FOCUS—PROBLEM

Harry Okamoto, Sally Broome, Kristina Duval, and Jocelyn Powers rented a home in the neighborhood of the university they were attending. The home was owned by an elderly widow who had moved to an apartment in a nearby city to be closer to her children following the death of her husband. The rent was mailed to her each month. After Okamoto and his roommates moved out at the end of their two-year lease, they wrote and asked for return of their $1,000 security deposit. A rental management company reported to the widow that paths were worn in the carpets, the paint around all light switches and door handles was scratched and stained, grease spatters on the walls around the kitchen stove and sink were permanent, there were permanent water stains on the drapes caused by outside sprinklers that had been showering the open windows, the toilet was "running" constantly and two faucets were dripping, the linoleum in the kitchen and bathrooms was curling at the edges and needed replacement, there was a hole in a window screen, and there was water damage to the subfloor around the shower in each bathroom. Can the widow use the security deposit to repair the items?

ordinary wear and tear Deterioration in a residential rental property that is attributable to the passage of time (for example, fading of draperies) and not to abuse by the tenant.

The widow probably cannot use the security deposit to repair these items. All of the items would occur ordinarily and gradually in any house occupied by four college students. These kinds of deterioration are called **ordinary wear and tear** in the law. Over time, interior paint will fade, discolor, and even crack; carpets will wear down, especially in high-traffic areas; curtains will sag, lose their shape, and discolor from the sun's rays and from oxidation; sediment in water will accumulate around rubber washers and cause faucets to leak; caulking around showers and tubs will discolor, crack, and ultimately leak; wood surfaces around door handles and cupboard pulls will mar from fingers and fingernails, and so forth. Sprinkler damage is not the tenant's responsibility, nor is the window screen damage unless caused by one of the tenants. Tenants are not legally responsible for correcting these types of damage.

Examples of damage beyond ordinary wear and tear, which usually are indeed the tenant's responsibility, include cigarette burns on furniture, permanent stains on carpets, chipped porcelain in sinks, burns on rugs and floors from fireplace embers, broken windows or damaged light fixtures, scratched and gouged walls, animal urine on carpeting or flooring, and graffiti on walls and ceiling.

Dirt is not damage, nor is it ordinary wear and tear, and so it is considered differently for purposes of security deposits. At the end of a rental tenancy, the tenant is legally obligated to leave the premises just as clean as when the tenancy began. If the tenant breaches this legal obligation, the landlord may use the security (i.e., cleaning) deposit to make the premises just as clean as when the tenancy began. The landlord cannot rightfully retain security deposits to make the premises cleaner than when the tenant took possession, even if the deposit is labeled a "cleaning deposit" in the paperwork. Sometimes, the distinction between cleanliness and damage is fuzzy, as when an oven has been used but left without cleaning over a long period of time, or when toilet bowl stains become permanent from lack of periodic cleaning. If the security deposit is inadequate to return the premises to as clean a condition as when the tenancy began, the tenant remains liable for any additional money that may be required.

Generally, the landlord and tenant are free to contract as they please. Because of their unequal bargaining power, however, courts will not enforce certain terms that frequently appear in landlord–tenant agreements because they are "against public policy." For example, a security deposit that is agreed to be nonrefundable nonetheless must be refunded to the extent it is not applied to some proper purpose, such as the repair of damage to the apartment.

LEGAL REMEDIES FOR TENANTS

Implied Warranty of Habitability

Under archaic principles of common law, a landlord had no continuing duty to maintain the rented premises; the tenant had the duty to maintain and repair. Under modern law, the landlord has a continuing duty to provide and to maintain habitability and to make repairs unless otherwise provided in the lease agreement. This duty, called the implied warranty of habitability, means that the landlord guarantees that there are no concealed defects in the facilities (i.e., those that are vital to the use of the premises for residential purposes) because of faulty original construction or deterioration from age or normal usage. This warranty applies to the condition of the premises at the time the rental arrangement is made.

LEGAL FOCUS—CASE

Becker fell against an untempered, frosted-glass shower door in the apartment he rented from IRM Corp. Becker broke and lacerated his arm. The landlord was not aware that the doors were made of untempered glass and therefore was not aware of any risk to tenants. Becker sued under a theory of strict product liability, arguing that the landlord should be held liable just like the manufacturer of any defective product. What was the result?

Becker v. IRM Corp., 38 Cal.3d 454, 698 P.2d 116, 213 Cal.Rptr. 213 (California, 1985).

Becker won. The California Supreme Court held that landlords were strictly liable (without fault) for damages caused by products in the apartments they rented. Courts in other states balked and refused to apply this new interpretation of law. Later, the California courts abandoned the rule, ruling that a tenant *cannot* reasonably expect that the landlord will have eliminated defects of which the landlord was unaware and which would not have been disclosed by a reasonable inspection. Thus, the implied warranty of habitability does not support an action for strict liability. In the *Becker* case, even if the landlord had inspected the apartment, the untempered type of glass would not have been apparent. The landlord therefore was not negligent, and Becker would lose if the case arose today. Still, a landlord must exercise due care in the management of the rental property to avoid foreseeable injury to tenants and others.

The implied warranty of habitability gives a tenant a reasonable expectation that the landlord has inspected the rental dwelling and corrected any defects disclosed by that inspection that would render the dwelling uninhabitable. The tenant further can expect that the landlord will maintain the property in a habitable condition by repairing promptly any conditions of which the landlord has actual or constructive notice that arise during the tenancy. Some states, however, reject the implied warranty of habitability.

LEGAL FOCUS—CASE

Robert Flain, visiting a friend who rented a home in Casper, Wyoming, fell down the rickety stairs leading to the basement and was seriously injured. There were no handrails on the dimly lit stairs. Flain sues the landlord for bodily injury from negligence. Can Flain win his case?

Ortega v. Flain, 902 P.2d 199 (Wyoming, 1995).

Flain cannot win the case in Wyoming, which follows the old common law rule under which a landlord owes no duty of care to tenants or their guests. Wyoming is a "Let the Tenant Beware" state, unlike the vast majority of states that have established an implied warranty of habitability. Under the modern rule, a jury would have decided whether the condition of the staircase violated an implied warranty of habitability. Even in Wyoming, the landlord owes a duty of reasonable care in maintaining the premises over which control is retained, such as hallways and parking lots.

Under the more modern view, the landlord is responsible for necessary maintenance and repairs arising during the lease term (e.g., stopped-up toilet, broken air conditioner, burned-out water heater, leaky faucet). The parties, however, are free to include a provision in their lease specifying that the tenant will make specified or all repairs. Unfortunately, in part due to their unequal bargaining power, the lessee-tenant frequently agrees to make all repairs, thereby effectively canceling any implied warranty of habitability. Unless so specified, the landlord has an ongoing duty to make repairs. Repairs made necessary because of the negligence of the tenant are, of course, the responsibility of the tenant.

Generally, the warranty of habitability applies to major physical defects in the property that affect the tenant's quality of life (e.g., a serious leak in the roof). The landlord has a reasonable time to repair such major defects. A defect that is merely unattractive or annoying, such as a crack in a wall, probably will not violate the warranty. Unless the crack is a structural defect or affects the residence's heating capabilities, it generally is not serious enough to make the property uninhabitable. In deciding whether a defect violates the landlord's warranty, courts may consider the following:

- Did the tenant cause the defect, or is the tenant otherwise responsible for it?
- How long has the defect existed?
- What is the age of the building? A newer building is expected to have fewer problems.

- What is the defect's impact—present and potential—on the tenant's health, safety, and activities, such as sleeping and eating?
- Is the defect in violation of housing, building, or sanitation codes?

The landlord is responsible for maintaining common areas, such as halls, stairways, and elevators. This duty requires repair of defects of which the landlord has actual knowledge and of those about which the landlord should know.

Tenants have duties as well. Lease agreements contain clauses requiring tenants to comply with the law and incorporate rules that purport to regulate conduct. The state has an obligation to provide for the health, safety, and welfare of the public, and thus has an interest in tenant life. State statutes may require tenants to keep premises as clean and sanitary as conditions of premises permit (slum property less sanitary than a suburban garden apartment); to dispose of all rubbish and trash; to pay for any fumigation necessary for removal of any infestation caused by the tenant (e.g., cockroaches, fleas, lice); to properly use all plumbing, heating, and appliances; to not intentionally trash the premises (doing so may be a crime); and to not engage in or permit drug-related activities in the premises. As a practical matter, police are not aware of any tenant violations until some commotion occurs, or until a landlord calls them to press criminal charges.* The police power also extends to homeowners, but in a slightly different way. For example, municipal ordinances ordinarily require trash to be disposed of, limit the kinds of animals owned (public health hazard), limit noise levels, and prohibit certain activities (practicing with firearms). But the renters in apartments may be regulated more closely because of the high density and, hence, proximity of families, the semipublic nature of the premises that can themselves invite mischief, as well as the property interest of landlords.

As already noted, courts and state legislatures consistently have been abandoning the old common law rules and have been imposing certain duties upon landlords to maintain and repair their premises reasonably, unless otherwise agreed. In this way, the common law is expanding continually, meeting new and changing circumstances.

covenant of quiet enjoyment
A promise usually implied from the landlord that others will not interfere with the tenant's right to occupy the premises.

Covenant of Quiet Enjoyment

The **covenant of quiet enjoyment** is a duty implied by law and declared by courts to be an incident of the landlord–tenant relationship. The historical covenant merely provides that the tenant will not be put out of possession (i.e., evicted) by any act or failure of the landlord. Courts have extended this principle so that any substantial interference with the tenant's use of the premises is considered a violation of the implied covenant of quiet enjoyment.

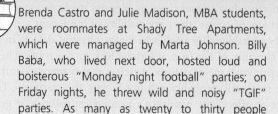

LEGAL FOCUS—PROBLEM

Brenda Castro and Julie Madison, MBA students, were roommates at Shady Tree Apartments, which were managed by Marta Johnson. Billy Baba, who lived next door, hosted loud and boisterous "Monday night football" parties; on Friday nights, he threw wild and noisy "TGIF" parties. As many as twenty to thirty people routinely attended these parties, and they often lasted until long after midnight. After repeated complaints to Johnson that they could not sleep or study, Castro and Madison suddenly moved out. Seven months remained on their lease and their rent was $1,200 per month. Can Johnson sue Castro and Madison for the unpaid rent?

*Recall from Chapter 6 that the attempt to obtain a monetary advantage by threatening prosecution of a crime is a variety of the felony called extortion. There is a world of difference between calling the police and threatening to call the police unless monetary restitution is made.

Johnson cannot sue if Castro and Madison provide documented strong evidence of the offensiveness of Baba's parties. The law treats certain serious and wrongful conduct, or neglect by a landlord, as a **constructive eviction**, which is equivalent to an actual wrongful, physical eviction. Violation of the covenant of quiet enjoyment is one example of wrongful conduct or neglect. Madison and Castro could sue their landlord Johnson for tort damages (e.g., mental distress and suffering) and moving costs on the theory of a wrongful eviction. Some courts would award them damages for any increase in rent they were required to pay for a similar apartment. In some states, they could ask for punitive damages, although the failure to provide peace and quiet does not appear to be particularly egregious conduct. Note that Castro and Madison would have no basis to sue Baba for damages. Baba was committing no tort even if he was breaking the published rules of the apartment by hosting noisy parties. In many cities, he probably was violating noise ordinances, which typically restrict the noise level allowed after a certain time at night (e.g., 10:00 P.M.). Frequently, such a violation constitutes the misdemeanor of "disturbing the peace." Violation of that noise ordinance, however, still does not create a private cause of action for his neighbors.

constructive eviction
Indirect eviction of a tenant by means of the landlord's failure to correct an intolerable interference or defects in the premises, which effectively drives the tenant out.

Less egregious conduct by a landlord also may be considered a constructive eviction, that is, a violation of the covenant of quiet enjoyment. For example, in cases in which a clogged sewer pipe caused foul odors, there was lack of heat, and the landlord permitted occupants of other parts of the buildings to carry on lewd activities, courts have found a violation of the implied covenant of quiet enjoyment. These examples do not mean that occasional noise is prohibited. But when persistent offensive and disturbing conduct reaches the level of a constructive eviction, the tenant becomes free to abandon the premises without further responsibility for rent and may sue the landlord for wrongful eviction. In most states, the tenant must vacate the premises before suing for a constructive eviction.

In addition to this private duty upon landlords to maintain rental premises, most cities and towns have housing ordinances designed to protect the health, safety, and welfare of renters and the public and to prevent the deterioration of dwellings to substandard or slum conditions. These ordinances may impose alleged hardships upon landlords, but they are constitutional exercises of the police power. Typically, for example, these ordinances require that flush toilets, lavatory sinks, bathtubs and showers, kitchen stoves and refrigerators, heating systems, and similar essentials be maintained by the landlord in good operating order.

Failure to comply with housing codes or ordinances may subject a landlord to government sanctions. But the landlord's obligation is to the municipality and not to the tenant, who, accordingly, cannot bring an action to enforce such codes and ordinances. The tenant is entitled to complain to the appropriate local official and wait for administrative enforcement of the housing code.

A **retaliatory eviction** (an eviction for revenge) occurs when a landlord evicts a tenant because the tenant insisted upon enforcement of some right, such as by complaining to a local official of a building code violation. Most states, by statute, specifically prohibit retaliatory evictions and provide remedies for occasions when they occur. Aggrieved tenants, however, must prove by a preponderance of the evidence that the eviction was motivated by revenge and not for valid reasons.

retaliatory eviction
An eviction carried out by a landlord primarily for revenge, or retaliation, against a particular tenant who has in some way angered the landlord.

The obvious defense for an aggressive "landlord's attorney" to assert in a case for retaliatory eviction is that the tenant broke the lease or violated the rules and deserved eviction. This explains why some apartments have strict rules that are enforced only when necessary to get rid of an undesirable tenant.

Many housing codes impose reciprocal duties of cleanliness and housekeeping upon the tenant, but enforcement is rare, as the landlord usually is reluctant to register a complaint that will invite inspection of the premises by an official.

If the landlord fails to maintain the premises, what remedy is available to the tenant? Under such circumstances, and depending on the terms of the lease and the state statutes involved, one of the following situations exists:

- The landlord is breaching an implied warranty of habitability or an implied covenant of quiet enjoyment (whether the duty was created by court decision or by statute).
- The landlord is violating a term in the rental agreement or lease.
- The tenant has the duty to repair and there is no remedy against the landlord.

If the landlord persists in violating a duty to maintain or repair, the tenant is free to declare the lease terminated and abandon the premises. This breach of duty will be a good defense for the tenant in any action the landlord might later pursue seeking unpaid rent.

More likely, however, the tenant desires to remain in possession as originally agreed and simply wants the landlord to fulfill the duty of maintaining, and if necessary repairing, the premises. Most states require the tenant to pay the rent and then sue for *redress*. Damages recoverable for breach of the covenant of quiet enjoyment or the implied warranty of habitability are measured by the difference between the rental value of the premises actually received and the rental value if the premises had been as "covenanted" or as "warranted." Thus, the costly testimony of expert witnesses as to their opinion of these values may be necessary. Such a suit brought in small claims court also may instigate a retaliatory eviction by the landlord and, thereby, escalate the legal proceedings beyond the willingness of the tenant to proceed. Unfortunately, there often is a practical side to legal remedies that often look better on paper than when applied in real life.

In most states, legislators have created new remedies for tenants. Some statutes permit the tenant to make necessary repairs and deduct their cost from the rent. The amount of the deduction from rent due usually is limited to a maximum of one month's rent. This remedy of "repair and deduct" is subject to various procedures and limitations. Some states have permitted **abatement**, temporary suspension of the duty of rent payment, as long as the premises remain uninhabitable.

abatement
The suspension of the duty of rent payment while the premises are uninhabitable.

A tenant facing eviction because of a failure to pay rent may admit the charge, but may claim legal justification because of the landlord's failure to maintain the premises. Where an implied warranty of habitability or an expanded covenant of quiet enjoyment exists, the tenant's contention is "relevant" and may constitute a valid defense to the summary proceedings for eviction. Every prospective renter should inquire as to which party will have the duty to maintain and repair. Where feasible, the tenant should negotiate to impose that burden upon the landlord, and have it stated in the terms of the lease; otherwise, the tenant should give long and careful thought to the potential financial burdens of making periodic repairs before blithely assuming that responsibility.

As noted earlier, some real estate scholars believe that forcing landlords to repair and maintain will hurt low-income tenants who are unable to afford increases in rent levels. The U.S. Department of Housing and Urban Development (HUD), however, now is involved extensively in financing and maintaining low-rent housing.

Landlord Negligence Causing Bodily Injury

The laws of torts apply to landlords and tenants just as they do to everybody else. Thus, if a landlord punches a tenant in the nose, a battery has occurred. But unlike other common situations, such as strangers driving automobiles on a freeway, landlords are in a special position of trust and responsibility for the safety of their tenants. In legal terms, landlords owe a duty of reasonable care for the safety of their tenants. States may adopt statutes that declare a specified duty of a landlord. For example, in California apartments, landlords have a duty to install and maintain deadbolt locks and must provide locking devices on windows and on all exterior doors that lead to common areas, such as lobbies.

The specific duties of landlords that are required by law often become an issue when tenants are injured by the criminal activities of third persons. On the one hand, landlords are not police officers and have no general responsibility to protect the public or tenants from criminal acts. Landlords, however, do have the duty to take all reasonably necessary management steps to protect tenants from unreasonable risks of criminal activity.

LEGAL FOCUS—CASE

Marisela Gomez, age twelve, was waiting for an elevator in the lobby of the 150-unit apartment building in New York City where she lived. She saw a man enter through the back door of the lobby, which was always ajar because it did not fit in its frame correctly. The man entered the elevator with Gomez and several other people, but he did not push a button to select a floor. When Gomez exited the elevator, the man followed, forced her to the building's roof, and then raped her. Gomez sued the landlord for negligently failing to maintain the back door. The trial court dismissed her case on the basis that there was no evidence that the assailant was an intruder. The assailant could have been another tenant, and thus the broken door would not be the proximate cause of the crime. The fact that no one recognized the assailant is not sufficient proof that he was an intruder—in a large apartment building, nobody would recognize every tenant or tenant's guest. Gomez appealed. What was the result on appeal?

Gomez v. New York City Housing Authority, 92 N.Y.2d 544, 706 N.E.2d 1163 (N.Y., 1998).

Gomez won on appeal. The court was persuaded that the man was an intruder because he made no attempt to conceal his identity although he knew there were other tenants about who might recognize a neighbor. The fact that the assailant did not push an elevator button also caused the court to view him as an intruder (although a tenant rapist who was following Gomez also would not know which button to push until she got off the elevator). The court held that a jury could find the landlord liable to Gomez for the negligent failure to maintain a properly locked rear door. The entrance of a criminal through an unlocked door is reasonably foreseeable, at least in high-crime areas. If doors to the lobby of the building were never locked, and if that fact was made known to prospective tenants, there would be no liability for the crimes of third parties (unless locked doors were required by statute). But, by providing locked doors, the landlord was obligated to keep them operating in good repair.

LEGAL FOCUS—CASE

Norma Burgos lived in a mid-rise apartment building with twenty-five units. One evening, she opened her door into the common area hallway, only to be accosted by two unmasked men who, after pushing her back into her apartment, beat and robbed her. She sued her landlord for negligence in failing to maintain functioning locks on any of the three entrances—the front door, back door, and roof door. The landlord defended on the basis that there was no proof that the assailants were "intruders" and thus no evidence that the unlocked doors were the proximate cause of Burgos's injuries. Who wins?

Burgos v. Aqueduct Realty Corp., 92 N.Y.2d 544, 706 N.E.2d 1163 (N.Y., 1998).

Burgos wins. Because the assailants were unmasked, the court reasoned, they probably were not residents of the building. Burgos does not need to prove absolutely that the assailants were strangers who gained access through the unlocked doors—only that it is more likely than not. Thus, the liability of a landlord in New York City under these circumstances depends on whether or not an assailant is wearing a mask. The premise is that tenants (for whom there would be no liability) would wear masks to avoid recognition, while strangers who entered through an unlocked door would not bother.

As noted, landlords are not guarantors of the safety of tenants from criminal acts by third persons. But when criminal acts are foreseeable, a landlord can be held liable for failing to take steps to prevent a crime, such as by failing to install sufficient exterior lighting. Whether or not criminal acts were foreseeable is influenced by the existence of similar criminal acts on or near the premises.

LEGAL FOCUS—PROBLEM

Norm Bates owns Bates Garden Apartments, which are managed by Bryan Walker. There are four buildings, a swimming pool, laundry room, and extensive landscaping. On the day that Aimee Morris asked for and received a rental application for Unit #15, the following circumstances existed:

- A pardoned sex offender and stalker lived in Unit #13.
- Over the preceding two years, no fewer than six master keys had become misplaced, stolen, or kept by former gardeners or maintenance workers.
- There were few night-lights above the parking area, and they were out of order.
- The chlorine level in the pool had not been checked for three months, and the sides were slimy to the touch.
- Bates had received an annual notification that the drinking water serving the area violated federal guidelines.
- There was lead in the hot water piping and in the paint used in most apartment units.
- The four apartment buildings, built by Bates's father some twenty-five years earlier, had asbestos insulation.
- The complex was located in an earthquake and flood zone, and renter's insurance therefore was more costly than otherwise.
- There were no safety locks on the sliding glass doors that led from bedrooms to patios.
- Last year, there had been a murder in Unit #15 involving a teenage gang member.
- Homicide police had visited the previous month inquiring about the tenant who lived in Unit #17. They assured Bates that the tenant was not a suspect yet.
- The manager, Walker, once had been convicted of voluntary manslaughter but had fully served his three-year sentence. Bates was unaware of this fact and also had no knowledge of the history of the gardener who carried a master key and hung out in the apartment workshop all day.
- The locks on Unit #15 had not been rekeyed during the residency of the preceding three tenants, the most recent of whom had been evicted for verbally harassing other tenants.

Which of the preceding circumstances does the law require landlords to reveal to prospective tenants?

This example is not as bizarre as it may first appear to be. The laws safeguarding prospective buyers of homes are more protective than the laws safeguarding prospective renters. As you will learn in Chapter 12, although the laws of the states are not uniform, taken together, they require disclosure to the buyer of most of the preceding circumstances. These same states do not require such advance disclosures to renters.

Although Morris may not have been told of these strange circumstances before she rented, she is owed reasonable care by her landlord. To put it differently, suppose that Morris rented Unit #15 and subsequently was injured gravely as the proximate result of action related to any of the listed circumstances. Could she sue and recover damages from Bates for negligently failing to inform her? The general answer is yes, even though she was not informed of the circumstances at the outset. Let's consider some laws that apply differently to renters than to buyers:

- Home sellers must often inform buyers of convicted sex offenders who are neighbors, or minimally how the buyers can learn the residence of nearby offenders. State legislators someday may apply Megan's Law (discussed in Chapter 6) to renters. In many states, finding out about nearby sex offenders is as easy as accessing the Internet.
- Home sellers in many states must inform buyers of earthquake and flood zones, of water quality, of the presence of lead or asbestos, and even whether or not water heaters are strapped to walls. Although ignored now, can it be too far in the new millennium before courts will protect prospective tenants with comparable zealousness?
- In Minnesota, owners of apartments are required by law to screen prospective managers and cannot hire persons who have been convicted of, for example, stalking, rape, or murder. Can we expect other states to follow suit? Of course, homeowners do not have managers, but many are subject to homeowner associations. Should they be screened?
- As noted, deadbolt locks often are required by law on apartments, as are smoke alarms, and locks on windows and doors to outside entrances to common areas. Homeowners must install smoke alarms but are free to provide whatever other security devices they choose.
- Home sellers in some states must inform buyers of any unnatural deaths that have occurred in the home (other than by AIDS), such as by murder or suicide. Renters often need not be informed even though they are just as likely to be affected psychologically as buyers.

In considering whether or not the law ought to protect renters to the same degree as it protects buyers, ask yourself whether you, as a renter, feel entitled to be informed of the items listed in the Bates Garden Apartments example. Under law, the landlord makes an implied (unwritten) representation that the premises are fit for use as a dwelling. Are the Bates Garden Apartments fit? There is a pertinent distinction between the nature of disclosures to buyers on the one hand and to renters on the other. Buyers are concerned about matters that affect the value of the home they are about to purchase, whereas renters are not. Renters are more concerned with disclosures that pertain to their safety and enjoyment of the premises. Perhaps that distinction will influence the evolving laws concerning what information landlords must provide to prospective renters.

There are unique risks of harm, especially to females, from living in apartments that typically do not have "neighborhood crime watch" programs, that are located in high-density locations, that often provide housing for the more transient and less affluent members of society, and that may be more likely to house convicted sex offenders than residential neighborhoods.

LEGAL FOCUS—PROBLEM

Rosa Hidalgo, a meticulous person, lived alone in a one-bedroom apartment near her university, where she was a sophomore. The apartment manager, Ben Willard, twenty-three years old, had several times been the subject of sex-related accusations, including peeping, stalking, and flashing, while he was a juvenile. Willard had been suspected, accused, investigated, and warned but never convicted. One afternoon, Hidalgo returned home from school and soon developed a sense of uneasiness—it was as if something in her apartment was not precisely the way it had been left. The next day, Hidalgo left concealed threads and buttons balancing on dresser drawers—when she returned, her greatest fears were realized—the buttons and threads had fallen. Someone had been in her dresser. What legal remedy does the terrified Hidalgo have?

None, as a practical matter. Hidalgo is unaware of the suspicious circumstances surrounding Willard, who may be innocent. Although Hidalgo has been injured mentally, an attorney would be very unlikely to sue the landlord on the basis of a general suspicion with the hope of finding evidence later. Unlike Morris in the preceding Bates example, Hidalgo had no tangible evidence nor physical injury to support a claim of wrongdoing upon which a case could be filed. Testimony might show that Willard had been hired negligently, or that the master keys had been managed carelessly, or that the locks on Hidalgo's door had not been changed. But without additional evidence, a lawsuit would be unlikely.* This dilemma points out the vulnerability of tenants, like Hidalgo, whose regular comings and goings are obvious to persons on the premises who possess master keys.

Recognizing the opportunity for abusive violations of tenant privacy, some states have enacted statutes addressing the problem. For example, Minnesota adopted the Tenant's Right to Privacy Act, under which a $100 fine, payable to the tenant, is imposed for each illegal entry. Apartment managers are entitled to enter and inspect the premises, or to make repairs, but only after reasonable notice is given to the tenant. Thus, statutes restricting entries by landlords may do little to help in situations like Hidalgo's in which an illegal entry is intended for illegal purposes. It would not be illegal or necessarily negligent for the apartment owner to hire someone with Willard's background as apartment manager. Minnesota also requires the screening of applicants for apartment manager jobs and makes it illegal to hire convicted felons. But even that law would not disqualify Willard.

LEGAL FOCUS—PROBLEM

Hei Ainy Lai owned a vicious dog, a Doberman, which she believed was necessary for her protection while she was in her apartment and outside while jogging. She paid additional rent each month for the privilege of keeping the dog. While the dog was exercising on the apartment lawn, it attacked and severely injured Albert East, a guest who was visiting his girlfriend who also lived in the complex. East sued the landlord for his injuries, primarily because Lai carried no personal liability insurance. What will the result be?

*You may recall that attorneys can obtain information by using written interrogatories and depositions. But those devices are available only after civil litigation has been commenced. Attorneys ethically cannot use a lawsuit as a device to search for evidence to justify the filing of the case. If that were done for Hidalgo, and if Willard were innocent, and if the keys had been maintained properly, the attorney personally might be held accountable by a lawsuit for malicious prosecution—a serious intentional tort.

East probably will win if the landlord knew, or should have known, the dangerous propensity of the dog.* As soon as an animal's dangerous propensity is known, a prudent landlord should request the tenant to immediately remove the animal from the premises. If the tenant fails to comply, his or her lease should be terminated by the landlord to avoid injury to others as well as personal liability. While eviction proceedings are under way, the landlord should seek the assistance of local officials and, if reasonably necessary under the circumstances, warn other tenants and others likely to be endangered, such as postal employees. The landlord would be wise to include a provision in the lease agreement that if pets exhibit any dangerous tendencies, they must be removed within a few days or the tenant shall be evicted. Some landlords refuse to rent to tenants with animals. The landlord is not responsible for injuries caused by tenants' pets that previously have exhibited no dangerous propensities or are not inherently dangerous.

LEGAL FOCUS—CASE

Lewis Crowell's father rented an apartment from the Dallas Housing Authority. The apartment contained a defective gas heater that leaked carbon monoxide gas. The lease contained an exculpatory clause stating the landlord would not be liable for any negligence. The father died of carbon monoxide poisoning, and the son sued the landlord. Is the clause enforceable? In other words, is the landlord relieved from legal responsibility?

Crowell v. Housing Authority, 495 S.W.2d 887 (Texas, 1973).

exculpatory clause
Provision in a contractual agreement (for example, a lease) by which a party agrees not to hold the other party responsible for her negligence.

An **exculpatory clause** is a provision in a lease or rental agreement under which the tenant agrees that the landlord shall not be liable for negligence. At common law, through the use of exculpatory clauses, landlords could effectively escape liability for personal injuries caused by their negligence in maintaining the premises or caused by physical defects in the premises. Liability could not be avoided for willful or wanton misconduct, for this would be against public policy. Legislatures in most states now prohibit broad exculpatory clauses, or severely limit their scope, and courts in the remaining states have modernized the common law by ruling that exculpatory clauses often are unenforceable, being against public policy. In this Texas case, the court held the exculpatory clause void against public policy and allowed the son to recover for the loss of his father.

Assigning and Subletting

sublease
The transfer by a tenant of less than the full, unexpired term of the lease to a subtenant.

A lease may prohibit the future transfer of possession of the rented premises by the resident to a substitute tenant. Such a transfer is either an assignment or, more commonly, a **sublease**. An assignment is the transfer of the full unexpired term of the lease, whereas a sublease is the transfer of less than the full term. The distinction, although potentially important, is ignored for purposes of this discussion.

The lessor usually does not want another person, of unknown desirability as a tenant, to appear suddenly as a subtenant. On the other hand, a tenant who has permission to assign has a practical escape route from the lease if it becomes necessary (e.g., when a change of employment occurs). A typical compromise is for the lessor to permit an assignment or sublease "subject to approval." If such a term is provided in the lease, the approval must not be unreasonably withheld by the lessor. Solid reasons to withhold approval of a prospective

*Lai is liable for the damages caused by her dog. If the landlord were held responsible and paid the claim, he or she could seek indemnification from Lai. But the problem is a practical one—with no liability insurance, the tenant is judgment-proof.

substitute tenant would be a poor credit record or a history of evictions from prior rental units. Following a proper assignment, the former tenant may be released from liability for future rent, although this is not necessarily so. For example, a tenant may choose to sublease to a new, substitute tenant but at a slightly reduced rent. The landlord, presented with a request to approve this arrangement, would no doubt ask the original tenant to remain responsible on the original lease and to personally make up any discounted rent. The landlord is bound legally to be reasonable in approving proposed subleases but is not required to accept discounted rent or any other material alteration in the original lease.

LEGAL FOCUS—PROBLEM

Jill Newton, Maria Medina, and Crissy Bell, juniors at Lighthouse University, signed a lease on a three-bedroom condominium at the beginning of the school year. They agreed to share the $1,200 per month rent plus all utilities equally. Consider each of the following situations:

1. Bell needed to drop out of school for a quarter but intended to return for the following quarter.
2. Bell flunked out of school and needed to return to her hometown.
3. Bell developed personality conflicts with her roommates and wanted out of the lease so she could move into campus housing.
4. What are Bell's options under each of the three above scenarios?

Under the first alternative, Bell could *sublease* to a substitute tenant who would agree to pay Bell's share of the rent and utilities. The landlord could refuse to permit the sublease, but only for good reason, such as if the proposed sublessee had a history of damaging apartments and fighting with landlords about repairs. Bell would remain responsible for her share of the rent and could continue making payments personally while collecting from her sublessee. Or Bell could permit her sublessee to make payments directly to her roommates. If Bell's subtenant agreed to pay only $350 rent each month, Bell would be responsible to make up the $50 per month deficiency. This arrangement would at least minimize her loss. Bell would return at the end of the sublease and resume her living arrangement with her roommates.

Under the second alternative, Bell could *assign* her lease to a substitute tenant who could agree to pay Bell's share of the rent and utilities until the end of the lease. Bell would have no right to return and resume living in the premises following assignment of the entire unexpired term of her lease. The landlord could, but need not, release Bell from the lease completely. Otherwise, the same consequences follow that pertain to the first alternative.

Under the third alternative, Bell has the power to simply move out and abandon her lease. She cannot "abandon" or avoid her legal obligations to pay rent, however. If Newton and Medina paid the entire $1,200 each month, they would have the right to sue Bell to recover rent (and utilities) they paid on her behalf. The landlord could evict Newton and Medina if they paid only $800 rent each month. Each individual tenant is fully responsible for the entire rent; if all the rent is not collected, the remedy of eviction is available to the landlord.

Under all three alternatives, Newton and Medina would have a significant interest in the course of action Bell selected. They would have to live with any substitute tenant and would undoubtedly be concerned about Bell's willingness to continue her obligations to pay the rent. Proposed roommates are well advised to consider the impact of possible future changes in their circumstances. Subleasing, in particular, should be recognized as placing the "tenant" into the role of "landlord" with obligations, restrictions, and so on. That is one reason why subletting should be approached cautiously and why many landlords forbid it.

HOW CAN A RENTER'S PROBLEMS BE MINIMIZED?

The bargaining power of renters may be slight in communities where vacancies are scarce. Lease and rental agreement forms commonly are supplied by the prospective landlord and favor the owner's legal position. And landlords tend to know more about the applicable laws and customs. How then may a prospective tenant minimize the risk of controversy, litigation, and victimization? Here are some suggestions:

- **Calculate the economics of the transaction.** In addition to the rent, the prospective tenant should inquire about all expenses that will be involved in the rental. Each utility service paid by the tenant (which may or may not include water, gas, electricity, sewage, heating oil, garbage and trash collection, and telephone) should be estimated. Increased commuting costs (in time and money) should be estimated. What penalty, if any, is levied for a tardy rent payment? Are rents increased each year, and if so, by how much? Ask when the last rent increase was made. Consider asking for a long-term lease to protect against future increases in rent, provided you are reasonably sure you will not be under pressure to move because of a job change or family situation. It sounds simple, but many make the mistake of miscalculating their total housing cost. Do not bite off more than you can comfortably chew.
- **Clarify the landlord's interpretation of the future disposition of all required security deposits.** Often, the landlord's forms are not sufficiently clear as to how security deposits are to be used. Ascertain how any deductions, if applicable, are to be calculated; when deposits will be refunded; what the landlord means by ordinary wear and tear; and whether full refunds will be made if there is no damage and the premises are left as clean as when you moved in. Ask when the dwelling was last painted on the inside, and who will be responsible for repainting, and when. Is interest paid on returned deposits? Make thorough notes while obtaining this information. Take date-stamped photos. On important items, later send the landlord a memo stating your understanding of the oral agreement, and keep a copy.
- **Ask about security and prior criminal activity in the building and vicinity.** Everyone expects to be safe and secure in his or her "castle." Unfortunately, some areas are more vulnerable than others to burglaries or even felonious assaults and rapes. The inquiry may prompt the installation of deadbolt locks, window security pins, exterior lighting, or other apparatus designed to reduce the chance of such occurrences, if they have not been installed previously. Although it is true that landlords could lie about this unfavorable information, they are unlikely to do so. If proven, such a lie would subject the landlord to the risk of substantial punitive damages that may not be covered by liability insurance. Landlords are reluctant to accept such serious risks.
- **Ask about master keys and authorized entry.** Many leases and rental agreements do not mention the circumstances under which the landlord may enter the rented premises in the absence of the tenant. Entry should be authorized for an emergency (e.g., a broken water pipe), but otherwise prior notice should be given to the tenant and an appointment made at a mutually convenient time, and for agreed-on purposes. This discussion should lead to the question of who has a master key and when the locks were last changed. It is not a major task to adjust a lock to reject prior keys. The landlord's manager or agent customarily will have a master key for emergencies. But there is no good reason why the gardener's master key that fits the maintenance shop also must fit your entry door.
- **Ask who has the duty to make needed repairs within the dwelling.** The landlord regularly should have assumed, or should now agree to assume, the responsibility for

making all repairs required as a result of normal wear and tear. The tenant should be required to make only those repairs necessitated by the tenant's negligence (e.g., carelessly allowing a spoon to lodge in a garbage disposal) or willfulness (e.g., throwing a beer bottle through a window).

- **Prepare a thorough inventory of the rented premises and their contents.** Complete this inventory (see Exhibit 11.2) before moving into the rented apartment or dwelling. Inspect the premises for both cleanliness and damage. List your findings room by room. Be accurate and do not exaggerate, a tactic that most likely would serve little purpose other than to anger the landlord. As soon as the inventory is prepared, deliver a signed copy to the landlord (or agent) and obtain a signed copy in return. Keep your copy with your valuable papers for future reference. If the landlord challenges the accuracy of the information, suggest a confirming joint inspection. Sometimes, color pictures are useful, especially if the premises are furnished.
- **If extraordinary unanticipated expenses compel a tardy payment of rent, advise the landlord in advance.** Often, late charges will be waived in exchange for such prompt and courteous notice; indeed, the desired mutual respect in your landlord and tenant relationship may even be strengthened. A partial payment of rent on time is recommended.
- **Upon departure at term's end, compare the premises to the inventory and ask for a joint inspection with the landlord.** The best times for discussing the condition of the premises (for cleanliness and for damage) are the day of arrival and the day of departure. Comparison of the premises to the previously prepared inventory helps to avoid misunderstandings and disputes. Usually, an agreement can be made on the spot as to the ultimate disposition of the security deposit.

The foregoing suggestions have been arranged in checklist form for quick review (see Exhibit 11.3).

EXHIBIT 11.2
Inventory of Rented Premises and Their Contents

Room	Damage	Cleanliness
Kitchen	Chip in counter near stove burners	Dust and debris behind refrigerator
		Linoleum clean but not waxed; several cuts and loose patches
		Encrusted stains in oven and on stove top
Living Room	Electrical outlet cracked	Windows spotted and streaked with dirt
	Hole in ceiling from former hanging object	Stain on carpet near front entry, about one square foot
	Holes in wallboard from picture hangers	
	Carpet torn near entry into kitchen	

Landlord ____________________

Tenant ____________________

EXHIBIT 11.3 Suggestions for Prospective Renters

BEFORE SIGNING A LEASE, FIND OUT ABOUT:

Projected Expenses (Stay Within Your Budget!)

- What are the personal expenses connected with living in the rental unit?
- What cash is due upon moving in (for example, prepaid rent, cleaning deposit, security deposit, telephone deposit)?
- What are the average utility rates? Are additional deposits required?

Deposits

- What is the disposition of all deposits at the end of the lease? Is a full refund possible?
- Is interest paid on deposits? Are deposits held in a separate account?
- Will your landlord or manager inspect the premises with you on the day of your departure at the end of the lease?

Condition of Premises

- What is the condition of each room: ceiling, walls, drapes, carpet, and all doors?
- What date was the unit last painted, the drapes cleaned, and the carpets professionally shampooed? Who pays for these items if they are necessary at the end of the lease?
- What is the operating condition of each appliance? (Check them out.)
- How does your landlord define "ordinary wear and tear"? Who is expected to pay for it at the end of the lease?
- How clean does the landlord expect the unit to be at the end of the lease? (Tell him or her that you will prepare a room-by-room checklist for both of you.)
- Are all lightbulbs new? Who must replace them? Are any exterior lights wired into the tenant's system, with the cost of electricity added to the tenant's electrical bill?
- What are policies regarding alterations, hanging framed paintings, pictures, bookcases, decals, adhesive shelf paper, and so on?

Safety

- Under what circumstances will the landlord enter your apartment in your absence?
- Who has master keys? When were the locks last changed? Are there deadbolt locks in the entry doors?
- What security measures are in effect? Is there a roving security patrol?
- Are fire extinguishers provided in or near your prospective unit?
- How soon do police and firefighters respond to a call in that area?
- What lighting exists in and around the unit at night? Are the parking areas well lit at night? (You should visit the prospective unit in the middle of the night to see for yourself.)
- What security problems have there been in the past? Assaults, burglaries, or thefts from cars?
- What is the policy about confidentiality of your rental application?
- Who are the neighboring tenants? Have there been any prior noise, safety, or other problems with them, or with traffic on fronting or nearby streets during rush hours?
- Are there safety pins or other devices for securing sliding glass doors?
- Are all windows equipped with screens? Are they in good condition?

Rights and Responsibilities

- What are the rules of the rental property regarding television and stereo use, swimming, parking, guests, parties, laundry facilities, and the like?
- Under what circumstances may a tenant break the lease? What about a job change, flunking out of college, illness, marriage, divorce, or birth of a child?
- Does a tenant have the option to substitute another person as tenant? What are criteria for the landlord's approval of a sub-lease, if required?
- When is the rent due? What is the delinquent rent penalty? What excuses are acceptable for late payments of rent without incurring any penalty, such as a check lost in the mail, a bank error, or an illness?
- In student housing, or other joint housing arrangements, is each of several roommates fully responsible for rent? (All occupants should sign the lease.)
- Who is responsible for repairs (for example, roof leaks, plumbing failure, sewer drain blockage, and garbage disposal and appliance breakdowns)? Has there been a history of such problems in your prospective unit?
- Who is to be telephoned if problems arise late at night, or on Sundays or holidays?
- What is the name and address of the owner (with the understanding that you will deal directly with the manager without disturbing the owner)?
- Who pays for utilities (electricity, gas, water, sewer, and refuse disposal)?
- What are the rules concerning pets?

(*continued*)

EXHIBIT 11.3 *(Continued)*

In Case of Disputes

- Will any disputes be handled by ADR or by court action?
- Will tenant's attorney fees be paid by the landlord if the tenant wins in a court proceeding? And vice versa?

Upon Signing A Lease and Before Moving in, Do:

- Make and date written notes of your understanding of your conversations with the landlord. Carefully enumerate subjects that do not appear to be covered in your lease.
- Prepare a detailed list of any damages on the premises (for example, chipped counters, stains, cuts or tears in the carpeting, cracks around door handles, tears or bends in screens, caulking cracks and stains in the bathroom, stains in the drapes, stains around heating and air conditioning vents, cracks in windows, and so forth). Be thorough because when you leave, the landlord will assuredly be.
- Prepare an inventory of all furniture and items on the premises, noting the condition of each.
- Prepare a list on cleanliness of the unit, room by room. Pay special attention to the kitchen appliances and bathroom facilities.
- Deliver a signed copy of these lists (but not your notes) to the landlord. Invite verification by personal inspection. Obtain a signed copy for your records.
- Keep yourself from being lulled into complacency by the personality of the landlord. After all, landlords change periodically, and you may be dealing with a different face when checkout time comes.

Before Moving Out, Do:

- Make the unit as clean as it was when you moved in, or hire a professional cleaner to do so.
- Compare the original damage list with the unit's present condition, arrange for repairs, or bargain with the landlord for an agreed-on amount of deduction from deposit.
- Insist on a personal inspection of your unit by the landlord in your presence, make notes of what is said, if possible, get the landlord to admit that the place is clean and the damage is as you indicate.
- Give your new mailing address to the landlord for your refund; ask when you can expect to receive it.

If following these suggestions does not prevent a serious misunderstanding with the landlord, the best recourse is alternative dispute resolution (ADR), if available. If ADR is not available, take the matter to the appropriate court, usually a small claims court. In many states, no attorney is necessary to do this, and whatever assistance is required may be obtained from a designated clerk or administrative official. All documents should be available for the court, including your personal notes taken at the time the lease was negotiated and the inventory prepared upon taking occupancy. This procedure is relatively inexpensive and usually will result in a satisfactory solution for the well-prepared tenant who has a valid claim. The successful tenant, depending on the state, may recover attorney fees (if they were actually paid) and double or triple the amount of deposits wrongfully retained by the landlord. In some states, landlords successfully avoid small claims suits by concealing their identity and address, which makes the service of process practically impossible. Only the resident manager is known to the tenant. But a persistent tenant can obtain needed information from the local tax assessor's office or from the record of fictitious business names maintained by the clerk of each county, which lists the true names of owners. In other states, the apartment manager is the agent for accepting process (service of small claims court papers) and that solves the problem. You should ask for this information when initially renting the apartment.

The specific laws governing renters and landlords vary from state to state in considerable detail. We have included a representative sample of them to broaden your understanding and sharpen your analytical skills. We believe, however, that the information contained in Exhibit 11.3 is so valuable that you should reproduce it for use in the future when renting accommodations.

CASE

Marina Point, Ltd. v. Wolfson

California Supreme Court, 30 Cal. 3d 721, 180 Cal.Rptr. 496 (California, 1982)

A landlord refused to rent an apartment to any family with a minor child. The landlord contended that middle-age persons, having worked long and hard, having raised their own children, and having paid both their taxes and their dues to society, deserve to spend their remaining years in a relatively quiet, peaceful, and tranquil environment of their own choice. This right is lost in the presence of children, who are rowdier, noisier, more mischievous, and more boisterous than adults.

The trial court agreed, holding that the exclusionary rental policy was reasonable and not arbitrary, and therefore not barred by a state statute that prohibited arbitrary discrimination in business establishments. On appeal, a majority of the California Supreme Court reversed the trial court and held the exclusion improper.

Justice Tobriner

[T]he basic rights guaranteed by (the California civil rights statute) would be drastically undermined if, as the landlord contends, a business enterprise could exclude from its premises or services entire classes of the public simply because the owner of the enterprise had some reason to believe that the class, taken as a whole, might present greater problems than other groups. Under such an approach, for example, members of entire occupations or avocations, e.g., sailors or motorcyclists, might find themselves excluded as a class from some places of public accommodation simply because that, as a statistical matter, members of their occupation or avocation were more likely than others to be involved in a disturbance.... [T]he exclusion of individuals ... on the basis of class or group affiliation basically conflicts with the individual nature of the right afforded by the (civil rights statute) of access to such enterprises.

... [T]he exclusionary practice at issue in this case is clearly distinguishable from the age-limited admission policies of retirement communities or housing complexes reserved for older citizens. Such facilities are designed for the elderly and in many instances have particular appurtenances and exceptional arrangements for their specified purposes.

Judgment reversed.

For Critical Analysis

1. In the foregoing case, there was no issue concerning due process or equal protection under the U.S. Constitution because there is no "state action" in the apartment rental business. The rule of the *Marina Point* case has been extended to apply to nonprofit homeowners associations that attempt to restrict condominium occupancy to adults. On the one hand, exclusion of children as a class is not permitted. On the other hand, however, housing accommodations exclusively for the elderly are permitted. What is the difference?

New Haverford Partnership v. Stroot

772 A.2d 792 (Delaware, 2001)

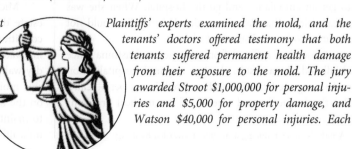

Elizabeth Stroot and Joletta Watson were tenants at the Haverford Place apartments in the early 1990s. They had continuing problems with water leaks and mold in their apartments, and as a result, both women's general health deteriorated. Numerous complaints failed to motivate the landlord to correct the problem. Plaintiffs' experts examined the mold, and the tenants' doctors offered testimony that both tenants suffered permanent health damage from their exposure to the mold. The jury awarded Stroot $1,000,000 for personal injuries and $5,000 for property damage, and Watson $40,000 for personal injuries. Each

award was reduced by 22 percent for contributory negligence. The landlord moved for remittitur, arguing it owes no common law duty to maintain the apartments. The landlord has appealed.*

BERGER, Justice

We hold that the Landlord Tenant Code imposes a duty on landlords to maintain the leased premises in a safe, sanitary condition and that an injured tenant may recover for personal injuries sustained as a result of landlord's negligent failure to do so. We also find no abuse of discretion in the trial court's contested evidentiary rulings or in its decision denying remittitur. Accordingly, we affirm.

Factual and Procedural Background

Stroot, whose health problems were more severe, was a 33 year old graduate student when she and a friend moved into a third floor apartment at Haverford Place in August 1992. Stroot immediately noticed mold around the windows and in the bathroom. Although she attempted to remove the mold by washing the affected areas with bleach, the mold kept returning. There also were leaks in Stroot's bedroom ceiling and in the kitchen sink and bathroom.

Stroot complained to the management and was told that the problem was caused by the upstairs tenants taking "sloppy" showers. Although the landlord made some effort to fix the upstairs shower, nothing was done to Stroot's apartment and the bathroom ceiling kept getting worse.

On the evening of May 16, 1994, Stroot's bathroom ceiling collapsed and water from the ceiling flooded her bathroom floor. The drywall debris and the exposed ceiling area were covered with black, green, orange and white mold. According to Stroot, the room was filled with a strong, nauseating odor. When she called maintenance, she was told that they could not do anything until the next morning. Stroot closed the bathroom door and slept in her apartment that night. By the next morning, she could not breathe. Stroot called her doctor, who told her to get an ambulance and go the hospital. When she was released later that day, Stroot decided that she could not continue to live at Haverford Place.

Stroot has suffered from allergies and asthma since childhood. As a result, she has required hospitalization and strong medications, such as prednisone, periodically. But the frequency and severity of her medical problems increased significantly after she moved to Haverford Place. During the 21 months that she lived at Haverford Place, Stroot was forced to go to the emergency room seven times for asthma attacks. In addition, she spent a total of nine days as an inpatient and received intravenous steroids twelve times.

[Discussion of tenant Watson's problems with mold is omitted.]

Plaintiffs offered the opinions of several experts to support their claims. Dr. Yang, a mycologist and microbiologist, inspected Haverford Place, took bulk samples and air samples, and interviewed residents. He opined that there was excessive and atypical mold growth in the apartment buildings; that it was caused by long term leaks; and that the widespread mold contamination posed a health risk to tenants. Dr. Johanning, a physician board-certified in environmental and occupational medicine, gathered similar data at Haverford Place. He also took blood samples from plaintiffs. Based on his analysis of this data, Johanning opined that the high concentration of toxic mold at Haverford Place significantly and permanently increased the severity of Stroot's asthma. He also opined that Stroot's cognitive deficits, diagnosed by Dr. Gordon, were caused by exposure to excessive and atypical molds. Johanning testified that Watson developed an allergy to Penicillium and permanent upper respiratory problems as a result of her exposure to the same molds.

Dr. Gordon, a neuropsychologist who has studied cognitive defects associated with exposure to atypical molds, evaluated Stroot and concluded that she suffers from significant cognitive impairment in the areas of attention, concentration, memory and executive functions. Gordon opined that these problems are permanent and were proximately caused by Stroot's exposure to atypical molds. Dr. Rose, a physician who is board-certified in pulmonary, occupational and environmental medicine, examined Stroot and opined that Stroot developed osteopenia as a result of her increased steroid usage while at Haverford Place. Dr. Rose also opined that Stroot's steroid usage increased her risk of developing tuberculosis.

Michael Lynn, an architect and partner in a real estate due diligence firm, performed a limited property condition assessment at Haverford Place. He noted standing water, roof joists covered with fungus, water-damaged dry wall covered with mold, and other evidence of excessive moisture. He opined that the deferred maintenance on the buildings was excessive and that landlord's failure to maintain the buildings was the proximate cause of the unhealthy and unsanitary conditions he observed.

*A judge's order reducing a judgment awarded by a jury.

Discussion

Landlord argues that its conduct does not give rise to any of the three causes of action that plaintiffs were allowed to present to the jury. [Also], Landlord complains that the jury verdict was so excessive as to shock the conscience and should have been reduced on its motion for remittitur. Each will be considered in turn.

Tort Liability of Landlord

Plaintiffs pursued three theories of tort liability: (i) ordinary or common law negligence based on Landlord's alleged failure to maintain safe and sanitary conditions in the apartments; (ii) negligence *per se* based on alleged violations of the New Castle County Code; and (iii) negligence *per se* based on alleged violations of the Landlord Tenant Code. The jury verdict form required a separate finding for each of the asserted forms of negligence, and the jury found for the plaintiffs on all three. Landlord argues that it has no duty that would support a claim for common law negligence, and that the statutes at issue do not give rise to a claim of negligence *per se*.

Landlord bases its common law negligence argument on the fact that, before the Landlord Tenant Code was enacted in 1972, landlords had no duty to maintain their buildings in a safe and sanitary condition. Although the Landlord Tenant Code imposes such a duty, Landlord says that the statute cannot be used to support a claim of common law negligence. Plaintiffs' only recourse, according to Landlord, is the Landlord Tenant Code, which purportedly abolishes all tort liability unless a plaintiff can establish negligence *per se*.

Landlord offers no authority for this position, which seems to be based on a misconception as to the meaning of the phrase "common law negligence." To state a claim for negligence one must allege that defendant owed plaintiff a duty of care; defendant breached that duty; and defendant's breach was the proximate cause of plaintiff's injury. The duty owed may be one recognized at common law or one imposed by statute. In either case, the elements of the negligence claim are the same. The phrase "common law" negligence is sometimes used, as it was in this case, to differentiate between ordinary negligence and negligence *per se*. It does not prevent a plaintiff from relying on a statute as the source of defendant's duty.

In sum, we find no error in the trial court's decision allowing plaintiffs to pursue an ordinary, or common law, negligence claim. Moreover, since the jury found in favor of plaintiffs on this claim, we need not address Landlord's arguments with respect to negligence *per se*. Assuming, without deciding, that it was error to allow the jury to consider the two negligence *per se* claims, they were duplicative of the ordinary negligence claim and the error, if any, was harmless.

Motion for Remittitur

Landlord argues that the amounts awarded to Watson and Stroot were so excessive that they shock the conscience. It points out that Watson's medical complaints were relatively mild and she had no observable symptoms after leaving Haverford Place. Stroot incurred $28,810 in medical expenses and suffered aggravation of her asthma and allergies. Her cognitive deficit, according to Landlord is mild and her increased risks of osteopenia and tuberculosis were not quantified. At best, according to Landlord, these injuries could support an award of $250,000, not the $1,000,000 set by the jury.

The trial court carefully considered these arguments:

The presumption in Delaware is that a jury verdict is "correct and just." A Motion for Remittitur ... may be granted ... only with great reluctance. This Court has the authority to grant a new trial if it finds that the verdict is based upon "passion, partiality, prejudice, mistake or misapprehension on the part of the jury." It has also been held that a verdict will not be set aside unless it is "so grossly excessive as to shock the Court's conscience and sense of justice; and unless the injustice of allowing the verdict is clear."

* * * * * *

The jury obviously accepted Dr. Johanning's and Dr. Rose's medical testimony in this case that despite other triggers which could cause her to have an asthma attack, Stroot's asthma was nevertheless significantly exacerbated or worsened by her exposure to microbial contamination at the apartment complex, and that her need for medication increased significantly after she moved to Haverford Place. The Court is satisfied that Stroot showed to a reasonable degree of medical probability that her asthma symptoms decreased, but did not return to her pre-exposure baseline, after she left the apartment complex.

* * * * * *

The Court also finds that the medical and scientific evidence presented at trial established ... that [Stroot's] osteopenia is causally related to her increased steroid use not only while living at Haverford Place, but also after she moved out. The evidence ... also showed that Stroot's increased need for steroids to suppress the asthma has increased her risk for developing active tuberculosis.

Further, the jury may have also chosen to accept Dr. Wayne Gordon's testimony ... that ... Stroot's cognitive deficits in three areas—attention, concentration, and executive functioning, were proximately caused by her long-term exposure to microbial contamination at Haverford Place.

* * * * * *

Given the permanent nature of Plaintiffs' injuries as well as the physical and emotional pain and suffering Stroot and Watson will have to endure for the remainder of their lives, the Court does not find the $1,000,000 verdict to Stroot, or the $40,000 verdict to Watson unreasonable, nor is its conscience shocked.

We accept the trial court's well reasoned analysis.

Conclusion

Based on the foregoing, the decision of the Superior Court is affirmed.

For Critical Analysis

1. The landlord in this case would have violated what duty owed the tenant?
2. The court opinion does not disclose the reasons for the reduction of damages based on plaintiff's contributory negligence. What do you suspect was the basis for the jury's reduction of damages?
3. What self-help remedies would the tenants have had in most states?
4. Why do you suppose the tenants did not simply move?
5. What is the treatment of mold and other similar conditions such as lead paint in your state?
6. Can a landlord legally reject as a tenant anyone who takes prednisone, who has been asthmatic since childhood, like Stroot?

CHAPTER QUESTIONS AND PROBLEMS

1. Arlene Hart, Sherry Francis, and Marguerite Bradley, college students, are roommates in an apartment they leased for one year. Their rent is $900 a month. If for an important reason (e.g., an ill family member, failure from school, or marriage) the women need to break their lease six months before its termination, may they do so? What are the consequences of "breaking" their lease? If only Bradley needs to leave, and the other two desire to remain, what are the probable consequences?
2. Several tenants, including Dorothy Detling, sued their landlord, C. E. Edelbrock, for damages, alleging that their leased premises were infested with rodents and roaches, were missing screens, and had exposed electrical wiring. They also alleged that the heating boiler was defective, that rubbish was strewn in passageways, and that the common area stairs were unstable. Does the landlord have a duty to prevent these kinds of conditions from occurring, or are such repairs and maintenance tasks the responsibility of the tenants? If you conclude that the landlord was at fault, must these tenants move out of the premises because they have been constructively evicted? [*Detling v. Edelbrock*, 671 S.W.2d 265 (Missouri, 1984).]
3. Assume that a landlord who was angry because a tenant's rent was unpaid entered the tenant's apartment with a master key, placed all of the tenant's possessions in a refuse-disposal container, and changed the locks on the door. What would be the tenant's legal remedy? Assume that a landlord's agent (i.e., an apartment manager) wrongfully entered and snooped through the tenant's personal belongings, but did not steal or damage anything. What would be the tenant's legal remedy?
4. Note that you have special permission to make a copy of Exhibit 11.3 without infringing on the publisher's legal copyright. Please make your personal copy now or at your earliest convenience. Even though you are probably settled in for the semester or school year, it is not too late to benefit from a careful, conscientious application of the questions in the exhibit to your own present living accommodations if you are currently a renter.

   Make the effort and take the time to ask and to answer every one of the questions that is applicable to you. (Ideally, of course, we wish you could have done this before you signed your lease or rental agreement.)

   After you have answered as many questions as you can (always in writing), talk to your landlord and, in a friendly manner, ask her or him to help you answer the remaining questions. (Blame us, the authors, for this assignment if any blame is forthcoming.)
5. Angela Jendralski, bitten by her neighbor's monkey, sued her landlord for damages for negligence. The

apartment lease forms did not allow the keeping of animals except small, caged birds. What should the result be? Would your answer be different if the lease permitted all pets? [*Jendralski v. Black*, 222 Cal.Rptr. 396 (1986).]

6. What arguments can you make to support the notion that tenants should earn interest on the portion of their security deposits that is refunded? Can you think of any opposing arguments?
7. Before making an apartment available for rent, the landlord legally must take which of the following actions?
   a. Provide a freshly painted unit
   b. Provide the unit with sterilized bathroom facilities
   c. Rekey the entry locks to the unit
   d. Deflea and deodorize the unit if a cat or dog had been kept in the premises
   e. Provide a clean oven
   f. Arrange for repair of all damages done by the previous tenant
   g. Disclose to prospective tenants any security problems that have occurred in the complex
   h. Provide the unit with a fire extinguisher
8. If a landlord files a court action against a former improvident tenant for unpaid rent and for damages to the rental unit and obtains a judgment for damages, how can the landlord "get blood out of a turnip"?
9. Notes jotted down on paper are not a contract and are not clauses in a written lease or rental agreement. Why then should prospective tenants who ask pertinent questions of a landlord who is offering rentals make written notation of the answers received?
10. Robert Calef leased a house from David West in the city of Flint, Michigan. Seven weeks into the lease term, Calef claims he tripped and fell when he stepped into a snow-covered hole located in the front yard. Calef claims that the hole had been created by West's removal of a fence post in the lawn. As the hole had been covered by snow during Calef's entire occupancy, he was unaware of the hazard. Suffering injuries including fractured humerus and ribs, Calef claims the landlord had a duty to warn him about the dangerous condition. West sought summary judgment based on an exculpatory clause signed by Calef. Does the exculpatory clause bar the claim by the tenant? [*Calef v. West*, 652 N.W.2d 496 (Mich. App., 2002).]

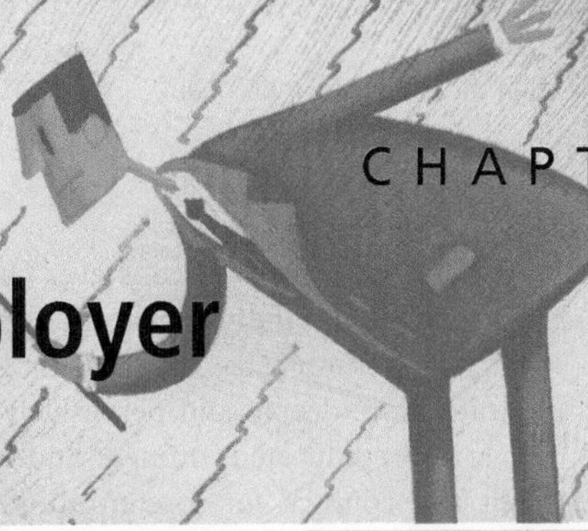

CHAPTER 12

Employee and Employer Rights and Duties

I'm a great believer in luck, and I find the harder I work the more I have of it.

Thomas Jefferson, 1743–1826

LEARNING OBJECTIVES

After reading and studying this chapter, you should be able to:

- Discuss and define the types of employment classifications: principal–agent, employer–employee, and employer–independent contractor.
- Explain and provide examples of the doctrine of *respondeat superior*.
- Identify the groups protected under the Civil Rights Act of 1964. Distinguish between disparate impact and disparate treatment theories of discrimination.
- Understand the nature of sexual harassment and the difference between *quid pro quo* and hostile environment sexual harassment.
- List necessary steps to a Title VII claim.
- Identify employer defenses to Title VII claims.
- Define a disability and suggest the limits of reasonable accommodation for the Americans with Disabilities Act of 1990 (ADA).
- Understand the development of different legal theories regarding wrongful termination.
- Identify basic rights and duties of employees.
- Understand the employment-at-will doctrine and its limiting exceptions.
- Identify some major legal issues of employee welfare in wages, retirement, family leave, privacy, and safety.
- Identify and discuss the major federal statutes affecting the labor/management relationship.
- Define "collective bargaining" and understand its ramifications. Understand the difference between a union and a nonunion workplace.
- Discuss the importance and limitations of arbitration clauses in employment contracts.

The American workplace is ever changing. Technological advancement has increased the capacity of the individual to do work while simultaneously replacing the need for workers in other job categories. Technology also has allowed personal communication to penetrate more deeply and pervasively into the workforce. Workers themselves have grown ever more educated, trained, and informed. Many manufacturing and service jobs have left the country for foreign shores. Job safety standards and expectations have been steadily raised for more than a century. We have added and continue to add layers of external obligations upon the employer to provide care for employees when not in the workplace. This change creates pressure and strain upon the employer–employee relationship and has helped make that relationship one of the most complicated and highly regulated ones in the United States.

We will examine the changing work environment to help understand the effect it has had on defining the American workplace. We study the obligations and rights of both the employer and the employee. This is probably a personal chapter for you. You may already have a job, and you most certainly plan to have one when you complete your studies. Whether as an employer or as an employee, (or as both!), you will find much of this chapter to be tremendously important to you personally.

THE CHANGING WORK ENVIRONMENT

The American workplace has been moving steadily toward managerial, professional, and service-oriented occupations. The Bureau of Labor Statistics' 2010–2020 employment projections indicate that the jobs with the highest predicted growth rates are those that involve professional services, technical skills in health care or services, and the information sector. College degrees were rare a hundred years ago, but now they are necessary for most of the best employment opportunities. In fact, occupations for which a master's degree is typically needed for entry, are expected to grow by almost 22 percent by 2020.

The pace of change in science and technology has increased in recent decades, stimulated by discoveries and inventions best exemplified by the computer. Among the most evident effects of this accelerated pace of change in employer–employee relations has been corporate downsizing: cutbacks in the number of middle-level managers and low-level line workers. Downsizing has been made possible by machines and technology that improve efficiency in all steps, from accounting through production, warehousing, and marketing. Concurrently, the internationalization of much business has expanded greatly world trade and intensified competition.

Technology has opened up the home, and the coffee shop, as extensions of the workplace. With the availability of computers, cell phones, and Internet access, workers in many jobs can be as productive outside of the office as inside. We enter the workforce armed with knowledge from the recent past that many common jobs may soon disappear and new job titles may require tasks and functions that today are unknown.

HOW DOES THE LAW AFFECT WORKERS AND THE WORKPLACE?

Legislation and court decisions affect or control a wide range of issues concerning employment.

- **Who may work?** Federal and state laws limit and strictly regulate labor of persons under eighteen years old. Thus, persons age sixteen or seventeen years are barred from hazardous work, including driving motor vehicles, mining, logging, and wrecking. Persons age fourteen or fifteen years may work in some office or sales jobs and in retail, food service, and gasoline service, but not during school hours or in such a way as to interfere with school. Under specified conditions, persons of any age may deliver newspapers; act in movies, theater, radio, or television; and work on any farm owned or operated by their parents. The secretary of labor prescribes other regulations. Many laws are designed to prevent discrimination in hiring, training, promoting, and dismissing employees simply because of their race, color, gender, national origin, religion, disability, or advanced age (forty to seventy years old).

- **What work may be done?** By statute, scores of occupations from commercial aviator to X-ray technician require a license obtainable only by persons who have prescribed education and experience and pass qualifying examinations. Many professionals are required to continue formal education to keep their skills current.
- **When may the work be done?** Generally, at least one day in each week is set aside for rest and recreation. The provision of a day of rest has been upheld by the U.S. Supreme Court as a valid state exercise of the police power in the interest of public health and general welfare. Reasonable exceptions to Sunday closing laws permit sale of commodities necessary for health and recreation. Annual vacations of one week or longer are not required by law but generally are provided as a fringe benefit. Most states, by statute or executive proclamation, observe some ten federal holidays that are designated by the president and Congress. Many states add one or more local legal holidays of their own. Time off, paid or otherwise, for these holidays is not required legally for employees of private employers, although to provide it is common.
- **Where may the work be done?** Extensive legislation and administrative regulations prescribe minimal acceptable environmental conditions in workplaces. Many states have **right-to-know laws**. These require disclosure to workers of information about any hazardous chemical substances they are likely to be exposed to on the job.

right-to-know laws
Federal and state laws requiring that information be collected and distributed about possible exposure to hazardous chemicals.

- **How may the work be done?** The Occupational Safety and Health Administration (OSHA) has a mission to ensure safe and healthful workplaces in America. The agency states that since its inception in 1971 workplace fatalities have been cut in half, and occupational injury and illness rates have declined forty percent, whereas the number of U.S. workers has doubled.
- **How many consecutive hours of work may be required in certain occupations?** Regulations control the maximum number of hours that certain employees, such as bus drivers and airline pilots, can be on duty without time off for sleep.
- **How much must be paid for labor?** At both the federal and state levels, minimum wage laws have been in effect since the Great Depression. They are coupled with regulations of the maximum hours of work that employers may demand without the payment of "time-and-a-half" for overtime.
- **Do workers have the legal right to unionize?** Federal and state laws guarantee most workers the right to organize into unions of their own choice and require employers to bargain collectively with the representatives of such unions over wages, hours, and a broad spectrum of conditions of employment.

The law's concern with the employment process is pervasive. It precedes hiring, applies during employment, continues through dismissal, and extends into retirement. Our public education system provides lifelong learning opportunities that facilitate useful employment. Without proper knowledge and skills, one is likely to be underemployed or unemployed throughout one's life. Legal involvement continues when jobs are lost because of an economic recession, and public funds pay unemployment compensation. Some workers wrongfully dismissed from employment may sue for damages under developing tort law.

LEGAL CLASSIFICATION OF EMPLOYEES

agency
Relationship in which, by mutual consent, an employee (the agent) is authorized to represent and bind an employer (the principal) in business dealings with third parties.

The world of work has been a prime concern of lawmakers over the centuries. Rules enforceable in court enable businesses to fulfill their needs of providing goods and services to many customers. They also govern the employer–employee relationship, of which there are three basic types: principal–agent, employer–ordinary employee, and contracting employer–independent contractor. These categories overlap, as we will learn in the next sections.

Principal–Agent Relationship

agent
A person employed by a principal to deal with third parties and to make contracts binding the principal to the third parties. An agent is a fiduciary of the principal.

principal
The person who empowers an agent to enter contract(s) on her or his behalf.

fiduciary
Someone who has an obligation to act with scrupulous good faith and honesty toward another.

Agency is described in technical language by the authoritative *Restatement of Agency* as "the fiduciary relation, which results from the manifestation of consent by one person to another that the other shall act on his behalf and subject to his control, and consent by the other, so to act." In less arcane terms, this means that the principal is a special type of employer who hires an **agent** to act for the **principal** in negotiating and transacting business with customers. The agent receives and accepts authority from the principal to carry out the principal's business as directed. Not all agents are employees and not all employees are agents.

Agents may be authorized to make contracts with customers on behalf of their principals. When made, the contracts are treated as legally binding between the customer and the employer, although negotiated by the agent. If every business customer had to deal directly with the owner, business as we know it could not exist. Agency law enables a business owner (as principal) to employ any number of persons (as agents) to enter into contracts with third parties for the sale or purchase of goods or services on behalf of the principal. Because an agent can legally bind his or her employer (the principal) to contracts that are made, the law declares the agent to be a *fiduciary* and imposes a high obligation of trustworthiness upon the agent.

A **fiduciary** relationship exists when the law requires one person to treat another with the most scrupulous good faith and honesty (e.g., an attorney toward a client, a trustee toward a beneficiary in a trust, and a partner toward another partner in a partnership). Obviously, a key to the expansion and success of business is to find and retain competent, honest, and industrious agents. The following hypothetical example illustrates how an agent may perform legal acts that bind the principal.

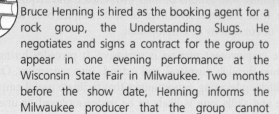

LEGAL FOCUS—PROBLEM

Bruce Henning is hired as the booking agent for a rock group, the Understanding Slugs. He negotiates and signs a contract for the group to appear in one evening performance at the Wisconsin State Fair in Milwaukee. Two months before the show date, Henning informs the Milwaukee producer that the group cannot appear as scheduled because "they'll be tied up in a two-week appearance in Vegas—a big break we just can't walk away from." Are the Understanding Slugs liable to the Milwaukee producer for damages for breach of the earlier contract?

Yes, the group is liable. It is legally bound by the acts of its agent just as the Milwaukee producer is liable under the contract to the group. Following are highlights of the agency relationship:

- Agency is a relationship between two persons: the *principal,* or employer who wants to get something done, and the *agent,* or employee who is authorized by the principal to do the specified job as a representative of the principal.
- The relationship is always *consensual.* Both principal and agent must expressly or impliedly consent to the relationship.
- The relationship is also usually—although not always—contractual, meaning that generally both parties give and receive consideration (see Chapter 8). For example, under an employment contract, Craig Marks serves as Molly Moore's agent (sales representative) in the Chicago territory. Marks enters into contracts on Moore's behalf and binds her to perform. She pays him a salary or commission for his services.
- An agency relationship can be gratuitous instead of contractual. For example, as a favor, Feria agrees to act as Lou Hockley's agent to buy two tickets to the big game. Hockley reimburses Feria for the price paid, but gives her no more than a "thank you" for the service. (Had Feria bought the tickets without Hockley's consent, Hockley would have no obligation to pay.)
- The agent represents and acts on behalf of the principal in dealings with third parties. The resulting contract is legally binding on the principal, provided that the agent acted within the scope of his or her authority as given by the principal. Usually, the agent is not bound to the third party to perform the contract.
- However, an agent who acts beyond the scope of his or her authority is personally liable to the third party. If in doubt as to the nature and scope of the agent's authority, the third party should check directly with the principal, asking (1) whether he or she is your agent and (2) what authority your agent has (e.g., to sell, to buy) and on what terms. The law presumes a duty on behalf of a third party to verify that an agent has the authority that he or she claims.

LEGAL FOCUS—PROBLEM

Several hospital workers were excited to find that former Major League Baseball pitcher Mickey Lolich was checking into St. Joseph's Medical Center. When the health care workers checked the identity of their patient, they found out it was not Lolich but someone named Leroy Fulton. Is Mickey Lolich liable for the health bills incurred by Leroy Fulton in his name?

If an agent exceeds his or her authority, the principal is ordinarily not liable. It is then also true that if a person attempts to pass himself or herself off as someone else, that person is liable but the "real" person, in this case Lolich, is not. Apparently, Leroy was also bumming beers and giving autographs. Do not assume that someone is who he or she claims to be without carefully checking. Leroy was arrested on suspicion of forgery and theft.

- The agent, in effect, walks in the shoes of the principal, even when out of the principal's presence. The principal has the continuing right to control the agent, but while alone, the agent may make a foolish contract and the principal must honor it as long as the agent's acts were authorized. Note that even if the agent violates explicit orders, the principal would be liable to affected innocent third parties (e.g., the agent sells goods below a minimum price set by the principal, or grants credit in violation of stated company policy). The principal is likewise responsible for most torts the agent committed while within the scope of authorized behavior under a doctrine called *respondeat superior* (discussed subsequently).

- An official notice (e.g., legal summons and complaint) given to a duly authorized agent legally is deemed to be a notice to the principal. Also, the agent is duty bound to perform as promised and to use reasonable care (which could be appropriate skilled care, as when the agent is a lawyer or real estate broker).
- Agency is a fiduciary relationship in which the agent must act in scrupulous good faith and honesty toward the principal, always placing the interests of the principal first. He or she must be loyal, never serving two adverse parties (e.g., the buyer and the seller in a transaction) at the same time, unless both are fully informed and give consent. Of course, an agent may be employed by a group of associated principals. Also, an attorney-at-law may be employed by two or more persons to prepare a partnership agreement as long as all clients give their informed consent, and the attorney treats them with impartiality and balanced fairness. Any agent must account to the principal for all receipts and disbursements and must never keep a secret profit. The burden of the fiduciary obligation is upon the agent and operates to safeguard the principal. The principal, although not a fiduciary, is still expected to deal fairly. For example, a company (the principal) must account to the agent for all receipts and commissions owed.

employee
A person who agrees by contract to perform work as directed and controlled by an employer in exchange for compensation (usually consisting of wages or salary and fringe benefits).

Employer–Ordinary Employee

An ordinary **employee** is a person hired to perform services for another, the employer, and the employee's physical conduct is controlled by, or is subject to control by, the employer. As mentioned, the employment relationship is a contractual relationship. Employees who transact business with third parties have a dual status; they are both ordinary employees and agents.

LEGAL FOCUS—PROBLEM

Donna Hunt owns a dress shop. She employs Myra Feldman, Roxanne Peters, and Nita Travis as salespeople and Kari Hudspeth as an in-house accountant. Hunt is the employer, and Feldman, Peters, Travis, and Hudspeth obviously work for her. Which of the employed parties are employees, and which are agents? Are the terms mutually exclusive?

Feldman, Peters, Travis, and Hudspeth are all employees. All are also agents. The classifications are not mutually exclusive, and many employees are agents and vice versa. The key to an employer–employee relationship is the extent of the employer's right to control the employee's acts. Ordinary employees often lack independent business discretion. The salespeople in the dress shop are told how to handle and display merchandise and how to record sales. When they actually sell the dresses, however, they act as agents as well as ordinary employees because they have been given the authority by Hunt to sell goods to customers. These sales are contracts between the customers and Hunt. Hudspeth, the accountant, has no authority to sell dresses but undoubtedly represents her employer in other ways. An employee is not an agent if she lacks authority to contract for or represent the employer to others. Obviously, most employees are also agents in some respect.

respondeat superior (Latin: "let the master answer")
A legal doctrine holding employers liable for injuries caused third persons by their employees who were negligent while acting within the course and scope of their employment.

The employer is liable to third parties for injuries caused by the negligence of employees while they are acting within the scope of their employment under a common law doctrine called ***respondeat superior***. This legal doctrine imposes vicarious—that is, indirect—liability on an employer for the wrongful acts of an agent or employee that occur while the agent or employee is on the job. Vicarious liability occurs even though the employer has not been careless. Because liability exists even without the fault of the employer, the doctrine is similar to the theory of strict liability in tort.

The discussion in this text refers to employer and employee, but the terms *principal* and *agent* and even *master* and *servant* also are used when discussing *respondeat superior*. If the appropriate control over the actor by the employer exists and the act is in the scope of employment, then liability exists, despite any inconsistency in the use of terms.

The doctrine of *respondeat superior* is justified by three supporting theories. The first concerns the issue of control. An employer has the right to control the acts of the agent or employee and is thus responsible for injuries arising out of such service. The second theory is economic in nature. Since the employer profits from the employee's or agent's service, he or she also should suffer the losses. The third reason is practical and is referred to as the *deep-pocket theory*. The employer is more likely to be able to pay for the losses than the employee or agent. In other words, the employer usually has more money; this is the origin of the saying "the employer has the deep pockets."

There are limitations on the employer's or principal's vicarious liability. An employer is responsible only for the wrongful conduct of an employee or agent occurring in the scope of the employment. Generally, the act must be of a kind the worker was employed to do. It also must have occurred within authorized time and space limits and must have been activated, at least in part, by a purpose to serve the employer.

Several questions are used to determine whether or not the employee's act occurred within the scope of employment. The answers assist a court or jury in determining whether the employee was on the job for purposes of the doctrine of *respondeat superior*.

- **Did the employer authorize the act?** If the answer is yes, then the act is probably within the scope of employment.
- **What were the time, place, and purpose of the act?** If it occurred on the worksite, then the employee was probably on the job. An employee commuting to or from work generally is not acting within the scope of employment.
- **Was the act one commonly performed by employees for the employer**? If yes, the employee was acting within the scope of employment.
- **To what extent was the employer's interest advanced by the act?** If the act ordinarily would benefit the employer, then the employee was acting within the scope of employment.
- **To what extent were the private interests of the employee involved?** If the act was primarily to benefit the employee, then perhaps the employee was not on the job. For example, an employee takes a break during the day and goes downtown to shoot a game of pool. An accident occurs while driving to the pool hall. The employee is probably not within the scope of employment.
- **Did the employer furnish the means or instrumentality (e.g., a truck or a machine) by which the injury was inflicted?** If the employee is using the employer's truck, he or she is more likely to be considered within the scope of employment.
- **Did the employer expect that the employee would do the act?** Had the employee done the act before? If the answer is yes to both questions, the employee is more likely to be within the scope of employment.

- **Did the act involve the commission of a serious crime?** If the act is a serious intentional wrong, the employee usually is not considered to be within the scope of employment, unless the employer requested or might reasonably expect that the employee would perform that wrongful act.

LEGAL FOCUS—PROBLEM

Walter Johnson was driving down Main Street on his way to deliver a package for Racehorse Delivery Service. Unfortunately, Johnson was distracted for a second and ran into the rear of Felicia Fresno's new Lexus automobile. Luckily, Fresno was not hurt, but the car suffered $10,000 in damages. Who is legally responsible for the harm to Fresno's car?

Johnson is, of course, liable for his own negligence. Because Johnson was an employee of Racehorse and because he injured another while driving the automobile on company business, Johnson was within the scope of his employment, making Racehorse Delivery also liable. Although Fresno can sue both Johnson and Racehorse, she will collect her actual damages only once; she will not receive twice that amount.

Many state and federal employment laws apply to employer–employee relationships. These laws cover such issues as Social Security, withholding of income taxes, workers' compensation benefits, unemployment compensation, workplace safety laws, employment discrimination, unionization, and the like. These laws do not apply to employer–independent contractor relationships, discussed next.

Contracting Employer–Independent Contractor

independent contractor
A person who is hired to do a specific job, and who retains control over how that job is done.

Independent contractors are not ordinary employees; they are engaged to accomplish some task, such as to build a warehouse. The party who contracts for their service has little control over how the job specified in the service contract is performed. The *Restatement of Agency* 2d §2 defines an independent contractor as

> *[A] person who contracts with another to do something for him but who is not controlled by the other nor subject to the other's right to control with respect to his physical conduct in the performance of the undertaking. He may or may not be an agent.*

If someone is an independent contractor rather than an employee, then the doctrine of *respondeat superior* does not apply, certain tax obligations of the employer do not arise, and obligations under various employment laws such as the Civil Rights Act of 1964 do not arise. Thus, when interviewing lawyers or real estate agents who are to be hired, a prospective client can ask questions that would not be permissible if directed to candidate employees. Questions such as "Are you married?" "Have you been arrested?" "Are you a Democrat?" "Do you believe in equality of the sexes?" "Do you contribute to the ACLU (American Civil Liberties Union)?" would all be legal questions to ask. Furthermore, the hiring principal could discriminate for or against candidates based on the answers to those questions. Interestingly, candidates to be engaged as independent contractors rarely submit résumés to their prospective principals.

In determining whether or not someone is an employee or an independent contractor, the following questions are important:

- **What control does the employer exercise over the details of the work?** Little or no control suggests the worker is an independent contractor.
- **Does the employed person work in an occupation or business distinct from that of the employer?** A different business suggests an independent contractor.
- **Is the work usually done under the employer's direction or by an unsupervised specialist?** Little or no supervision suggests an independent contractor.
- **Does the employer supply tools or equipment required at the place of work?** Not supplying tools or equipment suggests an independent contractor.
- **How long is the period of employment?** A shorter period of employment suggests that the employed person is an independent contractor.
- **What is the method of payment—by time period or upon completion of the job?** Payment upon completion of the agreed task suggests an independent contractor.
- **What degree of skill is required of the person employed?** A high degree of skill suggests an independent contractor.

How the employer or employed person for that matter refers to the relationship is not determinative or even particularly important. In other words, calling someone an independent contractor does not make that person an independent contractor. Building contractors and their subcontractors are examples of independent contractors. A property owner does not control the specific way in which either of these professionals performs the work. Truck drivers who own their equipment and hire out on an *ad hoc* basis are independent contractors. Truck drivers who drive company trucks, however, are usually ordinary employees. Collection agents and real estate brokers are usually independent contractors when hired to collect a debt for a business or sell a house for a homeowner. They are also employees for the collection agency and the real estate company unless the business is a sole proprietorship.

The relationship between a contracting employer and an independent contractor also may or may not be an agency relationship. Attorneys are often independent contractors who advise their clients and who also act as agents when they negotiate contracts with third parties on behalf of their clients.

The fact that the contracting employer has little or no control over the way in which the independent contractor does his or her work emphasizes the responsibility of the independent contractor to perform that work competently, although not as a fiduciary.

Yellow page community directories list many such independent contractors, from accountants to locksmiths to word-processing specialists. Many operate sizable firms and employ their own staffs of ordinary employees and agents. What is their appeal? Usually, they are experts in their specialized fields, and they perform jobs (such as painting houses) that are required only occasionally by the persons who employ them. An employer who hires independent contractors is relieved of the burdens of hiring and maintaining such specialists in a permanent workforce. Eliminated also are troublesome and costly chores of record keeping, payment of wages and workers' compensation insurance premiums, and the provision of fringe benefits such as medical insurance. As noted in the following section, however, the relationship can be misused. The nature of the relationship ultimately is determined by its legal characteristics, not how the parties designate it. In other words, as stated previously, simply being called an independent contractor does not necessarily make one an independent contractor. The relationship instead really may be an employer–ordinary employee relationship with its attendant consequences.

LEGAL FOCUS—PROBLEM

In response to increased competition, some Boston area restaurants contracted with Operations Management Group (OMG), a staffing agency, to move many of their existing employees to OMG's payroll as "independent contractors." The restaurants set the hourly rate the "independent contractors" would be paid and then reported to OMG the number of hours each person worked. OMG would issue the paychecks. When the individuals were on the job, restaurant supervisors directed them how to perform their jobs and had the authority to terminate the employees for poor performance. OMG exercised no supervision, but merely brokered the labor. Are these workers misclassified?

Yes, the workers are misclassified. The restaurants had misclassified employees as independent contractors to avoid paying overtime and benefits. The Department of Labor recovered more than $219,000 in back wages and damages for the misclassified employees.

In the early months of President Clinton's first term, another employee tax problem surfaced when it was determined that certain prospective presidential appointees had failed to pay Social Security taxes for their domestic help, presumably because of ignorance of the complex applicable law. Further investigation disclosed that the practice was widespread. It was estimated that three-quarters of all household employers had failed to pay applicable Social Security and Medicare taxes. The law passed in 1950 required such payments for domestic workers who earned more than $50 in a three-month period, or more than $200 in a year. In 1994, Congress approved a new "nanny tax" law that permits affected employers to pay their household employees' Social Security taxes as part of their own annual 1040 income tax returns, rather than file separate quarterly reports as in the past. The tax is payable on any domestic helper's wages that exceed $1,800 a year.

IS THERE A CONSTITUTIONAL RIGHT TO WORK?

Do you have a constitutional right to work for pay? The answer is no. The U.S. Constitution does not recognize any right to work for pay. In 1946, however, Congress enacted the Employment Act, which was a philosophical commitment to provide full employment by "all practical means" for persons who are able, willing, and seeking to work. Initially, these practical means included a federal job-finding program under the leadership of the U.S. Training and Employment Service; the gathering and interpreting of economic data; the advising of the president and Congress via the Council of Economic Advisers; and the strategic use of the fiscal weapons of federal taxing and spending, as well as the federal monetary weapons of controlling the supply of money and credit through actions of the Federal Reserve Board of Governors.

The United States has never achieved 100 percent employment. The reasons are numerous. Federal Reserve measures are limited in their accuracy and effectiveness. Some jobs are seasonal, as in farming and professional sports. Also, every year, thousands of high school and college graduates attempt to enter into, and must be absorbed by, the full-time job market. Additionally, the supply and demand for products and services are in a constant state of flux in our competitive business world, and countless variables affect the nation's economy. A theory that has gained support in recent years is that, in fact, there is a natural and unavoidable rate of unemployment.

LEGAL FOCUS—PROBLEM

Laura Lanier was pleased and honored when she was discharged from the U.S. Army, but now she needed a job in the private sector and could not find one. She heard that her state had enacted a "right-to-work" law, and so she went to a state employment office, described her skills as a truck driver, and demanded a job. "It's my legal right," she said. Must she be employed?

Civil Rights Act of 1964
Federal law (specifically Title VII) that makes it unlawful for employers of fifteen or more persons, engaged in interstate commerce, to discriminate with respect to employment against any individual because of such person's race, color, religion, sex, or national origin.

No, she does not have to be employed. *Right-to-work laws*, which have been enacted in many states, in no way guarantee every able and willing person a job. The term was coined to gain voter support for legislation outlawing union shops (discussed later in this chapter). Many believe that such laws actually are designed to weaken unions rather than to protect jobs or an authentic right to work. In states with right-to-work laws, a worker is not obligated to join or to pay dues to a union to get or keep a job. Note, however, that even in states without such laws, most workers do not belong to unions. In the preceding example, Lanier, as a veteran, legally may be given preferential treatment in competition with nonveterans for federal civil service jobs. (Many states and local governments allow some such bonus.) Thus, five points may be added to a veteran's score on qualifying tests for federal jobs, and ten points may be added if the applicant has a service-connected disability and was disabled while in uniform.

LAWS AGAINST DISCRIMINATION

LEGAL FOCUS—PROBLEM

Employees in G. R. Coleman's machine shop in a small New England town reflected the social makeup of the community. All were white, Anglo-American, Protestant, male, and highly skilled. Coleman was proud of his business and its products, and he ascribed much of its success to the homogeneity of the workforce. He therefore refused to hire Samara Fuguady when she applied for work in the mechanical drafting department. A native of southern Egypt, she was a naturalized American citizen, had extremely dark skin, and was a practicing Muslim. Fuguady had ten years of experience and excellent references. "It's not that I'm prejudiced," Coleman said, "but your presence would be disruptive and no one would be happy—least of all you." Is Coleman within his legal rights in refusing to hire Fuguady?

protected class
A classification of persons defined by one or more of these criteria: race, color, gender, national origin, age, or religion.

No, Coleman is not within his legal rights. The **Civil Rights Act of 1964 (Title VII)** makes it unlawful for an employer "to fail or refuse to hire or to discharge any individual, or otherwise to discriminate against any individual, with respect to compensation, terms, conditions, or privileges of employment because of such individual's race, color, religion, sex, or national origin." A group of people defined by one or more of these criteria (race, color, gender, national origin, or religion) is referred to as a **protected class**.

Coleman is using color, national origin, gender, and/or religion as a reason to not hire Fuguady—a clear case of illegal discrimination.

Title VII covers all employers and labor unions affecting interstate commerce with fifteen or more workers and all employment agencies. It also applies to all state and local governments. A special section of the law forbids discrimination in most federal government employment. Many states have passed legislation prohibiting discrimination among employers with fewer than fifteen employees. Discrimination is prohibited whether intentional or unintentional. To deal with the variety of complaints of discriminatory treatment, the following typology has evolved.

Types of Discrimination

disparate treatment
Less favorable treatment on the basis of race, color, religion, gender, age, or national origin.

disparate impact
An ostensibly neutral employment criterion that has an adverse discriminatory impact upon a protected group.

- **Disparate treatment** is intentional discrimination, and it may be proved by either direct or circumstantial evidence. The employer treats some people less favorably than others because of their race, color, religion, sex, or national origin. Proof of discriminatory motive is critical, although sometimes it can be inferred from differences in treatment.
- **Disparate impact** discrimination occurs when an employer uses a rule or practice that although appearing neutral adversely affects or excludes a protected group. Unlike a disparate treatment case which focuses upon the existence of discriminatory intent, the inquiry in a disparate impact case centers on the business justification for the employment practice.

Under Title VII, as amended, discrimination in employment practices is permitted only if in conformance with a bona fide (1) pre-Act seniority system, (2) merit system, (3) system that measures earnings by quantity or quality of production, or (4) system that is based on the results of a professionally developed ability test (or criteria) not designed or intended to discriminate on any of the barred bases, provided that the test is *job related*, meaning that persons who do well on the test do well on the job, and vice versa.

To win a case, a plaintiff generally needs to satisfy three requirements:

1. The plaintiff must prove a *prima facie* (on its face) case of discrimination.
2. The burden then shifts to the defendant to show some legitimate, nondiscriminatory reason for the employee's treatment or that its impact is a business necessity for the test or practice.
3. If a legitimate reason is shown, the plaintiff can counter that the reasons offered by the defendant were not the true reasons for the employer actions, but were a pretext for discrimination.

Remedies available to a successful plaintiff include reinstatement or hiring or front pay (future lost earnings for one not rehired), a court order to eliminate discriminatory practices, and a restoration of lost wages and damages. Although punitive damages are available, there is a statutory cap on total damages based on the number of employees working for the employer (e.g., $300,000 maximum for an employer of 500 employees). The prevailing plaintiff in a Title VII action ordinarily is entitled to recover attorneys' fees and costs. A prevailing defendant also can claim attorneys' fees and costs, but a plaintiff should not be assessed his opponent's attorney's fees unless the court finds that the claim to be frivolous, unreasonable, or groundless.

The Role of the EEOC

Congress made important amendments to the Civil Rights Act of 1964 with the Equal Employment Opportunity Act of 1972. For the first time, the federal Equal Employment Opportunity Commission (EEOC) was given power to bring civil actions itself to eliminate violations of the law. Formerly, it had to rely on informal methods, such as conferences and conciliation, which an employer could ignore. The individual victim often was unwilling or financially unable to take the grievance to court. Government was also added as a covered employer.

Title VII charges generally must be filed with the EEOC within 180 days of the alleged discriminatory act. In states or localities that have an antidiscrimination law and an agency authorized to grant or seek relief, a charge may be presented to that state or local agency instead of to the EEOC (the time requirements may differ). Strict time frames govern filing charges of employment discrimination: failure to file timely undermines the ability of the EEOC to act and may terminate an injured victim's right to file a private lawsuit. Filing a complaint with the EEOC or appropriate state equivalent and complying with EEOC rules is required before filing a private lawsuit.

LEGAL FOCUS—PROBLEM

Eric Baker agreed that "any dispute or claim" concerning his employment with Waffle House would be "settled by binding arbitration." As a condition of employment, all prospective employees are required to sign an application containing a similar mandatory arbitration agreement. Sixteen days after Baker began working as a grill operator he suffered a seizure at work and soon thereafter was discharged. Baker did not initiate arbitration proceedings, but instead filed a timely charge of discrimination with the EEOC alleging that his discharge violated federal law. Assuming the arbitration clause is fair and enforceable, can the EEOC bring an action against the company on Eric's behalf, or is arbitration his sole way to enforce the law?

EEOC v. Waffle House, Inc., 534 U.S. 279 (2002).

The EEOC can still bring the action in its own name and recover damages on behalf of someone subject to illegal discrimination in violation of the Civil Rights Act.

> *[T]he EEOC is authorized to bring suit in its own name and ... the EEOC has the prerogative, as a federal enforcement agency, to decide what relief is appropriately sought in a particular action brought by the EEOC. The Supreme Court rejected the argument that the EEOC is a mere proxy for the individuals for whom it seeks relief in its actions, ruling that the EEOC is the "master of its own case" and can decide to bring a claim for monetary damages in court, even though the individual for whom the EEOC seeks relief would be required to pursue his or her own claim in arbitration.*

Race and Color Discrimination

A company's standards, policies, or practices for selecting or promoting employees are illegal if they discriminate on the basis of race or color. Discrimination in employment conditions and benefits also is illegal. For example, an employer cannot grant higher annual bonuses to whites than to blacks.

LEGAL FOCUS—CASE

Julie Deffenbaugh, a white manager of the jewelry department at Walmart in Arlington, Texas, began dating Truce Williams, a black sales associate in another department. The store manager saw them together after work, obviously as a couple. The store manager told Deffenbaugh that she "would never move up with the company being associated with a black man and that Walmart frowned upon fraternization with[in] the company." Deffenbaugh responded that her personal business was not the company's concern, "because it did not affect [her] job performance." Later, her supervisor fired her, purportedly for shopping while on company time. Prior to the discovery of the interracial relationship, Deffenbaugh's employment record was spotless. Deffenbaugh sued Walmart, claiming that she was discharged because she was dating a black male. Walmart claimed that Deffenbaugh was not a member of a protected class because she was white and could not sue on the basis of Title VII. What was the result?

Deffenbaugh-Williams v. Wal-Mart, Inc., 156 F.3d 58 (5th Cir. 1998).

Deffenbaugh's jury verdict of $19,000 in compensatory damages was upheld, and a punitive damages award of $75,000 was allowed. Title VII prohibits discrimination in employment premised on an interracial relationship. "A reasonable juror could find that Deffenbaugh was discriminated against because of her race (white), if that discrimination was premised on the fact that she, a white person, had a relationship with a black person." A more complicated case and one more representative of the type of discrimination that African Americans have been subjected to is the case of *Roberts v. Texaco*. In 1996, this case, which involved the revelation of audiotapes featuring Texaco executives discussing the hiding of evidence and speaking of blacks in a disparaging way, made headlines nationwide. The case was settled for $176.1 million. The Texaco settlement was surpassed three years later when Coca-Cola agreed to pay the highest amount in history to settle a racial-discrimination lawsuit. It agreed to pay $192.5 million, including about $40,000 apiece to former and current black employees. The lawsuit accused Coca-Cola of erecting a corporate hierarchy in which black employees were clustered at the bottom of the pay scale, averaging $26,000 a year less than white workers.

A leading U.S. Supreme Court case unanimously held that it is a violation of the Civil Rights Act of 1964 for an employer to require a high school diploma and a passing score on a general intelligence test for employment or promotion when neither can be demonstrably related to job performance. This finding of disparate impact discrimination opened the door to some minority and nonminority members who lack the benefit of high school education but are willing and capable workers. Moreover, the Court held that employment and personnel management practices, procedures, or tests neutral on their face and even neutral in terms of intent are not maintainable if they operate to "freeze" the status quo of prior discriminatory employment practices. Thus, disparate hiring of relatively few women or minorities is illegal unless truly necessitated by lawful business purposes or requirements.

It does not matter whether or not an employer intends to discriminate in its hiring practices. If the requirements for employment operate to exclude minority groups and are unrelated to job performance, the requirements violate Title VII. The would-be employee must prove that the employer's policy has a disparate impact on qualified women or minorities in the particular workforce (*not* in the much wider labor market). To overcome these facts, the employer must then prove that the practice is required by business necessity and is essential for the job, a heavy burden of proof. The employer, however, is not compelled to hire and promote to meet specified quotas under 1991 amendments.

National-Origin Discrimination

It is unlawful under Title VII to discriminate against any employee or applicant on the basis of national origin. National origin includes birthplace, ancestry, culture, and linguistic characteristics common to a specific ethnic group. The Immigration Reform and Control Act of 1986 (IRCA)˙ also prohibits discrimination based on citizenship. The IRCA covers employers of four or more employees and proscribes discrimination against any person (other than an unauthorized alien) in hiring, discharge, or recruiting or referring for a fee because of national origin or citizenship status. While the IRCA prohibits discrimination on the basis of citizenship, it also requires verification of legal status of all workers. Employers are required to check workers' documents to confirm the identity and work eligibility of all persons hired. The U.S. Immigration and Naturalization Service (INS) requires employers to (1) hire only those persons authorized to work in the United States, (2) ask all new employees to show documents that establish both identity and work authorization, and (3) complete the INS Employment Eligibility Verification Form I-9 for every new employee—U.S. citizens and noncitizens alike.

LEGAL FOCUS—PROBLEM

Kwame Maafo, a Ghanaian-born black man, was employed in the laundry at a resort hotel. He made several unsuccessful attempts to transfer to the accounting department. Maafo had completed high school in Ghana and studied business at several universities in the United Kingdom. After emigrating to the United States, he also took classes at two community colleges and completed thirty units at State University in pursuit of a bachelor's degree in finance. Management told Maafo that his accent was a barrier to all positions in the accounting department. Maafo filed a discrimination claim. Is an accent sufficient reason to deny Maafo the transfer?

Odima v. Westin Tucson Hotel, 53 F.3d 1484 (9th Cir. 1995).

To succeed with a defense based on accent and English usage, the employer must show that Maafo's accent or manner of speaking would have a detrimental effect on job performance (that clear enunciation was a requisite job requirement and Maafo did not meet that requirement). A legitimate nondiscriminatory reason to not hire the applicant must be shown. In the case upon which this hypothetical is based, the court found that the plaintiff "speaks fluent, understandable English. His speech was clear and understandable during a whole day on the witness stand during which he underwent probing cross-examination." The hotel lost the case.

Whereas discrimination against a person on the basis of national origin is illegal, it is also illegal to hire an alien who is not authorized to work in the United States. All employers (agricultural and nonagricultural) are prohibited from knowingly employing aliens not legally entitled to work in the United States. The definition of "knowingly hiring" has expanded greatly in recent years. The applicable law now states:

> *Knowing is defined as including not only actual knowledge, but also constructive knowledge—knowledge which may fairly be inferred through notice of certain facts and certain circumstances which would lead a person, through the exercise of reasonable care, to know about certain conditions.*

Religious Discrimination

Title VII prohibits employers from discriminating on the basis of an employee's religious beliefs. Prohibited discrimination may be overt and blatant or a more subtle failure to reasonably accommodate an employee's religious beliefs. The plaintiff must establish four elements of a *prima facie* case of discrimination:

> *(1) he is a member of or practices a particular religion; (2) he is qualified to perform the job at issue; (3) he has suffered some adverse employment action; and (4) someone outside the protected class of which he is a member was treated differently.*

undue hardship
An action or accommodation that is excessively costly, extensive, substantial, or disruptive, or fundamentally would alter the nature or operation of the business.

Unlike the other categories included in Title VII, there is not an absolute prohibition against discrimination on the basis of religion. Instead, employers owe a duty to accommodate the employee's religious beliefs unless to do so would cause **undue hardship** on the employer (not more than a *de minimis* adjustment). Among other things, courts have found that it would be an undue hardship if an employer had to

- violate the seniority provision of a valid collective-bargaining agreement,
- pay out more than a *de minimis* cost (in terms of money or efficiency) to accommodate a worker who has religious conflicts, or
- force other employees who do not wish to do so to trade places with the employee who has a religious conflict.

LEGAL FOCUS—CASE

Officer Angelo Rodriguez, a patrol officer in the Chicago Police Department (CPD), was among those assigned to guard an abortion clinic during various demonstrations. A lifelong Roman Catholic, Officer Rodriguez believed clinic activities to be wrongful, and he requested that he not be assigned to guard the clinic. Rodriguez was offered a transfer to a district without an abortion clinic, but he refused. Thereupon, CPD refused to exempt Rodriguez from the duty, claiming department policy prohibited an officer from refusing any assignment. Must the employer agree not to assign Officer Rodriguez to such duty as an accommodation to his religion?

Rodriguez v. Chicago, 156 F.3d 771 (7th Cir. 1998).

The court held for the Chicago Police Department, stating that

> *[b]ecause the CPD provided Officer Rodriguez with the option of transferring to a district without an abortion clinic and such a transfer would have eliminated the conflict between his job responsibilities and his religious beliefs, we conclude that the City has satisfied its duty of reasonable accommodation under Title VII.*

LEGAL FOCUS—PROBLEM

The Blessed Mary Catholic Hospital hired Kobe Jackson to work as a lab technician. Some time after Jackson was hired, he became a born-again Christian. He then began to supplement the blood and urine tests he administered to patients with attempts to convert them to his view of Protestant Christianity. Hospital administrators asked him to stop, but he kept on spreading his message. He was fired. Can he claim protection under the Civil Rights Act for religious discrimination?

Silo v. CHW Medical Foundation, 45 P. 3d 1162 (Cal. 2000).

The Civil Rights Act requires employers to reasonably accommodate employees but does not require any and all accommodations. The accommodation need not be what the employee demands, and it need not be the least burdensome one to the employee. The Blessed Mary Catholic Hospital has a right to restrict Jackson's behavior on the job and perhaps even his on-site activities during his break or lunch time. When he refused his instructions, the hospital was within its legal rights to fire him. In particular, a religious institution can discriminate by hiring only members of its own religion even for secular (not religious) positions (e.g., receptionist or gardener). The religious institution also can discriminate on the basis of conduct or views inconsistent with a religion's tenets and teachings.

Gender Discrimination

The Equal Employment Opportunity Act of 1972 (EEOA), amending the Civil Rights Act of 1964, dramatically changed employment law relating to women. Before 1972, state law often prohibited the employment of women in certain jobs ostensibly for their own protection. For example, many state statutes barred women from working at night, working as a bartender, or working more than a certain number of hours per day or week. The EEOA struck down most of these limiting laws. Employers are forbidden to classify jobs as male or female, and they cannot have separate male and female seniority lists.

LEGAL FOCUS—BACKGROUND

Some 115 female flight attendants brought a class action suit against Pan American World Airways, Inc., in 1984. The women had been suspended, denied promotion, or fired for being overweight. The airline had used different tables of heights and weights, classifying men under the heading of "large frames" and women under "medium frames." The difference between the two sexes was eleven pounds for a person 5′7″ tall. Did the corporation's standards discriminate illegally against women?

Independent Union of Flight Attendants v. Pan American World Airways, Inc., No. C-88-3120-WWS, 1989 U.S. Dist. LEXIS 14759 (N.D. Ca. April 7, 1989).

Yes, the standard did discriminate. The federal district court in San Francisco found the weight standards to be discriminatory against the female employees, while reserving the issue of damages for later determination. Pan American began an appeal, but dropped it in 1989. Without admitting bias, it agreed to pay the attendants $2.35 million. It also adopted a more flexible weight policy with a new "large frame" category for women. Under its new policy, a 5′7″ woman of medium frame should weigh 139 pounds; for a 5′7″ woman with a large frame, the acceptable weight could be as much as 150 pounds. Moreover, the attendant could add up to three pounds upon reaching the age of thirty-five years, and again at ages forty-five and fifty-five years.

bona fide occupational qualifications (BFOQ)
Selection criteria that serve a legitimate business interest, which is justified although it has a disparate impact.

A defense to a sex discrimination case is the existence of a **bona fide occupational qualification (BFOQ)**. A BFOQ is a job requirement that, although discriminatory, is essential to the job in question. The BFOQ defense is available for gender, age, religion, and national origin discrimination but never for discrimination based on race or color.

LEGAL FOCUS—CASE

Four male corrections officers at the Women's Community Correctional Center (WCCC) on the Island of Oahu, Hawaii, filed a Title VII sexual discrimination claim after the WCCC assigned only female correction officers to six of forty-one available watch posts. The WCCC claimed that gender was a BFOQ because the protested watch sites were shower and toilet areas and the purpose of the restriction was to protect female inmates and to prevent allegations of sexual misconduct. Is gender a BFOQ in this case?

Robino v. Iranon, 145 F.3d 1109 (9th Cir. 1998).

The court said yes.

> *Each designated female-only post is residential and requires the ACO [Adult Corrections Officer] on duty to observe the inmates in the showers and toilet areas for the prison's own security or provides unsupervised access to the inmates. The state's legitimate penology interests outweigh whatever interests the male ACOs may have in standing the watches of their choice. Viewing the evidence in the light most favorable to the plaintiffs, the defendants have met their burden of demonstrating that their policy is reasonably necessary to the operation of the WCCC. The defendants have established these six female-only posts are a reasonable response to the concerns about inmate privacy and allegations of abuse by male ACOs.*

The following case illustrates how the well-intended protection of one group can hurt another.

LEGAL FOCUS—CASE

Johnson Controls, Inc., of Milwaukee, produces batteries. The manufacturing process exposes workers to levels of airborne lead considered harmful to a fetus and may cause birth defects. In 1982, Johnson instituted a program banning women from all jobs in the division where the airborne lead level was twenty-five micrograms per cubic meter or higher, unless they presented a doctor's certificate of sterility. It also barred women from jobs where the lead level was below twenty-five micrograms if the jobs could lead to promotion to more dangerous areas. Female employees working in the lead division were transferred to other divisions without loss of pay or seniority. The United Auto Workers union claimed that this was illegal sex discrimination and filed a complaint with the Equal Employment Opportunity Commission on behalf of seven involuntarily transferred women. A federal civil rights suit followed, and the district judge awarded summary judgment to Johnson Controls without trial, although a 1982 amendment to Title VII (the Pregnancy Discrimination Act) declared that "women affected by pregnancy or childbirth … shall be treated the same for all employment related purposes … as other persons not so affected but similar in their ability or inability to work." The UAW appealed. What was the outcome?

United Autoworkers v. Johnson Controls, Inc., 499 U.S. 187, 111 S.Ct. 1196 (1991).

The U.S. Supreme Court reversed the trial court, stating,

> *The PDA's (Pregnancy Discrimination Act) amendment to Title VII contains a BFOQ standard of its own: Unless pregnant employees differ from others in their ability or inability to work, they must be treated the same as other employees.… Title VII and the PDA simply do not allow a woman's dismissal because of her failure to submit to sterilization.*

LEGAL FOCUS—CASE

Macy applied for a position with the Bureau of Alcohol, Tobacco, Firearms & Explosives as a male. Macy later informed ATFE that she was transitioning from male to female. ATFE then informed Macy that another applicant had been hired because that applicant was farther along in the background check process. Macy filed a complaint against ATFE with the EEOC alleging that the real reason she was denied employment was because of her gender identity (transgender woman). Is Macy protected under Title VII?

Macy v. Holder, EEOC Appeal No. 0120120821 (Apr. 20, 2012).

sexual harassment
A form of illegal gender discrimination wherein (1) job opportunities, promotions, and the like are given on the basis of sexual favors or (2) the employee is subjected to a work environment where the employee must put up with sexual comments, jokes, or physical contact that is sexually offensive.

quid pro quo (Latin: "something for something")
Expression used in sexual harassment situations when sexual favors or demands are a term or condition of an individual's employment, or the basis for employment decisions affecting such individual.

hostile environment
Conduct by others in the workplace that has the purpose or effect of unreasonably interfering with an individual's work performance or creating an intimidating, hostile, or offensive working environment.

According to the EEOC, yes. The EEOC ruled that Title VII bars discrimination not only on the basis of biological sex, but also because of gender stereotyping, as well. The EEOC concluded that Macy potentially could establish sex discrimination either because the Bureau believed that biological men should look like men and wear male clothing, or because the Bureau was willing to hire a man, but not a woman. Whatever the facts established, transgender discrimination is discrimination based on sex in violation of Title VII, according to the EEOC. The Supreme Court, however, has not yet interpreted Title VII with respect to transgender discrimination.

Sexual Harassment

Sexual harassment in the workplace is a form of illegal gender discrimination that has garnered much publicity in recent years. Sexual harassment, a type of Title VII violation, occurs when job opportunities, promotions, and the like are given on the basis of sexual favors. Harassment also occurs when an employee is subjected to a work environment in which the employee must put up with sexual comments, jokes, or physical contact that is sexually offensive.

The EEOC has defined two types of sexual harassment in its guidelines:

1. ***Quid pro quo***.

   Unwelcome sexual advances, requests for sexual favors, and other verbal or physical conduct of a sexual nature constitute 'quid pro quo' sexual harassment when (1) submission to such conduct is made either explicitly or implicitly a term or condition of an individual's employment, or (2) submission to or rejection of such conduct by an individual is used as the basis for employment decisions affecting such individual.

   This form of harassment usually involves a supervisor–subordinate relationship because it requires the authority to grant an employee help in return for the unwelcome advance or punishment for the lack of cooperation.

2. **Hostile environment**. Conduct in a hostile environment "has the purpose or effect of unreasonably interfering with an individual's work performance or creating an intimidating, hostile, or offensive working environment." The EEOC considers several factors to determine whether or not a hostile environment exists for either gender:

   (1) whether the conduct was verbal or physical or both; (2) how frequently it was repeated; (3) whether the conduct was hostile or patently offensive; (4) whether the alleged harasser was a coworker or supervisor; (5) whether others joined in perpetrating the harassment; and (6) whether the harassment was directed at more than one individual. No one factor controls. An assessment is made based upon the totality of the circumstances.

Employers are liable for the actions of the supervisors because supervisors most likely control conditions of employment. When no tangible job consequences occur (like being fired or not promoted), an employee may still recover against the employer for unwelcome and threatening advances of a supervisor, subject to the employer's ability to prove an affirmative defense. This defense examines the reasonableness of the employer's conduct in conjunction with that of the plaintiff and questions:

- Whether or not the employer exercised reasonable care in order to prevent and promptly correct any sexually harassing behavior and
- Whether or not the employee unreasonably failed to take advantage of any preventative or corrective opportunities provided by the employer or otherwise failed to avoid the harm. Preventive precautions for the employer may include:
  - A well-publicized complaint-reporting system that employees trust.
  - Neutral, confidential, investigative procedures.
  - A provision in the firm's corporate Code of Ethics that states in unequivocal terms that discriminatory behavior will not be tolerated.
  - Required attendance at gender neutral training sessions on sexual harassment.

LEGAL FOCUS—CASE

Rena Weeks began work as Martin Greenstein's secretary on July 23, 1991. Greenstein was a partner at Baker & McKenzie, the world's largest law firm. "On August 8, the Thursday of her third week at the firm, Weeks had lunch with several persons, including Greenstein, at a local restaurant. As they left the restaurant, Greenstein gave her some M&M candies, which she put into the breast pocket of her blouse. As they walked to Greenstein's car, Greenstein pulled Weeks back, put his arm over her shoulder, put his hand in her breast pocket and dropped more candies into the pocket. He then put his knee in her lower back, pulled her shoulders back, and said, 'Let's see which breast is bigger.'" Is this behavior actionable sexual harassment for Greenstein and his employer, Baker & McKenzie?

Weeks v. Baker & McKenzie, 63 Cal.App. 4th 1128, 74 Cal.Rptr. 2d 510 (1998).

A San Francisco jury said yes, awarding Weeks $50,000 in compensatory damages. They said yes to this jury instruction:

> *Has plaintiff Rena Weeks proved by clear and convincing evidence that defendant Baker & McKenzie (a) had advance knowledge of the unfitness of defendant Martin R. Greenstein and with a conscious disregard of the rights or safety of others continued to employ him, or (b) ratified the conduct of Mr. Greenstein which is found to be oppression or malice?*

The jury awarded Weeks $7.1 million in total punitive damages. The trial court judge reduced the punitive damages award to $3.5 million, an amount later upheld on appeal. In upholding the punitive damages award against Baker & McKenzie, the court stated,

> *In all events, there is substantial evidence that at the time Weeks was hired, Baker & McKenzie and its relevant managing agents were well aware that Greenstein was likely to create a hostile work environment for women, and that Baker & McKenzie consistently failed to take measures reasonably designed to protect women from*

Greenstein's abuse. The failure to place reports of Greenstein's misconduct in his own personnel file so as to warn future supervisors of that conduct in and of itself demonstrates a conscious disregard for the rights and safety of other employees. No formal action was taken by the firm to prevent Greenstein from creating a hostile work environment.

Treating people in a nondiscriminatory fashion is clearly a laudable goal, but difficulty among people of good will can still arise. An employee wrongfully accused of discriminatory treatment may be discharged without a full and accurate investigation to protect the employer from sexual harassment claims. Except in limited circumstances, the wrongfully accused employee has no legal recourse. Employees protected by a just cause provision of a labor contract are among those with some protection. In union contracts, issues of employee discipline including discharge usually provide for a grievance mechanism, which culminates in a neutral arbitration. In the usual labor contract, an arbitrator decides whether or not the employee was a harasser and whether or not discipline is consistent with fair treatment under the contract.

The risk and complexity of civil rights lawsuits lead defendants to settle cases out of court. In 1992, State Farm Insurance settled a class action sex-discrimination lawsuit for $157 million to be paid to 814 women plaintiffs. The federal district court previously had ruled that State Farm had engaged in discriminatory practices. The court approved an agreement between State Farm and aggrieved employees whereby the company agreed that for the next ten years at least 50 percent of all sales agents hired would be women, to help remedy past violations. This affirmative action remedy was based on evidence of discriminatory practices that had occurred between 1970 and 1974, a period during which State Farm had hired 586 agents in California, but only one was a woman. Many women had applied for positions but had been rejected. One of the witnesses who worked as an insurance agent's assistant testified that when she applied for a sales agent job, she was told that a college degree was a prerequisite. Yet, at that time, State Farm was hiring male sales agents who did not have college degrees. Later, she was told that State Farm would not hire women as agents. At the time, this settlement was the largest in the history of civil rights litigation for any type of discrimination. Divided by the number of plaintiffs, however, the average award shrank to $19,287.

LEGAL FOCUS—CASE

Joseph Oncale worked as a roustabout for Sundowner Offshore Services on an oil platform in the Gulf of Mexico. On several occasions, he was forcibly subjected to sex-related, humiliating actions against him by three of his eight-man crew in front of the others. Two of the employees, Danny Pippen and John Lyons, also "physically assaulted Oncale in a sexual manner, and Lyons threatened him with rape." Oncale complained to a supervisor, but no help was forthcoming. Oncale quit and then filed a complaint against Sundowner alleging that he was discriminated against in his employment because of his sex, forcing him to resign. Is same-sex sexual harassment a form of discrimination protected by Title VII of the Civil Rights Act?

Joseph Oncale v. Sundowner Offshore Services, Incorporated, et al., 523 U.S. 75, 118 S.Ct. 998 (1998).

Yes, same-sex sexual harassment is a form of discrimination. Title VII's prohibition of discrimination "because of … sex" protects men as well as women but the *Oncale* case raised a different issue because the alleged harassment was same-gender harassment, in this case male on male. The court found that distinction unimportant.

> *We see no justification in the statutory language or our precedents for a categorical rule excluding same-sex harassment claims from the coverage of Title VII. As some courts have observed, male-on-male sexual harassment in the workplace was assuredly not the principal evil Congress was concerned with when it enacted Title VII. But statutory prohibitions often go beyond the principal evil to cover reasonably comparable evils, and it is ultimately the provisions of our laws rather than the principal concerns of our legislators by which we are governed. Title VII prohibits "discriminate[ion] ... because of ... sex" in the "terms" or "conditions" of employment.*

Equal Pay for Equal Work

LEGAL FOCUS—PROBLEM

Disappointed in her quest for civilian employment after leaving the Army, Laura Lanier enrolled in a private business school. Within a year, she was qualified as a computer operator. A wholesale hardware supply house hired her to work in its inventory control department. Her performance and output soon equaled that of several male computer operators who had been with the company for periods ranging from three to ten years. All of the men were paid more than Lanier. Was this a violation of federal equal pay legislation?

No, this is not a violation. The federal Equal Pay Act of 1963 specifically prohibits wage discrimination on the basis of gender for equal work in jobs that require equal skill, effort, and responsibility and that are performed under similar working conditions. The law, however, permits inequality in pay on the basis of (1) seniority, (2) merit, (3) quality or quantity of production, or (4) any factor other than gender (e.g., a shift differential, a higher rate maintained for an employee reassigned to a lower rate job because of "exigencies of the employer's needs," different level of responsibility, a training program, or higher sales commissions because of higher profits on goods sold). The employer, however, must act in good faith without unlawful discrimination in assignment and evaluation of work. Thus, in the *Lanier* case, there was no violation if the pay differentials were based on seniority.

For a variety of reasons, certain jobs tend to be held mostly by women—and most of these jobs pay less than most jobs held by men. When different pay scales are based on differences in work performed, there is no unlawful discrimination under present laws. Under the theory of **comparable worth**, however, jobs that have equal social and economic value should be paid equally. Thus, it is said, the services of a registered nurse who helps to keep you alive are worth at least as much as those of a licensed electrician who helps to provide light and power in your hospital room. The problem is that it is extremely difficult to measure with precision and fairness all the elements and variables that should determine the dollar value of different jobs at different times in different places. Presumably, the economic forces of supply and demand automatically should decide the question. Realistically, this function of the free market is distorted by such factors as traditional attitudes, long-established seniority rights, union pressures, government licensing regulations, and willingness or ability to make a commitment to long-term, full-time, career-type employment.

comparable worth
The theory that the same wage or salary should be paid for jobs that have equal societal and economic value based on such factors as required preparation, skill, effort, responsibility, and working conditions.

Lilly Ledbetter, an employee of Goodyear Tire and Rubber Company in Alabama, fought to close the gap between women's and men's wages. She filed suit against her employer alleging that several supervisors had given her poor evaluations because of her sex, and as a result, her pay had not increased as much as it would have if she had been evaluated fairly. She also claimed that those past pay decisions affected the amount of her pay throughout her employment, so that by the end of her employment, she was earning significantly less than her male colleagues. While the jury found these facts to be true, the statute of limitations under Title VII requires a complaint to be filed 180 days after the alleged unlawful employment practice occurred. The Supreme Court concluded that since Ledbetter alleged a series of discrete discriminatory acts, each of which was independently identifiable and actionable, a timely EEOC charge should have been filed with respect to each alleged violation. As a result, Ledbetter was not entitled to relief for any cumulative pay discrimination. In response, Congress passed the Lilly Ledbetter Fair Pay Act of 2009, which provides that the 180-day statute of limitations for filing an equal-pay lawsuit for pay discrimination resets with each new paycheck affected by that discriminatory action, and thus tolls (suspends) the running of Title VII's statute of limitation.

Age Discrimination

LEGAL FOCUS—BACKGROUND

The U.S. Department of Health and Human services reports that the sixty-five years and older population will increase by 36 percent between 2010 and 2020. Older workers are staying in the workforce longer, too. Between 1977 and 2007 the employment of workers over the age of sixty-five years increased 101 percent. What rights do these graying workers have under federal law when employers want to hire a less expensive youthful workforce?

Age Discrimination in Employment Act of 1967
Federal law that added "advanced age" (over age forty years) to attributes listed in the Civil Rights Act of 1964 that may not be used negatively in employment decisions.

Three years after the Civil Rights Act became law, Congress passed the **Age Discrimination in Employment Act of 1967 (ADEA)**, which prohibits "arbitrary age discrimination in employment" of persons forty years of age and older. It makes it unlawful for an employer in interstate commerce (including employment agencies and unions) to fail or refuse to hire or to discharge any individual, or otherwise to discriminate against persons with respect to compensation, terms, conditions, or privileges of employment, because of age. The ADEA applies to "a person (including a corporation) engaged in an industry affecting commerce who has twenty or more employees for each working day in each of twenty or more calendar weeks in the current or preceding calendar year."

LEGAL FOCUS—CASE

The new terms of a collective-bargaining agreement eliminated the employer's obligation to provide health benefits to retired employees, except for workers who were at least fifty years old. Employees between forty and fifty years of age alleged that the agreement violated the ADEA because it discriminated against them with respect to compensation, terms, conditions, or privileges of employment, because of their age. Is their allegation correct?

General Dynamics Land Systems, Inc. v. Cline, 540 U.S. 581 (2004).

No, their allegation is not correct. The Supreme Court concluded that the legislative history of the ADEA suggests that it was designed to protect relatively old workers from discrimination that works to the advantage of relatively young workers, and that the "enemy of 40 is 30, not 50."

Under the ADEA an

> *"employee" means an individual employed by any employer except that the term "employee" shall not include any person elected to public office in any State or political subdivision of any State by the qualified voters thereof, or any person chosen by such officer to be on such officer's personal staff, or an appointee on the policymaking level or an immediate adviser with respect to the exercise of the constitutional or legal powers of the office.*

The law also provides for mandatory retirement of certain executives over the age of sixty-five years under certain conditions.

The ADEA permits discrimination when age is a BFOQ reasonably necessary to the normal operation of the particular business, or in cases in which the differentiation is based on reasonable factors other than age, and it also recognizes the right of companies to discipline or even discharge a person for good cause. The ADEA is joined by the Workers Benefit Protection Act making it illegal for a business to use a worker's past-forty age as the basis for discriminatory treatment in awarding employee benefits.

LEGAL FOCUS—CASE

A radio station hired a market research firm, which evaluated its programming and proposed changes to its content to increase revenue and profits. As a result, a disc jockey's "oldies" programming air time was reduced and eventually eliminated. He complained that he was the victim of age discrimination. Was he?

Lit v. Infinity Broad. Corp., 2005 U.S. Dist. LEXIS 19927 (E.D. Pa. June 8, 2005).

No, he was not a victim of age discrimination. Program changes were attributable to a "reasonable factor other than age" given the employer's evidence that the station's reformatting was the result of extensive market research that led the station's executives to determine a new direction was necessary to keep the station successful.

Almost all states have enacted their own laws barring employment discrimination on the basis of race, sex, religion, national origin, and advanced age. Most states call for equal pay for equal work and also follow the federal model of protecting the employment rights of handicapped persons. Also, the developing tort law of wrongful dismissal (discussed later in the chapter) sometimes protects permanent employees against arbitrary discharge without good cause. Recently, the Supreme Court recognized that the disparate impact theory of discrimination was available to ADEA plaintiffs.

LEGAL FOCUS—CASE

The City of Jackson Mississippi sought to bring the starting salaries of police officers up to the regional average. It granted raises to all police officers and police dispatchers. Officers who had less than five years of service received proportionately greater raises when compared with their former pay than those with more seniority. Although some officers more than forty years old had less than five years of service, most of the older officers had more years, so the criteria for awarding raises disparately affected older officers. Does the raise criterion violate the ADEA?

Smith v. City of Jackson, 544 U.S. 228 (2005).

No, the criterion does not violate the ADEA. Although the Supreme Court recognized that the ADEA protects older workers from disparate impact discrimination, it also recognized that the Act permits differentiation based on reasonable factors other than age. In this case, the employer legitimately attempted to make salaries competitive across the board. The disparate impact resulted from the fact that because older workers were paid at a higher level, their percentage increase was lower.

What Is Meant by "Affirmative Action" in Employment Practices?

affirmative action programs Programs that require that preference in hiring be given to some statutorily protected group.

reverse discrimination Label given to the results of affirmative action programs by opponents who claim that such programs discriminate against male and white workers.

Because of many years of discrimination in employment against women and minorities, government administrators have made special efforts to provide these groups with more opportunities for gainful employment. By threatening to terminate lucrative supply and research contracts, federal government agencies have often pressured companies to adopt **affirmative action programs**. Essentially, these programs require positive efforts to hire and promote minorities and women, in percentages reflecting the makeup of the surrounding communities (sometimes referred to as the "potential applicant pool"). These efforts might include special outreach programs (recruiting), special training, and preferential hiring. Some have claimed this is **reverse discrimination** against qualified nonminority male employees and applicants. The presumption has been that such persons are better able to fend for themselves in the job market. It should be noted that Title VII neither requires nor denies affirmative action as a remedy for discriminatory practices.

No provision of Title VII provides for affirmative action; instead, it is a judicial remedy and sometimes administrative decision to correct historic discriminatory practices. Opponents of affirmative action say that the Civil Rights Act of 1964 calls for neutrality, with no discrimination for or against anyone. Proponents argue that with neutrality, corrective action might take several generations, and that is too long to correct historic discrimination.

The Supreme Court has not been as helpful as it might in determining the legality of affirmative action, perpetuating a contentious political debate over its efficacy and legality. In 1979, the Supreme Court gave its stamp of approval to a private, voluntary arrangement negotiated by the Kaiser Aluminum and Chemical Co. with the United Steelworkers Union. This program set up a skilled craft-training program with half the slots arbitrarily reserved for blacks and half for whites. At the time, although there was a 30 percent black population in the geographical area of the plant, fewer than 2 percent of the skilled craftworkers were black. Brian Weber, who was white, was passed over for skilled craft training and challenged the company and union plan as discriminatory. He lost. The Court's approval of this private, voluntary affirmative action plan to correct manifest racial imbalance automatically legitimized some 175,000 similar plans already in existence at that time and others that have been added since then. Moreover, one effect was to shield such employers from charges that the plans impliedly admitted prior bias for which they could be sued.

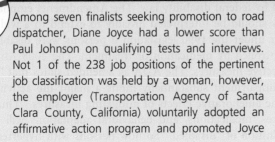

LEGAL FOCUS—CASE

Among seven finalists seeking promotion to road dispatcher, Diane Joyce had a lower score than Paul Johnson on qualifying tests and interviews. Not 1 of the 238 job positions of the pertinent job classification was held by a woman, however, the employer (Transportation Agency of Santa Clara County, California) voluntarily adopted an affirmative action program and promoted Joyce to the position. Johnson claimed this violated his rights under Title VII, and the trial court agreed. The court of appeals reversed, and Johnson appealed to the U.S. Supreme Court. How did it rule?

Johnson v. Transportation Agency, Santa Clara County, California, 480 U.S. 616, 107 S.Ct. 1442 (1987).

The judgment of the court of appeals was affirmed. The Court opined that the employer had acted reasonably in considering Joyce's gender because of "'a manifest imbalance' that reflected underrepresentation of women in 'traditionally segregated job categories.'" She was one of seven applicants, all classified as "qualified and eligible," and the agency director was authorized to promote any one of the seven. Johnson remains an employee who may seek other promotions in the future.

Amendments to Title VII in 1991 highlight the legal ambiguity of affirmative action:

> *Nothing in the amendments made by this Act shall be construed to require or encourage an employer to adopt hiring or promotion quotas on the basis of race, color, religion, sex or national origin: Provided, however, that nothing in the amendments made by this Act shall be construed to affect court-ordered remedies, affirmative action, or conciliation agreements that are otherwise in accordance with the law.*

In 1996, California voters passed a constitutional amendment by initiative, Proposition 209. The key provision of the initiative is that "[t]he state shall not discriminate against, or grant preferential treatment to, any individual or group on the basis of race, sex, color, ethnicity, or national origin in the operation of public employment, public education, or public contracting." Court challenges to the initiative have been unsuccessful. The effect of the initiative has been the curtailment of affirmative action programs like the one found in the preceding case.

Americans with Disabilities Act

Americans with Disabilities Act of 1990 (ADA)
Federal law that bars discrimination in the employment of capable handicapped persons by both private and public employers, and that requires reasonable accommodations for their special needs.

The **Americans with Disabilities Act of 1990 (ADA)** was hailed as a declaration of independence for some 43 million disabled Americans at the time of its enactment. The ADA applies to both the public and private sectors and went well beyond prior existing protective legislation at the state and federal levels. The ADA applies to practices in employment, public and private accommodations, transportation, and telecommunications facilities. Business firms and other establishments must improve access for the disabled if "readily achievable" without "undue hardship." This hardship could involve the nature and cost of the accommodation in comparison to the overall size of the firm and its financial resources.

Employers with fifteen or more employees are forbidden to discriminate in employment of disabled people who are capable of performing the essential functions of the job and are expected to make reasonable accommodations if necessary to allow them to do so. The ADA does not require employment of anyone who is unqualified for the job, nor does it require preferential treatment for the disabled. The 2008 amendments to the Act made several important changes to expand the scope of employees who are protected by federal disability law. The Amendments emphasized that the definition of disability should be interpreted broadly to extend to a wider class of individuals. It was unclear under the 1990 legislation if persons were disabled if their impairments could be controlled by medication or treatment. The 2008 Amendments addressed the use of corrective measures. The ADA as amended states that "the determination of whether an impairment substantially limits a major life activity shall be made without regard to the ameliorative effects of mitigating measures." Thus, persons who use adaptive measures, medications, and behavioral adaptations will no longer be excluded from the definition of "disabled." So now persons with hypertension may be covered, even though medication alleviates the potentially debilitating symptoms of such a condition.

The statutory definitions are critical in this legislation. The identification of members of the protected class in other antidiscrimination laws is established easily. Characteristics such as race, sex, and age are obvious. In contrast, the identification of that class of persons, who are disabled and deserving of protection from the effects of irrational discrimination based on nonperformance based criteria, is much more elusive. The key terms in this statute are not defined by medical encyclopedias or common usage, but rather by what Congress specifically has enunciated as their meaning.

Definitions

Determining what is a disability deserving of legal protection and defining reasonable accommodation have been among the most difficult tasks since enactment of the ADA. The definition of disability used is different from that used in workers' compensation, Social Security, and other laws providing benefits to people with a determined disability. Under the ADA, a qualified individual with a disability is a person who, with or without reasonable accommodation, can perform the essential functions of the employment position.

In other words, the statute is *not* unemployment insurance for employees who, because of a disability, are unable to perform job functions and need the financial support that a job would provide. Instead the statute protects employees who are able to perform job functions from arbitrary discrimination because of their disabilities. In short, the ADA prohibits discrimination because of a disability that does not interfere with job performance. It neither requires employers to hire persons with disabilities nor prohibits the termination of persons with disabilities who are unable to perform the essential functions of their job.

The definition of disability has three prongs:

- A physical or mental impairment that substantially limits one or more major life activities, such as
  - Cancer
  - Blindness
  - Deafness
  - Being HIV positive
  - Being a recovering substance abuser
- A record of such impairment
- Being regarded as having such an impairment (e.g., a birthmark)

"Substantially limits" means being unable to perform a major life activity that the average person in the general population can perform or being significantly restricted as to the condition, manner, or duration under which an individual can perform a major life activity as compared with the condition, manner, or duration under which the average person in the general population can perform that same major life activity. The amended Act also expands the definition of major life activities by including two nonexhaustive lists. The first list includes many activities that the EEOC has recognized, such as walking, as well as activities that EEOC has not specifically recognized, such as reading, bending, and communicating. The second list of major life activities includes major bodily functions, such as functions of the immune, endocrine, circulatory, and reproductive systems.

LEGAL FOCUS—CASE

Maria worked for a Community College as a student counselor, providing individual counseling to students, including career counseling, academic planning, as well as personal and crisis counseling. She suffers from post-traumatic stress disorder as a result of brain injury that incurred in a car accident. Her symptoms include unpredictable emotional outbursts that are exacerbated by stress. After several outbursts that included shouting at students and threatening her department head, she was terminated. Could her termination have been wrongful under the ADA?

Menchaca v. Maricopa Comm. College Dist., No. CV-07-1970-PHX-GMS, 2009 U.S. Dist. LEXIS 5510 (Jan. 23, 2009).

The termination possibly was wrongful. Working and caring for oneself constitute major life activities, and her ability to perform those functions was impaired as a result of the injury. A reasonable jury could conclude that her post-traumatic stress disorder, when activated by sufficient stressors, substantially limited her ability to interact at work and to care for herself. As a result, a job coach might be a reasonable accommodation to assist her with her communication skills.

Reasonable Accommodation

A qualified employee or applicant with a disability is one who with reasonable accommodation can perform the essential functions of the job in question. Reasonable accommodation may include, but is not limited to the following:

- Making existing facilities used by employees readily accessible to and usable by persons with disabilities.
- Restructuring jobs, modifying work schedules or loads, or reassigning to a vacant position.
- Acquiring or modifying equipment or devices; adjusting modifying examinations, training materials, or policies; and providing qualified readers or interpreters.

Reasonable accommodation may be necessary to apply for a job, to perform job functions, or to enjoy the benefits and privileges of employment that are enjoyed by people without disabilities. An employer is not required to lower production standards to make an accommodation and is not obligated to provide personal use items, such as eyeglasses or hearing aids.

An employee must provide notice to the employer of the disability and resulting limitations, if any. An employer is not charged with the responsibility to know each and every need of its workforce. The EEOC suggests that the determination of a reasonable accommodation should be resolved through an interactive process involving both the employer and the employee in which the employer (1) analyzes the job to determine its purpose and essential functions, (2) consults with the employee to ascertain the precise job-related limitations imposed by the individual's disability and how those limitations could be overcome with a reasonable accommodation, (3) identifies potential accommodations and assesses the effectiveness of each in consultation with the employee, and (4) selects and implements the accommodation that is most appropriate for the parties, considering the preferences of the individual.

undue hardship
An action or accommodation that is excessively costly, extensive, substantial, or disruptive, or fundamentally would alter the nature or operation of the business.

An employer does not have to provide a reasonable accommodation that would cause an **undue hardship** to the employer. The EEOC provides the following factors to determine undue hardship:

- The nature and cost of the accommodation needed
- The overall financial resources of the facility making the reasonable accommodation, the number of persons employed at this facility, and the effect on expenses and resources of the facility
- The overall financial resources, size, number of employees, and type and location of facilities of the employer (if the facility involved in the reasonable accommodation is part of a larger entity)
- The type of operation of the employer, including the structure and functions of the workforce, the geographic separateness, and the administrative or fiscal relationship of the facility involved in making the accommodation to the employer
- The impact of the accommodation on the operation of the facility

The plaintiff bears the burden of proving that a reasonable accommodation is possible. Once such proof is established, the burden shifts to the employer to show that the accommodation is not reasonable and would result in an undue hardship. For example, allowing time to conduct self-blood tests and carrying snacks could be a reasonable accommodation for diabetic school bus drivers.

LEGAL FOCUS—CASE

Michael Salley began working at Circuit City as a video sales counselor. Within two years, he became a store manager. Circuit City had a drug policy providing that managers "will work to ensure that employees are free from the effects of alcohol and illegal substances, whether consumed on or off Company property." Within a year of becoming a store manager, Salley told a superior of his significant drug activity and addiction, but said it was a thing of the past. Salley was assured that no action would be taken against him. Unfortunately, he suffered a relapse into drug and alcohol addiction. Circuit City discovered his drug use and other apparent violations of company drug policy, including missing work time because of drug use and alleged drug involvement with a subordinate, whose drug use he failed to report. Circuit City fired Salley two days after he signed a statement admitting his misconduct. Was Salley's firing in violation of the ADA?

Salley v. Circuit City Stores, Inc., 160 F.3d 977 (3rd Cir. 1998).

No, his firing did not violate the ADA. Although an employer is required to reasonably accommodate a person with a disability, it is not required to tolerate disobedience and violation of company rules:

> *[F]or purposes of [the ADA], the term "qualified individual with a disability" shall not include any employee or applicant who is currently engaging in the illegal use of drugs, when the covered entity acts on the basis of such use.*

The employee poses a hazard to the public and fellow employees. The court upheld Salley's dismissal, stating that "an employer may hold an alcoholic or drug-dependent employee" to the same qualification standards for employment or job performance and behavior that such entity holds other employees, even if any unsatisfactory performance or behavior is related to the drug use or alcoholism of such employee: "[No] reasonable jury could conclude that Salley was discharged for his disability rather than his drug use and concomitant violations of Circuit City's drug policy."

The ADA provides employers a limited defense of business necessity, such as a qualification standard that is "job related and consistent with business necessity" as well as a requirement that an individual not pose a direct threat to the health or safety of other individuals in the workplace. In other words, employers who refuse to place an employee in a position that poses a direct threat to the employee's own health and safety does not violate the ADA.

LEGAL FOCUS—CASE

Mario Echazabal worked for independent contractors at an oil refinery owned by Chevron U.S.A. Inc. He applied for a job directly with Chevron but an employment medical examination showed he had suffered a hepatitis C illness, which had damaged his liver. Chevron's medical staff was concerned that further exposure to toxins at Chevron's refinery would make his condition worse. Echazabal did not get the job at Chevron, and to make matters worse, Chevron asked the independent contractors to reassign him. They instead let him go. Echazabal sued under the ADA. Chevron defended, claiming that an EEOC regulation allowed it to refuse to hire someone whose disability on the job would pose a direct threat to other workers' health. Echazabal claimed the EEOC regulation was not consistent with the ADA. Who is correct, Chevron or Echazabal?

Chevron USA, Inc. v. Echazabal, 536 U.S. 73, 122 S.Ct. 2045 (2002).

Chevron is correct. The U.S. Supreme Court unanimously held that the ADA permits the EEOC's regulation allowing Chevron to refuse to hire someone for a task that endangers the worker's health.

As with other protected classes, certain questions and tests are prohibited. Among prohibited questions are those asking about the existence, nature, or severity of the disability. Job-related questions are allowed, such as "Can you keyboard or work with the newest software?" Passing a medical examination may be a prehiring qualification for a job as long as it is required of all applicants for the same job and is somehow job and business related. Although inquiries by the employer generally are prohibited, an individual seeking an accommodation for disabilities must let the employer know that an adjustment or change at work for a reason related to a medical condition is needed.

LEGAL FOCUS—PROBLEM

Jennifer interviewed for a job at a retail establishment. She had experience and training as a sales clerk, but was not hired. The prospective employer explained the reason for the decision: "You have your ears pierced twice and a visible tattoo. I know you say you have experience but at twenty-two, you're too young for my clientele. Besides, you graduated from the University of Texas, and I hate the Longhorns." Does Jennifer have a valid discrimination claim?

No, she does not have a valid claim. The prospective employer did not use any illegal criteria in reaching the decision. Remember, generally speaking, employers can hire, fire, promote, and demote for any reason, unless it is an illegal reason under state or federal law. Unless a law has made it made it illegal to discriminate because of a person's piercings, tattoos, youth, or alma mater, then the act is not illegal, although it may be unethical to hire, fire, promote, or demote for arbitrary non-performance-based criteria. It follows then, that documenting poor performance is not required to justify firing an employee, but compiling such a record is helpful for rebutting allegations of discrimination.

Exhibit 12.1 lists the major federal statutes prohibiting employment discrimination.

EXHIBIT 12.1
Major Federal Statutes Prohibiting Employment Discrimination

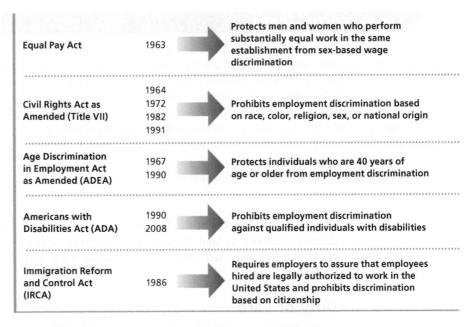

Equal Pay Act	1963	**Protects men and women who perform substantially equal work in the same establishment from sex-based wage discrimination**
Civil Rights Act as Amended (Title VII)	1964 1972 1982 1991	**Prohibits employment discrimination based on race, color, religion, sex, or national origin**
Age Discrimination in Employment Act as Amended (ADEA)	1967 1990	**Protects individuals who are 40 years of age or older from employment discrimination**
Americans with Disabilities Act (ADA)	1990 2008	**Prohibits employment discrimination against qualified individuals with disabilities**
Immigration Reform and Control Act (IRCA)	1986	**Requires employers to assure that employees hired are legally authorized to work in the United States and prohibits discrimination based on citizenship**

Source: Adapted from American Bar Association, Section of Law Practice Management (Chicago: ABA,1993).

WHAT ARE THE BASIC DUTIES OF EMPLOYEES?

Duty to Follow Lawful Instructions

LEGAL FOCUS—PROBLEM

Two weeks after being employed as a deckhand on Plato Pamasi's 180-foot yacht, *The Invincible*, Jake Morgan refused to obey an order of Chief Mate Ben Blight to swing over the side on a rope ladder and scrape and repaint a rusted section of the hull. Morgan argued that nothing had been said about such dirty and potentially dangerous duties when he was hired. Moreover, he said, "I'm too tired. Why don't you do it?" May he be fired without recourse?

Yes, he may be fired. Scraping and painting are customary duties of deckhands. This fact reasonably was implied, if not expressed explicitly, in their employment agreement. The agreement could have been expressed in words (spoken or written) or implied from conduct of the parties, or from customs of people in that occupation. Also, being too tired during working hours is no excuse for refusal to do a job. An employee is duty bound to obey reasonable orders and to comply with reasonable rules. Failure to follow a lawful order is insubordination, which is ground for discharge or other discipline. However, one cannot be required to do anything that is illegal, immoral, or contrary to public policy, nor can one be compelled to do work not covered by the employment contract. A worker may refuse to perform work that appears to be unreasonably dangerous.

LEGAL FOCUS—CASE

Two workers were instructed to clean a wire mesh screen suspended about 20 feet above the shop floor. The cleaning process required that the workers step above the screen to remove objects that had dropped onto the screen from overhead conveyor belts. Ten days before, a coworker had fallen to his death while doing similar work. The day before the same two workers brought alleged unsafe conditions to the attention of the company. After the workers refused the work instructions, written reprimands were placed in their employment files, and their pay was docked. The workers claimed they had the right to refuse work under these conditions without workplace penalty.

Whirlpool Corporation v. Marshall, Secretary of Labor, 445 U.S. 1, 100 S.Ct. 883 (1980).

The U.S. Labor Department and later the Supreme Court agreed with the workers' position, claiming authority to limit the employers discretion under the Occupational Safety and Health Act (the OSH Act), which seeks to guarantee a hazard-free working environment for employees.

Duty of Care

Every employee is duty bound to use reasonable skill in performing assigned work, to perform it conscientiously (i.e., to do an honest day's work for an honest day's wages), and to do nothing contrary to the interests of the employer. For example, one may not sabotage equipment, steal supplies, or sell company secrets to competitors.

LEGAL FOCUS—PROBLEM

Ed Block was a stationary engineer in charge of a battery of boilers at the Metropole Chemical Works. Safety valves would prevent a major explosion, but the equipment could be damaged seriously even if the fail-safe devices worked perfectly. All controls had to be monitored and regulated closely. One day Block's wife left him after a prolonged argument over their son, who had been arrested on a narcotics possession charge. Perhaps understandably, but not excusably, Block had consumed a large bottle of bourbon before he went to work on the swing shift. Within an hour, he was sound asleep at the control panel. The boilers soon overheated and shut down automatically. Repairs would cost at least $5,000, to say nothing of the cost of disrupted production and spoiled goods in process, worth perhaps another $50,000. Is Block liable for the loss?

Yes, Block is liable. Theoretically, an employee may be charged with the cost of the employer's products he or she spoils or the value of equipment damaged either intentionally or through negligence. Practically, most employers seldom go beyond dismissing the errant employee. They absorb such spoilage costs as part of the price of doing business and pass them along to consumers in higher prices for finished products. Insurance sometimes helps cover the costs.

Duty of Loyalty

Loyalty is a fundamental duty in an employment relationship. The employee has the duty to act to benefit the employer. He or she may not act for his or her personal interests or for those of a third party at the detriment of the employer and doing so is a conflict of interest.

The duty of loyalty also means that any information or knowledge learned through the employment relationship is confidential. It is a breach of loyalty to disclose such information during the relationship and even after it ends. An example of confidential information would be a list of customers that belongs to the employer.

An employee hired to sell something cannot be the buyer unless the employer specifically agrees. If an employee is selling an employer's product, he or she must report to the employer the true and accurate price obtained for the goods. If an employee's job is to buy goods or services for the employer, he or she cannot falsely report what was paid or pay an excess amount and then receive a return of some of the excess payment from the seller. In short, the employee's loyalty must be absolute. The actions must not result in any secret profit for the employee.

LEGAL FOCUS—EXAMPLE

Aztec Petroleum Corporation arranged to have Merle Douglas buy oil and gas leases on the company's behalf. In return for his services, Douglas was paid $5,000 plus a royalty interest in the leases purchased. Douglas purchased several leases for Aztec. He told Aztec that he paid more for the leases than he actually did. Through various tricks, Douglas kept much of the money Aztec gave him to pay for the leases. Douglas used the money for personal purchases, including two new cars and a boat. When Aztec refused to grant Douglas the promised royalty interest in the leases, Douglas sued. Because Douglas had breached his fiduciary duty (specifically the duty of loyalty) to Aztec, Aztec was not required to pay him any royalty.

WHAT ARE THE BASIC RIGHTS AND COMMON BENEFITS OF EMPLOYEES?

Every employee is entitled to compensation for services as agreed with the employer. If no figure is specified, the prevailing or customary wage applies, or whatever would be reasonable under the circumstances. Sometimes, as in many sales jobs, pay in the form of commissions is related to particular performance, such as a specified percentage of all sales made. A common variation is a contract that calls for payment of a minimum base salary, or "draw," to be offset by commissions earned. The employee retains any excess commissions. State laws commonly require payment every two weeks, or sometimes weekly.

Employment at Will and Limiting Exceptions

An employee is neither a slave nor an indentured servant bound to remain for a prescribed time. One has the power to quit at any time—simply leave the job. But there is no legal right to quit when to do so is a breach of a contract to work for a specified period of time. For this reason, an employee who quits before the contract ends may be liable for damages but will not be forced to continue services. This is an example of having the power to do something but not the right. In legal terms, the courts will not stop the employee from breaching the contract but instead will hold him or her responsible for any damages the employer suffers. Realistically, employers seldom sue their rank-and-file employees. A lawsuit is costly, other employees resent it, and any sizable judgment won often is uncollectible.

LEGAL FOCUS—PROBLEM

Sean Yashima was the star reporter for a leading Jacksonville, Florida, television station. Although pleased with his work, he wanted desperately to accept an offer from a Seattle television station to anchor the weekend news. Yashima is an on-the-rise newsreader and this was an opportunity to move from the fifty-third largest television market to the twelfth. Sean is in the eighteenth month of a three-year contract with the Jacksonville station. Can Yashima accept the new offer?

Yashima is an exception as an employee because most employees do not have term-of-time contracts. Because Yashima does have a term-of-time contract, he cannot accept the new offer unless the Jacksonville station releases him from his contract obligation. A highly valued employee who quits before the expiration of a specified term of a written contract to take a better job elsewhere cannot be compelled to return to his or her job. But a court of equity might grant the first employer an injunction barring the employee from working as a reporter for anyone else during the contract term. To defy the court order would mean citation for contempt and a possible fine, as well as a judgment for damages.

The second employer also might be guilty of the tort of interference with a contract or an economically advantageous situation. Some authors call this a *contort*—a contract tainted by a tort. The tort is **interference with an economically advantageous relationship** and is defined as the knowing and wrongful interference with the performance of an existing valid contract. Generally, a contract must exist between two parties, and the defendant must induce one of the parties to breach the contract. Thus, a computer software manufacturer might wrongfully induce a talented software designer to breach a fixed-term employment contract with the plaintiff and join the defendant's staff at a higher salary.

interference with an economically advantageous relationship
A knowing and wrongful interference with the promised performance of another person's contract.

Employment at Will

Instead of term-of-time contracts, most employment contracts are informal, stating no definite period of time. They also usually lack detailed express agreement as to the rights and duties of the parties. Such employment contracts are called **at-will employment**. Each party is free to terminate the relationship at any time without liability (other than payment by the employer for services rendered to date, or sometimes to the end of the pay period). Under such contracts, employers generally can fire or let employees go at will, and employees have the right to quit at will without liability.

In the past sixty years, major changes have occurred in the at-will employment doctrine. Among the changes to the doctrine are union contracts, federal and state statutes, public policy, implied contracts, and tort claims. Of course, contracts for a specified term (like Sean Yashima's) always have been an exception to the at-will doctrine. Specified term contracts in business usually exist only for top leadership, such as corporate presidents. The at-will doctrine still is an important part of employment law. As we discuss, however, the firing of most employees can no longer be for any reason.

at-will employment
A term used, for example, to indicate that an employment contract may be terminated at any time by either the employee or the employer without any liability (beyond payment for services rendered up to the time of departure or discharge).

Union Contracts

Most unions have successfully bargained for a **just cause** provision in employment contracts. A just cause clause in a contract means that the employer must have a legitimate provable reason to fire or perhaps even discipline any employee. The just cause provision thus limits the employer's ability to fire at will. Often, fired union employees have a right

just cause
An action based on reasonable grounds and fair treatment; lawful reasons for taking an action.

to an independent arbitration to examine the employer's reason for the firing or discipline and decide whether a firing was legitimate.

Federal and State Statutes

As discussed earlier in the chapter, federal statutes restrict an employer's ability to fire at will. Title VII of the Civil Rights Act of 1964, for example, prohibits discrimination on the basis of race, color, national origin, religion, and sex. An employee fired for discriminatory reasons has legal rights against the employer. Other federal statutes protect against discrimination on the basis of age, disability, or pregnancy.

State statutes also often prohibit discrimination and may provide additional remedies for employees. Sometimes, these laws prohibit other types of discrimination, such as discrimination based on sexual preference, marital status, and medical condition, or they prohibit firings because employees are requested or required to perform public responsibilities.

LEGAL FOCUS—EXAMPLE

Many states have laws that forbid an employer from firing an employee for certain specified public policy reasons. Examples include situations in which an employee is called for jury service, subpoenaed as a witness at a court or legislative proceeding, or called to serve in the National Guard.

Civil service statutes also protect more than half of the 15 million public workers—county, state, and federal. Civil service statutes require just cause before an employee is fired. College professors may have tenure, which is a form of just cause protection.

Public Policy

Sometimes, firing an employee violates a judicially recognized public policy. Many states will not allow an employee to be fired for performing an act encouraged by public need. An employee also should not be fired for refusing to perform an illegal or wrongful act. For example, employees who are discharged after refusing to lie in court about illegal company practices, such as illegal price fixing, have successfully challenged the employer's action.

What public policies are significant enough to warrant protection by the courts? This is a difficult question. The courts answer this question on a case-by-case basis. Employees fired because they filed a workers' compensation claim have been protected. In states that lack specific laws protecting workers who serve on juries, the courts have found such a firing to be a violation of public policy. Perhaps the most interesting application of the public policy exception is the protection of workers who act as **whistleblowers**. A whistleblower is someone who tells the public or the authorities about illegal or other wrongful activities in his or her organization.

whistleblower
A person who makes a disclosure about improper conduct by an organization or organization officer or official.

Implied Contract Theory

A few courts have found that an implied contract may exist to protect employees from arbitrary firing. The court may find that the acts of the employer and employee have created the contract. An employee fired in breach of these implied terms can sue for breach of contract.

LEGAL FOCUS—EXAMPLE

An employer's handbook or personnel bulletin may state that, as a matter of standard practice, workers will be dismissed only for good cause. If the employee is aware of this policy and works for the company relying on it, an implied contract may exist. The handbook or bulletin supplies the terms.

Oral statements, job evaluations, and other acts also may lead to an implied contract. This theory is most likely to be successful in cases involving long-term employees in which the work relationship has existed for ten, fifteen, and even twenty years. It is also true that in recent years employers have been careful in drafting their handbooks, making clear perhaps in several places that the employment relationship is at will. Implying a contract when express terms say it does not exist is not likely.

Tort Theory

In a few unusual cases, employers who fired an employee have been found to have committed a tort. If the firing is done in an abusive manner, an employer's actions might be found to be either the tort of intentional infliction of emotional distress or defamation.

LEGAL FOCUS—CASE

A restaurant had suffered a theft of supplies. The manager gathered the employees together at a special meeting. At the meeting, he announced that he would start firing waitresses alphabetically until the thief was identified. The first waitress, Debra Agis, was fired. She sued the restaurant claiming she suffered emotional distress as a result of her firing. Do these facts support a tort claim?

Agis v. Howard Johnson Co., 371 Mass. 140, 355 N.E.2d 315 (1976).

Yes, the facts support the claim. The highest court of Massachusetts said the manager's acts were actionable as the tort of intentional infliction of emotional distress.

Discharge is legal if it is for good or just cause (e.g., insubordination or intoxication of the worker on the job, lack of business, or bankruptcy for the employer). Despite these legal theories, an employee who has been discharged wrongfully often faces difficult obstacles to meaningful relief. One commentator stated, "The average employee who has been wrongfully terminated has as much chance of getting a jury trial as sprouting wings and flying to the moon." Although this is an exaggeration, it is certainly true that significant barriers exist to successful plaintiff resolution of such cases.

What Is the Minimum Wage?

The Fair Labor Standards Act of 1938 (FLSA) set a minimum standard hourly wage for industrial workers engaged in interstate commerce and set the maximum workweek at forty hours. The wage rate has been increased periodically (e.g., it was $0.25 in 1950); since 2009, the rate has been $7.25 for all workers who are at least twenty years old. Persons under twenty years may be hired for days for no less than $4.25 an hour. The Act is complex, with exemptions and exceptions specifically detailed in the law [e.g., employers of tipped employees (those customarily receiving $30 or more a month in tips) may consider those tips as part of the wages and may pay as low as $2.13 per hour]. Among those employees exempt from minimum pay requirements, as well as overtime provisions of FLSA, are executives, professional employees, academic employees, farm workers on small farms, casual babysitters, and administrative employees.

Legally, an employer must withhold federal income taxes (and, in some states, state income taxes) and Social Security taxes and pay them directly to the appropriate government agencies. By agreement with the employee, deductions are also common for such purposes as buying insurance, government savings bonds, or company stock; paying off company credit union loans; paying union dues; or putting money into savings accounts.

The law also mandates record-keeping requirements for employers to ensure their compliance with the FLSA.

If wages are not paid, an employee has the right to sue for money owed. Special legislation in most states and under federal bankruptcy laws gives the employee a preference or priority over the employer's other creditors.

LEGAL FOCUS—PROBLEM

Benny is a junior at State University. He signed up for an internship to get some experience before he went on the job market. While he will receive three hours of college credit for the internship, he will not receive any pay. Benny has to keep a log of his activities and work ten hours a week. Does this arrangement violate FLSA?

The arrangement may violate the FLSA. The U.S. Department of Labor considers six factors in evaluating internships in for-profit companies. Essentially, the experience should be similar to training that would be given in an educational environment and primarily for the benefit of the intern. The more an internship program is structured around a classroom or academic experience as opposed to the employer's actual operations, the more likely the internship will be viewed as an extension of the individual's educational experience and not as a violation of the FLSA.

Working Conditions

Occupational Safety and Health Act of 1970 (the OSH Act)
A federal law to ensure safe and healthful working conditions by authorizing enforcement of health and safety standards.

Every employee is entitled to reasonably safe working conditions. The federal **Occupational Safety and Health Act of 1970 (the OSH Act)** broadly requires the employer in interstate commerce to furnish employment and a place of employment that are free from recognized hazards that cause or are likely to cause death or serious physical harm. The enforcement arm of the act is the Occupational Safety and Health Administration (OSHA). According to OSHA, since its 1970 charter, the workplace death rate has been cut in half; still, about seventeen Americans die every day on the job.

The law extends to such diverse items as equipment, protective clothing, vapor and noise levels, and in-plant health facilities. The law requires that companies log injuries and correct unsafe conditions as well as notify employees of their rights to bring notice of unsafe conditions to the attention of OSHA. It provides for inspections, investigations, issuance of citations, judicial review, and penalties for violations. All states have a variety of similar local regulations governing production in intrastate commerce.

LEGAL FOCUS—PROBLEM

Carlos Gutierrez preferred to be a low-profile employee. In a previous job, however, he had been a safety inspector, and his new employer, Rivercity Cleaners, appeared to be in clear violation of several OSHA safety standards. After his supervisor refused to act, he notified the appropriate state OSHA. They inspected Rivercity and found violations related to protective equipment, portable fire extinguishers, electrical components and equipment, and walking-working surfaces. Rivercity fired Gutierrez for disloyalty. Does Gutierrez have any remedy?

Yes, he does. OSHA prohibits retaliation against workers who exercise their right to report unsafe working conditions. Workers must contact an OSHA office almost immediately after learning of the alleged discriminatory action to protect their rights. OSHA will investigate the complaint and upon finding merit will order reinstatement or other remedies.

Fringe Benefits

An employee has no constitutional right to fringe benefits, but legislation, competition, and union pressure have made them an integral part of most employment contracts. Such benefits are provided in addition to the regular wage or salary. Social Security, no doubt the most important fringe benefit, is mandated by the Social Security Act of 1935. Financed by taxes paid by both employers and employees, the massive Social Security program provides benefits to more than 40 million persons, a growing number that includes retirees (who generally start receiving pensions at the age of sixty-five years), dependent survivors of insured persons, and qualified disabled workers and disabled dependents. It also encompasses the Medicare program of health benefits for qualified retirees, their dependents, qualified disabled persons under sixty-five years, and qualified workers and their dependents of any age that need dialysis treatment or a kidney transplant.

Since the Social Security Act was enacted in 1935, people are living longer and are having fewer children, with the result that more and more people are receiving benefits while fewer and fewer are contributing. Furthermore, Congress repeatedly has increased benefits, extending them to additional groups and requiring increased payments to compensate for increases in the cost of living. As a result, to keep the program economically viable well beyond the year 2008, changes have been made and more will surely be made in Social Security taxes levied, in benefits paid, and in income taxes on benefits received by wealthier recipients.

Many private and public employers supplement Social Security retirement benefits with their own pension, stock-purchase, and profit-sharing plans. Some provide a simplified employee pension (SEP) plan, whereby they contribute to the employee's individual retirement account (IRA). Paid vacations and holidays and paid or subsidized medical and dental insurance are valuable fringe benefits for most employed persons. Some employers also offer a variety of less significant benefits. These include life insurance; legal aid plans; sick leave; prenatal, child, and elder care; maternity and paternity leave; adoption assistance; social, recreational, physical fitness, and continuing education programs; and employer-assisted housing. The dollar value of fringe benefits often equals as much as 20 to 30 percent of the monetary wages paid. The appeal of fringe benefits is enhanced by the fact that most are tax-free to the employees and tax-deductible as business expenses to the employers.

Employee Retirement Income Security Act (ERISA)
Federal legislation regulating private pension plans that supplement Social Security.

defined benefit plans
Plans that provide for the payment of determinable retirement income benefits.

Retirement Benefits

In every state, society intervenes when a worker is hurt on the job by providing for compensation under applicable workers' compensation laws. The worker who is permanently disabled, on or off the job, may qualify for Social Security disability payments, as may the worker's dependents. Upon reaching retirement age, the worker qualifies for Social Security benefit payments, and dependent survivors of a deceased worker may qualify for survivors' benefits under Social Security. If a private employer voluntarily has provided a private pension to supplement Social Security retirement payments, the worker is again protected by the federal **Employee Retirement Income Security Act (ERISA)**, which regulates **defined benefit plans**. A defined benefit plan is one in which the amount of the employee's retirement income is a promised fixed dollar amount or an amount determined in advance by a benefit formula. Under ERISA, the Pensions Benefit Guaranty Corporation (PBGC) was created "to guarantee payment of basic pension benefits earned by nearly 44 million American workers and retirees participating in more than 33,330 private-sector defined benefit pension plans."* Reserves come from insurance premiums paid by the participating private employers.

LEGAL FOCUS—PROBLEM

Durango Apparel, Inc., a corporation with manufacturing plants in Tennessee and Kentucky, had a pension plan covering more than 7,000 workers. The company filed for bankruptcy in March of 2001. The pension plan had assets of about $15 million and projected benefit liabilities totaling around $40 million. Will the workers' claims for pension benefits be lost in the bankruptcy proceeding?

No, the claims will not be lost in the bankruptcy. The PBGC took over the underfunded pension plan in March of 2002 to protect the workers' benefits. Although individuals were subject to a maximum pension benefit under federal law, PBGC projected that most workers and their dependents would receive full benefits.

individual retirement accounts (IRAs)
Federally authorized private pension plans in which qualified employees contribute a certain percentage of their income, tax-free, to their retirement accounts until retirement.

Roth IRA
A form of individual retirement account authorized by federal law that allows a taxpayer to contribute after-tax dollars to the account so that earnings are not taxed when withdrawn.

Individual Pension Plans

Because many private employers do not provide pension plans to supplement Social Security, the federal Internal Revenue Code allows qualified workers to individually set aside a certain percentage of earned income, tax-free until retirement, in conventional **individual retirement accounts (IRAs)** and **Roth IRAs**. IRAs are accounts that individual workers select and fund with pretax dollars. The employee gets a present tax break on the invested amount and a continuing income tax break on income earned over the years in the IRA account. However, income taxes are paid on the account principal and earnings when withdrawn after retirement. Thus, the regular IRA is a tax-deferred account.

A Roth IRA is very different, first because the income used to fund the account is after-tax income. Like the regular IRA, earnings on the account are not subject to income tax before retirement. The second big difference is the after-retirement treatment. Whereas income in a regular IRA's account is subject to income tax when withdrawn, a Roth IRA is free from any income tax obligation upon retirement. With a Roth IRA, the income is tax exempt.

Which is best? Variables such as tax rates (current and future), eligibility requirements, account fees, and so on, make the answer dependent on the individual employee's situation.

LEGAL FOCUS—BACKGROUND

Finley Cory invests $250 a month in a Roth IRA starting at the age of twenty years. He waits until age sixty-five years to make withdrawals, and the investment earns a 6 percent return compounded monthly. What will his tax-free investment be worth?

*Pension Benefit Guaranty Corp., http://www.pbgc.gov.

401(k) plans
Retirement savings account taking its name from the Internal Revenue Code of 1978. The plan is funded by employee contributions and (often) matching contributions from the employer. Contributions are taken from pretax salary, and the funds grow tax-free until withdrawn.

The power of compounding is astounding. After forty-five years, Cory's $250 a month investment ($135,000 total invested) in a tax-free Roth IRA would be worth $688,998. In all likelihood, as his income increases, Cory would invest additional funds in the account and the amount available at age sixty-five years would be much greater. And if he waited until age seventy years to retire, he will be almost a millionaire ($946,797) on this $3,000 a year investment alone.

Some employers contribute to their employees' retirement through **401(k) plans**. With these plans, companies may deposit cash or stock bonuses to a trust account for their employees' benefit. Also, the employee may fund these plans solely or partly through salary reduction. These deposited amounts are not taxed and like IRAs accrue income without tax consequences until distribution at retirement. Employees often have investment choices for the funds in these accounts; a popular choice has been stock in the company in which they work.

LEGAL FOCUS—BACKGROUND

The 2001 collapse of Enron Corporation, an energy provider company, caused many employees to rethink investment in company stock and Congress to consider limitations on how much employer stock should be in a 401(k) account. Sixty percent of Enron's 401(k) plan was invested in Enron shares, which fell to $0.26 from a peak of $90 in the previous year.

Self-employed persons may establish SEP-IRA or Keogh retirement plans, which serve the same purpose as IRAs or 401(k)s. All of these private arrangements provide retirement funds in addition to the maximum Social Security payments, which are meant to lay a minimum "floor" rather than an ideal customized "ceiling" for retirement needs.

Family and Medical Leave

Family and Medical Leave Act of 1993 (FMLA)
A federal law requiring employers with fifty or more employees to grant employees leave for certain family purposes related to child care and family health.

The **Family and Medical Leave Act of 1993 (FMLA)** requires employers with fifty or more employees to grant employees leave for certain family purposes related to child care and family health. All public agencies (state and local government) and local education agencies (schools) are covered even if they have fewer than fifty employees. The Act allows an employee to take up to twelve weeks' leave in any twelve-month period but does not require that the leave be paid, although the employer must continue any provided health benefits. The employer may require the employee to use paid benefits as part of the leave (e.g., the employee has three weeks of vacation available). Among the reasons deemed proper for family leave are the following:

- Caring for a child newly placed with the employee for adoption or foster care
- Caring for an immediate family member (spouse, child, or parent—but not a parent-in-law) with a serious health condition
- Being unable to work because of a serious health condition

After any leave is taken, the employee must be restored to the same or similar position in the company.

LEGAL FOCUS—CASE

Juanita Caldwell is a single mother with three children working for a Kentucky Fried Chicken franchisee. Before the events in question, records suggest she was an excellent employee. On Saturday morning, her three-year-old son, Kejuan, developed a high fever, pain in his ears, and congestion, later diagnosed as an ear infection. Caldwell promptly notified her supervisor before the start of her morning shift that she would be absent attending to Kejuan. Her supervisor approved the absence. When she returned for her next regular shift on Monday morning, the restaurant manager abruptly fired her without stating a reason. Caldwell sued, arguing that her termination violated the FMLA. The district court granted her employer a summary judgment, concluding that although the Act generally protects employees when the immediate family members have a "serious health condition," Kejuan's condition did not qualify. Caldwell appealed. Was her appeal successful?

Caldwell v. Holland of Texas, Inc., 208 F.3d 671, 676 (8th Cir. 2000).

Yes, her appeal was successful. The court of appeals reversed the trial court and remanded the case back to the trial court for further proceedings. The FMLA provides that a "serious health condition" occurs, under the regulations, when the family member suffers an "illness, injury, impairment, or physical or mental condition" that requires "in-patient care" or "continuing treatment" by a health care provider:

> *FMLA's purpose is to help working men and women balance the conflicting demands of work and personal life. The law requires courts to consider the seriousness of the afflicted individual's condition because the law was designed to prevent individuals like Juanita Caldwell from having to choose between their livelihood and treatment for their own or their family members' serious health conditions. Upon examining the seriousness of Kejuan's ear infection, which required surgery to prevent deafness, we hold that there is at least a question of fact as to whether Kejuan's condition was 'serious' under the regulations.*

The standard for one's own serious health condition is higher than that for a family member's serious health condition. Specifically, you may take leave to care for a family member who merely has a serious health condition. Your own health condition must be such that you are unable to perform the functions of your position.

LEGAL FOCUS—PROBLEM

ACME Company provides in its employee handbook that the FMLA applies to the company's employees. An employee seeking leave is denied, and the company claims as a defense that it employs fewer than fifty employees. Is this a good defense?

Douglas v. E.G. Baldwin & Associates, Inc., 150 F.3d 604 (6th Cir. 1998).

Yes, it is a good defense. Federal statutes apply to companies according to the jurisdictional requirements of the statute. As the Act applies only to employers with fifty or more employees, FMLA does not apply to ACME Company:

> *The agreement between the parties that ACME would comply with the requirements of the FMLA does not bring the parties within the Act itself, because to do so would effectively enable them to contract around the Court's lack of subject matter*

EXHIBIT 12.2
Selected Federal Statutes Protecting Employee Interests

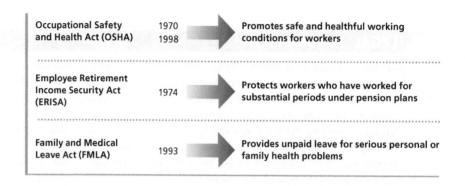

Occupational Safety and Health Act (OSHA)	1970 1998	**Promotes safe and healthful working conditions for workers**
Employee Retirement Income Security Act (ERISA)	1974	**Protects workers who have worked for substantial periods under pension plans**
Family and Medical Leave Act (FMLA)	1993	**Provides unpaid leave for serious personal or family health problems**

jurisdiction. Although such an agreement may have enhanced the terms of the contractual relationship between the parties, it does not provide the federal courts with jurisdiction to hear cases under the Act.

Exhibit 12.2 lists major federal statutes protecting employee safety, financial security, and family interests.

Health Care

Congress passed the Patient Protection and Affordable Care Act of 2010 to increase the number of Americans covered by health insurance and to decrease the cost of health care overall. Among other changes, the Act eliminates lifetime and unreasonable annual limits on benefits, provides assistance for those who are uninsured because of a preexisting condition, requires coverage of preventive services and immunizations, and extends dependent coverage up to age twenty-six years. Group health plans, such as those offered by employers, are covered under the Act, and employers can face penalties if they fail to make affordable health care available to their employees. By 2014, each state will establish an American Health Benefit Exchange to help individuals and small employers obtain coverage. For individuals who are not exempt, and who do not receive health insurance through an employer or government program like Medicare or Medicaid, the means of satisfying the Act's health insurance requirement is to purchase insurance from a private company. This particular provision was challenged on constitutional grounds and was upheld by the Supreme Court.

Privacy Rights

New technology can alter old habits and customs within a short time. For example, the introduction of computers and the Internet into our lives has aided business but at the expense of legal and ethical trade-offs. Many find the trade-offs disturbing, particularly in relation to privacy rights.

Computers make it possible to accumulate, store, and retrieve vast amounts of information. Virtually all institutions with which we deal—insurance companies, mail-order houses, banks, and credit card companies—gather information about us. They store that information in their computer files. Government agencies such as the U.S. Census Bureau, the Social Security Administration, and the Internal Revenue Service also collect and store data.

These businesses and agencies collect information on income, expenses, marital status, and other personal history and habits. Frequently, this personal information finds its way to present or potential employers. Seldom—if ever—do most persons give permission for, or even know about, the use of this information.

In recent years, the right to privacy has become a significant employment issue. As in many other areas of social life, the law attempts to balance competing interests to arrive at fair policies. Employers are interested in minimizing employee theft, loss of trade secrets, and misuse of company property while maximizing productivity; employees are interested in being treated with respect and dignity. Employers today must be careful not to violate their employees' rights to privacy and personal security. Areas of concern include drug testing, lie-detector tests, and electronic monitoring.

Employees must realize that they have limited privacy rights at the workplace. Personal e-mail, items kept in their desks, phone conversations, and the like may be subject to company monitoring and retrieval. Increasingly, employers are adopting technology, like Radio Frequency Identification Devices (RFID) and Global Positioning Systems (GPS) to monitor employee activities to ensure that employees are being vigilant in their activities at work and wasting neither their time nor company resources. GPS technology can be installed in company phones and cars, and RFID technology can be used to track employee movement at work as cards are scanned when entering and exiting buildings. The general balancing test between the rights of the employer to monitor the workforce and the privacy rights of employees centers on whether or not the employee has a reasonable expectation of privacy. Part of that inquiry hinges on whether or not the employer gave notice to employees that the technology was being used. If employers alert employees of their intention to track such information, the employee's expectation of privacy is diminished.

LEGAL FOCUS—CASE

A company installed GPS devices in their vehicles as part of an investigation into theft. An employee objected to the installation of a GPS devise in his company vehicle as an invasion of his privacy. What result?

Elgin v. St. Louis Coca-Cola Bottling Co., 2005 U.S. Dist. LEXIS 28976 (E.D. Mo. Nov. 14, 2005).

The court stated that use of the tracking device on the company car, even though it was assigned to the employee, did not constitute an invasion of privacy since the device revealed only the van's location on public streets, which could not be considered secret. Neither could its use be considered highly offensive to a reasonable person.

While the constitution protects privacy interests of citizens, it applies to *government* employees, not private employees. For protection against invasion of privacy by all other employers (like Walmart or IBM), a state or federal statute, or the common law of the state, must recognize a privacy right and provide a cause of action for its violation.

Drug Testing in the Workplace

Drug and alcohol abuse has been estimated to cost industry between $50 and $100 billion in absenteeism, impaired performance, and accidents each year. Naturally, employers are concerned about a decline in job performance and other harm resulting from drug abuse. Some employers therefore test employees to uncover drug use. But the tests are not always reliable. Even when tests are accurate, a question exists as to whether they violate employees' rights to privacy.

If the employer is a government agency, testing is subject to the requirements of the U.S. Constitution. Employees have a Fourth Amendment right to be "secure in their persons … against unreasonable searches and seizures." So the administration of drug tests is constitutional only if there is a reasonable basis for suspecting the employee's use of drugs—or if drug use in a particular government job could threaten public safety.

LEGAL FOCUS—CASE

The Department of Transportation required employees working on oil and gas pipelines to submit to random drug testing. All employees were subject to the rule whether they were suspected of drug use or not. Does the Department of Transportation's drug-testing rule violate employees' constitutional rights?

Electrical Workers Local 1245 v. Skinner, 913 F.2d 1454 (9th Cir. 1990).

No, it does not violate constitutional rights. The government's interest in promoting public safety was held to outweigh employees' privacy interests. Government also requires such testing for safety-sensitive occupations such as air and rail travel.

Constitutional limitations do not usually restrict private employers. Some state constitutions and statutes, however, do restrict and regulate private drug testing. Some collective-bargaining agreements regulate drug testing, specifying when and how it is or is not permitted. It often is required for participants in important competitive sporting events, such as track and field meets and certain Olympic events.

LEGAL FOCUS—PROBLEM

Donna Moran's employer maintained a drug-free workplace, requiring all employees to be subject to a random drug-testing program. Moran, a mechanical engineer and fifteen-year employee, was asked to report immediately for a urinalysis drug test. She refused and told her supervisor she had no intention of being tested and did not believe in the program. After additional unsuccessful attempts to get Moran to comply, the company fired her. Moran sought unemployment insurance and was denied because she lost her job due to "willful misconduct." Moran claims that the drug-testing policy is a humiliating invasion of her privacy and was adopted without the consent of the employees. Did the company have the right to require Moran to take the drug test, and can unemployment benefits be denied her?

Rebel v. Unemployment Compensation Board of Review, 555 Pa. 114, 723 A.2d 156 (1998).

Yes, the company had the right require the drug test, and, yes, unemployment benefits can be denied. Moran's reasons for declining the test are unknown, but the cost is clear. In the case upon which this scenario is based, the company's drug-testing program was upheld and the denial of unemployment compensation was deemed proper:

> *The avoidance of injury, as well as concern for vicarious liability that can accrue to the employer, are legitimate interests of the employer that must be accorded substantial weight. Appellant's objection that [the employer] adopted the testing program without having obtained the employees' consent is groundless. The creation of rules and requirements that govern the workplace is the prerogative of the employer.… We conclude that the testing program of [the employer] was narrowly tailored to meet the employer's needs and that it did not unduly intrude on appellant'sprivacy interests. Hence, it was reasonable. Appellant's failure to cooperate with the program was without good cause. Willful misconduct was properly found, and the denial of unemployment benefits was, therefore, proper.*

Lie-Detector Tests

At one time, many employers required job applicants and employees to take lie-detector tests (also called *polygraphs*) to determine whether or not the individual was answering questions asked by the employer honestly. Many employees considered these tests to be an invasion of their right to privacy and their privilege against self-incrimination. Other critics believe lie-detector tests create a dangerous fantasy that the truth can be ascertained, because most experts seriously doubt the tests' accuracy.

In 1988, Congress passed the Employee Polygraph Protection Act, which severely restricted the use of polygraphs. This Act prohibits certain employers from (1) requiring, suggesting, requesting, or causing employees or job applicants to take lie-detector tests; (2) using, accepting, referring to, or asking about the results of lie-detector tests taken by employees or applicants; and (3) taking or threatening negative employment-related action against employees or applicants based on results of lie-detector tests or because they refused to take the tests.

Some employers are exempted from these prohibitions, notably federal, state, and local government employers, certain security service firms, and companies manufacturing and distributing controlled substances. Other employers may use polygraph tests when investigating losses attributable to theft, including suspected embezzlement and theft of trade secrets. In all cases in which lie-detector tests are still permitted, however, stringent procedural requirements are imposed on employers. Employees always may refuse to submit to polygraph testing, but this may make them vulnerable to dismissal for good cause.

Monitoring Job Performance

Another workplace privacy issue involves the monitoring of employees' performance by employers. Today, some employers electronically monitor employees' use of computer terminals or company telephones. Some employers use video cameras to evaluate employees' performance.

Current federal law recognizes the right of employers to listen in on telephone conversations to monitor employees' performance, but state laws vary. An employer often may avoid state laws by simply informing employees subject to monitoring that the company may be listening. In areas such as this, there is very little case law, and an employer may wish to consider carefully whether the need to monitor employees' performance outweighs the employees' right to privacy, as well as the possible negative effect on general employee morale and productivity. If the company's monitoring is formally challenged, a court will balance the purposes of the search against its effect on the employees' privacy. The existence of other available methods for accomplishing the employer's goals will be considered as alternatives.

LEGAL FOCUS—PROBLEM

Fred Meyer's employer had assured all employees that their e-mail communications would not be accessed and used by the employer against its employees for disciplinary reasons. Meyer sent several work-related e-mails to his supervisor. The messages also included threats to "kill the backstabbing bastards" and referred to a planned holiday party as the "Jim Jones Kool-Aid affair." Meyer was fired. He sued, claiming his termination violated "public policy which precludes an employer from terminating an employee in violation of the employee's right to privacy as embodied in Pennsylvania common law." Was Meyer's lawsuit successful?

Smyth v. The Pillsbury Company, 914 F. Supp. 97 (E.D. Pa. 1996).

No, the lawsuit was not successful. In the case on which this hypothetical is based, the court found for the employer, stating,

We do not find a reasonable expectation of privacy in e-mail communications voluntarily made by an employee to his supervisor over the company e-mail system notwithstanding any assurances that such communications would not be intercepted by management. Once plaintiff communicated the alleged unprofessional comments to a second person (his supervisor) over an e-mail system, which was apparently utilized by the entire company, any reasonable expectation of privacy was lost. Significantly, the defendant did not require plaintiff, as in the case of a urinalysis or personal property search, to disclose any personal information about himself. Rather, plaintiff voluntarily communicated the alleged unprofessional comments over the company e-mail system. We find no privacy interests in such communications.

RIGHTS REGARDING UNIONS

Have workers always had the right to join with coworkers in unions? The answer is no. The history of relations between labor and capital is long and stormy. More precisely, in many cases, it is a record of relations between union leaders selected by workers and professional managers hired by the investors who are the owners of capital. In 1806, a group of Philadelphia boot and shoemakers (called *cordwainers*) who joined together were found guilty of common law criminal conspiracy and were fined. In another classic case about thirty-five years later, *Commonwealth v. Hunt*, the supreme court of Massachusetts rejected the idea that a combination of workers was criminal simply because of their concerted action. The proper test, the court said, was the purpose of the combination; if intended "to induce all those engaged in the same occupation to become members," it was lawful. "Such an association might be used to afford each other assistance in time of poverty, sickness, or distress; or to raise their intellectual, moral, and social condition, or to make improvement in their art; or for other proper purposes."

union
Association of workers formed to bargain collectively with employers over wages, hours, and conditions of employment.

picketing
Patrolling by strikers or sympathizers, generally at the entrances to a business plant, during a labor dispute.

Anti-Injunction Act of 1932
Federal law that restricts the issuance of injunctions in labor disputes, outlaws yellow dog contracts, and exempts unions from legal attack as monopolies.

yellow dog contracts
An employment contract in which a worker agrees not to join a union.

Nevertheless, **unions** continued to be harassed by court action instituted by employers who resisted any erosion of their decision-making power. For example, the federal Sherman Anti-Trust Act of 1890 was enacted to protect trade and commerce against unlawful restraints and monopolies of business firms, but it also was applied by courts to unions. Injunctions often were used to restrain concerted labor activity such as **picketing** (patrolling outside a business location to encourage workers to join the union, to gain recognition from the employer, or to gain sympathy and support from third parties during a strike). But the pendulum eventually did swing in the opposite direction to favor labor and union organization. For example, in 1940, the Supreme Court recognized peaceful picketing as a form of free speech protected by the First Amendment. In 1988, the Court upheld a local law that banned picketing in front of any particular or private home, but marching through a residential neighborhood or in front of an entire block of homes is not prohibited.

Statutes Governing Labor–Management Relations

During the Great Depression (1929–1939), many new socioeconomic laws were enacted as part of the New Deal of President Franklin D. Roosevelt. In the labor field, two important laws survived challenges to their constitutionality: the Anti-Injunction Act and the National Labor Relations Act.

The **Anti-Injunction Act of 1932** (popularly known as the Norris–La Guardia Act, after its prime movers) restricts the issuance of injunctions by the federal courts against unions peacefully striking in labor disputes. Together with the Clayton Act of 1914, it effectively exempts unions from prosecution as monopolistic trusts or conspiracies in restraint of trade. The Norris–La Guardia Act also outlawed **yellow dog contracts**,

EXHIBIT 12.3
Yellow Dog Contract

I, Alexander Krakner, in consideration of employment with Hardly Caring Corporation (HCC), covenant that I am not a member of a union nor have I ever been a member of a union. I further agree that while I am employed at HCC I will not become a member of a union nor will I assist or otherwise consort with those who purport to represent unions or are involved with any attempt to unionize HCC. I further agree that I will bring to the attention of HCC any contacts by a union of me or the names of any employees who I find out are engaging in union activities. I expressly agree that any violation of this agreement gives HCC the right to terminate my employment immediately.

Date: 11/17/30

Alexander Krakner, employee
Leavin Nutin Toochance, President of HCC

Wagner Act
A federal law that recognizes the right of workers to organize into unions of their own choice, and the duty of employers to bargain collectively with the unions over wages, hours, and conditions of employment. It provides a list of unfair labor practices by management.

under which an employee—as a condition of employment—agrees never to join a union (see Exhibit 12.3).

The **National Labor Relations Act of 1935 (Wagner Act)** recognizes the right of private-sector employees to form, join, or assist unions and to bargain collectively with employers through representatives of their own choosing. **Collective bargaining** is the right given to a union to bargain with the employer over the terms of employment, including wages, hours, job security, and benefits covering all members of the worker group. Once a union is recognized as the bargaining agent of a group of workers, the union has the exclusive authority to bargain for all members of the group. Accordingly, an employee is no longer free to bargain individually with the company. The recognized union not only has the right to bargain on behalf of all members of the group, but it also has a duty. It cannot refuse to represent a worker in the group even if he or she is not a member of the union. The pejorative term used by union members for such nonmembers is *freeloader*. The Wagner Act listed and outlawed five **unfair labor practices** of employers:

collective bargaining
The process of negotiation by representative (s) of the employees' union and representative(s) of an employer for an employment contract that provides terms and conditions of employment.

- Interference, restraint, or coercion with the organization or practice of union activities
- Wrongful domination of unions
- Encouragement or discouragement of unions by discriminating against union members
- Refusal to bargain with the union
- Discrimination against any employee seeking protection under the Act

LEGAL FOCUS—PROBLEM

Antonio Mondalli and Jack Smith were the two youngest and toughest workers at the Iceberg Cold Storage and Ice Company. When their request for a wage boost to match community levels was denied, they started to persuade other workers in the plant to join them in forming a local union or affiliating with the Teamsters Union. When Artemus Finley, owner-manager of Iceberg, heard of the talk, he promptly fired Mondalli and Smith. Do they have any recourse under the law?

unfair labor practices
Certain practices of employers and unions that are prohibited by federal or state law.

Yes, they do have recourse. They can file a complaint with the nearest office of the National Labor Relations Board. For intrastate businesses, in some states, they could apply to a comparable state board. In either case, the board could order their reinstatement with back pay.

Labor-Management Relations Act of 1947 (Taft-Hartley Act)
A federal law that lists unfair labor practices of unions. It outlaws the closed shop and the secondary boycott.

closed shop
A place of employment where workers must join a union before they can be hired. Made illegal by the Taft-Hartley Act.

The Pendulum Swings the Other Way

Some critics claimed that in applying the Wagner Act, the National Labor Relations Board favored the revitalized unions unfairly. And so the pendulum eventually swung back with law that restrained unions (but did not deprive them of their basic rights). The **Labor-Management Relations Act of 1947 (Taft-Hartley Act)** amended the Wagner Act and added a list of unfair labor practices of unions, including, most notably, coercion of employees in their right to join or to refuse to join a union. It outlawed the **closed shop**, which mandated that one must belong to the union before getting a job, and it banned **secondary boycotts**, in which pressure is brought by striking workers against neutral third parties who supply or buy from the affected employer. For example, workers on strike at a furniture factory may not legally picket the independent retail stores that sell the furniture.

In an **open shop**, a union may be recognized as the sole bargaining agent for all employees in the particular group or bargaining unit, but no workers are required to join the union.

LEGAL FOCUS—PROBLEM

Although a union had been selected by a majority of the workers in his department, Virgil Redman refused to join. There was no union-shop agreement, and he insisted on making his own "deal with the boss." "After all," he said, "I've been doing it that way for more than thirty years. We're both satisfied. I don't intend to stop now." May Redman make his own contract with his employer governing his compensation and other terms of employment?

secondary boycotts
Occurs when striking workers picket or use other pressure against a neutral third party who supplies or buys from the struck employer.

open shop
A company or department where union membership is not a requirement to get or keep a job.

No, he may not make his own contract with his employer. When a union is designated as the bargaining representative for workers in a given unit, collective bargaining requires the union to represent all workers in that unit, including nonmembers. This is true even when only a bare majority of eligible workers participated in the representation election, and consequently only a minority of the total workers voted for the union. The same phenomenon can be found in political and campus elections when there is a light turnout.

Legal Injunctions

The Taft-Hartley Act reintroduced the injunction against strikes, but made it available only at the request of the National Labor Relations Board or of the president of the United States in cases of disputes that endanger the national health and welfare. After an eighty-day cooling-off period in such cases, during which time the issues are investigated and reported by a public board, the strike may resume—to be ended possibly by government seizure and operation under an act of Congress. This extreme option is seldom utilized. Courts also may issue injunctions against illegal strikes or lockouts and illegal activity in connection with either, such as mass picketing or violence in a strike or lockout.

LEGAL FOCUS—PROBLEM

Loren Hilton was a rugged individualist, and as a matter of principle, he opposed joining any mutual help organization. He also was a highly skilled toolmaker. Some time after Advanced Avionics Corporation hired him, the company signed an agreement with the toolmakers' union that called for a union shop. Must Hilton now join the union if he wants to keep his job?

union shop
A place of employment where newly hired workers must join the union within thirty days of being hired.

Yes, he must join the union. In a **union shop**, an employee must join the union within thirty days of being hired. It is legal under the Taft-Hartley Act, although, as noted, some states have enacted right-to-work laws that outlaw this limited approach to union security and stability. Employers who accept the union shop reason that if they have to deal with a union, it may as well include all workers in the bargaining unit. There is likely to be less internal discord, and the union leaders, feeling more secure, are less likely to make outrageous demands or promises to justify their existence. Also, because the union provides benefits, the members understandably believe all workers should share the costs; thus, those who do not join the union are regarded contemptuously as freeloaders.

agency shop
A company or department in which all employees in the bargaining unit must pay union dues (or some comparable fee) irrespective of whether they are union members.

A variation of the union shop is the **agency shop**, in which all employees in the bargaining unit (nonmembers as well as members) support the union by paying a representative fee (usually a little less than union dues) as a condition of employment. Nonmembers must accept the union as their agent to conduct negotiations with the employer and to conclude employment contracts on behalf of all the employees within the bargaining unit. Many public-employee labor unions have agency-shop agreements that apply to nonmembers. The union cannot use any of such agency-shop dues for activities not directly related to collective bargaining.

Labor-Management Reporting and Disclosure Act of 1959 (Landrum-Griffin Act)
Federal law that mandates open, democratic internal government of unions.

The **Labor-Management Reporting and Disclosure Act of 1959 (the Landrum-Griffin Act)** sometimes is called the bill of rights of union members, because it guarantees their right to participate in union affairs, protects their freedom to speak up in union meetings, and requires that they be kept informed about the union's financial condition.

LEGAL FOCUS—PROBLEM

Raul Keroupian had joined the union at his plant shortly before the day of the meeting at which officers were to be selected. When nominations were made from the floor, someone moved to elect the entire incumbent slate by acclamation. Keroupian swallowed nervously, then stood up and said, "I don't think we can do that; it would be illegal." There were hoots and catcalls from the back of the room. Was he correct?

Yes, he was correct. Among other things, the Landrum-Griffin Act prescribes that every local labor organization must elect its officers at least once every three years by secret ballot among the members in good standing.

Exhibit 12.4 lists the major federal statutes pertaining to labor-management relations.

strike
A concerted refusal by employees to perform the services for which they were hired, generally to gain recognition of a union, or improvements in wages, hours, or conditions of employment.

Do Most Workers Engage in Strikes?

Only about 15 percent of the private workforce belongs to unions and unions normally call strikes, so that means that most workers do not engage in strikes. A **strike** is a concerted refusal by employees to perform the services for which they were hired. Strikers do not quit permanently; they consider themselves employees and plan to return to their old jobs when the strike ends. By then, they hope, their employer will have acceded to all

EXHIBIT 12.4
Major Federal Labor Law Statutes

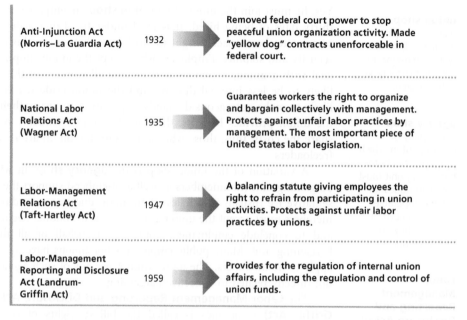

Statute	Year	Effect
Anti-Injunction Act (Norris–La Guardia Act)	1932	**Removed federal court power to stop peaceful union organization activity. Made "yellow dog" contracts unenforceable in federal court.**
National Labor Relations Act (Wagner Act)	1935	**Guarantees workers the right to organize and bargain collectively with management. Protects against unfair labor practices by management. The most important piece of United States labor legislation.**
Labor-Management Relations Act (Taft-Hartley Act)	1947	**A balancing statute giving employees the right to refrain from participating in union activities. Protects against unfair labor practices by unions.**
Labor-Management Reporting and Disclosure Act (Landrum-Griffin Act)	1959	**Provides for the regulation of internal union affairs, including the regulation and control of union funds.**

Source: Adapted from American Bar Association, Section of Law Practice Management (Chicago: ABA,1993).

lockout
A shutdown of operations by an employer in response to union demands or to achieve other changes in an employment contract.

or some of their demands. The strike is the ultimate weapon of unions, just as the ultimate weapon of employers is the **lockout**—a shutdown of operations in response to union activity or demands. Neither tactic is used casually or frequently, although the strike is much more common.

The number of major work stoppages has declined significantly since 1980. There were only 5 major work stoppages in 2009, idling 13,000 workers compared with a high of 424 work stoppages in 1974, idling 1,796,000 workers.

LEGAL FOCUS—PROBLEM

Pat McGillicuddy was unhappy with the wages, hours, work schedule, plant rules, heating and lighting of the workroom, fringe benefits (there were none), and supervision at his place of employment. One day, after weeks of grumbling and complaining to his coworkers, he got up from his workbench, put on his coat and hat, and shouted so that all in the large room could hear, "I strike!" Then he walked out the door and started to picket in front of the building. Was he on strike?

economic strike
A strike in which workers seek a change in wages, hours, and/or conditions of employment.

What Kinds of Strikes Are There?

Because there was no union ordering the strike nor combined action by a group of workers, McGillicuddy was not on strike. It is an individual's protest, and his employer can take the action to mean that he has quit and can be replaced.

When there is a union and it orders all members to walk out in an **economic strike** (over wages, hours, or conditions of employment), the employer legally may

strikebreakers
Persons hired to take the place of workers who are out on strike. If it is an economic strike, the strikebreakers may be retained as permanent replacements.

hire **strikebreakers** as permanent replacements. After the strike is over, however, if the jobs again become available (which is unlikely), the employer must rehire the strikers, provided they have not taken substantially equivalent permanent jobs elsewhere (which by the time the job becomes available is usually the case). On the other hand, when the strike is an **unfair labor practice strike** prompted by one or more unfair labor practices of the employer, the striking workers retain full rights to their jobs and must be restored to them when the strike ends. Moreover, the offending employer must pay back wages to the strikers.

LEGAL FOCUS—PROBLEM

The Snug Fit Shoe Corporation had a three-year contract with its production workers under a collective-bargaining agreement. The union vote approving the contract had been very close, and initial dissatisfaction gradually had turned into outspoken protest. After sixteen months, the workers defied their leaders and announced through a spokesperson: "We're on strike. To prevent strikebreakers from taking our jobs, we're going to stay right here in the plant." A sit-down strike had begun. Friends and relatives brought the strikers' sleeping bags and food for a long stay. Was the strike legal?

unfair labor practice strike
A strike in which the workers are protesting an unfair labor practice of their employer.

No, it was not legal. **Sit-down strikes**, in which workers retain possession of the employer's property, are illegal. Moreover, this was a **wildcat strike**, one that is in violation of the contract and of the union's own rules. As such, it constituted an unfair labor practice on the part of the workers, and the employer could hire permanent replacements for the strikers, who could be evicted by the police and be subject to punishment.

ARBITRATION OF EMPLOYMENT DISPUTES

sit-down strike
Illegal strike in which strikers remain in their places of employment but refuse to work.

Collective-bargaining agreements often provide for arbitration of disputes arising during the term of the labor agreement. For example, a common provision in a labor contract restricts management discretion in employee discipline and termination. The provision establishes that no discharge or discipline can occur except upon a showing of "just cause" (a limitation upon the common law "at will" doctrine) and in a specified fashion. If the subject union member is displeased with the discipline, he or she can grieve under agreed processes, which ultimately lead to a hearing by a neutral arbitrator.

LEGAL FOCUS—CASE

The manager of safety and security at a convalescence hospital became aware that "S," a PBX operator with some receptionist responsibilities, was wearing nose jewelry, namely a small silver hoop in her left nostril. The manager informed "S" not to wear this at work other than on breaks and lunch periods. An accommodation was later reached allowing "S" to wear a Band-Aid over the small hoop while working. "S" believed that the Band-Aid over her nose hoop violated provisions of the collective-bargaining agreement, and she filed a grievance. The case went to arbitration. How did the arbitrator rule?

103 Lab. Arb. (BNA) 988 (1994).

wildcat strike
An unlawful strike of union members that takes place without the approval of the union leaders.

Most disputes involving discipline over unusual hairstyles, body piercing, and clothing choices are resolved in the employer's favor. The employer's right to set dress standards is allowable management discretion unless it is a subterfuge for prohibited discrimination. In this case, the arbitrator noted that the company had dress guidelines prohibiting extremes in jewelry. The arbitrator gave great

> *deference to management's interpretation and application of its dress and grooming standards. [The company] did not violate the Agreement when it prohibited the Grievant from wearing a ring or hoop through her nose while on duty as a PBX Operator. Therefore, the grievance shall be denied.*

Whereas arbitration in union–labor contracts is common, is it common in nonunion employment situations? Until recently, the answer was no.

LEGAL FOCUS—CASE

Interstate/Johnson Lane Corporation (Interstate) hired Robert Gilmer as a manager of financial services in May 1981. Gilmer was required by his employer to register as a securities representative with the New York Stock Exchange (NYSE). His registration application provided for arbitration of any controversy arising out of a registered representative's employment or termination of employment. Interstate terminated Gilmer's employment at age sixty-two years. Thereafter, he filed a charge with the EEOC and brought suit in the district court, alleging that he had been discharged in violation of the Age Discrimination in Employment Act of 1967 (ADEA). Interstate moved to compel arbitration. Was Gilmer forced to arbitrate his ADEA claim?

Robert D. Gilmer v. Interstate/Johnson Lane Corporation, 500 U.S. 20, 111 S.Ct. 1647 (1991).

He was made to arbitrate his claim. Gilmer argued that U.S. Supreme Court precedent provided that employees were free to file civil rights suits without regard to agreements to arbitrate such claims and that Congress intended to protect ADEA claimants from a waiver of the judicial forum. The Court held otherwise, stating that earlier cases were restricted to collective-bargaining employment contracts:

> *An important concern therefore was the tension between collective representation and individual statutory rights, a concern not applicable to the present case. Finally, those cases were not decided under the FAA [Federal Arbitration Act], which reflects a "liberal federal policy favoring arbitration agreements." Therefore, those cases provide no basis for refusing to enforce Gilmer's agreement to arbitrate his ADEA claim.*

The U.S. Supreme Court required Gilmer to submit all his claims (including ADEA) to compulsory binding arbitration.

After the *Gilmer* case, courts began to uphold agreements to arbitrate nonunion employment disputes. Substantial concern about arbitration of employment disputes was raised by the National Employment Lawyers Association, which argued that such agreements lacked true consent by the employee and often limited employee rights. A special task force composed of individuals representing management, labor, employment, civil rights organizations, private administrative agencies, government, and the American Arbitration Association drafted "The Due Process Protocol for Mediation and Arbitration of Statutory Disputes Arising Out of the Employment Relationship." The Due Process Protocol "recognizes the dilemma inherent in the timing of an agreement to mediate and/or arbitrate statutory disputes" but does not take a position on whether an employer can require a predispute, binding arbitration program as a condition of employment.

The *Gilmer* case technically did not deal with an employment contract, although it appears no one except perhaps the U.S. Supreme Court believed that. Gilmer's arbitration agreement was in a securities exchange registration form, not an employment contract. Because of this, the Court did not address at that time the specific language of the Federal Arbitration Act (FAA), which states it does not apply to contracts of employment of "seamen, railroad employees, or any other class of workers engaged in foreign or interstate commerce." Ten years later, the Court held that the FAA does apply to all employment agreements, except those covering employees engaged in transportation. Companies can now ask their employees to waive their right to go to court and rely exclusively on arbitration to resolve workplace bias claims. An arbitration clause, however, does not preclude the EEOC from pursuing a claim on behalf of an employee.

LEGAL FOCUS—EXAMPLE

Greg Hendrickson was delighted to begin work for LA Billboards, Inc. Like most employees, he paid little attention to his six-page employment contract. Three years later, he was fired after he complained to his boss about business practices he said violated local ordinances. When Hendrickson contemplated filing a lawsuit for wrongful termination, he read his contract more carefully. The employment contract not only required he arbitrate any dispute, but it also forbade recovery of punitive damages and discovery. In addition, it ordered the payment of a nonrefundable $500 filing fee, that the matter be heard on the other coast at the company home office, that any back pay recovery be capped at $2,000, and that the employee share the costs of the arbitrator and the arbitration hearing room. Lastly, the arbitrator was to be selected from a list provided by LA Billboards.

Signing an arbitration clause may be nothing more than changing forums, which, although important, does not necessarily affect fundamental rights. On the other hand, giving up remedies and rights in the process could also be part of the contract. What restrictions might be enforceable is still in contention in U.S. courts, but it is clear that LA Billboards went too far. In the 2002 case *Circuit City Stores, Inc. v. Adams,** the Ninth Circuit Court of Appeals held that the Federal Arbitration Act, although allowing for the enforcement of employment arbitration clauses, does not allow enforcement of an unconscionable agreement. The contract in the *Circuit City* case was replete with "objectionable provisions pervading the entire contract." The court instructed employers that to be enforceable, a contract must:

- Provide for neutral arbitrators,
- Provide for more than minimal discovery,
- Require a written award,
- Provide for all of the types of relief that would otherwise be available in court, and
- Not require employees to pay either unreasonable costs or any arbitrators' fees or expenses as a condition of access to the arbitration forum.

**Circuit City Stores, Inc. v. Adams*, 279 F.3d 889 (9th Cir. 2002) cert. denied, 122 S.Ct. 2329 (2002).

CASE

Ricci V. Destefano

129 S.Ct. 2658 (2009)

In 2003, 118 New Haven firefighters took examinations to qualify for promotion to the rank of lieutenant or captain. Promotion examinations in New Haven were infrequent, so the stakes were high. The results would determine which firefighters would be considered for promotions during the next two years, and the order in which they would be considered. Many firefighters studied for months, at considerable personal and financial cost.

When the results of the exam showed that white candidates had outperformed minority candidates, a rancorous public debate ensued. Confronted with arguments both for and against certifying the test results—and threats of a lawsuit either way—the City threw out the results based on the statistical racial disparity. White firefighters and one Hispanic firefighter who passed the exams but were denied a chance at promotions by the City's refusal to certify the test results, sued the City alleging that discarding the test results discriminated against them based on their race in violation of Title VII of the Civil Rights Act of 1964. The defendants responded that certifying the test results might have been a Title VII violation for adopting a practice having a disparate impact on minority firefighters. The District Court granted summary judgment for the defendants, and the Second Circuit affirmed.

Judge Kennedy provided the opinion of the court:

The suit before us alleges that the City discriminated against the plaintiffs based on their race, in violation of Title VII of the Civil Rights Act of 1964.

The Civil Rights Act of 1964 did not include an express prohibition on policies or practices that produce a disparate impact. But in Griggs v. Duke Power the Court interpreted the Act to prohibit, in some cases, employers' facially neutral practices that, in fact, are "discriminatory in operation." The Griggs Court stated that the "touchstone" for disparate-impact liability is the lack of "business necessity": "If an employment practice which operates to exclude [minorities] cannot be shown to be related to job performance, the practice is prohibited." Under those precedents, if an employer met its burden by showing that its practice was job-related, the plaintiff was required to show a legitimate alternative that would have resulted in less discrimination. Twenty years after Griggs, the Civil Rights Act of 1991 was enacted. The Act included a provision codifying the prohibition on disparate-impact discrimination. That provision is now in force along with the disparate-treatment section already noted.

Under the disparate-impact statute, a plaintiff establishes a prima facie violation by showing that an employer uses "a particular employment practice that causes a disparate impact on the basis of race, color, religion, sex, or national origin." An employer may defend against liability by demonstrating that the practice is "job related for the position in question and consistent with business necessity." Even if the employer meets that burden, however, a plaintiff may still succeed by showing that the employer refuses to adopt an available alternative employment practice that has less disparate impact and serves the employer's legitimate needs.

Our analysis begins with this premise: The City's actions would violate the disparate-treatment prohibition of Title VII absent some valid defense. All the evidence demonstrates that the City chose not to certify the examination results because of the statistical disparity based on race—that is, how minority candidates had performed when compared to white candidates. As the District Court put it, the City rejected the test results because "too many whites and not enough minorities would be promoted were the lists to be certified." Without some other justification, this express, race-based decision making violates Title VII's command that employers cannot take adverse employment actions because of an individual's race.

The District Court did not adhere to this principle, however. It held that respondents' "motivation to avoid making promotions based on a test with a racially disparate impact ... does not, as a matter of law, constitute discriminatory intent. The City rejected the test results solely because the higher scoring candidates were white. The question is not whether that conduct was discriminatory but whether the City had a lawful justification for its race-based action.

We consider, therefore, whether the purpose to avoid disparate-impact liability excuses what otherwise would be prohibited disparate-treatment discrimination. Our task is to provide guidance to employers and courts for situations when these two prohibitions could be in conflict absent a rule to reconcile them.

With these principles in mind, we turn to the parties' proposed means of reconciling the statutory provisions. Petitioners take a strict approach, arguing that under Title VII, it cannot be permissible for an employer to take race-based adverse employment actions in order to avoid disparate-impact liability-even if the employer knows its practice violates the disparate-impact provision. We cannot accept petitioners' broad and inflexible formulation.

Petitioners next suggest that an employer in fact must be in violation of the disparate-impact provision before it can use compliance as a defense in a disparate-treatment suit. Again, this is overly simplistic and too restrictive of Title VII's purpose. The rule petitioners offer would run counter to what we have recognized as Congress's intent that "voluntary compliance" be "the preferred means of achieving the objectives of Title VII. Forbidding employers to act unless they know, with certainty, that a practice violates the disparate-impact provision would bring compliance efforts to a near standstill. Even in the limited situations when this restricted standard could be met, employers likely would hesitate before taking voluntary action for fear of later being proven wrong in the course of litigation and then held to account for disparate treatment.

At the opposite end of the spectrum, respondents assert that an employer's good-faith belief that its actions are necessary to comply with Title VII's disparate-impact provision should be enough to justify race-conscious conduct. But the original, foundational prohibition of Title VII bars employers from taking adverse action "because of ... race." Allowing employers to violate the disparate-treatment prohibition based on a mere good-faith fear of disparate-impact liability would encourage race-based action at the slightest hint of disparate impact.

If an employer cannot rescore a test based on the candidates' race, then it follows that it may not take the greater step of discarding the test altogether to achieve a more desirable racial distribution of promotion-eligible candidates—absent a strong basis in evidence that the test was deficient and that discarding the results is necessary to avoid violating the disparate-impact provision. Restricting an employer's ability to discard test results (and thereby discriminate against qualified candidates on the basis of their race) also is in keeping with Title VII's express protection of bona fide promotional examinations.

Title VII does not prohibit an employer from considering, before administering a test or practice, how to design that test or practice in order to provide a fair opportunity for all individuals, regardless of their race. And when, during the test-design stage, an employer invites comments to ensure the test is fair, that process can provide a common ground for open discussions toward that end. We hold only that, under Title VII, before an employer can engage in intentional discrimination for the asserted purpose of avoiding or remedying an unintentional disparate impact, the employer must have a strong basis in evidence to believe it will be subject to disparate-impact liability if it fails to take the race-conscious, discriminatory action.

The City argues that, even under the strong-basis-in-evidence standard, its decision to discard the examination results was permissible under Title VII. That is incorrect. Even if respondents were motivated by a desire to avoid committing disparate-impact discrimination, the record makes clear there is no support for the conclusion that respondents had an objective, strong basis in evidence to find the tests inadequate, with some consequent disparate-impact liability in violation of Title VII.

On this basis, we conclude that petitioners have met their obligation to demonstrate that there is no genuine issue as to any material fact and that they are entitled to judgment as a matter of law. In this Court, the City's only defense is that it acted to comply with Title VII's disparate-impact provision. To succeed on their motion, then, petitioners must demonstrate that there can be no genuine dispute that there was no strong basis in evidence for the City to conclude it would face disparate-impact liability if it certified the examination results.

The racial adverse impact here was significant, and petitioners do not dispute that the City was faced with a prima facie case of disparate-impact liability. On the captain exam, the pass rate for white candidates was 64 percent but was 37.5 percent for both black and Hispanic candidates. On the lieutenant exam, the pass rate for white candidates was 58.1 percent; for black candidates, 31.6 percent; and for Hispanic candidates, 20 percent. The pass rates of minorities, which were approximately one-half the pass rates for white candidates, fell well below the 80-percent standard set by the EEOC to implement the disparate-impact provision of Title VII. Based on how the passing candidates ranked and an application of the "rule of three," certifying the examinations would have meant that the City could not have considered black candidates for any of the then-vacant lieutenant or captain positions.

Based on the degree of adverse impact reflected in the results, respondents were compelled to take a hard look at the examinations to determine whether certifying the results would have had an impermissible disparate impact. The problem for respondents is that a prima facie case of disparate-impact liability is far from a strong basis in evidence that the City would have been liable under Title VII had it certified the results. That is because the City could be liable for disparate-impact discrimination only if the examinations were not job related and consistent with business necessity, or if there existed an equally valid, less-discriminatory alternative that served the City's needs but that the City refused to adopt. We conclude there is no strong basis in evidence to establish that the test was deficient in either of these respects.

There is no genuine dispute that the examinations were job-related and consistent with business necessity. The City's assertions to the contrary are blatantly contradicted by the record. The City turned a blind eye to evidence that supported the exams' validity. Respondents also lacked a strong basis in evidence of an equally valid, less-discriminatory testing alternative that the City, by certifying the examination results, would necessarily have refused to adopt. Respondents raise three arguments to the contrary, but each argument fails.

On the record before us, there is no genuine dispute that the City lacked a strong basis in evidence to believe it would face disparate-impact liability if it certified the examination results. In other words, there is no evidence—let alone the required strong basis in evidence—that the tests were flawed because they were not job-related or because other, equally valid and less discriminatory tests were available to the City. Fear of litigation alone cannot justify an employer's reliance on race to the detriment of individuals who passed the examinations and qualified for promotions. The City's discarding the test results was impermissible under Title VII, and summary judgment is appropriate for petitioners on their disparate-treatment claim.

The record in this litigation documents a process that, at the outset, had the potential to produce a testing procedure that was true to the promise of Title VII: No individual should face workplace discrimination based on race. Respondents thought about promotion qualifications and relevant experience in neutral ways. They were careful to ensure broad racial participation in the design of the test itself and its administration. As we have discussed at length, the process was open and fair.

The problem, of course, is that after the tests were completed, the raw racial results became the predominant rationale for the City's refusal to certify the results. The injury arises in part from the high, and justified, expectations of the candidates who had participated in the testing process on the terms the City had established for the promotional process. Many of the candidates had studied for months, at considerable personal and financial expense, and thus the injury caused by the City's reliance on raw racial statistics at the end of the process was all the more severe. Confronted with arguments both for and against certifying the test results—and threats of a lawsuit either way—the City was required to make a difficult inquiry. But its hearings produced no strong evidence of a disparate-impact violation, and the City was not entitled to disregard the tests based solely on the racial disparity in the results.

Our holding today clarifies how Title VII applies to resolve competing expectations under the disparate-treatment and disparate-impact provisions. If, after it certifies the test results, the City faces a disparate-impact suit, then in light of our holding today it should be clear that the City would avoid disparate-impact liability based on the strong basis in evidence that, had it not certified the results, it would have been subject to disparate-treatment liability.

The judgment of the Court of Appeals is reversed, and the cases are remanded for further proceedings consistent with this opinion. It is so ordered.

For Critical Analysis

1. What was the intent of the City in abandoning the test results? Was it to discriminate or to avoid discrimination. If the latter, then why there a question of whether the City's action is discriminatory?
2. Did the Court decide that the promotion test was not discriminatory despite its disparate results? If not, how the court be seen to have decided the case?
3. Under Title VII, are the results of promotion test solely determinative of its discriminatory character? If not, what is the criteria for allowing a promotion test?
4. The Court appears to be obligating the City to proceed with the promotions mandated by the test results despite the risk of liability for the City when it does so. Does this make sense to you? What prevents the court from resolving all the issues?

CHAPTER QUESTIONS AND PROBLEMS

1. Problems abound in the area of employment. The following questions involve some of the more difficult and challenging ones. What are your suggestions for answers and solutions?
   a. Do minimum-wage laws discourage employment of young persons, especially the unskilled, and thus encourage idleness and crime? Should the minimum-wage laws be eliminated or modified for minors and young adults?
   b. Subtle illegal discrimination because of sex, color, religion, age, and national origin still exists in many places. How can it be further reduced or eliminated? How can victims of discrimination facilitate that elimination?
   c. Should the federal government be the employer of last resort for those who cannot find jobs in the private sector? What meaningful work could such persons do?
   d. Should all states enact right-to-work laws?
   e. Should labor strikes and management lockouts be forbidden, and labor–management disputes be settled by compulsory arbitration?
   f. Are unions obsolescent or obsolete? If not, why, when, where, and how should union membership be encouraged? Should employers be required to rehire all strikers (after the strike is ended), even in an economic strike?
   g. Should comparable-worth laws be enacted at the federal and state levels? Would women be the only beneficiaries of such legislation?
   h. Since people live longer now than when the Social Security Act was enacted in 1935, should the normal retirement age be advanced from 65 to 70?
   i. Should racial and other special interest or minority quotas and affirmative action policies for employment and educational (e.g., college admission) opportunities be legally forbidden?
   j. The Civil Rights Act is silent as to gay rights. Does the federal statute provide civil rights protections to gays?
2. Generally, an employer has the right to fire an employee at will, even as the employee has the right to quit at will. Both parties by means of an express written and signed agreement can negate these rights, as, for example, when a college football coach is hired "for three years." An employer's power to fire may also be limited if there is an implied agreement not to discharge without cause. How could such an implied agreement be created?
3. A probationary police officer in the Globe, Arizona, police department was fired. The officer sued the city for wrongful discharge, claiming he was terminated because he had discovered that a man who had been arrested and convicted and was now serving time for vagrancy was doing so under a law that had been repealed. The officer told a court official of the situation, pointing out that the detention was illegal. The judicial official informed the police chief. The chief fired the officer, saying he did not appreciate "big city cops" coming to Globe to tell him how to run his department. A probationary civil service employee may generally be dismissed at will; a "just cause" need not be stated or proved. Was this firing nevertheless a wrongful discharge? [*Wagner v. City of Globe,* 150 Ariz. 82, 722 P.2d 250 (Arizona, 1986).]
4. Consider the following ethical issues:
   a. Is it legal for an employer to require an employee to lie when dealing with customers in order to make a sale?
   b. Should an auto mechanic be required by his employer to replace parts prematurely in order to boost the income of the shop?
   c. A carpet installer is asked by a customer to bypass his employer and install a carpet on his own time.
   d. The boss's son is making unwanted and unpleasant comments about his sexual intentions toward you. You keep it to yourself because you fear nothing will be done if you report the incidents.
5. Carolyn Garcia, nurse extraordinaire, was fired from her River County health clinic job when she refused to distribute "morning after" pills to patients. These pills are an emergency contraceptive medicine used to end a pregnancy in a manner similar to a miscarriage. Garcia sued River County alleging religious discrimination under Title VII of the Civil Rights Act and a violation of her First Amendment rights to free speech and religious practice. Do you think she prevailed in her lawsuit?
6. Delta Bibby had worked as a dental assistant in Dr. Harley Hayes's dental practice for three years. When Delta became pregnant, she approached Dr. Hayes about a leave. He scheduled an appointment to discuss the leave but when Bibby arrived, Dr. Hayes gave her a check for two weeks' severance pay and asked

for the keys to the office. Bibby asked Dr. Hayes why she was being fired. He replied: "My wife's jealousy has really gotten out of hand. She thinks I got you pregnant and she said either I let you go or forget the marriage. Sorry, but you have to go." Bibby and the dentist were innocent of any wrongdoing. Does Bibby have a gender discrimination case?

7. After a strike was legally called, Phil Thornbush joined coworkers on "picket duty" at their place of work, an intrastate business. There was no violence, and only two picketers at a given time marched in front of the plant, day and night. Thornbush and his partner were arrested and convicted under a state statute that made loitering and picketing a misdemeanor. They appealed, claiming the state violated their federal constitutional right to free speech. Should the convictions be reversed?
8. Several types of discrimination fall within the prohibitions of various civil rights acts. Which of the types of discrimination do you think occasions the most complaints by alleged victims?
   a. race
   b. gender
   c. national origin
   d. age
   e. disability
   f. religion
9. Two days after starting a new job, Dourly Popper was fired. He claims it was because he reported for jury service on the third day of work. His supervisor said it was because he refused to work overtime the first time he was asked. Can a probationary employee successfully sue for wrongful termination? What are his chances?
10. April Barber, an agent employed by Prototype, Inc., was driving her own car and rushing to an important luncheon meeting scheduled with a prospective customer. She saw the amber light in the signal ahead, but to stop and wait would delay her at least four minutes, and she was already late. So she pushed the accelerator down, even though the light had changed to red, and raced ahead at 50 mph through the intersection—*almost*. Before she got across, her car collided with Fred Lamare's truck, which had legally entered on the far right side. Lamare was injured, and the truck was demolished.
    a. Is Barber's employer, the principal Prototype, liable?
    b. Would the employer be liable if Barber were an ordinary employee?
    c. Would the employer be liable if Barber were an independent contractor?
    d. Would your answer be different in parts (a), (b), and (c) if April were violating not only the speed limit but also Prototype's explicit orders not to go faster than 35 mph in town?
    e. Is Barber personally liable to Lamare?
    f. Is Barber personally liable to Prototype?
11. It is important for employers to articulate and apply their employment policies consistently, even if federal law does not apply to the issue. Consider the following: a. You are the person in charge of hiring faculty in the History Department. Allie Applicant, a Native-American female, applied for a position and is a part of the qualified pool. She reported to HR that she had been previously convicted of petty larceny—she stole a street sign in college, but ultimately returned it. The criminal background check, however, revealed that she had been convicted of underage drinking as well, which she failed to report. Do you hire her? If not, why not? b. Adam Applicant, a Caucasian male, applied for a faculty position in the Political Science Department and is a part of the qualified pool. He reported to HR that he had been previously convicted of petty larceny—he stole a street sign in college but ultimately returned it. The criminal background check, however, revealed that he had been convicted of underage drinking as well, which he failed to report. Is there a potential issue if the History department hires Allie despite her conviction, but the Political Science department does not hire Adam because of his conviction?
12. Typically, medical and employment history, including salary, are considered to be private matters. But with the onslaught of social media outlets, what society considers appropriately private is changing rapidly. Suppose that a newspaper reported that a university official was "fired." On her Facebook page, that same person complained that she was "forced out." What effect would her Facebook admission have on her lawsuit against the newspaper for invasion of privacy by publishing a private fact concerning the termination of her employment?
13. The revolution in social media is affecting many aspects of the law, including employment relationships. For example, employees owe a duty of loyalty not to divulge the confidential information of their employers, such as customer lists. If the customers, however, are their *Linked In* contacts, how is the information confidential?

14. Recently, certain criteria employers use to select their workforce have come under increasing scrutiny by the EEOC and the subject of debate by academics.
    a. Credit histories are quintessentially private. Yet employers routinely include a credit check in their applicant screening process in an attempt to discern whether or not prospective employees possess such desirable traits as honesty and responsibility. Is it legal to discriminate based up on credit rating? Could the use of credit scores have a disparate impact on members of some protected classes? Is it ethical to use that information in making an employment decision? Does an applicant's poor credit rating translate into a lack of integrity any more than a good credit rating translates into ethical behavior and organizational skills? What factors could account for the low rating that have nothing to do with an employee's ability to perform the job?
    b. Often employers also will favor persons who are currently employed over persons who are unemployed, using employment as a signal of quality job performance. Is such discriminatory treatment illegal? Could it have a disparate impact on certain protected classes? Is it ethical? What are the societal ramifications of using employment status as selection criteria?
    c. Are criminal background checks illegal? Do they have a disparate impact on protected certain classes? What interest is the criminal background of a prospective employee to employers? Should arrests be used to disqualify candidates or only convictions? What effect, if any, might the use of criminal records in selecting employees have on the recidivist rate?
    d. What about employers who surf social media sites to find out information about job candidates? If the employer detects inappropriate photographs, evidence of alcohol or drug use, or perhaps information suggesting the applicant lied on the job application, the candidate may not be hired. Is such a practice legal or an invasion of the candidate's privacy? Is it ethical?

CHAPTER 13

Consumer Rights, Privacy and Protection

Many people want the government to protect the consumer. A much more urgent problem is to protect the consumer from the government.

Milton Friedman, *Economist,* 1912–2006

LEARNING OBJECTIVES

After reading and studying this chapter, you should be able to:

- Explain the foundation and purpose of consumer protection laws.
- Explain the data privacy protections provided consumers under federal law.
- Identify the gaps in privacy protection brought on by the modern digital age.
- Explain the scope and substance of California's Online Privacy Protection Act.
- Describe how to effectively manage the privacy of your online data.
- Describe the major federal consumer financial protection laws.
- Explain the scope and requirements of the Fair Debt Collections Practices Act and identify the remedies it provides for violations.
- Identify remedies available for violations of the Fair Debt Collections Practices Act.
- Explain the requirements of the Truth in Lending Act.

Consumer protection is a doctrine borne in the latter half of this past century. Various laws in the United States were created to protect consumers in response to various abuses, sometimes at the hands of aggressive businesses. Other laws govern privacy protections for all citizens. This chapter explains the laws that protect consumers in transactions, that give consumers extra rights against injury and harm, and that protect financial or consumer privacy rights. The emergence of the Internet, both as a place to socialize and communicate as well as a place to engage in commerce, has raised many new issues surrounding privacy. Laws and doctrines enacted before the digital age frequently have been found to be lacking in their ability to address or resolve these newer, digital age-driven issues. As a result, the past decade has seen a nearly continuous effort to add to or revise laws related to consumers and privacy. We will explore historical, traditional, and established consumer protection laws as well as the newest issues and the proposed or actual laws that address these new issues.

CONSUMER RIGHTS AND PROTECTION

consumer
A person who purchases goods or services.

What is a consumer and does a consumer differ from a citizen? In essence, every citizen of the United States is a consumer, but the class of consumers includes not just citizens, but all persons engaging in commerce in the United States. A **consumer** is a person who purchases goods or services. Many of those goods and services are fundamental to living a healthy and happy life. Food, shelter, and medicine are just three examples of goods or services that a consumer purchases that are basic needs. A healthy economy also requires that consumers feel safe engaging in transactions. Consumer protection laws thus not only benefit consumers directly but also benefit the entire country by ensuring that a confident consumer class engages in a robust and consistent level of commerce.

Consumer rights and protection flow from a myriad collection of laws, some of which are identified clearly as targeting consumers. Consider, for example, the Fair Debt Collections Practices Act (FDCPA), which protects consumers from abusive debt collection practices. Other laws that protect consumers might not be so obvious. The Privacy Act of 1974, for instance, protects the rights of citizens in general, but in part, also protects the privacy of consumers engaged in transactions. Privacy, in fact, is a basic right, very important to consumers, that is at risk when purchasing goods and services.

LEGAL FOCUS—EXAMPLE

Megan purchased a book at an online bookstore that provided advice on overcoming alcohol addiction. She had come to recognize that she had a drinking problem, but was not comfortable telling anyone else about it. Unbeknownst to her, however, the online bookstore was tracking the topics of books that its customers purchased and selling that information along with their customer contact information. One day she received a phone call from a telemarketer seeking to sign Megan up for an addiction seminar. Megan was horrified and had no idea how she had gotten on that company's list.

Megan's experience is not unique. It is possible that she actually authorized the sale of the information about her shopping interests by clicking a box when she set up her account with the online retailer or when she was completing the transaction. Privacy is given its own section in this chapter, because it is such an important topic and because there is a substantial body of law surrounding privacy rights.

Consumer Rights

In addition to privacy, consumer laws protect against many other potential problems or abuses. Discrimination in housing, transportation, and lending is protected. Lending, investment, and other monetary aspects of consumer life also are protected. Debt and debt collection have long been a topic of laws protecting consumers.

LEGAL FOCUS—PROBLEM

Mishka was in over his head, money-wise. He had substantial credit card debt, not to mention a car loan and student loans. Though he had a job, he was not earning enough to make even his minimum payments each month. As a result, he was behind in his car payments and also had watched the interest rate on his credit cards rise because of missing or late payments. Mishka was getting calls from the credit card companies almost every night, causing him to quit answering the phone. The pressure felt overwhelming. He wished he could stop all the calls. Does Mishka have the right to stop his credit card companies from calling him?

He may have the right to stop the calls, but he also may not want to do that. As will be explained further in the following section, the FDCPA gives Mishka the right to stop some calls and also limits the nature, timing, and frequency of phone calls that can be made. But, if he implements any such rights, he might force the creditors to sue him as their only other option.

As you study this chapter, try to recognize the types of problems that consumers often find themselves in and think to yourself how you could avoid them in the first place. Sometimes, the laws will help you, but nothing is better than being diligent and responsible about your personal data and your spending and debt accumulation. Being a savvy consumer is your first and best means of protection. First, we will evaluate consumer-related privacy protections and then we will examine transaction and debt protections afforded consumers.

CONSUMER PRIVACY

The right to privacy often is considered a fundamental human right. The U.S. Constitution, however, does not contain an express guarantee of the right to privacy. Several amendments, however, do recognize several rights that are privacy related. The Fourth Amendment, for instance, protects against unreasonable searches of the person, home, paper, and effects. The Ninth Amendment, with its broad general reservation to the people of rights not specifically listed in the bill of rights, often is thought to allow for the general right to privacy, although the Supreme Court has not yet made such a direct interpretation. Privacy, however, has been recognized in cases involving the Bill of Rights.

LEGAL FOCUS—CASE

In 1962, Estelle Griswold and a doctor named C. Lee Buxton opened a birth control clinic in New Haven Connecticut to sell contraceptives and thus challenge a law in Connecticut banning the sale of such devices. As desired, they were arrested and convicted of violating the law. Connecticut courts upheld their conviction and their appeal was heard by the Supreme Court in 1965. The Court found that the Connecticut law violated the "right to marital privacy," citing the "penumbras" and "emanations" of the Constitution generally.

Griswold v. Connecticut, 381 U.S. 479, 85 S. Ct. 1678; 14 L. Ed. 2d 510; 1965.

The Griswold decision, however, included four concurring opinions that added the Ninth Amendment and the Due Process Clause of the Fourteenth Amendment as being more specific constitutional rights protected. The Supreme Court revisited privacy-related rights again in the landmark 1973 case, *Roe. v. Wade*, involving abortion rights and as recently as 2003 in *Lawrence v. Texas*, a case involving the right to sexual conduct in one's home. Despite these hints at a general right to privacy being included in the Constitution, such a finding has never been made, and the Supreme Court easily could find, in its next case, a different interpretation. The Lawrence case, in fact, is a reversal of a 1986 case, *Bowers v. Hardwick*, a very short time period for such a stark reversal in Supreme Court interpretation of the Constitution.

Despite the ephemeral nature of the privacy under the U.S. Constitution, numerous laws—federal and in many states—recognize various privacy rights. Perhaps, even more important, many of these laws not only affect the right to privacy from government intrusion but also protect privacy as to other persons, businesses, and companies. Thus, the statutory recognition of privacy is strong and broader than the rights to privacy recognized to arise under the U.S. Constitution. This is especially true for the privacy rights related to consumers and consumer transactions.

consumer privacy The right to protect fiscal and consumer data and information about oneself.

Informational privacy The right to control the collection and sharing of data about oneself.

In its broadest sense, privacy includes many personal aspects of people's lives including their thoughts and feelings as well as "private" portions of their bodies. In the context of consumers and consumer activity, privacy takes on a narrower focus. **Consumer privacy** is the right to protect fiscal and consumer data and information about oneself. It is also sometimes called "financial privacy." A very similar, but broader, concept is "informational privacy." **Informational privacy** is the right to control the collection and sharing of data about oneself. This chapter is focused on the topic of consumer privacy. In the digital age, the privacy of consumer information has been threatened or breached constantly, and a body of laws now is designed to protect consumer data and information.

LEGAL FOCUS—EXAMPLE

Kin Thom practically lives his life online. He spends hours a day on his computer engaging in "conversations" on social media and news sites. He has profiles on many of those sites. He runs applications for some of them on his smart phone so he also can comment, converse, and even shop online from anywhere. He has registered his credit card, address, birthday, and sometimes his mother's maiden name and city of birth with various website operators. He wonders sometimes how secure his information really is but most of the time Kin just keeps posting, shopping, and moving along in his electronic life.

Kin is not abnormal, he is a quite typical consumer, or at least among younger consumers. Various protections are in place for his data, although they are not comprehensive. Also, many of the laws mandating various privacy requirements lack significant mandatory penalties or private enforcement provisions. Thus, Kin might decide, should important consumer data be disclosed or abused, that most of the damage done to his fiscal or personal well-being is not repairable nor compensable. He might conclude that he should have been more careful with how much information he provided and just exactly what all of those "disclosure statements" and "privacy" policies actually said.

We will go through the laws that exist to protect consumer privacy. What you are likely to conclude is that companies, businesses, and government are mostly just obligated to warn you, or give notice, of exactly what they will do with your data. Sometimes they are restricted in what data they can collect and in how they are supposed to act to preserve your data. Overall, the U.S. scheme has been called "patchwork" at best and often as "incomplete" in the effectiveness of its protection of privacy.

Privacy Act of 1974

The Privacy Act of 1974 was one of the first privacy laws implemented. It largely is focused on the government and ways that it might abuse privacy rights or disclose or share private information, including consumer information. The Privacy Act of 1974 created restrictions on what data government could gather or share and under what conditions it could do so. The purpose of the law was to ensure that individuals knew what information was gathered and to restrict when and how the government could gather it. It also was supposed to limit when information could be shared. There were large exceptions in the law, however, and many critics find the Privacy Act of 1974 to have little direct effect on preserving privacy. Another law was enacted a few years later that established firmer protections from government intrusion into financial information.

Right to Privacy Act of 1978

The Right to Financial Privacy Act of 1978 was designed to protect the confidentiality of personal financial records. It prohibits government access to the financial records of a customer of a financial institution unless certain requirements are met. The government agency seeking such records has to reasonably describe the records it seeks. Additionally, "no Government authority may have access to or obtain copies of, or the information contained in the financial records of any customer from a financial institution unless the financial records are reasonably described" unless the customer allows such access or certain approvals are made by a court (a search warrant or subpoena) or other such agency (such as an administrative subpoena or summons). The Right to Privacy Act of 1978 also prohibits financial institutions from requiring customers to authorize the release of financial records as a condition of doing business with them.

LEGAL FOCUS—PROBLEM

Mayor Bill Brown is deeply mired in a political crisis created by an annoying resident, Carol Kooky, who continually reveals to the press e-mails with the mayor's staff. Frustrated, he decides to start digging up dirt on Ms. Kooky. His private investigator goes to the bank that it seems she uses and attempts to get copies of her past two years of bank statements. The bank refuses, until the private investigator provides a copy of a letter from the mayor declaring that the private investigator is "deputized" and for all persons to provide full cooperation. The bank then gives in (especially since the mayor has been good for business) and provides the requested records. The statements reveal that one of Mayor Brown's staff has been getting checks paid by Ms. Kooky, and he promptly fires the staff member and confronts Carol Kooky, threatening to do more harm if she continues to harass him.

Was the bank correct in releasing the information? What remedies does Carol Kooky have?

No, the bank did not see a subpoena, search warrant, or an order by an agency. Nor did the letter describe the records the private investigator sought. The Right to Financial Privacy Act provides only a $100 per violation damages award, however. It was intended for large-scale intrusions by a government agency, not a rogue person who also happened to be in the government. Mayor Brown may have other civil liabilities or perhaps even criminal liability under other laws for actions that clearly appear to be abusive of a government position but that is not certain either. Carol Kooky probably will have a hard time showing any financial damage that results from his intrusion. She might have the same claims against the bank as well as other claims beyond those she might have against the mayor. Still, the Right to Financial Privacy Act of 1978 does prohibit this conduct, allows for class actions, and probably has reduced the willingness and frequency of unauthorized government intrusion into financial records of consumers.

Gramm-Leach-Bliley Act

In 1999, the United States enacted an additional and perhaps broader protection of consumer financial records in the form of the Gramm-Leach-Bliley Act, which protects the privacy of personally identifiable, nonpublic financial information by restricting when and how it can be disclosed to nonaffiliated third parties by financial institutions. Gramm-Leach-Bliley is also titled the Financial Services Modernization Act (FSMA). Gramm-Leach-Bliley requires notice of the categories of personal information the institution collects and disclosure of the categories of people the information will be disclosed to, the consumer's opt-out rights, and the institution's confidentiality policy. Gramm-Leach-Bliley also safeguards against the release of the information. The FSMA does not expressly create a private right of action for violations, although such violations may be useable with other claims. Largely, however, Gramm-Leach-Bliley is intended for the Federal Trade Commission (FTC) or other agency enforcement and customers are directed by the FTC to file a complaint as the primary means of seeking resolution. The law also allows states to pass stronger consumer privacy protections. The FTC adopted additional FSMA regulations in 2012.

Other Federal Consumer Privacy Laws

There is an eclectic mix of other federal consumer protection laws a few of which are relatively new. Following is a summary of these laws. Generally, the picture you should take away from these descriptions of federal consumer privacy protection is that it is very much like a tapestry of varying laws and protections, but a tapestry with holes in it. It is confusing to many and difficult for most to keep track of what privacy rights consumers have under what situations.

Children's Online Privacy Protection Act

Children certainly can be consumers, and when they are, some laws provide more protection solely for them. The 1998 Children's Online Privacy Protection Act restricts the manner in which website operators can interact with children and collect data from them. The FTC issued revised regulations in 2012 that further heightened the obligations of website operators and companies doing business online when collecting data from children or persons that might be underage. In particular, the age of thirteen years is a key threshold below which the collection of data is both limited and requires various notices and permissions.

Dodd-Frank Wall Street Reform and Consumer Protection Act

This law, usually just referred to as "Dodd-Frank" was enacted in 2010 in the fallout of the financial crisis that had unfolded beginning in 2008. Dodd-Frank, despite the powerful-sounding inclusion of "Consumer Protection" in its title has only a few specific provisions focused on consumers and very little related consumer privacy. But Title X of Dodd-Frank created a new government agency titled the Bureau of Consumer Financial Protection (BCFP), and it is possible that this brand new agency might just become a significant protector of consumer privacy in the coming years. You will learn more about this new agency in the Consumer Protection section of this chapter, which is the area that the bureau's efforts are more strongly focused.

Although the federal government has been enacting some privacy protection requirements, it is California's effort at establishing online consumer protection that appears to be leading the way toward more direct protection of consumer privacy.

California Online Privacy Protection Act

The federal government's efforts at protection of consumer privacy might be described as mixed at best, but one state, California, has taken a broader and stronger step as to online commerce. The California Online Privacy Protection Act was enacted in 2003 and reaches far beyond the borders of the state. To avoid confusing this law with the federal Children's Online Privacy Protection Act, we will refer to this law as CAL-OPPA. Under CAL-OPPA, commercial websites that collect personally identifiable information from California's residents are required to conspicuously post and comply with a privacy policy that meets certain requirements. Although, on its face, this would appear to be a law affecting only California business and California residents, the reality is that it affects a large portion of U.S. e-commerce.

CAL-OPPA is applicable to any individual or entity (corporation) that owns a commercial web page or an online service that collects and records confidential personal information from an individual living in California, visiting such web pages. The law, however, is not applicable to Internet service providers or similar entities that record data upon request from a third party.

The operator of a website must post a distinctive and easily found link to the website's privacy policy, commonly listed under the heading "Your California Privacy Rights." The privacy policy must detail the kinds of information gathered by the website, explain how the information may be shared with other parties, and, if such a process exists, describe the process the user can use to review and make changes to their stored information. It also must include the policy's effective date and a description of any changes since then.

Under CAL-OPPA, the owner or operator of a website is subject to private enforcement within thirty days of being notified that its privacy policy is not adequate or missing.

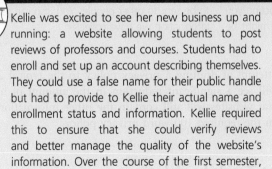

LEGAL FOCUS—PROBLEM

Kellie was excited to see her new business up and running: a website allowing students to post reviews of professors and courses. Students had to enroll and set up an account describing themselves. They could use a false name for their public handle but had to provide to Kellie their actual name and enrollment status and information. Kellie required this to ensure that she could verify reviews and better manage the quality of the website's information. Over the course of the first semester, she picked up about 100 accounts and about 400 reviews. Then one day she got an e-mail from a student complaining that he had been contacted by a professor about a negative review he had posted. The student was upset and noted to Kellie that she was lacking any privacy notice. The e-mail finished with the threat "I'm gonna sue you if you do not shut down your site right now!" How vulnerable is Kellie?

At this point, Kellie is not that vulnerable. She needs to promptly establish a privacy policy and disclose it conspicuously on her main page. If she does that within thirty days, her chances of having to deal with an effective lawsuit will be minimal. CAL-OPPA does not contain enforcement provisions of its own, but instead is intended to be enforced through California's Unfair Competition Law, which prohibits unlawful, unfair, or fraudulent business acts or practices. The law thus may be enforced by government officials or private parties, but only after giving thirty days' notice with the chance to fix the problem.

CAL-OPPA has a broad geographic reach, far beyond California's border. Neither the web server nor the company that operates the website have to be in California. The website only has to be accessible by California residents. The California Attorney General's office released a policy in 2013 that it would treat CAL-OPPA as being applicable to mobile devices when they access the Internet through a browser or an application.

At the time this edition was being prepared, controversial amendments to CAL-OPPA were enacted that increase the requirements of privacy policies. In fact, the new requirement can be said to be a decrease because the core new requirement is that the privacy policy must be no more than 100 words. It also now must be written in clear and concise language, be written at no greater than an eighth-grade reading level, and include a statement indicating whether the personally identifiable information could be sold or shared with others, and if so, how and with whom the information might be shared. Until this point, under CAL-OPPA, the privacy policies adopted and posted were usually several pages and thousands of words. One website reported that the average online privacy policy was 2,464 words. The Declaration of Independence, by comparison, is a mere 1,337 words. It was thought, probably accurately, that even consumers who started to read these policies were overwhelmed by the mass of words and gave up. The changes take effect January 1, 2014, and will bring about a significant change to the readability and conciseness of privacy policies for probably every website of U.S.-based companies and organizations. The following example is a sample 100-word, eighth-grade-compliant privacy policy prepared to show how limiting this requirement will be.

LEGAL FOCUS—EXAMPLE

Sample 100-Word Privacy Policy

Your California Privacy Rights

We will collect personally identifiable information about you, including your name, address, birthdate, account numbers, and personal likes and dislikes. We can and may share this information with other companies and persons interested in contacting you to offer other services or goods that you might be interested in. We will not inform you if we share that information. You can contact us by e-mail or regular mail by following the instructions on this web page to choose not to allow your information to be sent to other people. You also can review the information we have collected.

Compare this 100-word attempt at drafting a privacy policy to the typical 2,000-word privacy policy, and you will see a significant reduction in the amount of information provided. It is probable that websites will still contain the other information, but they simply will separate it from the required 100-word privacy policy.

California's Do-Not-Track Legislation

In 2013, California also enacted a significant new law that creates disclosure obligations regarding how websites will respond to "do-not-track" signals from browsers. These changes were adopted as new sections of CAL-OPPA. The new law requires that websites disclose through a conspicuous hyperlink, when and how the website "responds to Web browser 'do-not-track' signals or other mechanisms that provide consumers the ability to exercise choice regarding the collection of personally identifiable information about an individual consumer's online activities over time and across third-party websites or online services." Another new requirement is that the website or its operator must disclose what personal identifiable information it is collecting that relates to online consumer activity over time and across third party websites or online services.

CAL-OPPA has established a de facto online consumer privacy standard nationwide surpassing the direct accomplishments of the federal government to date. But the Obama Administration has put forward a proposal for a "bill of rights" for consumer privacy.

Consumer Privacy Bill of Rights

In 2012, the Obama Administration introduced a proposed Consumer Privacy Bill of Rights. This was touted as part of a "comprehensive blueprint to improve consumers' privacy protections and ensure that the Internet remains an engine for innovation and economic growth." To date, the proposal has not become a proposed law or a regulation issued by any agency. The Department of Commerce, home to the FTC, was tasked with beginning a conversation with companies, privacy advocates, and other stakeholders to develop and implement enforceable privacy policies based on the Consumer Privacy Bill of Rights. At the time this edition was being prepared that process was still unfolding.

The proposal was accompanied, however, by the announcement that several of the largest and most prominent website operators or online companies, including Google, Yahoo!, and Microsoft, had agreed to commit to "do-not-track" technology in web browsers to reduce online tracking of consumer activity. The companies also committed to not releasing consumers' browsing data to other companies that might use it for purposes other than advertising, such as employers making hiring decisions or insurers determining coverage. Finally, they committed to accepting FTC enforcement of these obligations.

LEGAL FOCUS—BACKGROUND

Consumer Privacy Bill of Rights*

- **Individual Control:** Consumers have a right to exercise control over what personal data organizations collect from them and how they use it.
- **Transparency:** Consumers have a right to easily understandable information about privacy and security practices.
- **Respect for Context:** Consumers have a right to expect that organizations will collect, use, and disclose personal data in ways that are consistent with the context in which consumers provide the data.
- **Security:** Consumers have a right to secure and responsible handling of personal data.
- **Access and Accuracy:** Consumers have a right to access and correct personal data in usable formats, in a manner that is appropriate to the sensitivity of the data and the risk of adverse consequences to consumers if the data are inaccurate.
- **Focused Collection:** Consumers have a right to reasonable limits on the personal data that companies collect and retain.
- **Accountability:** Consumers have a right to have personal data handled by companies with appropriate measures in place to ensure that they adhere to the Consumer Privacy Bill of Rights.

*From White House report titled "Consumer Data Privacy in a Networked World: A Framework for Protecting Privacy and Promoting Innovation in the Global Digital Economy," February 23, 2012.

The proposed Consumer Privacy Bill of Rights may or may not become law, but it, and California's Online Privacy Protection Act, have created growing pressure for a simpler but more compressive consumer privacy policy that reflects the digital age in which American's now live. You can expect continuing, if not frequent, new laws and changes to consumer privacy rights as you finish college and enter the workplace. As always, you rely mostly on yourself to protect your privacy. Be careful what data you surrender when you use websites and purchase goods and services online. Take the time to read privacy policies and note where you can opt out of disclosure of your data simply by clicking on a box. And, of course, you should know your consumer rights in general, which is the next section of this chapter.

CONSUMER PROTECTION

caveat emptor
A doctrine of transaction policy that means "let the buyer beware."

caveat venditor
A doctrine of transaction policy that means "let the seller beware."

Consumers in the United States who are involved in transactions are protected in numerous ways. Most models of capitalism include the principle of **caveat emptor** ("let the buyer beware"). Over the years (dating back at least to 1906, when the federal Pure Food and Drug Act was enacted), the government increasingly has been protecting consumers against unfair practices of a comparatively small group of unethical businesspersons and firms that always are present somewhere in the marketplace. In the 1960s and 1970s, several important federal consumer protection bills were added. Although abuses continue, legislation has given meaningful "teeth"—such as fines and prison terms—to the admonition, **caveat venditor** ("let the seller beware"). That phrase probably is an overstatement, as there remain many ways in which a careless buyer of goods and services can be harmed. But certainly also there are protections and rights that U.S. consumers should know and understand. The previous discussion of consumer privacy protection is a the most current and unfolding area of consumer protection law in the United States. The protection of consumers in transactions is all the more relevant in today's online, digital environment in which the entire buyer–seller interaction occurs through a website.

LEGAL FOCUS—EXAMPLE

Surrey needed to purchase his textbooks for the upcoming semester. He did a few searches and found an online "bookstore" that offered all of his textbooks at great prices. He ordered them, paying with his credit card. A week later he received a package that contained two of the five books he had ordered. Those two were in pretty bad condition. He tried calling the number he was given, but all he got was a recording. He e-mailed the bookstore and got a generic e-mail response. A week went by and still his other books had not arrived. School had started and so he purchased his remaining books at the school bookstore, at a substantially higher price. A month later, he still was not able to reach a human being at the online bookstore and never received a call back from his repeated voicemail messages.

Surrey could have, and should have, informed his credit card company that the merchant had not fulfilled its obligations. That would have created an obligation for the credit card company to force the merchant to prove it had delivered on its promises or face a chargeback. Consumer protection is focused on creating rules, such as credit card purchase rules. Those protections are even more relevant in today's online, digital world.

This section delves into consumer protection in transactions. In this regard, the law is being changed some and updated. We divide consumer protection into three categories that reflect the primary purpose or focus of the laws: Consumer Transactions, Consumer Lending and Credit Reporting, and Debt Collection.

As a warning, this area of the law is full of acronyms—a virtual alphabet soup. These acronyms are used pervasively, so we use them here as well. You already have read some of this information in the previous Consumer Privacy section of the chapter. You will become even more familiar with them as you proceed through the remainder of this chapter.

Consumer Transactions

A transaction usually involves a contract. If you have studied Chapter 8, then you understand that a contract makes an agreement enforceable. Most consumer purchases of goods and services involve a contract of varying complexity. The evolution of laws expressly designed to protect consumers in transactions actually began with the development of court-based doctrines to refuse to enforce certain contracts because of their inherent unfairness and the mismatched bargaining position they reflected.

adhesion contract
A contract drafted by a dominant party and then presented to the weaker party—the adhering party—on a take-it-or-leave-it basis.

When one party has vastly superior bargaining power over another, they often draft their contracts without consultation with the other party. Such a contract is called an **adhesion contract**, defined as a contract drafted by a dominant party and then presented to the weaker party—the adhering party—on a take-it-or-leave-it basis. If the powerful party used their bargaining advantage to include unfair or surprising terms in the contract, a court has the power to consider such terms or the entire contract unconscionable and to refuse to enforce it as against public policy. Unconscionable clauses—that is, those that "shock the conscience" of a court—are more likely to be found in adhesion contracts than contracts in which the parties truly bargained over terms.

LEGAL FOCUS—PROBLEM

A welfare recipient with a fourth-grade education agrees to purchase a refrigerator under a two-year installment contract with a high but legal interest rate. The total price of the refrigerator is $2,500. The same type of refrigerator usually sells for $400 on the market. Is it possible that this contract is unconscionable?

Some courts have held this type of contract to be unconscionable, even though courts generally do not inquire into the adequacy of the consideration. Besides courts, several agencies are focused on protecting consumers.

Consumer Product Safety Commission

Since 1972, the Consumer Product Safety Commission (CPSC) has been charged with overseeing the safety of all consumer products other than autos, trucks, airplanes, boats, food, drugs, and cosmetics (which are the concern of other federal agencies some of which are discussed in following sections or in other chapters).

LEGAL FOCUS—BACKGROUND

John D'Angelo, owner and president of Utility Free Inc., a Colorado-based distributor of alternative energy products, was sentenced to nearly two years in jail for violating two laws enforced by CPSC. D'Angelo pled guilty to fifteen counts of improperly shipping hazardous substances, including a highly corrosive, clear electrolyte solution. In December 1993, fifteen-year-old Justin Pulliam mistook the solution for water because D'Angelo had shipped it in a reused plastic one-gallon milk container that lacked appropriate warnings. The teenager drank it and died two weeks later from internal injuries.

Probably the most important task of the CPSC is recall or corrective action orders on products produced or sold in the United States.

LEGAL FOCUS—EXAMPLE

June 2006 Recall Announced by the U.S. Consumer Product Safety Commission

In cooperation with the U.S. Consumer Product Safety Commission (CPSC), Nexgrill Industries Inc., of City of Industry, California, is voluntarily recalling about 16,000 Nexgrill gas grills. The gas grill has a hose that connects the propane tank to the burner manifold. If this hose runs up too close to the firebox, the heat can cause the hose to detach from the burner manifold, causing a gas leak and a fire hazard.

The Food and Drug Administration

The Pure Food and Drug Act of 1906 is a legislative landmark in the area of consumer before-sale health protection. It marked the beginning of federal regulation of food and drugs in the United States. What caused the congressional action was the public outrage generated by a novel. Upton Sinclair's The *Jungle*, published in 1905, was an exposé of the Chicago meatpacking industry. The story was so revolting that no one who read it could remain unaffected. President Theodore Roosevelt demanded an immediate investigation of the Chicago meatpacking houses, supposedly after reading the following paragraph:

> *There was never the least attention paid to what was cut up for sausages; there would come all the way back from Europe old sausage that had been rejected, and that was mouldy and white—it would be dosed with borax and glycerine, and dumped into the hoppers, and made over again for home consumption. There would be meat that had tumbled out on the floor, in the dirt and sawdust, where the workers had tramped and spit uncounted billions of consumption germs.... It was too dark in these storage places to see well, but a man could run his hand over these piles of meat and sweep off handfuls of the dried dung of rats. These rats were nuisances, and the packers would put poisoned bread out for them; they would die, and then rats, bread and meat would go into the hoppers together. This is no fairy story and no joke; ... there were things that went into the sausage in comparison with which a poisoned rat was a tidbit.*

President Roosevelt ordered an investigation, and the labor commissioner confirmed Sinclair's observations. Both the long-stalled Pure Food and Drug Act and the Meat Inspection Act were passed immediately.

Under the authority of the federal Nutrition Labeling and Education Act of 1990, the Food and Drug Administration now requires that nutritional information (per serving) be provided on labels on canned and packaged foods. Examine the label on a can of your favorite soup, for example, and note the detailed listing of quantities therein of calcium, various types of fat, cholesterol, sodium, vitamins, and minerals. For many consumers, such information literally can be a lifesaver.

Federal Trade Commission

The FTC, created under the Federal Trade Commission Act of 1914 (FTCA), originally was concerned primarily with enforcement of the federal antitrust laws (i.e., the Sherman Anti-Trust Act of 1890 and the Clayton Act of 1914). The FTC sought to prevent among business corporations unfair methods of competition that could lead to monopolies. More recently, the FTC also has been active as the principal federal agency regulating advertising.

LEGAL FOCUS—BACKGROUND

On September 21, 1998, Judge Wilkie D. Ferguson, Jr., in U.S. District Court, Florida, granted the FTC's request for a stipulated final order and permanent injunction against the National Scholarship Foundation (NSF) to forbid advertising of student scholarship services. The FTC complaint stated that the NSF sent hundreds of thousands of postcards to potential college students and their families to solicit the NSF's scholarship search services. When a consumer called the listed 800 number, a company representative told the caller that the NSF could guarantee $1,000 worth of free grants and scholarships for a student if the caller paid a fee. In addition, the $189 fee would be refunded to anyone who did not receive $1,000 or more in scholarship money through the NSF within one year. The FTC charged that in fact the NSF did not fulfill its promise to find sources for its customers that led them to $1,000 minimum scholarship(s) and that the service provided was generally worthless. In addition, according to the FTC, the NSF rarely honored its refund guarantee.

Unfair or Deceptive Sales Presently, the FTCA, contains several provisions that protect consumers from abusive practices by business, most found in Section 5. Among other protections in Section 5 is a prohibition of "unfair and deceptive acts or practices." To be unfair, a company's action must meet a three-prong test:

1. The action must cause a substantial consumer injury.
2. The harm must outweigh any benefit.
3. The consumer must not have been able to reasonably avoid the injury.

LEGAL FOCUS—PROBLEM

Sherry walked into a store in a mall that had very pretty artwork. A salesman quickly introduced himself and began showing her the art. Eventually he sold Sherry on a farm landscape piece. A flyer posted next to the artwork claimed it was "original" and by an "artist that produces few pieces." It stated that the piece was likely to "increase in value" substantially. In fact the artwork was a copy of an original by an artist that churned out hundreds of pieces of art every year. Has Sherry been a victim of an unfair or deceptive business practice?

Yes, she has been a victim of an unfair business practice. Using the word original for a copy is probably enough to make the practice deceptive, but it is probably also unfair. Sherry probably paid much more than it was worth (injury), there is no benefit, and an unsophisticated buyer would not easily be able to ascertain the difference between an original and copy.

The FTC also can find a practice to be unfair because it violates a public policy. For instance, a mail order company was prohibited from filing collection suits in states that were a long way away from the state where the defendants lived. Deceptive practices also are not allowed.

LEGAL FOCUS—CASE

Audio Communications, Inc. runs ads on afternoon television telling kids they can talk to Santa Claus or the Easter Bunny if they call the number on the television screen. The number is a 900 toll call that costs a lot of money. When parents get the bills that result from these afternoon phone calls by their young children, they complain to the FTC. Does the FTC find that that Audio Communications violated Section 5 of the FTCA?

Yes, the company should have made it clear that the call would cost money and that the children needed to get the permission of their parents before calling (56 C.F.R. 22432, 1991).

Door to Door Sales

The FTC requires that consumers who make purchases from door-to-door sales have three business days to cancel the transaction with no obligation. Furthermore, the salesperson must notify the consumers that they have this right and have proof that they did so. This rule resulted in the cancellation of many encyclopedia purchases made from door-to-door salespersons. This rule was adopted to "level the playing field" because door-to-door salespersons can find their way into people's homes where they can use the pressure of not leaving to make sales happen.

Unordered Merchandise

If consumers receive merchandise that they did not order, they may treat it as a gift. This rule was adopted to curb a practice of sending goods to consumers and instructing them that they had to return them or pay for them. Companies then would follow up with pressure phone calls to complete the sale. This also helped counter one-time-only purchases that turn into a stream of continued deliveries without having agreed to have such an obligation to keep buying such goods.

Do-Not-Call Registry

In 2003, the FTC opened the National Do-Not-Call Registry required by Do-Not-Call Implementation Act of 2003. Consumers can sign up their telephone numbers for this registry and then be assured that telemarketers are prohibited from calling them unless they have a preexisting relationship that involved consent or agreement to receive such calls. Wireless and land-line phone numbers can be put on the list. There are exceptions: Nonprofit organizations can call numbers on list and surveys are allowed. Generally, however, the Do-Not-Call Registry has made for more relaxing evenings and reduced the ability of telemarketers to make pressure sales calls on consumers.

Consumer Leasing Act

The Consumer Leasing Act was enacted in 2001 and set minimum required written disclosures to lessors of cars, including the following:

- All required payments including deposits, down payments, taxes, balloon payments, and license fees and the total amount that will be paid by the end of the lease.
- The number and amount of monthly payments and how they are calculated.
- Insurance premiums that are required.
- Maintenance requirements.

Uniform Deceptive Trade Practices Act and State Consumer Laws

Many states provide a significant amount of consumer protection above and beyond federal protection. Many states have adopted the Uniform Deceptive Trade Practices Act or something very similar. The Uniform Deceptive Trade Practices prohibits unfair or fraudulent business practices and untrue or misleading advertising. The Act also allows for private causes of action and includes the potential for attorneys' fees to prevailing parties in cases in which the losing party "willfully engaged in the trade practice knowing it to be deceptive." This greatly enables the ability of an injured consumer to directly pursue claims against the rule-violating company. Many states also have a Department of Consumer Affairs devoted to regulating industries that focus on consumer goods and services and to protecting consumers who use goods and services from those industries.

Warranties

A **warranty** is an assurance, promise, or guarantee by one party that a particular statement of fact is true and may be relied on by the other party in a commercial transaction.

LEGAL FOCUS—BACKGROUND

Some devices, such as battery-operated toys costing $39.95, break down almost instantly upon exposure to the Earth's atmosphere. Other devices, such as stereo systems owned by your next-door neighbor's 13-year-old son who likes to listen to bands with names like 'Nerve Damage,' at a volume capable of disintegrating limestone, will continue to function perfectly for many years, even if you hit them with an ax.

—Dave Barry, humorist

Some warranties are implied by law and exist even if nothing is said about them; other warranties are expressed and may be oral, but they usually are stated in the written contract.

Uniform Commercial Code

Most warranty law is a function of state law. The Uniform Commercial Code (UCC) contains extensive provisions on warranties and most states have adopted those provisions. There is federal law covering warranties, most notable the Magnusson-Moss Warranty Act. Warranties can arise in a variety of situations, but this chapter focuses on the assurances given in the sale or lease of goods under the UCC because that is the aspect of warranties that most affects the consumer.

express warranty
A warranty created when a reasonable buyer would believe that a particular representation was part of the bargain.

An **express warranty** can exist even if a seller did not intend to make one. The UCC does not require that the seller "use formal words such as 'warrantor guarantee' or that they make a specific intention to make a warranty." It is necessary only that a reasonable buyer would believe that a particular representation was part of the bargain. An **implied warranty** is one that the law implies from the nature or circumstances of the transaction.

implied warranty
A warranty that the law implies from the nature or circumstances of the transaction.

Although warranties can arise in any sales or lease transaction, it is important to distinguish between merchants and casual sellers. A **merchant** is a professional seller who deals in goods of the kind, or otherwise by occupation holds himself or herself out as having knowledge or skill peculiar to the practice or goods involved in the transaction. Casual sellers are ordinary laypersons disposing of things they own.

merchant
A professional seller who deals in goods, or otherwise by occupation holds himself or herself out as having knowledge or skill peculiar to the good or service.

Under the UCC, either a merchant or a casual seller may explicitly make the following express warranties:

- **Warranty of conformity to description, sample, or model.** All goods supplied must conform to the sample or model shown at the time of the sale, or to the specifications provided.
- **Warranty of conformity to seller's statement or promise.** The seller who openly states or writes a factual assertion about the goods is bound by that assertion.

In addition to express warranties, sales by either a merchant or casual seller create each of these implied warranties:

- **Warranty of title.** The seller has the title to the goods as claimed and the right to transfer or sell them.
- **Warranty against encumbrances.** The goods delivered will be free of liens or encumbrances—creditors' claims—of which the buyer is not aware at the time of contracting.
- **Warranty of fitness for a particular purpose.** If the buyer indicates the purpose for which the goods are needed and then relies on the seller's selection, the goods will be reasonably fit for the intended stated purpose.

LEGAL FOCUS—PROBLEM

When Peggy Butler visited Mac's Sport Shack, she told the salesperson that she was planning a backpack trip into the Great Smoky Mountains. Butler insisted on being outfitted with "Pathfinder" brand moccasin boots and a "Kozy" brand sleeping bag. After several days in the wilderness using this gear, she realized that neither product fit her needs. Her ankles were swollen, and she caught pneumonia. Is Mac's Sport Shack liable on a breach of warranty of fitness for a particular purpose?

No, it is not liable. A warranty is not given when the buyer insists on a particular brand, as here. Possibly, Butler could hold the manufacturers liable if they had made express warranties as to the goods and these warranties were breached.

Merchant sellers alone make the following two additional implied warranties:

- **Warranty against infringement.** The goods sold are delivered free of any rightful claim of a third party under patent, copyright, or other legal protection.
- **Warranty of merchantability.** This is an extremely important warranty, promising that the goods are fit for the ordinary purposes for which such goods are used. Thus, a rocking chair (or stereo or toaster or umbrella) should function as such and last a reasonable length of time (which might be many years) under ordinary use.

LEGAL FOCUS—EXAMPLE

Goods that fail the warranty of merchantability include light-bulbs that explode when switched on, pajamas that burst into flames at slight contact with a stove burner, high-heeled shoes that break off under normal use, and shotgun shells that explode prematurely.

Contracts for sale or lease of used or secondhand goods involve only such obligation as is appropriate to such goods. This obligation includes the customary implied warranty of merchantability, but the price, age, and condition of the goods at the time of the sale are considered in determining the scope of the warranty. Obviously, such a warranty may be of little value to the buyer, especially if the goods are worn out or in poor condition.

LEGAL FOCUS—EXAMPLE

You need a gallon of paint to match the color of your bedroom walls, a light shade somewhere between coral and peach. You take a wall chip sample to your local hardware store and request a gallon of paint of that color. Instead, you are given a gallon of bright blue paint. The salesperson has not breached any warranty of implied merchantability—the bright blue paint may be of high quality and suitable for interior walls. The clerk, however, has breached an implied warranty of fitness for a particular purpose.

disclaimer
A statement made to avoid a warranty or otherwise eliminate a promise that might have been made about performance, capability, or future action.

consequential damages
Injury or harm occurring as a result, or consequence, of the failure of a party to correctly perform a promised act under a contract.

unconscionable
Something that is against public policy or otherwise so offensive that it shocks the conscience.

Disclaiming Warranties

A seller or lessor may generally *disclaim* (limit or negate) all warranties. Fortunately, because of competitive pressure, most sellers acknowledge they need to stand behind their products. To exclude the implied warranty of merchantability, the seller must conspicuously mention *merchantability* in the **disclaimer** or give notice of exclusion. A statement that the goods are sold "as is" or "with all faults" serves to exclude all other implied warranties. Most states, however, provide that **consequential damages** may *not* be limited or excluded if the exclusion is **unconscionable** (i.e., against public policy). Limitation of such damages "for injury to the person in the case of consumer goods is prima facie unconscionable." Also, if the goods are defective, the seller may be liable for damages under the tort doctrine of strict liability (see Chapter 7).

Formerly, sellers often were shielded from liability by legal requirements of *privity*, meaning that the plaintiff buyer seeking to enforce a warranty must be the party who contracted with the defendant seller. Thus, a consumer might sue a retailer who sold the defective product to him or her, but not the much wealthier manufacturer who made it. Most states have modified or rejected this doctrine and hold all merchants or manufacturers in the chain of distribution liable for any breach. Modernly, the warranty protection has been extended beyond the buyer to include all members of the buyer's family or household and any of the buyer's guests, where they reasonably might be expected to use such goods and where the defective goods cause physical injury. But in most states, innocent bystanders and others who are injured by a defective product must seek recovery on some other basis, such as strict product liability of manufacturers and intermediaries in a tort action, as noted previously.

LEGAL FOCUS—PROBLEM

While trying to persuade Marjorie Ayers to buy an expensive personal computer system, Leon Cannon said that all parts were guaranteed and would be replaced without any charge if found defective within five years. The written purchase contract that Ayers later signed spoke of only a one-year warranty against defects in materials and workmanship. Moreover, it said that the customer would have to pay for half of the usual labor charge. Which warranty terms actually apply to the purchase?

The one-year warranty terms apply—unless she can prove that the seller intentionally lied, that she was the victim of mistake or fraud, or that the written contract was incomplete. This is the result of the **parol evidence rule**, which presumes that the contracting parties have included all previous desired oral or written understandings in their final, integrated written agreement. Thus, it is not enough for a consumer to get all-important contracts in writing; one also should ensure that the writing includes all desired terms and any oral assurances and that they are stated correctly and completely, including a clear statement of any warranty protection.

parol evidence rule
A contract doctrine that presumes that the contracting parties have included all previous desired oral or written understandings in their final, integrated written agreement.

Magnuson-Moss Warranty Act

The federal Magnuson-Moss Warranty Act of 1975, designed to help protect ultimate consumers of personal, family, or household goods costing $10 or more, has added the concepts of *full and limited* warranties. Under the Act, no one is required to give a written warranty, but the seller who elects to do so must label it as either full or limited. If it is a *full warranty,* the seller agrees to fix the product within a reasonable time and without charge if it proves to be defective. If it cannot be fixed or if a reasonable number of attempts to fix it prove unsuccessful, the buyer has the choice of a full cash refund or a free replacement. (Some states have added *lemon laws,* which clarify and strengthen this rule.) No time limit may be placed on implied warranties in a full warranty. But if an otherwise full warranty has a time limit, it may be described, for example, as a "full five-year warranty." The seller must label any warranty that does not provide full protection a *limited warranty.* A warranty would be limited if, for example, the buyer had to pay any fee or transportation charge to utilize it. Implied warranties (e.g., of title or of merchantability) may not be disclaimed if any written warranty is given, but they may be defined and limited.

Typical language in an express warranty given by a representative manufacturer of consumer goods states that the product is warranted "against any defects due to faulty materials or workmanship for a one-year period after the original date of consumer purchase." In fairness to manufacturers, a warranty extended beyond the stated short period can be very costly to service. Buyers who neglect their possessions and fail to follow recommended maintenance schedules take unfair advantage of warranties. Yet, all buyers pay for the added protection that most do not need, because the added cost is distributed over the price in all sales. A better alternative for some may be the purchase of "extended warranty protection" for an additional period of time for an additional charge.

The FTC has independently imposed further regulations in cases in which the consumer good costs more than $15 (the law is more than thirty years old). The seller is required to disclose the name of the warrantors, the nature and limitations (if any) of the warranty, and the fact that the buyer has legal rights to specified procedures for the enforcement of the warranty.

Bureau of Consumer Financial Protection

The BCFP was created as part of the Dodd-Frank Wall Street Reform and Consumer Protection Act. The BCFP came into existence in 2011. As such a new agency it is still largely "getting to its feet" and has done little of substance that differs from what the FTC has or might have done. The BCFP, however, does have a different focus, one that suggests it may offer unique and perhaps valuable assistance to consumers. The BCFP is focused on the investment mechanisms from which consumers have to choose. It has jurisdiction over the banks, credit unions, and other institutions that offer such instruments. It serves to educate and perhaps also to regulate how those instruments are described, structured, or offered. Right now, the BCFP primarily is educating and taking complaints. You can visit them at their website at http://www.consumerfinance.gov.

Consumer Lending and Credit Reporting

In addition to laws protecting consumers in transactions, another body of law is focused on consumer credit. These laws are intended to ensure that consumers can borrow money in a safe, reliable manner. To ensure that, the laws focus on how credit is offered as well as on how the performance of consumers is reported, tracked, and ranked. After all, this latter aspect of the laws is necessary to ensure that credit is offered.

Truth in Lending Act

The most important section of the Consumer Credit Protection Act of 1968 is known as the Truth in Lending Act, which requires a full disclosure of the comparative costs of buying goods for cash or on credit. On credit sales and loans of money, the creditor must disclose, in writing and in advance of signing, the total dollar finance charge and the effective annual percentage rate (APR) of the interest or finance charge. Sellers may not mislead gullible customers, for example, by quoting a credit cost of "only 1.5 percent a month." They must disclose that the equivalent interest cost per year is 18 percent. The Act also provides for a three-day "cooling-off" period when a consumer agrees to borrow on the security of a second mortgage on a home. Under the law, the borrower may rescind and get back any money delivered to the creditor as long as he or she does it within the three days. The Act places no limit on the rate or amount of interest or carrying charge, although some consumer advocates think it should.

The cooling-off rule of the Truth in Lending Act does not apply to first mortgages (or first deeds) on homes, because such credit generally has not been the basis for exploitation of unsophisticated homeowners in need of funds and because the interest rates have been reasonable.

LEGAL FOCUS—PROBLEM

Staresh purchases a brand new luxurious couch on which to watch the first football games of the season. He buys it on credit from a store that both rents and sells furniture. When he gets home (the couch has not been delivered yet), his wife Tania is very upset and insists he cancel the contract, a right she says he has for three days. When Staresh goes back to the store, they explain that he cannot cancel it and whether he takes delivery of the couch or not, he is going to have to make all the required payments. They show him where he initialed a statement that essentially says just that. Can Staresh refuse to accept the couch and avoid liability for the debt?

He probably cannot do so and certainly cannot do so using the three-day rule. The three-day cooling-off period is a narrow exception that allows a party to escape a contract acceptance. Unfortunately, many consumers who have heard of the "three-day rule" think it applies to all consumer contracts. It does not. Staresh might prevail depending on the laws of his state, especially those on deceptive and unfair practices. He also might prevail just by writing to complain to a television news show or consumer advocacy agency or group.

Traditionally, *garnishment* (attachment of the salary or wages of a defaulting debtor) has been a principal remedy for unpaid creditors. To use this remedy, the creditor gets a court order (called a *writ of execution*) directing the debtor's employer to pay a certain portion of the employee's wages directly to the creditor until the judgment is paid in full. Sometimes, employers have fired workers who have gotten into such financial trouble. Under the federal Consumer Credit Protection Act, the amount garnished is subject to significant limitations. The Act further provides that an employer may not discharge an employee simply because wages have been garnished for any one indebtedness.

Fair Credit Reporting Act

The Fair Credit Reporting Act (FCRA) regulates the conditions under which disclosure of personal information may be made to third parties by consumer reporting agencies.

LEGAL FOCUS—PROBLEM

Fiona applies for a job. She fills out several forms. She is called in for an interview and it goes well. A week later, however, she gets a letter informing her that she was not selected. Curious, she calls the business manager back. The manager tells Fiona that her credit report showed significant problems and that she did not meet their creditworthiness criteria. Stunned Fiona asks how they got her credit report. The manager explains that she signed a form authorizing them to pull her credit report among other things they could do to investigate her. Was the company allowed to obtain and use a credit report in deciding not to hire Fiona?

Yes and no. The FCRA allows an employer or potential employer to obtain and review a credit report if the consumer gives consent. A state law might apply, and in either case, the manner in which Fiona gave consent might or might not comply with the law. Assuming her consent was obtained correctly, however, the company was within its rights to obtain and read her credit report. But before an adverse employment action can be taken based on such a report, the consumer must receive a copy of the report. That did not occur in Fiona's case. Although the Act does not restrict the amount or type of information that can be collected, it does give consumers the right to check their credit files for accuracy. The opportunity is provided to correct or explain inaccurate information, and the credit agency is under a duty to remove inaccurate or incomplete information. The national bureaus are required by law to have a joint reinvestigation system, so (in theory) a consumer trying to correct an incorrect credit report does not have to deal with all national providers. A recent amendment to the FCRA requires each of the nationwide consumer reporting companies—Equifax, Experian, and TransUnion—to provide a free copy of an individual's credit report once every twelve months. Violations of the FCRA are enforced by the FTC.

Fair Credit Billing Act

The Fair Credit Billing Act of 1974 is a response to problems that result when clerks with computers electronically provide invoices that may be erroneous. Consumers who believe (1) an accounting error has been made by the issuer of a credit card, (2) goods or services have not been delivered or accepted, (3) credit extensions have not been made or have been made incorrectly, or (4) payments or credits have been recorded incorrectly may notify the creditor in writing within sixty days after the issuer mailed them the first bill with the error. The creditor (or issuer of the card) must investigate and respond promptly, normally within thirty days of receipt. Within ninety days, the creditor must either eliminate the error or explain why it believes the bill was correct.

After notification, the creditor is barred temporarily from pressing for payment or reporting to a credit bureau, although statements may continue to be sent. Consumers are obligated legally to pay any part of the bill not in dispute. If the creditor admits an error, it cannot impose finance charges on the disputed amount. The creditor must submit a correct written notice of what is owed, and consumers must be given the usual time to pay before any finance charges or late-payment charges may be assessed. If it turns out that there was no error, consumers must pay finance charges on the disputed amount and make up any payments missed. The debtor who is not satisfied with the creditor's explanation is allowed a minimum of ten days after receiving the explanation in which to protest. Thereafter, whether or not such protest was made, the creditor may sue or use other collection procedures. If there was a second protest, however, the creditor who notified credit bureaus and other creditors must mention the dispute and inform the debtor of the identity of the addressees. These protections make the use of a credit card a wise choice on many purchases, especially with remote vendors.

Failure to comply with the stated rules makes the finance charges and first $30 of the disputed amount uncollectible, even if later events prove there was no creditor error.

The Credit Card Liability Act of 1970

The Credit Card Liability Act of 1970 amended the Truth in Lending Act to control certain practices of credit card companies. A consumer must apply for a credit card; it may not be thrust on the consumer without such request and consent. Moreover, the cardholder's liability for unauthorized use of the card by a thief or dishonest finder is limited to a maximum of $50 per card. And even this limited liability can be imposed only if all of the following apply:

- The cardholder requested and received the credit card, or signed or used it, or authorized another person to do so.
- The card issuer provided a self-addressed, prestamped notification to be mailed by the cardholder in the event of loss or theft of the card.
- The card issuer gave adequate notice of the $50 liability.
- The card issuer provided positive means of identification (e.g., signature or photo of the cardholder on the card).
- The unauthorized use took place before the cardholder notified the issuer that such use might take place.

Equal Credit Opportunity Act of 1974

The Equal Credit Opportunity Act of 1974 forbids discrimination in extension of credit because of sex, marital status, race, color, religion, national origin, or advanced age; because the applicants get all or part of their income from a public assistance welfare program; or because the applicant has in good faith exercised a right under the Consumer Credit Protection Act.

Debit Cards versus Credit Cards

In the past few years, the use of debit and automated teller machine (ATM) cards has increased significantly. A **debit card** deducts the amount of a purchase directly from your checking account. Its use is not dependent on any coding. An ATM card is used in an ATM, which may access a credit or a debit account to complete banking inquiries and fund transfers between accounts. Its use requires a code (personal identification number, or PIN). Technically, an ATM card is a subtype of a debit card. Although the use of these cards is pervasive, consumers appear to lack a good understanding of their legal significance.

debit card
an electronic card that allows consumers to pay for goods and services by directly applying funds from a deposit account.

Although they often look like credit cards, these cards are very different. Debit cards draw against an account the user has with a financial institution or a prior payment of money the user has made to the card issuer. They do not involve an extension of credit. Instead of "pay later," they represent "pay now."

Few of the consumer protections available when credit card disputes arise apply to debit card use. The transactions are essentially cash transactions. If the debit card is stolen, federal law limits the holder's maximum liability to $50 if the card loss is reported within two days of discovery. After two days, liability increases to $500; if the card loss is not reported within sixty days, the liability can be unlimited. In addition, because the money is taken directly from an account, checks can bounce with all attendant costs perhaps even before the consumer knows there is a problem. With a credit card, a bill is received; if charges are unauthorized, the consumer still has the money while working on the problem. With a debit card, you are working with your bank to get your money back.

Because debit card use provides a greater profit to banks than ATM use, many banks have sent debit cards to their customers in exchange for ATM-only cards. Although disclosures accompany these transactions, most consumers do not appreciate the distinction between an ATM card and a debit card that also acts as an ATM card. Many debit card providers offer more favorable terms to their customers than the law requires. Because debit cards carry significant additional risk over ATM cards or credit cards, be careful and shop around.

The Credit Card Accountability Responsibility and Disclosure Act of 2009

The Credit Card Accountability Responsibility and Disclosure Act or "The Credit CARD Act of 2009" took effect in February of 2010 and added new restrictions on when a credit card provider may increase interest rates. It also limits fees, to allocate payments to the highest interest rate debt first, and added many other various new protections for consumers regarding credit cards.

Debt Collection

The final category of laws grew out of the response to what had become a huge problem in the 1970s, a problem which resulted in complaints to Congress and state legislatures everywhere.

LEGAL FOCUS—EXAMPLE

Kayla was living a nightmare. After losing her job in the economic downturn, she had run out of the ability make payments on her credit cards. She was managing to find enough work to pay rent, utilities and buy food for her and her children but that was about it. Her children were wearing free clothes from the local assistance bank and she was desperate. Worse, most of her debts had been "sold" to debt collectors who were calling her house constantly. One company was particularly rude and cruel. They threatened to "jail" her, take away her children, and to make her life miserable. Kayla could not sleep or relax and the tension and stress of her environment was distracting her and preventing her from doing her best at getting a new job.

Unfortunately, this scenario is not and was not unusual. In the 1970s, this behavior was rampant. Congress responded with the Fair Debt Collection Practices Act and other laws following that. As you will read, consumer protection in this area is extensive and detailed. The case at the end of this chapter illustrates the potential for abusive practices in debt collection. The chapter finishes with an overview of bankruptcy laws as applied to consumers, which are the ultimate in debt collection protection. Sadly, the story in the previous example comes from a real-life example of a debt collection company shutdown in 2013. Abuse clearly continues, although it is substantially less common.

Fair Debt Collection Practices Act

Perhaps the single-most powerful registration protecting consumers who find themselves in financial trouble is the FDCPA. The FDCPA outlaws a variety of unreasonably harsh tactics used in the past by overly aggressive debt collectors. Following is a summary of some of the prohibited practices:

- **Making late night and early morning telephone calls.** Debt collectors cannot contact consumers by telephone outside of the hours of 8:00 A.M. to 9:00 P.M. local time.
- **Using obscene and abusive language.**
- **Threatening to notify employers.**
- **Representing oneself as being the police or an official government agent.**
- **Failing to cease communication upon request.**
- **Continuing communication when refused.** Debt collectors cannot continue to communicate with consumers after receiving written notice that the consumer wishes no further communication or refuses to pay the debt. There are a few certain exceptions, such as acknowledging the request to terminate communication or notifying the consumer that the collector intends to file a lawsuit or pursue other remedies.
- **Using the phone to harass.** Debt collectors cannot repeatedly call or engage any person in telephone conversation repeatedly or continuously with the intent to annoy, abuse, or harass.
- **Contacting at work.** Debt collectors cannot attempt to contact the consumer at work once they are advised it is unacceptable.
- **Contacting a consumer known to be represented by an attorney.**
- **Publishing the consumer's name or address on a "bad debt" list.**
- **Seeking excessive amounts.** Debt collectors cannot see unjustified amounts of money as payment of the debt.
- **Threatening arrest or other legal action that is either not permitted or not actually contemplated.**
- **Telling third parties about the consumer's debt.**
- **Contacting consumer by embarrassing media.** This includes using a postcard with any language or symbol other than the debt collector's name and address.
- **Reporting false information on a consumer's credit report.** Debt collectors also cannot threaten to do so.

There are more prohibitions. Nothing in the law prevents creditors from using legitimate methods and conventional legal remedies to collect overdue debts, but this list prevents debt collectors from most of the abusive practices used frequently in the past.

The FDCPA regulates the activities of "debt collectors" and generally does not apply to internal collectors, that is collections by the original creditor. The FDCPA defines a debt collector as

> *any person who uses any instrumentality of interstate commerce or the mails in any business the principal purpose of which is the collection of any debts, or who regularly collects or attempts to collect, directly or indirectly, debts owed or due or asserted to be owed or due another.*

Some states have adopted state consumer protection laws that mirror the FDCPA but that also regulate original creditors. There are exceptions to the definition of "debt collector." The Internal Revenue Service, notably, is not a debt collector, although rules applicable to their actions are similar to the restrictions in the FDCPA.

bankruptcy
A legal status in which a person has debts that so exceed their accounts or income that they cannot possibly pay them.

Bankruptcy Abuse Prevention and Consumer Protection Act
A 2005 law intended to curb perceived abuses of the bankruptcy system by individuals by setting new tests and requirements for eligibility to use the bankruptcy system.

Enforcement of the FDCPA The FTC has historically enforced the FDCPA, but the BCFP (see previous section) is now the administrative agency for the FDCPA. The FTC is still the enforcer of the FDCPA. More important, perhaps, the FDCPA has a strong private enforcement provision. Consumers may sue debt collectors in state or federal court to collect damages. Depending on the circumstances of the case, consumers can obtain not just actual damages but statutory minimum damages, attorneys' fees, and court costs. The FDCPA provides statutory damages of up to $1,000 plus reasonable attorneys' fees if a debt collector is proven to have violated the FDCPA. The collector, however, may escape statutory damages if the violation was unintentional and the result of a "bona fide error" that occurred despite procedures designed to avoid the error at issue. The case at the end of this chapter is a colorful story of a debt collection company accused of FDCPA violations.

chapter 7 bankruptcy
A type of bankruptcy proceeding wherein almost all debts of the debtor are erased and most all assets owned by debtor are surrendered to the creditors.

Bankruptcy

Consumers in the United States have the option of filing bankruptcy to absolve themselves of, or perhaps reorganize, their debts. **Bankruptcy** is a legal status in which a person has debts that so exceed their accounts or income that they cannot possibly pay them. Consumer bankruptcy filings prevent or stop creditors from pursuing debt collection and can, depending on the outcome of the proceeding, either release the consumer from any debt obligations or significantly modify or restructure how the debt is repaid. In 2005, the **Bankruptcy Abuse Prevention and Consumer Protection Act (BAPCPA)** was passed, which significantly changed how consumers could access and use bankruptcy as a debt collection protection measure.

chapter 11 bankruptcy
A type of bankruptcy proceeding wherein the debts of the debtor are reorganized and the debtor leaves the proceeding with a set payment plan that allows for sufficient available income to live.

Bankruptcy is administered exclusively by the federal government in a special federal court system, Bankruptcy Court. Consumers usually choose between a total liquidation bankruptcy, or **chapter 7 bankruptcy**, or a debt reorganization bankruptcy proceeding, or **chapter 11 bankruptcy**. BABCPA added a "means" test that restricts access to chapter 7 to those who lack a subsistence income, as that test measures it. When a consumer enters into bankruptcy, debt collection stops and the bankruptcy court determines the outcome of the consumer's debts. Bankruptcy is an extreme condition and should be entered into only after careful consideration of all options and the advice of financial advisors and attorneys. In cases in which it is necessary, however, it can result in a "fresh start" for a consumer who is overwhelmed by debt.

LEGAL FOCUS—PROBLEM

Aleem bought a brand new luxury recreational vehicle (RV) on credit from the RV sales company. After one year of barely making the payments and barely using the RV, Aleem realized he had made a mistake. He called the RV company to take the RV back, but they refused and reminded him that he had to make all eight years of payments still remaining. Angry, Aleem replied, "Well good luck getting another penny from me. I am going to sell the RV and claim bankruptcy and you won't get a penny." Is Aleem's plan very sound?

No, it is not a sound plan. First, Aleem probably does not have a clean title to the RV, so he cannot sell it unless it is done so illegally. Second, Aleem may or may not be eligible for bankruptcy, but making claims of planning on filing bankruptcy as a pressure tactic to a creditor is never a good idea.

CASE

Avila v. Rubin

7th Cir. Ct Ap. 1996

Raul Avila borrowed money for college from the Connecticut Student Loan Foundation. The Connecticut Student Loan Foundation had entered into an agreement with a debt collection company called Van Ru Credit Corporation and an attorney, Albert Rubin, who partly owned the collection company. The Connecticut Student Loan Foundation assigned the collection of Avila's debt to the collection company.

Terence T. Evans, Circuit Judge

Can a person, licensed to practice law, be in violation of the Fair Debt Collection Practices Act (FDCPA), for sending dunning collection letters that purport to be from an "attorney"? This we address today in this case involving Raul Avila, the Van Ru Credit Corporation, and Albert G. Rubin, an attorney-at-law from Skokie, Illinois. As Joe Friday would say, let's get to the facts. We will, but unlike Sergeant Friday, it won't be "just the facts" as we'll mix in some observations and findings along the way.

Avila is a student loan debtor living in Connecticut. Van Ru Credit Corporation is a collection agency in Skokie, Illinois. Rubin is an Illinois attorney. Although we were told at oral argument that Rubin and the Van Ru agency are separate, they actually seem to be as closely intertwined as lovers during an embrace. Here's the situation from which, we think, that conclusion is justified.

Rubin founded Van Ru and owns 80 percent of its corporate stock. The remainder is owned by Van Ru's president, who is Rubin's son. Rubin is Van Ru's chief executive officer, draws a large salary from the company, and, until eight years ago, managed Van Ru's day-to-day collection activities. Rubin is involved in the creation and modification of form letters, the most critical part of the debt collection operation.

In addition to his duties at Van Ru, Rubin has a law office which he calls Rubin & Associates. Rubin & Associates is located on the third floor of the "Van Ru Building." The Van Ru Building is owned by Van Ru Credit Services, Inc., and Rubin owns 75 percent of this firm. Rubin & Associates splits the third-floor space of the building with Van Ru. Rubin & Associates is comprised of Rubin, one other attorney, and some 35 "legal assistant collectors." The primary business of Rubin & Associates is to send form letters to delinquent debtors urging them to pay their debts and to refer the files of delinquent debtors to other attorneys for litigation. Neither Rubin nor the other attorney in his office actually litigates in Connecticut, and it is unclear (but we think doubtful) whether they litigate anywhere. Rubin & Associates receives all its business from Van Ru after Van Ru's efforts to collect debts are unsuccessful. Van Ru pays Rubin & Associates a monthly retainer for work that Rubin & Associates does on debtor accounts.

Rubin personally maintains offices in both the Van Ru and Rubin & Associates offices. Rubin works at Van Ru around 20 hours a week and spends some 30 hours each week working at Rubin & Associates. Van Ru and Rubin & Associates use the same computer system and internal account number to identify files. Van Ru and Rubin & Associates also utilize the same automated telephone dialing system to call delinquent debtors; employees from both entities sit next to each other when using the system. Van Ru and Rubin & Associates receive mail at the same post office box. Van Ru and Rubin & Associates use the same printer for their respective form letters. The two also use the same machine to fold and process form letters in preparation for mailing. The mailing machine processes Van Ru and Rubin & Associates letters simultaneously, resulting in stacks of mixed letters ready for mailing. The letters of both Van Ru and Rubin & Associates are placed in identical envelopes. The printer and mailing machine are operated, and the letters are handled, by employees of Pegasus Data Systems, Inc., a company located at the same address as Van Ru and Rubin & Associates. Rubin owns 50 percent of Pegasus.

Although Van Ru and Rubin & Associates utilize the same computer system, Van Ru employees do not issue Rubin & Associates letters or input data into a debtor's file after it is transferred to Rubin & Associates. Once a file is referred to Rubin & Associates, Van Ru's employees generally do not pursue collection activities against the debtor.

Avila allegedly owes money on a student loan to his creditor, the Connecticut Student Loan Foundation. The foundation has a written contract with Van Ru and an oral agreement with Rubin for debt collection services. The foundation forwarded Avila's account for collection to Van Ru via electronic data transmission. As is its practice, the foundation did not forward underlying documentation about Avila's loan. Van Ru sent Avila two demand or "dunning" letters in an attempt to collect the debt. Avila did not respond. Van Ru then "referred" Avila's account to Rubin & Associates. Rubin & Associates then cranked out three dunning letters to Avila on attorney letterhead in an attempt to collect the debt. The five form letters are the basis for this suit, filed by Avila against Van Ru and Rubin. Now let's look at the letters.

The first letter (we'll call it exhibit A), dated November 22, 1993, tells Avila that Van Ru intends to collect his debt. It informs Avila of his right to dispute the validity of the debt within 30 days. Ten days later, on December 2, 1993, Van Ru sent Avila a second letter, exhibit B, which demanded that Avila "commence immediate repayment of [the] loan" and threatened that "[i]f payment is not received, a civil suit may be initiated against you by your creditor."

The next three letters, which we'll call exhibits C, D, and E, were sent by Rubin & Associates on the following letterhead:

> Albert G. Rubin, Ltd.
> Attorney at Law

Exhibit C, dated January 4, 1994, tells Avila of his right to dispute or verify the debt. This information is immediately followed by the sentences: "If the above does not apply to you, we shall expect payment or arrangement for payment within ten (10) days from the date of this letter. If payment is not received, a civil suit may be initiated against you by your creditor for repayment of your loan." Exhibit A, the first letter from Van Ru, also contained this statement.

Exhibits D and E are letters from Rubin demanding payment from Avila and threatening a civil suit if payment is not forthcoming. Exhibits D and E do not notify Avila of a right to dispute the debt. Exhibits C through E are mass-produced collection letters "signed" with a mechanically reproduced facsimile of the signature of attorney "Albert G. Rubin."

Mr. Rubin reviews and approves the general form used on letters sent by Rubin & Associates. He does not, however, personally prepare, sign, or review any of the letters sent to targets, including Avila. This is understandable, for Rubin would probably be in the hospital with a severe case of writer's cramp if he did because some 270,000 such letters go out each year. That, by the way, comes out to 1,062 per working day, 133 per working hour.

The letters from attorney Rubin are actually the product of a non-attorney "legal assistant collector" who directs the computer to generate a letter on Rubin's attorney letterhead. Legal assistant collectors are provided with a training manual developed by Rubin to help them determine when an attorney debt collection letter is warranted. According to Rubin, the collectors use their "skill, judgment, and training" to determine when a letter should be sent.

Claiming that the letters, exhibits A–E, were violations of the FDCPA, Avila filed this suit in the spring of 1994. The parties filed joint motions for summary judgment on liability. Avila's motion carried the day as Rubin was held liable to the class under §§1692g and 1692e(3) and (9) of the FDCPA, and Van Ru was found liable as well under §1692g. Van Ru and Avila stipulated to damages of $20,000 and judgment in that amount was entered. Then, following a bench trial on the issue of statutory damages, judgment was entered for Avila against Rubin for $84,983. Rubin and Van Ru appeal.

A "validation notice" is required by law to be present in letters seeking to collect debts. Essentially, the notice must tell the target that she has 30 days to dispute the validity of all or a portion of the debt. If not disputed, the collector may assume the debt to be valid.

After some anguish, we held in *Gammon v. GC Servs. Ltd. Partnership*, that claims against debt collectors under the FDCPA are to be viewed through the eyes of the "unsophisticated consumer." We rejected what may be viewed as a somewhat lesser standard-the "least sophisticated consumer," used by other courts. We reiterate our standard today, but we don't want to be involved in the splitting of split hairs. Anyway it's viewed, the standard is low, close to the bottom of the sophistication meter.

Exhibits A and C, the first letters sent by Van Ru and Rubin, included the required 30-day debt verification notice. Both, however, followed the notice with the confusing statement we previously noted: "If the above does not apply to you, we shall expect payment or arrangement for payment to be made within ten (10) days from the date of this letter." The letter from Van Ru followed up on this statement by telling the debtor that "[t]his will avoid additional proceedings by our firm." The letter from Rubin followed up the statement by saying, "If payment is not received, a civil suit may be initiated against you by the creditor for repayment of your loan."We think that telling a debtor he has 30 days to dispute the debt and following that with a statement that "[i]f the above does not apply" you have ten days to pay up or real trouble will start is entirely inconsistent, and a failure to comply, with the FDCPA. We think the unsophisticated consumer would be scratching his head upon receipt of such a letter. He wouldn't have a clue as to what he was supposed to do before real trouble begins. A debt validation notice, to be valid, must be effective, and it cannot be cleverly couched in such a way as to eviscerate its message. To protect the uninformed, the naive, and the trusting—the sort of people who easily fit under the umbrella of the "unsophisticated consumer"—the notice cannot be as misleading and tricky as the one used here by Van Ru and Rubin. We think the validation notice was clearly overshadowed by the language that followed on its heels. So, like the district court, we believe that both Rubin and Van Ru are guilty of not complying with §1692g of the FDCPA.

We move now to the attorney letters, exhibits C, D, and E, noting first that §1692e of the FDCPA provides:

> *A debt collector may not use any false, deceptive, or misleading representation or means in connection with the collection of any debt. Without limiting the general application of the foregoing, the following conduct is a violation of this section:*

(3) The false representation or implication that any individual is an attorney or that any communication is from an attorney.
(9) The use or distribution of any written communication, which creates a false impression as to its source, authorization, or approval.

Avila contends that the three letters from Rubin constitute a false, deceptive, or misleading representation because the letters are not "from an attorney" as that term has been defined for the purposes of §1692e(3).

Rubin's dunning letters implore Avila to pay his debt. The form letters, as we noted, are mass-produced and are mechanically signed "Albert G. Rubin" under his "attorney" letterhead. As we also noted, 270,000 letters of this sort went out in the year prior to the filing of this suit.

The leading case on whether mass-produced mailings by an attorney violate the proscriptions of FDCPA is *Clomon v. Jackson*, 988 F.2d 1314 (2d Cir.1993). The facts of Clomon are similar to those presented here. In Clomon, a debt collection agency mailed dunning letters to debtors after receiving accounts on computer tape from the creditor. An attorney was employed part-time as general counsel for the agency. The agency's computer system caused each letter to be printed, folded, and placed in an envelope for mailing. The plaintiff received six form letters from the agency. The first letter was sent on the letterhead of an "account supervisor." The remaining five were sent on the attorney letterhead of the general counsel for the agency. Although the general counsel was indeed an attorney and employed by the agency, the letters were not actually signed by the attorney; instead, they bore the mechanically reproduced facsimile of his signature. The attorney letters implored the debtor to pay up and threatened legal action if payment was not forthcoming.

The attorney in Clomon personally approved the "form" of the letters and "approved the procedures according to which those letters were sent." The attorney had no direct personal involvement in the mailing of the letters to the plaintiff or to any other debtor. In short, the attorney "never considered the particular circumstances of Clomon's case prior to the mailing of the letters and he never participated personally in the mailing."

The Second Circuit held that the use of the attorney's letterhead and his signature on the collection letters was sufficient to give the consumer the false impression that the letters were communications from an attorney. The letters were false and misleading because although the attorney's name and signature were on them, they were not "from" the attorney in any meaningful sense of the word. In reaching its conclusion, the court found significant the fact that the attorney did not review each debtor's file, did not determine when particular letters should be sent, did not approve the sending of particular letters based upon the recommendations of others, did not see particular letters before they were sent, and did not know the identities of the persons to whom the letters were issued. Accordingly, it held that sending attorney dunning letters in this manner violated §1692e(3).

Clomon establishes that an attorney sending dunning letters must be directly and personally involved in the mailing of the letters in order to comply with the strictures of FDCPA. This may include reviewing the file of individual debtors to determine if and when a letter should be sent or approving the sending of letters based on the recommendations of others. Given these requirements, Clomon concluded that "there will be few, if any, cases in which a mass-produced collection letter bearing the facsimile of an attorney's signature will comply with the restrictions imposed by section 1692e."

The undisputed facts in our case establish that Rubin has no real involvement in the mailing of dunning letters to debtors. Like the attorney in Clomon, he has a cozy relationship with the "referring" collection agency. Rubin is not personally or directly involved in deciding when or to whom a dunning letter should be sent. There is no true "judgment" being rendered here by a real attorney. Like the attorney in Clomon, Rubin did not review the debtor's file; he did not determine when particular letters should be sent; he did not approve the sending of particular letters based upon the recommendation of others; he did not see particular letters before they were sent; and he did not even know the identities of the debtors to whom the letters were sent. Instead, Rubin said at his deposition that letters are only brought to his attention for advice and guidance when there is "some unusual problem or something different [or] out of the ordinary comes up."

Given these undisputed facts, the district court correctly concluded that Rubin violated §1692e(3) and (9) because his collection letters create the false and misleading impression that the communications were from an attorney when, in fact, they were not really "from" an attorney in any meaningful sense of the word.

An unsophisticated consumer, getting a letter from an "attorney," knows the price of poker has just gone up. And that clearly is the reason why the dunning campaign escalates from the collection agency, which might not strike fear in the heart of the consumer, to the attorney, who is better positioned to get the debtor's knees knocking.

A letter from an attorney implies that a real lawyer, acting like a lawyer usually acts, directly controlled or supervised the process through which the letter was sent. That's the essence of the connotation that accompanies the title of "attorney." A debt collection letter on an attorney's letterhead conveys authority. Consumers are inclined to more quickly react to an attorney's threat than to one coming from a debt collection agency. It is reasonable to believe that a dunning letter from an attorney threatening legal action will be more effective in collecting a debt than a letter from a collection agency. The attorney letter implies that the attorney has reached a considered, professional judgment that the debtor is delinquent and is a candidate for legal action. And the letter also implies that the attorney has some personal involvement in the decision to send the letter. Thus, if a debt collector (attorney or otherwise) wants to take advantage of the special connotation of the word "attorney" in the minds of delinquent consumer debtors to better effect collection of the debt, the debt collector should at least ensure that an attorney has become professionally involved in the debtor's file.

The defendants make two final arguments. First, they claim that mass mailing is economically efficient and necessary in the debt collection industry. This argument has been rejected by several courts. As Clomon stated, "[n]o mass mailing technique is permissible—regardless of how effective it might be-that technique constitutes a false, deceptive, or misleading communication." An attorney's signature implies the attorney has formed a professional judgment about the debtor's case; these implications will frequently be false in a mass mailing situation. Second, the defendants argue that holding Rubin liable will effectively condemn the use of paralegals and assistants in a law office. This argument is untenable. Paralegals do not (or should not) engage in the practice of law. Paralegals do not intake a new client, decide whether a lawsuit is warranted, prepare unreviewed pleadings, stamp the attorney's signature, and file the lawsuit, all without the considered approval of the attorney. Attorneys personally supervise and review paralegals' work, consider the case, and approve the recommendations or work.

Albert G. Rubin, acting as an attorney, was not the real "source" of the letters in this case. The true source of the "attorney" letters was the collection agent who pressed a button on the agency's computer. "Albert G. Rubin & Associates, Ltd." is a collection agency, not a law firm at all in any real sense of the term. The "law firm" does not have a retainer agreement with plaintiff's creditor. No attorney working in the "law firm" ever files a lawsuit or goes to court on behalf of a client. We agree with the district court and with the Second Circuit in Clomon. Rubin was correctly found to be on the wrong side of the FDCPA.

The judgments of the district court are affirmed.

For Critical Analysis

1. This debt collection case involved an attorney who appears to have been acting in a manner not in keeping with legal standards. Do you think the courts were influenced by the presence of a lawyer at the center of the potentially abusive practices?
2. What exactly did the collection company do that was a violation of the FDCPA? Were they just a bit too aggressive in some of their language choice? Do you think they would have ever merited an enforcement proceeding if not for the presence of the attorney?
3. What did the attorney do that was in violation of the FDCPA? Do you think the court was bothered by how close the company and the attorney were? Would they have been so closely questioning the attorney's actions if the attorney were not benefiting financially from the debt collection company's results?
4. How would you advise a debt collection company to limit their behavior to ensure that they stayed within the requirements of the FDCPA?
5. The court seems particularly concerned with the communications from and the role of the attorney. Can you think of a way for a lawyer to set up a debt collection company to avoid potential FDCPA violations simply from the nature of this case?

CHAPTER QUESTIONS AND PROBLEMS

1. Is consumer privacy meaningfully protected in the United States? What gaps exist that should or could be addressed by further national legislation?
2. How do you protect the privacy of your online data? Do you actually read privacy policies? Do you ever opt out of allowing your data to be shared? Is there certain information you simply will never share online for purposes of making a purchase or engaging in social media?
3. Do consumers need further protection in the market place or is the current mix of laws adequate for protection of consumers? Has the advent of electronic commerce and the use of the Internet to engage socially excessively opened up the risk of consumer injury?
4. Which of the following would or could be a violation of the Do-Not-Call Registry? Why or why not? What additional information might help you resolve some of the choices?
   a. Shelia is at dinner when a telemarketer calls her home number seeking donations to the church's fund for the homeless.
   b. Corinth receives a call from a company that repaired her car the year before attempting to schedule her to bring the car in for regularly scheduled maintenance.
   c. The state governor calls Henry on his cell to ask for additional donations to the governor's political campaign.
   d. A representative of a major political party calls Susie to ask her a series of questions regarding her satisfaction with the current state Senator.
5. You buy a chair for your living room at the local furniture store. After using it one week, the back of the chair comes loose from the base sending you falling to the floor where you injure your hip. Your friend takes the chair back to the furniture mart for you (since you cannot carry it anymore), but the salesman there insists that "all sales are final" and points out those words on your receipt and on a big sign behind the register. Being a good student, you remember learning about the warranty of merchantability and tell the salesman that the words "all sales are final" is not a disclaimer of that implied warranty. Are you correct? Does the merchant need to refund your money? Is the merchant responsible for your injury as well?
6. Severance was behind on his bills as he attempted to finish the semester without working. He had enough money available from his student loans to pay his rent and buy groceries, but not to make payments on his credit card. So he quit making the payments. When the credit card company called him to ask for payment, he told them to quit calling him, a right he had under the FDCPA. Was he correct? Was there something he could do to make them stop calling (short of catching up on his payments)?
7. Carl borrowed money from a store in a strip mall that offered "payday" loans and "check advances." He had to sign a lot of various papers, but once done, he received a loan for $2,000 against his pending paycheck, which would be for $3,100. A week later, he took his paycheck to the store. They cashed it and gave him $30.26. Infuriated, he insisted he should be given much more. He claimed the interest had to violate the law and that he was going to complain to the Better Business Bureau. The clerk behind the very thick glass patiently explained that most of the money he paid was a set-up and processing fee and that his interest was only 18 percent. The clerk also pointed out where Carl had acknowledged all of that. Can Carl succeed in getting more of his check back? Is the Better Business Bureau the right place to go to complain?
8. Upon taking a client out to dinner, Cynthia's credit card is declined. Embarrassed, she pays with another card. As soon as she gets home, she calls her credit card company to complain. When they inform her that she was over her limit, Cynthia knows something is wrong. When they start reviewing her recent charges, she realizes that someone has gotten her account information and has been purchasing goods online. How much is this going to cost her?
9. You find a large package on your doorstep. Inside of it is brand new computer. The package was addressed to someone that used to live at your address. Ecstatic, you recall learning about unordered merchandise and realize that you just got a computer as a gift. The first day you are using it, however, you spill a soda on it and ruin it. A week later the phone rings. It is the company that shipped it wanting you to return it. Are you now responsible for paying for the damage to the computer or are you protected under the Federal Trade Commission Act?
10. What consumer protection laws does your state have? What agency enforces them? Has your state adopted the Uniform Deceptive Trade Practices Act?

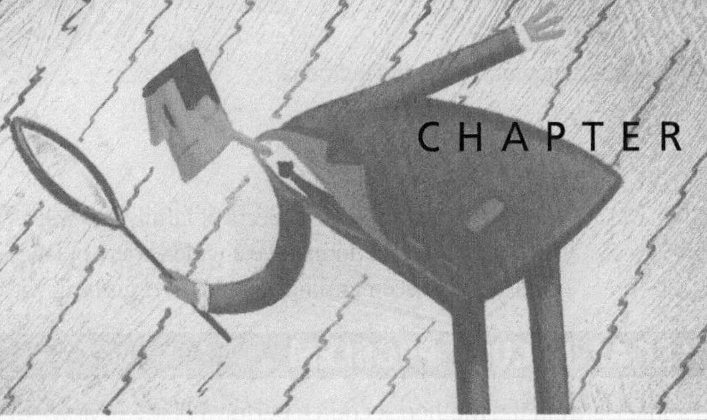

CHAPTER 14

Family Law

Love, the quest; marriage, the conquest; divorce, the inquest.

Helen Rolland, *Reflections of a Bachelor Girl*, 1903

LEARNING OBJECTIVES

After reading and studying this chapter, you should be able to:

- Discuss what legal topics fit within family law.
- Describe the typical legal requirements of marriage.
- Discuss civil unions and domestic partnerships.
- Describe the legal rights and obligations of marriage.
- Describe the common attributes of marital and community property.
- Discuss tort immunities of family members.
- Discuss the legal duties of parents and issues establishing maternity and paternity.
- Identify legal issues surrounding adoption.
- Discuss major issues regarding juvenile justice and protection of minors.
- Distinguish an annulment from a divorce and identify the grounds for each.
- Discuss issues surrounding alimony, property distribution, and child custody.
- Discuss marital property contracts and their likely enforceability.

Unquestionably some aspects of family law will affect your life. The legal implications of living as a family can and do involve a wide variety of laws. Many examples demonstrate the complexities existing between families and laws, beginning with the very definition of marriage.

LEGAL FOCUS—PROBLEM

Some clergy in the Methodist church perform "holy union" ceremonies for same-sex couples. Other pastors with a more conservative or fundamental view of the Bible vehemently object to this practice and threaten to withdraw from the church. Do these ceremonies create marriages?

Legal marriage must be created in conformity with state laws, all of which require marital licenses. Whether or not a union of a same-sex couple results in a marriage will depend on whether the state in which the ceremony is conducted allows marriage to include same-sex couples and grants a marriage license to those couples. In short, marriage is a legal status determined by state law. Same-sex "unions," however, increasingly are recognized by states as well. These unions also create families that are, in many states and in many ways, protected by law. For example, in those states, sexual orientation is not a valid basis for a landlord to refuse to rent living space. The key legal component, however, remains what rights, privileges, and responsibilities a state grants a union or a marriage.

In this chapter, you will learn about laws designed to protect family values as well as the potential involvement of family law in your daily lives. In general, family law has little to do with happy families. Rather, family law is about protecting the family unit, especially children. The laws defining marriage, the mechanics of divorce, and the basis for division of family assets upon divorce are all set forth in state statutes. Wide variations exist in family law from state to state because legislative viewpoints reflect substantially different cultural and societal values. Understandably, these viewpoints often clash on the sensitive and important principles applicable to the family. Religious beliefs, for example, probably conflict more frequently with family law than with any other category of law.

Family law is designed to protect family values. But differences of opinion as to those values can be significant. The debate over the definition of marriage and whether or not same-sex couples can marry is one such example. Family law faces what may be the most controversial issue ever—the genetic alteration of persons, which offers prospective parents the choice of specific characteristics in their offspring (so-called designer babies). Already, thorny issues of custody and the use of frozen and fertilized embryos following death or divorce have arisen in this blend of moral and legal issues.

As in other areas of law, when disputes arise between family members, we rely on lawyers for assistance in presenting our family issues to judges and courts for resolution. These "divorce" lawyers present family law issues to judges (without juries, as family law is "in equity") for resolution. These judges, who typically specialize in domestic matters, rely heavily on the recommendations of social service experts for such sensitive issues as child custody following the breakup of a marriage.

Our law is focusing increasingly on the protection of the fetus during pregnancy. The primary issue in society involving the unborn fetus has been the right of females to choose abortion. By the turn of the twentieth century, virtually every state had a law prohibiting or restricting abortion. It is noteworthy that women also did not have the right to vote. It was not until 1973 that the choice to abort a nonviable fetus became guaranteed under the U.S. Constitution.* But the issue of protection of the fetus is changing. Abortion no longer is the single issue.

*A fetus is viable when it theoretically could survive independent of its mother. In 1973, the law described viability as beginning after the first trimester (three months). *Roe v. Wade*, 410 U.S. 113, 93 S.Ct. 705 (1973).

The protection of children is also a function of family law. Child abuse is a violation of both criminal and family law, and it is covered in this chapter as well as Chapter 6 of this textbook. The scope of protective laws and issues covers a vast range of problems, from censorship of the Internet to the exclusionary zoning of "adult" bookstores; from sex, gore, and alcohol on television to metal detectors in grade schools. This area of family law is rich with controversy, with prospects for new legal solutions undoubtedly eluding us well into the twenty-first century.

Most rules of family law are found in civil law. But some also are found in criminal law because certain conduct involving family members is so reprehensible that society, through legislation, expresses its disapproval by imposing criminal penalties. Child abuse and spousal beating are examples of such conduct. Both criminal and civil statutes exist to protect and enhance marriage and the family. Examples of criminal laws designed to protect the family include those proscribing adultery, bigamy, seduction accomplished by false promise of marriage, and incest (i.e., sexual intercourse between closely related individuals and for whom marriage is forbidden by law). Examples of civil laws related to the family include divorce and child custody laws.

IS THE FEDERAL GOVERNMENT INVOLVED IN FAMILY LAW?

Although there is no national (federal) marriage or divorce law, a family member may become involved in a matter involving federal jurisdiction. For example, if American citizen Bruce Brown, husband and father, entered the United States at Nogales, Arizona, with contraband, such as marijuana, he would have committed a federal crime. If Brown is jailed, the question of how his family would be supported must be determined by principles of family law in the state of his residence. In addition, some federal laws are designed to protect the family when issues involving more than one state are raised. For example, the Child Abuse Prevention and Treatment Act of 1984 encourages states to adopt remedial statutes; the Omnibus Budget Reconciliation Act of 1981 provides for the interception of income tax refunds payable to parents who are delinquent in their support obligations; the Parental Kidnapping Act of 1984 provides special penalties for "child-snatching" parents; and more recently the Uniform Interstate Family Support Act of 1992 streamlines the forced collection of support. Also, the U.S. Supreme Court held that former spouses who reside in different states may sue each other in federal court for damages (but not for divorce, alimony, or child custody). Federal courts will accept jurisdiction in some family law matters that extend across state lines. In the following case, a federal court applied the Illinois law regarding a breach of promise to marry.

LEGAL FOCUS—PROBLEM

Sharon Wildey, an attorney, sued her fiancé, Richard Springs, III, for damages for ending their seven-week engagement, which had followed a whirlwind romance. She sued in federal court on the basis of diversity of citizenship. Sharon claimed she suffered depression and lost income by giving up her main client. Richard told Sharon that she could keep the $19,000 engagement ring and offered her $10,000 cash to help her "get through these times." She was thrice divorced and had four children; Richard was once divorced and had fathered three children. At the close of trial, Sharon's attorney asked the jury for damages of $365,000. What result do you predict?

Wildey v. Springs, 840 F. Supp. 1259 (N.D. Ill. 1994).

The federal court jury awarded Sharon $93,000 for pain and suffering, $60,000 for lost income, and $25,000 for counseling. This case was exceptional because few states permit legal actions seeking damages for breach of promise to marry on the general grounds that "pillow talk" cases should not be resolved in court.

No one doubts the sincerity of the intentions to protect families that underlie new federal laws. But many such national laws fail to live up to their expectations when adopted. For example, federal law bars the sale of cigarettes to persons under eighteen years of age, yet minors still are able to purchase them in many circumstances. With such regulation, the federal government also taxes cigarettes, as do many states. Are taxes on cigarettes likely to reduce their consumption by minors or more likely simply to raise funds? Alcohol similarly has been regulated and taxed, yet there is a perceived need for further federal laws to reduce driving under the influence and to protect the fetuses of minors from alcohol syndrome.

WHAT IS MARRIAGE?

[W]hilst marriage is often termed by text writers and in decisions of courts a civil contract ... it is something more than a mere contract. The consent of the parties is of course essential to its existence, but when the contract to marry is executed by the marriage, a relation between the parties is created which they cannot change. Marriage remains largely a matter of status, although that status is today more ambiguous than in the past.

From *Maynard v. Hill*, 125 U.S. 190, 8 S.Ct. 723 (1888)

marriage
Legal union as husband and wife.

Marriage is a status, the legal union of husband and wife, accomplished by means of a contract that is enforceable by courts. The legal relationship of marriage is based on state rather than federal law. When the status is created, the law grants enforceable rights to the parties and also imposes various mutual duties or obligations. Such official governance of the relationship is justified because marriage is recognized as essential for healthy, viable families and therefore the foundation of a healthy, viable society.

LEGAL FOCUS—PROBLEM

Alexis McVey and Martin Neiderhasen were exchanging wedding vows when Neiderhasen collapsed. He died of cardiac arrest in the ambulance. During their courtship, neither prepared a last will. Does McVey have any legal rights to inherit from Neiderhasen?

McVey has no rights of inheritance unless their vows were completed and their marriage proclaimed. The law treats McVey and Neiderhasen just as it does any other unmarried persons. Neiderhasen's parents would inherit from him. If the marriage existed for only a moment, McVey would have significant rights to his property in all states.

Statutes regulate the lawful creation of marriage. In most states, a license between adults is prescribed for marriage. Parental consent is required for a minor (person under eighteen years of age) to obtain a marriage license, but in special situations (e.g., an out-of-wedlock pregnancy), some state courts are authorized to approve the marriage of underage persons.

LEGAL FOCUS—PROBLEM

With her parents' blessings, Tina Akers and her boyfriend, Wayne Compton, went to the courthouse, obtained a license, and were married. Compton is twenty-nine years old, whereas Tina, eight months pregnant, is thirteen years old. Is this union a new legal family or an example of parental child abuse or predatory and even pedophiliac sexual abuse and statutory rape?

In Maryland, Tina and Wayne Compton and their newly born son, Austin, are a legal family. In other states, Wayne would have been charged with a crime, and the marriage would not have been valid. Tina's father married his wife Nancy when she was sixteen years old. They had eight children before their divorce. Although the marriage of very young teenagers was commonplace at the turn of the century, that practice gradually ended and largely disappeared following World War II.

All states prohibit marriage between members of the immediate family (ascendants–descendants, that is, parent and child) and siblings (brother and sister) on moral and genetic grounds. Most states also prohibit uncle–niece or aunt–nephew marriages, and some extend the prohibition to first cousins. A few states continue to proscribe matrimony for certain relationships of affinity (e.g., stepfather–stepdaughter). Statutes typically require that a person entering marriage be of sound mind—not be insane, an idiot, an imbecile, or a lunatic—although doctors have difficulty diagnosing mental illness, and confusion persists as to what such terms mean in law. Previously, most states required a health examination showing freedom from certain venereal diseases as a precondition to the issuance of a marriage license, but that requirement has been eliminated in the vast majority of states. Solemnization of the union generally is required by either a civil (justice of the peace or judge) or religious (minister, priest, rabbi, or the like) authority.

LEGAL FOCUS—PROBLEM

Pauline Bradshaw, while planning her marriage to George Hall, became curious about whether or not she must use George's surname. Is a wife legally required to take her husband's surname?

common law marriage
The bond formed when a man and a woman live together in the manner of a husband and a wife for the number of years prescribed by state law, though without observing the legal formalities of marriage. This form of marriage is legal in some states.

No, Pauline is not required by law to take her husband's surname. Wives customarily have taken the surname of their husbands in the United States, but this custom is not mandated under the law. Many women choose to use both family surnames in combination. Thus, Pauline could choose to be known as "Pauline Bradshaw-Hall." Pauline could choose to retain her name as Pauline Hall; George could change his name from George Hall to George Bradshaw.

Common Law Marriage

In states where it is legally recognized, a **common law marriage** may arise when a man and a woman continue to live together as husband and wife but without legal formalities (health examination, marriage license, and proper solemnization). Although this recognition was more prevalent in the past, only nine states will recognize new common law marriages today, and only a few others continue to recognize established common law marriages. For a common law marriage to exist, the parties must be legally qualified to marry, must cohabit for a certain period of time, must create the public impression that a marriage exists, and must intend that it exist.

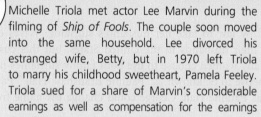

LEGAL FOCUS—PROBLEM

Sandra Jennings and actor William Hurt had a three-year intimate relationship while living in Manhattan. New York State does not recognize common law marriages. But Jennings and Hurt spent five weeks in South Carolina during Hurt's filming of *The Big Chill.* After they ended the relationship, Jennings sued Hurt in a New York court claiming that a common law marriage, by mutual agreement, had existed under South Carolina's law. Hurt often expressed his desire not to marry, and evidence of any agreement contrary to that desire was lacking. Jennings lost her case and appealed, contending, among other things, that the trial court wrongfully excluded Hurt's diaries from evidence. She also lost the appeal, prompting her attorney, Richard Golub, to publicly declare that the trial court judge, a woman, was so in love with Hurt that Jennings never had a chance.

Jennings v. Hurt, 160 App. Div. 2d 576, 554 N.Y.S.2d 220 (N. Y. 1990).

The law clearly requires considerable evidence in support of any determination that a common law marriage exists. But once the common law marriage is created, it is treated by the laws the same as all other conventional marriages. The vast majority of states do not recognize common law marriage. Article IV, Section 1 of the U.S. Constitution, however, provides: "Full faith and credit shall be given in each State to the public Acts, Records, and judicial Proceedings of every other State." Accordingly, states that by law do not permit common law marriages still must recognize a common law marriage that legally was created elsewhere as being valid.

The "Marvin Marriage"

LEGAL FOCUS—CASE

Michelle Triola met actor Lee Marvin during the filming of *Ship of Fools*. The couple soon moved into the same household. Lee divorced his estranged wife, Betty, but in 1970 left Triola to marry his childhood sweetheart, Pamela Feeley. Triola sued for a share of Marvin's considerable earnings as well as compensation for the earnings she allegedly sacrificed for Marvin's sake in giving up her career as a singer. Under Triola's theory, she would have shared one-half of Marvin's earnings from *Ship of Fools* and his estranged wife would receive the other one-half as community property. What was the result?

Marvin v. Marvin, 134 Cal.Rptr. 815, 18 Cal.3d 660, 557 P.2d. 106 (Calif. 1976).

Triola ultimately lost her case. But the celebrated trial between Michelle Triola and Lee Marvin highlighted a trend, in segments of our society, toward living together without the formality of a traditional marriage. The historical attitude of the courts had been to give no protection to either party of a so-called meretricious (based on pretense) relationship. Thus, upon separation, neither "pseudo-spouse" could obtain a share of the other party's earnings or accumulated wealth, or receive payments of alimony for continued support. Any contract that purported to create property or support rights in another person in exchange for participation in a meretricious relationship was declared void as against public policy.

Departing from tradition, the California Supreme Court held that adults who live together and engage in sexual relations, nonetheless, are competent to contract to combine earnings or to keep earnings and other property separate. The court stated that such an agreement might be express, implied (inferred from conduct), or based on "some other tacit understanding." The contract, however, could not be based on the exchange of sexual favors. The California Supreme Court remanded the case to the trial court to determine whether or not such an agreement existed between Triola and Marvin. The trial court rejected Triola's contention that a contract existed, but awarded her $104,000 for rehabilitative compensation, called "palimony" by the media. That award subsequently was reversed on a second appeal because there was no evidence of a contract, and Triola ultimately received nothing.

A rash of similar lawsuits followed in California, setting a trend for courts in other states to grant relief to "discarded" companions when the existence of a contract could be proved. But most state legislatures have been reluctant to enact protective laws for cohabiting persons, usually citing public policy as a reason for discouraging cohabitation without marriage. In effect, some courts have discarded public-policy objections and recognized the economic value of the pseudo-spouse as a homemaker. Thus, courts in many states now protect cohabitants by awarding division of property or payment of support through enforcement of an express (written or oral) or implied (inferred) agreement. Not all states recognize such agreements; some states deny all relief to cohabitants on the grounds of public policy.

In recent years, the legal status of nonmarried couples has made a major shift in public policy, although it appears that much of what has happened has not received publicity commensurate with its historic importance. Three groups have provided the impetus toward marital-type recognition for nonmarried couples. First, the number of cohabiting heterosexual couples has increased since the 1980s. Second, senior couples (many of whom are widows or widowers) do not marry for Medicare, Social Security, estate tax, and income tax reasons. Third, the gay rights movement has sought either the right to marry or an alternative to marriage for committed same-sex couples.

domestic partnerships
Unmarried couples who live together and seek economic and noneconomic benefits available to married couples.

civil union
A legal relationship, analogous to but different from a marriage, wherein the state recognizes that certain domestic rights, benefits, and duties exist between two unmarried persons.

Domestic Partnerships and Civil Unions

Married couples receive many financial benefits that are not available to unmarried couples who may have financial interdependence, shared living arrangements, and a commitment to mutual caring and love. Are such couples entitled to equal protection under law through equal access to financial benefits? Some states and Canadian provinces and several cities in the United States and Canada, by statute or ordinance, have created **domestic partnerships** or other similar means, such as **civil unions**, by which nonmarried couples can qualify for marriage-like benefits that previously had been reserved for heterosexual married couples. These laws vary significantly, as some restrict coverage to gay couples and others allow gay and opposite-gender couples to qualify. Some laws require or allow registration with the law-making body as a precondition to inclusion in the law's benefits and others do not. Coverage of these laws often is restricted to public employees. Benefits may include health insurance, bereavement leave, annuity and pension rights, and housing rights (as in rent-controlled apartments). Proponents are lobbying to expand these benefits to include adoption and inheritance rights, federal income tax equality, and veterans' benefits.

MORALS AND ETHICS

Right to Marry

Opponents of same-sex marriage frequently offer civil unions and domestic partnerships as being equivalent and equal to marriage. Advocates for same-sex marriage rights argue that such replacement relationships are no better than the "separate but equal" doctrine that came out of the Reconstruction Era following the Civil War. They argue that no replacement truly can be equal and that they have a right to enjoy exactly the same marriage benefits that heterosexual couples have. The tension over these two positions lies at the heart of most marriage issues. What do you think the answer should be? What is the driving belief that leads you to that answer? Can both sides of this issue be correct, or must one side be right and one side be wrong?

Opponents claim that a sexual relationship should not be a precondition to receiving such benefits nor should any of the typical characteristics of a loving marriage. Theoretically, they argue, an elderly woman and her live-in nurse should qualify or even a pair of fraternity brothers living as roommates.

Is Marriage Limited to Heterosexual Couples?

State laws traditionally restrict marriage to a man and a woman. Proponents of same-sex marriages argue that the heart of the public contract is an emotional, financial, and psychological bond between two people. That the two people cannot bear children is not relevant because no civil marriage license is granted on the condition that the couple must bear children. The question of what a marriage is or should be has been argued and carried in different directions over the past two decades, and it remains one of the most controversial topics in family law.

LEGAL FOCUS—PROBLEM

Nina Baehr and Genora Dancel applied for but were denied a marriage license in Hawaii. In court, they argued that they had a fundamental right to marry that was protected by the same constitutional right of privacy that legitimized abortion. Are Baehr and Dancel correct?

No, they are not correct. The Hawaii Supreme Court did rule, however, that by restricting marriage to opposite-sex couples only, a sex-based discrimination occurred that violated the Hawaii Constitution unless the state could demonstrate a "compelling interest" to do so. More than a dozen states immediately enacted definitions of marriage excluding same-sex couples as "against public policy." The fear was that if same-sex marriages became legal in Hawaii, then under the Full Faith and Credit Clause of the U.S. Constitution, all other states would be required to recognize such marriages, just as they must recognize common law marriages. Congress acted promptly by passing the Defense of Marriage Act of 1996 (DOMA), which allows states to refuse to recognize same-sex marriages performed under the laws of other states and also excludes a same-sex partner from the definition of "spouse" as that term is used in federal statutes. But does DOMA violate the Constitutional guarantees of equal protection under the law to same sex partners?

LEGAL FOCUS—PROBLEM

Edie Windsor married Thea Spyer, her partner of more than forty years, in Canada in 2007. The couple lived in New York, a state that recognizes same-sex marriages. When Spyer died, Windsor inherited her entire estate for which she had to pay $363,000 in federal estate taxes. Had she been married instead to a man, as a widow, she would have paid no taxes on the inheritance. Can Congress legally treat married same-sex couples differently from married heterosexual couples under federal tax law?

United States v. Windsor, 2013 U.S. LEXIS 4921; 81 U.S.L.W. 4633.

No, Congress may not treat differently such couples differently under federal law. The U.S. Supreme Court ruled that the section of DOMA, which denied equal treatment under federal law to couples whose marriage was recognized under their state law, was unconstitutional as a deprivation of the equal liberty of persons. The Court observed that DOMA attempted to reverse the long-established precept that allows states to regulate domestic relations as a legitimate exercise of their sovereign power and not the federal government. It further determined that DOMA forced same-sex couples in states that recognized same-sex marriage to live as married for the purpose of state law, but unmarried for the purpose of federal law.

The Supreme Court did not address the other provision of DOMA, which allows states the right to refuse to recognize same-sex marriages performed under the laws of other states. Therefore, if a same-sex couple is married in a state that recognizes same-sex marriage, and then moves to a state that does not recognize same-sex marriage, their marriage status is no longer recognized under either their new state's law or under federal law, because the DOMA decision on federal statutory protection only extended to same-sex marriages that were legal under state law.

As of early 2013, Connecticut, Delaware, Iowa, Maine, Maryland, Massachusetts, Minnesota, New Hampshire, New York, Rhode Island, Vermont, Washington, and the District of Columbia have legalized same-sex marriages. Some states have taken a different path and passed defense of marriage–type laws defining marriage as being between a man and a woman only. The law in states that recognize same-sex marriage still may forbid the granting of marriage licenses to couples from states in which the marriage would be illegal in the applicants' state of residency.

In California, a ban on gay marriage has been adopted twice and both times overruled in court. The most recent example involved Proposition 8, which established that only marriage between a man and a woman was to be considered valid in California. Proposition 8 survived the California Supreme Court, but was ruled unconstitutional by a federal district court that held it violated the Due Process and Equal Protection clauses of the Fourteenth Amendment to the U.S. Constitution. That decision was upheld by the U.S. Court of Appeals for the Ninth Circuit. State officials refused to defend Proposition 8 further and did not appeal the court's order. In light of the officials' decision not to appeal, proponents of the measure attempted to challenge the court's ruling. Subsequently, the Supreme Court held that the proponents of Proposition 8 did not have standing to contest the order because they had no direct stake in the outcome of the appeal. As a result, the decision as reported in *Perry et al. v. Schwarzenegger* (see case at the end of the chapter) stands, at least in that circuit court and on the basis of those facts.

The legal issues and social questions being raised by same-gender unions are significant and complicated. The quest for recognition of marital rights raises issues of adoption, child and partner support, health insurance, and property rights to name but a few.

LEGAL FOCUS—PROBLEM

Glen Rosengarten filed an action in Connecticut to dissolve a civil union created in Vermont with Peter Downes. At the time, Connecticut law did not provide for civil unions, and the lawsuit was filed claiming jurisdiction as a family law matter. Will the Connecticut court recognize the Vermont civil union and accept jurisdiction to dissolve it?

Rosengarten v. Downes, 802 A.2d 170 (Conn. App. 2002).

The Connecticut court dismissed the lawsuit holding that it was not a family relations matter under Connecticut law and that the court had no subject matter jurisdiction to dissolve a civil union. The court addressed the constitutional question of full faith and credit and added:

> *[W]here statute or policy of the forum State [where the lawsuit is brought] is set up as a defense to a suit brought under the statute of another State ... the conflict is to be resolved, not by giving automatic effect to the full faith and credit clause and thus compelling courts of each State to subordinate its own statutes to those of others but by appraising the governmental interest of each jurisdiction and deciding accordingly.*

WHAT ARE THE LEGAL CONSEQUENCES OF MARRIAGE?

Obligation of Support

The marital relationship implies a continuing and mutual obligation of support. Support includes food, shelter, clothing, medicine, and usually a wide range of consumer goods, all appropriate to the family's wealth and established standard of living. Management of the family budget is left to the wise or unwise (and sometimes spiteful) management of the spouses. It is a crime for parents willfully to fail to support their children. Moreover, some states have enacted statutes requiring adult children who have the financial means to support their indigent parents who receive government assistance. But courts seldom become involved in support disputes unless the marriage in question is in the process of dissolution or divorce. You will see, later in this chapter, that the family's budget (standard of living) before divorce is relevant to the issue of how much support (called *alimony*) should be imposed by law for the period following divorce.

LEGAL FOCUS—PROBLEM

Robert Hamilton became disabled and could not work. His wife, Sally, a trained legal secretary, had been serving as housewife and homemaker. Sally declared that she would not seek gainful employment to support her husband and would henceforth terminate the marriage. Is Sally required to go to work to support Robert if the marriage remains intact? What if the marriage is terminated?

Yes, Sally will be required to apply her earning skills in support of her husband whether or not the marriage remains intact. Also, in this hypothetical case, she could be required to use property owned in her name for his support. Sally would not necessarily be indentured for life, however; courts will terminate lifetime support in many circumstances. At some point, the balance of equities would weigh in favor of public support of the disabled Robert, and Sally would be released from that obligation.

The specific criteria often used by courts in setting the amount of required support following termination of the marriage, and the length of time support must be paid, are reviewed later in this chapter.

separate property
Property owned by a marital partner separate from the spouse, either brought into a marriage at the outset or acquired during marriage by gift or inheritance.

Property Rights

The legal rights of spouses to their marital property (assets of the family, as defined by statute) vary depending upon the applicable state law.

marital property
Property acquired during marriage in a marital property state.

Marital Property States

Under original common law theory, title to all property owned by a woman automatically was vested in her husband upon marriage. During marriage, the wife owned no property. Marriage created one entity: the husband. A creditor who successfully sued the wife received a judgment against the husband and thereby reached all of the family's nonexempt assets.

community property
All property acquired (in a community property state) by the husband or the wife during marriage other than by gift or inheritance, and other than as profits or income from separate property.

Today, most states have adopted a form of marital property law that distinguishes between separate and marital property. **Separate property** is property acquired before marriage or during marriage by gift or inheritance. The husband and wife are "partners" in all other property acquired during marriage, and that property is called **marital property**. Property earned (i.e., wages) by one spouse during marriage is marital property even if held in one spouse's name in a separate account. As you read about community property states and compare them with marital property states, the two types of property ownership will sound very much alike. For our purposes, the most important distinction occurs upon divorce. In a marital property state, courts are expected to divide the property equitably but not necessarily equally. In a **community property** state, the family property is considered equally owned and thus is awarded 50 percent to each spouse. More information about marital property division upon divorce is explained later in this chapter.

Community Property States

In community property states (e.g., Arizona, California, Idaho, Louisiana, Nevada, New Mexico, Texas, Washington, and Wisconsin), all property acquired by the husband or wife during marriage, other than by gift or inheritance, is community property. Unless agreed otherwise, the respective earnings of husband and wife during marriage are owned equally when received. Upon dissolution, accumulated earnings, as with all other community properties, are divided equally between spouses because the ownership of community property is equal. Whereas most U.S. law is based on English law, the civil law systems of Spain and France are the origin of community property law in the United States.

commingling
The mixing together of community property and separate property to the extent that the properties cannot be traced back to their original status. Commingled property becomes community property.

As stated earlier, separate property is property either brought into the marriage or acquired during marriage by gift or inheritance. Separate property retains its separate character as long as independent records are kept. For example, cash kept in a separate savings account will retain its separate property classification. **Commingling** of separate property and community property occurs when the two types are so combined that they reasonably cannot be traced back to their original status. In such cases, the separate property has been transmuted into community property and has lost its former status. An example is cash brought into the marriage and subsequently combined in the family checking account with monthly community earnings. The status of property as separate or community also can be altered by an agreement between the spouses.

LEGAL FOCUS—BACKGROUND

How romantic can you get? Not only did she consent to marry, but C. V. brought to the marriage her two mules. As the marriage and affection grew, so too did the mules. But a third party, Stringfellow, came between the two—not romantically but economically. Stringfellow successfully sued C. V.'s husband, but when he found the husband's coffers bare, he sought to satisfy the judgment by levying upon C. V.'s mules. Stringfellow claimed the mules' increase in value from $35 to $75 was due to the husband's care and thus was community property. The Texas Supreme Court sided with C. V., declaring that the animals were the same ones owned by her at her marriage. "She does not hold her separate property by so precarious a tenure as to depend upon the fluctuations of weight or the prices in the market."

Stringfellow v. Sorrels, 18 S.W. 689 (Tex. 1891).

Marriage property issues can arise in many ways, and state marital law is not as uniform as other areas of the law. Issues of property can be raised by creditors, gifts bestowed, death, and divorce, and treatment of the property is influenced by how the question arises. In this brief discussion, community property and marital property sound very much alike. But the devil is in the details, and much detail is sorted out in the dissolution of a marriage, where the differences in treatment of the two types of marriage property are considerable.

Gifts of Marital Property

Marital Property

In a marital property state, property is not classified as marital property until some event occurs that requires a classification, such as a divorce or death. At the time of the event, all existing property is classified as either marital or separate property. As a general rule, an asset transferred before the need to classify it is no longer eligible as marital property. In other words, gifts of property before a divorce or probate proceeding usually are not recaptured in the marital estate. The major exceptions to this general rule are when a transfer results in dissipation, waste, or conversion of assets with the intent to deprive the marital estate.

LEGAL FOCUS—EXAMPLE

James A. Szesny appealed an order of the divorce court that found him solely responsible for more than $82,000 in marital debt. The court found that during the marriage he went out at night without his wife and child; that he belonged to a health club; that he opened charge accounts without his wife's knowledge or permission; that he spent money on clothing for himself and at fine restaurants; that he gave money to his mother; that he borrowed money but did not use it to reduce the marital debt; and that he "in effect kited his account in consumer debts." The trial court also found that Taryn Szesny spent minimal amounts on clothing, ate in fast-food restaurants, and in one year was responsible for less than one-twelfth of their total expenses. In upholding the trial court's determination, the court stated, "Dissipation can occur prior to dissolution. The key is whether one spouse uses marital property for his or her own benefit for a purpose unrelated to the marriage."

Szesny v. Szesny, 197 Ill. App. 3d 966, 557 N.E.2d 222 (Ill. 1990).

Community Property

Because both spouses own an undivided one-half interest in the community property, neither spouse can defeat the other spouse's ownership rights by giving it away without consent.

LEGAL FOCUS—PROBLEM

In Bellevue, Washington, George Thompson was enamored with his secretary, Vickie Ehlers, and gave her a Jaguar XJS purchased with earnings from his accounting business. When his wife, Betty, learned of the gift, she insisted that the car be taken from Ehlers. Can this be done legally?

Yes, under the law, Betty may insist the car be taken. Whenever either spouse gives away community property without consent, the injured spouse can ask the court to set aside the transfer of property and order the property returned to the community. If, however, the automobile was "given" to the secretary in exchange for services legitimately rendered, then the "gift" would be in the nature of a bonus, or wage, and would not be set aside. Realistically, in the preceding hypothetical example, the marriage probably would have deteriorated to the extent that Betty Thompson would petition for a dissolution (divorce) rather than continue the marriage while pursuing a lawsuit to return an improper gift from the community. In any divorce decree, the court, in dividing the community property equally, would give Betty "credit" for her one-half value of the XJS.

Creditors of the Family

Marital Property

The extent to which creditors of one spouse can reach the family's marital property varies from state to state. Under the Uniform Marital Property Act (UMPA), which has been adopted only in Wisconsin but which has influenced other marital property states, all marital property can be reached by the creditors of either spouse. Courts in Maine have ruled in the absence of statute that all marital property can be reached by creditors of either spouse during the marriage. This rule reflects the trend. But courts in many states continue to rule that creditors of one spouse can reach only marital property that is held in that spouse's name. These states hold that property rights generally are based upon who holds title to the property, and creditors can reach only property held in the title of the debtor. Even in these states, however, property owners cannot change the title to property simply to avoid the claims of creditors. Such transfers can be set aside as being fraudulent.

Community Property

Unpaid creditors who obtain a judgment against either the husband or wife can reach all nonexempt community property to satisfy their claims. Property declared "exempt" by statute cannot be taken from anyone by any creditor (sufficient monies to obtain the necessaries of life are an example of exempt property). Accordingly, if a husband wrongfully punches a letter carrier, for example, severely injuring that person's eyesight, the victim can receive payment of the court judgment from the accumulated earnings of the defendant's wife or from any other nonexempt community property. Of course, the husband's separate property could be used to satisfy a judgment for torts committed during marriage and his personal debts incurred before his marriage; his wife's separate property could not. Reciprocally, the wife's separate property could be used to satisfy a judgment for her torts or other debts before marriage; her husband's separate property could not be used. Either spouse's marital earnings, however, may be diverted from the marriage and taken to satisfy premarital debts. To this extent, one does "marry" the pre-existing debts of the spouse.

One spouse is not responsible for the crimes or torts of the other, and separate property is immune from fines or civil judgments against the other spouse. Indirectly, of course, the innocent spouse is hurt if a fine is paid from community property or if, as a result of confinement, community property is not earned. Marriage does not shield one's separate property from his own creditors.

Civil Lawsuits between Family Members

One traditional concept embodied in the common law has been that marriage melded a man and woman into a single legal entity. It logically followed that one spouse could not sue the other spouse, other than to dissolve the entity (as through divorce). This common law rule, called **spousal immunity**, prohibits actions between spouses for torts, such as negligence and assault and battery. A justification for this immunity is to protect domestic tranquility. This doctrine does not prevent a victimized spouse from obtaining a divorce on grounds of adultery or extreme mental cruelty, but it does insulate many types of wrongful and abusive conduct by a family member. Consequently, the doctrine of spousal immunity currently is yielding to modern concepts and modifications by the courts (and legislatures) to permit lawsuits between spouses in various situations and to provide more equitable property distributions upon divorce.

spousal immunity
A doctrine of the common law that tort actions between spouses are prohibited because of a public policy to protect the harmony of the marital relationship from adversarial and disruptive legal proceedings.

Wives successfully have sued husbands for both compensatory and punitive damages for wife beating; for intentional infliction of mental distress in cases in which a husband tried to hire a professional killer to murder his wife; for fraudulently undervaluing and selling marital property; and for emotional distress when a husband had temper tantrums, doled out stingy amounts of cash, made his wife wear cheap clothes, and belittled her in front of their daughter.

LEGAL FOCUS—CASE

Shortly after her whirlwind courtship and wedding to Samuel B. McNeill, III, Jo McNeill falsely told her husband that she was an attorney, had a master's degree in accounting, was suffering from cancer, and had an outstanding premarital judgment against her that could affect their assets. In reliance on these false statements, Samuel deeded title of his separate property, an exclusive waterfront home in Huntington Beach, California, into their joint names. Later, Jo falsely told Sam that she had only ninety days to live, encouraged him to put "their" assets into a trust, and then gave him documents to sign that, in reality, transferred all of his assets to her. Soon thereafter, the marriage deteriorated, and Sam moved into a small rental cottage in Los Angeles near his work. Upon discovery of the truth, Sam sued his wife for fraud and also sought recovery of his property. What was the result?

In re Marriage of McNeill, 160 Cal.App. 3d 548, 206 Cal.Rptr. 641 (Calif. 1984).

The trial court ruled in favor of Sam. Misstatements of affection or feelings generally are not actionable, but none of the false statements made by Jo concerned her feelings about Sam. Children also may sue their parents in many states. For example, a daughter was permitted to sue her father for assault and rape; a child sued her mother for negligently failing to buckle the child's seatbelt; and a child injured in utero successfully sued her mother for negligence in jaywalking. Some courts apply the doctrine of parental immunity to prevent a child's civil lawsuit for sexual abuse and others allow them. These actions between spouses, as well as lawsuits between children and their parents, are called **domestic torts**.

domestic torts
Various tortuous acts in which the perpetrator and victim are family members.

Commentators argue that permitting lawsuits for injuries from domestic torts simply places another weapon in the hands of embittered and vengeful spouses. It drags soap operas into public courtrooms, implicitly forces the government (through its courts and legislatures) to prescribe what constitutes "normal" or "acceptable" interpersonal conduct, and exacerbates the litigation explosion. Others respond that spousal immunity should not be a shield against penalties for abusive conduct that would be compensable if the parties were strangers. The question of what conduct ought to be compensable is not easy to answer.

LEGAL FOCUS—CASE

A family court judge found that Mr. Hakkila's behavior in demeaning his wife, screaming at her, locking her out of the house, and refusing to have sex with her was "beyond the bounds of decency ... atrocious ... utterly intolerable" and constituted compensable negligent and intentional infliction of emotional distress. Should Mr. Hakkila be ordered to pay damages to his wife?

Hakkila v. Hakkila, 112 N.M. 172, 812 P.2d 1320 (N.M. 1991).

The case against Mr. Hakkila was thrown out on appeal. In New Mexico, family members can sue one another but only if the wrongful conduct is sufficiently outrageous: "the threshold of outrageousness should be set high enough ... that the social good from recognizing the tort will not be outweighed by unseemly and invasive litigation." That the husband insulted his wife in front of her friends by calling her an obscenity, mistreated her physically, locked her out of the house after she ripped the buttons off his shirt, called her "stupid" and "insane," and blamed their poor sexual relationship on her was held insufficiently outrageous to justify liability. Why must intentional conduct between spouses be sufficiently outrageous to justify civil liability? Presumably, the law should not require a degree of civility between spouses that is beyond their capacity. People need to vent to some extent. About half of the states where the question has arisen have honored emotional distress cases between spouses. The other half require extraordinarily outrageous behavior or the lawsuit is rejected.

Additionally, new attention has been given to lawsuits by children against abusive parents, even when many years have elapsed since the alleged wrongful conduct. Many states hold that actions by children are not barred by the statute of limitations because it does not begin to "run" until adult survivors of child abuse overcome their memory blocks and discover (usually in psychiatric or psychological therapy) the acts that took place when they were young children. Even grossly negligent conduct by mothers during pregnancy (e.g., drug, alcohol, or nicotine abuse or rejection of prenatal care) also may give rise to civil judgments for damages in favor of the injured children.

Sexual abuse and severe physical abuse of a child are serious crimes discussed later in this chapter. Child abuse also is a domestic tort that, like other civil cases, may be proven by a "preponderance of the evidence." This burden of proof is much easier to meet than the proof "beyond a reasonable doubt" that is required for conviction in criminal cases. Perhaps the most perplexing dilemma clouding this particular domestic tort is how to identify and reject unjustified claims for damages sought many years following commission of the alleged acts. Such claims are based on "recovered memory" that is recovered, perhaps after many years, during psychiatric therapy. The reliability of such recollections, the possibility that they were suggested rather than recollected, and the possibility of false claims are among the most difficult issues in such cases.

Claims of child abuse made during contested custody proceedings (as distinguished from claims made during civil litigation) are discussed later in this chapter. Not all abuse within families is by parents, nor are all civil lawsuits between family members designed to obtain money.

LEGAL FOCUS—PROBLEM

Merle Haggard, at the time age sixty, famous for singing "Okie from Muskogee" and "Workin' Man Blues," received a "continuous barrage of threats against his safety" from his then thirty-nine-year-old son, Marty. Marty believed that Merle "owed him and his mother a lot of money." What civil remedy is available to protect the senior Haggard?

Haggard obtained a restraining order from court barring Marty from harassing or even coming near him. Violation of such an injunction would be a contempt of court, for which jail is the usual sanction.

WHAT LAWS GOVERN PARENTHOOD?

Prenatal Laws

Perhaps the most controversial issue in family law is the question of abortion. Until 1973, an overwhelming majority of states prohibited abortion unless necessary to preserve the life or health of the mother. In that year, the leading and much-publicized case of *Roe v. Wade* was decided by the U.S. Supreme Court. It held that a pregnant female, married or single, in consultation with her physician, has an unqualified, absolute right to have an abortion during the first trimester (three months) of her pregnancy. This right could not be vetoed by the natural father, by a parent, or by a husband. During the second trimester, the right continued, but the abortion procedures could be regulated by the state, if it chooses, in ways that were related to maternal health (e.g., hospitalization). During the final trimester and when the fetus had become viable (capable of continuing its existence outside the womb naturally or by use of artificial life-support systems), the state could, if it chose to do so, prohibit abortion unless it was necessary for the health or preservation of the life of the mother. The mechanical trimester analysis of *Roe* subsequently shifted to the moment of viability, which because of medical advances may occur earlier, at perhaps twenty-three to twenty-four weeks, or even earlier.

In a more recent case, *Webster v. Reproductive Health Services* the U.S. Supreme Court held that a state may withhold the use of public employees and facilities to perform or assist abortions that are not necessary to save the mother's life. Also, whereas *Roe* held that there is a compelling state interest in protecting a fetus (through regulation) once it has become viable, in *Webster* the Court held that a state could regulate abortion before the fetus was viable by requiring medical tests to determine whether or not the point of viability had occurred.

In 1990, the U.S. Supreme Court upheld as being constitutionally permissible (1) an Ohio law requiring an unmarried minor to notify at least one parent of her intended abortion and (2) a Minnesota law requiring an unmarried minor to notify both parents. In both states, a minor may bypass parental notification by obtaining a judge's order. In 1992, the U.S. Supreme Court declared that although a state cannot prohibit an abortion before a fetus is viable, it nonetheless can require that candidates for abortion first consider information about available and legal alternatives. Although states can regulate abortions before viability, the Court stated that they cannot do so in a way that "places a substantial obstacle in the path of a woman's choice."

In *Stenberg v. Carhart* the U.S. Supreme Court struck down as being unconstitutional a Nebraska law making criminal the performance of dilation and evacuation (D&E) abortion. The Supreme Court held that restrictions on methods of abortion must be specific and must not ban the most commonly used and safest methods. In addition, any statute banning abortion must contain an exception for the woman's health.

All of the U.S. Supreme Court decisions authorizing abortion have been 5–4 votes. Since the most recent *Stenberg* decision, several judges have left the court and been replaced. Thus, the current Supreme Court could reverse course with the next abortion case presented before it.

Paternity

A legitimate child enjoys rights and sometimes duties of support, possesses rights of inheritance, and typically carries the father's surname. Such a child is the issue of her natural, married parents. Historically, an illegitimate child was a child born of an unmarried mother or born of an adulterous, incestuous, or bigamous relationship. Current statutes are inclusive and tend to resolve any doubt in favor of legitimacy through the application of a legal presumption of legitimacy.

The Uniform Parentage Act, last amended in 2002, has been adopted in some form by nineteen states and aims to provide workable and sound rules for determining the parentage of a child. The Act presumes the legal father of a child to be one of the following: an unrebutted presumed father (i.e., a man married to the birth mother at the time of conception, or a man who resided in the same household as the child during its first two years of life and openly held the child out as his own), a man who has acknowledged **paternity**, an adjudicated father as the result of a judgment in a paternity action, an adoptive father, a man who consents to an assisted reproduction, or an adjudicated father in a proceeding confirming a gestational agreement.

paternity
Establishing the father of a child. Often determined by a lawsuit to prove that a named person is the father of a child.

The presumption of legitimacy is difficult to overcome and usually will depend on the husband's showing of impotency or on a blood-typing analysis that all but conclusively proves that the husband could not be the child's father. With modern blood-typing techniques and analyses, experts can establish statistical probabilities as to whether or not a suspect could be the natural father. Such tests also can show a high probability that a specific man is the father. Every state has statutes providing for the admissibility of specified genetic tests in paternity cases. Blood tests are not absolutely conclusive. In one case, the defendant contended that he had never even met the mother of the child he was accused of fathering even though blood tests revealed he had a 99.99 percent probability of paternity. The court believed the persuasive man. DNA testing is even more conclusive and generally has become accepted.

LEGAL FOCUS—PROBLEM

Four poor children born out of wedlock to different mothers had their paternity established by DNA "sibling" testing of one another. Their deceased father was Larry Hillbloom, who crashed at sea, leaving no DNA readily available. Hillbloom had sex with the teenage mothers of the half-brothers and half-sisters while he was on various trips to the South Pacific. Hillbloom's will left everything to the University of California at Berkeley—nothing was said about any children. Can the illegitimate children inherit?

Yes, the children may inherit. Both legitimate and illegitimate children (once paternity is established) inherit in California unless specifically disinherited in the will. Not mentioning is not disinheriting. Thus, the four South Pacific children each received $90 million.

The basic handicaps of an illegitimate child are financial. Until paternity is established by a court, the child does not inherit as an heir and has no right to paternal support.

Adopted children are treated under the law the same as natural children. There is a trend to equalize the rights of illegitimate (whose paternity is established) and legitimate children as well. This trend reflects the facts that increasing numbers of children are born out of wedlock and that such children are innocent of any wrongdoing. Thus, the U.S. Supreme Court has held that states may not discriminate against illegitimate children and that states must require natural fathers to support both their legitimate and illegitimate children. Nor may a state create a right of action in favor of legitimate children for the wrongful death of a parent and exclude illegitimate children from the benefit of such a right. And illegitimate children may not be excluded from sharing equally with other children in the recovery of workers' compensation benefits for the death of their parent.

The Supreme Court declined to recognize an illegitimate child's right to claim inheritance. The question of inheritance rights of illegitimate children is left to the states. Some states (such as California, Arizona, and North Dakota) have adopted statutes that permit illegitimate children to inherit from their fathers, regardless of whether the father has acknowledged the child. In the absence of such a statute, the illegitimate child will inherit only from his mother. Custody of a child conceived out of wedlock remains with the mother as long as she is a suitable person. Otherwise, custody may be awarded to another suitable person, including the natural father.

Legal rights for nonmarital offspring have little meaning unless the natural father is identified. Statutory presumptions create paternity in many cases, but the mother or child may need to bring a civil paternity action to establish the child's natural parentage. If the mother prevails and paternity is established, the court's judgment will include an order of periodic support and reimbursement of her medical costs, expenses of pregnancy, and attorney fees. Once paternity is established, all states authorize their courts to order the payment of support because of state interest (welfare authorities may have the burden of support if the natural father is not held responsible). A few states also confer inheritance rights upon a child legitimated by a paternity proceeding. Even though a child has inheritance rights, any child may be intentionally disinherited by the will of a parent.

Surrogate-Mother Contracts

surrogate mother
A woman who is artificially inseminated, carries the fetus to term, and then relinquishes her parental rights to the biological father. Surrogacy services are performed pursuant to a contract in return for money.

To obtain a biologically related child, a husband and wife may desire to impregnate a contracting **surrogate mother**, who agrees to carry the fetus until birth and then relinquish her parental rights to the biological father. The natural father's wife then adopts the child. One type of surrogacy arrangement is gestational surrogacy, where the surrogate mother is not related genetically to the child. A fertilized egg is transferred into the surrogate mother's uterus to gestate until birth. The fertilized egg may or may not be genetically related to both the husband and wife, who may have used the sperm or egg of a donor. Another type of surrogacy agreement involves artificially inseminating the egg of the surrogate mother with sperm, such that the surrogate mother is also the biological mother of the child she carries.

LEGAL FOCUS—CASE

In 1985, William Stern and Mary Beth Whitehead entered into a surrogacy contract. It stated that Stern's wife, Elizabeth, was infertile, that they wanted a child, and that Whitehead was willing to serve as the mother with Stern as the father. The contract provided that Whitehead would become pregnant (through artificial insemination, using Stern's sperm), carry the child to term, bear it, deliver it to the Sterns, and thereafter do whatever was necessary to terminate her maternal rights so that Mrs. Stern thereafter could adopt the child. Stern agreed to pay $10,000 to Whitehead.

On March 27, 1986, Baby M was born; on March 30 she was delivered to the Sterns. Later that day, Whitehead underwent an emotional crisis; she was deeply disturbed, disconsolate, and stricken with unbearable sadness. She had to have her child. Fearing that she might commit suicide, the Sterns returned Baby M in exchange for Whitehead's promise to return the child in one week. The struggle over custody then began in the courts, and Melissa (Baby M) was returned to the Sterns pending final outcome of the litigation. Whitehead was permitted limited visitation. The trial court ruled in favor of the Sterns. Whitehead appealed. What was the result?

In re Baby M, 217 N.J. Super. 313, 525 A.2d 1128, *reversed*, 109 N.J. 396, 537 A.2d 1227 (1988).

The supreme court of New Jersey held that the surrogacy contract conflicted with the state's adoption laws, especially in calling for the payment of money and by providing for the irrevocable agreement of the natural mother to terminate her parental rights to facilitate the adoption. Also, the contract's basic premise, that the natural parents can decide in advance of birth which one is to have custody of the child, conflicts with the law that the child's best interests shall determine custody. Therefore, the court reasoned, the contract was void and unenforceable. The court then decided that custody with the Sterns was in the best interests of Melissa regardless of the invalidity of the contract. Whitehead lost custody but was awarded visitation rights.

After *In re Baby M*, legislatures in a number of states barred or severely limited the enforceability of surrogate contracts. But time and science march on, and assisted reproduction and gestational agreements became commonplace in the 1990s. The Uniform Parentage Act permits gestational agreements as do several states, either through case law or by passing surrogacy-friendly statutes. As noted earlier, several states have taken the opposite tack and prohibit surrogacy agreements.

LEGAL FOCUS—CASE

Crispina and Mark Calvert entered into a contract with Anna Johnson, who agreed to have their embryo (created by the sperm and egg of the Calverts) implanted into her uterus and to bear the child. The Calverts agreed to pay Anna $10,000 and to purchase a life insurance policy on Anna's life for this service. Several months into the pregnancy, Anna claimed that she had "bonded" with the fetus and filed suit to be declared the legal mother. What was the result?

Johnson v. Calvert, 5 Cal. 4th 84, 851 P.2d 776, 19 Cal.Rptr. 2d 494 (Calif. 1993).

The California Supreme Court held that the law recognizes both genetic consanguinity (of the same blood) and giving birth as two means of establishing a mother and child relationship. In this case, the two means did not coincide in one woman. Anna Johnson's attorney argued that the birth mother had the better case because the donor of the fertilized egg had never been pregnant and had never given birth. The court decided that the one who intended to bring about the birth of a child that she intended to raise as her own (Crispina Calvert in this case) is the natural mother.

In vitro fertilization (IVF) takes place in a petri dish (a glass dish with an overlapping cover for the culture of microorganisms), following which the fertilized egg is placed into the mother's uterus. It also is possible to freeze the fertilized embryo and implant it in the future.

LEGAL FOCUS—CASE

Maureen Kass, thirty-nine years old, could not have children naturally because while in her mother's womb, she was exposed to the drug DES. Maureen and her husband, Steven, caused five of her eggs to be artificially fertilized by his sperm, and then frozen. They signed a contract stating that, upon divorce, the eggs would be donated to research and ultimately destroyed. But following their divorce, Maureen changed her mind; Steven objected, saying he did not want to have a child by his former wife. Maureen contended that the law should protect her maternal rights to her fertilized egg. Who prevails?

Kass v. Kass, 91 N.Y.2d 554, 686 N.E.2d 174 (N.Y. 1998).

The New York Court of Appeals upheld the contract. The issue would not be so clear if there had been no contract to uphold. A male has no legal right to object to an abortion of the embryo; should he have a right to object to its gestation and birth before it has been implanted into a womb?

Cryopreservation of sperm makes artificial insemination possible without having to match ovulation cycles with sperm donations. The storage of large numbers of sperm samples permits infertile couples to select donor characteristics to assure a close match to the sterile husband's own makeup. Selection can be based on race, height, body type, eye color, intelligence, religious background, and even national origin. Because fertilized embryos can be frozen, for perhaps 100 years, women do not need to be subjected to surgery each time they need to get an egg—a dozen or more can be retrieved at one time.

At the beginning of the twenty-first century, an estimated 9,000 embryos were stock piled in the country's freezers. The number is much larger now. Some of these fertilized eggs are forgotten or abandoned. Legal issues arise when storage bills are not paid. What if one or more of the donors dies? Can abandoned embryos be foreclosed upon and be given or sold in the open market?

Today a thriving surrogacy industry exists in this country, and thousands of IVF children have been born. Typically, these surrogacy arrangements involve fertilization of the woman's own egg with a male client's sperm. Many arrangements, like the Crispina and Mark Calvert case, however, involve a couple's renting of a womb for nine months to produce their baby.

Legal issues presented in such cases concern the validity of the underlying contracts, forfeiture of parental rights by surrogate mothers, assurance of adoption by wives of the natural fathers, the best interests of the children, inheritance rights following the intestate death of either of the biological parents, and commercialization of the whole process.

In addition to legal issues, surrogacy raises many fundamental social, medical, and moral questions: Is surrogacy an acceptable positive solution to the problem of female infertility? Or is it an unnatural arrangement, and in effect a "forced baby sale" exploitive of poor women, even if they are paid for their cooperation? Should similar questions be asked about the use of fertility drugs, which have resulted in multiple births, even the birth of octuplets (eight siblings)?

Adoption

Adoption is governed primarily by state law, which provides a legal process for adopting a child, determines who may adopt and who may be adopted, establishes who must consent to an adoption, and who may have access to adoption records. Like custody determinations, adoption decisions are made in the "best interest of the child." When adoption occurs, the law applies the same parenting rules that apply to all natural parents.

LEGAL FOCUS—BACKGROUND

Steven Lofton is a registered pediatric nurse who has raised three foster children, including John Doe ("Doe"), since infancy. All three of Lofton's foster children tested positive for HIV at birth. Although the other two foster children developed AIDS, Doe no longer tests positive for HIV. For the past ten years, Lofton has cared for his foster children full time, administering medications and looking after them when they were sick. He has an Outstanding Foster Parenting award from a child placement agency. Doe was released for adoption in 1994, and Lofton applied to adopt. Under Florida law, however, Lofton automatically was disqualified because he is gay.

Lofton v. Kearney, 157 F. Supp. 2d 1372 (S.D. Fla. 2001), *affirmed*, 358 F.3d 804 (11th Cir. 2004).

Same-sex couples or gay persons are allowed to adopt a child in most states, but in Florida, a statute specifically bans homosexuals from being adoptive parents. A challenge to the statute was filed arguing that it violates the constitutional rights of children who need homes and gay people who want to adopt by denying each the equal protection of the law when the denial is based solely on sexual preference. In upholding the statute, the court recognized that a statutory classification that does not involve a suspect classification nor infringes on a fundamental right must be upheld against an equal protection challenge as long as there is a rational basis for the classification. The appeals court determined that Florida asserted a sufficient rational basis for the ban as part of a broader adoption policy designed to create adoptive homes that resemble the nuclear family to provide the stability that marriage affords and the presence of both male and female authority figures for optimal development and socialization.

Parental Rights and Liabilities

Freedom from governmental involvement in family affairs is a fundamental value in our society. Although it is not explicitly stated therein, the U.S. Constitution implies a right to marry, to establish a home and bring up children, to educate one's children as one chooses, and to ensure privacy—that is, to be left alone by the government in the private realm of family life. Parents thus have a constitutional right to autonomy in rearing their children, and the state cannot interfere except under "clear and convincing" proof of severe child abuse or abandonment. Parents also must exercise reasonable care, supervision, protection, and control over their minor children. Willful failure to do so may be a crime, a variation of the misdemeanor called contributing to the delinquency of a minor. Parents are not criminally responsible for negligent parenting if they make reasonable efforts to control their children but are unable to do so. No crime (or civil liability) is visited upon parents for their children's general incorrigibility and bad disposition.

In general, parents have the right to custody of their minor children and are free to raise them as they see fit. Does the following case fly in the face of this rule?

LEGAL FOCUS—PROBLEM

Gregory Kingsley, twelve years old, was living happily with his foster parents, George and Lizabeth Russ, who had eight children of their own. George Russ had noticed Gregory while visiting the Lake County Boys Ranch and soon applied to be his foster parent. (A foster family usually provides a temporary haven for a child until the child can be reunited with his family.) Before long, the Russes applied to formally adopt Gregory, but his natural mother, Rachel, objected. Gregory then contacted and hired his own attorney, Jerri Blair, to "sue his parents for divorce" so he could be adopted legally by the Russes. What was the outcome?

The state circuit court in Orlando, Florida, allowed Gregory Kingsley to "divorce" his natural parents, freeing him for adoption by George and Lizabeth. This case, however, does not contradict the broad rights of parents to raise their children as they see fit. The reality of the *Gregory Kingsley* case is that his parents, for various reasons, were not raising him at all.

Genetic Engineering and Family Planning: Legal Issues

You most certainly will be affected by and participate in society's response to what many refer to as the "Biotech Century." The accelerated pace of scientific discovery in biotechnology is the direct result of the marriage of the genetic and computer revolutions.

Private biotech corporations are interested in the potential profits from new medicine and vaccines that can be produced once the genetic code of disease is identified. This rapidly developing science soon will begin affecting the family and family law.

"Designer Babies" in the Future?

Ethical and legal issues arise when a human egg is fertilized in a petri dish and then is permitted to divide and grow in the dish before implantation into a surrogate's womb. What legal issues will arise when potential parents engage the services of geneticists to obtain "designer babies"?

With *in vitro* fertilization already an established process, genetic changes could be made in embryos outside the womb to correct deadly diseases, enhance mood, modify behavior, or change intelligence and physical traits. The "enhanced" embryo then would be planted in its mother's womb. The mapping of the entire human genome will allow the characteristics associated with specific genes to be studied and modified in the laboratory. Even though environmental factors bear strongly on behavior, so too do genetics, as demonstrated by twins who have been raised in radically different environments.

Human genome mapping, reproductive technologies, and genetic manipulation are by their nature the tools of *eugenics* (the movement to improve the human species through hereditary measures via "proper" mating). Eugenics was a popular movement at the beginning of the twentieth century, until it later was twisted by the insanities of Adolf Hitler. It was popularly believed that heredity was more influential than economic, cultural, or social factors in determining human behavior.

Indeed, many states enacted laws mandating sterilization under specified circumstances of family members who were criminals or "idiots." Like it or not, you are on the threshold of a new eugenics society. In germ-line therapy, genetic changes are made in the sperm, in the egg, or in embryonic cells after fertilization and are carried on to future generations. Whatever is excised by genetic surgery is gone forever from the heredity of that future family. Genetic therapy that prevents the inheritance of some negative characteristic by future generations will likely be the first therapy to be developed.

LEGAL FOCUS—PROBLEM

In 2010, Jean Luc Gelé and his bride Kristie Moore consider and then decide not to obtain a genetic review of their *in vitro* embryo before it is implanted. They choose to let "nature run its course." Their son Injo is subsequently born with a lifelong defect that easily could have been deleted from the fertilized egg by simple gene surgery. Are Gelé and Moore civilly liable to Injo for negligently failing to obtain genetic screening?

In considering your answer to this hypothetical situation, do not assume the family members are angry with each other. Sometimes, family suits are designed to obtain payment from an insurance company, as when a minor/passenger sues the parent/driver who is covered by insurance. Clearly, family law will be faced with difficult issues.

Parents sued their doctor for his inability to extract fluid from the wife's uterus that would have revealed the presence of Down syndrome. Had they known, they would have aborted the fetus. Would prospective parents abort a fetus that was predisposed to obesity? More than one-half of all adults and more than 25 percent of all children are overweight or obese. If lifelong illnesses are to be prevented by gene surgery, what about less serious characteristics? Would prospective parents choose to genetically eliminate myopia, dyslexia, left-handedness, or shortness? Already, sex screening is well established, and opportunities sometimes are taken through abortion to achieve gender balance in the family. Would these families choose gene therapy to improve the physical characteristics of their babies, thus producing designer babies? Such designer babies may be available only to the wealthy, who also may opt for gestation in an artificial womb to avoid the unpleasantries of pregnancy.

Should children have the legal right to be told of changes made to their genetic sources? For years, many children have had genetic roots different from their parents, because of adoption or sperm donation. Today, egg donation also is in widespread use, allowing women to overcome infertility. *In vitro* fertilization raises myriad legal issues when fertilized eggs stored in banks are abandoned by their owners, or when disagreements arise between their owners relative to their ultimate disposition. These issues already are in our courtrooms. In one bizarre example, a fertility doctor erroneously transplanted the embryo of an African American couple into Donna Fusano's uterus along with an embryo created by Donna and her husband, who are Caucasian. Twin boys were born of different races.

An overwhelming majority of parents of children conceived through sperm donation have not told their children, and many of those parents who have told them reportedly regret it. So far, children do not have a legal right to know the truth. In some states, such as New York, the identities of sperm and egg donors are not disclosed to recipients—but records are maintained.

Cloning Babies

For centuries, science has been domesticating, breeding, and hybridizing animals and plants. But nature always has imposed limits on combinations of species. In the twenty-first century, microscopic bits of DNA from two species that could not mate in nature can be spliced together to create new life forms, to modify existing life forms, or to produce biological chemicals, such as insulin.

In November 2001, scientists at Advanced Cell Technology in Worcester, Massachusetts, announced that they had cloned the first human embryo. In Congress, the House of Representatives passed legislation that would have made all types of human cloning a federal crime, but the bill died in the Senate. Cloning is forbidden by law in many countries, including England. England's law covers "reproductive cloning," however, not "therapeutic cloning." Therapeutic cloning is legal for scientists who have been granted a state license.

Concern about cloning is complicated by the different types of cloning. *Embryo cloning* occurs when cells are removed from a fertilized embryo and encouraged to develop into one or more duplicate embryos. Twins or triplets are formed, with identical DNA. *Adult DNA cloning* is what many think of when the term cloning is used. This type of cloning intends to produce a duplicate of the existing animal. This is the technique used to clone Dolly the sheep and other mammals. The DNA from an ovum is removed and replaced with the DNA from a cell removed from an adult animal. The fertilized ovum (pre-embryo) is implanted in a womb and allowed to develop into a new animal. The last type is therapeutic cloning. This procedure begins like adult DNA cloning, but stem cells are removed from the pre-embryo with the intent of producing tissue or a whole organ for transplant back into the person who supplied the DNA. The pre-embryo dies in the process.

Given the opportunity, would family members be willing to pay to clone themselves? Would they pay to produce genetically identical children? If a fetus is not protected by the Constitution, then presumably it has no legal standing to object to its alteration. Or does it? What if, following legal separation, one parent chooses to alter the embryo genetically and have it transplanted in a surrogate mother? These unanswered questions are meant only to typify the many and esoteric kinds of family law issues that will be surfacing in the near future.

STATE PROTECTION OF MINORS

Involvement of the state in family affairs is a modern trend. The purpose is protection of those family members who are least able to protect themselves. Out-of-wedlock births have contributed to a growing number of single-parent families, often requiring tax-supported public assistance. The state steps in when special needs arise, for example, to protect family members from serious harm caused by drug addiction or venereal disease, or in complications from difficult pregnancies. Finally, the state now engages in "co-parenting" through official acceptance of teenagers' decisions with regard to abortion and contraception.

Still another area of government protection of minors involves parental misconduct. Historically, parental immunity was considered necessary to preserve family harmony. For example, children could not sue their parents for personal injuries caused by parental negligence. In modern times, though, insurance covers damages caused by the negligent driving of the parent—at no apparent risk to family harmony. Thus, as indicated previously in this chapter, parents are liable to their children for serious misconduct, parental immunity being a rapidly fading concept.

As a general common law rule, parents are not liable for torts of their children causing injury to third persons. However, nearly half of the states have statutes creating parental liability up to certain specified limited amounts for their children's torts. Some states require a showing of willful conduct by the minor before their parents are responsible, up to a statutory maximum amount of money. Many states also create parental liability for malicious mischief when their children damage school or other public property.

LEGAL FOCUS—PROBLEM

Antoinette Walker is a police officer in Oakland, California, with responsibility to recruit new officers. She left her loaded handgun on her bedroom dresser where it was found by her ten-year-old son, who shot and wounded his twelve- year-old brother. No adult was at home. What family law issues have arisen?

Antoinette Walker could be charged with a crime—either misdemeanor or felony negligence in leaving a firearm readily available to minors. Handguns can be disabled by parents using trigger locks or simply by keeping them under lock and key. No crime was charged, however, raising the issue of selective enforcement—would an ordinary citizen have been prosecuted? The father, Walker's estranged husband, could sue in civil court for money damages or even to contest the existing custody arrangement. The wounded son may be entitled to recover damages from his mother for negligence. None of these actions, however, took place in this family tragedy, as often they do not. Family law has implications for injurious behavior among family members, but only when victims make complaints and attorneys bring their cases to court. Unfortunately, within families, many abuses exist that are known only to the victims and perpetrators.

Some children need protection from each other. Metal detectors are widely used in junior and senior high schools in major metropolitan areas. Some elementary schools use screening. This policy is believed necessary to protect students, teachers, and staff. When minor students commit serious crimes against other students, especially involving guns or knives, they are prosecuted in juvenile court, the same as with off-campus crime. But lesser antisocial behavior among students, such as physical bullying, is ignored by the law. Such bullying, if occurring between strangers at a downtown mall, for example, would be a criminal assault and battery. Persistent schoolyard abuse (e.g., pushing and slapping or teasing about physical or mental characteristics) can be more damaging to its victims than isolated incidents off campus. Yet, such incidents largely are ignored by police and left for administrative discipline by school officials.

State statutes impose the obligation on parents to support their children until adulthood, or until earlier emancipation when the minor child becomes self-supporting. Some states, however, provide for postminority (over age eighteen years) support by order of the divorce court or by statute. Even when postminority support is not required, states will enforce marital agreements that call for such support. The general purpose of postminority child support is to pay for college education. In most states, child support is a joint obligation, although it may be apportioned between the parents according to their respective financial circumstances. It is a crime to willfully fail to support a child, and almost all states have computerized methods for tracking down deadbeat parents. But finding deadbeat parents is not the only problem. Often, there simply is not enough money to go around.

LEGAL FOCUS—PROBLEM

Keith Jackson was elected school board president in San Francisco, overseeing 64,000 students and a $530 million budget. He receives $500 per month for his services. He previously had been hired by the district attorney to "track down deadbeat dads," but that job, for some unknown reason, lasted only three days. Keith is divorced and has two sons, ages six and twelve, for whom the court has ordered $643 monthly child support. Keith is in arrearage of more than $5,000 and is falling further behind each month. Should a father run for an elected office that pays less than a court order for support, or should he obtain employment that pays enough for child support?

A court could order Jackson to search for a job that pays adequately for child support and could jail him if he refused. Public service as an elected official is important, but perhaps it is not as indispensable as being a supportive father. The issue of child support is covered more fully later in this chapter.

Most parents choose to provide for their children, "the natural objects of their bounty," by will. A parent, however, intentionally may disinherit her child (or children) completely, even if the child is a dependent minor of tender years. This rule of absolute testamentary freedom originated in the common law. Nevertheless, state statutes commonly provide that the child must receive a share of the parental estate unless it is absolutely clear that disinheritance was planned. In other words, disinheritance of a child cannot occur through oversight by a parent. If a disinherited child is mentioned in the will (e.g., when a child is left a nominal amount), it is clear that the disinheritance was intentional and it will be upheld.

Emancipated Minors

emancipated minor
A minor legally allowed to handle her own financial affairs.

The term *emancipation* means setting free. Therefore, an **emancipated minor** is "set free" from his parents, meaning that the parents no longer have responsibility for or control over their emancipated child. Thus, parents also are set free, so to speak. Following emancipation, parents no longer have a legal duty to support or care for that child. Emancipated minors take on all of the rights and responsibilities of adults except for certain ones, such as being able to purchase alcoholic beverages legally. Nor is such a minor necessarily deprived of the benefits of juvenile court, discussed in the following section.

A number of states recognize the status of emancipation based on the lawful marriage of the minor, service in the military, or simply for becoming self-supporting. Some states provide a judicial procedure for a declaration of the emancipated status.

LEGAL FOCUS—PROBLEM

In the fall of 1998, seventeen-year-old Dominique Moceanu, a member of the 1996 gold medal U.S. Olympic gymnastics team, filed suit in Texas requesting, among other things, future independence from her parents, saying they squandered her fortune and oppressed her for years. "I want whatever I have earned to be under my control so I know how my earnings are being used, and I want to be able to train and compete in the sport I love for the right reason—because I love it—not because my father tells me I have to make more money." Has Moceanu stated sufficient grounds to become emancipated?

Yes, she has stated sufficient grounds to become emancipated. Before trial, Moceanu and her parents settled the lawsuit, and her parents agreed to the emancipation. The settlement was approved by court.

Juvenile Court Protection

> *I've been struck by the upside-down priorities of the juvenile-justice system. We are willing to spend the least amount of money to keep a kid at home, more to put him in a foster home, and the most to institutionalize him.*
>
> Marian Wright Edelman, American lawyer

Unfortunately, children sometimes are forced to live without adequate, or any, parental supervision; consequently, many juveniles become delinquent or even incorrigible. Legislatures have created juvenile court systems to protect minor children as well as the public in such situations. Unknown at the turn of the twentieth century, juvenile law and courts have burgeoned, especially following World War II. Today, there is much sentiment that juvenile laws and courts are too lenient and that more minors who engage in vicious crimes ought to be treated as adults.

Children are not under the jurisdiction of juvenile courts simply because they are minors; rather, juvenile courts become involved only when necessary. For example, minor children who need proper parental care or who are destitute (with no home and without the necessaries of life) are within the jurisdiction of the juvenile court system. They can be declared "dependents" of the court, which then is free to make a wide variety of possible orders for their care, supervision, custody, and support. A dependent child may be taken from the custody of her parents and, for example, be placed in a foster home (as in the *Gregory Kingsley* case) or the home of a relative, or be subject to any other arrangement deemed by the court to be in the child's best interest.

Also subject to the jurisdiction of juvenile courts are minor children who commit acts that would be crimes if committed by adults. Because juveniles may be confined against their will, they are entitled to many constitutional protections. For example, a minor in juvenile court has the right to representation by an attorney (without charge, if the minor is indigent) and cannot be compelled to be a witness against himself. The burden of proof is the same as in criminal cases—generally, that is, "beyond a reasonable doubt." However, no right to trial by jury exists in juvenile court, nor is there a right to bail (although prehearing release is common).

Ordinarily, juvenile court hearings are not open to the public. If the accused person is found to have committed the charged offense, the court will declare the minor a ward of the court. Juvenile courts can make various orders, such as probation, fines, or commitments to juvenile homes, ranches, camps, or special jails for youthful offenders.

Parents can and do take control of unruly, out-of-control children who are truants from school and otherwise incorrigible by hiring "professional escorts" (moonlighting police and probation officers) to take their children to "behavior modification" camps in other locations, sometimes as far away as Jamaica. These children can be taken against their will because parents have the right and responsibility to determine what is best for their children.

Under specified conditions (usually the passage of a specified number of years), juvenile courts officially will seal all records pertaining to a minor's case. The minor then has no official criminal record and will not be handicapped in the future when seeking employment.

Not all juvenile offenders are processed by juvenile courts. The nature of some youthful offenders, and the severity of their alleged misconduct (such as homicide, armed robbery, or rape), may lead the juvenile court to reject jurisdiction, thereby compelling the minor to stand trial as an adult and face harsher criminal procedures and possible penalties.

Sexual Abuse of Children

Sexual abuse of a child is a serious felony that is difficult to detect, usually occurring in complete privacy. The victimized child may be the only witness and may be reluctant or unable to testify adequately. Forced testimony by a child in open court may result in the child's suffering serious emotional distress that may affect adversely both the child and the usefulness of the information obtained.

Nearly all states have adopted statutes designed to protect child witnesses from further harm caused by the humiliation and stress of testifying in open court. To balance the goals of protecting the child and the constitutional rights of the accused, various techniques are evolving to obtain testimony from involved children outside the presence of the alleged abuser. For example, out-of-court statements (hearsay evidence) made privately by children to mental health or child protection professionals, who often use anatomically correct dolls, sometimes can be used in court.* This procedure assists many children who are unable to recall, report, or evaluate events accurately. Critics, however, point out that some experts, with the best of intentions, may come to faulty conclusions based on interpretations of the manner in which children manipulate dolls. Additional protective procedures include closed-circuit testimony from a private room, videotaping of such out-of-court testimony, and allowing admission of hearsay evidence that otherwise would be excluded from the trial. But some protective laws may clash with the Sixth Amendment to the U.S. Constitution.

The Sixth Amendment grants an accused the right to confront all witnesses. Thus, the U.S. Supreme Court has denied the use of a screen in court to shield a child from visual contact while testifying. But one exception to the right to eye-to-eye confrontation between the accused and the child while testifying in court has been approved by the U.S. Supreme Court. A 5–4 majority of justices held that the Sixth Amendment does not invariably require face-to-face confrontation between a defendant and an adverse witness. It concluded that public policy, including the interest in protecting child witnesses from trauma, can justify an exception to the normal "preference" for face-to-face confrontation. The Court upheld a Maryland statutory scheme permitting a child to testify from outside the courtroom via closed-circuit television.

Note that protection of the child from confrontation with the accused is a different problem from closing the trial to the public and press. Court proceedings almost always are open to the public; however, under appropriate circumstances, a judge can close the courtroom to protect a child from serious emotional injury.

Recall from Chapter 6 that proof of guilt in criminal cases must be "beyond a reasonable doubt." Such a high standard of proof is difficult to meet with testimony that is incomplete, inconsistent, or even contradictory. The age and maturity of a child can make prosecution especially difficult in sexual abuse cases. The best example of the difficulties in determining the guilt or innocence of the accused is the notorious *McMartin* case (one of the longest and most costly criminal trials in U.S. history), in which one defendant was found not guilty of molesting numerous children while responsible for their care in a preschool. The jury in the three-year trial dead locked on certain charges against the other defendant, and a retrial limited to those charges again resulted in a hung jury. Clearly, emotions were high, perhaps bordering on hysteria, in the local

*Admission into the record of such hearsay evidence is proper only when the "totality of circumstances" surrounding the testimony renders the witness particularly worthy of belief. Out-of-court hearsay was ruled not admissible in cases in which the doctor conducted an interview without a videotape, asked leading questions, and had a preconceived idea of what the child should be disclosing. *Idaho v. Wright*, 497 U.S. 805, 110 S.Ct. 3139 (1990).

community, and the consequences were serious with regard to everyone involved in such difficult, complex, and bewildering litigation.

In civil law divorce and child custody proceedings, more relaxed procedures and reduced standards of proof are applicable. For example, there is no right to trial by jury in divorce or custody matters.* Civil remedies also are quite different from criminal penalties for the sexual abuse of a child. Whereas jail is the probable result of a criminal conviction for child abuse, a court order that all visitation be supervised is one possible result of a civil proceeding. Monetary damages are another possible result of a civil remedy, as previously discussed.

LEGAL FOCUS—BACKGROUND

Vulnerable children with self-image problems get real pleasure and support from a song written in 1998 by songwriters Steven Seskin and Alan Shamblin. The song "Don't Laugh at Me" was recorded by several singers including Brad Paisley and Peter, Paul, and Mary. After hearing the song, Peter Yarrow of Peter, Paul and Mary was so moved that he established the Don't Laugh at Me Project. Children suffering from self-image problems, which often include victims of sexual abuse, children with disabilities, and children subject to bullying, have benefited from the song and project activities.

Maternal Abuse during Pregnancy

The U.S. Constitution has been interpreted to guarantee women the right to choose to abort their fetuses under most circumstances at any time before viability (the first moment following which the unborn child could survive without its mother). The right of privacy also guarantees women the right to live their lives during pregnancy any way they please—with certain reservations. There is no constitutional right for women to live their lives during pregnancy in such a way that their future children predictably will not be harmed.

LEGAL FOCUS—PROBLEM

Government fliers distributed at her high school warned Shirley Pinker that drinking alcohol during pregnancy was likely to cause serious health defects to babies. Several years later, she began drinking whiskey heavily during pregnancy. Has Pinker committed a crime?

If Pinker were a resident of South Dakota, she could be made to attend a hearing (without a jury) and then be ordered by a judge to a detox center or to a treatment center. Fetal alcohol syndrome can leave its victims mentally and physically disabled for their entire lives, and the law in South Dakota has intervened to protect these unborn family members. Fetal alcohol syndrome is about twenty times more prevalent in South Dakota (and some other states) and among certain ethnic groups.

The most pervasive abusive behavior by pregnant women consists of drug and alcohol use. This complex issue involves weighing the interest of society in healthy fetal life versus the mother's right to freedom of movement during part or all of her

*Only Texas permits trial by jury in divorce cases.

pregnancy. The difficulties of such a family law are described in the *Johnson* case found at the end of this chapter.

The issue arises in the context of civil proceedings to confine abusive mothers in treatment centers, hospitals, or even the homes of relatives. Proposed laws are pending in a dozen or more states that would legalize the involuntary commitment to some kind of treatment facility for most or all of the gestational period of drug or alcohol abusers. But what about pregnant women who make other choices that adversely affect their fetuses, such as poor food and medicine choices, poor or no prenatal care, and even smoking? Is a civil proceeding to incarcerate a person a veiled device to avoid the constitutional rights enjoyed by those people accused of crimes? Some states proposing incarceration of future mothers put the matter under the jurisdiction of the juvenile court, where many rules are different and where trial by jury is not available. Most constitutional rights, however, are not suspended simply because the juvenile court has jurisdiction. How can society prevent the birth of "cocaine babies"? Can the unborn fetus be confined in a place where it is safe from abuse by its mother, such as a health institution, a foster home, or even the home of a responsible friend?

LEGAL FOCUS—CASE

Darlene Brown was pregnant with a viable fetus and critically needed a blood transfusion, which she refused on religious grounds. Brown's refusal threatened the life of her unborn baby. Can the court order Brown to submit to a blood transfusion to save her viable fetus?

In re fetus Brown v. Darlene Brown, 228 Ill. Dec. 525, 294 Ill. App. 3d 159, 689 N.E.2d 397 (Ill. 1997).

No, the court cannot issue the order. At the turn of the twentieth century, fetuses were protected by the laws making abortion illegal. In the twenty-first century, the right of women to an abortion has been established. How that right will be reconciled with the rights of fetuses to be born free of harm from drug use or other abusive conduct by their mothers is evolving. In addition, states proscribing child abuse provide exceptions on religious grounds for behavior or conditions that otherwise might be considered abuse, absent the religious directive.

HOW MAY MARRIAGE BE TERMINATED?

Dissolution (Divorce)

divorce
Termination of a marriage relationship by court judgment. Divorce is called dissolution in some states.

no-fault divorce
A divorce granted by a court without either party having to prove fault in the other party.

As there is a need for marriage, so is there a need for **divorce** (also called *dissolution of marriage).* Divorce ends the marriage, but it does not terminate spousal responsibilities that arose from the marriage necessarily, such as the duties of child support and alimony. Divorce requires court proceedings, in which a judgment (or decree) in dissolution is rendered. Legislatures traditionally have permitted divorce for an "innocent" spouse from a "guilty" spouse; this "fault" basis of divorce, in some form or other, is still in effect in some states. All states, however, also provide for some variety of **no-fault divorce.**

In response to widespread disenchantment with fault systems of divorce, many states adopted some variety of no-fault divorce exclusively. The prevailing no-fault system requires proof of two elements: a breakdown of the marriage and the objective fact of physical separation of the spouses for some specified period of time, such as six months. This separation period offers the added benefit of preventing overly hasty divorces. Some states also retain the fault basis of divorce to provide immediate relief in severe cases or to allow judges to award unequal distributions of marital property. (Distributions of property and rights to spousal support upon divorce are covered subsequently in this chapter.) A breakdown is established by testimony that the marriage is irretrievably broken because of the attitude of one or both spouses or because of a long physical separation without a resumption of cohabitation. Following appropriate evidence of a breakdown, divorce then is available.

A primary advantage of no-fault divorce is that spouses are not required to "air their dirty laundry" in a courtroom, detailing each other's alleged misdeeds. Furthermore, there is no need for private detectives to track spouses thought to be unfaithful. In fault systems, on the other hand, the stakes can be much higher because the more innocent spouse can benefit through uneven distribution of marital property and perhaps through the award of a larger amount of support.

Under no-fault systems, an "innocent" spouse cannot prevent a divorce from occurring. People cannot be locked into marriage. But people facing divorce can use the law in retaliation.

LEGAL FOCUS—PROBLEM

The divorce proceedings by Donna Carroll, of Janesville, Wisconsin, prompted her husband to file criminal charges of adultery. The charges did little to save the marriage, but did cause Donna to perform forty hours of community service. Facing a criminal trial, up to two years in jail, and as much as a $10,000 fine, Donna entered a plea bargain. Can the fear of adultery charges be used by spouses to obtain larger divorce settlements?

Yes, it is legal to file such charges, which may have the effect of inspiring settlement. Adultery is still a crime in many states, including New York, Massachusetts, Connecticut, and Michigan. Enforcement of adultery statutes seldom occurs until a spouse brings charges during no-fault divorce proceedings. However, there is a fine line between using legal proceedings as a club and the crime of extortion. (You may recall from Chapter 6 that the coercion of money under threat of harm is a felony called extortion.) Adultery can be committed only with a member of the opposite sex, so a gay affair would not be considered adultery.

Some states permit civil remedies for alienation of affection. A third party can be sued by one spouse for "alienating" the affections of the other spouse—usually through sexual intercourse. Although the "alienated" spouse also may be guilty of the crime of adultery, the third-party interloper may be liable civilly in damages. This kind of "heart balm" lawsuit may be more of a vindication than a realistic legal remedy.

LEGAL FOCUS—EXAMPLE

Dorothy Hutelmyer sued secretary Lynne Cox for wrecking her marriage by sleeping with her husband Joseph. Dorothy was awarded a jury verdict of $1 million as damages, even though Cox testified that Joseph's marriage already was wrecked as evidenced by a lack of sexual relations for the preceding seven years. The North Carolina jury apparently rejected that contention in making the award. Adulteress Cox was broke, and even though she subsequently married Joseph Hutelmyer, he is not liable for her debts.

Recall our discussion of the modern trend to permit suits for damages in domestic torts. Critics of this development argue that they are "putting the fault back into no-fault divorces." Indeed, the family "dirty laundry" (e.g., wife beating) can be aired in court as the basis for tort litigation, even if it is shielded from the court by no-fault divorce laws. Of course, this criticism applies only to a limited number of divorce cases in which the alleged spousal misconduct is egregious enough to justify the filing of a separate domestic tort lawsuit.

Although no-fault divorce is generally available throughout the states, new schemes to strengthen the marital vows have been proposed. The current "quickie divorce" system, according to proponents of these plans, promotes irresponsibility because spouses can "walk away" from their marriages easily. Nearly one in two marriages are expected to end in divorce. Children of broken homes are more likely to do poorly in school, suffer relationship problems, have babies out of wedlock, and get into trouble with the law. Not all sociologists agree with these conclusions, but there is a national movement afoot to make divorce more difficult. A two-tier system under which no-fault divorce would not be available if minor children were involved has failed to become law in any state—but it is pending in some state legislatures. States also are considering longer predivorce waiting periods.

covenant marriage
A type of marriage in which couples agree to certain marital promises and limitations on their ability to terminate the marriage. States allowing covenant marriage provide it as optional.

Another scheme called the **covenant marriage** has been adopted in Arizona, Arkansas, and Louisiana. Louisiana's covenant marriage requires couples to engage in premarital counseling and a mandatory two-year waiting period before divorce. In Arizona, parties that select covenant marriage status agree to premarital counseling and a significant limitation on grounds for any divorce. Among the grounds available is "divorce by persuasion," under which both parties need to agree to the divorce. If one spouse disagrees, the other has to purchase a ticket out through financial incentives or failing that, revert back to a "fault" basis for divorce.

Although a couple may obtain a divorce without the services of an attorney, it usually is desirable to hire one in cases in which substantial family assets or liabilities must be distributed, or if child custody or visitation rights are contested. Many people with limited assets and no children obtain uncontested divorces by filling out appropriate forms without the assistance of any attorney. But many divorce attorneys in the world are responding to a perceived need. Unfortunately, this area of law is rife with opportunities for unethical behavior by attorneys. The nature of divorce renders the clients extraordinarily vulnerable, emotionally as well as financially. The topic of legal ethics has been discussed in Chapter 4, but it is appropriate to note here that at least one state—New York—has by court rule adopted special ethical standards for divorce lawyers. One rule prohibits charging "up-front" nonrefundable fees. Such fees, collected before representation is undertaken, necessarily tend to dissuade the client from discharging the lawyer even if she is doing a poor job. Another clause prohibits so-called "couch fees," that is, sexual favors from the client during representation. Yet another important clause requires written, instead of verbal, fee agreements. Contingent fees in divorce cases have long been prohibited, but they are permitted in domestic tort cases.

Annulment

Annulment is a declaration by a court that a purported marriage does not exist and never existed because of some defect present at the time of the marriage ceremony. Examples of such serious defects that could exist at the inception of the apparent marriage include incest, bigamy, mental incapacity, physical incapacity to consummate the marriage, insanity, and consent to marry resulting from fraud, dare, or intoxication.

LEGAL FOCUS—EXAMPLE

On January 5, 2004, pop star Britney Spears impulsively married a young man from her hometown, Jason Allan Alexander, at 5:30 A.M. on a Saturday morning after spending most of the night with him at a club in Las Vegas. As the story spread to entertainment and tabloid news outlets around the globe, it was quickly announced that she would seek an annulment. Ms. Spears' petition for annulment stated that she "lacked understanding of her actions to the extent that she was incapable of agreeing to the marriage." Can the court grant her request?

Yes, a court may grant her request, and did so less than fifty-five hours after the marriage. The former husband of Ms. Spears acknowledged that their decision was too impulsive.

When a defective marriage exists, only an innocent victim has the option to annul and must do so promptly upon discovery of the defect. Significant false statements (e.g., that one is pregnant or that one will attempt to have a child) justify an annulment; less significant false statements (e.g., that one is rich or that one is a virgin) do not.

Even though a marriage is annulled, in the eyes of the law, a child conceived before the annulment is deemed to be a legitimate child of the marriage that legally never existed.

LEGAL FOCUS—PROBLEM

On the second day of Mardi Gras in New Orleans, Carl Seither, twenty-one years old, met Maria Escovedo, seventeen years old, at a Dixieland jazz concert. Within a week, they were madly in love and decided to marry and begin a family of six children. They promptly applied for a marriage license and discovered that Louisiana enforced a three-day waiting period between the license and marriage dates. Impetuous, they drove to Texas and got married, although Escovedo had to lie about her age on their license. Within weeks, as their passions were cooling, Seither revealed that he "hated" children and that the divorce from his former wife was not yet final. What would Escovedo's attorney advise her?

Escovedo's lawyer would observe that Seither's lie about children was material and sufficient basis to annul the marriage. Furthermore, a declaration that the marriage was void also was possible because Seither's divorce was not final. Although without significance in most states, Seither was guilty of bigamy. Escovedo also committed a crime when she lied about her age, but the court would not refuse to grant an annulment for that reason. Most likely, Escovedo would not be prosecuted for that misdemeanor. Seither also committed the intentional tort of fraud and could be sued civilly by Escovedo. If she could persuade a jury that she suffered substantial mental distress, such as humiliation and loss of sexual naïveté because of Seither's wanton and malicious lies, Escovedo may recover substantial compensatory and punitive damages.

separation
The status of spouses who are by judicial decree living apart, that is, no longer cohabiting.

divorce from bed and board
A modification of the spousal relationship in which the parties are forbidden to cohabit but do not dissolve the marriage. Support may be paid, and property is divided as in a divorce.

"Bed and Board" Separation, Separate Maintenance, or Legal Separation

Many states provide for a partial termination of marriage. **Separation** *a mensa et thoro* (Latin: "from bed and board") allows spouses to live apart without fixing desertion upon one or the other. Support obligations are established, and property is divided by the court. The couple, however, is not divorced and neither can remarry. This remedy of **divorce from bed and board** derives from early English law when divorce was not available.

The remedy is appropriate where the spouses (1) do not intend to remarry, (2) desire a complete settlement of their economic affairs, (3) want to preserve entitlements under certain public laws (e.g., Social Security), and (4) are opposed to divorce on religious grounds. Separate maintenance and **legal separation** are similar to "bed and board" separation and provide the same benefits to the couple, except that property division normally is not adjudicated.

WHAT ARE A SPOUSE'S RIGHTS AND DUTIES UPON TERMINATION OF MARRIAGE?

Maintenance (Alimony)

legal separation
A court order permitting spouses to live apart with necessary related orders for child custody and child support, support of the wife (or husband), and division of property (as in dissolution), but the marriage endures.

maintenance
Payment by one spouse to the other spouse following dissolution of their marriage. Term used interchangeably with *alimony*.

Upon termination of the marriage by divorce, **maintenance** (often called *alimony* or *support*) may be ordered by the court in both dollars per month and in duration of payments. Rehabilitative, or limited-term, alimony terminates at the end of a specified time period, during which the recipient seeks education, training, or experience to become self-supporting. Permanent alimony or maintenance is indefinite in duration. Many couples who divorce arrive at a mutual agreement as to maintenance and thereby avoid the time, expense, and uncertainty of a court's decision. (Note that such marital agreements are subject to approval by the court.) But if the former spouses cannot agree, the judge, sitting as a court of equity and hence without a jury, considers all relevant factors and makes the award.

In 1979, the Supreme Court "de-sexed" alimony and held that gender-based alimony statutes were unconstitutional. Alimony is required from either spouse if the other is in genuine need. One is in need, for example, if she (or he) cannot be self-supporting or if there is a child whose situation precludes employment by the parent with custody. Generally, marital fault is not a factor in determining whether or not alimony should be awarded, although some states specifically consider fault.

The amount of alimony is related to the needs of the spouse receiving it and the ability of the other to pay. The following factors are considered by courts in setting and terminating alimony:

- Financial condition of the spouse seeking support as well as the ability of the other to pay
- Length of the marriage
- Age, health, education, and station in life of the parties
- Occupations, vocational skills, and employability of the parties
- Needs and opportunities for future income of the parties
- Contributions of each in acquiring or maintaining marital property (including non-economic contributions)
- Need of a custodial parent to occupy the marital home
- Tax consequences involved

LEGAL FOCUS—CASE

Thomas Wilson had been married about four years when his wife, Elma, was injured in a fall. Her injuries resulted in a permanent neurological deficit. She lacked "social judgment, common sense, and social intelligence." Two years later, the Wilsons agreed to divorce. Elma received $500 per month for two years, plus medical insurance for the same time. After those two years, Elma asked the court to extend alimony, anticipating further brain surgery and continued unemployment. The court extended alimony for one year, following which Elma asked for another extension, claiming no improvement in her condition or employment potential. What should the court order?

In re the Marriage of Wilson, 201 Cal.App. 3d 913, 247 Cal.Rptr. 522 (1988).

The trial court terminated the alimony, noting the shortness of the marriage and weighing society's obligation to assist Mrs. Wilson against Mr. Wilson's continuing obligation. In affirming the judgment, the appellate court observed that Mrs. Wilson was not a "displaced homemaker" but a "middle-aged bartender" with adult children. It further said, "While no one will dispute Elma's tragic disability, the clear trend is for trial courts to consider the totality of circumstances (in terminating support)."

In the 1970s, the push for equality between the sexes resulted in a shift of state laws from permanent to rehabilitative alimony. But regardless of notions of equality, the reality often is that some women, especially those in their forties and fifties, could not go back to school and become doctors or lawyers and compete with their former husbands' earning capacity. As a result, such displaced homemakers often suffer a severe drop in their standard of living following divorce. Many such women lack marketable job skills or even knowledge about the changing workplace. Moreover, they often face illegal gender and age discrimination. For these reasons, courts in Ohio, Maryland, Louisiana, New York, Pennsylvania, and Florida have begun to require permanent, rather than limited-time, alimony awards. Contrary opinions are offered that alimony should not be a "perpetual pension." Some believe that permanent alimony ought to be awarded to older women in marriages of long duration, but not to younger women who are capable of becoming self-supporting.

When circumstances change, alimony may be modified (even terminated) by petition to the court, which retains continuing jurisdiction until alimony finally is terminated. As previously noted, all relevant factors are considered by the court when hearing a petition to modify. Often, the changing factors relate to changes in the relative financial conditions of the former spouses. For example, a former husband can be reluctant to support his ex-wife while she is living with another man. Generally, cohabitation with another person is not in itself a sufficient basis for terminating alimony. Some states, however, do provide for modification or termination of alimony under such circumstances. These laws are equally operative if a former wife is paying support to her ex-husband.

LEGAL FOCUS—CASE

Dentist Hall agreed to a divorce settlement in which his wife received the home, furnishings, and vehicle totaling more than $100,000 in value, plus annual alimony of $15,000. Three years later, he petitioned the court to terminate alimony due to changed circumstances. Robert Jones, who was sharing Hall's former home with his former wife, contributed nothing toward rent or maintenance and engaged in sexual intercourse with her. The trial court terminated the alimony on the grounds that Hall should not be compelled to "support his divorced wife and her paramour in idleness and fornication." What was the result on appeal?

Hall v. Hall, 25 Ill. App. 3d 524, 323 N.E.2d 541 (Ill. 1975).

The judgment was reversed. Alimony may not be utilized as a club to regulate the ex-wife's sex life. On the other hand, the court did remand the case to the trial court for a reduction in alimony.

Fourteen states allow payment of spousal support in a lump sum. In these states, the spouse may pay the total support obligation at the time of the divorce. Although the payment burden could be steep, completed payment usually extinguishes any future support obligation or risk of modification of the support order. The obligation of permanent alimony ends with the death of either spouse. Remarriage of the spouse receiving alimony also automatically terminates the duty to pay.

Property Division in Equitable Distribution States

A divorcing couple can reach an agreement about how to divide their property and debts, and a judge normally will incorporate their agreement in the final divorce decree. But if the couple cannot agree, they can submit their property dispute to the court, which will use local state law to divide the property. Remember, most states are marital property states and these states provide for an "equitable" distribution of marital property upon divorce, either in the form of property division or maintenance. Note that equitable distribution in a marital property state does not mean equal distribution. The process is in three steps: (1) identification of marital property, (2) valuation of the assets, and (3) distribution to each spouse.

LEGAL FOCUS—CASE

James sued Sandra for a divorce, alleging incompatibility. Sandra counterclaimed, alleging incompatibility and adultery. She sought alimony, a division of the marital assets, and attorney fees. A judgment of divorce was entered, alimony was granted, and property was divided. The husband moved to set aside the property division, arguing that the trial court had abused its discretion in awarding the wife more than $2 million in marital assets. The wife moved to set aside the trial court's property division because she received an unequal share of an estate valued at more than $5 million. Should the judgment be set aside because it is unequal?

Long v. Long, 824 So.2d 778 (Ala. 2001).

Remember that in equitable distribution states, marital distributions need not be equal, just equitable. The Alabama Appellate Court upheld the trial court's decision, making these points:

1. The trial court is presumed correct because they are in the unique position of observing the witnesses to assess their demeanor and credibility.
2. Matters of alimony and property division are within the trial court's discretion, and its rulings are not to be disturbed except for abuse of discretion.
3. Awards of alimony and property division are interrelated, and the entire judgment must be considered in determining whether or not the trial court abused its discretion.
4. A division of marital property in a divorce case does not have to be equal, only equitable, and a determination of what is equitable rests within the sound discretion of the trial court.

The doctrine of equitable distribution awards a marital interest in all assets that were acquired with a material economic contribution by both spouses regardless of which spouse holds legal title. Savings or acquisitions from salaries or interest income and investment proceeds are obvious examples of marital property. One important property interest typically considered to be marital property is pension earned during the marriage, with an important caveat: The U.S. Supreme Court held that military pensions cannot be awarded to divorcing spouses; otherwise, important "military personnel objectives" would be threatened. For one example of such objectives, retirement (pension) payments are similar to a retainer, because retired military personnel may be required to return to duty at any time. As a result of this decision, Congress enacted the Federal Uniformed Services Former Spouses' Protection Act, which gave states the choice of whether or not to treat military pensions as marital property, with up to 50 percent of the pension going to the nonmilitary spouse if the marriage has lasted ten years or more. Most states do consider military pensions as marital property. Some married veterans, however, are entitled to either pension or disability payments, and because the former are taxable income and the latter are not, these veterans often elect disability pay. To the chagrin of some, disability pay cannot be considered marital property.

LEGAL FOCUS—CASE

The O'Briens' married life began in 1971. The action for divorce came during the holiday season of 1980, two months after the husband received his medical license. The New York trial court found that the wife contributed 76 percent of the family income while the husband did postgraduate work and attended medical school in Guadalajara, Mexico, and in New York. At the time of the divorce, the couple had few assets—or did they? Is the prospective value of the husband's career marital property?

O'Brien v. O'Brien, 66 N.Y.2d 576, 498 N.Y.S.2d 743, 489 N.E.2d 713 (N.Y. 1985).

It is also not clear whether or not one spouse should be awarded a property interest in the professional license or degree of the other. How should an advanced degree, such as a master's in business administration, or a professional license, such as a license to practice medicine, be treated upon divorce? Can they be assigned a dollar value and equitably distributed or divided? Suppose one spouse sacrifices his education to put his wife through medical school. Upon a divorce immediately following the wife's graduation, should the husband be awarded half of the dollar value of the degree or license? If so, how should it be valued? In the preceding New York case, it was held that a husband's medical license was marital property under the state's equitable distribution law. Following that decision, New York's highest court held that an academic degree obtained during marriage is also marital property subject to equitable distribution. In the states that equitably distribute marital property, division of property is based on such factors as length of the marriage, the parties' abilities to support themselves, and the property and income that were obtained during the marriage. Thus, a spouse has claim to an expected future stream of earnings resulting from an investment, or perhaps from an advanced degree.

In most states, "professional" goodwill, which may be defined loosely as enhanced earning power based upon special talents, reputation, business referral base, or uniqueness of services offered, is marital property that can be and is divided upon divorce. In some states, restitutional alimony instead of property division may be awarded to reimburse one spouse for contributions made to the other in earning a professional degree.

In many states, the nonmonetary contributions of a homemaker are considered to be the equivalent of the wage earner's monetary contributions. The starting point in making an equitable distribution is a presumption that equality is equity: An equal division is the most just.

LEGAL FOCUS—CASE

For thirty-two years, Lorna Jorgenson Wendt ran the household and raised the Wendts' two daughters. Her husband Gary, age fifty-five, chairman of GE Capital Services, testified that Lorna had no interest in business or his problems. Connecticut is an "equitable distribution" state, and the divorce judge must decide the worth of a stay-at-home wife. Lorna said, "I worked hard and I was very loyal." Gary said, "I worked hard. She didn't." The Wendt estate was valued as high as $100 million. What should the judge award to Lorna?

Wendt v. Wendt, 1998 WL 161165 (Conn. 1998).

Lorna was awarded a multimillion-dollar home in Stamford and a vacation home in Key Largo; $252,000 a year payable in monthly installments; and half of all stocks, bonds, and cash, all totaling about $20 million. In a community property state, Lorna would have received precisely one-half the total value of the family assets.

LEGAL FOCUS—CASE

Sam Burgess's premarital house appreciated in value during his marriage with Sally. On the advice of her attorney, Sally Burgess agreed to quitclaim deed all her rights, title, and interest, if any, in the house to Sam for a payment of $10. Did Sally lose her marital interest in the house?

Burgess v. Burgess, 710 P.2d 417 (Alaska 1985).

No, she did not lose her marital interest in the house. The court ruled that all increase in value of a premarital house is a marital asset if the nonowner spouse takes an active role in its upkeep and management. The court will not uphold an unconscionable agreement.

Assets, such as a promissory note requiring payment of money to the spouses, must be distributed in accordance with the court ordered distribution. One asset that may be distributed in kind is a cryogenically preserved (frozen) preembryo.

LEGAL FOCUS—CASE

When Junior L. and Mary Sue Davis divorced, they owned seven cryogenically preserved preembryos. Ms. Davis desired to carry the preembryos to term; Mr. Davis objected and did not want to become a father against his will. The trial court ruled that the preembryos were human beings and awarded custody to Ms. Davis. During lengthy appeals, Ms. Davis remarried and changed her mind, desiring to donate the preembryos to another couple. Who should receive the preembryos, and why?

Davis v. Davis, 842 S.W. 2d 588 (Tenn. 1992).

In a case of first impression, the Tennessee Supreme Court ruled against Ms. Davis, stating that preembryos do not enjoy protection as "persons" under federal law.

> *[There are] two rights of equal significance—the right to procreate and the right to avoid procreation. The equivalence of and inherent tension between these two interests are nowhere more evident than in the context of in vitro fertilization. None of the concerns about a woman's bodily integrity that have previously precluded men from controlling abortion decisions is applicable here. If the state's interests do not become sufficiently compelling in the abortion context until the end of the first trimester, after significant*

developmental stages have passed, there is no state interest in these preembryos. Ordinarily, the party wishing to avoid procreation should prevail, assuming that the other party has a reasonable possibility of achieving parenthood by means other than use of the pre-embryos in question. If no reasonable alternatives exist, then the argument in favor of using the pre-embryos to achieve pregnancy should be considered. However, if the party seeking control of the preembryos intends merely to donate them to another couple, the objecting party obviously has the greater interest and should prevail.

The trend is to minimize relative fault of the spouses as a factor in property division. Many states, however, consider economic fault (e.g., dissipation of marital assets pending divorce) in making an equitable division. The criteria used in most states in making an equitable distribution of marital property between the spouses are comparable to the factors (previously listed) that are relied on in setting alimony awards. Food stamps, other government assistance, and child support payments are not considered income to the recipient parent and therefore are not included as factors in dividing marital property.

Property Division in Community Property States

As stated earlier, community property is all property acquired by the husband and the wife during marriage other than by gift or inheritance. Community property must be distributed equally because each spouse is the "owner" of an undivided one-half interest. This characteristic is the most important one in distinguishing between community property and equitable distribution states.

Upon divorce, the court allocates the net value of each one-half interest to each spouse. If the community property physically cannot be distributed equally, it may be sold and the cash proceeds divided, or a promissory note may be made from one spouse to the other to equalize the values received from an unequal physical distribution. (A physical distribution of assets is called a distribution in kind.) As discussed earlier, professional licenses or degrees may be marital property (in both equitable distribution and community property states) and are good examples of property that cannot be distributed in kind.

In some community property states (e.g., Washington and Texas), the court may divide the marital property in any manner it deems "just and equitable," not necessarily equally. An unequal distribution of community property may act as a substitute for alimony.

All property either brought into the marriage or acquired by gift or inheritance is separate property, as mentioned earlier. Separate property typically is not subject to distribution by the court upon divorce and neither are its passive earnings (such as interest) if they are maintained separately with proper records. In a few states, however, all marital property is subject to distribution by the divorce court.

Child Custody

The legal standard for court award of child custody and visitation rights is the "best interests of the child." Often, parents are sensitive to their child's needs, and so they agree on custody and visitation. In such instances, courts normally comply with the parents' joint request. When both parents demand custody or argue about visitation rights, the court must attempt to determine the best interests of the child and make appropriate orders.

The Uniform Marriage and Divorce Act specifies several factors, including the following for determining custody arrangements in the best interests of the child: (1) the wishes of the parents and the child; (2) the child's adjustment to her home, school, and community; and (3) the mental and physical health of all individuals involved. Although courts consider the wishes of the child, they weigh their importance by the child's age and maturity. It is not appropriate to ask a child in open court which parent she chooses to live with because it is not reckoned to be in the child's best interest to have custody turn on the transitory desires of a child.

Children may be the parties most affected by divorce; they are undoubtedly the least able to protect their own rights, especially because the court receives most of its information about finances and emotional trauma from the parents. For this reason, one theory holds that children ought to be represented independently by their own attorney. Advocates of this theory applaud the case of Gregory Kingsley, previously discussed, who successfully "divorced" his parents by using his own attorney. A contrary theory holds that the illusion of power created by one's own attorney might be inimical to children's emotional well-being. Courts have the power to appoint a special guardian *ad litem* (Latin: "for the purpose of the suit") to protect the interests of the child.

The granting of meaningful visitation opportunities may be expected to temper the impact of a change in custody unless visitation is used by a vindictive spouse as a weapon to prolong the agonies of divorce for all concerned. In such situations, the court may prohibit visitation or strictly limit its terms. When divorced parents reside in different communities, split custody—where one parent has custody during summer, the other during the school year—may be an effective option.

joint custody
Responsibility shared by both parents, following a divorce, annulment, or separation, to guide and support their child(ren).

Joint custody, in which the parents share responsibility for the child, became the most widespread choice of courts in the 1980s. Many state legislatures expressed a preference for joint custody in their statutory guidelines under the theory that, ideally, children need two actively involved parents in their lives.

LEGAL FOCUS—PROBLEM

Matthew Anderson and Margie Stavros have court-ordered joint custody of their only child, Roger. Living within the same city, both parents share decision making on all important issues, such as those created by religion, school, and sports activities. Roger lives with Mom Monday to Thursday and with Dad Friday to Saturday. Sundays are alternated. Anderson earns more than Stavros and pays monthly child support. This arrangement is working smoothly, and both parents remain flexible. What happens when Stavros wants to move away to live with her new boyfriend and to take Roger with her?

This hypothetical example shows both the benefits and the possible disadvantages of joint custody. When parents cooperate and circumstances permit, joint custody is effective in providing the parental guidance needed by children. When parents are emotionally antagonistic, judges sometimes are asked to establish the specific custody changes on each vacation or holiday and to otherwise resolve normal parenting issues. The hiring of lawyers to dispute child custody issues further depletes the family funds available for the children. When one parent moves far away, the children necessarily lose the stability of a two-parent family. The emotional costs to the children and parents, as well as the financial costs, can be ruinous. Judges cannot be expected to solve all parenting issues by court orders. The toll upon children from marriages gone wrong cannot be measured or cured by the application of family law. Simply stated, children are not best served when joint custody is awarded to parents who continue their bitterness and disagreements after the divorce. In keeping with this experience, many states now have neither a preference nor a presumption for joint custody awards. The key to effective joint custody is joint cooperation between the parents.

Virtually everyone agrees that a mutually acceptable custody and visitation arrangement is the best method of minimizing the traumatic experience of divorce upon children. One method of achieving agreement is through mediation. Recall that mediation uses a professional, neutral third party who attempts to assist in the reconciliation of opposing views. Often, mediation is the only way divorcing parents can reach agreements. Studies indicate that children of mediated divorces appear to adjust better and their parents appear to retain less hostility. Indeed, many states require mediation proceedings whenever child custody is disputed. One concern about mandated mediation programs is that husband and wife may not have equal bargaining power, and one may give away some rights in reaching an agreement. This inequality may be especially significant in a forum in which full disclosure of financial matters is not enforced as rigorously as it is in court proceedings, where formal discovery procedures are available.

All rational attempts to base custody fairly in the best interests of the child are made difficult, if not impossible, when false charges of child abuse are made by one parent, or the child, against the other parent (usually the father). The false charging of child abuse is referred to as the Parental Alienation Syndrome (or PAS). Of course, false charges can be made by a husband against a wife as well.

Child Support

In addition to custody orders, the court granting a divorce must make orders providing for the future support of the minor children. Statutory guidelines for setting the appropriate amount of child support presently exist in most states as a result of the federal Family Support Act. State statutes typically consider the following factors:

- Child's necessities
- Parent's standard of living and circumstances
- Financial status of the parents
- Earning capacity of each parent
- Future educational plans of the child
- Child's age
- Earning ability and fiscal resources of the child
- Duty of each parent to support other people
- Value of care given by the custodial parent

States also frequently take into consideration the need for and cost of day care. Most of the criteria listed relate to finances—but the legal obligation of support cannot exceed the financial capacity of the parent to pay it. One criterion listed credits the custodial parent with the monetary value of the care that parent gives. Would the value of that care be greater if the custodial parent—if a woman—were a "homemaker" mom or a "career" mom? What is the monetary value of daily love and affection? These examples of questions, and others that may occur to you, help explain the variable degree of subjectivity underlying support awards.

Original support orders can be modified by petition to the court when circumstances change. A frequent argument is that remarriage constitutes a significant change in circumstance. Allocation of the earnings of an ex-spouse between a former family and a second-marriage family can be a sensitive issue. Traditionally, the common law position has been that children should not be made to suffer from the existence of a new family in their father's (or mother's) life. The modern view is contrary: Remarriage or a change in career may constitute a changed circumstance sufficient to justify a reduction in child support payments. Sometimes, a new career will offer lower wages (necessitating a reduction in child support) in exchange for higher potential earnings in the future.

Collection of child support payments is far more difficult than ordering them. When the parent who is delinquent in making child support payments (the obligor) resides in the same state as the child, the custodial parent has several options: Legal procedures (often called the *levy of a writ of execution*) permit the delinquent parent's assets to be taken, including bank accounts and real property. Certain portions of the debtor's assets, however, are exempt from execution and cannot be taken. Legal procedures necessary to obtain relief by writ of execution can become so complex as to be ineffective, especially when the debtor does not have substantial assets. If the delinquent parent is employed, a wage assignment is an alternative. Under this legal mechanism, a portion of the parent's wages is withheld from weekly or monthly earnings and is forwarded to the custodial parent.

A judgment ordering the payment of child support also can be enforced by contempt proceedings when the failure to support is willful. Theoretically, an obligor who has the ability to pay the ordered child support but purposefully fails to do so can be jailed for contempt, that is, for violating the court's order. Courts, however, are reluctant to jail an employable parent. Jail precludes employment and contributes to an already crowded correction system. On the other hand, the threat of jail, or a short sentence for contempt of court, may act as a catalyst in encouraging a delinquent obligor to make the required child support payments.

When the parent who is delinquent in making child support payments resides out of state, another difficult problem exists. How can the custodial parent enforce the payment of child support by a former spouse who resides in another state? To alleviate this problem, all states have adopted the Uniform Child Custody Jurisdiction and Enforcement Act. This law streamlines procedures and closes loopholes that had evolved under prior law. Under the uniform law, the prosecutor in the local state (residence of the custodial parent) initiates a formal legal proceeding in the foreign state (residence of the delinquent obligor), which will be prosecuted in the foreign state by its local prosecutor. The court in the foreign state enters a support order and enforces it under local laws (including the issuance of a writ of execution or contempt of court proceedings, if appropriate). Monies collected in the foreign state are forwarded to the custodial parent.

If the failure to make support payments is a crime, the foreign court can extradite (return) the delinquent obligor to the local state for criminal prosecution. The Child Support Recovery Act of 1992 made the willful failure to pay child support for more than one year a federal crime. The elements of the offense are that the defendant (1) has the ability to pay, (2) willfully fails to pay, (3) known past-due (child) support obligations, (4) which have remained unpaid for longer than one year or total more than $5,000, (5) for a child who resides in another state. This remedial legislation also created the National Commission on Child and Family Welfare, which has many enumerated duties related to child custody, visitation, and domestic violence.

When court-ordered child support payments become delinquent, they do not disappear; rather, they accumulate and may be collected at any time in the future, in the same manner that other money judgments are collected, such as by levy of writ of execution to take assets or portions of the debtor's wages. Accumulated child support liabilities are not discharged (eliminated) if the delinquent father successfully petitions for bankruptcy either.

Even with existing legal remedies that are available to enforce child support (and alimony) payments, collection remains a serious problem in most states. It is widely acknowledged that custodial parents generally receive inadequate child support regardless of court orders.

HOW MAY FAMILY LAW BE MODIFIED BY CONTRACT?

Premarital Agreements

antenuptial, premarital, or prenuptial agreement
A binding contract whereby two persons who are contemplating marriage specify certain future mutual rights and obligations as marriage partners.

A marital contract made before marriage is called an **antenuptial, premarital, or prenuptial agreement**. This type of agreement should be in writing to facilitate enforcement, and some states require that it be witnessed by a third person or notary public. Such contracts are increasingly popular as more and more persons prudently seek to establish and fix, before their nuptials, property division or support payments in the event that the marriage ends in divorce. Especially when either spouse has a disproportionately large estate of separate property, the premarital agreement can help to resolve future potential misunderstandings without costly litigation.

In response to this need, all states recognize premarital agreements. Approximately half of the states have adopted some version of the 1983 Uniform Premarital Agreement Act. Theoretically, premarital agreements can deal with (1) property and support rights during and after marriage; (2) the personal rights and obligations of the spouses during marriage; or (3) the education, care, and rearing of children. But the most common subjects of marital agreements are property divisions and support rights upon death or divorce.

In most states, upon death of a spouse, the surviving spouse has an elective right to choose between inheriting under the decedent's will or rejecting the inheritance and taking instead a portion of the decedent's estate as provided for by statute. Premarital agreements may alter this option. On the other hand, this "elective" choice is not available in community property states because the surviving spouse is protected through ownership of one-half of the community property. But this community property ownership interest also can be altered by premarital agreement. Even states that do not permit contracts that alter the incidents of divorce do permit contracts that alter property distributions upon death of one spouse.

Upon divorce, premarital agreements can alter court determinations concerning both property division and continuing support (alimony or maintenance). However, prenuptial agreements are void, as a matter of law, to the extent that they adversely affect the rights of minor children. Agreements affecting custody, care, or education of minor children can be valid but are subject to approval by the court. The court will void agreements if they adversely affect the children's best interests. Although about one-half of the states authorize premarital agreements that alter the legal incidents of divorce, some will not enforce agreements affecting support (alimony, maintenance, or child support).

LEGAL FOCUS—PROBLEM

Arlene Van Zandt, a talented and promising young actress, had received her first multimillion-dollar contract to perform the lead in a major movie production. She also was contemplating marriage to Bud Waleska, her off-again, on-again childhood sweetheart, who was a professional boxer with a low earning potential. Van Zandt decided to confer with an attorney concerning preparation of a premarital agreement. What might such a contract accomplish?

If Van Zandt and Waleska lived in a community property state and did not have a premarital agreement, Waleska would become the "owner" of one-half of Van Zandt's earnings after the marriage and would be entitled to his one-half of all community property acquired with her earnings upon any future divorce. The divorce court could not alter. A contract, on the other hand, could provide that all of Van Zandt's earnings would remain her separate property, and that upon divorce Waleska would be entitled to a cash payment of, say, $100,000. In an "equitable distribution" state, the court would allocate Van Zandt's earnings based on the factors discussed earlier in this chapter. But Van Zandt and Waleska also could agree in equitable distribution states that $100,000 would be distributed to Waleska upon any future divorce—and that would resolve the issue. In some states, Van Zandt and Waleska could agree that, upon any divorce, Van Zandt would pay alimony to Waleska in some specified amount for some specified time. Courts, however, would not enforce such a promise that attempted to set support payments unless it was fair under all the circumstances. An agreement would not be necessary relative to distribution of assets upon Van Zandt's unexpected death.

LEGAL FOCUS—CASE

She met him in Montreal in the summer of 1987. The meeting led to telephone calls and a fall visit and a later move to his Phoenix home before marriage in February 1988. The day before the Las Vegas marriage, both signed a premarital agreement stating in part that "all the earnings and accumulations resulting from the other's personal services, skill, efforts and work, together with all property acquired with funds and income derived therefrom, shall be the separate property of that spouse." In the property settlement portion of a dissolution action against baseball megastar Barry Bonds, Susann (Sun) Bonds sought to have the agreement set aside arguing it was unfair, she did not understand it when she signed it, and she was not represented by counsel. Was her argument a home run?

In re Marriage of Bonds, 24 Cal.4th 1, 5 P.3d 815, 99 Cal.Rptr. 2d 252 (Calif. 2000).

Like most baseball pitchers, a unanimous California Supreme Court gave Mr. Bonds a free pass in its interpretation of the Uniform Premarital Agreement Act. The court held that "although persons, once they are married, are in a fiduciary relationship to one another," the same confidential relationship does not exist before marriage. As to the fairness of the agreement, the court concluded that substantial evidence existed that Sun Bonds voluntarily signed the agreement and that she had ample opportunity to get independent legal advice, and that it was her duty to protect her own interests. Prenuptial agreements can be updated during the marriage to reflect the desires of the spouses as their circumstances change from time to time, but during the marriage, a fiduciary responsibility exists that raises fairness issues that would not have existed before the marriage.

As distinguished from prenuptial agreements, contracts made during marriage are called simply *marital contracts*, or *separation agreements* if they are entered while contemplating a forthcoming divorce. Marital contracts are intended to resolve the same sorts of future problems as premarital agreements and receive comparable enforcement by the courts.

Contracts signed immediately before the marriage ceremony may be voided by the court, but like the *Bonds* case, they also may be enforced. Courts will not enforce marital contracts of any kind that they conclude are unconscionable (unjust, unfair, or excessive).

Preceding marriage, there often is unequal bargaining power between the prospective spouses, and persons may overreach (take unfair advantage). A premarital contract prepared by the attorney of only one party should at least be reviewed and approved by counsel of the other party before signing. Legal representation minimizes the possibility of unfair overreaching and a possible subsequent declaration of invalidity by a court. This safeguard also increases the likelihood that all assets will be disclosed and taken into consideration before the contract is signed.

LEGAL FOCUS—PROBLEM

Sara was married to Sean, a multimillionaire, for about five years. Prior to the marriage, she signed a premarital agreement that awarded her a substantial though relatively modest amount in comparison to his net worth. The marriage produced two children, but the relationship became strained. Police were called to the marital home several times in response to allegations of domestic violence by Sara. Sara wants to file for divorce but is concerned about her financial support should the marriage end. Should substantiated allegations of domestic violence influence the decision to enforce the premarital agreement?

In addition to the terms of the agreement, spousal abuse is certainly a factor that should be considered in determining whether or not enforcement of the premarital agreement is unconscionable; in such circumstances, staying in the marriage may not be an option. Also, because there is a public policy against divorce, courts will not enforce premarital agreements that are unconscionable or that promote divorce. A premarital agreement drafted so as to absolve a breadwinner from all obligations after divorce, no doubt, would be declared unconscionable and therefore unenforceable. But note that in recent years at least a few cases have upheld premarital contracts that have waived a spouse's right to spousal support if a divorce occurs. As a general rule, courts are more likely to enforce premarital agreements that affect property rights than those that affect support rights.

Separation Agreements

As noted previously, a marital contract made during marriage, but when a divorce or dissolution is contemplated or is occurring, is called a *separation agreement.* These agreements are enforceable if each spouse fully discloses to the other spouse all financial information and if its provisions are not unconscionable. Public policy favors private settlement of disputes, and courts usually will approve separation agreements as a part of the divorce proceedings. Parties to separation agreements should obtain legal counsel before signing because ramifications of such contracts are not readily apparent to, or understood by, a layperson. For example, will payments from one spouse be taxable income to the other? Will agreed-upon support payments be subject to future modification by the court in case of changed circumstances (e.g., an unanticipated disability)? What would be the effect of a bankruptcy on the contractual obligations? Will the support provisions be enforceable by contempt powers of the court? What effect will a subsequent marriage of either spouse have upon the earlier separation agreement? The answers to these questions, as well as many others, may differ based on the needs and desires of the separating spouses and the law of the particular state. Accordingly, couples usually require the services of a qualified attorney to achieve results that are fair to both parties.

Cohabitation Agreements

Unmarried persons who live together as husband and wife may desire to protect their respective financial interests by entering into a *cohabitation agreement.* The first obstacle facing such a couple is the longstanding refusal of courts to enforce any contract purporting to exchange property for sexual favors.

LEGAL FOCUS—CASE

Mary Mullen orally agreed to "quit her job and be available to travel" in exchange for a man's promise to "take care of her for the rest of her life." Is the agreement enforceable?

Mullen v. Suchko, 279 Pa. Super. 499, 421 A.2d 310 (Penn. 1980).

Yes, the agreement is enforceable because the contract services do not necessarily include sexual favors. In a few states, such as New York, an agreement for a lifetime of support requires a writing. In still other states, the contract could be interpreted as including sexual favors and therefore violates public policy.

LEGAL FOCUS—CASE

Michele, aged twenty, orally promised to "account to" Charles, eighty years of age, "all of her waking moments; to be at his beck and call as he should desire," for which services he would pay her $1,000 a month for the rest of her life. Is this contract enforceable?

Rubenstein v. Kleven, 261 F.2d 921 (1st Cir. 1958).

This contract would not be enforceable in most states because it implies compensation in exchange for sexual favors, in violation of public policy. Public policy will not condone a contract that impliedly calls for the exchange of sexual favors.

The preceding examples demonstrate the difficulties in establishing consistent laws for the enforcement of cohabitation agreements. Cohabitation agreements that do not contemplate the exchange of property for sexual favors are enforceable in most states, whether express (written or oral) or implied. You may recall the case involving Michelle Triola and Lee Marvin from earlier in this chapter. The court was willing to enforce even an oral agreement concerning financial support. But Triola was unable to produce any evidence of such an agreement.

To increase the probability of enforcement of such an agreement, the parties would be well advised to obtain legal counsel for each person, fully disclose their respective financial resources, provide for a reasonable distribution of their properties upon any future parting of their ways, and express it all in writing.

CASE

Johnson v. State of Florida

602 So. 2d 1288 (1992)

Jennifer Johnson gave birth to a boy whose urine contained benzoylecgonine, a breakdown product of cocaine. Fifteen months later, Jennifer gave birth to a girl who also tested positive for a cocaine derivative in her urine. Florida has a statute that states: "it is unlawful for any person 18 years of age or older to deliver any controlled substance to a person under the age of 18 years.... Any person who violates this provision ... is guilty of a felony in the first degree." Johnson was convicted on two counts of delivering a controlled substance to her children. The theory of the prosecution was that Jennifer Johnson "delivered" cocaine to her two children via blood flowing through the children's umbilical cords in the 60- to 90-second period after they were expelled from her birth canal but before their umbilical cords were severed. Johnson could not be prosecuted for giving birth to a drug-dependent child because that is not a crime in Florida. Nor does Florida have a criminal statute prohibiting in utero transfers of controlled substances. Johnson's convictions were appealed to the Florida Supreme Court.

Opinion of the Court

Justice Harding delivered the opinion of the Court.... There can be no doubt that drug abuse is one of the most serious problems confronting our society today.... Of particular concern is the alarming rise in the number of babies born with cocaine in their systems as a result of cocaine use by pregnant women. Some experts estimate that as many as eleven percent of pregnant women have used an illegal drug during pregnancy, and of those women, seventy-five percent have used cocaine. Report of the American Medical Association Board of Trustees, Legal Interventions During Pregnancy, 264 *Journal of the American Medical Association* 2663 (Nov. 28, 1990). Others estimate that 375,000 newborns per year are born to women who are users of illicit drugs. American Public Health Association 1990 Policy Statement. It is well-established that the effects of cocaine use by a pregnant woman on her fetus and later on her newborn can be severe. On average, cocaine-exposed babies have lower birth weights, shorter body lengths at birth, and smaller head circumferences than normal infants. 264 *Journal of the American Medical Association* 2666 (Nov. 28, 1990). Cocaine use may also result in sudden infant death syndrome, neural-behavioral deficiencies as well as other medical problems and long-term developmental abnormalities. American Public Health Association 1990 Policy Statement.

The basic problem of damaging the fetus by drug use during pregnancy should not be addressed piecemeal, however, by prosecuting users who deliver their babies close in time to use of drugs and ignoring those who simply use drugs during their pregnancy. Florida could possibly have elected to make in utero transfers criminal. But it chose to deal with this problem in other ways. One way is to allow evidence of drug use by women as a ground for removal of the child to the custody of protective services, as was done in this case....

At Johnson's trial, Dr. Tompkins testified that a mother's blood passes nutrients, oxygen and chemicals to an unborn child by a diffusion exchange at the capillary level from the womb to the placenta. The umbilical cord then circulates the baby's blood (including the exchange from its mother) between the placenta and the child. Metabolized cocaine derivatives in the mother's blood thus diffuse from the womb to the placenta, and then reach the baby through its umbilical cord. Although the blood flow is somewhat restricted during the birthing process, a measurable amount of blood is transferred from the placenta to the baby through the umbilical cord during delivery and after birth.... Dr. Stephen Kandall, a neonatologist, testified for the defense ... that it is theoretically possible that cocaine or other substances can pass between a mother and her baby during the thirty-to-sixty second period after the child is born and before the umbilical cord is cut, but that the amount would be tiny.

... [I]n my view, the primary question in this case is whether [the statute] was intended by the Legislature to apply to the birthing process. Before Johnson can be prosecuted under this statute, it must be clear that the Legislature intended for it to apply to the delivery of cocaine derivatives to a newborn during a sixty-to-ninety second interval, before severance of the umbilical cord. I can find no case where "delivery" of a drug was based on an involuntary act such as diffusion and blood flow.... My review ... leads me to conclude in this case that the Legislature expressly chose to treat the problem as a public health problem and that it considered but rejected imposing criminal sanctions....

... The California Medical Association has noted: While unhealthy behavior cannot be condoned, to bring criminal charges against a pregnant woman for activities which may be harmful to her fetus is inappropriate. Such prosecution is counterproductive to the public interest as it may discourage a woman from seeking prenatal care or dissuade her from providing accurate information to health care providers out of fear of self-incrimination.

The conviction of Jennifer Johnson was reversed.

Not all state courts agree with the Florida Supreme Court. In 1992, Cornelia Whitner was sentenced to eight years in jail after her baby was born with traces of cocaine in its system. The South Carolina courts relied on a statute prohibiting child "endangerment." Other states rely upon drug laws, charging that women were delivering drugs through the umbilical cords, as in the Johnson case. The South Carolina Supreme Court ruled that a viable fetus is a person under the meaning of the child abuse law—thus a child had been endangered.

For Critical Analysis

1. What are the pros and cons of the position that a woman has either (or both) a natural law right or a right of privacy under the U.S. Constitution to control her body as she pleases both before and during her pregnancy?
2. If a theory of criminality in a proposed law is to be based on a child abuse statute, how would you define the term "criminal abuse"? For example, would you include smoking, abusive smoking, or prolonged exposure to secondhand smoke during pregnancy? Of accepting employment that meant standing at an assembly line for eight hours each workday? Of neglecting to obtain prenatal care? Of getting drunk?
3. If a theory of criminality in a proposed statute is to be based on a statute prohibiting the supplying of illegal drugs, how would you describe the extent of drug use that constitutes the crime? Would you include the occasional use of marijuana? Of cocaine? Of a misused prescription drug? Or would you reserve the determination until the newborn baby's blood could be tested? If so, would that be gambling with the health of the child?

Perry et al. v. Schwarzenegger

704 F.Supp.2d 921 (2010) United States District Court for the Northern District of California

Kristin Perry and Sandra Stier, two women in a relationship and raising four children, were denied a marriage license. Perry and Stier and another same-sex couple challenged Proposition 8, a November 2008 voter-enacted amendment to the California Constitution that provided "Only marriage between a man and a woman is valid or recognized in California." The plaintiffs alleged that Proposition 8 deprived them of due process and of equal protection of the laws contrary to the Fourteenth Amendment because it prevented them from getting married and enjoying the benefits of marriage. The California Supreme Court upheld the proposition and the plaintiffs appealed to Federal Court.

Decision of the Court

The Due Process Clause provides that no "State shall deprive any person of life, liberty, or property, without due process of law." Plaintiffs contend that the freedom to marry the person of one's choice is a fundamental right protected by the *Due Process Clause* and that Proposition 8 violates this fundamental right because it prevents each plaintiff from marrying the person of his or her choice.

The Equal Protection Clause provides that no state shall "deny to any person within its jurisdiction the equal protection of the laws." According to plaintiffs, Proposition 8 violates the Equal Protection Clause because it discriminates against gay men and lesbians by denying them a right to marry the person of their choice whereas heterosexual men and women may do so freely.

Plaintiffs argue that Proposition 8 should be subjected to heightened scrutiny under the Equal Protection Clause because gays and lesbians constitute a suspect class. Plaintiffs further contend that Proposition 8 is irrational because it singles out gays and lesbians for unequal treatment, as they and they alone may not marry the person of their choice.

Proponents' Defense of Proposition 8

The ballot argument submitted to the voters summarizes proponents' arguments in favor of Proposition 8 during the 2008 campaign. The argument states: "Proposition 8 is simple and straightforward. Proposition 8 is about preserving marriage; it's not an attack on the gay lifestyle. It protects our children from being taught in public schools that 'same-sex marriage' is the same as traditional marriage."

Proponents abandoned previous arguments from the campaign that had asserted the moral superiority of opposite-sex couples. Instead, in this litigation, proponents asserted that Proposition 8:

1. Maintains California's definition of marriage as excluding same-sex couples;
2. Affirms the will of California citizens to exclude same-sex couples from marriage;
3. Promotes stability in relationships between a man and a woman because they naturally (and at times unintentionally) produce children; and
4. Promotes "statistically optimal" child-rearing households; that is, households in which children are raised by a man and a woman married to each other.

Proponents argued that Proposition 8 should be evaluated solely by considering its language and its consistency with the "central purpose of marriage, in California and everywhere else to promote naturally procreative sexual relationships and to channel them into stable, enduring unions for the sake of producing and raising the next generation.

Proponents' procreation argument, is as follows: the state has an interest in encouraging sexual activity between people of the opposite sex to occur in stable marriages because such sexual activity may lead to pregnancy and children, and the state has an interest in encouraging parents to raise children in stable households. The state therefore, the argument goes, has an interest in encouraging all opposite-sex sexual activity, whether responsible or irresponsible, procreative or otherwise, to occur within a stable marriage, as this encourages the development of a social norm that opposite-sex sexual activity should occur within marriage.

The freedom to marry is recognized as a fundamental right protected by the Due Process Clause. The parties do not dispute that the right to marry is fundamental. The question presented here is whether plaintiffs seek to exercise the fundamental right to marry; or, because they are couples of the same sex, whether they seek recognition of a new right.

To determine whether a right is fundamental under the Due Process Clause, the court inquires into whether the right is rooted in our nation's history, legal traditions, and practices. Here, because the right to marry is fundamental, the court looks to the evidence presented at trial to determine: (1) the history, tradition and practice of marriage in the United States; and (2) whether plaintiffs seek to exercise their right to marry or seek to exercise some other right.

Race restrictions on marital partners were once common in most states but are now seen as archaic, shameful or even bizarre. When the Supreme Court invalidated race restrictions in *Loving*, the definition of the right to marry did not change. *388 US at 12.* Instead, the Court recognized that race restrictions, despite their historical prevalence, stood in stark contrast to the concepts of liberty and choice inherent in the right to marry.

The marital bargain in California traditionally required that a woman's legal and economic identity be subsumed by her husband's upon marriage under the doctrine of coverture; this once-unquestioned aspect of marriage now is regarded as antithetical to the notion of marriage as a union of equals. As states moved to recognize the equality of the sexes, they eliminated laws and practices like coverture that had made gender a proxy for a spouse's role within a marriage. Marriage was thus transformed from a male-dominated institution into an institution recognizing men and women as equals. Id. Yet, individuals retained the right to marry; that right did not become different simply because the institution of marriage became compatible with gender equality.

The evidence at trial shows that marriage in the United States traditionally has not been open to same-sex couples. The evidence suggests many reasons for this tradition of exclusion, including gender roles mandated through coverture, social disapproval of same-sex relationships, and the reality that the vast majority of people are heterosexual and have had no reason to challenge the restriction. That time has passed.

Plaintiffs do not seek recognition of a new right. Rather, plaintiffs ask California to recognize their relationships for what they are: marriages.

Because plaintiffs seek to exercise their fundamental right to marry, their claim is subject to strict scrutiny.

Under strict scrutiny, the state bears the burden of producing evidence to show that Proposition 8 is narrowly tailored to a compelling government interest.

Proposition 8 cannot withstand rational basis review. Still less can Proposition 8 survive the strict scrutiny required by plaintiffs' due process claim. The minimal evidentiary presentation made by proponents does not meet the heavy burden of production necessary to show that Proposition 8 is narrowly tailored to a compelling government interest. Accordingly, Proposition 8 violates the Due Process Clause of the Fourteenth Amendment.

Equal Protection

The Equal Protection Clause of the Fourteenth Amendment provides that no state shall deny to any person within its jurisdiction the equal protection of the laws. The guarantee of equal protection coexists, of course, with the reality that most legislation must classify for some purpose or another. When a law creates a classification but neither targets a suspect class nor burdens a fundamental right, the court presumes the law is valid and will uphold it as long as it is rationally related to some legitimate government interest.

Plaintiffs challenge Proposition 8 as violating the *Equal Protection Clause* because Proposition 8 discriminates both on the basis of sex and on the basis of sexual orientation. Sexual orientation discrimination can take the form of sex discrimination. Here, for example, Perry is prohibited from marrying Stier, a woman, because Perry is a woman. If Perry were a man, Proposition 8 would not prohibit the marriage. Thus, Proposition 8 operates to restrict Perry's choice of marital partner because of her sex. But Proposition 8 also operates to restrict Perry's choice of marital partner because of her sexual orientation; her desire to marry another woman arises only because she is a lesbian.

The evidence at trial shows that gays and lesbians experience discrimination based on unfounded stereotypes and prejudices specific to sexual orientation. Gays and lesbians have historically been targeted for discrimination because of their sexual orientation; that discrimination continues to the present. Sexual orientation discrimination is thus a phenomenon distinct from, but related to, sex discrimination.

Strict scrutiny is the appropriate standard of review to apply to legislative classifications based on sexual orientation. All classifications based on sexual orientation appear suspect, as the evidence shows that California would rarely, if ever, have a reason to categorize individuals based on their sexual orientation. Here, however, strict scrutiny is unnecessary. Proposition 8 fails to survive even rational basis review.

Proposition 8 cannot withstand any level of scrutiny under the Equal Protection Clause, as excluding same-sex couples from marriage is simply not rationally related to a legitimate state interest. One example of a legitimate state interest in not issuing marriage licenses to a particular group might be a scarcity of marriage licenses or county officials to issue them. But marriage licenses in California are not a limited commodity, and the existence of 18,000 same-sex married couples in California shows that the state has the resources to allow both same-sex and opposite-sex couples to wed.

A Private Moral View That Same-Sex Couples are Inferior to Opposite-Sex Couples is not a Proper Basis for Legislation

In the absence of a rational basis, what remains of proponents' case is an inference that Proposition 8 was premised on the belief that same-sex couples simply are not as good as opposite-sex couples. Whether that belief is based on moral disapproval of homosexuality, animus toward gays and lesbians or simply a belief that a relationship between a man and a woman is inherently better than a relationship between two men or two women, this belief is not a proper basis on which to legislate. The constitution cannot control private biases but neither can it tolerate them.

Moral disapproval alone is an improper basis on which to deny rights to gay men and lesbians. The evidence shows conclusively that Proposition 8 enacts, without reason, a private moral view that same-sex couples are inferior to opposite-sex couples. Because Proposition 8 disadvantages gays and lesbians without any rational justification, Proposition 8 violates the Equal Protection Clause of the Fourteenth Amendment.

Proposition 8 fails to advance any rational basis in singling out gay men and lesbians for denial of a marriage license. Indeed, the evidence shows Proposition 8 does nothing more than enshrine in the California Constitution the notion that opposite sex couples are superior to same-sex couples. Because California has no interest in discriminating against gay men and lesbians, and because Proposition 8 prevents California from fulfilling its constitutional obligation to provide marriages on an equal basis, the court concludes that Proposition 8 is unconstitutional.

Plaintiffs have demonstrated by overwhelming evidence that Proposition 8 violates their due process and equal protection rights and that they will continue to suffer these constitutional violations until state officials cease enforcement of

Proposition 8. California is able to issue marriage licenses to same-sex couples, as it has already issued 18,000 marriage licenses to same-sex couples and has not suffered any demonstrated harm as a result; more over, California officials have chosen not to defend Proposition 8 in these proceedings.

Because Proposition 8 is unconstitutional under both the Due Process and Equal Protection Clauses, the court orders entry of judgment permanently enjoining its enforcement; prohibiting the official defendants from applying or enforcing Proposition 8 and directing the official defendants that all persons under their control or supervision shall not apply or enforce Proposition 8.

IT IS SO ORDERED.
/s/ Vaughn R Walker
VAUGHN R WALKER
United States District Chief Judge

For Critical Analysis

1. The court took a strong position that Proposition 8 could not survive even a rational basis test but then went on to evaluate it under strict scrutiny. Can you distinguish the difference between these two standards in this case?
2. Does this case depend on the conclusion that gays and lesbians are members of a suspect class that government must protect?
3. Judge Walker compared the treatment of homosexuals under Proposition 8 to the historical treatment of women in marriage and on interracial couples under interracial marriage bans. Do you agree with those comparisons? Did the court make those comparisons in order to determine the purpose behind Proposition 8? Or was it for a different reason?

CHAPTER QUESTIONS AND PROBLEMS

1. Family law is in a state of change because of rapidly evolving social patterns. For example, there is an emergence of "informal marriage" (cohabitation with express or implied contract) alongside formal marriage (ceremonial or statutory). The domestic partnerships of homosexual couples also are a variety of "informal marriage." Both varieties of relationships, formal and informal marriage, often are terminated by choice, creating special legal consequences. Although you probably have not studied all of the implications that can flow from marriage, from your generalized knowledge, try to compare the implications of both types of relationships (formal marriage and cohabitation) on the following criteria:
   a. Federal and state income taxes
   b. Selection and use of surname
   c. Child support obligations
   d. Credit extension
   e. Expense of creating or ending the relationship
   f. Mutual support obligations
   g. Vicarious tort liability
   h. Recovery for lost consortium, or wrongful death
   i. Privilege not to testify against one another
   j. Immunities for sex crimes between spouses
   k. Division of assets upon death or termination of relationship
   l. Inheritance rights, absent a will
   m. Costs and coverage of health or life insurance
   n. Social Security benefits
   o. Privacy in business matters upon termination of marriage
   p. Workers' compensation benefits
   q. Care for a dying loved one
2. It has been said that divorce is "the great American tragedy." Among measures suggested to reduce the divorce rate are higher age requirements for marriage, computerized analysis of personalities and backgrounds of prospective spouses, longer mandatory waiting periods after a marriage license is obtained, mandatory "marriage license training" (including instruction in the financial, social, psychological, and sexual aspects of marriage), trial marriage for a probationary period, and government day care centers for infants and preschool children to free mothers from the burdens of child care. What do you think should be done, if anything?
3. Which of the following promises are enforceable if contained in a premarital agreement?
   a. Wife waives any claim for support upon any future divorce
   b. Husband agrees to raise children in a specified religion.
   c. Both agree to a specified variety of sexual activities with a specified frequency.
   d. Husband agrees to transfer certain valuable property to wife immediately upon marriage.
   e. Wife agrees that husband may have custody of the children, if any, upon any future divorce.

4. What legal rights accrue in your state to an unmarried woman who lives with a man for thirteen years "as husband and wife" who then is abandoned? Does it make any difference if she had received an oral promise of future support? What if they had a child? You may either refer to a legal encyclopedia in your library or surf the web. In either case, search under the subject index of "cohabitation," "same-sex marriage," and "domestic partnerships."
5. Does someone have a legal right to know that she is not genetically related to her father because her mother's egg was fertilized *in vitro* at a sperm bank? Should someone have a legal right to know the name of his genetic parent? Do you apply the same rationale to donors who someday want desperately to find their genetic children, perhaps to leave them millions of dollars?
6. What legal problems can you think of that might arise if a surrogate mother changed her mind immediately following birth and refused to release her child to the natural father, as she had contracted to do? For example, what if she moved to another state and assumed a new identity and life—would she be guilty of child-snatching (kidnapping by a relative) or only be responsible for breach of contract? Would your answer change if the surrogate mother was genetically related to the child (via her egg with *in vitro* fertilization)? Do any legal problems come to mind if a surrogate mother aborts the contracting parties' fetus?
7. Sharon Bottoms and April Wade were living together in a lesbian relationship. Sharon's mother, Kay, sought court-ordered custody of Sharon's two-year-old son, Tyler, on the grounds that Bottoms's relationship with Wade made her an unfit mother. What should be the result? Are children raised in a homosexual family thereby disadvantaged in some way?
8. Suppose that John and Mary Powers arrange to have their fertilized egg, or preembryo, frozen for future use. Suppose John is killed in an airplane crash. Should Mary have the legal right to bring the preembryo to birth? To hire a surrogate mother for that purpose? To have genetic surgery performed upon it to change its future behavioral characteristics? To donate it to gene research? To donate it to another couple? What should be the rights of the genetic donors to custody of a preembryo?
9. If one spouse puts the other spouse through medical school by working and by delaying his own formal education, and if divorce occurs soon after the doctor completes residency, how might a court's judgment take these factors into consideration? What difference would it make if divorce occurs before the medical license is obtained?
10. Should divorcing spouses be permitted to bring tort actions against each other for precisely the same conduct that would entitle strangers to sue each other? Can you think of any conduct between spouses that arguably should not justify a domestic tort? Should the same rules of liability between spouses be interpreted to include liability between parents and their children?
11. In 1958, Mildred Jeter, a black woman, and Richard Loving, a white man, both residents of Virginia, were married in the District of Columbia. When they returned home to Virginia, they were prosecuted and convicted of violating Virginia's statute prohibiting interracial marriages (miscegenation). The Lovings were sentenced to a one-year jail term, which would be suspended if they agreed to leave Virginia for a twenty-five-year period. (The statute was subsequently held to be unconstitutional. *Loving v. Virginia*, 388 U.S. 1 (1967)). Today, more than fifty years later, interracial marriages are not unusual and are accepted by society. Do you think that gay marriage in fifty years will be accepted by society and that laws prohibiting such unions will no longer exist either? Why or why not? Constitutionally, why are statutes banning interracial marriages and homosexual marriages evaluated differently?
12. The Indian Child Welfare Act was passed by Congress in 1978 in response to a finding that a high number of Native American children were removed from their homes and placed outside the tribal community. The statute provides that preference be given, in the absence of good cause to the contrary, to an adoptive placement with (1) a member of the child's extended family, (2) other members of the Indian child's tribe, or (3) other Indian families. In 2009, a South Carolina couple adopted a baby from her unwed biological mother, who was not Native American. The biological mother chose the couple to adopt her daughter and signed papers in which she renounced her parental rights. The baby's father, who was serving in the military four hours away, agreed to surrender his parental rights by text

message. Upon learning of the adoption, he changed his mind, claiming that he thought he was surrendering his rights to the biological mother, not to an adoptive couple. Should he be able to veto the adoption if he previously failed to support the child and her mother? Is the statutory preference a legitimate substitute for the traditional "best interest of the child" inquiry? *Couple v. Baby Girl*, 186 L. Ed. 2d 729 (2013), *rev'g* 398 S.C. 625, 731 S.E. 2d 550 (2012).

13. Pat Price, Sean's spouse, charges several purchases that remain unpaid. Creditors seek payment from Sean's separate property. Is Sean liable? Does it make any difference if the charges are for necessities?

CHAPTER 15

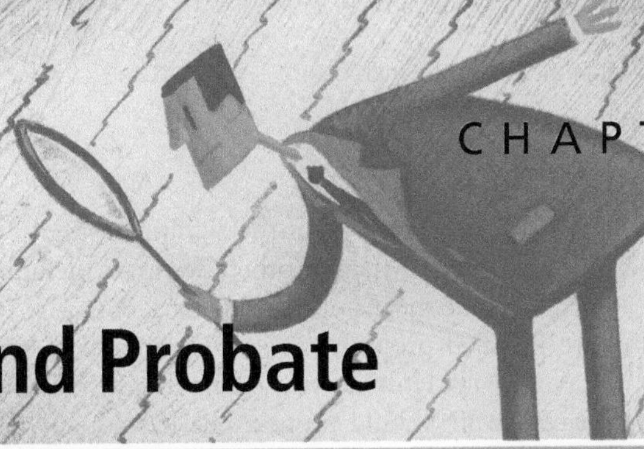

Wills, Trusts, and Probate

In youth my wings were strong and tireless, But I did not know the mountains. In age I knew the mountains, But my weary wings could not follow my vision—Genius is wisdom and youth.

"Headstone of Alexander Throckmorton," *Spoon River Anthology* (Edgar Lee Masters, 1864–1950)

LEARNING OBJECTIVES

After reading and studying this chapter, you should be able to:

- Define estate planning and describe the major concerns in planning an estate.
- Identify the major taxes and expenses that accompany transfers of property by gift or death.
- Identify the requisites of and the different types of valid wills. Understand the reasons why a person creates a will.
- Describe challenges that can be made to a will.
- Understand probate and describe its positive and negative aspects.
- Explain how property is distributed if a person dies without a valid will.
- Describe advance directives, living wills, directives to physicians, and durable powers of attorney for health care.
- Discuss the legal concepts of suicide and euthanasia and understand the moral debate over end-of-life issues.
- Identify the legal requisites of different types of trusts, including living trusts.
- Describe the use of conservatorship and guardianship.

Unfortunately, not all of the significant events in our lives are pleasant. Death will come to family members and others we love, including ourselves. But life goes on, and the law provides the means of assuring survivors that important financial matters of the deceased are handled properly. Are you prepared to share in these responsibilities? Who should have a will? How do you create a will? Do you need the services of an attorney to prepare a will? Should property be left equally, share and share alike, to heirs? When is a trust helpful in preparing for the financial aftermath of death? Is an attorney needed when a family member dies? Under what circumstances can a will be contested? How are family assets taxed when death occurs? What is a living will? A living trust? Can you leave instructions to prevent being hooked up to life-support systems if you suffer a stroke or are in an automobile accident and become too incapacitated to make such a decision? These issues and others are the subjects of this chapter.

LEGAL FOCUS—PROBLEM

Mary Trimble, age eighty-seven and bedridden, had been suffering from a painful, debilitating illness for two years. Medical opinion was that she would never improve. She asked her physician to help her commit suicide by lethal injection. She also asked her husband to take whatever means he could to end her life as mercifully as possible. Can Trimble's physician or husband legally give her the relief she seeks?

decedent
A deceased person.

heirs
Persons designated by law to receive the estate of a decedent who leaves no will.

estate planning
The process of arranging a person's property and estate, taking into account the laws of wills, taxes, insurance, property, and trusts so as to gain maximum benefit of all laws while carrying out the person's wishes for use of the property during his lifetime and disposition of the property upon his death.

No, they may not provide her the relief she seeks because most states prohibit assisted suicide. The U.S. Supreme Court has ruled that there is no constitutional right to die; therefore, state laws that make the act of assisting suicide a crime are valid and Trimble's physician or husband could be imprisoned if they ended her life, even at her request. This situation is quite different from those in which patients previously have signed a written directive that they desire that life-support equipment be avoided, or even removed once connected. Many people believe that laws should be expanded to include the choice of physician-assisted suicide.

In this chapter, we present the challenging laws of estate planning and probate matters. To most of us, the subject of death is unpleasant, so we avoid discussing it. We are willing, of course, to acknowledge that death happens. But it happens "to others, not to me! At least not yet!"

The inevitability of one's death calmly should be recognized as a reason for appropriate planning, starting at least by midlife. By law, upon death, title to the assets of a **decedent** (a more technical and less personal way of referring to a person who has died) must go to someone, generally through the procedures of a probate court. It is true that "You can't take it with you." But with prudent planning, and using such legal instruments as a will and perhaps a trust, you can arrange to have your property distributed consistently with your wishes. Moreover, your foresight can guarantee that your **heirs** (those persons who are entitled legally to your estate if you leave no will), as well as other intended beneficiaries will receive more property, and that the government death-tax collectors will receive less. The topic is important.

A hundred years ago, only the rich needed to do **estate planning** (wills and trusts), but today its importance has increased for the rich and middle class alike. Today, taxes are a significant potential burden on the passing of wealth to heirs, and many Americans have estates substantial enough to desire protection from high federal tax rates. In Congress, elimination of estate taxes has become a recurring theme, and the issue of whether or not estate taxes are good taxes that should remain a permanent source of government revenue is a political issue, not a legal one, and the ultimate resolution is anybody's guess. The complexity of the political fallout is, however, a legal and financial issue.

In 1913, the Sixteenth Amendment to the U.S. Constitution established the modern income tax. Until 1916, the federal government utilized death and gift taxes only in times of extraordinary revenue demands, such as wartime, although states used them as a substantial revenue source routinely. Many of the legal methods used in estate planning discussed in this chapter existed in the late-nineteenth century, but many did not. There were no living wills, medical directives, A and B trusts for tax planning, or "Avoid Probate" seminars and self-help books. And to advocate legally assisted suicide would have been suicidal. Property that could be transferred in the year 2013 includes such items as a computer, automobile, airplane, Microsoft common stock, high-definition television set, DVD collection, iPod, vacation-share condominium, and cryofreeze container complete with instructions. These gifts will not be found if you search the probate records of early 1900 wills. Instead, you will find horses, wagons, guns, family Bibles, books, tools, and (if lucky) the family farm. An attorney at the beginning of the last century needed to ask clients the names of all of their children born of any marriage or born outside of marriage (the last question asked with great delicacy). A twenty-first-century attorney must ask clients about frozen eggs and sperm when trying to establish potential heirs and estate claims. What will the attorneys of the year 2110 need to ask?

WHAT IS ESTATE PLANNING?

Estate planning is an ongoing analysis of what a person owns or expects to own (assets), and what he owes to others (liabilities). It involves short-range tactics and long-range strategies to maximize benefits for the individual and the estate (and dependents) while still alive, and for the heirs and other beneficiaries who will own the estate after the individual's death. As personal income and expenses change, and as needs and wants also change over the years, estate plans must change as well, or they can cause more harm than good. For example, estate plans typically must be adjusted following a divorce, the birth of a child, the receipt of a substantial inheritance, or changes in the number and circumstances of intended beneficiaries. An estate plan may involve continuing education, investing, saving for major purchases, borrowing for such things as a residence, and providing for retirement.

Estate plans usually include the following four major objectives:

- **To provide for the financial needs of the planner while alive.** If the planner is married, the financial needs of the spouse and other dependents are also an important concern.
- **To reflect the desires of the planner.** That is, the plan should provide appropriately for beneficiaries who are thought to be deserving, and possibly charities, while excluding potential beneficiaries who are deemed undeserving or not in need.
- **To minimize or legitimately avoid taxes.** Taxes include (1) income taxes payable both during life and after the planner's death, and (2) estate and inheritance taxes (**death taxes**) payable after the planner's death.
- **To minimize or avoid the delays, costs, and publicity of probate. Probate** is the process of proving the validity of a will in court, coupled with the ability to monitor the administration of the decedent's estate.

Even for persons of modest wealth and income, we cannot overstate the importance and value of proper estate planning. All aspects of such planning have legal consequences, but

death tax
Taxes imposed on the estate of the decedent (i.e., an estate tax on the privilege of giving) and on the gifts received by the donee(s) (i.e., an inheritance tax on the privilege of receiving).

probate
The process of proving the validity of a will in court, coupled with the related matter of administering the decedent's estate.

our focus is on the transfer of property to others before or after death, and on trusts and wills as they relate to probate.

WHAT TAX BURDENS CAN THE ESTATE PLANNER REDUCE OR AVOID?

estate tax
A tax imposed by the federal government and some states on the privilege of giving property to another person after death of the donor.

The federal government in modern history has imposed a death tax or **estate tax** on the total net assets of a person at death, which is a levy on the giving of property to others after death. In 2010, the Bush administration tax cuts eliminated the federal estate tax. The estate tax was reinstated on January 1, 2011, with a $5 million exemption and a 35 percent top rate for 2011 and a $5.12 million exemption and 35 percent top rate in 2012. In 2013, Congress continued the exemption at $5.25 million and set the rate at 40 percent. Surviving spouses can carry over each other's unused exemptions, so that means a wealthy couple could shield a combined $10.5 million in 2013. The tax remains controversial with proponents calling for a reduced exemption and an increased rate, and opponents calling for the elimination of the tax.

A declining number of states also levy death taxes. A few state governments impose these death taxes as a transfer tax on the estate and the property transferred at death. More states impose an **inheritance tax** upon the receiving of property from the estate of a decedent. The individual who inherits the property pays state inheritance tax. Inheritance and estate taxes together are called death taxes, as mentioned previously.

inheritance tax
A tax imposed by most states on the privilege of receiving property from a decedent.

Most modest estates are distributed free of federal tax. Large estates are taxed heavily, although appropriate estate planning can reduce and even eliminate this burden. Wealthy persons avoid taxes (both income and estate) by making exempt gifts, by utilizing trusts, and by making thoughtful wills. Wills and trusts also are used to direct property to preferred persons, called beneficiaries. The most common types of tax-reduction trusts are marital trusts and generation-skipping trusts; both are described later in this chapter.

Tax laws clearly affect behavior. The government often encourages certain conduct through the enactment of particular tax laws (e.g., a mortgage interest deduction would encourage homeownership). Tax laws also stimulate the creative energies of tax advisors, who seek ways to reduce tax burdens for their clients. Not all such tax-avoidance behaviors are desired by those legislators who draft tax laws. The result is that every few years tax laws are amended to encourage some social policies and to discourage others. It is an oft-repeated ritual of Congress.

MORALS AND ETHICS

It is not always clear that a "tax avoidance" strategy is legal. Many people, however, feel that if it is legal, then it is their moral duty to use the strategy. Such strategies often are called "loopholes," inferring that the avoidance strategy was not anticipated by legislators. Congress often reacts to them by enacting legislation that prohibits the strategy. An example of a loophole was the transfer of property to children through an irrevocable but temporary trust called a Clifford Trust. The transfer was irrevocable for at least ten years, during which time the income belonged to the child and was taxed at the child's much lower rate. After ten years, the property would return to the donor. The Tax Reform Act of 1986 closed this loophole by taxing income from a Clifford Trust to a child under fourteen years at the same rate as the donor would be taxed.

Taxes on Lifetime Gifts

unified estate and gift tax
A federal tax levied on the transfer of property through an estate at the time of death or on a taxable transfer by gift. The estate or the donor is responsible for payment of the tax. A unified credit is available to be applied against the transfer tax.

The federal estate tax provides for a **unified estate and gift tax**. In other words, both estate and gift taxes have the same tax rates and **exemptions**. By imposing a federal tax on gifts, federal law prevents a person from avoiding payment of death taxes by making large gifts, especially "deathbed gifts." This tax system requires the taxpayer to keep track of larger gifts and to combine the total value of these lifetime gifts with the value of property transferred at death. Taxes are based on the total value of these gifts, after the deduction of a *unified credit* (exemption), which has fluctuated significantly since 2001 and is $5.25 million in 2013.

In reality, most gifts are totally free of tax. An individual may make annual tax-free gifts of up to $14,000 to each of any number of *donees* (recipients of gifts). Such gifts are called *exemptions.* A husband and wife together may give $28,000 each year to any number of donees, their children. If a gift is $14,000 or less, the gift has no federal tax consequences and need not be declared. Use of the tax-free exclusion allows a considerable amount of money or property to be given tax-free over time.

MATTERS CONCERNING WILLS

What Is a Will?

estate tax exemption
A sum of money that can be transferred without tax implications. Once that amount is exceeded, taxes are imposed on any additional transferred amount.

A man who dies without a will has lawyers for his heirs.

—Anonymous

A **will** is the proper written legal expression of a person's wishes for the distribution of property after death. A person who dies with a will dies **testate**; without a will, the individual is considered to be **intestate**. Upon death without a will, state statutes control the distribution of property. Generally, statutes prefer descendants to ascendants. In other words, children or grandchildren, instead of parents or grandparents, will inherit from the deceased. If there are any lineals (grandparents, parents, children, grandchildren, and so on), then collaterals (aunts, uncles, siblings, or cousins) will not inherit. If a person dies without any heirs whatsoever, not even distant cousins, a typically rare event, then the decedent's assets escheat (transfer) to the state—usually the state of the decedent's permanent residence—to benefit the public in general.

will
Legal expression (usually in writing, signed, and witnessed) of a person's directions as to how property owned is to be disposed after death.

A person who dies leaving a will is called a **testator**. The court responsible for administering any legal problems surrounding a will usually is called a *probate court* and sometimes a *surrogate* or *chancery court.* A gift of real estate by will is a **devise**, and a gift of personal property by will is a **bequest or legacy**. When someone dies, a personal representative settles affairs of the estate. An **executor** is a personal representative named in a will. An **administrator** is the personal representative appointed by the court for a decedent without a will. An administrator also may be appointed if a person fails to name an executor in a will, or names an executor who lacks the capacity to serve, or writes a will that the court refuses to admit to probate (e.g., because it was not witnessed properly). A will that is "admitted to probate" has been accepted by the court as the valid last will of the decedent.

testate
The legal status of a person who died leaving a valid will.

intestate
The status of a person who died without leaving a valid will.

A will is a conditional document. Although valid when properly created, it has no immediate legal effect. It becomes operative at the testator's death. Hence, the will "speaks upon the author's death." Therefore, if the testator destroys it, or writes a more recent will, the older will is nullified automatically. This conditional feature makes a will a unique document, adding importance to proving its validity (a process called *authentication*) after the death of the testator.

LEGAL FOCUS—CASE

All baseball fans have heard of Shoeless Joe Jackson, a player of extraordinary skill. He is probably best remembered for his alleged involvement in the Black Sox scandal of 1919 and subsequent banishment from baseball. His will named his wife, Katie, as his beneficiary and executor. Her will named charities as residual beneficiaries; after her death, the charities sought declaration from the court that his signed and probated will (thus, a rare and valuable collectible) be considered property of her estate. The probate court denied the request, and the charities appealed. The circuit court agreed with the probate court judge and concluded that original wills, which are required by state law to be filed with the probate court, constitute public records. "[T]he probate code neither intends nor provides that the deliverer of a will, even if a devisee under it, gain ownership in the actual document." The court instead recognized that the court itself is the place of "permanent retention of original documents from decedent estates."

American Heart Association v. County of Greenville, 331 S.C. 498, 489 S.E.2d 921 (S.C. 1997).

testator
(1) Person who makes a valid will. (2) Person who dies leaving a valid will.

devise
A gift of real property by will.

bequest or legacy
A gift of personal property by will.

executor
A person named by a testator to dispose of her estate after death as directed in the will and in compliance with the law.

administrator
A person appointed by a court to supervise the disposition of the estate of a decedent who dies without leaving a valid will.

To be valid, wills normally must follow strictly state statutory requirements regarding both the right and the process of making a will. A will can serve other purposes besides the distribution of property; it can recommend appointment of a guardian for minor children or incapacitated adults, and it can nominate a personal representative to settle the legal affairs of the deceased. Indeed, a well-drafted will provides many important advantages:

- **Property is distributed as the testator wishes.** Gifts may be made to charities, distant relatives, friends, or employees. Some beneficiaries may receive more property, some less. Unique assets, such as family heirlooms, may go to specified beneficiaries.
- **The possibility of a disaster that kills both husband and wife, and possibly one or more children, can be anticipated and accommodated.** Although unlikely, modern means of transportation increases this danger. A properly drafted will can eliminate multiple costly tax-burdened probates that may be required when couples or adult family members die in close succession over a period of days or weeks from injuries sustained in a common calamity.
- **Death taxes may be avoided or reduced.** This goal is accomplished by taking the **marital deduction** (tax deduction allowed a surviving spouse that is not available to single persons) or by utilizing appropriate trusts. Also, the will may direct the executor to pay inheritance taxes, as well as estate taxes from the *residuary property* (property not identified specifically and given to a beneficiary) of the estate. Therefore, assuming assets are sufficient, gifts to named beneficiaries will not be reduced by death taxes.
- **Confusion is minimized when specific property owned by the testator is identified, and beneficiaries are designated correctly.** The will also minimizes the possibility of lawsuits among contending claimants—for example, a claim that "He gave it to me before he died."
- **The testator may nominate appropriate guardian(s) for minor children and their estates.** The will may name both a guardian of the person (handles personal decisions in lieu of parent) and a guardian of the estate (handles the child's assets). Nominations by a testator generally are honored, but the welfare of the child (or children) is the primary concern of the court. If a natural parent survives, this problem does not arise. If there is no nomination, the court makes the appointment independently.

marital deduction
A tax deduction allowing a surviving spouse to receive an estate from the deceased spouse free of federal estate tax.

- **A personal representative (usually called an executor) may be designated in the will to handle the estate.** Otherwise, or if the nominated executor refuses to serve, the probate court will name an administrator. A statutory commission, or fee, ultimately is payable to the personal representative from the assets in the estate, although it is common for the personal representative to waive the fee if he is also the principal beneficiary under the will. The reason personal representatives often waive fees is that such fees are taxable income. If they otherwise inherit the property, there may be a lesser tax or no tax. It is also important to note that the statutory fees to both personal representatives and the attorneys who assist them during probate proceedings are maximums, not prescribed fees. That is, beneficiaries can encourage competitive bids from probate attorneys as an additional way to maximize the estate.

fidelity bond
A bond insuring against losses caused by a fraudulent performance of duties by a personal representative.

If a will does not waive it, a **fidelity bond** is required. A fidelity bond insures against losses caused by the dishonest performance of duties by a personal representative (or by a guardian of the children, if one is named and accepts the task). Although the bond provides added protection, it is an expense to the estate. However, it often is prudent to require the posting of a fidelity bond for estates that consist of large amounts of cash. The judgment of trustworthy persons can be affected through control of large sums of cash, as opposed to other "less liquid" types of assets such as real property, automobiles, jewelry, or investments. Such a bond may be unnecessary altogether when the estate consists of no liquid assets or the executor is also the sole primary beneficiary. Also, it is common advice that if a person is not trustworthy enough to be appointed without a bond, that person should not be appointed.

- **The will can give funeral instructions.** Such directives also can and should be done in a letter of "last instructions" (described next), separate from the will and immediately available to a close relative or friend upon death.

Accompaniments to Wills

letter of last instructions
A document prepared by a person instructing his personal representative (executor or administrator) as to the nature and location of assets and liabilities and suggesting appropriate action to be taken immediately after death.

Ideally, a personal or family balance sheet, listing assets and liabilities, should accompany a will and be updated periodically. A **letter of last instructions**, as mentioned previously, should be prepared. This letter is not binding on the executor, but it is helpful in disclosing the location of assets and liabilities. It can indicate how the testator would like matters requiring immediate attention, such as a donation of body organs under the Uniform Anatomical Gift Act, to be handled. Note that letters of last instructions, or even explanations for survivors, can be prepared by the testator in many ways: in writing, in an audio recording, or even in a video recording. These instructions are not binding legally but can be useful in explaining why, for example, someone was disinherited.

Types of Gifts by Will

residuary clause
Any part of the will that allocates property not expressly disposed of by other provisions of the will.

Gifts made by a will can be specific, general, or residuary. A *specific* devise or bequest describes particular property—for example, a bequest of an inscribed gold watch or a collection of rare books. A *general* bequest usually specifies a sum of money but does not single out any particular item of property. Sometimes, a will provides that any assets remaining after specific gifts are made, and after debts are paid, are to be distributed through a **residuary clause**. Such a clause is useful because the testator can never be sure precisely what property will remain following payment of debts and taxes. Sample gift clauses in a will follow.

- A *specific bequest.* I give my grandfather's gold ring with the initials GSH to my son, Scott Bradshaw of Mountain Oaks, Colorado.

- A *general bequest.* I give the sum of twenty thousand dollars ($20,000) from my account number ZXY1117865 in First Hoosier Bank to the American Cancer Society, 1244 Normal, Decatur, Indiana.
- A *specific devise.* I give my real property situated in Shorewood County, Milwaukee, Wisconsin, and commonly known as 1278 University Lane, to my sister, Carolyn A. Hamilton.
- A *residuary gift.* I give the residue of my estate, both real and personal property, to my wife, Patricia A. Jenkins-Bradshaw.

How Does One Create a Valid Will?

A will must comply with statutory formalities that are designed to ensure that the testator understood his actions at the time the will was made. These formalities are intended to help prevent fraud. If not followed exactly, the will is void. The decedent's property then is distributed according to state laws of intestacy.

Three types of wills generally are recognized as valid: formal (or witnessed) typed or printed wills; informal (or holographic), handwritten wills; and, in a very limited situation, oral wills. An oral will, also called a nuncupative will, is valid only when the testator is in fear of imminent death (e.g., an accident victim with fatal injuries). In the few states recognizing a nuncupative will, usually two persons must hear the orally expressed intentions and the property subject to transfer must be a small sum (often $1,000). Because of these limitations and special requirements, nuncupative wills are not common.

What Is a Formal or Witnessed Will?

formal will
A typewritten or computer-printed will executed in compliance with law and signed or acknowledged by the testator in the presence of witnesses who also sign the document.

The **formal will** usually is drafted by a lawyer and generally is prepared on a computer, word processor, or typewriter. It must be signed at the end (subscribed) by the testator. The subscription must be made in the presence of witnesses, or in their presence, the testator must acknowledge that the will was made previously by her or under her direction. Most states require the following to create a valid formal will.

1. **The testator must have testamentary capacity.** The testator must be of legal age and sound mind *at the time the will is made.* The legal age for executing a will varies, but in most states eighteen years is the minimum age. Thus, a will of a twenty-one-year-old decedent, written when she was sixteen years of age, is invalid.

The concept of "being of sound mind" refers to the testator's ability to formulate and understand his plan to distribute property, coupled with an intent for the will to put into effect the distribution plan. Although the testator must be competent when the will is executed, illiteracy or physical or mental infirmity caused by old age (such as senility) does not prevent the making of a valid will. If there is physical or mental infirmity, it is advisable to have a medical doctor act as one witness who then can testify that the condition did not affect the soundness of the testator's mind at the execution of the will.

LEGAL FOCUS—PROBLEM

Michael Taylor signed a new will three days before he died of AIDS. The new will left most of his $3.5 million estate to a charitable trust for the decorative arts. The next largest gift was to his companion, who was to receive property worth about $400,000. His eighty-seven-year-old mother challenged the will. What is the result?

A San Francisco jury held that Taylor, in a weakened condition in the final days of his illness, was subjected to undue influence by his companion. He lacked the freedom of will necessary to express his true intent, and the will was declared void.

2. **The will must be in writing.** The writing itself can be informal as long as it complies with statutory requirements. A will can be handwritten in crayon or ink. It can be written on a scrap of paper, a paper bag, or a piece of cloth. A will also can refer to a memorandum that contains information necessary to carry out the will, although the memorandum is not a will.

LEGAL FOCUS—PROBLEM

Fran O'Hehir's will directed that a sum of money be divided among a group of charities named in a memorandum that she gave to Bob Meehum the same day she signed her will. Will the charities benefit from O'Hehir's bequest?

The list of charities legally is included or "incorporated by reference" into the will, but only if it was described sufficiently when the will was signed. This practice is not desirable and should be avoided because of the opportunities it presents for error or even fraud.

3. **The will must be signed by the testator.** It is a fundamental requirement in almost all jurisdictions that the testator's signature appear at the end of the will. Each state dictates what constitutes a legally sufficient signature. Initials, an "X" or other mark, and words like "Mom" have all been held valid when evidence demonstrates that the testator intended the marks to be a signature.
4. **A formal will must be witnessed.** A will must be witnessed by at least two witnesses or it is invalid. The number of witnesses, their qualifications, and how a will should be witnessed are set out in state statutes. Most states require that a witness be disinterested—that is, not a beneficiary under the will. There are no age requirements for witnesses, but they must be mentally competent.

attestation
The act of witnessing the signing of a document and thereafter signing, as evidence that you have witnessed it.

The purpose of statutes that require witnesses is to verify that the testator actually executed (signed) the will and had the requisite intent and capacity at that time. A witness does not have to read the contents of the will. Typically, the testator and witnesses all must sign in the sight or the presence of one another. The act of witnessing the signing of a will and thereafter signing the will to that effect is called **attestation**.

published
A legal rule of wills in some states requiring a declaration by the maker of the will to the witnesses that the document she is about to sign is indeed her will.

5. **Sometimes a will must be published.** A will is **published** by an oral declaration by the maker to the witnesses that the document they are about to sign is his "last will and testament."

Formalities required for wills are enforced strictly by probate courts and provide added assurance of validity. After all, the testator is dead when the will "speaks" and unable to challenge fraudulent claims. If witnesses also are dead at that time and unable to supply appropriate affidavits (sworn statements in writing), their handwriting on the will may be authenticated by other means. This complication usually is avoided through the use of witnesses who are younger than the testator.

statutory will
A form will authorized by state law with blanks to be completed by the testator.

One variation of a formal will is a **statutory will**, a standardized form of will authorized by the state, with blanks to be completed by the testator. Statutory wills were devised to provide for the simple and usual circumstances of persons who otherwise may die intestate. States authorizing such wills commonly provide that no changes to the preprinted form are permitted.

EXHIBIT 15.1
The Last Will and Testament of Warren E. Burger

LAST WILL AND TESTAMENT OF WARREN E. BURGER

I hereby make and declare the following to be my last will and testament.

1. My executors will first pay all claims against my estate;
2. The remainder of my estate will be distributed as follows; one-third to my daughter, Margaret Elizabeth Burger Rose and two-thirds to my son, Wade A. Burger;
3. I designate and appoint as executors of this will, Wade A. Burger and J. Michael Luttig.

IN WITNESS WEREOF, I have hereunto set my hand to this my Last Will and Testament this 9th day of June, 1994.

/s/Warren E. Burger

We hereby certify that in our presence on the date written above WARREN E. BURGER signed the foregoing instrument and declared it to be his Last Will and Testament and that at this request in his presence and in the presence of each other we have signed our names below as witnesses.

/s/Nathaniel E. Brady residing at 120 F St., NW, Washington, DC

/s/Alice M. Khu residing at 3041 Meeting St., Falls Church, VA

Wills can be complicated or simple. The will in Exhibit 15.1 is the actual complete will of the former chief justice of the United States Warren E. Burger, now deceased. Because of the size of his estate and the lack of planning and appropriate assignment of executor powers, his heirs undoubtedly lost substantial amounts of money to taxes and administrative costs. The irony of his lack of careful planning is real and instructive.

holographic will
An unwitnessed will. States that allow such a will usually require it to be written in longhand by the testator, signed, and dated.

What Is a Holographic Will?

An exception to the formal witnessed will exists in many states. A **holographic will** is a type of self-prepared will written, signed, and dated, all entirely in the handwriting of the testator. About half of the states recognize this type of will, although the exact requirements often vary slightly. If the will is appropriately witnessed and other formalities are observed, the document is considered a formal will even though it is handwritten by the testator.

LEGAL FOCUS—PROBLEM

Dave Decker, married to Dora May Decker and father of one child (female) named Dora June Decker, decided to make a holographic will. He carefully wrote on a blank sheet of paper, "I give all I own to Dora." He signed and dated the paper. As an afterthought, he took the document to his office and asked his friend Arthur Bamish to sign and date his paper as a witness. Is the document a valid will?

No, the will is not valid in this particular case. In many states, a person may prepare a valid holographic will without witnesses, in one's own handwriting, signed and dated by the testator. Even if Decker's state is one of these, his will is invalid. Why? Decker's wife and daughter were both named Dora. When he dies, the probate court cannot be sure to whom he intended to leave his property. Consequently, his will is void because of the uncertainty as to the identity of the beneficiary. Such ambiguity invalidates a will. Once a will is invalidated, state laws substitute a statutory will for the testator, more formally called statutes of succession. Under a state statutory will or law of succession, either the wife will inherit all the property, or both the wife and daughter will share in Decker's estate in a specified proportion depending on the nature of the state's property law and the statutory will.

Dave Decker also failed to meet an additional requirement of some states: that he declare to the witnesses that it is a will and specifically ask them to serve as witnesses. Decker did not tell his witness, Bamish, that the document was his will, nor did he sign, or acknowledge his signature, in Bamish's presence. (Recall that witnesses must sign in the presence of the testator. Some states also require that witnesses sign in the presence of each other.)

LEGAL FOCUS—EXAMPLE

The Tractor Will

If you happen to go to law school in Canada (who knows), you are sure to hear about Cecil George Harris of the McGee area of Saskatchewan province. On June 8, 1948, while Cecil was working on his tractor, he mistakenly put it in reverse and was pinned by the tractor. Fearful that he might not live through this experience, he used his jackknife (pocket knife) to etch in the fender of the tractor this message. "In case I die in this mess, I leave all to the wife. Cecil Geo. Harris." Although rescued by his wife and neighbors, he died of his injuries two days later. The fender was discovered and admitted to probate as a valid holographic will. It was entirely in the handwriting of the deceased, and it was signed. When the courthouse was closed in 1996, Chief Justice D. K. MacPherson of the Court of Queen's Bench ordered that the fender and knife be turned over to the College of Law of the University of Saskatchewan for public display. Don't miss it if you travel to Saskatoon, Saskatchewan, Canada.

In most states that permit holographic wills, the requirements must be followed precisely. A major criticism of holographic wills is the absence of witnesses. Probate courts are concerned, among other things, with the possibility of forgery and undue influence. As holographic wills usually are not witnessed, there is little protection against forgery or undue influence. Probate judges have ruled many attempted holographic wills to be invalid because they were partially typed (thus not entirely in the handwriting of the testator) or not dated.

A few states have liberalized the requirements for a holographic will, allowing typed or printed provisions as long as the signature and material provisions are in the handwriting of the testator. Even where holographic wills usually are acceptable, the wisdom of preparing one is questionable. Many people fail to express their intentions clearly. They also may fail to take advantage of readily available techniques to minimize estate taxes and other costs (such as appropriate executor powers and waiver of bond). A person who insists on proceeding without professional legal assistance would be well advised to study one of the self-help books containing standard forms and provisions.

What about a self-prepared digital will? Nevada passed a statute recognizing wills "written, created and stored in an electronic record," but the legislation does not require a specific electronic format. The electronic will, however, must contain the date and the testator's electronic signature, along with at least one authentication characteristic of the testator, such as a digitized signature, voice recognition, facial recognition, a retinal scan, a fingerprint, or other type of authentication. The will must be created and stored in such a manner that only one authoritative copy exists, the authoritative copy must be maintained and controlled by the testator or a custodian designated by the testator in the electronic will, and any attempted alteration of the authoritative copy must be readily identifiable. But what happens in states without such statutes?

LEGAL FOCUS—CASE

Javier Castro was hospitalized in Ohio for a life-threatening condition. As a Jehovah's Witness, he refused a blood transfusion that was needed for him to survive. He had no paper or a pencil, so in conversation with his brothers he dictated how he wanted his estate to be divided and his brother recorded his instructions on his electronic tablet using a stylus. Both of his brothers witnessed his signature. May the will be admitted to probate?

The Nevada electronic wills statute does not control the validity of wills in Ohio. Nevertheless, the probate court admitted the will and admonished the legislature to address the issue of electronic wills. While some self-prepared wills in whatever form may be enforceable, their legal effect is not often what the drafter intends.

LEGAL FOCUS—CASE

Shortly after Christine McCarthy and Stephen Kapcar married in 1972, Kapcar named McCarthy as beneficiary of an Aetna Life Insurance Co. group life insurance policy. Within a year of the marriage, Kapcar was diagnosed with multiple sclerosis. He developed severe tremors, underwent brain surgery to alleviate the tremors, and became legally blind in 1974. Within a few years, they separated; in 1978, Kapcar divorced McCarthy. Neither the divorce decree nor a property settlement mentioned the Aetna policy. Kapcar died in 1984 a quadriplegic, having spent the last seven years of his life unemployed and living with his father. According to the terms of a holographic will written in 1977, Kapcar stated that "I will all my personal belongings, stock certificates, bank accounts, insurance benefits, and any other earthly belongings to my father. This will voids my previous will bequeathing my belongings to Christine B. Kapcar." Kapcar never changed the named beneficiary (Christine) on the Aetna policy. Christine claimed the proceeds of the insurance policy. Did the holographic will transfer the interest in the life insurance policy to Kapcar's father?

McCarthy v. Aetna Life Insurance Co., 92 N.Y.2d 436, 704 N.E.2d 557, 681 N.Y.S.2d 790 (N.Y. 1998).

The admonition that people should seek legal counsel to prepare wills is not made simply to make lawyers money. Any competent attorney would have asked questions about Kapcar's assets, including life insurance policies, and Kapcar would have been directed to change the beneficiary according to his wishes. The predictable result in this case was that the self-prepared will was insufficient to change the beneficiary in the life insurance policy, and the divorced wife got the proceeds instead of the faithful father. To allow a change in beneficiary to be made by testamentary disposition alone would open up a serious question as to payment of life insurance policies and would run counter to the public interest that an insurance company pay the beneficiary designated in the policy as promptly after the death of the insured as reasonably may be done.

How Does One Revoke a Will?

The maker of a will may revoke it at any time during her lifetime. Revocation can be partial or complete, and it should follow certain specified formalities. A testator can revoke a will by a physical act such as intentionally burning, tearing, canceling, obliterating, or destroying it. Having someone else destroy the will at the maker's direction and in the maker's presence also revokes the will. The intention to destroy the will is essential.

codicil
A document prepared to change but not revoke an existing will.

Another document, called a **codicil**, may change a will. A codicil is a written instrument, separate from the will that amends or revokes provisions in the will. A codicil makes it unnecessary to redraft the entire will if its maker wants to change only part of it. A codicil also can be used to revoke an entire will. In either case, the codicil must be created with the same formalities required for the will, and it must refer to the will.

A second or new will can be executed to revoke the first. The second will must use specific language, such as "This will hereby revokes all prior wills." If the first will is not revoked, then some courts will admit both wills into probate. The second will is treated as a codicil. It is good idea to keep copies of prior wills—but they should be marked clearly and preferably initialed and dated to indicate that they are revoked and superseded by the will executed on (name the date).

Can a Probate Court Distribute Property Contrary to the Terms of a Will?

pretermitted heir
A child who was not specifically provided for in life and was not mentioned in a parent's will.

In most states, a failure to provide for a spouse or child can revoke a will partially, in which case a probate court can compel distribution of an estate contrary to the stated terms of a will. A **pretermitted heir** is a child either unintentionally left out of a will or born after the will is made. Most states have pretermitted heir statutes that give to a pretermitted child a statutory share of the testator's property. This statutory share overrides the will, unless the child received some gift in the will, or the exclusion was made deliberately, expressly, and clearly. If a child (or grandchild, if the child has died and there is a surviving grandchild) is not mentioned in the will, and no provision was made for the child outside the will, the law assumes that the omission was a mistake. A parent testator is free to ignore and exclude a child in his will but must do so expressly. Likewise, in some states spouses can be excluded from receiving the decedent's property, but only if the will specifies that the omission of the spouse is purposeful.

ademption
The elimination of a specific gift of property listed in a will because it no longer exists.

Sometimes, a testator identifies a specific gift of property in a will, but then disposes of it before the will "speaks." For example, the testator wills his savings account at the Texarkana Bank of Austin to Johnny Raye, but when the testator dies, no such account exists at the Texarkana Bank of Austin. Even if an account can be found at another bank in Austin, the gift fails. The executor is powerless to substitute other property to Johnny Raye. Instead, the testator's property will be distributed as otherwise specified in the will (e.g., in a residual disposition clause). This failure of a bequest is called **ademption**: disposing of something given to a donee in a will before the testator's death. Thus, the provision in the will is inoperative and impossible to carry out. The person for whom the gift originally was intended does not receive it, even though the will is valid.

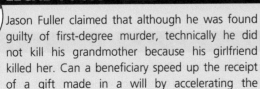

LEGAL FOCUS—CASE

Jason Fuller claimed that although he was found guilty of first-degree murder, technically he did not kill his grandmother because his girlfriend killed her. Can a beneficiary speed up the receipt of a gift made in a will by accelerating the testator's death, or as Sam Spade would say it, "Can you do the person in and still inherit"?

Estate of Walker v. Russell Eastern Star Home of Colorado, Inc., 847 P.2d 162 (Colo. 1992).

Because a will is a document subject to change at the whim of the testator, it has been the subject of much intrigue in fiction, and in life (or death). A potential heir can be written out of a will any time the testator wishes. States have passed laws to protect individuals from impatient and evil beneficiaries. For example, anyone convicted of a crime that caused the death of a testator cannot receive benefits under the will. Fuller's claim was based on the misplaced hope that the court would construe narrowly a so-called slayer statute. But the court interpreted the term "kills," as used in Colorado's statute, as referring to a person who causes the death of another by bringing about that effect.

Probate court is the place for proving the validity of a will. It is also where wills are challenged or contested. The usual grounds for challenging a will are as follows:

- The testator lacked capacity.
- The testator was subject to undue influence.
- The will was not executed properly.
- Someone defrauded the testator into executing this particular will.

To discourage the contesting of wills, drafters often include a *no-contest* or *incontestability clause* in the will. Such a clause might read as follows:

> *If any beneficiary under this Will in any manner, directly or indirectly, contests or attacks the Will or any of its provisions, any share of interest in my estate given that contesting beneficiary under the Will is revoked and shall be disposed of as if that contesting beneficiary had died before me.*

Such a clause discourages beneficiaries from asserting frivolous lawsuits contesting wills. When an entire will is ruled invalid, however, the incontestability clause as well as all other provisions is rendered void. The estate therefore would be distributed by intestate succession (see the following discussion), or in some cases, by the terms of a prior will.

What If the Testator Is the Victim of Undue Influence?

Valid wills express the maker's intention to transfer and distribute his property after death. If it can be shown that the will was the result of improper pressure brought by another person, the will is void because it truly does not express the maker's intention.

undue influence
Wrongful persuasion often by a beneficiary or other trusted individual that deprives the victim of decision-making freedom in making a will.

Undue influence is sometimes inferred by the court if the testator ignores blood relatives, who are normally the "natural objects of his bounty," and instead names a non-relative as a beneficiary. The likelihood of undue influence is greater if the beneficiary is a person who was in constant close physical contact with the deceased and therefore able to influence the making of the will. When a nurse or friend who cares for the deceased during a comparatively short span of time before the death benefits to the exclusion of close family members, questions of undue influence inevitably arise. Even a spouse may be suspected of undue influence if children from a former marriage are excluded.

LEGAL FOCUS—PROBLEM

J. Seward Johnson died in 1983 from prostate cancer, leaving his entire estate to his wife of twelve years, Barbara Piasecka Johnson. Mrs. Johnson had worked as a chambermaid and cook at the Johnson mansion before their marriage. Mr. Johnson's six children by a prior marriage contested the will, claiming that their father had been the victim of undue influence by his wife and had been "terrorized" into signing the will just before his death. The estate valuation exceeded $500 million. Did the children succeed in their will contest?

After a four-month legal battle in New York's surrogate court, the parties reached an out-of-court settlement. Mrs. Johnson received $350 million, and the remainder was divided among the children and a charitable oceanographic research foundation that had been founded by the testator in 1971.

Will-signing ceremonies are sometimes video recorded to show that the ritual prescribed by law was followed correctly. Such records also provide evidence as to the demeanor (behavior and possibly competence) of the testator and have been used effectively to defend challenges to the validity of wills.

What Happens to the Estate of a Person Who Dies without Leaving a Will?

Each state regulates how property is to be distributed when a resident of the state dies without leaving a will. Such laws attempt to carry out the presumed intent and wishes of the decedent. These statutes are called **intestacy laws** and, as briefly noted previously in the chapter, provide for the distribution of property to designated heirs.

intestacy laws
Statutory prescription for distribution of the estate among heirs of a decedent leaving no will.

The rules of descent vary from state to state. The law always provides that the debts of the decedent first must be paid with assets of the estate. Then there is usually a special statutory provision for the rights of the surviving spouse and children. When no children or grandchildren survive the decedent, the surviving spouse gets the entire estate.

LEGAL FOCUS—EXAMPLE

Freddie Allen dies intestate and is survived by his wife, Della, and his children, Duane and Tara. Allen's property passes according to intestacy laws. After Allen's outstanding debts are paid, his widow ordinarily will receive one-third to one-half interest in the property; Duane and Tara will receive equal shares of the remainder.

State distribution laws specify the order in which heirs of an intestate have claims against the estate. When there is no surviving spouse or child, then the grandchildren, brothers and sisters, and, in some states, parents of the decedent follow in that sequence to receive the entire estate.

Because state laws differ so widely, few generalizations can be made about the laws of descent and distribution. It is necessary to refer to the exact terms of the applicable statutes to answer questions about intestate distribution in any given state. Exhibit 15.2 shows a typical pattern of intestate distribution of property (in this case, in Indiana).

MATTERS CONCERNING PROBATE

Is it the eccentric nature of the customers or the probate system itself that generates so much attention? I think it is a little bit of both.

—Probate Judge Pat Gregory, Harris County, Texas

What Is Probate?

Probate is a court proceeding in which wills are proved to be valid or invalid and in which estates of decedents are administered and ultimately property is distributed. Probate serves several useful purposes. It provides an opportunity for unsecured

EXHIBIT 15.2 Intestate Distribution of Property under Indiana Law

Deceased	Survived by	Spouse	Parent(s)	Child(ren)	Siblings (Brothers and Sisters)	Grandparents
Husband or Wife	Spouse only	All property				
	Spouse and one or more children	$\frac{1}{2}$*		$\frac{1}{2}$†		
	Spouse, children, and parent(s)	$\frac{1}{2}$		$\frac{1}{2}$†		
	Spouse and parent(s) only	$\frac{3}{4}$	$\frac{1}{4}$			
	Child(ren) and parent(s) only			All property		
Widow, Widower, or Single or Divorced	Child(ren)			All property		
	Child(ren) and parent(s)			All property		
	Parent(s) only		All property			
	Parent(s) and siblings‡		$\frac{1}{2}$		$\frac{1}{2}$†,‡	
	Siblings				All property†	
	Grandparents only					All property
	No spouse, parent, issue, siblings or grandparents§					
	No relatives¶					

*Limitations exist for a childless spouse when children by the dependent's prior marriage survive.
†Descendants of a deceased take the deceased person's share.
‡Assumes both parents are living and there are two or more siblings. Each parent takes as a sibling but receives at least one-fourth interest. For example, one parent and one sibling each would receive one-half share. If there are one parent and six siblings, the parent would get one-fourth and the six siblings would divide the remaining three-fourths share.
§All property to aunts and uncles. If an aunt or uncle is deceased but leaves a surviving child, the child or children receives the aunt or uncle's share.
¶All property goes (escheats) to the state.
Source: Indiana code §29-1-2-1.

creditors of the decedent to submit claims for payment from the estate. If they fail to submit a claim, they risk having their debts canceled, with no future claims against the beneficiaries of the estate. Secured debts (i.e., a note secured by a testator's property) remain secured; thus, any beneficiary who receives the property receives it subject to the security interest held by the creditor.

Death taxes if owed also normally are paid as part of the probate process. If the court validates a will, then the net assets (after all debts and liabilities of the decedent are paid) are distributed to named beneficiaries. If there is no valid will, the probate court will accomplish similar tasks by complying with the state's law of intestate succession. Probate laws vary from state to state, although some states have adopted the Uniform Probate Code. Note that applicable death taxes are payable whether or not there is a probate proceeding.

Can Probate Be Avoided?

Probate has important disadvantages. It takes time: generally a minimum of six months, often one to two years, sometimes longer. During this time, title to property is uncertain, as it is not transferred to the beneficiaries pending proof of the will and payment of the debts of the estate. The trauma of a loved one's death may be exacerbated by the inability to use assets that the survivor badly needs. Appropriate planning and a well-chosen executor who is advised by a competent lawyer should minimize or eliminate problems caused by probate delay. In addition, the facts about the estate and its disposition become a matter of public record. Information about the estate and beneficiaries in probates of prominent persons, famous or infamous, often is publicized in the media.

LEGAL FOCUS—EXAMPLE

Vickie Lynn Marshall, otherwise known as Anna Nicole Smith the celebrity model, actress and centerfold, was the surviving widow of billionaire J. Howard Marshall II, who died without providing for her in his will. Vickie was twenty-six years old at the time of their wedding and J. Howard was eighty-nine years old. Vickie claimed that her husband intended to provide for her through a gift in the form of a trust; however, his son, Pierce Marshall, was the ultimate beneficiary of his father's estate plan to the exclusion of both Vicki and Pierce's brother Howard. Pierce claimed that Vickie defamed him when her lawyers told the press that he had engaged in forgery, fraud, and overreaching to gain control of his father's assets. She claimed that Pierce tortiously interfered with a gift she expected from her husband. The dispute endured fifteen years and proceeded in two states in probate and bankruptcy courts, going before the U.S. Supreme Court twice. Neither party was alive when the dispute eventually was resolved in favor of Pierce Marshall.

Probate fees are payable to the personal representative (executor or administrator) and to the attorney who handles the estate. As noted previously, sometimes the executor is a principal or sole beneficiary and will waive probate fees (which are taxable as earned income for income tax purposes) to increase the inheritance (which may be tax-free depending on size, or may be taxable at death tax rates that are lower than the executor's income tax bracket). Statutes establish the maximum fees that generally may be received by both the executor and the attorney. The amount of the lawyer's fee is negotiable, and an executor may reach an agreement in which the attorney agrees to accept a fee less than the statutory amount. The statutory fee, however, typically is the amount paid. Costs of appraisal, tax returns, and property management are extra. If unusual or extraordinary services are provided, such as defense against a claim that the will is invalid, a court usually will allow a higher fee. If a state does not provide a statutory fee, the usual practice is for the attorney to bill by the hour.

Many states have laws that allow distribution of assets without probate proceedings. Less formal methods of transferring title are used for estates with small property values. In some states, for example, merely filling out standard forms can transfer savings and checking accounts, title to cars, and certain other property. And summary proceedings often are available when there is only one heir, notably a spouse. Most states provide for a Transfer on Death (TOD) of securities free of probate under the Uniform Transfer-On-Death Security Registration Act. The securities need to be held in an account that provides for this type of transfer, and the specific details must be planned carefully. Many other states authorize Pay on Death (PODs), which allow bank accounts, government bonds, individual retirement accounts, and cars to name a beneficiary on their certificate of title, allowing for the property to bypass probate. With TODs or PODs, the beneficiary has no rights as long as the donor is alive. The donor is free to sell or give away the property or to name someone else as the beneficiary. TODs and

PODs are similar as they both involve property in which proof of ownership exists in some sort of certificate of title; the primary difference is that the TOD involves securities and a POD involves other types of personal property.

family settlement agreement
A law of probate in some states allowing family members to agree to settle among themselves the distribution of a decedent's assets.

A majority of states provide for **family settlement agreements**—private agreements among the beneficiaries. Once a will is admitted to probate, the family members can agree to settle among themselves the distribution of the decedent's assets. A court order still is needed, however, to protect the estate from possible future claims of creditors and to clear title to estate assets. The use of such summary procedures in estate administration saves time and money. The expenses of a personal representative's commission, attorneys' fees, and appraisers' fees thus can be eliminated or at least minimized.

Some persons with larger estates (not eligible for summary procedures) nonetheless try to avoid probate and its related costs. With proper estate planning, the size of the probate estate may be reduced substantially. The following are types of property transfers that bypass probate:

- Undivided interests in property owned by the decedent in joint tenancy (or tenancy by the entireties) goes to the survivor(s) without probate under the right of survivorship (see Chapter 9).
- In community property states, only one-half of the community property will go through probate because the surviving spouse already owns the other half.
- Life insurance proceeds are paid directly to beneficiaries, unless the estate is named as the beneficiary (e.g., to provide cash for payment of death taxes, thus avoiding forced liquidation of other assets, such as equity in a business).
- Certain U.S. government bonds are paid directly to the person listed on the front of the bond as POD ("paid on death").
- Property previously transferred to an *inter vivos* trust (discussed subsequently in the chapter) is not probated.

Not all of these methods are suitable for every estate, but they are alternatives to probate administration.

What Are the Duties of an Executor?

LEGAL FOCUS—PROBLEM

One day, Robert Yu received the sad news of the death of his wealthy uncle, Wilbur Yu. A few days later, he received some good news and some bad news. The good news: He was named a beneficiary in his uncle's will and was to receive 500 shares of Berkshire Hathaway Inc. class A common stock. The bad news (or so he regarded it): He was named executor of his uncle's will. Should he accept the appointment?

Yes, he should accept the appointment. If Yu declines, the court will appoint a substitute administrator. If he accepts the nomination, an attorney he selects to handle the estate in probate court will do the legal work and will guide him in the proper performance of his duties. Both Yu and the attorney will be entitled to payment authorized by statute, plus compensation for extraordinary time or expenditures (e.g., defending or pursuing litigation on behalf of the estate, or negotiating sales of real property). This compensation is usually adequate and even generous, at least for larger estates. Compensation usually is limited by statute based on the gross value of the estate (total value of assets without regard to liabilities). Executor and attorney fees are often the same for a complicated estate consisting of various business and assorted assets as they are for an estate consisting of one bank account, if the values of each estate are the same. This anomaly flows from the misunderstanding of most executors that the maximum attorney fees provided by statute are the standard fee. In fact, a lower fee can be paid if agreed to between the executor and the attorney.

LEGAL FOCUS—BACKGROUND

Baseball Hall of Famer Ted Williams of the Boston Red Sox died in July 2002. Immediately after his death, all tributes to his skills were replaced by a story about his body being stored in a chamber of liquid nitrogen (cryonics).* Apparently, Williams had been frozen at the request of his son, John Henry, and his daughter Claudia. His other daughter, Bobby-Jo, reportedly was appalled, claiming that his will and professed wishes called for cremation. Probate is where the final decision will be made, but the executor of his will makes the initial call. Once a body is cremated, cryonics no longer matters even to the most optimistic futurist.

The duties of an executor are important, although many of these services are provided by the lawyer employed by the executor to assist with administration of the estate:

1. Comply with decedent's special instructions for funeral and burial.
2. Locate witnesses to the will.
3. Notify heirs (i.e., persons who would get the estate if there were no will) and beneficiaries named in the will, preferably meeting with them, if convenient.
4. Arrange for a bond, if necessary, to cover faithful performance of his duties as executor.
5. Notify the post office to send the decedent's mail to the executor and discontinue telephone and other services as appropriate.
6. Open a bank account for the estate.
7. Assist the attorney in identifying creditors and arranging for payment of debts.
8. Identify, inventory, and safeguard all probate assets (obtain appropriate insurance and prevent relatives from plundering estate assets, if necessary).
9. Review nonprobate assets (joint tenancy and trusts) for appropriate action to ensure legal transfer.
10. Offer the will for probate in court and be appointed formally by the court as executor (referred to as *receiving letters testamentary*).
11. Review and take appropriate action regarding the decedent's financial records, including notification of death: leases, mortgages, notes, life, health and auto insurance

*"Cryonics is basically the science of turning us humans into popsicles upon our death with the hope of reviving us in the future and restoring us to our former, healthy selves again. Just after death, 'patients' who elect to take a shot at immortality are stored in a chamber of liquid nitrogen to prevent further physical decay." Adam Thierer, "Could Ted Williams Hit .400 Again in the Future?" *TechCentralStation*, 12 July 2002.

The remains of Ted William remain in cryonic preservation at the Alcor Life Extension Foundation in Scottsdale, Arizona. Ultimately the decision was not made by the probate court because the daughter who objected to the deposition of the corpse withdrew her objection before the probate court hearing. Richard Sandomir, "BASEBALL; Williams Children Agree to Keep Their Father Frozen," *New York Times*, 21 December 2002.

policies, pensions, Social Security, stocks, bonds, saving accounts, checking accounts, credit card companies, any memberships, and so on.

12. Collect any dividends, interest, or rent and pay any rent, interest, insurance premiums, or other obligations.
13. Have assets appraised when advisable or required.
14. If decedent had a business, act to continue proper operation if feasible and appropriate, or to sell and liquidate if necessary.
15. Publish statutorily required notice to creditors and review and pay claims.
16. Keep detailed records of receipts (income) and disbursements (expenses and debt payments).
17. Determine cash requirements for taxes (income and estate), probate expenses, valid claims, and cash bequests, and decide which assets are to be used or liquidated for these needs.
18. With the aid of an accountant, file income tax returns (final return of decedent, tax returns for the estate while administration continues) and death taxes (inheritance or estate) and make necessary payments.
19. Prepare a final estate accounting to submit to the court (listing assets, receipts, disbursements, sales with gains and losses, and reconciliation of beginning and ending balances).
20. Transfer title to real and personal property to beneficiaries (and sometimes trustees) in accordance with the probate court decree of distribution under the will and obtain receipts for them.
21. Obtain formal court approval of the settlement of the estate and final discharge as the executor.

living will
A document, usually authorized by state statute, that directs any attending physician to comply with the wishes of the drafter regarding the use of life-support systems in the treatment of a terminal illness.

WHAT ARE LIVING WILLS AND OTHER ADVANCE DIRECTIVES?

The population of the United States is aging, primarily thanks to some remarkable advances in medical practice and pharmacology as well as in diet. Increases in the number of aged persons influences social, political, and economic policy and related law. There has been a growing acceptance of a document called a **living will**, which allows an individual to instruct her family, and medical personnel, about the medical procedures to follow—or more particularly, to abstain from—under specified circumstances.

MORALS AND ETHICS

Courts often are challenged with the moral dilemma of deciding whether or not to remove life support from persons who enter into permanent comas without leaving living wills or instructions behind, as illustrated by the story of Nancy Cruzan. At age twenty-five Nancy lapsed into a permanent coma after an automobile accident. Five years after the accident, her parents sought a court order to remove a feeding tube from Cruzan, who had been in a vegetative state since the accident. Without medical assistance, Cruzan would die. After several years of court battles, a Missouri circuit court in 1987 granted Nancy Cruzan's parents' wishes and the feeding tubes were removed. Twelve days after the court order, Cruzan died. Among the reasons for the long court battle was the absence of any written evidence as to what Cruzan's desires might be. A living will would have provided the written evidence that her parents lacked.

Cruzan by Cruzan v. Director, Missouri Dept. of Health, 497 U.S. 261, 110 S.Ct. 2841 (1990).

advance medical directives (AMD)
Instructions prepared in advance of a life-threatening condition as to what care should be given or not given in the event of incapacitation.

incapacity
Lack of legal capacity to make important decisions.

directive to physicians
A signed document communicating the signer's wishes regarding the use of life-support systems in the treatment of a terminal illness.

durable power of attorney for health care
A document authorizing another person to make health care (and sometimes other) decisions for a person even after he has become incapacitated.

power of attorney
A document authorizing another person to act as one's agent. A general power of attorney authorizes the agent (called the attorney-in-fact) to do all acts not prohibited by law for another (called the principal).

All states now have passed statutes providing for **advance medical directives (AMD)**, instructions to others about the care persons wish, or do not wish, to receive if they become terminally ill or incapacitated. **Incapacity** is the lack of legal capacity to make important decisions. It can result from a serious illness, an accident causing a coma, or even old age if coupled with Alzheimer's disease or dementia. The most common AMD is the living will.

The term *living will* is misleading because a living will has nothing to do with the transfer of property after death. A less confusing term used in many states is **directive to physicians**, which in most states has an identical meaning. A related directive is the durable power of attorney for health care, discussed later. Whatever the name, it is a document directed to physicians to consider the ill or injured person's wishes regarding the use of life-support systems. All states provide for living wills, but the requirements vary. (A living will should not be confused with a living trust, which is discussed subsequently in the chapter.)

Some living will statutes require that the living will be created after a patient has learned of a terminal illness but not before. This type of living will obviously would not have assisted Cruzan's parents because her condition occurred without notice or time to plan. Also, Cruzan was not just permanently ill; she was brain dead in a permanent coma.

Living wills must be witnessed by two or more disinterested (meaning free from any selfish motive or interest) persons and prepared using a specific format or form. If a form is legally invalid in execution, it still may be used in court to show the desires of the ill person if he is unable to testify.

A **durable power of attorney for health care** is a more flexible document than the living will. It authorizes another person to make health care decisions for someone who is incapacitated. It is one type of power of attorney. A **power of attorney** is a common legal document allowing the creator, a principal, to empower another (agent) to act on her behalf, usually in regard to financial and property decisions. These documents can authorize another person to perform any act that the principal otherwise could do. They also can be limited in scope to authorize specified and limited acts, such as selling specific shares of stock. Note that the person nominated is known as the *attorney-in-fact* and need not be and usually is not an attorney-at-law. (The term *attorney* literally means "representative.") An ordinary power of attorney ends with the incapacity or death of the person giving the power; it automatically terminates at that point. The powers granted by a durable power of attorney, however, do not end with the incapacitation of its creator.

A durable power of attorney can be created in some states to authorize financial decisions, as well as health care decisions, but here we are discussing the *durable power of attorney for health care,* a phrase describing a document that limits the attorney-in-fact to health care decisions. Such durable powers of attorney often are created to be "springing" documents, written to provide power to the designated representative only upon the occurrence of a health care crisis. In other words, the power is given to the attorney-in-fact only upon the occurrence of certain specified events or conditions.

In any form, a durable power of attorney gives the attorney-in-fact, usually a close relative or friend, the power to make health care decisions for a person who becomes incapacitated through serious illness, accident, or any other means. The decisions authorized include life-and-death decisions, such as whether or not to order the withdrawal of life-support systems for the incapacitated party. The durable power is not necessarily restricted to life-and-death health decisions, however. For example, if a person who is incapacitated needs elective surgery, the durable power of attorney may allow the designated person to approve the surgery.

A durable power of attorney for health care typically requires the signature of at least one disinterested witness and must contain the exact required statutory language. Often, the signature of the creator of the power must be attested and certified by a notary public.*

As with a living will, a durable power of attorney can be revoked by the principal creator at any time before incapacity. Note that the durable power of attorney differs from the living will in two important ways: (1) it can be created at any time—one need not be terminally ill, and (2) it delegates extensive and critical decision-making powers to another person. Therefore, that person should be selected carefully. Although these documents are well advised and useful, they should be created with great care and thoughtful consideration.

LEGAL FOCUS—PROBLEM

Mabel Bradshaw was elderly and concerned about being able to handle her affairs in the future. She wished to grant a power of attorney to her daughter Ann, who then could manage her property and make decisions about her medical care if she, Bradshaw, became incapacitated. Would you advise Bradshaw to create a power of attorney or a durable power of attorney?

Bradshaw's wishes suggest that a durable power of attorney is more appropriate. This choice will permit her daughter to handle her health care decisions and to make decisions about her property and investments should she become unable to do so.

LEGAL FOCUS—CASE

A petition to remove the life-support system for George Vogel was accompanied by this affidavit of Dr. Jonathan Sumner:

> George Vogel suffered a major stroke that has left him in a vegetative state. He can move, but has no awareness; he further has no intellectual function. He is being kept alive solely by the use of a gastric tube through his nose in which material, in the consistency of eggnog, is fed into his body. George Vogel is not aware of his surroundings, nor is there any possibility that he will ever be in any other state other than the vegetative state that he presently suffers.

Testimony was also offered by his sister-in-law that Vogel, prior to his recent illness, had said "he did not wish to be kept alive by having tubes inserted into his body and that he would not wish to be kept alive solely by artificial means." A nonphysician guardian appointed by the court opposed the petition, stating that Vogel was neither brain dead ("his brain stem is operative") nor terminally ill. Vogel had not prepared any advance directive and he was not otherwise terminally ill. What was the order of the court?

Vogel v. Forman, 134 Misc.2d 395, 512 N.Y.S.2d 622 (N.Y. 1986).

*As law in this area varies from state to state, specific state statutes must be consulted before creating either a living will or durable power of attorney. Considerable thought also needs to be given to the selection of the attorney-in-fact. He or she should be someone you trust implicitly and who knows and is willing to abide by your wishes in trying times. In both the living will and either type of durable power of attorney, the instructions can be as detailed for the attorney-in-fact as one might wish, including exactly what to do in a variety of circumstances.

The court denied the petition, stating,

> *A distinction must be drawn between those who are unable to care for themselves due to infirmities of illness, age or other physical disabilities and those who are brain-dead or terminally ill, without hope of recovery and are being kept alive solely by use of artificial means made available by the techniques of modern medicine and technology. [I]t is a function of humanity to care for those who are unable to care for themselves by reason of illness, age or infirmities.*

Clearly, the legal response to Vogel's condition would have been different had he prepared an appropriate advance directive.

In 1991, the federal Patient Self-Determination Act became a law. It requires that, before being admitted to certain health care facilities participating in Medicare or Medicaid (including hospitals), patients must be informed of the right to execute advance directives and have an opportunity to inform the health care facility of their wishes regarding heroic measures to sustain life.

Natural Death Act
A statute that allows a person with a terminal condition to request that a physician remove life support.

States are establishing, and liberalizing, their statutes involving living wills and durable powers of attorney to allow persons greater flexibility.* Issues involving death are understandably difficult and sensitive, creating disagreements among persons with different values. Requirements for the creation and use of the document undoubtedly will continue to vary until a greater consensus emerges as to the proper way to deal with issues of natural death.

DOES A TERMINALLY ILL PERSON HAVE THE LEGAL RIGHT TO COMMIT SUICIDE?

LEGAL FOCUS—BACKGROUND

In the later years of the twentieth century, Dr. Jack Kevorkian, a retired pathologist and advocate for physician-assisted suicide, became a focal point for much of the debate about assisted suicide. He admittedly assisted in the suicide of several terminally ill patients. At least one source has credited Dr. Kevorkian with assisting in the death of more than 130 persons. He was charged with various homicide offenses in his home state of Michigan, with the charges usually being dropped or, in three instances, resulting in an acquittal by jury. In November 1998, the CBS television program *60 Minutes* used videotape provided by Dr. Kevorkian showing his participation in the death of Thomas Youk, a terminally ill fifty-two year-old ALS patient. (ALS is commonly referred to as Lou Gehrig's disease, a severe and progressive disorder of the nervous system for which there is no cure.) Youk was wheelchair bound, fed through a tube, and forced to use a machine to help him breathe, waiting to die an agonizing death when he requested that Dr. Kevorkian terminate his life. Millions of Americans witnessed physician-assisted suicide in prime time. This portrayed act led to Kevorkian's second-degree murder conviction in 1999 and a sentence of ten to twenty-five years in prison. He was paroled in 2007 and now advocates for assisted-suicide laws.

*Together, living will statutes and durable powers of attorney are often part of a "**Natural Death Act**" or "Rights of Terminally Ill" statute. Some states provide that family members or close friends can make medical decisions for incompetent patients who have not provided advance directives. Also, some states provide for nonhospital do-not-resuscitate (DNR) orders. The typical DNR order is written on an official form provided by the state department of health. Upon its presentation to a paramedic, emergency room technician, or any other health professional, all resuscitation efforts must be stopped.

suicide
The intentional killing of oneself.

euthanasia
The act of allowing one to die by withholding extraordinary medical measures, or putting to death by painless means a person suffering from an incurable disease or a condition of an extremely painful nature.

The issue of whether or not **suicide** (the taking of one's own life) is morally correct is one of many issues upon which Americans lack consensus. Most religions and certain legal rules generally label it a wrongful act. Currently, no state in the United States explicitly condones suicide; and only four states, Oregon, Washington, Montana, and Vermont allow assisted suicide under restricted conditions.

Euthanasia, also called mercy killing, is the affirmative act of bringing about the immediate death of another, allegedly in a painless way; it is generally administered by someone who thinks that the dying person wishes to die because of a terminal or extremely painful disease. The advance directives discussed earlier provide that only extraordinary and heroic measures to resuscitate can be refused or discontinued. Euthanasia involves an aggressive act of putting the patient to death perhaps without his prior authorization, an act most likely to be treated as some form of criminal homicide. The Oregon **Death with Dignity Act** is effectively a law legalizing euthanasia for the first time in the United States. A few other countries, such as the Netherlands, provide for legal euthanasia.

MATTERS CONCERNING TRUSTS

Put not your trust in money, but put your money in trust.

—Oliver Wendell Holmes, Jr., 1841–1935 (Associate Justice of the U.S. Supreme Court, 1902–1932)

What Are Trusts?

LEGAL FOCUS—PROBLEM

Marisa Fabor and her husband, Brandon, are worried. They fear that when their children, Kathy and Tom, inherit the family farm, they will sell it and squander the proceeds within a short time; the children "simply do not know the value of a dollar." What can the Fabors do to keep their children from squandering their inheritance?

Death with Dignity Act
A state statute that allows competent, terminally ill adult patients to obtain a physician's prescription for drugs to end their life.

One solution is the creation of a **trust**. A trust transfers legal title to property from the owner (called a **settlor** or sometimes called the *trustor* or *donor*) to another (called a **trustee**) to hold for the benefit of, and someday distribute to, the specified **beneficiary**. A trust becomes a separate legal entity, governed by its trustee. Thus, the trustee is anyone who holds property for the benefit of another, called the *trust beneficiary*. In the preceding situation, Marisa and Brandon would be the settlors, and Kathy and Tom would be the beneficiaries. The person or business firm selected by Marisa and Brandon to manage the trust would be the trustee. They could select themselves as co-trustees and name others as successor trustees upon their deaths.

How property is to be distributed is determined by the settlor and stated in the trust document. The trustee receives possession and legal title to the property for the duration of the trust, until it is distributed to the beneficiaries. Pending distribution, the beneficiary owns the equitable title to the property, which is a beneficial interest but without the right to possess or transfer the property. A trust can be created for any legal purpose consistent with public policy. Its essential elements are as follows:

1. The settlor must be competent to create a trust.
2. The settlor must intend to create a trust.

trust
A legal relationship in which one party (called trustor, settlor, or donor) transfers legal title in property to a second party (trustee) for the benefit of a third party (beneficiary or donee).

settlor
A person who establishes a trust. A settlor is also called a trustor.

trustee
A person who holds property in a trust for the benefit of another, the beneficiary.

beneficiary
A person or entity that is to receive assets or profits from an estate, trust, insurance policy, or other device when there is distribution.

3. The trust must be created for a proper purpose.
4. Money or property sufficiently identified to allow title to pass must be transferred to the trust.
5. A beneficiary must be designated.
6. Although a writing is not required to create a trust, it is expected.
7. The trust instrument should name a trustee with appropriate capacity.

If the Fabors transfer their farm to the First Bank of Minnesota, in trust, for the benefit of their children, the couple will have created a trust. This arrangement is illustrated in Exhibit 15.3.

A frequent use for trusts is to provide funds for a child's education. These trusts are created both in wills and as *inter vivos* trusts. The amount of assets or cash necessary to accomplish the purpose of this trust obviously changes over time. If Yale is your child's goal (or the parent's), note that the estimated cost of attending Yale in 2012–2013 is $58,600, which includes tuition ($42,300), room ($7,150), board ($5,850), and books and personal expenses ($3,300). If you could find a working time machine and travel back to 1900, you would find attending Yale a more reasonable $155 per year; room rent, $200; board, $200; books, $35 to $45; subscriptions, society dues, and so on, $100; and clothing and incidentals, $150—making a total of $850.

Who May Be a Trustee, and What Does a Trust Cost?

Any settlor who creates a trust may serve as her own trustee. Unless the trust is a living trust, however, the settlor usually chooses a competent and trustworthy relative or friend or a commercial trust company with its staff of experts. In addition, many financial corporations, such as banks, offer their services as commercial trustees. Anyone nominated as a trustee is free to decline to serve. If a successor or alternate is not named in the trust document, the court will usually name a trustee.

If compensation is not mentioned in the trust document, trustees have a right to be paid for their services. The fees are determined consistent with state law or as allowed by the probate court. The settlor can provide in the trust document how, or even whether or not, the trustee is to be paid for services. If the court sets the fee, it will determine

EXHIBIT 15.3
Trust Arrangement

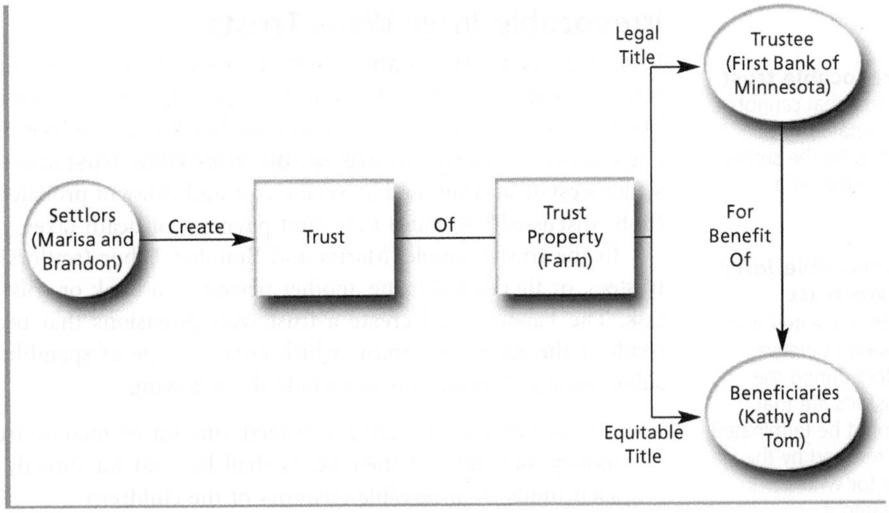

what is reasonable in view of the size of the estate, time required to administer it, services performed, and results achieved.

In trusts created during the settlor's life, like Marisa and Brandon Fabor's, the fees are negotiated. Common percentages are three-fourths of 1 percent of the fair market value of real estate and obligations secured by real estate, and three-fifths of 1 percent of the fair market value of other assets in the trust estate. The percentage may be less for a very large trust (e.g., one with assets in excess of $1 million). Corporate trustees frequently charge one-tenth of 1 percent as an "acceptance fee" when the trust takes effect, and a 1 percent "distribution fee" for all amounts they distribute. Trustees, like attorneys and personal representatives in probate proceedings, also are entitled to extra compensation for special services and expenses, such as defending the trust in a lawsuit.

What Are the Duties of a Trustee?

The trustee is a fiduciary to the beneficiary of the trust; that is, the trustee owes to the beneficiary a duty of highest care, honesty, and loyalty. The legal responsibilities of trustees are the same in both *inter vivos* and testamentary trusts, discussed shortly.

A trustee is duty bound to manage the assets of the trust properly. The trustee is accountable to the beneficiaries and must invest the property carefully. As a fiduciary, the trustee may not profit personally from the trust, other than by the payment provided for services rendered. Payment for duties performed as a trustee obviously is not considered a conflict of interest. Also, if the trustee is a beneficiary of the trust, receiving benefits from the trust consistent with the trust terms does not violate the duty of the trustee. Trustee duties are specified in state statutes, but they often are modified or further explained by the trust document.

ARE THERE DIFFERENT TYPES OF TRUSTS?

***inter vivos* trust**
A trust created during the lifetime of the settlor.

Two general categories of trusts are commonly used in estate planning. ***Inter vivos* trusts** (Latin: "among the living") are those created before death, such as that of the Fabors. *Inter vivos* trusts may be *revocable*, meaning they can be terminated (i.e., legally erased) at any time, or *irrevocable*, meaning they are permanent. A second general category of trust is the testamentary trust, which is created by will and which becomes effective upon the death of the testator.

Irrevocable *Inter Vivos* Trusts

irrevocable trust
A trust that cannot be terminated or revoked by the settlor who created it.

irrevocable *inter vivos* trust
A trust created and having operative effect during the trustor's life that cannot be terminated or revoked by the trustor who created it.

If the trust is an **irrevocable trust**, it cannot be revoked, nor can the property be returned to the settlor. Income from the trust is taxable to whoever receives it. Thus, shifting it in trust to someone in a lower tax bracket can reduce the amount of tax paid on one's income property. An **irrevocable *inter vivos* trust** also can keep property out of a settlor's estate at death and avoid the cost and delay of probate. A marital life estate trust (to be discussed later) also may limit payment of death taxes.

In the trust example, Marisa and Brandon Fabor (settlors) can name themselves as trustees, or they could name another person or a bank or trust company to perform the task. The Fabors could create a trust with provisions that become operative upon the death of the surviving spouse, which create a type of spendthrift trust that is discussed subsequently. Provisions may include the following:

- The children shall receive a limited amount of income from the trust as spending money, but most of their needs shall be paid for directly by the trustee (to shield such funds from possible creditors of the children).

- The children cannot give away or sell their rights in the trust.
- Creditors of the children cannot reach the trust principal.
- The trustee may spend part of the principal of the trust, if necessary, for the welfare of the children (using discretionary power to "invade the corpus" or use the "body" of the principal amount, in addition to interest or profit earned on the principal).
- The trustee shall transfer 25 percent of the trust to each child at age thirty years and the balance at age forty years. (The ages used here are arbitrary. The parents, depending on their opinion of when their children will have matured and could safely be given the assets, could select any age. Also, the trustee could be given the power to decide the time for appropriate distributions within some constraint.) Alternatively, the parents could direct that the principal remain intact and go to the then-living grandchildren. This option would eliminate a possible levy of estate taxes on the trust assets when their own children—the initial beneficiaries—die.

A major disadvantage of the irrevocable trust is that it cannot be changed to meet new circumstances. A will can be changed frequently to reflect new thoughts about how assets ought to be distributed upon death (of course, after death a will is irrevocable). And that distribution could be made under the terms of a testamentary trust included in their wills.

Revocable *Inter Vivos* Trusts

revocable *inter vivos* trust
A trust created and having operative effect during the trustor's life that may be terminated or revoked by the trustor who created it

The Fabors may be reluctant to make the trust irrevocable, because they might need the money for themselves before they die. Therefore, they might create a **revocable *inter vivos* trust**. Here they can change the terms, or beneficiaries, or terminate the trust at any time, regaining full control over the principal. All trust income would be taxable to them as owners, however, and the value of the trust principal would be taxed as part of the estate of the spouse who dies last. Death taxes would not be affected one way or the other by this trust. On the other hand, the trust assets will not be probated if the trust exists, is funded, and is not revoked prior to their deaths.

What Is a Living Trust?

living trust
A popular term for a revocable *inter vivos* trust whose primary purpose is to avoid probate.

The **living trust** is a popular term for a type of *inter vivos* trust designed to avoid probate. A person may desire to avoid probate because of its costs, and also to maintain privacy in the settlement of family affairs. The living trust is often less expensive than probate, and it is private. However, a living trust will not by itself reduce death taxes.

With the living trust, settlors transfer all of their property into a revocable living trust. To illustrate, assume that the trust is created jointly by husband and wife; the settlors can be joint trustees, or one alone may serve as the trustee. During their lives, they each may be the beneficiary of the trust. At the death of the first settlor, certain benefits of the trust shift to one or more other person(s), and the surviving settlor becomes the sole trustee, perhaps with the power to name a co-trustee.

LEGAL FOCUS—PROBLEM

Don and Pat Lee have a gross estate of $900,000 and a net estate (after payment of debts) of $800,000. They wish to avoid probate expenses for whichever of them is the surviving spouse. Ultimately, they wish to minimize shrinkage of estate assets for their only child, Kelly. They decide to create a living trust. Will it accomplish their goals?

Yes, it will accomplish their goals. They can create a living trust, transferring all or most of their property into the trust. For example, if they own real property, their ownership interest is conveyed by deed to the trust. Thereafter, the trust is legal owner of the real property. Other property, stocks, bonds, and pension contracts also are transferred to them as trustees of the trust.

The Lees can name themselves cotrustees with the surviving spouse also named as the successor trustee, anticipating the inevitability of death. (They might name additional successor trustees as well.) They also can name the beneficiary (or beneficiaries) who will receive distributions from the trust after the death of the settlors. At the death of the first spouse, the property will remain in the trust and the trust becomes irrevocable as to the decedent's property. At the death of the second spouse, the property will be distributed to the named beneficiary (or beneficiaries) in compliance with the terms of the trust.

Thus, the costs directly attributable to probate are not incurred. Deciding the cost savings, however, can be tricky and misleading. It is common and usual when the executor is the heir for executor fees to be waived, and if all or most of the property is community, and the spouse is the heir, he may elect an alternate procedure to probate, which eliminates most of the fees. Suppose Don dies first. When the property is probated at the time of Pat's death (assuming that her gross estate now totals $900,000), the probate fees would be $42,000. (An assumption is made that Pat has lived within her income and the estate is larger because Pat received Don's property.) It should be noted that the executor might waive his executor fee, so again the probate costs are probably overstated. If the property has been placed in the living trust, there are no probate fees at either death. Alternatively, there are only minimal fees to transfer the property to the surviving beneficiary (or beneficiaries). The total probate fee savings could be substantial. Although this example assumes a marital living trust, a living trust also would reduce probate fees for the estate of a single person.

There are costs involved when creating the trust, when transferring title to the property into the trust, when managing the trust, and when making its final distributions. Attorney and certified public accountant (CPA) fees may be incurred at every stage. In addition, probate fees are a deductible expense on the decedent's final income tax filing, and so the amount of savings by using the trust is somewhat overstated. Other reductions in probate fees can be made by waiving the executor's fees (common occurrence) and negotiating attorney fees below the statutory maximum. What the living trust does require is advance planning about fees that may be triggered upon death.

As a special caution, living trusts are marketed in ways that can lead to abuse. For example, the living trust often is sold in hotel seminars as a magic, painless way to save money for one's heirs. Sellers often overcharge for a form trust, failing to spend sufficient time with the client determining whether or not a living trust makes sense for that individual's estate plan, to appropriately transfer property into the trust, to provide for monitoring of the trust, and to arrange for how the settlors will have their future questions about the trust answered. Although a living trust may be a good idea for some, it is not automatically a good idea for everyone. Unless you are a sophisticated investor and estate planner, you should obtain competent professional advice about your particular situation.

The simple living trust makes the most sense for unconditional gifts to family members. The trustee is expected to be the settlor. (In a marital living trust, both spouses are joint trustees, with the surviving spouse being the successor trustee.) The trustee's duties are expected to be simple; the most important and complex of these duties is the distribution of the property. But the trust must be kept current, with title to property kept in the name of the trust, which can be an annoying burden to some persons. Valuations that are a normal part of probate and are certain to occur often are forgotten in private trust administration. Failure to appraise trust property and to obtain stepped-up valuations for assets can lead to significantly higher income taxes for heirs when inherited assets are ultimately sold.

The following situations are among those that suggest extreme caution in the creation of a living trust and necessitate the advice of an attorney:

- **A minor child is among the beneficiaries.** Special attention must be taken for the care of the minor child, and property should remain subject to the trust at least until the minor reaches the age of majority.
- **Long-term care of the settlors is contemplated** (e.g., a senior center or nursing home). This situation necessitates planning for the best and most appropriate use of assets to allow for maximum health care while preserving property for the heirs.
- **Long-term care of a beneficiary is contemplated** (e.g., a developmentally disabled child or a spouse who is mentally incapacitated). This situation necessitates a more complex trust and significant long-term responsibilities.
- **Conditional gifts to beneficiaries are contemplated** (e.g., in the Lee case, property to Kelly if she graduates from college). Conditional gifts create increased responsibilities for the trustee. If the trustee has discretionary powers, conflict between the beneficiary and the trustee is possible.
- **The value of the estate is significant, and estate taxes are to be paid** (e.g., a significant amount might be $2.5 million). Depending on whether the estate is liquid (i.e., cash, stocks, and bonds) or not (i.e., real property, most partnership interests, or a sole proprietorship business), determining and accumulating the money to pay the death taxes may complicate the duties of the trustee.
- **A substantial number of unsecured debts is expected.** One of the advantages of probate is the provision for an orderly method of paying debtors of the decedent—a living trust does not extinguish the debts of the settlor. Creditors expect to be paid, and without probate, the process may be awkward. Secured property (e.g., real property with a mortgage or an automobile with a secured interest) will be transferred subject to its indebtedness. Unsecured creditors have a claim against all property of the decedent. If the amount of debt is small, there will be little difficulty; if debts are significant, then careful plans should be made to pay them. Creditor claims complicate the trustee's duties and can cloud the title to property for intended beneficiaries for some time.
- **Personal trust assets are used from time to time as security for business loans.** Private lenders will inspect such trust documents and may well require changes to be made to the trust terms. If you later require additional financing, a second lender also may desire changes to the trust documents, which require approval of the first lender if it is willing. In any case, it gets complicated and the settlor loses control of the terms of the trust. This caution applies also to nonbusiness situations in which you intend that trust property act as security for a loan.

None of these situations makes a living trust inappropriate. Indeed, the same or similar problems arise when there is no trust. If complications are likely, however, then how the estate planner wishes these complications to be addressed should be considered in deciding whether or not a trust is appropriate and, if so, how it should be drafted.

Testamentary Trusts

testamentary trust
A trust created by a valid will.

A trust created in a will is called a **testamentary trust**. Although it is created when the will is made, the trust does not take effect until the settlor's death. If the will setting up a testamentary trust is invalid, then the trust also will be invalid. The property that was supposed to be in the trust will then pass according to intestacy laws, not according to the terms of the trust. Because the property is part of the decedent's estate, a testamentary trust does not avoid estate taxes or probate fees, nor provide the privacy of *inter vivos* trusts.

Marital Life Estate Trusts

marital life estate trust
Reciprocal trust executed by a husband and wife with the other spouse as a life beneficiary. These trusts also are called A and B trusts.

remainder interest
Any interest that is left after another interest in the property ends.

Don and Pat may wish to reduce federal death taxes on their estate. The living trust discussed earlier does not accomplish that goal. A **marital life estate trust**, also called an *A and B trust*, however, can reduce death taxes significantly to the ultimate benefit of the beneficiaries if it is created before the first spouse dies. In this trust, once the first spouse dies, the surviving spouse receives a life interest in the property and someone else (the designated beneficiary) has a **remainder interest** (the interest remaining after the life interest). An owner of a life interest can use the property for life, but cannot transfer it by contract or will. At the death of the owner of the life interest, the owner of the remainder interest (usually a child or children) automatically becomes the sole owner of the property. This trust, whether created *inter vivos* or by will, does restrict the freedom of the surviving spouse to use the property as he might wish. Anyone owning the remainder interest therefore is protected from diversion and unjustified dispersion of the trust property.

The effect of the trust is to reduce the size of the estate transferred upon the death of the second spouse. The net tax savings can be considerable. The larger the estate is, the larger the potential savings. There are, of course, additional costs of creating and maintaining the trust and a loss of deductions on the decedent's final tax return. Actual predicted savings for an individual should be determined in consultation with tax and estate planning advisors. The general admonition is to seek competent legal and tax advice for any kind of trust, which has significant, and sometimes undesirable, consequences to the settlors. Fortunately, such trusts usually are revocable by either settlor before either one dies, allowing the trust to be revoked or amended if circumstances or wishes change.

The Rule against Perpetuities

rule against perpetuities
A rule that requires remainder interests in property to vest (i.e., to take effect) no later than a life or any number of identified lives in being, plus twenty-one years.

As noted at the beginning of this chapter, there is an old saying that "you can't take it with you." The law cannot get around that truth, but instruments such as trusts and wills do the next best thing: They legitimately avoid probate fees and death taxes. Moreover, they allow persons to control who is to receive the property upon their death, and to instruct or restrict how that property may be used. However, the **rule against perpetuities** limits this control as it applies to trusts and other legal instruments that restrict the use and free transferability of property in the future. Under this rule, title in property must vest (i.e., some beneficiary must get full and unrestricted possession and ownership of the property) no later than a life or lives in being plus twenty-one years.

The details of this rule are complicated and beyond the scope of this text. But the purpose of the rule is simple and understandable. The rule against perpetuities is designed to prevent a trust from accumulating and compounding income for generations, by which time a small sum may have grown to a prodigious amount. It also keeps assets under the control of living persons rather than straitjacketed by donors long since dead.

The rule generally does not apply to charitable gifts. A gift of real property to a church, so long as no alcohol is served on the property, would not violate the rule. Such a restriction can last for hundreds of years, whereupon a violation (i.e., liquor is served on the land) could lead to a reversion of the property to the donor's heirs (who may well be hard to find and who will be surprised to learn of their interest).

Taxation of Generation-Skipping Trusts

generation-skipping trust
A trust created whereby the settlors of the first generation (parents) arrange for their child(ren) (the second generation) to receive the income while they are alive, but not the principal, which is reserved for the grandchild(ren) (the third generation) after the death of the second generation.

There are special rules to tax certain large generation-skipping transfers of wealth. Trusts usually are used for such transfers. For example, in a **generation-skipping trust**, a father (first generation) creates a trust under which his daughter (second generation) receives the income while she lives. When she dies, the principal goes to her child, a son (third generation). There is a death tax when the father dies, but no second tax when the daughter dies. The daughter's generation has been skipped as to estate tax liability because the daughter never received or controlled the principal. (Of course, when her child dies, any property from the trust still in his possession would be part of his estate for tax purposes.) This technique of tax avoidance is effective only for a trust that, on the death of the second-generation member (the daughter in our example), has a value less than any exemption threshold in effect at the time of the death. At the time this text was prepared that threshold was $5.25 million for 2013. Any value in excess of the exemption amount is taxed.

Are There Other Uses of Trusts?

LEGAL FOCUS—PROBLEM

H. Pauline Amesbury dearly loves her husband, who is fifteen years her senior and in his eighties. She is terminally ill and afraid that when she dies first, as is likely, he will be unable to manage the family estate alone. He might be talked into foolish investments, or worse, into remarriage to someone interested only in his money. What can Amesbury do to protect her husband against such developments?

She can create an *inter vivos* or testamentary trust, specifying that he shall receive the income during his lifetime and that the trustee may use the principal, if necessary, for his welfare. When he dies, the property will not appear in his estate, where it would increase his estate tax. Instead, it will be distributed as prescribed in Amesbury's trust, perhaps to go to their children, or even to be held for their grandchildren. The effect is the same as in the marital life estate trust, even if only one spouse creates the trust, as long as the settlor spouse is the first one to die.

power of appointment
Authority given to a person (the donee) under a trust or will to designate or appoint the person(s) who shall receive specified assets after a specified event, such as death of the donee.

The trust instrument could name charities or other beneficiaries selected by H. Pauline Amesbury herself, or designated by Mr. Amesbury if he is given a **power of appointment**—a designation in a will or trust giving him the power to decide who gets the money or property or to designate how the money or property will be used. This useful estate-planning tool allows the trust to postpone deciding which child or children or other beneficiaries receive what gifts. In these ways, a trust can frustrate would-be fortune hunters who prey on wealthy and unsophisticated beneficiaries.

Sometimes trusts make sense when the beneficiary is ill, mentally retarded, or very old. Settlors even may create a trust naming themselves as the beneficiaries and a bank

discretionary sprinkling and accumulation trust
A trust in which the trustee is authorized to decide who among the designated beneficiaries is to receive periodic payments of income or principal, and when.

charitable trust
A trust designed for the benefit of a segment of the public or of the public in general.

spendthrift trust
A trust created to provide for the maintenance of an improvident beneficiary by limiting his control of the corpus (the principal of the trust) and by barring access by creditors.

or trust company as the trustees, to spare themselves the burden of managing their estate. One also may create a trust and name it as beneficiary of insurance policies on one's life. This arrangement is often preferable to allowing the insurance proceeds to go as a lump sum to a beneficiary unequipped to handle such a sum.

A **discretionary sprinkling and accumulation trust** may be appropriate when flexibility is vital to meet the changing needs of family-member beneficiaries. The trustee is authorized to decide who among the designated beneficiaries is to receive periodic payments of income, or principal, or both. Beneficiaries who need more can be given more; those who need less get less. To help the trustee distribute the trust funds, the trust specifies guidelines, which might include maintaining a stated standard of living or comfort and general welfare for beneficiaries and allowing special payment for educational or medical fees. Income not paid is accumulated and ultimately distributed as part of the principal.

A trust designed for the benefit of a segment of the public or of the public in general is a **charitable trust**. It differs from a private trust in that the identities of the beneficiaries are uncertain. Usually, to be deemed a charitable trust, a trust must be created for charitable, educational, religious, or scientific purposes.

A trust created to provide for the maintenance of a beneficiary by preventing his improvidence with the bestowed funds is a **spendthrift trust**. Essentially, the beneficiary receives or is permitted to draw only a certain portion of the total amount of which he is the beneficial owner. Most states permit spendthrift trust provisions that prohibit creditors from taking possession of the assets of the trust before they are distributed to the beneficiaries.

A special type of trust that is created when a person deposits money in a bank in her own name as a trustee for another is called a **Totten trust**. This trust is tentative in that it is revocable at will until the depositor dies or completes the gift in her lifetime by some unequivocal act or declaration (e.g., delivery of the funds to the intended beneficiary). If the depositor should die before the beneficiary dies and if the depositor has not revoked the trust expressly or impliedly, a presumption arises that an absolute trust has been created for the benefit of the beneficiary. At the death of the depositor, the beneficiary obtains property rights to the balance on hand.

IS JOINT TENANCY AN EFFECTIVE WAY TO AVOID PROBATE?

Joint tenancy (or the similar tenancy by the entireties between spouses in some states) is a form of ownership for two or more persons to hold property (see Chapter 9). One of the most important aspects of joint tenancy is its *survivorship feature.*

LEGAL FOCUS—EXAMPLE

Al Brumley and Beth Alvarez own a house in joint tenancy. If Alvarez dies, Brumley automatically becomes the sole owner of the house immediately and without probate. Full title passes to Brumley even if Alvarez left a will that attempted to give her interest in the house to her mother, Sue Smith. Surviving joint tenants automatically receive the interests of a deceased joint-tenancy owner. As Brumley's interest is perfected at the moment of Alvarez's death, there is no interest left to convey by will.

Totten trust
A trust for bank depositors whereby they deposit money in a bank in the settlor's own name as a trustee for another person.

Depending on the circumstances and desires of the co-owners, this survivorship feature is either a reason to own property in joint tenancy or a reason not to own property in this manner. Because the ownership transfers automatically at the death of a joint tenant to the remaining tenant(s), joint-tenancy property is not subject to probate. Indeed, it is an effective way to avoid probate. Like most living trusts, however, a transfer by joint tenancy will not reduce death taxes because the transfer itself may be subject to such taxes because of its value. Other disadvantages to holding title to property in joint tenancy include the following:

- Either joint tenant can secretly terminate the tenancy while alive by conveying his interest to another person. The owner of the conveyed interest will not be a joint tenant but a tenant in common with the other joint owner(s).
- Creditors may terminate the tenancy by claims against the interest of one of the tenants. Such a claim may require sale of the asset to satisfy the claim. Such actions can tie up and cloud title to the property, even though the creditor's claim is generally good only against the debtor's interest in the property.
- The establishment of joint tenancy in property other than a bank account might be considered a gift. To the extent that its value exceeds $14,000 in a given year, the gift is a federal taxable event.
- Following the death of a joint tenant, there may be adverse capital gains treatment for the surviving tenant when the property subsequently is sold. Explanation of such complex tax consequences is beyond the scope of this text. The moral is as follows: If you are dealing with significant financial interests, seek legal and tax advice as to the most appropriate manner of joint ownership for you and your co-owners.

WHAT ARE CONSERVATORSHIPS AND GUARDIANSHIPS?

LEGAL FOCUS—PROBLEM

Peter White, seventy-eight years old, is a millionaire who sometimes acts in a way his family considers eccentric. His son Ed has been disturbed since Peter bought a large sailboat and announced his intention to sail to the South Pacific with an all-female crew. Ed contacted an attorney to inquire how he might stop his father from squandering the family fortune. Can Ed tie up his father's money?

conservatorship
A legal relationship created by a court to allow a person, the conservator, to manage the assets and personal affairs of another, the conservatee, who is not competent to manage her affairs.

No, he cannot tie up his father's money unless there is more to the story. Peter White appears to be capable of handling his own affairs, including his personal needs and financial resources. A conservatorship cannot and will not be declared simply to stop an eccentric person from overspending and thereby dissipating his estate. If the father was unable physically or mentally to handle his affairs (including the sailboat!), however, his son could petition the court to declare a **conservatorship**. A responsible person would be named the *conservator* to manage the assets and personal affairs of the *conservatee*. The pop star Britney Spears was placed under a conservatorship in 2008 after displaying erratic behavior. Her father successfully petitioned the court to be appointed conservator to manage affairs relating to her finances and career opportunities.

The conservator makes periodic reports to the court showing the business and personal transactions that have occurred. Although *conservatees* are without authority to handle their own affairs, they ordinarily can still make, or modify, a last will. A conservatee also may petition the court to modify the order or even to end the conservatorship based on changed circumstances.

guardianship
A court-established arrangement whereby an adult guardian is appointed to take care of the person or the estate of a minor.

An alternative procedure, called a **guardianship**, is available for those individuals who, for any reason, are unable to care for themselves or their estates. Usually, a guardianship is created to provide for a minor whose parents are dead, but an adult who is infirm judicially may be declared incompetent and placed in a guardianship. The person subject to a guardianship is called a *ward*. The person in charge of the ward's personal and financial affairs is called the *guardian*.

Under a typical guardianship statute, to declare one a ward, proof must show that the person is unable to provide for her own personal needs (food, clothing, shelter, medical care)—in other words, to manage her finances. Isolated incidents of negligence or improvidence will not suffice as evidence of the required standard of substantial inability. The alleged incompetent has the right to appear at the court hearing and to oppose the petition with the aid of counsel.

A proposed conservatee has similar rights, and either party may call for a jury trial if provided by state law. If the petition is granted, the court monitors the activities of the person in charge, requiring periodic reports. Both guardianships and conservatorships usually are costly to the estate of the protected party.

PRINCIPAL ELEMENTS OF ESTATE PLANNING

Although you probably have little personal need for an estate plan at this early stage of your life, the following guidelines may be valuable in the future, and perhaps now for members of your family. Also see Exhibit 15.4 for a useful checklist.

1. Prepare a personal or family balance sheet to show assets and liabilities. Keep accurate records of dates along with evidence of the acquisition costs of assets, including real property and its improvements (with receipts, for future tax purposes). Prepare a budget to monitor your earnings, spending, saving, and investing on a monthly and an annual basis.
2. Consider life insurance if appropriate for the needs of beneficiaries. (Be sure you understand the difference between term and ordinary life policies.) Select a suitable settlement option for each policy.
3. Consider creation of trusts (*inter vivos*, or testamentary, or both). Consider using a living trust to avoid probate and death taxes.
4. You (and your spouse, if married) should prepare a will specifying the recipients of all your possessions. Prepare a will even if you use a trust to avoid probate. Let your heirs celebrate if there is insufficient property to require probate because you effectively and economically transferred your estate by other means.
5. Write or record your final instructions. Leave a version of Exhibit 15.4 explaining where important records and assets are located.
6. Consider donating your body organs at death and prepare appropriate documents. Make your intentions known to others (e.g., on a card in your wallet, as such information should be accessible immediately).
7. Consider the execution of a living will or a durable power of attorney to permit implementation of your wishes if you become terminally ill or incapacitated.
8. Consider the transfer of certain assets into joint tenancy so that they will pass to the surviving joint tenant, avoiding probate. If married and living in a community property state, consider holding your jointly owned property as community property.

9. Make tax-free *inter vivos* gifts to reduce the size of your estate and thus reduce the level of income taxes and death taxes that will have to be paid upon your death. A salutary side effect is to help the donees when they need the money most and not later when unpredictable destiny forces a distribution by death.
10. Review pension plans to determine how much retirement income you can expect from all sources, including Social Security.
11. Consider investments in annuities to supplement a fixed income expected from pensions. Annuities can be created from the lump-sum proceeds of cash surrender values of life insurance policies.
12. Keep in mind the possible assistance obtainable from workers' compensation insurance and Social Security in case of accidental injury or death on the job, and from unemployment insurance, in case of forced idleness.
13. If one of your major assets is stock in a closely held corporation, prepare and execute a buy–sell agreement coupled with qualified plans for deferred compensation through profit sharing or company pension plans.
14. If one of your major assets is an interest in a partnership, prepare and execute a suitable buy–sell agreement and arrange for life insurance or some other means of providing cash to fund the purchase.
15. If one of your major assets is a sole proprietorship, provide a funded plan that will provide for the continuation of the company or liquidation under favorable circumstances.
16. Review and update your plan anytime there is a change in your personal status, or at least every few years. An outdated plan may be worse than no plan.

EXHIBIT 15.4
Important Papers Record

WHERE TO FIND MY IMPORTANT PAPERS

Name ________________ Social Security Number ________________

My valuable papers are stored locations (address plus where to look):

A. Residence ________________

B. Safe-deposit box(es) ________________

C. Other ________________

Items	A	B	C
My will (original)	____	____	____
Powers of appointment	____	____	____
Spouse's will (original)	____	____	____
Location and combination of safe	____	____	____
Trust agreements			
As settlor	____	____	____
As beneficiary	____	____	____
Life insurance policy(ies)	____	____	____
Insurance policy(ies)	____	____	____
Homeowner's insurance policy	____	____	____
Motor vehicle and other insurance policy(ies) (including boats)	____	____	____
Employment contract(s)	____	____	____
Partnership agreement(s)	____	____	____
List of checking, savings accounts	____	____	____
List of ATM & credit cards with numbers	____	____	____
List of online accounts (PayPal)	____	____	____
List of your e-mail addresses	____	____	____
Brokerage account records	____	____	____
Stock certificates	____	____	____
Bonds	____	____	____
Notes receivable	____	____	____
Notes payable	____	____	____

Items	A	B	C
Retirement papers	____	____	____
Deferred compensation; IRA papers	____	____	____
Titles and deeds	____	____	____
Notes (mortgages)	____	____	____
List of stored & loaned items (item, bailee, and address)	____	____	____
Motor vehicle ownership records	____	____	____
Birth certificates (mine, spouse's and children's)	____	____	____
Military enlistment and discharge papers	____	____	____
Marriage certificate(s)	____	____	____
Divorce/separation records	____	____	____
Contract(s)	____	____	____
Important receipts*	____	____	____
Important warranties	____	____	____
Other	____	____	____
	____	____	____
	____	____	____
	____	____	____
	____	____	____

*Including receipts for capital improvements to residence.

IMPORTANT NAMES, ADDRESSES AND PHONE NUMBERS

Beneficiaries under my will (list)

____

____

____

____

____

Attorney ________________

Accountant ________________

Insurance agent ________________

Stock broker ________________

Medical doctor ________________

Date prepared ________________

People to whom copies have been given ________________

1. ________________
2. ________________
3. ________________
4. ________________

CASE

Estate of Dorothy Southworth v. North Shore Animal League

Court of Appeal, 51 Cal.App. 4th 564, 59 Cal.Rptr. 2d 272 (Calif. 1996)

Dorothy Southworth requested information from the North Shore Animal League (NSAL) about its lifetime pet care program. NSAL sent Dorothy the information, included a request that Dorothy return an enclosed pet care registration card, and told Dorothy to contact her attorney about including a bequest to NSAL in her estate. Dorothy did not return the registration card to NSAL; however, after additional correspondence she did return a donor card to NSAL. In a blank space following the printed words, "I am not taking action now, but my intention is," Dorothy wrote, "my entire estate is to be left to North Shore Animal League" and she signed and dated the donor card. On January 14, 1994, Dorothy Southworth died without a will. NSAL asked that the donor card be admitted to pro bate as a holographic will, and the trial court ruled in its favor, stating that the card "substantially complies with all the Probate Code requirements for a holographic will." The intestate heirs, suppressing their natural love for animals, appealed.

Gilbert, Associate Justice

Decedent never married and had no children. On March 4, 1986, in response to decedent's request for information, NSAL sent a letter to her describing its lifetime pet care program and explaining how to register for it. NSAL asked that she return its enclosed pet care registration card, contact her attorney to include her bequest to NSAL in her estate and send a copy of the bequest to NSAL. NSAL informed her that "[e]ven if you don't currently have a will, we'll accept your Registration on good faith and maintain an Active file on your pet while you're arranging the Bequest." Decedent never returned the registration card to NSAL.

NSAL sent a donor card to the decedent. It stated: "Your newest gift to the North Shore Animal League will help get more homeless dogs and cats out of cages and into new homes." The donor card thanked her "for your interest in making a bequest to the League." It explained that she could change her life insurance policy or provide for animals in her will by calling her attorney. It sought gifts and legacies and asked her to complete and return the donor card.

On April 19, 1989, she returned the donor card to NSAL. [There had been other occasional contact in the intervening 3 years.] The card provided three options: a. naming NSAL as a beneficiary of a life insurance policy, b. changing one's will to leave securities or cash to NSAL, or c. not taking immediate action, but stating her intentions. On the card, the decedent circled printed option (c) which states: "I am not taking action now, but my intention is [in the blank space provided she wrote] My entire estate is to be left to North Shore Animal League."

The donor card also included a printed statement which reads, "The total amount that the animal shelter will someday receive is [she wrote in the blank space] $500,000." The card then stated, "I would like the money used for:

"Food and shelter for the animals
Adoption Fund to advertise for new owners
Spaying and Neutering Program
Unrestricted use[.]"

Decedent placed an "x" next to the food and spaying options listed. She signed and dated the donor card.

On May 10, 1989, NSAL sent a thank you letter to decedent for "letting us know that you will remember the North Shore Animal League in your will." The letter requested that decedent "have your attorney send us a copy of your will[.]"

The Neptune Society [where she had arranged for her cremation] asked for additional information to complete the death certificate, pursuant to amendments to the Probate Code. Decedent returned Neptune's supplemental form and stated that there are "[n]o living relatives" and to "[p]lease notify North Shore Animal League." She included NSAL's address, telephone numbers and the name of the executive director of NSAL. She signed the supplemental form and dated it October 20, 1989.

On September 2, 1992, NSAL sent a letter to decedent acknowledging that in March 1989 she wrote NSAL to state that she intended to take action leading to its becoming one of the beneficiaries of her estate. NSAL requested a meeting with decedent, thanking her for her "kind thoughts and generous support." She never responded to this request.

Jeanette Southworth, Jack Southworth, Michael Hulse and Arthur Hulse assigned part of their alleged interests in the estate to Francis V. See (hereinafter "See"). Jeanette and Jack are the surviving half-siblings of decedent. Michael and Arthur Hulse are the children of another half-sister of decedent who predeceased her.

The See contestants argued that the donor card should be denied admission into probate as a holographic will because not all of its material provisions are in the handwriting of the decedent and there is no showing of testamentary intent at the time she signed the card. NSAL argued that the donor card reflected decedent's testamentary intent and satisfied the statutory requirements for a holographic will.

The trial court concluded that decedent's handwritten statement on the donor card that "[m]y entire estate is to be left to North Shore Animal League" substantially complies with all the Probate Code requirements for a holographic will. The court viewed the preprinted parts of the donor card and the $500,000 sum written in to be immaterial. The court interpreted the preprinted words stating that "I am not taking action now, but my intention is ... "to mean that she did not want to immediately transfer her funds to NSAL, but intended to bequeath them upon her death. The trial court admitted the donor card to probate as the last will of the decedent. The See contestants appeal from the judgment.

Discussion

The facts are stipulated. "Where, as here, there is no conflict in the evidence, the validity of the holographic instrument must be determined entirely by reference to the applicable statutes and principles of law." Interpretation of statutes is a question of law and our fundamental task is to ascertain the intent of the Legislature.

Former Civil Code section 1277 stated that "[a] [h]olographic will is one that is *entirely written, dated and signed by the hand of the testator himself.* It is subject to no other form,... and need not be witnessed." (Emphasis added.) Section 1277 was strictly construed.

In 1931, the Legislature reenacted former Civil Code section 1277 as section 53 of the Probate Code and added a third sentence "... No address, date or other matter written, printed or stamped upon the document, which is not incorporated in the provisions which are in the handwriting of the decedent, shall be considered as any part of the will."

In *Estate of Black*, the decedent wrote out her will on three identical, commercially printed one-page will forms. In the blanks provided, she wrote her signature and place of domicile, and on the third page she inserted the name and gender of her executor, the date of the instrument and the city and state where she executed it. She either struck out or ignored other printed language regarding residuary gifts, the appointment of an executor, attesting witnesses and a testimonium clause.

"Using virtually all of the remaining space on each of the three pages, testatrix expressed in her own handwriting a detailed testamentary disposition of her estate, including specific devises and legacies to individuals and a charitable institution and a bequest of her residuary estate."

The trial court denied probate because the testatrix incorporated some of the printed language, even though it concerned perfunctory procedural matters in the form will. Our Supreme Court reversed because "none of the incorporated material is either material to the substance of the will or essential to its validity as a testamentary disposition...." (*Estate of Black,* 181 Cal.Rptr. 222.)

The Black court explained that "[t]he policy of the law is toward a construction favoring validity, in determining whether a will has been executed in conformity with statutory requirements." Moreover, we affirmed ([in the] Estate of Baker) "the tendency of both the courts and the Legislature ... toward greater liberality in accepting a writing as an holographic will...." "Substantial compliance with the statute, and not absolute precision is all that is required...." Courts are to use common sense in evaluating whether a document constitutes a holographic will.

The Black court recognized that "[i]f testators are to be encouraged by a statute like ours to draw their own wills, the courts should not adopt, upon purely technical reasoning, a construction which would result in invalidating such wills in half the cases." That sensible admonition is no less appropriate today. The law recognizes that such wills are generally made by people without legal training. The primary purpose of the statutory holographic will provisions is to prevent fraud. Because counterfeiting another's handwriting "is exceedingly difficult," these statutes require the material provisions of holographic wills to be in the testator's handwriting.

Whether a document should be admitted to probate as a holographic will depends on proof of its authorship and authenticity, and whether the words establish that it was intended to be the author's last will and testament at the time she wrote it.

Our high court explained that four questions are pertinent in evaluating whether a document should be invalidated as a holographic will due to printed language in the document: "Was the particular provision relevant to the substance of the will? Was it essential to the will's validity? Did the testator intend to incorporate the provision? Would invalidation of the holograph defeat the testator's intent?"

Accordingly, in 1983, the year after our Supreme Court decided Black, our Legislature replaced Probate Code section 53 with Probate Code section 6111. Section 6111 provides, in pertinent part, that "(a) A will ... is valid as a holographic will, whether or not witnessed, if the signature and the material provisions are in the hand writing of the testator." In 1990, the Legislature added subdivision (c) which provides that "Any statement of testamentary intent contained in a holographic will may be set forth either in the testator's own handwriting or as part of a commercially printed form will.

There is no question that the handwriting on the document at issue is that of Dorothy Southworth, and that she signed and dated it. Unlike Black, however, the document is not a commercially printed will form. It is a donor card for a charity. It was not drafted to serve as a will. The card provides the option of informing NSAL that the donor has or intends to instruct one's attorney to change her will.

Furthermore, the printed language Southworth incorporated from the donor card does not evince her present testamentary intent. Instead of striking the material printed words which state "I am not taking action now, but my intention is," she chose to incorporate those words with her handwritten statement, "My entire estate is to be left to North Shore Animal League." The material printed language together with her handwriting evince a future intent; not present testamentary intent.

Although other extrinsic evidence, such as her letter to NSAL of September 4, 1987, and the supplemental Neptune form she signed on October 20, 1989, shows that Southworth desired to leave her estate to NSAL, neither the donor card at issue nor the handwriting on it substantially complies with probate code requirements for holographic wills. Although courts may consider statements made before and after a holographic will is made and the surrounding circumstances, evidence of present testamentary intent provided by the instrument at issue is paramount.

Here, Southworth incorporated printed language stating that she was not taking any action when she executed it. It does not establish her testamentary intent at the time she executed it. It only states her intention to make a will in the future.

The judgment is reversed. The parties are to bear their own costs.

For Critical Analysis

1. What were the appellate court's reasons for holding there was no valid holographic will? Do you agree with the court? Explain.
2. What could NSAL have done, if anything, to increase its chances of inheriting from Ms. Southworth?
3. Identify the heirs who are claiming Ms. South worth's estate and their relation to Ms. Southworth. Why had Ms. Southworth told the Neptune Society she had no "living relatives"?
4. Are the rules for holographic wills too technical? Explain your answer.

McConnell v. Beverly Enterprises-Connecticut, Inc.

Supreme Court of Connecticut, 209 Conn. 692, 553 A.2d 596 (Conn. 1989)

The husband and children of a comatose, terminally ill patient brought an action seeking to terminate life-support services being provided to Carol M. McConnell by a private nursing home, Danbury Pavilion Healthcare. Carol McConnell was the fifty-seven-year-old wife of the plaintiff John E. McConnell and the mother of the three other coplaintiffs. By profession, she was a registered nurse. Her last nursing positions were as head nurse and manager of the emergency room at Danbury Hospital. On January 18, 1985, Mrs. McConnell sustained a severe head injury as the result of an automobile accident. She had not regained consciousness, despite excellent medical care. She was in an irreversible persistent vegetative state with no prospect of improvement. In the opinion of her attending physician, her condition was terminal. Her life was sustained by means of a gastrostomy tube through which she received nutrition and hydration. The superior court entered judgment for the patient's husband and

children, and the state attorney general and the patient's guardian ad litem took appeal.

Chief Justice Peters Wrote the Opinion

This case concerns the right of a family, on behalf of a patient who is presently in a terminal coma, to implement the patient's clearly expressed wish for the removal of a gastrostomy tube that is artificially providing nutrition and hydration for the patient.

[T]he Removal of Life Support Systems Act in which the legislature, cognizant of a common law right of self-determination and of a constitutional right to privacy, sought to provide a statutory mechanism to implement these important rights. We must decide what role this act plays in the present litigation. The trial court held that the plaintiffs were entitled to relief without regard to the act, which the court construed to be nonexclusive. The defendants, by contrast, maintain that the act governs and precludes the relief sought by the plaintiffs. There is, however, a middle ground, a construction of the act that is consistent with the plaintiffs' affirmative claims for relief.

Although the United States Constitution does not expressly provide a right to privacy, the United States Supreme Court has recognized a right to privacy in the penumbra of the Bill of Rights, specifically in the protection of the First, Third, Fourth and Fifth amendments. "[T]he Court has recognized that a right of personal privacy, or a guarantee of certain areas or zones of privacy, does exist under the Constitution." Justice Brandeis has referred to this right as "the right to be let alone—the most comprehensive of rights and the right most valued by civilized men." Although the court has recently construed this right to privacy narrowly; it has held that personal rights that are "implicit in the concept of ordered liberty"; or "deeply rooted in this Nation's history and tradition" are included in this guarantee of personal privacy. The court has found that contraception, procreation, marriage, and education implicate privacy rights.

The right to refuse medical treatment has been specifically recognized as a subject of constitutional protection. This court has also long held that "[e]very human being of adult years and sound mind has a right to determine what shall be done with his own body...." Court after court has recognized the existence of a right, in principle and in properly guarded circumstances, to the removal of medical treatments that artificially prolong life.

Many of the cases upholding a right of self-determination for terminally ill individuals have urged legislatures to enact guidelines for appropriate private decision-making in these heart-rending dilemmas. When the legislature has attempted to respond to this urgent request for statutory assistance, we have an obligation to pursue the applicability of statutory criteria before resorting to an exploration of residual common law rights, if any such rights indeed remain. We must therefore decide whether a reasonable construction of our act ever permits the removal of a gastrostomy tube.

Careful examination of our act discloses that the legislature approached the appropriate treatment for very sick patients by establishing three guiding principles. First, if a patient, in the eyes of his or her attending physician, is not in a terminal condition, "beneficial medical treatment and nutrition and hydration must be provided." Second, if a patient, to the contrary, is deemed by his or her physician to be in a terminal condition, life sustaining technology may be removed, in the exercise of the physician's best medical judgment, when that judgment has received the informed consent of the patient's next of kin or guardian and when it coincides with the expressed wishes of the patient. Third, even the removal of life sustaining technology must be done in a manner consistent with providing "comfort care and pain alleviation" for the patient. Under the act, the patient's attending physician must deem "the patient to be in a terminal condition." For the purposes of the act, "'[t]erminal condition' means the final stage of an incurable or irreversible medical condition which, in the opinion of the attending physician, will result in death." Dr. Robert Ruxin serves as Mrs. McConnell's attending physician and he testified that he deemed her to be in a terminal condition. While there was testimony to the contrary on this issue, the act places the responsibility for reaching the conclusion with the attending physician, contemplating a decision to discontinue treatment reached after consultation between the attending physician and the family or next of kin, unimpeded by courts, other medical experts or ethicists.

Ruxin reached his conclusion after numerous examinations of Mrs. McConnell. He deemed her to be in an incurable, irreversible, persistent vegetative state, a condition that ultimately will lead to her death. The trial court found Ruxin's testimony credible and we have discovered nothing in the trial transcripts to warrant disturbing this finding.

The statute requires that the attending physician obtain the informed consent of the patient's next of kin prior to removing a life support system. The fact that the rest of the McConnell family (husband John, daughters Kathleen and Amy, and son James), all over the age of majority, have brought this action indicates that they consent to the removal of the gastrostomy tube. Furthermore, the testimony of all four demonstrates positively that they reached their decision out of love and concern for their mother and wife and respect for her wishes. There is not a hint in the trial court testimony of any ulterior motive on the part of any of the plaintiffs.

Finally, pursuant to the act, the attending physician must consider "the patient's wishes as expressed by the patient directly, through his next of kin or legal guardian...." The trial court found clear and convincing evidence that Mrs. McConnell had expressed "forcefully and without wavering" that artificial means should not be employed to prolong her life. We conclude that the trial court did not err in this finding.

That Mrs. McConnell desired that her family not prolong her life should she ever suffer an injury that left her in a vegetative state could not have been clearer. She worked as a registered nurse in an emergency room, and therefore often saw the tragedy that befell those who suffered severe head injuries. The court heard testimony from a co-worker, Marie Kornhaas, that Mrs. McConnell did not believe in the use of respirators, feeding tubes or other life-sustaining systems, and that if she were ever placed on such a system, she hoped that Kornhaas would do what she could to stop it.

The trial court heard testimony from all of Mrs. McConnell's immediate family that she was extremely concerned about head injuries, warning her children often about the dangers of motorcycles and small cars. Her husband described her as having "a phobia about head injury." She had also been adamant that her own mother, when dying of cancer, not be placed on any life support system. Finally, each member of her immediate family testified absolutely, without hesitation, that Mrs. McConnell did not believe in life support systems, including gastrostomy tubes, for herself, that she would want the tube removed from her and that they sought to carry out her wishes. We therefore conclude that the record sustains those findings of fact by the trial court that are required by the act to be shown as a condition for the withdrawal of life support systems.

III

In his brief, the Attorney General raises the specter of suicide, claiming that the state has a compelling interest in preventing it and that to allow Mrs. McConnell to carry out her wish to discontinue food and nutrition would be to allow her to commit suicide. We are not persuaded that a suicide would occur in this case.

It is well established that the state may not base a criminal prosecution on the exercise of a constitutional right. Because we hold that the legislature in enacting the Removal of Life Support Systems Act sought to establish a workable mechanism by which individuals may implement their common law and constitutional rights, it follows that by exercising these rights, the individual cannot become criminally liable.

Furthermore, we agree with the majority of jurisdictions that have addressed this issue in holding that the removal of a gastrostomy tube is not the "death producing agent," set in motion with the intent of causing her own death. In exercising her right of self-determination, Mrs. McConnell merely seeks to be free of extraordinary mechanical devices and to allow nature to take its course. Thus, death will be by natural causes underlying the disease, not by self-inflicted injury.

There is no error.

In this opinion CALLAHAN, GLASS and COVELLO, J.J., concur.

For Critical Analysis

1. Why did the state attorney general oppose the family's wishes? Was it appropriate that he do so?
2. What does this sentence mean? "The trial court held that the plaintiffs were entitled to relief without regard to the act, which the court construed to be nonexclusive."
3. Do you agree with the doctor's diagnosis that Mrs. McConnell was in a "terminal condition"? Remember this diagnosis was made before removal of the gastrostomy tube—after removal it is clear she would be. How would Mrs. McConnell's situation be any more terminal than that of anyone else, including you?
4. Assume a person makes a conscious decision to stop taking nutrition and hydration (eating and drinking). Is that suicide? Is it illegal? At some point, the person would become unconscious before death; would it be wrongful to provide hydration and nutrition by a feeding tube against the person's wishes? If it were administered, could the person demand removal upon regaining consciousness?

CHAPTER QUESTIONS AND PROBLEMS

1. Joe Mariano never made a will. Now he is flat on his back in a hospital bed after being injured in a crash of his private plane. Both his arms are in casts, and he has extensive internal injuries. But his mind is alert, and he can talk. Realizing that the prognosis is bad, he calls for his lawyer. Can they prepare a formal, witnessed will, even though Mariano cannot write his name?
2. When Pauline Puffington died, she left her entire estate of $3 million to a trust for the care of her twelve dogs and fourteen cats. After the pets' deaths, the principal was to be paid to a designated society for the prevention of cruelty to animals. Relatives challenged the will, proving not only that she was eccentric and senile when she made it, but also that she was insane when she died. Can the will be enforced?
3. Mary Dorsett was convinced that making a will was tantamount to writing one's own death warrant. Even after she married and had given birth to the twins, she did nothing to ensure the economical transfer of her estate to her family after her death. She was a hard-working dentist and had acquired an estate of $1.5 million by age thirty years. Then she suddenly died of a heart attack. Under the state's law of intestacy, her husband received one-third of her separate property and the twins, age five years, shared the balance equally. What expenses and burdens might she have avoided for her widower?
4. Richard Kalfus murdered his wife, Domenica. He pled guilty and was sentenced to prison. Her husband and two infant children survived Domenica. She left no will. Under New Jersey's law of intestate succession, a husband is entitled to a one-third share of personal property if children also survive the deceased parent. The statute made no reference to the effect of wrongful acts by an heir. Is Richard entitled to his intestate share of Domenica's estate? [*Estate of Kalfus v. Kalfus,* 81 N.J. Super. 435, 195 A.2d 903 (N.J. 1963).]
5. Harry Gordon died at the age of eighty-three years. The sole beneficiary in his will was a charitable organization. The attorney who drafted Gordon's will was the regional vice president of the organization and his practice was located in the same building as the charity. All witnesses to the will were officers of the corporation, as were the executors. The original will was kept in the charity's offices. The will was executed seven years before Gordon's death. Would there be a presumption of undue influence? Was undue influence present? [*Herman v. Kogan,* 487 So.2d 48 (Fla. 1986).]
6. The will of Warren E. Burger, chief justice of the United States from 1969 until 1986, is included as Exhibit 15.1 in this chapter. He prepared the will himself. Is it a holographic will? What improvements to his will could you advise?
7. Discuss situations in which a directive to physician would apply. A durable power of attorney? What ethical dilemmas do these instruments create?
8. What is the difference between a revocable and an irrevocable trust? Identify a circumstance where each would be appropriate.
9. First Virginia Bank of Tidewater was the trustee of a testamentary marital trust. In the course of the bank's service as trustee, it invested $40,000 in real estate investment trusts. The investment became worthless. The beneficiaries of the trust brought suit, complaining that the bank had violated the Virginia statutory "prudent man rule," which guided trustees in careful investment of trust assets. The bank defended, alleging the settlor had granted the bank broad discretion, obviating the "prudent man rule." Language in the will authorized real estate investments and to hold or sell investments "without liability on the part of any fiduciary for depreciation in the value." Can a settlor supersede a statutory standard for a trustee? Did the testator settlor do so in this case? [*Hoffman v. First Virginia Bank of Tidewater,* 220 Va. 834, 263 S.E.2d 402 (Va. 1980).]
10. J. T. Payne executed a valid will on June 29, 1934. On April 24, 1956, a will with singed edges was offered to the probate court. Three of his children challenged the will, contending the deceased had revoked it. A witness at the trial testified that in July of 1934, J. T. Payne said, "I am going to get rid of this damn will right now," and he threw it on live coals in the fireplace. Payne's wife rescued the document and, with it still smoking on one end, put it into her apron. No language of the will offered in probate was obliterated or obscured. Can this be considered a valid will? [*Payne v. Payne,* 3213 Ga. 613, 100 S.E.2d 450 (Ga. 1957).]
11. Over a period of fifteen years, Clint and Mary Hamilton gave each of their three children $10,000 each ($30,000 annually) totaling $450,000 of gifts. Will Clint, Mary or their children be subject to federal tax liability on these gifts? Why or why not?

12. A rare coin collector left his entire estate valued at around $280,000 to an American neo-Nazi group linked to assassinations and bombings. His sister contested the will, arguing that it is invalid as being against public policy. Is such an argument valid?
13. In the Netherlands, euthanasia is understood to mean termination of life by a doctor at the request of a patient. The inclusion in the country's Criminal Code of a special ground for exemption from criminal liability means that doctors who terminate life on request or assist in a patient's suicide can no longer be prosecuted, provided that they satisfy the statutory due care criteria and notify the appropriate regional euthanasia review committee. Do you prefer this approach to end-of-life issues or that of the United States? Justify your position.
14. Sung Fong had two strong obsessions during a long, eventful life: to become a millionaire and to "go it alone." He never married and now, at age ninety years, has a net worth of more than $10 million, almost all in stocks and bonds. He has no enemies, explaining with a chuckle that he has outlived them all. He has no true friends and no known relatives. With his health failing rapidly, he added a third goal: to pay no death tax to the government. "Not one cent," he repeats. Can you tell him how to accomplish this last strange goal?
15. Answer each of the following questions. Check your answer with answers provided by experts by conducting an Internet search of estate planning websites.
    a. Why should I prepare a will?
    b. What happens if I die without a will?
    c. Does a will cover all my property?
    d. How do I change my will after it has been signed?
    e. What is probate? How can I avoid it?
    f. What does it mean when a will is contested?
    g. What does it mean to be an executor?
16. Terri Schiavo suffered severe brain damage in 1990 after she collapsed, presumably due to the physical stress of chronic bulimia. She suffered hypoxic encephalopathy, or brain damage caused by a lack of oxygen. Doctors determined that the unconscious woman was in a persistent vegetative state with no chance of recovering any cognitive abilities. Her husband wished to remove the feeding tubes that provided a nutrient solution to keep her alive, but her parents, the Schindlers, objected strenuously. They believed that she was responding to their visits, although the doctor said her noises and facial expressions were reflexes.

    Terri did not have any advance directives regarding her care as she was a young woman of twenty-six years when she became incapacitated. Therefore, the key issue was whether or not she would have wanted to remain connected to the feeding tubes. Her husband, Michael Schiavo, provided sufficient evidence to convince the county court that she would not have wanted to exist though the use of extraordinary measures. In 2001, Schiavo's feeding tube was removed, but then reinserted two days later when a court issued an order to resume her nourishment based on the discovery of evidence that seemed to rebut her husband's assertions.

    After another trial that examined medical evidence of her condition, the judge once again ordered the removal of the tube. But the state legislature responded with "Terri's Law," which gave Florida Governor Jeb Bush the authority to order the reinstatement of Terri's nutrition and hydration and provided for the appointment of an independent *guardian ad litem*. Subsequently, the Florida Supreme Court held that the statutory directive unconstitutionally interfered with powers reserved to the judicial branch.

    The feeding tube was removed again on March 18, 2005. Shortly thereafter President George Bush signed into law an extraordinary act passed by Congress that allowed the parents to seek review in federal court as to whether or not Terri Schiavo's constitutional rights had been protected adequately. Ultimately a federal court refused to reverse the decision of the county court, and Terri Schiavo passed away fourteen days later. The Schindlers called the removal of the tube "judicial homicide."

    What evidentiary burden should be met regarding the wishes of such an incapacitated person in order to remove her from life support? What kind of evidence would likely be forthcoming to demonstrate those wishes? How can conflicting testimony be resolved? If there is insufficient proof of the incapacitated person's wishes, what then should be done? Do you think there a societal predisposition to find proof that the person would not want extraordinary measures taken? Do you want extraordinary measures taken or know someone who would not want to be removed from life support? Do you think executive and legislative branches overreached in the Schiavo case? Why or why not, and why do you think her case captured the attention of all three branches of both state and federal government?

APPENDIX A

Case Brief

Case briefing is a long-used method of studying law. Its purpose is to have students identify the rules of law found in court cases and analyze how courts apply these rules of law to the facts of a case in an objective and rational manner. Case briefing hones analytic skills and heightens understanding of the role of courts in defining, interpreting, and applying law. This appendix explains one way to brief cases. There is no single standard for case briefing, but the following structure is common and will serve you well, both in studying the law now and in using the law in the future. It is worthwhile mastering. After explaining how a brief is constructed, a sample brief of the case *Eric J. v. Betty M.*, which appeared at the end of Chapter 1, is provided.

PURPOSES OF A BRIEF

The purposes of a brief are as follows:

1. Establishes a useful means of bringing the facts of a case back to memory in a short time, for whatever purpose, including classroom discussion.
2. Allows you to extract from a judicial decision its future value as precedent. In other words, it helps you find the principles of law that the case sets forth.
3. Allows for easier and smoother review of an area of law. Each brief takes a complex and long document (the case) and reduces it to its key facts, holding, and rationale (the brief). A collection of briefs can provide a comprehensive summary of an area of law.

ELEMENTS OF A BRIEF

A brief is primarily a self-teaching tool; as such, you should structure your briefs to meet your own needs. Various writers have proposed many formats. Use the one that makes the most sense to you. For an introductory law class, the purpose of a brief is more limited than for either a law student or a lawyer. Also, a brief should be brief. A long brief eliminates the most important role of a brief: the boiling down of a complex case to its essence.

Several basic components of a brief are present in almost all brief styles. If your brief style includes the following elements, you should do well:

- Facts
- Issue or issues
- Holding, including the rule of law
- Rationale

Facts

State the facts of the case in your own words. Indicate which facts are operative and which bear on the issues to be decided. Do not just repeat the judge's words. Be brief. Often a sign of how well you understand the case is your ability to identify the relative importance of facts. Some cases may have many extraneous facts that do not need to be in your brief. Most certainly, some facts will be more important than others. Your task is to frame the problem by describing the facts that count.

Issue

Issue spotting is the skill of recognizing in the facts a pattern that implies a certain type of issue. For instance, facts that describe two people both claiming ownership rights over a chair should spotlight an issue of ownership of personal property. In reading cases, often the parties and the court do this work for you. Ask yourself what legal questions are posed by the appealing party. The appealing party is alleging that an error of law was made. What is that error? What question is the court answering? Sometimes a court will see the issue differently than the parties and present a different twist on the issue. State the issue cleanly and crisply. Avoid stating it in technical or procedural terms. Some believe that beginning your issue statement with "Whether" will allow you to focus your statement.

> ***Example:*** *Whether Smith established legal ownership of the chair by physically possessing it for seven years.*

Holding

What is the ruling by the court? Who won? Answering these questions forces you to identify the outcome of the case. You must understand the procedural setting enough to know what happens as a result of the decision. For instance, if the court rules "in favor of the appellants," what does this mean? More important, you need to find the holding on the issue itself. How did the court decide the issue? What rule of law is provided by the case? Using the previous chair ownership example, a holding that resolves the issue might be as follows:

> ***Example:*** *The court found that Smith had not established ownership of the chair by virtue of possessing the chair for seven years.*

Notice how this statement ignores who owns the chair. A newspaper headline would be more focused on the personal story: "Smith Loses Chair to Green." In briefing a case, however, you are not a reporter; you are a student of the law. For that reason, you must stick to the issue and its resolution as the primary focus.

Rationale

The length of each part of the case brief need not be evenly distributed. In fact, the rationale section is usually the longest section. In the rationale section, you explain why the court ruled the way that it did. This means that you need to describe the court's reasoning, sometimes even quoting the court's choice of words. You also must explain which facts the court depended on and which ones it discounted or ignored. You also should note what prior decisions it looked at and whether it chose to follow them, overrule them, or differentiate them. The court also might interpret or cite particular statutes or other laws in reaching its decision. Finally, notice whether the court relies on public policy to reach its decision. Thus, the potential components to a court's rationale include the following:

- Facts, including which ones were dispositive and which ones not
- Prior cases that were followed, differentiated, or overruled
- Statutory law and how it was interpreted
- Public policy principles

Your task is to organize these components and explain how the court used them to reach its decision. You are trying to find the rule of law that may flow from this case. The rule of law is the "why" of the decision, not the "what." This distinction is important because unless you can determine the why of a case, it is difficult to use the case to predict the outcome of similar disputes when they arise.

Returning to the chair ownership issue, the holding does not tell us the "why" and, as such, it is not really that useful. The rationale of the court, however, might describe how the court relied on a long history that ownership is not automatically determined by mere possession, but instead it depends on how possession and control were lost by a previous owner.

REMEMBER

Almost all cases are appellate cases. Think about which appellate court they are from: state or federal? Is it a final court of appeal or an intermediate court? Consider when the case was decided—recently, or many years ago? Has the passage of time eroded the soundness of the decision? Finally, what do you think of the decision? Is it logical, just, fair, or otherwise? How does it fit with a textbook chapter or topic? Briefing cases can teach you about courts, moral viewpoints, and the seam between ethical values and the law.

BRIEF OF THE CASE OF *ERIC J. v. BETTY M.*

Here is a sample brief of the case of *Eric J. v. Betty M.* (Cal. Appellate Case 1999), which you read at the end of Chapter 1. Note that the "Facts" and the "Rationale" sections make up the bulk of the case brief. The facts have been retold in the author's own words and not all facts are recited. The Rationale section explains the court's holding and what it means as a rule of law. It cites the case law as well as the public policy that the court applied. The Rationale also explains how the court dealt with a possible contrary case.

Facts

Robert brought home his new girlfriend, Helen, and her eight-year-old son, Eric, to meet his mother, father, brothers, and sister and their spouses. The relationship between Robert and Helen continued and Helen and Eric were guests several times in different family homes. No family member told Helen that Robert had a criminal history of felony child molestation. It later was discovered that Robert sexually molested Eric during some of these visits at the family homes, all while Robert was on parole for child molestation. Robert was convicted of molesting Eric and sent back to prison. Helen filed suit against Robert's family, claiming they had a duty to warn her about Robert's criminal past and the potential danger to her child, and failing that duty, they were liable for money damages for the harm suffered by Eric. The trial court dismissed the case on a nonsuit motion.

Issue

Whether the trial court properly dismissed the negligence claim based on the premise that family members of a convicted child molester have no affirmative duty to disclose that information to the molester's girlfriend who has an eight-year-old boy.

Holding

The appellate court affirmed the trial court, holding that the family members had no affirmative duty to disclose the information.

Rationale

The appellate court placed great weight on the "no duty to aid" rule, developed "over the centuries" in courts. The court noted that a special relationship is required to create a duty to warn, give aid, or otherwise help another. Ultimately, the court found that no such special relationship existed and found no other reason to suggest that the family members had a duty to warn the girlfriend. The court cited several cases, including a California Supreme Court case, *Williams v. State of California*, that establish the "no duty to aid" rule. In short, a person who has not created the danger or risk is not liable simply for failing to take an affirmative action unless "some relationship" creates a "duty to act." The court rejected a case that seemed to rule the other way, *Soldano v. O'Daniels*, by explaining that the facts in that case clearly showed that the defendant actually had prevented someone else from rendering aid. The court also noted that any decision to find a duty to aid in this case would interfere with family relationships by creating "intolerable conflicts of interest." Impliedly, interfering with family relationships would go against public policy.

APPENDIX B

Legal Research

Understanding the Law, Seventh Edition, presents legal rules that help to solve a variety of problems that people commonly confront in their personal and business relations. When a legal problem or question arises, the law or laws applying to that particular situation in that particular jurisdiction must be determined. In our discussion of general rules of law, a rule presented may or may not apply in your particular state. Sometimes the rules of different states on a given matter may differ even fundamentally. If differences do exist, the decisive rule is the one that applies in the particular state involved.

Both lawyers and students of law conduct legal research to find the legal rule(s) that apply to specific problems, as well as those that form the body of a larger area of law. Today, most research is conducted using computers accessing the Internet and proprietary databases. In the very recent past, most legal research involved library time, and most printed books and resources still are being updated and maintained. Even lawyers still consult printed texts from time to time. Mostly, however, legal research involves electronic research.

Legal research is the search for authority to determine what the applicable law is, or to support your legal arguments; it is the search for **primary law**. Primary law consists of established rules from constitutions, statutes, administrative agency regulations and rules, treaties, and judicial decisions. Primary law is law stated without interpretation by comentators. It is law issued directly from an authoritative source, such as Congress or an appellate court. In important legal matters, one cites existing primary law in support of contentions made; if primary law of the appropriate jurisdiction is not available, one may present primary law from other jurisdictions or discussions of applicable law from secondary sources.

Law from other than primary sources is gathered from **secondary materials**, which include encyclopedias and other books that present the writer's opinion of what the law is or should be. This textbook is a secondary source. Secondary materials also assist a researcher in finding primary law and in understanding broad areas of the law.

This appendix discusses how to begin legal research, where to find law among electronic and hard copy sources, primary law, and some types of secondary sources of law.

WHERE TO BEGIN

There are many ways to begin legal research. Among the benefits of a formal legal education is knowledge about how and where to look for answers to legal questions. For example, a person may want to know if the cost of repairing a flood-damaged home is a deductible expense for income tax purposes. This is a legal question, a question of tax law, both federal and state. The inquirer is interested in applicable federal statutes and regulations and in the administrative interpretations and court enforcement of those laws. Once the answer is obtained for federal income taxes, a similar inquiry may be necessary with regard to state income taxes. State law may or may not treat the expense in the same way.

Jurisdiction

It is important to apply the concepts of jurisdiction at the beginning of your research. In some cases, it will be clear that you are interested in the answer from a particular state's perspective. At other times, you may be looking for a general answer. Because a single Internet search can produce results from nearly every jurisdiction in the world, you need to begin with some level of focus. But also consider that some circumstances might seem to have application only to one jurisdiction, for example, Illinois. Do not forget, however, that in the United States federal jurisdiction is always lurking and that it is possible another states' rules might apply as well.

Key Terms and Phrases

Once you have some sense of the probable jurisdictions involved, you then should analyze your fact situation for key terms, words, phrases, and issues. This time-tested method developed by the West Publishing Company can aid the identification of key terms, phrases, and issues.

Begin by asking yourself, "What words describe the parties concerned, the places or things involved, the basis of the action or issue, the possible defense or defenses, and the relief sought?"

Parties

Parties are persons of a particular class, occupation, or relation; for example, children, collectors, heirs, or any person who is either directly or indirectly necessary to a proper determination of the action.

Places and Things

Places and things are objects that necessarily must exist before any cause of action or dispute can arise; objects are perceptible through the senses; for example, automobiles, sidewalks, derricks, or garages are words describing the places or things that must exist before a cause of action alleging negligent use or defective condition can arise regarding them.

Basis of Action or Issue

A basis of action or an issue is some wrong suffered by reason of another's neglect of duty, for example, loss (of goods); some affirmative wrong, including boycott, ejection, or assault; some legal obligation ignored, such as stop, look, and listen; or the violation of some statutory or constitutional provision, like the eight-hour law, the Civil Rights Act, or restriction of free speech.

Defense

Defense is some reason in law or fact why the plaintiff should not recover; for example, failure of consideration, act of God, assumption of risk, or infancy.

Relief Sought

Relief sought is the legal remedy sought; for example, restraining order, restitution, damages, or annulment.

LEGAL RESEARCH IN THE ELECTRONIC AGE

Many lawyers practicing today learned to conduct legal research by reading paper versions of books, digests, and treatises, but nearly all lawyers have had to learn electronic research methods. Hard-copy versions of statutes still are used and necessary; however, most lawyers find electronic research to be a faster, cheaper, and more efficient way to determine the law. As explained in the section on primary law later in this appendix, ensuring that a statute you are reading in hard copy is the most current version requires a process of "updating," in which you check pocket parts and supplements. Electronic versions of the same statute are, by definition, supposed to be the most current. Thus, looking up the statute electronically can be a one-step process.

One important caution should guide you in electronic legal research. Many electronic sources of law are not official. Even those that are provided by a court system or a state legislature can contain errors and are not the official source of the law. Thus, to be certain that you have answered a legal question accurately, you may want or need to verify the critical law, regulation, ordinance, or case in its official print version.

Nevertheless, by using the Internet, you can access nearly every federal and state statute and regulation, most case law, and many local ordinances. If you have access to an electronic legal database such as Westlaw or Lexis Nexis, you have practically the entire legal universe at your fingertips.

Internet Search Engines and Legal Websites

Using Internet search engines is a good way to research your legal questions. Although nonlegal search engines, such as Google and Yahoo!, are useful, developing a familiarity with a search engine focused on the law should improve your research results. Following are a few websites that provide useful legal searching and databases. Since we first started providing a list of search engines, many websites have shifted from being information providers to being sites trying to connect browsers to lawyers. Thus, this list has thus shrunk some over the years.

- **Internet Legal Research Group:** http://www.ilrg.com
- **'Lectric Law Library:** http://www.lectlaw.com
- **Cornell Law School Legal Information Institute:** http://www.law.cornell.edu

Databases

A number of legal databases—collections of information useful to anyone doing legal research—can be accessed through several high-speed data delivery systems. The two most common systems are WestlawNext and LexisNexis. WestlawNext is a computer-assisted legal research service provided by Westlaw, part of Thomson Reuters. LexisNexis is a similar service provided by LexisNexis, a division of Reed Elsevier, Inc. Each system is accessed primarily by people who have accounts and access rights. Many university libraries provide access privileges for currently enrolled students to one or more of these databases.

Westlaw, LexisNexis, and similar computerized data search systems allow access to virtually all cases, statutes, and federal regulations. Access is almost immediate and requires a minimum of physical effort. Often, the latest cases can be found through a database before they are available at a local law school or law office library.

Electronic Codes, Statutes, Regulations, Ordinances, and Cases

Most sources of the primary law discussed later in this appendix are available electronically at government websites. Many court systems provide an indexed compilation of more recent cases on court websites. In short, you probably can find the website for a source of primary law provided by the government body responsible for creating or applying that law. As cautioned earlier, do not confuse the fact that the website is provided by a governmental body with a statement of its accuracy or authority. The only official version of the law you are researching resides in a hard-copy version. Thus, to ensure accuracy, you have to check the hard-copy version.

PRIMARY LAW

Primary law consists of court opinions, constitutions, statutes, and administrative regulations.

State Court Decisions

A court "decision" on a case or matter results in primary law only if it is "published" or released in written form as an opinion. For most state trial court cases, the judges do not write opinions, and decisions thus are not published. New York and a few other states do publish selected opinions of their trial courts, but decisions of the state trial courts generally are filed in the office of the clerk of the court, where they are available for public inspection. These decisions include findings of fact and conclusion of law, but they do not have the authority or "*stare decisis* effect" of appellate court decisions and related opinions.

Written decisions of appellate courts, on the other hand, usually are published and distributed. These "reported" decisions generally include opinions that give reasons for the judgments. Reported appellate decisions are published in volumes called *Reports*, which are numbered consecutively. State appellate court decisions are found in the state reports of that particular state. More and more states now are making appellate court opinions available on the Internet. At this time, however, most older cases still are available only in books and on private databases.

Additionally, state court opinions appear in regional units of the *National Reporter System*, published by West Publishing Company. Most lawyers and libraries have the West reporters because they report cases more quickly and are distributed more widely than the state-published reports. In fact, many states (e.g., Texas) have eliminated their own official reports in favor of West's *National Reporter System*. The *National Reporter System* divides the states into the following geographic areas: Atlantic (A. or A.2d), South Eastern (S.E. or S.E.2d), South Western (S.W. or S.W.2d), North Western (N.W. or N.W.2d), North Eastern (N.E. or N.E.2d), Southern (So. or So.2d), and Pacific (P. or P.2d).

After appellate decisions have been published, they normally are referred to (cited) by the name of the case; the volume, name, and page of the state's official reporter (if different from West's *National Reporter System*); the volume, unit, and page number of the *National Reporter*; and the volume, name, and page number of any other selected reporter. (Citing a reporter by volume number, name, and page number, in that order, is common to all citations.) This information is included in what is called the **citation**. When more than one reporter is cited for the same case, each reference is called a *parallel citation*. For example, consider the following case: *People v. Segal*, 54 N.Y. 2d 58, 429 N.E.2d 107 (N.Y. 1981). We see that the opinion in this case may be found in volume 54 of the official *New York Reporter*, Second Series, on page 58. The parallel citation is to Volume 429 of the *North Eastern Reporter*, Second Series, page 107. When reprinting appellate opinions in this text, in addition to the citation, we give the state of the court hearing the case and the year of the court's decision (N.Y. 1981).

Cases often are provided on websites maintained by the court system as well. Often, the court website will not contain older cases. Many courts still do not publish or post cases electronically, although the number of courts not doing this decreases every year. Other websites on the Internet also provide searchable databases of cases. Thus, you will be able to find most cases online.

A few states—including those with intermediate appellate courts, such as California, Illinois, and New York—have more than one reporter for opinions given by their courts.

Federal Court Decisions

Federal trial court decisions are published unofficially in West's *Federal Supplement* (F. Supp.), and decisions of the circuit courts of appeal are reported unofficially in West's *Federal Reporter* (F. or F.2d). Cases concerning federal bankruptcy law are published unofficially in West's *Bankruptcy Reporter* (Bankr.). Decisions of the U.S. Supreme Court are reported in West's *Supreme Court Reporter* (S.Ct.), and the *United States Reports* (U.S.).

The *United States Reports* is the official edition of all decisions of the U.S. Supreme Court for which there are written opinions. Published by the federal government, the series includes reports of Supreme Court cases dating from the term of August 1791, although originally many of the decisions were not reported in the early volumes.

West's *Supreme Court Reporter* is an unofficial edition dating from the Court's term in October 1882. Preceding each of its case reports is a summary of the case with *headnotes* (brief editorial statements of the law involved in the case, numbered to correspond to numbers in the report). The headnotes also are given classification numbers that serve to cross-reference each headnote to other headnotes on similar points throughout the *National Reporter System* and other West publications. This facilitates research of all relevant cases on a given point. This is important because, as may be evident from the doctrine of *stare decisis*, a lawyer's goal in undertaking legal research is to find an authority that is similar or "on all fours," which means that the facts are very close and the same questions of law are involved.

Case Titles

In the title of a case, such as *Ardmeyer v. Rau*, the *v.* or *vs.* stands for versus, which means "against." In the trial court, Ardmeyer was the plaintiff—the person who filed the suit. Rau was the defendant. If the case is appealed, however, the appellate court sometimes will place the name of the party appealing the decision first, so that the case may be called *Rau v. Ardmeyer*. Because some appellate courts retain the trial court order of names, it is often impossible to distinguish the plaintiff from the defendant by the title of a reported appellate court decision. The student must carefully read the facts of each case to identify the legal status of each party. Otherwise, the discussion by the appellate court is difficult to understand.

Terminology

The following terms and phrases frequently are encountered in court opinions and legal publications. Because it is important to understand what these terms and phrases mean, we define and discuss them here.

Decisions and Opinions

Most decisions reached by reviewing, or appellate, courts are explained in writing. A *decision* contains the opinion (the court's reasons for its decision), the rules of law that apply, and the judgment (outcome). There are four possible types of written *opinions* for any particular case decided by an appellate court. When all justices agree on an opinion, it is written for the entire court and is called a **unanimous opinion**. When there is not a unanimous opinion, a **majority opinion** is written, outlining the views of the majority of the justices deciding the case. Often, a justice who feels strongly about making or emphasizing a point that was not made or emphasized in the unanimous or majority opinion will write a **concurring opinion**. That means that the judge or justice agrees (concurs) with the judgment given in the unanimous or majority opinion, but for different reasons. In other than unanimous opinions, a judge or justice who does not agree (i.e., dissents) with the majority reasoning or holding often writes a **dissenting opinion**. The dissenting opinion is important because it may form the basis of the arguments used years later in overruling the precedent of the majority opinion.

Judges and Justices

The terms **judge** and **justice** usually are synonymous and represent two designations given to judges in various courts. All members of the U.S. Supreme Court, for example, are referred to as justices. Justice is the formal title usually given to judges of appellate courts, although this is not always so. Thus, in New York, a justice is a trial judge of the Trial Court (which is called the Supreme Court), whereas a member of the Court of Appeals (the state's highest court) is called a judge. The term *justice* is commonly abbreviated to J., and justices to JJ. A Supreme Court case might refer to Justice Kennedy as Kennedy, J.; or to Chief Justice Roberts as Roberts, C. J.

Appellants and Appellees

The **appellant** is the party who appeals a case to another court or jurisdiction from the court or jurisdiction in which the case originally was brought. Sometimes, an appellant who appeals from a judgment is referred to as the **petitioner**. The **appellee** is the party against whom the appeal is taken. Sometimes an appellee is referred to as the **respondent**.

Updating Case Law Research

Case law is printed or organized chronologically, by its decision date. One can never know by reading the case whether it has been reheard subsequently by the same court or reversed by a later higher court, or even whether the doctrines declared in the opinion have been rendered moot for later disputants by an act of the legislature. Yet that information is critical when relying on the holding of a court opinion. Imagine a lawyer's embarrassment (and perhaps malpractice) when citing an apparently leading dispositive case, when he is told by the opposing counsel that "the case was overruled two months ago."

Several indexes or services provide the primary protection against such errors as an overruled case. *Sheppard's Citations or Citators* and Westlaw's Keycite services are two such means of determining the currency of cases. These services track and then report when and where reported cases are cited. Assume you are interested in the case *Boyson v. Thorn* cited in 98 Cal. 578. You can find the case citation and a list of every published case in the United States that has cited *Boyson* since it was issued. The services also provide coding notes indicating among other things, whether the case has been overruled, criticized, or followed.

Constitutional Law

The federal government and the states have separate constitutions that define the general organization, powers, and limits of governments. The U.S. Constitution is the supreme law of the land. A law in violation of the Constitution, no matter what its source, will be declared unconstitutional and will not be enforced. Similarly, unless it conflicts with the U.S. Constitution, every state constitution is supreme within the borders of that state. The U.S. Constitution defines the powers and limitations of the federal government. All powers not granted to the federal government are retained by the states or by the people. Constitutions are published and available for research in the same publications that provide the text of federal and state **codes** (systematic collections of law, rules, or regulations). For a great website on U.S. Supreme Court cases and key issues the court has or is addressing, visit http://www.scotusblog.com.

Statutory Law

Statutes enacted by the U.S. Congress and the various state legislative bodies are another source of law, generally called **statutory law**. Statutory law also includes the ordinances passed by cities and counties. Today, legislative bodies and regulatory agencies exercise an ever-increasing role in lawmaking. Much of the work of modern courts is interpreting what the rule makers meant when a statute was enacted and applying it to a particular set of facts. When Congress passes laws, and the president signs them, they are collected in a publication titled *United States Statutes at Large*. When state legislatures pass laws, and state governors sign them, they are collected in similar state publications. These publications arrange laws chronologically by date of enactment. Most frequently, however, laws are cited in their codified form—that is, the form in which they appear in the federal and state codes.

In these codes, laws are compiled by subject. For example, the *United States Code* (U.S.C.) arranges all existing federal laws of a public and permanent nature by fifty subjects. Each of the subjects into which U.S.C. arranges the laws has a title and a title number. For example, laws related to commerce and trade are collected in Title 15, which is titled "Commerce and Trade." (Titles may be divided into chapters and subchapters. Within Title 15, for instance, Chapter 1 includes laws concerning monopolies.) Within each subdivision, statutes are assigned numbers, which are referred to as section numbers. A U.S.C. citation includes titles and section numbers. Thus, a reference to "15 U.S.C. Section 1" means that the statute can be found in Section 1 of Title 15. ("Section" also may be designated by the symbol §.)

Sometimes, a citation includes the abbreviation et seq. (e.g., 15 U.S.C. Section 1 et seq.). Et seq. (Latin: *et sequens*) means "and the following." This is a reference to sections that concern the same subject as the numbered section and follow it in sequence.

State codes follow the U.S.C. pattern of law arranged by subject. They may be called Codes, Revisions, Compilations, Consolidations, General Statutes, or Statutes, depending on the preference of the specific state. In some codes, subjects are designated by number. In others, they are designated by name. For example, "13 Pennsylvania Consolidated Statutes Section 1101" means the statute can be found in Section 1101 of Title 13 of the Pennsylvania code. "California Commercial Code Section 1101" means the statute can be found in Section 1101 under the commercial heading of the California code. Abbreviations may be used. For example, "13 Pennsylvania Consolidated Statutes Section 1101" may be abbreviated "13 Pa.C.S.§1101," and "California Commercial Code Section 1101" may be abbreviated "Cal. Com. Code §1101."

Commercial publications of these laws and regulations are available and are often more helpful than the official publications. For example, West Publishing Company publishes the *United States Code Annotated* (U.S.C.A.). U.S.C.A. contains the complete text of laws included in U.S.C, as well as notes of short summaries of court decisions that interpret and apply specific sections of the statutes, plus the text of presidential proclamations and executive orders. U.S.C.A. also includes research aids, such as cross-references to related statutes, historical notes, and library references. A citation to U.S.C.A. is similar to a citation to U.S.C. (e.g., 15 U.S.C.A. Section 1).

Most federal and state statutes are provided online on government websites. Many cities and counties also have placed their laws online. When looking up a statute online, it is useful to verify when the online source was last updated.

Commercial publishers provide comparable publications for state statutes. For example, in California, two private compilations of California statutory law exist, West's *Annotated Codes* and Deering's *Codes Annotated*. Each provides helpful features similar to those found in U.S.C.A.

Updating Statutory Law Research

There are two major benefits to placing statutes into organized codes. It is easier to index the law and thus to help those researchers who wish to find a specific provision of the law when they do not know the appropriate legal citation. The second benefit is provided by *pocket parts*. Once a code is published, it is almost immediately out of date. When the legislature passes a new statute or amends an existing one, the code must be changed. Publishing a new set of books each year to be temporarily current is wasteful and expensive beyond reason. Pocket parts meet the need of accuracy and efficiency. Several times during the course of the year, the publisher issues to purchasers of its book supplements that update the main text. These supplements commonly are placed in a pouch or pocket in the back inside cover of the book. They are indexed to correspond to the sections in the main body of the work.

To find an appropriate statute in the main text and then fail to check and examine any pocket part is a critical error in legal research. In annotated codes or constitutions, these pocket parts also provide summaries of new recent cases that have interpreted statutes listed in the main text.

When conducting statutory research online, it can be more challenging to ensure that the statutes are current. An online source of statutory law maintained by the government body that creates the statutes probably can be considered more reliable than a third-party website. When in doubt, the only way to ensure that you have found the current version of the statute is to consult the official publication as described previously. For a critical statute in your legal research, this is advisable.

Administrative Law

Rules and regulations adopted by federal administrative agencies are compiled in the *Code of Federal Regulations* (C.F.R.). Like U.S.C., C.F.R. is divided into fifty titles. Rules within each title are assigned section numbers. A full citation to C.F.R. includes title and section numbers. For example, a reference to "17 C.F.R. Section 230.504" means the rule can be found in Section 230.504 of Title 17. For many bodies of federal law, regulations that interpret, implement, and expand a statute are as important as the statute itself, if not more. Thus, when researching a statute, ensure that you find the regulations applicable to the statute as well. The entire C.F.R. is available online at http://www.gpoaccess.gov/cfr/index.html. Many federal agencies also provide their applicable regulations at the agency's website.

State administrative offices generally also have their regulations listed in a state administrative code. State agencies play a similar role in implementing state laws as federal agencies do for federal laws. Most state regulations are available online at state websites. Additionally, many state agencies provide regulations applicable to the agency at their websites.

Updating Administrative Law Research

The procedure for updating administrative law research is as follows: Check each book to see whether it provides pocket parts; if so, consult them. If the publication does not provide pocket parts, check the publication date; the older it is, the less confidence you can have in any source you have identified therein. State administrative regulations are sometimes available in loose-leaf form. If so, check the date on the page consulted and check the beginning of the volume to see when the last loose-leaf additions were made available to the library.

SECONDARY SOURCES OF LEGAL INFORMATION

Numerous legal publications meet different needs of lawyers, judges, and other people who are interested in the law. Some provide general discussions of the law; others provide excellent methods to find the appropriate and important primary law sources. Some of these sources are available only in hard copy and some are available online. The following are major secondary sources of law.

Dictionaries

Print dictionaries provide definitions of terms and pronunciation guides. The leading authoritative legal dictionaries are *Ballentine's Law Dictionary* and *Black's Law Dictionary*. West Publishing Company also publishes an elaborate dictionary called *Words and Phrases*. The definitions are taken from actual court opinions and feature pocket parts to keep the publication current.

Legal Encyclopedias

Encyclopedias report the whole of the law without commentary or analysis. Some encyclopedias are national in scope (*American Jurisprudence and Corpus Juris Secundum*); others are statewide (*California Jurisprudence*). These books are very useful starting points when you want a general overview of almost any important legal topic. They also often provide useful citations to important cases and statutes. When using an encyclopedia, be sure to check applicable pocket parts or supplemental books.

Topical Publications

Publishers offer topical publications in areas of legal practice for which great detail and current status may be critical. Taxation, employment law, and securities regulation exemplify areas for which topical publications are available. The publications are often loose-leaf, to facilitate insertion of current supplements. Again, when using topical publications, check for pocket parts or supplemental books.

Restatements of the Law

A *Restatement* is a product of extensive consultation and research by scholars, judges, and practitioners on specific areas of law, such as torts, contracts, and agency. Each *Restatement* includes a synthesis of state black letter law (i.e., principles accepted by appellate courts or included in statutes), commentaries, and examples of the application of listed rules of law to specific problems. Although a *Restatement* has no binding force of law, courts often cite *Restatement* provisions because of their clarity and precision in stating the law. Such citation gives the quoted *Restatement* rule the force of law in that particular jurisdiction. Here again, when using *Restatements*, check for pocket parts and or supplemental volumes.

Treatises and Texts

Treatises are books, limited in topical content, that cover either one area of law or a group of closely related areas of law. Treatises are usually more comprehensive than encyclopedias in their discussion of a given topic. They often contain critical commentary in addition to the expository text treatment. Other texts that serve this purpose are also available.

Digests

Digests are elaborate indexes to court decisions. They provide a synopsis of parts of the court opinions (usually the headnotes) and are arranged and indexed by topic and subtopic. Digests exist for federal court opinions (*Federal Digest and Supreme Court Digest*), for all state opinions (*American Digest System*), and for some populous states. Check for pocket parts.

Annotated Reports

Annotated reports are publications of selected cases accompanied by a thorough discussion, summary, and synthesis of other reported cases on the same or similar topic. They provide a valuable source for finding citations of similar cases. Annotated reports are updated but by different means depending on the policy of the publisher. Consult the source on how to find updated information.

Annotated Codes

Annotated codes are private publications that generally contain the entire applicable federal or state code and constitution, along with summary capsule annotations to cases that have construed or interpreted the statutes. Also included are references to legislative history and cross-references to related statutes. Check for pocket parts.

Law Journals

Law journals are periodicals that contain scholarly articles on the law written by professors, judges, practitioners, and sometimes law students. Leading law schools usually publish them, although professional associations such as the American Bar Association also sponsor such learned journals.

Self-Help Books

Many books are published by commercial publishers and professional organizations advising laypersons how to perform legal tasks. The quality of these books varies widely, but Nolo Press in Berkeley, California, has earned a reputation for providing high-quality self-help books at reasonable prices. Great care should be exercised in using self-help books. Pay particular attention to their publication dates.

Practice Books

Some books are published to assist lawyers in procedural requirements for performing certain legal tasks. They often are provided by continuing education organizations and give specific directions on how to perform certain legal tasks in areas, such as criminal procedure, family law, and wills and trusts. The books are usually too complicated for use by laypersons.

Glossary

A

abandoned property Property discarded by the true owner, who has no intention of reclaiming it.

abandonment When a tenant leaves rented premises with no intent to return or to honor legal obligations under the lease.

abatement The suspension of the duty of rent payment while the premises are uninhabitable.

absolute privilege Total protection from liability for defamation. Legislators enjoy it for statements made during official sessions, and judges and others enjoy it during judicial proceedings.

abstract of title A chronological history of recorded documents that affect the title to a parcel of real property.

acceleration clause A provision in a loan agreement that allows the lender to declare the entire unpaid balance due and payable immediately if a given event occurs.

acceptance Affirmative response to the terms of an offer, creating a contract.

accessory A person who, though not present at the scene of a crime, aided and abetted the principal in its commission.

accessory after the fact Person who harbors, conceals, or otherwise voluntarily and intentionally aids a known perpetrator of a crime to escape arrest or punishment

accessory before the fact Person who encourages or assists a perpetrator of a crime but is not present at its commission.

accord and satisfaction A party agrees (by accord) to accept some substitute for the promised performance of a contract, which is then provided (the satisfaction).

accusation Formal commencement of a criminal case by a specified public official such as a district attorney or by a grand jury.

action in equity A civil trial held without a jury when relief sought by the plaintiff is equitable in nature, such as an injunction, or a divorce or dissolution of a marriage.

actual cause The negligent person's carelessness is the reason for the loss by the victim; in other words, when injury to person or property results from the tortfeasor's action or failure to act.

ademption The elimination of a specific gift of property listed in a will because it no longer exists.

adhesion contract A contract drafted by a dominant party and then presented to the other party, the adhering party, on a "take it or leave it" basis.

administrative agency Collectively, subbranches of the executive branch of federal, state, and local governments. Administrative agencies may possess legislative, executive, and judicial powers in specialized technical areas where appropriate regulation requires action by experts.

administrative law The body of law concerned with the power of administrative agencies. Administrative law consists of rules, regulations, orders, and adjudications. Also the composite body of substantive law created by the various administrative agencies in the performance of their assigned tasks.

administrative law judge A government employee appointed to hear and decide matters in administrative agency hearings.

Administrative Procedure Act (APA) of 1946 Law that mandates procedures for federal administrative agencies.

administrator A person appointed by a court to supervise the disposition of the estate of a decedent who dies without leaving a valid will.

advance medical directives (AMD) Instructions prepared in advance of a life-threatening condition as to what care should be given or not given in the event of incapacitation.

adversarial system The jurisprudential system in which the parties to a legal dispute are opponents. Their attorneys advocate a great variety of theories of benefit to the cause of their clients both before and during the trial, and on any appeal.

adverse possessor A person who creates ownership of real property through its possession for a prescribed number of years without the consent of its owner.

affirm The confirmation of a lower court's judgment or order because the prior decision is deemed to be correct and free from prejudicial error.

affirmative action Policies and practices designed to ensure employment of women and of minorities until their percentages in the workforce approximate their percentages in the community.

affirmative action programs Programs that require that preference in hiring be given to some statutorily protected group.

Age Discrimination in Employment Act of 1967 Federal law that added "advanced age" (over age forty years) to attributes listed in the Civil Rights Act of 1964 that may not be used negatively in employment decisions.

agency Relationship in which, by mutual consent, an employee (the agent) is authorized to represent and bind an employer (the principal) in business dealings with third parties.

agency shop A company or department in which all employees in the bargaining unit must pay union dues (or some comparable fee) irrespective of whether they are union members.

agent A person employed by a principal to deal with third parties and to make contracts binding the principal to the third parties. An agent is a fiduciary of the principal.

aider or abettor One who encourages, incites, persuades, or sets another on to commit a crime.

alternative dispute resolution (ADR) Various methods of resolving disputes through means other than the judicial process.

American Arbitration Association (AAA) A private nonprofit organization with the purpose of providing education, training, and administrative assistance to parties who use nonjudicial methods—that is, alternative dispute resolution (ADR)—for resolving disputes.

American Land Title Association insurance policy A standardized form of extended title insurance coverage that is more comprehensive than the customary policy.

Americans with Disabilities Act of 1990 (ADA) Federal law that bars discrimination in the employment of capable handicapped persons by both private and public employers, and that requires reasonable accommodations for their special needs.

amortize To repay a note secured by mortgage through agreed-upon monthly payments of principal and interest over the life of the loan.

annualized percentage rate (APR) The rate of interest a borrower is paying to a mortgage lender when points and lender's fees are considered as interest rather than mere expenses of the transaction.

answer A document containing a defendant's denials, admissions or allegations of fact in response to a complaint.

antenuptial, premarital, or prenuptial agreement A binding contract whereby two persons who are contemplating marriage specify certain future mutual rights and obligations as marriage partners.

Anti-Injunction Act of 1932 Federal law that restricts the issuance of injunctions in labor disputes, outlaws yellow dog contracts, and exempts unions from legal attack as monopolies.

antideficiency laws State laws protecting a homeowner from payment of any deficiency (or unpaid balance) if a mortgage foreclosure sale fails to produce sufficient money to satisfy the underlying debt in full.

appeal Formal request to a higher court to review any action of a lower court.

appellant or petitioner The party who appeals to a higher court for review of a lower court ruling.

appellate court Court that reviews decisions of prior courts for substantive and procedural correctness.

appellee or respondent The party who, on appeal, defends the earlier court determination.

appraised value Opinion of a real estate expert "professional appraiser" of the fair market value of property, usually stated in a formal writing.

arbitrary and capricious Action taken impulsively or in bad faith and without good or valid reason.

arbitration An alternative to litigation whereby conflicting parties select a neutral third party (or parties) to hear and decide their dispute. Arbitration can be binding or nonbinding.

armed robbery Robbery committed with the use of a lethal weapon, such as a gun or a knife.

arraigned To be formally charged with a crime in a court of law and to make a plea.

arrest To take a person into custody in order to charge that person with commission of a crime.

arson The intentional and malicious burning of a building or other property for unlawful purposes.

assault The tort of creating apprehension in the mind of the victim that he or she is about to be touched in a harmful or an offensive way. There is no requirement that the actor have the present ability to inflict actual harm.

assessed value The value assigned to real property by a local official called an assessor for the purpose of levying a property tax.

assignment The transfer of some or all rights under a contract to another person.

assumption of mortgage An agreement by one person (usually a buyer) to assume (i.e., take upon herself) all the obligations of an existing secured real property loan of another person (usually the seller).

assumption of risk When a plaintiff with knowledge of the facts of a dangerous condition voluntarily exposes himself or herself to the particular risk of injury.

at-will employment A term used, for example, to indicate that an employment contract may be terminated at any time by either the employee or the employer without any liability (beyond payment for services rendered up to the time of departure or discharge).

attempt Intention of the accused to commit a crime and a substantial step toward its commission.

attestation The act of witnessing the signing of a document and thereafter signing, as evidence that you have witnessed it.

attorney–client privilege The right of clients to keep communications with their attorneys confidential and free from disclosure.

attorney-at-law A person licensed to practice law, and usually called a lawyer, attorney, counsel, or counselor.

attractive-nuisance doctrine The doctrine under which minors who trespass may collect damages if attracted on to the defendant's premises where they are injured by a man-made instrumentality that has special appeal to children (such as a railroad turntable or an unfenced swimming pool).

award The final decision of an arbitrator or other nonjudicial officer in the resolution of a dispute.

B

bad faith The deliberate failure to fulfill some duty or contractual obligation owed to another (e.g., a purposeful failure by an insurance company to pay a lawful claim).

bail Security posted with the court to ensure that the accused, if released before trial, will return voluntarily for further criminal proceedings.

bail bond A document signed by both the accused and a bail bondsman, binding the bail bondsman to pay a specified sum of money to the state if the accused fails to appear in court as directed.

bailee One who rightfully receives temporary possession of personal property from another, the bailor, in a bailment.

bailment A delivery of personal property to another by which that person has the right to temporary possession. Often, though not always, bailment is created by contract.

bailor One who transfers temporary possession of personal property to another, the bailee.

bankruptcy A legal status in which a person has debts that so exceed their accounts or income that they cannot possibly pay them.

Bankruptcy Abuse Prevention and Consumer Protection Act A 2005 law intended to curb perceived abuses of the bankruptcy system by individuals by setting new tests and requirements for eligibility to use the bankruptcy system.

battery Any harmful or offensive touching of another human being without excuse or consent. Usually (but not necessarily) battery involves violent infliction of injury.

beneficiary A person or entity that is to receive assets or profits from an estate, trust, insurance policy, or other device when there is distribution.

bequest or legacy A gift of personal property by will.

beyond a reasonable doubt The quantum evidence that fully satisfies and entirely convinces the jury in a criminal trial that the defendant is guilty as charged.

bias A preconceived belief affecting neutrality.

bilateral contract Agreement in which both parties exchange binding promises.

bill of attainder Act of the legislature inflicting capital punishment upon a named person or member of a specific group without trial and conviction. Forbidden by the U.S. Constitution.

Bill of Rights The first ten amendments to the U.S. Constitution.

blackmail Obtaining something of value from a person by threatening to reveal substantially true information about that person.

blight An extremely adverse condition affecting the value of real property, such as disrepair or garbage in the yard.

blue laws Statutes that regulate or prohibit commercial activities and amusements on Sundays.

bona fide occupational qualifications (BFOQ) Selection criteria that serve a legitimate business interest, which is justified although it has a disparate impact.

booked The administrative practice that occurs when an arrested person is brought to a police station following arrest but before incarceration in jail.

breach Failure without legal excuse to perform a promise made in a legally binding agreement.

briefs Written arguments addressed to the appellate court.

burden of proof The duty to produce evidence as a trial progresses.

burglary The crime of unlawfully entering premises, structures, or vehicles with intent to commit larceny (theft) or any other felony.

C

capital crime A crime for which the death penalty may be imposed in states where authorized and at the federal level.

capital punishment Death penalty for a crime.

carryback mortgage financing A credit sale of real property in which the seller takes a promissory note and security in the property (mortgage) from the buyer.

case law All reported judicial decisions; the law that comes from judges' opinions in lawsuits. Also referred to as court law, judge law, and sometimes common law.

case or controversy A requirement that courts may decide only cases in which an actual conflict between persons exists.

case-in-chief The case presented by each party in a trial.

caucus A private confidential meeting between disputants and a third-party neutral.

cause of action An existing right to seek and to receive judicial relief, assuming the factual allegations of the plaintiff are true.

caveat emptor A doctrine of transaction policy that means "let the buyer beware."

caveat venditor A doctrine of transaction policy that means "let the seller beware."

cease-and-desist A command from an administrative agency that the subject party refrain from specified activities.

challenge for cause Ability to exclude a prospective trial juror if bias or prejudice is indicated.

champerty An illegal agreement with a party to a suit for a portion of any recovery in exchange for paying the litigant's lawsuit expenses.

chapter 7 bankruptcy A type of bankruptcy proceeding wherein almost all debts of the debtor are erased and most all assets owned by debtor are surrendered to the creditors.

chapter 11 bankruptcy A type of bankruptcy proceeding wherein the debts of the debtor are reorganized and the debtor leaves the proceeding with a set payment plan that allows for sufficient available income to live.

charitable trust A trust designed for the benefit of a segment of the public or of the public in general.

citation, legal Abbreviated reference to a variety of legal authorities, including court cases.

civil dispute A lawsuit commenced for the purpose of resolving a civil conflict.

civil law The branch of law dealing with individual rights and duties and their enforcement. Civil law also refers to the total system of law, embracing civil and criminal matters, that was used in the ancient Roman Empire and copied on the continent of Europe in modern times. In ancient times, the law was defined by experts and imposed from above by the emperor. Roman civil law is contrasted to English *common law*.

Civil Rights Act of 1964 Federal law (specifically Title VII) that makes it unlawful for employers of fifteen or more persons, engaged in interstate commerce, to discriminate with respect to employment against any individual because of such person's race, color, religion, sex, or national origin.

civil union A legal relationship, analogous to but different from a marriage, wherein the state recognizes that certain domestic rights, benefits, and duties exist between two unmarried persons.

class action When all members of a group of persons who have suffered the same or similar injury join together in a single lawsuit against the alleged wrongdoer. The group must be so numerous that it is impracticable to bring all members before the court individually.

class actions When all members of a group of persons who have suffered the same or similar injury join together in a single lawsuit against the alleged wrongdoer. The group must be so numerous that it is impracticable to bring all members before the court individually.

closed shop A place of employment where workers must join a union before they can be hired. Made illegal by the Taft-Hartley Act.

closing costs Charges for various services that arise in connection with the purchase and sale of a home.

cloud on title Any dormant or actively pursued claim to the possession of or title to real property that is unresolved or contested.

code of ethics A systematic statement of agreed-on moral rules for a profession, business, or group.

codes Compilations of statutes that are grouped together by subject matter (e.g., a vehicle code).

codicil A document prepared to change but not revoke an existing will.

collaborative law practice A method whereby the parties agree to resolve their disputes without court intervention using interest-based negotiation practices.

collateral Money or other property made available as security by a debtor to a creditor, through physical possession or legal right, to guarantee repayment of a loan.

collective bargaining The process of negotiation by representative(s) of the employees' union and representative(s) of an employer for an employment contract that provides terms and conditions of employment.

collision insurance Automobile insurance that protects against the risk of loss from damages to one's own automobile in a collision regardless of who is at fault.

commerce The exchange of goods or commodities for payment in cash, credit, services, or other goods.

Commerce clause A part of the U.S. Constitution that provides Congress with the power to pass laws to provide for trade with foreign countries and among states.

commercial speech Oral, written, and other forms of communication used in advertising and in other business activities.

commingling The mixing together of community property and separate property to the extent that the properties cannot be traced back to their original status. Commingled property becomes community property.

common carrier A carrier that transports for payment all persons who apply for passage, assuming space is available and there is no legal excuse for refusal.

common law marriage The bond formed when a man and a woman live together in the manner of a husband and a wife for the number of years prescribed by state law, though without observing the legal formalities of marriage. This form of marriage is legal in some states.

common law: as a system of law The total system of law that originated in medieval England and was adopted by the United States at the time of the American Revolution. Expressed originally in opinions and judgments of the courts, it is judge-made law that reflects the customs and usages of the people. Contrasted to Roman civil law, it is found throughout the English-speaking world. Common law is sometimes called unwritten law.

common law: as a type of law That law that comes from the common courts as opposed to a legislature or court of equity.

community property All property acquired (in a community property state) by the husband or the wife during marriage other than by gift or inheritance, and other than as profits or income from separate property.

commutation Reduction, by a state governor or by the president, of punishment for a crime.

comparable worth The theory that the same wage or salary should be paid for jobs that have equal societal and economic value based on such factors as required preparation, skill, effort, responsibility, and working conditions.

comparative negligence Negligence of the plaintiff that does not bar recovery of damages but may reduce the amount of recovery proportionally.

compensatory damages Amount awarded by a court to make good or replace the actual loss suffered by a plaintiff. In the case of a breach of contract, this amount is equivalent to the actual dollar loss suffered because the defendant did not perform as promised.

competent parties Parties who are legally qualified (that is, have the capacity) to make a binding contractual agreement.

complaint A document stating the facts constituting an alleged cause of action.

complaint, criminal (a) A written statement filed by complainant containing facts that indicate a crime has been committed and that the accused committed it. (b) An accusation of a misdemeanor.

comprehensive insurance Automobile insurance that protects against losses from having one's car stolen or damaged other than by collision (for example, by falling trees, sandstorm).

compulsory process (a) The right guaranteed by the Sixth Amendment to every person accused of a crime to require witnesses to appear in his or her favor, by court order. (b) Official action to force a person to appear as a witness in court, at an administrative hearing, or before a legislature.

Conciliation Use of a third party to lower tensions, improve communications, and explore possible solutions to a conflict.

concurrent jurisdiction Power of more than one court to hear a case.

concurring opinion A written opinion wherein a judge agrees (concurs) with the result reached by another judge, but for different reasons from those stated by the other judge.

conditional or qualified privilege A partial immunity which protects one who makes a defamatory statement in the performance of a legal, moral, or social duty, to a person who has a corresponding duty or interest in receiving it.

confidentiality A private communication with an attorney-at-law in which the attorney is under a duty to keep the information secret.

conflict of interest When a client's interests are at odds with another's because the attorney serves, might serve, or is tempted to serve the other.

confusion Mixing of one person's personal property with another's, resulting in the goods becoming indistinguishable.

consequential damages Injury or harm occuring as a result, or consequence, of the failure of a party to correctly perform a promised act under a contract.

conservatorship A legal relationship created by a court to allow a person, the conservator, to manage the assets and personal affairs of another, the conservatee, who is not competent to manage her affairs.

consideration The price or inducement (e.g., reciprocal promises) to enter a contract.

consortium The reciprocal legal right of companionship, cooperation, aid, affection, and sexual relations of each spouse from and to the other.

conspiracy An agreement by two or more persons to commit a crime coupled with an overt act by one party toward commission of the agreed crime.

constitutionalism The principles of constitutional government; adherence to them, including, notably, restrictions and limitations on government power.

construction loan A short-term real estate loan, secured by mortgage, intended to finance building costs.

constructive delivery Acts that are the equivalent of actual delivery such as delivering the key to the safety deposit box with the present intent to give the person the contents of that box.

constructive eviction Indirect eviction of a tenant by means of the landlord's failure to correct an intolerable interference or defects in the premises, which effectively drives the tenant out.

consumer A person who purchases goods or services.

consumer privacy The right to protect fiscal and consumer data and information about oneself.

contempt of court Willful defiance of the authority of a court, affront to its dignity, or willful disobedience of its lawful orders.

contingency fee A fixed percentage of the monetary recovery obtained by a lawyer for a client. It is agreed on in advance and accepted in full payment for services rendered.

contract A legally enforceable agreement to do or not to do a specified thing.

contributory negligence The negligence of a plaintiff that helped to cause a tort. In states accepting the doctrine, a contributory negligence plaintiff usually is barred from claiming damages if injured.

conventional loan A home-purchase mortgage, the repayment of which is not guaranteed by an agency of the federal government.

conversion Unauthorized taking of the personal property of another and wrongfully exercising rights of ownership.

corpus delicti The two essential elements of every crime: evidence that (a) harm has occurred, (b) most probably because of a criminal act.

court (a) A government body that administers justice by applying laws to civil controversies and criminal offenses. (b) The place where trials are held.

court-annexed arbitration A type of nonbinding arbitration required by some courts be fore the parties may proceed to trial.

covenant marriage A type of marriage in which couples agree to certain marital promises and limitations on their ability to terminate the marriage. States allowing covenant marriage provide it as optional.

covenant not to compete A promise not to engage in a competing business or profession. Such covenants generally are illegal unless they are part of an otherwise-enforceable contract for the sale of a business or for employment. In such cases, they are legal only if they are drafted to be reasonable regarding time, scope, and geographic area and are necessary to protect the interests of the contracting parties.

covenant of quiet enjoyment A promise usually implied from the landlord that others will not interfere with the tenant's right to occupy the premises.

covenants, conditions, and restrictions (CC&Rs) A written set of limitations, in deeds or other recorded documents, on the future use of real property.

criminal assault The threat of violence upon another person.

criminal battery The unlawful application of force to another human being without excuse or consent.

criminal dispute A trial in which the government prosecutes a person charged with a crime.

criminal facilitation The crime of assisting another person in the commission of a crime.

criminal intent The requisite guilty state of mind [Latin *mens rea*: "guilty mind"] to hold a person responsible for a particular crime.

criminal law The branch of law dealing with crimes and their punishment.

criminal negligence Conduct that is without criminal intent and yet is so careless, or occurs in such reckless disregard of another's safety, that criminal penalties are prescribed by statute.

cruel and unusual punishment Criminal punishment in which the punishment is totally disproportionate to the offense, or the prisoner is subjected to inhuman torture or merciless abuse, or the method of the punishment is unacceptable to society, or the punishment is arbitrary.

culpability Behavior that is sufficiently wrongful to be at fault or to be responsible for proscribed conduct.

D

damages Money awarded by a court to a plaintiff for injury or economic loss caused by the defendant.

date rape Nonconsensual sexual intercourse by a friend or acquaintance.

***de novo* review** A complete reevaluation of an issue, finding, or case as if the original decision had never been made.

death tax Taxes imposed on the estate of the decedent (i.e., an estate tax on the privilege of giving) and on the gifts received by the donee(s) (i.e., an inheritance tax on the privilege of receiving).

Death with Dignity Act A state statute that allows competent, terminally ill adult patients to obtain a physician's prescription for drugs to end their life.

debit card an electronic card that allows consumers to pay for goods and services by directly applying funds from a deposit account.

decedent A deceased person.

deductible A provision in an insurance policy whereby the insured bears modest losses up to a prescribed sum (for example, \$50, \$100, or a little more) in exchange for reduced premiums.

Deductive logic A method of logical reasoning from two or more propositions to a conclusion. Inferences are drawn from a general premise to a specific premise. The conclusion is valid if the propositions on which the conclusion is based are true.

deed Any document used to transfer any ownership interest in real property. Many types of deeds are used in a variety of property transfers.

deed of trust A deed used by a borrower (called *trustor*) to transfer the legal title to real property to a disinterested stakeholder (the *trustee*) to hold as security or collateral for the benefit of the lender (the *beneficiary*).

defamation False statement injuring the reputation of the victim.

default Failure of a party to do what is legally required.

default judgment Court-awarded judgment based on the defendant's failure to answer the summons and complaint or to appear at the trial to contest the claim of the plaintiff.

defendant (a) In a civil trial, the person from whom money damages or other relief is sought by the plaintiff. (b) In a criminal trial, the accused.

deficiency judgment Judgment against a debtor for the unpaid balance still due after repossession and resale of goods that were sold on credit, or after judicial foreclosure of a real estate mortgage.

defined benefit plans Plans that provide for the payment of determinable retirement income benefits.

delegation Transfer of some or all contractual duties to another person.

deliberate The review, discussion, and weighing of evidence presented at a trial by a jury.

demurrer or motion to dismiss A motion filed by a defendant in response to a summons and complaint alleging the complaint, even if true, is insufficient to state a cause of action.

deposition Questioning of a witness or adverse party to an action, under oath, by the opposing attorney before the trial.

deregulation A process of eliminating, reducing, or restructuring the regulation of an industry.

design patent Issued for the visual ornamental characteristics embodied in, or applied to, an article of manufacture.

detention The brief stopping of a suspicious person by a police officer for the limited purpose of determining whether or not a crime has been or is being committed in the proximity of the detainee.

devise A gift of real property by will.

dicta Any part of a court opinion that is unnecessary to the resolution of dispute before the court. Such digression by a judge is not binding on later courts.

diminished capacity Reduced ability to exercise one's freedom of will or to choose between right and wrong.

directive to physicians A signed document communicating the signer's wishes regarding the use of life-support systems in the treatment of a terminal illness.

disclaimer A statement made to avoid a warranty or otherwise eliminate a promise that might have been made about performance, capability, or future action.

discovery Group of methods used during the period between commencement of a lawsuit and the date of trial to learn facts about the dispute.

discretionary sprinkling and accumulation trust A trust in which the trustee is authorized to decide who among the designated beneficiaries is to receive periodic payments of income or principal, and when.

disparate impact An ostensibly neutral employment criterion that has an adverse discriminatory impact upon a protected group.

disparate treatment Less favorable treatment on the basis of race, color, religion, gender, age, or national origin.

dissenting opinion A written opinion by a judge or judges who votes contrary to the majority opinion and holding of the court.

diversity of citizenship A basis of jurisdiction in federal courts requiring that plaintiff and defendant be involved in an actual controversy, that they be citizens of different states, and that a minimum of $75,000 be sought in damages.

divorce Termination of a marriage relationship by court judgment. Divorce is called dissolution in some states.

divorce from bed and board A modification of the spousal relationship in which the parties are forbidden to cohabit but do not dissolve the marriage. Support may be paid, and property is divided as in a divorce.

domestic partnerships Unmarried couples who live together and seek economic and noneconomic benefits available to married couples.

domestic torts Various tortuous acts in which the perpetrator and victim are family members.

donative intent Present intent to make a gift.

donee The person to whom a gift is made in life or by will.

donor A person who makes a gift in life or by will.

double jeopardy A second criminal prosecution against a person for the same single offense, after the person has been found innocent of the crime in the prior trial.

dramshop statute A state law making it a crime for a tavern proprietor or employee to serve intoxicants to an obviously inebriated customer.

Due Process The requirement that legal proceedings (including arrest, civil and criminal trials, and punishment) comply with the U.S. Constitution and other applicable substantive and procedural laws.

durable power of attorney for health care A document authorizing another person to make health care (and sometimes other) decisions for a person even after he has become incapacitated.

duress Any threat of, or actual, physical harm that deprives a person of the freedom of will to choose and decide.

duress Any threat of, or actual, physical harm that deprives a person of the freedom of will to choose and decide.

duty The obligation enforceable in court to recognize and respect the person, property, and rights of others. Legal duty is the reciprocal of *legal right*.

duty-based ethics The doctrine that actions are morally correct if they comply with existing obligations owed another or ourselves.

E

early neutral evaluation An ADR process providing disputing parties with an early and candid evaluation by an objective observer of the merits of a case.

easement The right to use the real property of another for a limited purpose (e.g., access to a beach or public road).

economic strike A strike in which workers seek a change in wages, hours, and/or conditions of employment.

emancipated minor A minor legally allowed to handle her own financial affairs.

embezzlement The crime of stealing property that, before the theft, was lawfully in the possession of the thief.

employee A person who agrees by contract to perform work as directed and controlled by an employer in exchange for compensation (usually consisting of wages or salary and fringe benefits).

Employee Retirement Income Security Act (ERISA) Federal legislation regulating private pension plans that supplement Social Security.

enabling statute A statute that creates an administrative agency and typically also authorizes it to perform specified actions.

encroachment Construction (e.g., building or fence) or vegetation (e.g., tree limb or ground cover) that physically intrudes upon or overlaps the real property of another.

entrapment A defense to criminal charges if the crime was induced by police encouragement, but not if police merely provided an opportunity for the accused to commit the criminal act.

Equal Protection The clause in the Fourteenth Amendment to the U.S. Constitution declaring that "no state shall … deny to any person within its jurisdiction the equal protection of the laws."

equitable maxims General rules applied by courts to cases in equity.

equitable owner An owner who has possession and use of the property although someone else may retain the legal title.

equity The net interest of a homeowner in the property, representing the excess of the value of the property over loans or other legal claims outstanding against it.

escrow An arrangement common in real estate transactions whereby the buyer and seller (and/or the borrower and lender) designate a neutral third party as an agent to carry out instructions for gathering and distributing documents and funds as necessary.

escrow agent A person paid to perform all the administrative tasks necessary to close a real estate escrow.

estate planning The process of arranging a person's property and estate, taking into account the laws of wills, taxes, insurance, property, and trusts so as to gain maximum benefit of all laws while carrying out the person's wishes for use of the property during his lifetime and disposition of the property upon his death.

estate tax A tax imposed by the federal government and some states on the privilege of giving property to another person after death of the donor.

estate tax exemption A sum of money that can be transferred without tax implications. Once that amount is exceeded, taxes are imposed on any additional transferred amount.

estray statutes Laws requiring finders of lost personal property to report their discovery to authorities.

ethics Standards of fair and honest conduct applied to social behavior.

euthanasia The act of allowing one to die by withholding extraordinary medical measures, or putting to death by painless means a person suffering from an incurable disease or a condition of an extremely painful nature.

evidence Everything presented by disputing parties and witnesses that the "finder of fact" is entitled to consider in arriving at a determination of the facts.

***ex parte* trial** A legal action in which only one side of the dispute is heard.

***ex post facto* laws** [Latin: "after the fact"] A statute that retroactively makes previously lawful conduct a crime. Such a statute is unconstitutional.

exclusionary rule The court-made rule that precludes the use in criminal court proceedings of any evidence improperly obtained by the prosecution.

exclusive jurisdiction The sole power a court has over the particular subject matter of a case.

exclusive listing Employment contract in which the owner of real property agrees to pay a licensed agent a certain commission regardless of who finds the buyer to whom the property is sold. Also called *an exclusive right to sell.*

exclusive-agency listing Employment contract between an owner of real property and a licensed agent in which the owner may find a buyer and sell the property without liability for payment of commission, but must pay the listing agent if that agent or any other licensed agent finds the buyer.

exculpatory clause Provision in a contractual agreement (for example, a lease) by which a party agrees not to hold the other party responsible for her negligence.

executed contract A contract that has been performed fully by both parties.

executive clemency A formal act of kindness, mercy, and leniency by a governor or by the president in commuting a criminal penalty or granting a pardon.

executive departments Generally, administrative bodies headed by single persons ultimately answerable to one person, the chief executive.

executor A person named by a testator to dispose of her estate after death as directed in the will and in compliance with the law.

executory contract A valid contract in which something remains to be done by either or both parties.

exempt assets Property that a debtor can protect against seizure resulting from execution of judgment by a judgment creditor or a trustee in a bankruptcy distribution.

exhaustion of remedies A doctrine requiring that a person attempt all available options within an administrative agency before taking a claim to a court.

expert fact-finding A nonbinding process in which an appointed expert investigates or hears facts on selected issues. At the conclusion, he or she makes findings of fact.

expert witness Anyone qualified by knowledge and skill, experience, training, or education to offer a credible and useful opinion upon some material issue in a trial.

express contract An agreement stated in words, spoken, or written.

express warranty A warranty created when a reasonable buyer would believe that a particular representation was part of the bargain.

extended coverage Coverage for title defects as described within the American Land Title Insurance form.

extortion Obtaining something of value from a person by force, intimidation, or undue or other illegal acts.

F

Fair Debt Collection Practices Act A federal law that outlaws certain unreasonably harsh collection practices previously used by professional debt collectors.

fair hearing An oral proceeding before an administrative agency to hear and decide some factual question related to agency action.

fair use A defense to claim of copyright infringement that allows the use of copyrighted material without owner's permission.

false arrest Taking custody of another, without proper legal authority, to be held or restrained in order to answer a civil claim or criminal charge. Because this action restrains the person's liberty, it is also *false imprisonment.*

false imprisonment The wrongful restraint of the personal liberty of another.

Family and Medical Leave Act of 1993 (FMLA) A federal law requiring employers with fifty or more employees to grant employees leave for certain family purposes related to child care and family health.

family purpose doctrine A law in some states that holds the owner of a motor vehicle vicariously responsible whenever a member of his immediate family or household drives and a third party is injured because of the negligence of the driver.

family settlement agreement A law of probate in some states allowing family members to agree to settle among themselves the distribution of a decedent's assets.

federalism A form of government consisting of a union of more or less self-governing states under an umbrella of federal government.

federalism A government consisting of a union of more or less self-governing states under an umbrella of federal government.

felony A serious crime (such as murder) that is punishable by death or imprisonment for more than one year.

fidelity bond A bond insuring against losses caused by a fraudulent performance of duties by a personal representative.

fiduciary Someone who has an obligation to act with scrupulous good faith and honesty toward another.

fiduciary relationship A relationship between two persons wherein one has an obligation to perform services with scrupulous good faith and honesty.

field sobriety test A simple test used to determine the reactions of a motor vehicle driver who is suspected of driving under the influence of alcohol or another drug. The test is administered at the scene of the arrest.

Fifth Amendment "No person shall be held to answer for a capital, or otherwise infamous crime, unless on a presentment or indictment of a Grand Jury, except in cases arising in the land or naval forces, or in the Militia, when in actual service in time of War or public danger; nor shall any person be subject for the same offence to be twice put in jeopardy of life or limb; nor shall be compelled in any criminal case to be a witness against himself, nor be deprived of life, liberty, or property, without due process of law; nor shall private property be taken for public use, without just compensation."

financial responsibility law A statute requiring that after an automobile accident of specified severity, driver not covered by insurance must post specified cash or equivalent bond.

First Amendment "Congress shall make no law respecting an establishment of religion, or prohibiting the free exercise thereof; or abridging the freedom of speech, or of the press; or of the right of the people peaceably to assemble, and to petition the Government for a redress of grievances."

first-degree murder Premeditated murder perpetrated with malice aforethought.

fixed-rate mortgage A traditional home purchase mortgage in which the interest rate and the monthly payment do not fluctuate during the life of the loan.

forcible eviction An illegal eviction technique, by which a landlord confronts a tenant, forcibly removes all personal items, and changes locks on the unit.

foreclosure Process by which secured real property is confiscated at the direction of the unpaid creditor and sold to the highest bidder.

foreclosure sale Sale of a debtor's real property to raise cash with which to reduce or retire the unpaid debt. A foreclosure sale may be of two varieties, by a court official following judicial foreclosure or by a trustee following nonjudicial foreclosure.

formal contract Agreement that must use prescribed language or be in prescribed form.

formal will A typewritten or computer-printed will executed in compliance with law and signed or acknowledged by the testator in the presence of witnesses who also sign the document.

401(k) plans Retirement savings account taking its name from the Internal Revenue Code of 1978. The plan is funded by employee contributions and (often) matching contributions from the employer. Contributions are taken from pretax salary, and the funds grow tax-free until withdrawn.

Fourteenth Amendment In part, "All persons born or naturalized in the United States, and subject to the jurisdiction thereof, are citizens of the United States and of the State wherein they reside. No State shall make or enforce any law which shall abridge the privileges or immunities of citizens of the United States; nor shall any State deprive any person of life, liberty, or property, without due process of law; nor deny to any person within its jurisdiction the equal protection of the laws."

fraud A knowingly false representation of a material fact, made through words or conduct, with intent to deceive a victim, who is induced to contract in reliance on the lie, and who is thereby injured.

fraud A knowingly false representation of a material fact, made through words or conduct, with intent to deceive a victim, who is induced to contract in reliance on the lie, and who is thereby injured.

free speech "Congress shall make no law … abridging the freedom of speech, or of the press; or the right of the people peaceably to assemble, and to petition the Government for a redress of grievances."

Freedom of Information Act (FOIA) A federal law requiring the federal government to disclose most public records to any person on request.

freedom of religion "Congress shall make no law respecting an establishment of religion, or prohibiting the free exercise thereof."

fungible Each item of personal property is identical to every other item.

G

garnishment A legal proceeding in which a plaintiff-creditor gets a court order compelling a third party to pay monies earned by the defendant to the plaintiff.

general damages Amount awarded by a court to pay the plaintiff for nonmonetary losses (e.g., pain and suffering) that resulted from an injury, without reference to any special circumstances of the plaintiff.

general intent In criminal law, the intent to do the prohibited act without the necessity of proving intent to cause the precise harm.

general jurisdiction Authorization of a court to hear and decide virtually any type of case occurring within the political boundaries of the geographic area in which it is located.

generation-skipping trust A trust created whereby the settlors of the first generation (parents) arrange for their child (ren) (the second generation) to receive the income while they are alive, but not the principal, which is reserved for the grandchild(ren) (the third generation) after the death of the second generation.

genuine assent When consent of both parties to be bound by a contract is given freely and is not negated by fraud, duress, undue influence, or certain mistakes.

gift A voluntary transfer of property ownership by one under no duty to transfer the ownership.

Good Samaritan laws Statutes that protect volunteers from liability for ordinary negligence while aiding persons in need.

goods Tangible, movable personal property.

Government in the Sunshine Act A federal law requiring that most meetings of federal agencies be open for public observation and that advance notice be given of agency meetings, listing the expected topics of discussion.

graduated-payment mortgage A home-purchase mortgage and promissory note that features artificially low monthly payments for the initial few years as an inducement for borrowers whose incomes and creditworthiness are expected to improve in the future.

grand jury An appointed body of citizens formed both to investigate the operations of government and to issue indictments against persons suspected of criminal conduct.

grand theft Theft of personal property of substantial value, as declared by statute.

grant deed A document that conveys the ownership of real property, and impliedly warrants that the grantor previously has not conveyed the property to another and that the property is free from undisclosed encumbrances.

gross negligence The failure of even slight or scant care.

guardianship A court-established arrangement whereby an adult guardian is appointed to take care of the person or the estate of a minor.

guest statutes Law that pertains to guests of a driver of a motor vehicle. In some states, a guest cannot sue the driver if injured, unless the driver is guilty of intoxication, willful misconduct, or gross negligence that causes the accident and resulting injury or death. In other states, a guest may sue the driver for ordinary negligence.

H

habeas corpus A legal writ or court order to release a prisoner from allegedly unlawful confinement so that he can appear before a court for proper remedial action. The petitioner seeks release.

hate crime Any crime for which the motivation was persecution of a victim because of race, religion, sexual orientation, or political beliefs.

hate speech Words spoken, written, or symbolized (e.g., by placing burning crosses on private lawns) that express irrational and false ideas that insult and demean certain persons or classes of persons.

heirs Persons designated by law to receive the estate of a decedent who leaves no will.

Hold harmless agreement or Exculpatory clause A hold harmless agreement or exculpatory clause releases one party to the agreement from liability.

holographic will An unwitnessed will. States that allow such a will usually require it to be written in longhand by the testator, signed, and dated.

home invasion burglary The intentional breaking and entering into a person's occupied residence using violent means to take property of the occupant.

homeowners policy Insurance that typically covers losses of the homeowner's property from specified casualties, such as fire and water damage, as well as the possible liability of the owner for specified damages she may cause to another person through negligent behavior (other than with a motor vehicle or boat).

homestead A declaration of a debtor's exemption in a specified amount of the equity of the homeowner's residence from levy and execution by a creditor.

homicide The killing of a human being by another human being.

hostile environment Conduct by others in the workplace that has the purpose or effect of unreasonably interfering with an individual's work performance or creating an intimidating, hostile, or offensive working environment.

I

identity theft The wrongful or false use of another person's identification or the commission of a crime using the identification of another.

impeach To discredit, dispute, disparage, or contradict a witness's testimony.

implied in fact contract Contractual agreement manifested by conduct or body language (e.g., purchase of items from vendors in noisy stadiums during sporting events).

implied warranty A warranty that the law implies from the nature or circumstances of the transaction.

impound account An account held by a mortgage lender in which to accumulate sufficient funds to pay all annual property taxes and property and liability insurance premiums.

***in personam* jurisdiction** The power of a court over a person.

in propria persona (in pro se) Term meaning the person represents herself or himself in a legal action with out the appearance of an attorney.

***in rem* jurisdiction** The power of a court to declare rights against the world rather than solely against the named defendant(s).

incapacity Lack of legal capacity to make important decisions.

incorporation doctrine The Supreme Court's utilization of the Fourteenth Amendment to find Bill of Rights limitations on state and local governments.

independent administrative agency An administrative body empowered to regulate some policy area led by officials who cannot be dismissed by the president of the United States except for good cause.

independent contractor A person who is hired to do a specific job, and who retains control over how that job is done.

indictment An accusation of felony filed by a grand jury.

individual retirement accounts (IRAs) Federally authorized private pension plans in which qualified employees contribute a certain percentage of their income, tax-free, to their retirement accounts until retirement.

information An accusation of a criminal offense.

Informational privacy The right to control the collection and sharing of data about oneself.

informed consent Actual and complete knowledge by a person of risks involved in a situation.

infraction Any minor crime (for example, parking violation) that is not punishable by incarceration, but only by fine. Accordingly, trial by jury is not required or permitted.

inheritance tax A tax imposed by most states on the privilege of receiving property from a decedent.

initiative An electoral process for making new statutes or changing the constitution by filing appropriate formal petitions to be voted on by legislature (and governor) or by the people. The initiative is not available in all states.

initiative process An electoral process for making new statutes or changing the constitution by filing appropriate formal petitions to be voted upon by legislature (and governor) or by the total electorate.

injunction An order of a court of equity to someone to do or not do some act.

inquisitorial system A legal system used in some countries that allows the judge to investigate, question witnesses, and seek out evidence before a trial.

insanity defense A defense to a crime based on some mental disease or defect.

insurable interest A sufficient interest in property such that its loss or destruction would cause an economic loss to the owner or possessor.

intangible property Property recognized by law even though it has no physical existence.

Intellectual property Information or property, such as patents or copyrights, that provides the owner a competitive advantage

intentional infliction of mental distress Outrageous conduct that causes mental, if not immediate physical, suffering by the victim.

intentional tort Occurs when the tortfeasor deliberately performs a wrongful act that injures an innocent victim.

***inter vivos* trust** A trust created during the lifetime of the settlor.

interest The price, usually expressed as an annualized rate (percentage), for use of a sum of money (principal) obtained from a lender.

interference with an economically advantageous relationship A knowing and wrongful interference with the promised performance of another person's contract.

international law The branch of law governing relations between and among sovereign nations.

interpleader A legal proceeding to resolve conflicting claims (e.g., conflicting claims to funds in an escrow account).

interrogatories A form of discovery consisting of written questions directed to a party or witness who is expected to reply with written answers under oath.

interstate Activity that crosses state boundaries.

intervening cause A cause of an accident or other injury that legally excuses the wrongdoer who originally sets a series of events in motion.

intestacy laws Statutory prescription for distribution of the estate among heirs of a decedent leaving no will.

intestate The status of a person who died without leaving a valid will.

intrastate Activity that occurs entirely within a state's boundaries.

invasion of privacy Violation of the right of every person who has done no wrong to be left alone.

invitee One who enters another's land with the permission (implied or express) of the owner or occupier, for a matter of business benefiting the owner or occupier.

involuntary manslaughter The unintentional killing of another person because of gross negligence, or as a result of dangerous and unlawful conduct.

irrelevant evidence Evidence that does not relate to or have a bearing upon a question of fact in dispute during a trial.

irrevocable *inter vivos* trust A trust created and having operative effect during the trustor's life that cannot be terminated or revoked by the trustor who created it.

irrevocable trust A trust that cannot be terminated or revoked by the settlor who created it.

J

joint custody Responsibility shared by both parents, following a divorce, annulment, or separation, to guide and support their child(ren).

joint tenancy A method of co-ownership of property by two or more persons. Upon the death of any co-owner, that person's percentage interest goes to the surviving joint tenant(s) regardless of the decedent's last will. This right of survivorship is the basic incident of joint-tenancy ownership.

judgment The final determination or decision of the court as to the rights and duties of the parties in a lawsuit.

judgment creditor A person who has won a judgment but has not been fully paid.

judgment debtor A person against whom a judgment for payment of money has been entered but who has not yet made or completed that payment.

judgment *non obstante veredicto* A decision by a judge that overrules the verdict of the jury.

judgment-proof Financial condition of a person who lacks the assets to pay any judgment rendered against him or her.

judicial activists Judges whose judicial philosophy includes treating the law as a vibrant and active source of rules. When faced with new issues (e.g., social), such judges are likely to see the Constitution as a flexible document and *stare decisis* as challengeable when they believe important social needs must be addressed.

judicial foreclosure The forced sale, following a court proceeding, of an owner's real property to raise money to satisfy the creditor's claim for the unpaid balance of the loan that is in default.

judicial review Power of the U.S. Supreme Court to declare unconstitutional an act of Congress, a presidential order, or a state law.

judicial review The power of the courts to review administrative agency action.

jurisdiction The power of a court to decide a controversy and to award appropriate relief.

jury A group of men and women sworn to declare the truth based on evidence presented to them.

jury instructions Rules of law and charges provided by the judge to the jury for guidance in reaching a verdict.

jury nullification The power of a jury in a criminal trial to disregard the law and unanimously find the defendant innocent, although there is ample evidence to support a verdict of guilty.

just cause An action based on reasonable grounds and fair treatment; lawful reasons for taking an action.

K

kangaroo court A farce trial—one that lacks proper procedure and fairness and where the outcome is predetermined. Origin of the term is thought to be the bizarre appearance of the animal after which it is named.

kidnapping The crime of unlawful seizure and transport of a victim against his will.

L

Labor-Management Relations Act of 1947 (Taft-Hartley Act) A federal law that lists unfair labor practices of unions. It outlaws the closed shop and the secondary boycott.

Labor-Management Reporting and Disclosure Act of 1959 (Landrum-Griffin Act) Federal law that mandates open, democratic internal government of unions.

landlord The owner of residential property who leases it to a tenant, or renter, in exchange for rent.

larceny The crime of stealing property from another.

larceny by trick Theft accomplished by deceit or subterfuge wherein the victim turns over property, especially money, to the perpetrator.

law A body of rules of conduct prescribed by controlling authority and having binding legal force.

lawsuit or litigation A court process at law or in equity to determine the legal merits of a controversy.

lease A contract, usually written, by which the relationship of landlord and tenant is created and a property interest is created.

legal assistant Someone with specialized training who assists an attorney. Also called a "paralegal".

legal ethics Rules promulgated by lawyer-governing bodies to proscribe standards of professional behavior and regulate lawyer and judicial conduct.

legal malpractice Violation of a duty of due care by a professional person.

legal owner An owner who has legal title, for example, as security for repayment of a loan or payment of the purchase price of real property or personal property, such as an automobile.

legal separation A court order permitting spouses to live apart with necessary related orders for child custody and child support, support of the wife (or husband), and division of property (as in dissolution), but the marriage endures.

legal service plans Insurance plans designed to make legal services available to members of unions or other organizations, such as business firms.

Legal Services Corporation (LSC) A federally funded corporation that distributes federal tax dollars to state programs that provide legal assistance in noncriminal proceedings to persons financially unable to afford such services.

lemon laws Statutes designed to assist the buyer of seriously defective goods to obtain a replacement or full refund.

lessee A party to a lease who pays rent to the landlord in exchange for the possession and use of real property, such as a person who rents an apartment. The lessee more commonly is called the tenant.

lessor A party to a lease who receives rent from a tenant in exchange for the possession and use of real property by the tenant. The lessor more commonly is called the *landlord.*

letter of last instructions A document prepared by a person instructing his personal representative (executor or administrator) as to the nature and location of assets and liabilities and suggesting appropriate action to be taken immediately after death.

liability insurance Coverage sold to protect against claims based on the insured's negligence that has caused bodily injury or property damage to the claimant.

libel A false statement of fact about a person in written or other permanent form causing harm to the reputation of that person and is further communicated to a third person.

license Permission to use copyrighted work granted by the holder of the copyright.

licensee A person who enters another's land with permission (implied or express) of the owner or possessor, for the visitor's convenience.

limited jurisdiction Limitation on a court as to the types of cases it can hear and decide.

liquidated damages Amount of damages that contracting parties previously have agreed would be fair payment in case of breach.

listing agent A licensed agent who enters into an employment contract with the owner of real property to hunt for a buyer of the property on specified terms.

living trust A popular term for a revocable *inter vivos* trust whose primary purpose is to avoid probate.

living will A document, usually authorized by state statute, that directs any attending physician to comply with the wishes of the drafter regarding the use of life-support systems in the treatment of a terminal illness.

loan origination fee A lump-sum fee paid by a mortgage borrower to the lender, who in turn pays all or a portion of it to the mortgage broker who introduced the borrower to the lender.

loan underwriting The process of evaluating the acceptability of a prospective borrower's loan application.

lobbying Efforts by individuals and representatives of special-interest groups to persuade legislators (and sometimes administrators) to enact, amend, or rescind specified laws.

lockout A shutdown of operations by an employer in response to union demands or to achieve other changes in an employment contract.

long-arm statute A state law authorizing a court to hear cases brought against nonresidents under specified circumstances.

lost property Property that is involuntarily left and forgotten by the owner.

M

maintenance Assisting a party to a lawsuit with money or otherwise, to prosecute or defend the lawsuit.

maintenance Payment by one spouse to the other spouse following dissolution of their marriage. Term used interchangeably with *alimony.*

majority opinion A written opinion by a judge outlining the views of the majority of the judges of the court deciding the case.

maker The creator of a promissory note.

malice The highest degree of criminal culpability, characterized by a cold and malignant heart and a mental predetermination to do the wrongful act without legal justification or excuse.

malpractice Violation of a duty of due care by a professional person.

manslaughter The unlawful killing of another person without malice aforethought. Usually classified as *voluntary* or *involuntary,* depending on the degree of culpability involved.

marital deduction A tax deduction allowing a surviving spouse to receive an estate from the deceased spouse free of federal estate tax.

marital life estate trust Reciprocal trust executed by a husband and wife with the other spouse as a life beneficiary. These trusts also are called A and B trusts.

marital property Property acquired during marriage in a marital property state.

market value The price property would bring if offered for sale in a fair market (not at auction or in a forced sale) by a willing and fully informed (but not compelled) seller, after ample time to find a willing and fully informed (but not compelled) buyer.

marriage Legal union as husband and wife.

mayhem The crime of unlawfully depriving the victim of some member of his body; disfiguring, disabling, or rendering the member useless or otherwise permanently disfiguring the body.

mechanic's lien A legal claim of a contractor or material supplier who helped or supplied materials to construct, improve, or repair a building.

med-arb An alternative dispute resolution (ADR) process that combines mediation and arbitration.

mediation The use of a neutral third party to assist parties in voluntarily resolving their dispute(s).

medical-payments insurance Coverage available in conjunction with automobile insurance—for example, to pay medical, surgical, dental, and funeral expenses suffered by the insured or any member of the insured's household who is injured while occupying or being struck by an automobile.

Megan's Law A state law that protects children and families by allowing or requiring law enforcement to publicize information about the identity and location of convicted sex offenders.

merchant A professional seller who deals in goods, or otherwise by occupation holds himself or herself out as having knowledge or skill peculiar to the good or service.

mini-trial A private, voluntary, informal form of dispute resolution in which attorneys for each disputant make a brief presentation of their best case before officials for each side who have authority to settle.

Miranda warnings Warnings directed to a suspect by police before a *custodial* (while in custody) interrogation may occur.

misdemeanor A crime punishable by fine or by incarceration in a county jail up to a year, or both.

mislaid property Property that has been voluntarily placed somewhere by the owner and then forgotten.

misrepresentation A false statement made intentionally, knowing it is not true. A negligent misrepresentation is a false statement made carelessly.

mock jury A panel of lay citizens selected and paid to mirror the role of an actual jury.

modify Appellate court alters the decision of a lower court.

moral problem solving Conflict-resolution process aimed at solving conflicts involving moral dilemmas through communication, education, and negotiation. The broad term describes interrelational rather than individual process.

moral reasoning A rational thought process directed at testing whether action is right or wrong. The conclusion is a determination of moral responsibility or culpability.

morals Values concerning right and wrong.

mortgage (or real mortgage) The contract in which the buyer of real property typically gives a lender a lien or claim against the real property that serves as collateral for a loan of money, often borrowed to pay part of the purchase price.

mortgage banker A business that makes real estate loans with its own capital, as well as with institutional funds, and then sells the loans in the secondary mortgage market.

mortgage broker A person licensed to engage in the business of bringing together borrowers and lenders of mortgage funds. Mortgage brokers typically are paid a commission based upon the volume of loans they originate.

mortgagee The lender of funds secured by a mortgage.

mortgagor The borrower of funds secured by a mortgage.

motion A formal request by counsel addressed to a court or other tribunal for a particular decision or act.

motion for a directed verdict Request to a judge by counsel to enter a particular verdict instead of allowing the jury to do so because there are insufficient facts to allow any other verdict.

motion for change of venue Request to a judge by counsel to transfer the trial to a different geographic location within the jurisdiction of the court.

motion for summary judgment Request to a judge by counsel to award judgment because there are no significant questions of fact in the lawsuit.

motion to produce Request to a judge by counsel to compel the opposing party to provide specified evidence to the court.

motive A reason for committing, or failing to perform, an act. Motive is not synonymous with criminal intent. Intent is essential for proof of crime; motive is not.

multiple listing service An organization of real estate brokers who exchange information about listings of property they have obtained.

murder The unlawful killing of a human being with malice aforethought.

mutual or bilateral mistake Where both parties to a contract labor under the same error about an important fact in their agreement.

N

Natural Death Act A statute that allows a person with a terminal condition to request that a physician remove life support.

natural law The higher law believed by some ethicists to be above and beyond man's power to change.

natural rights Inalienable rights of every human being that exist by virtue of natural law, notably to life, liberty, and property.

necessaries Goods and services ordinarily required by and appropriate to an incompetent person's station in life, yet not available and/or not provided by parent or guardian.

negative amortization A monthly increase in the unpaid principal balance of a mortgage loan resulting when the borrower does not make the required monthly interest payments in full.

negligence Failure to act as a reasonable, careful person would act under the same or similar circumstances, thereby causing injury that was foreseeable.

negligence *per se* The unexcused violation of a statute or ordinance which is automatically deemed to be negligent conduct without argument or proof as to the particular surrounding circumstances.

negotiated rulemaking A process to bring together representatives of a rulemaking agency and stakeholders to jointly prepare the text of a proposed rule in a consensus-seeking negotiation before the agency formally submits the rule to the rulemaking process.

Negotiation Communication between disputing parties for the purposes of persuasion and settlement or resolution.

neighbor law The body of laws and rules found in state statutes; in county and city ordinances; in covenants, conditions, and restrictions (CC&Rs); and in court decisions that govern the legal issues that arise between residential neighbors.

no-fault divorce A divorce granted by a court without either party having to prove fault in the other party.

no-fault insurance A type of automobile insurance, generally mandatory for all motorists in adopting states, that provides benefits to the insured, regardless of fault of parties to the accident.

nominal damages Insignificant amount (such as $1) awarded by a court when the defendant has violated the rights of the plaintiff but no monetary loss has been suffered or can be proved.

noncapital crime A homicide for which the death penalty may not be imposed even if such penalty is authorized for other crimes by the state in which the crime is committed.

nonjudicial foreclosure The involuntary sale, without court proceedings, of an owner's real property to raise money to satisfy the unpaid balance of the loan that is in default.

nonnormative statements Statements that reflect no value judgment.

nonowned automobile An automobile or trailer not owned by, or furnished for, the regular use of the named insured.

normative statements Statements that reflect what should be or how one should act.

notarized Signed in the presence of a person licensed by the state to perform identification services as a notary public.

novation A three-party agreement in which a creditor accepts a new party who agrees to assume the debt and to release the prior debtor.

nuisance Any unreasonable and continuous interference with the use and enjoyment of real property.

O

objective theory of contracts A theory that the words and conduct of an offeror mean whatever a reasonable person in the offeree's position would think they mean, as opposed to what the offeror actually may have meant.

Occupational Safety and Health Act of 1970 (the OSH Act) A federal law to ensure safe and healthful working conditions by authorizing enforcement of health and safety standards.

offer A promise by one person (the offeror) to do or to give consideration (something of value) in exchange for sought-for consideration through acceptance by another person (the offeree).

offeree In contracts, the party to whom an offer is made by the offeror.

offeror In contracts, the party who makes an offer.

ombudsperson A proactive neutral party who investigates and determines facts and suggests resolutions to disputes.

open shop A company or department where union membership is not a requirement to get or keep a job.

opening statement Summaries by counsel of plaintiff and of defendant indicating what they expect to prove in the ensuing trial.

option contract An agreement concerning the right to buy or sell something to another at a certain price within a certain time.

order of examination A judicially authorized inquiry as to the assets of a judgment debtor.

ordinance A written law enacted by a city or county (parish). An example is a zoning ordinance that governs the use of land.

ordinary wear and tear Deterioration in a residential rental property that is attributable to the passage of time (for example, fading of draperies) and not to abuse by the tenant.

P

pardon Release of a convicted criminal from all punishment for a crime through an act of the governor of the state or the president.

parol evidence rule A contract doctrine that presumes that the contracting parties have included all previous desired oral or written understandings in their final, integrated written agreement.

parole Release from a prison on specified conditions involving good behavior.

partnering A team-building process designed to improve contract performance and reduce or eliminate contract litigation through common understanding of goals and improved communication. The process is used in large, complicated, and expensive contracts and has its roots in the construction industry.

patent An exclusive privilege which allows the holder to manufacture, use, or sell a product for a fixed, non-renewable period of 20 years.

paternity Establishing the father of a child. Often determined by a lawsuit to prove that a named person is the father of a child.

payee Person in whose favor a check, draft, or promissory note is drawn.

peaceable eviction An improper eviction technique by which a landlord surreptitiously enters the absent tenant's apartment, removes the tenant's belongings, and changes locks to the unit. It is peaceable in the sense that no eye-to-eye, person-to-person confrontation takes place, as in a forcible eviction.

peremptory challenge Ability to exclude a prospective juror for any reason other than race or gender.

performance That which each party to a contract promises to do.

periodic tenancy Tenancy for a period often determined by frequency of rent payments; automatically renewed unless proper notice is given.

personal property All property that is not real property, that is, property other than land and things permanently attached to it.

personal property Movable property; any property that is not real property.

petty theft Theft of a thing of little value, as specified by statute.

picketing Patrolling by strikers or sympathizers, generally at the entrances to a business plant, during a labor dispute.

PITI An acronym for principal, interest, taxes, and insurance, which represent the four basic repetitive expenses of buying real property with borrowed funds.

plaintiff In trial, the person trying to recover money damages or other relief from a defendant.

plant patent Issued for a distinct and new variety of plant invented or discovered and asexually reproduced.

plea bargain A binding agreement in which an accused agrees to plead guilty (or *nolo contendere*) if the court agrees to a specified punishment in advance.

pleadings The complaint of the plaintiff and answer of the defendant in a lawsuit.

points A one-time charge made by a lender when a home loan is originated. One point is 1 percent of the loan.

police power The inherent power of the government to make laws and impose reasonable regulations for the health, safety, morals, or general welfare of the public, even when this limits individual freedom.

portfolio lender A lender of home purchase funds that does not expect to sell its mortgages in the secondary mortgage market. Because such lenders keep their loans within their own portfolio of loans, they can be more flexible (liberal) in terms of the loans they offer prospective homebuyers.

positive law (Chapter 2, types of law) Law enacted by government authority, such as legislatures, courts, and administrative agencies, as distinguished from natural law.

positive law (Chapter 1, concept of law) The rules members of a society are obliged to obey to avoid punishment or penalty imposed by the government.

possessory lien A lien that empowers a creditor to retain possession of the collateral until the debt is paid or until it is sold to the highest bidder in accordance with law.

power of appointment Authority given to a person (the donee) under a trust or will to designate or appoint the person (s) who shall receive specified assets after a specified event, such as death of the donee.

power of attorney A document authorizing another person to act as one's agent. A general power of attorney authorizes the agent (called the attorney-in-fact) to do all acts not prohibited by law for another (called the principal).

precedent A court decision on a question of law that gives authority or direction on a similar question of law in a later case with similar facts. See also *stare decisis*.

preliminary hearing An examination in open court by a judge to determine whether sufficient evidence exists to hold the accused for trial.

preponderance of evidence Standard of determining civil liability, that the weight of the evidence offered to prove a matter is more probable than not.

prescriptive easement An easement, usually of access, over the land of another person, created by a continuous, open (visible) use without the consent of the landowner for a long period of time, usually five years or more in most states.

presumption A rule of law permitting one to assume a fact is true until such time as there is a greater weight of evidence that disproves or outweighs the assumed fact.

pretermitted heir A child who was not specifically provided for in life and was not mentioned in a parent's will.

pretrial hearing or conference Hearing occurring before a trial.

prima facie [Latin: "on first appearance"] Term describing facts legally sufficient to establish a fact or a case unless disproved by some contrary evidence.

principal (Chapter 8, Contracts) The person who empowers an agent to enter contract(s) on her or his behalf.

principal (Chapter 6, Criminal Law) One who is present and participates in a crime or persuades another to commit a crime.

prior restraint Restraints on a publication before it is actually published.

private judging The use of a legally trained arbitrator who follows formal judicial procedures in hearing a case outside a court.

private law That body of law regulating the rights and duties that exist between private persons (including private corporations). Contract law is an example of private law.

private mortgage insurance (PMI) Insurance to protect a lender in the event that a borrower defaults in the repayment of a mortgage loan.

privilege A legal right to do or refrain from doing something enjoyed by only some persons or classes.

privilege against self-incrimination The right of any person, including one accused of a crime, to remain silent when what might be said could indicate criminal guilt.

privity of contract Applies to a direct contractual relationship between parties, as exists, for example, with a consumer-buyer dealing with the retail-seller but not with the wholesaler or manufacturer of the goods.

pro bono publico When an attorney provides legal services free of charge to poor but worthy clients or causes.

probable cause The standard by which a police officer may make an arrest, conduct a personal or property search, or obtain a warrant.

probate The process of proving the validity of a will in court, coupled with the related matter of administering the decedent's estate.

probation Release of a convicted criminal before sentence begins on condition of good behavior and under supervision of a probation officer. If this condition is violated, incarceration begins.

procedural law General principles and detailed rules that define the methods of administering substantive law.

process server A person who serves (delivers) a copy of the summons and complaint, or other legal document, upon a party or witness at the request of the opposing party to civil litigation.

product liability A general area of law holding manufacturers and sellers of goods liable to buyers, users, and perhaps bystanders for harm caused when goods are defective.

product liability Law holding manufacturers and sellers of goods liable to buyers, users, and perhaps bystanders for harm caused by defective goods.

professional ethics Written rules of conduct that are adopted by and binding upon members of a professional group.

promisee The person to whom a contractual promise is made.

promisor The person who makes a contractual promise.

promissory note A written promise to pay to a named person or to the bearer of the note a certain sum of money in the future.

property The legally protected rights and interests a person has in anything with an ascertainable value that is subject to ownership.

protected class A classification of persons defined by one or more of these criteria: race, color, gender, national origin, age, or religion.

proximate cause An action that, in natural and continuous sequence, unbroken by an intervening force or cause, produces the injury, and without which the effect or result would not have occurred. Furthermore, the result is not entirely outside the range of expectation or probability.

public defender A lawyer provided by the community for a person who is accused of a serious crime (felony) and cannot afford to hire counsel.

public interest law firm A nonprofit law firm that offers assistance in areas such as employment, minority rights, civil rights, political rights, family law, and environmental law.

public law That body of law directly concerned with public rights and obligations, such as constitutional, administrative, criminal, and international law.

published A legal rule of wills in some states requiring a declaration by the maker of the will to the witnesses that the document she is about to sign is indeed her will.

puffing Seller's talk; claims about the quality of goods, usually exaggerated; not considered fraud.

punitive damages Amount awarded by a court, to the victim of an intentional tort, in addition to compensatory damages; designed to punish the tortfeasor and serve as an example to others.

purchase agreement A contract by which a seller agrees to sell, and the buyer agrees to buy, a specified parcel of real property at a specified price and upon specified terms.

Q

quasi contract Not a true contract, but an obligation imposed on one party to prevent unjust enrichment of another. Also called "implied in law contract."

questions of fact Circumstances or matters surrounding and involved in a case that is being tried by a court.

questions of law Principles and rules of human conduct determined by the judge to be applicable in a case being tried by a court.

***quid pro quo* (Latin: "something for something")** Expression used in sexual harassment situations when sexual favors or demands are a term or condition of an individual's employment, or the basis for employment decisions affecting such individual.

quitclaim deed A deed to real property in which the transferor conveys whatever ownership interest he may possess, which may be none.

R

Racketeer Influenced and Corrupt Organizations Act (RICO) A federal law passed to control attempts by organized crime to invest money gained from illegal racketeering in legitimate business activities.

rape An unlawful act of sexual intercourse, against the will of the victim.

rape shield statute A statute that protects victims from courtroom questioning about prior sexual experiences with persons other than the defendant.

real estate agent A person licensed by the state to negotiate the buying and selling of real property while employed and supervised by a licensed real estate broker.

real estate broker One who acts as an intermediary for real estate transactions on behalf of others for a fee or commission.

real property Land and things permanently attached to it. Includes air space above, surface water, and subsurface waters, gases, and minerals.

recall A democratic process for removing public officials from their elective positions by a vote of the people taken after filing of a petition signed by the required number of qualified voters.

receiving stolen property The crime of knowingly receiving property of another.

recidivist A repeat criminal offender.

recognizance A written promise by the accused that if released without posting bail, that person will return voluntarily for further criminal proceedings.

recordation The act or process of recording title to real property in a public registry.

referendum A democratic process whereby a state legislature submits (refers) proposed or existing laws to the electorate for approval or rejection.

refinance loan A loan, secured by mortgage, the proceeds of which are used primarily to pay off, or retire, an existing mortgage loan. Refinancing occurs when interest rates drop, encouraging homeowners to pay off existing high interest rate loans with new lower interest rate loans.

registered owner The buyer of a car on credit, who, as the equitable owner, gets possession and use of the vehicle while making payments.

regulations Rules promulgated by an administrative agency under authority given to the agency by the enabling statute.

Regulatory Flexibility Act Federal law requiring federal agencies to consider the effects of their regulatory actions on small businesses and other small entities and to minimize any undue disproportionate burden.

regulatory offense A violation of a rule promulgated by an administrative agency.

relevant evidence Evidence that is related to the facts in dispute.

remainder interest Any interest that is left after another interest in the property ends.

remand Appellate court sends case back to a lower court to take some further action.

rent The tenant's payment to the landlord for the tenant's use of the landlord's real property.

rent control A law that places limits on the amount of rent a landlord can charge for an apartment.

rental agreement A contract, usually written, between a landlord and tenant. Technically, it is a lease.

reporter A set of books that contains the written opinions of justices of specified appellate courts. These volumes contain the decisional, or unwritten, law. Volumes in the reporters and the cases they contain are arranged in chronological order and accessible by case name or subject matter index.

reprieve Postponement, or stay of execution (i.e., of enforcement), of the judgment after conviction for a crime.

republic A system of government with the supreme power in the people, exercised by representatives chosen through the votes of qualified voters.

res ipsa loquitur A doctrine under which negligence is inferred when the instrumentality causing the injury was under control of the defendant and an injury occurred that normally would not occur in the absence of negligence by the defendant. This doctrine is frequently relied on by victims of medical malpractice.

rescission An equitable remedy that annuls a contract and returns the parties to the relationship they had before the contract was made.

rescission The unmaking of a contract by the mutual agreement of the parties.

residuary clause Any part of the will that allocates property not expressly disposed of by other provisions of the will.

respondeat superior (Latin: "let the master answer") A legal doctrine holding employers liable for injuries caused third persons by their employees who were negligent while acting within the course and scope of their employment.

retainer fee (a) A sum of money paid to an attorney for a promise to remain available to the client for consultation when needed and requested. (b) Fees paid in advance that are held in a trust account to be drawn down (taken) by the attorney as work progresses.

retaliatory eviction An eviction carried out by a landlord primarily for revenge, or retaliation, against a particular tenant who has in some way angered the landlord.

reverse Appellate court sets aside the decision of a lower court.

reverse discrimination Label given to the results of affirmative action programs by opponents who claim that such programs discriminate against male and white workers.

revocable *inter vivos* trust A trust created and having operative effect during the trustor's life that may be terminated or revoked by the trustor who created it

revocation The taking back of an offer.

right of redemption Right of a debtor to recover, within one year, the property sold at a judicial foreclosure sale.

right of reinstatement The right of a defaulting debtor to reinstate the loan by payment of all money due for prior months including late charges, even though the note and mortgage declare that the *entire* unpaid balance is immediately due in full upon any default.

right-to-know laws Federal and state laws requiring that information be collected and distributed about possible exposure to hazardous chemicals.

robbery The crime of stealing property from another person in her immediate presence through the use of force or fear.

Roth IRA A form of individual retirement account authorized by federal law that allows a taxpayer to contribute after-tax dollars to the account so that earnings are not taxed when withdrawn.

royalty A share in the proceeds paid to a copyright holder.

rule against perpetuities A rule that requires remainder interests in property to vest (i.e., to take effect) no later than a life or any number of identified lives in being, plus twenty-one years.

rule of law Principle that decisions should be made by the application of established laws without the intervention of individual discretion.

S

sale A contract in which title (ownership) of property passes from seller to buyer. Possession usually transfers at the time of sale.

second-degree murder A measurement in law of the degree of culpability of the perpetrator of a murder of less than first degree.

secondary boycotts Occurs when striking workers picket or use other pressure against a neutral third party who supplies or buys from the struck employer.

secured transaction Any transaction, regardless of form, that is intended to create a security interest in personal property.

security deposit A lump sum of cash paid by a tenant to his or her new landlord as security that the tenant will pay rent as agreed and will not damage the rented premises.

self-defense The legal right to use whatever force appears to be reasonably necessary to protect oneself (or specified others) from great and imminent bodily injury by an assailant.

separate property Property owned by a marital partner separate from the spouse, either brought into a marriage at the outset or acquired during marriage by gift or inheritance.

separation The status of spouses who are by judicial decree living apart, that is, no longer cohabiting.

separation of powers The granting of the various powers of government among three branches so that each branch checks the other two.

settlor A person who establishes a trust. A settlor is also called a trustor.

severalty Separate or individual ownership of property by one person or ownership as separate property by a married person.

sexual harassment A form of illegal gender discrimination wherein (1) job opportunities, promotions, and the like are given on the basis of sexual favors or (2) the employee is subjected to a work environment where the employee must put up with sexual comments, jokes, or physical contact that is sexually offensive.

shopkeeper's privilege Legal right of a storekeeper to detain suspected shoplifters for a reasonable time in a reasonable way when there is probable cause to believe a theft has taken place.

short sale The sale of property (such as a home) for less than the unpaid balance of a loan for which the property serves as security.

simple contract All oral and written contracts not classified as formal contracts.

sit-down strike Illegal strike in which strikers remain in their places of employment but refuse to work.

situational ethics The term used disparagingly to describe an "end-justifies-the-means" maxim supplanting duty or obligation.

slander Oral defamation; the speaking of false words to a third person tending to cause injury to the reputation of the victim.

slander *per se* Slander in itself; words not requiring proof of special damages.

small claims court A court with jurisdiction to decide civil controversies of a relatively minor nature.

solicitation The crime of encouraging another person to commit a crime.

Son-of-Sam Laws A law that limits the ability of a criminal offender to receive profits from the recounting of his crime.

special damages Amount awarded by a court to pay for monetary out-of-pocket losses resulting from the specific or special circumstances of the plaintiff (e.g., for medical expenses, loss of wages, and destruction of property).

specific intent In criminal law, the intent to accomplish the precise act and harm that the law prohibits.

specific performance An equitable remedy allowing a buyer to get possession and title to real property and to goods that are unique when the seller refuses to deliver under a valid sales contract.

spendthrift trust A trust created to provide for the maintenance of an improvident beneficiary by limiting his control of the corpus (the principal of the trust) and by barring access by creditors.

spite fence A fence erected primarily to vex, annoy, or "spite" a neighbor.

spousal immunity A doctrine of the common law that tort actions between spouses are prohibited because of a public policy to protect the harmony of the marital relationship from adversarial and disruptive legal proceedings.

stalking An unwelcome or intrusive long-term pattern of threat or harassment directed repeatedly toward a specific individual that triggers fear or concern in that person.

standard title insurance Customary title insurance coverage that does not include the special coverage included within the more expensive American Land Title Association policy, which includes physical inspection of the premises as well as a review of the official records in a title search.

standing to sue A person's right or capacity to bring a lawsuit because he or she has a legally protected interest at stake in the litigation.

stare decisis The common law doctrine that binds an inferior (subordinate) court to follow and apply decisions and interpretations of higher courts when similar cases arise. Also called the *doctrine of precedents.*

Statute of Frauds A state statute requiring certain types of contracts to be evidenced by writing and to be signed by the party to be charged, or by her or his authorized agent.

statute of limitations A statute that bars civil or criminal proceedings unless brought within a specified period of time after the act occurred.

statute of limitations A statute that bars civil or criminal proceedings unless brought within a specified period of time after the act occurred.

statute of repose A type of statute of limitations that specifies an absolute time from the date of sale during which the cause of action must be brought to collect damages for defects in the product.

statutes Laws enacted by Congress or by state legislatures.

statutory rape Sexual intercourse between an adult, usually eighteen years or older, and a consenting minor, usually seventeen years or younger.

statutory will A form will authorized by state law with blanks to be completed by the testator.

strict constructionists Judges whose reading of the law narrowly interprets legal words and who subscribe to interpreting the law consistent with the believed meaning given it by the drafters.

strict liability A tort theory available in special situations determined by public policy in which a person is held responsible for harm occurring to another without proof of fault (e.g., inherently dangerous activities, wild animals, explosives, sale of defective products).

strike A concerted refusal by employees to perform the services for which they were hired, generally to gain recognition of a union, or improvements in wages, hours, or conditions of employment.

strikebreakers Persons hired to take the place of workers who are out on strike. If it is an economic strike, the strikebreakers may be retained as permanent replacements.

subject matter jurisdiction The power of a court to hear and decide cases of the general type to which the subject in question belongs.

sublease The transfer by a tenant of less than the full, unexpired term of the lease to a subtenant.

subornation of perjury Crime of persuading another person to commit perjury.

subpoena An order directing a person to appear at a certain time and place for the purpose of giving testimony as a witness.

subpoena *duces tecum* A judicial order to bring specified documents or physical evidence to court.

subrogation The substitution of a third party for the creditor in a claim against a debtor.

substantial performance When a party to a contract honestly performs most essentials of the contract, but there is some minor omission or deviation that can be corrected, or compensated for in a reduction of the price.

substantive law General principles and detailed rules that define legal rights and duties.

suicide The intentional killing of oneself.

summary jury trial A nonbinding alternative dispute resolution (ADR) process in which parties present their cases to a private mock jury, which then gives the parties an advisory verdict.

summation The review of the evidence presented to the court by each lawyer in oral argument at the close of the trial.

summons A document issued by a clerk of the court inviting the defendant to respond to a complaint.

supremacy doctrine The judicial doctrine that holds that any state or federal law that is inconsistent with the U.S. Constitution is null and void.

surrogate mother A woman who is artificially inseminated, carries the fetus to term, and then relinquishes her parental rights to the biological father. Surrogacy services are performed pursuant to a contract in return for money.

survivor statutes Law allowing a lawsuit even after the death of the victim perhaps permitting recovery for damages to the victim.

sustained Agreement by the judge with request by an attorney-at-law.

syllogism A pattern of deductive logic that contains a major or general premise, a minor or specific premise, and a conclusion, always in that order. The conclusion follows from the premises but is not a premise itself.

T

tangible personal property Property in a physical form.

tangible property Property that has physical existence and can be touched. An automobile is tangible personal property; a house is tangible real property.

tax evasion The intentional and illegal violation of federal and state tax laws.

temporary insanity A passing or temporal mental disease or defect.

tenancy at sufferance Continued possession of land by a tenant without legal right.

tenancy at will Tenancy for as long as both parties agree; no notice of termination is required.

tenancy by the entirety A form of co-ownership of property between husband and wife in some states. As with joint-tenancy ownership, the spouses have a right of survivorship.

tenancy for years Tenancy for a specified time period stated by express contract.

tenancy in common A form of coownership of property by two or more persons. Upon the death of any co-owner, that person's percentage interest passes by intestate succession or by last will.

tenant A party to a lease who pays rent to the landlord in exchange for the possession and use of real property (e.g., a person who rents an apartment).

testamentary trust A trust created by a valid will.

testate The legal status of a person who died leaving a valid will.

testator (1) Person who makes a valid will. (2) Person who dies leaving a valid will.

theft The taking of property without the owner's consent. Depending on the nature or value of the property stolen, it is either petty theft (*misdemeanor*) or grand theft (*felony*).

third-party beneficiary A third party who receives the benefit of a contract between two other persons.

tort A private wrong committed by one person (the tortfeasor) that injures another (the victim) in person or property and for which society allows the legal remedy of monetary damages.

tortfeasor A wrongdoer who commits a private injury to another person by breaching a duty recognized by law.

Totten trust A trust for bank depositors whereby they deposit money in a bank in the settlor's own name as a trustee for another person.

trade secret Confidential data or other information that has economic value because it is not generally known.

trespass Wrongful interference with the real or personal property of another.

trespass to chattel A brief, temporary, unauthorized interference with the personal-property rights of another.

trial court The initial court that hears evidence and applies the law to decided facts.

trial *de novo* A new trial that takes place as if the first trial had not occurred.

trier of fact Jury or judge acting as the finder of issues of fact.

trust A legal relationship in which one party (called trustor, settlor, or donor) transfers legal title in property to a second party (trustee) for the benefit of a third party (beneficiary or donee).

trustee A person who holds property in a trust for the benefit of another, the beneficiary.

U

unanimous opinion A judicial decision with complete agreement by all judges.

unconscionable Something that is against public policy or otherwise so offensive that it shocks the conscience.

undue hardship An action or accommodation that is excessively costly, extensive, substantial, or disruptive, or fundamentally would alter the nature or operation of the business.

undue influence (Chapter 8, Contracts) Wrongful persuasion, often by a fiduciary or other trusted individual, that deprives the victim of freedom of will in making a contract.

undue influence (Chapter 15, wills) Wrongful persuasion often by a beneficiary or other trusted individual that deprives the victim of decision-making freedom in making a will.

unenforceable contract A valid contract that for some reason cannot be enforced, for example, because of the running of a statute of limitations.

unfair labor practice strike A strike in which the workers are protesting an unfair labor practice of their employer.

unfair labor practices Certain practices of employers and unions that are prohibited by federal or state law.

unified estate and gift tax A federal tax levied on the transfer of property through an estate at the time of death or on a taxable transfer by gift. The estate or the donor is responsible for payment of the tax. A unified credit is available to be applied against the transfer tax.

Uniform Commercial Code A uniform code drafted by the National Conference of Commissioners of Uniform State Laws governing the conduct of business, sales, warranties, and other commercial matters.

Uniform Electronic Transactions Act (UETA) A uniform state act providing a legal framework for electronic transactions giving electronic signatures and records the same validity and enforceability as manual signatures and paper-based transactions.

unilateral contract A contract in which the promisor seeks performance of a requested act. Upon performance of the act, the contract is formed and the promisor is obligated to fulfill the promise.

unilateral mistake A situation in which one of the parties to a contract labors under some error about an important fact in the agreement.

uninsured-motorist insurance Automobile insurance that protects against the risk of loss from bodily injury and property damage suffered by an insured driver because of the negligence of either an uninsured, an underinsured, or a hit-and-rundriver.

union Association of workers formed to bargain collectively with employers over wages, hours, and conditions of employment.

union shop A place of employment where newly hired workers must join the union within thirty days of being hired.

unlawful detainer A statutory remedy for a landlord to evict a renter who has defaulted in the payment of rent or who has broken the terms of the lease in some other manner. It is not a full-blown trial on all issues before a jury.

unwritten law A historically based reference to court- or judge-made law.

utilitarianism An ethical doctrine holding that determining right conduct is based on consequences; that the purpose of the behavior should be the greatest happiness of the greatest number.

utility patent Issued for the invention of a new and useful process, machine, manufacture, or composition of matter.

V

valid contract An agreement that complies with all requisites of the law for enforceability.

Variable interest-rate mortgage (VIRM) A home-purchase mortgage and promissory note in which the interest rate may fluctuate, up or down, in sync with a published index. Also called *adjustable-rate mortgage.*

vehicular manslaughter The wrongful killing of another person by a perpetrator driving a vehicle in a reckless and dangerous manner (e.g., in some cases while under the influence of alcohol or other drugs).

venue The local place, within the geographic boundaries of a larger jurisdiction, where a case is generally most appropriately tried.

verdict The expressed decision of the jury on questions of fact submitted to it for determination, based on evidence presented during trial.

Veterans Administration (VA) loan A home-purchase mortgage loan made to any eligible veteran by the federal Veterans

Administration. The VA was established in 1944 by the Serviceman's Readjustment Act to assist veterans in becoming homeowners.

vicarious liability The responsibility of one person for the wrongful acts of another.

violations Any minor crime (for example, parking violation) that is not punishable by incarceration, but only by fine. Accordingly, trial by jury is not required or permitted.

void agreement Without legal force or binding effect.

voidable contract An agreement that may be legally enforced or may be rejected by a party. For example, a contract between a minor and an adult is voidable or valid at the option of the minor.

voir dire Process of questioning prospective jurors to ascertain whether they have any bias that would make difficult or unlikely their impartiality in determining questions of fact during a trial.

voluntary manslaughter The wrongful and intentional killing of another person during the heat of passion, or under the influence of alcohol or drugs, or while engaged in some reckless and dangerous activity.

W

Wagner Act A federal law that recognizes the right of workers to organize into unions of their own choice, and the duty of employers to bargain collectively with the unions over wages, hours, and conditions of employment. It provides a list of unfair labor practices by management.

waive To give up a right.

warranty deed A type of deed with several warranties implied by law to protect the buyer.

whistleblower A person who makes a disclosure about improper conduct by an organization or organization officer or official.

white-collar crime Illegal acts committed usually without violence by persons of comparatively high social status and economic wealth.

wildcat strike An unlawful strike of union members that takes place without the approval of the union leaders.

will Legal expression (usually in writing, signed, and witnessed) of a person's directions as to how property owned is to be disposed after death.

work furlough A rehabilitative program for prisoners under which they may participate in part-time gainful employment even while they are serving time in a prison or jail.

workers' compensation Medical treatment, rehabilitation benefits, and disability payments for workers injured on the job.

writ of *certiorari* A procedural document whereby an appellate court exercises its discretionary power to accept jurisdiction of a pending case.

writ of execution Order of the court directing the sheriff to confiscate property of the defendant.

writ of *habeas corpus* [Latin: "you have the body"] A formal written order that an arrestee be brought before a court.

written law An old-fashioned reference to the statutes and ordinances of federal, state, and local governments, and the published rules of administrative agencies.

wrongful-death statutes A law allowing the heirs of a deceased person to sue whoever caused the decedent's death and to collect any court-awarded damages. The damage sued for is the damage to the heirs for the loss of the loved one's life.

Y

yellow dog contracts An employment contract in which a worker agrees not to join a union.

Index

A

B

C

D

E

F

G

H

K

L

M

N

O

P

Q

R

S

T

U